COLLINS
ITALIAN
DICTIONARY

FULLY REVISED AND UPDATED—
AMERICAN ENGLISH USAGE

Contributors

Catherine Love
Gabriella Bacchelli
P. L. Rossi
E. Bilucaglia

HARPER

An Imprint of HarperCollins*Publishers*

HARPER

An Imprint of HarperCollins*Publishers*
10 East 53rd Street
New York, New York 10022-5299

© William Collins Sons & Co. Ltd. 1990
© HarperCollins Publishers 2000, 2007
ISBN: 978-0-06-126049-0
ISBN-10: 0-06-126049-5

First Harper paperback printing: September 2007

HarperCollins® and Harper® are trademarks of HarperCollins Publishers.

Printed in the United States of America

Visit Harper paperbacks on the World Wide Web at www.harper collins.com

10 9 8 7 6 5 4

INDICE

CONTENTS

I marchi registrati

I termini che a nostro parere costituiscono un marchio registrato sono stati designati come tali. In ogni caso, né la presenza né l'assenza di tale designazione implicano alcuna valutazione del loro reale stato giuridico.

Note on trademarks

Entered words that we have reason to believe constitute trademarks have been designated as such. However, neither the presence nor the absence of such designation should be regarded as affecting the legal status of any trademark.

INTRODUZIONE

Vi ringraziamo di aver scelto il Dizionario inglese Collins e ci auguriamo che esso si riveli uno strumento utile e piacevole da usare nello studio, in vacanza e sul lavoro.

INTRODUCTION

We are delighted that you have decided to buy the Collins Italian Dictionary and hope you will enjoy and benefit from using it at school, at home, on holiday or at work.

William Collins' dream of knowledge for all began with the publication of his first book in 1819. A self-educated mill worker, he not only enriched millions of lives, but also founded a flourishing publishing house. Today, staying true to this spirit, Collins books are packed with inspiration, innovation, and practical expertise. They place you at the centre of a world of possibility and give you exactly what you need to explore it.

Language is the key to this exploration, and at the heart of Collins Dictionaries is language as it is really used. New words, phrases, and meanings spring up every day, and all of them are captured and analysed by the Collins Word Web. Constantly updated, and with over 2.5 billion entries, this living language resource is unique to our dictionaries.

Words are tools for life. And a Collins Dictionary makes them work for you.

Collins. Do more

ABBREVIAZIONI   ABBREVIATIONS

abbreviazione	*abbr*	abbreviation
aggettivo	*adj*	adjective
amministrazione	*Admin*	administration
avverbio	*adv*	adverb
aeronautica, viaggi aerei	*Aer*	flying, air travel
aggettivo	*ag*	adjective
agricoltura	*Agr*	agriculture
amministrazione	*Amm*	administration
anatomia	*Anat*	anatomy
architettura	*Archit*	architecture
articolo determinativo	*art def*	definite article
articolo indeterminativo	*art indef*	indefinite article
attributivo	*attrib*	attributive
ausiliare	*aus, aux*	auxiliary
automobile	*Aut*	motor car and motoring
avverbio	*av*	adverb
aeronautica, viaggi aerei	*Aviat*	flying, air travel
biologia	*Biol*	biology
botanica	*Bot*	botany
inglese britannico	*BRIT*	British English
consonante	C	consonant
chimica	*Chim, Chem*	chemistry
commercio, finanza	*Comm*	commerce, finance
comparativo	*compar*	comparative
informatica	*Comput*	computing
congiunzione	*cong, conj*	conjunction
edilizia	*Constr*	building
sostantivo usato come aggettivo, ma mai con funzione predicativa	*cpd*	compound element: noun used as adjective and which cannot follow the noun it qualifies
cucina	*Cuc, Culin*	cookery
davanti a	*dav*	before

vii

ABBREVIAZIONI

Italian	Abbr	
articolo determinativo	*def art*	
determinativo; articolo, aggettivo dimostrativo o indefinito ecc	*det*	
diminutivo	*dimin*	
diritto	*Dir*	
economia	*Econ*	
edilizia	*Edil*	
elettricità, elettronica	*Elettr, Elec*	
esclamazione	*escl, excl*	
femminile	*f*	
familiare (! da evitare)	*fam(!)*	
ferrovia	*Ferr*	
senso figurato	*fig*	
fisiologia	*Fisiol*	
fotografia	*Fot*	
verbo inglese la cui particella è inseparabile dal verbo	*fus*	
nella maggior parte dei sensi; generalmente	*gen*	
geografia, geologia	*Geo*	
geometria	*Geom*	
storia, storico	*Hist*	
impersonale	*impers*	
articolo indeterminativo	*indef art*	
familiare (! da evitare)	*inf(!)*	
infinito	*infin*	
informatica	*Inform*	

ABBREVIATIONS

- *def art* definite article
- *det* determiner: article, demonstrative etc
- *dimin* diminutive
- *Dir* law
- *Econ* economics
- *Edil* building
- *Elettr, Elec* electricity, electronics
- *escl, excl* exclamation
- *f* feminine
- *fam(!)* colloquial usage (! particularly offensive)
- *Ferr* railways
- *fig* figurative use
- *Fisiol* physiology
- *Fot* photography
- *fus* (phrasal verb) where the particle cannot be separated from the main verb
- *gen* in most or all senses; generally
- *Geo* geography, geology
- *Geom* geometry
- *Hist* history, historical
- *impers* impersonal
- *indef art* indefinite article
- *inf(!)* colloquial usage (! particularly offensive)
- *infin* infinitive
- *Inform* computing

ABBREVIAZIONI

		# ABBREVIATIONS
insegnamento, sistema scolastico e universitario	*Ins*	schooling, schools and universities
invariabile	*inv*	invariable
irregolare	*irreg*	irregular
grammatica, linguistica	*Ling*	grammar, linguistics
maschile	*m*	masculine
matematica	*Mat(h)*	mathematics
termine medico, medicina	*Med*	medical term, medicine
il tempo, meteorologia	*Meteor*	the weather, meteorology
maschile o femminile	*m/f*	masculine or feminine
esercito, linguaggio militare	*Mil*	military matters
musica	*Mus*	music
sostantivo	*n*	noun
nautica	*Naut*	sailing, navigation
numerale (aggettivo, sostantivo)	*num*	numeral adjective or noun
	o.s.	oneself
peggiorativo	*peg, pej*	derogatory, pejorative
fotografia	*Phot*	photography
fisiologia	*Physiol*	physiology
plurale	*pl*	plural
politica	*Pol*	politics
participio passato	*pp*	past participle
preposizione	*prep*	preposition
pronome	*pron*	pronoun
psicologia, psichiatria	*Psic, Psych*	psychology, psychiatry
tempo passato	*pt*	past tense
qualcosa	*qc*	
qualcuno	*qn*	
religione, liturgia	*Rel*	religions, church service
sostantivo	*s*	noun
	sb	somebody

ABBREVIAZIONI		ABBREVIATIONS
insegnamento, sistema scolastico e universitario	*Scol*	schooling, schools and universities
singolare	*sg*	singular
soggetto (grammaticale)	*sog*	(grammatical) subject
	sth	something
congiuntivo	*sub*	subjunctive
soggetto (grammaticale)	*subj*	(grammatical) subject
superlativo	*superl*	superlative
termine tecnico, tecnologia	*Tecn, Tech*	technical term, technology
telecomunicazioni	*Tel*	telecommunications
tipografia	*Tip*	typography, printing
televisione	*TV*	television
tipografia	*Typ*	typography, printing
università	*Univ*	university
inglese americano	*US*	American English
vocale	*V*	vowel
verbo	*vb*	verb
verbo o gruppo verbale con funzione intransitiva	*vi*	verb or phrasal verb used intransitively
verbo pronominale o riflessivo	*vpr*	pronominal or reflexive verb
verbo o gruppo verbale con funzione transitiva	*vt*	verb or phrasal verb used transitively
zoologia	*Zool*	zoology
marchio registrato	®	registered trademark
introduce un'equivalenza culturale	≈	introduces a cultural equivalent

TRASCRIZIONE FONETICA

Consonanti   Consonants

NB **p, b, t, d, k, g** sono seguite da un'aspirazione in inglese.

NB **p, b, t, d, k, g** are not aspirated in Italian.

padre	p	**p**up**py**
bam**b**ino	b	**b**a**by**
tu**tt**o	t	**t**en**t**
da**d**o	d	**d**ad**dy**
cane **ch**e	k	**c**or**k** **k**iss **ch**ord
gola **gh**iro	g	**g**a**g** **gu**ess
sano	s	**s**o ri**ce** ki**ss**
svago e**s**ame	z	cou**s**in bu**zz**
scena	ʃ	**sh**eep **s**ugar
	ʒ	plea**s**ure bei**ge**
pe**c**e lan**ci**are	tʃ	**ch**ur**ch**
giro **gi**oco	dʒ	**j**ud**ge** **g**eneral
a**f**a **f**aro	f	**f**arm ra**ff**le
vero bra**v**o	v	**v**ery re**v**
	θ	**th**in ma**th**s
	ð	**th**at o**th**er
letto a**l**a	l	**l**itt**l**e ba**ll**
g**li**	ʎ	mi**lli**on
rete a**r**co	ɾ	**r**at **r**a**r**e
ramo ma**d**re	m	**m**u**mm**y co**mb**
no fu**m**ante	n	**n**o ra**n**
gnomo	ɲ	ca**ny**on
	ŋ	si**ng**i**ng** ba**n**k
	h	**h**at re**h**eat
bu**i**o p**i**acere	j	**y**et
uomo g**u**aio	w	**w**all be**w**ail
	x	lo**ch**

Varie   Miscellaneous

per l'inglese: la "r" finale viene pronunciata se seguita da una vocale	ɾ	
precede la sillaba accentata	'	precedes the stressed syllable

PHONETIC TRANSCRIPTION

Vocali		Vowels
Vocali		**Vowels**
NB La messa in equivalenza di certi suoni indica solo una rassomiglianza approssimativa.		NB The pairing of some vowel sounds only indicates approximate equivalence.
vino idea	i iː	heel bead
	ɪ	hit pity
stella edera	e	
epoca eccetto	ɛ	set tent
mamma amore	a æ	bat apple
	ɑː	after car calm
	ɑ̃	fiancé
	ʌ	fun cousin
müsli	y	
	ə	over above
	əː	urn fern work
rosa occhio	ɔ	wash pot
	ɔː	born cork
ponte ognuno	o	
föhn	ø	
utile zucca	u	full soot
	uː	boon lewd

Dittonghi		Diphthongs
Dittonghi		**Diphthongs**
	ɪə	beer tier
	ɛə	tear fair there
	eɪ	date plaice day
	aɪ	life buy cry
	au	owl foul now
	əu	low no
	ɔɪ	boil boy oily
	uə	poor tour

ITALIAN PRONUNCIATION

Vowels

Where the vowel **e** or the vowel **o** appears in a stressed syllable it can be either open [ε], [ɔ] or closed [e], [o]. As the open or closed pronunciation of these vowels is subject to regional variation, the distinction is of little importance to the user of this dictionary. Phonetic transcription for headwords containing these vowels will therefore only appear where other pronunciation difficulties are present.

Consonants

c before "e" or "i" is pronounced like the *"tch"* in match.
ch is pronounced like the *"k"* in "kit".
g before "e" or "i" is pronounced like the *"j"* in "jet".
gh is pronounced like the *"g"* in "get".
gl before "e" or "i" is normally pronounced like the *"lli"* in "million", and in a few cases only like the *"gl"* in "glove".
gn is pronounced like the *"ny"* in "canyon"
sc before "e" or "i" is pronounced *"sh"*.
z is pronounced like the *"ts"* in "stetson", or like the *"d's"* in "bird's-eye".

Headwords containing the above consonants and consonantal groups have been given full phonetic transcription in this dictionary.

NB All double written consonants in Italian are fully sounded: e.g. the *tt* in "tutto" is pronounced as in "hat trick".

ITALIAN VERB FORMS

1 Gerundio 2 Participio passato 3 Presente 4 Imperfetto 5 Passato remoto
6 Futuro 7 Condizionale 8 Congiuntivo presente 9 Congiuntivo passato
10 Imperativo

andare 3 vado, vai, va, andiamo, andate, vanno 6 andrò ecc. 8 vada 10 va'!, vada!, andate!, vadano!

apparire 2 apparso 3 appaio, appari o apparisci, appare o apparisce, appaiono o appariscono 5 apparvi o apparsi, apparisti, apparve o apparì o apparse, apparvero o apparirono o apparsero 8 appaia o apparisca

aprire 2 aperto 3 apro 5 aprii, apristi 8 apra

AVERE 3 ho, hai, ha, abbiamo, avete, hanno 5 ebbi, avesti, ebbe, avemmo, aveste, ebbero 6 avrò ecc. 8 abbia ecc. 10 abbi!, abbia!, abbiate!, abbiano!

bere 1 bevendo 2 bevuto 3 bevo ecc. 4 bevevo ecc. 5 bevvi o bevetti, bevesti 6 berrò ecc. 8 beva ecc. 9 bevessi ecc.

cadere 5 caddi, cadesti 6 cadrò ecc.

cogliere 2 colto 3 colgo, colgono 5 colsi, cogliesti 8 colga

correre 2 corso 5 corsi, corresti

cuocere 2 cotto 3 cuocio, cociamo, cuociono 5 cossi, cocesti

dare 3 do, dai, dà, diamo, date, danno 5 diedi o detti, desti 6 darò ecc. 8 dia ecc. 9 dessi ecc. 10 da'!, dai!, date!, diano!

dire 1 dicendo 2 detto 3 dico, dici, dice, diciamo, dite, dicono 4 dicevo ecc. 5 dissi, dicesti 6 dirò ecc. 8 dica, diciamo, diciate, dicano 9 dicessi ecc. 10 di'!, dica!, dite!, dicano!

dolere 3 dolgo, duoli, duole, dolgono 5 dolsi, dolesti 6 dorrò ecc. 8 dolga

dovere 3 devo o debbo, devi, deve, dobbiamo, dovete, devono o debbono 6 dovrò ecc. 8 debba, dobbiamo, dobbiate, devano o debbano

ESSERE 2 stato 3 sono, sei, è, siamo, siete, sono 4 ero, eri, era, eravamo, eravate, erano 5 fui, fosti, fu, fummo, foste, furono 6 sarò ecc. 8 sia ecc. 9 fossi, fossi, fosse, fossimo, foste, fossero 10 sii!, sia!, siate!, siano!

fare 1 facendo 2 fatto 3 faccio, fai, fa, facciamo, fate, fanno 4 facevo ecc. 5 feci, facesti 6 farò ecc. 8 faccia ecc. 9 facessi ecc. 10 fa'!, faccia!, fate!, facciano!

FINIRE 1 finendo 2 finito 3 finisco, finisci, finisce, finiamo, finite, finiscono 4 finivo, finivi, finiva, finivamo, finivate, finivano 5 finii, finisti, finì, finimmo, fineste, finirono 6 finirò, finirai, finirà, finiremo, finirete, finiranno 7 finirei, finiresti, finirebbe, finiremmo, finireste, finirebbero 8 finisca, finisca, finisca, finiamo, finiate, finiscano 9 finissi, finissi, finisse, finissimo, finiste, finissero 10 finisci!, finisca!, finite!, finiscano!

giungere 2 giunto 5 giunsi, giungesti

leggere 2 letto 5 lessi, leggesti

mettere 2 messo 5 misi, mettesti

morire 2 morto 3 muoio, muori, muore, moriamo, morite, muoiono 6 morirò o morrò ecc. 8 muoia

muovere 2 mosso 5 mossi, movesti

nascere 2 nato 5 nacqui, nascesti

nuocere 2 nuociuto 3 nuoccio, nuoci, nuoce, nociamo o nuociamo, nuocete, nuocciono 4 nuocevo ecc. 5 nocqui, nuocesti 6 nuocerò ecc. 7 nuoccia

offrire 2 offerto 3 offro 5 offersi o offrii, offristi 8 offra

parere 2 parso 3 paio, paiamo, paiono 5 parvi o parsi, paresti 6 parrò ecc. 8 paia, paiamo, paiate, paiano

xiv

PARLARE 1 parlando 2 parlato 3 parlo, parli, parla, parliamo, parlate, parlano 4 parlavo, parlavi, parlava, parlavamo, parlavate, parlavano 5 parlai, parlasti, parlò, parlammo, parlaste, parlarono 6 parlerò, parlerai, parlerà, parleremo, parlerete, parleranno 7 parlerei, parleresti, parlerebbe, parleremmo, parlereste, parlerebbero 8 parli, parli, parli, parliamo, parliate, parlino 9 parlassi, parlassi, parlasse, parlassimo, parlaste, parlassero 10 parla!, parli!, parlate!, parlino!

piacere 2 piaciuto 3 piaccio, piacciamo, piacciono 5 piacqui, piacesti 8 piacci *ecc.*

porre 1 ponendo 2 posto 3 pongo, poni, pone, poniamo, ponete, pongono 4 ponevo *ecc.* 5 posi, ponesti 6 porrò *ecc.* 8 ponga, poniamo, poniate, pongano 9 ponessi *ecc.*

potere 3 posso, puoi, può, possiamo, potete, possono 6 potrò *ecc.* 8 possa, possiamo, possiate, possano

prendere 2 preso 5 presi, prendesti

ridurre 1 riducendo 2 ridotto 3 riduco *ecc.* 4 riducevo *ecc.* 5 ridussi, riducesti 6 ridurrò *ecc.* 8 riduca *ecc.* 9 riducessi *ecc.*

riempire 1 riempiendo 3 riempio, riempi, riempie, riempiono

rimanere 2 rimasto 3 rimango, rimangono 5 rimasi, rimanesti 6 rimarrò *ecc.* 8 rimanga

rispondere 2 risposto 5 risposi, rispondesti

salire 3 salgo, sali, salgono 8 salga

sapere 3 so, sai, sa, sappiamo, sapete, sanno 5 seppi, sapesti 6 saprò *ecc.* 8 sappia *ecc.* 10 sappi!, sappia!, sappiate!, sappiano!

scrivere 2 scritto 5 scrissi, scrivesti

sedere 3 siedo, siedi, siede, siedono 8 sieda

spegnere 2 spento 3 spengo, spengono 5 spensi, spegnesti 8 spenga

stare 2 stato 3 sto, stai, sta, stiamo, state, stanno 5 stetti, stesti 6 starò *ecc.* 8 stia *ecc.* 9 stessi *ecc.* 10 sta'!, stia!, state!, stiano!

tacere 2 taciuto 3 taccio, tacciono 5 tacqui, tacesti 8 taccia

tenere 3 tengo, tieni, tiene, tengono 5 tenni, tenesti 6 terrò *ecc.* 8 tenga

trarre 1 traendo 2 tratto 3 traggo, trai, trae, traiamo, traete, traggono 4 traevo *ecc.* 5 trassi, traesti 6 trarrò *ecc.* 8 tragga 9 traessi *ecc.*

udire 3 odo, odi, ode, odono 8 oda

uscire 3 esco, esci, esce, escono 8 esca

valere 2 valso 3 valgo, valgono 5 valsi, valesti 6 varrò *ecc.* 8 valga

vedere 2 visto *o* veduto 5 vidi, vedesti 6 vedrò *ecc.*

VENDERE 1 vendendo 2 venduto 3 vendo, vendi, vende, vendiamo, vendete, vendono 4 vendevo, vendevi, vendeva, vendevamo, vendevate, vendevano 5 vendei *o* vendetti, vendesti, vendé *o* vendette, vendemmo, vendeste, venderono *o* vendettero 6 venderò, venderai, venderà, venderemo, venderete, venderanno 7 venderei, venderesti, venderebbe, venderemmo, vendereste, venderebbero 8 venda, venda, venda, vendiamo, vendiate, vendano 9 vendessi, vendessi, vendesse, vendessimo, vendeste, vendessero 10 vendi!, venda!, vendete!, vendano!

venire 2 venuto 3 vengo, vieni, viene, vengono 5 venni, venisti 6 verrò *ecc.* 8 venga

vivere 2 vissuto 5 vissi, vivesti

volere 3 voglio, vuoi, vuole, vogliamo, volete, vogliono 5 volli, volesti 6 vorrò *ecc.* 8 voglia *ecc.* 10 vogli!, voglia!, vogliate!, vogliano!

ENGLISH VERB FORMS

present	pt	pp	present	pt	pp
arise	arose	arisen	feed	fed	fed
awake	awoke	awoken	feel	felt	felt
be (am, is, are; being)	was, were	been	fight	fought	fought
			find	found	found
bear	bore	born(e)	flee	fled	fled
beat	beat	beaten	fling	flung	flung
become	became	become	fly	flew	flown
begin	began	begun	forbid	forbade	forbidden
bend	bent	bent	forecast	forecast	forecast
bet	bet, betted	bet, betted	forget	forgot	forgotten
			forgive	forgave	forgiven
bid (at auction, cards)	bid	bid	forsake	forsook	forsaken
			freeze	froze	frozen
bid (say)	bade	bidden	get	got	got, (US) gotten
bind	bound	bound			
bite	bit	bitten	give	gave	given
bleed	bled	bled	go (goes)	went	gone
blow	blew	blown	grind	ground	ground
break	broke	broken	grow	grew	grown
breed	bred	bred	hang	hung	hung
bring	brought	brought	hang (execute)	hanged	hanged
build	built	built	have (has; having)	had	had
burn	burnt, burned	burnt, burned			
			hear	heard	heard
burst	burst	burst	hide	hid	hidden
buy	bought	bought	hit	hit	hit
can	could	(been able)	hold	held	held
cast	cast	cast	hurt	hurt	hurt
catch	caught	caught	keep	kept	kept
choose	chose	chosen	kneel	knelt, kneeled	knelt, kneeled
cling	clung	clung			
come	came	come	know	knew	known
cost	cost	cost	lay	laid	laid
cost (work out price of)	costed	costed	lead	led	led
			lean	leant, leaned	leant, leaned
creep	crept	crept			
cut	cut	cut	leap	leapt, leaped	leapt, leaped
deal	dealt	dealt			
dig	dug	dug	learn	learnt, learned	learnt, learned
do (does)	did	done			
draw	drew	drawn	leave	left	left
dream	dreamed, dreamt	dreamed, dreamt	lend	lent	lent
			let	let	let
			lie (lying)	lay	lain
drink	drank	drunk	light	lit, lighted	lit, lighted
drive	drove	driven			
dwell	dwelt	dwelt			
eat	ate	eaten	lose	lost	lost
fall	fell	fallen	make	made	made

present	pt	pp	present	pt	pp
may	might	—	spell	spelt, spelled	spelt, spelled
mean	meant	meant			
meet	met	met	spend	spent	spent
mistake	mistook	mistaken	spill	spilt, spilled	spilt, spilled
mow	mowed	mown, mowed			
			spin	spun	spun
must	(had to)	(had to)	spit	spat	spat
pay	paid	paid	split	split	split
put	put	put	spoil	spoiled, spoilt	spoiled, spoilt
quit	quit, quitted	quit, quitted			
			spread	spread	spread
read	read	read	spring	sprang	sprung
rid	rid	rid	stand	stood	stood
ride	rode	ridden	steal	stole	stolen
ring	rang	rung	stick	stuck	stuck
rise	rose	risen	sting	stung	stung
run	ran	run	stink	stank	stunk
saw	sawed	sawed, sawn	stride	strode	stridden
			strike	struck	struck, stricken
say	said	said			
see	saw	seen	strive	strove	striven
seek	sought	sought	swear	swore	sworn
sell	sold	sold	sweep	swept	swept
send	sent	sent	swell	swelled	swollen, swelled
set	set	set			
sew	sewed	sewn	swim	swam	swum
shake	shook	shaken	swing	swung	swung
shear	sheared	shorn, sheared	take	took	taken
			teach	taught	taught
shed	shed	shed	tear	tore	torn
shine	shone	shone	tell	told	told
shoot	shot	shot	think	thought	thought
show	showed	shown	throw	threw	thrown
shrink	shrank	shrunk	thrust	thrust	thrust
shut	shut	shut	tread	trod	trodden
sing	sang	sung	wake	woke, waked	woken, waked
sink	sank	sunk			
sit	sat	sat			
slay	slew	slain	wear	wore	worn
sleep	slept	slept	weave	wove, weaved	woven, weaved
slide	slid	slid			
sling	slung	slung	wed	wedded, wed	wedded, wed
slit	slit	slit			
smell	smelt, smelled	smelt, smelled			
			weep	wept	wept
sow	sowed	sown, sowed	win	won	won
			wind	wound	wound
speak	spoke	spoken	wring	wrung	wrung
speed	sped, speeded	sped, speeded	write	wrote	written

month; **pagato a ore** paid by the hour; **vendere qc a 2 euro il chilo** to sell sth at 2 euros a *o* per kilo

abbagli'ante [abbaʎ'ʎante] *ag* dazzling; **abbaglianti** *smpl* (*Aut*): **accendere gli abbaglianti** to put one's headlights on full (BRIT) *o* high (US) beam

abbagli'are [abbaʎ'ʎare] *vt* to dazzle; (*illudere*) to delude

abbai'are *vi* to bark

abbando'nare *vt* to leave, abandon, desert; (*trascurare*) to neglect; (*rinunciare a*) to abandon, give up; **abbandonarsi** *vpr* to let o.s. go; **abbandonarsi a** (*ricordi, vizio*) to give o.s. up to

abbas'sare *vt* to lower; (*radio*) to turn down; **abbassarsi** *vpr* (*chinarsi*) to stoop; (*livello, sole*) to go down; (*fig: umiliarsi*) to demean o.s.; **~ i fari** (*Aut*) to dip *o* dim (US) one's lights

ab'basso *escl* **~ il re!** down with the king!

abbas'tanza [abbas'tantsa] *av* (*a sufficienza*) enough; (*alquanto*) quite, rather, fairly; **non è ~ furbo** he's not shrewd enough; **un vino ~ dolce** quite a sweet wine; **averne ~ di qn/qc** to have had enough of sb/sth

ab'battere *vt* (*muro, casa*) to pull down; (*ostacolo*) to knock down; (*albero*) to fell; (: *vento*) to bring down; (*bestie da macello*) to slaughter; (*cane, cavallo*) to destroy, put down; (*selvaggina, aereo*) to shoot down; (*fig: malattia, disgrazia*) to lay low; **abbattersi** *vpr* (*avvilirsi*) to lose heart; **abbat'tuto, -a** *ag* (*fig*) depressed

abba'zia [abbat'tsia] *sf* abbey

'abbia *vb vedi* **avere**

abbi'ente *ag* well-to-do, well-off; **abbienti** *smpl* **gli abbienti** the well-to-do

abbiglia'mento [abbiʎʎa'mento] *sm* dress *no pl*; (*indumenti*) clothes *pl*; (*industria*) clothing industry

abbi'nare *vt* **~ (a)** to combine (with)

abboc'care *vi* (*pesce*) to bite; (*tubi*) to join; **~ (all'amo)** (*fig*) to swallow the bait

abbona'mento *sm* subscription; (*alle ferrovie ecc*) season ticket; **fare l'~** to take out a subscription (*o* season ticket)

abbo'narsi *vpr* **~ a un giornale** to take out a subscription to a newspaper; **~ al teatro/alle ferrovie** to take out a season ticket for the theatre/the train

abbon'dante *ag* abundant, plentiful; (*giacca*) roomy

abbon'danza [abbon'dantsa] *sf* abundance; plenty

abbor'dabile *ag* (*persona*) approachable; (*prezzo*) reasonable

---

a

A *abbr* (= *autostrada*) ≈ M (*motorway*)

 PAROLA CHIAVE

a (*a + il* = **al**, *a + lo* = **allo**, *a + l'* = **all'**, *a + la* = **alla**, *a + i* = **ai**, *a + gli* = **agli**, *a + le* = **alle**) *prep*

1 (*stato in luogo*) at; (: *in*) in; **essere alla stazione** to be at the station; **essere a casa/a scuola/a Roma** to be at home/at school/in Rome; **è a 10 km da qui** it's 10 km from here, it's 10 km away

2 (*moto a luogo*) to; **andare a casa/a scuola** to go home/to school

3 (*tempo*) at; (*epoca, stagione*) in; **alle cinque** at five (o'clock); **a mezzanotte/Natale** at midnight/Christmas; **al mattino** in the morning; **a maggio/primavera** in May/spring; **a cinquant'anni** at fifty (years of age); **a domani!** see you tomorrow!

4 (*complemento di termine*) to; **dare qc a qn** to give sth to sb

5 (*mezzo, modo*) with, by; **a piedi/cavallo** on foot/horseback; **fatto a mano** made by hand, handmade; **una barca a motore** a motorboat; **a uno a uno** one by one; **all'italiana** the Italian way, in the Italian fashion

6 (*rapporto*) a, per; (: *con prezzi*) at; **prendo 850 euro al mese** I get 850 euros a *o* per

abbotto'nare vt to button up, do up

abbracci'are [abbrat'tʃare] vt to embrace; (persona) to hug, embrace; (professione) to take up; (contenere) to include; **abbracciarsi** vpr to hug o embrace (one another); **ab'braccio** sm hug, embrace

abbrevi'are vt to shorten; (parola) to abbreviate

abbreviazi'one [abbrevjat'tsjone] sf abbreviation

abbron'zante [abbron'dzante] ag tanning, sun cpd

abbronzarsi vpr to tan, get a tan

abbron'zato, -a [abbron'dzato] ag (sun)tanned

abbrusto'lire vt (pane) to toast; (caffè) to roast; **abbrustolirsi** vpr to toast; (fig: al sole) to soak up the sun

abbuf'farsi vpr (fam): ~ (di qc) to stuff o.s. (with sth)

abdi'care vi to abdicate; ~ a to give up, renounce

a'bete sm fir (tree); **abete rosso** spruce

'abile ag (idoneo): ~ (a qc/a fare qc) fit (for sth/to do sth); (capace) able; (astuto) clever; (accorto) skilful; ~ al servizio militare fit for military service; **abilità** sf inv ability; cleverness; skill

a'bisso sm abyss, gulf

abi'tante sm/f inhabitant

abi'tare vt to live in, dwell in ▷ vi ~ in campagna/a Roma to live in the country/in Rome; **dove abita?** where do you live?; **abitazi'one** sf residence; house

'abito sm dress no pl; (da uomo) suit; (da donna) dress; (abitudine, disposizione, Rel) habit; **abiti** smpl (vestiti) clothes; **in ~ da sera** in evening dress

abitu'ale ag usual, habitual; (cliente) regular

abitual'mente av usually, normally

abitu'are vt ~ qn a to get sb used o accustomed to; **abituarsi a** to get used to, accustom o.s. to

abitudi'nario, -a ag of fixed habits ▷ sm/f regular customer

abi'tudine sf habit; **aver l'~ di fare qc** to be in the habit of doing sth; **d'~** usually; **per ~** from o out of habit

abo'lire vt to abolish; (Dir) to repeal

abor'tire vi (Med) to miscarry, have a miscarriage; (: deliberatamente) to have an abortion; (fig) to miscarry, fail; **a'borto** sm miscarriage; abortion

ABS [abiɛse] sigla m (= Anti-Blockier System) ABS

'abside sf apse

abu'sare vi ~ di to abuse, misuse; (alcool) to take to excess; (approfittare, violare) to take advantage of

abu'sivo, -a ag unauthorized, unlawful; **(occupante)** ~ (di una casa) squatter

▨ Attenzione! In inglese esiste la parola abusive che però vuol dire ingiurioso.

a.C. av abbr (= avanti Cristo) B.C.

a'cacia, -cie [a'katʃa] sf (Bot) acacia

ac'cadde vb vedi **accadere**

acca'demia sf (società) learned society; (scuola: d'arte, militare) academy

acca'dere vb impers to happen, occur

accal'dato ag hot

accalo'rarsi vpr (fig) to get excited

accampa'mento sm camp

accamparsi vpr to camp

acca'nirsi vpr (infierire) to rage; (ostinarsi) to persist; **acca'nito, -a** ag (odio, gelosia) fierce, bitter; (lavoratore) assiduous, dogged; (fumatore) inveterate

ac'canto av near, nearby; ~ a prep near, beside, close to

accanto'nare vt (problema) to shelve; (somma) to set aside

accappa'toio sm bathrobe

accarez'zare [akkaret'tsare] vt to caress, stroke, fondle; (fig) to toy with

acca'sarsi vpr to set up house; to get married

accasci'arsi [akkaʃ'ʃarsi] vpr to collapse; (fig) to lose heart

accat'tone, -a sm/f beggar

accaval'lare vt (gambe) to cross

acce'care [attʃe'kare] vt to blind ▷ vi to go blind

ac'cedere [at'tʃedere] vi ~ a to enter; (richiesta) to grant, accede to

accele'rare [attʃele'rare] vt to speed up ▷ vi (Aut) to accelerate; ~ il passo to quicken one's pace; **accelera'tore** sm (Aut) accelerator

ac'cendere [at'tʃɛndere] vt (fuoco, sigaretta) to light; (luce, televisione) to put on, switch on, turn on; (Aut: motore) to switch on; (Comm: conto) to open; (fig: suscitare) to inflame, stir up; **ha da ~?** have you got a light?; **non riesco ad ~ il riscaldamento** I can't turn the heating on; **accen'dino, accendi'sigaro** sm (cigarette) lighter

accen'nare [attʃen'nare] vt (Mus) to pick out the notes of; to hum ▷ vi ~ a (fig: alludere a) to hint at; (: far atto di) to make as if; ~ **un saluto** (con la mano) to make as if to wave; (col capo) to half nod; **accenna a piovere** it looks as if it's going to rain

ac'cenno [at'tʃenno] sm (cenno) sign; nod; (allusione) hint

accensi'one [attʃen'sjone] sf (vedi verbo) lighting; switching on; opening; (Aut) ignition

ac'cento [at't∫ɛnto] *sm* accent; (*Fonetica*, *fig*) stress; (*inflessione*) tone (of voice)

accentu'are [att∫entu'are] *vt* to stress, emphasize; **accentuarsi** *vpr* to become more noticeable

accerchi'are [att∫er'kjare] *vt* to surround, encircle

accerta'mento [att∫erta'mento] *sm* check; assessment

accer'tare [att∫er'tare] *vt* to ascertain; (*verificare*) to check; (*reddito*) to assess; **accertarsi** *vpr* **accertarsi (di)** to make sure (of)

ac'ceso, -a [at't∫eso] *pp di* **accendere** ▷ *ag* lit; on; open; (*colore*) bright

acces'sibile [att∫es'sibile] *ag* (*luogo*) accessible; (*persona*) approachable; (*prezzo*) reasonable

ac'cesso [at't∫ɛsso] *sm* (*anche Inform*) access; (*Med*) attack, fit; (*impulso violento*) fit, outburst

accessori *smpl* accessories

ac'cetta [at't∫etta] *sf* hatchet

accet'tabile [att∫et'tabile] *ag* acceptable

accet'tare [att∫et'tare] *vt* to accept; **accettate carte di credito?** do you accept credit cards?; **~ di fare qc** to agree to do sth; **accettazi'one** *sf* acceptance; (*locale di servizio pubblico*) reception; **accettazione bagagli** (*Aer*) check-in (desk)

acchiap'pare [akkjap'pare] *vt* to catch

acciaie'ria [att∫aje'ria] *sf* steelworks *sg*

acci'aio [at't∫ajo] *sm* steel

acciden'tato, -a [att∫iden'tato] *ag* (*terreno ecc*) uneven

accigli'ato, -a [att∫iʎ'ʎato] *ag* frowning

ac'cingersi [at't∫indʒersi] *vpr* **~ a fare qc** to be about to do sth

acciuf'fare [att∫uf'fare] *vt* to seize, catch

acci'uga, -ghe [at't∫uga] *sf* anchovy

ac'cludere *vt* to enclose

accocco'larsi *vpr* to crouch

accogli'ente [akkoʎ'ʎɛnte] *ag* welcoming, friendly

ac'cogliere [ak'koʎʎere] *vt* (*ricevere*) to receive; (*dare il benvenuto*) to welcome; (*approvare*) to agree to, accept; (*contenere*) to hold, accommodate

ac'colgo *ecc vb vedi* **accogliere**

ac'colsi *ecc vb vedi* **accogliere**

accoltel'lare *vt* to knife, stab

accomoda'mento *sm* agreement, settlement

accomo'dante *ag* accommodating

accomo'darsi *vpr* (*sedersi*) to sit down; (*entrare*) to come in; **s'accomodi!** (*venga avanti*) come in!; (*si sieda*) take a seat!

accompagna'mento [akkompaɲɲa'mento] *sm* (*Mus*) accompaniment

accompa'gnare [akkompaɲ'ɲare] *vt* to accompany, come o go with; (*Mus*) to accompany; (*unire*) to couple; **~ la porta** to close the door gently

accompagna'tore, -trice *sm/f* companion; **~ turistico** courier

acconcia'tura [akkont∫a'tura] *sf* hairstyle

accondiscen'dente [akkondi∫∫en'dɛnte] *ag* affable

acconsen'tire *vi* **~ (a)** to agree o consent (to)

acconten'tare *vt* to satisfy; **accontentarsi** *vpr* **accontentarsi di** to be satisfied with, content o.s. with

ac'conto *sm* part payment; **pagare una somma in ~** to pay a sum of money as a deposit

acco'rato, -a *ag* heartfelt

accorci'are [akkor't∫are] *vt* to shorten; **accorciarsi** *vpr* to become shorter

accor'dare *vt* to reconcile; (*colori*) to match; (*Mus*) to tune; (*Ling*): **~ qc con qc** to make sth agree with sth; (*Dir*) to grant; **accordarsi** *vpr* to agree, come to an agreement; (*colori*) to match

ac'cordo *sm* agreement; (*armonia*) harmony; (*Mus*) chord; **essere d'~** to agree; **andare d'~** to get on well together; **d'~!** all right!, agreed!; **accordo commerciale** trade agreement

ac'corgersi [ak'kordʒersi] *vpr* **~ di** to notice; (*fig*) to realize

ac'correre *vi* to run up

ac'corto, -a *pp di* **accorgersi** ▷ *ag* shrewd; **stare ~** to be on one's guard

accos'tare *vt* (*avvicinare*): **~ qc a** to bring sth near to, put sth near to; (*avvicinarsi a*) to approach; (*socchiudere: imposte*) to half-close; (: *porta*) to leave ajar ▷ *vi* (*Naut*) to come alongside; **accostarsi** *vpr* **accostarsi a** to draw near, approach; (*fig*) to support

accredi'tare *vt* (*notizia*) to confirm the truth of; (*Comm*) to credit; (*diplomatico*) to accredit

ac'credito *sm* (*Comm: atto*) crediting; (: *effetto*) credit

accucci'arsi [akkut't∫arsi] *vpr* (*cane*) to lie down

accu'dire *vt* (*anche: vi* **~ a**) to attend to

accumu'lare *vt* to accumulate; **accumularsi** *vpr* to accumulate; (*Finanza*) to accrue

accu'rato, -a *ag* (*diligente*) careful; (*preciso*) accurate

ac'cusa *sf* accusation; (*Dir*) charge; **la pubblica ~** the prosecution

accu'sare *vt* **~ qn di qc** to accuse sb of sth; (*Dir*) to charge sb with sth; **~ ricevuta di** (*Comm*) to acknowledge receipt of

accusa'tore, -'trice *sm/f* accuser ▷ *sm* (*Dir*) prosecutor

a'cerbo, -a [a'tʃerbo] *ag* bitter; (*frutta*) sour, unripe; (*persona*) immature

'acero ['atʃero] *sm* maple

a'cerrimo, -a [a'tʃerrimo] *ag* very fierce

a'ceto [a'tʃeto] *sm* vinegar

ace'tone [atʃe'tone] *sm* nail varnish remover

A.C.I. ['atʃi] *sigla m* = **Automobile Club d'Italia**

'acido, -a ['atʃido] *ag* (*sapore*) acid, sour; (*Chim*) acid ▷ *sm* (*Chim*) acid

'acino ['atʃino] *sm* berry; **acino d'uva** grape

'acne *sf* acne

'acqua *sf* water; (*pioggia*) rain; **acque** *sfpl* (*di mare, fiume ecc*) waters; **fare ~** (*Naut*) to leak, take in water; **~ in bocca!** mum's the word!; **acqua corrente** running water; **acqua dolce/salata** fresh/salt water; **acqua minerale/potabile/tonica** mineral/drinking/tonic water; **acque termali** thermal waters

a'cquaio *sm* sink

acqua'ragia [akkwa'radʒa] *sf* turpentine

a'cquario *sm* aquarium; (*dello zodiaco*): **A~** Aquarius

acquascooter [akkwas'kuter] *sm inv* Jet Ski®

ac'quatico, -a, -ci, -che *ag* aquatic; (*Sport, Scienza*) water *cpd*

acqua'vite *sf* brandy

acquaz'zone [akkwat'tsone] *sm* cloudburst, heavy shower

acque'dotto *sm* aqueduct; waterworks *pl*, water system

acque'rello *sm* watercolour

acqui'rente *sm/f* purchaser, buyer

acquis'tare *vt* to purchase, buy; (*fig*) to gain; **a'cquisto** *sm* purchase; **fare acquisti** to go shopping

acquo'lina *sf* **far venire l'~ in bocca a qn** to make sb's mouth water

a'crobata, -i, -e *sm/f* acrobat

a'culeo *sm* (*Zool*) sting; (*Bot*) prickle

a'cume *sm* acumen, perspicacity

a'custico, -a, ci, che *ag* acoustic ▷ *sf* (*scienza*) acoustics *sg*; (*di una sala*) acoustics *pl*; **cornetto ~** ear trumpet; **apparecchio ~** hearing aid

a'cuto, -a *ag* (*appuntito*) sharp, pointed; (*suono, voce*) shrill, piercing; (*Mat, Ling, Med*) acute; (*Mus*) high-pitched; (*fig: dolore,*

desiderio) intense; (*: perspicace*) acute, keen

a'dagio [a'dadʒo] *av* slowly ▷ *sm* (*Mus*) adagio; (*proverbio*) adage, saying

adatta'mento *sm* adaptation

adat'tare *vt* to adapt; (*sistemare*) to fit; **adattarsi** *vpr* **adattarsi (a)** (*ambiente, tempi*) to adapt (to); (*essere adatto*) to be suitable (for)

a'datto, -a *ag* **~ (a)** suitable (for), right (for)

addebi'tare *vt* **~ qc a qn** to debit sb with sth

ad'debito *sm* (*Comm*) debit

adden'tare *vt* to bite into

adden'trarsi *vpr* **~ in** to penetrate, go into

addestra'mento *sm* training

addes'trare *vt* to train

ad'detto, -a *ag* **~ a** (*persona*) assigned to; (*oggetto*) intended for ▷ *sm* employee; (*funzionario*) attaché; **gli addetti ai lavori** authorized personnel; (*fig*) those in the know; **addetto commerciale** commercial attaché; **addetto stampa** press attaché

ad'dio *sm, escl* goodbye, farewell

addirit'tura *av* (*veramente*) really, absolutely; (*perfino*) even; (*direttamente*) directly, right away

addi'tare *vt* to point out; (*fig*) to expose

addi'tivo *sm* additive

addizi'one *sf* addition

addob'bare *vt* to decorate; **ad'dobbo** *sm* decoration

addolo'rare *vt* to pain, grieve; **addolorarsi (per)** to be distressed (by)

addolo'rato, -a *ag* distressed, upset; **l'Addolorata** (*Rel*) Our Lady of Sorrows

ad'dome *sm* abdomen

addomi'nale *ag* abdominal; (**muscoli** *mpl*) **addominali** stomach muscles

addormen'tare *vt* to put to sleep; **addormentarsi** *vpr* to fall asleep, go to sleep

ad'dosso *av* on; **mettersi ~ il cappotto** to put one's coat on; **~ a** (*sopra*) on; (*molto vicino*) right next to; **stare ~ a qn** (*fig*) to breathe down sb's neck; **dare ~ a qn** (*fig*) to attack sb

adeguarsi *vpr* to adapt

adegu'ato, -a *ag* adequate; (*conveniente*) suitable; (*equo*) fair

a'dempiere *vt* to fulfil, carry out

ade'rente *ag* adhesive; (*vestito*) close-fitting ▷ *sm/f* follower

ade'rire *vi* (*stare attaccato*) to adhere, stick; **~ a** to adhere to, stick to; (*fig: società, partito*) to join; (*: opinione*) to support; (*richiesta*) to agree to

adesi'one *sf* adhesion; (*fig*) agreement,

acceptance; **ade'sivo, -a** ag, sm adhesive

a'desso av (ora) now; (or ora, poco fa) just now; (tra poco) any moment now

adia'cente [adja'tʃɛnte] ag adjacent

adi'bire vt (usare): **~ qc a** to turn sth into

adole'scente [adoleʃ'ʃɛnte] ag, sm/f adolescent

adope'rare vt to use

ado'rare vt to adore; (Rel) to adore, worship

adot'tare vt to adopt; (decisione, provvedimenti) to pass; **adot'tivo, -a** ag (genitori) adoptive; (figlio, patria) adopted; **adozi'one** sf adoption; **adozione a distanza** child sponsorship

adri'atico, -a, -ci, -che ag Adriatic ▷ sm **l'A~, il mare A~** the Adriatic, the Adriatic Sea

adu'lare vt to adulate, flatter

a'dultero, -a ag adulterous ▷ sm/f adulterer (adulteress)

a'dulto, -a ag adult; (fig) mature ▷ sm adult, grown-up

a'ereo, -a ag air cpd; (radice) aerial ▷ sm aerial; (aeroplano) plane; **aereo da caccia** fighter (plane); **aereo di linea** airliner; **aereo a reazione** jet (plane); **ae'robica** sf aerobics sg; **aero'nautica** sf (scienza) aeronautics sg; **aeronautica militare** air force

aero'porto sm airport; **all'~ per favore** to the airport, please

aero'sol sm inv aerosol

'afa sf sultriness

af'fabile ag affable

affaccen'dato, -a [affattʃen'dato] ag (persona) busy

affacci'arsi [affat'tʃarsi] vpr **~ (a)** to appear (at)

affa'mato, -a ag starving; (fig): **~ (di)** eager (for)

affan'noso, -a ag (respiro) difficult; (fig) troubled, anxious

af'fare sm (faccenda) matter, affair; (Comm) piece of business, (business) deal; (occasione) bargain; (Dir) case; (fam: cosa) thing; **affari** smpl (Comm) business sg; **Ministro degli Affari esteri** Foreign Secretary (BRIT), Secretary of State (US)

affasci'nante [affaʃʃi'nante] ag fascinating

affasci'nare [affaʃʃi'nare] vt to bewitch; (fig) to charm, fascinate

affati'care vt to tire; **affaticarsi** vpr (durar fatica) to tire o.s. out; **affati'cato, -a** ag tired

af'fatto av completely; **non ... ~** not ... at all; **niente ~** not at all

affer'mare vt (dichiarare) to maintain,

affirm; **affermarsi** vpr to assert o.s., make one's name known; **affer'mato, -a** ag established, well-known; **affermazi'one** sf affirmation, assertion; (successo) achievement

affer'rare vt to seize, grasp; (fig: idea) to grasp; **afferrarsi** vpr **afferrarsi a** to cling to

affet'tare vt (tagliare a fette) to slice; (ostentare) to affect

affetta'trice [affetta'tritʃe] sf meat slicer

affet'tivo, -a ag emotional, affective

af'fetto sm affection; **affettu'oso, -a** ag affectionate

affezio'narsi [affettsjo'narsi] vpr **~ a** to grow fond of

affezio'nato, -a [affettsjo'nato] ag **~ a qn/qc** fond of sb/sth; (attaccato) attached to sb/sth

affia'tato, -a ag **essere molto affiatati** to get on very well

affibbi'are vt (fig: dare) to give

affi'dabile ag reliable

affida'mento sm (Dir: di bambino) custody; (fiducia): **fare ~ su qn** to rely on sb; **non dà nessun ~** he's not to be trusted

affi'dare vt **~ qc o qn a qn** to entrust sth o sb to sb; **affidarsi** vpr **affidarsi a** to place one's trust in

affi'lare vt to sharpen

affi'lato, -a ag (gen) sharp; (volto, naso) thin

affinché [affin'ke] cong in order that, so that

affit'tare vt (dare in affitto) to let, rent (out); (prendere in affitto) to rent; **af'fitto** sm rent; (contratto) lease

af'fliggere [af'fliddʒere] vt to torment; **affliggersi** vpr to grieve

af'flissi ecc vb vedi **affliggere**

afflosci'arsi [affloʃ'ʃarsi] vpr to go limp

afflu'ente sm tributary

affo'gare vt, vi to drown

affol'lare vt to crowd; **affollarsi** vpr to crowd; **affol'lato, -a** ag crowded

affon'dare vt to sink

affran'care vt to free, liberate; (Amm) to redeem; (lettera) to stamp; (: meccanicamente) to frank (BRIT), meter (US)

af'fresco, -schi sm fresco

affrettarsi vpr to hurry; **~ a fare qc** to hurry o hasten to do sth

affret'tato, -a ag (veloce: passo, ritmo) quick, fast; (frettoloso: decisione) hurried, hasty; (: lavoro) rushed

affron'tare vt (pericolo ecc) to face; (nemico) to confront; **affrontarsi** vpr (reciproco) to come to blows

affumi'cato, -a *ag* (*prosciutto, aringa ecc*) smoked

affuso'lato, -a *ag* tapering

Af'ganistan *sm* **I'~** Afghanistan

a'foso, -a *ag* sultry, close

'Africa *sf* **I'~** Africa; **afri'cano, -a** *ag, sm/f* African

a'genda [a'dʒɛnda] *sf* diary

Attenzione! In inglese esiste la parola *agenda* che però vuol dire *ordine del giorno*.

a'gente [a'dʒɛnte] *sm* agent; **agente di cambio** stockbroker; **agente di polizia** police officer; **agente segreto** secret agent; **agen'zia** *sf* agency; (*succursale*) branch; **agenzia immobiliare** estate agent's (office) (BRIT), real estate office (US); **agenzia di collocamento/stampa** employment/press agency; **agenzia viaggi** travel agency

agevo'lare [adʒevo'lare] *vt* to facilitate, make easy

agevolazi'one [adʒevolat'tsjone] *sf* (*facilitazione economica*) facility; **agevolazione di pagamento** payment on easy terms; **agevolazioni creditizie** credit facilities; **agevolazioni fiscali** tax concessions

a'gevole [a'dʒevole] *ag* easy; (*strada*) smooth

agganci'are [aggan'tʃare] *vt* to hook up; (*Ferr*) to couple

ag'geggio [ad'dʒeddʒo] *sm* gadget, contraption

agget'tivo [addʒet'tivo] *sm* adjective

agghiacci'ante [aggjat'tʃante] *ag* chilling

aggior'nare [addʒor'nare] *vt* (*opera, manuale*) to bring up-to-date; (*seduta ecc*) to postpone; **aggiornarsi** *vpr* to bring (o keep) o.s. up-to-date; **aggior'nato, -a** *ag* up-to-date

aggi'rare [addʒi'rare] *vt* to go round; (*fig: ingannare*) to trick; **aggirarsi** *vpr* to wander about; **il prezzo s'aggira sul milione** the price is around the million mark

aggi'ungere [ad'dʒundʒere] *vt* to add

aggi'unsi *ecc* [ad'dʒunsi] *vb* vedi **aggiungere**

aggius'tare [addʒus'tare] *vt* (*accomodare*) to mend, repair; (*riassettare*) to adjust; (*fig: lite*) to settle

aggrap'parsi *vpr* **~ a** to cling to

aggra'vare *vt* (*aumentare*) to increase; (*appesantire: anche fig*) to weigh down, make heavy; (*pena*) to make worse; **aggravarsi** *vpr* to worsen, become worse

aggre'dire *vt* to attack, assault

aggressi'one *sf* aggression; (*atto*) attack, assault

aggres'sivo, -a *ag* aggressive

aggres'sore *sm* aggressor, attacker

aggrot'tare *vt* **~ le sopracciglia** to frown

aggrovigliarsi *vpr* (*fig*) to become complicated

aggu'ato *sm* trap; (*imboscata*) ambush; **tendere un ~ a qn** to set a trap for sb

agguer'rito, -a *ag* fierce

agi'ato, -a [a'dʒato] *ag* (*vita*) easy; (*persona*) well-off, well-to-do

'agile ['adʒile] *ag* agile, nimble

'agio ['adʒo] *sm* ease, comfort; **mettersi a proprio ~** to make o.s. at home o comfortable; **agi** *smpl* comforts; **mettersi a proprio ~** to make o.s. at home o comfortable; **dare ~ a qn di fare qc** to give sb the chance of doing sth

a'gire [a'dʒire] *vi* to act; (*esercitare un'azione*) to take effect; (*Tecn*) to work, function; **~ contro qn** (*Dir*) to take action against sb

agi'tare [adʒi'tare] *vt* (*bottiglia*) to shake; (*mano, fazzoletto*) to wave; (*fig: turbare*) to disturb; (: *incitare*) to stir (up); (: *dibattere*) to discuss; **agitarsi** *vpr* (*mare*) to be rough; (*malato, dormitore*) to toss and turn; (*bambino*) to fidget; (*emozionarsi*) to get upset; (*Pol*) to agitate; **agi'tato, -a** *ag* rough; restless; fidgety; upset, perturbed

'aglio ['aʎʎo] *sm* garlic

a'gnello [aɲ'ɲɛllo] *sm* lamb

'ago (*pl* **'aghi**) *sm* needle

ago'nistico, -a, -ci, -che *ag* athletic; (*fig*) competitive

agopun'tura *sf* acupuncture

a'gosto *sm* August

a'grario, -a *ag* agrarian, agricultural; (*riforma*) land *cpd*

a'gricolo, -a *ag* agricultural, farm *cpd*; **agricol'tore** *sm* farmer; **agricol'tura** *sf* agriculture, farming

agri'foglio [agri'fɔʎʎo] *sm* holly

agritu'rismo *sm* farm holidays *pl*

agrodolce *ag* bittersweet; (*salsa*) sweet and sour

a'grume *sm* (*spesso al pl: pianta*) citrus; (: *frutto*) citrus fruit

a'guzzo, -a [a'guttso] *ag* sharp

'ahi *escl* (*dolore*) ouch!

'Aia *sf* **I'~** the Hague

'aids *abbr m o f* Aids

airbag *sm inv* air bag

ai'rone *sm* heron

aiu'ola *sf* flower bed

aiu'tante *sm/f* assistant ▷ *sm* (*Mil*) adjutant; (*Naut*) master-at-arms; **aiutante di campo** aide-de-camp

aiu'tare *vt* to help; **~ qn (a fare)** to help sb

(to do); **aiutarsi** *vpr* to help each other; **~ qn in qc/a fare qc** to help sb with sth/to do sth; **può aiutarmi?** can you help me?

ai'uto *sm* help, assistance, aid; *(aiutante)* assistant; **venire in ~ di qn** to come to sb's aid; **aiuto chirurgo** assistant surgeon

'ala *(pl* **'ali)** *sf* wing; **fare ~** to fall back, make way; **ala destra/sinistra** *(Sport)* right/left wing

ala'bastro *sm* alabaster

a'lano *sm* Great Dane

'alba *sf* dawn

alba'nese *ag, sm/f, sm* Albanian

Alba'nia *sf* **l'~** Albania

albe'rato, -a *ag (viale, piazza)* lined with trees, tree-lined

al'bergo, -ghi *sm* hotel; **albergo della gioventù** youth hostel

'albero *sm* tree; *(Naut)* mast; *(Tecn)* shaft; **albero genealogico** family tree; **albero a gomiti** crankshaft; **albero maestro** mainmast; **albero di Natale** Christmas tree; **albero di trasmissione** transmission shaft

albi'cocca, -che *sf* apricot

'album *sm* album; **album da disegno** sketch book

al'bume *sm* albumen

'alce ['altʃe] *sm* elk

'alcol *sm inv* = **alcool**

al'colico, -a, -ci, -che *ag* alcoholic ▷ *sm* alcoholic drink

alcoliz'zato, -a [alcolid'dzato] *sm/f* alcoholic

'alcool *sm inv* alcohol

al'cuno, -a *(det: dav sm:* **alcun** + *C, V,* **alcuno** + *s impura, gn, pn, ps, x, z; dav sf:* **alcuna** + *C,* **alcun'** +*V) det (nessuno):* **non ... ~** no, not any; **alcuni, e** *det pl* some, a few; **non c'è alcuna fretta** there's no hurry, there isn't any hurry; **senza alcun riguardo** without any consideration ▷ *pron pl* **alcuni, e** some, a few

alfa'betico, -a, ci, che *ag* alphabetical

alfa'beto *sm* alphabet

'alga, -ghe *sf* seaweed *no pl,* alga

'algebra ['aldʒebra] *sf* algebra

Alge'ria [aldʒe'ria] *sf* **l'~** Algeria

alge'rino, -a [aldʒe'rino] *ag, sm/f* Algerian

ali'ante *sm (Aer)* glider

'alibi *sm inv* alibi

a'lice [a'litʃe] *sf* anchovy

ali'eno, -a *ag (avverso):* **~ (da)** opposed (to), averse (to) ▷ *sm/f* alien

alimen'tare *vt* to feed; *(Tecn)* to feed; to supply; *(fig)* to sustain ▷ *ag* food *cpd*; **alimentari** *smpl* foodstuffs; *(anche:*

negozio di alimentari) grocer's shop; **alimentazi'one** *sf* feeding; supplying; sustaining; *(gli alimenti)* diet

a'liquota *sf* share; *(d'imposta)* rate; **aliquota d'imposta** tax rate

alis'cafo *sm* hydrofoil

'alito *sm* breath

all. *abbr (= allegato)* encl.

allaccia'mento [allattʃa'mento] *sm (Tecn)* connection

allacci'are [allat'tʃare] *vt (scarpe)* to tie, lace (up); *(cintura)* to do up, fasten; *(luce, gas)* to connect; *(amicizia)* to form

allaccia'tura [allattʃa'tura] *sf* fastening

alla'gare *vt* to flood; **allagarsi** *vpr* to flood

allar'gare *vt* to widen; *(vestito)* to let out; *(aprire)* to open; *(fig: dilatare)* to extend; **allargarsi** *vpr (gen)* to widen; *(scarpe, pantaloni)* to stretch; *(fig: problema, fenomeno)* to spread

allar'mare *vt* to alarm

al'larme *sm* alarm; **allarme aereo** air-raid warning

allat'tare *vt* to feed

alle'anza [alle'antsa] *sf* alliance

alle'arsi *vpr* to form an alliance; **alle'ato, -a** *ag* allied ▷ *sm/f* ally

alle'gare *vt (accludere)* to enclose; *(Dir: citare)* to cite, adduce; *(denti)* to set on edge; **alle'gato, -a** *ag* enclosed ▷ *sm* enclosure; *(di e-mail)* attachment; **in allegato** enclosed

allegge'rire [alleddʒe'rire] *vt* to lighten, make lighter; *(fig: lavoro, tasse)* to reduce

alle'gria *sf* gaiety, cheerfulness

al'legro, -a *ag* cheerful, merry; *(un po' brillo)* merry, tipsy; *(vivace: colore)* bright ▷ *sm (Mus)* allegro

allena'mento *sm* training

alle'nare *vt* to train; **allenarsi** *vpr* to train; **alle'natore** *sm (Sport)* trainer, coach

allen'tare *vt* to slacken; *(disciplina)* to relax; **allentarsi** *vpr* to become slack; *(ingranaggio)* to work loose

aller'gia, -'gie [aller'dʒia] *sf* allergy; **al'lergico, -a, -ci, -che** *ag* allergic; **sono allergico alla penicillina** I'm allergic to penicillin

alles'tire *vt (cena)* to prepare; *(esercito, nave)* to equip, fit out; *(spettacolo)* to stage

allet'tante *ag* attractive, alluring

alle'vare *vt (animale)* to breed, rear; *(bambino)* to bring up

allevi'are *vt* to alleviate

alli'bito, -a *ag* astounded

alli'evo *sm* pupil; *(apprendista)* apprentice; *(Mil)* cadet

alliga'tore *sm* alligator

alline'are vt (persone, cose) to line up; (Tip) to align; (fig: economia, salari) to adjust, align; **allinearsi** vpr to line up; (fig: a idee): **allinearsi a** to come into line with

al'lodola sf (sky)lark

alloggi'are [allod'dʒare] vt to accommodate ▷ vi to live; **al'loggio** sm lodging, accommodation (BRIT), accommodations (US)

allonta'nare vt to send away, send off; (impiegato) to dismiss; (pericolo) to avert, remove; (estraniare) to alienate; **allontanarsi** vpr **allontanarsi (da)** to go away (from); (estraniarsi) to become estranged (from)

al'lora av (in quel momento) then ▷ cong (in questo caso) well then; (dunque) well then, so; **la gente d'~** people then o in those days; **da ~ in poi** from then on

al'loro sm laurel

'alluce ['allutʃe] sm big toe

alluci'nante [allutʃi'nante] ag awful; (fam) amazing

allucinazi'one [allutʃinat'tsjone] sf hallucination

al'ludere vi **~ a** to allude to, hint at

allu'minio sm aluminium (BRIT), aluminum (US)

allun'gare vt to lengthen; (distendere) to prolong, extend; (diluire) to water down; **allungarsi** vpr to lengthen; (ragazzo) to stretch, grow taller; (sdraiarsi) to lie down, stretch out

al'lusi ecc vb vedi **alludere**

allusi'one sf hint, allusion

alluvi'one sf flood

al'meno av at least ▷ cong **(se) ~** if only; **(se) ~ piovesse!** if only it would rain!

a'logeno, -a [a'lɔdʒeno] ag **lampada alogena** halogen lamp

a'lone sm halo

'Alpi sfpl **le ~** the Alps

alpi'nismo sm mountaineering, climbing; **alpi'nista, -i, -e** sm/f mountaineer, climber

al'pino, -a ag Alpine; mountain cpd; **alpini** smpl (Mil) Italian Alpine troops

alt escl halt!, stop!

alta'lena sf (a funi) swing; (in bilico) seesaw

al'tare sm altar

alter'nare vt to alternate; **alternarsi** vpr to alternate; **alterna'tiva** sf alternative; **alterna'tivo, -a** ag alternative

al'terno, -a ag alternate; **a giorni alterni** on alternate days, every other day

al'tero, -a ag proud

al'tezza [al'tettsa] sf height; width, breadth; depth; pitch; (Geo) latitude; (titolo) highness; (fig: nobiltà) greatness; **essere all'~ di** to be on a level with; (fig) to be up to o equal to

al'ticcio, -a, -ci, -ce [al'tittʃo] ag tipsy

alti'tudine sf altitude

'alto, -a ag high; (persona) tall; (tessuto) wide, broad; (sonno, acque) deep; (suono) high(-pitched); (Geo) upper; (settentrionale) northern ▷ sm top (part) ▷ av high; (parlare) aloud, loudly; **il palazzo è ~ 20 metri** the building is 20 metres high; **ad alta voce** aloud; **a notte alta** in the dead of night; **in ~** up, upwards; at the top; **dall'~ in o al basso** up and down; **degli alti e bassi** (fig) ups and downs; **alta fedeltà** high fidelity, hi-fi; **alta finanza/società** high finance/society; **alta moda** haute couture

altopar'lante sm loudspeaker

altopi'ano (pl altipi'ani) sm plateau, upland plain

altret'tanto, -a ag, pron as much; (pl) as many ▷ av equally; **tanti auguri! — grazie, ~** all the best! — thank you, the same to you

altri'menti av otherwise

 PAROLA CHIAVE

'altro, -a det **1** (diverso) other, different; **questa è un'altra cosa** that's another o a different thing

2 (supplementare) other; **prendi un altro cioccolatino** have another chocolate; **hai avuto altre notizie?** have you had any more o any other news?

3 (nel tempo): **l'altro giorno** the other day; **l'altr'anno** last year; **l'altro ieri** the day before yesterday; **domani l'altro** the day after tomorrow; **quest'altro mese** next month

4: **d'altra parte** on the other hand ▷ pron **1** (persona, cosa diversa o supplementare): **un altro, un'altra** another (one); **lo farà un altro** someone else will do it; **altri, e** others; **gli altri** (la gente) others, other people; **l'uno e l'altro** both (of them); **aiutarsi l'un l'altro** to help one another; **da un giorno all'altro** from day to day; (nel giro di 24 ore) from one day to the next; (da un momento all'altro) any day now

2 (sostantivato: solo maschile) something else; (: in espressioni interrogative) anything else; **non ho altro da dire** I have nothing else o I don't have anything else to say; **più che altro** above all; **se non altro** at least; **tra l'altro** among other things; **ci mancherebbe altro!** that's all we need!; **non faccio altro che lavorare** I do nothing but work; **contento?** — **altro che!** are you pleased? — and how!; *vedi* **senza**; **noialtri**; **voialtri**; **tutto**

al'trove *av* elsewhere, somewhere else
altru'ista, -i, -e *ag* altruistic
a'lunno, -a *sm/f* pupil
alve'are *sm* hive
al'zare [al'tsare] *vt* to raise, lift; (*issare*) to hoist; (*costruire*) to build, erect; **alzarsi** *vpr* to rise; (*dal letto*) to get up; (*crescere*) to grow tall (*o* taller); **~ le spalle** to shrug one's shoulders; **alzarsi in piedi** to stand up, get to one's feet
a'maca, -che *sf* hammock
amalga'mare *vt* to amalgamate; **amalgamarsi** *vpr* to amalgamate
a'mante *ag* **~ di** (*musica ecc*) fond of ▷ *sm/f* lover/mistress
a'mare *vt* to love; (*amico, musica, sport*) to like; **amarsi** *vpr* to love each other
amareggi'ato, -a [amared'dʒato] *ag* upset, saddened
ama'rena *sf* sour black cherry
ama'rezza [ama'rettsa] *sf* bitterness
a'maro, -a *ag* bitter ▷ *sm* bitterness; (*liquore*) bitters *pl*
amaz'zonico, -a, ci, che [amad'dzɔniko] *ag* Amazonian; Amazon *cpd*
ambasci'ata [ambaʃ'ʃata] *sf* embassy; (*messaggio*) message; **ambascia'tore, -'trice** *sm/f* ambassador/ambassadress
ambe'due *ag inv* **~ i ragazzi** both boys ▷ *pron inv* both
ambienta'lista, -i, e *ag* environmental ▷ *sm/f* environmentalist
ambien'tare *vt* to acclimatize; (*romanzo, film*) to set; **ambientarsi** *vpr* to get used to one's surroundings
ambi'ente *sm* environment; (*fig: insieme di persone*) milieu; (*stanza*) room
am'biguo, -a *ag* ambiguous
ambizi'one [ambit'tsjone] *sf* ambition; **ambizi'oso, -a** *ag* ambitious
'ambo *ag inv* both ▷ *sm* (*al gioco*) double
'ambra *sf* amber; **ambra grigia** ambergris
ambu'lante *ag* itinerant ▷ *sm* peddler
ambu'lanza [ambu'lantsa] *sf* ambulance; **chiamate un ~** call an ambulance
ambula'torio *sm* (*studio medico*) surgery
A'merica *sf* l'**~** America; l'**~ latina** Latin America; **ameri'cano, -a** *ag, sm/f* American
ami'anto *sm* asbestos
ami'chevole [ami'kevole] *ag* friendly
ami'cizia [ami'tʃittsja] *sf* friendship; **amicizie** *sfpl* (*amici*) friends
a'mico, -a, -ci, -che *sm/f* friend;

(*fidanzato*) boyfriend/girlfriend; **amico del cuore** bosom friend
'amido *sm* starch
ammac'care *vt* (*pentola*) to dent; (*persona*) to bruise
ammacca'tura *sf* dent; bruise
ammaes'trare *vt* (*animale*) to train
ammai'nare *vt* to lower, haul down
amma'larsi *vpr* to fall ill; **amma'lato, -a** *ag* ill, sick ▷ *sm/f* sick person; (*paziente*) patient
ammanet'tare *vt* to handcuff
ammas'sare *vt* (*ammucchiare*) to amass; (*raccogliere*) to gather together; **ammassarsi** *vpr* to pile up; to gather
ammat'tire *vi* to go mad
ammaz'zare [ammat'tsare] *vt* to kill; **ammazzarsi** *vpr* (*uccidersi*) to kill o s.; (*rimanere ucciso*) to be killed; **ammazzarsi di lavoro** to work o.s. to death
am'mettere *vt* to admit; (*riconoscere: fatto*) to acknowledge, admit; (*permettere*) to allow, accept; (*supporre*) to suppose
amminis'trare *vt* to run, manage; (*Rel, Dir*) to administer; **amministra'tore** *sm* administrator; (*di condominio*) flats manager; **amministratore delegato** managing director; **amministrazi'one** *sf* management; administration
ammi'raglio [ammi'raʎʎo] *sm* admiral
ammi'rare *vt* to admire; **ammirazi'one** *sf* admiration
am'misi *ecc vb vedi* **ammettere**
ammobili'ato, -a *ag* furnished
am'mollo *sm* **lasciare in ~** to leave to soak
ammo'niaca *sf* ammonia
ammo'nire *vt* (*avvertire*) to warn; (*rimproverare*) to admonish; (*Dir*) to caution
ammonizi'one [ammonit'tsjone] *sf* (*monito: anche Sport*) warning; (*rimprovero*) reprimand; (*Dir*) caution
ammon'tare *vi* **~ a** to amount to ▷ *sm* (*total*) amount
ammorbi'dente *sm* fabric conditioner
ammorbi'dire *vt* to soften
ammortizza'tore *sm* (*Aut, Tecn*) shock-absorber
ammucchi'are [ammuk'kjare] *vt* to pile up, accumulate
ammuf'fire *vi* to go mouldy (BRIT) *o* moldy (US)
ammuto'lire *vi* to be struck dumb
amne'sia *sf* amnesia
amnis'tia *sf* amnesty
'amo *sm* (*Pesca*) hook; (*fig*) bait
a'more *sm* love; **amori** *smpl* love affairs; **il tuo bambino è un ~** your baby's a darling; **fare l'~ o all'~** to make love; **per ~ o per forza** by hook or by crook; **amor proprio**

self-esteem, pride

amo'roso, -a *ag (affettuoso)* loving, affectionate; *(d'amore: sguardo)* amorous; *(: poesia, relazione)* love *cpd*

'ampio, -a *ag* wide, broad; *(spazioso)* spacious; *(abbondante: vestito)* loose; *(: gonna)* full; *(: spiegazione)* ample, full

am'plesso *sm* intercourse

ampli'are *vt (ingrandire)* to enlarge; *(allargare)* to widen; **ampliarsi** *vpr* to grow, increase

amplifica'tore *sm (Tecn, Mus)* amplifier

ampu'tare *vt (Med)* to amputate

A.N. *sigla f (=Alleanza Nazionale)* Italian right-wing party

anabbaglianti *smpl* dipped (BRIT) o dimmed (US) headlights

anaboliz'zante *ag* anabolic ▷ *sm* anabolic steroid

anal'colico, -a, -ci, -che *ag* non-alcoholic ▷ *sm* soft drink

analfa'beta, -i, -e *ag, sm/f* illiterate

anal'gesico, -a, -ci, -che [anal'dʒɛziko] *ag, sm* analgesic

a'nalisi *sf inv* analysis; *(Med: esame)* test; **analisi del sangue** blood test *sg*

analiz'zare [analid'dzare] *vt* to analyse; *(Med)* to test

a'nalogo, -a, -ghi, -ghe *ag* analogous

'ananas *sm inv* pineapple

anar'chia [anar'kia] *sf* anarchy; **a'narchico, -a, -ci, -che** *ag* anarchic(al) ▷ *sm/f* anarchist

anarco-insurreziona'lista *ag* anarcho-revolutionary

'A.N.A.S. *sigla f (= Azienda Nazionale Autonoma delle Strade)* national roads department

anato'mia *sf* anatomy

'anatra *sf* duck

'anca, -che *sf (Anat)* hip

'anche ['anke] *cong (inoltre, pure)* also, too; *(perfino)* even; **vengo anch'io** I'm coming too; **~ se** even if

an'cora *av* still; *(di nuovo)* again; *(di più)* some more; *(persino)*: **~ più forte** even stronger; **non ~** not yet; **~ una volta** once more, once again; **~ un po'** a little more; *(di tempo)* a little longer

an'dare *sm* a lungo **~** in the long run ▷ *vi* to go; *(essere adatto)*: **~ a** to suit; *(piacere)*: **il suo comportamento non mi va** I don't like the way he behaves; **ti va di ~ al cinema?** do you feel like going to the cinema?; **andarsene** to go away; **questa camicia va lavata** this shirt needs a wash o should be washed; **~ a cavallo** to ride; **~ in macchina/aereo** to go by car/plane; **~ a fare qc** to go and do sth; **~ a pescare/**

sciare to go fishing/skiing; **~ a male** to go bad; **come va?** *(lavoro, progetto)* how are things?; **come va? — bene, grazie!** how are you? — fine, thanks!; **va fatto entro oggi** it's got to be done today; **ne va della nostra vita** our lives are at stake; **an'data** *sf* going; *(viaggio)* outward journey; **biglietto di sola andata** single (BRIT) o one-way ticket; **biglietto di andata e ritorno** return (BRIT) o round-trip (US) ticket

andrò *ecc vb vedi* **andare**

a'neddoto *sm* anecdote

a'nello *sm* ring; *(di catena)* link; **anelli** *smpl (Ginnastica)* rings

a'nemico, -a, -ci, -che *ag* anaemic

aneste'sia *sf* anaesthesia

'angelo ['andʒelo] *sm* angel; **angelo custode** guardian angel

anghe'ria [ange'ria] *sf* vexation

angli'cano, -a *ag* Anglican

anglo'sassone *ag* Anglo-Saxon

'angolo *sm* corner; *(Mat)* angle; **angolo cottura** *(di appartamento ecc)* cooking area

an'goscia, -sce [an'gɔʃʃa] *sf* deep anxiety, anguish *no pl*

angu'illa *sf* eel

an'guria *sf* watermelon

'anice ['anitʃe] *sm (Cuc)* aniseed; *(Bot)* anise

'anima *sf* soul; *(abitante)* inhabitant; **non c'era ~ viva** there wasn't a living soul; **anima gemella** soul mate

ani'male *sm, ag* animal; **animale domestico** pet

anna'cquare *vt* to water down, dilute

annaffi'are *vt* to water; **annaffia'toio** *sm* watering can

an'nata *sf* year; *(importo annuo)* annual amount; **vino d'~** vintage wine

anne'gare *vt, vi* to drown

anne'rire *vt* to blacken ▷ *vi* to become black

annien'tare *vt* to annihilate, destroy

anniver'sario *sm* anniversary; **anniversario di matrimonio** wedding anniversary

'anno *sm* year; **ha 8 anni** he's 8 (years old)

anno'dare *vt* to knot, tie; *(fig: rapporto)* to form

annoi'are *vt* to bore; **annoiarsi** *vpr* to be bored

> Attenzione! In inglese esiste il verbo *to annoy* che però vuol dire *dare fastidio a*.

anno'tare *vt (registrare)* to note, note down; *(commentare)* to annotate

annu'ale *ag* annual

annu'ire *vi* to nod; *(acconsentire)* to agree

annul'lare *vt* to annihilate, destroy;

(*contratto, francobollo*) to cancel; (*matrimonio*) to annul; (*sentenza*) to quash; (*risultati*) to declare void

annunci'are [annun'tʃare] *vt* to announce; (*dar segni rivelatori*) to herald

an'nuncio [an'nuntʃo] *sm* announcement; (*fig*) sign; **annunci economici** classified advertisements, small ads; **annunci mortuari** (*colonna*) obituary column; **annuncio pubblicitario** advertisement

'annuo, -a *ag* annual, yearly

annu'sare *vt* to sniff, smell; **~ tabacco** to take snuff

a'nomalo, -a *ag* anomalous

a'nonimo, -a *ag* anonymous ▷ *sm* (*autore*) anonymous writer (*o painter ecc*); **società anonima** (*Comm*) joint stock company

anores'sia *sf* anorexia

ano'ressico, -a, ci, che *ag* anorexic

anor'male *ag* abnormal ▷ *sm/f* subnormal person

ANSA *sigla f* (= *Agenzia Nazionale Stampa Associata*) press agency

'ansia *sf* anxiety

ansi'mare *vi* to pant

ansi'oso, -a *ag* anxious

'anta *sf* (*di finestra*) shutter; (*di armadio*) door

An'tartide *sf* **l'~** Antarctica

an'tenna *sf* (*Radio, TV*) aerial; (*Zool*) antenna, feeler; (*Naut*) yard; **antenna parabolica** satellite dish

ante'prima *sf* preview; **anteprima di stampa** (*Inform*) print preview

anteri'ore *ag* (*ruota, zampa*) front; (*fatti*) previous, preceding

antiade'rente *ag* non-stick

antibi'otico, -a, -ci, -che *ag, sm* antibiotic

anti'camera *sf* anteroom; **fare ~** to wait (for an audience)

antici'pare [antitʃi'pare] *vt* (*consegna, visita*) to bring forward, anticipate; (*somma di denaro*) to pay in advance; (*notizia*) to disclose ▷ *vi* to be ahead of time; **an'ticipo** *sm* anticipation; (*di denaro*) advance; **in anticipo** early, in advance; **occorre che prenoti in anticipo?** do I need to book in advance?

an'tico, -a, -chi, -che *ag* (*quadro, mobili*) antique; (*dell'antichità*) ancient; **all'antica** old-fashioned

anticoncezio'nale [antikontʃettsjo'nale] *sm* contraceptive

anticonfor'mista, -i, -e *ag, sm/f* nonconformist

anti'corpo *sm* antibody

antidolo'rifico, -ci *sm* painkiller

anti'doping *sm* drug testing ▷ *ag inv* **test ~ drugs** (BRIT) *o* drug (US) test

an'tifona *sf* (*Mus, Rel*) antiphon; **capire l'~** (*fig*) to take the hint

anti'forfora *ag inv* anti-dandruff

anti'furto *sm* anti-theft device

anti'gelo [anti'dʒɛlo] *ag inv* (**liquido**) **~** (*per motore*) antifreeze; (*per cristalli*) de-icer

antiglobalizzazione [antiglobalidd zat'tsjone] *ag inv* **movimento ~** anti-globalization movement

An'tille *sfpl* **le ~** the West Indies

antin'cendio [antin'tʃendjo] *ag inv* fire cpd

anti'nebbia *sm inv* (*anche:* **faro ~:** *Aut*) fog lamp

antinfiamma'torio, -a *ag, sm* anti-inflammatory

antio'rario [antio'rarjo] *ag* **in senso ~** anticlockwise

anti'pasto *sm* hors d'œuvre

antipa'tia *sf* antipathy, dislike; **anti'patico, -a, -ci, -che** *ag* unpleasant, disagreeable

antiproi'ettile *ag inv* bulletproof

antiquari'ato *sm* antique trade; **un oggetto d'~** an antique

anti'quario *sm* antique dealer

anti'quato, -a *ag* antiquated, old-fashioned

anti'rughe *ag inv* (*crema, prodotto*) anti-wrinkle

antitraspi'rante *ag* antiperspirant

anti'vipera *ag inv* **siero ~** remedy for snake bites

antivirus [anti'virus] *sm inv* antivirus software *no pl* ▷ *ag inv* antivirus

antolo'gia, -'gie [antolo'dʒia] *sf* anthology

anu'lare *ag* ring cpd ▷ *sm* third finger

'anzi ['antsi] *av* (*invece*) on the contrary; (*o meglio*) or rather, or better still

anzi'ano, -a [an'tsjano] *ag* old; (*Amm*) senior ▷ *sm/f* old person; senior member

anziché [antsi'ke] *cong* rather than

a'patico, -a, -ci, -che *ag* apathetic

'ape *sf* bee

aperi'tivo *sm* apéritif

aperta'mente *av* openly

a'perto, -a *pp di* **aprire** ▷ *ag* open; **all'~** in the open (air); **è ~ al pubblico?** is it open to the public?; **quando è ~ il museo?** when is the museum open?

aper'tura *sf* opening; (*ampiezza*) width; (*Fot*) aperture; **apertura alare** wing span; **apertura mentale** open-mindedness

ap'nea *sf* **immergersi in ~** to dive without breathing apparatus

a'postrofo *sm* apostrophe

ap'paio *ecc vb vedi* **apparire**

ap'palto *sm* (*Comm*) contract; **dare/ prendere in ~ un lavoro** to let out/ undertake a job on contract

appannarsi *vpr* to mist over; to grow dim

apparecchi'are [apparek'kjare] *vt* to prepare; (*tavola*) to set ▷ *vi* to set the table

appa'recchio [appa'rekkjo] *sm* piece of apparatus, device; (*aeroplano*) aircraft *inv*; **apparecchio acustico** hearing aid; **apparecchio telefonico** telephone; **apparecchio televisivo** television set

appa'rente *ag* apparent

appa'rire *vi* to appear; (*sembrare*) to seem, appear

apparta'mento *sm* flat (*BRIT*), apartment (*US*)

appar'tarsi *vpr* to withdraw

apparte'nere *vi* ~ **a** to belong to

ap'parvi *ecc vb vedi* **apparire**

appassio'nare *vt* to thrill; (*commuovere*) to move; **appassionarsi** *vpr* **appassionarsi a qc** to take a great interest in sth; **appassio'nato, -a** *ag* passionate; (*entusiasta*) **appassionato (di)** keen (on)

appas'sire *vi* to wither

appas'sito, -a *ag* dead

ap'pello *sm* roll-call; (*implorazione, Dir*) appeal; **fare ~ a** to appeal to

ap'pena *av* (*a stento*) hardly, scarcely; (*solamente, da poco*) just ▷ *cong* as soon as; **(non) ~ furono arrivati ...** as soon as they had arrived ...; **~ ... che** *o* **quando** no sooner ... than

ap'pendere *vt* to hang (up)

appen'dice [appen'ditfe] *sf* appendix; **romanzo d'~** popular serial

appendi'cite [appendi'tfite] *sf* appendicitis

Appen'nini *smpl* **gli ~** the Apennines

appesan'tire *vt* to make heavy; **appesantirsi** *vpr* to grow stout

appe'tito *sm* appetite

appic'care *vt* ~ **il fuoco a** to set fire to, set on fire

appicci'care [appittfi'kare] *vt* to stick; **appiccicarsi** *vpr* to stick; (*fig: persona*) to cling

appiso'larsi *vpr* to doze off

applau'dire *vt, vi* to applaud; **ap'plauso** *sm* applause

appli'care *vt* to apply; (*regolamento*) to enforce; **applicarsi** *vpr* to apply o.s.

appoggi'are [appod'dʒare] *vt* (*mettere contro*): ~ **qc a qc** to lean *o* rest sth against sth; (*fig: sostenere*) to support; **appoggiarsi** *vpr* **appoggiarsi a** to lean against; (*fig*) to rely upon; **ap'poggio** *sm* support

apposita'mente *av* specially; (*apposta*) on purpose

ap'posito, -a *ag* appropriate

ap'posta *av* on purpose, deliberately

appos'tarsi *vpr* to lie in wait

ap'prendere *vt* (*imparare*) to learn

appren'dista, -i, -e *sm/f* apprentice

apprensi'one *sf* apprehension

apprez'zare [appret'tsare] *vt* to appreciate

appro'dare *vi* (*Naut*) to land; (*fig*): **non ~ a nulla** to come to nothing

approfit'tare *vi* ~ **di** to make the most of; (*peg*) to take advantage of

approfon'dire *vt* to deepen; (*fig*) to study in depth

appropri'ato, -a *ag* appropriate

approssima'tivo, -a *ag* approximate, rough; (*impreciso*) inexact, imprecise

appro'vare *vt* (*condotta, azione*) to approve of; (*candidato*) to pass; (*progetto di legge*) to approve

appunta'mento *sm* appointment; (*amoroso*) date; **darsi ~** to arrange to meet (one another); **ho un ~ con...** I have an appointment with ...; **vorrei prendere un ~** I'd like to make an appointment

ap'punto *sm* note; (*rimprovero*) reproach ▷ *av* (*proprio*) exactly, just; **per l'~!, ~!** exactly!

apribot'tiglie [apribot'tiλλe] *sm inv* bottle opener

a'prile *sm* April

a'prire *vt* to open; (*via, cadavere*) to open up; (*gas, luce, acqua*) to turn on ▷ *vi* to open; **aprirsi** *vpr* to open; **aprirsi a qn** to confide in sb, open one's heart to sb; **a che ora aprite?** what time do you open?

apris'catole *sm inv* tin (*BRIT*) *o* can opener

APT *sigla f* (= *Azienda di Promozione*) ≈ tourist board

aquagym [akkwa'dʒim] *sf* aquaerobics

'aquila *sf* (*Zool*) eagle; (*fig*) genius

aqui'lone *sm* (*giocattolo*) kite; (*vento*) North wind

A/R *abbr* = **andata e ritorno** (*biglietto*) return ticket (*BRIT*), round-trip ticket (*US*)

A'rabia Sau'dita *sf* **l'~** Saudi Arabia

'arabo, -a *ag, sm/f* Arab ▷ *sm* (*Ling*) Arabic

a'rachide [a'rakide] *sf* peanut

ara'gosta *sf* crayfish; lobster

a'rancia, -ce [a'rantʃa] *sf* orange; **aranci'ata** *sf* orangeade; **aranci'one** *inv* **(color) arancione** bright orange

a'rare *vt* to plough (*BRIT*), plow (*US*)

a'ratro *sm* plough (*BRIT*), plow (*US*)

a'razzo [a'rattso] *sm* tapestry

arbi'trare *vt* (*Sport*) to referee; to umpire; (*Dir*) to arbitrate

arbi'trario, -a ag arbitrary

'arbitro sm arbiter, judge; (Dir) arbitrator; (Sport) referee; (: Tennis, Cricket) umpire

ar'busto sm shrub

archeolo'gia [arkeolo'dʒia] sf arch(a)eology; **arche'ologo, -a, -gi, -ghe** sm/f arch(a)eologist

architet'tare [arkitet'tare] vt (fig: ideare) to devise; (: macchinare) to plan, concoct

archi'tetto [arki'tetto] sm architect; **architet'tura** sf architecture

ar'chivio [ar'kivjo] sm archives pl; (Inform) file

'arco sm (arma, Mus) bow; (Archit) arch; (Mat) arc

arcoba'leno sm rainbow

arcu'ato, -a ag curved, bent

'ardere vt, vi to burn

ar'desia sf slate

'area sf area; (Edil) land, ground; **area di rigore** (Sport) penalty area; **area di servizio** (Aut) service area

a'rena sf arena; (per corride) bullring; (sabbia) sand

are'narsi vpr to run aground

argente'ria [ardʒente'ria] sf silverware, silver

Argen'tina [ardʒen'tina] sf l'~ Argentina; **argen'tino, -a** ag, sm/f Argentinian

ar'gento [ar'dʒento] sm silver; **argento vivo** quicksilver

ar'gilla [ar'dʒilla] sf clay

'argine ['ardʒine] sm embankment, bank; (diga) dyke, dike

argo'mento sm argument; (motivo) motive; (materia, tema) subject

'aria sf air; (espressione, aspetto) air, look; (Mus: melodia) tune; (di opera) aria; **mandare all'~ qc** to ruin o upset sth; **all'~ aperta** in the open (air)

'arido, -a ag arid

arieggi'are [arjed'dʒare] vt (cambiare aria) to air; (imitare) to imitate

ari'ete sm ram; (Mil) battering ram; (dello zodiaco): **A~** Aries

a'ringa, -ghe sf herring inv

arit'metica sf arithmetic

'arma, -i sf weapon, arm; (parte dell'esercito) arm; **chiamare alle armi** to call up (BRIT), draft (US); **sotto le armi** in the army (o forces); **alle armi!** to arms!; **arma atomica/nucleare** atomic/nuclear weapon; **arma da fuoco** firearm; **armi di distruzione di massa** weapons of mass destruction

arma'dietto sm (di medicinali) medicine cabinet; (in palestra ecc) locker; (in cucina) (kitchen) cupboard

ar'madio sm cupboard; (per abiti) wardrobe; **armadio a muro** built-in cupboard

ar'mato, -a ag ~ **(di)** (anche fig) armed (with) ▷ sf (Mil) army; (Naut) fleet; **rapina a mano armata** armed robbery

arma'tura sf (struttura di sostegno) framework; (impalcatura) scaffolding; (Storia) armour no pl, suit of armour

armis'tizio [armis'tittsjo] sm armistice

armo'nia sf harmony

ar'nese sm tool, implement; (oggetto indeterminato) thing, contraption; **male in ~** (malvestito) badly dressed; (di salute malferma) in poor health; (povero) down-at-heel

'arnia sf hive

a'roma, -i sm aroma; fragrance; **aromi** smpl (Cuc) herbs and spices; **aromatera'pia** sf aromatherapy

'arpa sf (Mus) harp

arrabbi'are vi (cane) to be affected with rabies; **arrabbiarsi** vpr (essere preso dall'ira) to get angry, fly into a rage; **arrabbi'ato, -a** ag rabid, with rabies; furious, angry

arrampi'carsi vpr to climb (up)

arrangiarsi vpr to manage, do the best one can

arreda'mento sm (studio) interior design; (mobili ecc) furnishings pl

arre'dare vt to furnish

arre'ndersi vpr to surrender

arres'tare vt (fermare) to stop, halt; (catturare) to arrest; **arrestarsi** vpr (fermarsi) to stop; **ar'resto** sm (cessazione) stopping; (fermata) stop; (cattura, Med) arrest; **subire un arresto** to come to a stop o standstill; **mettere agli arresti** to place under arrest; **arresti domiciliari** house arrest sg

arre'trare vt, vi to withdraw; **arre'trato, -a** ag (lavoro) behind schedule; (paese, bambino) backward; (numero di giornale) back cpd; **arretrati** smpl arrears

arric'chire [arrik'kire] vt to enrich; **arricchirsi** vpr to become rich

arri'vare vi to arrive; (accadere) to happen, occur; ~ **a** (livello, grado ecc) to reach; **a che ora arriva il treno da Londra?** what time does the train from London arrive?; **non ci arrivo** I can't reach it; (fig: non capisco) I can't understand it

arrive'derci [arrive'dertʃi] escl goodbye!

arri'vista, -i, -e sm/f go-getter

ar'rivo sm arrival; (Sport) finish, finishing line

arro'gante ag arrogant

arros'sire vi (per vergogna, timidezza) to blush, flush; (per gioia, rabbia) to flush

arros'tire vt to roast; (pane) to toast; (ai

ferri) to grill

ar'rosto *sm, ag inv* roast

arroto'lare *vt* to roll up

arroton'dare *vt* (*forma, oggetto*) to round; (*stipendio*) to add to; (*somma*) to round off

arrugginito, -a [arruddʒin'nito] *ag* rusty

'arsi *vb vedi* ardere

'arte *sf* art; (*abilità*) skill

ar'teria *sf* artery; arteria stradale main road

'artico, -a, -ci, -che *ag* Arctic

articolazi'one *sf* articulation; (*Anat, Tecn*) joint

ar'ticolo *sm* article; articolo di fondo (*Stampa*) leader, leading article

artifici'ale [artifi'tʃale] *ag* artificial

artigia'nato [artidʒa'nato] *sm* craftsmanship; craftsmen *pl*

artigi'ano, -a [arti'dʒano] *sm/f* craftsman/woman

ar'tista, -i, -e *sm/f* artist; ar'tistico, -a, -ci, -che *ag* artistic

ar'trite *sf* (*Med*) arthritis

a'scella [aʃ'ʃella] *sf* (*Anat*) armpit

ascen'dente [aʃʃen'dɛnte] *sm* ancestor; (*fig*) ascendancy; (*Astr*) ascendant

ascen'sore [aʃʃen'sore] *sm* lift

a'scesso [aʃ'ʃɛsso] *sm* (*Med*) abscess

asciugaca'pelli [aʃʃugaka'pelli] *sm* hair-drier

asciuga'mano [aʃʃuga'mano] *sm* towel

asciu'gare [aʃʃu'gare] *vt* to dry; asciugarsi *vpr* to dry o.s.; (*diventare asciutto*) to dry

asci'utto, -a [aʃ'ʃutto] *ag* dry; (*fig: magro*) lean; (*: burbero*) curt; restare a bocca asciutta (*fig*) to be disappointed

ascol'tare *vt* to listen to

as'falto *sm* asphalt

'Asia *sf* l'~ Asia; asi'atico, -a, -ci, -che *ag, sm/f* Asiatic, Asian

a'silo *sm* refuge, sanctuary; ~ (d'infanzia) nursery(-school); asilo nido crèche; asilo politico political asylum

'asino *sm* donkey, ass

ASL *sigla f* (= Azienda Sanitaria Locale) local health centre

'asma *sf* asthma

as'parago, -gi *sm* asparagus *no pl*

aspet'tare *vt* to wait for; (*anche Comm*) to await; (*aspettarsi*) to expect ▷ *vi* to wait; aspettami, per favore wait for me, please

as'petto *sm* (*apparenza*) aspect, appearance, look; (*punto di vista*) point of view; di bell'~ good-looking

aspira'polvere *sm inv* vacuum cleaner

aspi'rare *vt* (*respirare*) to breathe in, inhale; (*apparecchi*) to suck (up) ▷ *vi* ~ a to

aspire to

aspi'rina *sf* aspirin

'aspro, -a *ag* (*sapore*) sour, tart; (*odore*) acrid, pungent; (*voce, clima, fig*) harsh; (*superficie*) rough; (*paesaggio*) rugged

assaggi'are [assad'dʒare] *vt* to taste; posso assaggiarlo? can I have a taste?; assaggino [assad'dʒino] *sm* assaggini (*Cuc*) selection of first courses; solo un assaggino just a little

as'sai *av* (*molto*) a lot, much; (: *con ag*) very; (*a sufficienza*) enough ▷ *ag inv* (*quantità*) a lot of, much; (*numero*) a lot of, many; ~ contento very pleased

as'salgo *ecc vb vedi* assalire

as'salire *vt* to attack, assail

assal'tare *vt* (*Mil*) to storm; (*banca*) to raid; (*treno, diligenza*) to hold up

as'salto *sm* attack, assault

assassi'nare *vt* to murder; to assassinate; (*fig*) to ruin; assas'sino, -a *ag* murderous ▷ *sm/f* murderer; assassin

'asse *sm* (*Tecn*) axle; (*Mat*) axis ▷ *sf* board; asse *sf* da stiro ironing board

assedi'are *vt* to besiege

asse'gnare [assen'ɲare] *vt* to assign, allot; (*premio*) to award

as'segno [as'seɲɲo] *sm* allowance; (*anche:* ~ bancario) cheque (BRIT), check (US); contro ~ cash on delivery; posso pagare con un ~? can I pay by cheque?; assegno circolare bank draft; assegni familiari ≈ child benefit *no pl*; assegno sbarrato crossed cheque; assegno di viaggio traveller's cheque; assegno a vuoto dud cheque; assegno di malattia/di invalidità sick pay/disability benefit

assem'blea *sf* assembly

assen'tarsi *vpr* to go out

as'sente *ag* absent; (*fig*) faraway, vacant; as'senza *sf* absence

asse'tato, -a *ag* thirsty, parched

assicu'rare *vt* (*accertare*) to ensure; (*infondere certezza*) to assure; (*fermare, legare*) to make fast, secure; (*fare un contratto di assicurazione*) to insure; assicurarsi *vpr* (*accertarsi*): assicurarsi (di) to make sure (of); (*contro il furto ecc*): assicurarsi (contro) to insure o.s. (against); assicurazi'one *sf* assurance; insurance

assi'eme *av* (*insieme*) together; ~ a (together) with

assil'lare *vt* to pester, torment

assis'tente *sm/f* assistant; assistente sociale social worker; assistente di volo (*Aer*) steward/stewardess

assis'tenza [assis'tentsa] *sf* assistance; ~ ospedaliera free hospital treatment;

~ sociale welfare services *pl*; **assistenza sanitaria** health service

as'sistere *vt* (*aiutare*) to assist, help; (*curare*) to treat ▷ *vi* **~ (a qc)** (*essere presente*) to be present (at sth), to attend (sth)

'**asso** *sm* ace; **piantare qn in ~** to leave sb in the lurch

associ'are [asso'tʃare] *vt* to associate; **associarsi** *vpr* to enter into partnership; **associarsi a** to become a member of, join; (*dolori, gioie*) to share in; **~ qn alle carceri** to take sb to prison

associazi'one [assotʃat'tsjone] *sf* association; (*Comm*) association, society; **~ a delinquere** (*Dir*) criminal association

as'solsi *ecc vb vedi* **assolvere**

assoluta'mente *av* absolutely

asso'luto, -a *ag* absolute

assoluzi'one [assolut'tsjone] *sf* (*Dir*) acquittal; (*Rel*) absolution

as'solvere *vt* (*Dir*) to acquit; (*Rel*) to absolve; (*adempiere*) to carry out, perform

assomigli'are [assomiʎ'ʎare] *vi* **~ a** to resemble, look like; **assomigliarsi** *vpr* to look alike; (*nel carattere*) to be alike

asson'nato, -a *ag* sleepy

asso'pirsi *vpr* to doze off

assor'bente *ag* absorbent ▷ *sm*: **assorbente interno** tampon; **assorbente esterno/igienico** sanitary towel

assor'bire *vt* to absorb

assor'dare *vt* to deafen

assorti'mento *sm* assortment

assor'tito, -a *ag* assorted; matched, matching

assuefazi'one [assuefat'tsjone] *sf* (*Med*) addiction

as'sumere *vt* (*impiegato*) to take on, engage; (*responsabilità*) to assume, take upon o.s.; (*contegno, espressione*) to assume, put on; (*droga*) to consume

as'sunsi *ecc vb vedi* **assumere**

assurdità *sf inv* absurdity; **dire delle ~** to talk nonsense

as'surdo, -a *ag* absurd

'**asta** *sf* pole; (*vendita*) auction

as'temio, -a *ag* teetotal ▷ *sm/f* teetotaller

■ Attenzione! In inglese esiste la parola *abstemious* che però vuol dire *moderato*.

aste'nersi *vpr* **~ (da)** to abstain (from), refrain (from); (*Pol*) to abstain (from)

aste'risco, -schi *sm* asterisk

'**astice** ['astitʃe] *sm* lobster

astig'matico, -a, ci, che *ag* astigmatic

asti'nenza [asti'nɛntsa] *sf* abstinence; **essere in crisi di ~** to suffer from withdrawal symptoms

as'tratto, -a *ag* abstract

'**astro...** *prefisso*; **astro'logia** [astrolo'dʒia] *sf* astrology; **astro'nauta, -i, -e** *sm/f* astronaut; **astro'nave** *sf* space ship; **astro'nomia** *sf* astronomy; **astro'nomico, -a, -ci, -che** *ag* astronomic(al)

as'tuccio [as'tuttʃo] *sm* case, box, holder

as'tuto, -a *ag* astute, cunning, shrewd

A'tene *sf* Athens

'**ateo, -a** *ag, sm/f* atheist

at'lante *sm* atlas

at'lantico, -a, -ci, -che *ag* Atlantic ▷ *sm* **l'A~, l'Oceano A~** the Atlantic, the Atlantic Ocean

at'leta, -i, -e *sm/f* athlete; **at'letica** *sf* athletics *sg*; **atletica leggera** track and field events *pl*; **atletica pesante** weightlifting and wrestling

atmos'fera *sf* atmosphere

a'tomico, -a, -ci, -che *ag* atomic; (*nucleare*) atomic, atom *cpd*, nuclear

'**atomo** *sm* atom

'**atrio** *sm* entrance hall, lobby

a'troce [a'trotʃe] *ag* (*che provoca orrore*) dreadful; (*terribile*) atrocious

attac'cante *sm/f* (*Sport*) forward

attacca'panni *sm* hook, peg; (*mobile*) hall stand

attac'care *vt* (*unire*) to attach; (*cucendo*) to sew on; (*far aderire*) to stick (on); (*appendere*) to hang (up); (*assalire: anche fig*) to attack; (*iniziare*) to begin, start; (*fig: contagiare*) to pass on ▷ *vi* to stick, adhere; **attaccarsi** *vpr* to stick, adhere; (*trasmettersi per contagio*) to be contagious; (*afferrarsi*): **attaccarsi (a)** to cling (to); (*fig: affezionarsi*): **attaccarsi (a)** to become attached (to); **~ discorso** to start a conversation; **at'tacco, -chi** *sm* (*azione offensiva: anche fig*) attack; (*Med*) attack, fit; (*Sci*) binding; (*Elettr*) socket

atteggia'mento [atteddʒa'mento] *sm* attitude

at'tendere *vt* to wait for, await ▷ *vi* **~ a** to attend to

atten'dibile *ag* (*storia*) credible; (*testimone*) reliable

atten'tato *sm* attack; **~ alla vita di qn** attempt on sb's life

at'tento, -a *ag* attentive; (*accurato*) careful, thorough; **stare ~ a qc** to pay attention to sth; **~!** be careful!

attenzi'one [atten'tsjone] *sf* attention; **~!** watch out!, be careful!; **attenzioni** *sfpl* (*premure*) attentions; **fare ~ a** to watch out for; **coprire qn di attenzioni** to lavish attentions on sb

atter'raggio [atter'raddʒo] *sm* landing

atter'rare vt to bring down ▷ vi to land

at'tesa sf waiting; (tempo trascorso aspettando) wait; **essere in ~ di qc** to be waiting for sth

at'tesi ecc vb vedi **attendere**

at'teso, -a pp di **attendere**

'attico, -ci sm attic

atti'llato, -a ag (vestito) close-fitting

'attimo sm moment; **in un ~** in a moment

atti'rare vt to attract

atti'tudine sf (disposizione) aptitude; (atteggiamento) attitude

attività sf inv activity; (Comm) assets pl

at'tivo, -a ag active; (Comm) profit-making, credit cpd ▷ sm (Comm) assets pl; **in ~** in credit

'atto sm act; (azione, gesto) action, act, deed; (Dir: documento) deed, document; **atti** smpl (di congressi ecc) proceedings; **mettere in ~** to put into action; **fare ~ di fare qc** to make as if to do sth; **atto di morte/di nascita** death/birth certificate

at'tore, -'trice sm/f actor/actress

at'torno av round, around, about; **~ a** round, around, about

attrac'care vt, vi (Naut) to dock, berth

at'tracco, -chi sm (Naut) docking no pl; berth

at'trae ecc vb vedi **attrarre**

attra'ente ag attractive

at'traggo ecc vb vedi **attrarre**

at'trarre vt to attract

at'trassi ecc vb vedi **attrarre**

attraver'sare vt to cross; (città, bosco, fig: periodo) to go through; (fiume) to run through

attra'verso prep through; (da una parte all'altra) across

attrazi'one [attrat'tsjone] sf attraction

at'trezzo sm tool, instrument; (Sport) piece of equipment

at'trice [at'tritʃe] sf vedi **attore**

attu'ale ag (presente) present; (di attualità) topical

   ▨ Attenzione! In inglese esiste la parola *actual* che però vuol dire *effettivo*.

attualità sf inv topicality; (avvenimento) current event

attual'mente av at the moment, at present

   ▨ Attenzione! In inglese esiste la parola *actually* che però vuol dire *effettivamente* oppure *veramente*.

attu'are vt to carry out

attu'tire vt to deaden, reduce

'audio sm (TV, Radio, Cine) sound

audiovi'sivo, -a ag audiovisual

audizi'one [audit'tsjone] sf hearing; (Mus) audition

augu'rare vt to wish; **augurarsi qc** to hope for sth

au'guri smpl best wishes; **fare gli ~ a qn** to give sb one's best wishes; **tanti ~!** best wishes!; (per compleanno) happy birthday!

'aula sf (scolastica) classroom; (universitaria) lecture theatre; (di edificio pubblico) hall

aumen'tare vt, vi to increase; **au'mento** sm increase

au'rora sf dawn

ausili'are ag, sm, sm/f auxiliary

Aus'tralia sf l'~ Australia; **australi'ano, -a** ag, sm/f Australian

'Austria sf l'~ Austria; **aus'triaco, -a, -ci, -che** ag, sm/f Austrian

au'tentico, -a, -ci, -che ag authentic, genuine

au'tista, -i sm driver

'auto sf inv car

autoabbron'zante sm, ag self-tan

autoade'sivo, -a ag self-adhesive ▷ sm sticker

autobio'grafico, -a, ci, che ag autobiographic(al)

'autobus sm inv bus

auto'carro sm lorry (BRIT), truck

autocertificazi'one [autotʃertifikat'tsjone] sf self-declaration

autodistrut'tivo, -a ag self-destructive

auto'gol sm inv own goal

au'tografo, -a ag, sm autograph

auto'grill® sm inv motorway restaurant

auto'matico, -a, -ci, -che ag automatic ▷ sm (bottone) snap fastener; (fucile) automatic

auto'mobile sf (motor) car

automobi'lista, -i, -e sm/f motorist

autono'leggio sm car hire

autono'mia sf autonomy; (di volo) range

au'tonomo, -a ag autonomous, independent

autop'sia sf post-mortem, autopsy

auto'radio sf inv (apparecchio) car radio; (autoveicolo) radio car

au'tore, -'trice sm/f author

autoreggente [autored'dʒente] ag **calze autoreggenti** hold ups

auto'revole ag authoritative; (persona) influential

autoricari'cabile ag **scheda ~** top-up card

autori'messa sf garage

autorità sf inv authority

autoriz'zare [autorid'dzare] vt (permettere) to authorize; (giustificare) to allow, sanction

autos'contro sm dodgem car (BRIT), bumper car (US)

autoscu'ola *sf* driving school
autos'tima *sf* self-esteem
autos'top *sm* hitchhiking;
  autostop'pista, -i, -e *sm/f* hitchhiker
autos'trada *sf* motorway (BRIT),
  highway (US); **autostrada informatica**
  information superhighway

※ **AUTOSTRADE**
※
※ You have to pay to use Italian
※ motorways. They are indicated by an "A"
※ followed by a number on a green sign.
※ The speed limit on Italian motorways
※ is 130 kph.

auto'velox® *sm inv* (police) speed camera
autovet'tura *sf* (motor) car
au'tunno *sm* autumn
avam'braccio [avam'brattʃo] (*pl (f)* **-cia**)
  sm forearm
avangu'ardia *sf* vanguard
a'vanti *av* (*stato in luogo*) in front; (*moto:
  andare, venire*) forward; (*tempo: prima*)
  before ▷ *prep* (*luogo*): **~ a** before, in front
  of; (*tempo*): **~ Cristo** before Christ ▷ *escl*
  (*entrate*) come (*o* go) in!; (*Mil*) forward!;
  (*coraggio*) come on! ▷ *sm inv* (*Sport*)
  forward; **~ e indietro** backwards and
  forwards; **andare ~** to go forward;
  (*continuare*) to go on; (*precedere*) to go
  (on) ahead; (*orologio*) to be fast; **essere ~
  negli studi** to be well advanced with one's
  studies
avan'zare [avan'tsare] *vt* (*spostare
  in avanti*) to move forward, advance;
  (*domanda*) to put forward; (*promuovere*)
  to promote; (*essere creditore*): **~ qc da qn** to be
  owed sth by sb ▷ *vi* (*andare avanti*) to move
  forward, advance; (*progredire*) to make
  progress; (*essere d'avanzo*) to be left, remain
ava'ria *sf* (*guasto*) damage; (*: meccanico*)
  breakdown
a'varo, -a *ag* avaricious, miserly ▷ *sm*
  miser

  PAROLA CHIAVE

a'vere *sm* (*Comm*) credit; **gli averi** (*ricchezze*)
  wealth *sg*
  ▷ *vt* **1** (*possedere*) to have; **ha due
  bambini/una bella casa** she has (got)
  two children/a lovely house; **ha i capelli
  lunghi** he has (got) long hair; **non ho da
  mangiare/bere** I've (got) nothing to eat/
  drink, I don't have anything to eat/drink
  2 (*indossare*) to wear, have on; **aveva una
  maglietta rossa** he was wearing *o* he had
  on a red tee-shirt; **ha gli occhiali** he wears

o has glasses
  3 (*ricevere*) to get; **hai avuto l'assegno?**
  did you get *o* have you had the cheque?
  4 (*età, dimensione*) to be; **ha 9 anni** he
  is 9 (years old); **la stanza ha 3 metri di
  lunghezza** the room is 3 metres in length;
  vedi **fame**; **paura** *ecc*
  5 (*tempo*): **quanti ne abbiamo oggi?**
  what's the date today?; **ne hai per molto?**
  will you be long?
  6 (*fraseologia*): **avercela con qn** to be
  angry with sb; **cos'hai?** what's wrong *o*
  what's the matter (with you)?; **non ha
  niente a che vedere** *o* **fare con me** it's
  got nothing to do with me
  ▷ *vb aus* **1** to have; **aver bevuto/
  mangiato** to have drunk/eaten
  2 (*+ da + infinito*): **avere da fare qc** to have
  to do sth; **non hai che da chiederlo** you
  only have to ask him

aviazi'one [avjat'tsjone] *sf* aviation; (*Mil*)
  air force
'avido, -a *ag* eager; (*peg*) greedy
avo'cado *sm* avocado
a'vorio *sm* ivory
Avv. *abbr* = **avvocato**
avvantaggi'are [avvantad'dʒare]
  vt to favour; **avvantaggiarsi** *vpr*
  **avvantaggiarsi negli affari/sui
  concorrenti** to get ahead in business/of
  one's competitors
avvele'nare *vt* to poison
av'vengo *ecc vb vedi* **avvenire**
avveni'mento *sm* event
avve'nire *vi, vb impers* to happen, occur
  ▷ *sm* future
av'venni *ecc vb vedi* **avvenire**
avven'tato, -a *ag* rash, reckless
avven'tura *sf* adventure; (*amorosa*) affair
avventu'rarsi *vpr* to venture
avventu'roso, -a *ag* adventurous
avve'rarsi *vpr* to come true
av'verbio *sm* adverb
avverrò *ecc vb vedi* **avvenire**
avver'sario, -a *ag* opposing ▷ *sm*
  opponent, adversary
avver'tenza [avver'tentsa] *sf*
  (*ammonimento*) warning; (*cautela*) care;
  (*premessa*) foreword; **avvertenze** *sfpl*
  (*istruzioni per l'uso*) instructions
avverti'mento *sm* warning
avver'tire *vt* (*avvisare*) to warn; (*rendere
  consapevole*) to inform, notify; (*percepire*)
  to feel
avvi'are *vt* (*mettere sul cammino*) to direct;
  (*impresa, trattative*) to begin, start; (*motore*)
  to start; **avviarsi** *vpr* to set off, set out
avvici'nare [avvitʃi'nare] *vt* to bring

near; (*trattare con: persona*) to approach;
avvicinarsi *vpr* **avvicinarsi (a qn/qc)** to
approach (sb/sth), draw near (to sb/sth)
avvi'lito, -a *ag* discouraged
avvin'cente *ag* captivating
avvi'sare *vt* (*far sapere*) to inform;
(*mettere in guardia*) to warn; **av'viso** *sm*
warning; (*annuncio*) announcement;
(: *affisso*) notice; (*inserzione pubblicitaria*)
advertisement; **a mio avviso** in my
opinion; **avviso di chiamata** (*servizio*)
call waiting; (*segnale*) call waiting signal;
avviso di garanzia (*Dir*) notification (*of
impending investigation and of the right to
name a defence lawyer*)

> Attenzione! In inglese esiste la parola
> *advice* che però vuol dire *consiglio*.

avvis'tare *vt* to sight
avvi'tare *vt* to screw down (*o* in)
avvo'cato, -'essa *sm/f* (*Dir*) barrister
(*BRIT*), lawyer; (*fig*) defender, advocate
av'volgere [av'vɔldʒere] *vt* to roll up;
(*avviluppare*) to wrap up; **avvolgersi** *vpr*
(*avvilupparsi*) to wrap o.s. up; **avvol'gibile**
sm roller blind (*BRIT*), blind
av'volsi *ecc vb vedi* **avvolgere**
avvol'toio *sm* vulture
aza'lea [addza'lea] *sf* azalea
azi'enda [ad'dzjɛnda] *sf* business, firm,
concern; **azienda agricola** farm
azi'one [at'tsjone] *sf* action; (*Comm*) share
a'zoto [ad'dzɔto] *sm* nitrogen
azzar'dare [addzar'dare] *vt* (*soldi, vita*) to
risk, hazard; (*domanda, ipotesi*) to hazard,
venture; **azzardarsi** *vpr* **azzardarsi a fare**
to dare (to) do
az'zardo [ad'dzardo] *sm* risk
azzec'care [attsek'kare] *vt* (*risposta ecc*)
to get right
azzuf'farsi [attsuf'farsi] *vpr* to come to
blows
az'zurro, -a [ad'dzurro] *ag* blue ▷ *sm*
(*colore*) blue; **gli azzurri** (*Sport*) the Italian
national team

'babbo *sm* (*fam*) dad, daddy; **Babbo
Natale** Father Christmas
baby'sitter ['beɪbɪsɪtə'] *sm/f inv* baby-
sitter
'bacca, -che *sf* berry
baccalà *sm* dried salted cod; (*fig: peg*)
dummy
bac'chetta [bak'ketta] *sf* (*verga*) stick, rod;
(*di direttore d'orchestra*) baton; (*di tamburo*)
drumstick; **~ magica** magic wand
ba'checa, -che [ba'kɛka] *sf* (*mobile*)
showcase, display case; (*Univ, in ufficio*)
notice board (*BRIT*), bulletin board (*US*)
baci'are [ba'tʃare] *vt* to kiss; **baciarsi** *vpr*
to kiss (one another)
baci'nella [batʃi'nɛlla] *sf* basin
ba'cino [ba'tʃino] *sm* basin; (*Mineralogia*)
field, bed; (*Anat*) pelvis; (*Naut*) dock
'bacio ['batʃo] *sm* kiss
'baco, -chi *sm* worm; **baco da seta**
silkworm
ba'dare *vi* (*fare attenzione*) to take care, be
careful; (*occuparsi di*): **~ a** to look after, take
care of; (*dar ascolto*): **~ a** to pay attention
to; **bada ai fatti tuoi!** mind your own
business!
'baffi *smpl* moustache *sg*; (*di animale*)
whiskers; **ridere sotto i ~** to laugh up
one's sleeve; **leccarsi i ~** to lick one's lips
bagagli'aio [bagaʎ'ʎajo] *sm* luggage van

(BRIT) o car (US); (Aut) boot (BRIT), trunk (US)

ba'gaglio [ba'gaʎʎo] sm luggage no pl, baggage no pl; **fare/disfare i bagagli** to pack/unpack; **i nostri bagagli non sono arrivati** our luggage has not arrived; **può mandare qualcuno a prendere i nostri bagagli?** could you send someone to collect our luggage?; **bagaglio a mano** hand luggage

bagli'ore [baʎ'ʎore] sm flash, dazzling light; **un ~ di speranza** a ray of hope

ba'gnante [baɲ'ɲante] sm/f bather

ba'gnare [baɲ'ɲare] vt to wet; (inzuppare) to soak; (innaffiare) to water; (fiume) to flow through; (: mare) to wash, bathe; **bagnarsi** vpr to get wet; (al mare) to go swimming o bathing; (in vasca) to have a bath

ba'gnato, -a [baɲ'ɲato] ag wet

ba'gnino [baɲ'ɲino] sm lifeguard

'bagno ['baɲɲo] sm bath; (stanza) bathroom; (toilette) toilet; **bagni** smpl (stabilimento) baths; **fare il ~** to have a bath; (nel mare) to go swimming o bathing; **dov'è il ~?** where's the toilet?; **fare il ~ a qn** to give sb a bath; **mettere a ~** to soak; **~ schiuma** bubble bath

bagnoma'ria [baɲɲoma'ria] sm **cuocere a ~** to cook in a double saucepan

bagnoschi'uma [baɲɲoskj'uma] sm inv bubble bath

'baia sf bay

balbet'tare vi to stutter, stammer; (bimbo) to babble ▷ vt to stammer out

bal'canico, -a, ci, che ag Balkan

bal'cone sm balcony; **avete una camera con ~?** do you have a room with a balcony?

bal'doria sf **fare ~** to have a riotous time

ba'lena sf whale

ba'leno sm flash of lightning; **in un ~** in a flash

bal'lare vt, vi to dance

balle'rina sf dancer; ballet dancer; (scarpa) ballet shoe

balle'rino sm dancer; ballet dancer

bal'letto sm ballet

'ballo sm dance; (azione) dancing no pl; **essere in ~** (fig: persona) to be involved; (: cosa) to be at stake

balne'are ag seaside cpd; (stagione) bathing

'balsamo sm (aroma) balsam; (lenimento, fig) balm

bal'zare [bal'tsare] vi to bounce; (lanciarsi) to jump, leap; **'balzo** sm bounce; jump, leap; (del terreno) crag

bam'bina ag, sf vedi **bambino**

bam'bino, -a sm/f child

'bambola sf doll

bambù sm bamboo

ba'nale ag banal, commonplace

ba'nana sf banana

'banca, -che sf bank; **banca dati** data bank

banca'rella sf stall

banca'rotta sf bankruptcy; **fare ~** to go bankrupt

ban'chetto [ban'ketto] sm banquet

banchi'ere [ban'kjere] sm banker

ban'china [ban'kina] sf (di porto) quay; (per pedoni, ciclisti) path; (di stazione) platform; **~ cedevole** (Aut) soft verge (BRIT) o shoulder (US)

'banco, -chi sm bench; (di negozio) counter; (di mercato) stall; (di officina) (work-)bench; (Geo, banca) bank; **banco di corallo** coral reef; **banco degli imputati** dock; **banco di prova** (fig) testing ground; **banco dei testimoni** witness box; **banco dei pegni** pawnshop; **banco di nebbia** bank of fog

'Bancomat® sm inv automated banking; (tessera) cash card

banco'nota sf banknote

'banda sf band; (di stoffa) band, stripe; (lato, parte) side; **~ perforata** punch tape

bandi'era sf flag, banner

ban'dito sm outlaw, bandit

'bando sm proclamation; (esilio) exile, banishment; **~ alle chiacchiere!** that's enough talk!; **bando di concorso** announcement of a competition

bar sm inv bar

'bara sf coffin

ba'racca, -che sf shed, hut; (peg) hovel; **mandare avanti la ~** to keep things going

ba'rare vi to cheat

'baratro sm abyss

ba'ratto sm barter

ba'rattolo sm (di latta) tin; (di vetro) jar; (di coccio) pot

'barba sf beard; **farsi la ~** to shave; **farla in ~ a qn** (fig) to do sth to sb's face; **che ~!** what a bore!

barbabi'etola sf beetroot (BRIT), beet (US); **barbabietola da zucchero** sugar beet

barbi'ere sm barber

bar'bone sm (cane) poodle; (vagabondo) tramp

'barca, -che sf boat; **barca a motore** motorboat; **barca a remi** rowing boat; **barca a vela** sail(ing) boat

barcol'lare vi to stagger

ba'rella sf (lettiga) stretcher

ba'rile sm barrel, cask

ba'rista, -i, -e sm/f barman/maid; (proprietario) bar owner

ba'rocco, -a, -chi, -che *ag, sm* baroque
ba'rometro *sm* barometer
ba'rone *sm* baron; **baro'nessa** *sf* baroness
'barra *sf* bar; (*Naut*) helm; (*linea grafica*) line, stroke
bar'rare *vt* to bar
barri'carsi *vpr* to barricade o.s.
barri'era *sf* barrier; (*Geo*) reef
ba'ruffa *sf* scuffle
barzel'letta [bardzel'letta] *sf* joke, funny story
ba'sare *vt* to base, found; **basarsi** *vpr* **basarsi su** (*fatti, prove*) to be based o founded on; (: *persona*) to base one's arguments on
'basco, -a, -schi, -sche *ag* Basque ▷ *sm* (*copricapo*) beret
'base *sf* base; (*fig: fondamento*) basis; (*Pol*) rank and file; **di ~** basic; **in ~ a** on the basis of, according to; **a ~ di caffè** coffee-based
'baseball ['beisbɔ:l] *sm* baseball
ba'sette *sfpl* sideburns
ba'silica, -che *sf* basilica
ba'silico *sm* basil
basket ['basket] *sm* basketball
bas'sista, -i, -e *sm/f* bass player
'basso, -a *ag* low; (*di statura*) short; (*meridionale*) southern ▷ *sm* bottom, lower part; (*Mus*) bass; **la bassa Italia** southern Italy
bassorili'evo *sm* bas-relief
bas'sotto, -a *ag* squat ▷ *sm* (*cane*) dachshund
'basta *escl* (that's) enough!, that will do!
bas'tardo, -a *ag* (*animale, pianta*) hybrid, crossbreed; (*persona*) illegitimate, bastard; (*peg*) ▷ *sm/f* illegitimate child, bastard (*peg*)
bas'tare *vi, vb impers* to be enough, be sufficient; **~ a qn** to be enough for sb; **basta chiedere** *o* **che chieda a un vigile** you have only to *o* need only ask a policeman; **basta così, grazie** that's enough, thanks
basto'nare *vt* to beat, thrash
baston'cino [baston'tʃino] *sm* (*Sci*) ski pole; **bastoncini di pesce** fish fingers
bas'tone *sm* stick; **~ da passeggio** walking stick
bat'taglia [bat'taʎʎa] *sf* battle; fight
bat'tello *sm* boat
bat'tente *sm* (*imposta: di porta*) wing, flap; (: *di finestra*) shutter; (*batacchio: di porta*) knocker; (: *di orologio*) hammer; **chiudere i battenti** (*fig*) to shut up shop
'battere *vt* to beat; (*grano*) to thresh; (*percorrere*) to scour ▷ *vi* (*bussare*) to knock; (*urtare*): **~ contro** to hit *o* strike against;

(*pioggia, sole*) to beat down; (*cuore*) to beat; (*Tennis*) to serve; **battersi** *vpr* to fight; **~ le mani** to clap; **~ i piedi** to stamp one's feet; **~ a macchina** to type; **~ bandiera italiana** to fly the Italian flag; **~ in testa** (*Aut*) to knock; **in un batter d'occhio** in the twinkling of an eye
batte'ria *sf* battery; (*Mus*) drums *pl*
bat'terio *sm* bacterium
batte'rista, -i, -e *sm/f* drummer
bat'tesimo *sm* (*rito*) baptism; christening
battez'zare [batted'dzare] *vt* to baptize; to christen
batti'panni *sm inv* carpet-beater
battis'trada *sm inv* (*di pneumatico*) tread; (*di gara*) pacemaker
'battito *sm* beat, throb; **battito cardiaco** heartbeat
bat'tuta *sf* blow; (*di macchina da scrivere*) stroke; (*Mus*) bar; beat; (*Teatro*) cue; (*frase spiritosa*) witty remark; (*di caccia*) beating; (*Polizia*) combing, scouring; (*Tennis*) service
ba'tuffolo *sm* wad
ba'ule *sm* trunk; (*Aut*) boot (BRIT), trunk (US)
'bava *sf* (*di animale*) slaver, slobber; (*di lumaca*) slime; (*di vento*) breath
bava'glino [bavaʎ'ʎino] *sm* bib
ba'vaglio [ba'vaʎʎo] *sm* gag
'bavero *sm* collar
ba'zar [bad'dzar] *sm inv* bazaar
BCE *sigla f* (= *Banca centrale europea*) ECB
be'ato, -a *ag* blessed; (*fig*) happy; **~ te!** lucky you!
bec'care *vt* to peck; (*fig: raffreddore*) to catch; **beccarsi** *vpr* (*fig*) to squabble; **beccarsi qc** to catch sth
beccherò *ecc* [bekke'rɔ] *vb vedi* beccare
'becco, -chi *sm* beak, bill; (*di caffettiera ecc*) spout; lip
be'fana *sf* hag, witch; **la B~** old woman who, according to legend, brings children their presents at the Epiphany; (*Epifania*) Epiphany

❉ BEFANA

The **Befana** is a national holiday on the feast of the Epiphany. It takes its name from **la Befana**, the old woman who, according to Italian legend comes down the chimney during the night leaving gifts for children who have been good, and coal for those who have not.

bef'fardo, -a *ag* scornful, mocking
'begli ['beʎʎi] *ag vedi* **bello**
'bei *ag vedi* **bello**

beige [bɛʒ] *ag inv* beige
bel *ag vedi* **bello**
be'lare *vi* to bleat
'**belga, -gi, -ghe** *ag, sm/f* Belgian
'**Belgio** ['bɛldʒo] *sm* **il ~** Belgium
'**bella** *sf* (*Sport*) decider; *vedi anche* **bello**
bel'lezza [bel'lettsa] *sf* beauty

 PAROLA CHIAVE

'**bello, -a** (*ag: dav sm* **bel** + C, **bell'** + V,
bello + *s impura, gn, pn, ps, x, z, pl* **bei** +
C, **begli** + *s impura ecc o* V) *ag* **1** (*oggetto,
donna, paesaggio*) beautiful, lovely; (*uomo*)
handsome; (*tempo*) beautiful, fine, lovely;
le belle arti fine arts
2 (*quantità*): **una bella cifra** a considerable
sum of money; **un bel niente** absolutely
nothing
3 (*rafforzativo*): **è una truffa bella e
buona!** it's a real fraud!; **è bell'e finito** it's
already finished
▷ *sm* **1** (*bellezza*) beauty; (*tempo*) fine
weather
2: **adesso viene il bello** now comes the
best bit; **sul più bello** at the crucial point;
cosa fai di bello? are you doing anything
interesting?
▷ *av* **fa bello** the weather is fine, it's fine

'**belva** *sf* wild animal
belve'dere *sm inv* panoramic viewpoint
benché [ben'ke] *cong* although
'**benda** *sf* bandage; (*per gli occhi*) blindfold;
ben'dare *vt* to bandage; to blindfold
'**bene** *av* well; (*completamente, affatto*):
è ben difficile it's very difficult ▷ *ag inv*
gente ~ well-to-do people ▷ *sm* good;
beni *smpl* (*averi*) property *sg*, estate *sg*;
io sto ~/poco ~ I'm well/not very well;
va ~ all right; **volere un ~ dell'anima a
qn** to love sb very much; **un uomo per ~**
a respectable man; **fare ~** to do the right
thing; **fare ~ a** (*salute*) to be good for; **fare
del ~ a qn** to do sb a good turn; **beni di
consumo** consumer goods
bene'detto, -a *pp di* **benedire** ▷ *ag*
blessed, holy
bene'dire *vt* to bless; to consecrate
benedu'cato, -a *ag* well-mannered
benefi'cenza [benefi'tʃentsa] *sf* charity
bene'ficio [bene'fitʃo] *sm* benefit; **con ~
d'inventario** (*fig*) with reservations
be'nessere *sm* well-being
benes'tante *ag* well-to-do
be'nigno, -a [be'niɲɲo] *ag* kind, kindly;
(*critica ecc*) favourable; (*Med*) benign
benve'nuto, -a *ag, sm* welcome; **dare il ~
a qn** to welcome sb

ben'zina [ben'dzina] *sf* petrol (BRIT), gas
(US); **fare ~** to get petrol (BRIT) o gas (US);
sono rimasto senza ~ I have run out of
petrol (BRIT) o gas (US); **benzina verde**
unleaded (petrol); **benzi'naio** *sm* petrol
(BRIT) o gas (US) pump attendant
'**bere** *vt* to drink; **darla a ~ a qn** (*fig*) to fool
sb; **vuoi qualcosa da ~?** would you like
a drink?
ber'lina *sf* (*Aut*) saloon (car) (BRIT), sedan
(US)
Ber'lino *sf* Berlin
ber'muda *smpl* (*calzoncini*) Bermuda
shorts
ber'noccolo *sm* bump; (*inclinazione*) flair
ber'retto *sm* cap
berrò *ecc vb vedi* **bere**
ber'saglio [ber'saʎʎo] *sm* target
besciamella [beʃʃa'mɛlla] *sf* béchamel
sauce
bes'temmia *sf* curse; (*Rel*) blasphemy
bestemmi'are *vi* to curse, swear; to
blaspheme ▷ *vt* to curse, swear at; to
blaspheme
'**bestia** *sf* animal; **andare in ~** (*fig*) to fly
into a rage; **besti'ale** *ag* beastly; animal
cpd; (*fam*): **fa un freddo bestiale** it's
bitterly cold; **besti'ame** *sm* livestock;
(*bovino*) cattle *pl*
be'tulla *sf* birch
be'vanda *sf* drink, beverage
'**bevo** *ecc vb vedi* **bere**
be'vuto, -a *pp di* **bere**
'**bevvi** *ecc vb vedi* **bere**
bianche'ria [bjanke'ria] *sf* linen; **~
da donna** ladies' underwear, lingerie;
biancheria femminile lingerie;
biancheria intima underwear
bi'anco, -a, -chi, -che *ag* white; (*non
scritto*) blank ▷ *sm* white; (*intonaco*)
whitewash ▷ *sm/f* white, white man/
woman; **in ~** (*foglio, assegno*) blank; (*notte*)
sleepless; **in ~ e nero** (*TV, Fot*) black and
white; **mangiare in ~** to follow a bland
diet; **pesce in ~** boiled fish; **andare in
~** (*non riuscire*) to fail; **bianco dell'uovo**
egg-white
biasi'mare *vt* to disapprove of, censure
'**Bibbia** *sf* (*anche fig*) bible
bibe'ron *sm inv* feeding bottle
'**bibita** *sf* (soft) drink
biblio'teca, -che *sf* library; (*mobile*)
bookcase
bicarbo'nato *sm* **~ (di sodio)** bicarbonate
(of soda)
bicchi'ere [bik'kjɛre] *sm* glass
bici'cletta [bitʃi'kletta] *sf* bicycle; **andare
in ~** to cycle
bidè *sm inv* bidet

bi'dello, -a *sm/f* (*Ins*) janitor
bi'done *sm* drum, can; (*anche:* ~ **dell'immondizia**) (dust)bin; (*fam: truffa*) swindle; **fare un ~ a qn** (*fam*) to let sb down; to cheat sb
bien'nale *ag* biennial

bifamili'are *sf* ≈ semi-detached house
bifor'carsi *vpr* to fork
bigiotte'ria [bidʒotte'ria] *sf* costume jewellery; (*negozio*) jeweller's (*selling only costume jewellery*)
bigliet'taio, -a *sm/f* (*in treno*) ticket inspector; (*in autobus*) conductor
bigliette'ria [biʎʎette'ria] *sf* (*di stazione*) ticket office; booking office; (*di teatro*) box office
bigli'etto [biʎ'ʎetto] *sm* (*per viaggi, spettacoli ecc*) ticket; (*cartoncino*) card; (*anche:* ~ **di banca**) (bank)note; **biglietto d'auguri** greetings card; **biglietto da visita** visiting card; **biglietto d'andata e ritorno** return (ticket), round-trip ticket (*us*); **biglietto di sola andata** single (ticket)
bignè [biɲ'ɲe] *sm inv* cream puff
bigo'dino *sm* roller, curler
bi'gotto, -a *ag* over-pious ▷ *sm/f* church fiend
bi'kini *sm inv* bikini
bi'lancia, -ce [bi'lantʃa] *sf* (*pesa*) scales *pl*; (: *di precisione*) balance; (*dello zodiaco*): **B~** Libra; **bilancia commerciale** balance of trade; **bilancia dei pagamenti** balance of payments
bi'lancio [bi'lantʃo] *sm* (*Comm*) balance(-sheet); (*statale*) budget; **fare il ~ di** (*fig*) to assess; **bilancio consuntivo** (*final*) balance; **bilancio preventivo** budget
bili'ardo *sm* billiards *sg*; billiard table
bi'lingue *ag* bilingual
bilo'cale *sm* two-room flat (*Brit*) o apartment (*us*)
bi'nario, -a *ag* (*sistema*) binary ▷ *sm* (*railway*) track o line; (*piattaforma*) platform; **da che ~ parte il treno per Londra?** which platform does the train for

London go from?; **binario morto** dead-end track
bi'nocolo *sm* binoculars *pl*
bio... *prefisso*: **biodegra'dabile** *ag* biodegradable; **biodi'namico, -a, -ci, -che** *ag* biodynamic; **biogra'fia** *sf* biography; **biolo'gia** *sf* biology
bio'logico, -a, -ci, -che *ag* (*scienze, fenomeni ecc*}) biological; (*agricoltura, prodotti*) organic; **guerra biologica** biological warfare
bi'ondo, -a *ag* blond, fair
biotecnologia [biotekno lo'dʒia] *sf* biotechnology
biri'chino, -a [biri'kino] *ag* mischievous ▷ *sm/f* scamp, little rascal
bi'rillo *sm* skittle (*BRIT*), pin (*us*)
'biro® *sf inv* biro®
'birra *sf* beer; **a tutta ~** (*fig*) at top speed; **birra chiara/scura** ≈ lager/stout; **birre'ria** *sf* ≈ bierkeller
bis *escl, sm inv* encore
bis'betico, -a, -ci, -che *ag* ill-tempered, crabby
bisbigli'are [bisbiʎ'ʎare] *vt, vi* to whisper
'bisca, -sche *sf* gambling-house
'biscia, -sce ['biʃʃa] *sf* snake; **biscia d'acqua** grass snake
biscot'tato, -a *ag* crisp; **fette biscottate** rusks
bis'cotto *sm* biscuit
bisessu'ale *ag, sm/f* bisexual
bises'tile *ag* **anno ~** leap year
bis'nonno, -a *sm/f* great grandfather/ grandmother
biso'gnare [bizoɲ'ɲare] *vb impers* **bisogna che tu parta/lo faccia** you'll have to go/do it; **bisogna parlargli** we'll (o I'll) have to talk to him
bi'sogno [bi'zoɲɲo] *sm* need; **ha ~ di qualcosa?** do you need anything?
bis'tecca, -che *sf* steak, beefsteak
bisticci'are [bistit'tʃare] *vi* to quarrel, bicker; **bisticciarsi** *vpr* to quarrel, bicker
'bisturi *sm* scalpel
'bivio *sm* fork; (*fig*) dilemma
biz'zarro, -a [bid'dzarro] *ag* bizarre, strange
blate'rare *vi* to chatter
blin'dato, -a *ag* armoured
bloc'care *vt* to block; (*isolare*) to isolate, cut off; (*porto*) to blockade; (*prezzi, beni*) to freeze; (*meccanismo*) to jam; **bloccarsi** *vpr* (*motore*) to stall; (*freni, porta*) to jam, stick; (*ascensore*) to stop, get stuck
blocche'rò *ecc* [blokke'rɔ] *vb vedi* **bloccare**
bloc'chetto [blok'ketto] *sm* notebook; (*di biglietti*) book

'blocco, -chi sm block; (Mil) blockade; (dei fitti) restriction; (quadernetto) pad; (fig: unione) coalition; (il bloccare) blocking; isolating, cutting-off; blockading; freezing; jamming; **in ~** (nell'insieme) as a whole; (Comm) in bulk; **blocco cardiaco** cardiac arrest; **blocco stradale** road block

blu ag inv, sm dark blue

'blusa sf (camiciotto) smock; (camicetta) blouse

'boa sm inv (Zool) boa constrictor; (sciarpa) feather boa ▷ sf buoy

bo'ato sm rumble, roar

bob [bɔb] sm inv bobsleigh

'bocca, -che sf mouth; **in ~ al lupo!** good luck!

boc'caccia, -ce [bok'kattʃa] sf (malalingua) gossip; **fare le boccacce** to pull faces

boc'cale sm jug; **boccale da birra** tankard

boc'cetta [bot'tʃetta] sf small bottle

'boccia, -ce ['bottʃa] sf bottle; (da vino) decanter, carafe; (palla) bowl; **gioco delle bocce** bowls sg

bocci'are [bot'tʃare] vt (proposta, progetto) to reject; (Ins) to fail; (Bocce) to hit

bocci'olo [bot'tʃɔlo] sm bud

boc'cone sm mouthful, morsel

boicot'tare vt to boycott

'bolla sf bubble; (Med) blister; **bolla di consegna** (Comm) delivery note; **bolla papale** papal bull

bol'lente ag boiling; boiling hot

bol'letta sf bill; (ricevuta) receipt; **essere in ~** to be hard up

bollet'tino sm bulletin; (Comm) note; **bollettino meteorologico** weather report; **bollettino di spedizione** consignment note

bollicina [bolli'tʃina] sf bubble

bol'lire vt, vi to boil

bolli'tore sm (Cuc) kettle; (per riscaldamento) boiler

'bollo sm stamp; **bollo per patente** driving licence tax; **bollo postale** postmark

'bomba sf bomb; **bomba atomica** atom bomb; **bomba a mano** hand grenade; **bomba ad orologeria** time bomb

bombarda'mento sm bombardment; bombing

bombar'dare vt to bombard; (da aereo) to bomb

'bombola sf cylinder

bombo'letta sf aerosol

bomboni'era sf box of sweets (as souvenir at weddings, first communions etc)

bo'nifico, -ci sm (riduzione, abbuono)

discount; (versamento a terzi) credit transfer

bontà sf goodness; (cortesia) kindness; **aver la ~ di fare qc** to be good o kind enough to do sth

borbot'tare vi to mumble

'borchia ['borkja] sf stud

bor'deaux [bɔr'dɔ] ag inv, sm inv maroon

'bordo sm (Naut) ship's side; (orlo) edge; (striscia di guarnizione) border, trim; **a ~ di** (nave, aereo) aboard, on board; (macchina) in

bor'ghese [bor'geze] ag (spesso peg) middle-class; bourgeois; **abito ~** civilian dress

'borgo, -ghi sm (paesino) village; (quartiere) district; (sobborgo) suburb

boro'talco sm talcum powder

bor'raccia, -ce [bor'rattʃa] sf canteen, water-bottle

'borsa sf bag; (anche: ~ da signora) handbag; (Econ): **la B~ (valori)** the Stock Exchange; **borsa dell'acqua calda** hot-water bottle; **borsa nera** black market; **borsa della spesa** shopping bag; **borsa di studio** grant; **borsel'lino** sm purse; **bor'setta** sf handbag

'bosco, -schi sm wood

bos'niaco, -a, ci, che ag, sm/f Bosnian

'Bosnia Erze'govina ['bɔsnja erdze'govina] sf **la ~** Bosnia Herzegovina

Bot, bot sigla m inv (= buono ordinario del Tesoro) short-term Treasury bond

bo'tanica sf botany

bo'tanico, -a, -ci, -che ag botanical ▷ sm botanist

'botola sf trap door

'botta sf blow; (rumore) bang

'botte sf barrel, cask

bot'tega, -ghe sf shop; (officina) workshop

bot'tiglia [bot'tiʎʎa] sf bottle; **bottiglie'ria** sf wine shop

bot'tino sm (di guerra) booty; (di rapina, furto) loot

'botto sm bang; crash; **di ~** suddenly

bot'tone sm button; **attaccare ~ a qn** (fig) to buttonhole sb

bo'vino, -a ag bovine; **bovini** smpl cattle

box [bɔks] sm inv (per cavalli) horsebox; (per macchina) lock-up; (per macchina da corsa) pit; (per bambini) playpen

boxe [bɔks] sf boxing

'boxer ['bɔkser] sm inv (cane) boxer ▷ smpl (mutande): **un paio di ~** a pair of boxer shorts

BR sigla fpl = **Brigate Rosse**

brac'cetto [brat'tʃetto] sm **a ~** arm in arm

braccia'letto sm bracelet, bangle

bracci'ata [brat'tʃata] *sf* (*nel nuoto*) stroke

'braccio ['brattʃo] (*pl(f)* **braccia**) *sm* (*Anat*) arm; (*pl(m)* **bracci**: *di gru, fiume*) arm; (: *di edificio*) wing; **braccio di mare** sound; **bracci'olo** *sm* (*appoggio*) arm

'bracco, -chi *sm* hound

'brace ['bratʃe] *sf* embers *pl*

braci'ola [bra'tʃɔla] *sf* (*Cuc*) chop

'branca, -che *sf* branch

'branchia ['brankja] *sf* (*Zool*) gill

'branco, -chi (*di cani, lupi*) pack; (*di pecore*) flock; (*peg: di persone*) gang, pack

bran'dina *sf* camp bed (*BRIT*), cot (*US*)

'brano *sm* piece; (*di libro*) passage

Bra'sile *sm* **il ~** Brazil; **brasili'ano, -a** *ag, sm/f* Brazilian

'bravo, -a *ag* (*abile*) clever, capable, skilful; (*buono*) good, honest; (: *bambino*) good; (*coraggioso*) brave; **~!** well done!; (*a teatro*) bravo!

bra'vura *sf* cleverness, skill

Bre'tagna [bre'taɲɲa] *sf* **la ~** Brittany

bre'tella *sf* (*Aut*) link; **bretelle** *sfpl* (*di calzoni*) braces

bretone *ag, sm/f* Breton

'breve *ag* brief, short; **in ~** in short

brevet'tare *vt* to patent

bre'vetto *sm* patent; **brevetto di pilotaggio** pilot's licence (*BRIT*) o license (*US*)

'bricco, -chi *sm* jug; **bricco del caffè** coffeepot

briciola ['britʃola] *sf* crumb

briciolo ['britʃolo] *sm* (*specie fig*) bit

'briga, -ghe *sf* (*fastidio*) trouble, bother; **pigliarsi la ~ di fare qc** to take the trouble to do sth

bri'gata *sf* (*Mil*) brigade; (*gruppo*) group, party; **Brigate Rosse** (*Pol*) Red Brigades

'briglia ['briʎʎa] *sf* rein; **a ~ sciolta** at full gallop; (*fig*) at full speed

bril'lante *ag* bright; (*anche fig*) brilliant; (*che luccica*) shining ▷ *sm* diamond

bril'lare *vi* to shine; (*mina*) to blow up ▷ *vt* (*mina*) to set off

'brillo, -a *ag* merry, tipsy

'brina *sf* hoarfrost

brin'dare *vi* **~ a qn/qc** to drink to o toast sb/sth

'brindisi *sm inv* toast

bri'oche [bri'ɔʃ] *sf inv* brioche

bri'tannico, -a, -ci, -che *ag* British

'brivido *sm* shiver; (*di ribrezzo*) shudder; (*fig*) thrill

brizzo'lato, -a [brittso'lato] *ag* (*persona*) going grey; (*barba, capelli*) greying

'brocca, -che *sf* jug

'broccoli *smpl* broccoli *sg*

'brodo *sm* broth; (*per cucinare*) stock;

brodo ristretto consommé

bron'chite [bron'kite] *sf* (*Med*) bronchitis

bronto'lare *vi* to grumble; (*tuono, stomaco*) to rumble

'bronzo ['brondzo] *sm* bronze

'browser ['brauzer] *sm inv* (*Inform*) browser

brucia'pelo [brutʃa'pelo]: **a ~** *av* point-blank

bruci'are [bru'tʃare] *vt* to burn; (*scottare*) to scald ▷ *vi* to burn; **bruciarsi** *vpr* to burn o.s.; (*fallire*) to ruin one's chances; **~ le tappe** (*fig*) to shoot ahead; **bruciarsi la carriera** to ruin one's career

'bruco, -chi *sm* caterpillar; grub

'brufolo *sm* pimple, spot

'brullo, -a *ag* bare, bleak

'bruno, -a *ag* brown, dark; (*persona*) dark(-haired)

'brusco, -a, -schi, -sche *ag* (*sapore*) sharp; (*modi, persona*) brusque, abrupt; (*movimento*) abrupt, sudden

bru'sio *sm* buzz, buzzing

bru'tale *ag* brutal

'brutto, -a *ag* ugly; (*cattivo*) bad; (*malattia, strada, affare*) nasty, bad; **~ tempo** bad weather

Bru'xelles [bry'sɛl] *sf* Brussels

BSE [biesse'e] *sigla f* (= *encefalopatia spongiforme bovina*) BSE

'buca, -che *sf* hole; (*avvallamento*) hollow; **buca delle lettere** letterbox

buca'neve *sm inv* snowdrop

bu'care *vt* (*forare*) to make a hole (*o* holes) in; (*pungere*) to pierce; (*biglietto*) to punch; **bucarsi** *vpr* (*di eroina*) to mainline; **~ una gomma** to have a puncture

bu'cato *sm* (*operazione*) washing; (*panni*) wash, washing

'buccia, -ce ['buttʃa] *sf* skin, peel

bucherò *ecc* [buke'rɔ] *vb vedi* **bucare**

'buco, -chi *sm* hole

bud'dismo *sm* Buddhism

bu'dino *sm* pudding

'bue *sm* ox; **carne di ~** beef

bu'fera *sf* storm

'buffo, -a *ag* funny; (*Teatro*) comic

bu'gia, -'gie [bu'dʒia] *sf* lie; **dire una ~** to tell a lie; **bugi'ardo, -a** *ag* lying, deceitful ▷ *sm/f* liar

'buio, -a *ag* dark ▷ *sm* dark, darkness

'bulbo *sm* (*Bot*) bulb; **bulbo oculare** eyeball

Bulga'ria *sf* **la ~** Bulgaria

'bulgaro, -a *ag, sm/f, sm* Bulgarian

buli'mia *sf* bulimia; **bu'limico, -a, -ci, -che** *ag* bulimic

bul'lone *sm* bolt

buona'notte *escl* good night! ▷ *sf* **dare la**

~ a to say good night to
buona'sera *escl* good evening!
buongi'orno [bwon'dʒorno] *escl* good morning (o afternoon)!
buongus'taio, -a *sm/f* gourmet

 PAROLA CHIAVE

bu'ono, -a (*ag: dav sm* buon + CoV, buono + *s impura, gn, pn, ps, x, z; dav sf* buon' + V) *ag*
1 (*gen*) good; **un buon pranzo/ristorante** a good lunch/restaurant; **(stai) buono!** behave!
2 (*benevolo*): **buono (con)** good (to), kind (to)
3 (*giusto, valido*) right; **al momento buono** at the right moment
4 (*adatto*): **buono a/da** fit for/to; **essere buono a nulla** to be no good o use at anything
5 (*auguri*): **buon anno!** happy New Year!; **buon appetito!** enjoy your meal!; **buon compleanno!** happy birthday!; **buon divertimento!** have a nice time!; **buona fortuna!** good luck!; **buon riposo!** sleep well!; **buon viaggio!** bon voyage!, have a good trip!
6: **a buon mercato** cheap; **di buon'ora** early; **buon senso** common sense; **alla buona** *ag* simple
▷ *av* in a simple way, without any fuss ▷ *sm*
1 (*bontà*) goodness, good
2 (*Comm*) voucher, coupon; **buono di cassa** cash voucher; **buono di consegna** delivery note; **buono del Tesoro** Treasury bill

buon'senso *sm* = buon senso
burat'tino *sm* puppet
'burbero, -a *ag* surly, gruff
buro'cratico, -a, ci, che *ag* bureaucratic
burocra'zia [burokrat'tsia] *sf* bureaucracy
bur'rasca, -sche *sf* storm
'burro *sm* butter
bur'rone *sm* ravine
bus'sare *vi* to knock
'bussola *sf* compass
'busta *sf* (*da lettera*) envelope; (*astuccio*) case; **in ~ aperta/chiusa** in an unsealed/sealed envelope; **busta paga** pay packet
busta'rella *sf* bribe, backhander
bus'tina *sf* (*piccola busta*) envelope; (*di cibi, farmaci*) sachet; (*Mil*) forage cap; **bustina di tè** tea bag
'busto *sm* bust; (*indumento*) corset, girdle; **a mezzo ~** (*foto*) half-length
but'tare *vt* to throw; (*anche*: **~ via**) to throw away; **~ giù** (*scritto*) to scribble

down; (*cibo*) to gulp down; (*edificio*) to pull down, demolish; (*pasta, verdura*) to put into boiling water; **buttarsi** *vpr* (*saltare*) to jump; **buttarsi dalla finestra** to jump out of the window
byte ['bait] *sm inv* byte

C

to drop; (*anche:* **~ dal sonno**) to be falling asleep on one's feet; **~ dalle nuvole** (*fig*) to be taken aback

cadrò ecc vb vedi **cadere**

ca'duta sf fall; **la ~ dei capelli** hair loss

caffè sm inv coffee; (*locale*) café; **caffè corretto** espresso coffee with a shot of spirits; **caffè macchiato** coffee with a dash of milk; **caffè macinato** ground coffee

caffel'latte sm inv white coffee

caffetti'era sf coffeepot

'cagna ['kaɲɲa] sf (*Zool, peg*) bitch

CAI sigla m = **Club Alpino Italiano**

cala'brone sm hornet

cala'maro sm squid

cala'mita sf magnet

calamità sf inv calamity, disaster

ca'lare vt (*far discendere*) to lower; (*Maglia*) to decrease ▷ vi (*discendere*) to go (o come) down; (*tramontare*) to set, go down; **~ di peso** to lose weight

cal'cagno [kal'kaɲɲo] sm heel

cal'care sm (*incrostazione*) (lime)scale

'calce ['kaltʃe] sm in **~** at the foot of the page ▷ sf lime; **calce viva** quicklime

calci'are [kal'tʃare] vt, vi to kick; **calcia'tore** sm footballer

'calcio ['kaltʃo] sm (*pedata*) kick; (*sport*) football, soccer; (*di pistola, fucile*) butt; (*Chim*) calcium; **calcio d'angolo** (*Sport*) corner (kick); **calcio di punizione** (*Sport*) free kick; **calcio di rigore** penalty

calco'lare vt to calculate, work out, reckon; (*ponderare*) to weigh (up); **calcola'tore, -'trice** ag calculating ▷ sm calculator; (*fig*) calculating person; **calcolatore elettronico** computer; **calcola'trice** sf calculator

'calcolo sm (*anche Mat*) calculation; (*infinitesimale ecc*) calculus; (*Med*) stone; **fare i propri calcoli** (*fig*) to weigh the pros and cons; **per ~** out of self-interest

cal'daia sf boiler

'caldo, -a ag warm; (*molto caldo*) hot; (*fig: appassionato*) keen; hearty ▷ sm heat; **ho ~** I'm warm; I'm hot; **fa ~** it's warm; it's hot

caleidos'copio sm kaleidoscope

calen'dario sm calendar

'calibro sm (*di arma*) calibre, bore; (*Tecn*) callipers pl; (*fig*) calibre; **di grosso ~** (*fig*) prominent

'calice ['kalitʃe] sm goblet; (*Rel*) chalice

Cali'fornia sf California

californi'ano, -a ag Californian

calligra'fia sf (*scrittura*) handwriting; (*arte*) calligraphy

'callo sm callus; (*ai piedi*) corn

'calma sf calm

---

ca'bina sf (*di nave*) cabin; (*da spiaggia*) beach hut; (*di autocarro, treno*) cab; (*di aereo*) cockpit; (*di ascensore*) cage; **cabi'nato** sm cabin cruiser; **cabina di pilotaggio** cockpit; **cabina telefonica** call o (tele)phone box

ca'cao sm cocoa

'caccia ['kattʃa] sf hunting; (*con fucile*) shooting; (*inseguimento*) chase; (*cacciagione*) game ▷ sm inv (*aereo*) fighter; (*nave*) destroyer; **caccia grossa** big-game hunting; **caccia all'uomo** manhunt

cacci'are [kat'tʃare] vt to hunt; (*mandar via*) to chase away; (*ficcare*) to shove, stick ▷ vi to hunt; **cacciarsi** vpr **dove s'è cacciata la mia borsa?** where has my bag got to?; **cacciarsi nei guai** to get into trouble; **~ fuori qc** to whip o pull sth out; **~ un urlo** to let out a yell; **caccia'tore** sm hunter; **cacciatore di frodo** poacher

caccia'vite [kattʃa'vite] sm inv screwdriver

'cactus sm inv cactus

ca'davere sm (*dead*) body, corpse

'caddi ecc vb vedi **cadere**

ca'denza [ka'dɛntsa] sf cadence; (*ritmo*) rhythm; (*Mus*) cadenza

ca'dere vi to fall; (*denti, capelli*) to fall out; (*tetto*) to fall in; **questa gonna cade bene** this skirt hangs well; **lasciar ~** (*anche fig*)

cal'mante sm tranquillizer
cal'mare vt to calm; (lenire) to soothe;
calmarsi vpr to grow calm, calm down;
(vento) to abate; (dolori) to ease
'calmo, -a ag calm, quiet
'calo sm (Comm: di prezzi) fall; (: di volume)
shrinkage; (: di peso) loss
ca'lore sm warmth; heat; **in ~** (Zool) on
heat
calo'ria sf calorie
calo'rifero sm radiator
calo'roso, -a ag warm
calpes'tare vt to tread on, trample on; **"è
vietato ~ l'erba"** "keep off the grass"
ca'lunnia sf slander; (scritta) libel
cal'vizie [kal'vittsje] sf baldness
'calvo, -a ag bald
'calza ['kaltsa] sf (da donna) stocking;
(da uomo) sock; **fare la ~** to knit; **calze di
nailon** nylons, (nylon) stockings
calza'maglia [kaltsa'maʎʎa] sf tights pl;
(per danza, ginnastica) leotard
calzet'tone [kaltset'tone] sm heavy knee-
length sock
cal'zino [kal'tsino] sm sock
calzo'laio [kaltso'lajo] sm shoemaker;
(che ripara scarpe) cobbler
calzon'cini [kaltson'tʃini] smpl shorts;
calzoncini da bagno (swimming) trunks
cal'zone [kal'tsone] sm trouser leg; (Cuc)
savoury turnover made with pizza dough;
calzoni smpl (pantaloni) trousers (BRIT),
pants (US)
camale'onte sm chameleon
cambia'mento sm change
cambi'are vt to change; (modificare)
to alter, change; (barattare): **~ (qc con
qn/qc)** to exchange (sth with sb/for
sth) ▷ vi to change, alter; **cambiarsi**
vpr (d'abito) to change; **~ casa** to move
(house); **~ idea** to change one's mind;
~ treno to change trains; **dove posso
~ dei soldi?** where can I change some
money?; **ha da ~?** have you got any
change?; **posso cambiarlo, per favore?**
could I change this, please?
cambiava'lute sm inv exchange office
'cambio sm change; (modifica) alteration,
change; (scambio, Comm) exchange; (corso
dei cambi) rate (of exchange); (Tecn, Aut)
gears pl; **in ~ di** in exchange for; **dare il ~ a
qn** to take over from sb
'camera sf room; (anche: **~ da letto**)
bedroom; (Pol) chamber, house; **camera
ardente** mortuary chapel; **camera d'aria**
inner tube; (di pallone) bladder; **camera
di commercio** Chamber of Commerce;
Camera dei Deputati Chamber of
Deputies, ≈ House of Commons (BRIT),

≈ House of Representatives (US); **camera a
gas** gas chamber; **camera a un letto/due
letti** single/twin-bedded room; **camera
matrimoniale** double room; **camera
oscura** (Fot) dark room

> Attenzione! In inglese esiste la parola
> camera, che però significa macchina
> fotografica.

came'rata, -i, -e sm/f companion, mate
▷ sf dormitory
cameri'era sf (domestica) maid; (che
serve a tavola) waitress; (che fa le camere)
chambermaid
cameri'ere sm (man)servant; (di
ristorante) waiter
came'rino sm (Teatro) dressing room
'camice ['kamitʃe] sm (Rel) alb; (per medici
ecc) white coat
cami'cetta [kami'tʃetta] sf blouse
ca'micia, -cie [ka'mitʃa] sf (da uomo)
shirt; (da donna) blouse; **camicia di forza**
straitjacket; **camicia da notte** (da donna)
nightdress; (da uomo) nightshirt
cami'netto sm hearth, fireplace
ca'mino sm chimney; (focolare) fireplace,
hearth
'camion sm inv lorry (BRIT), truck (US)
camio'nista, -i sm lorry driver (BRIT),
truck driver (US)
cam'mello sm (Zool) camel; (tessuto)
camel hair
cammi'nare vi to walk; (funzionare) to
work, go
cam'mino sm walk; (sentiero) path;
(itinerario, direzione, tragitto) way; **mettersi
in ~** to set o start off
camo'milla sf camomile; (infuso)
camomile tea
ca'moscio [ka'moʃʃo] sm chamois; **di ~**
(scarpe, borsa) suede cpd
cam'pagna [kam'paɲɲa] sf country,
countryside; (Pol, Comm, Mil) campaign;
in ~ in the country; **andare in ~** to go to
the country; **fare una ~** to campaign;
campagna pubblicitaria advertising
campaign
cam'pana sf bell; (anche: **~ di vetro**) bell
jar; **campa'nello** sm (all'uscio, da tavola)
bell
campa'nile sm bell tower, belfry
cam'peggio sm camping; (terreno) camp
site; **fare (del) ~** to go camping
camper ['kamper] sm inv motor caravan
(BRIT), motor home (US)
campio'nario, -a ag **fiera campionaria**
trade fair ▷ sm collection of samples
campio'nato sm championship
campi'one, -'essa sm/f (Sport) champion
▷ sm (Comm) sample

'campo sm field; (Mil) field; (accampamento) camp; (spazio delimitato: sportivo ecc) ground; field; (di quadro) background; **i campi** (campagna) the countryside; **campo da aviazione** airfield; **campo di battaglia** (Mil, fig) battlefield; **campo di concentramento** concentration camp; **campo da golf** golf course; **campo profughi** refugee camp; **campo sportivo** sports ground; **campo da tennis** tennis court; **campo visivo** field of vision

'Canada sm **il ~** Canada; **cana'dese** ag, sm/f Canadian ▷ sf (anche: **tenda canadese**) ridge tent

ca'naglia [ka'naʎʎa] sf rabble, mob; (persona) scoundrel, rogue

ca'nale sm (anche fig) channel; (artificiale) canal

'canapa sf hemp; **canapa indiana** (droga) cannabis

cana'rino sm canary

cancel'lare [kantʃel'lare] vt (con la gomma) to rub out, erase; (con la penna) to strike out; (annullare) to annul, cancel; (disdire) to cancel

cancelle'ria [kantʃelle'ria] sf chancery; (materiale per scrivere) stationery

can'cello [kan'tʃello] sm gate

'cancro sm (Med) cancer; (dello zodiaco): **C~** Cancer

candeg'gina [kanded'dʒina] sf bleach

can'dela sf candle; **candela (di accensione)** (Aut) spark(ing) plug

cande'labro sm candelabra

candeli'ere sm candlestick

candi'dare vt to present as candidate; **candidarsi** vpr to present o.s. as candidate

candi'dato, -a sm/f candidate; (aspirante a una carica) applicant

'candido, -a ag white as snow; (puro) pure; (sincero) sincere, candid

can'dito, -a ag candied

'cane sm dog; (di pistola, fucile) cock; **fa un freddo ~** it's bitterly cold; **non c'era un ~** there wasn't a soul; **cane da caccia/da guardia** hunting/guard dog; **cane lupo** Alsatian; **cane pastore** sheepdog

ca'nestro sm basket

can'guro sm kangaroo

ca'nile sm kennel; (di allevamento) kennels pl; **canile municipale** dog pound

'canna sf (pianta) reed; (: indica, da zucchero) cane; (bastone) stick, cane; (di fucile) barrel; (di organo) pipe; (fam: droga) joint; **canna fumaria** chimney flue; **canna da pesca** (fishing) rod; **canna da zucchero** sugar cane

cannel'loni smpl pasta tubes stuffed with sauce and baked

cannocchi'ale [kannok'kjale] sm telescope

can'none sm (Mil) gun; (Storia) cannon; (tubo) pipe, tube; (piega) box pleat; (fig) ace

can'nuccia, -ce [kan'nuttʃa] sf (drinking) straw

ca'noa sf canoe

'canone sm canon, criterion; (mensile, annuo) rent; fee

canot'taggio [kanot'taddʒo] sm rowing

canotti'era sf vest

ca'notto sm small boat, dinghy; canoe

can'tante sm/f singer

can'tare vt, vi to sing; **cantau'tore, -'trice** sm/f singer-composer

canti'ere sm (Edil) (building) site; (cantiere navale) shipyard

can'tina sf cellar; (bottega) wine shop; **cantina sociale** cooperative winegrowers' association

▓ Attenzione! In inglese esiste la parola *canteen*, che però significa *mensa*.

'canto sm song; (arte) singing; (Rel) chant; chanting; (poesia) poem, lyric; (parte di una poesia) canto; (parte, lato): **da un ~** on the one hand; **d'altro ~** on the other hand

canzo'nare [kantso'nare] vt to tease

can'zone [kan'tsone] sf song; (Poesia) canzone

'caos sm inv chaos; **ca'otico, -a, -ci, -che** ag chaotic

CAP sigla m = **codice di avviamento postale**

ca'pace [ka'patʃe] ag able, capable; (ampio, vasto) large, capacious; **sei ~ di farlo?** can you o are you able to do it?; **capacità** sf inv ability; (Dir, di recipiente) capacity

ca'panna sf hut

capan'none sm (Agr) barn; (fabbricato industriale) (factory) shed

ca'parbio, -a ag stubborn

ca'parra sf deposit, down payment

ca'pello sm hair; **capelli** smpl (capigliatura) hair sg

ca'pezzolo [ka'pettsolo] sm nipple

ca'pire vt to understand; **non capisco** I don't understand

capi'tale ag (mortale) capital; (fondamentale) main, chief ▷ sf (città) capital ▷ sm (Econ) capital

capi'tano sm captain

capi'tare vi (giungere casualmente) to happen to go, find o.s.; (accadere) to happen; (presentarsi: cosa) to turn up, present itself ▷ vb impers to happen; **mi è capitato un guaio** I've had a spot of trouble

capi'tello *sm* (Archit) capital
ca'pitolo *sm* chapter
capi'tombolo *sm* headlong fall, tumble
'capo *sm* head; (*persona*) head, leader; (: *in ufficio*) head, boss; (: *in tribù*) chief; (*di oggetti*) head; top; end; (Geo) cape; **andare a ~** to start a new paragraph; **da ~** over again; **capo di bestiame** head *inv* of cattle; **capo di vestiario** item of clothing; **Capo'danno** *sm* New Year; **capo'giro** *sm* dizziness *no pl*; **capola'voro, -i** *sm* masterpiece; **capo'linea** (*pl* **capi'linea**) *sm* terminus; **capostazi'one** (*pl* **capistazi'one**) *sm* station master
capo'tavola (*pl(m)* **capi'tavola**) *pl(f)* inv *sm/f* (*persona*) head of the table; **sedere a ~** to sit at the head of the table
capo'volgere [kapo'vɔldʒere] *vt* to overturn; (*fig*) to reverse; **capovolgersi** *vpr* to overturn; (*barca*) to capsize; (*fig*) to be reversed
'cappa *sf* (*mantello*) cape, cloak; (*del camino*) hood
cap'pella *sf* (Rel) chapel
cap'pello *sm* hat
'cappero *sm* caper
cap'pone *sm* capon
cap'potto *sm* (over)coat
cappuc'cino [kapput'tʃino] *sm* (*frate*) Capuchin monk; (*bevanda*) cappuccino, frothy white coffee
cap'puccio [kap'puttʃo] *sm* (*copricapo*) hood; (*della biro*) cap
'capra *sf* (she-)goat
ca'priccio [ka'prittʃo] *sm* caprice, whim; (*bizza*) tantrum; **fare i capricci** to be very naughty; **capricci'oso, -a** *ag* capricious, whimsical; naughty
Capri'corno *sm* Capricorn
capri'ola *sf* somersault
capri'olo *sm* roe deer
'capro *sm* **~ espiatorio** scapegoat
ca'prone *sm* billy-goat
'capsula *sf* capsule; (*di arma, per bottiglie*) cap
cap'tare *vt* (Radio, TV) to pick up; (*cattivarsi*) to gain, win
carabini'ere *sm* member of Italian military police force

CARABINIERI

Originally part of the armed forces, the **carabinieri** are police who perform both military and civil duties. They include paratroopers and mounted divisions.

ca'raffa *sf* carafe

Ca'raibi *smpl* **il mar dei ~** the Caribbean (Sea)
cara'mella *sf* sweet
ca'rattere *sm* character; (*caratteristica*) characteristic, trait; **avere un buon ~** to be good-natured; **carattere jolly** wild card; **caratte'ristica, -che** *sf* characteristic, trait, peculiarity; **caratte'ristico, -a, -ci, -che** *ag* characteristic
car'bone *sm* coal
carbu'rante *sm* (motor) fuel
carbura'tore *sm* carburettor
carce'rato, -a [kartʃe'rato] *sm/f* prisoner
'carcere ['kartʃere] *sm* prison; (*pena*) imprisonment
carci'ofo [kar'tʃɔfo] *sm* artichoke
cardel'lino *sm* goldfinch
car'diaco, -a, -ci, -che *ag* cardiac, heart *cpd*
cardi'nale *ag, sm* cardinal
'cardine *sm* hinge
'cardo *sm* thistle
ca'rente *ag* **~ di** lacking in
cares'tia *sf* famine; (*penuria*) scarcity, dearth
ca'rezza [ka'rettsa] *sf* caress
'carica, -che *sf* (*mansione ufficiale*) office, position; (Mil, Tecn, Elettr) charge; **ha una forte ~ di simpatia** he's very likeable; *vedi anche* **carico**
caricabatte'ria *sm inv* battery charger
cari'care *vt* (*merce, Inform*) to load; (*orologio*) to wind up; (*batteria, Mil*) to charge
'carico, -a, -chi, -che *ag* (*che porta un peso*): **~ di** loaded o laden with; (*fucile*) loaded; (*orologio*) wound up; (*batteria*) charged; (*colore*) deep; (*caffè, tè*) strong ▷ *sm* (*il caricare*) loading; (*ciò che si carica*) load; (*fig: peso*) burden, weight; **persona a ~** dependent; **essere a ~ di qn** (*spese ecc*) to be charged to sb
'carie *sf* (*dentaria*) decay
ca'rino, -a *ag* (*grazioso*) lovely, pretty, nice; (*riferito a uomo, anche simpatico*) nice
carità *sf* charity; **per ~!** (*escl di rifiuto*) good heavens, no!
carnagi'one [karna'dʒone] *sf* complexion
'carne *sf* flesh; (*bovina, ovina ecc*) meat; **non mangio ~** I don't eat meat; **carne di maiale/manzo/pecora** pork/beef/ mutton; **carne in scatola** tinned o canned meat; **carne tritata** o **macinata** mince (BRIT), hamburger meat (US), minced (BRIT) o ground (US) meat

carne'vale sm carnival

'caro, -a ag (amato) dear; (costoso) dear, expensive; **è troppo ~** it's too dear
ca'rogna [ka'roɲɲa] sf carrion; (anche: fig: fam) swine
ca'rota sf carrot
caro'vana sf caravan
car'poni av on all fours
car'rabile ag suitable for vehicles; **"passo ~"** "keep clear"
carreggi'ata [karred'dʒata] sf carriageway (BRIT), (road)way
car'rello sm trolley; (Aer) undercarriage; (Cinema) dolly; (di macchina da scrivere) carriage
carri'era sf career; **fare ~** to get on; **a gran ~** at full speed
carri'ola sf wheelbarrow
'carro sm cart, wagon; **carro armato** tank; **carro attrezzi** breakdown van
car'rozza [kar'rɔttsa] sf carriage, coach
carrozze'ria [karrottse'ria] sf body, coachwork (BRIT); (officina) coachbuilder's workshop (BRIT), body shop
carroz'zina [karrot'tsina] sf pram (BRIT), baby carriage (US)
'carta sf paper; (al ristorante) menu; (Geo) map; plan; (documento) card; (costituzione) charter; **carte** sfpl (documenti) papers, documents; **alla ~** (al ristorante) à la carte; **carta assegni** bank card; **carta assorbente** blotting paper; **carta bollata** o **da bollo** official stamped paper; **carta (da gioco)** playing card; **carta di credito** credit card; **carta (geografica)** map; **carta d'identità** identity card; **carta igienica** toilet paper; **carta d'imbarco** (Aer, Naut) boarding card; **carta da lettere** writing paper; **carta da pacchi** wrapping paper; **carta da parati** wallpaper; **carta libera** (Amm) unstamped paper; **carta stradale** road map; **carta verde** (Aut) green card; **carta vetrata** sandpaper; **carta da visita** visiting card
car'taccia, -ce [kar'tattʃa] sf waste paper
carta'pesta sf papier-mâché
car'tella sf (scheda) card; (Inform, custodia: di cartone) folder; (: di uomo d'affari ecc)

briefcase; (: di scolaro) schoolbag, satchel; **cartella clinica** (Med) case sheet
cartel'lino sm (etichetta) label; (su porta) notice; (scheda) card; **timbrare il ~** (all'entrata) to clock in; (all'uscita) to clock out; **cartellino di presenza** clock card, timecard
car'tello sm sign; (pubblicitario) poster; (stradale) sign, signpost; (Econ) cartel; (in dimostrazioni) placard; **cartello stradale** sign; **cartel'lone** sm (della tombola) scoring frame; (Teatro) playbill; **tenere il cartellone** (spettacolo) to have a long run; **cartellone pubblicitario** advertising poster
car'tina sf (Aut, Geo) map; **può indicarmelo sulla ~?** can you show it to me on the map?
car'toccio [kar'tɔttʃo] sm paper bag
cartole'ria sf stationer's (shop)
carto'lina sf postcard; **cartolina postale** ready-stamped postcard
car'tone sm cardboard; (Arte) cartoon; **cartoni animati** (Cinema) cartoons
car'tuccia, -ce [kar'tuttʃa] sf cartridge
'casa sf house; (in senso astratto) home; (Comm) firm, house; **essere a ~** to be at home; **vado a ~ mia/tua** I'm going home/ to your house; **vino della ~** house wine; **casa di cura** nursing home; **casa editrice** publishing house; **Casa delle Libertà** centre-right coalition; **casa di riposo** (old people's) home, care home; **case popolari** ≈ council houses (o flats) (BRIT), ≈ public housing units (US); **casa dello studente** student hostel
ca'sacca, -che sf military coat; (di fantino) blouse
casa'linga, -ghe sf housewife
casa'lingo, -a, -ghi, -ghe ag household, domestic; (fatto a casa) home-made; (semplice) homely; (amante della casa) home-loving
cas'care vi to fall; **cas'cata** sf fall; (d'acqua) cascade, waterfall
casche'rò ecc [kaske'rɔ] vb vedi **cascare**
'casco, -schi sm helmet; (del parrucchiere) hair-drier; (di banane) bunch; **casco blu** (Mil) blue helmet (UN soldier)
casei'ficio [kazei'fitʃo] sm creamery
ca'sella sf pigeon-hole; **casella postale** post office box
ca'sello sm (di autostrada) toll-house
ca'serma sf barracks pl
ca'sino (fam) sm brothel; (confusione) row, racket
casi'nò sm inv casino
'caso sm chance; (fatto, vicenda) event, incident; (possibilità) possibility; (Med,

Ling) case; **a ~** at random; **per ~** by chance, by accident; **in ogni ~, in tutti i casi** in any case, at any rate; **al ~** should the opportunity arise; **nel ~ che** in case; **~ mai** if by chance; **caso limite** borderline case

caso'lare *sm* cottage

'caspita *escl (di sorpresa)* good heavens!; *(di impazienza)* for goodness' sake!

'cassa *sf* case, crate, box; *(bara)* coffin; *(mobile)* chest; *(involucro: di orologio ecc)* case; *(macchina)* cash register, till; *(luogo di pagamento)* checkout (counter); *(fondo)* fund; *(istituto bancario)* bank; **cassa automatica prelievi** cash dispenser; **cassa continua** night safe; **cassa mutua** *o* **malattia** health insurance scheme; **cassa integrazione: mettere in cassa integrazione** ≈ to lay off; **cassa di risparmio** savings bank; **cassa toracica** *(Anat)* chest

cassa'forte *(pl* **casse'forti)** *sf* safe; **lo potrebbe mettere nella ~?** could you put this in the safe, please?

cassa'panca *(pl* **cassa'panche** *o* **casse'panche)** *sf* settle

casseru'ola *sf* saucepan

cas'setta *sf* box; *(per registratore)* cassette; *(Cinema, Teatro)* box-office takings *pl*; **film di ~** box-office draw; **cassetta di sicurezza** strongbox; **cassetta delle lettere** letterbox

cas'setto *sm* drawer

cassi'ere, -a *sm/f* cashier; *(di banca)* teller

casso'netto *sm* wheelie-bin

cas'tagna [kas'taɲɲa] *sf* chestnut

cas'tagno [kas'taɲɲo] *sm* chestnut (tree)

cas'tano, -a *ag* chestnut (brown)

cas'tello *sm* castle; *(Tecn)* scaffolding

casti'gare *vt* to punish; **cas'tigo, -ghi** *sm* punishment

cas'toro *sm* beaver

casu'ale *ag* chance *cpd*; *(Inform)* random *cpd*

catalizza'tore [kataliddza'tore] *sm (anche fig)* catalyst; *(Aut)* catalytic converter

ca'talogo, -ghi *sm* catalogue

catarifran'gente [katarifran'dʒɛnte] *sm (Aut)* reflector

ca'tarro *sm* catarrh

ca'tastrofe *sf* catastrophe, disaster

cate'goria *sf* category

ca'tena *sf* chain; **catena di montaggio** assembly line; **catene da neve** *(Aut)* snow chains; **cate'nina** *sf (gioiello)* (thin) chain

cate'ratta *sf* cataract; *(chiusa)* sluice-gate

ca'tino *sm* basin

ca'trame *sm* tar

'cattedra *sf* teacher's desk; *(di docente)* chair

catte'drale *sf* cathedral

catti'veria *sf* malice, spite; naughtiness; *(atto)* spiteful act; *(parole)* malicious *o* spiteful remark

cat'tivo, -a *ag* bad; *(malvagio)* bad, wicked; *(turbolento: bambino)* bad, naughty; *(: mare)* rough; *(odore, sapore)* nasty, bad

cat'tolico, -a, -ci, -che *ag, sm/f* (Roman) Catholic

cattu'rare *vt* to capture

'causa *sf* cause; *(Dir)* lawsuit, case, action; **a ~ di, per ~ di** because of; **fare** *o* **muovere ~ a qn** to take legal action against sb

cau'sare *vt* to cause

cau'tela *sf* caution, prudence

'cauto, -a *ag* cautious, prudent

cauzi'one [kaut'tsjone] *sf* security; *(Dir)* bail

'cava *sf* quarry

caval'care *vt (cavallo)* to ride; *(muro)* to sit astride; *(ponte)* to span; **caval'cata** *sf* ride; *(gruppo di persone)* riding party

cavalca'via *sm inv* flyover

cavalci'oni [kaval'tʃoni]: **a ~ di** *prep* astride

cavali'ere *sm* rider; *(feudale, titolo)* knight; *(soldato)* cavalryman; *(al ballo)* partner

caval'letta *sf* grasshopper

caval'letto *sm (Fot)* tripod; *(da pittore)* easel

ca'vallo *sm* horse; *(Scacchi)* knight; *(Aut: anche: ~ vapore)* horsepower; *(dei pantaloni)* crotch; **a ~** on horseback; **a ~ di** astride, straddling; **cavallo di battaglia** *(fig)* hobby-horse; **cavallo da corsa** racehorse; **cavallo a dondolo** rocking horse

ca'vare *vt (togliere)* to draw out, extract, take out; *(: giacca, scarpe)* to take off; *(: fame, sete, voglia)* to satisfy; **cavarsela** to manage, get on all right; *(scamparla)* to get away with it

cava'tappi *sm inv* corkscrew

ca'verna *sf* cave

'cavia *sf* guinea pig

cavi'ale *sm* caviar

ca'viglia [ka'viʎʎa] *sf* ankle

'cavo, -a *ag* hollow ▷ *sm (Anat)* cavity; *(corda, Elettr, Tel)* cable

cavo'letto *sm* **~ di Bruxelles** Brussels sprout

cavolfi'ore *sm* cauliflower

'cavolo *sm* cabbage; *(fam)*: **non m'importa un ~** I don't give a damn

C.C.D. *sigla m* (= *Centro Cristiano Democratico*) *Italian political party of the centre*

CD *sm inv* CD; (*lettore*) CD player

CD-Rom [tʃidi'rom] *sm inv* CD-ROM

C.D.U. *sigla m* (= *Cristiano Democratici Uniti*) *Italian centre-right political party*

ce [tʃe] *pron, av vedi* **ci**

Ce'cenia [tʃe'tʃenja] *sf* **la ~** Chechnya

ce'ceno, -a [tʃe'tʃeno] *sm/f, ag* Chechen

'ceco, -a, -chi, -che ['tʃɛko] *ag, sm/f* Czech; **la Repubblica Ceca** the Czech Republic

'cedere ['tʃedere] *vt* (*concedere posto*) to give up; (*Dir*) to transfer, make over ▷ *vi* (*cadere*) to give way, subside; **~ (a)** to surrender (to), yield (to), give in (to)

'cedola ['tʃedola] *sf* (*Comm*) coupon; voucher

'ceffo ['tʃeffo] (*peg*) *sm* ugly mug

cef'fone [tʃef'fone] *sm* slap, smack

cele'brare [tʃele'brare] *vt* to celebrate

'celebre ['tʃelebre] *ag* famous, celebrated

ce'leste [tʃe'leste] *ag* celestial; heavenly; (*colore*) sky-blue

'celibe ['tʃelibe] *ag* single, unmarried

'cella ['tʃella] *sf* cell; **cella frigorifera** cold store

'cellula ['tʃellula] *sf* (*Biol, Elettr, Pol*) cell; **cellu'lare** *sm* cellphone

cellu'lite [tʃellu'lite] *sf* cellulite

cemen'tare [tʃemen'tare] *vt* (*anche fig*) to cement

ce'mento [tʃe'mento] *sm* cement; **cemento armato** reinforced concrete

'cena ['tʃena] *sf* dinner; (*leggera*) supper

ce'nare [tʃe'nare] *vi* to dine, have dinner

'cenere ['tʃenere] *sf* ash

'cenno ['tʃenno] *sm* (*segno*) sign, signal; (*gesto*) gesture; (*col capo*) nod; (*con la mano*) wave; (*allusione*) hint, mention; (*breve esposizione*) short account; **far ~ di sì/no** to nod (one's head)/shake one's head

censi'mento [tʃensi'mento] *sm* census

cen'sura [tʃen'sura] *sf* censorship; censor's office; (*fig*) censure

cente'nario, -a [tʃente'narjo] *ag* (*che ha cento anni*) hundred-year-old; (*che ricorre ogni cento anni*) centennial, centenary *cpd* ▷ *sm/f* centenarian ▷ *sm* centenary

cen'tesimo, -a [tʃen'tezimo] *ag, sm* hundredth; (*di euro, dollaro*) cent

cen'tigrado, -a [tʃen'tigrado] *ag* centigrade; **20 gradi centigradi** 20 degrees centigrade

cen'timetro [tʃen'timetro] *sm* centimetre

centi'naio [tʃenti'najo] (*pl(f)* **-aia**) *sm* **un ~ (di)** a hundred; about a hundred

'cento ['tʃɛnto] *num* a hundred, one hundred

cento'mila [tʃento'mila] *num* a o one hundred thousand; **te l'ho detto ~ volte** (*fig*) I've told you a thousand times

cen'trale [tʃen'trale] *ag* central ▷ *sf*: **centrale telefonica** (telephone) exchange; **centrale elettrica** electric power station; **centrali'nista** *sm/f* operator; **centra'lino** *sm* (telephone) exchange; (*di albergo ecc*) switchboard; **centralizzato, -a** [tʃentralid'dzato] *ag* central

cen'trare [tʃen'trare] *vt* to hit the centre of; (*Tecn*) to centre

cen'trifuga [tʃen'trifuga] *sf* spin-drier

'centro ['tʃɛntro] *sm* centre; **centro civico** civic centre; **centro commerciale** shopping centre; (*città*) commercial centre

'ceppo ['tʃeppo] *sm* (*di albero*) stump; (*pezzo di legno*) log

'cera ['tʃera] *sf* wax; (*aspetto*) appearance

ce'ramica, -che [tʃe'ramika] *sf* ceramic; (*Arte*) ceramics *sg*

cerbi'atto [tʃer'bjatto] *sm* (*Zool*) fawn

cer'care [tʃer'kare] *vt* to look for, search for ▷ *vi* **~ di fare qc** to try to do sth; **stiamo cercando un albergo/ristorante** we're looking for a hotel/restaurant

cercherò *ecc* [tʃerke'rɔ] *vb vedi* **cercare**

'cerchia ['tʃerkja] *sf* circle

cerchietto [tʃer'kjetto] *sm* (*per capelli*) hairband

'cerchio ['tʃerkjo] *sm* circle; (*giocattolo, di botte*) hoop

cereali [tʃere'ali] *smpl* cereal *sg*

ceri'monia [tʃeri'mɔnja] *sf* ceremony

ce'rino [tʃe'rino] *sm* wax match

'cernia ['tʃernja] *sf* (*Zool*) stone bass

cerni'era [tʃer'njɛra] *sf* hinge; **cerniera lampo** zip (fastener) (BRIT), zipper (US)

'cero ['tʃero] *sm* (church) candle

ce'rotto [tʃe'rotto] *sm* sticking plaster

certa'mente [tʃerta'mente] *av* certainly

certifi'cato *sm* certificate; **certificato medico** medical certificate; **certificato di nascita/di morte** birth/death certificate

 PAROLA CHIAVE

'certo, -a ['tʃerto] *ag* (*sicuro*): **certo (di/ che)** certain o sure (of/that)
▷ *det* **1** (*tale*) certain; **un certo signor Smith** a (certain) Mr Smith
2 (*qualche: con valore intensivo*) some; **dopo un certo tempo** after some time; **un fatto di una certa importanza** a matter of some importance; **di una certa età**

past one's prime, not so young
▷ pron **certi, e** *pl* some ▷ *av* (*certamente*) certainly; (*senz'altro*) of course; **di certo** certainly; **no (di) certo!, certo che no!** certainly not!; **sì certo** yes indeed, certainly

cer'vello, -i [tʃerˈvɛllo] (*Anat*) (*pl*(*f*) **-a**) *sm* brain; **cervello elettronico** computer
'cervo, -a [ˈtʃɛrvo] *sm/f* stag/doe ▷ *sm* deer; **cervo volante** stag beetle
ces'puglio [tʃesˈpuʎʎo] *sm* bush
ces'sare [tʃesˈsare] *vi, vt* to stop, cease; **~ di fare qc** to stop doing sth
ces'tino [tʃesˈtino] *sm* basket; (*per la carta straccia*) wastepaper basket; **cestino da viaggio** (*Ferr*) packed lunch (*o* dinner)
'cesto [ˈtʃesto] *sm* basket
'ceto [ˈtʃɛto] *sm* (social) class
cetrio'lino [tʃetrioˈlino] *sm* gherkin
cetri'olo [tʃetriˈɔlo] *sm* cucumber
Cfr. *abbr* (= *confronta*) cf.
CGIL *sigla f* (= *Confederazione Generale Italiana del Lavoro*) trades union organization
chat line [tʃætˈlaen] *sf inv* chat room
chattare [tʃatˈtare] *vi* (*Inform*) to chat online

PAROLA CHIAVE

che [ke] *pron* **1** (*relativo: persona: soggetto*) who; (*: oggetto*) whom, that; (*: cosa, animale*) which, that; **il ragazzo che è venuto** the boy who came; **l'uomo che io vedo** the man (whom) I see; **il libro che è sul tavolo** the book which *o* that is on the table; **il libro che vedi** the book (which *o* that) you see; **la sera che ti ho visto** the evening I saw you
2 (*interrogativo, esclamativo*) what; **che (cosa) fai?** what are you doing?; **a che (cosa) pensi?** what are you thinking about?; **non sa che (cosa) fare** he doesn't know what to do; **ma che dici!** what you are saying!
3 (*indefinito*): **quell'uomo ha un che di losco** there's something suspicious about that man; **un certo non so che** an indefinable something
▷ *det* **1** (*interrogativo: tra tanti*) what; (*: tra pochi*) which; **che tipo di film preferisci?** what sort of film do you prefer?; **che vestito ti vuoi mettere?** what (*o* which) dress do you want to put on?
2 (*esclamativo: seguito da aggettivo*) how; (*: seguito da sostantivo*) what; **che buono!** how delicious!; **che bel vestito!** what a lovely dress!
▷ *cong* **1** (*con proposizioni subordinate*) that;

credo che verrà I think he'll come; **voglio che tu studi** I want you to study; **so che tu c'eri** I know (that) you were there; **non che, non che sia sbagliato, ma ...** not that it's wrong, but ...
2 (*finale*) so that; **vieni qua, che ti veda** come here, so (that) I can see you
3 (*temporale*): **arrivai che eri già partito** you had already left when I arrived; **sono anni che non lo vedo** I haven't seen him for years
4 (*in frasi imperative, concessive*): **che venga pure!** let him come by all means!; **che tu sia benedetto!** may God bless you!
5 (*comparativo: con più, meno*) than; *vedi anche* **più; meno; così** *ecc*

chemiotera'pia [kemjoteraˈpia] *sf* chemotherapy
chero'sene [keroˈzɛne] *sm* kerosene

PAROLA CHIAVE

chi [ki] *pron* **1** (*interrogativo: soggetto*) who; (*: oggetto*) who, whom; (*: oggetto*) who, whom; **chi è?** who is it?; **di chi è questo libro?** whose book is this?, whose is this book?; **con chi parli?** who are you talking to?; **a chi pensi?** who are you thinking about?; **chi di voi?** which of you?; **non so a chi rivolgermi** I don't know who to ask
2 (*relativo*) whoever, anyone who; **dillo a chi vuoi** tell whoever you like
3 (*indefinito*): **chi ... chi ...** some ... others ...; **chi dice una cosa, chi dice un'altra** some say one thing, others say another

chiacchie'rare [kjakkjeˈrare] *vi* to chat; (*discorrere futilmente*) to chatter; (*far pettegolezzi*) to gossip; **chi'acchiere** *sfpl* **fare due** *o* **quattro chiacchiere** to have a chat
chia'mare [kjaˈmare] *vt* to call; (*rivolgersi a qn*) to call (in), send for; **chiamarsi** *vpr* (*aver nome*) to be called; **come ti chiami?** what's your name?; **mi chiamo Paolo** my name is Paolo, I'm called Paolo; **~ alle armi** to call up; **~ in giudizio** to summon; **chia'mata** *sf* (*Tel*) call; (*Mil*) call-up
chia'rezza [kjaˈrettsa] *sf* clearness; clarity
chia'rire [kjaˈrire] *vt* to make clear; (*fig: spiegare*) to clear up, explain
chi'aro, -a [ˈkjaro] *ag* clear; (*luminoso*) clear, bright; (*colore*) pale, light
chi'asso [ˈkjasso] *sm* uproar, row
chi'ave [ˈkjave] *sf key* ▷ *ag inv* key *cpd*; **posso avere la mia ~?** can I have my key?; **chiave d'accensione** (*Aut*) ignition key;

chiave di volta keystone; **chiave inglese** monkey wrench

chi'azza ['kjattsa] *sf* stain; splash

'chicco, -chi ['kikko] *sm* grain; *(di caffè)* bean; **chicco d'uva** grape

chi'edere ['kjɛdere] *vt (per sapere)* to ask; *(per avere)* to ask for ▷ *vi* ~ **di qn** to ask after sb; *(al telefono)* to ask for *o* want sb; ~ **qc a qn** to ask sb sth; to ask sb for sth; **chiedersi** *vpr* **chiedersi (se)** to wonder (whether)

chi'esa ['kjɛza] *sf* church

chi'esi *ecc* ['kjɛzi] *vb vedi* **chiedere**

'chiglia [ki'ʎʎa] *sf* keel

'chilo ['kilo] *sm* kilo; **chi'lometro** *sm* kilometre

'chimica ['kimika] *sf* chemistry

'chimico, -a, -ci, -che ['kimiko] *ag* chemical ▷ *sm/f* chemist

chi'nare [ki'nare] *vt* to lower, bend; **chinarsi** *vpr* to stoop, bend

chi'occiola ['kjɔttʃola] *sf* snail; *(di indirizzo e-mail)* at sign, @; **scala a ~** spiral staircase

chi'odo ['kjɔdo] *sm* nail; *(fig)* obsession; **chiodo di garofano** *(Cuc)* clove

chi'osco, -schi ['kjɔsko] *sm* kiosk, stall

chi'ostro ['kjɔstro] *sm* cloister

chiro'mante [kiro'mante] *sm/f* palmist

chirur'gia [kirur'dʒia] *sf* surgery; **chirurgia estetica** cosmetic surgery; **chi'rurgo, -ghi** *o* **gi** *sm* surgeon

chissà [kis'sa] *av* who knows, I wonder

chi'tarra [ki'tarra] *sf* guitar

chitar'rista, -i, e [kitar'rista] *sm/f* guitarist, guitar player

chi'udere ['kjudere] *vt* to close, shut; *(luce, acqua)* to put off, turn off; *(definitivamente: fabbrica)* to close down, shut down; *(strada)* to close; *(recingere)* to enclose; *(porre termine a)* to end ▷ *vi* to close, shut; to close down, shut down; to end; **chiudersi** *vpr* to shut, close; *(ritirarsi: anche fig)* to shut o.s. away; *(ferita)* to close up; **a che ora chiudete?** what time do you close?

chi'unque [ki'unkwe] *pron (relativo)* whoever; *(indefinito)* anyone, anybody; ~ **sia** whoever it is

'chiusi *ecc* ['kjusi] *vb vedi* **chiudere**

chi'uso, -a ['kjuso] *pp di* **chiudere** ▷ *sf (di corso d'acqua)* sluice, lock; *(recinto)* enclosure; *(di discorso ecc)* conclusion, ending; **chiu'sura** *sf (vedi* **chiudere)** closing; shutting; closing *o* shutting down; enclosing; putting *o* turning off; ending; *(dispositivo)* catch; fastening; fastener; **chiusura lampo®** zip (fastener) (BRIT), zipper (US)

C.I. *abbr* = **carta d'identità**

 PAROLA CHIAVE

ci [tʃi] *(dav lo, la, li, le, ne diventa ce)* *pron* **1** *(personale: complemento oggetto)* us; (: *a noi: complemento di termine)* (to) us; (: *riflessivo)* ourselves; (: *reciproco)* each other, one another; *(impersonale):* **ci si veste** we get dressed; **ci ha visti** he's seen us; **non ci ha dato niente** he gave us nothing; **ci vestiamo** we get dressed; **ci amiamo** we love one another *o* each other

2 *(dimostrativo: di ciò, su ciò, in ciò ecc)* about *(o* on *o* of) it; **non so cosa farci** I don't know what to do about it; **che c'entro io?** what have I got to do with it? ▷ *av (qui)* here; *(lì)* there; *(moto attraverso luogo):* **ci passa sopra un ponte** a bridge passes over it; **non ci passa più nessuno** nobody comes this way any more; **esserci** *vedi* **essere**

cia'batta [tʃa'batta] *sf* slipper; *(pane)* ciabatta

ciam'bella [tʃam'bɛlla] *sf (Cuc)* ring-shaped cake; *(salvagente)* rubber ring

ci'ao ['tʃao] *escl (all'arrivo)* hello!; *(alla partenza)* cheerio! (BRIT), bye!

cias'cuno, -a [tʃas'kuno] *(det: dav sm:* **ciascun** +*C, V,* **ciascuno** +*s impura, gn, pn, ps, x, z; dav sf:* **ciascuna** +*C,* **ciascun'** +*V)* *det* every, each; *(ogni)* every ▷ *pron* each (one); *(tutti)* everyone, everybody

ci'barie [tʃi'barje] *sfpl* foodstuffs

cibernauta, -i, -e [tʃiber'nauta] *sm/f* Internet surfer

ciberspazio [tʃiber'spattsjo] *sm* cyberspace

'cibo ['tʃibo] *sm* food

ci'cala [tʃi'kala] *sf* cicada

cica'trice [tʃika'tritʃe] *sf* scar

'cicca ['tʃikka] *sf* cigarette end

'ciccia ['tʃittʃa] *(fam)* *sf* fat

cicci'one, -a [tʃit'tʃone] *sm/f (fam)* fatty

cicla'mino [tʃikla'mino] *sm* cyclamen

ci'clismo [tʃi'klizmo] *sm* cycling; **ci'clista, -i, -e** *sm/f* cyclist

'ciclo ['tʃiklo] *sm* cycle; *(di malattia)* course

ciclomo'tore [tʃiklomo'tore] *sm* moped

ci'clone [tʃi'klone] *sm* cyclone

ci'cogna [tʃi'koɲɲa] *sf* stork

ci'eco, -a, -chi, -che ['tʃɛko] *ag* blind ▷ *sm/f* blind man/woman

ci'elo ['tʃɛlo] *sm* sky; *(Rel)* heaven

'cifra ['tʃifra] *sf (numero)* figure; numeral; *(somma di denaro)* sum, figure; *(monogramma)* monogram, initials *pl*; *(codice)* code, cipher

'ciglio, -i ['tʃiʎʎo] *(delle palpebre)* *(pl(f)* **ciglia)** *sm (margine)* edge, verge; (eye)lash; (eye)lid; *(sopracciglio)* eyebrow

'cigno ['tʃiɲɲo] *sm* swan

cigo'lare [tʃigo'lare] *vi* to squeak, creak

'Cile ['tʃile] *sm* **il ~** Chile

ci'leno, -a [tʃi'lɛno] *ag, sm/f* Chilean

cili'egia, -gie o **ge** [tʃi'ljɛdʒa] *sf* cherry

cilie'gina [tʃilje'dʒina] *sf* glacé cherry

cilin'drata [tʃilin'drata] *sf (Aut) (cubic)* capacity; **una macchina di grossa ~** a big-engined car

ci'lindro [tʃi'lindro] *sm* cylinder; *(cappello)* top hat

'cima ['tʃima] *sf (sommità)* top; *(di monte)* top, summit; *(estremità)* end; **in ~ a** at the top of; **da ~ a fondo** from top to bottom; *(fig)* from beginning to end

'cimice ['tʃimitʃe] *sf (Zool)* bug; *(puntina)* drawing pin (BRIT), thumbtack (US)

cimini'era [tʃimi'njɛra] *sf* chimney; *(di nave)* funnel

cimi'tero [tʃimi'tɛro] *sm* cemetery

'Cina ['tʃina] *sf* **la ~** China

cin'cin [tʃin'tʃin] *escl* cheers!

'cinema ['tʃinema] *sm inv* cinema

ci'nese [tʃi'nese] *ag, sm/f, sm* Chinese *inv*

'cinghia ['tʃingja] *sf* strap; *(cintura, Tecn)* belt

cinghi'ale [tʃin'gjale] *sm* wild boar

cinguet'tare [tʃingwet'tare] *vi* to twitter

'cinico, -a, -ci, -che ['tʃiniko] *ag* cynical ▷ *sm/f* cynic

cin'quanta [tʃin'kwanta] *num* fifty; **cinquan'tesimo, -a** *num* fiftieth

cinquan'tina [tʃinkwan'tina] *sf (serie)*: **una ~ (di)** about fifty; *(età)*: **essere sulla ~** to be about fifty

'cinque ['tʃinkwe] *num* five; **avere ~ anni** to be five (years old); **il ~ dicembre 1998** the fifth of December 1998; **alle ~ (ora)** at five (o'clock)

cinque'cento [tʃinkwe'tʃɛnto] *num* five hundred ▷ *sm* **il C~** the sixteenth century

cin'tura [tʃin'tura] *sf* belt; **cintura di salvataggio** lifebelt (BRIT), life preserver (US); **cintura di sicurezza** *(Aut, Aer)* safety o seat belt

cintu'rino [tʃintu'rino] *sm* strap; **~ dell'orologio** watch strap

ciò [tʃɔ] *pron* this; that; **~ che** what; **~ nonostante** o **nondimeno** nevertheless, in spite of that

ci'occa, -che ['tʃɔkka] *sf (di capelli)* lock

ciocco'lata [tʃokko'lata] *sf* chocolate; *(bevanda)* (hot) chocolate; **cioccola'tino** *sm* chocolate

cioè [tʃo'ɛ] *av* that is (to say)

ci'otola ['tʃɔtola] *sf* bowl

ci'ottolo ['tʃɔttolo] *sm* pebble; *(di strada)* cobble(stone)

ci'polla [tʃi'polla] *sf* onion; *(di tulipano ecc)* bulb

cipol'lina [tʃipol'lina] *sf* **cipolline sottaceto** pickled onions

ci'presso [tʃi'prɛsso] *sm* cypress (tree)

'cipria ['tʃiprja] *sf (face)* powder

'Cipro ['tʃipro] *sm* Cyprus

'circa ['tʃirka] *av* about, roughly ▷ *prep* about, concerning; **a mezzogiorno ~** about midday

'circo, -chi ['tʃirko] *sm* circus

circo'lare [tʃirko'lare] *vi* to circulate; *(Aut)* to drive (along), move (along) ▷ *ag* circular ▷ *sf (Amm)* circular; *(di autobus)* circle (line)

'circolo ['tʃirkolo] *sm* circle

circon'dare [tʃirkon'dare] *vt* to surround; **circondarsi** *vpr* **circondarsi di** to surround o.s. with

circonvallazi'one [tʃirkonvallat'tsjone] *sf* ring road (BRIT), beltway (US); *(per evitare una città)* by-pass

circos'petto, -a [tʃirkos'pɛtto] *ag* circumspect, cautious

circos'tante [tʃirkos'tante] *ag* surrounding, neighbouring

circos'tanza [tʃirkos'tantsa] *sf* circumstance; *(occasione)* occasion

cir'cuito [tʃir'kuito] *sm* circuit

CISL *sigla f (= Confederazione Italiana Sindacati Lavoratori)* trades union organization

cis'terna [tʃis'tɛrna] *sf* tank, cistern

'cisti ['tʃisti] *sf* cyst

cis'tite [tʃis'tite] *sf* cystitis

ci'tare [tʃi'tare] *vt (Dir)* to summon; *(autore)* to quote; *(a esempio, modello)* to cite

ci'tofono [tʃi'tɔfono] *sm* entry phone; *(in uffici)* intercom

città [tʃit'ta] *sf inv* town; *(importante)* city; **città universitaria** university campus

cittadi'nanza [tʃittadi'nantsa] *sf* citizens *pl*; *(Dir)* citizenship

citta'dino, -a [tʃitta'dino] *ag* town *cpd*; city *cpd* ▷ *sm/f (di uno Stato)* citizen; *(abitante di città)* townsman, city dweller

ci'uccio ['tʃuttʃo] *sm (fam)* comforter, dummy (BRIT), pacifier (US)

ci'uffo ['tʃuffo] *sm* tuft

ci'vetta [tʃi'vetta] *sf (Zool)* owl; *(fig: donna)* coquette, flirt ▷ *ag inv* **auto/nave ~** decoy car/ship

'civico, -a, -ci, -che ['tʃiviko] *ag* civic; *(museo)* municipal, town *cpd*

ci'vile [tʃi'vile] *ag* civil; *(non militare)* civilian; *(nazione)* civilized ▷ *sm* civilian

civiltà [tʃivil'ta] *sf* civilization; *(cortesia)* civility

'clacson *sm inv* (*Aut*) horn

clandes'tino, -a *ag* clandestine; (*Pol*) underground, clandestine; (*immigrato*) illegal ▷ *sm/f* stowaway; *(anche:* **immigrato ~**) illegal immigrant

'classe *sf* class; **di ~** (*fig*) with class; of excellent quality; **classe operaia** working class; **classe turistica** (*Aer*) economy class

'classico, -a, -ci, -che *ag* classical; *(tradizionale: moda)* classic(al) ▷ *sm* classic; classical author

clas'sifica *sf* classification; (*Sport*) placings *pl*

classifi'care *vt* to classify; (*candidato, compito*) to grade; **classificarsi** *vpr* to be placed

'clausola *sf* (*Dir*) clause

clavi'cembalo [klavi'tʃembalo] *sm* harpsichord

cla'vicola *sf* (*Anat*) collar bone

clic'care *vi* (*Inform*): **~ su** to click on

cli'ente *sm/f* customer, client

'clima, -i *sm* climate; **climatizzatore** *sm* air conditioning system

'clinica, -che *sf* (*scienza*) clinical medicine; *(casa di cura)* clinic, nursing home; *(settore d'ospedale)* clinic

clo'nare *vt* to clone; **clonazione** [klona'tsjone] *sf* cloning

'cloro *sm* chlorine

club *sm inv* club

c.m. *abbr* = **corrente mese**

cm *abbr* (= *centimetro*) cm

coalizi'one [koalit'tsjone] *sf* coalition

'COBAS *sigla mpl* (= *Comitati di base*) independent trades unions

'coca *sf* (*bibita*) Coke®; (*droga*) cocaine

coca'ina *sf* cocaine

cocci'nella [kottʃi'nɛlla] *sf* ladybird (BRIT), ladybug (US)

cocci'uto, -a [kot'tʃuto] *ag* stubborn, pigheaded

'cocco, -chi *sm* (*pianta*) coconut palm; (*frutto*): **noce di ~** coconut ▷ *sm/f* (*fam*) darling

cocco'drillo *sm* crocodile

cocco'lare *vt* to cuddle, fondle

cocerò *ecc* [kotʃe'rɔ] *vb vedi* **cuocere**

co'comero *sm* watermelon

'coda *sf* tail; (*fila di persone, auto*) queue (BRIT), line (US); (*di abiti*) train; **con la ~ dell'occhio** out of the corner of one's eye; **mettersi in ~** to queue (up) (BRIT), line up (US); to join the queue (BRIT) *o* line (US); **coda di cavallo** (*acconciatura*) ponytail

co'dardo, -a *ag* cowardly ▷ *sm/f* coward

'codice ['koditʃe] *sm* code; **codice di avviamento postale** postcode (BRIT), zip code (US); **codice a barre** bar code; **codice civile** civil code; **codice fiscale** tax code; **codice penale** penal code; **codice segreto** (*di tessera magnetica*) PIN (number); **codice della strada** highway code

coe'rente *ag* coherent

coe'taneo, -a *ag, sm/f* contemporary

'cofano *sm* (*Aut*) bonnet (BRIT), hood (US); (*forziere*) chest

'cogliere ['kɔʎʎere] *vt* (*fiore: frutto*) to pick, gather; (*sorprendere*) to catch, surprise; (*bersaglio*) to hit; (*fig: momento opportuno ecc*) to grasp, seize, take; (*: capire*) to grasp; **~ qn in flagrante** *o* **in fallo** to catch sb red-handed

co'gnato, -a [koɲ'ɲato] *sm/f* brother-/sister-in-law

co'gnome [koɲ'ɲome] *sm* surname

coinci'denza [kointʃi'dɛntsa] *sf* coincidence; (*Ferr, Aer, di autobus*) connection

coin'cidere [koin'tʃidere] *vi* to coincide

coin'volgere [koin'vɔldʒere] *vt* **~ in** to involve in

cola'pasta *sm inv* colander

co'lare *vt* (*liquido*) to strain; (*pasta*) to drain; (*oro fuso*) to pour ▷ *vi* (*sudore*) to drip; (*botte*) to leak; (*cera*) to melt; **~ a picco** *vt, vi* (*nave*) to sink

colazi'one [kolat'tsjone] *sf* breakfast; **fare ~** to have breakfast; **a che ora è servita la ~?** what time is breakfast?

co'lera *sm* (*Med*) cholera

'colgo *ecc vb vedi* **cogliere**

'colica *sf* (*Med*) colic

co'lino *sm* strainer

'colla *sf* glue; (*di farina*) paste

collabo'rare *vt* to collaborate; **~ a** to collaborate on; (*giornale*) to contribute to; **collabora'tore, -'trice** *sm/f* collaborator; contributor; **collaboratore esterno** freelance; **collaboratrice familiare** home help

col'lana *sf* necklace; (*collezione*) collection, series

col'lant [kɔ'lã] *sm inv* tights *pl*

col'lare *sm* collar

col'lasso *sm* (*Med*) collapse

collau'dare *vt* to test, try out

col'lega, -ghi, -ghe *sm/f* colleague

collega'mento *sm* connection; (*Mil*) liaison

colle'gare *vt* to connect, join, link; **collegarsi** *vpr* (*Radio, TV*) to link up; **collegarsi con** (*Tel*) to get through to

col'legio [kol'lɛdʒo] *sm* college; (*convitto*)

boarding school; **collegio elettorale** (*Pol*) constituency

'**collera** *sf* anger

col'lerico, -a, -ci, -che *ag* quick-tempered, irascible

col'letta *sf* collection

col'letto *sm* collar

collezio'nare [kollettsjo'nare] *vt* to collect

collezi'one [kollet'tsjone] *sf* collection

col'lina *sf* hill

col'lirio *sm* eyewash

'**collo** *sm* neck; (*di abito*) neck, collar; (*pacco*) parcel; **collo del piede** instep

colloca'mento *sm* (*impiego*) employment; (*disposizione*) placing, arrangement

collo'care *vt* (*libri, mobili*) to place; (*Comm: merce*) to find a market for

collocazi'one [kollokat'tsjone] *sf* placing; (*di libro*) classification

col'loquio *sm* conversation, talk; (*ufficiale, per un lavoro*) interview; (*Ins*) preliminary oral exam

col'mare *vt ~ di* (*anche fig*) to fill with; (*dare in abbondanza*) to load o overwhelm with

co'lombo, -a *sm/f* dove; pigeon

co'lonia *sf* colony; (*per bambini*) holiday camp; **(acqua di) ~** (eau de) cologne

co'lonna *sf* column; **colonna sonora** (*Cinema*) sound track; **colonna vertebrale** spine, spinal column

colon'nello *sm* colonel

colo'rante *sm* colouring

colo'rare *vt* to colour; (*disegno*) to colour in

co'lore *sm* colour; **a colori** in colour, colour *cpd*; **farne di tutti i colori** to get up to all sorts of mischief; **vorrei un ~ diverso** I'd like a different colour

colo'rito, -a *ag* coloured; (*viso*) rosy, pink; (*linguaggio*) colourful ▷ *sm* (*tinta*) colour; (*carnagione*) complexion

'**colpa** *sf* fault; (*biasimo*) blame; (*colpevolezza*) guilt; (*azione colpevole*) offence; (*peccato*) sin; **di chi è la ~?** whose fault is it?; **è ~ sua** it's his fault; **per ~ di** through, owing to; **col'pevole** *ag* guilty

col'pire *vt* to hit, strike; (*fig*) to strike; **rimanere colpito da qc** to be amazed o struck by sth

'**colpo** *sm* (*urto*) knock; (: *affettivo*) blow, shock; (: *aggressivo*) blow; (*di pistola*) shot; (*Med*) stroke; (*rapina*) raid; **di ~** suddenly; **fare ~** to make a strong impression; **colpo d'aria** chill; **colpo in banca** bank job o raid; **colpo basso** (*Pugilato, fig*) punch below the belt; **colpo di fulmine** love at

first sight; **colpo di grazia** coup de grâce; **colpo di scena** (*Teatro*) coup de théâtre; (*fig*) dramatic turn of events; **colpo di sole** sunstroke; **colpo di Stato** coup d'état; **colpo di telefono** phone call; **colpo di testa** (sudden) impulse o whim; **colpo di vento** gust (of wind); **colpi di sole** (*nei capelli*) highlights

'**colsi** *ecc vb vedi* **cogliere**

coltel'lata *sf* stab

col'tello *sm* knife; **coltello a serramanico** clasp knife

colti'vare *vt* to cultivate; (*verdura*) to grow, cultivate

'**colto, -a** *pp di* **cogliere** ▷ *ag* (*istruito*) cultured, educated

'**coma** *sm inv* coma

comanda'mento *sm* (*Rel*) commandment

coman'dante *sm* (*Mil*) commander, commandant; (*di reggimento*) commanding officer; (*Naut, Aer*) captain

coman'dare *vi* to be in command ▷ *vt* to command; (*imporre*) to order, command; **~ a qn di fare** to order sb to do

combaci'are [komba'tʃare] *vi* to meet; (*fig: coincidere*) to coincide

com'battere *vt, vi* to fight

combi'nare *vt* to combine; (*organizzare*) to arrange; (*fam: fare*) to make, cause; **combinazi'one** *sf* combination; (*caso fortuito*) coincidence; **per combinazione** by chance

combus'tibile *ag* combustible ▷ *sm* fuel

 PAROLA CHIAVE

'**come** *av* **1** (*alla maniera di*) like; **ti comporti come lui** you behave like him o like he does; **bianco come la neve** (as) white as snow; **come se** as if, as though

2 (*in qualità di*) as a; **lavora come autista** he works as a driver

3 (*interrogativo*) how; **come ti chiami?** what's your name?; **come sta?** how are you?; **com'è il tuo amico?** what is your friend like?; **come?** (*prego?*) pardon?, sorry?; **come mai?** how come?; **come mai non ci hai avvertiti?** why on earth didn't you warn us?

4 (*esclamativo*): **come sei bravo!** how clever you are!; **come mi dispiace!** I'm terribly sorry!

▷ *cong* **1** (*in che modo*) how; **mi ha spiegato come l'ha conosciuto** he told me how he met him

2 (*correlativo*) as; (*con comparativi di maggioranza*) than; **non è bravo come pensavo** he isn't as clever as I thought; **è**

meglio di come pensassi it's better than I thought
3 (*appena che, quando*) as soon as; **come arrivò, iniziò a lavorare** as soon as he arrived, he set to work; *vedi* **così**; **tanto**

'comico, -a, -ci, -che *ag* (*Teatro*) comic; (*buffo*) comical ▷ *sm* (*attore*) comedian, comic actor
cominci'are [komin'tʃare] *vt*, *vi* to begin, start; **~ a fare/col fare** to begin to do/by doing; **a che ora comincia il film?** when does the film start?
comi'tato *sm* committee
comi'tiva *sf* party, group
co'mizio [ko'mittsjo] *sm* (*Pol*) meeting, assembly
com'media *sf* comedy; (*opera teatrale*) play; (: *che fa ridere*) comedy; (*fig*) playacting *no pl*
commemo'rare *vt* to commemorate
commen'tare *vt* to comment on; (*testo*) to annotate; (*Radio, TV*) to give a commentary on
commerci'ale [kommer'tʃale] *ag* commercial, trading; (*peg*) commercial
commercia'lista, -i, e [kommertʃa'lista] *sm/f* (*laureato*) graduate in economics and commerce; (*consulente*) business consultant
commerci'ante [kommer'tʃante] *sm/f* trader, dealer; (*negoziante*) shopkeeper
commerci'are [kommer'tʃare] *vt*, *vi* **~ in** to deal o trade in
com'mercio [kom'mɛrtʃo] *sm* trade, commerce; **essere in ~** (*prodotto*) to be on the market o on sale; **essere nel ~** (*persona*) to be in business; **commercio al dettaglio/all'ingrosso** retail/wholesale trade; **commercio elettronico** e-commerce
com'messo, -a *pp di* **commettere** ▷ *sm/f* shop assistant (BRIT), sales clerk (US) ▷ *sm* (*impiegato*) clerk; **commesso viaggiatore** commercial traveller
commes'tibile *ag* edible
com'mettere *vt* to commit
com'misi *ecc vb vedi* **commettere**
commissari'ato *sm* (*Amm*) commissionership; (: *sede*) commissioner's office; **commissariato di polizia** police station
commis'sario *sm* commissioner; (*di pubblica sicurezza*) ≈ (police) superintendent (BRIT), ≈ (police) captain (US); (*Sport*) steward; (*membro di commissione*) member of a committee o board
commissi'one *sf* (*incarico*) errand;

(*comitato, percentuale*) commission; (*Comm: ordinazione*) order; **commissioni** *sfpl* (*acquisti*) shopping *sg*; **commissioni bancarie** bank charges; **commissione d'esame** examining board
com'mosso, -a *pp di* **commuovere**
commo'vente *ag* moving
commozi'one [kommot'tsjone] *sf* emotion, deep feeling; **commozione cerebrale** (*Med*) concussion
commu'overe *vt* to move, affect; **commuoversi** *vpr* to be moved
como'dino *sm* bedside table
comodità *sf inv* comfort; convenience
'comodo, -a *ag* comfortable; (*facile*) easy; (*conveniente*) convenient; (*utile*) useful, handy ▷ *sm* comfort; convenience; **con ~** at one's convenience o leisure; **fare il proprio ~** to do as one pleases; **far ~** to be useful o handy
compa'gnia [kompaɲ'nia] *sf* company; (*gruppo*) gathering
com'pagno, -a [kom'paɲɲo] *sm/f* (*di classe, gioco*) companion; (*Pol*) comrade
com'paio *ecc vb vedi* **comparire**
compa'rare *vt* to compare
compara'tivo, -a, sm comparative
compa'rire *vi* to appear
com'parvi *ecc vb vedi* **comparire**
compassi'one *sf* compassion, pity; **avere ~ di qn** to feel sorry for sb, to pity sb
com'passo *sm* (pair of) compasses *pl*; callipers *pl*
compa'tibile *ag* (*scusabile*) excusable; (*conciliabile, Inform*) compatible
compa'tire *vt* (*aver compassione di*) to sympathize with, feel sorry for; (*scusare*) to make allowances for
com'patto, -a *ag* compact; (*roccia*) solid; (*folla*) dense; (*fig: gruppo, partito*) united
compen'sare *vt* (*equilibrare*) to compensate for, make up for; **~ qn di** (*rimunerare*) to pay o remunerate sb for; (*risarcire*) to pay compensation to sb for; (*fig: fatiche, dolori*) to reward sb for; **com'penso** *sm* compensation payment, remuneration; reward; **in compenso** (*d'altra parte*) on the other hand
compe'rare *vt* = **comprare**
'compere *sfpl* **fare ~** to do the shopping
compe'tente *ag* competent; (*mancia*) apt, suitable
com'petere *vi* to compete, vie; (*Dir: spettare*): **~ a** to lie within the competence of; **competizi'one** *sf* competition
compi'angere [kom'pjandʒere] *vt* to sympathize with, feel sorry for
'compiere *vt* (*concludere*) to finish, complete; (*adempiere*) to carry out, fulfil;

compiersi vpr (avverarsi) to be fulfilled, come true; **~ gli anni** to have one's birthday

compi'lare vt (modulo) to fill in; (dizionario, elenco) to compile

'compito sm (incarico) task, duty; (dovere) duty; (Ins) exercise; (: a casa) piece of homework; **fare i compiti** to do one's homework

comple'anno sm birthday

comples'sità sf complexity

comples'sivo, -a ag (globale) comprehensive, overall; (totale: cifra) total

com'plesso, -a ag complex ▷ sm (Psic, Edil) complex; (Mus: corale) ensemble; (: orchestrina) band; (: di musica pop) group; **in** o **nel ~** on the whole; **complesso alberghiero** hotel complex; **complesso edilizio** building complex; **complesso vitaminico** vitamin complex

completa'mente av completely

comple'tare vt to complete

com'pleto, -a ag complete; (teatro, autobus) full ▷ sm suit; **al ~** full; (tutti presenti) all present; **completo da sci** ski suit

compli'care vt to complicate; **complicarsi** vpr to become complicated

'complice ['komplitʃe] sm/f accomplice

complicità [komplitʃi'ta] sf inv complicity; **un sorriso/uno sguardo di ~** a knowing smile/look

complimen'tarsi vpr **~ con** to congratulate

compli'mento sm compliment; **complimenti** smpl (cortesia eccessiva) ceremony sg; (ossequi) regards, compliments; **complimenti!** congratulations!; **senza complimenti!** don't stand on ceremony!; make yourself at home!; help yourself!

complot'tare vi to plot, conspire

com'plotto sm plot, conspiracy

com'pone ecc vb vedi **comporre**

compo'nente sm/f member ▷ sm component

com'pongo ecc vb vedi **comporre**

componi'mento sm (Dir) settlement; (Ins) composition; (poetico, teatrale) work

com'porre vt (musica, testo) to compose; (mettere in ordine) to arrange; (Dir: lite) to settle; (Tip) to set; (Tel) to dial; **comporsi** vpr **comporsi di** to consist of, be composed of

comporta'mento sm behaviour

compor'tare vt (implicare) to involve; **comportarsi** vpr to behave

com'posi ecc vb vedi **comporre**

composi'tore, -'trice sm/f composer;

(Tip) compositor, typesetter

com'posto, -a pp di **comporre** ▷ ag (persona) composed, self-possessed; (: decoroso) dignified; (formato da più elementi) compound cpd ▷ sm compound

com'prare vt to buy; **dove posso ~ delle cartoline?** where can I buy some postcards?

com'prendere vt (contenere) to comprise, consist of; (capire) to understand

compren'sibile ag understandable

comprensi'one sf understanding

compren'sivo, -a ag (prezzo): **~ di** inclusive of; (indulgente) understanding

Attenzione! In inglese esiste la parola comprehensive, che però in genere significa compound.

com'preso, -a pp di **comprendere** ▷ ag (incluso) included; **il servizio è ~?** is service included?

com'pressa sf (Med: garza) compress; (: pastiglia) tablet; vedi anche **compresso**

com'primere vt (premere) to press; (Fisica) to compress; (fig) to repress

compro'messo, -a pp di **compromettere** ▷ sm compromise

compro'mettere vt to compromise; **compromettersi** vpr to compromise o s.

com'puter sm inv computer

comu'nale ag municipal, town cpd, ≈ borough cpd

co'mune ag common; (consueto) common, everyday; (di livello medio) average; (ordinario) ordinary ▷ sm (Amm) town council; (: sede) town hall ▷ sf (di persone) commune; **fuori del ~** out of the ordinary; **avere in ~** to have in common, share; **mettere in ~** to share

comuni'care vt (notizia) to pass on, convey; (malattia) to pass on; (ansia ecc) to communicate; (trasmettere: calore ecc) to transmit, communicate; (Rel) to administer communion to ▷ vi to communicate

comuni'cato sm communiqué; **comunicato stampa** press release

comunicazi'one [komunikat'tsjone] sf communication; (annuncio) announcement; (Tel): **dare la ~ a qn** to put sb through; **ottenere la ~** to get through; **comunicazione (telefonica)** (telephone) call

comuni'one sf communion; **comunione di beni** (Dir) joint ownership of property

comu'nismo sm communism

comunità sf inv community; **Comunità Europea** European Community

co'munque cong however, no matter how ▷ av (in ogni modo) in any case; (tuttavia) however, nevertheless

con *prep* with; **partire col treno** to leave by train; **~ mio grande stupore** to my great astonishment; **~ tutto ciò** for all that

con'cedere [kon'tʃedere] *vt* (*accordare*) to grant; (*ammettere*) to admit, concede; **concedersi qc** to treat o.s. to sth, to allow o.s. sth

concentrarsi *vpr* to concentrate

concentrazi'one *sf* concentration

conce'pire [kontʃe'pire] *vt* (*bambino*) to conceive; (*progetto, idea*) to conceive (of); (*metodo, piano*) to devise

con'certo [kon'tʃɛrto] *sm* (*Mus*) concert; (: *componimento*) concerto

con'cessi *ecc* [kon'tʃɛssi] *vb vedi* **concedere**

con'cetto [kon'tʃɛtto] *sm* (*pensiero, idea*) concept; (*opinione*) opinion

concezi'one [kontʃet'tsjone] *sf* conception

con'chiglia [kon'kiʎʎa] *sf* shell

conci'are [kon'tʃare] *vt* (*pelli*) to tan; (*tabacco*) to cure; (*fig: ridurre in cattivo stato*) to beat up; **conciarsi** *vpr* (*sporcarsi*) to get in a mess; (*vestirsi male*) to dress badly

concili'are [kontʃi'ljare] *vt* to reconcile; (*contravvenzione*) to pay on the spot; (*sonno*) to be conducive to, induce; **conciliarsi qc** to gain o win sth (for o.s.); **conciliarsi qn** to win sb over; **conciliarsi con** to be reconciled with

con'cime [kon'tʃime] *sm* manure; (*chimico*) fertilizer

con'ciso, -a [kon'tʃizo] *ag* concise, succinct

concitta'dino, -a [kontʃitta'dino] *sm/f* fellow citizen

con'cludere *vt* to conclude; (*portare a compimento*) to conclude, finish, bring to an end; (*operare positivamente*) to achieve ▷ *vi* (*essere convincente*) to be conclusive; **concludersi** *vpr* to come to an end, close

concor'dare *vt* (*tregua, prezzo*) to agree on; (*Ling*) to make agree ▷ *vi* to agree

con'corde *ag* (*d'accordo*) in agreement; (*simultaneo*) simultaneous

concor'rente *sm/f* competitor; (*Ins*) candidate; **concor'renza** *sf* competition

concorrenzi'ale [konkorren'tsjale] *ag* competitive

con'correre *vi* **~ (in)** (*Mat*) to converge o meet (in); **~ (a)** (*competere*) to compete (for); (: *Ins: a una cattedra*) to apply (for); (*partecipare: a un'impresa*) to take part (in), contribute (to); **con'corso, -a** *pp di* **concorrere** ▷ *sm* competition; (*Ins*) competitive examination; **concorso di colpa** (*Dir*) contributory negligence

con'creto, -a *ag* concrete

con'danna *sf* sentence; conviction; condemnation

condan'nare *vt* (*Dir*): **~ a** to sentence to; **~ per** to convict of; (*disapprovare*) to condemn

conden'sare *vt* to condense

condi'mento *sm* seasoning; dressing

con'dire *vt* to season; (*insalata*) to dress

condi'videre *vt* to share

condizio'nale [kondittsjo'nale] *ag* conditional ▷ *sm* (*Ling*) conditional ▷ *sf* (*Dir*) suspended sentence

condizio'nare [kondittsjo'nare] *vt* to condition; **ad aria condizionata** air-conditioned; **condiziona'tore** *sm* air conditioner

condizi'one [kondit'tsjone] *sf* condition

condogli'anze [kondoʎ'ʎantse] *sfpl* condolences

condo'minio *sm* joint ownership; (*edificio*) jointly-owned building

con'dotta *sf* (*modo di comportarsi*) conduct, behaviour; (*di un affare ecc*) handling; (*di acqua*) piping; (*incarico sanitario*) country medical practice controlled by a local authority

condu'cente [kondu'tʃɛnte] *sm* driver

con'duco *ecc vb vedi* **condurre**

con'durre *vt* to conduct; (*azienda*) to manage; (*accompagnare: bambino*) to take; (*automobile*) to drive; (*trasportare: acqua, gas*) to convey, conduct; (*fig*) to lead ▷ *vi* to lead

con'dussi *ecc vb vedi* **condurre**

confe'renza [konfe'rɛntsa] *sf* (*discorso*) lecture; (*riunione*) conference; **conferenza stampa** press conference

con'ferma *sf* confirmation

confer'mare *vt* to confirm

confes'sare *vt* to confess; **confessarsi** *vpr* to confess; **andare a confessarsi** (*Rel*) to go to confession

con'fetto *sm* sugared almond; (*Med*) pill
Attenzione! In inglese esiste la parola **confetti**, che però significa *coriandoli*.

confet'tura *sf* (*gen*) jam; (*di arance*) marmalade

confezio'nare [konfettsjo'nare] *vt* (*vestito*) to make (up); (*merci, pacchi*) to package

confezi'one [konfet'tsjone] *sf* (*di abiti: da uomo*) tailoring; (: *da donna*) dressmaking; (*imballaggio*) packaging; **confezioni per signora** ladies' wear; **confezioni da uomo** menswear; **confezione regalo** gift pack

confic'care *vt* **~ qc in** to hammer o drive sth into; **conficcarsi** *vpr* to stick

confi'dare *vi* **~ in** to confide in, rely on ▷ *vt* to confide; **confidarsi con qn** to confide in sb

configu'rare vt (Inform) to set

configurazi'one [konfigurat'tsjone] sf configuration; (Inform) setting

confi'nare vi ~ **con** to border on ▷ vt (Pol) to intern; (fig) to confine

Confin'dustria sigla f (= Confederazione Generale dell'Industria Italiana) employers' association, ≈ CBI (BRIT)

con'fine sm boundary; (di paese) border, frontier

confis'care vt to confiscate

con'flitto sm conflict

conflu'enza [konflu'ɛntsa] sf (di fiumi) confluence; (di strade) junction

con'fondere vt to mix up, confuse; (imbarazzare) to embarrass; **confondersi** vpr (mescolarsi) to mingle; (turbarsi) to be confused; (sbagliare) to get mixed up

confor'tare vt to comfort, console

confron'tare vt to compare

con'fronto sm comparison; **in** o **a ~ di** in comparison with, compared to; **nei miei** (o **tuoi** ecc) **confronti** towards me (o you ecc)

con'fusi ecc vb vedi **confondere**

confusi'one sf confusion; (chiasso) racket, noise; (imbarazzo) embarrassment

con'fuso, -a pp di **confondere** ▷ ag (vedi confondere) confused; embarrassed

conge'dare [kondʒe'dare] vt to dismiss; (Mil) to demobilize; **congedarsi** vpr to take one's leave

con'gegno sm device, mechanism

conge'lare [kondʒe'lare] vt to freeze; **congelarsi** vpr to freeze; **congela'tore** sm freezer

congesti'one [kondʒes'tjone] sf congestion

conget'tura [kondʒet'tura] sf conjecture

con'giungere [kon'dʒundʒere] vt to join (together); **congiungersi** vpr to join (together)

congiunti'vite [kondʒunti'vite] sf conjunctivitis

congiun'tivo [kondʒun'tivo] sm (Ling) subjunctive

congi'unto, -a [kon'dʒunto] pp di **congiungere** ▷ ag (unito) joined ▷ sm/f relative

congiunzi'one [kondʒun'tsjone] sf (Ling) conjunction

congi'ura [kon'dʒura] sf conspiracy

congratu'larsi vpr ~ **con qn per qc** to congratulate sb on sth

congratulazi'oni [kongratulat'tsjoni] sfpl congratulations

con'gresso sm congress

C.O.N.I. sigla m (= Comitato Olimpico Nazionale Italiano) Italian Olympic Games Committee

coni'are vt to mint, coin; (fig) to coin

co'niglio [ko'niλλo] sm rabbit

coniu'gare vt (Ling) to conjugate; **coniugarsi** vpr to get married

'coniuge ['kɔnjudʒe] sm/f spouse

connazio'nale [konnattsjo'nale] sm/f fellow-countryman/woman

connessi'one sf connection

con'nettere vt to connect, join ▷ vi (fig) to think straight

'cono sm cone; **cono gelato** ice-cream cone

co'nobbi ecc vb vedi **conoscere**

cono'scente [konoʃʃente] sm/f acquaintance

cono'scenza [konoʃʃentsa] sf (il sapere) knowledge no pl; (persona) acquaintance; (facoltà sensoriale) consciousness no pl; **perdere ~** to lose consciousness

co'noscere [ko'noʃʃere] vt to know; **ci siamo conosciuti a Firenze** we (first) met in Florence; **conoscersi** vpr to know o.s.; (reciproco) to know each other; (incontrarsi) to meet; **~ qn di vista** to know sb by sight; **farsi ~** (fig) to make a name for o s.; **conosci'uto, -a** pp di **conoscere** ▷ ag well-known

con'quista sf conquest

conquis'tare vt to conquer; (fig) to gain, win

consa'pevole ag ~ **di** aware o conscious of

'conscio, -a, -sci, -sce ['kɔnʃo] ag ~ **di** aware o conscious of

consecu'tivo, -a ag consecutive; (successivo: giorno) following, next

con'segna [kon'seɲɲa] sf delivery; (merce consegnata) consignment; (custodia) care, custody; (Mil: ordine) orders pl; (: punizione) confinement to barracks; **pagamento alla ~** cash on delivery; **dare qc in ~ a qn** to entrust sth to sb

conse'gnare [konse'ɲɲare] vt to deliver; (affidare) to entrust, hand over; (Mil) to confine to barracks

consegu'enza [konse'gwɛntsa] sf consequence; **per** o **di ~** consequently

con'senso sm approval, consent; **consenso informato** informed consent

consen'tire vi ~ **a** to consent o agree to ▷ vt to allow, permit

con'serva sf (Cuc) preserve; **conserva di frutta** jam; **conserva di pomodoro** tomato purée

conser'vante sm (per alimenti) preservative

conser'vare vt (Cuc) to preserve; (custodire) to keep; (: dalla distruzione ecc) to preserve, conserve

conserva'tore, -'trice *sm/f* (*Pol*) conservative

conserva'torio *sm* (*di musica*) conservatory

conservazi'one [konservat'tsjone] *sf* preservation; conservation

conside'rare *vt* to consider; (*reputare*) to consider, regard; **considerarsi** *vpr* to consider o.s.

consigli'are [konsiʎ'ʎare] *vt* (*persona*) to advise; (*metodo, azione*) to recommend, advise, suggest; **mi può ~ un buon ristorante?** can you recommend a good restaurant?; **con'siglio** *sm* (*suggerimento*) advice *no pl*, piece of advice; (*assemblea*) council; **consiglio d'amministrazione** board; **Consiglio d'Europa** Council of Europe; **Consiglio dei Ministri** (*Pol*): **il Consiglio dei Ministri** ≈ the Cabinet

consis'tente *ag* thick; solid; (*fig*) sound, valid

con'sistere *vi* **~ in** to consist of

conso'lare *ag* consular ▷ *vt* (*confortare*) to console, comfort; (*rallegrare*) to cheer up; **consolarsi** *vpr* to be comforted; to cheer up

conso'lato *sm* consulate

consolazi'one [konsolat'tsjone] *sf* consolation, comfort

'console *sm* consul

conso'nante *sf* consonant

'consono, -a *ag* **~ a** consistent with, consonant with

con'sorte *sm/f* consort

consta'tare *vt* to establish, verify

consu'eto, -a *ag* habitual, usual

consu'lente *sm/f* consultant

consul'tare *vt* to consult; **consultarsi** *vpr* **consultarsi con qn** to seek the advice of sb

consul'torio *sm* **~ familiare** family planning clinic

consu'mare *vt* (*logorare: abiti, scarpe*) to wear out; (*usare*) to consume, use up; (*mangiare, bere*) to consume; (*Dir*) to consummate; **consumarsi** *vpr* to wear out; to be used up; (*anche fig*) to be consumed; (*combustibile*) to burn out

con'tabile *ag* accounts *cpd*, accounting ▷ *sm/f* accountant

contachi'lometri [kontaki'lɔmetri] *sm inv* ≈ mileometer

conta'dino, -a *sm/f* countryman/ woman, farm worker; (*peg*) peasant

contagi'are [konta'dʒare] *vt* to infect

contagi'oso, -a *ag* infectious; contagious

conta'gocce [konta'gottʃe] *sm inv* (*Med*) dropper

contami'nare *vt* to contaminate

con'tante *sm* cash; **pagare in contanti** to pay cash; **non ho contanti** I haven't got any cash

con'tare *vt* to count; (*considerare*) to consider ▷ *vi* to count, be of importance; **~ su qn** to count o rely on sb; **~ di fare qc** to intend to do sth; **conta'tore** *sm* meter

contat'tare *vt* to contact

con'tatto *sm* contact

'conte *sm* count

conteggi'are [konted'dʒare] *vt* to charge, put on the bill

con'tegno [kon'teɲɲo] *sm* (*comportamento*) behaviour; (*atteggiamento*) attitude; **darsi un ~** to act nonchalant; to pull o.s. together

contemporanea'mente *av* simultaneously; at the same time

contempo'raneo, -a *ag, sm/f* contemporary

conten'dente *sm/f* opponent, adversary

conte'nere *vt* to contain; **conteni'tore** *sm* container

conten'tezza [konten'tettsa] *sf* contentment

con'tento, -a *ag* pleased, glad; **~ di** pleased with

conte'nuto *sm* contents *pl*; (*argomento*) content

con'tessa *sf* countess

contes'tare *vt* (*Dir*) to notify; (*fig*) to dispute

con'testo *sm* context

continen'tale *ag, sm/f* continental

conti'nente *ag* continent ▷ *sm* (*Geo*) continent; (*: terra ferma*) mainland

contin'gente [kontin'dʒɛnte] *ag* contingent ▷ *sm* (*Comm*) quota; (*Mil*) contingent

continua'mente *av* (*senza interruzione*) continuously, nonstop; (*ripetutamente*) continually

continu'are *vt* to continue (with), go on with ▷ *vi* to continue, go on; **~ a fare qc** to go on o continue doing sth

continuità *sf* continuity

con'tinuo, -a *ag* (*numerazione*) continuous; (*pioggia*) continual, constant; (*Elettr*): **corrente continua** direct current; **di ~** continually

'conto *sm* (*calcolo*) calculation; (*Comm, Econ*) account; (*di ristorante, albergo*) bill; (*fig: stima*) consideration, esteem; **il ~, per favore** can I have the bill, please?; **lo metta sul mio ~** put it on my bill; **fare i conti con qn** to settle one's account with sb; **fare ~ su qn/qc** to count o rely on sb; **rendere ~ a qn di qc** to be accountable to sb for sth; **tener ~ di qn/qc** to take sb/sth into account; **per ~ di** on behalf of; **per ~ mio** as far as I'm concerned; **a conti fatti, in fin dei conti** all things considered; **conto corrente** current account; **conto alla rovescia** countdown

con'torno *sm* (*linea*) outline, contour; (*ornamento*) border; (*Cuc*) vegetables *pl*

con'torto, -a *pp di* **contorcere**

contrabbandi'ere, -a *sm/f* smuggler

contrab'bando *sm* smuggling, contraband; **merce di ~** contraband, smuggled goods *pl*

contrab'basso *sm* (*Mus*) (double) bass

contraccambi'are *vt* (*favore ecc*) to return

contraccet'tivo, -a [kontrattʃet'tivo] *ag, sm* contraceptive

contrac'colpo *sm* rebound; (*di arma da fuoco*) recoil; (*fig*) repercussion

contrad'dire *vt* to contradict; **contraddirsi** *vpr* to contradict o.s.; (*uso reciproco: persone*) to contradict each other *o* one another; (: *testimonianze ecc*) to be contradictory

contraf'fare *vt* (*persona*) to mimic; (*alterare: voce*) to disguise; (*firma*) to forge, counterfeit

contraria'mente *av* **~ a** contrary to

contrari'are *vt* (*contrastare*) to thwart, oppose; (*irritare*) to annoy, bother

con'trario, -a *ag* opposite; (*sfavorevole*) unfavourable ▷ *sm* opposite; **essere ~ a qc** (*persona*) to be against sth; **in caso ~** otherwise; **avere qc in ~** to have some objection; **al ~ on** the contrary

contrasse'gnare [kontrassen'ɲare] *vt* to mark

contras'tare *vt* (*avversare*) to oppose; (*impedire*) to bar; (*negare: diritto*) to contest, dispute ▷ *vi* **~ (con)** (*essere in disaccordo*) to contrast (with); (*lottare*) to struggle (with)

contrat'tacco *sm* counterattack

contrat'tare *vt, vi* to negotiate

contrat'tempo *sm* hitch

con'tratto, -a *pp di* **contrarre** ▷ *sm* contract

contravvenzi'one [kontravven'tsjone] *sf* contravention; (*ammenda*) fine

contrazi'one [kontrat'tsjone] *sf* contraction; (*di prezzi ecc*) reduction

contribu'ente *sm/f* taxpayer; ratepayer (BRIT), property tax payer (US)

contribu'ire *vi* to contribute

'contro *prep* against; **~ di me/lui** against me/him; **pastiglie ~ la tosse** throat lozenges; **~ pagamento** (*Comm*) on payment ▷ *prefisso*: **controfi'gura** *sf* (*Cinema*) double

control'lare *vt* (*accertare*) to check; (*sorvegliare*) to watch, control; (*tenere nel proprio potere, fig*: *dominare*) to control; **controllarsi** *vpr* to control o.s.; **con'trollo** *sm* check; watch; control; **controllo delle nascite** birth control; **control'lore** *sm* (*Ferr, Autobus*) (ticket) inspector

contro'luce [kontro'lutʃe] *sf inv* (*Fot*) backlit shot ▷ *av* **(in) ~** against the light; (*fotografare*) into the light

contro'mano *av* **guidare ~** to drive on the wrong side of the road; (*in un senso unico*) to drive the wrong way up a one-way street

controprodu'cente [kontroprodu'tʃɛnte] *ag* counterproductive

contro'senso *sm* (*contraddizione*) contradiction in terms; (*assurdità*) nonsense

controspio'naggio [kontrospio'naddʒo] *sm* counterespionage

contro'versia *sf* controversy; (*Dir*) dispute

contro'verso, -a *ag* controversial

contro'voglia [kontro'vɔʎʎa] *av* unwillingly

contusi'one *sf* (*Med*) bruise

convale'scente [konvaleʃ'ʃɛnte] *ag, sm/f* convalescent

convali'dare *vt* (*Amm*) to validate; (*fig: sospetto, dubbio*) to confirm

con'vegno [kon'veɲɲo] *sm* (*incontro*) meeting; (*congresso*) convention, congress; (*luogo*) meeting place

conve'nevoli *smpl* civilities

conveni'ente *ag* suitable; (*vantaggioso*) profitable; (: *prezzo*) cheap

> Attenzione! In inglese esiste la parola *convenient*, che però significa *comodo*.

conve'nire *vi* (*riunirsi*) to gather, assemble; (*concordare*) to agree; (*tornare utile*) to be worthwhile ▷ *vb impers* **conviene fare questo** it is advisable to do this; **conviene andarsene** we should go; **ne convengo** I agree

con'vento *sm* (*di frati*) monastery; (*di suore*) convent

convenzio'nale [konventsjo'nale] *ag* conventional

convenzi'one [konven'tsjone] *sf* (*Dir*) agreement; (*nella società*) convention

conver'sare *vi* to have a conversation, converse

conversazi'one [konversat'tsjone] *sf* conversation; **fare ~** to chat, have a chat

conversi'one *sf* conversion; **conversione ad U** (*Aut*) U-turn

conver'tire *vt* (*trasformare*) to change; (*Pol, Rel*) to convert; **convertirsi** *vpr* **convertirsi (a)** to be converted (to)

con'vesso, -a *ag* convex

convin'cente [konvin'tʃɛnte] *ag* convincing

con'vincere [kon'vintʃere] *vt* to convince; **~ qn di qc** to convince sb of sth; **~ qn a fare qc** to persuade sb to do sth; **convincersi** *vpr* **convincersi (di qc)** to convince o.s. (of sth); **~ qn di qc** to convince sb of sth; **~ qn a fare qc** to convince sb to do sth

convi'vente *sm/f* common-law husband/wife

con'vivere *vi* to live together

convo'care *vt* to call, convene; *(Dir)* to summon

convulsi'one *sf* convulsion

coope'rare *vi* **~ (a)** to cooperate (in); **coopera'tiva** *sf* cooperative

coordi'nare *vt* to coordinate

co'perchio [ko'pɛrkjo] *sm* cover; *(di pentola)* lid

co'perta *sf* cover; *(di lana)* blanket; *(da viaggio)* rug; *(Naut)* deck

coper'tina *sf* *(Stampa)* cover, jacket

co'perto, -a *pp di* **coprire** ▷ *ag* covered; *(cielo)* overcast ▷ *sm* place setting; *(posto a tavola)* place; *(al ristorante)* cover charge; **~ di** covered in o with

coper'tone *sm* *(Aut)* rubber tyre

coper'tura *sf* *(anche Econ, Mil)* cover; *(di edificio)* roofing

'copia *sf* copy; **brutta/bella ~** rough/final copy

copi'are *vt* to copy

copi'one *sm* *(Cinema, Teatro)* script

'coppa *sf* *(bicchiere)* goblet; *(per frutta, gelato)* dish; *(trofeo)* cup, trophy; **coppa dell'olio** oil sump (BRIT) o pan (US)

'coppia *sf* *(di persone)* couple; *(di animali, Sport)* pair

coprifu'oco, -chi *sm* curfew

copri'letto *sm* bedspread

copripiu'mino *sm* duvet cover

co'prire *vt* to cover; *(occupare: carica, posto)* to hold; **coprirsi** *vpr* *(cielo)* to cloud over; *(vestirsi)* to wrap up, cover up; *(Econ)* to cover o.s.; **coprirsi di** *(macchie, muffa)* to become covered in

coque [kɔk] *sf* **uovo alla ~** boiled egg

co'raggio [ko'raddʒo] *sm* courage, bravery; **~!** *(forza!)* come on!; *(animo!)* cheer up!

co'rallo *sm* coral

Co'rano *sm* *(Rel)* Koran

co'razza [ko'rattsa] *sf* armour; *(di animali)* carapace, shell; *(Mil)* armour(-plating)

'corda *sf* cord; *(fune)* rope; *(spago, Mus)* string; **dare ~ a qn** to let sb have his *(o* her) way; **tenere sulla ~ qn** to keep sb on tenterhooks; **tagliare la ~** to slip away, sneak off; **corda vocale** vocal cords

cordi'ale *ag* cordial, warm ▷ *sm* *(bevanda)* cordial

'cordless ['kɔːdlɪs] *sm inv* cordless phone

cor'done *sm* cord, string; *(linea: di polizia)* cordon; **cordone ombelicale** umbilical cord

Co'rea *sf* **la ~** Korea

coreogra'fia *sf* choreography

cori'andolo *sm* *(Bot)* coriander; **coriandoli** *smpl* confetti *sg*

cor'nacchia [kor'nakkja] *sf* crow

corna'musa *sf* bagpipes *pl*

cor'netta *sf* *(Mus)* cornet; *(Tel)* receiver

cor'netto *sm* *(Cuc)* croissant; *(gelato)* cone

cor'nice [kor'nitʃe] *sf* frame; *(fig)* setting, background

cornici'one [korni'tʃone] *sm* *(di edificio)* ledge; *(Archit)* cornice

'corno *(pl(f) -a)* *sm* *(Zool)* horn; *(pl(m) -i: Mus)* horn; **fare le corna a qn** to be unfaithful to sb

Corno'vaglia [korno'vaʎʎa] *sf* **la ~** Cornwall

cor'nuto, -a *ag* *(con corna)* horned; *(fam!: marito)* cuckolded ▷ *sm* *(fam!)* cuckold; *(: insulto)* bastard *(!)*

'coro *sm* chorus; *(Rel)* choir

co'rona *sf* crown; *(di fiori)* wreath

'corpo *sm* body; *(militare, diplomatico)* corps *inv*; **prendere ~** to take shape; **a ~ a ~** hand-to-hand; **corpo di ballo** corps de ballet; **corpo insegnante** teaching staff

corpora'tura *sf* build, physique

cor'reggere [kor'rɛddʒere] *vt* to correct; *(compiti)* to correct, mark

cor'rente *ag* *(acqua: di fiume)* flowing; *(: di rubinetto)* running; *(moneta, prezzo)* current; *(comune)* everyday ▷ *sm* **essere al ~ (di)** to be well-informed (about); **mettere al ~ (di)** to inform (of) ▷ *sf* *(d'acqua)* current, stream; *(spiffero)* draught; *(Elettr, Meteor)* current; *(fig)* trend, tendency; **la vostra lettera del 5 ~ mese** *(Comm)* your letter of the 5th of this month; **corrente alternata/continua** alternate/direct current; **corrente'mente** *av* commonly; **parlare una lingua correntemente** to speak a language fluently

'correre *vi* to run; *(precipitarsi)* to rush; *(partecipare a una gara)* to race, run; *(fig: diffondersi)* to go round ▷ *vt* *(Sport: gara)* to compete in; *(rischio)* to run; *(pericolo)* to face; **~ dietro a qn** to run after sb; **corre voce che ...** it is rumoured that ...

cor'ressi *ecc vb vedi* **correggere**

correzi'one [korret'tsjone] *sf* correction; marking; **correzione di bozze** proofreading

corri'doio *sm* corridor; *(in aereo, al cinema)*

aisle; **vorrei un posto sul ~** I'd like an aisle seat

corri'dore sm (Sport) runner; (: su veicolo) racer

corri'era sf coach (BRIT), bus

corri'ere sm (diplomatico, di guerra, postale) courier; (Comm) carrier

corri'mano sm handrail

corrispon'dente ag corresponding ▷ sm/f correspondent

corrispon'denza [korrispon'dɛntsa] sf correspondence

corris'pondere vi (equivalere): **~ (a)** to correspond (to) ▷ vt (stipendio) to pay; (fig: amore) to return

cor'rodere vt to corrode

cor'rompere vt to corrupt; (comprare) to bribe

cor'roso, -a pp di **corrodere**

cor'rotto, -a pp di **corrompere** ▷ ag corrupt

corru'gare vt to wrinkle; **~ la fronte** to knit one's brows

cor'ruppi ecc vb vedi **corrompere**

corruzi'one [korrut'tsjone] sf corruption; bribery

'corsa sf running no pl; (gara) race; (di autobus, taxi) journey, trip; **fare una ~** to run, dash; (Sport) to run a race; **corsa campestre** cross-country race

'corsi ecc vb vedi **correre**

cor'sia sf (Aut, Sport) lane; (di ospedale) ward

'Corsica sf **la ~** Corsica

cor'sivo sm cursive (writing); (Tip) italics pl

'corso, -a pp di **correre** ▷ sm course; (strada cittadina) main street; (di unità monetaria) circulation; (di titoli, valori) rate, price; **in ~** in progress, under way; (annata) current; **corso d'acqua** river, stream; (artificiale) waterway; **corso d'aggiornamento** refresher course; **corso serale** evening class

'corte sf (court)yard; (Dir, regale) court; **fare la ~ a qn** to court sb; **corte marziale** court-martial

cor'teccia, -ce [kor'tettʃa] sf bark

corteggi'are [korted'dʒare] vt to court

cor'teo sm procession

cor'tese ag courteous; **per cortesia ...** excuse me, please ...

cor'tile sm (court)yard

cor'tina sf curtain; (anche fig) screen

'corto, -a ag short; **essere a ~ di qc** to be short of sth; **corto circuito** short-circuit

'corvo sm raven

'cosa sf thing; (faccenda) affair, matter, business no pl; **(che) ~?** what?; **(che)**

cos'è? what is it?; **a ~ pensi?** what are you thinking about?

'coscia, -sce ['kɔʃʃa] sf thigh; **coscia di pollo** (Cuc) chicken leg

cosci'ente [koʃʃɛnte] ag conscious; **~ di** conscious o aware of

PAROLA CHIAVE

così av **1** (in questo modo) like this, (in) this way; (in tal modo) so; **le cose stanno così** this is the way things stand; **non ho detto così!** I didn't say that!; **come stai? — (e) così** how are you? — so-so; **e così via** and so on; **per così dire** so to speak

2 (tanto) so; **così lontano** so far away; **un ragazzo così intelligente** such an intelligent boy

▷ ag inv (tale): **non ho mai visto un film così** I've never seen such a film ▷ cong **1** (perciò) so, therefore

2: **così ... come** as ... as; **non è così bravo come te** he's not as good as you; **così ... che** so ... that

cosid'detto, -a ag so-called

cos'metico, -a, -ci, -che ag, sm cosmetic

cos'pargere [kos'pardʒere] vt **~ di** to sprinkle with

cos'picuo, -a ag considerable, large

cospi'rare vi to conspire

'cossi ecc vb vedi **cuocere**

'costa sf (tra terra e mare) coast(line); (litorale) shore; (Anat) rib; **la C~ Azzurra** the French Riviera

cos'tante ag constant; (persona) steadfast ▷ sf constant

cos'tare vi, vt to cost; **quanto costa?** how much does it cost?; **~ caro** to be expensive, cost a lot

cos'tata sf (Cuc) large chop

costeggi'are [kosted'dʒare] vt to be close to; to run alongside

costi'ero, -a ag coastal, coast cpd

costitu'ire vt (comitato, gruppo) to set up, form; (elementi, parti: comporre) to make up, constitute; (rappresentare) to constitute; (Dir) to appoint; **costituirsi** vpr **costituirsi alla polizia** to give o s. up to the police

costituzi'one [kostitut'tsjone] sf setting up; building up; constitution

'costo sm cost; **a ogni o qualunque ~, a tutti i costi** at all costs

'costola sf (Anat) rib

cos'toso, -a ag expensive, costly

cos'tringere [kos'trindʒere] vt **~ qn a fare qc** to force sb to do sth

costru'ire vt to construct, build;

costruzi'one sf construction, building

cos'tume sm (uso) custom; (foggia di vestire, indumento) costume; **costume da bagno** bathing o swimming costume (BRIT), swimsuit; (da uomo) bathing o swimming trunks pl

co'tenna sf bacon rind

coto'letta sf (di maiale, montone) chop; (di vitello, agnello) cutlet

co'tone sm cotton; **cotone idrofilo** cotton wool (BRIT), absorbent cotton (US)

'cotta sf (fam: innamoramento) crush

'cottimo sm **lavorare a ~** to do piecework

'cotto, -a pp di **cuocere** ▷ ag cooked; (fam: innamorato) head-over-heels in love; **ben ~** (carne) well done

cot'tura sf cooking; (in forno) baking; (in umido) stewing

co'vare vt to hatch; (fig: malattia) to be sickening for; (: odio, rancore) to nurse ▷ vi (fuoco, fig) to smoulder

'covo sm den

co'vone sm sheaf

'cozza ['kɔttsa] sf mussel

coz'zare vi **~ contro** to bang into, collide with

'crampo sm cramp; **ho un ~ alla gamba** I've got cramp in my leg

'cranio sm skull

cra'tere sm crater

cra'vatta sf tie

cre'are vt to create

'crebbi ecc vb vedi **crescere**

cre'dente sm/f (Rel) believer

cre'denza [kre'dɛntsa] sf belief; (armadio) sideboard

'credere vt to believe ▷ vi **~ in, ~ a** to believe in; **~ qn onesto** to believe sb (to be) honest; **~ che** to believe o think that; **credersi furbo** to think one is clever

'credito sm (anche Comm) credit; (reputazione) esteem, repute; **comprare a ~** to buy on credit

'crema sf cream; (con uova, zucchero ecc) custard; **crema pasticciera** confectioner's custard; **crema solare** sun cream

cre'mare vt to cremate

'crepa sf crack

cre'paccio [kre'pattʃo] sm large crack, fissure; (di ghiacciaio) crevasse

crepacu'ore sm broken heart

cre'pare vi (fam: morire) to snuff it, kick the bucket; **~ dalle risa** to split one's sides laughing

crêpe [krɛp] sf inv pancake

cre'puscolo sm twilight, dusk

'crescere ['kreʃʃere] vi to grow ▷ vt (figli) to raise

cre'sima sf (Rel) confirmation

'crespo, -a ag (capelli) frizzy; (tessuto) puckered ▷ sm crêpe

'cresta sf crest; (di polli, uccelli) crest, comb

'creta sf chalk; clay

creti'nata sf (fam): **dire/fare una ~** to say/do a stupid thing

cre'tino, -a ag stupid ▷ sm/f idiot, fool

CRI sigla f = **Croce Rossa Italiana**

cric sm inv (Tecn) jack

cri'ceto [kri'tʃɛto] sm hamster

crimi'nale ag, sm/f criminal

criminalità sf crime; **criminalità organizzata** organized crime

'crimine sm (Dir) crime

crip'tare vt (TV: programma) to encrypt

crisan'temo sm chrysanthemum

'crisi sf inv crisis; (Med) attack, fit; **crisi di nervi** attack o fit of nerves

cris'tallo sm crystal; **cristalli liquidi** liquid crystals

cristia'nesimo sm Christianity

cristi'ano, -a ag, sm/f Christian

'Cristo sm Christ

cri'terio sm criterion; (buon senso) (common) sense

'critica, -che sf criticism; **la ~** (attività) criticism; (persone) the critics pl; vedi anche **critico**

criti'care vt to criticize

'critico, -a, -ci, -che ag critical ▷ sm critic

cro'ato, -a ag, sm/f Croatian, Croat

Croa'zia [kroa'ttsja] sf Croatia

croc'cante ag crisp, crunchy

'croce ['krotʃe] sf cross; **in ~** (di traverso) crosswise; (fig) on tenterhooks; **Croce Rossa** Red Cross

croci'ata [kro'tʃata] sf crusade

croci'era [kro'tʃɛra] sf (viaggio) cruise; (Archit) transept

croci'fisso, -a pp di **crocifiggere**

crol'lare vi to collapse; **'crollo** sm collapse; (di prezzi) slump, sudden fall; **crollo in Borsa** slump in prices on the Stock Exchange

cro'mato, -a ag chromium-plated

'cromo sm chrome, chromium

'cronaca, -che sf (Stampa) news sg; (: rubrica) column; (TV, Radio) commentary; **fatto** o **episodio di ~** news item; **cronaca nera** crime news sg; crime column

'cronico, -a, -ci, -che ag chronic

cro'nista, -i sm (Stampa) reporter

cro'nometro sm chronometer; (a scatto) stopwatch

'crosta sf crust

cros'tacei [kros'tatʃei] smpl shellfish

cros'tata sf (Cuc) tart

cros'tino sm (Cuc) crouton; (: da antipasto) canapé

cruci'ale [kru'tʃale] *ag* crucial
cruci'verba *sm inv* crossword (puzzle)
cru'dele *ag* cruel
'**crudo, -a** *ag* (*non cotto*) raw; (*aspro*) harsh, severe
cru'miro (*peg*) *sm* blackleg (BRIT), scab
'**crusca** *sf* bran
crus'cotto *sm* (*Aut*) dashboard
CSI *sigla f inv* (= *Comunità Stati Indipendenti*) CIS
CSM [tʃiesse'emme] *sigla m* (= *consiglio superiore della magistratura*) Magistrates' Board of Supervisors
'**Cuba** *sf* Cuba
cu'bano, -a *ag, sm/f* Cuban
cu'betto *sm*; **cubetto di ghiaccio** ice cube
'**cubico, -a, -ci, -che** *ag* cubic
cu'bista, -i, -e *ag* (*Arte*) Cubist ▷ *sf* (*in discoteca*) podium dancer
'**cubo, -a** *ag* cubic ▷ *sm* cube; **elevare al ~** (*Mat*) to cube
cuc'cagna [kuk'kaɲɲa] *sf* **paese della ~** land of plenty; **albero della ~** greasy pole (*fig*)
cuc'cetta [kut'tʃetta] *sf* (*Ferr*) couchette; (*Naut*) berth
cucchiai'ata [kukja'jata] *sf* spoonful
cucchia'ino [kukkja'ino] *sm* teaspoon; coffee spoon
cucchi'aio [kuk'kjajo] *sm* spoon
'**cuccia, -ce** ['kuttʃa] *sf* dog's bed; **a ~!** down!
'**cucciolo** ['kuttʃolo] *sm* cub; (*di cane*) puppy
cu'cina [ku'tʃina] *sf* (*locale*) kitchen; (*arte culinaria*) cooking, cookery; (*le vivande*) food, cooking; (*apparecchio*) cooker; **cucina componibile** fitted kitchen; **cuci'nare** *vt* to cook
cu'cire [ku'tʃire] *vt* to sew, stitch; **cuci'trice** *sf* stapler
cucù *sm inv* cuckoo
'**cuffia** *sf* bonnet, cap; (*da infermiera*) cap; (*da bagno*) (bathing) cap; (*per ascoltare*) headphones *pl*, headset
cu'gino, -a [ku'dʒino] *sm/f* cousin

 PAROLA CHIAVE

'**cui** *pron* **1** (*nei complementi indiretti: persona*) whom; (: *oggetto, animale*) which; **la persona/le persone a cui accennavi** the person/people you were referring to o to whom you were referring; **i libri di cui parlavo** the books I was talking about o about which I was talking; **il quartiere in cui abito** the district where I live; **la ragione per cui** the reason why
2 (*inserito tra articolo e sostantivo*) whose;

la donna i cui figli sono scomparsi the woman whose children have disappeared; **il signore, dal cui figlio ho avuto il libro** the man from whose son I got the book

culi'naria *sf* cookery
'**culla** *sf* cradle
cul'lare *vt* to rock
'**culmine** *sm* top, summit
'**culto** *sm* (*religione*) religion; (*adorazione*) worship, adoration; (*venerazione: anche fig*) cult
cul'tura *sf* culture; education, learning; **cultu'rale** *ag* cultural
cultu'rismo *sm* body-building
cumula'tivo, -a *ag* cumulative; (*prezzo*) inclusive; (*biglietto*) group *cpd*
'**cumulo** *sm* (*mucchio*) pile, heap; (*Meteor*) cumulus
cu'netta *sf* (*avvallamento*) dip; (*di scolo*) gutter
cu'ocere ['kwɔtʃere] *vt* (*alimenti*) to cook; (*mattoni ecc*) to fire ▷ *vi* to cook; **~ al forno** (*pane*) to bake; (*arrosto*) to roast; **cu'oco, -a, -chi, -che** *sm/f* cook; (*di ristorante*) chef
cu'oio *sm* leather; **cuoio capelluto** scalp
cu'ore *sm* heart; **cuori** *smpl* (*Carte*) hearts; **avere buon ~** to be kind-hearted; **stare a ~ a qn** to be important to sb
'**cupo, -a** *ag* dark; (*suono*) dull; (*fig*) gloomy, dismal
'**cupola** *sf* dome; cupola
'**cura** *sf* care; (*Med: trattamento*) (course of) treatment; **aver ~ di** (*occuparsi di*) to look after; **a ~ di** (*libro*) edited by; **cura dimagrante** diet
cu'rare *vt* (*malato, malattia*) to treat; (: *guarire*) to cure; (*aver cura di*) to take care of; (*testo*) to edit; **curarsi** *vpr* to take care of o.s.; (*Med*) to follow a course of treatment; **curarsi di** to pay attention to
curio'sare *vi* to look round, wander round; (*tra libri*) to browse; **~ nei negozi** to look o wander round the shops
curiosità *sf inv* curiosity; (*cosa rara*) curio, curiosity
curi'oso, -a *ag* curious; **essere ~ di** to be curious about
cur'sore *sm* (*Inform*) cursor
'**curva** *sf* curve; (*stradale*) bend, curve
cur'vare *vt* to bend ▷ *vi* (*veicolo*) to take a bend; (*strada*) to bend, curve; **curvarsi** *vpr* to bend; (*legno*) to warp
'**curvo, -a** *ag* curved; (*piegato*) bent
cusci'netto [kuʃʃi'netto] *sm* pad; (*Tecn*) bearing ▷ *ag inv* **stato ~** buffer state; **cuscinetto a sfere** ball bearing
cu'scino [kuʃ'ʃino] *sm* cushion;

(*guanciale*) pillow

cus'tode *sm/f* keeper, custodian

cus'todia *sf* care; (*Dir*) custody; (*astuccio*) case, holder

custo'dire *vt* (*conservare*) to keep; (*assistere*) to look after, take care of; (*fare la guardia*) to guard

CV *abbr* (= *cavallo vapore*) h.p.

cybercaffè [tʃiberka'fe] *sm inv* cybercafé

cybernauta, -i, -e *sm/f* Internet surfer

cyberspazio *sm* cyberspace

d

 PAROLA CHIAVE

da (*da+il = dal, da+lo = dallo, da+l' = dall', da+la = dalla, da+i = dai, da+gli = dagli, da+le = dalle*) *prep* **1** (*agente*) by; **dipinto da un grande artista** painted by a great artist

2 (*causa*) with; **tremare dalla paura** to tremble with fear

3 (*stato in luogo*) at; **abito da lui** I'm living at his house o with him; **sono dal giornalaio/da Francesco** I'm at the newsagent's/Francesco's (house)

4 (*moto a luogo*) to; (*moto per luogo*) through; **vado da Pietro/dal giornalaio** I'm going to Pietro's (house)/to the newsagent's; **sono passati dalla finestra** they came in through the window

5 (*provenienza, allontanamento*) from; **arrivare/partire da Milano** to arrive/depart from Milan; **scendere dal treno/dalla macchina** to get off the train/out of the car; **si trova a 5 km da qui** it's 5 km from here

6 (*tempo: durata*) for; (: *a partire da: nel passato*) since; (: *nel futuro*) from; **vivo qui da un anno** I've been living here for a year; **è dalle 3 che ti aspetto** I've been waiting for you since 3 (o'clock); **da oggi in poi** from today onwards; **da bambino** as a

child, when I (o he *ecc*) was a child
7 (*modo, maniera*) like; **comportarsi da uomo** to behave like a man; **l'ho fatto da me** I did it (by) myself
8 (*descrittivo*): **una macchina da corsa** a racing car; **una ragazza dai capelli biondi** a girl with blonde hair; **un vestito da 60 euro** a 60 euros dress

dà *vb vedi* **dare**

dac'capo *av* (*di nuovo*) (once) again; (*dal principio*) all over again, from the beginning

'dado *sm* (*da gioco*) dice o die; (*Cuc*) stock (BRIT) o bouillon (US) cube; (*Tecn*) (screw)nut; **dadi** *smpl* (*game of*) dice; **giocare a dadi** to play dice

'daino *sm* (fallow) deer *inv*; (*pelle*) buckskin

dal'tonico, -a, -ci, -che *ag* colour-blind

'dama *sf* lady; (*nei balli*) partner; (*gioco*) draughts *sg* (BRIT), checkers *sg* (US)

damigi'ana [dami'dʒana] *sf* demijohn

da'nese *ag* Danish ▷ *sm/f* Dane ▷ *sm* (*Ling*) Danish

Dani'marca *sf* **la ~** Denmark

dannazi'one *sf* damnation

danneggi'are [danned'dʒare] *vt* to damage; (*rovinare*) to spoil; (*nuocere*) to harm

'danno *sm* damage; (*a persona*) harm, injury; **danni** *smpl* (*Dir*) damages; **dan'noso, -a** *ag* **dannoso (a, per)** harmful (to), bad (for)

Da'nubio *sm* **il ~** the Danube

'danza ['dantsa] *sf* **la ~** dancing; **una ~** a dance

dan'zare [dan'tsare] *vt, vi* to dance

dapper'tutto *av* everywhere

dap'prima *av* at first

'dare *sm* (*Comm*) debit ▷ *vt* to give; (*produrre: frutti, suono*) to produce ▷ *vi* (*guardare*): **~ su** to look (out) onto; **darsi** *vpr* **darsi a** to dedicate o.s. to; **darsi al commercio** to go into business; **darsi al bere** to take to drink; **~ da mangiare a qn** to give sb sth to eat; **~ per certo qc** to consider sth certain; **~ per morto qn** to give sb up for dead; **darsi per vinto** to give in

'data *sf* date; **~ limite d'utilizzo** *or* **di consumo** best-before date; **data di nascita** date of birth; **data di scadenza** expiry date

'dato, -a *ag* (*stabilito*) given ▷ *sm* datum; **dati** *smpl* data *pl*; **~ che** given that; **un ~ di fatto** a fact; **dati sensibili** personal information

da'tore, -'trice *sm/f*; **datore di lavoro** employer

'dattero *sm* date

dattilogra'fia *sf* typing

datti'lografo, -a *sm/f* typist

da'vanti *av* in front; (*dirimpetto*) opposite ▷ *ag inv* front ▷ *sm* front; **~ a** in front of; facing, opposite; (*in presenza di*) before, in front of

davan'zale [davan'tsale] *sm* windowsill

dav'vero *av* really, indeed

d.C. *adv abbr* (= *dopo Cristo*) A.D.

'dea *sf* goddess

'debbo *ecc vb vedi* **dovere**

'debito, -a *ag* due, proper ▷ *sm* debt; (*Comm: dare*) debit; **a tempo ~** at the right time

'debole *ag* weak, feeble; (*suono*) faint; (*luce*) dim ▷ *sm* weakness; **debo'lezza** *sf* weakness

debut'tare *vi* to make one's debut

deca'denza [deka'dɛntsa] *sf* decline; (*Dir*) loss, forfeiture

decaffei'nato, -a *ag* decaffeinated

decapi'tare *vt* to decapitate, behead

decappot'tabile *ag, sf* convertible

de'cennio [de'tʃɛnnjo] *sm* decade

de'cente [de'tʃɛnte] *ag* decent, respectable, proper; (*accettabile*) satisfactory, decent

de'cesso [de'tʃɛsso] *sm* death

de'cidere [de'tʃidere] *vt* **~ qc** to decide on sth; (*questione, lite*) to settle sth; **~ di fare/ che** to decide to do/that; **~ di qc** (*cosa*) to determine sth; **decidersi (a fare)** to decide (to do), make up one's mind (to do)

deci'frare [detʃi'frare] *vt* to decode; (*fig*) to decipher, make out

deci'male [detʃi'male] *ag* decimal

'decimo, -a ['dɛtʃimo] *num* tenth

de'cina [de'tʃina] *sf* ten; (*circa dieci*): **una ~ (di)** about ten

de'cisi *ecc* [de'tʃizi] *vb vedi* **decidere**

decisi'one [detʃi'zjone] *sf* decision; **prendere una ~** to make a decision

deci'sivo, -a [detʃi'zivo] *ag* (*gen*) decisive; (*fattore*) deciding

de'ciso, -a [de'tʃizo] *pp di* **decidere**

decli'nare *vi* (*pendio*) to slope down; (*fig: diminuire*) to decline ▷ *vt* to decline

declinazi'one *sf* (*Ling*) declension

de'clino *sm* decline

decodifica'tore *sm* (*Tel*) decoder

decol'lare *vi* (*Aer*) to take off; **de'collo** *sm* take-off

deco'rare *vt* to decorate; **decorazi'one** *sf* decoration

de'creto *sm* decree; **decreto legge** *decree with the force of law*

'dedica, -che *sf* dedication

dedi'care *vt* to dedicate; **dedicarsi** *vpr* **dedicarsi a** to devote o.s. to

dedicherò *ecc* [dedike'rɔ] *vb vedi* **dedicare**

'dedito, -a *ag* ~ **a** (*studio ecc*) dedicated *o* devoted to; (*vizio*) addicted to

de'duco *ecc vb vedi* **dedurre**

de'durre *vt* (*concludere*) to deduce; (*defalcare*) to deduct

de'dussi *ecc vb vedi* **dedurre**

defici'ente [defi'tʃɛnte] *ag* (*mancante*): ~ **di** deficient in; (*insufficiente*) insufficient ▷ *sm/f* mental defective; (*peg: cretino*) idiot

'deficit ['dɛfitʃit] *sm inv* (Econ) deficit

defi'nire *vt* to define; (*risolvere*) to settle; **defini'tiva** *sf* **in** ~ (*dopotutto*) in the end; (*dunque*) hence; **defini'tivo, -a** *ag* definitive, final; **definizi'one** *sf* definition; settlement

defor'mare *vt* (*alterare*) to put out of shape; (*corpo*) to deform; (*pensiero, fatto*) to distort; **deformarsi** *vpr* to lose its shape

de'forme *ag* deformed; disfigured

de'funto, -a *ag* late *cpd* ▷ *sm/f* deceased

degene'rare [dedʒene'rare] *vi* to degenerate

de'gente [de'dʒɛnte] *sm/f* (*in ospedale*) in-patient

deglu'tire *vt* to swallow

de'gnare [deɲ'ɲare] *vt* ~ **qn della propria presenza** to honour sb with one's presence; **degnarsi** *vpr* **degnarsi di fare qc** to deign *o* condescend to do sth

'degno, -a *ag* dignified; ~ **di** worthy of; ~ **di lode** praiseworthy

de'grado *sm*; **degrado urbano** urban decline

'delega, -ghe *sf* (*procura*) proxy

dele'terio, -a *ag* damaging; (*per salute ecc*) harmful

del'fino *sm* (Zool) dolphin; (Storia) dauphin; (*fig*) probable successor

deli'cato, -a *ag* delicate; (*salute*) delicate, frail; (*fig: gentile*) thoughtful, considerate; (: *che dimostra tatto*) tactful

delin'quente *sm/f* criminal, delinquent; **delinquente abituale** regular offender, habitual offender; **delin'quenza** *sf* criminality, delinquency; **delinquenza minorile** juvenile delinquency

deli'rare *vi* to be delirious, rave; (*fig*) to rave

de'lirio *sm* delirium; (*ragionamento insensato*) raving; (*fig*): **andare/mandare in** ~ to go/send into a frenzy

de'litto *sm* crime

delizi'oso, -a *ag* delightful; (*cibi*) delicious

delta'plano *sm* hang-glider; **volo col** ~ hang-gliding

delu'dente *ag* disappointing

de'ludere *vt* to disappoint; **delusi'one** *sf* disappointment; **de'luso, -a** *pp di* deludere

'demmo *vb vedi* **dare**

demo'cratico, -a, -ci, -che *ag* democratic

democra'zia [demokrat'tsia] *sf* democracy

demo'lire *vt* to demolish

de'monio *sm* demon, devil; **il D~** the Devil

de'naro *sm* money

densità *sf inv* density

'denso, -a *ag* thick, dense

den'tale *ag* dental

'dente *sm* tooth; (*di forchetta*) prong; **al** ~ (Cuc: *pasta*) al dente; **denti del giudizio** wisdom teeth; **denti da latte** milk teeth; **denti'era** *sf* (set of) false teeth *pl*

denti'fricio [denti'fritʃo] *sm* toothpaste

den'tista, -i, -e *sm/f* dentist

'dentro *av* inside; (*in casa*) indoors; (*fig: nell'intimo*) inwardly ▷ *prep* ~ **(a)** in; **piegato in** ~ folded over; **qui/là** ~ in here/ there; ~ **di sé** (*pensare, brontolare*) to oneself

de'nuncia, -ce *o* **cie** [de'nuntʃa] *sf* denunciation; declaration; **denuncia dei redditi** (income) tax return

denunci'are [denun'tʃare] *vt* to denounce; (*dichiarare*) to declare; (*persona, smarrimento ecc*) report; **vorrei** ~ **un furto** I'd like to report a theft

denu'trito, -a *ag* undernourished

denutrizi'one [denutrit'tsjone] *sf* malnutrition

deodo'rante *sm* deodorant

depe'rire *vi* to waste away

depi'larsi *vpr* ~ **(le gambe)** (*con rasoio*) to shave (one's legs); (*con ceretta*) to wax (one's legs)

depila'torio, -a *ag* hair-removing *cpd*, depilatory

dépli'ant [depli'ã] *sm inv* leaflet; (*opuscolo*) brochure

deplo'revole *ag* deplorable

de'pone, de'pongo *ecc vb vedi* **deporre**

de'porre *vt* (*depositare*) to put down; (*rimuovere: da una carica*) to remove; (: *re*) depose; (Dir) to testify

depor'tare *vt* to deport

de'posi *ecc vb vedi* **deporre**

deposi'tare *vt* (*gen, Geo, Econ*) to deposit; (*lasciare*) to leave; (*merci*) to store; **depositarsi** *vpr* (*sabbia, polvere*) to settle

de'posito *sm* deposit; (*luogo*) warehouse; depot; (: *Mil*) depot; **deposito bagagli** left-luggage office

deposizi'one [depozit'tsjone] *sf* deposition; (*da una carica*) removal

depra'vato, -a *ag* depraved ▷ *sm/f* degenerate

depre'dare *vt* to rob, plunder

depressi'one sf depression

de'presso, -a pp di **deprimere** ▷ ag depressed

deprez'zare [depret'tsare] vt (Econ) to depreciate

depri'mente ag depressing

de'primere vt to depress

depu'rare vt to purify

depu'tato sm (Pol) deputy, ≈ Member of Parliament (BRIT), ≈ Member of Congress (US)

deragli'are [deraʎˈʎare] vi to be derailed; **far ~** to derail

de'ridere vt to mock, deride

de'risi ecc vb vedi **deridere**

de'riva sf (Naut, Aer) drift; **andare alla ~** (anche fig) to drift

deri'vare vi **~ da** to derive from ▷ vt to derive; (corso d'acqua) to divert

derma'tologo, -a, -gi, -ghe sm/f dermatologist

deru'bare vt to rob

des'crivere vt to describe; **descrizi'one** sf description

de'serto, -a ag deserted ▷ sm (Geo) desert; **isola deserta** desert island

deside'rare vt to want, wish for; (sessualmente) to desire; **~ fare/che qn faccia** to want o wish to do/sb to do; **desidera fare una passeggiata?** would you like to go for a walk?

desi'derio sm wish; (più intenso, carnale) desire

deside'roso, -a ag **~ di** longing o eager for

desi'nenza [deziˈnɛntsa] sf (Ling) ending, inflexion

de'sistere vi **~ da** to give up, desist from

deso'lato, -a ag (paesaggio) desolate; (persona: spiacente) sorry

dessi ecc vb vedi **dare**

deste ecc vb vedi **dare**

desti'nare vt to destine; (assegnare) to appoint, assign; (indirizzare) to address; **~ qc a qn** to intend to give sth to sb, intend sth to have sth; **destina'tario, -a** sm/f (di lettera) addressee

destinazi'one [destinat'tsjone] sf destination; (uso) purpose

des'tino sm destiny, fate

destitu'ire vt to dismiss, remove

'destra sf (mano) right hand; (parte) right (side); (Pol): **la ~** the Right; **a ~** (essere) on the right; (andare) to the right

destreggi'arsi [destredˈdʒarsi] vpr to manoeuvre (BRIT), maneuver (US)

des'trezza [desˈtrettsa] sf skill, dexterity

'destro, -a ag right, right-hand

dete'nuto, -a sm/f prisoner

deter'gente [deterˈdʒɛnte] ag (crema, latte) cleansing ▷ sm cleanser

■ Attenzione! In inglese esiste la parola detergent che però significa detersivo.

determi'nare vt to determine

determina'tivo, -a ag determining; **articolo ~** (Ling) definite article

determi'nato, -a ag (gen) certain; (particolare) specific; (risoluto) determined, resolute

deter'sivo sm detergent

detes'tare vt to detest, hate

de'trae, de'traggo ecc vb vedi **detrarre**

de'trarre vt **~ (da)** to deduct (from), take away (from)

de'trassi ecc vb vedi **detrarre**

'detta sf **a ~ di** according to

det'taglio [detˈtaʎʎo] sm detail; (Comm): **il ~** retail; **al ~** (Comm) retail; separately

det'tare vt to dictate; **~ legge** (fig) to lay down the law; **det'tato** sm dictation

'detto, -a pp di **dire** ▷ ag (soprannominato) called, known as; (già nominato) above-mentioned ▷ sm saying; **~ fatto** no sooner said than done

devas'tare vt to devastate; (fig) to ravage

devi'are vi **~ (da)** to turn off (from) ▷ vt to divert; **deviazi'one** sf (anche Aut) diversion

'devo ecc vb vedi **dovere**

de'volvere vt (Dir) to transfer, devolve

de'voto, -a ag (Rel) devout, pious; (affezionato) devoted

devozi'one [devotˈtsjone] sf devoutness; (anche Rel) devotion

⬤ **PAROLA CHIAVE**

di (di+il = **del**, di+lo = **dello**, di+l' = **dell'**, di+la = **della**, di+i = **dei**, di+gli = **degli**, di+le = **delle**) prep **1** (possesso, specificazione) of; (composto da, scritto da) by; **la macchina di Paolo/mio fratello** Paolo's/my brother's car; **un amico di mio fratello** a friend of my brother's, one of my brother's friends; **un quadro di Botticelli** a painting by Botticelli

2 (caratterizzazione, misura) of; **una casa di mattoni** a brick house, a house made of bricks; **un orologio d'oro** a gold watch; **un bimbo di 3 anni** a child of 3, a 3-year-old child

3 (causa, mezzo, modo) with; **tremare di paura** to tremble with fear; **morire di cancro** to die of cancer; **spalmare di burro** to spread with butter

4 (argomento) about, of; **discutere di sport** to talk about sport

5 (luogo: provenienza) from; out of; **essere**

di Roma to be from Rome; **uscire di casa** to come out of o leave the house **6** (tempo) in; **d'estate/d'inverno** in (the) summer/winter; **di notte** by night, at night; **di mattina/sera** in the morning/evening; **di lunedì** on Mondays ▷ det (una certa quantità di) some; (: negativo) any; (interrogativo) any; some; **del pane** (some) bread; **delle caramelle** (some) sweets; **degli amici miei** some friends of mine; **vuoi del vino?** do you want some o any wine?

dia'bete sm diabetes sg
dia'betico, -a, ci, che ag, sm/f diabetic
dia'framma, -i sm (divisione) screen; (Anat, Fot, contraccettivo) diaphragm
di'agnosi [di'aɲɲozi] sf diagnosis sg
diago'nale ag, sf diagonal
dia'gramma, -i sm diagram
dia'letto sm dialect
di'alisi sf dialysis sg
di'alogo, -ghi sm dialogue
dia'mante sm diamond
di'ametro sm diameter
diaposi'tiva sf transparency, slide
di'ario sm diary
diar'rea sf diarrhoea
di'avolo sm devil
di'battito sm debate, discussion
'dice ['ditʃe] vb vedi **dire**
di'cembre [di'tʃɛmbre] sm December
dice'ria [ditʃe'ria] sf rumour, piece of gossip
dichia'rare [dikja'rare] vt to declare; **dichiararsi** vpr to declare o.s.; (innamorato) to declare one's love; **dichiararsi vinto** to acknowledge defeat; **dichiarazi'one** sf declaration; **dichiarazione dei redditi** statement of income; (modulo) tax return
dician'nove [ditʃan'nɔve] num nineteen
dicias'sette [ditʃas'sɛtte] num seventeen
dici'otto [di'tʃɔtto] num eighteen
dici'tura [ditʃi'tura] sf words pl, wording
'dico ecc vb vedi **dire**
didasca'lia sf (di illustrazione) caption; (Cine) subtitle; (Teatro) stage directions pl
di'eci ['djɛtʃi] num ten
di'edi ecc vb vedi **dare**
'diesel ['dizəl] sm inv diesel engine
dies'sino, -a sm/f member of the DS political party
di'eta sf diet; **essere a ~** to be on a diet
di'etro av behind; (in fondo) at the back ▷ prep behind; (tempo: dopo) after ▷ sm back, rear ▷ ag inv back cpd; **le zampe di ~** the hind legs; **~ richiesta** on demand; (scritta) on application

di'fendere vt to defend; **difendersi** vpr (cavarsela) to get by; **difendersi da/contro** to defend o.s. from/against; **difendersi dal freddo** to protect o.s. from the cold; **difen'sore, -a** sm/f defender; **avvocato difensore** counsel for the defence; **di'fesa** sf defence
di'fesi ecc vb vedi **difendere**
di'fetto sm (mancanza): **~ di** lack of; shortage of; (di fabbricazione) fault, flaw, defect; (morale) fault, failing, defect; (fisico) defect; **far ~** to be lacking; **in ~** at fault; in the wrong; **difet'toso, -a** ag defective, faulty
diffe'rente ag different
diffe'renza [diffe'rɛntsa] sf difference; **a ~ di** unlike
diffe'rire vt to postpone, defer ▷ vi to be different
diffe'rita sf **in ~** (trasmettere) prerecorded
dif'ficile [dif'fitʃile] ag difficult; (persona) hard to please, difficult (to please); (poco probabile): **è ~ che sia libero** it is unlikely that he'll be free ▷ sm difficult part; difficulty; **difficoltà** sf inv difficulty
diffi'dente ag suspicious, distrustful
diffi'denza sf suspicion, distrust
dif'fondere vt (luce, calore) to diffuse; (notizie) to spread, circulate; **diffondersi** vpr to spread
dif'fusi ecc vb vedi **diffondere**
dif'fuso, -a pp di **diffondere** ▷ ag (malattia, fenomeno) widespread
'diga, -ghe sf dam; (portuale) breakwater
dige'rente [didʒe'rɛnte] ag (apparato) digestive
dige'rire [didʒe'rire] vt to digest; **digesti'one** sf digestion; **diges'tivo, -a** ag digestive ▷ sm (after-dinner) liqueur
digi'tale [didʒi'tale] ag digital; (delle dita) finger cpd, digital ▷ sf (Bot) foxglove
digi'tare [didʒi'tare] vt, vi (Inform) to key (in)
digiu'nare [didʒu'nare] vi to starve o.s.; (Rel) to fast; **digi'uno, -a** ag **essere digiuno** not to have eaten ▷ sm fast; **a digiuno** on an empty stomach
dignità [diɲɲi'ta] sf inv dignity
'DIGOS ['digos] sigla f (= Divisione Investigazioni Generali e Operazioni Speciali) police department dealing with political security
digri'gnare [digriɲ'ɲare] vt **~ i denti** to grind one's teeth
dilapi'dare vt to squander, waste
dila'tare vt to dilate; (gas) to cause to expand; (passaggio, cavità) to open (up); **dilatarsi** vpr to dilate; (Fisica) to expand
dilazio'nare [dilattsjo'nare] vt to delay,

defer

i'lemma, -i sm dilemma

ilet'tante sm/f dilettante; (anche Sport) amateur

ili'gente [dili'dʒɛnte] ag (scrupoloso) diligent; (accurato) careful, accurate

ilu'ire vt to dilute

ilun'garsi vpr (fig): ~ **su** to talk at length on o about

iluvi'are vb impers to pour (down)

i'luvio sm downpour; (inondazione, fig) flood

ima'grante ag slimming cpd

ima'grire vi to get thinner, lose weight

ime'nare vt to wave, shake; **dimenarsi** vpr to toss and turn; (fig) to struggle; ~ **la coda** (cane) to wag its tail

imensi'one sf dimension; (grandezza) size

imenti'canza [dimenti'kantsa] sf forgetfulness; (errore) oversight, slip; **per ~** inadvertently

imenti'care vt to forget; **ho dimenticato la chiave/il passaporto** I forgot the key/my passport; **dimenticarsi** vpr **dimenticarsi di qc** to forget sth

imesti'chezza [dimesti'kettsa] sf familiarity

i'mettere vt ~ **qn da** to dismiss sb from; (dall'ospedale) to discharge sb from; **dimettersi** vpr **dimettersi (da)** to resign (from)

imez'zare [dimed'dzare] vt to halve

iminu'ire vt to reduce, diminish; (prezzi) to bring down, reduce ▷ vi to decrease, diminish; (rumore) to die down, die away; (prezzi) to fall, go down

iminu'tivo, -a ag, sm diminutive

iminuzi'one sf decreasing, diminishing

i'misi ecc vb vedi **dimettere**

imissi'oni sfpl resignation sg; **dare o presentare le ~** to resign, hand in one's resignation

imos'trare vt to demonstrate, show; (provare) to prove, demonstrate; **dimostrarsi** vpr **dimostrarsi molto abile** to show o.s. o prove to be very clever; **dimostra 30 anni** he looks about 30 (years old); **dimostrazi'one** sf demonstration; proof

i'namica sf dynamics sg

i'namico, -a, -ci, -che ag dynamic

ina'mite sf dynamite

i'namo sf inv dynamo

ino'sauro sm dinosaur

intorni smpl outskirts; **nei ~ di** in the vicinity o neighbourhood of

i'io (pl **'dei**) sm god; **D~** God; **gli dei** the gods; **D~ mio!** my goodness!, my God!

diparti'mento sm department

dipen'dente ag dependent ▷ sm/f employee; **dipendente statale** state employee

di'pendere vi ~ **da** to depend on; (finanziariamente) to be dependent on; (derivare) to come from, be due to

di'pesi ecc vb vedi **dipendere**

di'pingere [di'pindʒere] vt to paint

di'pinsi ecc vb vedi **dipingere**

di'pinto, -a pp di **dipingere** ▷ sm painting

di'ploma, -i sm diploma

diplo'matico, -a, -ci, -che ag diplomatic ▷ sm diplomat

diploma'zia [diplomat'tsia] sf diplomacy

di'porto: imbarcazione da ~ sf pleasure craft

dira'dare vt to thin (out); (visite) to reduce, make less frequent; **diradarsi** vpr to disperse; (nebbia) to clear (up)

'dire vt to say; (segreto, fatto) to tell; ~ **qc a qn** to tell sb sth; ~ **a qn di fare qc** to tell sb to do sth; ~ **di sì/no** to say yes/no; **si dice che ...** they say that ...; **si ~bbe che ...** it looks (o sounds) as though ...; **dica, signora?** (in un negozio) yes, Madam, can I help you?; **come si dice in inglese...?** what's the English (word) for ...?

di'ressi ecc vb vedi **dirigere**

di'retta sf vedi **diretto**

di'retto, -a pp di **dirigere** ▷ ag direct ▷ sm (Ferr) through train

diret'tore, -'trice sm/f (di azienda) director: manager/ess; (di scuola elementare) head (teacher) (BRIT), principal (US); **direttore d'orchestra** conductor; **direttore vendite** sales director o manager

direzi'one [diret'tsjone] sf board of directors; management; (senso di movimento) direction; **in ~ di** in the direction of, towards

diri'gente [diri'dʒɛnte] sm/f executive; (Pol) leader ▷ ag **classe ~** ruling class

di'rigere [di'ridʒere] vt to direct; (impresa) to run, manage; (Mus) to conduct; **dirigersi** vpr **dirigersi verso o a** to make o head for

dirim'petto av opposite; ~ **a** opposite, facing

di'ritto, -a ag straight; (onesto) straight, upright ▷ av straight, directly; **andare ~** to go straight on ▷ sm right side; (Tennis) forehand; (Maglia) plain stitch; (prerogativa) right; (leggi, scienza): **il ~** law; **diritti** smpl (tasse) duty sg; **stare ~** to stand up straight; **aver ~ a qc** to be entitled to sth; **diritti d'autore** royalties

dirotta'mento sm; **dirottamento**

(aereo) hijack

dirot'tare vt (nave, aereo) to change the course of; (aereo sotto minaccia) to hijack; (traffico) to divert ▷ vi (nave, aereo) to change course; **dirotta'tore, -'trice** sm/f hijacker

di'rotto, -a ag (pioggia) torrential; (pianto) unrestrained; **piovere a ~** to pour; **piangere a ~** to cry one's heart out

di'rupo sm crag, precipice

di'sabile sm/f disabled person ▷ ag disabled; **i disabili** the disabled

disabi'tato, -a ag uninhabited

disabitu'arsi vpr **~ a** to get out of the habit of

disac'cordo sm disagreement

disadat'tato, -a ag (Psic) maladjusted

disa'dorno, -a ag plain, unadorned

disagi'ato, -a [diza'dʒato] ag poor, needy; (vita) hard

di'sagio [di'zadʒo] sm discomfort; (disturbo) inconvenience; (fig: imbarazzo) embarrassment; **essere a ~** to be ill at ease

disappro'vare vt to disapprove of; **disapprovazi'one** sf disapproval

disap'punto sm disappointment

disar'mare vt, vi to disarm; **di'sarmo** sm (Mil) disarmament

di'sastro sm disaster

disas'troso, -a ag disastrous

disat'tento, -a ag inattentive; **disattenzl'one** sf carelessness, lack of attention

disavven'tura sf misadventure, mishap

dis'capito sm **a ~ di** to the detriment of

dis'carica, -che sf (di rifiuti) rubbish tip o dump

di'scendere [diʃ'ʃɛndere] vt to go (o come) down ▷ vi to go (o come) down; (strada) to go down; (smontare) to get off; **~ da** (famiglia) to be descended from; **~ dalla macchina/dal treno** to get out of the car/out of o off the train; **~ da cavallo** to dismount, get off one's horse

di'scesa [diʃ'ʃesa] sf descent; (pendio) slope; **in ~** (strada) downhill cpd, sloping; **discesa libera** (Sci) downhill (race)

disci'plina [diʃʃi'plina] sf discipline

'disco, -schi sm disc; (Sport) discus; (fonografico) record; (Inform) disk; **disco orario** (Aut) parking disc; **disco rigido** (Inform) hard disk; **disco volante** flying saucer

disco'grafico, -a, ci, che ag record cpd, recording cpd ▷ sm record producer; **casa discografica** record(ing) company

dis'correre vi **~ (di)** to talk (about)

dis'corso, -a pp di **discorrere** ▷ sm speech; (conversazione) conversation, talk

disco'teca, -che sf (raccolta) record library; (locale) disco

discre'panza [diskre'pantsa] sf disagreement

dis'creto, -a ag discreet; (abbastanza buono) reasonable, fair

discriminazi'one [diskriminat'tsjone] sf discrimination

dis'cussi ecc vb vedi **discutere**

discussi'one sf discussion; (litigio) argument; **fuori ~** out of the question

dis'cutere vt to discuss, debate; (contestare) to question ▷ vi (conversare): **~ (di)** to discuss; (litigare) to argue

dis'detta sf (di prenotazione ecc) cancellation; (sfortuna) bad luck

dis'dire vt (prenotazione) to cancel; (Dir): **~ un contratto d'affitto** to give notice (to quit); **vorrei ~ la mia prenotazione** I want to cancel my booking

dise'gnare [disen'ɲare] vt to draw; (progettare) to design; (fig) to outline

disegna'tore, -'trice sm/f designer

di'segno [di'seɲɲo] sm drawing; design; outline; **disegno di legge** (Dir) bill

diser'bante sm weed-killer

diser'tare vt, vi to desert

dis'fare vt to undo; (valigie) to unpack; (meccanismo) to take to pieces; (neve) to melt; **disfarsi** vpr to come undone; (neve) to melt; **~ il letto** to strip the bed; **disfarsi di qn** (liberarsi) to get rid of sb; **dis'fatto, -a** pp di **disfare**

dis'gelo [diz'dʒɛlo] sm thaw

dis'grazia [diz'grattsja] sf (sventura) misfortune; (incidente) accident, mishap

disgu'ido sm hitch; **disguido postale** error in postal delivery

disgus'tare vt to disgust

dis'gusto sm disgust; **disgus'toso, -a** ag disgusting

disidra'tare vt to dehydrate

disimpa'rare vt to forget

disinfet'tante ag, sm disinfectant

disinfet'tare vt to disinfect

disini'bito, -a ag uninhibited

disinstal'lare vt (software) to uninstall

disinte'grare vt, vi to disintegrate; **disintegrarsi** vpr to disintegrate

disinteres'sarsi vpr **~ di** to take no interest in

disinte'resse sm indifference; (generosità) unselfishness

disintossicarsi vpr to clear out one's system; (alcolizzato, drogato) to be treated for alcoholism (o drug addiction)

disin'volto, -a ag casual, free and easy

dismi'sura sf excess; **a ~** to excess, excessively

disoccu'pato, -a ag unemployed ▷ sm/f unemployed person; **disoccupazi'one** sf unemployment

diso'nesto, -a ag dishonest

disordi'nato, -a ag untidy; (privo di misura) irregular, wild

di'sordine sm (confusione) disorder, confusion; (sregolatezza) debauchery; **disordini** smpl (Pol ecc) disorder sg; (tumulti) riots

disorien'tare vt to disorientate

disorien'tato, -a ag disorientated

'dispari ag inv odd, uneven

dis'parte: in ~ av (da lato) aside, apart; **tenersi o starsene in ~** to keep to o.s., hold o.s. aloof

dispendi'oso, -a ag expensive

dis'pensa sf pantry, larder; (mobile) sideboard; (Dir) exemption; (Rel) dispensation; (fascicolo) number, issue

dispe'rato, -a ag (persona) in despair; (caso, tentativo) desperate

disperazi'one sf despair

dis'perdere vt (disseminare) to disperse; (Mil) to scatter, rout; (fig: consumare) to waste, squander; **disperdersi** vpr to disperse; to scatter; **dis'perso, -a** pp di **disperdere** ▷ sm/f missing person

dis'petto sm spite no pl, spitefulness no pl; **fare un ~ a qn** to play a (nasty) trick on sb; **a ~ di** in spite of; **dispet'toso, -a** ag spiteful

dispia'cere [dispja'tʃere] sm (rammarico) regret, sorrow; (dolore) grief; **dispiaceri** smpl (preoccupazioni) troubles, worries vi ~ **a** to displease vb impers **mi dispiace (che)** I am sorry (that); **le dispiace se...?** do you mind if...?

dis'pone, dis'pongo ecc vb vedi **disporre**

dispo'nibile ag available

dis'porre vt (sistemare) to arrange; (preparare) to prepare; (Dir) to order; (persuadere): **~ qn a** to incline o dispose sb towards ▷ vi (decidere) to decide; (usufruire): **~ di** to use, have at one's disposal; (essere dotato): **~ di** to have

dis'posi ecc vb vedi **disporre**

disposi'tivo sm (meccanismo) device

disposizi'one [dispozit'tsjone] sf arrangement, layout; (stato d'animo) mood; (tendenza) bent, inclination; (comando) order; (Dir) provision, regulation; **a ~ di qn** at sb's disposal

dis'posto, -a pp di **disporre**

disprez'zare [dispret'tsare] vt to despise

dis'prezzo [dis'prettso] sm contempt

'disputa sf dispute, quarrel

dispu'tare vt (contendere) to dispute, contest; (gara) to take part in ▷ vi to

quarrel; **~ di** to discuss; **disputarsi qc** to fight for sth

'disse vb vedi **dire**

dissente'ria sf dysentery

dissen'tire vi ~ **(da)** to disagree (with)

disse'tante ag refreshing

'dissi vb vedi **dire**

dissimu'lare vt (fingere) to dissemble; (nascondere) to conceal

dissi'pare vt to dissipate; (scialacquare) to squander, waste

dissu'adere vt ~ **qn da** to dissuade sb from

distac'care vt to detach, separate; (Sport) to leave behind; **distaccarsi** vpr to be detached; (fig) to stand out; **distaccarsi da** (fig: allontanarsi) to grow away from

dis'tacco, -chi sm (separazione) separation; (fig: indifferenza) detachment; (Sport): **vincere con un ~ di ...** to win by a distance of ...

dis'tante av far away ▷ ag ~ **(da)** distant (from), far away (from)

dis'tanza [dis'tantsa] sf distance

distanzi'are [distan'tsjare] vt to space out, place at intervals; (Sport) to outdistance; (fig: superare) to outstrip, surpass

dis'tare vi **distiamo pochi chilometri da Roma** we are only a few kilometres (away) from Rome; **quanto dista il centro da qui?** how far is the town centre?

dis'tendere vt (coperta) to spread out; (gambe) to stretch (out); (mettere a giacere) to lay; (rilassare: muscoli, nervi) to relax; **distendersi** vpr (rilassarsi) to relax; (sdraiarsi) to lie down

dis'tesa sf expanse, stretch

dis'teso, -a pp di **distendere**

distil'lare vt to distil

distille'ria sf distillery

dis'tinguere vt to distinguish; **distinguersi** vpr (essere riconoscibile) to be distinguished; (emergere) to stand out, be conspicuous, distinguish o.s.

dis'tinta sf (nota) note; (elenco) list; **distinta di versamento** pay-in slip

distin'tivo, -a ag distinctive; distinguishing ▷ sm badge

dis'tinto, -a pp di **distinguere** ▷ ag (dignitoso ed elegante) distinguished; **"distinti saluti"** (in lettera) yours faithfully

distinzi'one [distin'tsjone] sf distinction

dis'togliere [dis'tɔʎʎere] vt ~ **da** to take away from; (fig) to dissuade from

distorsi'one sf (Med) sprain; (Fisica, Ottica) distortion

dis'trarre vt to distract; (divertire) to entertain, amuse; **distrarsi** vpr (non *fare attenzione*) to be distracted, let one's mind wander; (*svagarsi*) to amuse o enjoy o.s.; **dis'tratto, -a** *pp di* **distrarre** ▷ *ag* absent-minded; (*disattento*) inattentive; **distrazi'one** *sf* absent-mindedness; inattention; (*svago*) distraction, entertainment

dis'tretto *sm* district

distribu'ire *vt* to distribute; (*Carte*) to deal (out); (*posta*) to deliver; (*lavoro*) to allocate, assign; (*ripartire*) to share out; **distribu'tore** *sm* (*di benzina*) petrol (BRIT) o gas (US) pump; (*Aut, Elettr*) distributor; **distributore automatico** vending machine

distri'care *vt* to disentangle, unravel; **districarsi** *vpr* (*tirarsi fuori*): **districarsi da** to get out of, disentangle o.s. from

dis'truggere [dis'truddʒere] *vt* to destroy; **distruzi'one** *sf* destruction

distur'bare *vt* to disturb, trouble; (*sonno, lezioni*) to disturb, interrupt; **disturbarsi** *vpr* to put o.s. out

dis'turbo *sm* trouble, bother, inconvenience; (*indisposizione*) (slight) disorder, ailment; **scusi il ~** I'm sorry to trouble you

disubbidi'ente *ag* disobedient

disubbi'dire *vi* **~ (a qn)** to disobey (sb)

disu'mano, -a *ag* inhuman

di'tale *sm* thimble

'dito (*pl(f)* **'dita**) *sm* finger; (*misura*) finger, finger's breadth; **dito (del piede)** toe

'ditta *sf* firm, business

ditta'tore *sm* dictator

ditta'tura *sf* dictatorship

dit'tongo, -ghi *sm* diphthong

di'urno, -a *ag* day *cpd*, daytime *cpd*

'diva *sf vedi* **divo**

di'vano *sm* sofa; divan; **divano letto** bed settee, sofa bed

divari'care *vt* to open wide

di'vario *sm* difference

diven'tare *vi* to become; **~ famoso/professore** to become famous/a teacher

diversifi'care *vt* to diversify, vary; to differentiate; **diversificarsi** *vpr* **diversificarsi (per)** to differ (in)

diversità *sf inv* difference, diversity; (*varietà*) variety

diver'sivo *sm* diversion, distraction

di'verso, -a *ag* (*differente*): **~ (da)** different (from); **diversi, -e** *det pl* several, various; (*Comm*) sundry *pron pl* several (people), many (people)

diver'tente *ag* amusing

diverti'mento *sm* amusement, pleasure; (*passatempo*) pastime, recreation

diver'tire *vt* to amuse, entertain;

divertirsi *vpr* to amuse o enjoy o.s.

di'videre *vt* (*anche Mat*) to divide; (*distribuire, ripartire*) to divide (up), split (up); **dividersi** *vpr* (*separarsi*) to separate; (*strade*) to fork

divi'eto *sm* prohibition; **"~ di sosta"** (Aut) "no parking"

divinco'larsi *vpr* to wriggle, writhe

di'vino, -a *ag* divine

di'visa *sf* (*Mil ecc*) uniform; (*Comm*) foreign currency

di'visi *ecc vb vedi* **dividere**

divisi'one *sf* division

'divo, -a *sm/f* star

divo'rare *vt* to devour

divorzi'are [divor'tsjare] *vi* **~ (da qn)** to divorce (sb)

di'vorzio [di'vɔrtsjo] *sm* divorce

divul'gare *vt* to divulge, disclose; (*rendere comprensibile*) to popularize

dizio'nario [ditsjo'narjo] *sm* dictionary

DJ [di'dʒei] *sigla m/f* (= *Disk Jockey*) DJ

do *sm* (*Mus*) C; (: *solfeggiando*) do(h)

dobbi'amo *vb vedi* **dovere**

D.O.C. [dɔk] *abbr* (= *denominazione di origine controllata*) *label guaranteeing the quality of wine*

'doccia, -ce ['dottʃa] *sf* (*bagno*) shower; **fare la ~** to have a shower

do'cente [do'tʃente] *ag* teaching ▷ *sm/f* teacher; (*di università*) lecturer

'docile ['dɔtʃile] *ag* docile

documen'tario *sm* documentary

documentarsi *vpr* **~ (su)** to gather information o material (about)

docu'mento *sm* document; **documenti** *smpl* (*d'identità ecc*) papers

dodi'cesimo, -a [dodi'tʃezimo] *num* twelfth

'dodici ['doditʃi] *num* twelve

do'gana *sf* (*ufficio*) customs *pl*; (*tassa*) (customs) duty; **passare la ~** to go through customs; **dogani'ere** *sm* customs officer

'doglie ['dɔʎʎe] *sfpl* (*Med*) labour *sg*, labour pains

'dolce ['doltʃe] *ag* sweet; (*carattere, persona*) gentle, mild; (*fig: mite: clima*) mild; (*non ripido: pendio*) gentle ▷ *sm* (*sapore dolce*) sweetness, sweet taste; (*Cuc: portata*) sweet, dessert; (: *torta*) cake; **dolcifi'cante** *sm* sweetener

'dollaro *sm* dollar

Dolo'miti *sfpl* **le ~** the Dolomites

do'lore *sm* (*fisico*) pain; (*morale*) sorrow, grief; **dolo'roso, -a** *ag* painful; sorrowful, sad

do'manda *sf* (*interrogazione*) question; (*richiesta*) demand; (: *cortese*) request;

(*Dir: richiesta scritta*) application; (*Econ*): **la ~** demand; **fare una ~ a qn** to ask sb a question; **fare ~ (per un lavoro)** to apply (for a job)

doman'dare vt (*per avere*) to ask for; (*per sapere*) to ask; (*esigere*) to demand; **domandarsi** vpr to wonder; to ask o.s.; **~ qc a qn** to ask sb for sth; to ask sb sth

do'mani av tomorrow ▷ sm **il ~** (*il futuro*) the future; (*il giorno successivo*) the next day; **~ l'altro** the day after tomorrow

do'mare vt to tame

doma'tore, -'trice sm/f (*gen*) tamer; **domatore di cavalli** horsebreaker; **domatore di leoni** lion tamer

domat'tina av tomorrow morning

do'menica, -che sf Sunday; **di** o **la ~** on Sundays

do'mestico, -a, -ci, -che ag domestic ▷ sm/f servant, domestic

domi'cilio [domi'tʃiljo] sm (*Dir*) domicile, place of residence

domi'nare vt to dominate; (*fig: sentimenti*) to control, master ▷ vi to be in the dominant position

do'nare vt to give, present; (*per beneficenza ecc*) to donate ▷ vi (*fig*): **~ a** to suit, become; **~ sangue** to give blood; **dona'tore, -'trice** sm/f donor; **donatore di sangue/di organi** blood/organ donor

dondo'lare (*cullare*) to rock; **dondolarsi** vpr to swing, sway; **'dondolo** sm **sedia/cavallo a dondolo** rocking chair/horse

'donna sf woman; **donna di casa** housewife; home-loving woman; **donna di servizio** maid

donnai'olo sm ladykiller

'donnola sf weasel

'dono sm gift

doping ['dɔpiŋ] sm doping

'dopo av (*tempo*) afterwards; (*più tardi*) later; (*luogo*) after, next ▷ prep after ▷ cong (*temporale*): **~ aver studiato** after having studied; **~ mangiato va a dormire** after having eaten o after a meal he goes for a sleep ▷ ag inv **il giorno ~** the following day; **un anno ~** a year later; **~ di me/lui** after me/him; **~, a ~!** see you later!

dopo'barba sm inv after-shave

dopodo'mani av the day after tomorrow

doposcì [dopoʃ'ʃi] sm inv après-ski outfit

dopo'sole sm inv aftersun (lotion)

dopo'tutto av (*tutto considerato*) after all

doppi'aggio [dop'pjaddʒo] sm (*Cinema*) dubbing

doppi'are vt (*Naut*) to round; (*Sport*) to lap; (*Cinema*) to dub

'doppio, -a ag double; (*fig: falso*) double-dealing, deceitful ▷ sm (*quantità*): **il ~**

(di) twice as much (o many), double the amount (o number) of; (*Sport*) doubles pl ▷ av double

doppi'one sm duplicate (copy)

doppio'petto sm double-breasted jacket

dormicchi'are [dormik'kjare] vi to doze

dormigli'one, -a [dormiʎ'ʎone] sm/f sleepyhead

dor'mire vt, vi to sleep; **andare a ~** to go to bed; **dor'mita** sf **farsi una dormita** to have a good sleep

dormi'torio sm dormitory

dormi'veglia [dormi'veʎʎa] sm drowsiness

'dorso sm back; (*di montagna*) ridge, crest; (*di libro*) spine; **a ~ di cavallo** on horseback

do'sare vt to measure out; (*Med*) to dose

'dose sf quantity, amount; (*Med*) dose

do'tato, -a ag ~ **di** (*attrezzature*) equipped with; (*bellezza, intelligenza*) endowed with; **un uomo ~** a gifted man

'dote sf (*di sposa*) dowry; (*assegnata a un ente*) endowment; (*fig*) gift, talent

Dott. abbr (= *dottore*) Dr.

dotto'rato sm degree; **dottorato di ricerca** doctorate, doctor's degree

dot'tore, -essa sm/f doctor; **chiamate un ~** call a doctor

⊛ **DOTTORE**
⊛
⊛ In Italy, anyone who has a degree in any
⊛ subject can use the title **dottore**. Thus
⊛ a person who is addressed as **dottore** is
⊛ not necessarily a doctor of medicine.

dot'trina sf doctrine

Dott.ssa abbr (= *dottoressa*) Dr.

'dove av (*gen*) where; (*in cui*) where, in which; (*dovunque*) wherever ▷ cong (*mentre, laddove*) whereas; **~ sei?/vai?** where are you?/are you going?; **dimmi dov'è** tell me where it is; **di ~ sei?** where are you from?; **per ~ si passa?** which way should we go?; **la città ~ abito** the town where o in which I live; **siediti ~ vuoi** sit wherever you like

do'vere sm (*obbligo*) duty ▷ vt (*essere debitore*): **~ qc (a qn)** to owe (sb) sth ▷ vi (*seguito dall'infinito: obbligo*) to have to; **rivolgersi a chi di ~** to apply to the appropriate authority o person; **lui deve farlo** he has to do it, he must do it; **quanto le devo?** how much do I owe you?; **è dovuto partire** he had to leave; **ha dovuto pagare** he had to pay; (: *intenzione*): **devo partire domani** I'm (due) to leave tomorrow; (: *probabilità*): **dev'essere tardi** it must be late; **come**

si deve (*lavorare, comportarsi*) properly;
una persona come si deve a respectable
person

dove'roso, -a *ag* (*right and*) proper

dovrò *ecc vb vedi* **dovere**

do'vunque *av* (*in qualunque luogo*)
wherever; (*dappertutto*) everywhere; **~ io
vada** wherever I go

do'vuto, -a *ag* (*causato*): **~ a** due to

doz'zina [dod'dzina] *sf* dozen; **una ~ di
uova** a dozen eggs

dozzi'nale [doddzi'nale] *ag* cheap,
second-rate

'drago, -ghi *sm* dragon

'dramma, -i *sm* drama; **dram'matico, -a,
-ci, -che** *ag* dramatic

'drastico, -a, -ci, -che *ag* drastic

'dritto, -a *ag, av* = **diritto**

'droga, -ghe *sf* (*sostanza aromatica*) spice;
(*stupefacente*) drug; **droghe leggere/
pesanti** soft/hard drugs

drogarsi *vpr* to take drugs

dro'gato, -a *sm/f* drug addict

droghe'ria [droge'ria] *sf* grocer's shop
(*BRIT*), grocery (store) (*US*)

drome'dario *sm* dromedary

DS [di'esse] *sigla mpl* (= *Democratici di
Sinistra*) *Italian left-wing party*

'dubbio, -a *ag* (*incerto*) doubtful, dubious;
(*ambiguo*) dubious ▷ *sm* (*incertezza*) doubt;
avere il ~ che to be afraid that, suspect
that; **mettere in ~ qc** to question sth

dubi'tare *vi* **~ di** to doubt; (*risultato*) to be
doubtful of

Dub'lino *sf* Dublin

'duca, -chi *sm* duke

du'chessa [du'kessa] *sf* duchess

'due *num* two

due'cento [due'tʃento] *num* two hundred
▷ *sm* **il D~** the thirteenth century

due'pezzi [due'pettsi] *sm* (*costume
da bagno*) two-piece swimsuit; (*abito
femminile*) two-piece suit

'dunque *cong* (*perciò*) so, therefore;
(*riprendendo il discorso*) well (then) ▷ *sm inv*
venire al ~ to come to the point

du'omo *sm* cathedral

▨ Attenzione! In inglese esiste la parola
dome, che però significa *cupola*.

dupli'cato *sm* duplicate

'duplice ['duplitʃe] *ag* double, twofold; **in
~ copia** in duplicate

du'rante *prep* during

du'rare *vi* to last; **~ fatica a** to have
difficulty in

du'rezza [du'rettsa] *sf* hardness;
stubbornness; harshness; toughness

'duro, -a *ag* (*pietra, lavoro, materasso,
problema*) hard; (*persona: ostinato*)
stubborn, obstinate; (*severo*) harsh, hard;
(*voce*) harsh; (*carne*) tough ▷ *sm* hardness;
(*difficoltà*) hard part; (*persona*) tough
guy; **tener ~** to stand firm, hold out; **~
d'orecchi** hard of hearing

DVD [divu'di] *sigla m* (= *digital versatile (or)
video disc*) DVD; (*lettore*) DVD player

e (*davV spesso* **ed**) *cong* and; **e lui?** what about him?; **e compralo!** well buy it then!

E *abbr* (= *est*) E

è *vb vedi* **essere**

eb'bene *cong* well (then)

'ebbi *ecc vb vedi* **avere**

e'braico, -a, -ci, -che *ag* Hebrew, Hebraic ▷ *sm* (*Ling*) Hebrew

e'breo, -a *ag* Jewish ▷ *sm/f* Jew/ess

EC *abbr* (= *Eurocity*) fast train connecting Western European cities

ecc. *av abbr* (= *eccetera*) etc

eccel'lente [ettʃel'lɛnte] *ag* excellent

ec'centrico, -a, -ci, -che [et'tʃɛntriko] *ag* eccentric

ecces'sivo, -a [ettʃes'sivo] *ag* excessive

ec'cesso [et'tʃɛsso] *sm* excess; **all'~** (*gentile, generoso*) to excess, excessively; **eccesso di velocità** (*Aut*) speeding

ec'cetera [et'tʃɛtera] *av* et cetera, and so on

ec'cetto [et'tʃɛtto] *prep* except, with the exception of; **~ che** except, other than; **~ che (non)** unless

eccezio'nale [ettʃetsjo'nale] *ag* exceptional

eccezi'one [ettʃet'tsjone] *sf* exception; (*Dir*) objection; **a ~ di** with the exception of, except for; **d'~** exceptional

ecci'tare [ettʃi'tare] *vt* (*curiosità, interesse*) to excite, arouse; (*folla*) to incite; **eccitarsi** *vpr* to get excited; (*sessualmente*) to become aroused

'ecco *av* (*per dimostrare*): **~ il treno!** here's o here comes the train!; (*dav pron*): **~mi!** here I am!; **~ne uno!** here's one (of them)!; (*dav pp*): **~ fatto!** there, that's it done!

ec'come *av* rather; **ti piace? — ~!** do you like it? — I'll say! o and how! o rather! (BRIT)

e'clisse *sf* eclipse

'eco (*pl*(*m*) **'echi**) *sm o f* echo

ecogra'fia *sf* (*Med*) scan

ecolo'gia [ekolo'dʒia] *sf* ecology

eco'logico, -a, ci, che [eko'lɔdʒiko] *ag* ecological

econo'mia *sf* economy; (*scienza*) economics *sg*; (*risparmio: azione*) saving; **fare ~** to economize, make economies; **eco'nomico, -a, -ci, -che** *ag* economic; (*poco costoso*) economical

ecstasy ['ekstazi] *sf* Ecstasy

'edera *sf* ivy

e'dicola *sf* newspaper kiosk o stand (US)

edi'ficio [edi'fitʃo] *sm* building

e'dile *ag* building *cpd*

Edim'burgo *sf* Edinburgh

edi'tore, -'trice *ag* publishing *cpd* ▷ *sm/f* publisher

> ■ Attenzione! In inglese esiste la parola *editor*, che però significa *redattore*.

edizi'one [edit'tsjone] *sf* edition; (*tiratura*) printing; **edizione straordinaria** special edition

edu'care *vt* to educate; (*gusto, mente*) to train; **~ qn a fare** to train sb to do; **edu'cato, -a** *ag* polite, well-mannered; **educazi'one** *sf* education; (*familiare*) upbringing; (*comportamento*) (good) manners *pl*; **educazione fisica** (*Ins*) physical training o education

> ■ Attenzione! In inglese esiste la parola *educated*, che però significa *istruito*.

educherò *ecc* [eduke'rɔ] *vb vedi* **educare**

effemi'nato, -a *ag* effeminate

efferve'scente [effervef'ʃɛnte] *ag* effervescent

effet'tivo, -a *ag* (*reale*) real, actual; (*impiegato, professore*) permanent; (*Mil*) regular ▷ *sm* (*Mil*) strength; (*di patrimonio ecc*) sum total

ef'fetto *sm* effect; (*Comm: cambiale*) bill; (*fig: impressione*) impression; **in effetti** in fact, actually; **effetto serra** greenhouse effect; **effetti personali** personal effects, personal belongings

effi'cace [effi'katʃe] *ag* effective

effici'ente [effi'tʃɛnte] *ag* efficient

E'geo [e'dʒɛo] *sm* **l'~, il mare ~** the Aegean (Sea)

E'gitto [e'dʒitto] *sm* **I'~** Egypt

egizi'ano, -a [edʒit'tsjano] *ag, sm/f* Egyptian

'egli ['eʎʎi] *pron* he; **~ stesso** he himself

ego'ismo *sm* selfishness, egoism; **ego'ista, -i, -e** *ag* selfish, egoistic ▷ *sm/f* egoist

Egr. *abbr* = **egregio**

e'gregio, -a, -gi, -gie [e'grɛdʒo] *ag* (*nelle lettere*): **E~ Signore** Dear Sir

E.I. *abbr* = **Esercito Italiano**

elabo'rare *vt* (*progetto*) to work out, elaborate; (*dati*) to process

elasticiz'zato, -a [elastitʃid'dzato] *ag* stretch *cpd*

e'lastico, -a, -ci, -che *ag* elastic; (*fig: andatura*) springy; (: *decisione, vedute*) flexible ▷ *sm* (*di gomma*) rubber band; (*per il cucito*) elastic *no pl*

ele'fante *sm* elephant

ele'gante *ag* elegant

e'leggere [e'lɛddʒere] *vt* to elect

elemen'tare *ag* elementary; **le (scuole) elementari** *sfpl* primary (BRIT) o grade (US) school

ele'mento *sm* element; (*parte componente*) element, component, part; **elementi** *smpl* (*della scienza ecc*) elements, rudiments

ele'mosina *sf* charity, alms *pl*; **chiedere l'~** to beg

elen'care *vt* to list

elencherò *ecc* [elenke'rɔ] *vb vedi* **elencare**

e'lenco, -chi *sm* list; **elenco telefonico** telephone directory

e'lessi *ecc vb vedi* **eleggere**

eletto'rale *ag* electoral, election *cpd*

elet'tore, -'trice *sm/f* voter, elector

elet'trauto *sm inv* workshop for car electrical repairs; (*tecnico*) car electrician

elettri'cista, -i [elettri'tʃista] *sm* electrician

elettricità [elettritʃi'ta] *sf* electricity

e'lettrico, -a, -ci, -che *ag* electric(al)

elettriz'zante [elettrid'dzante] *ag* (*fig*) electrifying, thrilling

elettriz'zare [elettrid'dzare] *vt* to electrify; **elettrizzarsi** *vpr* to become charged with electricity

e'lettro... *prefisso*: **elettrodo'mestico, -a, -ci, -che** *ag* **apparecchi elettrodomestici** domestic (electrical) appliances; **elet'tronico, -a, -ci, -che** *ag* electronic

elezi'one [elet'tsjone] *sf* election; **elezioni** *sfpl* (*Pol*) election(s)

'elica, -che *sf* propeller

eli'cottero *sm* helicopter

elimi'nare *vt* to eliminate

elisoc'corso *sm* helicopter ambulance

el'metto *sm* helmet

elogi'are [elo'dʒare] *vt* to praise

elo'quente *ag* eloquent

e'ludere *vt* to evade

e'lusi *ecc vb vedi* **eludere**

e-mail [i'meil] *sf inv* (*messaggio, sistema*) e-mail ▷ *ag inv* (*indirizzo*) e-mail

emargi'nato, -a [emardʒi'nato] *sm/f* outcast; **emarginazione** [emardʒinat'tsjone] *sf* marginalization

embri'one *sm* embryo

emenda'mento *sm* amendment

emer'genza [emer'dʒɛntsa] *sf* emergency; **in caso di ~** in an emergency

e'mergere [e'mɛrdʒere] *vi* to emerge; (*sommergibile*) to surface; (*fig: distinguersi*) to stand out

e'mersi *ecc vb vedi* **emergere**

e'mettere *vt* (*suono, luce*) to give out, emit; (*onde radio*) to send out; (*assegno, francobollo, ordine*) to issue

emi'crania *sf* migraine

emi'grare *vi* to emigrate

emis'fero *sm* hemisphere; **emisfero australe** southern hemisphere; **emisfero boreale** northern hemisphere

e'misi *ecc vb vedi* **emettere**

emit'tente *ag* (*banca*) issuing; (*Radio*) broadcasting, transmitting ▷ *sf* (*Radio*) transmitter

emorra'gia, -'gie [emorra'dʒia] *sf* haemorrhage

emor'roidi *sfpl* haemorrhoids *pl* (BRIT), hemorrhoids *pl* (US)

emo'tivo, -a *ag* emotional

emozio'nante [emottsjo'nante] *ag* exciting, thrilling

emozionare [emottsjo'nare] *vt* (*commuovere*) to move; (*agitare*) to make nervous; (*elettrizzare*) to excite; **emozionarsi** *vpr* to be moved; to be nervous; to be excited; **emozionato, -a** [emottsjo'nato] *ag* (*commosso*) moved; (*agitato*) nervous; (*elettrizzato*) excited

emozi'one [emot'tsjone] *sf* emotion; (*agitazione*) excitement

enciclope'dia [entʃiklope'dia] *sf* encyclopaedia

endove'noso, -a *ag* (*Med*) intravenous

'E.N.E.L. ['enel] *sigla m* (= *Ente Nazionale per l'Energia Elettrica*) national electricity company

ener'getico, -a, ci, che [ener'dʒɛtiko] *ag* (*risorse, crisi*) energy *cpd*; (*sostanza, alimento*) energy-giving

ener'gia, -'gie [ener'dʒia] *sf* (*Fisica*) energy; (*fig*) energy, strength, vigour; **energia eolica** wind power; **energia solare** solar energy, solar power;

e'**nergico, -a, -ci, -che** *ag* energetic, vigorous

'**enfasi** *sf* emphasis; (*peg*) bombast, pomposity

en'**nesimo, -a** *ag* (*Mat, fig*) nth; **per l'ennesima volta** for the umpteenth time

e'**norme** *ag* enormous, huge

'**ente** *sm* (*istituzione*) body, board, corporation; (*Filosofia*) being; **enti pubblici** public bodies; **ente di ricerca** research organization

en'**trambi, -e** *pron pl* both (of them) ▷ *ag pl* **~ i ragazzi** both boys, both of the boys

en'**trare** *vi* to go (*o* come) in; **~ in** (*luogo*) to enter, go (*o* come) into; (*trovar posto, poter stare*) to fit into; (*essere ammesso a: club ecc*) to join, become a member of; **~ in automobile** to get into the car; **far ~ qn** (*visitatore ecc*) to show sb in; **questo non c'entra** (*fig*) that's got nothing to do with it; **en'trata** *sf* entrance, entry; **dov'è l'entrata?** where's the entrance?; **entrate** *sfpl* (*Comm*) receipts, takings; (*Econ*) income *sg*

'**entro** *prep* (*temporale*) within

entusias'**mare** *vt* to excite, fill with enthusiasm; **entusiasmarsi** *vpr* **entusiasmarsi (per qc/qn)** to become enthusiastic (about sth/sb); **entusi'asmo** *sm* enthusiasm; **entusi'asta, -i, -e** *ag* enthusiastic ▷ *sm/f* enthusiast

epa'**tite** *sf* hepatitis

epide'**mia** *sf* epidemic

epiles'**sia** *sf* epilepsy

epi'**lettico, -a, ci, che** *ag, sm/f* epileptic

epi'**sodio** *sm* episode

'**epoca, -che** *sf* (*periodo storico*) age, era; (*tempo*) time; (*Geo*) age

ep'**pure** *cong* and yet, nevertheless

EPT *sigla m* (= *Ente Provinciale per il Turismo*) district tourist bureau

equa'**tore** *sm* equator

equazi'**one** [ekwat'tsjone] *sf* (*Mat*) equation

e'**questre** *ag* equestrian

equi'**librio** *sm* balance, equilibrium; **perdere l'equilibrare** to lose one's balance

e'**quino, -a** *ag* horse *cpd*, equine

equipaggia'**mento** [ekwipaddʒa'mento] *sm* (*operazione: di nave*) equipping, fitting out; (: *di spedizione, esercito*) equipping, kitting out; (*attrezzatura*) equipment

equipaggi'**are** [ekwipad'dʒare] *vt* (*di persone*) to man; (*di mezzi*) to equip; **equipaggiarsi** *vpr* to equip o.s.; **equi'paggio** *sm* crew

equitazi'**one** [ekwitat'tsjone] *sf* (horse-)riding

equiva'**lente** *ag, sm* equivalent

e'**quivoco, -a, -ci, -che** *ag* equivocal, ambiguous; (*sospetto*) dubious ▷ *sm* misunderstanding; **a scanso di equivoci** to avoid any misunderstanding; **giocare sull'~** to equivocate

'**equo, -a** *ag* fair, just

'**era** *sf* era

'**era** *ecc vb vedi* **essere**

'**erba** *sf* grass; **in ~** (*fig*) budding; **erbe aromatiche** herbs; **erba medica** lucerne; **er'baccia, -ce** *sf* weed

erboriste'**ria** *sf* (*scienza*) study of medicinal herbs; (*negozio*) herbalist's (shop)

e'**rede** *sm/f* heir; **eredità** *sf* (*Dir*) inheritance; (*Biol*) heredity; **lasciare qc in eredità a qn** to leave *o* bequeath sth to sb; **eredi'tare** *vt* to inherit; **eredi'tario, -a** *ag* hereditary

ere'**mita, -i** *sm* hermit

er'**gastolo** *sm* (*Dir: pena*) life imprisonment

'**erica** *sf* heather

er'**metico, -a, -ci, -che** *ag* hermetic

'**ernia** *sf* (*Med*) hernia

'**ero** *vb vedi* **essere**

e'**roe** *sm* hero

ero'**gare** *vt* (*somme*) to distribute; (*gas, servizi*) to supply

e'**roico, -a, -ci, -che** *ag* heroic

ero'**ina** *sf* heroine; (*droga*) heroin

erosi'**one** *sf* erosion

e'**rotico, -a, -ci, -che** *ag* erotic

er'**rato, -a** *ag* wrong

er'**rore** *sm* error, mistake; (*morale*) error; **per ~** by mistake; **ci dev'essere un ~** there must be some mistake; **errore giudiziario** miscarriage of justice

eruzi'**one** [erut'tsjone] *sf* eruption

esacer'**bare** [ezatʃer'bare] *vt* to exacerbate

esage'**rare** [ezadʒe'rare] *vt* to exaggerate ▷ *vi* to exaggerate; (*eccedere*) to go too far

esal'**tare** *vt* to exalt; (*entusiasmare*) to excite, stir

e'**same** *sm* examination; (*Ins*) exam, examination; **fare** *o* **dare un ~** to sit *o* take an exam; **esame di guida** driving test; **esame del sangue** blood test

esami'**nare** *vt* to examine

esaspe'**rare** *vt* to exasperate; to exacerbate

esatta'**mente** *av* exactly; accurately, precisely

esat'**tezza** [ezat'tettsa] *sf* exactitude, accuracy, precision

e'**satto, -a** *pp di* **esigere** ▷ *ag* (*calcolo, ora*) correct, right, exact; (*preciso*) accurate,

precise; (puntuale) punctual
esau'dire vt to grant, fulfil
esauri'ente ag exhaustive
esauri'mento sm exhaustion;
  esaurimento nervoso nervous
  breakdown
esau'rire vt (stancare) to exhaust, wear
  out; (provviste, miniera) to exhaust;
  esaurirsi vpr to exhaust o s., wear o.s.
  out; (provviste) to run out; **esau'rito, -a**
  ag exhausted; (merci) sold out; **registrare**
  il tutto esaurito (Teatro) to have a full
  house; **e'sausto, -a** ag exhausted
'esca (pl **'esche**) sf bait
'esce ['eʃʃe] vb vedi **uscire**
eschi'mese [eski'mese] ag, sm/f Eskimo
'esci ['eʃʃi] vb vedi **uscire**
escla'mare vi to exclaim, cry out
esclama'tivo, -a ag **punto ~** exclamation
  mark
esclamazi'one sf exclamation
es'cludere vt to exclude
es'clusi ecc vb vedi **escludere**
esclusi'one sf exclusion; **a ~ di, fatta**
  ~ di except (for), apart from; **senza ~**
  (alcuna) without exception; **procedere**
  per ~ to follow a process of elimination;
  senza ~ di colpi (fig) with no holds barred;
  esclusione sociale social exclusion
esclu'siva sf (Dir, Comm) exclusive o sole
  rights pl
esclusiva'mente av exclusively, solely
esclu'sivo, -a ag exclusive
es'cluso, -a pp di **escludere**
'esco vb vedi **uscire**
escogi'tare [eskodʒi'tare] vt to devise,
  think up
'escono vb vedi **uscire**
escursi'one sf (gita) excursion, trip;
  (: a piedi) hike, walk; (Meteor) range;
  escursione termica temperature range
esecuzi'one [ezekut'tsjone] sf execution,
  carrying out; (Mus) performance;
  esecuzione capitale execution
esegu'ire vt to carry out, execute; (Mus) to
  perform, execute
e'sempio sm example; **per ~** for example,
  for instance; **fare un ~** to give an example;
  esem'plare ag exemplary ▷ sm example;
  (copia) copy
eserci'tare [ezertʃi'tare] vt (professione)
  to practise (BRIT), practice (US); (allenare:
  corpo, mente) to exercise, train; (diritto)
  to exercise; (influenza, pressione) to exert;
  esercitarsi vpr to practise; **esercitarsi**
  alla lotta to practise fighting
e'sercito [e'zertʃito] sm army
eser'cizio [ezer'tʃittsjo] sm practice,
  exercising; (fisico: di matematica) exercise;

(Econ) financial year; (azienda) business,
  concern; **in ~** (medico ecc) practising;
  esercizio pubblico (Comm) commercial
  concern
esi'bire vt to exhibit, display; (documenti)
  to produce, present; **esibirsi** vpr (attore)
  to perform; (fig) to show off; **esibizi'one**
  sf exhibition; (di documento) presentation;
  (spettacolo) show, performance
esi'gente [ezi'dʒɛnte] ag demanding
e'sigere [e'zidʒere] vt (pretendere) to
  demand; (richiedere) to demand, require;
  (imposte) to collect
'esile ag (persona) slender, slim; (stelo) thin;
  (voce) faint
esili'are vt to exile; **e'silio** sm exile
esis'tenza [ezis'tɛntsa] sf existence
e'sistere vi to exist
esi'tare vi to hesitate
'esito sm result, outcome
'esodo sm exodus
esone'rare vt to exempt
e'sordio sm debut
esor'tare vt **~ qn a fare** to urge sb to do
e'sotico, -a, -ci, -che ag exotic
es'pandere vt to expand; (confini) to
  extend; (influenza) to extend, spread;
  espandersi vpr to expand; **espansi'one**
  sf expansion; **espansione di memoria**
  (Inform) memory upgrade; **espan'sivo, -a**
  ag expansive, communicative
espatri'are vi to leave one's country
espedi'ente sm expedient
es'pellere vt to expel
esperi'enza [espe'rjɛntsa] sf experience
esperi'mento sm experiment
es'perto, -a ag, sm expert
espi'rare vt, vi to breathe out
es'plicito, -a [es'plitʃito] ag explicit
es'plodere vi (anche fig) to explode ▷ vt
  to fire
esplo'rare vt to explore
esplosi'one sf explosion
es'pone ecc vb vedi **esporre**
es'pongo, es'poni ecc vb vedi **esporre**
es'porre vt (merci) to display; (quadro)
  to exhibit, show; (fatti, idee) to explain,
  set out; (porre in pericolo, Fot) to expose;
  esporsi vpr **esporsi a** (sole, pericolo) to
  expose o s. to; (critiche) to lay o.s. open to
espor'tare vt to export
es'pose ecc vb vedi **esporre**
esposizi'one [espozit'tsjone] sf
  displaying; exhibiting; setting out;
  (anche Fot) exposure; (mostra) exhibition;
  (narrazione) explanation, exposition
es'posto, -a pp di **esporre** ▷ ag **~ a nord**
  facing north ▷ sm (Amm) statement,
  account; (: petizione) petition

espressi'one sf expression
espres'sivo, -a ag expressive
es'presso, -a pp di **esprimere** ▷ ag express ▷ sm (lettera) express letter; (anche: **treno ~**) express train; (anche: **caffè ~**) espresso
es'primere vt to express; **esprimersi** vpr to express o.s.
es'pulsi ecc vb vedi **espellere**
espulsi'one sf expulsion
es'senza [es'sɛntsa] sf essence; **essenzi'ale** ag essential; **l'essenziale** the main o most important thing

PAROLA CHIAVE

'**essere** sm being; **essere umano** human being
▷ vb copulativo **1** (con attributo, sostantivo) to be; **sei giovane/simpatico** you are o you're young/nice; **è medico** he is o he's a doctor
2 (+ di: appartenere) to be; **di chi è la penna?** whose pen is it?; **è di Carla** it is o it's Carla's, it belongs to Carla
3 (+ di: provenire) to be; **è di Venezia** he is o he's from Venice
4 (data, ora): **è il 15 agosto/lunedì** it is o it's the 15th of August/Monday; **che ora è?, che ore sono?** what time is it?; **è l'una** it is o it's one o'clock; **sono le due** it is o it's two o'clock
5 (costare): **quant'è?** how much is it?; **sono 10 euro** it's 10 euros
▷ vb aus **1** (attivo): **essere arrivato/ venuto** to have arrived/come; **è già partita** she has already left
2 (passivo) to be; **essere fatto da** to be made by; **è stata uccisa** she has been killed
3 (riflessivo): **si sono lavati** they washed, they got washed
4 (+ da + infinito): **è da farsi subito** it must be o is to be done immediately
▷ vb **1** (esistere, trovarsi) to be; **sono a casa** I'm at home; **essere in piedi/seduto** to be standing/sitting
2 **esserci**: **c'è** there is; **ci sono** there are; **che c'è** what's the matter?, what is it?; **ci sono!** (fig: ho capito) I get it!; vedi anche **ci**
▷ vb impers **è tardi/Pasqua** it's late/ Easter; **è possibile che venga** he may come; **è così** that's the way it is

'**essi** pron mpl vedi **esso**
'**esso, -a** pron it; (riferito a persona: soggetto) he/she; (: complemento) him/her
est sm east
es'tate sf summer

esteri'ore ag outward, external
es'terno, -a ag (porta, muro) outer, outside; (scala) outside; (alunno, impressione) external ▷ sm outside, exterior ▷ sm/f (allievo) day pupil; **all'~** outside; **per uso ~** for external use only; **esterni** smpl (Cinema) location shots
'**estero, -a** ag foreign ▷ sm **all'~** abroad
es'teso, -a pp di **estendere** ▷ ag extensive, large; **scrivere per ~** to write in full
es'tetico, -a, -ci, -che ag aesthetic ▷ sf (disciplina) aesthetics sg; (bellezza) attractiveness; **este'tista, -i, -e** sm/f beautician
es'tinguere vt to extinguish, put out; (debito) to pay off; **estinguersi** vpr to go out; (specie) to become extinct
es'tinsi ecc vb vedi **estinguere**
estin'tore sm (fire) extinguisher
estinzi'one sf putting out; (di specie) extinction
estir'pare vt (pianta) to uproot, pull up; (fig: vizio) to eradicate
es'tivo, -a ag summer cpd
es'torcere [es'tɔrtʃere] vt **~ qc (a qn)** to extort sth (from sb)
estradizi'one [estradit'tsjone] sf extradition
es'trae, es'traggo ecc vb vedi **estrarre**
es'traneo, -a ag foreign ▷ sm/f stranger; **rimanere ~ a qc** to take no part in sth
es'trarre vt to extract; (minerali) to mine; (sorteggiare) to draw
es'trassi ecc vb vedi **estrarre**
estrema'mente av extremely
estre'mista, -i, e sm/f extremist
estremità sf inv extremity, end ▷ sfpl (Anat) extremities
es'tremo, -a ag extreme; (ultimo: ora, tentativo) final, last ▷ sm extreme; (di pazienza, forze) limit, end; **estremi** smpl (Amm: dati essenziali) details, particulars; **l'~ Oriente** the Far East
estro'verso, -a ag, sm extrovert
età sf inv age; **all'~ di 8 anni** at the age of 8, at 8 years of age; **ha la mia ~** he (o she) is the same age as me o as I am; **raggiungere la maggiore ~** to come of age; **essere in ~ minore** to be under age
'**etere** sm ether
eternità sf eternity
e'terno, -a ag eternal
etero'geneo, -a [etero'dʒɛneo] ag heterogeneous
eterosessu'ale ag, sm/f heterosexual
'**etica** sf ethics sg; vedi anche **etico**
eti'chetta [eti'ketta] sf label; (cerimoniale): **l'~** etiquette

'etico, -a, -ci, -che *ag* ethical
eti'lometro *sm* Breathalyzer®
etimolo'gia, -'gie [etimolo'dʒia] *sf*
etymology
Eti'opia *sf* l'~ Ethiopia
'etnico, -a, -ci, -che *ag* ethnic
e'trusco, -a, -schi, -sche *ag, sm/f*
Etruscan
'ettaro *sm* hectare (= 10,000 m²)
'etto *sm abbr* (= ettogrammo) 100 grams
'euro *sm inv* (divisa) euro
Eu'ropa *sf* l'~ Europe
europarlamen'tare *sm/f* Member of the
European Parliament, MEP
euro'peo, -a *ag, sm/f* European
eutana'sia *sf* euthanasia
evacu'are *vt* to evacuate
e'vadere *vi* (fuggire): ~ **da** to escape from
  ▷ *vt* (sbrigare) to deal with, dispatch; (tasse)
  to evade
evapo'rare *vi* to evaporate
e'vasi *ecc vb vedi* **evadere**
evasi'one *sf* (vedi evadere) escape;
dispatch; **evasione fiscale** tax evasion
eva'sivo, -a *ag* evasive
e'vaso, -a *pp di* **evadere** ▷ *sm* escapee
e'vento *sm* event
eventu'ale *ag* possible

> Attenzione! In inglese esiste la parola
> *eventual*, che però significa *finale*.

eventual'mente *av* if necessary

> Attenzione! In inglese esiste la
> parola *eventually*, che però significa
> *alla fine*.

evi'dente *ag* evident, obvious
eviden'temente *av* evidently;
(palesemente) obviously, evidently
evi'tare *vt* to avoid; ~ **di fare** to avoid
doing; ~ **qc a qn** to spare sb sth
evoluzi'one [evolut'tsjone] *sf* evolution
e'volversi *vpr* to evolve
ev'viva *escl* hurrah!; ~ **il re!** long live the
king!, hurrah for the king!
ex *prefisso* ex, former
'extra *ag inv* first-rate; top-quality ▷ *sm*
inv extra; **extracomuni'tario, -a** *ag* from
outside the EC ▷ *sm/f* non-EC citizen
extrater'restre *ag, sm/f* extraterrestrial

f

fa *vb vedi* **fare** ▷ *sm inv* (Mus) F;
(: solfeggiando la scala) fa ▷ *av* **10 anni fa** 10
years ago
'fabbrica *sf* factory; **fabbri'care** *vt* to
build; (produrre) to manufacture, make;
(fig) to fabricate, invent

> Attenzione! In inglese esiste la parola
> *fabric*, che però significa *stoffa*.

fac'cenda [fat'tʃɛnda] *sf* matter, affair;
(cosa da fare) task, chore
fac'chino [fak'kino] *sm* porter
'faccia, -ce ['fattʃa] *sf* face; (di moneta,
medaglia) side; **faccia a faccia** face to face
facci'ata [fat'tʃata] *sf* façade; (di pagina)
side
'faccio ['fattʃo] *vb vedi* **fare**
fa'cessi *ecc* [fa'tʃessi] *vb vedi* **fare**
fa'cevo *ecc* [fa'tʃevo] *vb vedi* **fare**
'facile ['fatʃile] *ag* easy; (disposto): ~ **a**
inclined to, prone to; (probabile): **è ~ che
piova** it's likely to rain
facoltà *sf inv* (autorità) power
facolta'tivo, -a *ag* optional; (fermata
d'autobus) request *cpd*
'faggio ['faddʒo] *sm* beech
fagi'ano [fa'dʒano] *sm* pheasant
fagio'lino [fadʒo'lino] *sm* French (BRIT) o
string bean
fagi'olo [fa'dʒolo] *sm* bean
'fai *vb vedi* **fare**

'fai-da-'te *sm inv* DIY, do-it-yourself

'falce ['faltʃe] *sf* scythe; **falci'are** *vt* to cut; *(fig)* to mow down

falcia'trice [faltʃa'tritʃe] *sf (per fieno)* reaping machine; *(per erba)* mowing machine

'falco, -chi *sm* hawk

'falda *sf* layer, stratum; *(di cappello)* brim; *(di cappotto)* tails *pl*; *(di monte)* lower slope; *(di tetto)* pitch

fale'gname [faleɲ'ɲame] *sm* joiner

falli'mento *sm* failure; bankruptcy

fal'lire *vi (non riuscire)*: **~ (in)** to fail (in); *(Dir)* to go bankrupt ▷ *vt (colpo, bersaglio)* to miss

'fallo *sm* error, mistake; *(imperfezione)* defect, flaw; *(Sport)* foul; fault; **senza ~** without fail

falò *sm inv* bonfire

falsifi'care *vt* to forge; *(monete)* to forge, counterfeit

'falso, -a *ag* false; *(errato)* wrong; *(falsificato)* forged; fake; *(: oro, gioielli)* imitation *cpd* ▷ *sm* forgery; **giurare il ~** to commit perjury

'fama *sf* fame; *(reputazione)* reputation, name

'fame *sf* hunger; **aver ~** to be hungry

fa'miglia [fa'miʎʎa] *sf* family

famili'are *ag (della famiglia)* family *cpd*; *(ben noto)* familiar; *(rapporti, atmosfera)* friendly; *(Ling)* informal, colloquial ▷ *sm/f* relative, relation

fa'moso, -a *ag* famous, well-known

fa'nale *sm (Aut)* light, lamp (BRIT); *(luce stradale, Naut)* light; *(di faro)* beacon

fa'natico, -a, -ci, -che *ag* fanatical; *(del teatro, calcio ecc)*: **~ di** o **per** mad o crazy about ▷ *sm/f* fanatic; *(tifoso)* fan

'fango, -ghi *sm* mud

'fanno *vb vedi* **fare**

fannul'lone, -a *sm/f* idler, loafer

fantasci'enza [fantaʃ'ʃɛntsa] *sf* science fiction

fanta'sia *sf* fantasy, imagination; *(capriccio)* whim, caprice ▷ *ag inv* **vestito ~** patterned dress

fan'tasma, -i *sm* ghost, phantom

fan'tastico, -a, -ci, -che *ag* fantastic; *(potenza, ingegno)* imaginative

fan'tino *sm* jockey

fara'butto *sm* crook

fard *sm inv* blusher

 PAROLA CHIAVE

'fare *sm* **1** *(modo di fare)*: **con fare distratto** absent-mindedly; **ha un fare simpatico** he has a pleasant manner

2: **sul far del giorno/della notte** at daybreak/nightfall

▷ *vt* **1** *(fabbricare, creare)* to make; *(: casa)* to build; *(: assegno)* to make out; **fare un pasto/una promessa/un film** to make a meal/a promise/a film; **fare rumore** to make a noise

2 *(effettuare: lavoro, attività, studi)* to do; *(: sport)* to play; **cosa fa?** *(adesso)* what are you doing?; *(di professione)* what do you do?; **fare psicologia/italiano** *(Ins)* to do psychology/Italian; **fare un viaggio** to go on a trip o journey; **fare una passeggiata** to go for a walk; **fare la spesa** to do the shopping

3 *(funzione)* to be; *(Teatro)* to play, be; **fare il medico** to be a doctor; **fare il malato** *(fingere)* to act the invalid

4 *(suscitare: sentimenti)*: **fare paura a qn** to frighten sb; **(non) fa niente** *(non importa)* it doesn't matter

5 *(ammontare)*: **3 più 3 fa 6** 3 and 3 are o make 6; **fanno 3 euro** that's 3 euros; **Roma fa 2.000.000 di abitanti** Rome has 2,000,000 inhabitants; **che ora fai?** what time do you make it?

6 *(+ infinito)*: **far fare qc a qn** *(obbligare)* to make sb do sth; *(permettere)* to let sb do sth; **fammi vedere** let me see; **far partire il motore** to start (up) the engine; **far riparare la macchina/costruire una casa** to get o have the car repaired/a house built

7: **farsi: farsi una gonna** to make o.s. a skirt; **farsi un nome** to make a name for o s.; **farsi la permanente** to get a perm; **farsi tagliare i capelli** to get one's hair cut; **farsi operare** to have an operation

8 *(fraseologia)*: **farcela** to succeed, manage; **non ce la faccio più** I can't go on; **ce la faremo** we'll make it; **me l'hanno fatta!** *(imbrogliare)* I've been done!; **lo facevo più giovane** I thought he was younger; **fare sì/no con la testa** to nod/shake one's head

▷ *vi* **1** *(agire)* to act, do; **fate come volete** do as you like; **fare presto** to be quick; **fare da** to act as; **non c'è niente da fare** it's no use; **saperci fare con qn/qc** to know how to deal with sb/sth; **faccia pure!** go ahead!

2 *(dire)* to say; **"davvero?" fece** "really?" he said

3: **fare per** *(essere adatto)* to be suitable for; **fare per qc** to be about to do sth; **fece per andarsene** he made as if to leave

4: **farsi: si fa così** you do it like this, this is the way it's done; **non si fa così!** *(rimprovero)* that's no way to behave!; **la festa non si fa** the party is off

5: **fare a gara con qn** to compete o vie
with sb; **fare a pugni** to come to blows;
fare in tempo a fare to be in time to do
▷ vb impers **fa bel tempo** the weather
is fine; **fa caldo/freddo** it's hot/cold;
fa notte it's getting dark ▷ vpr **farsi 1**
(*diventare*) to become; **farsi prete** to
become a priest; **farsi grande/vecchio** to
grow tall/old
2 (*spostarsi*): **farsi avanti/indietro** to
move forward/back
3 (*fam: drogarsi*) to be a junkie

far'falla sf butterfly

fa'rina sf flour

farma'cia, -'cie [farma'tʃia] sf pharmacy;
(*negozio*) chemist's (shop) (BRIT),
pharmacy; **farma'cista, -i, -e** sm/f
chemist (BRIT), pharmacist

'farmaco, -ci o **chi** sm drug, medicine

'faro sm (*Naut*) lighthouse; (*Aer*) beacon;
(*Aut*) headlight

'fascia, -sce ['faʃʃa] sf band, strip; (*Med*)
bandage; (*di sindaco, ufficiale*) sash; (*parte
di territorio*) strip, belt; (*di contribuenti ecc*)
group, band; **essere in fasce** (*anche fig*)
to be in one's infancy; **fascia oraria** time
band

fasci'are [faʃ'ʃare] vt to bind; (*Med*) to
bandage

fa'scicolo [faʃ'ʃikolo] sm (*di documenti*)
file, dossier; (*di rivista*) issue, number;
(*opuscolo*) booklet, pamphlet

'fascino ['faʃino] sm charm, fascination

fa'scismo [faʃ'ʃizmo] sm fascism

'fase sf phase; (*Tecn*) stroke; **fuori ~**
(*motore*) rough

fas'tidio sm bother, trouble; **dare ~ a
qn** to bother o annoy sb; **sento ~ allo
stomaco** my stomach's upset; **avere
fastidi con la polizia** to have trouble o
bother with the police; **fastidi'oso, -a** ag
annoying, tiresome

   Attenzione! In inglese esiste la parola
fastidious, che però significa *pignolo*.

'fata sf fairy

fa'tale ag fatal; (*inevitabile*) inevitable; (*fig*)
irresistible

fa'tica, -che sf hard work, toil; (*sforzo*)
effort; (*di metalli*) fatigue; **a ~** with
difficulty; **fare ~ a fare qc** to have a
job doing sth; **fati'coso, -a** ag tiring,
exhausting; (*lavoro*) laborious

'fatto, -a pp di **fare** ▷ ag **un uomo ~** a
grown man; **~ a mano/in casa** hand-
/home-made ▷ sm fact; (*azione*) deed;
(*avvenimento*) event, occurrence; (*di
romanzo, film*) action, story; **cogliere qn
sul ~** to catch sb red-handed; **il ~ sta** o **è**

che the fact remains o is that; **in ~ di** as for,
as far as … is concerned

fat'tore sm (*Agr*) farm manager; (*Mat,
elemento costitutivo*) factor; **fattore di
protezione** (*di lozione solare*) factor; **vorrei
una crema solare con ~ di protezione 15**
I'd like a factor 15 suntan cream

fatto'ria sf farm; farmhouse

   Attenzione! In inglese esiste la parola
factory, che però significa *fabbrica*.

fatto'rino sm errand-boy; (*di ufficio*) office-
boy; (*d'albergo*) porter

fat'tura sf (*Comm*) invoice; (*di abito*)
tailoring; (*malia*) spell

fattu'rato sm (*Comm*) turnover

'fauna sf fauna

'fava sf broad bean

'favola sf (*fiaba*) fairy tale; (*d'intento morale*)
fable; (*fandonia*) yarn; **favo'loso, -a** ag
fabulous; (*incredibile*) incredible

fa'vore sm favour; **per ~** please; **fare un ~
a qn** to do sb a favour

favo'rire vt to favour; (*il commercio,
l'industria, le arti*) to promote, encourage;
vuole ~? won't you help yourself?;
favorisca in salotto please come into the
sitting room

fax sm inv fax; **mandare qc via ~** to fax sth

fazzo'letto [fattso'letto] sm
handkerchief; (*per la testa*) (head)scarf;
fazzoletto di carta tissue

feb'braio sm February

'febbre sf fever; **aver la ~** to have a high
temperature; **febbre da fieno** hay fever

'feci ecc ['fɛtʃi] vb vedi **fare**

fecondazi'one [fekondat'tsjone] sf
fertilization; **fecondazione artificiale**
artificial insemination

fe'condo, -a ag fertile

'fede sf (*credenza*) belief, faith; (*Rel*)
faith; (*fiducia*) faith, trust; (*fedeltà*)
loyalty; (*anello*) wedding ring; (*attestato*)
certificate; **aver ~ in qn** to have faith in sb;
in buona/cattiva ~ in good/bad faith; **"in
~"** (*Dir*) "in witness whereof"; **fe'dele** ag
fedele (a) faithful (to) ▷ sm/f follower; **i
fedeli** (*Rel*) the faithful

'federa sf pillowslip, pillowcase

fede'rale ag federal

'fegato sm liver; (*fig*) guts pl, nerve

'felce ['feltʃe] sf fern

fe'lice [fe'litʃe] ag happy; (*fortunato*) lucky;
felicità sf happiness

felici'tarsi [felitʃi'tarsi] vpr (*congratularsi*):
~ con qn per qc to congratulate sb on sth

fe'lino, -a ag, sm feline

'felpa sf sweatshirt

'femmina sf (*Zool, Tecn*) female; (*figlia*)
girl, daughter; (*spesso peg*) woman;

femmi'nile *ag* feminine; (*sesso*) female; (*lavoro, giornale, moda*) woman's ▷ *sm* (*Ling*) feminine

'femore *sm* thighbone, femur

fe'nomeno *sm* phenomenon

feri'ale *ag* giorno ~ weekday

'ferie *sfpl* holidays (BRIT), vacation *sg* (US); **andare in ~** to go on holiday o vacation

fe'rire *vt* to injure; (*deliberatamente: Mil ecc*) to wound; (*colpire*) to hurt; **ferirsi** *vpr* to hurt o.s., injure o.s.; **fe'rita** *sf* injury, wound; **fe'rito, -a** *sm/f* wounded o injured man/woman

fer'maglio [fer'maʎʎo] *sm* clasp; (*per documenti*) clip

fer'mare *vt* to stop, halt; (*Polizia*) to detain, hold ▷ *vi* to stop; **fermarsi** *vpr* to stop, halt; **fermarsi a fare qc** to stop to do sth; **può fermarsi qui/all'angolo?** could you stop here/at the corner?

fer'mata *sf* stop; **fermata dell'autobus** bus stop

fer'menti *smpl* ~ **lattici** probiotic bacteria

fer'mezza [fer'mettsa] *sf* (*fig*) firmness, steadfastness

'fermo, -a *ag* still, motionless; (*veicolo*) stationary; (*orologio*) not working; (*saldo: anche fig*) firm; (*voce, mano*) steady ▷ *escl* stop!; keep still! ▷ *sm* (*chiusura*) catch, lock; (*Dir*) **fermo di polizia** police detention

fe'roce [fe'rɔtʃe] *ag* (*animale*) fierce, ferocious; (*persona*) cruel, fierce; (*fame, dolore*) raging; **le bestie feroci** wild animals

ferra'gosto *sm* (*festa*) feast of the Assumption; (*periodo*) August holidays *pl*

🔹 FERRAGOSTO

🔹
🔹 **Ferragosto**, August 15th, is a national
🔹 holiday. Marking the Feast of the
🔹 Assumption, its origins are religious
🔹 but in recent years it has simply become
🔹 the most important public holiday of
🔹 the summer season. Most people take
🔹 some extra time off work and head out
🔹 of town to the holiday resorts.

ferra'menta *sfpl* **negozio di ~** ironmonger's (BRIT), hardware shop o store (US)

'ferro *sm* iron; **una bistecca ai ferri** a grilled steak; **ferro battuto** wrought iron; **ferro da calza** knitting needle; **ferro di cavallo** horseshoe; **ferro da stiro** iron

ferro'via *sf* railway (BRIT), railroad (US); **ferrovi'ario, -a** *ag* railway *cpd* (BRIT), railroad *cpd* (US); **ferrovi'ere** *sm*

railwayman (BRIT), railroad man (US)

'fertile *ag* fertile

'fesso, -a *pp di* **fendere** ▷ *ag* (*fam: sciocco*) crazy, cracked

fes'sura *sf* crack, split; (*per gettone, moneta*) slot

'festa *sf* (*religiosa*) feast; (*pubblica*) holiday; (*compleanno*) birthday; (*onomastico*) name day; (*ricevimento*) celebration, party; **far ~** to have a holiday; to live it up; **far ~ a qn** to give sb a warm welcome

festeggi'are [fested'dʒare] *vt* to celebrate; (*persona*) to have a celebration for

fes'tivo, -a *ag* (*atmosfera*) festive; **giorno ~** holiday

'feto *sm* foetus (BRIT), fetus (US)

'fetta *sf* slice

fettuc'cine [fettut'tʃine] *sfpl* (*Cuc*) ribbon-shaped pasta

FF.SS. *abbr* = **Ferrovie dello Stato**

FI *sigla* = **Firenze** ▷ *abbr* (= *Forza Italia*) *Italian centre-right political party*

fi'aba *sf* fairy tale

fi'acca *sf* weariness; (*svogliatezza*) listlessness

fi'acco, -a, -chi, -che *ag* (*stanco*) tired, weary; (*svogliato*) listless; (*debole*) weak; (*mercato*) slack

fi'accola *sf* torch

fi'ala *sf* phial

fi'amma *sf* flame

fiam'mante *ag* (*colore*) flaming; **nuovo ~** brand new

fiam'mifero *sm* match

fiam'mingo, -a, -ghi, -ghe *ag* Flemish ▷ *sm/f* Fleming ▷ *sm* (*Ling*) Flemish; **i Fiamminghi** the Flemish

fi'anco, -chi *sm* side; (*Mil*) flank; **di ~** sideways, from the side; **a ~ a ~** side by side

fi'asco, -schi *sm* flask; (*fig*) fiasco; **fare ~** to fail

fia'tare *vi* (*fig: parlare*): **senza ~** without saying a word

fi'ato *sm* breath; (*resistenza*) stamina; **avere il ~ grosso** to be out of breath; **prendere ~** to catch one's breath

'fibbia *sf* buckle

'fibra *sf* fibre; (*fig*) constitution

fic'care *vt* to push, thrust, drive; **ficcarsi** *vpr* (*andare a finire*) to get to

ficcherò *ecc* [fikke'rɔ] *vb vedi* **ficcare**

'fico, -chi *sm* (*pianta*) fig tree; (*frutto*) fig; **fico d'India** prickly pear; **fico secco** dried fig

fidanza'mento [fidantsa'mento] *sm* engagement

fidan'zarsi [fidan'tsarsi] *vpr* to get engaged; **fidan'zato, -a** *sm/f* fiancé/

fiancée

fi'darsi *vpr* ~ **di** to trust; **fi'dato, -a** *ag* reliable, trustworthy

fi'ducia [fi'dutʃa] *sf* confidence, trust; **incarico di ~** position of trust, responsible position; **persona di ~** reliable person

fie'nile *sm* barn; hayloft

fi'eno *sm* hay

fi'era *sf* fair

fi'ero, -a *ag* proud; (*audace*) bold

'fifa (*fam*) *sf* **aver ~** to have the jitters

fig. *abbr* (= *figura*) fig.

'figlia ['fiʎʎa] *sf* daughter

figli'astro, -a [fiʎ'ʎastro] *sm/f* stepson/ daughter

'figlio ['fiʎʎo] *sm* son; (*senza distinzione di sesso*) child; **figlio di papà** spoilt, wealthy young man; **figlio unico** only child

fi'gura *sf* figure; (*forma, aspetto esterno*) form, shape; (*illustrazione*) picture, illustration; **far ~** to look smart; **fare una brutta ~** to make a bad impression

figu'rina *sf* figurine; (*cartoncino*) picture card

'fila *sf* row, line; (*coda*) queue; (*serie*) series, string; **di ~** in succession; **fare la ~** to queue; **in ~ indiana** in single file

fi'lare *vt* to spin ▷ *vi* (*baco, ragno*) to spin; (*formaggio fuso*) to go stringy; (*discorso*) to hang together; (*fam: amoreggiare*) to go steady; (*muoversi a forte velocità*) to go at full speed; **~ diritto** (*fig*) to toe the line; **~ via** to dash off

filas'trocca, -che *sf* nursery rhyme

filate'lia *sf* philately, stamp collecting

fi'letto *sm* (*di vite*) thread; (*di carne*) fillet

fili'ale *ag* filial ▷ *sf* (*di impresa*) branch

film *sm inv* film

'filo *sm* (*anche fig*) thread; (*filato*) yarn; (*metallico*) wire; (*di lama, rasoio*) edge; **per ~ e per segno** in detail; **con un ~ di voce** in a whisper; **filo d'erba** blade of grass; **filo interdentale** dental floss; **filo di perle** string of pearls; **filo spinato** barbed wire

fi'lone *sm* (*di minerali*) seam, vein; (*pane*) ≈ Vienna loaf; (*fig*) trend

filoso'fia *sf* philosophy; **fi'losofo, -a** *sm/f* philosopher

fil'trare *vt, vi* to filter

'filtro *sm* filter; **filtro dell'olio** (*Aut*) oil filter

fi'nale *ag* final ▷ *sm* (*di opera*) end, ending; (*: Mus*) finale ▷ *sf* (*Sport*) final; **final'mente** *av* finally, at last

fi'nanza [fi'nantsa] *sf* finance; **finanze** *sfpl* (*di individuo, Stato*) finances

finché [fin'ke] *cong* (*per tutto il tempo che*) as long as; (*fino al momento in cui*) until; **aspetta ~ io (non) sia ritornato** wait until I get back

'fine *ag* (*lamina, carta*) thin; (*capelli, polvere*) fine; (*vista, udito*) keen, sharp; (*persona: raffinata*) refined, distinguished; (*osservazione*) subtle ▷ *sf* end ▷ *sm* aim, purpose; (*esito*) result, outcome; **secondo ~** ulterior motive; **in** *o* **alla ~** in the end, finally

fi'nestra *sf* window; **fines'trino** *sm* window; **vorrei un posto vicino al finestrino** I'd like a window seat

'fingere ['findʒere] *vt* to feign; (*supporre*) to imagine, suppose; **fingersi** *vpr* **fingersi ubriaco/pazzo** to pretend to be drunk/ mad; **~ di fare** to pretend to do

fi'nire *vt* to finish ▷ *vi* to finish, end; **quando finisce lo spettacolo?** when does the show finish?; **~ di fare** (*compiere*) to finish doing; (*smettere*) to stop doing; **~ in galera** to end up *o* finish up in prison

finlan'dese *ag, sm* (*Ling*) Finnish ▷ *sm/f* Finn

Fin'landia *sf* **la ~** Finland

'fino, -a *ag* (*capelli, seta*) fine; (*oro*) pure; (*fig: acuto*) shrewd ▷ *av* (*spesso troncato in* **fin**: *pure, anche*) even ▷ *prep* (*spesso troncato in* **fin**: *tempo*) **fin quando?** till when?; (*: luogo*): **fin qui** as far as here; **~ a** (*tempo*) until, till; (*luogo*) as far as, (up) to; **fin da domani** from tomorrow onwards; **fin da ieri** since yesterday; **fin dalla nascita** from *o* since birth

fi'nocchio [fi'nɔkkjo] *sm* fennel; (*fam: peg: omosessuale*) queer

fi'nora *av* up till now

'finsi *ecc vb vedi* **fingere**

'finta *sf* pretence, sham; (*Sport*) feint; **far ~ (di fare)** to pretend (to do)

'finto, -a *pp di* **fingere** ▷ *ag* false; artificial

finzi'one [fin'tsjone] *sf* pretence, sham

fi'occo, -chi *sm* (*di nastro*) bow; (*di stoffa, lana*) flock; (*di neve*) flake; (*Naut*) jib; **coi fiocchi** (*fig*) first-rate; **fiocchi di avena** oatflakes; **fiocchi di granturco** cornflakes

fi'ocina ['fjɔtʃina] *sf* harpoon

fi'oco, -a, -chi, -che *ag* faint, dim

fi'onda *sf* catapult

fio'raio, -a *sm/f* florist

fi'ore *sm* flower; **fiori** *smpl* (*Carte*) clubs; **a fior d'acqua** on the surface of the water; **avere i nervi a fior di pelle** to be on edge; **fior di latte** cream; **fiori di campo** wild flowers

fioren'tino, -a *ag* Florentine

fio'retto *sm* (*Scherma*) foil

fio'rire *vi* (*rosa*) to flower; (*albero*) to blossom; (*fig*) to flourish

Fi'renze [fi'rɛntse] *sf* Florence

'firma sf signature

Attenzione! In inglese esiste la parola firm, che però significa ditta.

fir'mare vt to sign; **un abito firmato** a designer suit; **dove devo ~?** where do I sign?

fisar'monica, -che sf accordion

fis'cale ag fiscal, tax cpd; **medico ~ doctor** employed by Social Security to verify cases of sick leave

fischi'are [fis'kjare] vi to whistle ▷ vt to whistle; (attore) to boo, hiss

fischi'etto [fis'kjetto] sm (strumento) whistle

'fischio ['fiskjo] sm whistle

'fisco sm tax authorities pl, ≈ Inland Revenue (BRIT), ≈ Internal Revenue Service (US)

'fisica sf physics sg

'fisico, -a, -ci, -che ag physical ▷ sm/f physicist ▷ sm physique

fisiotera'pia sf physiotherapy

fisiotera'pista sm/f physiotherapist

fis'sare vt to fix, fasten; (guardare intensamente) to stare at; (data, condizioni) to fix, establish, set; (prenotare) to book; **fissarsi** vpr **fissarsi su** (sguardo, attenzione) to focus on; (fig: idea) to become obsessed with

'fisso, -a ag fixed; (stipendio, impiego) regular ▷ av **guardare ~ qc/qn** to stare at sth/sb

'fitta sf sharp pain; vedi anche **fitto**

fit'tizio, -a ag fictitious, imaginary

'fitto, -a ag thick, dense; (pioggia) heavy ▷ sm depths pl, middle; (affitto, pigione) rent

fi'ume sm river

fiu'tare vt to smell, sniff; (animale) to scent; (fig: inganno) to get wind of, smell; **~ tabacco/cocaina** to take snuff/cocaine

fla'grante ag **cogliere qn in ~** to catch sb red-handed

fla'nella sf flannel

flash [flaʃ] sm inv (Fot) flash; (giornalistico) newsflash

'flauto sm flute

fles'sibile ag pliable; (fig: che si adatta) flexible

flessibili'tà sf (anche fig) flexibility

flessi'one sf (gen) bending; (Ginnastica: a terra) sit-up; (: in piedi) forward bend; (: sulle gambe) knee-bend; (diminuzione) slight drop, slight fall; (Ling) inflection; **fare una ~** to bend; **una ~ economica** a downward trend in the economy

'flettere vt to bend

'flipper sm inv pinball machine

F.lli abbr (= fratelli) Bros.

'flora sf flora

'florido, -a ag flourishing; (fig) glowing with health

'floscio, -a, -sci, -sce ['flɔʃʃo] ag (cappello) floppy, soft; (muscoli) flabby

'flotta sf fleet

'fluido, -a ag, sm fluid

flu'oro sm fluorine

'flusso sm flow; (Fisica, Med) flux; **~ e ri~** ebb and flow

fluvi'ale ag river cpd, fluvial

FMI sigla m (= Fondo Monetario Internazionale) IMF

'foca, -che sf (Zool) seal

fo'caccia, -ce [fo'kattʃa] sf kind of pizza; (dolce) bun

'foce ['fotʃe] sf (Geo) mouth

foco'laio sm (Med) centre of infection; (fig) hotbed

foco'lare sm hearth, fireside; (Tecn) furnace

'fodera sf (di vestito) lining; (di libro, poltrona) cover

'fodero sm (di spada) scabbard; (di pugnale) sheath; (di pistola) holster

'foga sf enthusiasm, ardour

'foglia ['fɔʎʎa] sf leaf; **foglia d'argento/ d'oro** silver/gold leaf

'foglio ['fɔʎʎo] sm (di carta) sheet (of paper); (di metallo) sheet; **foglio di calcolo** (Inform) spreadsheet; **foglio rosa** (Aut) provisional licence; **foglio di via** (Dir) expulsion order; **foglio volante** pamphlet

'fogna ['foɲɲa] sf drain, sewer

föhn [føːn] sm inv hair dryer

'folla sf crowd, throng

'folle ag mad, insane; (Tecn) idle; **in ~** (Aut) in neutral

fol'lia sf folly, foolishness; foolish act; (pazzia) madness, lunacy

'folto, -a ag thick

fon sm inv hair dryer

fondamen'tale ag fundamental, basic

fonda'mento sm foundation; **fondamenta** sfpl (Edil) foundations

fon'dare vt to found; (fig: dar base): **~ qc su** to base sth on

fon'dente ag **cioccolato ~** plain o dark chocolate

'fondere vt (neve) to melt; (metallo) to fuse, melt; (fig: colori) to merge, blend; (: imprese, gruppi) to merge ▷ vi to melt; **fondersi** vpr to melt; (fig: partiti, correnti) to unite, merge

'fondo, -a ag deep ▷ sm (di recipiente, pozzo) bottom; (di stanza) back; (quantità di liquido che resta, deposito) dregs pl; (sfondo) background; (unità immobiliare) property, estate; (somma di denaro) fund; (Sport) long-distance race; **fondi** *smpl* (*denaro*) funds; **a notte fonda** at dead of night; **in ~ a** at the bottom of; at the back of; (*strada*) at the end of; **andare a ~** (*nave*) to sink; **conoscere a ~** to know inside out; **dar ~ a** (*fig: provviste, soldi*) to use up; **in ~** (*fig*) after all, all things considered; **andare fino in ~ a** (*fig*) to examine thoroughly; **a ~ perduto** (*Comm*) without security; **fondi di magazzino** old *o* unsold stock *sg*; **fondi di caffè** coffee grounds; **fondo comune di investimento** investment trust

fondo'tinta *sm inv* (*cosmetico*) foundation

fo'netica *sf* phonetics *sg*

fon'tana *sf* fountain

'fonte *sf* spring, source; (*fig*) source ▷ *sm*: **fonte battesimale** (*Rel*) font; **fonte energetica** source of energy

fo'raggio [fo'raddʒo] *sm* fodder, forage

fo'rare *vt* to pierce, make a hole in; (*pallone*) to burst; (*biglietto*) to punch; **~ una gomma** to burst a tyre (BRIT) *o* tire (US)

'forbici ['fɔrbitʃi] *sfpl* scissors

'forca, -che *sf* (*Agr*) fork, pitchfork; (*patibolo*) gallows *sg*

for'chetta [for'ketta] *sf* fork

for'cina [for'tʃina] *sf* hairpin

fo'resta *sf* forest

foresti'ero, -a *ag* foreign ▷ *sm/f* foreigner

'forfora *sf* dandruff

'forma *sf* form; (*aspetto esteriore*) form, shape; (*Dir: procedura*) procedure; (*per calzature*) last; (*stampo da cucina*) mould

formag'gino [formad'dʒino] *sm* processed cheese

for'maggio [for'maddʒo] *sm* cheese

for'male *ag* formal

for'mare *vt* to form, shape, make; (*numero di telefono*) to dial; (*fig: carattere*) to form, mould; **formarsi** *vpr* to form, take shape; **for'mato** *sm* format, size; **formazi'one** *sf* formation; (*fig: educazione*) training; **formazione professionale** vocational training

for'mica¹, -che *sf* ant

formica®² ['fɔrmika] *sf* (*materiale*) Formica®

formi'dabile *ag* powerful, formidable; (*straordinario*) remarkable

'formula *sf* formula; **formula di cortesia** courtesy form

formu'lare *vt* to formulate; to express

for'naio *sm* baker

for'nello *sm* (*elettrico, a gas*) ring; (*di pipa*) bowl

for'nire *vt* **~ qn di qc, ~ qc a qn** to provide *o* supply sb with sth, supply sth to sb

'forno *sm* (*di cucina*) oven; (*panetteria*) bakery; (*Tecn: per calce ecc*) kiln; (: *per metalli*) furnace; **forno a microonde** microwave oven

'foro *sm* (*buco*) hole; (*Storia*) forum; (*tribunale*) (law) court

'forse *av* perhaps, maybe; (*circa*) about; **essere in ~** to be in doubt

'forte *ag* strong; (*suono*) loud; (*spesa*) considerable, great; (*passione, dolore*) great, deep ▷ *av* strongly; (*velocemente*) fast; (*a voce alta*) loud(ly); (*violentemente*) hard ▷ *sm* (*edificio*) fort; (*specialità*) forte, strong point; **essere ~ in qc** to be good at sth

for'tezza [for'tettsa] *sf* (*morale*) strength; (*luogo fortificato*) fortress

for'tuito, -a *ag* fortuitous, chance

for'tuna *sf* (*destino*) fortune, luck; (*buona sorte*) success, fortune; (*eredità, averi*) fortune; **per ~** luckily, fortunately; **di ~** makeshift, improvised; **atterraggio di ~** emergency landing; **fortu'nato, -a** *ag* lucky, fortunate; (*coronato da successo*) successful

'forza ['fɔrtsa] *sf* strength; (*potere*) power; (*Fisica*) force; **forze** *sfpl* (*fisiche*) strength *sg*; (*Mil*) forces *escl* come on!; **per ~** against one's will; (*naturalmente*) of course; **a viva ~** by force; **a ~ di** by dint of; **~ maggiore** circumstances beyond one's control; **la ~ pubblica** the police *pl*; **forze armate** armed forces; **forze dell'ordine** the forces of law and order; **Forza Italia** *Italian centre-right political party*; **forza di pace** peacekeeping force

for'zare [for'tsare] *vt* to force; **~ qn a fare** to force sb to do

for'zista, -i, e [for'tsista] *ag* of Forza Italia ▷ *sm/f* member (*o* supporter) of Forza Italia

fos'chia [fos'kia] *sf* mist, haze

'fosco, -a, -schi, -sche *ag* dark, gloomy

'fosforo *sm* phosphorous

'fossa *sf* pit; (*di cimitero*) grave; **fossa biologica** septic tank

fos'sato *sm* ditch; (*di fortezza*) moat

fos'setta *sf* dimple

'fossi *ecc vb vedi* **essere**

'fossile *ag, sm* fossil

'fosso *sm* ditch; (*Mil*) trench

'foste *ecc vb vedi* **essere**

'foto *sf* photo; **può farci una ~, per favore?** would you take a picture of us, please? ▷ *prefisso*: **foto ricordo** souvenir photo; **foto tessera** passport(-type) photo; **foto'camera** *sf* **fotocamera digitale** digital camera; **foto'copia** *sf* photocopy; **fotocopi'are** *vt* to photocopy; **fotocopia'trice** [fotokopja'tritʃe] *sf* photocopier; **fotogra'fare** *vt* to photograph; **fotogra'fia** *sf* (*procedimento*) photography; (*immagine*) photograph; **fare una fotografia** to take a photograph; **una fotografia a colori/in bianco e nero** a colour/black and white photograph; **foto'grafico, -a, ci, che** *ag* photographic; **macchina fotografica** camera; **fo'tografo, -a** *sm/f* photographer; **fotoro'manzo** *sm* romantic picture story

fou'lard [fu'lar] *sm inv* scarf

fra *prep* = **tra**

'fradicio, -a, -ci, -ce ['fraditʃo] *ag* (*molto bagnato*) soaking (wet); **ubriaco ~** blind drunk

'fragile ['fradʒile] *ag* fragile; (*fig: salute*) delicate

'fragola *sf* strawberry

fra'grante *ag* fragrant

frain'tendere *vt* to misunderstand

fram'mento *sm* fragment

'frana *sf* landslide; (*fig: persona*): **essere una ~** to be useless

fran'cese [fran'tʃeze] *ag* French ▷ *sm/f* Frenchman/woman ▷ *sm* (*Ling*) French; **i Francesi** the French

'Francia ['frantʃa] *sf* **la ~** France

'franco, -a, -chi, -che *ag* (*Comm*) free; (*sincero*) frank, open, sincere ▷ *sm* (*moneta*) franc; **farla franca** (*fig*) to get off scot-free; **prezzo ~ fabbrica** ex-works price; **franco di dogana** duty-free

franco'bollo *sm* (*postage*) stamp

'frangia, -ge ['frandʒa] *sf* fringe

frap'pé *sm* milk shake

'frase *sf* (*Ling*) sentence; (*locuzione, espressione, Mus*) phrase; **frase fatta** set phrase

'frassino *sm* ash (tree)

frastagli'ato, -a [frastaʎ'ʎato] *ag* (*costa*) indented, jagged

frastor'nare *vt* to daze; to befuddle

frastu'ono *sm* hubbub, din

'frate *sm* friar, monk

fratel'lastro *sm* stepbrother; (*con genitore in comune*) half-brother

fra'tello *sm* brother; **fratelli** *smpl* brothers; (*nel senso di fratelli e sorelle*) brothers and sisters

fra'terno, -a *ag* fraternal, brotherly

frat'tempo *sm* **nel ~** in the meantime, meanwhile

frat'tura *sf* fracture; (*fig*) split, break

frazi'one [frat'tsjone] *sf* fraction; (*di comune*) small town

'freccia, -ce ['frettʃa] *sf* arrow; **freccia di direzione** (*Aut*) indicator

fred'dezza [fred'dettsa] *sf* coldness

'freddo, -a *ag, sm* cold; **fa ~** it's cold;

aver ~ to be cold; **a ~** (*fig*) deliberately; **freddo'loso, -a** *ag* sensitive to the cold

fre'gare *vt* to rub; (*fam: truffare*) to take in, cheat; (: *rubare*) to swipe, pinch; **fregarsene** (*fam!*): **chi se ne frega?** who gives a damn (about it)?

fregherò *ecc* [frege'rɔ] *vb vedi* **fregare**

fre'nare *vt* (*veicolo*) to slow down; (*cavallo*) to rein in; (*lacrime*) to restrain, hold back ▷ *vi* to brake; **frenarsi** *vpr* (*fig*) to restrain o s., control o s.

'freno *sm* brake; (*morso*) bit; **tenere a ~** to restrain; **freno a disco** disc brake; **freno a mano** handbrake

frequen'tare *vt* (*scuola, corso*) to attend; (*locale, bar*) to go to, frequent; (*persone*) to see (often)

frequen'tato, -a *ag* (*locale*) busy

fre'quente *ag* frequent; **di ~** frequently

fres'chezza [fres'kettsa] *sf* freshness

'fresco, -a, -schi, -sche *ag* fresh; (*temperatura*) cool; (*notizia*) recent, fresh ▷ *sm* **godere il ~** to enjoy the cool air; **stare ~** (*fig*) to be in for it; **mettere al ~** to put in a cool place

'fretta *sf* hurry, haste; **in ~** in a hurry; **in ~ e furia** in a mad rush; **aver ~** to be in a hurry

'friggere ['friddʒere] *vt* to fry ▷ *vi* (*olio ecc*) to sizzle

'frigido, -a ['fridʒido] *ag* (*Med*) frigid

'frigo *sm* fridge

frigo'bar *sm inv* minibar

frigo'rifero, -a *ag* refrigerating ▷ *sm* refrigerator

fringu'ello *sm* chaffinch

'frissi *ecc vb vedi* **friggere**

frit'tata *sf* omelette; **fare una ~** (*fig*) to make a mess of things

frit'tella *sf* (*Cuc*) fritter

'fritto, -a *pp di* **friggere** ▷ *ag* fried ▷ *sm* fried food; **fritto misto** mixed fry

frit'tura *sf* (*Cuc*): **frittura di pesce** mixed fried fish

'frivolo, -a *ag* frivolous

frizi'one [frit'tsjone] *sf* friction; (*sulla pelle*) rub, rub-down; (*Aut*) clutch

friz'zante [frid'dzante] *ag* (*anche fig*) sparkling

fro'dare *vt* to defraud, cheat

'frode *sf* fraud; **frode fiscale** tax evasion

'fronda *sf* (*leafy*) branch; (*di partito politico*) internal opposition; **fronde** *sfpl* (*di albero*) foliage *sg*

fron'tale *ag* frontal; (*scontro*) head-on

'fronte *sf* (*Anat*) forehead; (*di edificio*) front, façade ▷ *sm* (*Mil, Pol, Meteor*) front; **a ~, di ~** facing, opposite; **di ~ a** (*posizione*) opposite, facing, in front of; (*a paragone di*) compared with

fronti'era sf border, frontier

'frottola sf fib

fru'gare vi to rummage ▷ vt to search

frugherò ecc [fruge'rɔ] vb vedi **frugare**

frul'lare vt (Cuc) to whisk ▷ vi (uccelli) to flutter; **frul'lato** sm milk shake; fruit drink; **frulla'tore** sm electric mixer

fru'mento sm wheat

fru'scio [fruʃ'ʃio] sm rustle; rustling; (di acque) murmur

'frusta sf whip; (Cuc) whisk

frus'tare vt to whip

frus'trato, -a ag frustrated

'frutta sf fruit; (portata) dessert; **frutta candita** candied fruit; **frutta secca** dried fruit

frut'tare vi to bear dividends, give a return

frut'teto sm orchard

frutti'vendolo, -a sm/f greengrocer (BRIT), produce dealer (US)

'frutto sm fruit; (fig: risultato) result(s); (Econ: interesse) interest; (: reddito) income; **frutti di bosco** berries; **frutti di mare** seafood sg

FS abbr = **Ferrovie dello Stato**

fu vb vedi **essere** ▷ ag inv **il fu Paolo Bianchi** the late Paolo Bianchi

fuci'lare [futʃi'lare] vt to shoot

fu'cile [fu'tʃile] sm rifle, gun; (da caccia) shotgun, gun

'fucsia sf fuchsia

'fuga sf escape, flight; (di gas, liquidi) leak; (Mus) fugue; **fuga di cervelli** brain drain

fug'gire [fud'dʒire] vi to flee, run away; (fig: passar veloce) to fly ▷ vt to avoid

'fui vb vedi **essere**

fu'liggine [fu'liddʒine] sf soot

'fulmine sm thunderbolt; lightning no pl

fu'mare vi to smoke; (emettere vapore) to steam ▷ vt to smoke; **le dà fastidio se fumo?** do you mind if I smoke?; **fuma'tore, -'trice** sm/f smoker

fu'metto sm comic strip; **giornale** sm, **a fumetti** comic

'fummo vb vedi **essere**

'fumo sm smoke; (vapore) steam; (il fumare tabacco) smoking; **fumi** smpl (industriali ecc) fumes; **i fumi dell'alcool** the after-effects of drink; **vendere ~** to deceive, cheat; **fumo passivo** passive smoking

'fune sf rope, cord; (più grossa) cable

'funebre ag (rito) funeral; (aspetto) gloomy, funereal

fune'rale sm funeral

'fungere ['fundʒere] vi **~ da** to act as

'fungo, -ghi sm fungus; (commestibile) mushroom; **fungo velenoso** toadstool

funico'lare sf funicular railway

funi'via sf cable railway

'funsi ecc vb vedi **fungere**

funzio'nare [funtsjo'nare] vi to work, function; (fungere): **~ da** to act as; **come funziona?** how does this work?; **la TV non funziona** the TV isn't working

funzio'nario [funtsjo'narjo] sm official; **funzionario statale** civil servant

funzi'one [fun'tsjone] sf function; (carica) post, position; (Rel) service; **in ~** (meccanismo) in operation; **in ~ di** (come) as; **fare la ~ di qn** (farne le veci) to take sb's place

fu'oco, -chi sm fire; (fornello) ring; (Fot, Fisica) focus; **dare ~ a qc** to set fire to sth; **far ~** (sparare) to fire; **al ~!** fire!; **fuoco d'artificio** firework

fuorché [fwor'ke] cong, prep except

fu'ori av outside; (all'aperto) outdoors, outside; (fuori di casa, Sport) out; (esclamativo) get out! ▷ prep **~ (di)** out of, outside ▷ sm outside; **lasciar ~ qc/qn** to leave sth/sb out; **far ~ qn** (fam) to kill sb, do sb in; **essere ~ di sé** to be beside o.s.; **~ luogo** (inopportuno) out of place, uncalled for; **~ mano** out of the way, remote; **~ pericolo** out of danger; **~ uso** old-fashioned; obsolete; **fuorigi'oco** sm offside; **fuori'strada** sm (Aut) cross-country vehicle

'furbo, -a ag clever, smart; (peg) cunning

fu'rente ag **~ (contro)** furious (with)

fur'fante sm rascal, scoundrel

fur'gone sm van

'furia sf (ira) fury, rage; (fig: impeto) fury, violence; (fretta) rush; **a ~ di** by dint of; **andare su tutte le furie** to get into a towering rage; **furi'bondo, -a** ag furious

furi'oso, -a ag furious

'furono vb vedi **essere**

fur'tivo, -a ag furtive

'furto sm theft; **vorrei denunciare un ~** I'd like to report a theft; **furto con scasso** burglary

'fusa sfpl **fare le ~** to purr

fu'seaux smpl inv leggings

'fusi ecc vb vedi **fondere**

fu'sibile sm (Elettr) fuse

fusi'one sf (di metalli) fusion, melting; (colata) casting; (Comm) merger; (fig) merging

'fuso, -a pp di **fondere** ▷ sm (Filatura) spindle; **fuso orario** time zone

fus'tino sm (di detersivo) tub

'fusto sm stem; (Anat, di albero) trunk; (recipiente) drum, can

fu'turo, -a ag, sm future

'gabbia sf cage; (da imballaggio) crate; **gabbia dell'ascensore** lift (BRIT) o elevator (US) shaft; **gabbia toracica** (Anat) rib cage

gabbi'ano sm (sea)gull

gabi'netto sm (Med ecc) consulting room; (Pol) ministry; (WC) toilet, lavatory; (Ins: di fisica ecc) laboratory

'gaffe [gaf] sf inv blunder

ga'lante ag gallant, courteous; (avventura) amorous

ga'lassia sf galaxy

ga'lera sf (Naut) galley; (prigione) prison

'galla sf **a ~** afloat; **venire a ~** to surface, come to the surface; (fig: verità) to come out

galleggi'are [galled'dʒare] vi to float

galle'ria sf (traforo) tunnel; (Archit, d'arte) gallery; (Teatro) circle; (strada coperta con negozi) arcade

'Galles sm **il ~** Wales

gal'lina sf hen

'gallo sm cock

galop'pare vi to gallop

ga'loppo sm gallop; **al o di ~** at a gallop

'gamba sf leg; (asta: di lettera) stem; **in ~** (in buona salute) well; (bravo, sveglio) bright, smart; **prendere qc sotto ~** (fig) to treat sth too lightly

gambe'retto sm shrimp

'gambero sm (di acqua dolce) crayfish; (di mare) prawn

'gambo sm stem; (di frutta) stalk

'gamma sf (Mus) scale; (di colori, fig) range

'gancio ['gantʃo] sm hook

'gara sf competition; (Sport) competition; contest; match; (: corsa) race; **fare a ~** to compete, vie

ga'rage [ga'raʒ] sm inv garage

garan'tire vt to guarantee; (debito) to stand surety for; (dare per certo) to assure

garan'zia [garan'tsia] sf guarantee; (pegno) security

gar'bato, -a ag courteous, polite

gareggi'are [gared'dʒare] vi to compete

garga'rismo sm gargle; **fare i gargarismi** to gargle

ga'rofano sm carnation; **chiodo di ~** clove

'garza ['gardza] sf (per bende) gauze

gar'zone [gar'dzone] sm (di negozio) boy

gas sm inv gas; **sento odore di ~** I can smell gas; **a tutto ~** at full speed; **dare ~** (Aut) to accelerate

ga'solio sm diesel (oil)

gas'sato, -a ag fizzy

gast'rite sf gastritis

gastrono'mia sf gastronomy

gat'tino sm kitten

'gatto, -a sm/f cat, tomcat/she-cat; **gatto delle nevi** (Aut, Sci) snowcat; **gatto selvatico** wildcat

'gazza ['gaddza] sf magpie

gel [dʒɛl] sm inv gel

ge'lare [dʒe'lare] vt, vi, vb impers to freeze

gelate'ria [dʒelate'ria] sf ice-cream shop

gela'tina [dʒela'tina] sf gelatine; **gelatina esplosiva** dynamite; **gelatina di frutta** fruit jelly

ge'lato, -a [dʒe'lato] ag frozen ▷ sm ice cream

'gelido, -a ['dʒɛlido] ag icy, ice-cold

'gelo ['dʒɛlo] sm (temperatura) intense cold; (brina) frost; (fig) chill

gelo'sia [dʒelo'sia] sf jealousy

ge'loso, -a [dʒe'loso] ag jealous

'gelso ['dʒɛlso] sm mulberry (tree)

gelso'mino [dʒɛlso'mino] sm jasmine

ge'mello, -a [dʒe'mɛllo] ag, sm/f twin; **gemelli** smpl (di camicia) cufflinks; (dello zodiaco): **Gemelli** Gemini sg

'gemere ['dʒɛmere] vi to moan, groan; (cigolare) to creak

'gemma ['dʒɛmma] sf (Bot) bud; (pietra preziosa) gem

gene'rale [dʒene'rale] ag, sm general; **in ~** (per sommi capi) in general terms; (di solito) usually, in general

gene'rare [dʒene'rare] vt (dar vita) to give birth to; (produrre) to produce; (causare)

genere | 74

to arouse; (Tecn) to produce, generate; **generazi'one** sf generation

'genere ['dʒɛnere] sm kind, type, sort; (Biol) genus; (merce) article, product; (Ling) gender; (Arte, Letteratura) genre; **in ~** generally, as a rule; **genere umano** mankind; **generi alimentari** foodstuffs

ge'nerico, -a, -ci, -che [dʒe'nɛriko] ag generic; (vago) vague, imprecise

'genero ['dʒɛnero] sm son-in-law

gene'roso, -a [dʒene'roso] ag generous

ge'netica [dʒe'nɛtika] sf genetics sg

ge'netico, -a, -ci, -che [dʒe'nɛtiko] ag genetic

gen'giva [dʒen'dʒiva] sf (Anat) gum

geni'ale [dʒen'jale] ag (persona) of genius; (idea) ingenious, brilliant

'genio ['dʒɛnjo] sm genius; **andare a ~ a qn** to be to sb's liking, appeal to sb

geni'tore [dʒeni'tore] sm parent, father o mother; **i miei genitori** my parents, my father and mother

gen'naio [dʒen'najo] sm January

'Genova ['dʒɛnova] sf Genoa

'gente ['dʒɛnte] sf people pl

gen'tile [dʒen'tile] ag (persona, atto) kind; (: garbato) courteous, polite; (nelle lettere): **G~ Signore** Dear Sir; (: sulla busta): **G~ Signor Fernando Villa** Mr Fernando Villa

genu'ino, -a [dʒenu'ino] ag (prodotto) natural; (persona, sentimento) genuine, sincere

geogra'fia [dʒeogra'fia] sf geography

geolo'gia [dʒeolo'dʒia] sf geology

ge'ometra, -i, -e [dʒe'ɔmetra] sm/f (professionista) surveyor

geome'tria [dʒeome'tria] sf geometry

ge'ranio [dʒe'ranjo] sm geranium

gerar'chia [dʒerar'kia] sf hierarchy

'gergo, -ghi ['dʒɛrgo] sm jargon; slang

geria'tria [dʒerja'tria] sf geriatrics sg

Ger'mania [dʒer'manja] sf **la ~** Germany; **la ~ occidentale/orientale** West/East Germany

'germe ['dʒɛrme] sm germ; (fig) seed

germogli'are [dʒermoʎ'ʎare] vi to sprout; to germinate

gero'glifico, -ci [dʒero'glifiko] sm hieroglyphic

ge'rundio [dʒe'rundjo] sm gerund

'gesso ['dʒɛsso] sm chalk; (Scultura, Med, Edil) plaster; (statua) plaster figure; (minerale) gypsum

gesti'one [dʒes'tjone] sf management

ges'tire [dʒes'tire] vt to run, manage

'gesto ['dʒɛsto] sm gesture

Gesù [dʒe'zu] sm Jesus

gesu'ita, -i [dʒezu'ita] sm Jesuit

get'tare [dʒet'tare] vt to throw; (anche:

~ via) to throw away o out; (Scultura) to cast; (Edil) to lay; (acqua) to spout; (grido) to utter; **gettarsi** vpr **gettarsi in** (fiume) to flow into; **~ uno sguardo su** to take a quick look at

'getto ['dʒɛtto] sm (di gas, liquido, Aer) jet; **a ~ continuo** uninterruptedly; **di ~** (fig) straight off, in one go

get'tone [dʒet'tone] sm token; (per giochi) counter; (: roulette ecc) chip; **gettone telefonico** telephone token

ghiacci'aio [gjat'tʃajo] sm glacier

ghiacci'ato, -a ag frozen; (bevanda) ice-cold

ghi'accio ['gjattʃo] sm ice

ghiacci'olo [gjat'tʃɔlo] sm icicle; (tipo di gelato) ice lolly (BRIT), Popsicle® (US)

ghi'aia ['gjaja] sf gravel

ghi'anda ['gjanda] sf (Bot) acorn

ghi'andola ['gjandola] sf gland

ghi'otto, -a ['gjotto] ag greedy; (cibo) delicious, appetizing

ghir'landa [gir'landa] sf garland, wreath

'ghiro ['giro] sm dormouse

'ghisa ['giza] sf cast iron

già [dʒa] av already; (ex, in precedenza) formerly ▷ escl of course!, yes indeed!

gi'acca, -che ['dʒakka] sf jacket; **giacca a vento** windcheater (BRIT), windbreaker (US)

giacché [dʒak'ke] cong since, as

giac'cone [dʒak'kone] sm heavy jacket

gi'ada ['dʒada] sf jade

giagu'aro [dʒa'gwaro] sm jaguar

gi'allo ['dʒallo] ag yellow; (carnagione) sallow ▷ sm yellow; (anche: **romanzo ~**) detective novel; (anche: **film ~**) detective film; **giallo dell'uovo** yolk

Giamaica [dʒa'maika] sf **la ~** Jamaica

Giap'pone [dʒap'pone] sm Japan; **giappo'nese** ag, sm/f, sm Japanese inv

giardi'naggio [dʒardi'naddʒo] sm gardening

giardini'ere, -a [dʒardi'njɛre] sm/f gardener

giar'dino [dʒar'dino] sm garden; **giardino d'infanzia** nursery school; **giardino pubblico** public gardens pl, (public) park; **giardino zoologico** zoo

giavel'lotto [dʒavel'lɔtto] sm javelin

gigabyte [dʒiga'bait] sm inv gigabyte

gi'gante, -'essa [dʒi'gante] sm/f giant ▷ ag giant, gigantic; (Comm) giant-size

'giglio ['dʒiʎʎo] sm lily

gilè [dʒi'lɛ] sm inv waistcoat

gin [dʒin] sm inv gin

gine'cologo, -a, -gi, -ghe [dʒine'kɔlogo] sm/f gynaecologist

gi'nepro [dʒi'nepro] sm juniper

gi'nestra [dʒi'nɛstra] *sf* (*Bot*) broom

Gi'nevra [dʒi'nevra] *sf* Geneva

gin'nastica *sf* gymnastics *sg*; (*esercizio fisico*) keep-fit exercises; (*Ins*) physical education

gi'nocchio [dʒi'nɔkkjo] (*pl(m)* **gi'nocchi**, *o pl(f)* **gi'nocchia**) *sm* knee; **stare in ~** to kneel, be on one's knees; **mettersi in ~** to kneel (down)

gio'care [dʒo'kare] *vt* to play; (*scommettere*) to stake, wager, bet; (*ingannare*) to take in ▷ *vi* to play; (*a roulette ecc*) to gamble; (*fig*) to play a part, be important; **~ a** (*gioco, sport*) to play; (*cavalli*) to bet on; **giocarsi la carriera** to put one's career at risk; **gioca'tore, -'trice** *sm/f* player; gambler

gio'cattolo [dʒo'kattolo] *sm* toy

giocherò *ecc* [dʒoke'rɔ] *vb vedi* **giocare**

gi'oco, -chi ['dʒɔko] *sm* game; (*divertimento, Tecn*) play; (*al casinò*) gambling; (*Carte*) hand; (*insieme di pezzi ecc necessari per un gioco*) set; **per ~** for fun; **fare il doppio ~ con qn** to double-cross sb; **i Giochi Olimpici** the Olympic Games; **gioco d'azzardo** game of chance; **gioco degli scacchi** chess set

giocoli'ere [dʒoko'ljɛre] *sm* juggler

gi'oia ['dʒɔja] *sf* joy, delight; (*pietra preziosa*) jewel, precious stone

gioielle'ria [dʒojelle'ria] *sf* jeweller's craft; jeweller's (shop)

gioiell'iere, -a [dʒojel'ljɛre] *sm/f* jeweller

gioi'ello [dʒo'jɛllo] *sm* jewel, piece of jewellery; **i miei gioielli** my jewels *o* jewellery; **gioielli** *smpl* (*anelli, collane ecc*) jewellery; **i gioielli della Corona** the crown jewels

Gior'dania [dʒor'danja] *sf* **la ~** Jordan

giorna'laio, -a [dʒorna'lajo] *sm/f* newsagent (*BRIT*), newsdealer (*US*)

gior'nale [dʒor'nale] *sm* (*news*) paper; (*diario*) journal, diary; (*Comm*) journal; **giornale di bordo** log; **giornale radio** radio news *sg*

giornali'ero, -a [dʒorna'ljɛro] *ag* daily; (*che varia: umore*) changeable ▷ *sm* day labourer

giorna'lismo [dʒorna'lizmo] *sm* journalism

giorna'lista, -i, -e [dʒorna'lista] *sm/f* journalist

gior'nata [dʒor'nata] *sf* day; **giornata lavorativa** working day

gi'orno ['dʒorno] *sm* day; (*opposto alla notte*) day, daytime; (*anche: luce del ~*) daylight; **al ~** per day; **di ~** by day; **al ~ d'oggi** nowadays

gi'ostra ['dʒɔstra] *sf* (*per bimbi*) merry-go-round; (*torneo storico*) joust

gi'ovane ['dʒovane] *ag* young; (*aspetto*) youthful ▷ *sm/f* youth/girl, young man/ woman; **i giovani** young people

gio'vare [dʒo'vare] *vi* **~ a** (*essere utile*) to be useful to; (*far bene*) to be good for ▷ *vb impers* (*essere bene, utile*) to be useful; **giovarsi di qc** to make use of sth

giovedì [dʒove'di] *sm inv* Thursday; **di *o* il ~** on Thursdays

gioventù [dʒoven'tu] *sf* (*periodo*) youth; (*i giovani*) young people *pl*, youth

G.I.P. [dʒip] *sigla m inv* (= *Giudice per le Indagini Preliminari*) judge for preliminary enquiries

gira'dischi [dʒira'diski] *sm inv* record player

gi'raffa [dʒi'raffa] *sf* giraffe

gi'rare [dʒi'rare] *vt* (*far ruotare*) to turn; (*percorrere, visitare*) to go round; (*Cinema*) to shoot; to make; (*Comm*) to endorse ▷ *vi* to turn; (*più veloce*) to spin; (*andare in giro*) to wander, go around; **girarsi** *vpr* to turn; **~ attorno a** to go round; to revolve round; **al prossimo incrocio giri a destra/sinistra** turn right/left at the next junction; **far ~ la testa a qn** to make sb dizzy; (*fig*) to turn sb's head

girar'rosto [dʒirar'rɔsto] *sm* (*Cuc*) spit

gira'sole [dʒira'sole] *sm* sunflower

gi'revole [dʒi'revole] *ag* revolving, turning

gi'rino [dʒi'rino] *sm* tadpole

'giro ['dʒiro] *sm* (*circuito, cerchio*) circle; (*di chiave, manovella*) turn; (*viaggio*) tour, excursion; (*passeggiata*) stroll, walk; (*in macchina*) drive; (*in bicicletta*) ride; (*Sport: della pista*) lap; (*di denaro*) circulation; (*Carte*) hand; (*Tecn*) revolution; **prendere in ~ qn** (*fig*) to pull sb's leg; **fare un ~** to go for a walk (*o* a drive *o* a ride); **andare in ~** to go about, walk around; **a stretto ~ di posta** by return of post; **nel ~ di un mese** in a month's time; **essere nel ~** (*fig*) to belong to a circle (of friends); **giro d'affari** (*Comm*) turnover; **giro di parole** circumlocution; **giro di prova** (*Aut*) test drive; **giro turistico** sightseeing tour; **giro'collo** *sm* **a girocollo** crew-neck *cpd*

gironzo'lare [dʒirondzo'lare] *vi* to stroll about

'gita ['dʒita] *sf* excursion, trip; **fare una ~** to go for a trip, go on an outing

gi'tano, -a [dʒi'tano] *sm/f* gipsy

giù [dʒu] *av* down; (*dabbasso*) downstairs; **in ~** downwards, down; **~ di lì** (*pressappoco*) thereabouts; **bambini dai 6 anni in ~** children aged 6 and under; **~ per, cadere ~ per le scale** to fall down the stairs; **essere ~** (*fig: di salute*) to be run down; (: *di spirito*) to be depressed

giub'botto [dʒub'bɔtto] *sm* jerkin; **giubbotto antiproiettile** bulletproof vest; **giubbotto salvagente** life jacket

giudi'care [dʒudi'kare] *vt* to judge; *(accusato)* to try; *(lite)* to arbitrate in; ~ **qn/qc bello** to consider sb/sth (to be) beautiful

gi'udice ['dʒudit∫e] *sm* judge; **giudice conciliatore** justice of the peace; **giudice istruttore** examining (BRIT) *o* committing (US) magistrate; **giudice popolare** member of a jury

giu'dizio [dʒu'dittsjo] *sm* judgment; *(opinione)* opinion; *(Dir)* judgment, sentence; *(: processo)* trial; *(: verdetto)* verdict; **aver ~** to be wise *o* prudent; **citare in ~** to summons

gi'ugno ['dʒuɲɲo] *sm* June

gi'ungere ['dʒundʒere] *vi* to arrive ▷ *vt* *(mani ecc)* to join; ~ **a** to arrive at, reach

gi'ungla ['dʒungla] *sf* jungle

gi'unsi *ecc* ['dʒunsi] *vb vedi* **giungere**

giura'mento [dʒura'mento] *sm* oath; **giuramento falso** perjury

giu'rare [dʒu'rare] *vt* to swear ▷ *vi* to swear, take an oath

giu'ria [dʒu'ria] *sf* jury

giu'ridico, -a, -ci, -che [dʒu'ridiko] *ag* legal

giustifi'care [dʒustifi'kare] *vt* to justify; **giustificazi'one** *sf* justification; *(Ins)* (note of) excuse

gius'tizia [dʒus'tittsja] *sf* justice; **giustizi'are** *vt* to execute, put to death

gi'usto, -a ['dʒusto] *ag* *(equo)* fair, just; *(vero)* true, correct; *(adatto)* right, suitable; *(preciso)* exact, correct ▷ *av* *(esattamente)* exactly, precisely; *(per l'appunto, appena)* just; **arrivare ~** to arrive just in time; **ho ~ bisogno di te** you're just the person I need

glaci'ale [gla't∫ale] *ag* glacial

gli [ʎi] *(davV, s impura, gn, pn, ps, x, z) det mpl* the ▷ *pron* *(a lui)* to him; *(a esso)* to it; *(in coppia con lo, la, li, le, ne: a lui, a lei, a loro ecc)*: ~**ele do** I'm giving them to him *(o her o* them); *vedi anche* **il**

glo'bale *ag* overall

'globo *sm* globe

'globulo *sm* *(Anat)*: **globulo rosso/bianco** red/white corpuscle

'gloria *sf* glory

'gnocchi ['ɲɔkki] *smpl* *(Cuc)* small dumplings made of semolina pasta or potato

'gobba *sf* *(Anat)* hump; *(protuberanza)* bump

'gobbo, -a *ag* hunchbacked; *(ricurvo)* round-shouldered ▷ *sm/f* hunchback

'goccia, -ce ['gɔtt∫a] *sf* drop; **goccio'lare** *sf*

vi, vt to drip

go'dere *vi* *(compiacersi)*: ~ **(di)** to be delighted (at), rejoice (at); *(trarre vantaggio)*: ~ **di** benefit from ▷ *vt* to enjoy; **godersi la vita** to enjoy life; **godersela** to have a good time, enjoy o.s.

godrò *ecc vb vedi* **godere**

'goffo, -a *ag* clumsy, awkward

'gola *sf* *(Anat)* throat; *(golosità)* gluttony, greed; *(di camino)* flue; *(di monte)* gorge; **fare ~** *(anche fig)* to tempt

golf *sm inv* *(Sport)* golf; *(maglia)* cardigan

'golfo *sm* gulf

go'loso, -a *ag* greedy

gomi'tata *sf* **dare una ~ a qn** to elbow sb; **farsi avanti a (forza *o* furia di) gomitate** to elbow one's way through; **fare a gomitate per qc** to fight to get sth

'gomito *sm* elbow; *(di strada ecc)* sharp bend

go'mitolo *sm* ball

'gomma *sf* rubber; *(per cancellare)* rubber, eraser; *(di veicolo)* tyre (BRIT), tire (US); **gomma americana *o* da masticare** chewing gum; **gomma a terra** flat tyre (BRIT) *o* tire (US); **ho una ~ a terra** I've got a flat tyre; **gom'mone** *sm* rubber dinghy

gonfi'are *vt* *(pallone)* to blow up, inflate; *(dilatare, ingrossare)* to swell; *(fig: notizia)* to exaggerate; **gonfiarsi** *vpr* to swell; *(fiume)* to rise; **'gonfio, -a** *ag* swollen; *(stomaco)* bloated; *(vela)* full; **gonfi'ore** *sm* swelling

'gonna *sf* skirt; **gonna pantalone** culottes *pl*

'gorgo, -ghi *sm* whirlpool

gorgogli'are [gorgoʎ'ʎare] *vi* to gurgle

go'rilla *sm inv* gorilla; *(guardia del corpo)* bodyguard

'gotico, -a, ci, che *ag, sm* Gothic

'gotta *sf* gout

gover'nare *vt* *(stato)* to govern, rule; *(pilotare, guidare)* to steer; *(bestiame)* to tend, look after

go'verno *sm* government

GPL *sigla m* (= *Gas di Petrolio Liquefatto*) LPG

GPS *sigla m* (= *Global Positioning System*) GPS

graci'dare [grat∫i'dare] *vi* to croak

'gracile ['grat∫ile] *ag* frail, delicate

gradazi'one [gradat'tsjone] *sf* *(sfumatura)* gradation; **gradazione alcolica** alcoholic content, strength

gra'devole *ag* pleasant, agreeable

gradi'nata *sf* flight of steps; *(in teatro, stadio)* tiers *pl*

gra'dino *sm* step; *(Alpinismo)* foothold

gra'dire *vt* *(accettare con piacere)* to accept; *(desiderare)* to wish, like; **gradisce una tazza di tè?** would you like a cup of tea?

'grado *sm* *(Mat, Fisica ecc)* degree; *(stadio)*

degree, level; (*Mil, sociale*) rank; **essere in ~ di fare** to be in a position to do
gradu'ale *ag* gradual
graf'fetta *sf* paper clip
graffi'are *vt* to scratch; **graffiarsi** *vpr* to get scratched; (*con unghie*) to scratch o.s.
'graffio *sm* scratch
gra'fia *sf* spelling; (*scrittura*) handwriting
'grafico, -a, -ci, -che *ag* graphic ▷ *sm* graph; (*persona*) graphic designer
gram'matica, -che *sf* grammar
'grammo *sm* gram(me)
'grana *sf* (*granello, di minerali, corpi spezzati*) grain; (*fam: seccatura*) trouble; (: *soldi*) cash ▷ *sm inv* Parmesan (cheese)
gra'naio *sm* granary, barn
gra'nata *sf* (*proiettile*) grenade
Gran Bre'tagna [-bre'taɲɲa] *sf* **la ~** Great Britain
'granchio ['grankjo] *sm* crab; (*fig*) blunder; **prendere un ~** (*fig*) to blunder
'grande (*qualche volta* **gran** + *C,* **grand'** + *V*) *ag* (*grosso, largo, vasto*) big, large; (*alto*) tall; (*lungo*) long; (*in sensi astratti*) great ▷ *sm/f* (*persona adulta*) adult, grown-up; (*chi ha ingegno e potenza*) great man/woman; **fare le cose in ~** to do things in style; **una gran bella donna** a very beautiful woman; **non è una gran cosa** *o* **un gran che** it's nothing special; **non ne so gran che** I don't know very much about it
gran'dezza [gran'dettsa] *sf* (*dimensione*) size; magnitude; (*fig*) greatness; **in ~ naturale** life-size(d)
grandi'nare *vb impers* to hail
'grandine *sf* hail
gra'nello *sm* (*di cereali, uva*) seed; (*di frutta*) pip; (*di sabbia, sale ecc*) grain
gra'nito *sm* granite
'grano *sm* (*in quasi tutti i sensi*) grain; (*frumento*) wheat; (*di rosario, collana*) bead; **grano di pepe** peppercorn
gran'turco *sm* maize
'grappa *sf* rough, strong brandy
'grappolo *sm* bunch, cluster
gras'setto *sm* (*Tip*) bold (type)
'grasso, -a *ag* fat; (*cibo*) fatty; (*pelle*) greasy; (*terreno*) rich; (*fig: guadagno, annata*) plentiful ▷ *sm* (*di persona, animale*) fat; (*sostanza che unge*) grease
'grata *sf* grating
gra'ticola *sf* grill
'gratis *av* free, for nothing
grati'tudine *sf* gratitude
'grato, -a *ag* grateful; (*gradito*) pleasant, agreeable
gratta'capo *sm* worry, headache
grattaci'elo [gratta'tʃɛlo] *sm* skyscraper
gratta e vinci ['gratta e 'vintʃi] *sm*

inv (*biglietto*) scratchcard; (*lotteria*) scratchcard lottery
grat'tare *vt* (*pelle*) to scratch; (*raschiare*) to scrape; (*pane, formaggio, carote*) to grate; (*fam: rubare*) to pinch ▷ *vi* (*stridere*) to grate; (*Aut*) to grind; **grattarsi** *vpr* to scratch o.s.; **grattarsi la pancia** (*fig*) to twiddle one's thumbs
grat'tugia, -gie [grat'tudʒa] *sf* grater; **grattugi'are** *vt* to grate; **pane grattugiato** breadcrumbs *pl*
gra'tuito, -a *ag* free; (*fig*) gratuitous
'grave *ag* (*danno, pericolo, peccato ecc*) grave, serious; (*responsabilità*) heavy, grave; (*contegno*) grave, solemn; (*voce, suono*) deep, low-pitched; (*Ling*): **accento ~** grave accent; **un malato ~** a person who is seriously ill
grave'mente *av* (*ammalato, ferito*) seriously
gravi'danza [gravi'dantsa] *sf* pregnancy
gravità *sf* seriousness; (*anche Fisica*) gravity
gra'voso, -a *ag* heavy, onerous
'grazia ['grattsja] *sf* grace; (*favore*) favour; (*Dir*) pardon
'grazie ['grattsje] *escl* thank you!; **~ mille!** *o* **tante!** *o* **infinite!** thank you very much!; **~ a** thanks to
grazi'oso, -a [grat'tsjoso] *ag* charming, delightful; (*gentile*) gracious
'Grecia ['grɛtʃa] *sf* **la ~** Greece; **'greco, -a, -ci, -che** *ag, sm/f, sm* Greek
'gregge ['greddʒe] (*pl(f)* -**i**) *sm* flock
grem'biule *sm* apron; (*sopravveste*) overall
'grembo *sm* lap; (*ventre della madre*) womb
'grezzo, -a ['greddzo] *ag* raw, unrefined; (*diamante*) rough, uncut; (*tessuto*) unbleached
gri'dare *vi* (*per chiamare*) to shout, cry (out); (*strillare*) to scream, yell ▷ *vt* to shout (out), yell (out); **~ aiuto** to cry *o* shout for help
'grido (*pl(m)* -**i**, *o pl(f)* -**a**) *sm* shout, cry; scream, yell; (*di animale*) cry; **di ~** famous
'grigio, -a, -gi, -gie ['gridʒo] *ag, sm* grey
'griglia ['griʎʎa] *sf* (*per arrostire*) grill; (*Elettr*) grid; (*inferriata*) grating; **alla ~** (*Cuc*) grilled
gril'letto *sm* trigger
'grillo *sm* (*Zool*) cricket; (*fig*) whim
'grinta *sf* grim expression; (*Sport*) fighting spirit
gris'sino *sm* bread-stick
Groen'landia *sf* **la ~** Greenland
gron'daia *sf* gutter
gron'dare *vi* to pour; (*essere bagnato*): **~ di** to be dripping with ▷ *vt* to drip with
'groppa *sf* (*di animale*) back, rump; (*fam:*

dell'uomo) back, shoulders *pl*

gros'sezza [gros'settsa] *sf* size; thickness

gros'sista, -i, -e *sm/f* (*Comm*) wholesaler

'**grosso, -a** *ag* big, large; (*di spessore*) thick; (*grossolano: anche fig*) coarse; (*grave, insopportabile*) serious, great; (*tempo, mare*) rough ▷ *sm* **il ~ di** the bulk of; **un pezzo ~** (*fig*) a VIP, a bigwig; **farla grossa** to do something very stupid; **dirle grosse** to tell tall stories; **sbagliarsi di ~** to be completely wrong

'**grotta** *sf* cave; grotto

grot'tesco, -a, -schi, -sche *ag* grotesque

gro'viglio [gro'viʎʎo] *sm* tangle; (*fig*) muddle

gru *sf inv* crane

'**gruccia, -ce** ['gruttʃa] *sf* (*per camminare*) crutch; (*per abiti*) coat-hanger

'**grumo** *sm* (*di sangue*) clot; (*di farina ecc*) lump

'**gruppo** *sm* group; **gruppo sanguigno** blood group

GSM *sigla m* (= *Global System for Mobile Communication*) GSM

guada'gnare [gwada'ɲɲare] *vt* (*ottenere*) to gain; (*soldi, stipendio*) to earn; (*vincere*) to win; (*raggiungere*) to reach

gua'dagno [gwa'daɲɲo] *sm* earnings *pl*; (*Comm*) profit; (*vantaggio, utile*) advantage, gain; **guadagno lordo/netto** gross/net earnings *pl*

gu'ado *sm* ford; **passare a ~** to ford

gu'ai *escl* **~ a te (o lui ecc)!** woe betide you (*o him ecc*)!

gu'aio *sm* trouble, mishap; (*inconveniente*) trouble, snag

gua'ire *vi* to whine, yelp

gu'ancia, -ce ['gwantʃa] *sf* cheek

guanci'ale [gwan'tʃale] *sm* pillow

gu'anto *sm* glove

guarda'linee *sm inv* (*Sport*) linesman

guar'dare *vt* (*con lo sguardo: osservare*) to look at; (*film, televisione*) to watch; (*custodire*) to look after, take care of ▷ *vi* to look; (*badare*): **~ a** to pay attention to; (*luoghi: esser orientato*): **~ a** to face; **guardarsi** *vpr* to look at o.s.; **guardarsi da** (*astenersi*) to refrain from; (*stare in guardia*) to beware of; **guardarsi dal fare** to take care not to do; **guarda di non sbagliare** try not to make a mistake; **~ a vista qn** to keep a close watch on sb

guarda'roba *sm inv* wardrobe; (*locale*) cloakroom

gu'ardia *sf* (*individuo, corpo*) guard; (*sorveglianza*) watch; **fare la ~ a qc/qn** to guard sth/sb; **stare in ~** (*fig*) to be on one's guard; **di ~** (*medico*) on call; **guardia carceraria** (*prison*) warder; **guardia del**

corpo bodyguard; **Guardia di finanza** (*corpo*) customs *pl*; (*persona*) customs officer; **guardia medica** emergency doctor service

GUARDIA DI FINANZA

The **Guardia di Finanza** is a military body which deals with infringements of the laws governing income tax and monopolies. It reports to the Ministers of Finance, Justice or Agriculture, depending on the function it is performing.

guardi'ano, -a *sm/f* (*di carcere*) warder; (*di villa ecc*) caretaker; (*di museo*) custodian; (*di zoo*) keeper; **guardiano notturno** night watchman

guarigi'one [gwari'dʒone] *sf* recovery

gua'rire *vt* (*persona, malattia*) to cure; (*ferita*) to heal ▷ *vi* to recover, be cured; to heal (up)

guar'nire *vt* (*ornare: abiti*) to trim; (*Cuc*) to garnish

guasta'feste *sm/f inv* spoilsport

guastarsi *vpr* (*cibo*) to go bad; (*meccanismo*) to break down; (*tempo*) to change for the worse

gu'asto, -a *ag* (*non funzionante*) broken; (: *telefono ecc*) out of order; (*andato a male*) bad, rotten; (: *dente*) decayed, bad; (*fig: corrotto*) depraved ▷ *sm* breakdown; (*avaria*) failure; **guasto al motore** engine failure

gu'erra *sf* war; (*tecnica: atomica, chimica ecc*) warfare; **fare la ~ (a)** to wage war (against); **guerra mondiale** world war; **guerra preventiva** preventive war

'**gufo** *sm* owl

gu'ida *sf* (*libro*) guidebook; (*persona*) guide; (*comando, direzione*) guidance, direction; (*Aut*) driving; (*tappeto: di tenda, cassetto*) runner; **avete una ~ in italiano?** do you have a guidebook in Italian?; **c'è una ~ che parla italiano?** is there an Italian-speaking guide?; **guida a destra/a sinistra** (*Aut*) right-/left-hand drive; **guida telefonica** telephone directory; **guida turistica** tourist guide

gui'dare *vt* to guide; (*squadra, rivolta*) to lead; (*auto*) to drive; (*aereo, nave*) to pilot; **sai ~?** can you drive?; **guida'tore, -trice** *sm/f* (*conducente*) driver

guin'zaglio [gwin'tsaʎʎo] *sm* leash, lead

'**guscio** ['guʃʃo] *sm* shell

gus'tare *vt* (*cibi*) to taste; (: *assaporare con piacere*) to enjoy, savour; (*fig*) to enjoy, appreciate ▷ *vi*: **~ a** to please; **non mi**

gusta affatto I don't like it at all
'gusto sm taste; (sapore) flavour;
(godimento) enjoyment; **che gusti avete?**
which flavours do you have?; **al ~ di
fragola** strawberry-flavoured; **mangiare
di ~** to eat heartily; **prenderci ~: ci ha
preso ~** he's acquired a taste for it, he's
got to like it; **gus'toso, -a** ag tasty; (fig)
agreeable

H, h ['akka] sf o m inv (lettera) H, h ▷ abbr
(= ora) hr; (= etto, altezza) h; **H come hotel**
≈ H for Harry (BRIT), H for How (US)
ha, 'hai [a, ai] vb vedi **avere**
ha'cker [hæ'kəᵣ] sm inv hacker
hall [hɔl] sf inv hall, foyer
hamburger [am'burger] sm inv (carne)
hamburger; (panino) burger
'handicap ['handikap] sm inv handicap;
handicap'pato, -a ag handicapped ▷ sm/
f handicapped person, disabled person
'hanno ['anno] vb vedi **avere**
hard discount [ardi'kaunt] sm inv
discount supermarket
hard disk [ar'disk] sm inv hard disk
hardware ['ardwer] sm inv hardware
hascisch [aʃ'ʃiʃ] sm hashish
Hawaii [a'vai] sfpl **le ~** Hawaii sg
help [ɛlp] sm inv (Inform) help
'herpes ['ɛrpes] sm (Med) herpes sg; **herpes
zoster** shingles sg
'hi-fi ['haifai] sm inv, ag inv hi-fi
ho [ɔ] vb vedi **avere**
'hobby ['hɔbi] sm inv hobby
'hockey ['hɔki] sm hockey; **hockey su
ghiaccio** ice hockey
home page ['houm'pɛidʒ] sf inv home
page
Hong Kong ['ɔkɔg] sf Hong Kong
'hostess ['houstis] sf inv air hostess (BRIT)

o stewardess

hot dog ['hɔtdɔg] *sm inv* hot dog

ho'tel *sm inv* hotel

humour ['hjuːmə] *sm inv* (sense of) humour

'humus *sm* humus

husky ['aski] *sm inv* (*cane*) husky *m inv*

i *det mpl* the

IC *abbr* (= *Intercity*) Intercity

ICI ['itʃi] *sigla f* (= *Imposta Comunale sugli Immobili*) ≈ Council Tax

i'cona *sf* (*Rel, Inform, fig*) icon

i'dea *sf* idea; (*opinione*) opinion, view; (*ideale*) ideal; **dare l'~ di** to seem, look like; **neanche** *o* **neppure per ~!** certainly not!; **idea fissa** obsession

ide'ale *ag, sm* ideal

ide'are *vt* (*immaginare*) to think up, conceive; (*progettare*) to plan

i'dentico, -a, -ci, -che *ag* identical

identifi'care *vt* to identify; **identificarsi** *vpr* **identificarsi (con)** to identify o.s. (with)

identità *sf inv* identity

ideolo'gia, -'gie [ideolo'dʒia] *sf* ideology

idio'matico, -a, -ci, -che *ag* idiomatic; **frase idiomatica** idiom

idi'ota, -i, -e *ag* idiotic ▷ *sm/f* idiot

'idolo *sm* idol

idoneità *sf* suitability

i'doneo, -a *ag* **~ a** suitable for, fit for; (*Mil*) fit for; (*qualificato*) qualified for

i'drante *sm* hydrant

idra'tante *ag* moisturizing ▷ *sm* moisturizer

i'draulico, -a, -ci, -che *ag* hydraulic ▷ *sm* plumber

idroe'lettrico, -a, -ci, -che *ag*
hydroelectric

i'drofilo, -a *ag vedi* **cotone**

i'drogeno [i'drɔdʒeno] *sm* hydrogen

idrovo'lante *sm* seaplane

i'ena *sf* hyena

i'eri *av, sm* yesterday; **il giornale di ~**
yesterday's paper; **~ l'altro** the day before
yesterday; **~ sera** yesterday evening

igi'ene [i'dʒɛne] *sf* hygiene; **igiene
pubblica** public health; **igi'enico, -a, -ci,
-he** *ag* hygienic; (*salubre*) healthy

i'gnaro, -a [iɲ'ɲaro] *ag* **~ di** unaware of,
ignorant of

i'gnobile [iɲ'ɲɔbile] *ag* despicable, vile

igno'rante [iɲɲo'rante] *ag* ignorant

igno'rare [iɲɲo'rare] *vt* (*non sapere,
conoscere*) to be ignorant *o* unaware of,
not to know; (*fingere di non vedere, sentire*)
to ignore

i'gnoto, -a [iɲ'ɲɔto] *ag* unknown

 PAROLA CHIAVE

il (*pl*(*m*) **i**; *diventa* **lo** (*pl* **gli**) *davanti a s impura,
gn, pn, ps, x, z;* **l'** a (*pl* **le**)) *det m* **1** the; **il
libro/lo studente/l'acqua** the book/the
student/the water; **gli scolari** the pupils
2 (*astrazione*): **il coraggio/l'amore/la
giovinezza** courage/love/youth
3 (*tempo*): **il mattino/la sera** in the
morning/evening; **il venerdì** *ecc*
(*abitualmente*) on Fridays *ecc*; (*quel
giorno*) on (the) Friday *ecc*; **la settimana
prossima** next week
4 (*distributivo*) a, an; **2 euro il chilo/paio** 2
euros a *o* per kilo/pair
5 (*partitivo*) some, any; **hai messo lo
zucchero?** have you added sugar?; **hai
comprato il latte?** did you buy (some *o*
any) milk?
6 (*possesso*): **aprire gli occhi** to open one's
eyes; **rompersi la gamba** to break one's
leg; **avere i capelli neri/il naso rosso** to
have dark hair/a red nose
7 (*con nomi propri*): **il Petrarca** Petrarch; **il
Presidente Bush** President Bush; **dov'è la
Francesca?** where's Francesca?
8 (*con nomi geografici*): **il Tevere** the Tiber;
l'Italia Italy; **il Regno Unito** the United
Kingdom; **l'Everest** Everest

ille'gale *ag* illegal

illeg'gibile [illed'dʒibile] *ag* illegible

ille'gittimo, -a [ille'dʒittimo] *ag*
illegitimate

il'leso, -a *ag* unhurt, unharmed

illimi'tato, -a *ag* boundless; unlimited

ill.mo *abbr* = **illustrissimo**

il'ludere *vt* to deceive, delude; **illudersi**
vpr to deceive o s., delude o.s.

illumi'nare *vt* to light up, illuminate; (*fig*)
to enlighten; **illuminarsi** *vpr* to light up; **~
a giorno** to floodlight; **illuminazi'one** *sf*
lighting; illumination; floodlighting; (*fig*)
flash of inspiration

il'lusi *ecc vb vedi* **illudere**

illusi'one *sf* illusion; **farsi delle illusioni**
to delude o s.; **illusione ottica** optical
illusion

il'luso, -a *pp di* **illudere**

illus'trare *vt* to illustrate; **illustrazi'one**
sf illustration

il'lustre *ag* eminent, renowned;
illus'trissimo, -a *ag* (*negli indirizzi*) very
revered

imbal'laggio [imbal'laddʒo] *sm* packing
no pl

imbal'lare *vt* to pack; (*Aut*) to race

imbalsa'mare *vt* to embalm

imbambo'lato, -a *ag* (*sguardo*) vacant,
blank

imbaraz'zante [imbarat'tsante] *ag*
embarrassing, awkward

imbaraz'zare [imbarat'tsare] *vt* (*mettere
a disagio*) to embarrass; (*ostacolare
movimenti*) to hamper

imbaraz'zato, -a [imbarat'tsato] *ag*
embarrassed; **avere lo stomaco ~** to have
an upset stomach

imba'razzo [imba'rattso] *sm* (*disagio*)
embarrassment; (*perplessità*) puzzlement,
bewilderment; **imbarazzo di stomaco**
indigestion

imbar'care *vt* (*passeggeri*) to embark;
(*merci*) to load; **imbarcarsi** *vpr* **imbarcarsi
su** to board; **imbarcarsi per l'America** to
sail for America; **imbarcarsi in** (*fig: affare
ecc*) to embark on

imbarcazi'one [imbarkat'tsjone]
sf (small) boat, (small) craft *inv*;
imbarcazione di salvataggio lifeboat

im'barco, -chi *sm* embarkation; loading;
boarding; (*banchina*) landing stage

imbas'tire *vt* (*cucire*) to tack; (*fig:
abbozzare*) to sketch, outline

im'battersi *vpr* **~ in** (*incontrare*) to bump
o run into

imbat'tibile *ag* unbeatable, invincible

imbavagli'are [imbavaʎ'ʎare] *vt* to gag

imbe'cille [imbe'tʃille] *ag* idiotic ▷ *sm/f*
idiot; (*Med*) imbecile

imbian'care *vt* to whiten; (*muro*) to
whitewash ▷ *vi* to become *o* turn white

imbian'chino [imbjan'kino] *sm* (house)
painter, painter and decorator

imboc'care *vt* (*bambino*) to feed; (*entrare:
strada*) to enter, turn into

imbocca'tura sf mouth; (di strada, porto) entrance; (Mus, del morso) mouthpiece

imbos'cata sf ambush

imbottigli'are [imbottiʎ'ʎare] vt to bottle; (Naut) to blockade; (Mil) to hem in; **imbottigliarsi** vpr to be stuck in a traffic jam

imbot'tire vt to stuff; (giacca) to pad; **imbottirsi** vpr **imbottirsi di** (rimpinzarsi) to stuff o.s. with; **imbot'tito, -a** ag stuffed; (giacca) padded; **panino imbottito** filled roll

imbra'nato, -a ag clumsy, awkward ▷ sm/f clumsy person

imbrogli'are [imbroʎ'ʎare] vt to mix up; (fig: raggirare) to deceive, cheat; (: confondere) to confuse, mix up; **imbrogli'one, -a** sm/f cheat, swindler

imbronci'ato, -a ag sulky

imbu'care vt to post; **dove posso ~ queste cartoline?** where can I post these cards?

imbur'rare vt to butter

im'buto sm funnel

imi'tare vt to imitate; (riprodurre) to copy; (assomigliare) to look like

immagazzi'nare [immagaddzi'nare] vt to store

immagi'nare [immadʒi'nare] vt to imagine; (supporre) to suppose; (inventare) to invent; **s'immagini!** don't mention it!, not at all!; **imaginazi'one** sf imagination; (cosa immaginata) fancy

im'magine [im'madʒine] sf image; (rappresentazione grafica, mentale) picture

imman'cabile ag certain; unfailing

im'mane ag (smisurato) enormous; (spaventoso) terrible

immangi'abile [imman'dʒabile] ag inedible

immatrico'lare vt to register; **immatricolarsi** vpr (Ins) to matriculate, enrol

imma'turo, -a ag (frutto) unripe; (persona) immature; (prematuro) premature

immedesi'marsi vpr ~ **in** to identify with

immediata'mente av immediately, at once

immedi'ato, -a ag immediate

im'menso, -a ag immense

im'mergere [im'mɛrdʒere] vt to immerse, plunge; **immergersi** vpr to plunge; (sommergibile) to dive, submerge; (dedicarsi a): **immergersi in** to immerse o.s. in

immeri'tato, -a ag undeserved

immersi'one sf immersion; (di sommergibile) submersion, dive; (di palombaro) dive

im'mettere vt ~ **(in)** to introduce (into); ~ **dati in un computer** to enter data on a computer

immi'grato, -a sm/f immigrant

immi'nente ag imminent

immischiarsi vpr ~ **in** to interfere o meddle in

im'mobile ag motionless, still; **immobili'are** ag (Dir) property cpd

immon'dizia [immon'dittsja] sf dirt, filth; (spesso al pl: spazzatura, rifiuti) rubbish no pl, refuse no pl

immo'rale ag immoral

immor'tale ag immortal

im'mune ag (esente) exempt; (Med, Dir) immune

immu'tabile ag immutable; unchanging

impacchet'tare [impakket'tare] vt to pack up

impacci'ato, -a ag awkward, clumsy; (imbarazzato) embarrassed

im'pacco, -chi sm (Med) compress

impadro'nirsi vpr ~ **di** to seize, take possession of; (fig: apprendere a fondo) to master

impa'gabile ag priceless

impa'lato, -a ag (fig) stiff as a board

impalca'tura sf scaffolding

impalli'dire vi to turn pale; (fig) to fade

impa'nato, -a ag (Cuc) coated in breadcrumbs

impanta'narsi vpr to sink (in the mud); (fig) to get bogged down

impappi'narsi vpr to stammer, falter

impa'rare vt to learn

impar'tire vt to bestow, give

imparzi'ale [impar'tsjale] ag impartial, unbiased

impas'sibile ag impassive

impas'tare vt (pasta) to knead

impastic'carsi vpr to pop pills

im'pasto sm (l'impastare: di pane) kneading; (: di cemento) mixing; (pasta) dough; (anche fig) mixture

im'patto sm impact

impau'rire vt to scare, frighten ▷ vi (anche: **impaurirsi**) to become scared o frightened

impazi'ente [impat'tsjɛnte] ag impatient

impaz'zata [impat'tsata] sf **all'~** (precipitosamente) at breakneck speed

impaz'zire [impat'tsire] vi to go mad; ~ **per qn/qc** to be crazy about sb/sth

impec'cabile ag impeccable

impedi'mento sm obstacle, hindrance

impe'dire vt (vietare): ~ **a qn di fare** to prevent sb from doing; (ostruire) to obstruct; (*impacciare*) to hamper, hinder

impegnarsi *vpr* (*vincolarsi*): **~ a fare** to undertake to do; (*mettersi risolutamente*): **~ in qc** to devote o.s. to sth; **~ con qn** (*accordarsi*) to come to an agreement with sb

impegna'tivo, -a *ag* binding; (*lavoro*) demanding, exacting

impe'gnato, -a *ag* (*occupato*) busy; (*fig: romanzo, autore*) committed, engagé

im'pegno [im'peɲɲo] *sm* (*obbligo*) obligation; (*promessa*) promise, pledge; (*zelo*) diligence, zeal; (*compito, d'autore*) commitment

impel'lente *ag* pressing, urgent

impen'narsi *vpr* (*cavallo*) to rear up; (*Aer*) to nose up; (*fig*) to bridle

impensie'rire *vt* to worry; **impensierirsi** *vpr* to worry

impera'tivo, -a *ag, sm* imperative

impera'tore, -'trice *sm/f* emperor/ empress

imperdo'nabile *ag* unforgivable, unpardonable

imper'fetto, -a *ag* imperfect ▷ *sm* (*Ling*) imperfect (tense)

imperi'ale *ag* imperial

imperi'oso, -a *ag* (*persona*) imperious; (*motivo, esigenza*) urgent, pressing

imperme'abile *ag* waterproof ▷ *sm* raincoat

im'pero *sm* empire; (*forza, autorità*) rule, control

imperso'nale *ag* impersonal

imperso'nare *vt* to personify; (*Teatro*) to play, act (the part of)

imperter'rito, -a *ag* fearless, undaunted; impassive

imperti'nente *ag* impertinent

'impeto *sm* (*moto, forza*) force, impetus; (*assalto*) onslaught; (*fig: impulso*) impulse; (: *slancio*) transport; **con ~** energetically; vehemently

impet'tito, -a *ag* stiff, erect

impetu'oso, -a *ag* (*vento*) strong, raging; (*persona*) impetuous

impi'anto *sm* (*installazione*) installation; (*apparecchiature*) plant; (*sistema*) system; **impianto elettrico** wiring; **impianto di risalita** (*Sci*) ski lift; **impianto di riscaldamento** heating system; **impianto sportivo** sports complex

impic'care *vt* to hang; **impiccarsi** *vpr* to hang o.s.

impicci'arsi [impit'tʃarsi] *vpr* (*immischiarsi*): **~ (in)** to meddle (in); **impicciati degli affari tuoi!** mind your own business!

impicci'one, -a [impit'tʃone] *sm/f* busybody

impie'gare *vt* (*usare*) to use, employ; (*spendere: denaro, tempo*) to spend; (*investire*) to invest; **impie'gato, -a** *sm/f* employee

impi'ego, -ghi *sm* (*uso*) use; (*occupazione*) employment; (*posto di lavoro*) (regular) job, post; (*Econ*) investment

impieto'sire *vt* to move to pity; **impietosirsi** *vpr* to be moved to pity

impigli'arsi *vpr* to get caught up *o* entangled

impi'grirsi *vpr* to grow lazy

impli'care *vt* to imply; (*coinvolgere*) to involve

im'plicito, -a [im'plitʃito] *ag* implicit

implo'rare *vt* to implore; (*pietà ecc*) to beg for

impolve'rarsi *vpr* to get dusty

impo'nente *ag* imposing, impressive

im'pongo *ecc vb vedi* **imporre**

impo'nibile *ag* taxable ▷ *sm* taxable income

impopo'lare *ag* unpopular

im'porre *vt* to impose; (*costringere*) to force, make; (*far valere*) to impose, enforce; **imporsi** *vpr* (*persona*) to assert o.s.; (*cosa: rendersi necessario*) to become necessary; (*aver successo: moda, attore*) to become popular; **~ a qn di fare** to force sb to do, make sb do

impor'tante *ag* important; **impor'tanza** *sf* importance; **dare importanza a qc** to attach importance to sth; **darsi importanza** to give o.s. airs

impor'tare *vt* (*introdurre dall'estero*) to import ▷ *vi* to matter, be important ▷ *vb impers* (*essere necessario*) to be necessary; (*interessare*) to matter; **non importa!** it doesn't matter!; **non me ne importa!** I don't care!

im'porto *sm* (*total*) amount

importu'nare *vt* to bother

im'posi *ecc vb vedi* **imporre**

imposizi'one [impozit'tsjone] *sf* imposition; order, command; (*onere, imposta*) tax

imposses'sarsi *vpr* **~ di** to seize, take possession of

impos'sibile *ag* impossible; **fare l'~** to do one's utmost, do all one can

im'posta *sf* (*di finestra*) shutter; (*tassa*) tax; **imposta sul reddito** income tax; **imposta sul valore aggiunto** value added tax (*BRIT*), sales tax (*US*)

impos'tare *vt* (*imbucare*) to post; (*preparare*) to plan, set out; (*avviare*) to begin, start off; (*voce*) to pitch

impostazi'one [impostat'tsjone] *sf*
(*di lettera*) posting (BRIT); mailing (US);
(*di problema, questione*) formulation,
statement; (*di lavoro*) organization,
planning; (*di attività*) setting up; (*Mus:
di voce*) pitch; **impostazioni** *sfpl* (*di
computer*) settings

impo'tente *ag* weak, powerless; (*anche
Med*) impotent

imprati'cabile *ag* (*strada*) impassable;
(*campo da gioco*) unplayable

impre'care *vi* to curse, swear; **~ contro** to
hurl abuse at

imprecazi'one [imprekat'tsjone] *sf*
abuse, curse

impre'gnare [impreɲ'ɲare] *vt* **~ (di)**
(*imbevere*) to soak o impregnate (with);
(*riempire*) to fill (with)

imprendi'tore *sm* (*industriale*)
entrepreneur; (*appaltatore*) contractor;
piccolo ~ small businessman

im'presa *sf* (*iniziativa*) enterprise; (*azione*)
exploit; (*azienda*) firm, concern

impressio'nante *ag* impressive;
upsetting

impressio'nare *vt* to impress; (*turbare*) to
upset; (*Fot*) to expose; **impressionarsi** *vpr*
to be easily upset

impressi'one *sf* impression; (*fig:
sensazione*) sensation, feeling; (*stampa*)
printing; **fare ~** (*colpire*) to impress;
(*turbare*) to frighten, upset; **fare
buona/cattiva ~ a** to make a good/bad
impression on

impreve'dibile *ag* unforeseeable;
(*persona*) unpredictable

impre'visto, -a *ag* unexpected,
unforeseen ▷ *sm* unforeseen event; **salvo
imprevisti** unless anything unexpected
happens

imprigio'nare [impridʒo'nare] *vt* to
imprison

impro'babile *ag* improbable, unlikely

im'pronta *sf* imprint, impression, sign;
(*di piede, mano*) print; (*fig*) mark, stamp;
impronta digitale fingerprint

improvvisa'mente *av* suddenly;
unexpectedly

improvvi'sare *vt* to improvise

improv'viso, -a *ag* (*imprevisto*)
unexpected; (*subitaneo*) sudden; **all'~**
unexpectedly; suddenly

impru'dente *ag* unwise, rash

impu'gnare [impuɲ'ɲare] *vt* to grasp,
grip; (*Dir*) to contest

impul'sivo, -a *ag* impulsive

im'pulso *sm* impulse

impun'tarsi *vpr* to stop dead, refuse to
budge; (*fig*) to be obstinate

impu'tato, -a *sm/f* (*Dir*) accused,
defendant

 PAROLA CHIAVE

in (*in* + *il* = **nel**, *in* + *lo* = **nello**, *in* + *l'* = **nell'**, *in*
+ *la* = **nella**, *in* + *i* = **nei**, *in* + *gli* = **negli**, *in* + *le*
= **nelle**) *prep* **1** (*stato in luogo*) in; **vivere in
Italia/città** to live in Italy/town; **essere in
casa/ufficio** to be at home/the office; **se
fossi in te** if I were you

2 (*moto a luogo*) to; (: *dentro*) into; **andare
in Germania/città** to go to Germany/
town; **andare in ufficio** to go to the office;
entrare in macchina/casa to get into the
car/go into the house

3 (*tempo*) in; **nel 1989** in 1989; **in giugno/
estate** in June/summer

4 (*modo, maniera*) in; **in silenzio** in silence;
in abito da sera in evening dress; **in
guerra** at war; **in vacanza** on holiday;
Maria Bianchi in Rossi Maria Rossi née
Bianchi

5 (*mezzo*) by; **viaggiare in autobus/treno**
to travel by bus/train

6 (*materia*) made of; **in marmo** made of
marble, marble *cpd*; **una collana in oro** a
gold necklace

7 (*misura*) in; **siamo in quattro** there are
four of us; **in tutto** in all

8 (*fine*): **dare in dono** to give as a gift;
spende tutto in alcool he spends all his
money on drink; **in onore di** in honour of

inabi'tabile *ag* uninhabitable

inacces'sibile [inattʃes'sibile] *ag* (*luogo*)
inaccessible; (*persona*) unapproachable

inaccet'tabile [inattʃet'tabile] *ag*
unacceptable

ina'datto, -a *ag* **~ (a)** unsuitable o unfit
(for)

inadegu'ato, -a *ag* inadequate

inaffi'dabile *ag* unreliable

inami'dato, -a *ag* starched

inar'care *vt* (*schiena*) to arch; (*sopracciglia*)
to raise

inaspet'tato, -a *ag* unexpected

inas'prire *vt* (*disciplina*) to tighten up,
make harsher; (*carattere*) to embitter;
inasprirsi *vpr* to become harsher; to
become bitter; to become worse

inattac'cabile *ag* (*anche fig*) unassailable;
(*alibi*) cast-iron

inatten'dibile *ag* unreliable

inat'teso, -a *ag* unexpected

inattu'abile *ag* impracticable

inau'dito, -a *ag* unheard of

inaugu'rare *vt* to inaugurate, open;
(*monumento*) to unveil

inaugurazi'one [inaugurat'tsjone] *sf* inauguration; unveiling

incal'lito, -a *ag* calloused; (*fig*) hardened, inveterate; (: *insensibile*) hard

incande'scente [inkandeʃʃɛnte] *ag* incandescent, white-hot

incan'tare *vt* to enchant, bewitch; **incantarsi** *vpr* (*rimanere intontito*) to be spellbound; to be in a daze; (*meccanismo: bloccarsi*) to jam; **incan'tevole** *ag* charming, enchanting

in'canto *sm* spell, charm, enchantment; (*asta*) auction; **come per ~** as if by magic; **mettere all'~** to put up for auction

inca'pace [inka'patʃe] *ag* incapable

incarce'rare [inkartʃe'rare] *vt* to imprison

incari'care *vt* **~ qn di fare** to give sb the responsibility of doing; **incaricarsi di** to take care o charge of

in'carico, -chi *sm* task, job

incarta'mento *sm* dossier, file

incar'tare *vt* to wrap (in paper)

incas'sare *vt* (*merce*) to pack (in cases); (*gemma: incastonare*) to set; (*Econ: riscuotere*) to collect; (*Pugilato: colpi*) to take, stand up to; **in'casso** *sm* cashing, encashment; (*introito*) takings *pl*

incas'trare *vt* to fit in, insert; (*fig: intrappolare*) to catch; **incastrarsi** *vpr* (*combaciare*) to fit together; (*restare bloccato*) to become stuck

incate'nare *vt* to chain up

in'cauto, -a *ag* imprudent, rash

inca'vato, -a *ag* hollow; (*occhi*) sunken

incendi'are [intʃen'djare] *vt* to set fire to; **incendiarsi** *vpr* to catch fire, burst into flames

in'cendio [in'tʃendjo] *sm* fire

inceneri'tore [intʃeneri'tore] *sm* incinerator

in'censo [in'tʃenso] *sm* incense

incensu'rato, -a [intʃensu'rato] *ag* (*Dir*): **essere ~** to have a clean record

incenti'vare [intʃenti'vare] *vt* (*produzione, vendite*) to boost; (*persona*) to motivate

incen'tivo [intʃen'tivo] *sm* incentive

incepparsi *vpr* to jam

incer'tezza [intʃer'tettsa] *sf* uncertainty

in'certo, -a [in'tʃɛrto] *ag* uncertain; (*irresoluto*) undecided, hesitating ▷ *sm* uncertainty

in'cetta [in'tʃetta] *sf* buying up; **fare ~ di qc** to buy up sth

inchi'esta [in'kjesta] *sf* investigation, inquiry

inchinarsi *vpr* to bend down; (*per riverenza*) to bow; (: *donna*) to curtsy

inchio'dare [inkjo'dare] *vt* to nail (down); **~ la macchina** (*Aut*) to jam on the brakes

inchi'ostro [in'kjɔstro] *sm* ink; **inchiostro simpatico** invisible ink

inciam'pare [intʃam'pare] *vi* to trip, stumble

inci'dente [intʃi'dɛnte] *sm* accident; **ho avuto un ~** I've had an accident; **incidente automobilistico** o **d'auto** car accident; **incidente diplomatico** diplomatic incident

in'cidere [in'tʃidere] *vi* **~ su** to bear upon, affect ▷ *vt* (*tagliare incavando*) to cut into; (*Arte*) to engrave; to etch; (*canzone*) to record

in'cinta [in'tʃinta] *ag f* pregnant

incipri'are [intʃi'prjare] *vt* to powder

incipriarsi ▷ *vpr* to powder one's face

in'circa [in'tʃirka] *av* **all'~** more or less, very nearly

in'cisi *ecc* [in'tʃizi] *vb vedi* **incidere**

incisi'one [intʃi'zjone] *sf* cut; (*disegno*) engraving; etching; (*registrazione*) recording; (*Med*) incision

in'ciso, -a [in'tʃizo] *pp di* **incidere** ▷ *sm* **per ~** incidentally, by the way

inci'tare [intʃi'tare] *vt* to incite

inci'vile [intʃi'vile] *ag* uncivilized; (*villano*) impolite

incl. *abbr* (= *incluso*) encl.

incli'nare *vt* to tilt; **inclinarsi** *vpr* (*barca*) to list; (*aereo*) to bank

in'cludere *vt* to include; (*accludere*) to enclose; **in'cluso, -a** *pp di* **includere** ▷ *ag* included; enclosed

incoe'rente *ag* incoherent; (*contraddittorio*) inconsistent

in'cognita [in'koɲɲita] *sf* (*Mat, fig*) unknown quantity

in'cognito, -a [in'koɲɲito] *ag* unknown ▷ *sm* **in ~** incognito

incol'lare *vt* to glue, gum; (*unire con colla*) to stick together

inco'lore *ag* colourless

incol'pare *vt* **~ qn di** to charge sb with

in'colto, -a *ag* (*terreno*) uncultivated; (*trascurato: capelli*) neglected; (*persona*) uneducated

in'colume *ag* safe and sound, unhurt

incom'benza [inkom'bɛntsa] *sf* duty, task

in'combere *vi* (*sovrastare minacciando*): **~ su** to threaten, hang over

incominci'are [inkomin'tʃare] *vi, vt* to begin, start

incompe'tente *ag* incompetent

incompi'uto, -a *ag* unfinished, incomplete

incom'pleto, -a *ag* incomplete

incompren'sibile *ag* incomprehensible

inconce'pibile [inkontʃe'pibile] *ag*

inconceivable

inconcili'abile [inkontʃi'ljabile] *ag* irreconcilable

inconclu'dente *ag* inconclusive; (*persona*) ineffectual

incondizio'nato, -a [inkondittsjo'nato] *ag* unconditional

inconfon'dibile *ag* unmistakable

inconsa'pevole *ag* ~ **di** unaware of, ignorant of

in'conscio, -a, -sci, -sce [in'kɔnʃo] *ag* unconscious ▷ *sm* (*Psic*): **l'~** the unconscious

inconsis'tente *ag* insubstantial; unfounded

inconsu'eto, -a *ag* unusual

incon'trare *vt* to meet; (*difficoltà*) to meet with; **incontrarsi** *vpr* to meet

in'contro *av* ~ **a** (*verso*) towards ▷ *sm* meeting; (*Sport*) match; meeting; **incontro di calcio** football match

inconveni'ente *sm* drawback, snag

incoraggia'mento [inkoraddʒa'mento] *sm* encouragement

incoraggi'are [inkorad'dʒare] *vt* to encourage

incornici'are [inkorni'tʃare] *vt* to frame

incoro'nare *vt* to crown

in'correre *vi* ~ **in** to meet with, run into

incosci'ente [inkoʃ'ʃɛnte] *ag* (*inconscio*) unconscious; (*irresponsabile*) reckless, thoughtless

incre'dibile *ag* incredible, unbelievable

in'credulo, -a *ag* incredulous, disbelieving

incremen'tare *vt* to increase; (*dar sviluppo a*) to promote

incre'mento *sm* (*sviluppo*) development; (*aumento numerico*) increase, growth

incresci'oso, -a [inkreʃ'ʃoso] *ag* (*incidente ecc*) regrettable

incrimi'nare *vt* (*Dir*) to charge

incri'nare *vt* to crack; (*fig: rapporti, amicizia*) to cause to deteriorate; **incrinarsi** *vpr* to crack; to deteriorate

incroci'are [inkro'tʃare] *vt* to cross; (*incontrare*) to meet ▷ *vi* (*Naut, Aer*) to cruise; **incrociarsi** *vpr* (*strade*) to cross, intersect; (*persone, veicoli*) to pass each other; ~ **le braccia/le gambe** to fold one's arms/cross one's legs

in'crocio [in'krotʃo] *sm* (*anche Ferr*) crossing; (*di strade*) crossroads

incuba'trice [inkuba'tritʃe] *sf* incubator

'incubo *sm* nightmare

incu'rabile *ag* incurable

incu'rante *ag* ~ **(di)** heedless (of), careless (of)

incurio'sire *vt* to make curious; **incuriosirsi** *vpr* to become curious

incursi'one *sf* raid

incur'vare *vt* to bend, curve; **incurvarsi** *vpr* to bend, curve

incusto'dito, -a *ag* unguarded, unattended

in'cutere *vt* ~ **timore/rispetto a qn** to strike fear into sb/command sb's respect

'indaco *sm* indigo

indaffa'rato, -a *ag* busy

inda'gare *vt* to investigate

in'dagine [in'dadʒine] *sf* investigation, inquiry; (*ricerca*) research, study; **indagine di mercato** market survey

indebi'tarsi *vpr* to run o get into debt

indebo'lire *vt, vi* (*anche*: **indebolirsi**) to weaken

inde'cente [inde'tʃɛnte] *ag* indecent

inde'ciso, -a [inde'tʃizo] *ag* indecisive; (*irresoluto*) undecided

indefi'nito, -a *ag* (*anche Ling*) indefinite; (*impreciso, non determinato*) undefined

in'degno, -a [in'deɲɲo] *ag* (*atto*) shameful; (*persona*) unworthy

indemoni'ato, -a *ag* possessed (by the devil)

in'denne *ag* unhurt, uninjured

indenniz'zare [indennid'dzare] *vt* to compensate

indetermina'tivo, -a *ag* (*Ling*) indefinite

'India *sf* **l'~** India; **indi'ano, -a** *ag* Indian ▷ *sm/f* (*d'India*) Indian; (*d'America*) Native American, (American) Indian

indi'care *vt* (*mostrare*) to show, indicate; (*: col dito*) to point to, point out; (*consigliare*) to suggest, recommend; **indica'tivo, -a** *ag* indicative ▷ *sm* (*Ling*) indicative (mood); **indicazi'one** *sf* indication; (*informazione*) piece of information

'indice ['inditʃe] *sm* index; (*fig*) sign; (*dito*) index finger, forefinger; **indice di gradimento** (*Radio, TV*) popularity rating

indicherò *ecc* [indike'rɔ] *vb vedi* **indicare**

indi'cibile [indi'tʃibile] *ag* inexpressible

indietreggi'are [indietred'dʒare] *vi* to draw back, retreat

indi'etro *av* back; (*guardare*) behind, back; (*andare, cadere: anche*: **all'~**) backwards; **rimanere** ~ to be left behind; **essere** ~ (*col lavoro*) to be behind; (*orologio*) to be slow; **rimandare qc** ~ to send sth back

indi'feso, -a *ag* (*città ecc*) undefended; (*persona*) defenceless

indiffe'rente *ag* indifferent

in'digeno, -a [in'didʒeno] *ag* indigenous, native ▷ *sm/f* native

indigesti'one [indidʒes'tjone] *sf* indigestion

indi'gesto, -a [indi'dʒɛsto] *ag* indigestible

indi'gnare [indiɲ'ɲare] vt to fill with indignation; **indignarsi** vpr to get indignant

indimenti'cabile ag unforgettable

indipen'dente ag independent

in'dire vt (concorso) to announce; (elezioni) to call

indi'retto, -a ag indirect

indiriz'zare [indirit'tsare] vt (dirigere) to direct; (mandare) to send; (lettera) to address

indi'rizzo [indi'rittso] sm address; (direzione) direction; (avvio) trend, course; **il mio ~ è...** my address is ...

indis'creto, -a ag indiscreet

indis'cusso, -a ag unquestioned

indispen'sabile ag indispensable, essential

indispet'tire vt to irritate, annoy ▷ vi (anche: **indispettirsi**) to get irritated o annoyed

individu'ale ag individual

individu'are vt (dar forma distinta a) to characterize; (determinare) to locate; (riconoscere) to single out

indi'viduo sm individual

indizi'ato, -a ag suspected ▷ sm/f suspect

in'dizio [in'dittsjo] sm (segno) sign, indication; (Polizia) clue; (Dir) piece of evidence

'indole sf nature, character

indolen'zito, -a [indolen'tsito] ag stiff, aching; (intorpidito) numb

indo'lore ag painless

indo'mani sm **l'~** the next day, the following day

Indo'nesia sf **l'~** Indonesia

indos'sare vt (mettere indosso) to put on; (avere indosso) to have on; **indossa'tore, -'trice** sm/f model

indottri'nare vt to indoctrinate

indovi'nare vt (scoprire) to guess; (immaginare) to imagine, guess; (il futuro) to foretell; **indovi'nello** sm riddle

indubbia'mente av undoubtedly

in'dubbio, -a ag certain, undoubted

in'duco ecc vb vedi **indurre**

indugi'are [indu'dʒare] vi to take one's time, delay

in'dugio [in'dudʒo] sm (ritardo) delay; **senza ~** without delay

indul'gente [indul'dʒente] ag indulgent; (giudice) lenient

indu'mento sm article of clothing, garment

indu'rire vt to harden ▷ vi (anche: **indurirsi**) to harden, become hard

in'durre vt **~ qn a fare qc** to induce o persuade sb to do sth; **~ qn in errore** to mislead sb

in'dussi ecc vb vedi **indurre**

in'dustria sf industry; **industri'ale** ag industrial ▷ sm industrialist

inecce'pibile [inettʃe'pibile] ag unexceptionable

i'nedito, -a ag unpublished

ine'rente ag **~ a** concerning, regarding

i'nerme ag unarmed; defenceless

inerpi'carsi vpr **~ (su)** to clamber (up)

i'nerte ag inert; (inattivo) indolent, sluggish

ine'satto, -a ag (impreciso) inexact; (erroneo) incorrect; (Amm: non riscosso) uncollected

inesis'tente ag non-existent

inesperi'enza [inespe'rjentsa] sf inexperience

ines'perto, -a ag inexperienced

inevi'tabile ag inevitable

i'nezia [i'nettsja] sf trifle, thing of no importance

infagot'tare vt to bundle up, wrap up; **infagottarsi** vpr to wrap up

infal'libile ag infallible

infa'mante ag defamatory

in'fame ag infamous; (fig: cosa, compito) awful, dreadful

infan'gare vt to cover with mud; (fig: reputazione) to sully; **infangarsi** vpr to get covered in mud; to be sullied

infan'tile ag child cpd; childlike; (adulto, azione) childish; **letteratura ~** children's books pl

in'fanzia [in'fantsja] sf childhood; (bambini) children pl; **prima ~** babyhood, infancy

infari'nare vt to cover with (o sprinkle with o dip in) flour; **infarina'tura** sf (fig) smattering

in'farto sm (Med) heart attack

infasti'dire vt to annoy, irritate; **infastidirsi** vpr to get annoyed o irritated

infati'cabile ag tireless, untiring

in'fatti cong actually, as a matter of fact

> Attenzione! In inglese esiste l'espressione in fact che però vuol dire in effetti.

infatu'arsi vpr **~ di** to become infatuated with, fall for

infe'dele ag unfaithful

infe'lice [infe'litʃe] ag unhappy; (sfortunato) unlucky, unfortunate; (inopportuno) inopportune, ill-timed; (mal riuscito: lavoro) bad, poor

inferi'ore ag lower; (per intelligenza, qualità) inferior ▷ sm/f inferior; **~ a** (numero, quantità) less o smaller than;

(*meno buono*) inferior to; **~ alla media** below average; **inferiorità** *sf* inferiority
inferme'ria *sf* infirmary; (*di scuola, nave*) sick bay
infermi'ere, -a *sm/f* nurse
infermità *sf inv* illness; infirmity; **infermità mentale** mental illness; (*Dir*) insanity
in'fermo, -a *ag* (*ammalato*) ill; (*debole*) infirm
infer'nale *ag* infernal; (*proposito, complotto*) diabolical
in'ferno *sm* hell
inferri'ata *sf* grating
infes'tare *vt* to infest
infet'tare *vt* to infect; **infettarsi** *vpr* to become infected; **infezi'one** *sf* infection
infiam'mabile *ag* inflammable
infiam'mare *vt* to set alight; (*fig, Med*) to inflame; **infiammarsi** *vpr* to catch fire; (*Med*) to become inflamed; **infiammazi'one** *sf* (*Med*) inflammation
infie'rire *vi* **~ su** (*fisicamente*) to attack furiously; (*verbalmente*) to rage at
infi'lare *vt* (*ago*) to thread; (*mettere: chiave*) to insert; (: *anello, vestito*) to slip o put on; (*strada*) to turn into, take; **infilarsi** *vpr* **infilarsi in** to slip into; (*indossare*) to slip on; **~ l'uscio** to slip in; to slip out
infil'trarsi *vpr* to penetrate, seep through; (*Mil*) to infiltrate
infil'zare [infil'tsare] *vt* (*infilare*) to string together; (*trafiggere*) to pierce
'infimo, -a *ag* lowest
in'fine *av* finally; (*insomma*) in short
infinità *sf* infinity; (*in quantità*): **un'~ di** an infinite number of
infi'nito, -a *ag* infinite; (*Ling*) infinitive ▷ *sm* infinity; (*Ling*) infinitive; **all'~** (*senza fine*) endlessly
infinocchi'are [infinok'kjare] (*fam*) *vt* to hoodwink
infischi'arsi [infis'kjarsi] *vpr* **~ di** not to care about
in'fisso, -a (*pp*) *di* **infiggere** *sm* fixture; (*di porta, finestra*) frame
inflazi'one [inflat'tsjone] *sf* inflation
in'fliggere [in'fliddʒere] *vt* to inflict
in'flissi *ecc vb vedi* **infliggere**
influ'ente *ag* influential; **influ'enza** *sf* influence; (*Med*) influenza, flu
influen'zare [influen'tsare] *vt* to influence, have an influence on
influ'ire *vi* **~ su** to influence
in'flusso *sm* influence
infon'dato, -a *ag* unfounded, groundless
in'fondere *vt* **~ qc in qn** to instill sth in sb
infor'mare *vt* to inform, tell; **informarsi**

vpr **informarsi (di** o **su)** to inquire (about)
infor'matica *sf* computer science
informa'tivo, -a *ag* informative
infor'mato, -a *ag* informed; **tenersi ~** to keep o.s. (well-)informed
informa'tore *sm* informer
informazi'one [informat'tsjone] *sf* piece of information; **prendere informazioni sul conto di qn** to get information about sb; **chiedere un'~** to ask for (some) information
in'forme *ag* shapeless
informico'larsi *vpr* to have pins and needles
infortu'nato, -a *ag* injured, hurt ▷ *sm/f* injured person
infor'tunio *sm* accident; **infortunio sul lavoro** industrial accident, accident at work
infra'dito *sm inv* (*calzatura*) flip flop (BRIT), thong (US)
infrazi'one [infrat'tsjone] *sf* **~ a** breaking of, violation of
infredda'tura *sf* slight cold
infreddo'lito, -a *ag* cold, chilled
infu'ori *av* out; **all'~** outwards; **all'~ di** (*eccetto*) except, with the exception of
infuri'arsi *vpr* to fly into a rage
infusi'one *sf* infusion
in'fuso, -a *pp di* **infondere** ▷ *sm* infusion
Ing. *abbr* = **ingegnere**
ingaggi'are [ingad'dʒare] *vt* (*assumere con compenso*) to take on, hire; (*Sport*) to sign on; (*Mil*) to engage
ingan'nare *vt* to deceive; (*fisco*) to cheat; (*eludere*) to dodge, elude; (*fig: tempo*) to while away ▷ *vi* (*apparenza*) to be deceptive; **ingannarsi** *vpr* to be mistaken, be wrong
in'ganno *sm* deceit, deception; (*azione*) trick; (*menzogna, frode*) cheat, swindle; (*illusione*) illusion
inge'gnarsi [indʒeɲ'ɲarsi] *vpr* to do one's best, try hard; **~ per vivere** to live by one's wits
inge'gnere [indʒeɲ'ɲɛre] *sm* engineer; **~ civile/navale** civil/naval engineer; **ingegne'ria** *sf* engineering; **ingegnere genetica** genetic engineering
in'gegno [in'dʒeɲɲo] *sm* (*intelligenza*) intelligence, brains *pl*; (*capacità creativa*) ingenuity; (*disposizione*) talent; **inge'gnoso, -a** *ag* ingenious, clever
ingelo'sire [indʒelo'zire] *vt* to make jealous ▷ *vi* (*anche*: **ingelosirsi**) to become jealous
in'gente [in'dʒɛnte] *ag* huge, enormous
ingenuità [indʒenui'ta] *sf* ingenuousness

in'genuo, -a [in'dʒɛnuo] *ag* naïve
▪ Attenzione! In inglese esiste la parola *ingenious*, che però significa *ingegnoso*.

inge'rire [indʒe'rire] *vt* to ingest

inges'sare [indʒes'sare] *vt* (*Med*) to put in plaster; **ingessa'tura** *sf* plaster

Inghil'terra [ingil'tɛrra] *sf* l'~ England

inghiot'tire [ingjot'tire] *vt* to swallow

ingial'lire [indʒal'lire] *vi* to go yellow

inginocchi'arsi [indʒinok'kjarsi] *vpr* to kneel (down)

ingiù [in'dʒu] *av* down, downwards

ingi'uria [in'dʒurja] *sf* insult; (*fig: danno*) damage

ingius'tizia [indʒus'tittsja] *sf* injustice

ingi'usto, -a [in'dʒusto] *ag* unjust, unfair

in'glese *ag* English ▷ *sm/f* Englishman/ woman ▷ *sm* (*Ling*) English; **gli Inglesi** the English; **andarsene** o **filare all'~** to take French leave

ingoi'are *vt* to gulp (down); (*fig*) to swallow (up)

ingol'farsi *vpr* to flood

ingom'brante *ag* cumbersome

ingom'brare *vt* (*strada*) to block; (*stanza*) to clutter up

in'gordo, -a *ag* ~ **di** greedy for; (*fig*) greedy o avid for

in'gorgo, -ghi *sm* blockage, obstruction; (*anche*: ~ **stradale**) traffic jam

ingoz'zarsi *vpr* ~ (**di**) to stuff o s. (with)

ingra'naggio [ingra'naddʒo] *sm* (*Tecn*) gear; (*di orologio*) mechanism; **gli ingranaggi della burocrazia** the bureaucratic machinery

ingra'nare *vi* to mesh, engage ▷ *vt* to engage; ~ **la marcia** to get into gear

ingrandi'mento *sm* enlargement; extension

ingran'dire *vt* (*anche Fot*) to enlarge; (*estendere*) to extend; (*Ottica, fig*) to magnify ▷ *vi* (*anche*: **ingrandirsi**) to become larger o bigger; (*aumentare*) to grow, increase; (*espandersi*) to expand

ingras'sare *vt* to make fat; (*animali*) to fatten; (*lubrificare*) to oil, lubricate ▷ *vi* (*anche*: **ingrassarsi**) to get fat, put on weight

in'grato, -a *ag* ungrateful; (*lavoro*) thankless, unrewarding

ingredi'ente *sm* ingredient

in'gresso *sm* (*porta*) entrance; (*atrio*) hall; (*l'entrare*) entrance, entry; (*facoltà di entrare*) admission; **ingresso libero** admission free

ingros'sare *vt* to increase; (*folla, livello*) to swell ▷ *vi* (*anche*: **ingrossarsi**) to increase; to swell

in'grosso *av* **all'~** (*Comm*) wholesale;

(*all'incirca*) roughly, about

ingua'ribile *ag* incurable

'inguine *sm* (*Anat*) groin

ini'bire *vt* to forbid, prohibit; (*Psic*) to inhibit; **inibirsi** *vpr* to restrain o s.

ini'bito, -a *ag* inhibited ▷ *sm/f* inhibited person

iniet'tare *vt* to inject; **iniezi'one** *sf* injection

ininterrotta'mente *av* non-stop, continuously

ininter'rotto, -a *ag* unbroken; uninterrupted

inizi'ale [init'tsjale] *ag, sf* initial

inizi'are [init'tsjare] *vi, vt* to begin, start; **a che ora inizia il film?** when does the film start?; ~ **qn a** to initiate sb into; (*pittura ecc*) to introduce sb to; ~ **a fare qc** to start doing sth

inizia'tiva [inittsja'tiva] *sf* initiative; **iniziativa privata** private enterprise

i'nizio [i'nittsjo] *sm* beginning; **all'~** at the beginning, at the start; **dare ~ a qc** to start sth, get sth going

innaffi'are *ecc* = **annaffiare** *ecc*

innamo'rarsi *vpr* ~ (**di qn**) to fall in love (with sb); **innamo'rato, -a** *ag* (*che nutre amore*): **innamorato** (**di**) in love (with); (*appassionato*): **innamorato di** very fond of ▷ *sm/f* lover; sweetheart

innanzi'tutto *av* first of all

in'nato, -a *ag* innate

innatu'rale *ag* unnatural

inne'gabile *ag* undeniable

innervo'sire *vt* ~ **qn** to get on sb's nerves; **innervosirsi** *vpr* to get irritated o upset

innes'care *vt* to prime

'inno *sm* hymn; **inno nazionale** national anthem

inno'cente [inno'tʃɛnte] *ag* innocent

in'nocuo, -a *ag* innocuous, harmless

innova'tivo, -a *ag* innovative

innume'revole *ag* innumerable

inol'trare *vt* (*Amm*) to pass on, forward

i'noltre *av* besides, moreover

inon'dare *vt* to flood

inoppor'tuno, -a *ag* untimely, ill-timed; inappropriate; (*momento*) inopportune

inorri'dire *vt* to horrify ▷ *vi* to be horrified

inosser'vato, -a *ag* (*non notato*) unobserved; (*non rispettato*) not observed, not kept

inossi'dabile *ag* stainless

INPS *sigla m* (= *Istituto Nazionale Previdenza Sociale*) social security service

inqua'drare *vt* (*foto, immagine*) to frame; (*fig*) to situate, set

inqui'eto, -a *ag* restless; (*preoccupato*) worried, anxious

inqui'lino, -a sm/f tenant

inquina'mento sm pollution

inqui'nare vt to pollute

insabbi'are vt (fig: pratica) to shelve; **insabbiarsi** vpr (arenarsi: barca) to run aground; (fig: pratica) to be shelved

insac'cati smpl (Cuc) sausages

insa'lata sf salad; **insalata mista** mixed salad; **insalata russa** (Cuc) Russian salad (comprised of cold diced cooked vegetables in mayonnaise); **insalati'era** sf salad bowl

insa'nabile ag (piaga) which cannot be healed; (situazione) irremediable; (odio) implacable

insa'puta sf **all'~ di qn** without sb knowing

inse'diarsi vpr to take up office; (popolo, colonia) to settle

in'segna [in'seɲɲa] sf sign; (emblema) sign, emblem; (bandiera) flag, banner

insegna'mento [inseɲɲa'mento] sm teaching

inse'gnante [inseɲ'ɲante] ag teaching ▷ sm/f teacher

inse'gnare [inseɲ'ɲare] vt, vi to teach; **~ a qn qc** to teach sb sth; **~ a qn a fare qc** to teach sb (how) to do sth

insegui'mento sm pursuit, chase

insegu'ire vt to pursue, chase

insena'tura sf inlet, creek

insen'sato, -a ag senseless, stupid

insen'sibile ag (nervo) insensible; (persona) indifferent

inse'rire vt to insert; (Elettr) to connect; (allegare) to enclose; (annuncio) to put in, place; **inserirsi** vpr (fig): **inserirsi in** to become part of

inservi'ente sm/f attendant

inserzi'one [inser'tsjone] sf insertion; (avviso) advertisement; **fare un'~ sul giornale** to put an advertisement in the paper

insetti'cida, -i [insetti'tʃida] sm insecticide

in'setto sm insect

insi'curo, -a ag insecure

insi'eme av together ▷ prep **~ a o con** together with ▷ sm whole; (Mat, servizio, assortimento) set; (Moda) ensemble, outfit; **tutti ~** all together; **tutto ~** all together; (in una volta) at one go; **nell'~** on the whole; **d'~** (veduta ecc) overall

in'signe [in'siɲɲe] ag (persona) famous, distinguished; (città, monumento) notable

insignifi'cante [insiɲɲifi'kante] ag insignificant

insinu'are vt (introdurre): **~ qc in** to slip o slide sth into; (fig) to insinuate, imply; **insinuarsi** vpr **insinuarsi in** to seep into;

(fig) to creep into; to worm one's way into

in'sipido, -a ag insipid

insis'tente ag insistent; persistent

in'sistere vi **~ su qc** to insist on sth; **~ in qc/a fare** (perseverare) to persist in sth/in doing

insoddis'fatto, -a ag dissatisfied

insoffe'rente ag intolerant

insolazi'one [insolat'tsjone] sf (Med) sunstroke

inso'lente ag insolent

in'solito, -a ag unusual, out of the ordinary

inso'luto, -a ag (non risolto) unsolved

in'somma av (in conclusione) in short; (dunque) well ▷ escl for heaven's sake!

in'sonne ag sleepless; **in'sonnia** sf insomnia, sleeplessness

insonno'lito, -a ag sleepy, drowsy

insoppor'tabile ag unbearable

in'sorgere [in'sordʒere] vi (ribellarsi) to rise up, rebel; (apparire) to come up, arise

in'sorsi ecc vb vedi **insorgere**

insospet'tire vt to make suspicious ▷ vi (anche: **insospettirsi**) to become suspicious

inspi'rare vt to breathe in, inhale

in'stabile ag (carico, indole) unstable; (tempo) unsettled; (equilibrio) unsteady

instal'lare vt to install

instan'cabile ag untiring, indefatigable

instau'rare vt to introduce, institute

insuc'cesso [insut'tʃesso] sm failure, flop

insuffici'ente [insuffi'tʃente] ag insufficient; (compito, allievo) inadequate; **insuffici'enza** sf insufficiency; inadequacy; (Ins) fail; **insufficienza di prove** (Dir) lack of evidence; **insufficienza renale** renal insufficiency

insu'lina sf insulin

in'sulso, -a ag (sciocco) inane, silly; (persona) dull, insipid

insul'tare vt to insult, affront

in'sulto sm insult, affront

intac'care vt (fare tacche) to cut into; (corrodere) to corrode; (fig: cominciare ad usare: risparmi) to break into; (: ledere) to damage

intagli'are [intaʎ'ʎare] vt to carve

in'tanto av (nel frattempo) meanwhile, in the meantime; (per cominciare) just to begin with; **~ che** while

inta'sare vt to choke (up), block (up); (Aut) to obstruct, block; **intasarsi** vpr to become choked o blocked

intas'care vt to pocket

in'tatto, -a ag intact; (puro) unsullied

intavo'lare vt to start, enter into

inte'grale ag complete; (pane, farina)

wholemeal (BRIT), whole-wheat (US);
(Mat): **calcolo ~** integral calculus

inte'grante ag **parte ~** integral part

inte'grare vt to complete; (Mat) to
integrate; **integrarsi** vpr (persona) to
become integrated

integra'tore sm **integratori alimentari**
nutritional supplements

integrità sf integrity

'integro, -a ag (intatto, intero) complete,
whole; (retto) upright

intelaia'tura sf frame; (fig) structure,
framework

intel'letto sm intellect; **intellettu'ale** ag,
sm/f intellectual

intelli'gente [intelli'dʒɛnte] ag
intelligent

intem'perie sfpl bad weather sg

in'tendere vt (avere intenzione): **~ fare qc**
to intend o mean to do sth; (comprendere)
to understand; (udire) to hear; (significare)
to mean; **intendersi** vpr (conoscere):
intendersi di to know a lot about, be
a connoisseur of; (accordarsi) to get on
(well); **intendersela con qn** (avere una
relazione amorosa) to have an affair with sb;
intendi'tore, -'trice sm/f connoisseur,
expert

inten'sivo, -a ag intensive

in'tenso, -a ag intense

in'tento, -a ag (teso, assorto): **~ (a)** intent
(on), absorbed (in) ▷ sm aim, purpose

intenzio'nale [intentsjo'nale] ag
intentional

intenzi'one [inten'tsjone] sf intention;
(Dir) intent; **avere ~ di fare qc** to intend to
do sth, have the intention of doing sth

interat'tivo, -a ag interactive

intercet'tare [intertʃet'tare] vt to
intercept

intercity [ɪntəsɪ'ti] sm inv (Ferr) ≈ intercity
(train)

inter'detto, -a pp di **interdire** ▷ ag
forbidden, prohibited; (sconcertato)
dumbfounded ▷ sm (Rel) interdict

interes'sante ag interesting; **essere in
stato ~** to be expecting (a baby)

interes'sare vt to interest; (concernere) to
concern, be of interest to; (far intervenire):
~ qn a to draw sb's attention to ▷ vi **~ a**
to interest, matter to; **interessarsi** vpr
(mostrare interesse): **interessarsi a** to take
an interest in, be interested in; (occuparsi):
interessarsi di to take care of

inte'resse sm (anche Comm) interest

inter'faccia, -ce [inter'fattʃa] sf (Inform)
interface

interfe'renza [interfe'rɛntsa] sf
interference

interfe'rire vi to interfere

interiezi'one [interjet'tsjone] sf
exclamation, interjection

interi'ora sfpl entrails

interi'ore ag interior, inner, inside,
internal; (fig) inner

inter'medio, -a ag intermediate

inter'nare vt (arrestare) to intern; (Med) to
commit (to a mental institution)

inter'nauta sm/f Internet user

internazio'nale [internattsjo'nale] ag
international

'Internet ['internet] sf Internet; **in ~** on
the Internet

in'terno, -a ag (di dentro) internal,
interior, inner; (: mare) inland; (nazionale)
domestic; (allievo) boarding ▷ sm inside,
interior; (di paese) interior; (fodera) lining;
(di appartamento) flat (number); (Tel)
extension ▷ sm/f (Ins) boarder; **interni**
smpl (Cinema) interior shots; **all'~** inside;
Ministero degli Interni Ministry of the
Interior, ≈ Home Office (BRIT), Department
of the Interior (US)

in'tero, -a ag (integro, intatto) whole,
entire; (completo, totale) complete;
(numero) whole; (non ridotto: biglietto) full;
(latte) full-cream

interpel'lare vt to consult

interpre'tare vt to interpret; **in'terprete**
sm/f interpreter; (Teatro) actor/actress,
performer; (Mus) performer; **ci potrebbe
fare da interprete?** could you act as an
interpreter for us?

interregio'nale [interredʒo'nale] sm
train that travels between two or more regions
of Italy, stopping frequently

interro'gare vt to question; (Ins) to test;
interrogazi'one sf questioning no pl; (Ins)
oral test

inter'rompere vt to interrupt; (studi,
trattative) to break off, interrupt;
interrompersi vpr to break off, stop

interrut'tore sm switch

interruzi'one [interrut'tsjone] sf
interruption; break

interur'bana sf trunk o long-distance call

inter'vallo sm interval; (spazio) space, gap

interve'nire vi (partecipare): **~ a** to
take part in; (intromettersi: anche Pol)
to intervene; (Med: operare) to operate;
inter'vento sm participation;
(intromissione) intervention; (Med)
operation; **fare un intervento nel corso
di** (dibattito, programma) to take part in

inter'vista sf interview; **intervis'tare** vt
to interview

intes'tare vt (lettera) to address;
(proprietà): **~ a** to register in the name of;

~ un assegno a qn to make out a cheque to sb
intestato, -a ag (proprietà, casa, conto) in the name of; (assegno) made out to; **carta intestata** headed paper
intes'tino sm (Anat) intestine
intimidazi'one [intimidat'tsjone] sf intimidation
intimi'dire vt to intimidate ▷ vi (intimidirsi) to grow shy
intimità sf intimacy; privacy; (familiarità) familiarity
'**intimo, -a** ag intimate; (affetti, vita) private; (fig: profondo) inmost ▷ sm (persona) intimate o close friend; (dell'animo) bottom, depths pl; **parti intime** (Anat) private parts
in'tingolo sm sauce; (pietanza) stew
intito'lare vt to give a title to; (dedicare) to dedicate; **intitolarsi** vpr (libro, film) to be called
intolle'rabile ag intolerable
intolle'rante ag intolerant
in'tonaco, -ci o **chi** sm plaster
into'nare vt (canto) to start to sing; (armonizzare) to match; **intonarsi** vpr (colori) to go together; **intonarsi a** (carnagione) to suit; (abito) to go with, match
inton'tito, -a ag stunned, dazed; **~ dal sonno** stupid with sleep
in'toppo sm stumbling block, obstacle
in'torno av around; **~ a** (attorno a) around; (riguardo, circa) about
intossi'care vt to poison; **intossicazi'one** sf poisoning
intralci'are [intral'tʃare] vt to hamper, hold up
intransi'tivo, -a ag, sm intransitive
intrapren'dente ag enterprising, go-ahead
intra'prendere vt to undertake
intrat'tabile ag intractable
intratte'nere vt to entertain; to engage in conversation; **intrattenersi** vpr to linger; **intrattenersi su qc** to dwell on sth
intrave'dere vt to catch a glimpse of; (fig) to foresee
intrecci'are [intret'tʃare] vt (capelli) to plait, braid; (intessere: anche fig) to weave, interweave, intertwine
intri'gante ag scheming ▷ sm/f schemer, intriguer
in'trinseco, -a, -ci, -che ag intrinsic
in'triso, -a ag **~ (di)** soaked (in)
intro'durre vt to introduce; (chiave ecc): **~ qc in** to insert sth into; (persone: far entrare) to show in; **introdursi** vpr (moda, tecniche) to be introduced; **introdursi in** (persona:

penetrare) to enter; (: entrare furtivamente) to steal o slip into; **introduzi'one** sf introduction
in'troito sm income, revenue
intro'mettersi vpr to interfere, meddle; (interporsi) to intervene
in'truglio [in'truʎʎo] sm concoction
intrusi'one sf intrusion; interference
in'truso, -a sm/f intruder
intu'ire vt to perceive by intuition; (rendersi conto) to realize; **in'tuito** sm intuition; (perspicacia) perspicacity
inu'mano, -a ag inhuman
inumi'dire vt to dampen, moisten; **inumidirsi** vpr to become damp o wet
i'nutile ag useless; (superfluo) pointless, unnecessary
inutil'mente av unnecessarily; (senza risultato) in vain
inva'dente ag (fig) interfering, nosey
in'vadere vt to invade; (affollare) to swarm into, overrun; (acque) to flood
inva'ghirsi [inva'girsi] vpr **~ di** to take a fancy to
invalidità sf infirmity; disability; (Dir) invalidity
in'valido, -a ag (infermo) infirm, invalid; (al lavoro) disabled; (Dir: nullo) invalid ▷ sm/f invalid; disabled person
in'vano av in vain
invasi'one sf invasion
inva'sore, invadi'trice [invadi'tritʃe] ag invading ▷ sm invader
invecchi'are [invek'kjare] vi (persona) to grow old; (vino, popolazione) to age; (moda) to become dated ▷ vt to age; (far apparire più vecchio) to make look older
in'vece [in'vetʃe] av instead; (al contrario) on the contrary; **~ di** instead of
inve'ire vi **~ contro** to rail against
inven'tare vt to invent; (pericoli, pettegolezzi) to make up, invent
inven'tario sm inventory; (Comm) stocktaking no pl
inven'tore sm inventor
invenzi'one [inven'tsjone] sf invention; (bugia) lie, story
inver'nale ag winter cpd; (simile all'inverno) wintry
in'verno sm winter
invero'simile ag unlikely
inversi'one sf inversion; reversal; "**divieto d'~**" (Aut) "no U-turns"
in'verso, -a ag opposite; (Mat) inverse ▷ sm contrary, opposite; **in senso ~** in the opposite direction; **in ordine ~** in reverse order
inver'tire vt to invert, reverse; **~ la marcia** (Aut) to do a U-turn

investi'gare *vt, vi* to investigate; **investiga'tore, -'trice** *sm/f* investigator, detective; **investigatore privato** private investigator

investi'mento *sm* (*Econ*) investment

inves'tire *vt* (*denaro*) to invest; (*veicolo: pedone*) to knock down; (: *altro veicolo*) to crash into; (*apostrofare*) to assail; (*incaricare*): **~ qn di** to invest sb with

invi'are *vt* to send; **invi'ato, -a** *sm/f* envoy; (*Stampa*) correspondent; **inviato speciale** (*Pol*) special envoy; (*di giornale*) special correspondent

in'vidia *sf* envy; **invidi'are** *vt* **invidiare qn (per qc)** to envy sb for sth; **invidiare qc a qn** to envy sb sth; **invidi'oso, -a** *ag* envious

in'vio, -'vii *sm* sending; (*insieme di merci*) consignment; (*tasto*) Return (key), Enter (key)

invipe'rito, -a *ag* furious

invi'sibile *ag* invisible

invi'tare *vt* to invite; **~ qn a fare** to invite sb to do; **invi'tato, -a** *sm/f* guest; **in'vito** *sm* invitation

invo'care *vt* (*chiedere: aiuto, pace*) to cry out for; (*appellarsi: la legge, Dio*) to appeal to, invoke

invogli'are [invoʎ'ʎare] *vt* **~ qn a fare** to tempt sb to do, induce sb to do

involon'tario, -a *ag* (*errore*) unintentional; (*gesto*) involuntary

invol'tino *sm* (*Cuc*) roulade

in'volto *sm* (*pacco*) parcel; (*fagotto*) bundle

in'volucro *sm* cover, wrapping

inzup'pare [intsup'pare] *vt* to soak; **inzupparsi** *vpr* to get soaked

'io *pron* I ▷ *sm inv* **I'~** the ego, the self; **~ stesso(a)** I myself

i'odio *sm* iodine

I'onio *sm* **Io ~, il mar ~** the Ionian (Sea)

ipermer'cato *sm* hypermarket

ipertensi'one *sf* high blood pressure, hypertension

iper'testo *sm* hypertext

ip'nosi *sf* hypnosis; **ipnotiz'zare** *vt* to hypnotize

ipocri'sia *sf* hypocrisy

i'pocrita, -i, -e *ag* hypocritical ▷ *sm/f* hypocrite

ipo'teca, -che *sf* mortgage

i'potesi *sf inv* hypothesis

'ippica *sf* horseracing

'ippico, -a, -ci, -che *ag* horse *cpd*

ippocas'tano *sm* horse chestnut

ip'podromo *sm* racecourse

ippo'potamo *sm* hippopotamus

'ipsilon *sf o m inv* (*lettera*) Y, y; (: *dell'alfabeto greco*) epsilon

IR *abbr* (= *Interregionale*) long distance train which stops frequently

ira'cheno, -a [ira'kɛno] *ag, sm/f* Iraqi

I'ran *sm* **I'~** Iran

irani'ano, -a *ag, sm/f* Iranian

I'raq *sm* **I'~** Iraq

'iride *sf* (*arcobaleno*) rainbow; (*Anat, Bot*) iris

'iris *sm inv* iris

Ir'landa *sf* **I'~** Ireland; **I'~ del Nord** Northern Ireland, Ulster; **la Repubblica d'~** Eire, the Republic of Ireland; **irlan'dese** *ag* Irish ▷ *sm/f* Irishman/woman; **gli Irlandesi** the Irish

iro'nia *sf* irony; **i'ronico, -a, -ci, -che** *ag* ironic(al)

irragio'nevole [irradʒo'nevole] *ag* irrational; unreasonable

irrazio'nale [irrattsjo'nale] *ag* irrational

irre'ale *ag* unreal

irrego'lare *ag* irregular; (*terreno*) uneven

irremo'vibile *ag* (*fig*) unshakeable, unyielding

irrequi'eto, -a *ag* restless

irresis'tibile *ag* irresistible

irrespon'sabile *ag* irresponsible

irri'gare *vt* (*annaffiare*) to irrigate; (*fiume ecc*) to flow through

irrigi'dire [irridʒi'dire] *vt* to stiffen; **irrigidirsi** *vpr* to stiffen

irri'sorio, -a *ag* derisory

irri'tare *vt* (*mettere di malumore*) to irritate, annoy; (*Med*) to irritate; **irritarsi** *vpr* (*stizzirsi*) to become irritated *o* annoyed; (*Med*) to become irritated

ir'rompere *vi* **~ in** to burst into

irru'ente *ag* (*fig*) impetuous, violent

ir'ruppi *ecc vb vedi* **irrompere**

irruzi'one [irrut'tsjone] *sf* **fare ~ in** to burst into; (*polizia*) to raid

is'crissi *ecc vb vedi* **iscrivere**

is'critto, -a *pp di* **iscrivere** ▷ *sm/f* member; **per o in ~** in writing

is'crivere *vt* to register, enter; (*persona*): **~ (a)** to register (in), enrol (in); **iscriversi** *vpr* **iscriversi (a)** (*club, partito*) to join; (*università*) to register *o* enrol (at); (*esame, concorso*) to register *o* enter (for); **iscrizi'one** *sf* (*epigrafe ecc*) inscription; (*a scuola, società*) enrolment, registration; (*registrazione*) registration

Is'lam *sm* **I'~** Islam

Is'landa *sf* **I'~** Iceland

islan'dese *ag* Icelandic ▷ *sm/f* Icelander ▷ *sm* (*Ling*) Icelandic

'isola *sf* island; **isola pedonale** (*Aut*) pedestrian precinct

isola'mento *sm* isolation; (*Tecn*) insulation

iso'lante *ag* insulating ▷ *sm* insulator

iso'lare vt to isolate; (Tecn) to insulate; (: acusticamente) to soundproof; **isolarsi** vpr to isolate o.s.; **iso'lato, -a** ag isolated; insulated ▷ sm (gruppo di edifici) block

ispet'tore sm inspector

ispezio'nare [ispettsjo'nare] vt to inspect

'ispido, -a ag bristly, shaggy

ispi'rare vt to inspire

Isra'ele sm I'~ Israel; **israeli'ano, -a** ag, sm/f Israeli

is'sare vt to hoist

istan'taneo, -a ag instantaneous ▷ sf (Fot) snapshot

is'tante sm instant, moment; **all'~, sull'~** instantly, immediately

is'terico, -a, -ci, -che ag hysterical

isti'gare vt to incite

is'tinto sm instinct

istitu'ire vt (fondare) to institute, found; (porre: confronto) to establish; (intraprendere: inchiesta) to set up

isti'tuto sm institute; (di università) department; (ente, Dir) institution; **istituto di bellezza** beauty salon; **istituto di credito** bank, banking institution; **istituto di ricerca** research institute

istituzi'one [istitut'tsjone] sf institution

'istmo sm (Geo) isthmus

'istrice ['istritʃe] sm porcupine

istru'ito, -a ag educated

istrut'tore, -'trice sm/f instructor ▷ ag **giudice ~** vedi **giudice**

istruzi'one sf education; training; (direttiva) instruction; **istruzioni** sfpl (norme) instructions; **istruzioni per l'uso** instructions for use; **~ obbligatoria** (Scol) compulsory education

l'talia sf I'~ Italy

itali'ano, -a ag Italian ▷ sm/f Italian ▷ sm (Ling) Italian; **gli italiani** the Italians

itine'rario sm itinerary

'ittico, -a, -ci, -che ag fish cpd; fishing cpd

Iugos'lavia = **Jugoslavia**

IVA ['iva] sigla f (= imposta sul valore aggiunto) VAT

J

jazz [dʒaz] sm jazz

jeans [dʒinz] smpl jeans

jeep® [dʒip] sm inv jeep

'jogging ['dʒɔgiŋ] sm jogging; **fare ~** to go jogging

'jolly ['dʒɔli] sm inv joker

joystick [dʒois'tik] sm inv joystick

ju'do [dʒu'dɔ] sm judo

Jugos'lavia [jugoz'lavja] sf (Storia): **la ~** Yugoslavia; **la ex-~** former Yugoslavia; **jugos'lavo, -a** ag, sm/f (Storia) Yugoslav(ian)

K l

K, k ['kappa] *sf o m inv* (lettera) K, k ▷ *abbr*
  (= *kilo-, chilo-*) k; (*Inform*) K; **K come**
  Kursaal ≈ K for King
kamikaze [kami'kaddze] *sm inv* kamikaze
karaoke [ka'raoke] *sm inv* karaoke
karatè *sm* karate
ka'yak [ka'jak] *sm inv* kayak
Kenia ['kɛnja] *sm* il ~ Kenya
kg *abbr* (= *chilogrammo*) kg
'killer *sm inv* gunman, hired gun
kitsch [kitʃ] *sm* kitsch
'kiwi ['kiwi] *sm inv* kiwi fruit
km *abbr* (= *chilometro*) km
K.O. [kappa'o] *sm inv* knockout
ko'ala [ko'ala] *sm inv* koala (bear)
koso'varo, -a [koso'varo] *ag, sm/f*
  Kosovan
Ko'sovo *sm* Kosovo
'krapfen *sm inv* (*Cuc*) doughnut
Kuwait [ku'vait] *sm* il ~ Kuwait

l' *det vedi* **la; lo; il**
la (*dav V* **l'**) *det f* the ▷ *pron* (*oggetto: persona*)
  her; (: *cosa*) it; (: *forma di cortesia*) you; *vedi*
  anche **il**
là *av* there; **di là** (*da quel luogo*) from there;
  (*in quel luogo*) in there; (*dall'altra parte*)
  over there; **di là di** beyond; **per di là** that
  way; **più in là** further on; (*tempo*) later
  on; **fatti in là** move up; **là dentro/**
  sopra/sotto in/up (*o* on)/under there;
  vedi anche **quello**
'labbro (*pl(f)* **labbra**) (*solo nel senso Anat*)
  sm lip
labi'rinto *sm* labyrinth, maze
labora'torio *sm* (*di ricerca*) laboratory;
  (*di arti, mestieri*) workshop; **laboratorio**
  linguistico language laboratory
labori'oso, -a *ag* (*faticoso*) laborious;
  (*attivo*) hard-working
'lacca, -che *sf* lacquer
'laccio ['lattʃo] *sm* noose; (*legaccio, tirante*)
  lasso; (*di scarpa*) lace; **laccio emostatico**
  tourniquet
lace'rare [latʃe'rare] *vt* to tear to shreds,
  lacerate; **lacerarsi** *vpr* to tear
'lacrima *sf* tear; **in lacrime** in tears;
  lacri'mogeno, -a *ag* **gas lacrimogeno**
  tear gas
la'cuna *sf* (*fig*) gap
'ladro *sm* thief

laggiù [lad'dʒu] *av* down there; (*di là*) over there

la'gnarsi [laɲ'ɲarsi] *vpr* ~ **(di)** to complain (about)

'lago, -ghi *sm* lake

la'guna *sf* lagoon

'laico, -a, -ci, -che *ag* (*apostolato*) lay; (*vita*) secular; (*scuola*) non-denominational ▷ *sm/f* layman/woman

'lama *sm inv* (Zool) llama; (Rel) lama ▷ *sf* blade

lamentarsi *vpr* (*emettere lamenti*) to moan, groan; (*rammaricarsi*) ~ **(di)** to complain (about)

lamen'tela *sf* complaining *no pl*

la'metta *sf* razor blade

'lamina *sf* (*lastra sottile*) thin sheet (*o* layer *o* plate); **lamina d'oro** gold leaf; gold foil

'lampada *sf* lamp; **lampada a gas** gas lamp; **lampada da tavolo** table lamp

lampa'dario *sm* chandelier

lampa'dina *sf* light bulb; **lampadina tascabile** pocket torch (BRIT) *o* flashlight (US)

lam'pante *ag* (*fig: evidente*) crystal clear, evident

lampeggi'are [lamped'dʒare] *vi* (*luce, fari*) to flash ▷ *vb impers* **lampeggia** there's lightning; **lampeggia'tore** *sm* (Aut) indicator

lampi'one *sm* street light *o* lamp (BRIT)

'lampo *sm* (Meteor) flash of lightning; (*di luce: fig*) flash

lam'pone *sm* raspberry

'lana *sf* wool; **pura ~ vergine** pure new wool; **lana d'acciaio** steel wool; **lana di vetro** glass wool

lan'cetta [lan'tʃetta] *sf* (*indice*) pointer, needle; (*di orologio*) hand

'lancia [ˈlantʃa] *sf* (*arma*) lance; (: *picca*) spear; (*di pompa antincendio*) nozzle; (*imbarcazione*) launch; **lancia di salvataggio** lifeboat

lanciafi'amme [lantʃaˈfjamme] *sm inv* flamethrower

lanci'are [lan'tʃare] *vt* to throw, hurl, fling; (Sport) to throw; (*far partire: automobile*) to get up to full speed; (*bombe*) to drop; (*razzo, prodotto, moda*) to launch; **lanciarsi** *vpr* **lanciarsi contro/su** to throw *o* hurl *o* fling o.s. against/on; **lanciarsi in** (*fig*) to embark on

lanci'nante [lantʃiˈnante] *ag* (*dolore*) shooting, throbbing; (*grido*) piercing

'lancio [ˈlantʃo] *sm* throwing *no pl*; throw; dropping *no pl*; drop; launching *no pl*; launch; **lancio del disco** (Sport) throwing the discus; **lancio del peso** putting the shot

'languido, -a *ag* (*fiacco*) languid, weak; (*tenero, malinconico*) languishing

lan'terna *sf* lantern; (*faro*) lighthouse

'lapide *sf* (*di sepolcro*) tombstone; (*commemorativa*) plaque

'lapsus *sm inv* slip

'lardo *sm* bacon fat, lard

lar'ghezza [larˈgettsa] *sf* width; breadth; looseness; generosity; **larghezza di vedute** broad-mindedness

'largo, -a, -ghi, -ghe *ag* wide; broad; (*maniche*) wide; (*abito: troppo ampio*) loose; (*fig*) generous ▷ *sm* width; breadth; (*mare aperto*): **il ~** the open sea ▷ *sf* **stare** *o* **tenersi alla larga (da qn/qc)** to keep one's distance (from sb/sth), keep away (from sb/sth); **~ due metri** two metres wide; **~ di spalle** broad-shouldered; **di manica larga** generous, open-handed; **su larga scala** on a large scale; **di larghe vedute** broad-minded; **al ~ di Genova** off the coast of) Genoa; **farsi ~ tra la folla** to push one's way through the crowd

'larice [ˈlaritʃe] *sm* (Bot) larch

larin'gite [larinˈdʒite] *sf* laryngitis

'larva *sf* larva; (*fig*) shadow

la'sagne [laˈzaɲɲe] *sfpl* lasagna *sg*

lasci'are [laʃˈʃare] *vt* to leave; (*abbandonare*) to leave, abandon, give up; (*cessare di tenere*) to let go of ▷ *vb aus* **~ fare qn** to let sb do; **~ andare** *o* **correre** *o* **perdere** to let things go their own way; **~ stare qc/qn** to leave sth/sb alone; **lasciarsi** *vpr* (*persone*) to part; (*coppia*) to split up; **lasciarsi andare** to let o.s. go

'laser [ˈlazer] *ag, sm inv* **(raggio) ~** laser (beam)

lassa'tivo, -a *ag, sm* laxative

'lasso *sm*; **lasso di tempo** interval, lapse of time

lassù *av* up there

'lastra *sf* (*di pietra*) slab; (*di metallo, Fot*) plate; (*di ghiaccio, vetro*) sheet; (*radiografica*) X-ray (plate)

lastri'cato *sm* paving

late'rale *ag* lateral, side *cpd*; (*uscita, ingresso ecc*) side *cpd* ▷ *sm* (Calcio) half-back

la'tino, -a *ag, sm* Latin

lati'tante *sm/f* fugitive (from justice)

lati'tudine *sf* latitude

'lato, -a *ag* (*fig*) wide, broad ▷ *sm* side; (*fig*) aspect, point of view; **in senso ~** broadly speaking

'latta *sf* tin (plate); (*recipiente*) tin, can

lat'tante *ag* unweaned

'latte *sm* milk; **latte detergente** cleansing milk *o* lotion; **latte intero** full-cream milk;

latte a lunga conservazione UHT milk, long-life milk; **latte magro** o **scremato** skimmed milk; **latte in polvere** dried o powdered milk; **latte solare** suntan lotion; **latti'cini** smpl dairy products
lat'tina sf (di birra ecc) can
lat'tuga, -ghe sf lettuce
'laurea sf degree; **laurea in ingegneria** engineering degree; **laurea in lettere** ≈ arts degree

⬥ **LAUREA**

⬥
⬥ The **laurea** is awarded to students
⬥ who successfully complete their
⬥ degree courses. Traditionally,
⬥ this takes between four and six
⬥ years; a major element of the final
⬥ examinations is the presentation
⬥ and discussion of a dissertation. A
⬥ shorter, more vocational course of
⬥ study, taking from two to three years,
⬥ is also available; at the end of this time
⬥ students receive a diploma called the
⬥ **laurea breve**.

laure'arsi vpr to graduate
laure'ato, -a ag, sm/f graduate
'lauro sm laurel
'lauto, -a ag (pranzo, mancia) lavish
'lava sf lava
la'vabo sm washbasin
la'vaggio [la'vaddʒo] sm washing no pl; **lavaggio del cervello** brainwashing no pl; **lavaggio a secco** dry-cleaning
la'vagna [la'vaɲɲa] sf (Geo) slate; (di scuola) blackboard
la'vanda sf (anche Med) wash; (Bot) lavender; **lavande'ria** sf laundry; **lavanderia automatica** launderette; **lavanderia a secco** dry-cleaner's; **lavan'dino** sm sink
lavapi'atti sm/f dishwasher
la'vare vt to wash; **lavarsi** vpr to wash, have a wash; **~ a secco** to dry-clean; **lavarsi le mani/i denti** to wash one's hands/clean one's teeth
lava'secco sm o finv dry cleaner's
lavasto'viglie [lavasto'viʎʎe] sm o finv (macchina) dishwasher
lava'trice [lava'tritʃe] sf washing machine
lavo'rare vi to work; (fig: bar, studio ecc) to do good business ▷ vt to work; **lavorarsi qn** (persuaderlo) to work on sb; **~ a to** work on; **~ a maglia** to knit; **lavora'tivo, -a** ag working; **lavora'tore, -'trice** sm/f worker ▷ ag working

la'voro sm work; (occupazione) job, work no pl; (opera) piece of work, job; (Econ) labour; **che ~ fa?** what do you do?; **lavori forzati** hard labour sg; **lavoro interinale** o **in affitto** temporary work
le det fpl the ▷ pron (oggetto) them; (: a lei, a essa) (to) her; (: forma di cortesia) (to) you; vedi anche **il**
le'ale ag loyal; (sincero) sincere; (onesto) fair
'lecca 'lecca sm inv lollipop
leccapi'edi (peg) sm/finv toady, bootlicker
lec'care vt to lick; (gatto: latte ecc) to lick o lap up; (fig) to flatter; **leccarsi i baffi** to lick one's lips
leccherò ecc [lekke'rɔ] vb vedi **leccare**
'leccio ['lettʃo] sm holm oak, ilex
leccor'nia sf titbit, delicacy
'lecito, -a ['lɛtʃito] ag permitted, allowed
'lega, -ghe sf league; (di metalli) alloy
le'gaccio [le'gattʃo] sm string, lace
le'gale ag legal ▷ sm lawyer; **legaliz'zare** vt to authenticate; (regolarizzare) to legalize
le'game sm (corda, fig: affettivo) tie, bond; (nesso logico) link, connection
le'gare vt (prigioniero, capelli, cane) to tie (up); (libro) to bind; (Chim) to alloy; (fig: collegare) to bind, join ▷ vi (far lega) to unite; (fig) to get on well
le'genda [le'dʒɛnda] sf (di carta geografica ecc) = **leggenda**
'legge ['leddʒe] sf law
leg'genda [led'dʒɛnda] sf (narrazione) legend; (di carta geografica ecc) key, legend
'leggere ['leddʒere] vt, vi to read
legge'rezza [leddʒe'rettsa] sf lightness; thoughtlessness; fickleness
leg'gero, -a [led'dʒɛro] ag light; (agile, snello) nimble, agile, light; (tè, caffè) weak; (fig: non grave, piccolo) slight; (: spensierato) thoughtless; (: incostante) fickle; free and easy; **alla leggera** thoughtlessly
leg'gio, -'gii [led'dʒio] sm lectern; (Mus) music stand
legherò ecc [lege'rɔ] vb vedi **legare**
legisla'tivo, -a [ledʒizla'tivo] ag legislative
legisla'tura [ledʒizla'tura] sf legislature
le'gittimo, -a [le'dʒittimo] ag legitimate; (fig: giustificato, lecito) justified, legitimate; **legittima difesa** (Dir) self-defence
'legna ['leɲɲa] sf firewood
'legno ['leɲɲo] sm wood; (pezzo di legno) piece of wood; **di ~** wooden; **legno compensato** plywood
'lei pron (soggetto) she; (oggetto: per dare rilievo, con preposizione) her; (forma di cortesia: anche: L~) you ▷ sm **dare del ~**

a qn to address sb as "lei"; **~ stessa** she herself; you yourself

lenta'mente *av* slowly

'lente *sf* (Ottica) lens *sg*; **lenti a contatto** *o* **corneali** contact lenses; **lenti (a contatto) morbide/rigide** soft/hard contact lenses; **lente d'ingrandimento** magnifying glass; **lenti** *sfpl* (occhiali) lenses

len'tezza [len'tettsa] *sf* slowness
len'ticchia [len'tikkja] *sf* (Bot) lentil
len'tiggine [len'tiddʒine] *sf* freckle
'lento, -a *ag* slow; (molle: fune) slack; (non stretto: vite, abito) loose ▷ *sm* (ballo) slow dance
'lenza ['lɛntsa] *sf* fishing-line
lenzu'olo [len'tswɔlo] *sm* sheet
le'one *sm* lion; (dello zodiaco): **L~** Leo
lepo'rino, -a *ag* **labbro ~** harelip
'lepre *sf* hare
'lercio, -a, -ci, -cie ['lɛrtʃo] *ag* filthy
lesi'one *sf* (Med) lesion; (Dir) injury, damage; (Edil) crack
les'sare *vt* (Cuc) to boil
'lessi *ecc vb vedi* **leggere**
'lessico, -ci *sm* vocabulary; lexicon
'lesso, -a *ag* boiled ▷ *sm* boiled meat
le'tale *ag* lethal; fatal
leta'maio *sm* dunghill
le'tame *sm* manure, dung
le'targo, -ghi *sm* lethargy; (Zool) hibernation
'lettera *sf* letter; **lettere** *sfpl* (letteratura) literature *sg*; (studi umanistici) arts (subjects); **alla ~** literally; **in lettere** in words, in full
letteral'mente *av* literally
lette'rario, -a *ag* literary
lette'rato, -a *ag* well-read, scholarly
lettera'tura *sf* literature
let'tiga, -ghe *sf* (barella) stretcher
let'tino *sm* cot (BRIT), crib (US); **lettino solare** sunbed
'letto, -a *pp di* **leggere** ▷ *sm* bed; **andare a ~** to go to bed; **letto a castello** bunk beds *pl*; **letto a una piazza** single; **letto a due piazze** *o* **matrimoniale** double bed
let'tore, -'trice *sm/f* reader; (Ins) (foreign language) assistant (BRIT), (foreign) teaching assistant (US) ▷ *sm* (Tecn): **~ ottico** optical character reader; **lettore**

CD CD player; **lettore DVD** DVD player
let'tura *sf* reading

leuce'mia [leutʃe'mia] *sf* leukaemia
'leva *sf* lever; (Mil) conscription; **far ~ su qn** to work on sb; **leva del cambio** (Aut) gear lever
le'vante *sm* east; (vento) East wind; **il L~** the Levant
le'vare *vt* (occhi, braccio) to raise; (sollevare, togliere: tassa, divieto) to lift; (indumenti) to take off, remove; (rimuovere) to take away; (: dal di sopra) to take off; (: dal di dentro) to take out
leva'toio, -a *ag* **ponte ~** drawbridge
lezi'one [let'tsjone] *sf* lesson; (Univ) lecture; **fare ~** to teach; to lecture; **dare una ~ a qn** to teach sb a lesson; **lezioni private** private lessons
li *pron pl* (oggetto) them
lì *av* there; **di o da lì** from there; **per di lì** that way; **di lì a pochi giorni** a few days later; **lì per lì** there and then; at first; **essere lì (lì) per fare** to be on the point of doing, be about to do; **lì dentro** in there; **lì sotto** under there; **lì sopra** on there; up there; *vedi anche* **quello**
liba'nese *ag, sm/f* Lebanese *inv*
Li'bano *sm* **il ~** the Lebanon
'libbra *sf* (peso) pound
li'beccio [li'bettʃo] *sm* south-west wind
li'bellula *sf* dragonfly
libe'rale *ag, sm/f* liberal
liberaliz'zare [liberalid'dzare] *vt* to liberalize
libe'rare *vt* (rendere libero: prigioniero) to release; (: popolo) to free, liberate; (sgombrare: passaggio) to clear; (: stanza) to vacate; (produrre: energia) to release; **liberarsi** *vpr* **liberarsi di qc/qn** to get rid of sth/sb; **liberazi'one** *sf* liberation, freeing; release; rescuing

'libero, -a *ag* free; (strada) clear; (non occupato: posto ecc) vacant; free; not taken; empty; not engaged; **~ di fare qc** free to do sth; **~ da** free from; **è ~ questo posto?** is this seat free?; **~ arbitrio** free will; **~ professionista** self-employed professional person; **~ scambio** free trade;

libertà sf inv freedom; (tempo disponibile) free time ▷ sfpl (licenza) liberties; **in libertà provvisoria/vigilata** released without bail/on probation

'**Libia** sf la ~ Libya; '**libico, -a, -ci, -che** ag, sm/f Libyan

li'bidine sf lust

li'braio sm bookseller

li'brarsi vpr to hover

libre'ria sf (bottega) bookshop; (mobile) bookcase

⚠ Attenzione! In inglese esiste la parola library, che però significa biblioteca.

li'bretto sm booklet; (taccuino) notebook; (Mus) libretto; **libretto degli assegni** cheque book; **libretto di circolazione** (Aut) logbook; **libretto di risparmio** (savings) bank-book, passbook; **libretto universitario** student's report book

'**libro** sm book; **libro di cassa** cash book; **libro mastro** ledger; **libro paga** payroll; **libro di testo** textbook

li'cenza [li'tʃɛntsa] sf (permesso) permission, leave; (di pesca, caccia, circolazione) permit, licence; (Mil) leave; (Ins) school leaving certificate; (libertà) liberty; licence; licentiousness; **andare in ~** (Mil) to go on leave

licenzia'mento [litʃentsja'mento] sm dismissal

licenzi'are [litʃen'tsjare] vt (impiegato) to dismiss; (Comm: per eccesso di personale) to make redundant; (Ins) to award a certificate to; **licenziarsi** vpr (impiegato) to resign, hand in one's notice; (Ins) to obtain one's school-leaving certificate

li'ceo [li'tʃɛo] sm (Ins) secondary (BRIT) o high (US) school (for 14- to 19-year-olds)

'**lido** sm beach, shore

Liechtenstein ['liktənstain] sm il ~ Liechtenstein

li'eto, -a ag happy, glad; **"molto ~"** (nelle presentazioni) "pleased to meet you"

li'eve ag light; (di poco conto) slight; (sommesso: voce) faint, soft

lievi'tare vi (anche fig) to rise ▷ vt to leaven

li'evito sm yeast; **lievito di birra** brewer's yeast

'**ligio, -a, -gi, -gie** ['lidʒo] ag faithful, loyal

'**lilla** sm inv lilac

'**lillà** sm inv lilac

'**lima** sf file; **lima da unghie** nail file

limac'cioso, -a [limat'tʃoso] ag slimy; muddy

li'mare vt to file (down); (fig) to polish

limi'tare vt to limit, restrict; (circoscrivere) to bound, surround; **limitarsi** vpr **limitarsi nel mangiare** to limit one's

eating; **limitarsi a qc/a fare qc** to limit o s. to sth/to doing sth

'**limite** sm limit; (confine) border, boundary; **limite di velocità** speed limit

limo'nata sf lemonade (BRIT), (lemon) soda (US); lemon squash (BRIT), lemonade (US)

li'mone sm (pianta) lemon tree; (frutto) lemon

'**limpido, -a** ag clear; (acqua) limpid, clear

'**lince** ['lintʃe] sf lynx

linci'are vt to lynch

'**linea** sf line; (di mezzi pubblici di trasporto: itinerario) route; (: servizio) service; **a grandi linee** in outline; **mantenere la ~** to look after one's figure; **aereo di ~** airliner; **nave di ~** liner; **volo di ~** scheduled flight; **linea aerea** airline; **linea di partenza/ d'arrivo** (Sport) starting/finishing line; **linea di tiro** line of fire

linea'menti smpl features; (fig) outlines

line'are ag linear; (fig) coherent, logical

line'etta sf (trattino) dash; (d'unione) hyphen

lin'gotto sm ingot, bar

'**lingua** sf (Anat, Cuc) tongue; (idioma) language; **mostrare la ~** to stick out one's tongue; **di ~ italiana** Italian-speaking; **che lingue parla?** what languages do you speak?; **una ~ di terra** a spit of land; **lingua madre** mother tongue

lingu'aggio [lin'gwaddʒo] sm language

lingu'etta sf (di strumento) reed; (di scarpa, Tecn) tongue; (di busta) flap

'**lino** sm (pianta) flax; (tessuto) linen

li'noleum sm inv linoleum, lino

liposuzi'one [liposut'tsjone] sf liposuction

lique'fatto, -a pp di **liquefare**

liqui'dare vt (società, beni: persona: uccidere) to liquidate; (persona: sbarazzarsene) to get rid of; (conto, problema) to settle; (Comm: merce) to sell off, clear; **liquidazi'one** sf liquidation; settlement; clearance sale

liquidità sf liquidity

'**liquido, -a** ag, sm liquid; **liquido per freni** brake fluid

liqui'rizia [likwi'rittsja] sf liquorice

li'quore sm liqueur

'**lira** sf (Storia: unità monetaria) lira; (Mus) lyre; **lira sterlina** pound sterling

'**lirico, -a, -ci, -che** ag lyric(al); (Mus) lyric; **cantante/teatro ~** opera singer/house

Lis'bona sf Lisbon

'**lisca, -sche** sf (di pesce) fishbone

lisci'are [liʃʃare] vt to smooth; (fig) to flatter

'**liscio, -a, -sci, -sce** ['liʃʃo] ag smooth;

(*capelli*) straight; (*mobile*) plain; (*bevanda alcolica*) neat; (*fig*) straightforward, simple ▷ *av* **andare ~** to go smoothly; **passarla liscia** to get away with it

'liso, -a *ag* worn out, threadbare

'lista *sf* (*elenco*) list; **lista elettorale** electoral roll; **lista delle spese** shopping list; **lista dei vini** wine list; **lista delle vivande** menu

lis'tino *sm* list; **listino dei cambi** (foreign) exchange rate; **listino dei prezzi** price list

'lite *sf* quarrel, argument; (*Dir*) lawsuit

liti'gare *vi* to quarrel; (*Dir*) to litigate

li'tigio [li'tidʒo] *sm* quarrel

lito'rale *ag* coastal, coast *cpd* ▷ *sm* coast

'litro *sm* litre

livel'lare *vt* to level, make level

li'vello *sm* level; (*fig*) level, standard; **ad alto ~** (*fig*) high-level; **livello del mare** sea level

'livido, -a *ag* livid; (*per percosse*) bruised, black and blue; (*cielo*) leaden ▷ *sm* bruise

Li'vorno *sf* Livorno, Leghorn

'lizza ['littsa] *sf* lists *pl*; **scendere in ~** to enter the lists

lo (*dav s impura, gn, pn, ps, x, z; dav V* **l'**) *det m* the ▷ *pron* (*oggetto: persona*) him; (: *cosa*) it; **lo sapevo** I knew it; **lo so** I know; **sii buono, anche se lui non lo è** be good, even if he isn't; *vedi anche* **il**

lo'cale *ag* local ▷ *sm* room; (*luogo pubblico*) premises *pl*; **locale notturno** nightclub; **località** *sf inv* locality

lo'canda *sf* inn

locomo'tiva *sf* locomotive

locuzi'one [lokut'tsjone] *sf* phrase, expression

lo'dare *vt* to praise

'lode *sf* praise; (*Ins*): **laurearsi con 110 e ~** ≈ to graduate with a first-class honours degree (BRIT), graduate summa cum laude (US)

'loden *sm inv* (*stoffa*) loden; (*cappotto*) loden overcoat

lo'devole *ag* praiseworthy

loga'ritmo *sm* logarithm

'loggia, -ge ['lɔddʒa] *sf* (*Archit*) loggia; (*circolo massonico*) lodge; **loggi'one** *sm* (*di teatro*): **il loggione** the Gods *sg*

'logico, -a, -ci, -che ['lɔdʒiko] *ag* logical

logo'rare *vt* to wear out; (*sciupare*) to waste; **logorarsi** *vpr* to wear out; (*fig*) to wear o s. out

'logoro, -a *ag* (*stoffa*) worn out, threadbare; (*persona*) worn out

Lombar'dia *sf* **la ~** Lombardy

lom'bata *sf* (*taglio di carne*) loin

lom'brico, -chi *sm* earthworm

londi'nese *ag* London *cpd* ▷ *sm/f* Londoner

'Londra *sf* London

lon'gevo, -a [lon'dʒevo] *ag* long-lived

longi'tudine [londʒi'tudine] *sf* longitude

lonta'nanza [lonta'nantsa] *sf* distance; absence

lon'tano, -a *ag* (*distante*) distant, faraway; (*assente*) absent; (*vago: sospetto*) slight, remote; (*tempo: remoto*) far-off, distant; (*parente*) distant, remote ▷ *av* far; **è lontana la casa?** is it far to the house?, is the house far from here?; **è ~ un chilometro** it's a kilometre away o a kilometre from here; **più ~** farther; **da** o **di ~** from a distance; **~ da** a long way from; **è molto ~ da qui?** is it far from here?; **alla lontana** slightly, vaguely

lo'quace [lo'kwatʃe] *ag* talkative, loquacious; (*fig: gesto ecc*) eloquent

'lordo, -a *ag* dirty, filthy; (*peso, stipendio*) gross

'loro *pron pl* (*oggetto, con preposizione*) them; (*complemento di termine*) to them; (*soggetto*) they; (*forma di cortesia: anche:* **L~**) you; to you; (*forma di cortesia: anche:* **L~**) your ▷ *pron* theirs; (*forma di cortesia: anche:* **L~**) yours; **~ stessi(e)** they themselves; you yourselves

'losco, -a, -schi, -sche *ag* (*fig*) shady, suspicious

'lotta *sf* struggle, fight; (*Sport*) wrestling; **lotta libera** all-in wrestling; **lot'tare** *vi* to fight, struggle; to wrestle

lotte'ria *sf* lottery; (*di gara ippica*) sweepstake

'lotto *sm* (*gioco*) (state) lottery; (*parte*) lot; (*Edil*) site

⊛ **Lotto**

⊛ The **Lotto** is an official lottery run by the
⊛ Italian Finance Ministry. It consists of
⊛ a weekly draw of numbers and is very
⊛ popular.

lozi'one [lot'tsjone] *sf* lotion

lubrifi'cante *sm* lubricant

lubrifi'care *vt* to lubricate

luc'chetto [luk'ketto] *sm* padlock

lucci'care [luttʃi'kare] *vi* to sparkle, glitter, twinkle

'luccio ['luttʃo] *sm* (*Zool*) pike

'lucciola ['luttʃola] *sf* (*Zool*) firefly; glowworm

'luce ['lutʃe] *sf* light; (*finestra*) window; **alla ~ di** by the light of; **fare ~ su qc** (*fig*) to shed o throw light on sth; **~ del sole/della luna**

sun/moonlight

lucer'nario [lutʃer'narjo] *sm* skylight

lu'certola [lu'tʃertola] *sf* lizard

iuci'dare [lutʃi'dare] *vt* to polish

lucida'trice [lutʃida'tritʃe] *sf* floor polisher

'lucido, -a ['lutʃido] *ag* shining, bright; (*lucidato*) polished; (*fig*) lucid ▷ *sm* shine, lustre; (*disegno*) tracing; **lucido per scarpe** shoe polish

'lucro *sm* profit, gain

'luglio ['luʎʎo] *sm* July

'lugubre *ag* gloomy

'lui *pron* (*soggetto*) he; (*oggetto: per dare rilievo, con preposizione*) him; **~ stesso** he himself

lu'maca, -che *sf* slug; (*chiocciola*) snail

lumi'noso, -a *ag* (*che emette luce*) luminous; (*cielo, colore, stanza*) bright; (*sorgente*) of light, light *cpd*; (*fig: sorriso*) bright, radiant

'luna *sf* moon; **luna nuova/piena** new/full moon; **luna di miele** honeymoon; **siamo in ~ di miele** we're on honeymoon

'luna park *sm inv* amusement park, funfair

lu'nare *ag* lunar, moon *cpd*

lu'nario *sm* almanac; **sbarcare il ~** to make ends meet

lu'natico, -a, -ci, -che *ag* whimsical, temperamental

lunedì *sm inv* Monday; **di** *o* **il ~** on Mondays

lun'ghezza [lun'gettsa] *sf* length; **lunghezza d'onda** (*Fisica*) wavelength

'lungo, -a, -ghi, -ghe *ag* long; (*lento: persona*) slow; (*diluito: caffè, brodo*) weak, watery, thin ▷ *sm* length ▷ *prep* along; **~ 3 metri** 3 metres long; **a ~** for a long time; **a ~ andare** in the long run; **di gran lunga** (*molto*) by far; **andare in ~** *o* **per le lunghe** to drag on; **saperla lunga** to know what's what; **in ~ e in largo** far and wide, all over; **~ il corso dei secoli** throughout the centuries

lungo'mare *sm* promenade

lu'notto *sm* (*Aut*) rear *o* back window; **lunotto termico** heated rear window

lu'ogo, -ghi *sm* place; (*posto: di incidente ecc*) scene, site; (*punto, passo di libro*) passage; **in ~ di** instead of; **in primo ~** in the first place; **aver ~** to take place; **dar ~ a** to give rise to; **luogo di nascita** birthplace; (*Amm*) place of birth; **luogo di provenienza** place of origin; **luogo comune** commonplace

'lupo, -a *sm/f* wolf

'luppolo *sm* (*Bot*) hop

'lurido, -a *ag* filthy

lusin'gare *vt* to flatter

Lussem'burgo *sm* (*stato*): **il ~** Luxembourg ▷ *sf* (*città*) Luxembourg

'lusso *sm* luxury; **di ~** luxury *cpd*; **lussu'oso, -a** *ag* luxurious

lus'suria *sf* lust

lus'trino *sm* sequin

'lutto *sm* mourning; **essere in/portare il ~** to be in/wear mourning

m

m. *abbr* = **mese; metro; miglia; monte**

ma *cong* but; **ma insomma!** for goodness sake!; **ma no!** of course not!

'macabro, -a *ag* gruesome, macabre

macché [mak'ke] *escl* not at all!, certainly not!

macche'roni [makke'roni] *smpl* macaroni *sg*

'macchia ['makkja] *sf* stain, spot; (*chiazza di diverso colore*) spot, splash, patch; (*tipo di boscaglia*) scrub; **alla ~** (*fig*) in hiding; **macchi'are** *vt* (*sporcare*) to stain, mark; **macchiarsi** *vpr* (*persona*) to get to s. dirty; (*stoffa*) to stain; to get stained *o* marked

macchi'ato, -a [mak'kjato] *ag* (*pelle, pelo*) spotted; **~ di** stained with; **caffè ~** coffee with a dash of milk

'macchina ['makkina] *sf* machine; (*motore, locomotiva*) engine; (*automobile*) car; (*fig: meccanismo*) machinery; **andare in ~** (*Aut*) to go by car; (*Stampa*) to go to press; **macchina da cucire** sewing machine; **macchina fotografica** camera; **macchina da presa** cine *o* movie camera; **macchina da scrivere** typewriter; **macchina a vapore** steam engine

macchi'nario [makki'narjo] *sm* machinery

macchi'nista, -i [makki'nista] *sm* (*di treno*) engine-driver; (*di nave*) engineer

Macedonia [matʃe'dɔnja] *sf* **la ~** Macedonia

mace'donia [matʃe'dɔnja] *sf* fruit salad

macel'laio [matʃel'lajo] *sm* butcher

macelle'ria *sf* butcher's (shop)

ma'cerie [ma'tʃɛrje] *sfpl* rubble *sg*, debris *sg*

ma'cigno [ma'tʃiɲɲo] *sm* (*masso*) rock, boulder

maci'nare [matʃi'nare] *vt* to grind; (*carne*) to mince (BRIT), grind (US)

macrobi'otico, -a *ag* macrobiotic ▷ *sf* macrobiotics *sg*

Ma'donna *sf* (*Rel*) Our Lady

mador'nale *ag* enormous, huge

'madre *sf* mother; (*matrice di bolletta*) counterfoil ▷ *ag inv* mother *cpd*; **ragazza ~** unmarried mother; **scena ~** (*Teatro*) principal scene; (*fig*) terrible scene

madre'lingua *sf* mother tongue, native language

madre'perla *sf* mother-of-pearl

ma'drina *sf* godmother

maestà *sf inv* majesty

ma'estra *sf vedi* **maestro**

maes'trale *sm* north-west wind, mistral

ma'estro, -a *sm/f* (*Ins: anche:* **~ di scuola o elementare**) primary (BRIT) *o* grade school (US) teacher; (*esperto*) expert ▷ *sm* (*artigiano, fig: guida*) master; (*Mus*) maestro ▷ *ag* (*principale*) main; (*di grande abilità*) masterly, skilful; **maestra d'asilo** nursery teacher; **~ di cerimonie** master of ceremonies

'mafia *sf* Mafia

'maga *sf* sorceress

ma'gari *escl* (*esprime desiderio*): **~ fosse vero!** if only it were true!; **ti piacerebbe andare in Scozia? — ~!** would you like to go to Scotland? — and how! ▷ *av* (*anche*) even; (*forse*) perhaps

magaz'zino [magad'dzino] *sm* warehouse; **grande ~** department store
▷ Attenzione! In inglese esiste la parola *magazine* che però significa *rivista*.

'maggio ['maddʒo] *sm* May

maggio'rana [maddʒo'rana] *sf* (*Bot*) (sweet) marjoram

maggio'ranza [maddʒo'rantsa] *sf* majority

maggior'domo [maddʒor'dɔmo] *sm* butler

maggi'ore [mad'dʒore] *ag* (*comparativo: più grande*) bigger, larger; taller; greater; (*: più vecchio: sorella, fratello*) older, elder; (*: di grado superiore*) senior; (*: più importante: Mil, Mus*) major; (*superlativo*) biggest, largest; tallest; greatest; oldest; eldest ▷ *sm/f* (*di grado*) superior; (*di età*) elder;

(*Mil*) major; (: *Aer*) squadron leader; **la maggior parte** the majority; **andare per la ~** (*cantante ecc*) to be very popular; **maggio'renne** *ag* of age ▷ *sm/f* person who has come of age

ma'gia [ma'dʒia] *sf* magic; **'magico, -a, -ci, -che** *ag* magic; (*fig*) fascinating, charming, magical

magis'trato [madʒis'trato] *sm* magistrate

'maglia ['maʎʎa] *sf* stitch; (*lavoro ai ferri*) knitting *no pl*; (*tessuto, Sport*) jersey; (*maglione*) jersey, sweater; (*di catena*) link; (*di rete*) mesh; **maglia diritta/rovescia** plain/purl; **magli'etta** *sf* (*canottiera*) vest; (*tipo camicia*) T-shirt

magli'one *sm* sweater, jumper

ma'gnetico, -a, -ci, -che *ag* magnetic

ma'gnifico, -a, -ci, -che [maɲ'ɲifiko] *ag* magnificent, splendid; (*ospite*) generous

ma'gnolia [maɲ'nɔlja] *sf* magnolia

'mago, -ghi *sm* (*stregone*) magician, wizard; (*illusionista*) magician

ma'grezza [ma'grettsa] *sf* thinness

'magro, -a *ag* (*very*) thin, skinny; (*carne*) lean; (*formaggio*) low-fat; (*fig: scarso, misero*) meagre, poor; (: *meschino: scusa*) poor, lame; **mangiare di ~** not to eat meat

'mai *av* (*nessuna volta*) never; (*talvolta*) ever; **non ... ~** never; **~ più** never again; **non sono ~ stato in Spagna** I've never been to Spain; **come ~?** why (*o* how) on earth?; **chi/dove/quando ~?** whoever/wherever/whenever?

mai'ale *sm* (*Zool*) pig; (*carne*) pork

maio'nese *sf* mayonnaise

'mais *sm inv* maize

mai'uscolo, -a *ag* (*lettera*) capital; (*fig*) enormous, huge

mala'fede *sf* bad faith

malan'dato, -a *ag* (*persona: di salute*) in poor health; (: *di condizioni finanziarie*) badly off; (*trascurato*) shabby

ma'lanno *sm* (*disgrazia*) misfortune; (*malattia*) ailment

mala'pena *sf* **a ~** hardly, scarcely

ma'laria *sf* (*Med*) malaria

ma'lato, -a *ag* ill, sick; (*gamba*) bad; (*pianta*) diseased ▷ *sm/f* sick person; (*in ospedale*) patient; **malat'tia** *sf* (*infettiva ecc*) illness, disease; (*cattiva salute*) illness, sickness; (*di pianta*) disease

mala'vita *sf* underworld

mala'voglia [mala'vɔʎʎa] *sf* **di ~** unwillingly, reluctantly

Mala'ysia *sf* Malaysia

mal'concio, -a, -ci, -ce [mal'kontʃo] *ag* in a sorry state

malcon'tento *sm* discontent

malcos'tume *sm* immorality

mal'destro, -a *ag* (*inabile*) inexpert, inexperienced; (*goffo*) awkward

'male *av* badly ▷ *sm* (*ciò che è ingiusto, disonesto*) evil; (*danno, svantaggio*) harm; (*sventura*) misfortune; (*dolore fisico, morale*) pain, ache; **di ~ in peggio** from bad to worse; **sentirsi ~** to feel ill; **far ~** (*dolere*) to hurt; **far ~ alla salute** to be bad for one's health; **far del ~ a qn** to hurt o harm sb; **restare** *o* **rimanere ~** to be sorry; to be disappointed; to be hurt; **andare a ~** to go bad; **come va? — non c'è ~** how are you? — not bad; **avere mal di gola/testa** to have a sore throat/a headache; **aver ~ ai piedi** to have sore feet; **mal d'auto** carsickness; **mal di cuore** heart trouble; **male di dente** toothache; **mal di mare** seasickness

male'detto, -a *pp di* **maledire** ▷ *ag* cursed, damned; (*fig: fam*) damned, blasted

male'dire *vt* to curse; **maledizi'one** *sf* curse; **maledizione!** damn it!

maledu'cato, -a *ag* rude, ill-mannered

maleducazi'one [maledukat'tsjone] *sf* rudeness

ma'lefico, -a, -ci, -che *ag* (*influsso, azione*) evil

ma'lessere *sm* indisposition, slight illness; (*fig*) uneasiness

malfa'mato, -a *ag* notorious

malfat'tore, -'trice *sm/f* wrongdoer

mal'fermo, -a *ag* unsteady, shaky; (*salute*) poor, delicate

mal'grado *prep* in spite of, despite ▷ *cong* although; **mio** (*o* **tuo** *ecc*) **~** against my (*o* your *ecc*) will

ma'ligno, -a [ma'liɲɲo] *ag* (*malvagio*) malicious, malignant; (*Med*) malignant

malinco'nia *sf* melancholy, gloom; **malin'conico, -a, -ci, -che** *ag* melancholy

malincu'ore: a ~ *av* reluctantly, unwillingly

malin'teso, -a *ag* misunderstood; (*riguardo, senso del dovere*) mistaken, wrong ▷ *sm* misunderstanding; **c'è stato un ~** there's been a misunderstanding

ma'lizia [ma'littsja] *sf* (*malignità*) malice; (*furbizia*) cunning; (*espediente*) trick; **malizi'oso, -a** *ag* malicious; cunning; (*vivace, birichino*) mischievous

malme'nare *vt* to beat up

ma'locchio [ma'lɔkkjo] *sm* evil eye

ma'lora *sf* **andare in ~** to go to the dogs

ma'lore *sm* (*sudden*) illness

mal'sano, -a *ag* unhealthy

'malta *sf* (*Edil*) mortar

mal'tempo *sm* bad weather

'malto sm malt

maltrat'tare vt to ill-treat

malu'more sm bad mood; (irritabilità) bad temper; (discordia) ill feeling; **di ~** in a bad mood

'malva sf (Bot) mallow ▷ ag, sm inv mauve

mal'vagio, -a, -gi, -gie [mal'vadʒo] ag wicked, evil

malvi'vente sm criminal

malvolenti'eri av unwillingly, reluctantly

'mamma, -e sf mummy, mum; **~ mia!** my goodness!

mam'mella sf (Anat) breast; (di vacca, capra ecc) udder

mam'mifero sm mammal

ma'nata sf (colpo) slap; (quantità) handful

man'canza [man'kantsa] sf lack; (carenza) shortage, scarcity; (fallo) fault; (imperfezione) failing, shortcoming; **per ~ di tempo** through lack of time; **in ~ di meglio** for lack of anything better

man'care vi (essere insufficiente) to be lacking; (venir meno) to fail; (sbagliare) to be wrong, make a mistake; (non esserci) to be missing, not to be there; (essere lontano): **~ (da)** to be away (from) ▷ vt to miss; **~ di** to lack; **~ a** (promessa) to fail to keep; **tu mi manchi** I miss you; **mancò poco che morisse** he very nearly died; **mancano ancora 10 sterline** we're still £10 short; **manca un quarto alle 6** it's a quarter to 6

mancherò ecc [manke'rɔ] vb vedi **mancare**

'mancia, -ce ['mantʃa] sf tip; **quanto devo lasciare di ~?** how much should I tip?; **~ competente** reward

manci'ata [man'tʃata] sf handful

man'cino, -a [man'tʃino] ag (braccio) left; (persona) left-handed; (fig) underhand

manda'rancio [manda'rantʃo] sm clementine

man'dare vt to send; (far funzionare: macchina) to drive; (emettere) to send out; (: grido) to give, utter, let out; **~ a chiamare qn** to send for sb; **~ avanti** (fig: famiglia) to provide for; (: fabbrica) to run, look after; **~ giù** to send down; (anche fig) to swallow; **~ via** to send away; (licenziare) to fire

manda'rino sm mandarin (orange); (cinese) mandarin

man'data sf (quantità) lot, batch; (di chiave) turn; **chiudere a doppia ~** to double-lock

man'dato sm (incarico) commission; (Dir: provvedimento) warrant; (di deputato ecc) mandate; (ordine di pagamento) postal o money order; **mandato d'arresto** warrant for arrest

man'dibola sf mandible, jaw

'mandorla sf almond; **'mandorlo** sm almond tree

'mandria sf herd

maneggi'are [maned'dʒare] vt (creta, cera) to mould, work, fashion; (arnesi, utensili) to handle; (: adoperare) to use; (fig: persone, denaro) to handle, deal with; **ma'neggio** sm moulding; handling; use; (intrigo) plot, scheme; (per cavalli) riding school

ma'nesco, -a, -schi, -sche ag free with one's fists

ma'nette sfpl handcuffs

manga'nello sm club

mangi'are [man'dʒare] vt to eat; (intaccare) to eat into o away; (Carte, Scacchi ecc) to take ▷ vi to eat ▷ sm eating; (cibo) food; (cucina) cooking; **possiamo ~ qualcosa?** can we have something to eat?; **mangiarsi le parole** to mumble; **mangiarsi le unghie** to bite one's nails

man'gime [man'dʒime] sm fodder

'mango, -ghi sm mango

ma'nia sf (Psic) mania; (fig) obsession, craze; **ma'niaco, -a, -ci, -che** ag suffering from a mania; **maniaco (di)** obsessed (by), crazy (about)

'manica sf sleeve; (fig: gruppo) gang, bunch; (Geo): **la M~, il Canale della M~** the (English) Channel; **essere di ~ larga/stretta** to be easy-going/strict; **manica a vento** (Aer) wind sock

mani'chino [mani'kino] sm (di sarto, vetrina) dummy

'manico, -ci sm handle; (Mus) neck

mani'comio sm mental hospital; (fig) madhouse

mani'cure sm o f inv manicure ▷ sf inv manicurist

mani'era sf way, manner; (stile) style, manner; **maniere** sfpl (comportamento) manners; **in ~ che** so that; **in ~ da** so as to; **in tutte le maniere** at all costs

manifes'tare vt to show, display; (esprimere) to express; (rivelare) to reveal, disclose ▷ vi to demonstrate; **manifestazi'one** sf show, display; expression; (sintomo) sign, symptom; (dimostrazione pubblica) demonstration; (cerimonia) event

mani'festo, -a ag obvious, evident ▷ sm poster, bill; (scritto ideologico) manifesto

ma'niglia [ma'niʎʎa] sf handle; (sostegno: negli autobus ecc) strap

manipo'lare vt to manipulate; (alterare: vino) to adulterate

man'naro: lupo ~ sm werewolf

'mano, -i sf hand; (strato: di vernice ecc) coat; **di prima ~** (notizia) first-hand; **di**

seconda ~ second-hand; **man** ~ little by little, gradually; **man** ~ **che** as; **darsi** o **stringersi la** ~ to shake hands; **mettere le mani avanti** (*fig*) to safeguard o.s.; **restare a mani vuote** to be left empty-handed; **venire alle mani** to come to blows; **a** ~ by hand; **mani in alto!** hands up!

mano'dopera *sf* labour

ma'nometro *sm* gauge, manometer

mano'mettere *vt* (*alterare*) to tamper with; (*aprire indebitamente*) to break open illegally

ma'nopola *sf* (*dell'armatura*) gauntlet; (*guanto*) mitt; (*di impugnatura*) hand-grip; (*pomello*) knob

manos'critto, -a *ag* handwritten ▷ *sm* manuscript

mano'vale *sm* labourer

mano'vella *sf* handle; (*Tecn*) crank

ma'novra *sf* manoeuvre (*BRIT*), maneuver (*US*); (*Ferr*) shunting

man'sarda *sf* attic

mansi'one *sf* task, duty, job

mansu'eto, -a *ag* gentle, docile

man'tello *sm* cloak; (*fig: di neve ecc*) blanket, mantle; (*Zool*) coat

mante'nere *vt* to maintain; (*adempiere: promesse*) to keep, abide by; (*provvedere a*) to support, maintain; **mantenersi** *vpr* **mantenersi calmo/giovane** to stay calm/young

'Mantova *sf* Mantua

manu'ale *ag* manual ▷ *sm* (*testo*) manual, handbook

ma'nubrio *sm* handle; (*di bicicletta ecc*) handlebars *pl*; (*Sport*) dumbbell

manutenzi'one [manuten'tsjone] *sf* maintenance, upkeep; (*d'impianti*) maintenance, servicing

'manzo ['mandzo] *sm* (*Zool*) steer; (*carne*) beef

'mappa *sf* (*Geo*) map; **mappa'mondo** *sm* map of the world; (*globo girevole*) globe

mara'tona *sf* marathon

'marca, -che *sf* (*Comm: di prodotti*) brand; (*contrassegno, scontrino*) ticket, check; **prodotto di** ~ (*di buona qualità*) high-class product; **marca da bollo** official stamp

mar'care *vt* (*munire di contrassegno*) to mark; (*a fuoco*) to brand; (*Sport: gol*) to score; (*: avversario*) to mark; (*accentuare*) to stress; ~ **visita** (*Mil*) to report sick

marcherò *ecc* [marke'rɔ] *vb vedi* **marcare**

mar'chese, -a [mar'keze] *sm/f* marquis o marquess/marchioness

marchi'are [mar'kjare] *vt* to brand

'marcia, -ce ['martʃa] *sf* (*anche Mus, Mil*) march; (*funzionamento*) running; (*il

camminare) walking; (*Aut*) gear; **mettere in** ~ to start; **mettersi in** ~ to get moving; **far** ~ **indietro** (*Aut*) to reverse; (*fig*) to back-pedal

marciapi'ede [martʃa'pjɛde] *sm* (*di strada*) pavement (*BRIT*), sidewalk (*US*); (*Ferr*) platform

marci'are [mar'tʃare] *vi* to march; (*andare: treno, macchina*) to go; (*funzionare*) to run, work

'marcio, -a, -ci, -ce ['martʃo] *ag* (*frutta, legno*) rotten, bad; (*Med*) festering; (*fig*) corrupt, rotten

mar'cire [mar'tʃire] *vi* (*andare a male*) to go bad, rot; (*suppurare*) to fester; (*fig*) to rot, waste away

'marco, -chi *sm* (*unità monetaria*) mark

'mare *sm* sea; **in** ~ at sea; **andare al** ~ (*in vacanza ecc*) to go to the seaside; **il M~ del Nord** the North Sea

ma'rea *sf* tide; **alta/bassa** ~ high/low tide

mareggi'ata [mared'dʒata] *sf* heavy sea

mare'moto *sm* seaquake

maresci'allo [mareʃʃallo] *sm* (*Mil*) marshal; (*: sottufficiale*) warrant officer

marga'rina *sf* margarine

marghe'rita [marge'rita] *sf* (*ox-eye*) daisy, marguerite; (*di stampante*) daisy wheel

'margine ['mardʒine] *sm* margin; (*di bosco, via*) edge, border

mariju'ana [mæri'wa:nə] *sf* marijuana

ma'rina *sf* navy; (*costa*) coast; (*quadro*) seascape; **marina mercantile/militare** navy/merchant navy (*BRIT*) o marine (*US*)

mari'naio *sm* sailor

mari'nare *vt* (*Cuc*) to marinate; ~ **la scuola** to play truant

ma'rino, -a *ag* sea *cpd*, marine

mario'netta *sf* puppet

ma'rito *sm* husband

ma'rittimo, -a *ag* maritime, sea *cpd*

marmel'lata *sf* jam; (*di agrumi*) marmalade

mar'mitta *sf* (*recipiente*) pot; (*Aut*) silencer; **marmitta catalitica** catalytic converter

'marmo *sm* marble

mar'motta *sf* (*Zool*) marmot

maroc'chino, -a [marok'kino] *ag, sm/f* Moroccan

Ma'rocco *sm* **il** ~ Morocco

mar'rone *ag inv* brown ▷ *sm* (*Bot*) chestnut

> Attenzione! In inglese esiste la parola *maroon*, che però indica un altro colore, il rosso bordeaux.

mar'supio *sm* pouch; (*per denaro*) bum bag; (*per neonato*) sling

martedì *sm inv* Tuesday; **di** o **il** ~ on

Tuesdays; **martedì grasso** Shrove Tuesday
martel'lare vt to hammer ▷ vi (pulsare) to
throb; (: cuore) to thump
mar'tello sm hammer; (: di uscio) knocker;
martello pneumatico pneumatic drill
'martire sm/f martyr
mar'xista, -i, -e ag, sm/f Marxist
marza'pane [martsa'pane] sm marzipan
'marzo ['martso] sm March
mascal'zone [maskal'tsone] sm rascal,
scoundrel
mas'cara sm inv mascara
ma'scella [maʃʃella] sf (Anat) jaw
'maschera ['maskera] sf mask;
(travestimento) disguise; (: per un
ballo ecc) fancy dress; (Teatro, Cinema)
usher/usherette; (personaggio del teatro)
stock character; **masche'rare** vt to
mask; (travestire) to disguise; to dress
up; (fig: celare) to hide, conceal; (Mil) to
camouflage; **mascherarsi da** to disguise
o.s. as; to dress up as; (fig) to masquerade
as
mas'chile [mas'kile] ag masculine; (sesso,
popolazione) male; (abiti) men's; (per ragazzi:
scuola) boys'
mas'chilista, -i, -e ag, sm/f (uomo) (male)
chauvinist, sexist; (donna) sexist
'maschio, -a ['maskjo] ag (Biol) male;
(virile) manly ▷ sm (anche Zool, Tecn) male;
(uomo) man; (ragazzo) boy; (figlio) son
masco'lino, -a ag masculine
'massa sf mass; (di errori ecc): **una ~ di**
heaps of, masses of; (di gente) mass,
multitude; (Elettr) earth; **in ~** (Comm) in
bulk; (tutti insieme) en masse; **adunata in ~**
mass meeting; **di ~** (cultura, manifestazione)
mass cpd
mas'sacro sm massacre, slaughter; (fig)
mess, disaster
massaggi'are [massad'dʒare] vt to
massage
mas'saggio [mas'saddʒo] sm massage;
massaggio cardiaco cardiac massage
mas'saia sf housewife
masse'rizie [masse'rittsje] sfpl
(household) furnishings
mas'siccio, -a, -ci, -ce [mas'sittʃo]
ag (oro, legno) solid; (palazzo) massive;
(corporatura) stout ▷ sm (Geo) massif
'massima sf (sentenza, regola) maxim;
(Meteor) maximum temperature; **in linea
di ~** generally speaking; vedi **massimo**
massi'male sm maximum
'massimo, -a ag, sm maximum; **al ~** at
(the) most
'masso sm rock, boulder
masteriz'zare [masterid'dzare] vt (CD,
DVD) to burn

masterizza'tore [masteriddza'tore] sm
CD burner o writer
masti'care vt to chew
'mastice ['mastitʃe] sm mastic; (per vetri)
putty
mas'tino sm mastiff
ma'tassa sf skein
mate'matica sf mathematics sg
mate'matico, -a, -ci, -che ag
mathematical ▷ sm/f mathematician
materas'sino sm mat; **materassino
gonfiabile** air bed
mate'rasso sm mattress; **materasso a
molle** spring o interior-sprung mattress
ma'teria sf (Fisica) matter; (Tecn, Comm)
material, matter no pl; (disciplina) subject;
(argomento) subject matter, material; **in ~
di** (per quanto concerne) on the subject of;
materie prime raw materials
materi'ale ag material; (fig: grossolano)
rough, rude ▷ sm material; (insieme di
strumenti ecc) equipment no pl, materials pl
maternità sf motherhood, maternity;
(reparto) maternity ward
ma'terno, -a ag (amore, cura ecc) maternal,
motherly; (nonno) maternal; (lingua, terra)
mother cpd
ma'tita sf pencil; **matite colorate**
coloured pencils; **matita per gli occhi**
eyeliner (pencil)
ma'tricola sf (registro) register; (numero)
registration number; (nell'università)
freshman, fresher
ma'trigna [ma'triɲɲa] sf stepmother
matrimoni'ale ag matrimonial, marriage
cpd
matri'monio sm marriage, matrimony;
(durata) marriage, married life; (cerimonia)
wedding
mat'tina sf morning
'matto, -a ag mad, crazy; (fig: falso) false,
imitation ▷ sm/f madman/woman; **avere
una voglia matta di qc** to be dying for sth
mat'tone sm brick; (fig): **questo libro/
film è un ~** this book/film is heavy going
matto'nella sf tile
matu'rare vi (anche: **maturarsi**: frutta,
grano) to ripen; (ascesso) to come to a head;
(fig: persona, idea, Econ) to mature ▷ vt to
ripen, to (make) mature
maturità sf maturity; (di frutta)
ripeness, maturity; (Ins) school-leaving
examination, ≈ GCE A-levels (BRIT)
ma'turo, -a ag mature; (frutto) ripe,
mature
max. abbr (= massimo) max
maxischermo [maxis'kermo] sm giant
screen
'mazza ['mattsa] sf (bastone) club;

(*martello*) sledge-hammer; (*Sport: da golf*) club; (: *da baseball, cricket*) bat

maz'zata [mat'tsata] *sf* (*anche fig*) heavy blow

'mazzo ['mattso] *sm* (*di fiori, chiavi ecc*) bunch; (*di carte da gioco*) pack

me *pron* me; **me stesso(a)** myself; **sei bravo quanto me** you are as clever as I (am) o as me

mec'canico, -a, -ci, -che *ag* mechanical ▷ *sm* mechanic; **può mandare un ~?** can you send a mechanic?

mecca'nismo *sm* mechanism

me'daglia [me'daʎʎa] *sf* medal

me'desimo, -a *ag* same; (*in persona*): **io ~** I myself

'media *sf* average; (*Mat*) mean; (*Ins: voto*) end-of-term average; **le medie** *sfpl* = **scuola media**; **in ~** on average; *vedi anche* **medio**

medi'ante *prep* by means of

media'tore, -'trice *sm/f* mediator; (*Comm*) middle man, agent

medi'care *vt* to treat; (*ferita*) to dress

medi'cina [medi'tʃina] *sf* medicine; **medicina legale** forensic medicine

'medico, -a, -ci, -che *ag* medical ▷ *sm* doctor; **chiamate un ~** call a doctor; **medico generico** general practitioner, GP

medie'vale *ag* medieval

'medio, -a *ag* average; (*punto, ceto*) middle; (*altezza, statura*) medium ▷ *sm* (*dito*) middle finger; **licenza media** *leaving certificate awarded at the end of 3 years of secondary education*; **scuola media** *first 3 years of secondary school*

medi'ocre *ag* mediocre, poor

medi'tare *vt* to ponder over, meditate on; (*progettare*) to plan, think out ▷ *vi* to meditate

mediter'raneo, -a *ag* Mediterranean; **il (mare) M~** the Mediterranean (Sea)

me'dusa *sf* (*Zool*) jellyfish

mega'byte *sm inv* (*Comput*) megabyte

me'gafono *sm* megaphone

'meglio ['meʎʎo] *av, ag inv* better; (*con senso superlativo*) best ▷ *sm* (*la cosa migliore*): **il ~** the best (thing); **faresti ~ ad andartene** you had better leave; **alla ~** as best one can; **andar di bene in ~** to get better and better; **fare del proprio ~** to do one's best; **per il ~** for the best; **aver la ~ su qn** to get the better of sb

'mela *sf* apple; **mela cotogna** quince

mela'grana *sf* pomegranate

melan'zana [melan'dzana] *sf* aubergine (BRIT), eggplant (US)

melato'nina *sf* melatonin

'melma *sf* mud, mire

'melo *sm* apple tree

melo'dia *sf* melody

me'lone *sm* (*musk*)melon

'membro *sm* member (*pl(f)* **membra**) (*arto*) limb

memo'randum *sm inv* memorandum

me'moria *sf* memory; **memorie** *sfpl* (*opera autobiografica*) memoirs; **a ~** (*imparare, sapere*) by heart; **a ~ d'uomo** within living memory

mendi'cante *sm/f* beggar

 PAROLA CHIAVE

'meno *av* **1** (*in minore misura*) less; **dovresti mangiare meno** you should eat less, you shouldn't eat so much

2 (*comparativo*): **meno ... di** not as ... as, less ... than; **sono meno alto di te** I'm not as tall as you (are), I'm less tall than you (are); **meno ... che** not as ... as, less ... than; **meno che mai** less than ever; **è meno intelligente che ricco** he's more rich than intelligent; **meno fumo più mangio** the less I smoke the more I eat

3 (*superlativo*) least; **il meno dotato degli studenti** the least gifted of the students; **è quello che compro meno spesso** it's the one I buy least often

4 (*Mat*) minus; **8 meno 5** 8 minus 5, 8 take away 5; **sono le 8 meno un quarto** it's a quarter to 8; **meno 5 gradi** 5 degrees below zero, minus 5 degrees; **1 euro in meno** 1 euro less

5 (*fraseologia*): **quanto meno poteva telefonare** he could at least have phoned; **non so se accettare o meno** I don't know whether to accept or not; **fare a meno di qc/qn** to do without sth/sb; **non potevo fare a meno di ridere** I couldn't help laughing; **meno male!** thank goodness!; **meno male che sei arrivato** it's a good job that you've come

▷ *ag inv* (*tempo, denaro*) less; (*errori, persone*) fewer; **ha fatto meno errori di tutti** he made fewer mistakes than anyone, he made the fewest mistakes of all ▷ *sm inv* **1**: **il meno** (*il minimo*) the least; **parlare del più e del meno** to talk about this and that

2 (*Mat*) minus

▷ *prep* (*eccetto*) except (for), apart from; **a meno che, a meno di** unless; **a meno che non piova** unless it rains; **non posso, a meno di prendere ferie** I can't, unless I take some leave

meno'pausa *sf* menopause

'mensa *sf* (*locale*) canteen; (: *Mil*) mess; (: *nelle università*) refectory

men'sile *ag* monthly ▷ *sm* (*periodico*) monthly (magazine); (*stipendio*) monthly salary

'mensola *sf* bracket; (*ripiano*) shelf; (*Archit*) corbel

'menta *sf* mint; (*anche:* **~ piperita**) peppermint; (*bibita*) peppermint cordial; (*caramella*) mint, peppermint

men'tale *ag* mental; **mentalità** *sf inv* mentality

'mente *sf* mind; **imparare/sapere qc a ~** to learn/know sth by heart; **avere in ~ qc** to have sth in mind; **passare di ~ a qn** to slip sb's mind

men'tire *vi* to lie

'mento *sm* chin

'mentre *cong* (*temporale*) while; (*avversativo*) whereas

menù *sm inv* menu; **ci può portare il ~?** could we see the menu?; **menù turistico** set menu

menzio'nare [mentsjo'nare] *vt* to mention

men'zogna [men'tsɔɲɲa] *sf* lie

mera'viglia [mera'viλλa] *sf* amazement, wonder; (*persona, cosa*) marvel, wonder; **a ~** perfectly, wonderfully; **meravigli'are** *vt* to amaze, astonish; **meravigliarsi (di)** to marvel (at); (*stupirsi*) to be amazed (at), be astonished (at); **meravigli'oso, -a** *ag* wonderful, marvellous

mer'cante *sm* merchant; **mercante d'arte** art dealer

merca'tino *sm* (*rionale*) local street market; (*Econ*) unofficial stock market

mer'cato *sm* market; **mercato dei cambi** exchange market; **mercato nero** black market

'merce ['mertʃe] *sf* goods *pl*, merchandise

mercé [mer'tʃe] *sf* mercy

merce'ria [mertʃe'ria] *sf* (*articoli*) haberdashery (BRIT), notions *pl* (US); (*bottega*) haberdasher's shop (BRIT), notions store (US)

mercoledì *sm inv* Wednesday; **di o il ~ on** Wednesdays; **mercoledì delle Ceneri** Ash Wednesday

mer'curio *sm* mercury

me'renda *sf* afternoon snack

meren'dina *sf* snack

meridi'ana *sf* (*orologio*) sundial

meridi'ano, -a *ag* meridian; midday *cpd*, noonday ▷ *sm* meridian

meridio'nale *ag* southern ▷ *sm/f* southerner

meridi'one *sm* south

me'ringa, -ghe *sf* (*Cuc*) meringue

meri'tare *vt* to deserve, merit ▷ *vb impers* **merita andare** it's worth going

meri'tevole *ag* worthy

'merito *sm* merit; (*valore*) worth; **in ~ a** as regards, with regard to; **dare ~ a qn di** to give sb credit for; **finire a pari ~** to finish joint first (*o second ecc*); to tie

mer'letto *sm* lace

'merlo *sm* (*Zool*) blackbird; (*Archit*) battlement

mer'luzzo [mer'luttso] *sm* (*Zool*) cod

mes'chino, -a [mes'kino] *ag* wretched; (*scarso*) scanty, poor; (*persona: gretta*) mean; (: *limitata*) narrow-minded, petty

mesco'lare *vt* to mix; (*vini, colori*) to blend; (*mettere in disordine*) to mix up, muddle up; (*carte*) to shuffle

'mese *sm* month

'messa *sf* (*Rel*) mass; (*il mettere*): **messa in moto** starting; **messa in piega** set; **messa a punto** (*Tecn*) adjustment; (*Aut*) tuning; (*fig*) clarification; **messa in scena** = **messinscena**

messag'gero [messad'dʒero] *sm* messenger

messaggino [messad'dʒino] *sm* (*di telefonino*) text (message)

mes'saggio [mes'saddʒo] *sm* message; **posso lasciare un ~?** can I leave a message?; **ci sono messaggi per me?** are there any messages for me?; **messaggio di posta elettronica** e-mail message

messag'gistica [messad'dʒistica] *sf* **~ immediata** (*Inform*) instant messaging; **programma di ~ immediata** instant messenger

mes'sale *sm* (*Rel*) missal

messi'cano, -a *ag, sm/f* Mexican

'Messico *sm* **il ~** Mexico

messin'scena [messin'ʃena] *sf* (*Teatro*) production

'messo, -a *pp di* **mettere** ▷ *sm* messenger

mesti'ere *sm* (*professione*) job; (: *manuale*) trade; (: *artigianale*) craft; (*fig: abilità nel lavoro*) skill, technique; **essere del ~** to know the tricks of the trade

'mestolo *sm* (*Cuc*) ladle

mestruazi'one [mestruat'tsjone] *sf* menstruation

'meta *sf* destination; (*fig*) aim, goal

metà *sf inv* half; (*punto di mezzo*) middle; **dividere qc a ~ per ~** to divide sth in half, halve sth; **fare a ~ (di qc con qn)** to go halves (with sb in sth); **a ~ prezzo** at half price; **a ~ strada** halfway

meta'done *sm* methadone

me'tafora *sf* metaphor

me'tallico, -a, -ci, -che *ag* (*di metallo*) metal *cpd*; (*splendore, rumore ecc*) metallic

me'tallo *sm* metal

metalmec'canico, -a, -ci, -che ag
engineering cpd ▷ sm engineering worker
me'tano sm methane
me'ticcio, -a, -ci, -ce [me'tittʃo] sm/f
half-caste, half-breed
me'todico, -a, -ci, -che ag methodical
'metodo sm method
'metro sm metre; (nastro) tape measure;
(asta) (metre) rule
metropoli'tana sf underground, subway
'mettere vt to put; (abito) to put on;
(: portare) to wear; (installare: telefono) to
put in; (fig: provocare): **~ fame/allegria a
qn** to make sb hungry/happy; (supporre):
mettiamo che ... let's suppose o say
that ...; **mettersi** vpr (persona) to put
o.s.; (oggetto) to go; (disporsi: faccenda) to
turn out; **mettersi a sedere** to sit down;
mettersi a letto to get into bed; (per
malattia) to take to one's bed; **mettersi il
cappello** to put on one's hat; **mettersi a**
(cominciare) to begin to, start to; **mettersi
al lavoro** to set to work; **mettersi con qn**
(in società) to team up with sb; (in coppia)
to start going out with sb; **metterci:
metterci molta cura/molto tempo** to
take a lot of care/a lot of time; **ci ho messo
3 ore per venire** it's taken me 3 hours to
get here; **mettercela tutta** to do one's
best; **~ a tacere qn/qc** to keep sb/sth
quiet; **~ su casa** to set up house; **~ su un
negozio** to start a shop; **~ via** to put away
mezza'notte [meddza'nɔtte] sf midnight
'mezzo, -a ['mɛddzo] ag half; **un ~ litro/
panino** half a litre/roll ▷ av half-; **~ morto**
half-dead ▷ sm (metà) half; (parte centrale:
di strada ecc) middle; (per raggiungere un fine)
means sg; (veicolo) vehicle; (nell'indicare
l'ora): **le nove e ~** half past nine; **~giorno e
~** half past twelve; **mezzi** smpl (possibilità
economiche) means; **di mezza età** middle-
aged; **un soprabito di mezza stagione**
a spring (o autumn) coat; **di ~** middle, in
the middle; **andarci di ~** (patir danno) to
suffer; **levarsi o togliersi di ~** to get out of
the way; **in ~ a** in the middle of; **per o a ~
di** by means of; **mezzi di comunicazione
di massa** mass media pl; **mezzi pubblici**
public transport sg; **mezzi di trasporto**
means of transport
mezzogi'orno [meddzo'dʒorno] sm
midday, noon; **a ~** at 12 (o'clock) o midday o
noon; **il ~ d'Italia** southern Italy
mi (dav lo, la, li, le, ne diventa **me**) pron
(oggetto) me; (complemento di termine)
to me; (riflessivo) myself ▷ sm (Mus) E;
(: solfeggiando la scala) mi
miago'lare vi to miaow, mew
'mica av (fam): **non ... ~** not ... at all; **non**

sono ~ stanco I'm not a bit tired; **non sarà
~ partito?** he wouldn't have left, would
he?; **~ male** not bad
'miccia, -ce ['mittʃa] sf fuse
micidi'ale [mitʃi'djale] ag fatal;
(dannosissimo) deadly
micro'fibra sf microfibre
mi'crofono sm microphone
micros'copio sm microscope
mi'dollo (pl(f) **midolla**) sm (Anat) marrow;
midollo osseo bone marrow
mi'ele sm honey
'miglia ['miʎʎa] sfpl di **miglio**
migli'aio [miʎ'ʎajo] ((pl)f **migliaia**) sm
thousand; **un ~ (di)** about a thousand; **a
migliaia** by the thousand, in thousands
'miglio ['miʎʎo] sm (Bot) millet (pl(f)
miglia) (unità di misura) mile; **~ marino** o
nautico nautical mile
migliora'mento [miʎʎora'mento] sm
improvement
miglio'rare [miʎʎo'rare] vt, vi to improve
migli'ore [miʎ'ʎore] ag (comparativo)
better; (superlativo) best ▷ sm **il ~** the best
(thing) ▷ sm/f **il(la) ~** the best (person); **il
miglior vino di questa regione** the best
wine in this area
'mignolo ['miɲɲolo] sm (Anat) little finger,
pinkie; (: dito del piede) little toe
Mi'lano sf Milan
miliar'dario, -a sm/f millionaire
mili'ardo sm thousand million, billion (US)
mili'one sm million; **mille euro** one
thousand euros
mili'tante ag, sm/f militant
mili'tare vi (Mil) to be a soldier, serve; (fig:
in un partito) to be a militant ▷ ag military
▷ sm serviceman; **fare il ~** to do one's
military service
'mille (pl **mila**) num a o one thousand; **dieci
mila** ten thousand
mil'lennio sm millennium
millepi'edi sm inv centipede
mil'lesimo, -a ag, sm thousandth
milli'grammo sm milligram(me)
mil'limetro sm millimetre
'milza ['miltsa] sf (Anat) spleen
mimetiz'zare [mimetid'dzare] vt to
camouflage; **mimetizzarsi** vpr to
camouflage o.s.
'mimo sm (attore, componimento) mime
mi'mosa sf mimosa
min. abbr (= minuto, minimo) min.
'mina sf (esplosiva) mine; (di matita) lead
mi'naccia, -ce [mi'nattʃa] sf threat;
minacci'are vt to threaten; **minacciare
qn di morte** to threaten to kill sb;
minacciare di fare qc to threaten to do
sth

mi'nare vt (Mil) to mine; (fig) to undermine

mina'tore sm miner

mine'rale ag, sm mineral

mine'rario, -a ag (delle miniere) mining; (dei minerali) ore cpd

mi'nestra sf soup; **minestra in brodo** noodle soup; **minestra di verdure** vegetable soup

minia'tura sf miniature

mini'bar sm inv minibar

mini'era sf mine

mini'gonna sf miniskirt

'minimo, -a ag minimum, least, slightest; (piccolissimo) very small, slight; (il più basso) lowest, minimum ▷ sm minimum; **al ~** at least; **girare al ~** (Aut) to idle

minis'tero sm (Pol, Rel) ministry; (governo) government; **M~ delle Finanze** Ministry of Finance, ≈ Treasury

mi'nistro sm (Pol, Rel) minister

mino'ranza [mino'rantsa] sf minority

mi'nore ag (comparativo) less; (più piccolo) smaller; (numero) lower; (inferiore) lower, inferior; (meno importante) minor; (più giovane) younger; (superlativo) least; smallest; lowest; youngest ▷ sm/f = **minorenne**

mino'renne ag under age ▷ sm/f minor, person under age

mi'nuscolo, -a ag (scrittura, carattere) small; (piccolissimo) tiny ▷ sf small letter

mi'nuto, -a ag tiny, minute; (pioggia) fine; (corporatura) delicate, fine ▷ sm (unità di misura) minute; **al ~** (Comm) retail

'mio (f'mia, pl mi'ei or 'mie) det **il ~, la mia** ecc my ▷ pron **il ~, la mia** ecc mine; **i miei** my family; **un ~ amico** a friend of mine

mi'ope ag short-sighted

'mira sf (anche fig) aim; **prendere la ~** to take aim; **prendere di ~ qn** (fig) to pick on sb

mi'racolo sm miracle

mi'raggio [mi'raddʒo] sm mirage

mi'rare vi **~ a** to aim at

mi'rino sm (Tecn) sight; (Fot) viewer, viewfinder

mir'tillo sm bilberry (BRIT), blueberry (US), whortleberry

mi'scela [miʃ'ʃela] sf mixture; (di caffè) blend

'mischia ['miskja] sf scuffle; (Rugby) scrum, scrummage

mis'cuglio [mis'kuʎʎo] sm mixture, hotchpotch, jumble

'mise vb vedi **mettere**

mise'rabile ag (infelice) miserable, wretched; (povero) poverty-stricken; (di scarso valore) miserable

mi'seria sf extreme poverty; (infelicità) misery

miseri'cordia sf mercy, pity

'misero, -a ag miserable, wretched; (povero) poverty-stricken; (insufficiente) miserable

'misi vb vedi **mettere**

mi'sogino [mi'zɔdʒino] sm misogynist

'missile sm missile

missio'nario, -a ag, sm/f missionary

missi'one sf mission

misteri'oso, -a ag mysterious

mis'tero sm mystery

'misto, -a ag mixed; (scuola) mixed, coeducational ▷ sm mixture

mis'tura sf mixture

mi'sura sf measure; (misurazione, dimensione) measurement; (taglia) size; (provvedimento) measure, step; (moderazione) moderation; (Mus) time; (: divisione) bar; (fig: limite) bounds pl, limit; **nella ~ in cui** inasmuch as, insofar as; **(fatto) su ~** made to measure

misu'rare vt (ambiente, stoffa) to measure; (terreno) to survey; (abito) to try on; (pesare) to weigh; (fig: parole ecc) to weigh up; (: spese, cibo) to limit ▷ vi to measure; **misurarsi** vpr **misurarsi con qn** to have a confrontation with sb; to compete with sb

'mite ag mild

'mitico, -a, ci, che ag mythical

'mito sm myth; **mitolo'gia, -'gie** sf mythology

'mitra sf (Rel) mitre ▷ sm inv (arma) sub-machine gun

mit'tente sm/f sender

mm abbr (= millimetro) mm

'mobile ag mobile; (parte di macchina) moving; (Dir: beni) movable, personal ▷ sm (arredamento) piece of furniture; **mobili** smpl (mobilia) furniture sg

mocas'sino sm moccasin

'moda sf fashion; **alla ~, di ~** fashionable, in fashion

modalità sf inv formality

mo'della sf model

mo'dello sm model; (stampo) mould ▷ ag inv model cpd

'modem sm inv modem

modera'tore, -'trice sm/f moderator

mo'derno, -a ag modern

mo'desto, -a ag modest

'modico, -a, -ci, -che ag reasonable, moderate

mo'difica, -che sf modification

modifi'care vt to modify, alter

'modo sm way, manner; (mezzo) means, way; (occasione) opportunity; (Ling) mood; (Mus) mode; **modi** smpl (comportamento) manners; **a suo ~, a ~ suo** in his own way;

ad *o* **in ogni ~** anyway; **di** *o* **in ~ che** so that; **in ~ da** so as to; **in tutti i modi** at all costs; (*comunque sia*) anyway; (*in ogni caso*) in any case; **in qualche ~** somehow or other; **per ~ di dire** so to speak; **modo di dire** turn of phrase

'**modulo** *sm* (*modello*) form; (*Archit, lunare, di comando*) module

'**mogano** *sm* mahogany

'**mogio, -a, -gi, -gie** ['mɔdʒo] *ag* down in the dumps, dejected

'**moglie** ['moʎʎe] *sf* wife

mo'ine *sfpl* cajolery *sg*; (*leziosità*) affectation *sg*

mo'lare *sm* (*dente*) molar

'**mole** *sf* mass; (*dimensioni*) size; (*edificio grandioso*) massive structure

moles'tare *vt* to bother, annoy; **mo'lestia** *sf* annoyance, bother; **recar molestia a qn** to bother sb; **molestie sessuali** sexual harassment *sg*

'**molla** *sf* spring; **molle** *sfpl* (*per camino*) tongs

mol'lare *vt* to release, let go; (*Naut*) to ease; (*fig: ceffone*) to give ▷ *vi* (*cedere*) to give in

'**molle** *ag* soft; (*muscoli*) flabby

mol'letta *sf* (*per capelli*) hairgrip; (*per panni stesi*) clothes peg

'**mollica, -che** *sf* crumb, soft part

mol'lusco, -schi *sm* mollusc

'**molo** *sm* mole, breakwater; jetty

moltipli'care *vt* to multiply; **moltiplicarsi** *vpr* to multiply; to increase in number; **moltiplicazi'one** *sf* multiplication

PAROLA CHIAVE

'**molto, -a** *det* (*quantità*) a lot of, much; (*numero*) a lot of, many; **molto pane/carbone** a lot of bread/coal; **molta gente** a lot of people, many people; **molti libri** a lot of books, many books; **non ho molto tempo** I haven't got much time; **per molto (tempo)** for a long time ▷ *av* **1** a lot, (very) much; **viaggia molto** he travels a lot; **non viaggia molto** he doesn't travel much *o* a lot

2 (*intensivo: con aggettivi, avverbi*) very; (*: con participio passato*) (very) much; **molto buono** very good; **molto migliore, molto meglio** much *o* a lot better ▷ *pron* much, a lot

momentanea'mente *av* at the moment, at present

momen'taneo, -a *ag* momentary, fleeting

mo'mento *sm* moment; **da un ~ all'altro** at any moment; (*all'improvviso*) suddenly; **al ~ di fare** just as I was (*o* you were *o* he was *ecc*) doing; **per il ~** for the time being; **dal ~ che** ever since; (*dato che*) since; **a momenti** (*da un momento all'altro*) any time *o* moment now; (*quasi*) nearly

'**monaca, -che** *sf* nun

'**Monaco** *sf* Monaco; **Monaco (di Baviera)** Munich

'**monaco, -ci** *sm* monk

monar'chia *sf* monarchy

monas'tero *sm* (*di monaci*) monastery; (*di monache*) convent

mon'dano, -a *ag* (*anche fig*) worldly; (*anche:* **dell'alta società**) society *cpd*; fashionable

mondi'ale *ag* (*campionato, popolazione*) world *cpd*; (*influenza*) world-wide

'**mondo** *sm* world; (*grande quantità*): **un ~ di** lots of, a host of; **il bel ~** high society

mo'nello, -a *sm/f* street urchin; (*ragazzo vivace*) scamp, imp

mo'neta *sf* coin; (*Econ: valuta*) currency; (*denaro spicciolo*) (small) change; **moneta estera** foreign currency; **moneta legale** legal tender

mongol'fiera *sf* hot-air balloon

'**monitor** *sm inv* (*Tecn, TV*) monitor

monolo'cale *sm* studio flat

mono'polio *sm* monopoly

mo'notono, -a *ag* monotonous

monovo'lume *ag inv*, *sf inv* (**automobile**) **~** people carrier, MPV

mon'sone *sm* monsoon

monta'carichi [monta'kariki] *sm inv* hoist, goods lift

mon'taggio [mon'taddʒo] *sm* (*Tecn*) assembly; (*Cinema*) editing

mon'tagna [mon'taɲɲa] *sf* mountain; (*zona montuosa*): **la ~** the mountains *pl*; **andare in ~** to go to the mountains; **montagne russe** roller coaster *sg*, big dipper *sg* (BRIT)

monta'naro, -a *ag* mountain *cpd* ▷ *sm/f* mountain dweller

mon'tano, -a *ag* mountain *cpd*; alpine

mon'tare *vt* to go up (*o* come) up; (*cavallo*) to ride; (*apparecchiatura*) to set up, assemble; (*Cuc*) to whip; (*Zool*) to cover; (*incastonare*) to mount, set; (*Cinema*) to edit; (*Fot*) to mount ▷ *vi* to go (*o* come) up; (*a cavallo*): **~ bene/male** to ride well/badly; (*aumentare di livello, volume*) to rise

monta'tura *sf* assembling *no pl*; (*di occhiali*) frames *pl*; (*di gioiello*) mounting, setting; (*fig*): **montatura pubblicitaria** publicity stunt

'**monte** *sm* mountain; **a ~** upstream; **mandare a ~ qc** to upset sth, cause sth to fail; **il M~ Bianco** Mont Blanc; **monte di pietà** pawnshop; **monte premi** prize

mon'tone sm (Zool) ram; **carne di ~** mutton

montu'oso, -a ag mountainous

monu'mento sm monument

mo'quette [mɔ'kɛt] sf inv fitted carpet

'mora sf (del rovo) blackberry; (del gelso) mulberry; (Dir) delay; (: somma) arrears pl

mo'rale ag moral ▷ sf (scienza) ethics sg, moral philosophy; (complesso di norme) moral standards pl, morality; (condotta) morals pl; (insegnamento morale) moral ▷ sm morale; **essere giù di ~** to be feeling down

'morbido, -a ag soft; (pelle) soft, smooth
  Attenzione! In inglese esiste la parola morbid, che però significa morboso.

mor'billo sm (Med) measles sg

'morbo sm disease

mor'boso, -a ag (fig) morbid

'mordere vt to bite; (addentare) to bite into

mori'bondo, -a ag dying, moribund

mo'rire vi to die; (abitudine, civiltà) to die out; **~ di fame** to die of hunger; (fig) to be starving; **~ di noia/paura** to be bored/scared to death; **fa un caldo da ~** it's terribly hot

mormo'rare vi to murmur; (brontolare) to grumble

'moro, -a ag dark(-haired), dark(-complexioned)

'morsa sf (Tecn) vice; (fig: stretta) grip

morsi'care vt to nibble (at), gnaw (at); (insetto) to bite

'morso, -a pp di **mordere** ▷ sm bite; (di insetto) sting; (parte della briglia) bit; **morsi della fame** pangs of hunger

morta'della sf (Cuc) mortadella (type of salted pork meat)

mor'taio sm mortar

mor'tale ag, sm mortal

'morte sf death

'morto, -a pp di **morire** ▷ ag dead ▷ sm/f dead man/woman; **i morti** the dead; **fare il ~** (nell'acqua) to float on one's back; **il Mar M~** the Dead Sea

mo'saico, -ci sm mosaic

'Mosca sf Moscow

'mosca, -sche sf fly; **mosca cieca** blind-man's-buff

mosce'rino [moʃʃe'rino] sm midge, gnat

mos'chea [mos'kɛa] sf mosque

'moscio, -a, -sci, -sce ['mɔʃʃo] ag (fig) lifeless

mos'cone sm (Zool) bluebottle; (barca) pedalo; (: a remi) kind of pedalo with oars

'mossa sf movement; (nel gioco) move

'mossi ecc vb vedi **muovere**

'mosso, -a pp di **muovere** ▷ ag (mare) rough; (capelli) wavy; (Fot) blurred

mos'tarda sf mustard; **mostarda di Cremona** pickled fruit with mustard

'mostra sf exhibition, show; (ostentazione) show; **in ~** on show; **far ~ di** (fingere) to pretend; **far ~ di sé** to show off

mos'trare vt to show; **può mostrarmi dov'è, per favore?** can you show me where it is, please?

'mostro sm monster; **mostru'oso, -a** ag monstrous

mo'tel sm inv motel

moti'vare vt (causare) to cause; (giustificare) to justify, account for

mo'tivo sm (causa) reason, cause; (movente) motive; (letterario) (central) theme; (disegno) motif, design, pattern; (Mus) motif; **per quale ~?** why?, for what reason?

'moto sm (anche Fisica) motion; (movimento, gesto) movement; (esercizio fisico) exercise; (sommossa) rising, revolt; (commozione) feeling, impulse ▷ sf inv (motocicletta) motorbike; **mettere in ~** to set in motion; (Aut) to start up

motoci'clista, -i, -e sm/f motorcyclist

mo'tore, -'trice ag motor; (Tecn) driving ▷ sm engine, motor; **a ~** motor cpd, power-driven; **~ a combustione interna/a reazione** internal combustion/jet engine; **motore di ricerca** (Inform) search engine; **moto'rino** sm moped; **motorino di avviamento** (Aut) starter

motos'cafo sm motorboat

'motto sm (battuta scherzosa) witty remark; (frase emblematica) motto, maxim

'mouse ['maus] sm inv (Inform) mouse

mo'vente sm motive

movi'mento sm movement; (fig) activity, hustle and bustle; (Mus) tempo, movement

mozi'one [mot'tsjone] sf (Pol) motion

mozza'rella [mottsa'rɛlla] sf mozzarella, a moist Neapolitan curd cheese

mozzi'cone [mottsi'kone] sm stub, butt, end; (anche: **~ di sigaretta**) cigarette end

'mucca, -che sf cow; **mucca pazza** mad cow disease

'mucchio ['mukkjo] sm pile, heap; (fig): **un ~ di** lots of, heaps of

'muco, -chi sm mucus

'muffa sf mould, mildew

mug'gire [mud'dʒire] vi (vacca) to low, moo; (toro) to bellow; (fig) to roar

mu'ghetto [mu'getto] sm lily of the valley

mu'lino sm mill; **mulino a vento** windmill

'mulo sm mule

'multa sf fine

multi'etnico, -a, -ci, -che *ag* multiethnic

multirazziale [multirat'tsjale] *ag* multiracial

multi'sala *ag inv* multiscreen

multivitami'nico, -a, -ci, -che *ag* **complesso ~** multivitamin

'mummia *sf* mummy

'mungere ['mundʒere] *vt (anche fig)* to milk

munici'pale [munitʃi'pale] *ag* municipal; town *cpd*

muni'cipio [muni'tʃipjo] *sm* town council, corporation; *(edificio)* town hall

munizi'oni [munit'tsjoni] *sfpl (Mil)* ammunition *sg*

'munsi *ecc vb vedi* **mungere**

mu'oio *ecc vb vedi* **morire**

mu'overe *vt* to move; *(ruota, macchina)* to drive; *(sollevare: questione, obiezione)* to raise, bring up; *(: accusa)* to make, bring forward; **muoversi** *vpr* to move; **muoviti!** hurry up!, get a move on!

'mura *sfpl vedi* **muro**

mu'rale *ag* wall *cpd*; mural

mura'tore *sm* mason; bricklayer

'muro *sm* wall

'muschio ['muskjo] *sm (Zool)* musk; *(Bot)* moss

musco'lare *ag* muscular, muscle *cpd*

'muscolo *sm (Anat)* muscle

mu'seo *sm* museum

museru'ola *sf* muzzle

'musica *sf* music; **musica da ballo/ camera** dance/chamber music; **musi'cale** *ag* musical; **musi'cista, -i, -e** *sm/f* musician

'müsli ['mysli] *sm* muesli

'muso *sm* muzzle; *(di auto, aereo)* nose; **tenere il ~** to sulk

mussul'mano, -a *ag, sm/f* Muslim, Moslem

'muta *sf (di animali)* moulting; *(di serpenti)* sloughing; *(per immersioni subacquee)* diving suit; *(gruppo di cani)* pack

mu'tande *sfpl (da uomo)* (under)pants

'muto, -a *ag (Med)* dumb; *(emozione, dolore, Cinema)* silent; *(Ling)* silent, mute; *(carta geografica)* blank; **~ per lo stupore** *ecc* speechless with amazement *ecc*

'mutuo, -a *ag (reciproco)* mutual ▷ *sm (Econ)* (long-term) loan

n

N *abbr (= nord)* N

n. *abbr (= numero)* no.

'nafta *sf* naphtha; *(per motori diesel)* diesel oil

nafta'lina *sf (Chim)* naphthalene; *(tarmicida)* mothballs *pl*

'naia *sf (Mil) slang term for national service*

na'if [na'if] *ag inv* naïve

'nanna *sf (linguaggio infantile)*: **andare a ~** to go to beddy-byes

'nano, -a *ag, sm/f* dwarf

napole'tano, -a *ag, sm/f* Neapolitan

'Napoli *sf* Naples

nar'ciso [nar'tʃizo] *sm* narcissus

nar'cotico, -ci *sm* narcotic

na'rice [na'ritʃe] *sf* nostril

nar'rare *vt* to tell the story of, recount; **narra'tiva** *sf (branca letteraria)* fiction

na'sale *ag* nasal

'nascere ['naʃʃere] *vi (bambino)* to be born; *(pianta)* to come o spring up; *(fiume)* to rise, have its source; *(sole)* to rise; *(dente)* to come through; *(fig: derivare, conseguire)*: **~ da** to arise from, be born out of; **è nata nel 1952** she was born in 1952; **'nascita** *sf* birth

nas'condere *vt* to hide, conceal; **nascondersi** *vpr* to hide; **nascon'diglio** *sm* hiding place; **nascon'dino** *sm (gioco)* hide-and-seek; **nas'cosi** *ecc vb*

vedi **nascondere**; **nas'costo, -a** *pp di*
nascondere ▷ *ag* hidden; **di nascosto**
secretly
na'sello *sm* (*Zool*) hake
'**naso** *sm* nose
'**nastro** *sm* ribbon; (*magnetico, isolante,*
Sport) tape; **nastro adesivo** adhesive
tape; **nastro trasportatore** conveyor belt
nas'turzio [nas'turtsjo] *sm* nasturtium
na'tale *ag* of one's birth ▷ *sm* (*Rel*): **N~**
Christmas; (*giorno della nascita*) birthday;
nata'lizio, -a *ag* (*del Natale*) Christmas *cpd*
'**natica, -che** *sf* (*Anat*) buttock
'**nato, -a** *pp di* **nascere** ▷ *ag* **un attore ~ a**
born actor; **nata Pieri** née Pieri
na'tura *sf* nature; **pagare in ~** to pay in
kind; **natura morta** still life
natu'rale *ag* natural
natural'mente *av* naturally; (*certamente,*
sì) of course
natu'rista, -i, e *ag, sm/f* naturist, nudist
naufra'gare *vi* (*nave*) to be wrecked;
(*persona*) to be shipwrecked; (*fig*) to fall
through; '**naufrago, -ghi** *sm* castaway,
shipwreck victim
'**nausea** *sf* nausea; **nause'ante** *ag* (*odore*)
nauseating; (*sapore*) disgusting; (*fig*)
sickening
'**nautico, -a, -ci, -che** *ag* nautical
na'vale *ag* naval
na'vata *sf* (*anche*: **~ centrale**) nave; (*anche*:
~ laterale) aisle
'**nave** *sf* ship, vessel; **nave cisterna**
tanker; **nave da guerra** warship; **nave**
passeggeri passenger ship
na'vetta *sf* shuttle; (*servizio di*
collegamento) shuttle (service)
navi'cella [navi'tʃɛlla] *sf* (*di aerostato*)
gondola; **navicella spaziale** spaceship
navi'gare *vi* to sail; **~ in Internet** to surf
the Net; **navigazi'one** *sf* navigation
nazio'nale [nattsjo'nale] *ag* national ▷ *sf*
(*Sport*) national team; **nazionalità** *sf inv*
nationality
nazi'one [nat'tsjone] *sf* nation
naziskin ['nɑːtsiskin] *sm inv* Nazi
skinhead
NB *abbr* (= *nota bene*) NB

 PAROLA CHIAVE

ne *pron* **1** (*di lui, lei, loro*) of him/her/them;
about him/her/them; **ne riconosco la**
voce I recognize his (*o* her) voice
2 (*di questa, quella cosa*) of it; about it; **ne**
voglio ancora I want some more (of it *o*
them); **non parliamone più!** let's not talk
about it any more!
3 (*con valore partitivo*): **hai dei libri? — sì,**

ne ho have you any books? — yes, I have
(some); **hai del pane? — no, non ne ho**
have you any bread? — no, I haven't any;
quanti anni hai? — ne ho 17 how old are
you? — I'm 17
▷ *av* (*moto da luogo: da lì*) from there; **ne**
vengo ora I've just come from there

né *cong* **né ... né** neither ... nor; **né l'uno**
né l'altro lo vuole neither of them wants
it; **non parla né l'italiano né il tedesco**
he speaks neither Italian nor German, he
doesn't speak either Italian or German;
non piove né nevica it isn't raining or
snowing
ne'anche [ne'anke] *av, cong* not even;
non ... ~ not even; **~ se volesse**
potrebbe venire he couldn't come even
if he wanted to; **non l'ho visto — ~ io**
I didn't see him — neither did I *o* I didn't
either; **~ per idea** *o* **sogno!** not on your
life!
'**nebbia** *sf* fog; (*foschia*) mist
necessaria'mente [netʃessarjamente]
av necessarily
neces'sario, -a [netʃes'sarjo] *ag*
necessary
necessità [netʃessi'ta] *sf inv* necessity;
(*povertà*) need, poverty
necro'logio [nekro'lɔdʒo] *sm* obituary
notice
ne'gare *vt* to deny; (*rifiutare*) to deny,
refuse; **~ di aver fatto/che** to deny
having done/that; **nega'tivo, -a** *ag, sf, sm*
negative
negherò *ecc* [nege'rɔ] *vb vedi* **negare**
negli'gente [negli'dʒɛnte] *ag* negligent,
careless
negozi'ante [negot'tsjante] *sm/f* trader,
dealer; (*bottegaio*) shopkeeper (BRIT),
storekeeper (US)
negozi'are [negot'tsjare] *vt* to negotiate
▷ *vi* **~ in** to trade *o* deal in; **negozi'ato** *sm*
negotiation
ne'gozio [ne'gɔttsjo] *sm* (*locale*) shop
(BRIT), store (US)
'**negro, -a** *ag, sm/f* Negro
ne'mico, -a, -ci, -che *ag* hostile; (*Mil*)
enemy *cpd* ▷ *sm/f* enemy; **essere ~ di** to be
strongly averse *o* opposed to
nem'meno *av, cong* **= neanche**
'**neo** *sm* mole; (*fig*) (slight) flaw
'**neon** *sm* (*Chim*) neon
neo'nato, -a *ag* newborn ▷ *sm/f* newborn
baby
neozelan'dese [neoddzelan'dese] *ag*
New Zealand *cpd* ▷ *sm/f* New Zealander
'**Nepal** *sm* **il ~** Nepal
nep'pure *av, cong* **= neanche**

'nero, -a ag black; (scuro) dark ▷ sm black; **il Mar N~** the Black Sea

'nervo sm (Anat) nerve; (Bot) vein; **avere i nervi** to be on edge; **dare sui nervi a qn** to get on sb's nerves; **ner'voso, -a** ag nervous; (irritabile) irritable ▷ sm (fam): **far venire il nervoso a qn** to get on sb's nerves

'nespola sf (Bot) medlar; (fig) blow, punch

'nesso sm connection, link

PAROLA CHIAVE

nes'suno, -a (det: dav sm **nessun** +C, V, **nessuno** +s impura, gn, pn, ps, x, z; dav sf **nessuna** +C, **nessun'** +V) det **1** (non uno) no; (, espressione negativa +) any; **non c'è nessun libro** there isn't any book, there is no book; **nessun altro** no one else, nobody else; **nessun'altra cosa** nothing else; **in nessun luogo** nowhere
2 (qualche) any; **hai nessuna obiezione?** do you have any objections?
▷ pron **1** (non uno) no one, nobody; (, espressione negativa +) any(one); (: cosa) none; (, espressione negativa +) any; **nessuno è venuto, non è venuto nessuno** nobody came
2 (qualcuno) anyone, anybody; **ha telefonato nessuno?** did anyone phone?

net'tare vt to clean

net'tezza [net'tettsa] sf cleanness, cleanliness; **nettezza urbana** cleansing department

'netto, -a ag (pulito) clean; (chiaro) clear, clear-cut; (deciso) definite; (Econ) net

nettur'bino sm dustman (BRIT), garbage collector (US)

neu'trale ag neutral

neutro, -a ag neutral; (Ling) neuter ▷ sm (Ling) neuter

neve sf snow; **nevi'care** vb impers to snow; **nevi'cata** sf snowfall

ne'vischio [ne'viskjo] sm sleet

ne'voso, -a ag snowy; snow-covered

nevral'gia [nevral'dʒia] sf neuralgia

nevras'tenico, -a, -ci, -che ag (Med) neurasthenic; (fig) hot-tempered

ne'vrosi sf neurosis

ne'vrotico, -a, ci, che ag, sm/f (anche fig) neurotic

nicchia ['nikkja] sf niche; (naturale) cavity, hollow; **nicchia di mercato** (Comm) niche market

nicchi'are [nik'kjare] vi to shilly-shally, hesitate

nichel ['nikel] sm nickel

nico'tina sf nicotine

'nido sm nest; **a ~ d'ape** (tessuto ecc) honeycomb cpd

PAROLA CHIAVE

ni'ente pron **1** (nessuna cosa) nothing; **niente può fermarlo** nothing can stop him; **niente di niente** absolutely nothing; **nient'altro** nothing else; **nient'altro che** nothing but, just, only; **niente affatto** not at all, not in the least; **come se niente fosse** as if nothing had happened; **cose da niente** trivial matters; **per niente** (gratis, invano) for nothing
2 (qualcosa): **hai bisogno di niente?** do you need anything?
3: **non ... niente** nothing; (espressione negativa +) anything; **non ho visto niente** I saw nothing, I didn't see anything; **non ho niente da dire** I have nothing o haven't anything to say
▷ sm nothing; **un bel niente** absolutely nothing; **basta un niente per farla piangere** the slightest thing is enough to make her cry ▷ av (in nessuna misura): **non ... niente** not ... at all; **non è (per) niente buono** it isn't good at all

Ni'geria [ni'dʒɛrja] sf **la ~** Nigeria

'ninfa sf nymph

nin'fea sf water lily

ninna-'nanna sf lullaby

'ninnolo sm (gingillo) knick-knack

ni'pote sm/f (di zii) nephew/niece; (di nonni) grandson/daughter, grandchild

'nitido, -a ag clear; (specchio) bright

ni'trire vi to neigh

ni'trito sm (di cavallo) neighing no pl; neigh; (Chim) nitrite

nitroglice'rina [nitroglitʃe'rina] sf nitroglycerine

no av (risposta) no; **vieni o no?** are you coming or not?; **perché no?** why not?; **lo conosciamo? — tu no ma io sì** do we know him? — you don't but I do; **verrai, no?** you'll come, won't you?

'nobile ag noble ▷ sm/f noble, nobleman/woman

'nocca, -che sf (Anat) knuckle

'noccio ecc ['nɔttʃo] vb vedi **nuocere**

nocci'ola [not'tʃɔla] ag inv (colore) hazel, light brown ▷ sf hazelnut

nocci'olina [nottʃo'lina] sf: **nocciolina americana** peanut

'nocciolo ['nɔttʃolo] sm (di frutto) stone; (fig) heart, core

'noce ['notʃe] sm (albero) walnut tree ▷ sf (frutto) walnut; **noce di cocco** coconut; **noce moscata** nutmeg

no'cevo ecc [no'tʃevo] vb vedi **nuocere**

no'civo, -a [no'tʃivo] ag harmful, noxious

'nocqui ecc vb vedi **nuocere**

'nodo sm (di cravatta, legname, Naut) knot; (Aut, Ferr) junction; (Med, Astr, Bot) node; (fig: legame) bond, tie; (: punto centrale) heart, crux; **avere un ~ alla gola** to have a lump in one's throat

no-'global sm/f anti-globalization protester ▷ ag (movimento, manifestante) anti-globalization

'noi pron (soggetto) we; (oggetto: per dare rilievo, con preposizione) us; **~ stessi(e)** we ourselves; (oggetto) ourselves

'noia sf boredom; (disturbo, impaccio) bother no pl, trouble no pl; **avere qn/qc a ~** not to like sb/sth; **mi è venuto a ~** I'm tired of it; **dare ~ a** to annoy; **avere delle noie con qn** to have trouble with sb

noi'oso, -a ag boring; (fastidioso) annoying, troublesome

▓ Attenzione! In inglese esiste la parola noisy, che però significa rumoroso.

noleggi'are [noled'dʒare] vt (prendere a noleggio) to hire (BRIT), rent; (dare a noleggio) to hire out (BRIT), rent (out); (aereo, nave) to charter; **vorrei ~ una macchina** I'd like to hire a car; **no'leggio** sm hire (BRIT), rental; charter

'nomade ag nomadic ▷ sm/f nomad

'nome sm name; (Ling) noun; **in/a ~ di** in the name of; **di o per ~** (chiamato) called, named; **conoscere qn di ~** to know sb by name; **nome d'arte** stage name; **nome di battesimo** Christian name; **nome di famiglia** surname

no'mignolo [no'miɲɲolo] sm nickname

'nomina sf appointment

nomi'nale ag nominal; (Ling) noun cpd

nomi'nare vt to name; (eleggere) to appoint; (citare) to mention

nomina'tivo, -a ag (Ling) nominative; (Econ) registered ▷ sm (Ling: anche: **caso ~**) nominative (case); (Amm) name

non av not ▷ prefisso non-; vedi **affatto**, **appena** ecc

nonché [non'ke] cong (tanto più, tanto meno) let alone; (e inoltre) as well as

noncu'rante ag **~ (di)** careless (of), indifferent (to)

'nonno, -a sm/f grandfather/mother; (in senso più familiare) grandma/grandpa; **i nonni** the grandparents

non'nulla sm inv **un ~** nothing, a trifle

'nono, -a ag, sm ninth

nonos'tante prep in spite of, notwithstanding ▷ cong although, even though

nontiscordardimé sm inv (Bot) forget-me-not

nord sm North ▷ ag inv north; northern; **il Mare del N~** the North Sea; **nor'dest** sm north-east; **nor'dovest** sm north-west

'norma sf (principio) norm; (regola) regulation, rule; (consuetudine) custom, rule; **a ~ di legge** according to law, as laid down by law; **norme per l'uso** instructions for use; **norme di sicurezza** safety regulations

nor'male ag normal; standard cpd

normal'mente av normally

norve'gese [norve'dʒese] ag, sm/f, sm Norwegian

Nor'vegia [nor'vedʒa] sf **la ~** Norway

nostal'gia [nostal'dʒia] sf (di casa, paese) homesickness; (del passato) nostalgia

nos'trano, -a ag local; national; home-produced

'nostro, -a det **il (la) ~(-a)** ecc our ▷ pron **il (la) ~(-a)** ecc ours ▷ sm **il ~** our money; our belongings; **i nostri** our family; our own people; **è dei nostri** he's one of us

'nota sf (segno) mark; (comunicazione scritta, Mus) note; (fattura) bill; (elenco) list; **degno di ~** noteworthy, worthy of note

no'taio sm notary

no'tare vt (segnare: errori) to mark; (registrare) to note (down), write down; (rilevare, osservare) to note, notice; **farsi ~** to get o.s. noticed

no'tevole ag (talento) notable, remarkable; (peso) considerable

no'tifica, -che sf notification

no'tizia [no'tittsja] sf (piece of) news sg; (informazione) piece of information; **notizi'ario** sm (Radio, TV, Stampa) news sg

'noto, -a ag (well-)known

notorietà sf fame; notoriety

no'torio, -a ag well-known; (peg) notorious

not'tambulo, -a sm/f night-bird; (fig)

not'tata sf night

'notte sf night; **di ~** at night; (durante la notte) in the night, during the night; **notte bianca** sleepless night

not'turno, -a ag nocturnal; (servizio, guardiano) night cpd

no'vanta num ninety; **novan'tesimo, -a** num ninetieth

'nove num nine

nove'cento [nove'tʃento] num nine hundred ▷ sm **il N~** the twentieth century

no'vella sf (Letteratura) short story

no'vello, -a ag (piante, patate) new; (insalata, verdura) early; (sposo) newly-married

no'vembre sm November

novità sf inv novelty; (innovazione)

innovation; (*cosa originale, insolita*) something new; (*notizia*) (piece of) news *sg*; **le ~ della moda** the latest fashions

nozi'one [not'tsjone] *sf* notion, idea

nozze ['nɔttse] *sfpl* wedding *sg*, marriage *sg*; **nozze d'argento/d'oro** silver/golden wedding *sg*

nubile *ag* (*donna*) unmarried, single

nuca *sf* nape of the neck

nucle'are *ag* nuclear

nucleo *sm* nucleus; (*gruppo*) team, unit, group; (*Mil, Polizia*) squad; **nucleo familiare** family unit

nu'dista, -i, -e *sm/f* nudist

nudo, -a *ag* (*persona*) bare, naked, nude; (*membra*) bare, naked; (*montagna*) bare ▷ *sm* (*Arte*) nude

nulla *pron, av* = **niente** ▷ *sm* = **il nulla** nothing

nullità *sf inv* nullity; (*persona*) nonentity

nullo, -a *ag* useless, worthless; (*Dir*) null (and void); (*Sport*): **incontro ~** draw

nume'rale *ag, sm* numeral

nume'rare *vt* to number

nu'merico, -a, -ci, -che *ag* numerical

numero *sm* number; (*romano, arabo*) numeral; (*di spettacolo*) act, turn; **numero civico** house number; **numero di scarpe** shoe size; **numero di telefono** telephone number; **nume'roso, -a** *ag* numerous, many; (*con sostantivo sg*) large

nu'occio *ecc* ['nwɔttʃo] *vb vedi* **nuocere**

nu'ocere ['nwɔtʃere] *vi* **~ a** to harm, damage

nu'ora *sf* daughter-in-law

nuo'tare *vi* to swim; (*galleggiare: oggetti*) to float; **nuota'tore, -'trice** *sm/f* swimmer; **nu'oto** *sm* swimming

nu'ova *sf* (*notizia*) (piece of) news *sg*; *vedi anche* **nuovo**

nuova'mente *av* again

Nu'ova Ze'landa [-dze'landa] *sf* **la ~** New Zealand

nu'ovo, -a *ag* new; **di ~** again; **~ fiammante** *o* **di zecca** brand-new

nutri'ente *ag* nutritious, nourishing

nutri'mento *sm* food, nourishment

nu'trire *vt* to feed; (*fig: sentimenti*) to harbour, nurse; **nutrirsi** *vpr* **nutrirsi di** to feed on, to eat

nuvola *sf* cloud; **nuvo'loso, -a** *ag* cloudy

nuzi'ale [nut'tsjale] *ag* nuptial; wedding *cpd*

nylon ['nailən] *sm* nylon

o (*dav V spesso* **od**) *cong* or; **o ... o** either ... or; **o l'uno o l'altro** either (of them)

O *abbr* (= *ovest*) W

'oasi *sf inv* oasis

obbedi'ente *ecc* = **ubbidiente** *ecc*

obbli'gare *vt* (*costringere*): **~ qn a fare** to force *o* oblige sb to do; (*Dir*) to bind; **obbliga'torio, -a** *ag* compulsory, obligatory; **'obbligo, -ghi** *sm* obligation; (*dovere*) duty; **avere l'obbligo di fare** to be obliged to do; **essere d'obbligo** (*discorso, applauso*) to be called for

o'beso, -a *ag* obese

obiet'tare *vt* **~ che** to object that; **~ su qc** to object to sth, raise objections concerning sth

obiet'tivo, -a *ag* objective ▷ *sm* (*Ottica, Fot*) lens *sg*, objective; (*Mil, fig*) objective

obiet'tore *sm* objector; **obiettore di coscienza** conscientious objector

obiezi'one [objet'tsjone] *sf* objection

obi'torio *sm* morgue, mortuary

o'bliquo, -a *ag* oblique; (*inclinato*) slanting; (*fig*) devious, underhand

oblite'rare *vt* (*biglietto*) to stamp; (*francobollo*) to cancel

oblò *sm inv* porthole

'oboe *sm* (*Mus*) oboe

'oca (*pl* **'oche**) *sf* goose

occasi'one *sf* (*caso favorevole*) opportunity;

(*causa, motivo, circostanza*) occasion; (*Comm*) bargain; **d'~** (*a buon prezzo*) bargain *cpd*; (*usato*) secondhand

occhi'aia [ok'kjaja] *sf* **avere le occhiaie** to have shadows under one's eyes

occhi'ali [ok'kjali] *smpl* glasses, spectacles; **occhiali da sole/da vista** sunglasses/(prescription) glasses

occhi'ata [ok'kjata] *sf* look, glance; **dare un'~ a** to have a look at

occhi'ello [ok'kjɛllo] *sm* buttonhole; (*asola*) eyelet

'occhio ['ɔkkjo] *sm* eye; **~!** careful!, watch out!; **a ~ nudo** with the naked eye; **a quattr'occhi** privately, tête-à-tête; **dare all'~ o nell'~ a qn** to catch sb's eye; **fare l'~ a qc** to get used to sth; **tenere d'~ qn** to keep an eye on sb; **vedere di buon/mal ~ qc** to look favourably/unfavourably on sth

occhio'lino [okkjo'lino] *sm* **fare l'~ a qn** to wink at sb

occiden'tale [ottʃiden'tale] *ag* western ▷ *sm/f* Westerner

occi'dente [ottʃi'dɛnte] *sm* west; (*Pol*): **l'O~** the West; **a ~** in the west

occor'rente *ag* necessary ▷ *sm* all that is necessary

occor'renza [okkor'rɛntsa] *sf* necessity, need; **all'~** in case of need

oc'correre *vi* to be needed, be required ▷ *vb impers* **occorre farlo** it must be done; **occorre che tu parta** you must leave, you'll have to leave; **mi occorrono i soldi** I need the money

Attenzione! In inglese esiste il verbo *to occur*, che però significa *succedere*.

oc'culto, -a *ag* hidden, concealed; (*scienze, forze*) occult

occu'pare *vt* to occupy; (*manodopera*) to employ; (*ingombrare*) to occupy, take up; **occuparsi** *vpr* to occupy o.s., keep o.s. busy; (*impiegarsi*) to get a job; **occuparsi di** (*interessarsi*) to take an interest in; (*prendersi cura di*) to look after, take care of; **occu'pato, -a** *ag* (*Mil, Pol*) occupied; (*persona: affaccendato*) busy; (*posto, sedia*) taken; (*toilette, Tel*) engaged; **la linea è occupata** the line's engaged; **è occupato questo posto?** is this seat taken?; **occupazi'one** *sf* occupation; (*impiego, lavoro*) job; (*Econ*) employment

o'ceano [o'tʃeano] *sm* ocean

'ocra *sf* ochre

'OCSE *sigla f* (= *Organizzazione per la Cooperazione e lo Sviluppo Economico*) OECD (*Organization for Economic Cooperation and Development*)

ocu'lare *ag* ocular, eye *cpd*; **testimone ~** eye witness

ocu'lato, -a *ag* (*attento*) cautious, prudent; (*accorto*) shrewd

ocu'lista, -i, -e *sm/f* eye specialist, oculist

odi'are *vt* to hate, detest

odi'erno, -a *ag* today's, of today; (*attuale*) present

'odio *sm* hatred; **avere in ~ qc/qn** to hate o detest sth/sb; **odi'oso, -a** *ag* hateful, odious

odo'rare *vt* (*annusare*) to smell; (*profumare*) to perfume, scent ▷ *vi* **~ (di)** to smell (of)

o'dore *sm* smell; **odori** *smpl* (*Cuc*) (aromatic) herbs

of'fendere *vt* to offend; (*violare*) to break, violate; (*insultare*) to insult; (*ferire*) to hurt; **offendersi** *vpr* (*con senso reciproco*) to insult one another; (*risentirsi*): **offendersi (di)** to take offence (at), be offended (by)

offe'rente *sm* (*in aste*): **al maggior ~** to the highest bidder

of'ferta *sf* offer; (*donazione, anche Rel*) offering; (*in gara d'appalto*) tender; (*in aste*) bid; (*Econ*) supply; **fare un'~** to make an offer; to tender; to bid; **"offerte d'impiego"** "situations vacant"; **offerta speciale** special offer

of'fesa *sf* insult, affront; (*Mil*) attack; (*Dir*) offence; *vedi anche* **offeso**

of'feso, -a *pp di* **offendere** ▷ *ag* offended; (*fisicamente*) hurt, injured ▷ *sm/f* offended party; **essere ~ con qn** to be annoyed with sb; **parte offesa** (*Dir*) plaintiff

offi'cina [offi'tʃina] *sf* workshop

of'frire *vt* to offer; **offrirsi** *vpr* (*proporsi*) to offer (o.s.), volunteer; (*occasione*) to present itself; (*esporsi*): **offrirsi a** to expose o.s. to; **ti offro da bere** I'll buy you a drink

offus'care *vt* to obscure, darken; (*fig: intelletto*) to dim, cloud; (: *fama*) to obscure overshadow; **offuscarsi** *vpr* to grow dark to cloud, grow dim; to be obscured

ogget'tivo, -a [oddʒet'tivo] *ag* objective

og'getto [od'dʒɛtto] *sm* object; (*materia, argomento*) subject (matter); **oggetti smarriti** lost property *sg*

'oggi ['ɔddʒi] *av, sm* today; **~ a otto** a week today; **oggigi'orno** *av* nowadays

OGM *sigla m* (= *organismo geneticamente modificato*) GMO

'ogni ['oɲɲi] *det* every, each; (*tutti*) all; (*con valore distributivo*) every; **~ uomo è mortale** all men are mortal; **viene ~ due giorni** he comes every two days; **~ cosa** everything; **ad ~ costo** at all costs, at any price; **in ~ luogo** everywhere; **~ tanto** every so often; **~ volta che** every time that

Ognis'santi [oɲɲis'santi] *sm* All Saints' Day

o'gnuno [oɲ'ɲuno] *pron* everyone,

everybody

O'landa sf l'~ Holland; **olan'dese** ag Dutch ▷ sm (Ling) Dutch ▷ sm/f Dutchman/woman; **gli Olandesi** the Dutch

ole'andro sm oleander

oleo'dotto sm oil pipeline

ole'oso, -a ag oily; (che contiene olio) oil-yielding

ol'fatto sm sense of smell

oli'are vt to oil

oli'era sf oil cruet

Olim'piadi sfpl Olympic games; **o'limpico, -a, -ci, -che** ag Olympic

'olio sm oil; **sott'~** (Cuc) in oil; **~ di fegato di merluzzo** cod liver oil; **olio d'oliva** olive oil; **olio di semi** vegetable oil

o'liva sf olive; **o'livo** sm olive tree

'olmo sm elm

OLP sigla f (= Organizzazione per la Liberazione della Palestina) PLO

ol'traggio [ol'traddʒo] sm outrage; offence, insult; **~ a pubblico ufficiale** (Dir) insulting a public official; **oltraggio al pudore** (Dir) indecent behaviour

ol'tranza [ol'trantsa] sf **a ~** to the last, to the bitter end

'oltre av (più in là) further; (di più: aspettare) longer, more ▷ prep (di là da) beyond, over, on the other side of; (più di) more than, over; (in aggiunta a) besides; (eccetto): **~ a** except, apart from; **oltrepas'sare** vt to go beyond, exceed

o'maggio [o'maddʒo] sm (dono) gift; (segno di rispetto) homage, tribute; **omaggi** smpl (complimenti) respects; **rendere ~ a** to pay homage o tribute to; **in ~** (copia, biglietto) complimentary

ombe'lico, -chi sm navel

'ombra sf (zona non assolata, fantasma) shade; (sagoma scura) shadow; **sedere all'~** to sit in the shade; **restare nell'~** (fig) to remain in obscurity

om'brello sm umbrella; **ombrel'lone** sm beach umbrella

om'bretto sm eye shadow

O.M.C. sigla f (= Organizzazione Mondiale del Commercio) WTO

ome'lette [ɔmə'lɛt] sf inv omelet(te)

ome'lia sf (Rel) homily, sermon

omeopa'tia sf homoeopathy

omertà sf conspiracy of silence

o'mettere vt to omit, leave out; **~ di fare** to omit o fail to do

omi'cida, -i, -e [omi'tʃida] ag homicidal, murderous ▷ sm/f murderer/eress

omi'cidio [omi'tʃidjo] sm murder; **omicidio colposo** culpable homicide

o'misi ecc vb vedi **omettere**

omissi'one sf omission; **omissione di soccorso** (Dir) failure to stop and give assistance

omogeneiz'zato [omodʒeneid'dzato] sm baby food

omo'geneo, -a [omo'dʒɛneo] ag homogeneous

o'monimo, -a sm/f namesake ▷ sm (Ling) homonym

omosessu'ale ag, sm/f homosexual

O.M.S. sigla f (= Organizzazione Mondiale della Sanità) WHO

On. abbr (Pol) = **onorevole**

'onda sf wave; **mettere** o **mandare in ~** (Radio, TV) to broadcast; **andare in ~** (Radio, TV) to go on the air; **onde corte/lunghe/medie** short/long/medium wave

'onere sm burden; **oneri fiscali** taxes

onestà sf honesty

o'nesto, -a ag (probo, retto) honest; (giusto) fair; (casto) chaste, virtuous

ONG sigla f inv **Organizzazione Non Governativa** NGO

onnipo'tente ag omnipotent

ono'mastico, -ci sm name-day

ono'rare vt to honour; (far onore a) to do credit to

ono'rario, -a ag honorary ▷ sm fee

o'nore sm honour; **in ~ di** in honour of; **fare gli onori di casa** to play host (o hostess); **fare ~ a** to honour; (pranzo) to do justice to; (famiglia) to be a credit to; **farsi ~** to distinguish o.s.; **ono'revole** ag honourable ▷ sm/f (Pol) ≈ Member of Parliament (BRIT), ≈ Congressman/woman (US)

on'tano sm (Bot) alder

'O.N.U. ['ɔnu] sigla f (= Organizzazione delle Nazioni Unite) UN, UNO

o'paco, -a, -chi, -che ag (vetro) opaque; (metallo) dull, matt

o'pale sm o f opal

'opera sf work; (azione rilevante) action, deed, work; (Mus) work; opus; (: melodramma) opera; (: teatro) opera house; (ente) institution, organization; **opere pubbliche** public works; **opera d'arte** work of art; **opera lirica** (grand) opera

ope'raio, -a ag working-class; workers' ▷ sm/f worker; **classe operaia** working class

ope'rare vt to carry out, make; (Med) to operate on ▷ vi to operate, work; (rimedio) to act, work; (Med) to operate; **operarsi** vpr (Med) to have an operation; **operarsi d'appendicite** to have one's appendix out; **operazi'one** sf operation

ope'retta sf (Mus) operetta, light opera

opini'one sf opinion; **opinione pubblica** public opinion

'oppio sm opium

op'pongo ecc vb vedi **opporre**

op'porre vt to oppose; **opporsi** vpr **opporsi (a qc)** to oppose (sth); to object (to sth); ~ **resistenza/un rifiuto** to offer resistance/refuse

opportu'nista, -i, -e sm/f opportunist

opportunità sf inv opportunity; (convenienza) opportuneness, timeliness

oppor'tuno, -a ag timely, opportune

op'posi ecc vb vedi **opporre**

opposizi'one [oppozit'tsjone] sf opposition; (Dir) objection

op'posto, -a pp di **opporre** ▷ ag opposite; (opinioni) conflicting ▷ sm opposite, contrary; **all'~** on the contrary

oppressi'one sf oppression

oppri'mente ag (caldo, noia) oppressive; (persona) tiresome; (deprimente) depressing

op'primere vt (premere, gravare) to weigh down; (estenuare: caldo) to suffocate, oppress; (tiranneggiare: popolo) to oppress

op'pure cong (or else)

op'tare vi ~ **per** to opt for

o'puscolo sm booklet, pamphlet

opzi'one [op'tsjone] sf option

'ora sf (60 minuti) hour; (momento) time; **che ~ è?, che ore sono?** what time is it?; **a che ~ apre il museo/negozio?** what time does the museum/shop open?; **non veder l'~ di fare** to long to do, look forward to doing; **di buon'~** early; **alla buon'~!** at last!; ~ **legale** o **estiva** summer time (BRIT), daylight saving time (US); **ora di cena** dinner time; **ora locale** local time; **ora di pranzo** lunchtime; **ora di punta** (Aut) rush hour

o'racolo sm oracle

o'rale ag, sm oral

o'rario, -a ag hourly; (fuso, segnale) time cpd; (velocità) per hour ▷ sm timetable, schedule; (di ufficio, visite ecc) hours pl, time(s pl); **in ~** on time

o'rata sf (Zool) sea bream

ora'tore, -'trice sm/f speaker; orator

'orbita sf (Astr, Fisica) orbit; (Anat) (eye-)socket

or'chestra [or'kɛstra] sf orchestra

orchi'dea [orki'dɛa] sf orchid

or'digno [or'diɲɲo] sm (esplosivo) explosive device

ordi'nale ag, sm ordinal

ordi'nare vt (mettere in ordine) to arrange, organize; (Comm) to order; (prescrivere: medicina) to prescribe; (comandare): **posso ~ per favore?** can I order now please?; ~ **a qn di fare qc** to order o command sb to do sth; (Rel) to ordain

ordi'nario, -a ag (comune) ordinary; everyday; standard; (grossolano) coarse, common ▷ sm ordinary; (Ins: di università) full professor

ordi'nato, -a ag tidy, orderly

ordinazi'one [ordinat'tsjone] sf (Comm) order; (Rel) ordination; **eseguire qc su ~** to make sth to order

'ordine sm order; (carattere): **d'~ pratico** of a practical nature; **all'~** (Comm: assegno) to order; **di prim'~** first-class; **fino a nuovo ~** until further notice; **essere in ~** (documenti) to be in order; (stanza, persona) to be tidy; **mettere in ~** to put in order, tidy (up); **l'~ pubblico** law and order; **ordini (sacri)** (Rel) holy orders; **ordine del giorno** (di seduta) agenda; (Mil) order of the day; **ordine di pagamento** (Comm) order for payment

orec'chino [orek'kino] sm earring

o'recchio [o'rekkjo] (pl(f) **o'recchie**) sm (Anat) ear

orecchi'oni [orek'kjoni] smpl (Med) mumps sg

o'refice [o'rɛfitʃe] sm goldsmith; jeweller; **orefice'ria** sf (arte) goldsmith's art; (negozio) jeweller's (shop)

'orfano, -a ag orphan(ed) ▷ sm/f orphan; ~ **di padre/madre** fatherless/motherless

orga'netto sm barrel organ; (fam: armonica a bocca) mouth organ; (: fisarmonica) accordion

or'ganico, -a, -ci, -che ag organic ▷ sm personnel, staff

organi'gramma, -i sm organization chart

orga'nismo sm (Biol) organism; (corpo umano) body; (Amm) body, organism

organiz'zare [organid'dzare] vt to organize; **organizzarsi** vpr to get organized; **organizzazi'one** sf organization

'organo sm organ; (di congegno) part; (portavoce) spokesman, mouthpiece

'orgia, -ge ['ɔrdʒa] sf orgy

or'goglio [or'ɡoʎʎo] sm pride; **orgogli'oso, -a** ag proud

orien'tale ag oriental; eastern; east

orienta'mento sm positioning; orientation; direction; **senso di ~** sense of direction; **perdere l'~** to lose one's bearings; **orientamento professionale** careers guidance

orientarsi vpr to find one's bearings; (fig: tendere) to tend, lean; (: indirizzarsi): ~ **verso** to take up, go in for

ori'ente sm east; **l'O~** the East, the Orient; **a ~** in the east

o'rigano sm oregano

origi'nale [oridʒi'nale] ag original; (bizzarro) eccentric ▷ sm original

origi'nario, -a [oridʒi'narjo] ag original; **essere ~ di** to be a native of; (provenire da) to originate from; to be native to

o'rigine [o'ridʒine] sf origin; **all'~** originally; **d'~ inglese** of English origin; **dare ~ a** to give rise to

origli'are [oriʎ'ʎare] vi **~ (a)** to eavesdrop (on)

o'rina sf urine

ori'nare vi to urinate ▷ vt to pass

orizzon'tale [oriddzon'tale] ag horizontal

oriz'zonte [orid'dzonte] sm horizon

'orlo sm edge, border; (di recipiente) rim, brim; (di vestito ecc) hem

'orma sf (di persona) footprint; (di animale) track; (impronta, traccia) mark, trace

or'mai av by now, by this time; (adesso) now; (quasi) almost, nearly

ormeggi'are [ormed'dʒare] vt (Naut) to moor

or'mone sm hormone

ornamen'tale ag ornamental, decorative

or'nare vt to adorn, decorate; **ornarsi** vpr **ornarsi (di)** to deck o.s. (out) (with)

ornitolo'gia [ornitolo'dʒia] sf ornithology

'oro sm gold; **d'~, in ~** gold cpd; **d'~** (colore, occasione) golden; (persona) marvellous

oro'logio [oro'lɔdʒo] sm clock; (da tasca, da polso) watch; **orologio al quarzo** quartz watch; **orologio da polso** wristwatch

o'roscopo sm horoscope

or'rendo, -a ag (spaventoso) horrible, awful; (bruttissimo) hideous

or'ribile ag horrible

or'rore sm horror; **avere in ~ qn/qc** to loathe o detest sb/sth; **mi fanno ~** I loathe o detest them

orsacchi'otto [orsak'kjɔtto] sm teddy bear

'orso sm bear; **orso bruno/bianco** brown/polar bear

or'taggio [or'taddʒo] sm vegetable

or'tensia sf hydrangea

or'tica, -che sf (stinging) nettle

orti'caria sf nettle rash

'orto sm vegetable garden, kitchen garden; (Agr) market garden (BRIT), truck farm (US); **orto botanico** botanical garden(s) (pl)

orto'dosso, -a ag orthodox

ortogra'fia sf spelling

orto'pedico, -a, -ci, -che ag orthopaedic ▷ sm orthopaedic specialist

orzai'olo [ordza'jɔlo] sm (Med) stye

'orzo ['ordzo] sm barley

o'sare vt, vi to dare; **~ fare** to dare (to) do

oscenità [oʃʃeni'ta] sf inv obscenity

o'sceno, -a [oʃ'ʃeno] ag obscene; (ripugnante) ghastly

oscil'lare [oʃʃil'lare] vi (pendolo) to swing; (dondolare: al vento ecc) to rock; (variare) to fluctuate; (Tecn) to oscillate; (fig): **~ fra** to waver o hesitate between

oscu'rare vt to darken, obscure; (fig) to obscure; **oscurarsi** vpr (cielo) to darken, cloud over; (persona): **si oscurò in volto** his face clouded over

oscurità sf (vedi ag) darkness; obscurity

os'curo, -a ag dark; (fig) obscure; humble, lowly ▷ sm **all'~** in the dark; **tenere qn all'~ di qc** to keep sb in the dark about sth

ospe'dale sm hospital; **dov'è l'~ più vicino?** where's the nearest hospital?

ospi'tale ag hospitable

ospi'tare vt to give hospitality to; (albergo) to accommodate

'ospite sm/f (persona che ospita) host/hostess; (persona ospitata) guest

os'pizio [os'pittsjo] sm (per vecchi ecc) home

osser'vare vt to observe, watch; (esaminare) to examine; (notare, rilevare) to notice, observe; (Dir: la legge) to observe, respect; (mantenere: silenzio) to keep, observe; **far ~ qc a qn** to point sth out to sb; **osservazi'one** sf observation; (di legge ecc) observance; (considerazione critica) observation, remark; (rimprovero) reproof; **in osservazione** under observation

ossessio'nare vt to obsess, haunt; (tormentare) to torment, harass

ossessi'one sf obsession

os'sia cong that is, to be precise

'ossido sm oxide; **ossido di carbonio** carbon monoxide

ossige'nare [ossidʒe'nare] vt to oxygenate; (decolorare) to bleach; **acqua ossigenata** hydrogen peroxide

os'sigeno sm oxygen

'osso (pl(f) **ossa**) (nel senso Anat) sm bone; **d'~** (bottone ecc) of bone, bone cpd; **osso di seppia** cuttlebone

ostaco'lare vt to block, obstruct

os'tacolo sm obstacle; (Equitazione) hurdle, jump

os'taggio [os'taddʒo] sm hostage

os'tello sm; **ostello della gioventù** youth hostel

osten'tare vt to make a show of, flaunt

oste'ria sf inn

os'tetrico, -a, -ci, -che ag obstetric ▷ sm obstetrician

'ostia sf (Rel) host; (per medicinali) wafer

'ostico, -a, -ci, -che ag (fig) harsh; hard, difficult; unpleasant

os'tile ag hostile

osti'narsi *vpr* to insist, dig one's heels in; **~ a fare** to persist (obstinately) in doing; **osti'nato, -a** *ag* (*caparbio*) obstinate; (*tenace*) persistent, determined

'ostrica, -che *sf* oyster

Attenzione! In inglese esiste la parola *ostrich*, che però significa *struzzo*.

ostru'ire *vt* to obstruct, block

o'tite *sf* ear infection

ot'tanta *num* eighty

ot'tavo, -a *num* eighth

otte'nere *vt* to obtain, get; (*risultato*) to achieve, obtain

'ottica *sf* (*scienza*) optics *sg*; (*Fot: lenti, prismi ecc*) optics *pl*

'ottico, -a, -ci, -che *ag* (*della vista: nervo*) optic; (*dell'ottica*) optical ▷ *sm* optician

ottima'mente *av* excellently, very well

otti'mismo *sm* optimism; **otti'mista, -i, -e** *sm/f* optimist

'ottimo, -a *ag* excellent, very good

'otto *num* eight

ot'tobre *sm* October

otto'cento [otto'tʃɛnto] *num* eight hundred ▷ *sm* l'O~ the nineteenth century

ot'tone *sm* brass; **gli ottoni** (*Mus*) the brass

ottu'rare *vt* to close (up); (*dente*) to fill; **il lavandino è otturato** the sink is blocked; **otturarsi** *vpr* to become o get blocked up; **otturazi'one** *sf* closing (up); (*dentaria*) filling

ot'tuso, -a *ag* (*Mat, fig*) obtuse; (*suono*) dull

o'vaia *sf* (*Anat*) ovary

o'vale *ag, sm* oval

o'vatta *sf* cotton wool; (*per imbottire*) padding, wadding

'ovest *sm* west

o'vile *sm* pen, enclosure

ovulazi'one [ovulat'tsjone] *sf* ovulation

'ovulo *sm* (*Fisiol*) ovum

o'vunque *av* = dovunque

ovvi'are *vi* ~ a to obviate

'ovvio, -a *ag* obvious

ozi'are [ot'tsjare] *vi* to laze, idle

'ozio ['ɔttsjo] *sm* idleness; (*tempo libero*) leisure; **ore d'~** leisure time; **stare in ~** to be idle

o'zono [o'dzɔno] *sm* ozone

p

P *abbr* (= *parcheggio*) P; (*Aut*: = *principiante*) L

p. *abbr* (= *pagina*) p.

pac'chetto [pak'ketto] *sm* packet; **pacchetto azionario** (*Comm*) shareholding

'pacco, -chi *sm* parcel; (*involto*) bundle; **pacco postale** parcel

'pace ['patʃe] *sf* peace; **darsi ~** to resign o.s.; **fare la ~ con** to make it up with

pa'cifico, -a, -ci, -che [pa'tʃi:fiko] *ag* (*persona*) peaceable; (*vita*) peaceful; (*fig: indiscusso*) indisputable; (: *ovvio*) obvious, clear ▷ *sm* il P~, l'Oceano P~ the Pacific (Ocean)

paci'fista, -i, -e [patʃi'fista] *sm/f* pacifist

pa'della *sf* frying pan; (*per infermi*) bedpan

padigli'one [padiʎ'ʎone] *sm* pavilion

'Padova *sf* Padua

'padre *sm* father

pa'drino *sm* godfather

padro'nanza [padro'nantsa] *sf* command, mastery

pa'drone, -a *sm/f* master/mistress; (*proprietario*) owner; (*datore di lavoro*) employer; **essere ~ di sé** to be in control of o.s.; **padrone(a) di casa** master/ mistress of the house; (*per gli inquilini*) landlord/lady

pae'saggio [pae'zaddʒo] *sm* landscape

pa'ese *sm* (*nazione*) country, nation; (*terra*) country, land; (*villaggio*) village, (small) town; **i Paesi Bassi** the Netherlands; **paese di provenienza** country of origin

'paga, -ghe *sf* pay, wages *pl*

paga'mento *sm* payment

pa'gare *vt* to pay; (*acquisto, fig: colpa*) to pay for; (*contraccambiare*) to repay, pay back ▷ *vi* to pay; **quanto l'hai pagato?** how much did you pay for it?; **posso ~ con la carta di credito?** can I pay by credit card?; **~ in contanti** to pay cash

pa'gella [pa'dʒella] *sf* (*Ins*) report card

pagherò [page'rɔ] *sm inv* acknowledgement of a debt, IOU

'pagina ['padʒina] *sf* page; **pagine bianche** phone book, telephone directory; **pagine gialle** Yellow Pages

'paglia ['paʎʎa] *sf* straw

pagli'accio [paʎ'ʎattʃo] *sm* clown

pagli'etta [paʎ'ʎetta] *sf* (*cappello per uomo*) (straw) boater; (*per tegami ecc*) steel wool

pa'gnotta [paɲ'ɲɔtta] *sf* round loaf

'paio (*pl*(*f*) **'paia**) *sm* pair; **un ~ di** (*alcuni*) a couple of

'Pakistan *sm* **il ~** Pakistan

'pala *sf* shovel; (*di remo, ventilatore, elica*) blade; (*di ruota*) paddle

pa'lato *sm* palate

pa'lazzo [pa'lattso] *sm* (*reggia*) palace; (*edificio*) building; **palazzo di giustizia** courthouse; **palazzo dello sport** sports stadium

'palco, -chi *sm* (*Teatro*) box; (*tavolato*) platform, stand; (*ripiano*) layer

palco'scenico, -ci [palkoʃ'ʃeniko] *sm* (*Teatro*) stage

pa'lese *ag* clear, evident

Pales'tina *sf* **la ~** Palestine

palesti'nese *ag, sm/f* Palestinian

pa'lestra *sf* gymnasium; (*esercizio atletico*) exercise, training; (*fig*) training ground, school

pa'letta *sf* spade; (*per il focolare*) shovel; (*del capostazione*) signalling disc

pa'letto *sm* stake, peg; (*spranga*) bolt

'palio (*gara*) *sm* **il P~** horse race run at Siena; **mettere qc in ~** to offer sth as a prize

PALIO

The **palio** is a horse race which takes place in a number of Italian towns, the most famous being the one in Siena. This is usually held twice a year on July 2nd and August 16th in the Piazza del Campo in Siena. 10 of the 17 **contrade** or districts take part, each represented by a horse and rider. The winner is the first horse to complete the course, whether it has a rider or not.

'palla *sf* ball; (*pallottola*) bullet; **palla di neve** snowball; **palla ovale** rugby ball; **pallaca'nestro** *sf* basketball; **palla'mano** *sf* handball; **pallanu'oto** *sf* water polo; **palla'volo** *sf* volleyball

palleggi'are [palled'dʒare] *vi* (*Calcio*) to practise with the ball; (*Tennis*) to knock up

pallia'tivo *sm* palliative; (*fig*) stopgap measure

'pallido, -a *ag* pale

pal'lina *sf* (*bilia*) marble

pallon'cino [pallon'tʃino] *sm* balloon; (*lampioncino*) Chinese lantern

pal'lone *sm* (*palla*) ball; (*Calcio*) football; (*aerostato*) balloon; **gioco del ~** football

pal'lottola *sf* pellet; (*proiettile*) bullet

'palma *sf* (*Anat*) = **palmo**; (*Bot, simbolo*) palm; **palma da datteri** date palm

'palmo *sm* (*Anat*) palm; **restare con un ~ di naso** to be badly disappointed

'palo *sm* (*legno appuntito*) stake; (*sostegno*) pole; **fare da o il ~** (*fig*) to act as look-out

palom'baro *sm* diver

pal'pare *vt* to feel, finger

'palpebra *sf* eyelid

pa'lude *sf* marsh, swamp

pan'cetta [pan'tʃetta] *sf* (*Cuc*) bacon

pan'china [pan'kina] *sf* garden seat; (*di giardino pubblico*) (park) bench

'pancia, -ce ['pantʃa] *sf* belly, stomach; **mettere** *o* **fare ~** to be getting a paunch; **avere mal di ~** to have stomachache *o* a sore stomach

panci'otto [pan'tʃɔtto] *sm* waistcoat

'pancreas *sm inv* pancreas

'panda *sm inv* panda

'pane *sm* bread; (*pagnotta*) loaf (of bread); (*forma*) **un ~ di burro** a pat of butter; **guadagnarsi il ~** to earn one's living; **pane a cassetta** sliced bread; **pane di Spagna** sponge cake; **pane integrale** wholemeal bread; **pane tostato** toast

panette'ria *sf* (*forno*) bakery; (*negozio*) baker's (shop), bakery

panetti'ere, -a *sm/f* baker

panet'tone *sm* a kind of spiced brioche with sultanas, eaten at Christmas

pangrat'tato *sm* breadcrumbs *pl*

'panico, -a, -ci, -che *ag, sm* panic

pani'ere *sm* basket

pani'ficio [pani'fitʃo] *sm* (*forno*) bakery; (*negozio*) baker's (shop), bakery

pa'nino *sm* roll; **panino caldo** toasted sandwich; **panino imbottito** filled roll;

panna | 124

sandwich

'panna *sf* (*Cuc*) cream; (*Tecn*) = **panne**; **panna da cucina** cooking cream; **panna montata** whipped cream

'panne *sf inv* **essere in ~** (*Aut*) to have broken down

pan'nello *sm* panel; **pannello solare** solar panel

'panno *sm* cloth; **panni** *smpl* (*abiti*) clothes; **mettiti nei miei panni** (*fig*) put yourself in my shoes

pan'nocchia [pan'nɔkkja] *sf* (*di mais ecc*) ear

panno'lino *sm* (*per bambini*) nappy (*BRIT*), diaper (*US*)

pano'rama, -i *sm* panorama

panta'loni *smpl* trousers (*BRIT*), pants (*US*), pair *sg*, of trousers *o* pants

pan'tano *sm* bog

pan'tera *sf* panther

pan'tofola *sf* slipper

'Papa, -i *sm* pope

papà *sm inv* dad(dy)

pa'pavero *sm* poppy

'pappa *sf* baby cereal; **pappa reale** royal jelly

pappa'gallo *sm* parrot; (*fig: uomo*) Romeo, wolf

pa'rabola *sf* (*Mat*) parabola; (*Rel*) parable

para'bolico, -a, ci, che *ag* (*Mat*) parabolic; *vedi anche* **antenna**

para'brezza [para'breddza] *sm inv* (*Aut*) windscreen (*BRIT*), windshield (*US*)

paraca'dute *sm inv* parachute

para'diso *sm* paradise

parados'sale *ag* paradoxical

para'fulmine *sm* lightning conductor

pa'raggi [pa'raddʒi] *smpl* **nei ~** in the vicinity, in the neighbourhood

parago'nare *vt* **~ con/a** to compare with/to

para'gone *sm* comparison; (*esempio analogo*) analogy, parallel; **reggere al ~** to stand comparison

pa'ragrafo *sm* paragraph

pa'ralisi *sf* paralysis

paral'lelo, -a *ag* parallel ▷ *sm* (*Geo*) parallel; (*comparazione*): **fare un ~ tra** to draw a parallel between

para'lume *sm* lampshade

pa'rametro *sm* parameter

para'noia *sf* paranoia; **para'noico, -a, -ci, -che** *ag, sm/f* paranoid

para'occhi [para'ɔkki] *smpl* blinkers

para'petto *sm* balustrade

pa'rare *vt* (*addobbare*) to adorn, deck; (*proteggere*) to shield, protect; (*scansare: colpo*) to parry; (*Calcio*) to save ▷ *vi* **dove**

vuole andare a ~? what are you driving at?

pa'rata *sf* (*Sport*) save; (*Mil*) review, parade

para'urti *sm inv* (*Aut*) bumper

para'vento *sm* folding screen; **fare da ~ a qn** (*fig*) to shield sb

par'cella [par'tʃella] *sf* account, fee (*of lawyer etc*)

parcheggi'are [parked'dʒare] *vt* to park; **posso ~ qui?** can I park here?; **parcheggiatore, -trice** [parkeddʒa'tore] *sm/f* (*Aut*) parking attendant

par'cheggio *sm* parking *no pl*; (*luogo*) car park; (*singolo posto*) parking space

par'chimetro [par'kimetro] *sm* parking meter

'parco, -chi *sm* park; (*spazio per deposito*) depot; (*complesso di veicoli*) fleet

par'cometro *sm* (pay-and-display) ticket machine

pa'recchio, -a [pa'rekkjo] *det* quite a lot of; (*tempo*) quite a lot of, a long

pareggi'are [pared'dʒare] *vt* to make equal; (*terreno*) to level, make level; (*bilancio, conti*) to balance ▷ *vi* (*Sport*) to draw; **pa'reggio** *sm* (*Econ*) balance; (*Sport*) draw

pa'rente *sm/f* relative, relation

▨ Attenzione! In inglese esiste la parola *parent*, che però significa *genitore*.

paren'tela *sf* (*vincolo di sangue, fig*) relationship

pa'rentesi *sf* (*segno grafico*) bracket, parenthesis; (*frase incisa*) parenthesis; (*digressione*) parenthesis, digression

pa'rere *sm* (*opinione*) opinion; (*consiglio*) advice, opinion; **a mio ~** in my opinion ▷ *vi* to seem, appear ▷ *vb impers* **pare che** it seems *o* appears that, they say that; **mi pare che** it seems to me that; **mi pare di sì** I think so; **fai come ti pare** do as you like; **che ti pare del mio libro?** what do you think of my book?

pa'rete *sf* wall

'pari *ag inv* (*uguale*) equal, same; (*in giochi*) equal; drawn, tied; (*Mat*) even ▷ *sm inv* (*Pol: di Gran Bretagna*) peer ▷ *sm/f inv* peer, equal; **copiato ~ ~** copied word for word; **alla ~** on the same level; **ragazza alla ~** au pair girl; **mettersi alla ~ con** to place o.s. on the same level as; **mettersi in ~ con** to catch up with; **andare di ~ passo con qn** to keep pace with sb

Pa'rigi [pa'ridʒi] *sf* Paris

pari'gino, -a [pari'dʒino] *ag, sm/f* Parisian

parità *sf* parity, equality; (*Sport*) draw, tie

parlamen'tare *ag* parliamentary ▷ *sm/f* ≈ Member of Parliament (*BRIT*), ≈ Congressman/woman (*US*) ▷ *vi* to negotiate, parley

parla'mento *sm* parliament

parlan'tina (*fam*) *sf* talkativeness; **avere ~** to have the gift of the gab

par'lare *vi* to speak, talk; (*confidare cose segrete*) to talk ▷ *vt* to speak; **~ (a qn) di** to speak o talk (to sb) about; **posso ~ con…?** can I speak to …?; **parla italiano?** do you speak Italian?; **non parlo inglese** I don't speak English

parmigi'ano [parmi'dʒano] *sm* (*grana*) Parmesan (cheese)

pa'rola *sf* word; (*facoltà*) speech; **parole** *sfpl* (*chiacchiere*) talk *sg*; **chiedere la ~** to ask permission to speak; **prendere la ~** to take the floor; **parola d'onore** word of honour; **parola d'ordine** (*Mil*) password; **parole incrociate** crossword (puzzle) *sg*; **paro'laccia, -ce** *sf* bad word, swearword

parrò *ecc vb vedi* **parere**

par'rocchia [par'rɔkkja] *sf* parish; parish church

par'rucca, -che *sf* wig

parrucchi'ere, -a [parruk'kjɛre] *sm/f* hairdresser ▷ *sm* barber

'parte *sf* part; (*lato*) side; (*quota spettante a ciascuno*) share; (*direzione*) direction; (*Pol*) party; faction; (*Dir*) party; **a ~** *ag* separate ▷ *av* separately; **scherzi a ~** joking aside; **a ~ ciò** apart from that; **da ~** (*in disparte*) to one side, aside; **d'altra ~** on the other hand; **da ~ di** (*per conto di*) on behalf of; **da ~ mia** as far as I'm concerned, as for me; **da ~ a ~** right through; **da ogni ~** on all sides, everywhere; (*moto da luogo*) from all sides; **da nessuna ~** nowhere; **da questa ~** (*in questa direzione*) this way; **prendere ~ a qc** to take part in sth; **mettere da ~** to put aside; **mettere qn a ~ di** to inform sb of

parteci'pare [partetʃi'pare] *vi* **~ a** to take part in, participate in; (*utili ecc*) to share in; (*spese ecc*) to contribute to; (*dolore, successo di qn*) to share (in)

parteggi'are [parted'dʒare] *vi* **~ per** to side with, be on the side of

par'tenza [par'tɛntsa] *sf* departure; (*Sport*) start; **essere in ~** to be about to leave, be leaving

parti'cipio [parti'tʃipjo] *sm* participle

partico'lare *ag* (*specifico*) particular; (*proprio*) personal, private; (*speciale*) special, particular; (*caratteristico*) distinctive, characteristic; (*fuori dal comune*) peculiar ▷ *sm* detail, particular; **in ~** in particular, particularly

par'tire *vi* to go, leave; (*allontanarsi*) to go (o drive ecc) away o off; (*petardo, colpo*) to go off; (*avere inizio, Sport*) to start; **sono partita da Roma alle 7** I left Rome at 7; **a che ora parte il treno/l'autobus?** what time does the train/bus leave?; **il volo parte da Ciampino** the flight leaves from Ciampino; **a ~ da** from

par'tita *sf* (*Comm*) lot, consignment; (*Econ: registrazione*) entry, item; (*Carte, Sport: gioco*) game; (: *competizione*) match, game; **partita di caccia** hunting party; **partita IVA** VAT registration number

par'tito *sm* (*Pol*) party; (*decisione*) decision, resolution; (*persona da maritare*) match

'parto *sm* (*Med*) delivery, (child)birth; labour

'parvi *ecc vb vedi* **parere**

parzi'ale [par'tsjale] *ag* (*limitato*) partial; (*non obiettivo*) biased, partial

pasco'lare *vt, vi* to graze

'pascolo *sm* pasture

'Pasqua *sf* Easter; **Pas'quetta** *sf* Easter Monday

pas'sabile *ag* fairly good, passable

pas'saggio [pas'saddʒo] *sm* passing *no pl*, passage; (*traversata*) crossing *no pl*, passage; (*luogo, prezzo della traversata, brano di libro ecc*) passage; (*su veicolo altrui*) lift (BRIT), ride; (*Sport*) pass; **di ~** (*persona*) passing through; **può darmi un ~ fino alla stazione?** can you give me a lift to the station?; **passaggio a livello** level (BRIT) o grade (US) crossing; **passaggio pedonale** pedestrian crossing

passamon'tagna [passamon'taɲɲa] *sm inv* balaclava

pas'sante *sm/f* passer-by ▷ *sm* loop

passa'porto *sm* passport

pas'sare *vi* (*andare*) to go; (*veicolo, pedone*) to pass (by), go by; (*fare una breve sosta: postino ecc*) to come, call; (: *amico: per fare una visita*) to call o drop in; (*sole, aria, luce*) to get through; (*trascorrere: giorni, tempo*) to pass, go by; (*fig: proposta di legge*) to be passed; (: *dolore*) to pass, go away; (*Carte*) to pass ▷ *vt* (*attraversare*) to cross; (*trasmettere: messaggio*): **~ qc a qn** to pass sth to sb; (*dare*): **~ qc a qn** to pass sth to sb, give sb sth; (*trascorrere: tempo*) to spend; (*superare: esame*) to pass; (*triturare: verdura*) to strain; (*approvare*) to pass, approve; (*oltrepassare, sorpassare: anche fig*) to go

beyond; pass; (fig: subire) to go through;
mi passa il sale/l'olio per favore? could
you pass the salt/oil please?; **~ da ... a**
to pass from ... to; **~ di padre in figlio** to
be handed down o to pass from father to
son; **~ per** (anche fig) to go through; **~ per
stupido/un genio** to be taken for a fool/a
genius; **~ sopra** (anche fig) to pass over; **~
attraverso** (anche fig) to go through; **~
storia** to pass into history; **~ a un esame**
to go up (to the next class) after an exam;
~ inosservato to go unnoticed; **~ di
moda** to go out of fashion; **le passo il Signor X**
(al telefono) here is Mr X; I'm putting you
through to Mr X; **lasciar ~ qn/qc** to let
sb/sth through; **come te la passi?** how
are you getting on o along?

passa'tempo sm pastime, hobby

pas'sato, -a ag past; (sfiorito) faded
▷ sm past; (Ling) past (tense); **passato
prossimo/remoto** (Ling) present perfect/
past historic; **passato di verdura** (Cuc)
vegetable purée

passeg'gero, -a [passed'dʒero] ag
passing ▷ sm/f passenger

passeggi'are [passed'dʒare] vi to go
for a walk; (in veicolo) to go for a drive;
passeggi'ata sf walk; drive; (luogo)
promenade; **fare una passeggiata** to
go for a walk (o drive); **passeg'gino** sm
pushchair (BRIT), stroller (US)

passe'rella sf footbridge; (di nave, aereo)
gangway; (pedana) catwalk

'passero sm sparrow

passi'one sf passion

pas'sivo, -a ag passive ▷ sm (Ling)
passive; (Econ) debit; (: complesso dei debiti)
liabilities pl

'passo sm step; (andatura) pace; (rumore)
(foot)step; (orma) footprint; (passaggio, fig:
brano) passage; (valico) pass; **a ~ d'uomo**
at walking pace; **~ (a) ~** step by step; **fare
due o quattro passi** to go for a walk o a
stroll; **di questo ~** at this rate; **"passo
carraio"** "vehicle entrance — keep clear"

'pasta sf (Cuc) dough; (: impasto per dolce)
pastry; (: anche: **~ alimentare**) pasta;
(massa molle di materia) paste; (fig: indole)
nature; **paste** sfpl (pasticcini) pastries;
pasta in brodo noodle soup; **pasta
sfoglia** puff pastry o paste (US)

pastasci'utta [pastaʃ'ʃutta] sf pasta

pas'tella sf batter

pas'tello sm pastel

pasticce'ria [pastittʃe'ria] sf (pasticcini)
pastries pl, cakes pl; (negozio) cake shop;
(arte) confectionery

pasticci'ere, -a [pastit'tʃere] sm/f
pastrycook; confectioner

pastic'cino [pastit'tʃino] sm petit four

pas'ticcio [pas'tittʃo] sm (Cuc) pie; (lavoro
disordinato, imbroglio) mess; **trovarsi nei
pasticci** to get into trouble

pas'tiglia [pas'tiʎʎa] sf pastille, lozenge

pas'tina sf small pasta shapes used in soup

'pasto sm meal

pas'tore sm shepherd; (Rel) pastor,
minister; (anche: **cane ~**) sheepdog;
pastore tedesco (Zool) Alsatian, German
shepherd

pa'tata sf potato; **patate fritte** chips
(BRIT), French fries; **pata'tine** sfpl (potato)
crisps; **patatine fritte** chips

pa'tente sf licence; **patente di guida**
driving licence (BRIT), driver's license (US);
patente a punti driving licence with penalty
points

> Attenzione! In inglese esiste la
> parola patent, che però significa
> brevetto.

paternità sf paternity, fatherhood

pa'tetico, -a, -ci, -che ag pathetic;
(commovente) moving, touching

pa'tibolo sm gallows sg, scaffold

'patina sf (su rame ecc) patina; (sulla lingua)
fur, coating

pa'tire vt, vi to suffer

pa'tito, -a sm/f enthusiast, fan, lover

patolo'gia [patolo'dʒia] sf pathology

'patria sf homeland

pa'trigno [pa'triɲno] sm stepfather

patri'monio sm estate, property; (fig)
heritage

pa'trono sm (Rel) patron saint; (socio di
patronato) patron; (Dir) counsel

patteggi'are [patted'dʒare] vt, vi to
negotiate; (Dir) to plea-bargain

patti'naggio [patti'naddʒo] sm skating;
pattinaggio a rotelle/sul ghiaccio
roller-/ice-skating

patti'nare vi to skate; **~ sul ghiaccio**
to ice-skate; **pattina'tore, -'trice**
sm/f skater; **'pattino** sm skate; (di slitta)
runner; (Aer) skid; (Tecn) sliding block;
pattini in linea Rollerblades®; **pattini da
ghiaccio/a rotelle** ice/roller skates

'patto sm (accordo) pact, agreement;
(condizione) term, condition; **a ~ che** on
condition that

pat'tuglia [pat'tuʎʎa] sf (Mil) patrol

pattu'ire vt to reach an agreement on

pattumi'era sf (dust)bin (BRIT), ashcan
(US)

pa'ura sf fear; **aver ~ di/di fare/che** to be
frightened o afraid of/of doing/that; **far ~
a** to frighten; **per ~ di/che** for fear of/that;
pau'roso, -a ag (che fa paura) frightening;
(che ha paura) fearful, timorous

'pausa *sf (sosta)* break; *(nel parlare, Mus)* pause

pavi'mento *sm* floor

> Attenzione! In inglese esiste la parola *pavement*, che però significa *marciapiede*.

pa'vone *sm* peacock

pazien'tare [pattsjen'tare] *vi* to be patient

pazi'ente [pat'tsjɛnte] *ag, sm/f* patient; **pazi'enza** *sf* patience

paz'zesco, -a, -schi, -sche [pat'tsesko] *ag* mad, crazy

paz'zia [pat'tsia] *sf (Med)* madness, insanity; *(azione)* folly; *(di azione, decisione)* madness, folly

'pazzo, -a ['pattso] *ag (Med)* mad, insane; *(strano)* wild, mad ▷ *sm/f* madman/ woman; **~ di** *(gioia, amore ecc)* mad o crazy with; **~ per qc/qn** mad o crazy about sth/sb

PC [pit'tʃi] *sigla m inv* (= *personal computer*) PC; **PC portatile** laptop

pec'care *vi* to sin; *(fig)* to err

pec'cato *sm* sin; **è un ~ che** it's a pity that; **che ~!** what a shame o pity!

peccherò *ecc* [pekke'rɔ] *vb vedi* **peccare**

'pece ['petʃe] *sf* pitch

Pe'chino [pe'kino] *sf* Beijing

'pecora *sf* sheep; **peco'rino** *sm* sheep's milk cheese

pe'daggio [pe'daddʒo] *sm* toll

pedago'gia [pedago'dʒia] *sf* pedagogy, educational methods *pl*

peda'lare *vi* to pedal; *(andare in bicicletta)* to cycle

pe'dale *sm* pedal

pe'dana *sf* footboard; *(Sport: nel salto)* springboard; *(: nella scherma)* piste

pe'dante *ag* pedantic ▷ *sm/f* pedant

pe'data *sf (impronta)* footprint; *(colpo)* kick; **prendere a pedate qn/qc** to kick sb/sth

pedi'atra, -i, -e *sm/f* paediatrician

pedi'cure *sm/f inv* chiropodist

pe'dina *sf (della dama)* draughtsman (BRIT), draftsman (US); *(fig)* pawn

pedi'nare *vt* to shadow, tail

pe'dofilo, -a *ag, sm/f* paedophile

pedo'nale *ag* pedestrian

pe'done, -a *sm/f* pedestrian ▷ *sm (Scacchi)* pawn

'peggio ['pɛddʒo] *av, ag inv* worse ▷ *sm o f* **il o la ~** the worst; **alla ~** at worst, if the worst comes to the worst; **peggio'rare** *vt* to make worse, worsen ▷ *vi* to grow worse, worsen; **peggi'ore** *ag (comparativo)* worse; *(superlativo)* worst ▷ *sm/f* **il(la) peggiore** the worst (person)

'pegno ['peɲɲo] *sm (Dir)* security, pledge; *(nei giochi di società)* forfeit; *(fig)* pledge, token; **dare in ~ qc** to pawn sth

pe'lare *vt (spennare)* to pluck; *(spellare)* to skin; *(sbucciare)* to peel; *(fig)* to make pay through the nose

pe'lato, -a *ag* **pomodori pelati** tinned tomatoes

'pelle *sf* skin; *(di animale)* skin, hide; *(cuoio)* leather; **avere la ~ d'oca** to have goose pimples o goose flesh

pellegri'naggio [pellegri'naddʒo] *sm* pilgrimage

pelle'rossa *(pl* **pelli'rosse)** *sm/f* Red Indian

pelli'cano *sm* pelican

pel'liccia, -ce [pel'littʃa] *sf (mantello di animale)* coat, fur; *(indumento)* fur coat; **pelliccia ecologica** fake fur

pel'licola *sf (membrana sottile)* film, layer; *(Fot, Cinema)* film

'pelo *sm* hair; *(pelame)* coat, hair; *(pelliccia)* fur; *(di tappeto)* pile; *(di liquido)* surface; **per un ~: per un ~ non ho perduto il treno** I very nearly missed the train; **c'è mancato un ~ che affogasse** he escaped drowning by the skin of his teeth; **pe'loso, -a** *ag* hairy

'peltro *sm* pewter

pe'luche [pə'lyʃ] *sm* plush; **giocattoli di ~** soft toys

pe'luria *sf* down

'pena *sf (Dir)* sentence; *(punizione)* punishment; *(sofferenza)* sadness *no pl*, sorrow; *(fatica)* trouble *no pl*, effort; *(difficoltà)* difficulty; **far ~** to be pitiful; **mi fai ~** I feel sorry for you; **prendersi** o **darsi la ~ di fare** to go to the trouble of doing; **pena di morte** death sentence; **pena pecuniaria** fine; **pe'nale** *ag* penal

pen'dente *ag* hanging; leaning ▷ *sm (ciondolo)* pendant; *(orecchino)* drop earring

'pendere *vi (essere appeso)*: **~ da** to hang from; *(essere inclinato)* to lean; *(fig: incombere)*: **~ su** to hang over

pen'dio, -'dii *sm* slope, slant; *(luogo in pendenza)* slope

'pendola *sf* pendulum clock

pendo'lare *sm/f* commuter

pendo'lino *sm* high-speed train

pene'trante *ag* piercing, penetrating

pene'trare *vi* to come o get in ▷ *vt* to penetrate; **~ in** to enter; *(proiettile)* to penetrate; *(: acqua, aria)* to go o come into

penicil'lina [penitʃil'lina] *sf* penicillin

pe'nisola *sf* peninsula

penitenzi'ario [peniten'tsjarjo] *sm* prison

'penna sf (di uccello) feather; (per scrivere) pen; **penne** sfpl (Cuc) quills (type of pasta); **penna a sfera** ballpoint pen; **penna stilografica** fountain pen

penna'rello sm felt(-tip) pen

pen'nello sm brush; (per dipingere) (paint)brush; **a ~** (perfettamente) to perfection, perfectly; **pennello per la barba** shaving brush

pe'nombra sf half-light, dim light

pen'sare vi to think ▷ vt to think; (inventare, escogitare) to think out; **~ a** to think of; (amico, vacanze) to think of o about; (problema) to think about; **~ di fare qc** to think of doing sth; **ci penso io** I'll see to o take care of it

pensi'ero sm thought; (modo di pensare, dottrina) thinking no pl; (preoccupazione) worry, care, trouble; **stare in ~ per qn** to be worried about sb; **pensie'roso, -a** ag thoughtful

'pensile ag hanging

pensio'nato, -a sm/f pensioner

pensi'one sf (al prestatore di lavoro) pension; (vitto e alloggio) board and lodging; (albergo) boarding house; **andare in ~** to retire; **mezza ~** half board; **pensione completa** full board

pen'tirsi vpr **~ di** to repent of; (rammaricarsi) to regret, be sorry for

'pentola sf pot; **pentola a pressione** pressure cooker

pe'nultimo, -a ag last but one (BRIT), next to last, penultimate

penzo'lare [pendzo'lare] vi to dangle, hang loosely

'pepe sm pepper; **pepe in grani/ macinato** whole/ground pepper

peperon'cino [peperon'tʃino] sm chilli pepper

pepe'rone sm pepper, capsicum; (piccante) chili

pe'pita sf nugget

PAROLA CHIAVE

per prep **1** (moto attraverso luogo) through; **i ladri sono passati per la finestra** the thieves got in (o out) through (o out) the window; **l'ho cercato per tutta la casa** I've searched the whole house o all over the house for it

2 (moto a luogo) for, to; **partire per la Germania/il mare** to leave for Germany/ the sea; **il treno per Roma** the Rome train, the train for o to Rome

3 (stato in luogo): **seduto/sdraiato per terra** sitting/lying on the ground

4 (tempo) for; **per anni/lungo tempo** for years/a long time; **per tutta l'estate** throughout the summer, all summer long; **lo rividi per Natale** I saw him again at Christmas; **lo faccio per lunedì** I'll do it for Monday

5 (mezzo, maniera) by; **per lettera/via aerea/ferrovia** by letter/airmail/rail; **prendere qn per un braccio** to take sb by the arm

6 (causa, scopo) for; **assente per malattia** absent because of o through o owing to illness; **ottimo per il mal di gola** excellent for sore throats

7 (limitazione) for; **è troppo difficile per lui** it's too difficult for him; **per quel che mi riguarda** as far as I'm concerned; **per poco che sia** however little it may be; **per questa volta ti perdono** I'll forgive you this time

8 (prezzo, misura) for; (distributivo) a, per; **venduto per 3 milioni** sold for 3 million; **1 euro per persona** 1 euro a o per person; **uno per volta** one at a time; **uno per uno** one by one; **5 per cento** 5 per cent; **3 per 4 fa 12** 3 times 4 equals 12; **dividere/ moltiplicare 12 per 4** to divide/multiply 12 by 4

9 (in qualità di) as; (al posto di) for; **avere qn per professore** to have sb as a teacher; **ti ho preso per Mario** I mistook you for Mario, I thought you were Mario; **dare per morto qn** to give sb up for dead

10 (seguito da vb: finale): **per fare qc** so as to do sth, in order to do sth; (: causale): **per aver fatto qc** for having done sth; (: consecutivo): **è abbastanza grande per andarci da solo** he's big enough to go on his own

'pera sf pear

per'bene ag inv respectable, decent ▷ av (con cura) properly, well

percentu'ale [pertʃentu'ale] sf percentage

perce'pire [pertʃe'pire] vt (sentire) to perceive; (ricevere) to receive

PAROLA CHIAVE

perché [per'ke] av why; **perché no?** why not?; **perché non vuoi andarci?** why don't you want to go?; **spiegami perché l'hai fatto** tell me why you did it

▷ cong **1** (causale) because; **non posso uscire perché ho da fare** I can't go out because o as I've a lot to do

2 (finale) in order that, so that; **te lo do perché tu lo legga** I'm giving it to you so (that) you can read it

3 (*consecutivo*): **è troppo forte perché si possa batterlo** he's too strong to be beaten
▷ *sm inv* reason; **il perché di** the reason for

perciò [per'tʃɔ] *cong* so, for this (*o* that) reason

per'correre *vt* (*luogo*) to go all over; (: *paese*) to travel up and down, go all over; (*distanza*) to cover

per'corso, -a *pp di* **percorrere** ▷ *sm* (*tragitto*) journey; (*tratto*) route

percu'otere *vt* to hit, strike

percussi'one *sf* percussion; **strumenti a ~** (*Mus*) percussion instruments

'perdere *vt* to lose; (*lasciarsi sfuggire*) to miss; (*sprecare: tempo, denaro*) to waste ▷ *vi* to lose; (*serbatoio ecc*) to leak; **perdersi** *vpr* (*smarrirsi*) to get lost; (*svanire*) to disappear, vanish; **mi sono perso** I'm lost; **ho perso il portafoglio/passaporto** I've lost my wallet/passport; **abbiamo perso il treno** we missed our train; **saper ~** to be a good loser; **lascia ~!** forget it!, never mind!

perdigi'orno [perdi'dʒorno] *sm/f inv* idler, waster

'perdita *sf* loss; (*spreco*) waste; (*fuoriuscita*) leak; (*Comm*) loss; **a ~ d'occhio** as far as the eye can see

perdo'nare *vt* to pardon, forgive; (*scusare*) to excuse, pardon

per'dono *sm* forgiveness; (*Dir*) pardon

perduta'mente *av* desperately, passionately

pe'renne *ag* eternal, perpetual, perennial; (*Bot*) perennial

perfetta'mente *av* perfectly; **sai ~ che ...** you know perfectly well that ...

per'fetto, -a *ag* perfect ▷ *sm* (*Ling*) perfect (tense)

perfeziona'mento [perfettsjona'mento] *sm* **~ (di)** improvement (in), perfection (of); **corso di ~** proficiency course

perfezio'nare [perfettsjo'nare] *vt* to improve, perfect; **perfezionarsi** *vpr* to improve

perfezi'one [perfet'tsjone] *sf* perfection

per'fino *av* even

perfo'rare *vt* to perforate, to punch a hole (*o* holes) in; (*banda, schede*) to punch; (*trivellare*) to drill

perga'mena *sf* parchment

perico'lante *ag* precarious

pe'ricolo *sm* danger; **mettere in ~** to endanger, put in danger; **perico'loso, -a** *ag* dangerous

perife'ria *sf* (*di città*) outskirts *pl*

pe'rifrasi *sf* circumlocution

pe'rimetro *sm* perimeter

peri'odico, -a, -ci, -che *ag* periodic(al); (*Mat*) recurring ▷ *sm* periodical

pe'riodo *sm* period

peripe'zie [peripet'tsie] *sfpl* ups and downs, vicissitudes

pe'rito, -a *ag* expert, skilled ▷ *sm/f* expert; (*agronomo, navale*) surveyor; **perito chimico** qualified chemist

peri'zoma, -i [peri'dzoma] *sm* G-string

'perla *sf* pearl; **per'lina** *sf* bead

perlus'trare *vt* to patrol

perma'loso, -a *ag* touchy

perma'nente *ag* permanent ▷ *sf* permanent wave, perm; **perma'nenza** *sf* permanence; (*soggiorno*) stay

perme'are *vt* to permeate

per'messo, -a *pp di* **permettere** ▷ *sm* (*autorizzazione*) permission, leave; (*dato a militare, impiegato*) leave; (*licenza*) licence, permit; (*Mil: foglio*) pass; **~?, è ~?** (*posso entrare?*) may I come in?; (*posso passare?*) excuse me; **permesso di lavoro/pesca** work/fishing permit; **permesso di soggiorno** residence permit

per'mettere *vt* to allow, permit; **~ a qn qc/di fare qc** to allow sb sth/to do sth; **permettersi qc/di fare qc** to allow o.s. sth/to do sth; (*avere la possibilità*) to afford sth/to do sth

per'misi *ecc vb vedi* **permettere**

per'nacchia [per'nakkja] (*fam*) *sf* **fare una ~** to blow a raspberry

per'nice [per'nitʃe] *sf* partridge

'perno *sm* pivot

pernot'tare *vi* to spend the night, stay overnight

'pero *sm* pear tree

però *cong* (*ma*) but; (*tuttavia*) however, nevertheless

perpendico'lare *ag, sf* perpendicular

per'plesso, -a *ag* perplexed; uncertain, undecided

perqui'sire *vt* to search; **perquisizi'one** *sf* (*police*) search

'perse *ecc vb vedi* **perdere**

persecuzi'one [persekut'tsjone] *sf* persecution

persegui'tare *vt* to persecute

perseve'rante *ag* persevering

'persi *ecc vb vedi* **perdere**

persi'ana *sf* shutter; **persiana avvolgibile** roller shutter

per'sino *av* = **perfino**

persis'tente *ag* persistent

'perso, -a *pp di* **perdere**

per'sona *sf* person; (*qualcuno*): **una ~** someone, somebody; (*espressione interrogativa +*) anyone *o* anybody

perso'naggio [perso'naddʒo] *sm* (*persona*

ragguardevole) personality, figure; *(tipo)* character, individual; *(Letteratura)* character

perso'nale *ag* personal ▷ *sm* staff; personnel; *(figura fisica)* build

personalità *sf inv* personality

perspi'cace [perspi'katʃe] *ag* shrewd, discerning

persu'adere *vt* ~ **qn (di qc/a fare) to** persuade sb (of sth/to do)

per'tanto *cong (quindi)* so, therefore

'pertica, -che *sf* pole

perti'nente *ag* ~ **(a)** relevant (to), pertinent (to)

per'tosse *sf* whooping cough

perturbazi'one [perturbat'tsjone] *sf* disruption; perturbation; **perturbazione atmosferica** atmospheric disturbance

per'vadere *vt* to pervade

per'verso, -a *ag* depraved; perverse

perver'tito, -a *sm/f* pervert

p.es. *abbr (= per esempio)* e.g.

pe'sante *ag* heavy; **è troppo ~** it's too heavy

pe'sare *vt* to weigh ▷ *vi (avere un peso)* to weigh; *(essere pesante)* to be heavy; *(fig)* to carry weight; **~ su** *(fig)* to lie heavy on; to influence; to hang over; **pesarsi** *vpr* to weigh o.s.; **~ le parole** to weigh one's words; **~ sulla coscienza** to weigh on sb's conscience; **mi pesa ammetterlo** I don't like admitting it; **tutta la responsabilità pesa su di lui** all the responsibility rests on him; **è una situazione che mi pesa** I find the situation difficult; **il suo parere pesa molto** his opinion counts for a lot

'pesca *(pl* **pesche)** *(: frutto) sf* peach; *(il pescare)* fishing; **andare a ~** to go fishing; **~ con la lenza** angling; **pesca di beneficenza** *(lotteria)* lucky dip

pes'care *vt (pesce)* to fish for; to catch; *(qc nell'acqua)* to fish out; *(fig: trovare)* to get hold of, find; **andare a ~** to go fishing

pesca'tore *sm* fisherman; angler

'pesce ['peʃʃe] *sm* fish *gen inv*; **Pesci** *(dello zodiaco)* Pisces; **pesce d'aprile!** April Fool!; **pesce rosso** goldfish; **pesce spada** swordfish; **pesce'cane** *sm* shark

pesche'reccio [peske'rettʃo] *sm* fishing boat

pesche'ria [peske'ria] *sf* fishmonger's (shop) *(BRIT)*, fish store *(US)*

pescherò *ecc* [peske'rɔ] *vb vedi* **pescare**

'peso *sm* weight; *(Sport)* shot; **rubare sul ~** to give short weight; **essere di ~ a qn** *(fig)* to be a burden to sb; **peso lordo/netto** gross/net weight; **peso massimo/medio** *(Pugilato)* heavy/middleweight

pessi'mismo *sm* pessimism; **pessi'mista,**

-i, -e *ag* pessimistic ▷ *sm/f* pessimist

'pessimo, -a *ag* very bad, awful

pes'tare *vt* to tread on, trample on; *(sale, pepe)* to grind; *(uva, aglio)* to crush; *(fig: picchiare)*: **~ qn** to beat sb up

'peste *sf* plague; *(persona)* nuisance, pest

pes'tello *sm* pestle

'petalo *sm (Bot)* petal

pe'tardo *sm* firecracker, banger *(BRIT)*

petizi'one [petit'tsjone] *sf* petition

petroli'era *sf (nave)* oil tanker

pe'trolio *sm* oil, petroleum; *(per lampada, fornello)* paraffin

> Attenzione! In inglese esiste la parola *petrol* che però significa *benzina*.

pettego'lare *vi* to gossip

pettego'lezzo [pettego'leddzo] *sm* gossip *no pl;* **fare pettegolezzi** to gossip

pet'tegolo, -a *ag* gossipy ▷ *sm/f* gossip

petti'nare *vt* to comb (the hair of); **pettinarsi** *vpr* to comb one's hair; **pettina'tura** *sf (acconciatura)* hairstyle

'pettine *sm* comb; *(Zool)* scallop

petti'rosso *sm* robin

'petto *sm* chest; *(seno)* breast, bust; *(Cuc: di carne bovina)* brisket; *(: di pollo ecc)* breast; **a doppio ~** *(abito)* double-breasted

petu'lante *ag* insolent

'pezza ['pettsa] *sf* piece of cloth; *(toppa)* patch; *(cencio)* rag, cloth

pez'zente [pet'tsɛnte] *sm/f* beggar

'pezzo ['pettso] *sm (gen)* piece; *(brandello, frammento)* piece, bit; *(di macchina, arnese ecc)* part; *(Stampa)* article; *(di tempo)*: **aspettare un ~** to wait quite a while o some time; **in** *o* **a pezzi** in pieces; **andare in pezzi** to break into pieces; **un bel ~ d'uomo** a fine figure of a man; **abito a due pezzi** two-piece suit; **pezzo di cronaca** *(Stampa)* report; **pezzo grosso** *(fig)* bigwig; **pezzo di ricambio** spare part

pi'accio *ecc* ['pjattʃo] *vb vedi* **piacere**

pia'cente [pja'tʃɛnte] *ag* attractive

pia'cere [pja'tʃere] *vi* to please; **una ragazza che piace** a likeable girl; an attractive girl; **~ a: mi piace** I like it; **quei ragazzi non mi piacciono** I don't like those boys; **gli ~bbe andare al cinema** he would like to go to the cinema ▷ *sm* pleasure; *(favore)* favour; **"~!"** *(nelle presentazioni)* "pleased to meet you!"; **~ (di conoscerla)** nice to meet you; **con ~** certainly, with pleasure; **per ~!** please; **fare un ~ a qn** to do sb a favour; **pia'cevole** *ag* pleasant, agreeable

pi'acqui *ecc vb vedi* **piacere**

pi'aga, -ghe *sf (lesione)* sore; *(ferita: anche fig)* wound; *(fig: flagello)* scourge, curse; *(: persona)* pest, nuisance

piagnuco'lare [pjaɲɲukoˈlare] vi to whimper

pianeggi'ante [pjanedˈdʒante] ag flat, level

piane'rottolo sm landing

pia'neta sm (Astr) planet

pi'angere [ˈpjandʒere] vi to cry, weep; (occhi) to water ▷ vt to cry, weep; (lamentare) to bewail, lament; **~ la morte di qn** to mourn sb's death

pianifi'care vt to plan

pia'nista, -i, -e sm/f pianist

pi'ano, -a ag (piatto) flat, level; (Mat) plane; (chiaro) clear, plain ▷ av (adagio) slowly; (a bassa voce) softly; (con cautela) slowly, carefully ▷ sm (Mat) plane; (Geo) plain; (livello) level, plane; (di edificio) floor; (programma) plan; (Mus) piano; **a che ~ si trova?** what floor is it on?; **pian ~** very slowly; (poco a poco) little by little; **in primo/secondo ~** in the foreground/ background; **di primo ~** (fig) prominent, high-ranking

piano'forte sm piano, pianoforte

piano'terra sm inv ground floor

pi'ansi ecc vb vedi **piangere**

pi'anta sf (Bot) plant; (Anat: anche: **~ del piede**) sole (of the foot); (grafico) plan; (topografica) map; **in ~ stabile** on the permanent staff; **pian'tare** vt to plant; (conficcare) to drive o hammer in; (tenda) to put up, pitch; (fig: lasciare) to leave, desert; **piantarsi** vpr **piantarsi davanti a qn** to plant o.s. in front of sb; **piantala!** (fam) cut it out!

pianter'reno sm = **pianoterra**

pia'nura sf plain

pi'astra sf plate; (di pietra) slab; (di fornello) hotplate; **panino alla ~** = toasted sandwich; **piastra di registrazione** tape deck

pias'trella sf tile

pias'trina sf (Mil) identity disc

piatta'forma sf (anche fig) platform

piat'tino sm saucer

pi'atto, -a ag flat; (fig: scialbo) dull ▷ sm (recipiente, vivanda) dish; (portata) course; (parte piana) flat (part); **piatti** smpl (Mus) cymbals; **piatto fondo** soup dish; **piatto forte** main course; **piatto del giorno** dish of the day, plat du jour; **piatto del giradischi** turntable; **piatto piano** dinner plate

pi'azza [ˈpjattsa] sf square; (Comm) market; **far ~ pulita** to make a clean sweep; **piazza d'armi** (Mil) parade ground; **piaz'zale** sm (large) square

piaz'zola [pjatˈtsɔla] sf (Aut) lay-by; (di tenda) pitch

pic'cante ag hot, pungent; (fig) racy; biting

pic'chetto [pikˈketto] sm (Mil, di scioperanti) picket; (di tenda) peg

picchi'are [pikˈkjare] vt (persona: colpire) to hit, strike; (: prendere a botte) to beat (up); (battere) to beat; (sbattere) to bang ▷ vi (bussare) to knock; (: con forza) to bang; (colpire) to hit, strike; (sole) to beat down; **picchi'ata** sf (Aer) dive

'picchio [ˈpikkjo] sm woodpecker

pic'cino, -a [pitˈtʃino] ag tiny, very small

picci'one [pitˈtʃone] sm pigeon

'picco, -chi sm peak; **a ~** vertically

'piccolo, -a ag small; (oggetto, mano, di età: bambino) small, little; (dav sostantivo: di breve durata: viaggio) short; (fig) mean, petty ▷ sm/f child, little one

pic'cone sm pick(-axe)

pic'cozza [pikˈkɔttsa] sf ice-axe

pic'nic sm inv picnic

pi'docchio [piˈdɔkkjo] sm louse

pi'ede sm foot; (di mobile) leg; **in piedi** standing; **a piedi** on foot; **a piedi nudi** barefoot; **su due piedi** (fig) at once; **prendere ~** (fig) to gain ground, catch on; **sul ~ di guerra** (Mil) ready for action; **piede di porco** crowbar

pi'ega, -ghe sf (piegatura, Geo) fold; (di gonna) pleat; (di pantaloni) crease; (grinza) wrinkle, crease; **prendere una brutta ~** (fig) to take a turn for the worse

pie'gare vt to fold; (braccia, gambe, testa) to bend ▷ vi to bend; **piegarsi** vpr to bend; (fig): **piegarsi (a)** to yield (to), submit (to)

piegherò ecc [pjegeˈrɔ] vb vedi **piegare**

pie'ghevole ag pliable, flexible; (porta) folding

Pie'monte sm **il ~** Piedmont

pi'ena sf (di fiume) flood, spate

pi'eno, -a ag full; (muro, mattone) solid ▷ sm (colmo) height, peak; (carico) full load; **~ di** full of; **in ~ giorno** in broad daylight; **il ~, per favore** (Aut) fill it up, please

piercing [ˈpirsing] sm piercing; **farsi il ~ all'ombelico** to have one's navel pierced

pietà sf pity; (Rel) piety; **senza ~** pitiless, merciless; **avere ~ di** (compassione) to pity, feel sorry for; (misericordia) to have pity o mercy on

pie'tanza [pjeˈtantsa] sf dish, course

pie'toso, -a ag (compassionevole) pitying, compassionate; (che desta pietà) pitiful

pi'etra sf stone; **pietra preziosa** precious stone, gem

'piffero sm (Mus) pipe

pigi'ama, -i [piˈdʒama] sm pyjamas pl

pigli'are [piʎˈʎare] vt to take, grab; (afferrare) to catch

ˈpigna [ˈpiɲɲa] sf pine cone
piˈgnolo, -a [piˈɲɲɔlo] ag pernickety
piˈgrizia [piˈgrittsja] sf laziness
ˈpigro, -a ag lazy
PIL sigla m (= prodotto interno lordo) GDP
ˈpila sf (catasta, di ponte) pile; (Elettr) battery; (torcia) torch (BRIT), flashlight
piˈlastro sm pillar
ˈpile [ˈpail] sm inv fleece
ˈpillola sf pill; **prendere la ~** to be on the pill
piˈlone sm (di ponte) pier; (di linea elettrica) pylon
piˈlota, -i, -e sm/f pilot; (Aut) driver ▷ ag inv pilot cpd; **pilota automatico** automatic pilot
pinacoˈteca, -che sf art gallery
piˈneta sf pinewood
ping-ˈpong [pɪŋˈpɔŋ] sm table tennis
pinguˈino sm (Zool) penguin
ˈpinna sf (di pesce) fin; (di cetaceo, per nuotare) flipper
ˈpino sm pine (tree); **piˈnolo** sm pine kernel
ˈpinza [ˈpintsa] sf pliers pl; (Med) forceps pl; (Zool) pincer
pinzette [pin'tsette] sfpl tweezers
piˈoggia, -ge [ˈpjɔddʒa] sf rain; **pioggia acida** acid rain
ˈpiolo sm peg; (di scala) rung
piomˈbare vi to fall heavily; (gettarsi con impeto): **~ su** to fall upon, assail ▷ vt (dente) to fill; **piombaˈtura** sf (di dente) filling
piomˈbino sm (sigillo) lead seal; (del filo a piombo) plummet; (Pesca) sinker
piˈombo sm (Chim) lead; **a ~** (cadere) straight down; **senza ~** (benzina) unleaded
pioniˈere, -a sm/f pioneer
ˈpioppo sm poplar
piˈovere vb impers to rain ▷ vi (fig: scendere dall'alto) to rain down; (lettere, regali) to pour into; **pioviggiˈnare** vb impers to drizzle; **pioˈvoso, -a** ag rainy
piˈovra sf octopus
piˈovve ecc vb vedi **piovere**
ˈpipa sf pipe
pipì (fam) sf **fare ~** to have a wee (wee)
pipiˈstrello sm (Zool) bat
piˈramide sf pyramid
piˈrata, -i sm pirate; **pirata della strada** hit-and-run driver; **pirata informatica** hacker
Pireˈnei smpl **i ~** the Pyrenees
piˈromane sm/f pyromaniac; arsonist
piˈroscafo sm steamer, steamship
piˈscina [piʃˈʃina] sf (swimming) pool; (stabilimento) (swimming) baths pl
piˈsello sm pea

pisoˈlino sm nap
ˈpista sf (traccia) track, trail; (di stadio) track; (di pattinaggio) rink; (da sci) run; (Aer) runway; (di circo) ring; **pista da ballo** dance floor
pisˈtacchio [pisˈtakkjo] sm pistachio (tree); pistachio (nut)
pisˈtola sf pistol, gun
pisˈtone sm piston
piˈtone sm python
pitˈtore, -ˈtrice sm/f painter; **pittoˈresco, -a, -schi, -sche** ag picturesque
pitˈtura sf painting; **pittuˈrare** vt to paint

○ **PAROLA CHIAVE**

più av 1 (in maggiore quantità) more; **più del solito** more than usual; **in più, di più** more; **ne voglio di più** I want some more; **ci sono 3 persone in o di più** there are 3 more o extra people; **più o meno** more or less; **per di più** (inoltre) what's more, moreover
2 (comparativo) more; (aggettivo corto +) ...er; **più ... di/che** more ... than; **lavoro più di te/Paola** I work harder than you/ Paola; **è più intelligente che ricco** he's more intelligent than rich
3 (superlativo) most; (aggettivo corto +) ...est; **il più grande/intelligente** the biggest/most intelligent; **è quello che compro più spesso** that's the one I buy most often; **al più presto** as soon as possible; **al più tardi** at the latest
4 (negazione): **non ... più** no more, no longer; **non ho più soldi** I've got no more money, I don't have any more money; **non lavoro più** I'm no longer working, I don't work any more; **a più non posso** (gridare) at the top of one's voice; (correre) as fast as one can
5 (Mat) plus; **4 più 5 fa 9** 4 plus 5 equals 9; **più 5 gradi** 5 degrees above freezing, plus 5 ▷ prep plus ▷ ag inv 1: **più ... (di)** more ... (than); **più denaro/tempo** more money/time; **più persone di quante ci aspettassimo** more people than we expected
2 (numerosi, diversi) several; **l'aspettai per più giorni** I waited for it for several days ▷ sm 1 (la maggior parte): **il più è fatto** most of it is done
2 (Mat) plus (sign)
3: **i più** the majority

piˈuma sf feather; **piuˈmino** sm (eider)down; (per letto) eiderdown; (: tipo *danese*) duvet, continental quilt; (*giacca*) quilted jacket (*with goose-feather padding*); (*per cipria*) powder puff; (*per spolverare*) feather duster

piut'tosto *av* rather; **~ che** (*anziché*) rather than

'pizza ['pittsa] *sf* pizza; **pizze'ria** *sf place where pizzas are made, sold or eaten*

pizzi'care [pittsi'kare] *vt* (*stringere*) to nip, pinch; (*pungere*) to sting; to bite; (*Mus*) to pluck ▷ *vi* (*prudere*) to itch, be itchy; (*cibo*) to be hot o spicy

'pizzico, -chi ['pittsiko] *sm* (*pizzicotto*) pinch, nip; (*piccola quantità*) pinch, dash; (*d'insetto*) sting; bite

pizzi'cotto [pittsi'kotto] *sm* pinch, nip

'pizzo ['pittso] *sm* (*merletto*) lace; (*barbetta*) goatee beard

plagi'are [pla'dʒare] *vt* (*copiare*) to plagiarize

plaid [plɛd] *sm inv* (*travelling*) rug (BRIT), lap robe (US)

pla'nare *vi* (*Aer*) to glide

'plasma *sm* plasma

plas'mare *vt* to mould, shape

'plastica, -che *sf* (*arte*) plastic arts *pl*; (*Med*) plastic surgery; (*sostanza*) plastic; **plastica facciale** face lift

'platano *sm* plane tree

pla'tea *sf* (*Teatro*) stalls *pl*

'platino *sm* platinum

plau'sibile *ag* plausible

pleni'lunio *sm* full moon

'plettro *sm* plectrum

pleu'rite *sf* pleurisy

'plico, -chi *sm* (*pacco*) parcel; **in ~ a parte** (*Comm*) under separate cover

plo'tone *sm* (*Mil*) platoon; **plotone d'esecuzione** firing squad

plu'rale *ag, sm* plural

PM *abbr* (*Pol*) = **Pubblico Ministero**; (= *Polizia Militare*) MP (*Military Police*)

po' *av, sm vedi* **poco**

⭕ **PAROLA CHIAVE**

'poco, -a, -chi, -che *ag* (*quantità*) little, not much; (*numero*) few, not many; **poco pane/denaro/spazio** little o not much bread/money/space; **poche persone/idee** few o not many people/ideas; **ci vediamo tra poco** (*sottinteso: tempo*) see you soon

▷ *av* **1** (*in piccola quantità*) little, not much; (*numero limitato*) few, not many; **guadagna poco** he doesn't earn much, he earns little

2 (*con ag, av*) (a) little, not very; **sta poco bene** he isn't very well; **è poco più vecchia di lui** she's a little o slightly older than him

3 (*tempo*): **poco dopo/prima** shortly afterwards/before; **il film dura poco** the film doesn't last very long; **ci vediamo molto poco** we don't see each other very often, we hardly ever see each other

4: **un po'** a little, a bit; **è un po' corto** it's a little o a bit short; **arriverà fra un po'** he'll arrive shortly o in a little while

5: **a dir poco** to say the least; **a poco a poco** little by little; **per poco non cadevo** I nearly fell; **è una cosa da poco** it's nothing, it's of no importance; **una persona da poco** a worthless person ▷ *pron* (a) little

po'dere *sm* (*Agr*) farm

'podio *sm* dais, platform; (*Mus*) podium

po'dismo *sm* (*Sport*) track events *pl*

poe'sia *sf* (*arte*) poetry; (*componimento*) poem

po'eta, -'essa *sm/f* poet/poetess

poggi'are [pod'dʒare] *vt* to lean, rest; (*posare*) to lay, place; **poggia'testa** *sm inv* (*Aut*) headrest

'poggio ['poddʒo] *sm* hillock, knoll

'poi *av* then; (*alla fine*) finally, at last; **e ~** (*inoltre*) and besides; **questa ~ (è bella)!** (*ironico*) that's a good one!

poiché [poi'ke] *cong* since, as

'poker *sm* poker

po'lacco, -a, -chi, -che *ag* Polish ▷ *sm/f* Pole

po'lare *ag* polar

po'lemica, -che *sf* controversy

po'lemico, -a, -ci, -che *ag* polemic(al), controversial

po'lenta *sf* (*Cuc*) sort of thick porridge made with maize flour

polio(mie'lite) *sf* polio(myelitis)

'polipo *sm* polyp

polisti'rolo *sm* polystyrene

po'litica, -che *sf* politics *sg*; (*linea di condotta*) policy; (*anche*: **politico**); **politica'mente** *av* politically; **politicamente corretto** politically correct

po'litico, -a, -ci, -che *ag* political ▷ *sm/f* politician

poli'zia [polit'tsia] *sf* police; **polizia giudiziaria** ≈ Criminal Investigation Department (BRIT); ≈ Federal Bureau of Investigation (US); **polizia stradale** traffic police; **polizi'esco, -a, -schi, -sche** *ag* police *cpd*; (*film, romanzo*) detective *cpd*; **polizi'otto** *sm* policeman; **cane poliziotto** police dog; **donna poliziotto**

policewoman; **poliziotto di quartiere** local police officer

'**polizza** ['pɔlittsa] sf (Comm) bill; **~ di assicurazione** insurance policy; **polizza di carico** bill of lading
pol'laio sm henhouse
'**pollice** ['pollitʃe] sm thumb
'**polline** sm pollen
'**pollo** sm chicken
pol'mone sm lung; **polmone d'acciaio** (Med) iron lung; **polmo'nite** sf pneumonia; **polmonite atipica** SARS
'**polo** sm (Geo, Fisica) pole; (gioco) polo; **polo nord/sud** North/South Pole
Po'lonia sf **la ~** Poland
'**polpa** sf flesh, pulp; (carne) lean meat
pol'paccio [pol'pattʃo] sm (Anat) calf
polpas'trello sm fingertip
pol'petta sf (Cuc) meatball
'**polpo** sm octopus
pol'sino sm cuff
'**polso** sm (Anat) wrist; (pulsazione) pulse; (fig: forza) drive, vigour
pol'trire vi to laze about
pol'trona sf armchair; (Teatro: posto) seat in the front stalls (BRIT) o orchestra (US)
'**polvere** sf dust; (sostanza ridotta minutissima) powder, dust; **latte in ~** dried o powdered milk; **caffè in ~** instant coffee; **sapone in ~** soap powder; **polvere da sparo/pirica** gunpowder
po'mata sf ointment, cream
po'mello sm knob
pome'riggio [pome'riddʒo] sm afternoon
'**pomice** ['pɔmitʃe] sf pumice
'**pomo** sm (mela) apple; (ornamentale) knob; (di sella) pommel; **pomo d'Adamo** (Anat) Adam's apple
pomo'doro sm tomato; **pomodori pelati** skinned tomatoes
'**pompa** sf pump; (sfarzo) pomp (and ceremony); **pompe funebri** funeral parlour sg (BRIT); undertaker's sg; **pompa di benzina** petrol (BRIT) o gas (US) pump; (distributore) filling o gas (US) station; **pom'pare** vt to pump; (trarre) to pump out; (gonfiare d'aria) to pump up
pom'pelmo sm grapefruit
pompi'ere sm fireman

po'nente sm west
pongo, poni ecc vb vedi **porre**
'**ponte** sm bridge; (di nave) deck; (: anche: **~ di comando**) bridge; (impalcatura) scaffold; **fare il ~** (fig) to take the extra day off (between 2 public holidays); **governo ~** interim government; **ponte aereo** airlift; **ponte levatoio** drawbridge; **ponte sospeso** suspension bridge
pon'tefice [pon'tɛfitʃe] sm (Rel) pontiff
'**popcorn** ['pɔpkɔːn] sm inv popcorn
popo'lare ag popular; (quartiere, clientela) working-class ▷ vt (rendere abitato) to populate; **popolarsi** vpr to fill with people, get crowded; **popolazi'one** sf population
'**popolo** sm people
'**poppa** sf (di nave) stern; (seno) breast
porcel'lana [portʃel'lana] sf porcelain, china; piece of china
porcel'lino, -a [portʃel'lino] sm/f piglet; **porcellino d'India** guinea pig
porche'ria [porke'ria] sf filth, muck; (fig: oscenità) obscenity; (: azione disonesta) dirty trick; (: cosa mal fatta) rubbish
por'cile [por'tʃile] sm pigsty
por'cino, -a [por'tʃino] ag of pigs, pork cpd ▷ sm (fungo) type of edible mushroom
'**porco, -ci** sm pig; (carne) pork
porcos'pino sm porcupine
'**porgere** ['pɔrdʒere] vt to hand, give; (tendere) to hold out
pornogra'fia sf pornography; **porno'grafico, -a, -ci, -che** ag pornographic
'**poro** sm pore
'**porpora** sf purple
'**porre** vt (mettere) to put; (collocare) to place; (posare) to lay (down), put (down); (fig: supporre): **poniamo (il caso) che ...** let's suppose that ...
'**porro** sm (Bot) leek; (Med) wart
'**porsi** ecc vb vedi **porgere**
'**porta** sf door; (Sport) goal; **portaba'gagli** sm inv (facchino) porter; (Aut, Ferr) luggage rack; **porta-CD** [portatʃi'di] sm inv (mobile) CD rack; (astuccio) CD holder; **porta'cenere** sm inv ashtray; **portachi'avi** sm inv keyring; **porta'erei** sf inv (nave) aircraft carrier; **portafi'nestra** (pl **portefi'nestre**) sf French window; **porta'foglio** sm wallet; (Pol, Borsa) portfolio; **non trovo il portafoglio** I can't find my wallet; **portafor'tuna** sm inv lucky charm; mascot
por'tale sm (di chiesa, Inform) portal
porta'mento sm carriage, bearing
portamo'nete sm inv purse

por'tante *ag* (*muro ecc*) supporting, load-bearing

portan'tina *sf* sedan chair; (*per ammalati*) stretcher

portaom'brelli *sm inv* umbrella stand

porta'pacchi [porta'pakki] *sm inv* (*di moto, bicicletta*) luggage rack

por'tare *vt* (*sostenere, sorreggere: peso, bambino, pacco*) to carry; (*indossare: abito, occhiali*) to wear; (: *capelli lunghi*) to have; (*avere: nome, titolo*) to have, bear; (*recare*): **~ qc a qn** to take (*o* bring) sth to sb; (*fig: sentimenti*) to bear

portasiga'rette *sm inv* cigarette case

por'tata *sf* (*vivanda*) course; (*Aut*) carrying (*o* loading) capacity; (*di arma*) range; (*volume d'acqua*) (rate of) flow; (*fig: limite*) scope, capability; (: *importanza*) impact, import; **alla ~ di tutti** (*conoscenza*) within everybody's capabilities; (*prezzo*) within everybody's means; **a/fuori ~ (di)** within/out of reach (of); **a ~ di mano** within (arm's) reach

por'tatile *ag* portable

por'tato, -a *ag* (*incline*): **~ a** inclined *o* apt to

portau'ovo *sm inv* eggcup

porta'voce [porta'votʃe] *sm/f inv* spokesman/woman

por'tento *sm* wonder, marvel

porti'era *sf* (*Aut*) door

porti'ere *sm* (*portinaio*) concierge, caretaker; (*di hotel*) porter; (*nel calcio*) goalkeeper

porti'naio, -a *sm/f* concierge, caretaker

portine'ria *sf* caretaker's lodge

'porto, -a *pp di* **porgere** ▷ *sm* (*Naut*) harbour, port ▷ *sm inv* port (wine); **porto d'armi** (*documento*) gun licence

Porto'gallo *sm* **il ~** Portugal; **porto'ghese** *ag, sm/f, sm* Portuguese *inv*

por'tone *sm* main entrance, main door

portu'ale *ag* harbour *cpd*, port *cpd* ▷ *sm* dock worker

porzi'one [por'tsjone] *sf* portion, share; (*di cibo*) portion, helping

'posa *sf* (*Fot*) exposure; (*atteggiamento, di modello*) pose

po'sare *vt* to put (down), lay (down) ▷ *vi* (*ponte, edificio, teoria*): **~ su** to rest on; (*Fot: atteggiarsi*) to pose; **posarsi** *vpr* (*aereo*) to land; (*uccello*) to alight; (*sguardo*) to settle

po'sata *sf* piece of cutlery

pos'critto *sm* postscript

'posi *ecc vb vedi* **porre**

posi'tivo, -a *ag* positive

posizi'one [pozit'tsjone] *sf* position; **prendere ~** (*fig*) to take a stand; **luci di ~** (*Aut*) sidelights

pos'porre *vt* to place after; (*differire*) to postpone, defer

posse'dere *vt* to own, possess; (*qualità, virtù*) to have, possess

posses'sivo, -a *ag* possessive

pos'sesso *sm* ownership *no pl*; possession

posses'sore *sm* owner

pos'sibile *ag* possible ▷ *sm* **fare tutto il ~** to do everything possible; **nei limiti del ~** as far as possible; **al più tardi ~** as late as possible; **possibilità** *sf inv* possibility ▷ *sfpl* (*mezzi*) means; **aver la possibilità di fare** to be in a position to do; to have the opportunity to do

possi'dente *sm/f* landowner

possi'edo *ecc vb vedi* **possedere**

'posso *ecc vb vedi* **potere**

'posta *sf* (*servizio*) post, postal service; (*corrispondenza*) post, mail; (*ufficio postale*) post office; (*nei giochi d'azzardo*) stake; **Poste** *sfpl* (*amministrazione*) post office; **c'è ~ per me?** are there any letters for me?; **ministro delle Poste e Telecomunicazioni** Postmaster General; **posta aerea** airmail; **posta elettronica** E-mail, e-mail, electronic mail; **posta ordinaria** ≈ second-class mail; **posta prioritaria** ≈ first-class post; **pos'tale** *ag* postal, post office *cpd*

posteggi'are [posted'dʒare] *vt, vi* to park; **pos'teggio** *sm* car park (BRIT), parking lot (US); (*di taxi*) rank (BRIT), stand (US)

'poster *sm inv* poster

posteri'ore *ag* (*dietro*) back; (*dopo*) later ▷ *sm* (*fam: sedere*) behind

postici'pare [postitʃi'pare] *vt* to defer, postpone

pos'tino *sm* postman (BRIT), mailman (US)

'posto, -a *pp di* **porre** ▷ *sm* (*sito, posizione*) place; (*impiego*) job; (*spazio libero*) room, space; (*di parcheggio*) space; (*sedile: al teatro, in treno ecc*) seat; (*Mil*) post; **a ~** (*in ordine*) in place, tidy; (*fig*) settled; (: *persona*) reliable; **vorrei prenotare due posti** I'd like to book two seats; **al ~ di** in place of; **sul ~** on the spot; **mettere a ~** to tidy (up), put in order; (*faccende*) to straighten out; **posto di blocco** roadblock; **posto di lavoro** job; **posti in piedi** (*in teatro, in autobus*) standing room; **posto di polizia** police station

po'tabile *ag* drinkable; **acqua ~** drinking water

po'tare *vt* to prune

po'tassio *sm* potassium

po'tente *ag* (*nazione*) strong, powerful; (*veleno, farmaco*) potent, strong; **po'tenza** *sf* power; (*forza*) strength

potenzi'ale [poten'tsjale] *ag, sm*
potential

 PAROLA CHIAVE

po'tere *sm* power; **al potere** (*partito ecc*)
in power; **potere d'acquisto** purchasing
power
▷ *vb aus* **1** (*essere in grado di*) can, be able
to; **non ha potuto ripararlo** he couldn't
o he wasn't able to repair it; **non è potuto
venire** he couldn't *o* he wasn't able to
come; **spiacente di non poter aiutare**
sorry not to be able to help
2 (*avere il permesso*) can, may, be allowed
to; **posso entrare?** can *o* may I come in?;
si può sapere dove sei stato? where on
earth have you been?
3 (*eventualità*) may, might, could;
potrebbe essere vero it might *o* could be
true; **può aver avuto un incidente** he
may *o* might *o* could have had an accident;
può darsi perhaps; **può darsi** *o* **essere
che non venga** he may *o* might not come
4 (*augurio*): **potessi almeno parlargli!** if
only I could speak to him!
5 (*suggerimento*): **potresti almeno
scusarti!** you could at least apologize!
▷ *vt* can, be able to; **può molto per noi** he
can do a lot for us; **non ne posso più** (*per
stanchezza*) I'm exhausted; (*per rabbia*) I
can't take any more

potrò *ecc vb vedi* **potere**
'povero, -a *ag* poor; (*disadorno*) plain, bare
▷ *sm/f* poor man/woman; **i poveri** the
poor; **~ di** lacking in, having little; **povertà**
sf poverty
poz'zanghera [pot'tsangera] *sf* puddle
'pozzo ['pottso] *sm* well; (*cava: di carbone*)
pit; (*di miniera*) shaft; **pozzo petrolifero**
oil well
P.R.A. [pra] *sigla m* (= *Pubblico Registro
Automobilistico*) ≈ DVLA
pran'zare [pran'dzare] *vi* to dine, have
dinner; to lunch, have lunch
'pranzo ['prandzo] *sm* dinner; (*a
mezzogiorno*) lunch
'prassi *sf* usual procedure
'pratica, -che *sf* practice; (*esperienza*)
experience; (*conoscenza*) knowledge,
familiarity; (*tirocinio*) training, practice;
(*Amm: affare*) matter, case; (*: incartamento*)
file, dossier; **in ~** (*praticamente*) in practice;
mettere in ~ to put into practice
prati'cabile *ag* (*progetto*) practicable,
feasible; (*luogo*) passable, practicable
pratica'mente *av* (*in modo pratico*)
in a practical way, practically; (*quasi*)

practically, almost
prati'care *vt* to practise; (*Sport: tennis ecc*)
to play; (*: nuoto, scherma ecc*) to go in for;
(*eseguire: apertura, buco*) to make; **~ uno
sconto** to give a discount
'pratico, -a, -ci, -che *ag* practical; **~ di**
(*esperto*) experienced *o* skilled in; (*familiare*)
familiar with
'prato *sm* meadow; (*di giardino*) lawn
preav'viso *sm* notice; **telefonata con ~**
personal *o* person to person call
pre'cario, -a *ag* precarious; (*Ins*)
temporary
precauzi'one [prekaut'tsjone] *sf* caution,
care; (*misura*) precaution
prece'dente [pretʃe'dɛnte] *ag* previous
▷ *sm* precedent; **il discorso/film ~** the
previous *o* preceding speech/film; **senza
precedenti** unprecedented; **precedenti
penali** criminal record *sg*; **prece'denza** *sf*
priority, precedence; (*Aut*) right of way
pre'cedere [pre'tʃedere] *vt* to precede, go
(*o come*) before
precipi'tare [pretʃipi'tare] *vi* (*cadere*) to
fall headlong; (*fig: situazione*) to get out
of control ▷ *vt* (*gettare dall'alto in basso*)
to hurl, fling; (*fig: affrettare*) to rush;
precipitarsi *vpr* (*gettarsi*) to hurl *o* fling
o.s.; (*affrettarsi*) to rush; **precipi'toso, -a**
ag (*caduta, fuga*) headlong; (*fig: avventato*)
rash, reckless; (*: affrettato*) hasty, rushed
preci'pizio [pretʃi'pittsjo] *sm* precipice; **a
~** (*fig: correre*) headlong
precisa'mente [pretʃiza'mente] *av* (*gen*)
precisely; (*con esattezza*) exactly
preci'sare [pretʃi'zare] *vt* to state, specify;
(*spiegare*) to explain (in detail)
precisi'one [pretʃi'zjone] *sf* precision,
accuracy
pre'ciso, -a [pre'tʃizo] *ag* (*esatto*) precise;
(*accurato*) accurate, precise; (*deciso: idee*)
precise, definite; (*uguale*): **2 vestiti precisi**
2 dresses exactly the same; **sono le 9
precise** it's exactly 9 o'clock
pre'cludere *vt* to block, obstruct
pre'coce [pre'kɔtʃe] *ag* early; (*bambino*)
precocious; (*vecchiaia*) premature
precon'cetto [prekon'tʃetto] *sm*
preconceived idea, prejudice
precur'sore *sm* forerunner, precursor
'preda *sf* (*bottino*) booty; (*animale, fig*) prey;
essere ~ di to fall prey to; **essere in ~ a** to
be prey to
'predica, -che *sf* sermon; (*fig*) lecture,
talking-to
predi'care *vt, vi* to preach
predi'cato *sm* (*Ling*) predicate
predi'letto, -a *pp di* **prediligere** ▷ *ag, sm/f*
favourite

predi'ligere [predi'lidʒere] vt to prefer, have a preference for

pre'dire vt to foretell, predict

predis'porre vt to get ready, prepare; ~ **qn a qc** to predispose sb to sth

predizi'one [predit'tsjone] sf prediction

prefazi'one [prefat'tsjone] sf preface, foreword

prefe'renza [prefe'rɛntsa] sf preference

prefe'rire vt to prefer, like better; ~ **il caffè al tè** to prefer coffee to tea, like coffee better than tea

pre'figgersi [pre'fiddʒersi] vpr ~ **uno scopo** to set o.s. a goal

pre'fisso, -a pp di **prefiggere** ▷ sm (Ling) prefix; (Tel) dialling (BRIT) o dial (US) code; **qual è il ~ telefonico di Londra?** what is the dialling code for London?

pre'gare vi to pray ▷ vt (Rel) to pray to; (implorare) to beg; (chiedere): ~ **qn di fare** to ask sb to do; **farsi ~** to need coaxing o persuading

pre'gevole [pre'dʒevole] ag valuable

pregherò ecc [prege'rɔ] vb vedi **pregare**

preghi'era [pre'gjera] sf (Rel) prayer; (domanda) request

pregi'ato, -a [pre'dʒato] ag (di valore) valuable; **vino ~** vintage wine

'pregio ['prɛdʒo] sm (stima) esteem, regard; (qualità) (good) quality, merit; (valore) value, worth

pregiudi'care [predʒudi'kare] vt to prejudice, harm, be detrimental to

pregiu'dizio [predʒu'dittsjo] sm (idea errata) prejudice; (danno) harm no pl

'prego escl (a chi ringrazia) don't mention it!; (invitando qn ad accomodarsi) please sit down!; (invitando qn ad andare prima) after you!

pregus'tare vt to look forward to

prele'vare vt (denaro) to withdraw; (campione) to take; (polizia) to take, capture

preli'evo sm (di denaro) withdrawal; (Med): **fare un ~ (di)** to take a sample (of); **prelievo di sangue: fare un ~ di sangue** to take a blood sample

prelimi'nare ag preliminary

'premere vt to press ▷ vi ~ **su** to press down on; (fig) to put pressure on; ~ **a** (fig: importare) to matter to

pre'mettere vt to put before; (dire prima) to start by saying, state first

premi'are vt to give a prize to; (fig: merito, onestà) to reward

premiazi'one [premjat'tsjone] sf prize giving

'premio sm prize; (ricompensa) reward; (Comm) premium; (Amm: indennità) bonus

pre'misi ecc vb vedi **premettere**

premu'nirsi vpr ~ **di** to provide o.s. with; ~ **contro** to protect o.s. from, guard o.s. against

pre'mura sf (fretta) haste, hurry; (riguardo) attention, care; **premure** sfpl (attenzioni, cure) care sg; **aver ~** to be in a hurry; **far ~ a qn** to hurry sb; **usare ogni ~ nei riguardi di qn** to be very attentive to sb; **premu'roso, -a** ag thoughtful, considerate

'prendere vt to take; (andare a prendere) to get, fetch; (ottenere) to get; (guadagnare) to get, earn; (catturare: ladro, pesce) to catch; (collaboratore, dipendente) to take on; (passeggero) to pick up; (chiedere: somma, prezzo) to charge, ask; (trattare: persona) to handle ▷ vi (colla, cemento) to set; (pianta) to take; (fuoco: nel camino) to catch; (voltare): ~ **a destra** to turn (to the) right; **prendersi** vpr (azzuffarsi): **prendersi a pugni** to come to blows; **dove si prende il traghetto per...** where do we get the ferry to ...; **prendi qualcosa?** (da bere, da mangiare) would you like something to eat (o drink)?; **prendo un caffè** I'll have a coffee; ~ **qn/qc per** (scambiare) to take sb/sth for; ~ **fuoco** to catch fire; ~ **parte a** to take part in; **prendersi cura di qn/qc** to look after sb/sth; **prendersela** (adirarsi) to get annoyed; (preoccuparsi) to get upset, worry

preno'tare vt to book, reserve; **vorrei ~ una camera doppia** I'd like to book a double room; **ho prenotato un tavolo al nome di ...** I booked a table in the name of ...; **prenotazi'one** sf booking, reservation; **ho confermato la prenotazione per fax/e-mail** I confirmed my booking by fax/e-mail

preoccu'pare vt to worry; to preoccupy; **preoccuparsi** vpr **preoccuparsi di qn/qc** to worry about sb/sth; **preoccuparsi per qn** to be anxious for sb; **preoccupazi'one** sf worry, anxiety

prepa'rare vt to prepare; (esame, concorso) to prepare for; **prepararsi** vpr (vestirsi) to get ready; **prepararsi a qc/a fare** to get ready o prepare (o.s.) for sth/to do; ~ **da mangiare** to prepare a meal; **prepara'tivi** smpl preparations

preposizi'one [prepozit'tsjone] sf (Ling) preposition

prepo'tente ag (persona) domineering, arrogant; (bisogno, desiderio) overwhelming, pressing ▷ sm/f bully

'presa sf taking no pl; catching no pl; (di città) capture; (indurimento: di cemento) setting; (appiglio, Sport) hold; (di acqua, gas) (supply) point; (piccola quantità: di sale *ecc*) pinch; (*Carte*) trick; **far ~** (*colla*) to set; **far ~ sul pubblico** to catch the public's imagination; **essere alle prese con** (*fig*) to be struggling with; **presa d'aria** air inlet; **presa (di corrente)** (*Elettr*) socket; (*: al muro*) point

pre'sagio [pre'zadʒo] *sm* omen

'presbite *ag* long-sighted

pres'crivere *vt* to prescribe

'prese *ecc vb vedi* **prendere**

presen'tare *vt* to present; (*far conoscere*): **~ qn (a)** to introduce sb (to); (*Amm: inoltrare*) to submit; **presentarsi** *vpr* (*recarsi, farsi vedere*) to present o.s., appear; (*farsi conoscere*) to introduce o.s.; (*occasione*) to arise; **presentarsi come candidato** (*Pol*) to stand as a candidate; **presentarsi bene/male** to have a good/poor appearance

pre'sente *ag* present; (*questo*) this ▷ *sm* present; **i presenti** those present; **aver ~ qc/qn** to remember sth/sb; **aver ~ qc/qn** (*persone*) people present; **aver ~ qc/qn** to remember sth/sb; **tenere ~ qn/qc** to keep sth/sb in mind

presenti'mento *sm* premonition

pre'senza [pre'zɛntsa] *sf* presence; (*aspetto esteriore*) appearance; **presenza di spirito** presence of mind

pre'sepio, pre'sepe *sm* crib

preser'vare *vt* to protect; to save; **preserva'tivo** *sm* sheath, condom

'presi *ecc vb vedi* **prendere**

'preside *sm/f* (*Ins*) head (teacher) (*BRIT*), principal (*US*); (*di facoltà universitaria*) dean; **preside di facoltà** (*Univ*) dean of faculty

presi'dente *sm* (*Pol*) president; (*di assemblea, Comm*) chairman; **presidente del consiglio** prime minister

presi'edere *vt* to preside over ▷ *vi* **~ a** to direct, be in charge of

pressap'poco *av* about, roughly

pres'sare *vt* to press

pressi'one *sf* pressure; **far ~ su qn** to put pressure on sb; **pressione sanguigna** blood pressure; **pressione atmosferica** atmospheric pressure

'presso *av* (*vicino*) nearby, close at hand ▷ *prep* (*vicino a*) near; (*accanto a*) beside, next to; (*in casa di*): **~ qn** at sb's home; (*nelle lettere*) care of, c/o; (*alle dipendenze di*): **lavora ~ di noi** he works for o with us ▷ *smpl* **nei pressi di** near, in the vicinity of

pres'tante *ag* good-looking

pres'tare *vt* **~ (qc a qn)** to lend (sb sth o sth to sb); **prestarsi** *vpr* (*offrirsi*): **prestarsi a fare** to offer to do; (*essere adatto*): **prestarsi a** to lend itself to, be suitable for; **mi può ~ dei soldi?** can you

lend me some money?; **~ aiuto** to lend a hand; **~ attenzione** to pay attention; **~ fede a qc/qn** to give credence to sth/sb; **~ orecchio** to listen; **prestazi'one** *sf* (*Tecn, Sport*) performance

prestigia'tore, -'trice [prestidʒa'tore] *sm/f* conjurer

pres'tigio [pres'tidʒo] *sm* (*fama*) prestige; (*illusione*): **gioco di ~** conjuring trick

'prestito *sm* lending *no pl*; loan; **dar in ~** to lend; **prendere in ~** to borrow

'presto *av* (*tra poco*) soon; (*in fretta*) quickly; (*di buon'ora*) early; **a ~** see you soon; **fare ~ a fare qc** to hurry up and do sth; (*non costare fatica*) to have no trouble doing sth; **si fa ~ a criticare** it's easy to criticize

pre'sumere *vt* to presume, assume

pre'sunsi *ecc vb vedi* **presumere**

presuntu'oso, -a *ag* presumptuous

presunzi'one [prezun'tsjone] *sf* presumption

'prete *sm* priest

preten'dente *sm/f* pretender ▷ *sm* (*corteggiatore*) suitor

pre'tendere *vt* (*esigere*) to demand, require; (*sostenere*): **~ che** to claim that; **pretende di aver sempre ragione** he thinks he's always right

> ▨ Attenzione! In inglese esiste il verbo *to pretend*, che però significa *far finta*.

pre'tesa *sf* (*esigenza*) claim, demand; (*presunzione, sfarzo*) pretentiousness; **senza pretese** unpretentious

pre'testo *sm* pretext, excuse

preva'lere *vi* to prevail

preve'dere *vt* (*indovinare*) to foresee; (*presagire*) to foretell; (*considerare*) to make provision for

preve'nire *vt* (*anticipare*) to forestall; to anticipate; (*evitare*) to avoid, prevent

preven'tivo, -a *ag* preventive ▷ *sm* (*Comm*) estimate

prevenzi'one [preven'tsjone] *sf* prevention; (*preconcetto*) prejudice

previ'dente *ag* showing foresight; prudent; **previ'denza** *sf* foresight; **istituto di previdenza** provident institution; **previdenza sociale** social security (*BRIT*), welfare (*US*)

pre'vidi *ecc vb vedi* **prevedere**

previsi'one *sf* forecast, prediction; **previsioni meteorologiche** weather forecast *sg*; **previsioni del tempo** weather forecast *sg*

pre'visto, -a *pp di* **prevedere** ▷ *sm* **più/meno del ~** more/less than expected

prezi'oso, -a [pret'tsjoso] *ag* precious; invaluable ▷ *sm* jewel; valuable

prez'zemolo [pret'tsemolo] *sm* parsley

'prezzo ['prɛttso] *sm* price; **prezzo d'acquisto/di vendita** buying/selling price

prigi'one [pri'dʒone] *sf* prison; **prigioni'ero, -a** *ag* captive ▷ *sm/f* prisoner

'prima *sf* (*Teatro*) first night; (*Cinema*) première; (*Aut*) first gear; *vedi anche* **primo** ▷ *av* before; (*in anticipo*) in advance, beforehand; (*per l'addietro*) at one time, formerly; (*più presto*) sooner, earlier; (*in primo luogo*) first ▷ *cong* **~ di fare/che parta** before doing/he leaves; **~ di** before; **~ o poi** sooner or later

pri'mario, -a *ag* primary; (*principale*) chief, leading, primary ▷ *sm* (*Med*) chief physician

prima'tista, -i, e *sm/f* (*Sport*) record holder

pri'mato *sm* supremacy; (*Sport*) record

prima'vera *sf* spring

primi'tivo, -a *ag* primitive; original

pri'mizie [pri'mittsje] *sfpl* early produce *sg*

'primo, -a *ag* first; (*fig*) initial; basic; prime ▷ *sm/f* first (one) ▷ *sm* (*Cuc*) first course; (*in date*): **il ~ luglio** the first of July; **le prime ore del mattino** the early hours of the morning; **ai primi di maggio** at the beginning of May; **viaggiare in prima** to travel first-class; **in ~ luogo** first of all, in the first place; **di prim'ordine** *o* **prima qualità** first-class, first-rate; **in un ~ tempo** at first; **prima donna** leading lady; (*di opera lirica*) prima donna

primordi'ale *ag* primordial

'primula *sf* primrose

princi'pale [printʃi'pale] *ag* main, principal ▷ *sm* manager, boss

principal'mente [printʃipal'mente] *av* mainly, principally

'principe ['printʃipe] *sm* prince; **principe ereditario** crown prince; **princi'pessa** *sf* princess

principi'ante [printʃi'pjante] *sm/f* beginner

prin'cipio [prin'tʃipjo] *sm* (*inizio*) beginning, start; (*origine*) origin, cause; (*concetto, norma*) principle; **al** *o* **in ~** at first; **per ~** on principle; **principi** *smpl* (*concetti fondamentali*) principles; **una questione di ~** a matter of principle

priorità *sf* priority

priori'tario, -a *ag* having priority, of utmost importance

pri'vare *vt* **~ qn di** to deprive sb of; **privarsi di** to go *o* do without

pri'vato, -a *ag* private ▷ *sm/f* private citizen; **in ~** in private

privilegi'are [privile'dʒare] *vt* to grant a privilege to

privilegi'ato, -a [privile'dʒato] *ag* (*individuo, classe*) privileged; (*trattamento, Comm: credito*) preferential; **azioni ~e** preference shares (*BRIT*), preferred stock (*US*)

privi'legio [privi'lɛdʒo] *sm* privilege

'privo, -a *ag* **~ di** without, lacking

pro *prep* for, on behalf of ▷ *sm inv* (*utilità*) advantage, benefit; **a che ~?** what's the use?; **il ~ e il contro** the pros and cons

pro'babile *ag* probable, likely; **probabilità** *sf inv* probability

probabil'mente *av* probably

pro'blema, -i *sm* problem

pro'boscide [pro'bɔʃʃide] *sf* (*di elefante*) trunk

pro'cedere [pro'tʃɛdere] *vi* to proceed; (*comportarsi*) to behave; (*iniziare*): **~ a** to start; **~ contro** (*Dir*) to start legal proceedings against; **proce'dura** *sf* (*Dir*) procedure

proces'sare [protʃes'sare] *vt* (*Dir*) to try

processi'one [protʃes'sjone] *sf* procession

pro'cesso [pro'tʃɛsso] *sm* (*Dir*) trial; proceedings *pl*; (*metodo*) process

pro'cinto [pro'tʃinto] *sm* **in ~ di fare** about to do, on the point of doing

procla'mare *vt* to proclaim

procre'are *vt* to procreate

procu'rare *vt* **~ qc a qn** (*fornire*) to get *o* obtain sth for sb; (*causare: noie ecc*) to bring *o* give sb sth

pro'digio [pro'didʒo] *sm* marvel, wonder; (*persona*) prodigy

pro'dotto, -a *pp di* **produrre** ▷ *sm* product; **prodotti agricoli** farm produce *sg*

pro'duco *ecc vb vedi* **produrre**

pro'durre *vt* to produce

pro'dussi *ecc vb vedi* **produrre**

produzi'one *sf* production; (*rendimento*) output

Prof. *abbr* (= *professore*) Prof.

profa'nare *vt* to desecrate

profes'sare *vt* to profess; (*medicina ecc*) to practise

professio'nale *ag* professional

professi'one *sf* profession; **professio'nista, -i, -e** *sm/f* professional

profes'sore, -'essa *sm/f* (*Ins*) teacher; (: *di università*) lecturer; (: *titolare di cattedra*) professor

pro'filo *sm* profile; (*breve descrizione*) sketch, outline; **di ~** in profile

pro'fitto *sm* advantage, profit, benefit; (*fig: progresso*) progress; (*Comm*) profit

profondità *sf inv* depth

pro'fondo, -a *ag* deep; (*rancore,*

meditazione) profound ▷ *sm* depth(*s pl*), bottom; **quanto è profonda l'acqua?** how deep is the water?; **~ 8 metri** 8 metres deep

'profugo, -a, -ghi, -ghe *sm/f* refugee
profu'mare *vt* to perfume ▷ *vi* to be fragrant; **profumarsi** *vpr* to put on perfume o scent
profu'mato, -a *ag* (*fiore, aria*) fragrant; (*fazzoletto, saponetta*) scented; (*pelle*) sweet-smelling; (*persona*) with perfume on
profume'ria *sf* perfumery; (*negozio*) perfume shop
pro'fumo *sm* (*prodotto*) perfume, scent; (*fragranza*) scent, fragrance
proget'tare [prodʒet'tare] *vt* to plan; (*edificio*) to plan, design; **pro'getto** *sm* plan; (*idea*) plan, project; **progetto di legge** bill
pro'gramma, -i *sm* programme; (*TV, Radio*) programmes *pl*; (*Ins*) syllabus, curriculum; (*Inform*) program; **program'mare** *vt* (*TV, Radio*) to put on; (*Inform*) to program; (*Econ*) to plan; **programma'tore, -'trice** *sm/f* (*Inform*) computer programmer
progre'dire *vi* to progress, make progress
pro'gresso *sm* progress *no pl*; **fare progressi** to make progress
proi'bire *vt* to forbid, prohibit
proiet'tare *vt* (*gen, Geom, Cinema*) to project; (: *presentare*) to show, screen; (*luce, ombra*) to throw, cast, project; **proi'ettile** *sm* projectile, bullet (*o shell ecc*); **proiet'tore** *sm* (*Cinema*) projector; (*Aut*) headlamp; (*Mil*) searchlight; **proiezi'one** *sf* (*Cinema*) projection; showing
prolife'rare *vi* (*fig*) to proliferate
pro'lunga, -ghe *sf* (*di cavo ecc*) extension
prolun'gare *vt* (*discorso, attesa*) to prolong; (*linea, termine*) to extend
prome'moria *sm inv* memorandum
pro'messa *sf* promise
pro'mettere *vt* to promise ▷ *vi* to be o look promising; **~ a qn di fare** to promise sb that one will do
promi'nente *ag* prominent
pro'misi *ecc vb vedi* **promettere**
promon'torio *sm* promontory, headland
promozi'one [promot'tsjone] *sf* promotion
promu'overe *vt* to promote
proni'pote *sm/f* (*di nonni*) great-grandchild, great-grandson/granddaughter; (*di zii*) great-nephew/niece
pro'nome *sm* (*Ling*) pronoun
pron'tezza [pron'tettsa] *sf* readiness; quickness, promptness

'pronto, -a *ag* ready; (*rapido*) fast, quick, prompt; **quando saranno pronte le mie foto?** when will my photos be ready?; **~!** (*Tel*) hello!; **~ all'ira** quick-tempered; **pronto soccorso** (*cure*) first aid; (*reparto*) A&E (*BRIT*), ER (*US*)
prontu'ario *sm* manual, handbook
pro'nuncia [pro'nuntʃa] *sf* pronunciation
pronunci'are [pronun'tʃare] *vt* (*parola, sentenza*) to pronounce; (*dire*) to utter; (*discorso*) to deliver; **come si pronuncia?** how do you pronounce it?
propa'ganda *sf* propaganda
pro'pendere *vi* **~ per** to favour, lean towards
propi'nare *vt* to administer
pro'porre *vt* (*suggerire*): **~ qc (a qn)** to suggest sth (to sb); (*candidato*) to put forward; (*legge, brindisi*) to propose; **~ di fare** to suggest o propose doing; **proporsi di fare** to propose o intend to do; **proporsi una meta** to set o s. a goal
proporzio'nale [proportsjo'nale] *ag* proportional
proporzi'one [propor'tsjone] *sf* proportion; **in ~ a** in proportion to; **proporzioni** *sfpl* (*dimensioni*) proportions; **di vaste proporzioni** huge
pro'posito *sm* (*intenzione*) intention, aim; (*argomento*) subject, matter; **a ~ di** regarding, with regard to; (: *apposta*) deliberately, on purpose; **a ~** by the way; **capitare a ~** (*cosa, persona*) to turn up at the right time
proposizi'one [propozit'tsjone] *sf* (*Ling*) clause; (: *periodo*) sentence
pro'posta *sf* proposal; (*suggerimento*) suggestion; **proposta di legge** bill
proprietà *sf inv* (*ciò che si possiede*) property *gen no pl*, estate; (*caratteristica*) property; (*correttezza*) correctness; **proprietà privata** private property; **proprie'tario, -a** *sm/f* owner; (*di albergo ecc*) proprietor, owner; (*per l'inquilino*) landlord/lady
'proprio, -a *ag* (*possessivo*) own; (: *impersonale*) one's; (*esatto*) exact, correct, proper; (*senso, significato*) literal; (*Ling: nome*) proper; (*particolare*): **~ di** characteristic of, peculiar to ▷ *av* (*precisamente*) just, exactly; (*davvero*) really; (*affatto*): **non ... ~** not ... at all; **l'ha visto con i (suoi) propri occhi** he saw it with his own eyes
proro'gare *vt* to extend; (*differire*) to postpone, defer
'prosa *sf* prose
pro'sciogliere [proʃʃɔʎʎere] *vt* to release; (*Dir*) to acquit
prosciu'gare [proʃʃu'gare] *vt* (*terreni*) to

drain, reclaim; **prosciugarsi** *vpr* to dry up
prosci'utto [proʃˈʃutto] *sm* ham;
  prosciutto cotto/crudo cooked/cured
  ham
prosegui'mento *sm* continuation; **buon
  ~!** all the best!; (*a chi viaggia*) enjoy the rest
  of your journey!
prosegu'ire *vt* to carry on with, continue
  ▷ *vi* to carry on, go on
prospe'rare *vi* to thrive
prospet'tare *vt* (*esporre*) to point out,
  show; **prospettarsi** *vpr* to look, appear
prospet'tiva *sf* (*Arte*) perspective; (*veduta*)
  view; (*fig: previsione, possibilità*) prospect
pros'petto *sm* (*Disegno*) elevation; (*veduta*)
  view, prospect; (*facciata*) façade, front;
  (*tabella*) table; (*sommario*) summary;
  prospetto informativo prospectus
prossimità *sf* nearness, proximity; **in ~ di**
  near (to), close to
'**prossimo, -a** *ag* (*vicino*): **~ a** near (to),
  close to; (*che viene subito dopo*) next;
  (*parente*) close ▷ *sm* neighbour, fellow man
prostitu'irsi *vpr* to prostitute o.s.
prosti'tuta *sf* prostitute
protago'nista, -i, -e *sm/f* protagonist
pro'teggere [proˈteddʒere] *vt* to protect
prote'ina *sf* protein
pro'tendere *vt* to stretch out
pro'testa *sf* protest
protes'tante *ag, sm/f* Protestant
protes'tare *vt, vi* to protest
pro'tetto, -a *pp di* **proteggere**
protezi'one [protetˈtsjone] *sf* protection;
  (*patrocinio*) patronage
pro'totipo *sm* prototype
pro'trarre *vt* (*prolungare*) to prolong;
  protrarsi *vpr* to go on, continue
protube'ranza [protubeˈrantsa] *sf*
  protuberance, bulge
'**prova** *sf* (*esperimento, cimento*) test,
  trial; (*tentativo*) attempt, try; (*Mat,
  testimonianza, documento ecc*) proof; (*Dir*)
  evidence *no pl*, proof; (*Ins*) exam, test;
  (*Teatro*) rehearsal; (*di abito*) fitting; **a ~ di** (*in
  testimonianza di*) as proof of; **a ~ di fuoco**
  fireproof; **fino a ~ contraria** until it is
  proved otherwise; **mettere alla ~** to put
  to the test; **giro di ~** test *o* trial run; **prova
  generale** (*Teatro*) dress rehearsal
pro'vare *vt* (*sperimentare*) to test; (*tentare*)
  to try, attempt; (*assaggiare*) to try, taste;
  (*sperimentare in sé*) to experience; (*sentire*)
  to feel; (*cimentare*) to put to the test;
  (*dimostrare*) to prove; (*abito*) to try on; **~ a
  fare** to try *o* attempt to do
proveni'enza [proveˈnjentsa] *sf* origin,
  source
prove'nire *vi* **~ da** to come from

pro'venti *smpl* revenue *sg*
pro'verbio *sm* proverb
pro'vetta *sf* test tube; **bambino in ~**
  test-tube baby
pro'vider [proˈvaider] *sm inv* (*Inform*)
  service provider
pro'vincia, -ce *o* **cie** [proˈvintʃa] *sf*
  province
pro'vino *sm* (*Cinema*) screen test;
  (*campione*) specimen
provo'cante *ag* (*attraente*) provocative
provo'care *vt* (*causare*) to cause, bring
  about; (*eccitare: riso, pietà*) to arouse;
  (*irritare, sfidare*) to provoke; **provocazi'one**
  sf provocation
provve'dere *vi* (*disporre*): **~ (a)** to provide
  (for); (*prendere un provvedimento*) to take
  steps, act; **provvedi'mento** *sm* measure;
  (*di previdenza*) precaution
provvi'denza [provviˈdentsa] *sf* **la ~**
  providence
provvigi'one [provviˈdʒone] *sf* (*Comm*)
  commission
provvi'sorio, -a *ag* temporary
prov'viste *sfpl* supplies
'**prua** *sf* (*Naut*) bow(s) (*pl*), prow
pru'dente *ag* cautious, prudent;
  (*assennato*) sensible, wise; **pru'denza** *sf*
  prudence, caution; wisdom
'**prudere** *vi* to itch, be itchy
'**prugna** [ˈpruɲɲa] *sf* plum; **prugna secca**
  prune
pru'rito *sm* itchiness *no pl*; itch
P.S. *abbr* (= *postscriptum*) P.S.; (*Polizia*)
  = **Pubblica Sicurezza**
pseu'donimo *sm* pseudonym
psica'nalisi *sf* psychoanalysis
psicana'lista, -i, -e *sm/f* psychoanalyst
'**psiche** [ˈpsike] *sf* (*Psic*) psyche
psichi'atra, -i, -e [psiˈkjatra] *sm/f*
  psychiatrist; **psichi'atrico, -a, -ci, -che** *ag*
  psychiatric
psicolo'gia [psikoloˈdʒia] *sf* psychology;
  psico'logico, -a, -ci, -che *ag*
  psychological; **psi'cologo, -a, -gi, -ghe**
  sm/f psychologist
psico'patico, -a, -ci, -che *ag*
  psychopathic ▷ *sm/f* psychopath
pubbli'care *vt* to publish
pubblicazi'one [pubblikatˈtsjone] *sf*
  publication
pubblicità [pubblitʃiˈta] *sf* (*diffusione*)
  publicity; (*attività*) advertising; (*annunci nei
  giornali*) advertisements *pl*
'**pubblico, -a, -ci, -che** *ag* public;
  (*statale: scuola ecc*) state *cpd* ▷ *sm* public;
  (*spettatori*) audience; **in ~** in public; **P~
  Ministero** Public Prosecutor's Office; **la
  Pubblica Sicurezza** the police; **pubblico**

funzionario civil servant
'pube *sm* (Anat) pubis
pubertà *sf* puberty
'pudico, -a, -ci, -che *ag* modest
pu'dore *sm* modesty
pue'rile *ag* childish
pugi'lato [pudʒi'lato] *sm* boxing
'pugile ['pudʒile] *sm* boxer
pugna'lare [puɲɲa'lare] *vt* to stab
pu'gnale [puɲ'ɲale] *sm* dagger
'pugno ['puɲɲo] *sm* fist; (colpo) punch; (quantità) fistful
'pulce ['pultʃe] *sf* flea
pul'cino [pul'tʃino] *sm* chick
pu'lire *vt* to clean; (lucidare) to polish; **pu'lito, -a** *ag* (anche fig) clean; (ordinato) neat, tidy; **puli'tura** *sf* cleaning; **pulitura a secco** dry cleaning; **puli'zia** *sf* cleaning; cleanness; **fare le pulizie** to do the cleaning o the housework; **pulizia etnica** ethnic cleansing
'pullman *sm inv* coach
pul'lover *sm inv* pullover, jumper
pullu'lare *vi* to swarm, teem
pul'mino *sm* minibus
'pulpito *sm* pulpit
pul'sante *sm* (push-)button
pul'sare *vi* to pulsate, beat
pul'viscolo *sm* fine dust; **pulviscolo atmosferico** specks *pl* of dust
'puma *sm inv* puma
pun'gente [pun'dʒɛnte] *ag* prickly; stinging; (anche fig) biting
'pungere ['pundʒere] *vt* to prick; (insetto, ortica) to sting; (: freddo) to bite
pungigli'one [pundʒiʎ'ʎone] *sm* sting
pu'nire *vt* to punish; **punizi'one** *sf* punishment; (Sport) penalty
'punsi *ecc vb vedi* **pungere**
'punta *sf* point; (parte terminale) tip, end; (di monte) peak; (di costa) promontory; (minima parte) touch, trace; **in ~ di piedi** on tip-toe; **ore di ~** peak hours; **uomo di ~** front-rank o leading man
pun'tare *vt* (piedi a terra, gomiti sul tavolo) to plant; (dirigere: pistola) to point; (scommettere) to bet ▷ *vi* (mirare): **~ a** to aim at; **~ su** (dirigersi) to head o make for; (fig: contare) to count o rely on
pun'tata *sf* (gita) short trip; (scommessa) bet; (parte di opera) instalment; **romanzo a puntate** serial
punteggia'tura [puntedddʒa'tura] *sf* (Ling) punctuation
pun'teggio [pun'teddʒo] *sm* score
puntel'lare *vt* to support
pun'tello *sm* prop, support
pun'tina *sf*; **puntina da disegno** drawing pin

pun'tino *sm* dot; **fare qc a ~** to do sth properly
'punto, -a *pp di* **pungere** ▷ *sm* (segno, macchiolina) dot; (Ling) full stop; (di indirizzo e-mail) dot; (Mat, momento, di punteggio: fig: argomento) point; (posto) spot; (a scuola) mark; (nel cucire, nella maglia, Med) stitch ▷ *av* **non ... ~** not at all; **punto cardinale** point of the compass, cardinal point; **punto debole** weak point; **punto esclamativo** exclamation mark; **punto interrogativo** question mark; **punto nero** (comedone) blackhead; **punto di partenza** (anche fig) starting point; **punto di riferimento** landmark; (fig) point of reference; **punto (di) vendita** retail outlet; **punto e virgola** semicolon; **punto di vista** (fig) point of view
puntu'ale *ag* punctual
pun'tura *sf* (di ago) prick; (Med) puncture; (: iniezione) injection; (dolore) sharp pain; **puntura d'insetto** sting, bite

▌ Attenzione! In inglese esiste la parola puncture, che si usa per indicare la foratura di una gomma.

punzecchi'are [puntsek'kjare] *vt* to prick; (fig) to tease
può *ecc*, **-pu'oi** *vb vedi* **potere**
pu'pazzo [pu'pattso] *sm* puppet
pu'pilla *sf* (Anat) pupil
purché [pur'ke] *cong* provided that, on condition that
'pure *cong* (tuttavia) and yet, nevertheless; (anche se) even if ▷ *av* (anche) too, also; **pur di** (al fine di) just to; **faccia ~!** go ahead!, please do!
purè *sm* (Cuc) purée; (: di patate) mashed potatoes
pu'rezza [pu'rettsa] *sf* purity
pur'gante *sm* (Med) purgative, purge
purga'torio *sm* purgatory
purifi'care *vt* to purify; (metallo) to refine
'puro, -a *ag* pure; (acqua) clear, limpid; (vino) undiluted; **puro'sangue** *sm/f inv* thoroughbred
pur'troppo *av* unfortunately
pus *sm* pus
'pustola *sf* pimple
puti'ferio *sm* rumpus, row
putre'fatto, -a *pp di* **putrefare**
puz'zare [put'tsare] *vi* to stink
'puzzo ['puttso] *sm* stink, foul smell
'puzzola ['puttsola] *sf* polecat
puzzo'lente [puttso'lɛnte] *ag* stinking
pvc [pivi'tʃi] *sigla m* (= polyvinyl chloride) PVC

q *abbr* (= quintale) q.

qua *av* here; **in ~** (verso questa parte) this way; **da un anno in ~** for a year now; **da ~ndo in ~?** since when?; **per di ~** (passare) this way; **al di ~ di** (fiume, strada) on this side of; **~ dentro/fuori** ecc in/out here ecc; vedi anche **questo**

qua'derno *sm* notebook; (per scuola) exercise book

qua'drante *sm* quadrant; (di orologio) face

qua'drare *vi* (bilancio) to balance, tally; (descrizione) to correspond ▷ *vt* (Mat) to square; **non mi quadra** I don't like it; **qua'drato, -a** *ag* square; (fig: equilibrato) level-headed, sensible; (: peg) square ▷ *sm* (Mat) square; (Pugilato) ring; **5 al quadrato** 5 squared

quadri'foglio [kwadri'fɔʎʎo] *sm* four-leaf clover

quadri'mestre *sm* (periodo) four-month period; (Ins) term

'quadro *sm* (pittura) painting, picture; (quadrato) square; (tabella) table, chart; (Tecn) board, panel; (Teatro) scene; (fig: scena, spettacolo) sight; (: descrizione) outline, description; **quadri** *smpl* (Pol) party organizers; (Mil) cadres; (Comm) managerial staff; (Carte) diamonds

'quadruplo, -a *ag, sm* quadruple

quaggiù [kwad'dʒu] *av* down here

'quaglia ['kwaʎʎa] *sf* quail

PAROLA CHIAVE

'qualche ['kwalke] *det* **1** some, a few; (in interrogative) any; **ho comprato qualche libro** I've bought some *o* a few books; **qualche volta** sometimes; **hai qualche sigaretta?** have you any cigarettes?
2 (uno): **c'è qualche medico?** is there a doctor?; **in qualche modo** somehow
3 (un certo, parecchio) some; **un personaggio di qualche rilievo** a figure of some importance
4: **qualche cosa** = **qualcosa**

qual'cosa *pron* something; (in espressioni interrogative) anything; **qualcos'altro** something else; anything else; **~ di nuovo** something new; anything new; **~ da mangiare** something to eat; anything to eat; **c'è ~ che non va?** is there something *o* anything wrong?

qual'cuno *pron* (persona) someone, somebody; (: in espressioni interrogative) anyone, anybody; (alcuni) some; **~ è favorevole a noi** some are on our side; **qualcun altro** someone *o* somebody else; anyone *o* anybody else

PAROLA CHIAVE

'quale (spesso troncato in qual) *det* **1** (interrogativo) what; (: scegliendo tra due o più cose o persone) which; **quale uomo/ denaro?** what man/money?, which man/ money?; **quali sono i tuoi programmi?** what are your plans?; **quale stanza preferisci?** which room do you prefer?
2 (relativo: come): **il risultato fu quale ci si aspettava** the result was as expected
3 (esclamativo) what; **quale disgrazia!** what bad luck!
▷ *pron* **1** (interrogativo) which; **quale dei due scegli?** which of the two do you want?
2 (relativo): **il (la) quale** (persona: soggetto) who; (: oggetto, con preposizione) whom; (cosa) which; (possessivo) whose; **suo padre, il quale è avvocato, ...** his father, who is a lawyer, ...; **il signore con il quale parlavo** the gentleman to whom I was speaking; **l'albergo al quale ci siamo fermati** the hotel where we stayed *o* which we stayed at; **la signora della quale ammiriamo la bellezza** the lady whose beauty we admire
3 (relativo: in elenchi) such as, like; **piante**

quali l'edera plants like o such as ivy;
quale sindaco di questa città as mayor
of this town

qua'lifica, -che sf qualification; (titolo)
title

qualifi'cato, -a ag (dotato di qualifica)
qualified; (esperto, abile) skilled; **non mi
ritengo ~ per questo lavoro** I don't think
I'm qualified for this job; **è un medico
molto ~** he is a very distinguished doctor

qualificazi'one sf **gara di ~** (Sport)
qualifying event

qualità sf inv quality; **in ~ di** in one's
capacity as

qua'lora cong in case, if

qual'siasi det inv = **qualunque**

qua'lunque det inv any; (quale che sia)
whatever; (discriminativo) whichever;
(posposto: mediocre) poor, indifferent;
ordinary; **mettiti un vestito ~** put on any
old dress; **~ cosa** anything; **~ cosa accada**
whatever happens; **a ~ costo** at any cost,
whatever the cost; **l'uomo ~** the man in the
street; **~ persona** anyone, anybody

'quando cong, av when; **~ sarò ricco** when
I'm rich; **da ~** (dacché) since; (interrogativo):
da ~ sei qui? how long have you been
here?; **quand'anche** even if

quantità sf inv quantity; (gran numero):
una ~ di a great deal of; a lot of; **in grande
~** in large quantities

PAROLA CHIAVE

'quanto, -a det **1** (interrogativo: quantità)
how much; (: numero) how many; **quanto
pane/denaro?** how much bread/money?;
quanti libri/ragazzi? how many books/
boys?; **quanto tempo?** how long?; **quanti
anni hai?** how old are you?
2 (esclamativo): **quante storie!** what a lot
of nonsense!; **quanto tempo sprecato!**
what a waste of time!
3 (relativo: quantità) as much … as;
(: numero) as many … as; **ho quanto
denaro mi occorre** I have as much money
as I need; **prendi quanti libri vuoi** take as
many books as you like
▷ pron **1** (interrogativo: quantità) how much;
(: numero) how many; (: tempo) how long;
quanto mi dai? how much will you give
me?; **quanti me ne hai portati?** how
many did you bring me?; **da quanto sei
qui?** how long have you been here?; **quanti
ne abbiamo oggi?** what's the date today?
2 (relativo: quantità) as much as; (: numero)
as many as; **farò quanto posso** I'll do as
much as I can; **possono venire quanti**

sono stati invitati all those who have
been invited can come
▷ av **1** (interrogativo: con ag, av) how;
(: con vb) how much; **quanto stanco ti
sembrava?** how tired did he seem to you?;
quanto corre la tua moto? how fast can
your motorbike go?; **quanto costa?** how
much does it cost?; **quant'è?** how much
is it?
2 (esclamativo: con ag, av) how; (: con vb)
how much; **quanto sono felice!** how
happy I am!; **sapessi quanto abbiamo
camminato!** if you knew how far we've
walked!; **studierò quanto posso** I'll study
as much as o all I can; **quanto prima** as
soon as possible
3: **in quanto** (in qualità di) as; (perché, per il
fatto che) as, since; **(in) quanto a** (per ciò
che riguarda) as for, as regards
4: **per quanto** (nonostante, anche se)
however; **per quanto si sforzi, non ce
la farà** try as he may, he won't manage
it; **per quanto sia brava, fa degli errori**
however good she may be, she makes
mistakes; **per quanto io sappia** as far as
I know

qua'ranta num forty
quaran'tena sf quarantine
quaran'tesimo, -a num fortieth
quaran'tina sf **una ~ (di)** about forty
'quarta sf (Aut) fourth (gear); vedi anche
quarto
quar'tetto sm quartet(te)
quarti'ere sm district, area; (Mil) quarters
pl; **quartier generale** headquarters pl
'quarto, -a ag fourth ▷ sm fourth; (quarta
parte) quarter; **le 6 e un ~** a quarter past
six; **quarti di finale** quarter final; **quarto
d'ora** quarter of an hour
'quarzo ['kwartso] sm quartz
'quasi av almost, nearly ▷ cong (anche: ~
che) as if; **(non) … ~ mai** hardly ever; **~ ~
me ne andrei** I've half a mind to leave
quassù av up here
quat'tordici [kwat'torditʃi] num fourteen
quat'trini smpl money sg, cash sg
'quattro num four; **in ~ e quattr'otto** in
less than no time; **quattro'cento** num
four hundred ▷ sm **il Quattrocento** the
fifteenth century

PAROLA CHIAVE

'quello, -a (dav sm **quel** + C, **quell'** + V,
quello + s impura, gn, pn, ps, x, z; pl **quei** +
C, **quegli** + V o s impura, gn, pn, ps, x, z; dav sf
quella + C, **quell'** + V; pl **quelle**) det that;
those pl; **quella casa** that house; **quegli**

uomini those men; **voglio quella camicia (lì** o **là)** I want that shirt
▷ *pron* **1** (*dimostrativo*) that (one), those (ones) *pl*; (*ciò*) that; **conosci quella?** do you know that woman?; **prendo quello bianco** I'll take the white one; **chi è quello?** who's that?; **prendi quello (lì** o **là)** take that one (there)
2 (*relativo*): **quello(a) che** (*persona*) the one (who); (*cosa*) the one (which), the one (that); **quelli(e) che** (*persone*) those who; (*cose*) those which; **è lui quello che non voleva venire** he's the one who didn't want to come; **ho fatto quello che potevo** I did what I could

'**quercia, -ce** ['kwɛrtʃa] *sf* oak (tree); (*legno*) oak
que'rela *sf* (*Dir*) (legal) action
que'sito *sm* question, query; problem
questio'nario *sm* questionnaire
questi'one *sf* problem, question; (*controversia*) issue; (*litigio*) quarrel; **in ~** in question; **è ~ di tempo** it's a matter o question of time

 PAROLA CHIAVE

'**questo, -a** *det* **1** (*dimostrativo*) this; these *pl*; **questo libro (qui** o **qua)** this book; **io prendo questo cappotto, tu quello** I'll take this coat, you take that one; **quest'oggi** today; **questa sera** this evening
2 (*enfatico*): **non fatemi più prendere di queste paure** don't frighten me like that again
▷ *pron* (*dimostrativo*) this (one); these (ones) *pl*; (*ciò*) this; **prendo questo (qui** o **qua)** I'll take this one; **preferisci questi o quelli?** do you prefer these (ones) or those (ones)?; **questo intendevo io** this is what I meant; **vengono Paolo e Luca: questo da Roma, quello da Palermo** Paolo and Luca are coming: the former from Palermo, the latter from Rome

ques'tura *sf* police headquarters *pl*
qui *av* here; **da** o **di ~** from here; **di ~ in avanti** from now on; **di ~ a poco/una settimana** in a little while/a week's time; **~ dentro/sopra/vicino** in/up/near here; *vedi anche* **questo**
quie'tanza [kwje'tantsa] *sf* receipt
qui'ete *sf* quiet, quietness; calmness; stillness; peace
qui'eto, -a *ag* quiet; (*notte*) calm, still; (*mare*) calm
'**quindi** *av* then ▷ *cong* therefore, so

'**quindici** ['kwinditʃi] *num* fifteen; **~ giorni** a fortnight (BRIT), two weeks
quindi'cina [kwindi'tʃina] *sf* (*serie*): **una ~ (di)** about fifteen; **fra una ~ di giorni** in a fortnight
quinta *sf vedi* **quinto**
quin'tale *sm* quintal (100 kg)
'**quinto, -a** *num* fifth
quiz [kwidz] *sm inv* (*domanda*) question; (*anche*): **gioco a ~** quiz game
'**quota** *sf* (*parte*) quota, share; (*Aer*) height, altitude; (*Ippica*) odds *pl*; **prendere/perdere ~** (*Aer*) to gain/lose height o altitude; **quota d'iscrizione** enrolment fee; (*a club*) membership fee
quotidi'ano, -a *ag* daily; (*banale*) everyday ▷ *sm* (*giornale*) daily (paper)
quozi'ente [kwot'tsjɛnte] *sm* (*Mat*) quotient; **quoziente d'intelligenza** intelligence quotient, IQ

r

R, r ['ɛrre] *sf o m (lettera)* R, r; **R come Roma** ≈ R for Robert (BRIT), R for Roger (US)

'rabbia *sf (ira)* anger, rage; *(accanimento, furia)* fury; *(Med: idrofobia)* rabies *sg*

rab'bino *sm* rabbi

rabbi'oso, -a *ag* angry, furious; *(facile all'ira)* quick-tempered; *(forze, acqua ecc)* furious, raging; *(Med)* rabid, mad

rabbo'nire *vt* to calm down

rabbrivi'dire *vi* to shudder, shiver

raccapez'zarsi [rakkapet'tsarsi] *vpr* **non ~** to be at a loss

raccapricci'ante [rakkaprit'tʃante] *ag* horrifying

raccatta'palle *sm inv (Sport)* ballboy

raccat'tare *vt* to pick up

rac'chetta [rak'ketta] *sf (per tennis)* racket; *(per ping-pong)* bat; **racchetta da neve** snowshoe; **racchetta da sci** ski stick

racchi'udere [rak'kjudere] *vt* to contain

rac'cogliere [rak'kɔʎʎere] *vt* to collect; *(raccattare)* to pick up; *(frutti, fiori)* to pick, pluck; *(Agr)* to harvest; *(approvazione, voti)* to win

rac'colta *sf* collecting *no pl*; collection; *(Agr)* harvesting *no pl*, gathering *no pl*; harvest, crop; *(adunata)* gathering; **raccolta differenziata** *(dei rifiuti)* separate collection of different kinds of household waste

rac'colto, -a *pp di* **raccogliere** ▷ *ag*

(persona: pensoso) thoughtful; *(luogo: appartato)* secluded, quiet ▷ *sm (Agr)* crop, harvest

raccoman'dabile *ag* (highly) commendable; **è un tipo poco ~** he is not to be trusted

raccoman'dare *vt* to recommend; *(affidare)* to entrust; *(esortare)*: **~ a qn di non fare** to tell o warn sb not to do; **raccoman'data** *sf (anche:* **lettera raccomandata)** recorded-delivery letter

raccon'tare *vt* **~ (a qn)** *(dire)* to tell (sb); *(narrare)* to relate (to sb), tell (sb) about; **rac'conto** *sm* telling *no pl*, relating *no pl*; *(fatto raccontato)* story, tale; **racconti per bambini** children's stories

rac'cordo *sm (Tecn: giunto)* connection, joint; *(Aut)*: **raccordo anulare** *(Aut)* ring road (BRIT), beltway (US); **raccordo autostradale** slip road (BRIT), entrance (o exit) ramp (US); **raccordo ferroviario** siding; **raccordo stradale** link road

racimo'lare [ratʃimo'lare] *vt (fig)* to scrape together, glean

'rada *sf (natural)* harbour

'radar *sm* radar

raddoppi'are *vt, vi* to double

raddriz'zare [raddrit'tsare] *vt* to straighten; *(fig: correggere)* to put straight, correct

'radere *vt (barba)* to shave off; *(mento)* to shave; *(fig: rasentare)* to graze; to skim; **radersi** *vpr* to shave (o.s.); **~ al suolo** to raze to the ground

radi'are *vt* to strike off

radia'tore *sm* radiator

radiazi'one [radjat'tsjone] *sf (Fisica)* radiation; *(cancellazione)* striking off

radi'cale *ag* radical ▷ *sm (Ling)* root

ra'dicchio [ra'dikkjo] *sm* chicory

ra'dice [ra'ditʃe] *sf* root

'radio *sf inv* radio ▷ *sm (Chim)* radium; **radioat'tivo, -a** *ag* radioactive; **radio'cronaca, -che** *sf* radio commentary; **radiogra'fia** *sf* radiography; *(foto)* X-ray photograph

radi'oso, -a *ag* radiant

radios'veglia [radjoz'veʎʎa] *sf* radio alarm

'rado, -a *ag (capelli)* sparse, thin; *(visite)* infrequent; **di ~** rarely

radu'nare *vt* to gather, assemble; **radunarsi** *vpr* to gather, assemble

ra'dura *sf* clearing

raf'fermo, -a *ag* stale

'raffica, -che *sf (Meteor)* gust (of wind); *(di colpi: scarica)* burst of gunfire

raffigu'rare *vt* to represent

raffi'nato, -a *ag* refined

raffor'zare [raffor'tsare] *vt* to reinforce

raffredda'mento *sm* cooling

raffred'dare *vt* to cool; *(fig)* to dampen, have a cooling effect on; **raffreddarsi** *vpr* to grow cool *o* cold; *(prendere un raffreddore)* to catch a cold; *(fig)* to cool (off)

raffred'dato, -a *ag (Med)*: **essere ~** to have a cold

raffred'dore *sm (Med)* cold

raf'fronto *sm* comparison

'rafia *sf (fibra)* raffia

rafting ['rafting] *sm* white-water rafting

ra'gazza [ra'gattsa] *sf* girl; *(fam: fidanzato)* girlfriend; **nome da ~** maiden name; **ragazza madre** unmarried mother

ra'gazzo [ra'gattso] *sm* boy; *(fam: fidanzato)* boyfriend; **ragazzi** *smpl (figli)* kids; **ciao ragazzi!** *(gruppo)* hi guys!

raggi'ante [rad'dʒante] *ag* radiant, shining

'raggio ['raddʒo] *sm (di sole ecc)* ray; *(Mat, distanza)* radius; *(di ruota ecc)* spoke; **raggio d'azione** range; **raggi X** X-rays

raggi'rare [raddʒi'rare] *vt* to take in, trick

raggi'ungere [rad'dʒundʒere] *vt* to reach; *(persona: riprendere)* to catch up (with); *(bersaglio)* to hit; *(fig: meta)* to achieve

raggomito'larsi *vpr* to curl up

raggranel'lare *vt* to scrape together

raggrup'pare *vt* to group (together)

ragiona'mento [radʒona'mento] *sm* reasoning *no pl*; arguing *no pl*; argument

ragio'nare [radʒo'nare] *vi* to reason; **~ di** *(discorrere)* to talk about

ragi'one [ra'dʒone] *sf* reason; *(dimostrazione, prova)* argument, reason; *(diritto)* right; **aver ~** to be right; **aver ~ di qn** to get the better of sb; **dare ~ a qn** to agree with sb; to prove sb right; **perdere la ~** to become insane; *(fig)* to take leave of one's senses; **in ~ di** at the rate of; to the amount of; according to; **a o con ~** rightly, justly; **a ragion veduta** after due consideration; **ragione sociale** *(Comm)* corporate name

ragione'ria [radʒone'ria] *sf* accountancy; accounts department

ragio'nevole [radʒo'nevole] *ag* reasonable

ragioni'ere, -a [radʒo'njɛre] *sm/f* accountant

ragli'are [raʎ'ʎare] *vi* to bray

ragna'tela [raɲɲa'tela] *sf* cobweb, spider's web

'ragno ['raɲɲo] *sm* spider

ragù *sm inv (Cuc)* meat sauce; stew

RAI-TV [raiti'vu] *sigla f* = **Radio televisione italiana**

ralle'grare *vt* to cheer up; **rallegrarsi** *vpr*

to cheer up; *(provare allegrezza)* to rejoice; **rallegrarsi con qn** to congratulate sb

rallen'tare *vt* to slow down; *(fig)* to lessen, slacken ▷ *vi* to slow down

rallenta'tore *sm (Cinema)* slow-motion camera; **al ~** *(anche fig)* in slow motion

raman'zina [raman'dzina] *sf* lecture, telling-off

'rame *sm (Chim)* copper

rammari'carsi *vpr* **~ (di)** *(rincrescersi)* to be sorry (about), regret; *(lamentarsi)* to complain (about)

rammen'dare *vt* to mend; *(calza)* to darn

'ramo *sm* branch

ramo'scello [ramo'ʃʃello] *sm* twig

'rampa *sf* flight (of stairs); **rampa di lancio** launching pad

rampi'cante *ag (Bot)* climbing

'rana *sf* frog

'rancido, -a ['rantʃido] *ag* rancid

ran'core *sm* rancour, resentment

ran'dagio, -a, -gi, -gie *o* **ge** [ran'dadʒo] *ag (gatto, cane)* stray

ran'dello *sm* club, cudgel

'rango, -ghi *sm (condizione sociale, Mil, riga)* rank

rannicchi'arsi [rannik'kjarsi] *vpr* to crouch, huddle

rannuvo'larsi *vpr* to cloud over, become overcast

'rapa *sf (Bot)* turnip

ra'pace [ra'patʃe] *ag (animale)* predatory; *(fig)* rapacious, grasping ▷ *sm* bird of prey

ra'pare *vt (capelli)* to crop, cut very short

rapida'mente *av* quickly, rapidly

rapidità *sf* speed

'rapido, -a *ag* fast; *(esame, occhiata)* quick, rapid ▷ *sm (Ferr)* express (train)

rapi'mento *sm* kidnapping; *(fig)* rapture

ra'pina *sf* robbery; **rapina in banca** bank robbery; **rapina a mano armata** armed robbery; **rapi'nare** *vt* to rob; **rapina'tore, -'trice** *sm/f* robber

ra'pire *vt (cose)* to steal; *(persone)* to kidnap; *(fig)* to enrapture, delight; **rapi'tore, -'trice** *sm/f* kidnapper

rap'porto *sm (resoconto)* report; *(legame)* relationship; *(Mat, Tecn)* ratio; **rapporti sessuali** sexual intercourse *sg*

rappre'saglia [rappre'saʎʎa] *sf* reprisal, retaliation

rappresen'tante *sm/f* representative

rappresen'tare *vt* to represent; *(Teatro)* to perform; **rappresentazi'one** *sf* representation; performing *no pl*; *(spettacolo)* performance

rara'mente *av* seldom, rarely

rare'fatto, -a *ag* rarefied

'raro, -a *ag* rare

ra'sare vt (barba ecc) to shave off; (siepi, erba) to trim, cut; **rasarsi** vpr to shave (o.s.)

raschi'are [ras'kjare] vt to scrape; (macchia, fango) to scrape off ▷ vi to clear one's throat

ra'sente prep ~ (a) close to, very near

'raso, -a pp di **radere** ▷ ag (barba) shaved; (capelli) cropped; (con misure di capacità) level; (pieno: bicchiere) full to the brim ▷ sm (tessuto) satin; **un cucchiaio** ~ a level spoonful; **raso terra** close to the ground

ra'soio sm razor; **rasoio elettrico** electric shaver o razor

ras'segna [ras'seɲɲa] sf (Mil) inspection, review; (esame) inspection; (resoconto) review, survey; (pubblicazione letteraria ecc) review; (mostra) exhibition, show; **passare in ~** (Mil, fig) to review

rassegnarsi vpr (accettare): ~ (a qc/a fare) to resign o.s. (to sth/to doing)

rassicu'rare vt to reassure

rasso'dare vt to harden, stiffen; **rassodarsi** vpr to harden, to strengthen

rassomigli'anza [rassomiʎ'ʎantsa] sf resemblance

rassomigli'are [rassomiʎ'ʎare] vi ~ **a** to resemble, look like

rastrel'lare vt to rake; (fig: perlustrare) to comb

ras'trello sm rake

'rata sf (quota) instalment; **pagare a rate** to pay by instalments o on hire purchase (BRIT)

ratifi'care vt (Dir) to ratify

'ratto sm (Dir) abduction; (Zool) rat

rattop'pare vt to patch

rattris'tare vt to sadden; **rattristarsi** vpr to become sad

'rauco, -a, -chi, -che ag hoarse

rava'nello sm radish

ravi'oli smpl ravioli sg

ravvi'vare vt to revive; (fig) to brighten up, enliven

razio'nale [rattsjo'nale] ag rational

razio'nare [rattsjo'nare] vt to ration

razi'one [rat'tsjone] sf ration; (porzione) portion, share

'razza ['rattsa] sf race; (Zool) breed; (discendenza, stirpe) stock, race; (sorta) sort, kind

razzi'ale [rat'tsjale] ag racial

raz'zismo [rat'tsizmo] sm racism, racialism

raz'zista, -i, -e [rat'tsista] ag, sm/f racist, racialist

'razzo ['raddzo] sm rocket

R.C. sigla m (= partito della Rifondazione Comunista) left-wing Italian political party

re sm inv king; (Mus) D; (: solfeggiando) re

rea'gire [rea'dʒire] vi to react

re'ale ag real; (di, da re) royal ▷ sm **il ~** reality

realiz'zare [realid'dzare] vt (progetto ecc) to realize, carry out; (sogno, desiderio) to realize, fulfil; (scopo) to achieve; (Comm: titoli ecc) to realize; (Calcio ecc) to score; **realizzarsi** vpr to be realized

real'mente av really, actually

realtà sf inv reality

re'ato sm offence

reat'tore sm (Fisica) reactor; (Aer: aereo) jet; (: motore) jet engine

reazio'nario, -a [reattsjo'narjo] ag (Pol) reactionary

reazi'one [reat'tsjone] sf reaction

'rebus sm inv rebus; (fig) puzzle; enigma

recapi'tare vt to deliver

re'capito sm (indirizzo) address; (consegna) delivery; **recapito a domicilio** home delivery (service); **recapito telefonico** phone number

re'cedere [re'tʃedere] vi to withdraw

recensi'one [retʃen'sjone] sf review

re'cente [re'tʃente] ag recent; **di ~** recently; **recente'mente** av recently

re'cidere [re'tʃidere] vt to cut off, chop off

recin'tare [retʃin'tare] vt to enclose, fence off

re'cinto [re'tʃinto] sm enclosure; (ciò che recinge) fence; surrounding wall

recipi'ente [retʃi'pjente] sm container

re'ciproco, -a, -ci, -che [re'tʃiproko] ag reciprocal

'recita ['rɛtʃita] sf performance

reci'tare [retʃi'tare] vt (poesia, lezione) to recite; (dramma) to perform; (ruolo) to play o act (the part of)

recla'mare vi to complain ▷ vt (richiedere) to demand

re'clamo sm complaint

recli'nabile ag (sedile) reclining

reclusi'one sf (Dir) imprisonment

'recluta sf recruit

re'condito, -a ag secluded; (fig) secret, hidden

'record ag inv record cpd ▷ sm inv record; **in tempo ~, a tempo di ~** in record time; **detenere il ~ di** to hold the record for; **record mondiale** world record

recriminazi'one [rekriminat'tsjone] sf recrimination

recupe'rare vt (rientrare in possesso di) to recover, get back; (tempo perduto) to make up for; (Naut) to salvage; (: naufraghi) to rescue; (delinquente) to rehabilitate; ~ **lo svantaggio** (Sport) to close the gap

redargu'ire vt to rebuke

re'dassi ecc vb vedi **redigere**
reddi'tizio, -a [reddi'tittsjo] ag profitable
'**reddito** sm income; (dello Stato) revenue; (di un capitale) yield
re'digere [re'didʒere] vt to write; (contratto) to draw up
'**redini** sfpl reins
'**reduce** ['rɛdutʃe] ag ~ **da** returning from, back from ▷ sm/f survivor
refe'rendum sm inv referendum
referenze [refe'rɛntse] sfpl references
re'ferto sm medical report
rega'lare vt to give (as a present), make a present of
re'galo sm gift, present
re'gata sf regatta
'**reggere** ['rɛddʒere] vt (tenere) to hold; (sostenere) to support, bear, hold up; (portare) to carry, bear; (resistere) to withstand; (dirigere: impresa) to manage, run; (governare) to rule, govern; (Ling) to take, be followed by ▷ vi (resistere): ~ **a** to stand up to, hold out against; (sopportare): ~ **a** to stand; (durare) to last; (fig: teoria ecc) to hold water; **reggersi** vpr (stare ritto) to stand
'**reggia, -ge** ['rɛddʒa] sf royal palace
reggi'calze [reddʒi'kaltse] sm inv suspender belt
reggi'mento [reddʒi'mento] sm (Mil) regiment
reggi'seno [reddʒi'seno] sm bra
re'gia, -'gie [re'dʒia] sf (TV, Cinema ecc) direction
re'gime [re'dʒime] sm (Pol) regime; (Dir: aureo, patrimoniale ecc) system; (Med) diet; (Tecn) (engine) speed
re'gina [re'dʒina] sf queen
regio'nale [redʒo'nale] ag regional ▷ sm local train (stopping frequently)
regi'one [re'dʒone] sf region; (territorio) region, district, area
re'gista, -i, -e [re'dʒista] sm/f (TV, Cinema ecc) director
regis'trare [redʒis'trare] vt (Amm) to register; (Comm) to enter; (notare) to note, take note of; (canzone, conversazione: strumento di misura) to record; (mettere a punto) to adjust, regulate; (bagagli) to check in; **registra'tore** sm (strumento) recorder, register; (magnetofono) tape recorder; **registratore di cassa** cash register; **registratore a cassette** cassette recorder
re'gistro [re'dʒistro] sm (libro, Mus, Tech) register; ledger; logbook; (Dir) registry
re'gnare [reɲ'ɲare] vi to reign, rule
'**regno** ['reɲɲo] sm kingdom; (periodo) reign; (fig) realm; **il R~ Unito** the United

Kingdom; **regno animale/vegetale** animal/vegetable kingdom
'**regola** sf rule; **a ~ d'arte** duly; perfectly; **in ~** in order
rego'labile ag adjustable
rego'mento sm (complesso di norme) regulations pl; (di debito) settlement; **regolamento di conti** (fig) settling of scores
rego'lare ag regular; (in regola: domanda) in order, lawful ▷ vt to regulate, control; (apparecchio) to adjust, regulate; (questione, conto, debito) to settle; **regolarsi** vpr (moderarsi): **regolarsi nel bere/nello spendere** to control one's drinking/spending; (comportarsi) to behave, act
rela'tivo, -a ag relative
relazi'one [relat'tsjone] sf (fra cose, persone) relation(ship); (resoconto) report, account
rele'gare vt to banish; (fig) to relegate
religi'one [reli'dʒone] sf religion
re'liquia sf relic
re'litto sm wreck; (fig) down-and-out
re'mare vi to row
remini'scenze [reminiʃ'ʃɛntse] sfpl reminiscences
remis'sivo, -a ag submissive, compliant
'**remo** sm oar
re'moto, -a ag remote
'**rendere** vt (ridare) to return, give back; (: saluto ecc) to return; (produrre) to yield, bring in; (esprimere, tradurre) to render; ~ **qc possibile** to make sth possible; **rendersi** vpr **rendersi utile** to make o.s. useful; **rendersi conto di qc** to realize sth; ~ **qc possibile** to make sth possible; ~ **grazie a qn** give thanks to sb; ~ **omaggio a qn** to pay homage to sb; ~ **un servizio a qn** to do sb a service; ~ **una testimonianza** to give evidence; **non so se rendo l'idea** I don't know if I'm making myself clear
rendi'mento sm (reddito) yield; (di manodopera, Tecn) efficiency; (capacità di produrre) output; (di studenti) performance
'**rendita** sf (di individuo) private o unearned income; (Comm) revenue; **rendita annua** annuity
'**rene** sm kidney
'**renna** sf reindeer inv
re'parto sm department, section; (Mil) detachment
repel'lente ag repulsive
repen'taglio [repen'taʎʎo] sm **mettere a ~ to** jeopardize, risk
repen'tino, -a ag sudden, unexpected
reper'torio sm (Teatro) repertory; (elenco) index, (alphabetical) list
'**replica, -che** sf repetition; reply, answer;

(*obiezione*) objection; (*Teatro, Cinema*) repeat performance; (*copia*) replica

repli'care vt (*ripetere*) to repeat; (*rispondere*) to answer, reply

repressi'one sf repression

re'presso, -a pp di **reprimere**

re'primere vt to suppress, repress

re'pubblica, -che sf republic

reputazi'one [reputat'tsjone] sf reputation

requi'sire vt to requisition

requi'sito sm requirement

'resa sf (*l'arrendersi*) surrender; (*restituzione, rendimento*) return; **resa dei conti** rendering of accounts; (*fig*) day of reckoning

'resi ecc vb vedi **rendere**

resi'dente ag resident; **residenzi'ale** ag residential

re'siduo, -a ag residual, remaining ▷ sm remainder; (*Chim*) residue

'resina sf resin

resis'tente ag (*che resiste*): ~ **a** resistant to; (*forte*) strong; (*duraturo*) long-lasting, durable; ~ **al caldo** heat-resistant;

resis'tenza sf resistance; (*di persona: fisica*) stamina, endurance; (: *mentale*) endurance, resistance

⬙ **RESISTENZA**
⬙
⬙ The **Resistenza** in Italy fought against
⬙ the Nazis and the Fascists during the
⬙ Second World War. Members of the
⬙ **Resistenza** spanned a wide political
⬙ spectrum and played a vital role in the
⬙ Liberation and in the formation of the
⬙ new democratic government at the end
⬙ of the war.

re'sistere vi to resist; ~ **a** (*assalto, tentazioni*) to resist; (*dolore: pianta*) to withstand; (*non patir danno*) to be resistant to

reso'conto sm report, account

res'pingere [res'pindʒere] vt to drive back, repel; (*rifiutare*) to reject; (*Ins: bocciare*) to fail

respi'rare vi to breathe; (*fig*) to get one's breath; to breathe again ▷ vt to breathe (in), inhale; **respirazi'one** sf breathing; **respirazione artificiale** artificial respiration; **res'piro** sm breathing no pl; (*singolo atto*) breath; (*fig*) respite, rest; **mandare un respiro di sollievo** to give a sigh of relief

respon'sabile ag responsible ▷ sm/f person responsible; (*capo*) person in charge; ~ **di** responsible for; (*Dir*) liable

for; **responsabilità** sf inv responsibility; (*legale*) liability

res'ponso sm answer

'ressa sf crowd, throng

'ressi ecc vb vedi **reggere**

res'tare vi (*rimanere*) to remain, stay; (*avanzare*) to be left, remain; ~ **orfano/cieco** to become o be left an orphan/become blind; ~ **d'accordo** to agree; **non resta più niente** there's nothing left; **restano pochi giorni** there are only a few days left

restau'rare vt to restore

res'tio, -a, -'tii, -'tie ag ~ **a** reluctant to

restitu'ire vt to return, give back; (*energie, forze*) to restore

'resto sm remainder, rest; (*denaro*) change; (*Mat*) remainder; **resti** smpl (*di cibo*) leftovers; (*di città*) remains; **del** ~ moreover, besides; **tenga pure il** ~ keep the change; **resti mortali** (mortal) remains

res'tringere [res'trindʒere] vt to reduce; (*vestito*) to take in; (*stoffa*) to shrink; (*fig*) to restrict, limit; **restringersi** vpr (*strada*) to narrow; (*stoffa*) to shrink

'rete sf net; (*fig*) trap, snare; (*di recinzione*) wire netting; (*Aut, Ferr, di spionaggio ecc*) network; **segnare una** ~ (*Calcio*) to score a goal; **la R~** the Web; **rete ferroviaria** railway network; **rete del letto** (sprung) bed base; **rete stradale** road network; **rete (televisiva)** (*sistema*) network; (*canale*) channel

reti'cente [reti'tʃɛnte] ag reticent

retico'lato sm grid; (*rete*) wire netting; (*di filo spinato*) barbed wire (fence)

'retina sf (*Anat*) retina

re'torico, -a, -ci, -che ag rhetorical

retribu'ire vt to pay

'retro sm inv back ▷ av (*dietro*): **vedi** ~ see over(leaf)

retro'cedere [retro'tʃedere] vi to withdraw ▷ vt (*Calcio*) to relegate; (*Mil*) to degrade

re'trogrado, -a ag (*fig*) reactionary, backward-looking

retro'marcia [retro'martʃa] sf (*Aut*) reverse; (: *dispositivo*) reverse gear

retro'scena [retro'ʃɛna] sm inv (*Teatro*) backstage; **i** ~ (*fig*) the behind-the-scenes activities

retrovi'sore sm (*Aut*) (rear-view) mirror

'retta sf (*Mat*) straight line; (*di convitto*) charge for bed and board; (*fig: ascolto*): **dar** ~ **a** to listen to, pay attention to

rettango'lare ag rectangular

ret'tangolo, -a ag right-angled ▷ sm rectangle

ret'tifica, -che sf rectification, correction

'rettile sm reptile

retti'lineo, -a ag rectilinear

'retto, -a pp di **reggere** ▷ ag straight; (Mat): **angolo ~** right angle; (onesto) honest, upright; (giusto, esatto) correct, proper, right

ret'tore sm (Rel) rector; (di università) ≈ chancellor

reuma'tismo sm rheumatism

revisi'one sf auditing no pl; audit; servicing no pl; overhaul; review; revision; **revisione di bozze** proofreading

revi'sore sm; **revisore di bozze** proofreader; **revisore di conti** auditor

revival [ri'vaival] sm inv revival

'revoca sf revocation

revo'care vt to revoke

re'volver sm inv revolver

ri'abbia ecc vb vedi **riavere**

riabili'tare vt to rehabilitate

rianimazi'one [rianimat'tsjone] sf (Med) resuscitation; **centro di ~** intensive care unit

ria'prire vt to reopen, open again; **riaprirsi** vpr to reopen, open again

ri'armo sm (Mil) rearmament

rias'sumere vt (riprendere) to resume; (impiegare di nuovo) to re-employ; (sintetizzare) to summarize; **rias'sunto, -a** pp di **riassumere** ▷ sm summary

riattac'care vt (attaccare di nuovo): **~ (a)** (manifesto, francobollo) to stick back (on); (bottone) to sew back (on); (quadro, chiavi) to hang back up (on); **~ (il telefono o il ricevitore)** to hang up (the receiver)

ria'vere vt to have again; (avere indietro) to get back; (riacquistare) to recover; **riaversi** vpr to recover

riba'dire vt (fig) to confirm

ri'balta sf flap; (Teatro: proscenio) front of the stage; (fig) limelight; **luci della ~** footlights pl

ribal'tabile ag (sedile) tip-up

ribal'tare vt, vi (anche: **ribaltarsi**) to turn over, tip over

ribas'sare vt to lower, bring down ▷ vi to come down, fall

ri'battere vt to return, hit back; (confutare) to refute; **~ che** to retort that

ribel'larsi vpr: **~ (a)** to rebel (against); **ri'belle** ag (soldati) rebel; (ragazzo) rebellious ▷ sm/f rebel

'ribes sm inv currant; **ribes nero** blackcurrant; **ribes rosso** redcurrant

ri'brezzo [ri'breddzo] sm disgust, loathing; **far ~ a** to disgust

ribut'tante ag disgusting, revolting

rica'dere vi to fall again; (scendere a terra: fig: nel peccato ecc) to fall back; (vestiti, capelli ecc) to hang (down); (riversarsi: fatiche, colpe): **~ su** to fall on; **rica'duta** sf (Med) relapse

rica'mare vt to embroider

ricambi'are vt to change again; (contraccambiare) to repay, return; **ri'cambio** sm exchange, return; (Fisiol) metabolism

ri'camo sm embroidery

ricapito'lare vt to recapitulate, sum up

ricari'care vt (arma, macchina fotografica) to reload; (pipa) to refill; (orologio) to rewind; (batteria) to recharge

ricat'tare vt to blackmail; **ri'catto** sm blackmail

rica'vare vt (estrarre) to draw out, extract; (ottenere) to obtain, gain

ric'chezza [rik'kettsa] sf wealth; (fig) richness

'riccio, -a ['rittʃo] ag curly ▷ sm (Zool) hedgehog; **riccio di mare** sea urchin; **'ricciolo** sm curl

'ricco, -a, -chi, -che ag rich; (persona, paese) rich, wealthy ▷ sm/f rich man/woman; **i ricchi** the rich; **~ di** full of; rich in

ri'cerca, -che [ri'tʃerka] sf search; (indagine) investigation, inquiry; (studio): **la ~** research; **una ~** piece of research; **ricerca di mercato** market research

ricer'care [ritʃer'kare] vt (motivi, cause) to look for, try to determine; (successo, piacere) to pursue; (onore, gloria) to seek; **ricer'cato, -a** ag (apprezzato) much sought-after; (affettato) studied, affected ▷ sm/f (Polizia) wanted man/woman

ricerca'tore, -'trice [ritʃerka'tore] sm/f (Ins) researcher

ri'cetta [ri'tʃetta] sf (Med) prescription; (Cuc) recipe; **mi può fare una ~ medica?** could you write me a prescription?

ricettazi'one [ritʃettat'tsjone] sf (Dir) receiving (stolen goods)

ri'cevere [ri'tʃevere] vt to receive; (stipendio, lettera) to get, receive; (accogliere: ospite) to welcome; (vedere: cliente, rappresentante ecc) to see; **ricevi'mento** sm receiving no pl; (festa) reception; **ricevi'tore** sm (Tecn) receiver; **rice'vuta** sf receipt; **posso avere una ricevuta, per favore?** can I have a receipt, please?; **ricevuta fiscale** receipt for tax purposes; **ricevuta di ritorno** (Posta) advice of receipt

richia'mare [rikja'mare] vt (chiamare indietro, ritelefonare) to call back; (ambasciatore, truppe) to recall; (rimproverare) to reprimand; (attirare) to attract, draw; **può ~ più tardi?** can you call back later?; **richiamarsi a** (riferirsi a) to refer to

richi'edere [ri'kjɛdere] vt to ask again for; (chiedere indietro): **~ qc** to ask for sth back; (chiedere: per sapere) to ask; (: per avere) to ask for; (Amm: documenti) to apply for; (esigere) to need, require; **richi'esta** sf (domanda) request; (Amm) application, request; (esigenza) demand, request; **a richiesta** on request

rici'clare [ritʃi'klare] vt to recycle

'ricino ['ritʃino] sm **olio di ~** castor oil

ricognizi'one [rikoɲɲit'tsjone] sf (Mil) reconnaissance; (Dir) recognition, acknowledgement

ricominci'are [rikomin'tʃare] vt, vi to start again, begin again

ricom'pensa sf reward

ricompen'sare vt to reward

riconciliarsi vpr to be reconciled

ricono'scente [rikonoʃ'ʃɛnte] ag grateful

rico'noscere [riko'noʃʃere] vt to recognize; (Dir: figlio, debito) to acknowledge; (ammettere: errore) to admit, acknowledge

rico'perto, -a pp di **ricoprire**

ricopi'are vt to copy

rico'prire vt (coprire) to cover; (occupare: carica) to hold

ricor'dare vt to remember, recall; (richiamare alla memoria): **~ qc a qn** to remind sb of sth; **ricordarsi** vpr **ricordarsi (di)** to remember; **ricordarsi di qc/di aver fatto** to remember sth/having done

ri'cordo sm memory; (regalo) keepsake, souvenir; (di viaggio) souvenir

ricor'rente ag recurrent, recurring; **ricor'renza** sf recurrence; (festività) anniversary

ri'correre vi (ripetersi) to recur; **~ a** (rivolgersi) to turn to; (: Dir) to appeal to; (servirsi di) to have recourse to

ricostitu'ente ag (Med): **cura ~** tonic

ricostru'ire vt (casa) to rebuild; (fatti) to reconstruct

ri'cotta sf soft white unsalted cheese made from sheep's milk

ricove'rare vt to give shelter to; **~ qn in ospedale** to admit sb to hospital

ri'covero sm shelter, refuge; (Mil) shelter; (Med) admission (to hospital)

ricreazi'one [rikreat'tsjone] sf recreation, entertainment; (Ins) break

ri'credersi vpr to change one's mind

ridacchi'are [ridak'kjare] vi to snigger

ri'dare vt to return, give back

'ridere vi to laugh; (deridere, beffare): **~ di** to laugh at, make fun of

ri'dicolo, -a ag ridiculous, absurd

ridimensio'nare vt to reorganize; (fig) to see in the right perspective

ri'dire vt to repeat; (criticare) to find fault with; to object to; **trova sempre qualcosa da ~** he always manages to find fault

ridon'dante ag redundant

ri'dotto, -a pp di **ridurre** ▷ ag (biglietto) reduced; (formato) small

ri'duco ecc vb vedi **ridurre**

ri'durre vt (anche Chim, Mat) to reduce; (prezzo, spese) to cut, reduce; (accorciare: opera letteraria) to abridge; (: Radio, TV) to adapt; **ridursi** vpr (diminuirsi) to be reduced, shrink; **ridursi a** to be reduced to; **ridursi pelle e ossa** to be reduced to skin and bone; **ri'dussi** ecc vb vedi **ridurre**; **ridut'tore** sm (Elec) adaptor; **riduzi'one** sf reduction; abridgement; adaptation; **ci sono riduzioni per i bambini/gli studenti?** is there a reduction for children/students?

ri'ebbi ecc vb vedi **riavere**

riem'pire vt to fill (up); (modulo) to fill in o out; **riempirsi** vpr to fill (up); **~ qc di** to fill sth (up) with

rien'tranza [rien'trantsa] sf recess; indentation

rien'trare vi (entrare di nuovo) to go (o come) back in; (tornare) to return; (fare una rientranza) to go in, curve inwards; to be indented; (riguardare): **~ in** to be included among, form part of

riepilo'gare vt to summarize ▷ vi to recapitulate

ri'esco ecc vb vedi **riuscire**

ri'fare vt to do again; (ricostruire) to make again; (nodo) to tie again, do up again; (imitare) to imitate, copy; **rifarsi** vpr (risarcirsi): **rifarsi di** to make up for; (vendicarsi): **rifarsi di qc su qn** to get one's own back on sb for sth; (riferirsi): **rifarsi a** to go back to; to follow; **~ il letto** to make the bed; **rifarsi una vita** to make a new life for o.s.

riferi'mento sm reference; **in** o **con ~ a** with reference to

rife'rire vt (riportare) to report ▷ vi to do a report; **riferirsi** vpr **riferirsi a** to refer to

rifi'nire vt to finish off, put the finishing touches to

rifiu'tare vt to refuse; **~ di fare** to refuse to do; **rifi'uto** sm refusal; **rifiuti** smpl (spazzatura) rubbish sg, refuse sg

riflessi'one sf (Fisica, meditazione) reflection; (il pensare) thought, reflection; (osservazione) remark

rifles'sivo, -a ag (persona) thoughtful, reflective; (Ling) reflexive

ri'flesso, -a *pp di* **riflettere** ▷ *sm (di luce, allo specchio)* reflection; *(Fisiol)* reflex; **di o per ~** indirectly

riflessologia [riflesso'lodʒia] *sf* reflexology

ri'flettere *vt* to reflect ▷ *vi* to think; **riflettersi** *vpr* to be reflected; **~ su** to think over

riflet'tore *sm* reflector; *(proiettore)* floodlight; searchlight

ri'flusso *sm* flowing back; *(della marea)* ebb; **un'epoca di ~** an era of nostalgia

ri'forma *sf* reform; **la R~** *(Rel)* the Reformation

riforma'torio *sm (Dir)* community home (BRIT), reformatory (US)

riforni'mento *sm* supplying, providing; restocking; **rifornimenti** *smpl (provviste)* supplies, provisions

rifor'nire *vt (provvedere):* **~ di** to supply o provide with; *(fornire di nuovo: casa ecc)* to restock; **rifornirsi** *vpr* **rifornirsi di qc** to stock up on sth

rifugi'arsi [rifu'dʒarsi] *vpr* to take refuge; **rifugi'ato, -a** *sm/f* refugee

ri'fugio [ri'fudʒo] *sm* refuge, shelter; *(in montagna)* shelter; **rifugio antiaereo** air-raid shelter

'riga, -ghe *sf* line; *(striscia)* stripe; *(di persone, cose)* line, row; *(regolo)* ruler; *(scriminatura)* parting; **mettersi in ~** to line up; **a righe** *(foglio)* lined; *(vestito)* striped

ri'gare *vt (foglio)* to rule ▷ *vi* **~ diritto** *(fig)* to toe the line

rigatti'ere *sm* junk dealer

righerò *ecc* [rige'rɔ] *vb vedi* **rigare**

'rigido, -a ['ridʒido] *ag* rigid, stiff; *(membra ecc: indurite)* stiff; *(Meteor)* harsh, severe; *(fig)* strict

rigogli'oso, -a [rigoʎ'ʎoso] *ag (pianta)* luxuriant; *(fig: commercio, sviluppo)* thriving

ri'gore *sm (Meteor)* harshness, rigours *pl*; *(fig)* severity, strictness; *(anche:* **calcio di ~)** penalty; **di ~** compulsory; **a rigor di termini** strictly speaking

riguar'dare *vt* to look at again; *(considerare)* to regard, consider; *(concernere)* to regard, concern; **riguardarsi** *vpr (aver cura di sé)* to look after o.s.

rigu'ardo *sm (attenzione)* care; *(considerazione)* regard, respect; **~ a** concerning, with regard to; **non aver riguardi nell'agire/nel parlare** to act/speak freely

rilasci'are [rilaʃ'ʃare] *vt (rimettere in libertà)* to release; *(Amm: documenti)* to issue

rilassarsi *vpr* to relax; *(fig: disciplina)* to become slack

rile'gare *vt (libro)* to bind

ri'leggere [ri'leddʒere] *vt* to reread, read again; *(rivedere)* to read over

ri'lento: a ~ *av* slowly

rile'vante *ag* considerable; important

rile'vare *vt (ricavare)* to find; *(notare)* to notice; *(mettere in evidenza)* to point out; *(venire a conoscere: notizia)* to learn; *(raccogliere: dati)* to gather, collect; *(Topografia)* to survey; *(Mil)* to relieve; *(Comm)* to take over

rili'evo *sm (Arte, Geo)* relief; *(fig: rilevanza)* importance; *(Topografia)* survey; **dar ~ a o mettere in ~ qc** *(fig)* to bring sth out, highlight sth

rilut'tante *ag* reluctant

'rima *sf* rhyme; *(verso)* verse

riman'dare *vt* to send again; *(restituire, rinviare)* to send back, return; *(differire):* **~ qc (a)** to postpone sth o put sth off (till); *(fare riferimento):* **~ qn a** to refer sb to; **essere rimandato** *(Ins)* to have to repeat one's exams

ri'mando *sm (rinvio)* return; *(dilazione)* postponement; *(riferimento)* cross-reference

rima'nente *ag* remaining ▷ *sm* rest, remainder; **i rimanenti** *(persone)* the rest of them, the others

rima'nere *vi (restare)* to remain, stay; *(avanzare)* to be left, remain; *(restare stupito)* to be amazed; *(restare, mancare):* **rimangono poche settimane a Pasqua** there are only a few weeks left till Easter; **rimane da vedere se** it remains to be seen whether; *(diventare):* **~ vedovo** to be left a widower; *(trovarsi):* **~ sorpreso** to be surprised

rimangi'are [riman'dʒare] *vt* to eat again; **~rsi la parola/una promessa** *(fig)* to go back on one's word/one's promise

ri'mango *ecc vb vedi* **rimanere**

rimargi'narsi *vpr* to heal

rimbal'zare [rimbal'tsare] *vi* to bounce back, rebound; *(proiettile)* to ricochet

rimbam'bito, -a *ag* senile, in one's dotage

rimboc'care *vt (coperta)* to tuck in; *(maniche, pantaloni)* to turn o roll up

rimbom'bare *vi* to resound

rimbor'sare *vt* to pay back, repay

rimedi'are *vi* **~ a** to remedy ▷ *vt (fam: procurarsi)* to get o scrape together

ri'medio *sm (medicina)* medicine; *(cura, fig)* remedy, cure

ri'mettere *vt (mettere di nuovo)* to put back; *(indossare di nuovo):* **~ qc** to put sth back on, put sth on again; *(affidare)* to entrust; *(: decisione)* to refer; *(condonare)* to remit; *(Comm: merci)* to deliver; *(: denaro)* to remit; (*vomitare*) to bring up; (*perdere*: *anche*: **rimetterci**) to lose; **rimettersi al bello** (*tempo*) to clear up; **rimettersi in salute** to get better, recover one's health

ri'misi ecc vb vedi **rimettere**

'rimmel® sm inv mascara

rimoder'nare vt to modernize

rimorchi'are [rimor'kjare] vt to tow; (*fig*: *ragazza*) to pick up

ri'morchio [ri'mɔrkjo] sm tow; (*veicolo*) trailer

ri'morso sm remorse

rimozi'one [rimot'tsjone] sf removal; (*da un impiego*) dismissal; (*Psic*) repression

rimpatri'are vi to return home ▷ vt to repatriate

rimpi'angere [rim'pjandʒere] vt to regret; (*persona*) to miss; **rimpi'anto, -a** pp di **rimpiangere** ▷ sm regret

rimpiaz'zare [rimpjat'tsare] vt to replace

rimpiccio'lire [rimpittʃo'lire] vt to make smaller ▷ vi (*anche*: **rimpicciolirsi**) to become smaller

rimpinzarsi [rimpin'tsarsi] vpr **~ (di qc)** to stuff o.s. (with sth)

rimprove'rare vt to rebuke, reprimand

rimu'overe vt to remove; (*destituire*) to dismiss

Rinasci'mento [rinaʃʃi'mento] sm **il ~** the Renaissance

ri'nascita [ri'naʃʃita] sf rebirth, revival

rinca'rare vt to increase the price of ▷ vi to go up, become more expensive

rinca'sare vi to go home

rinchi'udere [rin'kjudere] vt to shut (o lock) up; **rinchiudersi** vpr **rinchiudersi in** to shut o.s. up in; **rinchiudersi in se stesso** to withdraw into o.s.

rin'correre vt to chase, run after; **rin'corsa** sf short run

rin'crescere [rin'kreʃʃere] vb impers **mi rincresce che/di non poter fare** I'm sorry that/I can't do, I regret that/being unable to do

rinfacci'are [rinfat'tʃare] vt (*fig*): **~ qc a qn** to throw sth in sb's face

rinfor'zare [rinfor'tsare] vt to reinforce, strengthen ▷ vi (*anche*: **rinforzarsi**) to grow stronger

rinfres'care vt (*atmosfera, temperatura*) to cool (down); (*abito, pareti*) to freshen up ▷ vi (*tempo*) to grow cooler; **rinfrescarsi** vpr (*ristorarsi*) to refresh o.s.; (*lavarsi*) to freshen up; **rin'fresco, -schi** sm (*festa*) party; **rinfreschi** smpl refreshments

rin'fusa sf **alla ~** in confusion, higgledy-piggledy

ringhi'are [rin'gjare] vi to growl, snarl

ringhi'era [rin'gjɛra] sf railing; (*delle scale*)

banister(s) (*pl*)

ringiova'nire [rindʒova'nire] vt (*vestito, acconciatura ecc*): **~ qn** to make sb look younger; (: *vacanze ecc*) to rejuvenate ▷ vi (*anche*: **ringiovanirsi**) to become (o look) younger

ringrazia'mento [ringrattsja'mento] sm thanks pl

ringrazi'are [ringrat'tsjare] vt to thank; **~ qn di qc** to thank sb for sth

rinne'gare vt (*fede*) to renounce; (*figlio*) to disown, repudiate

rinnova'mento sm renewal; (*economico*) revival

rinno'vare vt to renew; (*ripetere*) to repeat, renew

rinoce'ronte [rinotʃe'ronte] sm rhinoceros

rino'mato, -a ag renowned, celebrated

rintracci'are [rintrat'tʃare] vt to track down

rintro'nare vi to boom, roar ▷ vt (*assordare*) to deafen; (*stordire*) to stun

rinunci'are [rinun'tʃare] vi **~ a** to give up, renounce; **~ a fare qc** to give up doing sth

rinvi'are vt (*rimandare indietro*) to send back, return; (*differire*): **~ qc (a)** to postpone sth o put sth off (till); to adjourn sth (till); (*fare un rimando*): **~ qn a** to refer sb to

rin'vio, -'vii sm (*rimando*) return; (*differimento*) postponement; (: *di seduta*) adjournment; (*in un testo*) cross-reference; **rinvio a giudizio** (*Dir*) indictment

riò ecc vb vedi **riavere**

ri'one sm district, quarter

riordi'nare vt (*rimettere in ordine*) to tidy; (*riorganizzare*) to reorganize

riorganiz'zare [riorganid'dzare] vt to reorganize

ripa'gare vt to repay

ripa'rare vt (*proteggere*) to protect, defend; (*correggere*: *male, torto*) to make up for; (: *errore*) to put right; (*aggiustare*) to repair ▷ vi (*mettere rimedio*): **~ a** to make up for; **ripararsi** vpr (*rifugiarsi*) to take refuge o shelter; **dove lo posso far ~?** where can I get this repaired?; **riparazi'one** sf (*di un torto*) reparation; (*di guasto, scarpe*) repairing no pl; repair; (*risarcimento*) compensation

ri'paro sm (*protezione*) shelter, protection; (*rimedio*) remedy

ripar'tire vt (*dividere*) to divide up; (*distribuire*) to share out ▷ vi to set off again; to leave again

ripas'sare vi to come (o go) back ▷ vt (*scritto, lezione*) to go over (again)

ripen'sare vi to think; (*cambiare pensiero*)

to change one's mind; (*tornare col pensiero*): **~ a** to recall

ripercu'otersi *vpr* **~ su** (*fig*) to have repercussions on

ripercussi'one *sf* (*fig*): **avere una ~ o delle ripercussioni su** to have repercussions on

ripes'care *vt* (*pesce*) to catch again; (*persona, cosa*) to fish out; (*fig: ritrovare*) to dig out

ri'petere *vt* to repeat; (*ripassare*) to go over; **può ~ per favore?** can you repeat that please?; **ripetizi'one** *sf* repetition; (*di lezione*) revision; **ripetizioni** *sfpl* (*Ins*) private tutoring *o* coaching *sg*

ripi'ano *sm* (*di mobile*) shelf

ri'picca *sf* **per ~** out of spite

'ripido, -a *ag* steep

ripie'gare *vt* to refold; (*piegare più volte*) to fold (up) ▷ *vi* (*Mil*) to retreat, fall back; (*fig: accontentarsi*): **~ su** to make do with

ripi'eno, -a *ag* full; (*Cuc*) stuffed; (*: panino*) filled ▷ *sm* (*Cuc*) stuffing

ri'pone, ri'pongo *ecc vb vedi* **riporre**

ri'porre *vt* (*porre al suo posto*) to put back, replace; (*mettere via*) to put away; (*fiducia, speranza*): **~ qc in qn** to place *o* put sth in sb

ripor'tare *vt* (*portare indietro*) to bring (*o* take) back; (*riferire*) to report; (*citare*) to quote; (*vittoria*) to gain; (*successo*) to have; (*Mat*) to carry; **riportarsi a** (*anche fig*) to go back to; (*riferirsi a*) to refer to; **~ danni** to suffer damage

ripo'sare *vt, vi* to rest; **riposarsi** *vpr* to rest

ri'posi *ecc vb vedi* **riporre**

ri'poso *sm* rest; (*Mil*): **~!** at ease!; **a ~** (*in pensione*) retired; **giorno di ~** day of rest

ripos'tiglio [ripos'tiλλo] *sm* lumber-room

ri'prendere *vt* (*prigioniero, fortezza*) to recapture; (*prendere indietro*) to take back; (*ricominciare: lavoro*) to resume; (*andare a prendere*) to fetch, come back for; (*riassumere: impiegati*) to take on again, re-employ; (*rimproverare*) to tell off; (*restringere: abito*) to take in; (*Cinema*) to shoot; **riprendersi** *vpr* to recover; (*correggersi*) to correct o.s.; **ri'presa** *sf* recapture; resumption; (*economica, da malattia, emozione*) recovery; (*Aut*) acceleration *no pl*; (*Teatro, Cinema*) rerun; (*Cinema: presa*) shooting *no pl*; shot; (*Sport*) second half; (*: Pugilato*) round; **a più riprese** on several occasions, several times; **ripresa cinematografica** shot

ripristi'nare *vt* to restore

ripro'durre *vt* to reproduce; **riprodursi** *vpr* (*Biol*) to reproduce; (*riformarsi*) to form again

ripro'vare *vt* (*provare di nuovo: gen*) to try

again; (*vestito*) to try on again; (*: sensazione*) to experience again ▷ *vi* (*tentare*): **~ (a fare qc)** to try (to do sth) again; **riproverò più tardi** I'll try again later

ripudi'are *vt* to repudiate, disown

ripu'gnante [ripuɲ'ɲante] *ag* disgusting, repulsive

ri'quadro *sm* square; (*Archit*) panel

ri'saia *sf* paddy field

risa'lire *vi* (*ritornare in su*) to go back up; **~ a** (*ritornare con la mente*) to go back to; (*datare da*) to date back to, go back to

risal'tare *vi* (*fig: distinguersi*) to stand out; (*Archit*) to project, jut out

risa'puto, -a *ag* **è ~ che ...** everyone knows that ..., it is common knowledge that ...

risarci'mento [risartʃi'mento] *sm* **~ (di)** compensation (for); **risarcimento danni** damages

risar'cire [risar'tʃire] *vt* (*cose*) to pay compensation for; (*persona*): **~ qn di qc** to compensate sb for sth

ri'sata *sf* laugh

riscalda'mento *sm* heating; **riscaldamento centrale** central heating

riscal'dare *vt* (*scaldare*) to heat; (*: mani, persona*) to warm; (*minestra*) to reheat; **riscaldarsi** *vpr* to warm up

ris'catto *sm* ransom; redemption

rischia'rare *vt* (*illuminare*) to light up; (*colore*) to make lighter; **rischiararsi** *vpr* (*tempo*) to clear up; (*cielo*) to clear; (*fig: volto*) to brighten up; **rischiararsi la voce** to clear one's throat

rischi'are [ris'kjare] *vt* to risk ▷ *vi* **~ di fare qc** to run the risk of doing sth

'rischio ['riskjo] *sm* risk; **rischi'oso, -a** *ag* risky, dangerous

riscia'cquare [riʃʃa'kware] *vt* to rinse

riscon'trare *vt* (*rilevare*) to find

ris'cuotere *vt* (*ritirare: somma*) to collect; (*: stipendio*) to draw, collect; (*assegno*) to cash; (*fig: successo ecc*) to win, earn

'rise *ecc vb vedi* **ridere**

risenti'mento *sm* resentment

risen'tire *vt* to hear again; (*provare*) to feel ▷ *vi* **~ di** to feel (*o* show) the effects of; **risentirsi** *vpr* **risentirsi di** *o* **per** to take offence at, resent; **risen'tito, -a** *ag* resentful

ri'serbo *sm* reserve

ri'serva *sf* reserve; (*di caccia, pesca*) preserve; (*restrizione, di indigeni*) reservation; **di ~** (*provviste ecc*) in reserve

riser'vare *vt* (*tenere in serbo*) to keep, put aside; (*prenotare*) to book, reserve; **ho riservato un tavolo a nome...** I booked a table in the name of ...; **riser'vato,**

-a ag (prenotato: fig: persona) reserved; (confidenziale) confidential

'risi ecc vb vedi **ridere**

risi'edere vi ~ a o in to reside in

'risma sf (di carta) ream; (fig) kind, sort

'riso (pl(f) **risa**) (: il ridere) sm **il ~** laughter; (pianta) rice ▷ pp di **ridere**

riso'lino sm snigger

ri'solsi ecc vb vedi **risolvere**

ri'solto, -a pp di **risolvere**

riso'luto, -a ag determined, resolute

risoluzi'one [risolut'tsjone] sf solving no pl; (Mat) solution; (decisione, di schermo, immagine) resolution

ri'solvere vt (difficoltà, controversia) to resolve; (problema) to solve; (decidere): ~ **di fare** to resolve to do; **risolversi** vpr (decidersi): **risolversi a fare** to make up one's mind to do; (andare a finire): **risolversi in** to end up, turn out; **risolversi in nulla** to come to nothing

riso'nanza [riso'nantsa] sf resonance; **aver vasta ~** (fig: fatto ecc) to be known far and wide

ri'sorgere [ri'sordʒere] vi to rise again; **risorgi'mento** sm revival; **il Risorgimento** (Storia) the Risorgimento

◉ **RISORGIMENTO**

◉
◉ The **Risorgimento** was the political
◉ movement which led to the
◉ proclamation of the Kingdom of Italy
◉ in 1861, and eventually to unification
◉ in 1871.

ri'sorsa sf expedient, resort; **risorse umane** human resources

ri'sorsi ecc vb vedi **risorgere**

ri'sotto sm (Cuc) risotto

risparmi'are vt to save; (non uccidere) to spare ▷ vi to save; ~ **qc a qn** to spare sb sth

ris'parmio sm saving no pl; (denaro) savings pl; **risparmi** smpl (denaro) savings

rispec'chiare [rispek'kjare] vt to reflect

rispet'tabile ag respectable

rispet'tare vt to respect; **farsi ~** to command respect

rispet'tivo, -a ag respective

ris'petto sm respect; **rispetti** smpl (saluti) respects, regards; ~ **a** (in paragone a) compared to; (in relazione a) as regards, as for

ris'pondere vi to answer, reply; (freni) to respond; ~ **a** (domanda) to answer, reply to; (persona) to answer; (invito) to reply to; (provocazione: veicolo, apparecchio) to respond to; (corrispondere a) to correspond to; (: speranze, bisogno) to answer; ~ **di** to

answer for; **ris'posta** sf answer, reply; **in risposta a** in reply to

'rissa sf brawl

ris'tampa sf reprinting no pl; reprint

risto'rante sm restaurant; **mi può consigliare un buon ~?** can you recommend a good restaurant?

ris'tretto, -a pp di **restringere** ▷ ag (racchiuso) enclosed, hemmed in; (angusto) narrow; (limitato): ~ **(a)** restricted o limited (to); (Cuc: brodo) thick; (: caffè) extra strong

ristruttu'rare vt (azienda) to reorganize; (edificio) to restore; (appartamento) to alter; (crema, balsamo) to repair

risucchi'are [risuk'kjare] vt to suck in

risul'tare vi (dimostrarsi) to prove (to be), turn out (to be); (riuscire): ~ **vincitore** to emerge as the winner; ~ **da** (provenire) to result from, be the result of; **mi risulta che ...** I understand that ...; **non mi risulta** not as far as I know; **risul'tato** sm result

risuo'nare vi (rimbombare) to resound

risurrezi'one [risurret'tsjone] sf (Rel) resurrection

risusci'tare [risuʃʃi'tare] vt to resuscitate, restore to life; (fig) to revive, bring back ▷ vi to rise (from the dead)

ris'veglio [riz've\ʎʎo] sm waking up; (fig) revival

ris'volto sm (di giacca) lapel; (di pantaloni) turn-up; (di manica) cuff; (di tasca) flap; (di libro) inside flap; (fig) implication

ritagli'are [rita\ʎ'\ʎare] vt (tagliar via) to cut out

ritar'dare vi (persona, treno) to be late; (orologio) to be slow ▷ vt (rallentare) to slow down; (impedire) to delay, hold up; (differire) to postpone, delay

ri'tardo sm delay; (di persona aspettata) lateness no pl; (fig: mentale) backwardness; **in ~** late; **il volo ha due ore di ~** the flight is two hours late; **scusi il ~** sorry I'm late

ri'tegno [ri'teɲɲo] sm restraint

rite'nere vt (trattenere) to hold back; (: somma) to deduct; (giudicare) to consider, believe

ri'tengo, ri'tenni ecc vb vedi **ritenere**

riterrò, ritiene ecc vb vedi **ritenere**

riti'rare vt to withdraw; (Pol: richiamare) to recall; (andare a prendere: pacco ecc) to collect, pick up; **ritirarsi** vpr to withdraw; (da un'attività) to retire; (stoffa) to shrink; (marea) to recede

'ritmo sm rhythm; (fig) rate; (: della vita) pace, tempo

'rito sm rite; **di ~** usual, customary

ritoc'care vt (disegno, fotografia) to touch up; (testo) to alter

ritor'nare vi to return, go (o come)

back, to get back; (*ripresentarsi*) to recur; (*ridiventare*): ~ **ricco** to become rich again ▷ vt (*restituire*) to return, give back; **quando ritorniamo?** when do we get back?

ritor'nello sm refrain

ri'torno sm return; **essere di ~** to be back; **avere un ~ di fiamma** (*Aut*) to backfire; (*fig: persona*) to be back in love again

ri'trarre vt (*trarre indietro, via*) to withdraw; (*distogliere: sguardo*) to turn away; (*rappresentare*) to portray, depict; (*ricavare*) to get, obtain

ritrat'tare vt (*disdire*) to retract, take back; (*trattare nuovamente*) to deal with again

ri'tratto, -a pp di **ritrarre** ▷ sm portrait

ritro'vare vt to find; (*salute*) to regain; (*persona*) to find; to meet again; **ritrovarsi** vpr (*essere, capitare*) to find o.s.; (*raccapezzarsi*) to find one's way; (*con senso reciproco*) to meet (again)

'ritto, -a ag (*in piedi*) standing, on one's feet; (*levato in alto*) erect, raised; (: *capelli*) standing on end; (*posto verticalmente*) upright

ritu'ale ag, sm ritual

riuni'one sf (*adunanza*) meeting; (*riconciliazione*) reunion

riu'nire vt (*ricongiungere*) to join (together); (*riconciliare*) to reunite, bring together (again); **riunirsi** vpr (*adunarsi*) to meet; (*tornare insieme*) to be reunited

riu'scire [riuʃ'ʃire] vi (*uscire di nuovo*) to go out again, go back out; (*aver esito: fatti, azioni*) to go, turn out; (*aver successo*) to succeed, be successful; (*essere, apparire*) to be, prove; (*raggiungere il fine*) to manage, succeed; ~ **a fare qc** to manage to do o succeed in doing o to be able to do sth

'riva sf (*di fiume*) bank; (*di lago, mare*) shore

ri'vale sm/f rival; **rivalità** sf rivalry

rivalu'tare vt (*Econ*) to revalue

rive'dere vt to see again; (*ripassare*) to revise; (*verificare*) to check

rivedrò ecc vb vedi **rivedere**

rive'lare vt to reveal; (*divulgare*) to reveal, disclose; (*dare indizio*) to reveal, show; **rivelarsi** vpr (*manifestarsi*) to be revealed; **rivelarsi onesto** ecc to prove to be honest ecc; **rivelazi'one** sf revelation

rivendi'care vt to claim, demand

rivendi'tore, -'trice sm/f retailer; **rivenditore autorizzato** (*Comm*) authorized dealer

ri'verbero sm (*di luce, calore*) reflection; (*di suono*) reverberation

rivesti'mento sm covering; coating

rives'tire vt to dress again; (*ricoprire*) to cover; to coat; (*fig: carica*) to hold

ri'vidi ecc vb vedi **rivedere**

ri'vincita [ri'vintʃita] sf (*Sport*) return match; (*fig*) revenge

ri'vista sf review; (*periodico*) magazine, review; (*Teatro*) revue; variety show

ri'volgere [ri'vɔldʒere] vt (*attenzione, sguardo*) to turn, direct; (*parole*) to address; **rivolgersi** vpr to turn round; (*fig: dirigersi per informazioni*) **rivolgersi a** to go and see, go and speak to; (: *ufficio*) to enquire at

ri'volsi ecc vb vedi **rivolgere**

ri'volta sf revolt, rebellion

rivol'tella sf revolver

rivoluzio'nare [rivoluttsjo'nare] vt to revolutionize

rivoluzio'nario, -a [rivoluttsjo'narjo] ag, sm/f revolutionary

rivoluzi'one [rivolut'tsjone] sf revolution

riz'zare [rit'tsare] vt to raise, erect; **rizzarsi** vpr to stand up; (*capelli*) to stand on end

'roba sf stuff, things pl; (*possessi, beni*) belongings pl, things pl, possessions pl; ~ **da mangiare** things pl to eat, food; ~ **da matti** sheer madness o lunacy

'robot sm inv robot

ro'busto, -a ag robust, sturdy; (*solido: catena*) strong

roc'chetto [rok'ketto] sm reel, spool

'roccia, -ce ['rɔttʃa] sf rock; **fare ~** (*Sport*) to go rock climbing

'roco, -a, chi, che ag hoarse

ro'daggio [ro'daddʒo] sm running (*BRIT*) o breaking (*US*) in; **in ~** running (*BRIT*) o breaking (*US*) in

rodi'tore sm (*Zool*) rodent

rodo'dendro sm rhododendron

ro'gnone [roɲ'ɲone] sm (*Cuc*) kidney

'rogo, -ghi sm (*per cadaveri*) (funeral) pyre; (*supplizio*): **il ~** the stake

rol'lio sm roll(ing)

'Roma sf Rome

Roma'nia sf **la ~** Romania

ro'manico, -a, -ci, -che ag Romanesque

ro'mano, -a ag, sm/f Roman

ro'mantico, -a, -ci, -che ag romantic

romanzi'ere [roman'dzjere] sm novelist

ro'manzo, -a [ro'mandzo] ag (*Ling*) romance cpd ▷ sm novel; **romanzo d'appendice** serial (story); **romanzo giallo/poliziesco** detective story; **romanzo rosa** romantic novel

'rombo sm rumble, thunder, roar; (*Mat*) rhombus; (*Zool*) turbot; brill

'rompere vt to break; (*fidanzamento*) to break off ▷ vi to break; **rompersi** vpr to break; **mi rompe le scatole** (*fam*) he (o she) is a pain in the neck; **rompersi un braccio** to break an arm; **mi si è rotta**

la macchina my car has broken down;
rompis'catole (fam) sm/f inv pest, pain
in the neck

'rondine sf (Zool) swallow

ron'zare [ron'dzare] vi to buzz, hum

ron'zio [ron'dzio] sm buzzing

'rosa sf rose ▷ ag inv, sm pink; **ro'sato, -a**
ag pink, rosy ▷ sm (vino) rosé (wine)

rosicchi'are [rosik'kjare] vt to gnaw (at);
(mangiucchiare) to nibble (at)

rosma'rino sm rosemary

roso'lare vt (Cuc) to brown

roso'lia sf (Med) German measles sg,
rubella

ro'sone sm rosette; (vetrata) rose window

'rospo sm (Zool) toad

ros'setto sm (per labbra) lipstick

'rosso, -a ag, sm, sm/f red; **il mar R~** the
Red Sea; **rosso d'uovo** egg yolk

rosticce'ria [rostitt ʃe'ria] sf shop selling
roast meat and other cooked food

ro'taia sf rut, track; (Ferr) rail

ro'tella sf small wheel; (di mobile) castor

roto'lare vt, vi to roll; **rotolarsi** vpr to roll
(about)

'rotolo sm roll; **andare a rotoli** (fig) to go
to rack and ruin

ro'tondo, -a ag round

'rotta sf (Aer, Naut) course, route; (Mil)
rout; **a ~ di collo** at breakneck speed;
essere in ~ con qn to be on bad terms
with sb

rotta'mare vt to scrap

rottamazione [rottama'tsjone] sf (come
incentivo) the scrapping of old vehicles in
return for incentives

rot'tame sm fragment, scrap, broken bit;
rottami smpl (di nave, aereo ecc) wreckage
sg

'rotto, -a pp di **rompere** ▷ ag broken;
(calzoni) torn, split; **per il ~ della cuffia** by
the skin of one's teeth

rot'tura sf breaking no pl; break; breaking
off; (Med) fracture, break

rou'lotte [ru'lɔt] sf caravan

ro'vente ag red-hot

'rovere sm oak

ro'vescia [ro'veʃʃa] sf **alla ~** upside-down;
inside-out; **oggi mi va tutto alla ~**
everything is going wrong (for me) today

rovesci'are [roveʃʃare] vt (versare in
giù) to pour; (: accidentalmente) to spill;
(capovolgere) to turn upside down; (gettare
a terra) to knock down; (: fig: governo)
to overthrow; (piegare all'indietro: testa)
to throw back; **rovesciarsi** vpr (sedia,
macchina) to overturn; (barca) to capsize;
(liquido) to spill; (fig: situazione) to be
reversed

ro'vescio, -sci [ro'veʃʃo] sm other side,
wrong side; (della mano) back; (di moneta)
reverse; (pioggia) sudden downpour; (fig)
setback; (Maglia: anche: **punto ~**) purl
(stitch); (Tennis) backhand (stroke); **a ~**
upside-down; inside-out; **capire qc a ~** to
misunderstand sth

ro'vina sf ruin; **andare in ~** (andare a pezzi)
to collapse; (fig) to go to rack and ruin;
rovine sfpl (ruderi) ruins; **mandare in ~**
to ruin

rovi'nare vi to collapse, fall down ▷ vt
(danneggiare: fig) to ruin; **rovinarsi** vpr
(persona) to ruin o.s.; (oggetto, vestito) to
be ruined

rovis'tare vt (casa) to ransack; (tasche) to
rummage in (o through)

'rovo sm (Bot) blackberry bush, bramble
bush

'rozzo, -a ['roddzo] ag rough, coarse

ru'bare vt to steal; **~ qc a qn** to steal sth
from sb; **mi hanno rubato il portafoglio**
my wallet has been stolen

rubi'netto sm tap, faucet (us)

ru'bino sm ruby

ru'brica, -che sf (Stampa) column;
(quadernetto) index book; address book;
rubrica d'indirizzi address book; **rubrica
telefonica** list of telephone numbers

'rudere sm (rovina) ruins pl

rudimen'tale ag rudimentary, basic

rudi'menti smpl rudiments; basic
principles; basic knowledge sg

ruffi'ano sm pimp

'ruga, -ghe sf wrinkle

'ruggine ['ruddʒine] sf rust

rug'gire [rud'dʒire] vi to roar

rugi'ada [ru'dʒada] sf dew

ru'goso, -a ag wrinkled

rul'lino sm (Fot) spool; (: pellicola) film;
vorrei un ~ da 36 pose I'd like a 36-
exposure film

'rullo sm (di tamburi) roll; (arnese cilindrico,
Tip) roller; **rullo compressore** steam
roller; **rullo di pellicola** roll of film

rum sm rum

ru'meno, -a ag, sm/f, sm Romanian

rumi'nare vt (Zool) to ruminate

ru'more sm **un ~** a noise, a sound; **il ~**
noise; **non riesco a dormire a causa del
~** I can't sleep for the noise; **rumo'roso,
-a** ag noisy

Attenzione! In inglese esiste la
parola rumour, che però significa voce
nel senso di diceria.

ru'olo sm (Teatro: fig) role, part; (elenco)
roll, register, list; **di ~** permanent, on the
permanent staff

ru'ota sf wheel; **ruota anteriore/**

posteriore front/back wheel; **ruota di scorta** spare wheel

ruo'tare vt, vi to rotate

'rupe sf cliff

'ruppi ecc vb vedi **rompere**

ru'rale ag rural, country cpd

ru'scello [ruʃʃɛllo] sm stream

'ruspa sf excavator

rus'sare vi to snore

'Russia sf **la ~** Russia; **'russo, -a** ag, sm/f, sm Russian

'rustico, -a, -ci, -che ag rustic; (fig) rough, unrefined

rut'tare vi to belch; **'rutto** sm belch

'ruvido, -a ag rough, coarse

S

S. abbr (= sud) S; (= santo) St

sa vb vedi **sapere**

'sabato sm Saturday; **di** o **il ~** on Saturdays

'sabbia sf sand; **sabbie mobili** quicksand(s); **sabbi'oso, -a** ag sandy

'sacca, -che sf bag; (bisaccia) haversack; **sacca da viaggio** travelling bag

sacca'rina sf saccharin(e)

saccheggi'are [sakked'dʒare] vt to sack, plunder

sac'chetto [sak'ketto] sm (small) bag, (small) sack; **sacchetto di carta/di plastica** paper/plastic bag

'sacco, -chi sm bag; (per carbone ecc) sack; (Anat, Biol) sac; (tela) sacking; (saccheggio) sack(ing); (fig: grande quantità): **un ~ di** lots of, heaps of; **sacco a pelo** sleeping bag; **sacco per i rifiuti** bin bag

sacer'dote [satʃer'dɔte] sm priest

sacrifi'care vt to sacrifice; **sacrificarsi** vpr to sacrifice o.s.; (privarsi di qc) to make sacrifices

sacri'ficio [sakri'fitʃo] sm sacrifice

'sacro, -a ag sacred

'sadico, -a, -ci, -che ag sadistic ▷ sm/f sadist

sa'etta sf arrow; (fulmine) thunderbolt; flash of lightning

sa'fari sm inv safari

sag'gezza [sad'dʒettsa] sf wisdom

'saggio, -a, -gi, -ge ['saddʒo] *ag* wise
▷ *sm* (*persona*) sage; (*esperimento*) test; (*fig: prova*) proof; (*campione*) sample; (*scritto*) essay

Sagit'tario [sadʒit'tarjo] *sm* Sagittarius

'sagoma *sf* (*profilo*) outline, profile; (*forma*) form, shape; (*Tecn*) template; (*bersaglio*) target; (*fig: persona*) character

'sagra *sf* festival

sagres'tano *sm* sacristan; sexton

sagres'tia *sf* sacristy

Sa'hara [sa'ara] *sm* **il (deserto del) ~** the Sahara (Desert)

'sai *vb vedi* **sapere**

'sala *sf* hall; (*stanza*) room; (*Cinema: Yyy: di proiezione*) cinema; **sala d'aspetto** waiting room; **sala da ballo** ballroom; **sala giochi** amusement arcade; **sala operatoria** operating theatre; **sala da pranzo** dining room; **sala per concerti** concert hall

sa'lame *sm* salami *no pl*, salami sausage

sala'moia *sf* (*Cuc*) brine

sa'lato, -a *ag* (*sapore*) salty; (*Cuc*) salted, salt *cpd*; (*fig: prezzo*) steep, stiff

sal'dare *vt* (*congiungere*) to join, bind; (*parti metalliche*) to solder; (: *con saldatura autogena*) to weld; (*conto*) to settle, pay

'saldo, -a *ag* (*resistente, forte*) strong, firm; (*fermo*) firm, steady, stable; (*fig*) firm, steadfast ▷ *sm* (*svendita*) sale; (*di conto*) settlement; (*Econ*) balance; **saldi** *smpl* (*Comm*) sales; **essere ~ nella propria fede** (*fig*) to stick to one's guns

'sale *sm* salt; (*fig*): **ha poco ~ in zucca** he doesn't have much sense; **sale fino** table salt; **sale grosso** cooking salt

'salgo *ecc vb vedi* **salire**

'salice ['salitʃe] *sm* willow; **salice piangente** weeping willow

sali'ente *ag* (*fig*) salient, main

sali'era *sf* salt cellar

sa'lire *vi* to go (*o come*) up; (*aereo ecc*) to climb, go up; (*passeggero*) to get on; (*sentiero, prezzi, livello*) to go up, rise ▷ *vt* (*scale, gradini*) to go (*o come*) up; **~ su** to climb (up); **~ sul treno/sull'autobus** to board the train/the bus; **~ in macchina** to get into the car; **sa'lita** *sf* climb, ascent; (*erta*) hill, slope; **in salita** *ag, av* uphill

sa'liva *sf* saliva

'salma *sf* corpse

'salmo *sm* psalm

sal'mone *sm* salmon

sa'lone *sm* (*stanza*) sitting room, lounge; (*in albergo*) lounge; (*su nave*) lounge, saloon; (*mostra*) show, exhibition; **salone di bellezza** beauty salon

sa'lotto *sm* lounge, sitting room; (*mobilio*) lounge suite

sal'pare *vi* (*Naut*) to set sail; (*anche*: **~ l'ancora**) to weigh anchor

'salsa *sf* (*Cuc*) sauce; **salsa di pomodoro** tomato sauce

sal'siccia, -ce [sal'sittʃa] *sf* pork sausage

sal'tare *vi* to jump, leap; (*esplodere*) to blow up, explode; (: *valvola*) to blow; (*venir via*) to pop off; (*non aver luogo: corso ecc*) to be cancelled ▷ *vt* to jump (over), leap (over); (*fig: pranzo, capitolo*) to skip, miss (out); (*Cuc*) to sauté; **far ~** to blow up; to burst open; **~ fuori** (*fig: apparire all'improvviso*) to turn up

saltel'lare *vi* to skip; to hop

'salto *sm* jump; (*Sport*) jumping; **fare un ~** to jump, leap; **fare un ~ da qn** to pop over to sb's (place); **salto in alto/lungo** high/long jump; **salto con l'asta** pole vaulting; **salto mortale** somersault

saltu'ario, -a *ag* occasional, irregular

sa'lubre *ag* healthy, salubrious

salume'ria *sf* delicatessen

sa'lumi *smpl* salted pork meats

salu'tare *ag* healthy; (*fig*) salutary, beneficial ▷ *vt* (*incontrandosi*) to greet; (*congedandosi*) to say goodbye to; (*Mil*) to salute

sa'lute *sf* health; **~!** (*a chi starnutisce*) bless you!; (*nei brindisi*) cheers!; **bere alla ~ di qn** to drink (to) sb's health

sa'luto *sm* (*gesto*) wave; (*parola*) greeting; (*Mil*) salute

salvada'naio *sm* money box, piggy bank

salva'gente [salva'dʒɛnte] *sm* (*Naut*) lifebuoy; (*ciambella*) life belt; (*giubbotto*) life jacket; (*stradale*) traffic island

salvaguar'dare *vt* to safeguard

sal'vare *vt* to save; (*trarre da un pericolo*) to rescue; (*proteggere*) to protect; **salvarsi** *vpr* to save o.s.; to escape; **salvaschermo** [salvas'kermo] *sm* (*Inform*) screen saver; **salvaslip** [salva'zlip] *sm inv* panty liner; **salva'taggio** *sm* rescue

'salve (*fam*) *escl* hi!

'salvia *sf* (*Bot*) sage

salvi'etta *sf* napkin; **salvietta umidificata** baby wipe

'salvo, -a *ag* safe, unhurt, unharmed; (*fuori pericolo*) safe, out of danger ▷ *sm* **in ~** safe ▷ *prep* (*eccetto*) except; **mettere qc in ~** to put sth in a safe place; **~ che** (*a meno che*) unless; (*eccetto che*) except (that); **~ imprevisti** barring accidents

sam'buco *sm* elder (tree)

'sandalo *sm* (*Bot*) sandalwood; (*calzatura*) sandal

'sangue *sm* blood; **farsi cattivo ~** to fret, get in a state; **sangue freddo** (*fig*) sang-froid, calm; **a ~ freddo** in cold blood;

sangui'nare vi to bleed

sanità sf health; (salubrità) healthiness; **Ministero della S~** Department of Health; **sanità mentale** sanity

sani'tario, -a ag health cpd; (condizioni) sanitary ▷ sm (Amm) doctor; **sanitari** smpl (impianti) bathroom o sanitary fittings

'**sanno** vb vedi **sapere**

'**sano, -a** ag healthy; (denti, costituzione) healthy, sound; (integro) whole, unbroken; (fig: politica, consigli) sound; **~ di mente** sane; **di sana pianta** completely, entirely; **~ e salvo** safe and sound

'**santo, -a** ag holy; (fig) saintly; (seguito da nome proprio) saint ▷ sm/f saint; **la Santa Sede** the Holy See

santu'ario sm sanctuary

sanzi'one [san'tsjone] sf sanction; (penale, civile) sanction, penalty

sa'pere vt to know; (essere capace di): **so nuotare** I know how to swim, I can swim ▷ vi **~ di** (aver sapore) to taste of; (aver odore) to smell of ▷ sm knowledge; **far ~ qc a qn** to inform sb about sth, let sb know sth; **mi sa che non sia vero** I don't think that's true; **non lo so** I don't know; **non so l'inglese** I don't speak English; **sa dove posso…?** do you know where I can …?

sa'pone sm soap; **sapone da bucato** washing soap

sa'pore sm taste, flavour; **sapo'rito, -a** ag tasty

sappi'amo vb vedi **sapere**

saprò ecc vb vedi **sapere**

sarà ecc vb vedi **essere**

saraci'nesca [saratʃi'neska] sf (serranda) rolling shutter

sar'castico, -a, ci, che ag sarcastic

Sar'degna [sar'deɲɲa] sf **la ~** Sardinia

sar'dina sf sardine

sa'rei ecc vb vedi **essere**

SARS sigla f (Med: = severe acute respiratory syndrome) SARS

'**sarta** sf vedi **sarto**

'**sarto, -a** sm/f tailor/dressmaker

'**sasso** sm stone; (ciottolo) pebble; (masso) rock

sas'sofono sm saxophone

sas'soso, -a ag stony; pebbly

'**Satana** sm Satan

sa'tellite sm, ag satellite

'**satira** sf satire

'**sauna** sf sauna

sazi'are [sat'tsjare] vt to satisfy, satiate; **saziarsi** vpr **saziarsi (di)** to eat one's fill (of); (fig): **saziarsi di** to grow tired o weary of

'**sazio, -a** ['sattsjo] ag **~ (di)** sated (with), full (of); (fig: stufo) fed up (with), sick (of);

sono ~ I'm full (up)

sba'dato, -a ag careless, inattentive

sbadigli'are [zbadiʎ'ʎare] vi to yawn; **sba'diglio** sm yawn

sbagli'are [zbaʎ'ʎare] vt to make a mistake in, get wrong ▷ vi to make a mistake, be mistaken, be wrong; (operare in modo non giusto) to err; **sbagliarsi** vpr to make a mistake, be mistaken, be wrong; **~ strada/la mira** to take the wrong road/ miss one's aim

sbagli'ato, -a [zbaʎ'ʎato] ag (gen) wrong; (compito) full of mistakes; (conclusione) erroneous

'**sbaglio** sm mistake, error; (morale) error; **fare uno ~** to make a mistake

sbalor'dire vt to stun, amaze ▷ vi to be stunned, be amazed

sbal'zare [zbal'tsare] vt to throw, hurl ▷ vi (balzare) to bounce; (saltare) to leap, bound

sban'dare vi (Naut) to list; (Aer) to bank; (Aut) to skid

sba'raglio [zba'raʎʎo] sm rout; defeat; **gettarsi allo ~** to risk everything

sbaraz'zarsi [zbarat'tsarsi] vpr **~ di** to get rid of, rid o.s. of

sbar'care vt (passeggeri) to disembark; (merci) to unload ▷ vi to disembark

'**sbarra** sf bar; (di passaggio a livello) barrier; (Dir): **presentarsi alla ~** to appear before the court

sbar'rare vt (strada ecc) to block, bar; (assegno) to cross; **~ il passo** to bar the way; **~ gli occhi** to open one's eyes wide

'**sbattere** vt (porta) to slam, bang; (tappeti, ali, Cuc) to beat; (urtare) to knock, hit ▷ vi (porta, finestra) to bang; (agitarsi: ali, vele ecc) to flap; **me ne sbatto!** (fam) I don't give a damn!

sba'vare vi to dribble; (colore) to smear, smudge

'**sberla** sf slap

sbia'dire vi, vt to fade; **sbia'dito, -a** ag faded; (fig) colourless, dull

sbian'care vt to whiten; (tessuto) to bleach ▷ vi (impallidire) to grow pale o white

sbirci'ata [zbir'tʃata] sf **dare una ~ a qc** to glance at sth, have a look at sth

sbloc'care vt to unblock, free; (freno) to release; (prezzi, affitti) to decontrol; **sbloccarsi** vpr (gen) to become unblocked; (passaggio, strada) to clear, become unblocked

sboc'care vi **~ in** (fiume) to flow into; (strada) to lead into; (persona) to come (out) into; (fig: concludersi) to end (up) in

sboc'cato, -a ag (persona) foul-mouthed; (linguaggio) foul

sbocci'are [zbot'tʃare] vi (fiore) to bloom,

open (out)

sbol'lire vi (fig) to cool down, calm down

'sbornia (fam) sf **prendersi una ~** to get plastered

sbor'sare vt (denaro) to pay out

sbot'tare vi **~ in una risata/per la collera** to burst out laughing/explode with anger

sbotto'nare vt to unbutton, undo

sbrai'tare vi to yell, bawl

sbra'nare vt to tear to pieces

sbricio'lare [zbritʃo'lare] vt to crumble; **sbriciolarsi** vpr to crumble

sbri'gare vt to deal with; **sbrigarsi** vpr to hurry (up)

'sbronza ['zbrontsa] (fam) sf (ubriaco): **prendersi una ~** to get plastered

sbron'zarsi [zbron'tsarsi] vpr (fam) to get sozzled

'sbronzo, -a ['zbrontso] (fam) ag plastered

sbruf'fone, -a sm/f boaster

sbu'care vi to come out, emerge; (improvvisamente) to pop out (o up)

sbucci'are [zbut'tʃare] vt (arancia, patata) to peel; (piselli) to shell; **sbucciarsi un ginocchio** to graze one's knee

sbucherò ecc [zbuke'rɔ] vb vedi **sbucare**

sbuf'fare vi (persona, cavallo) to snort; (ansimare) to puff, pant; (treno) to puff

sca'broso, -a ag (fig: difficile) difficult, thorny; (: imbarazzante) embarrassing; (: sconcio) indecent

scacchi smpl (gioco) chess sg; **a ~** (tessuto) check(ed)

scacchi'era [skak'kjɛra] sf chessboard

scacci'are [skat'tʃare] vt to chase away o out, drive away o out

'scaddi ecc vb vedi **scadere**

sca'dente ag shoddy, of poor quality

sca'denza [ska'dɛntsa] sf (di cambiale, contratto) maturity; (di passaporto) expiry date; **a breve/lunga ~** short-/long-term; **data di ~** expiry date

sca'dere vi (contratto ecc) to expire; (debito) to fall due; (valore, forze, peso) to decline, go down

sca'fandro sm (di palombaro) diving suit; (di astronauta) space-suit

scaf'fale sm shelf; (mobile) set of shelves

'scafo sm (Naut, Aer) hull

scagio'nare [skadʒo'nare] vt to exonerate, free from blame

'scaglia ['skaʎʎa] sf (Zool) scale; (scheggia) chip, flake

scagli'are [skaʎ'ʎare] vt (lanciare: anche fig) to hurl, fling; **scagliarsi** (anche: **vr**): **scagliarsi su** o **contro** to hurl o fling o.s. at; (fig) to rail at

'scala sf (a gradini ecc) staircase, stairs pl; (a pioli, di corda) ladder; (Mus, Geo, di colori, valori, fig) scale; (Mus, Geo, di colori, valori, fig) scale; **scale** sfpl (scalinata) stairs; **su vasta ~/~ ridotta** on a large/small scale; **~ mobile (dei salari)** index-linked pay scale; **scala a libretto** stepladder; **scala mobile** escalator; (Econ) sliding scale

⬙ **SCALA**

⬙
Milan's world-famous **la Scala** theatre
⬙ first opened its doors in 1778 with a
⬙ performance of Salieri's opera, "L'Europa
⬙ riconosciuta". It suffered serious
⬙ damage in the bombing of Milan in 1943
⬙ and reopened in 1946 with a concert
⬙ conducted by Toscanini. It also has a
⬙ famous classical dance school.

sca'lare vt (Alpinismo, muro) to climb, scale; (debito) to scale down, reduce

scalda'bagno [skalda'baɲɲo] sm water-heater

scal'dare vt to heat; **scaldarsi** vpr to warm up, heat up; (al fuoco, al sole) to warm o.s.; (fig) to get excited

scal'fire vt to scratch

scali'nata sf staircase

sca'lino sm (anche fig) step; (di scala a pioli) rung

'scalo sm (Naut) slipway; (: porto d'approdo) port of call; (Aer) stopover; **fare ~ (a)** (Naut) to call (at), put in (at); (Aer) to land (at), make a stop (at); **scalo merci** (Ferr) goods (BRIT) o freight yard

scalop'pina sf (Cuc) escalope

scal'pello sm chisel

scal'pore sm noise, row; **far ~** (notizia) to cause a sensation o a stir

'scaltro, -a ag cunning, shrewd

'scalzo, -a ['skaltso] ag barefoot

scambi'are vt to exchange; (confondere): **~ qn/qc per** to take o mistake sb/sth for; **mi hanno scambiato il cappello** they've given me the wrong hat; **scambiarsi** vpr (auguri, confidenze, visite) to exchange; **~ qn/qc per** (confondere) to mistake sth/sb for

'scambio sm exchange; (Ferr) points pl; **fare (uno) ~** to make a swap

scampa'gnata [skampaɲ'ɲata] sf trip to the country

scam'pare vt (salvare) to rescue, save; (evitare: morte, prigione) to escape ▷ vi **~ (a qc)** to survive (sth), escape (sth); **scamparla bella** to have a narrow escape

'scampo sm (salvezza) escape; (Zool) prawn; **cercare ~ nella fuga** to seek safety in flight

'scampolo sm remnant

scanala'tura sf (incavo) channel, groove

scandagli'are [skanda⋋'⋋are] vt (Naut) to sound; (fig) to sound out; to probe

scandaliz'zare [skandalid'dzare] vt to shock, scandalize; **scandalizzarsi** vpr to be shocked

'scandalo sm scandal

Scandi'navia sf **la ~** Scandinavia; **scandi'navo, -a** ag, sm/f Scandinavian

scanner ['skanner] sm inv (Inform) scanner

scansafa'tiche [skansafa'tike] sm/f inv idler, loafer

scan'sare vt (rimuovere) to move (aside), shift; (schivare: schiaffo) to dodge; (sfuggire) to avoid; **scansarsi** vpr to move aside

scan'sia sf shelves pl; (per libri) bookcase

'scanso sm **a ~ di** in order to avoid, as a precaution against

scanti'nato sm basement

scapacci'one [skapat'tʃone] sm clout

scapes'trato, -a ag dissolute

'scapola sf shoulder blade

'scapolo sm bachelor

scappa'mento sm (Aut) exhaust

scap'pare vi (fuggire) to escape; (andare via in fretta) to rush off; **lasciarsi ~ un'occasione** to let an opportunity go by; **~ di prigione** to escape from prison; **~ di mano** (oggetto) to slip out of one's hands; **~ di mente a qn** to slip sb's mind; **mi scappò detto** I let it slip; **scappa'toia** sf way out

scara'beo sm beetle

scarabocchi'are [skarabok'kjare] vt to scribble, scrawl; **scara'bocchio** sm scribble, scrawl

scara'faggio [skara'faddʒo] sm cockroach

scaraman'zia [skaraman'tsia] sf **per ~** for luck

scaraven'tare vt to fling, hurl; **scaraventarsi** vpr to fling o.s.

scarce'rare [skartʃe'rare] vt to release (from prison)

scardi'nare vt **~ una porta** to take a door off its hinges

scari'care vt (merci, camion ecc) to unload; (passeggeri) to set down, put off; (arma) to unload; (: sparare, Elettr) to discharge; (corso d'acqua) to empty, pour; (fig: liberare da un peso) to unburden, relieve; (da Internet) to download; **scaricarsi** vpr (orologio) to run o wind down; (batteria, accumulatore) to go flat o dead; (fig: rilassarsi) to unwind; (: sfogarsi) to let off steam

'scarico, -a, -chi, -che ag unloaded; (orologio) run down; (accumulatore) dead, flat ▷ sm (di merci, materiali) unloading; (di immondizie) dumping, tipping (BRIT); (Tecn: deflusso) draining; (: dispositivo) drain; (Aut) exhaust

scarlat'tina sf scarlet fever

scar'latto, -a ag scarlet

'scarpa sf shoe; **scarpe da ginnastica/ tennis** gym/tennis shoes

scar'pata sf escarpment

scarpi'era sf shoe rack

scar'pone sm boot; **scarponi da montagna** climbing boots; **scarponi da sci** ski-boots

scarseggi'are [skarsed'dʒare] vi to be scarce; **~ di** to be short of, lack

'scarso, -a ag (insufficiente) insufficient, meagre; (povero: annata) poor, lean; (Ins: voto) poor; **~ di** lacking in; **3 chili scarsi** just under 3 kilos, barely 3 kilos

scar'tare vt (pacco) to unwrap; (idea) to reject; (Mil) to declare unfit for military service; (carte da gioco) to discard; (Calcio) to dodge (past) ▷ vi to swerve

'scarto sm (cosa scartata: anche Comm) reject; (di veicolo) swerve; (differenza) gap, difference

scassi'nare vt to break, force

scate'nare vt (fig) to incite, stir up; **scatenarsi** vpr (temporale) to break; (rivolta) to break out; (persona: infuriarsi) to rage

'scatola sf box; (di latta) tin (BRIT), can; **cibi in ~** tinned (BRIT) o canned foods; **scatola cranica** cranium; **scato'lone** sm (big) box

scat'tare vt (fotografia) to take ▷ vi (congegno, molla ecc) to be released; (balzare) to spring up; (Sport) to put on a spurt; (fig: per l'ira) to fly into a rage; **~ in piedi** to spring to one's feet

'scatto sm (dispositivo) release; (: di arma da fuoco) trigger mechanism; (rumore) click; (balzo) jump, start; (Sport) spurt; (fig: di ira ecc) fit; (: di stipendio) increment; **di ~** suddenly

scaval'care vt (ostacolo) to pass (o climb) over; (fig) to get ahead of, overtake

sca'vare vt (terreno) to dig; (legno) to hollow out; (pozzo, galleria) to bore; (città sepolta ecc) to excavate

'scavo sm excavating no pl; excavation

'scegliere ['ʃeʎʎere] vt to choose, select

sce'icco, -chi [ʃe'ikko] sm sheik

'scelgo ecc ['ʃelgo] vb vedi **scegliere**

scel'lino [ʃel'lino] sm shilling

'scelta ['ʃelta] sf choice; selection; **di prima ~** top grade o quality; **frutta o formaggi a ~** choice of fruit or cheese

'scelto, -a ['ʃelto] pp di **scegliere** ▷ ag (gruppo) carefully selected; (frutta, verdura) choice, top quality; (Mil: specializzato) crack cpd, highly skilled

'scemo, -a [ˈʃemo] *ag* stupid, silly

'scena [ˈʃɛna] *sf* (*gen*) scene; (*palcoscenico*) stage; **le scene** (*fig: teatro*) the stage; **fare una ~** to make a scene; **andare in ~** to be staged *o* put on *o* performed; **mettere in ~** to stage

sce'nario [ʃeˈnarjo] *sm* scenery; (*di film*) scenario

sce'nata [ʃeˈnata] *sf* row, scene

'scendere [ˈʃendere] *vi* to go (*o* come) down; (*strada, sole*) to go down; (*notte*) to fall; (*passeggero: fermarsi*) to get out, alight; (*fig: temperatura, prezzi*) to go *o* come down, fall, drop ▷ *vt* (*scale, pendio*) to go (*o* come) down; **~ dalle scale** to go (*o* come) down the stairs; **~ dal treno** to get off *o* out of the train; **dove devo ~?** where do I get off?; **~ dalla macchina** to get out of the car; **~ da cavallo** to dismount, get off one's horse

sceneggi'ato [ʃenedˈdʒato] *sm* television drama

'scettico, -a, -ci, -che [ˈʃettiko] *ag* sceptical

'scettro [ˈʃettro] *sm* sceptre

'scheda [ˈskɛda] *sf* (index) card; **scheda elettorale** ballot paper; **scheda ricaricabile** (*Tel*) top-up card; **scheda telefonica** phone card; **sche'dario** *sm* file; (*mobile*) filing cabinet

sche'dina [skeˈdina] *sf* ≈ pools coupon (BRIT)

'scheggia, -ge [ˈskeddʒa] *sf* splinter, sliver

'scheletro [ˈskɛletro] *sm* skeleton

'schema, -i [ˈskɛma] *sm* (*diagramma*) diagram, sketch; (*progetto, abbozzo*) outline, plan

'scherma [ˈskerma] *sf* fencing

scher'maglia [skerˈmaʎʎa] *sf* (*fig*) skirmish

'schermo [ˈskermo] *sm* shield, screen; (*Cinema, TV*) screen

scher'nire [skerˈnire] *vt* to mock, sneer at

scher'zare [skerˈtsare] *vi* to joke

'scherzo [ˈskertso] *sm* joke; (*tiro*) trick; (*Mus*) scherzo; **è uno ~!** (*una cosa facile*) it's child's play!, it's easy!; **per ~** in jest; for a joke *o* a laugh; **fare un brutto ~ a qn** to play a nasty trick on sb

schiaccia'noci [skjattʃaˈnotʃi] *sm inv* nutcracker

schiacci'are [skjatˈtʃare] *vt* (*dito*) to crush; (*noci*) to crack; **~ un pisolino** to have a nap; **schiacciarsi** *vpr* (*appiattirsi*) to get squashed; (*frantumarsi*) to get crushed

schiaffeggi'are [skjaffedˈdʒare] *vt* to slap

schi'affo [ˈskjaffo] *sm* slap

schiantarsi *vpr* to break (up), shatter

schia'rire [skjaˈrire] *vt* to lighten, make lighter; **schiarirsi** *vpr* to grow lighter; (*tornar sereno*) to clear, brighten up; **schiarirsi la voce** to clear one's throat

schiavitù [skjaviˈtu] *sf* slavery

schi'avo, -a [ˈskjavo] *sm/f* slave

schi'ena [ˈskjɛna] *sf* (*Anat*) back; **schie'nale** *sm* (*di sedia*) back

schi'era [ˈskjɛra] *sf* (*Mil*) rank; (*gruppo*) group, band

schiera'mento [skjeraˈmento] *sm* (*Mil, Sport*) formation; (*fig*) alliance

schie'rare [skjeˈrare] *vt* (*esercito*) to line up, draw up, marshal; **schierarsi** *vpr* to line up; (*fig*): **schierarsi con** *o* **dalla parte di/contro qn** to side with/oppose sb

'schifo [ˈskifo] *sm* disgust; **fare ~** (*essere fatto male, dare pessimi risultati*) to be awful; **mi fa ~** it makes me sick, it's disgusting; **quel libro è uno ~** that book's rotten; **schi'foso, -a** *ag* disgusting, revolting; (*molto scadente*) rotten, lousy

schioc'care [skjokˈkare] *vt* (*frusta*) to crack; (*dita*) to snap; (*lingua*) to click; **~ le labbra** to smack one's lips

schiudersi *vpr* to open

schi'uma [ˈskjuma] *sf* foam; (*di sapone*) lather; (*di latte*) froth; (*fig: feccia*) scum

schi'vare [skiˈvare] *vt* to dodge, avoid

'schivo, -a [ˈskivo] *ag* (*ritroso*) stand-offish, reserved; (*timido*) shy

schiz'zare [skitˈtsare] *vt* (*spruzzare*) to spurt, squirt; (*sporcare*) to splash, spatter; (*fig: abbozzare*) to sketch ▷ *vi* to spurt, squirt; (*saltar fuori*) to dart up (*o* off *ecc*)

schizzi'noso, -a [skittsiˈnoso] *ag* fussy, finicky

'schizzo [ˈskittso] *sm* (*di liquido*) spurt; splash, spatter; (*abbozzo*) sketch

sci [ʃi] *sm* (*attrezzo*) ski; (*attività*) skiing; **sci d'acqua** water-skiing; **sci di fondo** cross-country skiing, ski touring (US); **sci nautico** water-skiing

'scia [ˈʃia] (*pl* **scie**) *sf* (*di imbarcazione*) wake; (*di profumo*) trail

scià [ʃa] *sm inv* shah

sci'abola [ˈʃabola] *sf* sabre

scia'callo [ʃaˈkallo] *sm* jackal

sciac'quare [ʃakˈkware] *vt* to rinse

scia'gura [ʃaˈgura] *sf* disaster, calamity; misfortune

scialac'quare [ʃalakˈkware] *vt* to squander

sci'albo, -a [ˈʃalbo] *ag* pale, dull; (*fig*) dull, colourless

sci'alle [ˈʃalle] *sm* shawl

scia'luppa [ʃaˈluppa] *sf*; **scialuppa di salvataggio** lifeboat

sci'ame [ˈʃame] *sm* swarm

sci'are [ʃiˈare] *vi* to ski

sci'arpa [ˈʃarpa] *sf* scarf; (*fascia*) sash

scia'tore, -'trice [ʃiaˈtore] *sm/f* skier

sci'atto, -a [ˈʃatto] *ag* (*persona*) slovenly, unkempt

scien'tifico, -a, -ci, -che [ʃenˈtifiko] *ag* scientific

sci'enza [ˈʃɛntsa] *sf* science; (*sapere*) knowledge; **scienze** *sfpl* (*Ins*) science *sg*; **scienze naturali** natural sciences; **scienzi'ato, -a** *sm/f* scientist

'scimmia [ˈʃimmja] *sf* monkey

scimpanzé [ʃimpanˈtse] *sm inv* chimpanzee

scin'tilla [ʃinˈtilla] *sf* spark; **scintil'lare** *vi* to spark; (*acqua, occhi*) to sparkle

scioc'chezza [ʃokˈkettsa] *sf* stupidity *no pl*; stupid *o* foolish thing; **dire sciocchezze** to talk nonsense

sci'occo, -a, -chi, -che [ˈʃɔkko] *ag* stupid, foolish

sci'ogliere [ˈʃɔʎʎere] *vt* (*nodo*) to untie; (*capelli*) to loosen; (*persona, animale*) to untie, release; (*fig: persona*) **~ da** to release from; (*neve*) to melt; (*nell'acqua: zucchero ecc*) to dissolve; (*fig: mistero*) to solve; (*porre fine a: contratto*) to cancel; (: *società, matrimonio*) to dissolve; (: *riunione*) to bring to an end; **sciogliersi** *vpr* to loosen, come untied; to melt; to dissolve; (*assemblea ecc*) to break up; **~ i muscoli** to limber up; **scioglilingua** [ʃoʎʎiˈlingwa] *sm inv* tongue-twister

sci'olgo *ecc* [ˈʃɔlgo] *vb vedi* **sciogliere**

sci'olto, -a [ˈʃɔlto] *pp di* **sciogliere** ▷ *ag* loose; (*agile*) agile, nimble; supple; (*disinvolto*) free and easy; **versi sciolti** (*Poesia*) blank verse

sciope'rare [ʃopeˈrare] *vi* to strike, go on strike

sci'opero [ˈʃopero] *sm* strike; **fare ~** to strike; **sciopero bianco** work-to-rule (BRIT), slowdown (US); **sciopero selvaggio** wildcat strike; **sciopero a singhiozzo** on-off strike

scio'via [ʃioˈvia] *sf* ski lift

scip'pare [ʃipˈpare] *vt* **~ qn** to snatch sb's bag; **mi hanno scippato** they snatched my bag

sci'rocco [ʃiˈrɔkko] *sm* sirocco

sci'roppo [ʃiˈroppo] *sm* syrup

'scisma, -i [ˈʃizma] *sm* (*Rel*) schism

scissi'one [ʃisˈsjone] *sf* (*anche fig*) split, division; (*Fisica*) fission

sciu'pare [ʃuˈpare] *vt* (*abito, libro, appetito*) to spoil, ruin; (*tempo, denaro*) to waste

scivo'lare [ʃivoˈlare] *vi* to slide *o* glide along; (*involontariamente*) to slip, slide; **'scivolo** *sm* slide; (*Tecn*) chute; **scivo'loso, -a** *ag* slippery

scle'rosi *sf* sclerosis

scoc'care *vt* (*freccia*) to shoot ▷ *vi* (*guizzare*) to shoot up; (*battere: ora*) to strike

scoccherò *ecc* [skokkeˈrɔ] *vb vedi* **scoccare**

scocci'are [skotˈtʃare] (*fam*) *vt* to bother, annoy; **scocciarsi** *vpr* to be bothered *o* annoyed

sco'della *sf* bowl

scodinzo'lare [skodintsoˈlare] *vi* to wag its tail

scogli'era [skoʎˈʎɛra] *sf* reef; cliff

'scoglio [ˈskɔʎʎo] *sm* (*al mare*) rock

scoi'attolo *sm* squirrel

scola'pasta *sm inv* colander

scolapi'atti *sm inv* drainer (*for plates*)

sco'lare *ag* **età scolare** school age ▷ *vt* to drain ▷ *vi* to drip

scola'resca *sf* schoolchildren *pl*, pupils *pl*

sco'laro, -a *sm/f* pupil, schoolboy/girl

Attenzione! In inglese esiste la parola *scholar*, che però significa *studioso*.

sco'lastico, -a, -ci, -che *ag* school *cpd*; scholastic

scol'lato, -a *ag* (*vestito*) low-cut, low-necked; (*donna*) wearing a low-cut dress (*o* blouse *ecc*)

scolla'tura *sf* neckline

scolle'gare *vt* (*fili, apparecchi*) to disconnect

'scolo *sm* drainage

scolo'rire *vt* to fade; to discolour; **scolorirsi** *vpr* to fade; to become discoloured; (*impallidire*) to turn pale

scol'pire *vt* to carve, sculpt

scombusso'lare *vt* to upset

scom'messa *sf* bet, wager

scom'mettere *vt, vi* to bet

scomo'dare *vt* to trouble, bother; to disturb; **scomodarsi** *vpr* to put o.s. out; **scomodarsi a fare** to go to the bother *o* trouble of doing

'scomodo, -a *ag* uncomfortable; (*sistemazione, posto*) awkward, inconvenient

scompa'rire *vi* (*sparire*) to disappear, vanish; (*fig*) to be insignificant

scomparti'mento *sm* compartment; **uno ~ per non-fumatori** a non-smoking compartment

scompigli'are [skompiʎˈʎare] *vt* (*cassetto, capelli*) to mess up, disarrange; (*fig: piani*) to upset

scomuni'care *vt* to excommunicate

'sconcio, -a, -ci, -ce [ˈskontʃo] *ag* (*osceno*) indecent, obscene ▷ *sm* disgrace

scon'figgere [skonˈfiddʒere] *vt* to defeat, overcome

sconfi'nare *vi* to cross the border; (*in proprietà privata*) to trespass; (*fig*): **~ da** to stray o digress from

scon'fitta sf defeat

scon'forto sm despondency

sconge'lare [skondʒe'lare] vt to defrost

scongiu'rare [skondʒu'rare] vt (implorare) to entreat, beseech, implore; (eludere: pericolo) to ward off, avert; **scongi'uro** sm entreaty; (esorcismo) exorcism; **fare gli scongiuri** to touch wood (BRIT), knock on wood (US)

scon'nesso, -a ag incoherent

sconosci'uto, -a [skonoʃʃuto] ag unknown; new, strange ▷ sm/f stranger; unknown person

sconsigli'are [skonsiʎ'ʎare] vt ~ qc a qn to advise sb against sth; ~ qn dal fare qc to advise sb not to do o against doing sth

sconso'lato, -a ag inconsolable; desolate

scon'tare vt (Comm: detrarre) to deduct; (: debito) to pay off; (: cambiale) to discount; (pena) to serve; (colpa, errori) to pay for, suffer for

scon'tato, -a ag (previsto) foreseen, taken for granted; **dare per ~ che** to take it for granted that

scon'tento, -a ag ~ (di) dissatisfied (with) ▷ sm dissatisfaction

'sconto sm discount; **fare uno ~** to give a discount; **ci sono sconti per studenti?** are there discounts for students?

scon'trarsi vpr (treni ecc) to crash, collide; (venire ad uno scontro, fig) to clash; ~ **con** to crash into, collide with

scon'trino sm ticket; (di cassa) receipt; **potrei avere lo ~ per favore?** can I have a receipt, please?

'scontro sm clash, encounter; crash, collision

scon'troso, -a ag sullen, surly; (permaloso) touchy

sconveni'ente ag unseemly, improper

scon'volgere [skon'vɔldʒere] vt to throw into confusion, upset; (turbare) to shake, disturb, upset; **scon'volto, -a** pp di **sconvolgere**

scooter ['skuter] sm inv scooter

'scopa sf broom; (Carte) Italian card game; **sco'pare** vt to sweep

sco'perta sf discovery

sco'perto, -a pp di **scoprire** ▷ ag uncovered; (capo) uncovered, bare; (macchina) open; (Mil) exposed, without cover; (conto) overdrawn

'scopo sm aim, purpose; **a che ~?** what for?

scoppi'are vi (spaccarsi) to burst; (esplodere) to explode; (fig) to break out; ~ **in pianto** o **a piangere** to burst out crying;

~ **dalle risa** o **dal ridere** to split one's sides laughing

scoppiet'tare vi to crackle

'scoppio sm explosion; (di tuono, arma ecc) crash, bang; (fig: di risa, ira) fit, outburst; (: di guerra) outbreak; **a ~ ritardato** delayed-action

sco'prire vt to discover; (liberare da ciò che copre) to uncover; (: monumento) to unveil; **scoprirsi** vpr to put on lighter clothes; (fig) to give o s. away

scoraggi'are [skorad'dʒare] vt to discourage; **scoraggiarsi** vpr to become discouraged, lose heart

scorcia'toia [skortʃa'toja] sf short cut

'scorcio ['skortʃo] sm (Arte) foreshortening; (di secolo, periodo) end, close; **scorcio panoramico** vista

scor'dare vt to forget; **scordarsi** vpr **scordarsi di qc/di fare** to forget sth/to do

'scorgere ['skɔrdʒere] vt to make out, distinguish, see

scorpacci'ata [skorpat'tʃata] sf **fare una ~ (di)** to stuff o.s. (with), eat one's fill (of)

scorpi'one sm scorpion; (dello zodiaco): **S~** Scorpio

'scorrere vt (giornale, lettera) to run o skim through ▷ vi (liquido, fiume) to run, flow; (fune) to run; (cassetto, porta) to slide easily; (tempo) to pass (by)

scor'retto, -a ag incorrect; (sgarbato) impolite; (sconveniente) improper

scor'revole ag (porta) sliding; (fig: stile) fluent, flowing

'scorsi ecc vb vedi **scorrere**

'scorso, -a pp di **scorrere** ▷ ag last

scor'soio, -a ag **nodo ~** noose

'scorta sf (di personalità, convoglio) escort; (provvista) supply, stock

scor'tese ag discourteous, rude

'scorza ['skɔrdza] sf (di albero) bark; (di agrumi) peel, skin

sco'sceso, -a [skoʃ'ʃeso] ag steep

'scossa sf jerk, jolt, shake; (Elettr: fig) shock; **scossa di terremoto** earth tremor

'scosso, -a pp di **scuotere** ▷ ag (turbato) shaken, upset

scos'tante ag (fig) off-putting (BRIT), unpleasant

scotch [skɔtʃ] sm inv (whisky) Scotch; (nastro adesivo) Scotch tape®, Sellotape®

scot'tare vt (ustionare) to burn; (: con liquido bollente) to scald ▷ vi to burn; (caffè) to be too hot; **scottarsi** vpr to burn/scald o.s.; (fig) to have one's fingers burnt; **scotta'tura** sf burn; scald

'scotto, -a ag overcooked ▷ sm (fig):

pagare lo ~ (di) to pay the penalty (for)
sco'vare vt to drive out, flush out; (fig) to discover
'Scozia ['skɔttsja] sf **la ~** Scotland; **scoz'zese** ag Scottish ▷ sm/f Scot
scredi'tare vt to discredit
screen saver ['skriːn'seɪvər] sm inv (Inform) screen saver
scre'mato, -a ag skimmed; **parzialmente ~** semi-skimmed
screpo'lato, -a ag (labbra) chapped; (muro) cracked
'screzio ['skrɛttsjo] sm disagreement
scricchio'lare [skrikkjo'lare] vi to creak, squeak
'scrigno ['skriɲɲo] sm casket
scrimina'tura sf parting
'scrissi ecc vb vedi **scrivere**
'scritta sf inscription
'scritto, -a pp di **scrivere** ▷ ag written ▷ sm writing; (lettera) letter, note
scrit'toio sm writing desk
scrit'tore, -'trice sm/f writer
scrit'tura sf writing; (Comm) entry; (contratto) contract; (Rel): **la Sacra S~** the Scriptures pl
scrittu'rare vt (Teatro, Cinema) to sign up, engage; (Comm) to enter
scriva'nia sf desk
'scrivere vt to write; **come si scrive?** how is it spelt?, how do you write it?
scroc'cone, -a sm/f scrounger
'scrofa sf (Zool) sow
scrol'lare vt to shake; **scrollarsi** vpr (anche fig) to give o.s. a shake; (anche: **~ le spalle/il capo**) to shrug one's shoulders/shake one's head
'scrupolo sm scruple; (meticolosità) care, conscientiousness
scrupo'loso, -a ag scrupulous; conscientious
scru'tare vt to scrutinize; (intenzioni, causa) to examine, scrutinize
scu'cire [sku'tʃire] vt (orlo ecc) to unpick, undo; **scucirsi** vpr to come unstitched
scude'ria sf stable
scu'detto sm (Sport) (championship) shield; (distintivo) badge
'scudo sm shield
sculacci'are [skulat'tʃare] vt to spank
scul'tore, -'trice sm/f sculptor
scul'tura sf sculpture
scu'ola sf school; **scuola elementare/materna** primary (BRIT) o grade (US) /nursery school; **scuola guida** driving school; **scuola media** secondary (BRIT) o high (US) school; **scuola dell'obbligo** compulsory education; **scuola tecnica** technical college; **scuole serali** evening classes, night school sg
scu'otere vt to shake
'scure sf axe
'scuro, -a ag dark; (fig: espressione) grim ▷ sm darkness; dark colour; (imposta) (window) shutter; **verde/rosso** ecc **~** dark green/red ecc
'scusa sf apology; (pretesto) excuse; **chiedere ~ a qn (per)** to apologize to sb (for); **chiedo ~** I'm sorry; (disturbando ecc) excuse me
scu'sare vt to excuse; **scusarsi** vpr **scusarsi (di)** to apologize (for); **(mi) scusi** I'm sorry; (per richiamare l'attenzione) excuse me
sde'gnato, -a [zdeɲ'ɲato] ag indignant, angry
'sdegno ['zdeɲɲo] sm scorn, disdain
sdolci'nato, -a [zdoltʃi'nato] ag mawkish, oversentimental
sdrai'arsi vpr to stretch out, lie down
'sdraio sm **sedia a ~** deck chair
sdruccio'levole [zdruttʃo'levole] ag slippery

 PAROLA CHIAVE

se pron vedi **si**
▷ cong **1** (condizionale, ipotetica) if; **se nevica non vengo** I won't come if it snows; **sarei rimasto se me l'avessero chiesto** I would have stayed if they'd asked me; **non puoi fare altro se non telefonare** all you can do is phone; **se mai** if, if ever; **siamo noi se mai che le siamo grati** it is we who should be grateful to you; **se no** (altrimenti) or (else), otherwise
2 (in frasi dubitative, interrogative indirette) if, whether; **non so se scrivere o telefonare** I don't know whether o if I should write or phone

sé pron (gen) oneself; (esso, essa, lui, lei, loro) itself; himself; herself; themselves; **sé stesso(a)** pron oneself; itself; himself; herself
seb'bene cong although, though
sec. abbr (= secolo) c.
'secca sf (del mare) shallows pl; vedi anche **secco**
sec'care vt to dry; (prosciugare) to dry up; (fig: importunare) to annoy, bother ▷ vi to dry; to dry up; **seccarsi** vpr to dry; to dry up; (fig) to grow annoyed
sec'cato, -a ag (fig: infastidito) bothered, annoyed; (: stufo) fed up
secca'tura sf (fig) bother no pl, trouble no pl
seccherò ecc [sekke'rɔ] vb vedi **seccare**

secchi'ello sm bucket; **secchiello del ghiaccio** ice bucket

'secchio ['sekkjo] sm bucket, pail

'secco, -a, -chi, -che ag dry; (fichi, pesce) dried; (foglie, ramo) withered; (magro: persona) thin, skinny; (fig: risposta, modo di fare) curt, abrupt; (: colpo) clean, sharp ▷ sm (siccità) drought; **restarci** ~ (fig: morire sul colpo) to drop dead; **mettere in** ~ (barca) to beach; **rimanere a** ~ (fig) to be left in the lurch

seco'lare ag age-old, centuries-old; (laico, mondano) secular

'secolo sm century; (epoca) age

se'conda sf (Aut) second (gear); **viaggiare in** ~ to travel second-class; vedi anche **secondo**; **seconda colazione** lunch

secon'dario, -a ag secondary

se'condo, -a ag second ▷ sm second; (di pranzo) main course ▷ prep according to; (nel modo prescritto) in accordance with; ~ **me** in my opinion, to my mind; **di seconda mano** second-hand; **a seconda di** according to; in accordance with; **seconda classe** second-class

'sedano sm celery

seda'tivo, -a ag, sm sedative

'sede sf seat; (di ditta) head office; (di organizzazione) headquarters pl; **sede centrale** head office; **sede sociale** registered office

seden'tario, -a ag sedentary

se'dere vi to sit, be seated

'sedia sf chair; **sedia elettrica** electric chair; **sedia a rotelle** wheelchair

'sedici ['seditʃi] num sixteen

se'dile sm seat; (panchina) bench

sedu'cente [sedu'tʃɛnte] ag seductive; (proposta) very attractive

se'durre vt to seduce

se'duta sf session, sitting; (riunione) meeting; **seduta spiritica** séance; **seduta stante** (fig) immediately

seduzi'one [sedut'tsjone] sf seduction; (fascino) charm, appeal

SEeO abbr (= salvo errori e omissioni) E and OE

'sega, -ghe sf saw

'segale sf rye

se'gare vt to saw; (recidere) to saw off

'seggio ['sɛddʒo] sm seat; **seggio elettorale** polling station

'seggiola ['sɛddʒola] sf chair; **seggio'lone** sm (per bambini) highchair

seggio'via [seddʒo'via] sf chairlift

segherò ecc [sege'rɔ] vb vedi **segare**

segna'lare [seɲɲa'lare] vt (manovra ecc) to signal; to indicate; (annunciare) to announce; to report; (fig: far conoscere) to point out; (: persona) to single out

se'gnale [seɲ'ɲale] sm signal; (cartello): **segnale acustico** acoustic o sound signal; **segnale d'allarme** alarm; (Ferr) communication cord; **segnale orario** (Radio) time signal; **segnale stradale** road sign

segna'libro [seɲɲa'libro] sm (anche Inform) bookmark

se'gnare [seɲ'ɲare] vt to mark; (prendere nota) to note; (indicare) to indicate, mark; (Sport: goal) to score

'segno ['seɲɲo] sm sign; (impronta, contrassegno) mark; (limite) limit, bounds pl; (bersaglio) target; **fare ~ di sì/no** to nod (one's head)/shake one's head; **fare ~ a qn di fermarsi** to motion (to) sb to stop; **cogliere** o **colpire nel** ~ (fig) to hit the mark; **segno zodiacale** star sign

segre'tario, -a sm/f secretary; **segretario comunale** town clerk; **Segretario di Stato** Secretary of State

segre'teria sf (di ditta, scuola) (secretary's) office; (d'organizzazione internazionale) secretariat; (Pol ecc: carica) office of Secretary; **segreteria telefonica** answering service

se'greto, -a ag secret ▷ sm secret; secrecy no pl; **in** ~ in secret, secretly

segu'ace [se'gwatʃe] sm/f follower, disciple

segu'ente ag following, next

segu'ire vt to follow; (frequentare: corso) to attend ▷ vi to follow; (continuare: testo) to continue

segui'tare vt to continue, carry on with ▷ vi to continue, carry on

'seguito sm (scorta) suite, retinue; (discepoli) followers pl; (favore) following; (continuazione) continuation; (conseguenza) result; **di** ~ at a stretch, on end; **in** ~ later on; **in** ~ **a, a** ~ **di** following; (a causa di) as a result of, owing to

'sei vb vedi **essere** ▷ num six

sei'cento [sei'tʃɛnto] num six hundred ▷ sm **il S~** the seventeenth century

selci'ato [sel'tʃato] sm cobbled surface

selezio'nare [selettsjo'nare] vt to select

selezi'one [selet'tsjone] sf selection

'sella sf saddle

sel'lino sm saddle

selvag'gina [selvad'dʒina] sf (animali) game

sel'vaggio, -a, -gi, -ge [sel'vaddʒo] ag wild; (tribù) savage, uncivilized; (fig) savage, brutal ▷ sm/f savage

sel'vatico, -a, -ci, -che ag wild

se'maforo sm (Aut) traffic lights pl

sem'brare vi to seem ▷ vb impers **sembra che** it seems that; **mi sembra che** it seems to me that, I think (that); **~ di essere** to seem to be

'seme sm seed; (sperma) semen; (Carte) suit

se'mestre sm half-year, six-month period

semifi'nale sf semifinal

semi'freddo sm ice-cream cake

semi'nare vt to sow

semi'nario sm seminar; (Rel) seminary

seminter'rato sm basement; (appartamento) basement flat

'semola sf; **semola di grano duro** durum wheat

semo'lino sm semolina

'semplice ['semplitʃe] ag simple; (di un solo elemento) single

'sempre av always; (ancora) still; **posso ~ tentare** I can always o still try; **da ~** always; **per ~** forever; **una volta per ~** once and for all; **~ che** provided (that); **~ più** more and more; **~ meno** less and less

sempre'verde ag, sm o f (Bot) evergreen

'senape sf (Cuc) mustard

se'nato sm senate; **sena'tore, -'trice** sm/f senator

'senno sm judgment, (common) sense; **col ~ di poi** with hindsight

'seno sm (Anat: petto, mammella) breast; (: grembo, fig) womb; (: cavità) sinus

sen'sato, -a ag sensible

sensazio'nale [sensattsjo'nale] ag sensational

sensazi'one [sensat'tsjone] sf feeling, sensation; **avere la ~ che** to have a feeling that; **fare ~** to cause a sensation, create a stir

sen'sibile ag sensitive; (ai sensi) perceptible; (rilevante, notevole) appreciable, noticeable; **~ a** sensitive to

Attenzione! In inglese esiste la parola sensible, che però significa ragionevole.

'senso sm (Fisiol, istinto) sense; (impressione, sensazione) feeling, sensation; (significato) meaning, sense; (direzione) direction; **sensi** smpl (coscienza) consciousness sg; (sensualità) senses; **ciò non ha ~** that doesn't make sense; **fare ~ a** (ripugnare) to disgust, repel; **in ~ orario/ antiorario** clockwise/anticlockwise; **senso di colpa** sense of guilt; **senso comune** common sense; **senso unico** (strada) one-way; **senso vietato** (Aut) no entry

sensu'ale ag sensual; sensuous

sen'tenza [sen'tɛntsa] sf (Dir) sentence; (massima) maxim

senti'ero sm path

sentimen'tale ag sentimental; (vita, avventura) love cpd

senti'mento sm feeling

senti'nella sf sentry

sen'tire vt (percepire al tatto, fig) to feel; (udire) to hear; (ascoltare) to listen to; (odore) to smell; (avvertire con il gusto, assaggiare) to taste ▷ vi **~ di** (avere sapore) to taste of; (avere odore) to smell of; **sentirsi** vpr (uso reciproco) to be in touch; **sentirsi bene/male** to feel well/unwell o ill; **non mi sento bene** I don't feel well; **sentirsi di fare qc** (essere disposto) to feel like doing sth

sen'tito, -a ag (sincero) sincere, warm; **per ~ dire** by hearsay

'senza ['sɛntsa] prep, cong without; **~ dir nulla** without saying a word; **fare ~ qc** to do without sth; **~ di me** without me; **~ che io lo sapessi** without me o my knowing; **senz'altro** of course, certainly; **~ dubbio** no doubt; **~ scrupoli** unscrupulous; **~ amici** friendless

sepa'rare vt to separate; (dividere) to divide; (tenere distinto) to distinguish; **separarsi** vpr (coniugi) to separate, part; (amici) to part, leave each other; **separarsi da** (coniuge) to separate o part from; (amico, socio) to part company with; (oggetto) to part with; **sepa'rato, -a** ag (letti, conto ecc) separate; (coniugi) separated

seppel'lire vt to bury

'seppi ecc vb vedi **sapere**

'seppia sf cuttlefish ▷ ag inv sepia

se'quenza [se'kwentsa] sf sequence

seques'trare vt (Dir) to impound; (rapire) to kidnap; **se'questro** sm (Dir) impoundment; **sequestro di persona** kidnapping

'sera sf evening; **di ~** in the evening; **domani ~** tomorrow evening, tomorrow night; **se'rale** ag evening cpd; **se'rata** sf evening; (ricevimento) party

ser'bare vt to keep; (mettere da parte) to put aside; **~ rancore/odio verso qn** to bear sb a grudge/hate sb

serba'toio sm tank; (cisterna) cistern

'Serbia sf **la ~** Serbia

'serbo ag Serbian ▷ sm/f Serbian, Serb ▷ sm (Ling) Serbian; (il serbare): **mettere/ tenere o avere in ~ qc** to put/keep sth aside

se'reno, -a ag (tempo, cielo) clear; (fig) serene, calm

ser'gente [ser'dʒɛnte] sm (Mil) sergeant

'serie sf inv (successione) series inv; (gruppo, collezione) set; (Sport) division; league; (Comm): **modello di ~/fuori ~** standard/

custom-built model; **in ~** in quick
succession; (Comm) mass cpd
serietà sf seriousness; reliability
'serio, -a ag serious; (impiegato)
responsible, reliable; (ditta, cliente) reliable,
dependable; **sul ~** (davvero) really, truly;
(seriamente) seriously, in earnest
ser'pente sm snake; **serpente a sonagli**
rattlesnake
'serra sf greenhouse; hothouse
ser'randa sf roller shutter
serra'tura sf lock
server ['sɛrver] sm inv (Inform) server
ser'vire vt to serve; (clienti: al ristorante)
to wait on; (: al negozio) to serve, attend
to; (fig: giovare) to aid, help; (Carte) to
deal ▷ vi (Tennis) to serve; (essere utile):
~ a qn to be of use to sb; **~ a qc/a fare**
(utensile ecc) to be used for sth/for doing;
~ (a qn) da to serve as (for sb); **servirsi**
vpr (usare): **servirsi di** to use; (prendere:
cibo): **servirsi (di)** to help o.s. to (to);
serviti pure! help yourself!; (essere cliente
abituale): **servirsi da** to be a regular
customer at, go to
servizi'evole [servit'tsjevole] ag obliging,
willing to help
ser'vizio [ser'vittsjo] sm service; (al
ristorante: sul conto) service (charge);
(Stampa, TV, Radio) report; (da tè, caffè ecc)
set, service; **servizi** smpl (di casa) kitchen
and bathroom; (Econ) services; **essere di**
~ to be on duty; **fuori ~** (telefono ecc) out
of order; **~ compreso** service included;
servizio militare military service;
servizio di posate set of cutlery; **servizi**
segreti secret service sg; **servizio da tè**
tea set
ses'santa num sixty; **sessan'tesimo, -a**
num sixtieth
sessi'one sf session
'sesso sm sex; **sessu'ale** ag sexual,
sex cpd
ses'tante sm sextant
'sesto, -a ag, sm sixth
'seta sf silk
'sete sf thirst; **avere ~** to be thirsty
'setola sf bristle
'setta sf sect
set'tanta num seventy; **settan'tesimo, -a**
num seventieth
set'tare vt (Inform) to set up
'sette num seven
sette'cento [sette'tʃɛnto] num seven
hundred ▷ sm **il S~** the eighteenth
century
set'tembre sm September
settentrio'nale ag northern
settentri'one sm north

setti'mana sf week; **settima'nale** ag,
sm weekly

'settimo, -a ag, sm seventh
set'tore sm sector
severità sf severity
se'vero, -a ag severe
sevizi'are [sevit'tsjare] vt to torture
sezio'nare [settsjo'nare] vt to divide into
sections; (Med) to dissect
sezi'one [set'tsjone] sf section
sfacchi'nata [sfakki'nata] sf (fam) chore,
drudgery no pl
sfacci'ato, -a [sfat'tʃato] ag (maleducato)
cheeky, impudent; (vistoso) gaudy
sfa'mare vt to feed; (cibo) to fill;
sfamarsi vpr to satisfy one's hunger,
fill o.s. up
sfasci'are [sfaʃʃare] vt (ferita) to
unbandage; (distruggere) to smash,
shatter; **sfasciarsi** vpr (rompersi) to
smash, shatter
sfavo'revole ag unfavourable
'sfera sf sphere
sfer'rare vt (fig: colpo) to land, deal;
(: attacco) to launch
'sfida sf challenge
sfi'dare vt to challenge; (fig) to defy, brave
sfi'ducia [sfi'dutʃa] sf distrust, mistrust
sfi'gato, -a (fam) ag (sfortunato) unlucky
sfigu'rare vt (persona) to disfigure; (quadro,
statua) to deface ▷ vi (far cattiva figura) to
make a bad impression
sfi'lare vt (ago) to unthread; (abito, scarpe)
to slip off ▷ vi (truppe) to march past;
(atleti) to parade; **sfilarsi** vpr (perle ecc)
to come unstrung; (orlo, tessuto) to fray;
(calza) to run, ladder; **sfi'lata** sf march
past; parade; **sfilata di moda** fashion
show
'sfinge ['sfindʒe] sf sphinx
sfi'nito, -a ag exhausted
sfio'rare vt to brush (against); (argomento)
to touch upon
sfio'rire vi to wither, fade
sfo'cato, -a ag (Fot) out of focus
sfoci'are [sfo'tʃare] vi **~ in** to flow into; (fig:
malcontento) to develop into
sfode'rato, -a ag (vestito) unlined
sfogarsi vpr (sfogare la propria rabbia) to
give vent to one's anger; (confidarsi): **~**
(con) to pour out one's feelings (to); **non**

sfogarti su di me! don't take your bad temper out on me!

sfoggi'are [sfod'dʒare] vt, vi to show off

'**sfoglia** ['sfoʎʎa] sf sheet of pasta dough; **pasta ~** (Cuc) puff pastry

sfogli'are [sfoʎ'ʎare] vt (libro) to leaf through

'**sfogo, -ghi** sm (eruzione cutanea) rash; (fig) outburst; **dare ~ a** (fig) to give vent to

sfon'dare vt (porta) to break down; (scarpe) to wear a hole in; (cesto, scatola) to burst, knock the bottom out of; (Mil) to break through ▷ vi (riuscire) to make a name for o.s.

'**sfondo** sm background

sfor'mato sm (Cuc) type of soufflé

sfor'tuna sf misfortune, ill luck no pl; **avere ~** to be unlucky; **sfortu'nato, -a** ag unlucky; (impresa, film) unsuccessful

sforzarsi vpr **~ di** o **a** o **per fare** to try hard to do

'**sforzo** ['sfɔrtso] sm effort; (tensione eccessiva, Tecn) strain; **fare uno ~** to make an effort

sfrat'tare vt to evict; '**sfratto** sm eviction

sfrecci'are [sfret'tʃare] vi to shoot o flash past

sfre'gare vt (strofinare) to rub; (graffiare) to scratch; **sfregarsi le mani** to rub one's hands; **~ un fiammifero** to strike a match

sfregi'are [sfre'dʒare] vt to slash, gash; (persona) to disfigure; (quadro) to deface

sfre'nato, -a ag (fig) unrestrained, unbridled

sfron'tato, -a ag shameless

sfrutta'mento sm exploitation

sfrut'tare vt (terreno) to overwork, exhaust; (miniera) to exploit, work; (fig: operai, occasione, potere) to exploit

sfug'gire [sfud'dʒire] vi to escape; **~ a** (custode) to escape (from); (morte) to escape; **~ a qn** (dettaglio, nome) to escape sb; **~ di mano a qn** to slip out of sb's hand (o hands)

sfu'mare vt (colori, contorni) to soften, shade off ▷ vi to shade (off), fade; (fig: svanire) to vanish, disappear; (: speranze) to come to nothing

sfuma'tura sf shading off no pl; (tonalità) shade, tone; (fig) touch, hint

sfuri'ata sf (scatto di collera) fit of anger; (rimprovero) sharp rebuke

sga'bello sm stool

sgabuz'zino [sgabud'dzino] sm lumber room

sgambet'tare vi to kick one's legs about

sgam'betto sm **far lo ~ a qn** to trip sb up; (fig) to oust sb

sganci'are [zgan'tʃare] vt to unhook; (Ferr) to uncouple; (bombe: da aereo) to release, drop; (fig: fam: soldi) to fork out; **sganciarsi** vpr (fig): **sganciarsi (da)** to get away (from)

sganghe'rato, -a [zgange'rato] ag (porta) off its hinges; (auto) ramshackle; (risata) wild, boisterous

sgar'bato, -a ag rude, impolite

'**sgarbo** sm **fare uno ~ a qn** to be rude to sb

sgargi'ante [zgar'dʒante] ag gaudy, showy

sgattaio'lare vi to sneak away o off

sge'lare [zdʒe'lare] vi, vt to thaw

sghignaz'zare [zgiɲɲat'tsare] vi to laugh scornfully

sgob'bare (fam) vi (scolaro) to swot; (operaio) to slog

sgombe'rare vt (tavolo, stanza) to clear; (piazza, città) to evacuate ▷ vi to move

'**sgombro, -a** ag **~ (di)** clear (of), free (from) ▷ sm (Zool) mackerel; (anche: **sgombero**) clearing; vacating; evacuation; (: trasloco) removal

sgonfi'are vt to let down, deflate; **sgonfiarsi** vpr to go down

'**sgonfio, -a** ag (pneumatico, pallone) flat

'**sgorbio** sm blot; scribble

sgra'devole ag unpleasant, disagreeable

sgra'dito, -a ag unpleasant, unwelcome

sgra'nare vt (piselli) to shell; **~ gli occhi** to open one's eyes wide

sgranchire [zgran'kire] vt (anche: **sgranchirsi**) to stretch; **~ le gambe** to stretch one's legs

sgranocchi'are [zgranok'kjare] vt to munch

'**sgravio** sm **~ fiscale** tax relief

sgrazi'ato, -a [zgrat'tsjato] ag clumsy, ungainly

sgri'dare vt to scold

sgual'cire [zgwal'tʃire] vt to crumple (up), crease

sgual'drina (peg) sf slut

sgu'ardo sm (occhiata) look, glance; (espressione) look (in one's eye)

sguaz'zare [zgwat'tsare] vi (nell'acqua) to splash about; (nella melma) to wallow; **~ nell'oro** to be rolling in money

sguinzagli'are [zgwintsaʎ'ʎare] vt to let off the leash; (fig: persona): **~ qn dietro a qn** to set sb on sb

sgusci'are [zguʃ'ʃare] vt to shell ▷ vi (sfuggire di mano) to slip; **~ via** to slip o slink away

'**shampoo** ['ʃampo] sm inv shampoo

shiatzu [ʃi'atstsu] sm inv shiatsu

shock [ʃɔk] *sm inv* shock

 PAROLA CHIAVE

si (*dav lo, la, li, le, ne diventa* **se**) *pron* **1**
(*riflessivo: maschile*) himself; (*: femminile*)
herself; (*: neutro*) itself; (*: impersonale*)
oneself; (*: pl*) themselves; **lavarsi** to wash
(oneself); **si è tagliato** he has cut himself;
si credono importanti they think a lot of
themselves
2 (*riflessivo: con complemento oggetto*):
lavarsi le mani to wash one's hands; **si
sta lavando i capelli** he (*o* she) is washing
his (*o* her) hair
3 (*reciproco*) one another, each other; **si
amano** they love one another *o* each other
4 (*passivo*): **si ripara facilmente** it is easily
repaired
5 (*impersonale*): **si dice che ...** they *o*
people say that ...; **si vede che è vecchio**
one *o* you can see that it's old
6 (*noi*) we; **tra poco si parte** we're leaving
soon

sì *av* yes; **un giorno sì e uno no** every
other day

'sia *cong* **~ ... ~** (*o ... o*): **~ che lavori, ~ che
non lavori** whether he works or not;
(*tanto ... quanto*): **verranno ~ Luigi ~ suo
fratello** both Luigi and his brother will be
coming

si'amo *vb vedi* **essere**

si'cario *sm* hired killer

sicché [sik'ke] *cong* (*perciò*) so (that),
therefore; (*e quindi*) (and) so

siccità [sittʃi'ta] *sf* drought

sic'come *cong* since, as

Si'cilia [si'tʃilja] *sf* **la ~** Sicily

si'cura *sf* safety catch; (*Aut*) safety lock

sicu'rezza [siku'rettsa] *sf* safety; security;
(*fiducia*) confidence; (*certezza*) certainty; **di
~ safety** *cpd*; **la ~ stradale** road safety

si'curo, -a *ag* safe; (*ben difeso*) secure;
(*fiducioso*) confident; (*certo*) sure, certain;
(*notizia, amico*) reliable; (*esperto*) skilled
▷ *av* (*anche*: **di ~**) certainly; **essere/
mettere al ~** to be safe/put in a safe place;
~ di sé self-confident, sure of o.s.; **sentirsi
~** to feel safe *o* secure

si'edo *ecc vb vedi* **sedere**

si'epe *sf* hedge

si'ero *sm* (*Med*) serum; **sieronega'tivo,
-a** *ag* HIV-negative; **sieroposi'tivo, -a** *ag*
HIV-positive

si'ete *vb vedi* **essere**

si'filide *sf* syphilis

Sig. *abbr* (= *signore*) Mr

siga'retta *sf* cigarette

'sigaro *sm* cigar

Sigg. *abbr* (= *signori*) Messrs

sigil'lare [sidʒil'lare] *vt* to seal

si'gillo [si'dʒillo] *sm* seal

'sigla *sf* initials *pl*; acronym, abbreviation;
sigla automobilistica abbreviation of
province on vehicle number plate; **sigla
musicale** signature tune

Sig.na *abbr* (= *signorina*) Miss

signifi'care [siɲɲifi'kare] *vt* to mean;
signifi'cato *sm* meaning

si'gnora [siɲ'ɲora] *sf* lady; **la ~ X** Mrs X;
buon giorno S~/Signore/Signorina
good morning; (*deferente*) good morning
Madam/Sir/Madam; (*quando si conosce
il nome*) good morning Mrs/Mr/Miss X;
Gentile S~/Signore/Signorina (*in una
lettera*) Dear Madam/Sir/Madam; **il signor
Rossi e ~** Mr Rossi and his wife; **signore e
signori** ladies and gentlemen

si'gnore [siɲ'ɲore] *sm* gentleman;
(*padrone*) lord, master; (*Rel*): **il S~** the Lord;
il signor X Mr X; **i signori Bianchi** (*coniugi*)
Mr and Mrs Bianchi; *vedi anche* **signora**

signo'rile [siɲɲo'rile] *ag* refined

signo'rina [siɲɲo'rina] *sf* young lady; **la ~
X** Miss X; *vedi anche* **signora**

Sig.ra *abbr* (= *signora*) Mrs

silenzia'tore [silentsja'tore] *sm* silencer

si'lenzio [si'lentsjo] *sm* silence; **fare ~** to
be quiet, stop talking; **silenzi'oso, -a** *ag*
silent, quiet

si'licio [si'litʃo] *sm* silicon

sili'cone *sm* silicone

'sillaba *sf* syllable

si'luro *sm* torpedo

simboleggi'are [simboled'dʒare] *vt* to
symbolize

'simbolo *sm* symbol

'simile *ag* (*analogo*) similar; (*di questo tipo*):
un uomo ~ such a man, a man like this;
libri simili such books; **~ a** similar to; **i suoi
simili** one's fellow men; one's peers

simme'tria *sf* symmetry

simpa'tia *sf* (*qualità*) pleasantness;
(*inclinazione*) liking; **avere ~ per qn** to like
sb, have a liking for sb; **sim'patico, -a, -ci,
-che** *ag* (*persona*) nice, pleasant, likeable;
(*casa, albergo ecc*) nice, pleasant

> Attenzione! In inglese esiste la
> parola *sympathetic*, che però significa
> *comprensivo*.

simpatiz'zare [simpatid'dzare] *vi* **~ con**
to take a liking to

simu'lare *vt* to sham, simulate; (*Tecn*) to
simulate

simul'taneo, -a *ag* simultaneous

sina'goga, -ghe *sf* synagogue

sincerità [sintʃeri'ta] *sf* sincerity

sin'cero, -a [sin'tʃero] *ag* sincere; genuine; heartfelt

sinda'cale *ag* (trade-)union *cpd*

sinda'cato *sm* (*di lavoratori*) (trade) union; (*Amm, Econ, Dir*) syndicate, trust, pool

'sindaco, -ci *sm* mayor

sinfo'nia *sf* (*Mus*) symphony

singhioz'zare [singjot'tsare] *vi* to sob; to hiccup

singhi'ozzo [sin'gjottso] *sm* sob; (*Med*) hiccup; **avere il ~** to have the hiccups; **a ~** (*fig*) by fits and starts

single ['singol] *ag inv, sm/f inv* single

singo'lare *ag* (*insolito*) remarkable, singular; (*Ling*) singular ⊳ *sm* (*Ling*) singular; (*Tennis*): **~ maschile/femminile** men's/women's singles

'singolo, -a *ag* single, individual ⊳ *sm* (*persona*) individual; (*Tennis*) = **singolare**

si'nistra *sf* (*Pol*) left (wing); **a ~** on the left; (*direzione*) to the left

si'nistro, -a *ag* left, left-hand; (*fig*) sinister ⊳ *sm* (*incidente*) accident

si'nonimo *sm* synonym; **~ di** synonymous with

sin'tassi *sf* syntax

'sintesi *sf* synthesis; (*riassunto*) summary, résumé

sin'tetico, -a, -ci, -che *ag* synthetic

sintetiz'zare [sintetid'dzare] *vt* to synthesize; (*riassumere*) to summarize

sinto'matico, -a, -ci, -che *ag* symptomatic

'sintomo *sm* symptom

sintonizzarsi *vpr* **~ su** to tune in to

si'pario *sm* (*Teatro*) curtain

si'rena *sf* (*apparecchio*) siren; (*nella mitologia, fig*) siren, mermaid

'Siria *sf* **la ~** Syria

si'ringa, -ghe *sf* syringe

'sismico, -a, -ci, -che *ag* seismic

sis'tema, -i *sm* system; method, way; **sistema nervoso** nervous system; **sistema operativo** (*Inform*) operating system; **sistema solare** solar system

siste'mare *vt* (*mettere a posto*) to tidy, put in order; (*risolvere: questione*) to sort out, settle; (*procurare un lavoro a*) to find a job for; (*dare un alloggio a*) to settle, find accommodation for; **sistemarsi** *vpr* (*problema*) to be settled; (*persona: trovare alloggio*) to find accommodation (BRIT) o accommodations (US); (*: trovarsi un lavoro*) to get fixed up with a job; **ti sistemo io!** I'll soon sort you out!

siste'matico, -a, -ci, -che *ag* systematic

sistemazi'one [sistemat'tsjone] *sf* arrangement; order; settlement; employment; accommodation (BRIT),

accommodations (US)

'sito *sm* **~ Internet** website

situazi'one [situat'tsjone] *sf* situation

ski-lift ['ski:lift] *sm inv* ski tow

slacci'are [zlat'tʃare] *vt* to undo, unfasten

slanci'ato, -a [zlan'tʃato] *ag* slender

'slancio *sm* dash, leap; (*fig*) surge; **di ~** impetuously

'slavo, -a *ag* Slav(onic), Slavic

sle'ale *ag* disloyal; (*concorrenza ecc*) unfair

sle'gare *vt* to untie

slip [zlip] *sm inv* briefs pl

'slitta *sf* sledge; (*trainata*) sleigh

slit'tare *vi* to slip, slide; (*Aut*) to skid

s.l.m. *abbr* (= *sul livello del mare*) a.s.l.

slo'gare *vt* (*Med*) to dislocate

sloggi'are [zlod'dʒare] *vt* (*inquilino*) to turn out ⊳ *vi* to move out

Slo'vacchia [zlo'vakkja] *sf* Slovakia

slo'vacco, -a, -chi, -che *ag, sm/f* Slovak

Slovenia [zlo'vɛnja] *sf* Slovenia

slo'veno, -a *ag, sm/f* Slovene, Slovenian ⊳ *sm* (*Ling*) Slovene

smacchi'are [zmak'kjare] *vt* to remove stains from; **smacchia'tore** *sm* stain remover

'smacco, -chi *sm* humiliating defeat

smagli'ante [zmaʎ'ʎante] *ag* brilliant, dazzling

smaglia'tura [zmaʎʎa'tura] *sf* (*su maglia, calza*) ladder; (*della pelle*) stretch mark

smalizi'ato, -a [zmalit'tsjato] *ag* shrewd, cunning

smalti'mento *sm* (*di rifiuti*) disposal

smal'tire *vt* (*merce*) to sell off; (*rifiuti*) to dispose of; (*cibo*) to digest; (*peso*) to lose; (*rabbia*) to get over; **~ la sbornia** to sober up

'smalto *sm* (*anche: di denti*) enamel; (*per ceramica*) glaze; **smalto per unghie** nail varnish

smantel'lare *vt* to dismantle

smarri'mento *sm* loss; (*fig*) bewilderment; dismay

smar'rire *vt* to lose; (*non riuscire a trovare*) to mislay; **smarrirsi** *vpr* (*perdersi*) to lose one's way, get lost; (*: oggetto*) to go astray

smasche'rare [zmaske'rare] *vt* to unmask

SME *sigla m* (= *Sistema Monetario Europeo*) EMS (*European Monetary System*)

smen'tire *vt* (*negare*) to deny; (*testimonianza*) to refute; **smentirsi** *vpr* to be inconsistent

sme'raldo *sm* emerald

'smesso, -a *pp di* **smettere**

'smettere *vt* to stop; (*vestiti*) to stop wearing ⊳ *vi* to stop, cease; **~ di fare** to stop doing

'smilzo, -a ['zmiltso] *ag* thin, lean

sminu'ire *vt* to diminish, lessen; (*fig*) to belittle

sminuz'zare [zminut'tsare] *vt* to break into small pieces; to crumble

'smisi *ecc* *vb vedi* **smettere**

smis'tare *vt* (*pacchi ecc*) to sort; (*Ferr*) to shunt

smisu'rato, -a *ag* boundless, immeasurable; (*grandissimo*) immense, enormous

smóking ['smɔukɪŋ] *sm inv* dinner jacket

smon'tare *vt* (*mobile, macchina ecc*) to take to pieces, dismantle; (*fig: scoraggiare*) to dishearten ▷ *vi* (*scendere: da cavallo*) to dismount; (: *da treno*) to get off; (*terminare il lavoro*) to stop (work); **smontarsi** *vpr* to lose heart; to lose one's enthusiasm

'smorfia *sf* grimace; (*atteggiamento lezioso*) simpering; **fare smorfie** to make faces; to simper

'smorto, -a *ag* (*viso*) pale, wan; (*colore*) dull

smor'zare [zmor'tsare] *vt* (*suoni*) to deaden; (*colori*) to tone down; (*luce*) to dim; (*sete*) to quench; (*entusiasmo*) to dampen; **smorzarsi** *vpr* (*suono, luce*) to fade; (*entusiasmo*) to dampen

SMS *sigla m inv* (= *short message service*) text (message)

smu'overe *vt* to move, shift; (*fig: commuovere*) to move; (: *dall'inerzia*) to rouse, stir

snatu'rato, -a *ag* inhuman, heartless

'snello, -a *ag* (*agile*) agile; (*svelto*) slender, slim

sner'vante *ag* (*attesa, lavoro*) exasperating

snob'bare *vt* to snub

sno'dare *vt* (*rendere agile, mobile*) to loosen; **snodarsi** *vpr* to come loose; (*articolarsi*) to bend; (*strada, fiume*) to wind

sno'dato, -a *ag* (*articolazione, persona*) flexible; (*fune ecc*) undone

so *vb vedi* **sapere**

sobbar'carsi *vpr* ~ **a** to take on, undertake

'sobrio, -a *ag* sober

socchi'udere [sok'kjudere] *vt* (*porta*) to leave ajar; (*occhi*) to half-close; **socchi'uso, -a** *pp di* **socchiudere**

soc'correre *vt* to help, assist

soccorri'tore, -'trice *sm/f* rescuer

soc'corso, -a *pp di* **soccorrere** ▷ *sm* help, aid, assistance; **soccorso stradale** breakdown service

soci'ale [so'tʃale] *ag* social; (*di associazione*) club *cpd*, association *cpd*

socia'lismo [sotʃa'lizmo] *sm* socialism; **socia'lista, -i, -e** *ag, sm/f* socialist

società [sotʃe'ta] *sf inv* society; (*sportiva*) club; (*Comm*) company; ~ **a responsabilità**

limitata *type of limited liability company*; **società per azioni** limited (BRIT) *o* incorporated (US) company

soci'evole [so'tʃevole] *ag* sociable

'socio ['sɔtʃo] *sm* (*Dir, Comm*) partner; (*membro di associazione*) member

'soda *sf* (*Chim*) soda; (*bibita*) soda (water)

soddisfa'cente [soddisfa'tʃɛnte] *ag* satisfactory

soddis'fare *vt, vi* ~ **a** to satisfy; (*impegno*) to fulfil; (*debito*) to pay off; (*richiesta*) to meet, comply with; **soddis'fatto, -a** *pp di* **soddisfare** ▷ *ag* satisfied; **soddisfatto di** happy *o* satisfied with; pleased with; **soddisfazi'one** *sf* satisfaction

'sodo, -a *ag* firm, hard; (*uovo*) hard-boiled ▷ *av* (*picchiare, lavorare*) hard; (*dormire*) soundly

sofà *sm inv* sofa

soffe'renza [soffe'rɛntsa] *sf* suffering

sof'ferto, -a *pp di* **soffrire**

soffi'are *vt* to blow; (*notizia, segreto*) to whisper ▷ *vi* to blow; (*sbuffare*) to puff (and blow); **soffiarsi il naso** to blow one's nose; ~ **qc/qn a qn** (*fig*) to pinch *o* steal sth/sb from sb; ~ **via qc** to blow sth away

soffi'ata *sf* (*fam*) tip-off; **fare una ~ alla polizia** to tip off the police

'soffice ['sɔffitʃe] *ag* soft

'soffio *sm* (*di vento*) breath; **soffio al cuore** heart murmur

sof'fitta *sf* attic

sof'fitto *sm* ceiling

soffo'cante *ag* suffocating, stifling

soffo'care *vi* (*anche*: **soffocarsi**) to suffocate, choke ▷ *vt* to suffocate, choke; (*fig*) to stifle, suppress

sof'frire *vt* to suffer, endure; (*sopportare*) to bear, stand ▷ *vi* to suffer; to be in pain; ~ **(di) qc** (*Med*) to suffer from sth

sof'fritto, -a *pp di* **soffriggere** ▷ *sm* (*Cuc*) fried mixture of herbs, bacon and onions

sofisti'cato, -a *ag* sophisticated; (*vino*) adulterated

'software ['sɔftwɛa] *sm* ~ **applicativo** applications package

sogget'tivo, -a [soddʒet'tivo] *ag* subjective

sog'getto, -a [sod'dʒetto] *ag* ~ **a** (*sottomesso*) subject to; (*esposto: a variazioni, danni ecc*) subject *o* liable to ▷ *sm* subject

soggezi'one [soddʒet'tsjone] *sf* subjection; (*timidezza*) awe; **avere ~ di qn** to stand in awe of sb; to be ill at ease in sb's presence

soggi'orno *sm* (*invernale, marino*) stay; (*stanza*) living room

'soglia ['sɔʎʎa] *sf* doorstep; (*anche fig*)

threshold

'sogliola ['sɔʎʎola] *sf* (*Zool*) sole

so'gnare [soɲ'ɲare] *vt, vi* to dream; **~ a occhi aperti** to daydream

'sogno ['soɲɲo] *sm* dream

'soia *sf* (*Bot*) soya

sol *sm* (*Mus*) G; (: *solfeggiando*) so(h)

so'laio *sm* (*soffitta*) attic

sola'mente *av* only, just

so'lare *ag* solar, sun *cpd*

'solco, -chi *sm* (*scavo*, *fig*: *ruga*) furrow; (*incavo*) rut, track; (*di disco*) groove

sol'dato *sm* soldier; **soldato semplice** private

soldi *smpl* (*denaro*) money *sg*; **non ho ~** I haven't got any money

'sole *sm* sun; (*luce*) sun(light); (*tempo assolato*) sun(shine); **prendere il ~** to sunbathe

soleggi'ato, -a [soled'dʒato] *ag* sunny

so'lenne *ag* solemn

soli'dale *ag* **essere ~ (con)** to be in agreement (with)

solidarietà *sf* solidarity

'solido, -a *ag* solid; (*forte, robusto*) sturdy, solid; (*fig*: *ditta*) sound, solid ▷ *sm* (*Mat*) solid

so'lista, -i, -e *ag* solo ▷ *sm/f* soloist

solita'mente *av* usually, as a rule

soli'tario, -a *ag* (*senza compagnia*) solitary, lonely; (*solo, isolato*) solitary, lone; (*deserto*) lonely ▷ *sm* (*gioiello, gioco*) solitaire

'solito, -a *ag* usual; **essere ~ fare** to be in the habit of doing; **di ~** usually; **più tardi del ~** later than usual; **come al ~** as usual

soli'tudine *sf* solitude

sol'letico *sm* tickling; **soffrire il ~** to be ticklish

solleva'mento *sm* raising; lifting; revolt; **sollevamento pesi** (*Sport*) weight-lifting

solle'vare *vt* to lift, raise; (*fig*: *persona*: *alleggerire*): **~ (da)** to relieve (of); (: *dar conforto*) to comfort, relieve; (: *questione*) to raise; (: *far insorgere*) to stir (to revolt); **sollevarsi** *vpr* to rise up; (*fig*: *riprendersi*) to recover; (: *ribellarsi*) to rise up

solli'evo *sm* relief; (*conforto*) comfort

'solo, -a *ag* alone; (*in senso spirituale*: *isolato*) lonely; (*unico*) **un ~ libro** only one book, a single book; (*con ag numerale*): **veniamo noi tre soli** just *o* only the three of us are coming ▷ *av* (*soltanto*) only, just; **non ~ ... ma anche** not only ... but also; **fare qc da ~** to do o sth (all) by oneself

sol'tanto *av* only

so'lubile *ag* (*sostanza*) soluble

soluzi'one [solut'tsjone] *sf* solution

sol'vente *ag, sm* solvent

so'maro *sm* ass, donkey

somigli'anza [somiʎ'ʎantsa] *sf* resemblance

somigli'are [somiʎ'ʎare] *vi* **~ a** to be like, resemble; (*nell'aspetto fisico*) to look like; **somigliarsi** *vpr* to be (o look) alike

'somma *sf* (*Mat*) sum; (*di denaro*) sum (of money)

som'mare *vt* to add up; (*aggiungere*) to add; **tutto sommato** all things considered

som'mario, -a *ag* (*racconto, indagine*) brief; (*giustizia*) summary ▷ *sm* summary

sommer'gibile [sommer'dʒibile] *sm* submarine

som'merso, -a *pp di* **sommergere**

sommità *sf inv* summit, top; (*fig*) height

som'mossa *sf* uprising

'sonda *sf* (*Med, Meteor, Aer*) probe; (*Mineralogia*) drill ▷ *ag inv* **pallone** *m* **~** weather balloon

son'daggio [son'daddʒo] *sm* sounding; probe; boring, drilling; (*indagine*) survey; **sondaggio d'opinioni** opinion poll

son'dare *vt* (*Naut*) to sound; (*atmosfera, piaga*) to probe; (*Mineralogia*) to bore, drill; (*fig*: *opinione ecc*) to survey, poll

so'netto *sm* sonnet

son'nambulo, -a *sm/f* sleepwalker

sonnel'lino *sm* nap

son'nifero *sm* sleeping drug (*o pill*)

'sonno *sm* sleep; **prendere ~** to fall asleep; **aver ~** to be sleepy

'sono *vb vedi* **essere**

so'noro, -a *ag* (*ambiente*) resonant; (*voce*) sonorous, ringing; (*onde, film*) sound *cpd*

sontu'oso, -a *ag* sumptuous; lavish

sop'palco, -chi *sm* mezzanine

soppor'tare *vt* (*subire*: *perdita, spese*) to bear, sustain; (*soffrire*: *dolore*) to bear, endure; (*cosa*: *freddo*) to withstand; (*persona*: *freddo, vino*) to take; (*tollerare*) to put up with, tolerate

> Attenzione! In inglese esiste il verbo *to support*, che però non significa *sopportare*.

sop'primere *vt* (*carica, privilegi, testimone*) to do away with; (*pubblicazione*) to suppress; (*parola, frase*) to delete

'sopra *prep* (*gen*) on; (*al di sopra di, più in alto di*) above; over; (*riguardo a*) on, about ▷ *av* on top; (*attaccato, scritto*) on it; (*al di sopra*) above; (*al piano superiore*) upstairs; **donne ~ i 30 anni** women over 30 (years of age); **abito di ~** I live upstairs; **dormirci ~** (*fig*) to sleep on it

so'prabito *sm* overcoat

soprac'ciglio [soprat'tʃiʎʎo] (*pl(f)* **soprac'ciglia**) *sm* eyebrow

sopraf'fare *vt* to overcome, overwhelm

sopral'luogo, -ghi *sm* (*di esperti*)

inspection; (di polizia) on-the-spot investigation

sopram'mobile sm ornament

soprannatu'rale ag supernatural

sopran'nome sm nickname

so'prano, -a sm/f (persona) soprano ▷ sm (voce) soprano

soprappensi'ero av lost in thought

sopras'salto sm **di ~** with a start; suddenly

soprasse'dere vi **~ a** to delay, put off

soprat'tutto av (anzitutto) above all; (specialmente) especially

sopravvalu'tare vt to overestimate

soprav'vento sm **avere/prendere il ~ su** to have/get the upper hand over

sopravvis'suto, -a pp di **sopravvivere**

soprav'vivere vi to survive; (continuare a vivere): **~ (in)** to live on (in); **~ a** (incidente ecc) to survive; (persona) to outlive

so'pruso sm abuse of power; **subire un ~** to be abused

soq'quadro sm **mettere a ~** to turn upside-down

sor'betto sm sorbet, water ice

sor'dina sf **in ~** softly; (fig) on the sly

'sordo, -a ag deaf; (rumore) muffled; (dolore) dull; (odio, rancore) veiled ▷ sm/f deaf person; **sordo'muto, -a** ag deaf-and-dumb ▷ sm/f deaf-mute

so'rella sf sister; **sorel'lastra** sf stepsister; (con genitore in comune) half-sister

sor'gente [sor'dʒɛnte] sf (d'acqua) spring; (di fiume, Fisica, fig) source

'sorgere ['sordʒere] vi to rise; (scaturire) to spring, rise; (fig: difficoltà) to arise

sorni'one, -a ag sly

sorpas'sare vt (Aut) to overtake; (fig) to surpass; (: eccedere) to exceed, go beyond; **~ in altezza** to be higher than; (persona) to be taller than

sorpren'dente ag surprising

sor'prendere vt (cogliere: in flagrante ecc) to catch; (stupire) to surprise; **sorprendersi** vpr **sorprendersi (di)** to be surprised (at); **sor'presa** sf surprise; **fare una sorpresa a qn** to give sb a surprise; **sor'preso, -a** pp di **sorprendere**

sor'reggere [sor'rɛddʒere] vt to support, hold up; (fig) to sustain; **sorreggersi** vpr (tenersi ritto) to stay upright

sor'ridere vi to smile; **sor'riso, -a** pp di **sorridere** ▷ sm smile

'sorsi ecc vb vedi **sorgere**

'sorso sm sip

'sorta sf sort, kind; **di ~** whatever, of any kind, at all

'sorte sf (fato) fate, destiny; (evento fortuito)

chance; **tirare a ~** to draw lots

sor'teggio [sor'teddʒo] sm draw

sorvegli'ante [sorveʎ'ʎante] sm/f (di carcere) guard, warder (BRIT); (di fabbrica ecc) supervisor

sorvegli'anza [sorveʎ'ʎantsa] sf watch; supervision; (Polizia, Mil) surveillance

sorvegli'are [sorveʎ'ʎare] vt (bambino, bagagli, prigioniero) to watch, keep an eye on; (malato) to watch over; (territorio, casa) to watch o keep watch over; (lavori) to supervise

sorvo'lare vt (territorio) to fly over ▷ vi **~ su** (fig) to skim over

S.O.S. sigla m mayday, SOS

'sosia sm inv double

sos'pendere vt (appendere) to hang (up); (interrompere, privare di una carica) to suspend; (rimandare) to defer; (appendere) to hang

sospet'tare vt to suspect ▷ vi **~ di** to suspect; (diffidare) to be suspicious of

sos'petto, -a ag suspicious ▷ sm suspicion; **sospet'toso, -a** ag suspicious

sospi'rare vi to sigh ▷ vt to long for, yearn for; **sos'piro** sm sigh

'sosta sf (fermata) stop, halt; (pausa) pause, break; **senza ~** non-stop, without a break

sostan'tivo sm noun, substantive

sos'tanza [sos'tantsa] sf substance; **sostanze** sfpl (ricchezze) wealth sg, possessions; **in ~** in short, to sum up

sos'tare vi (fermarsi) to stop (for a while), stay; (fare una pausa) to take a break

sos'tegno [sos'teɲɲo] sm support

soste'nere vt to support; (prendere su di sé) to take on, bear; (resistere) to withstand, stand up to; (affermare): **~ che** to maintain that; **sostenersi** vpr to hold o.s. up, support o.s.; (fig) to keep up one's strength; **~ gli esami** to sit exams

sostenta'mento sm maintenance, support

sostitu'ire vt (mettere al posto di): **~ qn/qc a** to substitute sb/sth for; (prendere il posto di: persona) to substitute for; (: cosa) to take the place of

sosti'tuto, -a sm/f substitute

sostituzi'one [sostitut'tsjone] sf substitution; **in ~ di** as a substitute for, in place of

sotta'ceti [sotta'tʃeti] smpl pickles

sot'tana sf (sottoveste) underskirt; (gonna) skirt; (Rel) soutane, cassock

sotter'fugio [sotter'fudʒo] sm subterfuge

sotter'raneo, -a ag underground ▷ sm cellar

sotter'rare vt to bury

sot'tile ag thin; (figura, caviglia) thin, slim,

slender; (*fine: polvere, capelli*) fine; (*fig: leggero*) light; (: *vista*) sharp, keen; (: *olfatto*) fine, discriminating; (: *mente*) subtle; shrewd ▷ *sm* **non andare per il ~** not to mince matters

sottin'teso, -a *pp di* **sottintendere** ▷ *sm* allusion; **parlare senza sottintesi** to speak plainly

'**sotto** *prep* (*gen*) under; (*più in basso di*) below ▷ *av* underneath, beneath; below; **(al piano) di ~** downstairs; **~ forma di** in the form of; **~ il monte** at the foot of the mountain; **siamo ~ Natale** it's nearly Christmas; **~ la pioggia/il sole** in the rain/ sun(shine); **~ terra** underground; **chiuso ~ vuoto** vacuum-packed

sotto'fondo *sm* background; **sottofondo musicale** background music

sottoline'are *vt* to underline; (*fig*) to emphasize, stress

sottoma'rino, -a *ag* (*flora*) submarine; (*cavo, navigazione*) underwater ▷ *sm* (*Naut*) submarine

sottopas'saggio [sottopas'saddʒo] *sm* (*Aut*) underpass; (*pedonale*) subway, underpass

sotto'porre *vt* (*costringere*) to subject; (*fig: presentare*) to submit; **sottoporsi** *vpr* to submit; **sottoporsi a** (*subire*) to undergo

sottos'critto, -a *pp di* **sottoscrivere**

sotto'sopra *av* upside-down

sotto'terra *av* underground

sotto'titolo *sm* subtitle

sottovalu'tare *vt* to underestimate

sotto'veste *sf* underskirt

sotto'voce [sotto'votʃe] *av* in a low voice

sottovu'oto *av* **confezionare ~** to vacuum-pack ▷ *ag* **confezione** *f* **~** vacuum packed

sot'trarre *vt* (*Mat*) to subtract, take away; **~ qn/qc a** (*togliere*) to remove sb/sth from; (*salvare*) to save o rescue sb/sth from; **~ qc a qn** (*rubare*) to steal sth from sb; **sottrarsi** *vpr* **sottrarsi a** (*sfuggire*) to escape; (*evitare*) to avoid; **sottrazi'one** *sf* subtraction; removal

souve'nir [suv(ə)'nir] *sm inv* souvenir

sovi'etico, -a, -ci, -che *ag* Soviet ▷ *sm/f* Soviet citizen

sovrac'carico, -a, chi, che *ag* **~ (di)** overloaded (with) ▷ *sm* excess load; **~ di lavoro** extra work

sovraffol'lato, -a *ag* overcrowded

sovrannatu'rale *ag* = **soprannatu'rale**

so'vrano, -a *ag* sovereign; (*fig: sommo*) supreme ▷ *sm/f* sovereign, monarch

sovrap'porre *vt* to place on top of, put on top of

sovvenzi'one [sovven'tsjone] *sf* subsidy, grant

'**sozzo, -a** ['sottso] *ag* filthy, dirty

S.P.A. *abbr* = **società per azioni**

spac'care *vt* to split, break; (*legna*) to chop; **spaccarsi** *vpr* to split, break; **spacca'tura** *sf* split

spaccherò *ecc* [spakke'rɔ] *vb vedi* **spaccare**

spacci'are [spat'tʃare] *vt* (*vendere*) to sell (off); (*mettere in circolazione*) to circulate; (*droga*) to peddle, push; **spacciarsi** *vpr* **spacciarsi per** (*farsi credere*) to pass o s. off as, pretend to be; **spaccia'tore, -'trice** *sm/f* (*di droga*) pusher; (*di denaro falso*) dealer; '**spaccio** *sm* (*di merce rubata, droga*): **spaccio (di)** trafficking (in); **spaccio (di)** passing (of); (*vendita*) sale; (*bottega*) shop

'**spacco, -chi** *sm* (*fenditura*) split, crack; (*strappo*) tear; (*di gonna*) slit

spac'cone *sm/f* boaster, braggart

'**spada** *sf* sword

spae'sato, -a *ag* disorientated, lost

spa'ghetti [spa'getti] *smpl* (*Cuc*) spaghetti *sg*

'**Spagna** ['spaɲɲa] *sf* **la ~** Spain; **spa'gnolo, -a** *ag* Spanish ▷ *sm/f* Spaniard ▷ *sm* (*Ling*) Spanish; **gli Spagnoli** the Spanish

'**spago, -ghi** *sm* string, twine

spai'ato, -a *ag* (*calza, guanto*) odd

spalan'care *vt* to open wide; **spalancarsi** *vpr* to open wide

spa'lare *vt* to shovel

'**spalla** *sf* shoulder; (*fig: Teatro*) stooge; **spalle** *sfpl* (*dorso*) back

spalli'era *sf* (*di sedia ecc*) back; (*di letto: da capo*) head(board); (: *da piedi*) foot(board); (*Ginnastica*) wall bars *pl*

spal'lina *sf* (*bretella*) strap; (*imbottitura*) shoulder pad

spal'mare *vt* to spread

'**spalti** *smpl* (*di stadio*) terracing

'spandere *vt* to spread; (*versare*) to pour (out)

spa'rare *vt* to fire ▷ *vi* (*far fuoco*) to fire; (*tirare*) to shoot; **spara'toria** *sf* exchange of shots

sparecchi'are [sparek'kjare] *vt* **~ (la tavola)** to clear the table

spa'reggio [spa'reddʒo] *sm* (*Sport*) play-off

'**spargere** ['spardʒere] *vt* (*sparpagliare*) to scatter; (*versare: vino*) to spill; (: *lacrime, sangue*) to shed; (*diffondere*) to spread; (*emanare*) to give off (o out); **spargersi** *vpr* to spread

spa'rire *vi* to disappear, vanish

spar'lare *vi* **~ di** to run down, speak ill of

'**sparo** *sm* shot

spar'tire vt (eredità, bottino) to share out; (avversari) to separate

spar'tito sm (Mus) score

sparti'traffico sm inv (Aut) central reservation (BRIT), median (strip) (US)

sparvi'ero sm (Zool) sparrowhawk

spasi'mante sm suitor

spassio'nato, -a ag dispassionate, impartial

'**spasso** sm (divertimento) amusement, enjoyment; **andare a ~** to go out for a walk; **essere a ~** (fig) to be out of work; **mandare qn a ~** (fig) to give sb the sack

'**spatola** sf spatula; (di muratore) trowel

spa'valdo, -a ag arrogant, bold

spaventa'passeri sm inv scarecrow

spaven'tare vt to frighten, scare; **spaventarsi** vpr to be frightened, be scared; to get a fright; **spa'vento** sm fear, fright; **far spavento a qn** to give sb a fright; **spaven'toso, -a** ag frightening, terrible; (fig: fam) tremendous, fantastic

spazientirsi [spattsjen'tirsi] vpr to lose one's patience

'**spazio** [spattsjo] sm space; **spazio aereo** airspace; **spazi'oso, -a** ag spacious

spazzaca'mino [spattsaka'mino] sm chimney sweep

spazza'neve [spattsa'neve] sm inv snowplough

spaz'zare [spat'tsare] vt to sweep; (foglie ecc) to sweep up; (cacciare) to sweep away; **spazza'tura** sf sweepings pl; (immondizia) rubbish; **spaz'zino** sm street sweeper

'**spazzola** ['spattsola] sf brush; **spazzola da capelli** hairbrush; **spazzola per abiti** clothesbrush; **spazzo'lare** vt to brush; **spazzo'lino** sm (small) brush; **spazzolino da denti** toothbrush

specchi'arsi [spek'kjarsi] vpr to look at o.s. in a mirror; (riflettersi) to be mirrored, be reflected

specchi'etto [spek'kjetto] sm (tabella) table, chart; **specchietto da borsetta** pocket mirror; **specchietto retrovisore** (Aut) rear-view mirror

'**specchio** ['spekkjo] sm mirror

speci'ale [spe'tʃale] ag special; **specia'lista, -i, -e** sm/f specialist; **specialità** sf inv speciality; (branca di studio) special field, speciality; **vorrei assaggiare una specialità del posto** I'd like to try a local speciality; **special'mente** av especially, particularly

'**specie** ['spetʃe] sf inv (Biol, Bot, Zool) species inv; (tipo) kind, sort ▷ av especially, particularly; **una ~ di** a kind of; **fare ~ a qn** to surprise sb; **la ~ umana** mankind

specifi'care [spetʃifi'kare] vt to specify, state

spe'cifico, -a, -ci, -che [spe'tʃifiko] ag specific

specu'lare vi **~ su** (Comm) to speculate in; (sfruttare) to exploit; (meditare) to speculate on; **speculazi'one** sf speculation

spe'dire vt to send

'**spegnere** ['speɲɲere] vt (fuoco, sigaretta) to put out, extinguish; (apparecchio elettrico) to turn o switch off; (gas) to turn off; (fig: suoni, passioni) to stifle; (debito) to extinguish; **spegnersi** vpr to go out; to go off; (morire) to pass away; **puoi ~ la luce?** could you switch off the light?; **non riesco a ~ il riscaldamento** I can't turn the heating off

spellarsi vpr to peel

'**spendere** vt to spend

'**spengo** ecc vb vedi **spegnere**

'**spensi** ecc vb vedi **spegnere**

spensie'rato, -a ag carefree

'**spento, -a** pp di **spegnere** ▷ ag (suono) muffled; (colore) dull; (sigaretta) out; (civiltà, vulcano) extinct

spe'ranza [spe'rantsa] sf hope

spe'rare vt to hope for ▷ vi **~ in** to trust in; **~ che/di fare** to hope that/to do; **lo spero, spero di sì** I hope so

sper'duto, -a ag (isolato) out-of-the-way; (persona: smarrita, a disagio) lost

sperimen'tale ag experimental

sperimen'tare vt to experiment with, test; (fig) to test, put to the test

'**sperma, -i** sm sperm

spe'rone sm spur

sperpe'rare vt to squander

'**spesa** sf (somma di denaro) expense; (costo) cost; (acquisto) purchase; (fam: acquisto del cibo quotidiano) shopping; **spese postali** postage sg; **spese di viaggio** travelling expenses

'**spesso, -a** ag (fitto) thick; (frequente) frequent ▷ av often; **spesse volte** frequently, often

spes'sore sm thickness

Spett. abbr vedi **spettabile**

spet'tabile (abbr: Spett.: in lettere) ag **~ Ditta X** Messrs X and Co.

spet'tacolo sm (rappresentazione) performance, show; (vista, scena) sight; **dare ~ di sé** to make an exhibition o a spectacle of o.s.

spet'tare vi **~ a** (decisione) to be up to; (stipendio) to be due to; **spetta a te decidere** it's up to you to decide

spetta'tore, -'trice sm/f (Cinema, Teatro) member of the audience; (di avvenimento) onlooker, witness

spettego'lare vi to gossip

spetti'nato, -a *ag* dishevelled

'spettro *sm (fantasma)* spectre; *(Fisica)* spectrum

'spezie ['spɛttsje] *sfpl (Cuc)* spices

spez'zare [spet'tsare] *vt (rompere)* to break; *(fig: interrompere)* to break up; **spezzarsi** *vpr* to break

spezza'tino [spettsa'tino] *sm (Cuc)* stew

spezzet'tare [spettset'tare] *vt* to break up *(o chop)* into small pieces

'spia *sf* spy; *(confidente della polizia)* informer; *(Elettr)* indicating light; warning light; *(fessura)* peep-hole; *(fig: sintomo)* sign, indication

spia'cente [spja'tʃɛnte] *ag* sorry; **essere ~ di qc/di fare qc** to be sorry about sth/for doing sth

spia'cevole [spja'tʃevole] *ag* unpleasant

spi'aggia, -ge ['spjaddʒa] *sf* beach; **spiaggia libera** public beach

spia'nare *vt (terreno)* to level, make level; *(edificio)* to raze to the ground; *(pasta)* to roll out; *(rendere liscio)* to smooth (out)

spi'are *vt* to spy on

spi'azzo ['spjattso] *sm* open space; *(radura)* clearing

'spicchio ['spikkjo] *sm (di agrumi)* segment; *(di aglio)* clove; *(parte)* piece, slice

spicci'arsi *vpr* to hurry up

'spiccioli *smpl* (small) change; **mi dispiace, non ho ~** sorry, I don't have any change

'spicco, -chi *sm* **di ~** outstanding; *(tema)* main, principal; **fare ~** to stand out

spie'dino *sm (utensile)* skewer; *(pietanza)* kebab

spi'edo *sm (Cuc)* spit

spie'gare *vt (far capire)* to explain; *(tovaglia)* to unfold; *(vele)* to unfurl; **spiegarsi** *vpr* to explain o.s., make o.s. clear; **~ qc a qn** to explain sth to sb; **spiegazi'one** *sf* explanation

spiegherò *ecc* [spjege'rɔ] *vb vedi* **spiegare**

spie'tato, -a *ag* ruthless, pitiless

spiffe'rare *(fam)* *vt* to blurt out, blab

'spiffero *sm* draught (BRIT), draft (US)

'spiga, -ghe *sf (Bot)* ear

spigli'ato, -a [spiʎ'ʎato] *ag* self-possessed, self-confident

'spigolo *sm* corner; *(Mat)* edge

'spilla *sf* brooch; *(da cravatta, cappello)* pin; **~ di sicurezza** *o* **da balia** safety pin

'spillo *sm* pin; **spillo da balia** *o* **di sicurezza** safety pin

spi'lorcio, -a, -ci, -ce [spi'lortʃo] *ag* mean, stingy

'spina *sf (Bot)* thorn; *(Zool)* spine, prickle; *(di pesce)* bone; *(Elettr)* plug; *(di botte)* bunghole; **birra alla ~** draught beer; **spina dorsale** *(Anat)* backbone

spinaci [spi'natʃi] *smpl* spinach *sg*

spi'nello *sm (Droga: gergo)* joint

'spingere ['spindʒere] *vt* to push; *(condurre: anche fig)* to drive; *(stimolare)*: **~ qn a fare** to urge *o* press sb to do

spi'noso, -a *ag* thorny, prickly

'spinsi *ecc vb vedi* **spingere**

'spinta *sf (urto)* push; *(Fisica)* thrust; *(fig: stimolo)* incentive, spur; *(: appoggio)* string-pulling *no pl*; **dare una ~ a qn** *(fig)* to pull strings for sb

'spinto, -a *pp di* **spingere**

spio'naggio [spio'naddʒo] *sm* espionage, spying

spion'cino [spion'tʃino] *sm* peephole

spi'raglio [spi'raʎʎo] *sm (fessura)* chink, narrow opening; *(raggio di luce, fig)* glimmer, gleam

spi'rale *sf* spiral; *(contraccettivo)* coil; **a ~** spiral(-shaped)

spiri'tato, -a *ag* possessed; *(fig: persona, espressione)* wild

spiri'tismo *sm* spiritualism

'spirito *sm (Rel, Chim, disposizione d'animo, di legge ecc, fantasma)* spirit; *(pensieri, intelletto)* mind; *(arguzia)* wit; *(umorismo)* humour, wit; **lo S~ Santo** the Holy Spirit *o* Ghost

spirito'saggine [spirito'saddʒine] *sf* witticism; *(peg)* wisecrack

spiri'toso, -a *ag* witty

spiritu'ale *ag* spiritual

'splendere *vi* to shine

'splendido, -a *ag* splendid; *(splendente)* shining; *(sfarzoso)* magnificent, splendid

splen'dore *sm* splendour; *(luce intensa)* brilliance, brightness

spogli'are [spoʎ'ʎare] *vt (svestire)* to undress; *(privare, fig: depredare)*: **~ qn di qc** to deprive sb of sth; *(togliere ornamenti: anche fig)*: **~ qn/qc di** to strip sb/sth of; **spogliarsi** *vpr* to undress, strip; **spogliarsi di** *(ricchezze ecc)* to deprive o.s. of, give up; *(pregiudizi)* to rid o.s. of; **spoglia'rello** [spoʎʎa'rɛllo] *sm* striptease; **spoglia'toio** *sm* dressing room; *(di scuola ecc)* cloakroom; *(Sport)* changing room

'spola *sf (bobina di filo)* cop; **fare la ~ (fra)** to go to and fro *o* shuttle (between)

spolve'rare *vt (anche Cuc)* to dust; *(con spazzola)* to brush; *(con battipanni)* to beat; *(fig)* to polish off ▷ *vi* to dust

spon'taneo, -a *ag* spontaneous; *(persona)* unaffected, natural

spor'care *vt* to dirty, make dirty; *(fig)* to sully, soil; **sporcarsi** *vpr* to get dirty

spor'cizia [spor'tʃittsja] *sf (stato)* dirtiness; *(sudiciume)* dirt, filth; *(cosa* *sporca* dirt *no pl*, something dirty

'sporco, -a, -chi, -che *ag* dirty, filthy

spor'genza [spor'dʒentsa] *sf* projection

'sporgere ['spɔrdʒere] *vt* to put out, stretch out ▷ *vi* (*venire in fuori*) to stick out; **sporgersi** *vpr* to lean out; **~ querela contro qn** (*Dir*) to take legal action against sb

'sporsi *ecc vb vedi* **sporgere**

sport *sm inv* sport

spor'tello *sm* (*di treno, auto ecc*) door; (*di banca, ufficio*) window, counter; **sportello automatico** (*Banca*) cash dispenser, automated telling machine

spor'tivo, -a *ag* (*gara, giornale, centro*) sports *cpd*; (*persona*) sporty; (*abito*) casual; (*spirito, atteggiamento*) sporting

'sposa *sf* bride; (*moglie*) wife

sposa'lizio [spoza'littsjo] *sm* wedding

spo'sare *vt* to marry; (*fig: idea, fede*) to espouse; **sposarsi** *vpr* to get married, marry; **sposarsi con qn** to marry sb, get married to sb; **spo'sato, -a** *ag* married

'sposo *sm* (bride)groom; (*marito*) husband

spos'sato, -a *ag* exhausted, weary

spos'tare *vt* to move, shift; (*cambiare: orario*) to change; **spostarsi** *vpr* to move; **può ~ la macchina, per favore?** can you move your car please?

'spranga, -ghe *sf* (*sbarra*) bar

spre'care *vt* to waste

spre'gevole [spre'dʒevole] *ag* contemptible, despicable

'spremere *vt* to squeeze

spremia'grumi *sm inv* lemon squeezer

spre'muta *sf* fresh juice; **spremuta d'arancia** fresh orange juice

sprez'zante [spret'tsante] *ag* scornful, contemptuous

sprofon'dare *vi* to sink; (*casa*) to collapse; (*suolo*) to give way, subside

spro'nare *vt* to spur (on)

sproporzio'nato, -a [sproportsjo'nato] *ag* disproportionate, out of all proportion

sproporzi'one [spropor'tsjone] *sf* disproportion

spro'posito *sm* blunder; **a ~** at the wrong time; (*rispondere, parlare*) irrelevantly

sprovve'duto, -a *ag* inexperienced, naïve

sprov'visto, -a *ag* (*mancante*): **~ di** lacking in, without; **alla sprovvista** unawares

spruz'zare [sprut'tsare] *vt* (*a nebulizzazione*) to spray; (*aspergere*) to sprinkle; (*inzaccherare*) to splash

'spugna ['spuɲɲa] *sf* (*Zool*) sponge; (*tessuto*) towelling

'spuma *sf* (*schiuma*) foam; (*bibita*) fizzy drink

spu'mante *sm* sparkling wine

spun'tare *vt* (*coltello*) to break the point of; (*capelli*) to trim ▷ *vi* (*uscire: germogli*) to sprout; (*: capelli*) to begin to grow; (*: denti*) to come through; (*apparire*) to appear (suddenly)

spun'tino *sm* snack

'spunto *sm* (*Teatro, Mus*) cue; (*fig*) starting point; **dare lo ~ a** (*fig*) to give rise to

spu'tare *vt* to spit out; (*fig*) to belch (out) ▷ *vi* to spit

'squadra *sf* (*strumento*) (set) square; (*gruppo*) team, squad; (*di operai*) gang, squad; (*Mil*) squad; (*: Aer, Naut*) squadron; (*Sport*) team; **lavoro a squadre** teamwork

squagli'arsi [skwaʎ'ʎarsi] *vpr* to melt; (*fig*) to sneak off

squa'lifica *sf* disqualification

squalifi'care *vt* to disqualify

'squallido, -a *ag* wretched, bleak

'squalo *sm* shark

'squama *sf* scale

squarcia'gola [skwartʃa'gola]: **a ~** *av* at the top of one's voice

squattri'nato, -a *ag* penniless

squili'brato, -a *ag* (*Psic*) unbalanced

squil'lante *ag* shrill, sharp

squil'lare *vi* (*campanello, telefono*) to ring (out); (*tromba*) to blare; **'squillo** *sm* ring, ringing *no pl*; blare; **ragazza f squillo** *inv* call girl

squi'sito, -a *ag* exquisite; (*cibo*) delicious; (*persona*) delightful

squit'tire *vi* (*uccello*) to squawk; (*topo*) to squeak

sradi'care *vt* to uproot; (*fig*) to eradicate

srego'lato, -a *ag* (*senza ordine: vita*) disorderly; (*smodato*) immoderate; (*dissoluto*) dissolute

S.r.l. *abbr* = **società a responsabilità limitata**

sroto'lare *vt*, **sroto'larsi** ▷ *vpr* to unroll

SS *sigla* = **strada statale**

S.S.N. *abbr* (= *Servizio Sanitario Nazionale*) ≈ NHS

sta *ecc vb vedi* **stare**

'stabile *ag* stable, steady; (*tempo: non variabile*) settled; (*Teatro: compagnia*) resident ▷ *sm* (*edificio*) building

stabili'mento *sm* (*edificio*) establishment; (*fabbrica*) plant, factory

stabi'lire *vt* to establish; (*fissare: prezzi, data*) to fix; (*decidere*) to decide; **stabilirsi** *vpr* (*prendere dimora*) to settle

stac'care *vt* (*levare*) to detach, remove; (*separare: anche fig*) to separate, divide; (*strappare*) to tear off (o out); (*scandire: parole*) to pronounce clearly; (*Sport*) to leave behind; **staccarsi** *vpr* (*bottone ecc*) to come off; (*scostarsi*): **staccarsi (da)**

to move away (from); (fig: separarsi):
staccarsi da to leave; **non ~ gli occhi da
qn** not to take one's eyes off sb

'**stadio** sm (Sport) stadium; (periodo, fase)
phase, stage

'**staffa** sf (di sella, Tecn) stirrup; **perdere le
staffe** (fig) to fly off the handle

staf'**fetta** sf (messo) dispatch rider; (Sport)
relay race

stagio'**nale** [stadʒo'nale] ag seasonal

stagio'**nato, -a** [stadʒo'nato] ag (vedi vb)
seasoned; matured; (scherzoso: attempato)
getting on in years

stagi'**one** [sta'dʒone] sf season; **alta/
bassa ~** high/low season

sta**gista, -i, -e** [sta'dʒ[gh]ista] sm/f
trainee, intern (us)

'**stagno, -a** ['staɲɲo] ag watertight; (a
tenuta d'aria) airtight ▷ sm (acquitrino)
pond; (Chim) tin

sta'**gnola** [staɲ'ɲɔla] sf tinfoil

'**stalla** sf (per bovini) cowshed; (per cavalli)
stable

stal'**lone** sm stallion

stamat'**tina** av this morning

stam'**becco, -chi** sm ibex

'**stampa** sf (Tip, Fot: tecnica) printing;
(impressione, copia fotografica) print;
(insieme di quotidiani, giornalisti ecc) press

stam'**pante** sf (Inform) printer

stam'**pare** vt to print; (pubblicare) to
publish; (coniare) to strike, coin; (imprimere:
anche fig) to impress

stampa'**tello** sm block letters pl

stam'**pella** sf crutch

'**stampo** sm mould; (fig: indole) type, kind,
sort

sta'**nare** vt to drive out

stan'**care** vt to tire, make tired; (annoiare)
to bore; (infastidire) to annoy; **stancarsi
vpr** to get tired, tire o.s. out; **stancarsi (di)**
to grow weary (of), grow tired (of)

stan'**chezza** [stan'kettsa] sf tiredness,
fatigue

'**stanco, -a, -chi, -che** ag tired; **~ di** tired
of, fed up with

stan'**ghetta** [stan'getta] sf (di occhiali) leg;
(Mus, di scrittura) bar

'**stanno** vb vedi **stare**

sta'**notte** av tonight; (notte passata) last
night

'**stante** prep **a sé ~** (appartamento, casa)
independent, separate

stan'**tio, -a, -'tii, -'tie** ag stale; (burro)
rancid; (fig) old

stan'**tuffo** sm piston

'**stanza** ['stantsa] sf room; (Poesia) stanza;
stanza da bagno bathroom; **stanza da
letto** bedroom

stap'**pare** vt to uncork; to uncap

'**stare** vi (restare in un luogo) to stay, remain;
(abitare) to stay, live; (essere situato) to be,
be situated; (anche: **~ in piedi**) to be, stand;
(essere, trovarsi) to be; (dipendere): **se stesse
in me** if it were up to me, if it depended on
me; (seguito da gerundio): **sta studiando**
he's studying; **starci** (esserci spazio): **nel
baule non ci sta più niente** there's no
more room in the boot; (accettare) to
accept; **ci stai?** is that okay with you?; **~
a** (attenersi a) to follow, stick to; (seguito
dall'infinito): **stiamo a discutere** we're
talking; (toccare a): **sta a te giocare** it's
your turn to play; **~ per fare qc** to be about
to do sth; **come sta?** how are you?; **io sto
bene/male** I'm very well/not very well; **~
a qn** (abiti ecc) to fit sb; **queste scarpe mi
stanno strette** these shoes are tight for
me; **il rosso ti sta bene** red suits you

starnu'**tire** vi to sneeze; **star'nuto** sm
sneeze

sta'**sera** av this evening, tonight

sta'**tale** ag state cpd; (government cpd
▷ sm/f state employee, local authority
employee; (nell'amministrazione) ≈ civil
servant; **strada statale** ≈ trunk (Brit) o
main road

sta'**tista, -i** sm statesman

sta'**tistica** sf statistics sg

'**stato, -a** pp di **essere; stare** ▷ sm
(condizione) state, condition; (Pol) state;
(Dir) status; **essere in ~ d'accusa** (Dir)
to be committed for trial; **~ d'assedio/
d'emergenza** state of siege/emergency;
~ civile (Amm) marital status; **gli Stati
Uniti (d'America)** the United States (of
America); **stato d'animo** mood; **stato
maggiore** (Mil) staff

'**statua** sf statue

statuni'**tense** ag United States cpd, of the
United States

sta'**tura** sf (Anat) height, stature; (fig)
stature

sta'**tuto** sm (Dir) statute; constitution

sta'**volta** av this time

stazio'**nario, -a** [stattsjo'narjo] ag
stationary; (fig) unchanged

stazi'**one** [stat'tsjone] sf station;
(balneare, termale) resort; **stazione degli
autobus** bus station; **stazione balneare**
seaside resort; **stazione ferroviaria**
railway (Brit) o railroad (US) station;
stazione invernale winter sports resort;
stazione di polizia police station (in small
town); **stazione di servizio** service o petrol
(Brit) o filling station

'**stecca, -che** sf stick; (di ombrello) rib; (di
sigarette) carton; (Med) splint; (stonatura):

fare una ~ to sing (o play) a wrong note

stec'cato sm fence

'**stella** sf star; **stella alpina** (Bot) edelweiss; **stella cadente** shooting star; **stella di mare** (Zool) starfish

'**stelo** sm stem; (asta) rod; **lampada a ~** standard lamp

'**stemma, -i** sm coat of arms

'**stemmo** vb vedi **stare**

stempi'ato, -a ag with a receding hairline

'**stendere** vt (braccia, gambe) to stretch (out); (tovaglia) to spread (out); (bucato) to hang out; (mettere a giacere) to lay (down); (spalmare: colore) to spread; (mettere per iscritto) to draw up; **stendersi** vpr (coricarsi) to stretch out, lie down; (estendersi) to extend, stretch

stenogra'fia sf shorthand

sten'tare vi **~ a fare** to find it hard to do, have difficulty doing

'**stento** sm (fatica) difficulty; **stenti** smpl (privazioni) hardship sg, privation sg; **a ~** with difficulty, barely

'**sterco** sm dung

stereo ['stɛreo] ag inv stereo ▷ sm inv (impianto) stereo

'**sterile** ag sterile; (terra) barren; (fig) futile, fruitless

steriliz'zare [sterilid'dzare] vt to sterilize

ster'lina sf pound (sterling)

stermi'nare vt to exterminate, wipe out

stermi'nato, -a ag immense; endless

ster'minio sm extermination, destruction

'**sterno** sm (Anat) breastbone

ste'roide sm steroid

ster'zare [ster'tsare] vt, vi (Aut) to steer; '**sterzo** sm steering; (volante) steering wheel

'**stessi** ecc vb vedi **stare**

'**stesso, -a** ag same; (rafforzativo: in persona, proprio): **il re ~** the king himself o in person ▷ pron **lo(la) ~(a)** the same (one); **i suoi stessi avversari lo ammirano** even his enemies admire him; **fa lo ~** it doesn't matter; **per me è lo ~** it's all the same to me, it doesn't matter to me; vedi **io**; **tu** ecc

ste'sura sf drafting no pl, drawing up no pl; draft

'**stetti** ecc vb vedi **stare**

'**stia** ecc vb vedi **stare**

sti'lare vt to draw up, draft

'**stile** sm style; **stile libero** freestyle; **sti'lista, -i** sm designer

stilo'grafica, -che sf (anche: **penna ~**) fountain pen

'**stima** sf esteem; valuation; assessment, estimate

sti'mare vt (persona) to esteem, hold in high regard; (terreno, casa ecc) to value; (stabilire in misura approssimativa) to estimate, assess; (ritenere): **~ che** to consider that; **stimarsi fortunato** to consider o.s. (to be) lucky

stimo'lare vt to stimulate; (incitare): **~ qn (a fare)** to spur sb on (to do)

'**stimolo** sm (anche fig) stimulus

'**stingere** ['stindʒere] vt, vi (anche: **stingersi**) to fade; '**stinto, -a** pp di **stingere**

sti'pare vt to cram, pack; **stiparsi** vpr (accalcarsi) to crowd, throng

sti'pendio sm salary

'**stipite** sm (di porta, finestra) jamb

stipu'lare vt (redigere) to draw up

sti'rare vt (abito) to iron; (distendere) to stretch; (strappare: muscolo) to strain; **stirarsi** vpr to stretch (o.s.)

stiti'chezza [stiti'kettsa] sf constipation

'**stitico, -a, -ci, -che** ag constipated

'**stiva** sf (di nave) hold

sti'vale sm boot

'**stizza** ['stittsa] sf anger, vexation

'**stoffa** sf material, fabric; (fig): **aver la ~ di** to have the makings of

'**stomaco, -chi** sm stomach; **dare di ~ to** vomit, be sick

sto'nato, -a ag (persona) off-key; (strumento) off-key, out of tune

stop sm inv (Tel) stop; (Aut: cartello) stop sign; (: fanalino d'arresto) brake-light

'**storcere** ['stɔrtʃere] vt to twist; **storcersi** vpr to writhe, twist; **~ il naso** (fig) to turn up one's nose; **storcersi la caviglia** to twist one's ankle

stor'dire vt (intontire) to stun, daze; **stor'dito, -a** ag stunned

'**storia** sf (scienza, avvenimenti) history; (racconto, bugia) story; (faccenda, questione) business no pl; (pretesto) excuse, pretext; **storie** sfpl (smancerie) fuss sg; '**storico, -a, -ci, -che** ag historic(al) ▷ sm historian

stori'one sm (Zool) sturgeon

'**stormo** sm (di uccelli) flock

'**storpio, -a** ag crippled, maimed

'**storsi** ecc vb vedi **storcere**

'**storta** sf (distorsione) sprain, twist

'**storto, -a** pp di **storcere** ▷ ag (chiodo) twisted, bent; (gamba, quadro) crooked

sto'viglie [sto'viʎʎe] sfpl dishes pl, crockery

strabico, -a, -ci, -che ag squint-eyed; (occhi) squint

strac'chino [strak'kino] sm type of soft cheese

stracci'are [strat'tʃare] vt to tear; **stracciarsi** vpr to tear

'**straccio, -a, -ci, -ce** ['strattʃo] ag **carta straccia** waste paper ▷ sm rag; (per pulire) cloth, duster; **stracci** smpl (peg: indumenti) rags; **si è ridotto a uno** ~ he's worn himself out; **non ha uno ~ di lavoro** he's not got a job of any sort

'**strada** sf road; (di città) street; (cammino, via, fig) way; **che ~ devo prendere per andare a …?** which road do I take for …?; **farsi ~** (fig) to do well for o s.; **essere fuori** ~ (fig) to be on the wrong track; ~ **facendo** on the way; **strada senza uscita** dead end; **stra'dale** ag road cpd

strafalci'one [strafal'tʃone] sm blunder, howler

stra'fare vi to overdo it

strafot'tente ag è ~ he doesn't give a damn, he couldn't care less

'**strage** ['stradʒe] sf massacre, slaughter

stralu'nato, -a ag (occhi) rolling; (persona) beside o.s., very upset

'**strambo, -a** ag strange, queer

strampa'lato, -a ag odd, eccentric

stra'nezza [stra'nettsa] sf strangeness

strango'lare vt to strangle

strani'ero, -a ag foreign ▷ sm/f foreigner

Attenzione! In inglese esiste la parola stranger, che però significa sconosciuto oppure estraneo.

'**strano, -a** ag strange, odd

straordi'nario, -a ag extraordinary; (treno ecc) special ▷ sm (lavoro) overtime

strapi'ombo sm overhanging rock; **a ~** overhanging

strap'pare vt (gen) to tear, rip; (pagina ecc) to tear off, tear out; (sradicare) to pull up; (togliere): ~ **qc a qn** to snatch sth from sb; (fig) to wrest sth from sb; **strapparsi** vpr (lacerarsi) to rip, tear; (rompersi) to break; **strapparsi un muscolo** to tear a muscle; '**strappo** sm pull, tug; tear, rip; **fare uno strappo alla regola** to make an exception to the rule; **strappo muscolare** torn muscle

strari'pare vi to overflow

'**strascico, -chi** ['straʃʃiko] sm (di abito) train; (conseguenza) after-effect

strata'gemma, -i [strata'dʒɛmma] sm stratagem

strate'gia, -'gie [strate'dʒia] sf strategy; **stra'tegico, -a, -ci, -che** ag strategic

'**strato** sm layer; (rivestimento) coat, coating; (Geo, fig) stratum; (Meteor) stratus; **strato d'ozono** ozone layer

strat'tone sm tug, jerk; **dare uno ~ a qc** to tug o jerk sth, give sth a tug o jerk

strava'gante ag odd, eccentric

stra'volto, -a pp di **stravolgere**

'**strazio** sm torture; (fig: cosa fatta male): **essere uno ~** to be appalling

'**strega, -ghe** sf witch

stre'gare vt to bewitch

stre'gone sm (mago) wizard; (di tribù) witch doctor

strepi'toso, -a ag clamorous, deafening; (fig: successo) resounding

stres'sante ag stressful

stres'sato, -a ag under stress

stretch [stretʃ] ag inv stretch

'**stretta** sf (di mano) grasp; (finanziaria) squeeze; (fig: dolore, turbamento) pang; **una ~ di mano** a handshake; **essere alle strette** to have one's back to the wall; vedi anche **stretto**

stretta'mente av tightly; (rigorosamente) strictly

'**stretto, -a** pp di **stringere** ▷ ag (corridoio, limiti) narrow; (gonna, scarpe, nodo, curva) tight; (intimo: parente, amico) close; (rigoroso: osservanza) strict; (preciso: significato) precise, exact ▷ sm (braccio di mare) strait; **a denti stretti** with clenched teeth; **lo ~ necessario** the bare minimum; **stret'toia** sf bottleneck; (fig) tricky situation

stri'ato, -a ag streaked

'**stridulo, -a** ag shrill

stril'lare vt, vi to scream, shriek; '**strillo** sm scream, shriek

strimin'zito, -a [strimin'tsito] ag (misero) shabby; (molto magro) skinny

strimpel'lare vt (Mus) to strum

'**stringa, -ghe** sf lace

strin'gato, -a ag (fig) concise

'**stringere** ['strindʒere] vt (avvicinare due cose) to press (together), squeeze (together); (tenere stretto) to hold tight, clasp, clutch; (pugno, mascella, denti) to clench; (labbra) to compress; (avvitare) to tighten; (abito) to take in; (scarpe) to pinch, be tight for; (fig: concludere: patto) to make; (: accelerare: passo, tempo) to quicken ▷ vi (essere stretto) to be tight; (tempo: incalzare) to be pressing

'**strinsi** ecc vb vedi **stringere**

'**striscia, -sce** ['striʃʃa] sf (di carta, tessuto ecc) strip; (riga) stripe; **strisce (pedonali)** zebra crossing sg

strisci'are [striʃ'ʃare] vt (piedi) to drag; (muro, macchina) to graze ▷ vi to crawl, creep

'**striscio** ['striʃʃo] sm graze; (Med) smear; **colpire di ~** to graze

strisci'one [striʃ'ʃone] sm banner

strito'lare vt to grind

striz'zare [strit'tsare] vt (panni) to wring (out); **~ l'occhio** to wink

'**strofa** sf strophe

strofi'naccio [strofi'nattʃo] sm duster, cloth; (per piatti) dishcloth; (per pavimenti)

floorcloth

strofi'nare *vt* to rub

stron'care *vt* to break off; (*fig: ribellione*) to suppress, put down; (*: film, libro*) to tear to pieces

'stronzo ['strontso] *sm* (*sterco*) turd; (*fig faml: persona*) shit (!)

stroz'zare [strot'tsare] *vt* (*soffocare*) to choke, strangle

struccarsi *vpr* to remove one's make-up

strumen'tale *ag* (*Mus*) instrumental

strumentaliz'zare [strumentalid'dzare] *vt* to exploit, use to one's own ends

stru'mento *sm* (*arnese, fig*) instrument, tool; (*Mus*) instrument; **~ a corda** *o* **ad arco/a fiato** stringed/wind instrument

'strutto *sm* lard

strut'tura *sf* structure

'struzzo ['struttso] *sm* ostrich

stuc'care *vt* (*muro*) to plaster; (*vetro*) to putty; (*decorare con stucchi*) to stucco

'stucco, -chi *sm* plaster; (*da vetri*) putty; (*ornamentale*) stucco; **rimanere di ~** (*fig*) to be dumbfounded

stu'dente, -'essa *sm/f* student; (*scolaro*) pupil, schoolboy/girl

studi'are *vt* to study

'studio *sm* studying; (*ricerca, saggio, stanza*) study; (*di professionista*) office; (*di artista, Cinema, TV, Radio*) studio; **studi** *smpl* (*Ins*) studies; **studio medico** doctor's surgery (BRIT) *o* office (US)

studi'oso, -a *ag* studious, hard-working ▷ *sm/f* scholar

'stufa *sf* stove; **stufa elettrica** electric fire *o* heater

stu'fare *vt* (*Cuc*) to stew; (*fig: fam*) to bore; **stufarsi** *vpr* (*fam*) **stufarsi (di)** (*fig*) to get fed up (with); **'stufo, -a** (*fam*) *ag* **essere stufo di** to be fed up with, be sick and tired of

stu'oia *sf* mat

stupefa'cente [stupefa'tʃɛnte] *ag* stunning, astounding ▷ *sm* drug, narcotic

stupe'fatto, -a *pp di* **stupefare**

stu'pendo, -a *ag* marvellous, wonderful

stupi'daggine [stupi'daddʒine] *sf* stupid thing (to do *o* say)

stupidità *sf* stupidity

'stupido, -a *ag* stupid

stu'pire *vt* to amaze, stun ▷ *vi* **stupirsi; ~ (di)** to be amazed (at), be stunned (by)

stu'pore *sm* amazement, astonishment

stu'prare *vt* to rape

'stupro *sm* rape

stu'rare *vt* (*lavandino*) to clear

stuzzica'denti [stuttsika'dɛnti] *sm* toothpick

stuzzi'care [stuttsi'kare] *vt* (*ferita ecc*)

to poke (at), prod (at); (*fig*) to tease; (*: appetito*) to whet; (*: curiosità*) to stimulate; **~ i denti** to pick one's teeth

PAROLA CHIAVE

su (*su +il* = **sul**, *su +lo* = **sullo**, *su +l'* = **sull'**, *su +la* = **sulla**, *su +i* = **sui**, *su +gli* = **sugli**, *su +le* = **sulle**) *prep* **1** (*gen*) on; (*moto*) on(to); (*in cima a*) on (top of); **mettilo sul tavolo** put it on the table; **un paesino sul mare** a village by the sea

2 (*argomento*) about, on; **un libro su Cesare** a book on *o* about Caesar

3 (*circa*) about; **costerà sui 3 milioni** it will cost about 3 million; **una ragazza sui 17 anni** a girl of about 17 (years of age)

4: **su misura** made to measure; **su richiesta** on request; **3 casi su dieci** 3 cases out of 10

▷ *av* **1** (*in alto, verso l'alto*) up; **vieni su** come on up; **guarda su** look up; **su le mani!** hands up!; **in su** (*verso l'alto*) up(wards); (*in poi*) onwards; **dai 20 anni in su** from the age of 20 onwards

2 (*addosso*) on; **cos'hai su?** what have you got on?

▷ *escl* come on!; **su coraggio!** come on, cheer up!

su'bacqueo, -a *ag* underwater ▷ *sm* skin-diver

sub'buglio [sub'buλλo] *sm* confusion, turmoil

'subdolo, -a *ag* underhand, sneaky

suben'trare *vi* **~ a qn in qc** to take over sth from sb

su'bire *vt* to suffer, endure

'subito *av* immediately, at once, straight away

subodo'rare *vt* (*insidia ecc*) to smell, suspect

subordi'nato, -a *ag* subordinate; (*dipendente*); **~ a** dependent on, subject to

suc'cedere [sut'tʃedere] *vi* (*prendere il posto di qn*); **~ a** to succeed; (*venire dopo*): **~ a** to follow; (*accadere*) to happen; **cos'è successo?** what happened?; **succes'sivo, -a** *ag* successive; **suc'cesso, -a** *pp di* **succedere** ▷ *sm* (*esito*) outcome; (*buona riuscita*) success; **di successo** (*libro, personaggio*) successful

succhi'are [suk'kjare] *vt* to suck (up); **succhi'otto** *sm* (*per bambino*) dummy

succhi'otto [suk'kjɔtto] *sm* dummy (BRIT), pacifier (US), comforter (US)

suc'cinto, -a [sut'tʃinto] *ag* (*discorso*) succinct; (*abito*) brief

'succo, -chi *sm* juice; (*fig*) essence, gist;

succo di frutta/pomodoro fruit/tomato juice

succur'sale sf branch (office)

sud sm south ▷ ag inv south; (lato) south, southern

Su'dafrica sm il ~ South Africa; **sudafri'cano, -a** ag, sm/f South African

Suda'merica sm il ~ South America

su'dare vi to perspire, sweat; ~ **freddo** to come out in a cold sweat

su'dato, -a ag (persona, mani) sweaty; (fig: denaro) hard-earned ▷ sf (anche fig) sweat; **una vittoria sudata** a hard-won victory; **ho fatto una bella sudata per finirlo in tempo** it was a real sweat to get it finished in time

suddi'videre vt to subdivide

su'dest sm south-east

'sudicio, -a, -ci, -ce ['suditʃo] ag dirty, filthy

su'dore sm perspiration, sweat

su'dovest sm south-west

suffici'ente [suffi'tʃɛnte] ag enough, sufficient; (borioso) self-important; (Ins) satisfactory; **suffici'enza** sf self-importance; pass mark; **a sufficienza** enough; **ne ho avuto a sufficienza!** I've had enough of this!

suf'fisso sm (Ling) suffix

sugge'rimento [suddʒeri'mento] sm suggestion; (consiglio) piece of advice, advice no pl

sugge'rire [suddʒe'rire] vt (risposta) to tell; (consigliare) to advise; (proporre) to suggest; (Teatro) to prompt

suggestio'nare [suddʒestjo'nare] vt to influence

sugges'tivo, -a [suddʒes'tivo] ag (paesaggio) evocative; (teoria) interesting, attractive

'sughero ['sugero] sm cork

'sugo, -ghi sm (succo) juice; (di carne) gravy; (condimento) sauce; (fig) gist, essence

sui'cida, -i, -e [sui'tʃida] ag suicidal ▷ sm/f suicide

suici'darsi [suitʃi'darsi] vpr to commit suicide

sui'cidio [sui'tʃidjo] sm suicide

su'ino, -a ag **carne suina** pork ▷ sm pig

sul'tano, -a sm/f sultan/sultana

'suo (f'sua, pl 'sue, su'oi) det il ~, **la sua** ecc (di lui) his; (di lei) her; (di esso) its; (con valore indefinito) one's, his/her; (anche: **S~**: forma di cortesia) your ▷ pron **il ~, la sua** ecc his; hers; yours; **i ~ i** his (o her o one's o your) family

su'ocero, -a ['swɔtʃero] sm/f father/mother-in-law

su'ola sf (di scarpa) sole

su'olo sm (terreno) ground; (terra) soil

suo'nare vt (Mus) to play; (campana) to ring; (ore) to strike; (clacson, allarme) to sound ▷ vi to play; (telefono, campana) to ring; (ore) to strike; (clacson, fig: parole) to sound

suone'ria sf alarm

su'ono sm sound

su'ora sf (Rel) sister

'super sf (anche: **benzina ~**) ≈ four-star (petrol) (BRIT), premium (US)

supe'rare vt (oltrepassare: limite) to exceed, surpass; (percorrere) to cover; (attraversare: fiume) to cross; (sorpassare: veicolo) to overtake; (fig: essere più bravo di) to surpass, outdo; (: difficoltà) to overcome; (: esame) to get through; ~ **qn in altezza/peso** to be taller/heavier than sb; **ha superato la cinquantina** he's over fifty (years of age)

su'perbia sf pride; **su'perbo, -a** ag proud; (fig) magnificent, superb

superfici'ale [superfi'tʃale] ag superficial

super'ficie, -ci [super'fitʃe] sf surface

su'perfluo, -a ag superfluous

superi'ore ag (piano, arto, classi) upper; (più elevato: temperatura, livello) ~ **(a)** higher (than); (migliore) ~ **(a)** superior (to)

superla'tivo, -a ag, sm superlative

supermer'cato sm supermarket

su'perstite ag surviving ▷ sm/f survivor

superstizi'one [superstit'tsjone] sf superstition; **superstizi'oso, -a** ag superstitious

super'strada sf ≈ (toll-free) motorway

su'pino, -a ag supine

supplemen'tare ag extra; (treno) relief cpd; (entrate) additional

supple'mento sm supplement

sup'piente sm/f temporary member of staff, supply (o substitute) teacher

'supplica, -che sf (preghiera) plea; (domanda scritta) petition, request

suppli'care vt to implore, beseech

sup'plizio [sup'plittsjo] sm torture

sup'pongo, sup'poni ecc vb vedi **supporre**

sup'porre vt to suppose

sup'porto sm (sostegno) support

sup'posta sf (Med) suppository

su'premo, -a ag supreme

surge'lare [surdʒe'lare] vt to (deep-)freeze

surge'lato, -a [surdʒe'lato] ag (deep-)frozen ▷ smpl **i surgelati** frozen food sg

sur'plus sm inv (Econ) surplus

surriscal'dare vt to overheat

suscet'tibile [suʃʃet'tibile] ag (sensibile) touchy, sensitive

susci'tare [suʃʃi'tare] vt to provoke,

arouse

su'sina sf plum

susseguirsi vpr to follow one another

sus'sidio sm subsidy; **sussidi didattici** teaching aids

sussul'tare vi to shudder

sussur'rare vt, vi to whisper, murmur; **sus'surro** sm whisper, murmur

svagarsi vpr to amuse o.s.; to enjoy o.s.

'svago, -ghi sm (riposo) relaxation; (ricreazione) amusement; (passatempo) pastime

svaligi'are [zvali'dʒare] vt to rob, burgle (BRIT), burglarize (US)

svalutarsi vpr (Econ) to be devalued

svalutazi'one sf devaluation

sva'nire vi to disappear, vanish

svantaggi'ato, -a [zvantad'dʒato] ag at a disadvantage

svan'taggio [zvan'taddʒo] sm disadvantage; (inconveniente) drawback, disadvantage

svari'ato, -a ag varied; various

'svastica sf swastika

sve'dese ag Swedish ▷ sm/f Swede ▷ sm (Ling) Swedish

'sveglia ['zveʎʎa] sf waking up; (orologio) alarm (clock); **sveglia telefonica** alarm call

svegli'are [zveʎ'ʎare] vt to wake up; (fig) to awaken, arouse; **svegliarsi** vpr to wake up; (fig) to be revived, reawaken; **vorrei essere svegliato alle 7, per favore** could I have an alarm call at 7 am, please?

'sveglio, -a ['zveʎʎo] ag awake; (fig) quick-witted

sve'lare vt to reveal

'svelto, -a ag (passo) quick; (mente) quick, alert; **alla svelta** quickly

'svendere vt to sell off, clear

'svendita sf (Comm) (clearance) sale

'svengo ecc vb vedi **svenire**

sveni'mento sm fainting fit, faint

sve'nire vi to faint

sven'tare vt to foil, thwart

sven'tato, -a ag (distratto) scatterbrained; (imprudente) rash

svento'lare vt, vi to wave, flutter

sven'tura sf misfortune

sverrò ecc vb vedi **svenire**

sves'tire vt to undress; **svestirsi** vpr to get undressed

'Svezia ['zvɛttsja] sf **la ~** Sweden

svi'are vt to divert; (fig) to lead astray

svi'gnarsela [zviɲ'ɲarsela] vpr to slip away, sneak off

svilup'pare vt to develop; **svilupparsi** vpr to develop; **può ~ questo rullino?** can you develop this film?

svi'luppo sm development

'svincolo sm (stradale) motorway (BRIT) o expressway (US) intersection

'svista sf oversight

svi'tare vt to unscrew

'Svizzera ['zvittsera] sf **la ~** Switzerland

'svizzero, -a ['zvittsero] ag, sm/f Swiss

svogli'ato, -a [zvoʎ'ʎato] ag listless; (pigro) lazy

'svolgere ['zvɔldʒere] vt to unwind; (srotolare) to unroll; (fig: argomento) to develop; (: piano, programma) to carry out; **svolgersi** vpr to unwind; to unroll; (fig: aver luogo) to take place; (: procedere) to go on

'svolsi ecc vb vedi **svolgere**

'svolta sf (atto) turning no pl; (curva) turn, bend; (fig) turning-point

svol'tare vi to turn

svuo'tare vt to empty (out)

T, t [ti] sf o m inv (lettera) T, t; **T come Taranto** ≈ T for Tommy

t abbr = **tonnellata**

tabacche'ria [tabakke'ria] sf tobacconist's (shop)

ta'bacco, -chi sm tobacco

ta'bella sf (tavola) table; (elenco) list

tabel'lone sm (pubblicitario) billboard; (con orario) timetable board

TAC sigla f (Med: = Tomografia Assiale Computerizzata) CAT

tac'chino [tak'kino] sm turkey

'tacco, -chi sm heel; **tacchi a spillo** stiletto heels

taccu'ino sm notebook

ta'cere [ta'tʃere] vi to be silent o quiet; (smettere di parlare) to fall silent ▷ vt to keep to oneself, say nothing about; **far ~ qn** to make sb be quiet; (fig) to silence sb

ta'chimetro [ta'kimetro] sm speedometer

'tacqui ecc vb vedi **tacere**

ta'fano sm horsefly

'taglia ['taʎʎa] sf (statura) height; (misura) size; (riscatto) ransom; (ricompensa) reward; **taglia forte** (di abito) large size

taglia'carte [taʎʎa'karte] sm inv paperknife

tagli'ando [taʎ'ʎando] sm coupon

tagli'are [taʎ'ʎare] vt to cut; (recidere, interrompere) to cut off; (intersecare) to cut across, intersect; (carne) to carve; (vini) to blend ▷ vi to cut; (prendere una scorciatoia) to take a short-cut; **tagliarsi** vpr to cut o s.; **mi sono tagliato** I've cut myself; **~ corto** (fig) to cut short; **~ la corda** (fig) to sneak off; **~ i ponti (con)** (fig) to break off relations (with); **~ la strada a qn** to cut across sb; **mi sono tagliato** I've cut myself

taglia'telle [taʎʎa'tɛlle] sfpl tagliatelle pl

taglia'unghie [taʎʎa'ungje] sm inv nail clippers pl

tagli'ente [taʎ'ʎɛnte] ag sharp

'taglio ['taʎʎo] sm cutting no pl; cut; (parte tagliente) cutting edge; (di abito) cut, style; (di stoffa: lunghezza) length; (di vini) blending; **di ~** on edge, edgeways; **banconote di piccolo/grosso ~** notes of small/large denomination; **taglio cesareo** Caesarean section

tailan'dese ag, sm/f, sm Thai

Tai'landia sf **la ~** Thailand

'talco sm talcum powder

 PAROLA CHIAVE

'tale det 1 (simile, così grande) such; **un(a) tale ...** such (a) ...; **non accetto tali discorsi** I won't allow such talk; **è di una tale arroganza** he is so arrogant; **fa una tale confusione!** he makes such a mess! 2 (persona o cosa indeterminata) such-and-such; **il giorno tale all'ora tale** on such-and-such a day at such-and-such a time; **la tal persona** that person; **ha telefonato una tale Giovanna** somebody called Giovanna phoned 3 (nelle similitudini): **tale ... tale** like ... like; **tale padre tale figlio** like father, like son; **hai il vestito tale quale il mio** your dress is just o exactly like mine ▷ pron (indefinito: persona): **un(a) tale** someone; **quel (o quella) tale** that person, that man (o woman); **il tal dei tali** what's-his-name

tale'bano sm Taliban

ta'lento sm talent

talis'mano sm talisman

tallon'cino [tallon'tʃino] *sm* counterfoil
tal'lone *sm* heel
tal'mente *av* so
'talpa *sf* (*Zool*) mole
tal'volta *av* sometimes, at times
tambu'rello *sm* tambourine
tam'buro *sm* drum
Ta'migi [ta'midʒi] *sm* **il ~** the Thames
tampo'nare *vt* (*otturare*) to plug; (*urtare: macchina*) to crash o ram into
tam'pone *sm* (*Med*) wad, pad; (*per timbri*) ink-pad; (*respingente*) buffer; **tampone assorbente** tampon
'tana *sf* lair, den
'tanga *sm inv* G-string
tan'gente [tan'dʒɛnte] *ag* (*Mat*): **~ a** tangential to ▷ *sf* tangent; (*quota*) share
tangenzi'ale [tandʒen'tsjale] *sf* (*Aut*) bypass
'tanica *sf* (*contenitore*) jerry can

PAROLA CHIAVE

'tanto, -a *det* **1** (*molto: quantità*) a lot of, much; (: *numero*) a lot of, many; (*così tanto: quantità*) so much, such a lot of; (: *numero*) so many, such a lot of; **tante volte** so many times, so often; **tanti auguri!** all the best!; **tante grazie** many thanks; **tanto tempo** so long, such a long time; **ogni tanti chilometri** every so many kilometres

2: **tanto … quanto** (*quantità*) as much … as; (*numero*) as many … as; **ho tanta pazienza quanta ne hai tu** I have as much patience as you have o as you; **ha tanti amici quanti nemici** he has as many friends as he has enemies

3 (*rafforzativo*) such; **ho aspettato per tanto tempo** I waited so long o for such a long time
▷ *pron* **1** (*molto*) much, a lot; (*così tanto*) so much, such a lot; **tanti, e** many, a lot; so many, such a lot; **credevo ce ne fosse tanto** I thought there was (such) a lot, I thought there was plenty

2: **tanto quanto** (*denaro*) as much as; (*cioccolatini*) as many as; **ne ho tanto quanto basta** I have as much as I need; **due volte tanto** twice as much

3 (*indeterminato*) so much; **tanto per l'affitto, tanto per il gas** so much for the rent, so much for the gas; **costa un tanto al metro** it costs so much per metre; **di tanto in tanto, ogni tanto** every so often; **tanto vale che …** I (*o we ecc*) may as well …; **tanto meglio!** so much the better!; **tanto peggio per lui!** so much the worse for him!

▷ *av* **1** (*molto*) very; **vengo tanto volentieri** I'd be very glad to come; **non ci vuole tanto a capirlo** it doesn't take much to understand it

2 (*così tanto: con ag, av*) so; (: *con vb*) so much, such a lot; **è tanto bella!** she's so beautiful!; **non urlare tanto** don't shout so much; **sto tanto meglio adesso** I'm so much better now; **tanto … che** so … (that); **tanto … da** so … as

3: **tanto … quanto** as … as; **conosco tanto Carlo quanto suo padre** I know both Carlo and his father; **non è poi tanto complicato quanto sembri** it's not as difficult as it seems; **tanto più insisti, tanto più non mollerà** the more you insist, the more stubborn he'll be; **quanto più … tanto meno** the more … the less

4 (*solamente*) just; **tanto per cambiare/scherzare** just for a change/a joke; **una volta tanto** for once

5 (*a lungo*) (for) long
▷ *cong* after all

'tappa *sf* (*luogo di sosta, fermata*) stop, halt; (*parte di un percorso*) stage, leg; (*Sport*) lap; **a tappe** in stages
tap'pare *vt* to plug, stop up; (*bottiglia*) to cork; **tapparsi** *vpr* **tapparsi in casa** to shut o.s. up at home; **tapparsi la bocca** to shut up; **tapparsi le orecchie** to turn a deaf ear
tappa'rella *sf* rolling shutter
tappe'tino *sm* (*per auto*) car mat; **tappetino antiscivolo** (*da bagno*) non-slip mat
tap'peto *sm* carpet; (*anche*: **tappetino**) rug; (*Sport*): **andare al ~** to go down for the count; **mettere sul ~** (*fig*) to bring up for discussion
tappez'zare [tappet'tsare] *vt* (*con carta*) to paper; (*rivestire*): **~ qc (di)** to cover sth (with); **tappezze'ria** *sf* (*tessuto*) tapestry; (*carta da parati*) wallpaper; (*arte*) upholstery; **far da tappezzeria** (*fig*) to be a wallflower
'tappo *sm* stopper; (*in sughero*) cork
tar'dare *vi* to be late ▷ *vt* to delay; **~ a fare** to delay doing
'tardi *av* late; **più ~** later (on); **al più ~** at the latest; **sul ~** (*verso sera*) late in the day; **far ~** to be late; (*restare alzato*) to stay up late; **è troppo ~** it's too late
'targa, -ghe *sf* plate; (*Aut*) number (*BRIT*) o license (*US*) plate; **tar'ghetta** *sf* (*su bagaglio*) name tag; (*su porta*) nameplate
ta'riffa *sf* (*gen*) rate, tariff; (*di trasporti*) fare; (*elenco*) price list; tariff
'tarlo *sm* woodworm

'tarma sf moth

tarocchi smpl (gioco) tarot sg

tarta'ruga, -ghe sf tortoise; (di mare) turtle; (materiale) tortoiseshell

tar'tina sf canapé

tar'tufo sm (Bot) truffle

'tasca, -sche sf pocket; **tas'cabile** ag (libro) pocket cpd

'tassa sf (imposta) tax; (doganale) duty; (per iscrizione: a scuola ecc) fee; **tassa di circolazione** road tax; **tassa di soggiorno** tourist tax

tas'sare vt to tax; to levy a duty on

tas'sello sm plug; wedge

tassì sm inv = **taxi**; **tas'sista, -i, -e** sm/f taxi driver

'tasso sm (di natalità, d'interesse ecc) rate; (Bot) yew; (Zool) badger; **tasso di cambio/ d'interesse** rate of exchange/interest

tas'tare vt to feel; **~ il terreno** (fig) to see how the land lies

tasti'era sf keyboard

'tasto sm key; (tatto) touch, feel

tas'toni av **procedere (a) ~** to grope one's way forward

'tatto sm (senso) touch; (fig) tact; **duro al ~** hard to the touch; **aver ~** to be tactful, have tact

tatu'aggio [tatu'addʒo] sm tattooing; (disegno) tattoo

tatu'are vt to tattoo

'tavola sf table; (asse) plank, board; (lastra) tablet; (quadro) panel (painting); (illustrazione) plate; **tavola calda** snack bar; **tavola rotonda** (fig) round table; **tavola a vela** windsurfer

tavo'letta sf tablet, bar; **a ~** (Aut) flat out

tavo'lino sm small table; (scrivania) desk

'tavolo sm table; **un ~ per 4 per favore** a table for 4, please

'taxi sm inv taxi; **può chiamarmi un ~ per favore?** can you call me a taxi, please?

'tazza ['tattsa] sf cup; **una ~ di caffè/tè** a cup of coffee/tea; **tazza da tè/caffè** tea/coffee cup

TBC abbr f (= tubercolosi) TB

te pron (soggetto: in forme comparative, oggetto) you

tè sm inv tea; (trattenimento) tea party

tea'trale ag theatrical

te'atro sm theatre

techno ['tɛkno] ag inv (musica) techno

'tecnica, -che sf technique; (tecnologia) technology

'tecnico, -a, -ci, -che ag technical ▷ sm/f technician

tecnolo'gia [teknolo'dʒia] sf technology

te'desco, -a, -schi, -sche ag, sm/f, sm German

te'game sm (Cuc) pan

'tegola sf tile

tei'era sf teapot

tel. abbr (= telefono) tel.

'tela sf (tessuto) cloth; (per vele, quadri) canvas; (dipinto) canvas, painting; **di ~** (calzoni) (heavy) cotton cpd; (scarpe, borsa) canvas cpd; **tela cerata** oilcloth

te'laio sm (apparecchio) loom; (struttura) frame

tele'camera sf television camera

teleco'mando sm remote control

tele'cronaca sf television report

telefo'nare vi to telephone, ring; to make a phone call ▷ vt to telephone; **~ a** to phone up, ring up, call up

telefo'nata sf (telephone) call; **~ a carico del destinatario** reverse charge (BRIT) o collect (US) call

tele'fonico, -a, -ci, -che ag (tele)phone cpd

telefon'ino sm mobile phone

te'lefono sm telephone; **telefono a gettoni** ≈ pay phone

telegior'nale [teledʒor'nale] sm television news (programme)

tele'gramma, -i sm telegram

telela'voro sm teleworking

Tele'pass® sm inv automatic payment card for use on Italian motorways

telepa'tia sf telepathy

teles'copio sm telescope

teleselezi'one [teleselet'tsjone] sf direct dialling

telespetta'tore, -'trice sm/f (television) viewer

tele'vendita sf teleshopping

televisi'one sf television

televi'sore sm television set

'tema, -i sm theme; (Ins) essay, composition

te'mere vt to fear, be afraid of; (essere sensibile a: freddo, calore) to be sensitive to ▷ vi to be afraid; (essere preoccupato): **~ per** to worry about, fear for; **~ di/che** to be afraid of/that

temperama'tite sm inv pencil sharpener

tempera'mento sm temperament

tempera'tura sf temperature

tempe'rino sm penknife

tem'pesta sf storm; **tempesta di sabbia/ neve** sand/snowstorm

'tempia sf (Anat) temple

'tempio sm (edificio) temple

'tempo sm (Meteor) weather; (cronologico) time; (epoca) time, times pl; (di film, gioco: parte) part; (Mus) time; (: battuta) beat; (Ling) tense; **che ~ fa?** what's the weather like?; **un ~** once; **~ fa** some time ago; **al ~**

stesso o **a un ~** at the same time; **per ~** early; **ha fatto il suo ~** it has had its day; **primo/secondo ~** (*Teatro*) first/second part; (*Sport*) first/second half; **in ~ utile** in due time o course; **a ~ pieno** full-time; **tempo libero** free time

tempo'rale *ag* temporal ▷ *sm* (*Meteor*) (thunder)storm

tempo'raneo, -a *ag* temporary

te'nace [te'natʃe] *ag* strong, tough; (*fig*) tenacious

te'naglie [te'naʎʎe] *sfpl* pincers *pl*

'tenda *sf* (*riparo*) awning; (*di finestra*) curtain; (*per campeggio ecc*) tent

ten'denza [ten'dɛntsa] *sf* tendency; (*orientamento*) trend; **avere ~ a** o **per qc** to have a bent for sth

'tendere *vt* (*allungare al massimo*) to stretch, draw tight; (*porgere: mano*) to hold out; (*fig: trappola*) to lay, set ▷ *vi* **~ a qc/a fare** to tend towards sth/to do; **~ l'orecchio** to prick up one's ears; **il tempo tende al caldo** the weather is getting hot; **un blu che tende al verde** a greenish blue

'tendine *sm* tendon, sinew

ten'done *sm* (*da circo*) tent

'tenebre *sfpl* darkness *sg*

te'nente *sm* lieutenant

te'nere *vt* to hold; (*conservare, mantenere*) to keep; (*ritenere, considerare*) to consider; (*spazio: occupare*) to take up, occupy; (*seguire: strada*) to keep to ▷ *vi* to hold; (*colori*) to be fast; (*dare importanza*): **~ a** to care about; **~ a fare** to want to do, be keen to do; **tenersi** *vpr* (*stare in una determinata posizione*) to stand; (*stimarsi*) to consider o.s.; (*aggrapparsi*): **tenersi a** to hold on to; (*attenersi*): **tenersi a** to stick to; **~ una conferenza** to give a lecture; **~ conto di qc** to take sth into consideration; **~ presente qc** to bear sth in mind

'tenero, -a *ag* tender; (*pietra, cera, colore*) soft; (*fig*) tender, loving

'tengo *ecc vb vedi* **tenere**

'tenni *ecc vb vedi* **tenere**

'tennis *sm* tennis

ten'nista, -i, e *sm/f* tennis player

te'nore *sm* (*tono*) tone; (*Mus*) tenor; **tenore di vita** (*livello*) standard of living

tensi'one *sf* tension

ten'tare *vt* (*indurre*) to tempt; (*provare*): **~ qc/di fare** to attempt o try sth/to do; **tenta'tivo** *sm* attempt; **tentazi'one** *sf* temptation

tenten'nare *vi* to shake, be unsteady; (*fig*) to hesitate, waver

ten'toni *av* **andare a ~** (*anche fig*) to grope one's way

'tenue *ag* (*sottile*) fine; (*colore*) soft; (*fig*)

slender, slight

te'nuta *sf* (*capacità*) capacity; (*divisa*) uniform; (*abito*) dress; (*Agr*) estate; **~ d'aria** airtight; **tenuta di strada** roadholding power

teolo'gia [teolo'dʒia] *sf* theology

teo'ria *sf* theory

te'pore *sm* warmth

tep'pista, -i *sm* hooligan

tera'pia *sf* therapy; **terapia intensiva** intensive care

tergicris'tallo [terdʒikris'tallo] *sm* windscreen (BRIT) o windshield (US) wiper

tergiver'sare [terdʒiver'sare] *vi* to shilly-shally

ter'male *ag* thermal; **stazione** *sf* **~** spa

'terme *sfpl* thermal baths

termi'nale *ag, sm* terminal

termi'nare *vt* to end; (*lavoro*) to finish ▷ *vi* to end

'termine *sm* term; (*fine, estremità*) end; (*di territorio*) boundary, limit; **contratto a ~** (*Comm*) forward contract; **a breve/lungo ~** short-/long-term; **parlare senza mezzi termini** to talk frankly, not to mince one's words

ter'mometro *sm* thermometer

'termos *sm inv* **= thermos®**

termosi'fone *sm* radiator

ter'mostato *sm* thermostat

'terra *sf* (*gen, Elettr*) earth; (*sostanza*) soil, earth; (*opposto al mare*) land *no pl*; (*regione, paese*) land; (*argilla*) clay; **terre** *sfpl* (*possedimento*) lands, land *sg*; **a** o **per ~** (*stato*) on the ground (o floor); (*moto*) to the ground, down; **mettere a ~** (*Elettr*) to earth

terra'cotta *sf* terracotta; **vasellame** *sm* **di ~** earthenware

terra'ferma *sf* dry land, terra firma; (*continente*) mainland

ter'razza [ter'rattsa] *sf* terrace

ter'razzo [ter'rattso] *sm* **= terrazza**

terre'moto *sm* earthquake

ter'reno, -a *ag* (*vita, beni*) earthly ▷ *sm* (*suolo, fig*) ground; (*Comm*) land *no pl*, plot (of land); site; (*Sport, Mil*) field

ter'restre *ag* (*superficie*) of the earth, earth's; (*di terra: battaglia, animale*) land *cpd*; (*Rel*) earthly, worldly

ter'ribile *ag* terrible, dreadful

terrifi'cante *ag* terrifying

ter'rina *sf* tureen

territori'ale *ag* territorial

terri'torio *sm* territory

ter'rore *sm* terror; **terro'rismo** *sm* terrorism; **terro'rista, -i, -e** *sm/f* terrorist

terroriz'zare [terrorid'dzare] *vt* to terrorize

terza ['tɛrtsa] sf (Scol: elementare) ≈ third year at primary school; (: media) ≈ second year at secondary school; (: superiore) ≈ fifth year at secondary school; (Aut) third gear

ter'zino [ter'tsino] sm (Calcio) fullback, back

'terzo, -a ['tɛrtso] ag third ▷ sm (frazione) third; (Dir) third party; **terza pagina** (Stampa) Arts page; **terzi** smpl (altri) others, other people

'teschio ['tɛskjo] sm skull

'tesi¹ sf thesis; **tesi di laurea** degree thesis

'tesi ecc² vb vedi **tendere**

'teso, -a pp di **tendere** ▷ ag (tirato) taut, tight; (fig) tense

te'soro sm treasure; **il Ministero del T~** the Treasury

'tessera sf (documento) card

tes'suto sm fabric, material; (Biol) tissue

test ['tɛst] sm inv test

'testa sf head; (di cose: estremità, parte anteriore) head, front; **di ~** (vettura ecc) front; **tenere ~ a qn** (nemico ecc) to stand up to sb; **fare di ~ propria** to go one's own way; **in ~** (Sport) in the lead; **~ o croce?** heads or tails?; **avere la ~ dura** to be stubborn; **testa d'aglio** bulb of garlic; **testa di serie** (Tennis) seed, seeded player

testa'mento sm (atto) will; **l'Antico/il Nuovo T~** (Rel) the Old/New Testament

tes'tardo, -a ag stubborn, pig-headed

tes'tata sf (parte anteriore) head; (intestazione) heading

tes'ticolo sm testicle

testi'mone sm/f (Dir) witness; **testimone oculare** eye witness

testimoni'are vt to testify; (fig) to bear witness to, testify to ▷ vi to give evidence, testify

'testo sm text; **fare ~** (opera, autore) to be authoritative; **questo libro non fa ~** this book is not essential reading

tes'tuggine [tes'tuddʒine] sf tortoise; (di mare) turtle

'tetano sm (Med) tetanus

'tetto sm roof; **tet'toia** sf roofing; canopy

tettuccio [tet'tuttʃo] sm **~ apribile** (Aut) sunroof

'Tevere sm **il ~** the Tiber

TG, Tg abbr = **telegiornale**

'thermos® ['tɛrmos] sm inv vacuum o Thermos® flask

ti pron (dav lo, la, li, le, ne diventa **te**) ▷ pron (oggetto) you; (complemento di termine) (to) you; (riflessivo) yourself

'Tibet sm **il ~** Tibet

'tibia sf tibia, shinbone

tic sm inv tic, (nervous) twitch; (fig)

mannerism

ticchet'tio [tikket'tio] sm (di macchina da scrivere) clatter; (di orologio) ticking; (della pioggia) patter

'ticket sm inv (su farmaci) prescription charge

ti'ene ecc vb vedi **tenere**

ti'epido, -a ag lukewarm, tepid

'tifo sm (Med) typhus; (fig): **fare il ~ per** to be a fan of

ti'fone sm typhoon

ti'foso, -a sm/f (Sport ecc) fan

tigì [ti'dʒi] sm inv TV news

'tiglio ['tiʎʎo] sm lime (tree), linden (tree)

'tigre sf tiger

tim'brare vt to stamp; (annullare: francobolli) to postmark; **~ il cartellino** to clock in

'timbro sm stamp; (Mus) timbre, tone

'timido, -a ag shy; timid

'timo sm thyme

ti'mone sm (Naut) rudder

ti'more sm (paura) fear; (rispetto) awe

'timpano sm (Anat) eardrum; (Mus)

'tingere ['tindʒere] vt to dye

'tinsi ecc vb inv vedi **tingere**

tin'nare vi to tinkle

tinto'ria sf (lavasecco) dry cleaner's (shop)

tin'tura sf (operazione) dyeing; (colorante) dye; **tintura di iodio** tincture of iodine

'tipico, -a, -ci, -che ag typical

'tipo sm type; (genere) kind, type; (fam) chap, fellow; **che ~ di...?** what kind of ...?

tipogra'fia sf typography; (procedimento) letterpress (printing); (officina) printing house

TIR sigla m (= Transports Internationaux Routiers) International Heavy Goods Vehicle

ti'rare vt (gen) to pull; (estrarre): **~ qc da** to take o pull sth out of; to get sth out of; to extract sth from; (chiudere: tenda ecc) to draw, pull; (tracciare, disegnare) to draw, trace; (lanciare: sasso, palla) to throw; (stampare) to print; (pistola, freccia) to fire ▷ vi (pipa, camino) to draw; (vento) to blow; (abito) to be tight; (fare fuoco) to fire; (fare del tiro, Calcio) to shoot; **~ avanti** vi to struggle on ▷ vt to keep going; **~ fuori** (estrarre) to take out, pull out; **~ giù** (abbassare) to bring down, to lower; (da scaffale ecc.) to take down; **~ su** to pull up; (capelli) to put up; (fig: bambino) to bring up; **tirarsi** vpr **tirarsi indietro** to draw back; (fig) to back out; **~ a indovinare** to take a guess; **~ sul prezzo** to bargain; **tirar dritto** to keep right on going; **tirati su!** (fig) cheer up!; **~ via** (togliere) to take off

tira'tura sf (azione) printing; (di libro) (print) run; (di giornale) circulation

'tirchio, -a ['tirkjo] ag mean, stingy

'tiro sm shooting no pl, firing no pl; (colpo, sparo) shot; (di palla: lancio) throwing no pl; throw; (fig) trick; **cavallo da ~** draught (BRIT) o draft (US) horse; **tiro a segno** target shooting; (luogo) shooting range; **tiro con l'arco** archery

tiro'cinio [tiro'tʃinjo] sm apprenticeship; (professionale) training

ti'roide sf thyroid (gland)

Tir'reno sm **il (mar) ~** the Tyrrhenian Sea

ti'sana sf herb tea

tito'lare sm/f incumbent; (proprietario) owner; (Calcio) regular player

'titolo sm title; (di giornale) headline; (diploma) qualification; (Comm) security; (: azione) share; **a che ~?** for what reason?; **a ~ di amicizia** out of friendship; **a ~ di premio** as a prize; **titolo di credito** share; **titoli di stato** government securities; **titoli di testa** (Cinema) credits

titu'bante ag hesitant, irresolute

toast [toust] sm inv toasted sandwich (generally with ham and cheese)

toc'cante ag touching

toc'care vt to touch; (tastare) to feel; (fig: riguardare) to concern; (: commuovere) to touch, move; (: pungere) to hurt, wound; (: far cenno a: argomento) to touch on, mention ▷ vi **~ a** (accadere) to happen to; (spettare) to be up to; **~ (il fondo)** (in acqua) to touch the bottom; **tocca a te difenderci** it's up to you to defend us; **a chi tocca?** whose turn is it?; **mi toccò pagare** I had to pay

toccherò ecc [tokke'rɔ] vb vedi **toccare**

'togliere ['tɔʎʎere] vt (rimuovere) to take away (o off), remove; (riprendere, non concedere più) to take away, remove; (Mat) to take away, subtract; **~ qc a qn** to take sth (away) from sb; **ciò non toglie che** nevertheless, be that as it may; **togliersi il cappello** to take off one's hat

toi'lette [twa'lɛt] sf inv toilet; (mobile) dressing table; **dov'è la ~?** where's the toilet?

'Tokyo sf Tokyo

'tolgo ecc vb vedi **togliere**

tolle'rare vt to tolerate

'tolsi ecc vb vedi **togliere**

'tomba sf tomb

tom'bino sm manhole cover

'tombola sf (gioco) tombola; (ruzzolone) tumble

'tondo, -a ag round

'tonfo sm splash; (rumore sordo) thud; (caduta): **fare un ~** to take a tumble

tonifi'care vt (muscoli, pelle) to tone up; (irrobustire) to invigorate, brace

tonnel'lata sf ton

'tonno sm tuna (fish)

'tono sm (gen) tone; (Mus: di pezzo) key; (di colore) shade, tone

ton'silla sf tonsil

'tonto, -a ag dull, stupid

to'pazio [to'pattsjo] sm topaz

'topo sm mouse

'toppa sf (serratura) keyhole; (pezza) patch

to'race [to'ratʃe] sm chest

'torba sf peat

'torcere ['tɔrtʃere] vt to twist; **torcersi** vpr to twist, writhe

'torcia, -ce ['tɔrtʃa] sf torch; **torcia elettrica** torch (BRIT), flashlight (US)

torci'collo [tortʃi'kɔllo] sm stiff neck

'tordo sm thrush

To'rino sf Turin

tor'menta sf snowstorm

tormen'tare vt to torment; **tormentarsi** vpr to fret, worry o.s.

tor'nado sm tornado

tor'nante sm hairpin bend

tor'nare vi to return, go (o come) back; (ridiventare: anche fig) to become (again); (riuscire giusto, esatto: conto) to work out; (risultare) to turn out (to be), prove (to be); **~ utile** to prove o turn out (to be) useful; **~ a casa** to go (o come) home; **torno a casa martedì** I'm going home on Tuesday

tor'neo sm tournament

'tornio sm lathe

'toro sm bull; (dello zodiaco): **T~** Taurus

'torre sf tower; (Scacchi) rook, castle; **torre di controllo** (Aer) control tower

tor'rente sm torrent

torri'one sm keep

tor'rone sm nougat

'torsi ecc vb vedi **torcere**

torsi'one sf twisting; torsion

'torso sm torso, trunk; (Arte) torso

'torsolo sm (di cavolo ecc) stump; (di frutta) core

'torta sf cake

tortel'lini smpl (Cuc) tortellini

'torto, -a pp di **torcere** ▷ ag (ritorto) twisted; (storto) twisted, crooked ▷ sm (ingiustizia) wrong; (colpa) fault; **a ~** wrongly; **aver ~** to be wrong

tor'tora sf turtle dove

tor'tura sf torture; **tortu'rare** vt to torture

to'sare vt (pecora) to shear; (siepe) to clip

Tos'cana sf **la ~** Tuscany

'tosse sf cough; **ho la ~** I've got a cough

'tossico, -a, -ci, -che ag toxic

tossicodipen'dente sm/f drug addict

tos'sire vi to cough

tosta'pane sm inv toaster

to'tale ag, sm total

toto'calcio [toto'kaltʃo] sm gambling pool betting on football results, ≈ (football) pools pl (BRIT)

to'vaglia [to'vaʎʎa] sf tablecloth; **tovagli'olo** sm napkin

tra prep (di due persone, cose) between; (di più persone, cose) among(st); (tempo: entro) within, in; ~ **5 giorni** in 5 days' time; **sia detto ~ noi ...** between you and me ...; **litigano ~ (di) loro** they're fighting amongst themselves; ~ **breve** soon; ~ **sé e sé** (parlare ecc) to oneself

traboc'care vi to overflow

traboc'chetto [trabok'ketto] sm (fig) trap

'traccia, -ce ['trattʃa] sf (segno, striscia) trail, track; (orma) tracks pl; (residuo, testimonianza) trace, sign; (abbozzo) outline

tracci'are [trat'tʃare] vt to trace, mark (out); (disegnare) to draw; (fig: abbozzare) to outline

tra'chea [tra'kɛa] sf windpipe, trachea

tra'colla sf shoulder strap; **borsa a ~** shoulder bag

tradi'mento sm betrayal; (Dir, Mil) treason

tra'dire vt to betray; (coniuge) to be unfaithful to; (doveri: mancare) to fail in; (rivelare) to give away, reveal; **tradirsi** vpr to give o.s. away

tradizio'nale [tradittsjo'nale] ag traditional

tradizi'one [tradit'tsjone] sf tradition

tra'durre vt to translate; (spiegare) to render, convey; **me lo può ~?** can you translate this for me?; **traduzi'one** sf translation

'trae vb vedi **trarre**

traffi'cante sm/f dealer; (peg) trafficker

traffi'care vi (commerciare): ~ **(in)** to trade (in), deal (in); (affaccendarsi) to busy o.s. ▷ vt (peg) to traffic in

'traffico, -ci sm traffic; (commercio) trade, traffic; **traffico di armi/droga** arms/drug trafficking

tra'gedia [tra'dʒɛdja] sf tragedy

'traggo ecc vb vedi **trarre**

tra'ghetto [tra'getto] sm ferry(boat)

'tragico, -a, -ci, -che ['tradʒiko] ag tragic

tra'gitto [tra'dʒitto] sm (passaggio) crossing; (viaggio) journey

tragu'ardo sm (Sport) finishing line; (fig) goal, aim

'trai ecc vb vedi **trarre**

traiet'toria sf trajectory

trai'nare vt to drag, haul; (rimorchiare) to tow

tralasci'are [tralaʃʃare] vt (studi) to neglect; (dettagli) to leave out, omit

tra'liccio [tra'littʃo] sm (Elettr) pylon

tram sm inv tram

'trama sf (filo) weft, woof; (fig: argomento, maneggio) plot

traman'dare vt to pass on, hand down

tram'busto sm turmoil

tramez'zino [tramed'dzino] sm sandwich

'tramite prep through

tramon'tare vi to set, go down; **tra'monto** sm setting; (del sole) sunset

trampo'lino sm (per tuffi) springboard, diving board; (per lo sci) ski-jump

tra'nello sm trap

'tranne prep except (for), but (for); ~ **che** unless

tranquil'lante sm (Med) tranquillizer

tranquillità sf calm, stillness; quietness; peace of mind

tranquilliz'zare [trankwillid'dzare] vt to reassure

> Attenzione! In inglese esiste il verbo to tranquillize, che però significa "calmare con un tranquillante".

tran'quillo, -a ag calm, quiet; (bambino, scolaro) quiet; (sereno) with one's mind at rest; **sta' ~** don't worry

transazi'one [transat'tsjone] sf compromise; (Dir) settlement; (Comm) transaction, deal

tran'senna sf barrier

transgenico, -a, -ci, -che [trans'dʒɛniko] ag genetically modified

tran'sigere [tran'sidʒere] vi (venire a patti) to compromise, come to an agreement

transi'tabile ag passable

transi'tare vi to pass

transi'tivo, -a ag transitive

'transito sm transit; **di ~** (merci) in transit; (stazione) transit cpd; **"divieto di ~"** "no entry"

'trapano sm (utensile) drill; (Med) trepan

trape'lare vi to leak, drip; (fig) to leak out

tra'pezio [tra'pɛttsjo] sm (Mat) trapezium; (attrezzo ginnico) trapeze

trapian'tare vt to transplant; **trapi'anto** sm transplanting; (Med) transplant; **trapianto cardiaco** heart transplant

'trappola sf trap

tra'punta sf quilt

'trarre vt to draw, pull; (portare) to take; (prendere, tirare fuori) to take (out), draw; (derivare) to obtain; ~ **origine da qc** to have its origins o originate in sth

trasa'lire vi to start, jump

trasan'dato, -a ag shabby

trasci'nare [traʃʃi'nare] vt to drag; **trascinarsi** vpr to drag o.s. along; (fig) to drag on

tras'correre vt (tempo) to spend, pass ▷ vi to pass

tras'crivere vt to transcribe

trascu'rare vt to neglect; (non considerare) to disregard

trasferi'mento sm transfer; (trasloco) removal, move; **trasferimento di chiamata** (Tel) call forwarding

trasfe'rire vt to transfer; **trasferirsi** vpr to move; **tras'ferta** sf transfer; (indennità) travelling expenses pl; (Sport) away game

trasfor'mare vt to transform, change; **trasformarsi** vpr to be transformed; **trasformarsi in qc** to turn into sth; **trasforma'tore** sm (Elec) transformer

trasfusi'one sf (Med) transfusion

trasgre'dire vt to disobey, contravene

traslo'care vt to move, transfer; **tras'loco, -chi** sm removal

tras'mettere vt (passare): **~ qc a qn** to pass sth on to sb; (mandare) to send; (Tecn, Tel, Med) to transmit; (TV, Radio) to broadcast; **trasmissi'one** sf (gen, Fisica, Tecn) transmission; (passaggio) transmission, passing on; (TV, Radio) broadcast

traspa'rente ag transparent

traspor'tare vt to carry, move; (merce) to transport, convey; **lasciarsi ~ (da qc)** (fig) to let o.s. be carried away (by sth); **tras'porto** sm transport

'trassi ecc vb vedi **trarre**

trasver'sale ag transverse, cross(-); running at right angles

'tratta sf (Econ) draft; (di persone): **la ~ delle bianche** the white slave trade

tratta'mento sm treatment; (servizio) service

trat'tare vt (gen) to treat; (commerciare) to deal in; (svolgere: argomento) to discuss, deal with; (negoziare) to negotiate ▷ vi **~ di** to deal with; **~ con** (persona) to deal with; **si tratta di ...** it's about ...

tratte'nere vt (far rimanere: persona) to detain; (intrattenere: ospiti) to entertain; (tenere, frenare, reprimere) to hold back, keep back; (astenersi dal consegnare) to hold, keep; (detrarre: somma) to deduct; **trattenersi** vpr (astenersi) to restrain o.s., stop o.s.; (soffermarsi) to stay, remain

trat'tino sm dash; (in parole composte) hyphen

'tratto, -a pp di **trarre** ▷ sm (di penna, matita) stroke; (parte) part, piece; (di strada) stretch; (di mare, cielo) expanse; (di tempo) period (of time)

trat'tore sm tractor

tratto'ria sf restaurant

'trauma, -i sm trauma

tra'vaglio [tra'vaʎʎo] sm (angoscia) pain, suffering; (Med) pains pl

trava'sare vt to decant

tra'versa sf (trave) crosspiece; (via) side street; (Ferr) sleeper (BRIT), (railroad) tie (US); (Calcio) crossbar

traver'sata sf crossing; (Aer) flight, trip; **quanto dura la ~?** how long does the crossing take?

traver'sie sfpl mishaps, misfortunes

tra'verso, -a ag oblique; **di ~** ag askew ▷ av sideways; **andare di ~** to go down the wrong way; **guardare di ~** to look askance at

travesti'mento sm disguise

travestirsi vpr to disguise o.s.

tra'volgere [tra'vɔldʒere] vt to sweep away, carry away; (fig) to overwhelm

tre num three

'treccia, -ce ['trettʃa] sf plait, braid

tre'cento [tre'tʃɛnto] num three hundred ▷ sm **il T~** the fourteenth century

'tredici ['treditʃi] num thirteen

'tregua sf truce; (fig) respite

tre'mare vi **~ di** (freddo ecc) to shiver o tremble with; (paura, rabbia) to shake o tremble with

tre'mendo, -a ag terrible, awful

> Attenzione! In inglese esiste la parola _tremendous_, che però significa _enorme_ oppure _fantastico, strepitoso_.

'tremito sm trembling no pl; shaking no pl; shivering no pl

'treno sm train; **è questo il ~ per...?** is this the train for ...?; **treno di gomme** set of tyres (BRIT) o tires (US); **treno merci** goods (BRIT) o freight train; **treno viaggiatori** passenger train

☀ TRENI

> ☀
> ☀ There are various types of train in
> ☀ Italy. For short journeys there are
> ☀ the "Regionali" (R), which generally
> ☀ operate within a particular region,
> ☀ and the "Interregionali" (IR), which
> ☀ operate beyond regional boundaries.
> ☀ Medium- and long-distance passenger
> ☀ journeys are carried out by "Intercity" (I)
> ☀ and "Eurocity" (EC) trains. The "Eurostar"
> ☀ service (ES) offers fast connections
> ☀ between the major Italian cities. Night
> ☀ services are operated by "Intercity
> ☀ Notte" (ICN), "Euronight" (EN) and by
> ☀ "Espressi" (EXP).

'trenta num thirty; **tren'tesimo, -a** num thirtieth; **tren'tina** sf **una trentina (di)** thirty or so, about thirty

'**trepidante** *ag* anxious
tri'angolo *sm* triangle
tribù *sf inv* tribe
tri'buna *sf* (*podio*) platform; (*in aule ecc*) gallery; (*di stadio*) stand
tribu'nale *sm* court
tri'ciclo [tri't∫iklo] *sm* tricycle
tri'foglio [tri'fɔʎʎo] *sm* clover
'triglia ['triʎʎa] *sf* red mullet
tri'mestre *sm* period of three months; (*Ins*) term, quarter (*us*); (*Comm*) quarter
trin'cea [trin't∫ɛa] *sf* trench
trion'fare *vi* to triumph, win; ~ **su** to triumph over, overcome; **tri'onfo** *sm* triumph
tripli'care *vt* to triple
'**triplo, -a** *ag* triple; treble ▷ *sm* **il ~ (di)** three times as much (as); **la spesa è tripla** it costs three times as much
'trippa *sf* (*Cuc*) tripe
'triste *ag* sad; (*luogo*) dreary, gloomy
tri'tare *vt* to mince, grind (*us*)
trivi'ale *ag* vulgar, low
tro'feo *sm* trophy
'**tromba** *sf* (*Mus*) trumpet; (*Aut*) horn; **tromba d'aria** whirlwind; **tromba delle scale** stairwell
trom'bone *sm* trombone
trom'bosi *sf* thrombosis
tron'care *vt* to cut off; (*spezzare*) to break off
'**tronco, -a, -chi, -che** *ag* cut off; broken off; (*Ling*) truncated; (*fig*) cut short ▷ *sm* (*Bot, Anat*) trunk; (*fig: tratto*) section; **licenziare qn in ~** to fire sb on the spot
'trono *sm* throne
tropi'cale *ag* tropical

 PAROLA CHIAVE

'**troppo, -a** *det* (*in eccesso: quantità*) too much; (: *numero*) too many; **c'era troppa gente** there were too many people; **fa troppo caldo** it's too hot
▷ *pron* (*in eccesso: quantità*) too much; (: *numero*) too many; **ne hai messo troppo** you've put in too much; **meglio troppi che pochi** better too many than too few
▷ *av* (*eccessivamente: con ag, av*) too; (: *con vb*) too much; **troppo amaro/tardi** too bitter/late; **lavora troppo** he works too much; **costa troppo** it costs too much; **di troppo** too much; too many; **qualche tazza di troppo** a few cups too many; **2 euro di troppo** 2 euros too much; **essere di troppo** to be in the way

'**trota** *sf* trout
'**trottola** *sf* spinning top

tro'vare *vt* to find; (*giudicare*): **trovo che** I find o think that; **trovarsi** *vpr* (*reciproco: incontrarsi*) to meet; (*essere, stare*) to be; (*arrivare, capitare*) to find o.s.; **non trovo più il portafoglio** I can't find my wallet; **andare a ~ qn** to go and see sb; **~ qn colpevole** to find sb guilty; **trovarsi bene** (*in un luogo, con qn*) to get on well
truc'care *vt* (*falsare*) to fake; (*attore ecc*) to make up; (*travestire*) to disguise; (*Sport*) to fix; (*Aut*) to soup up; **truccarsi** *vpr* to make up (one's face)
'**trucco, -chi** *sm* trick; (*cosmesi*) make-up
'**truffa** *sf* fraud, swindle; **truf'fare** *vt* to swindle, cheat
truffa'tore, -'trice *sm/f* swindler, cheat
'**truppa** *sf* troop
tu *pron* you; **tu stesso(a)** you yourself; **dare del tu a qn** to address sb as "tu"
'**tubo** *sm* tube; pipe; **tubo digerente** (*Anat*) alimentary canal, digestive tract; **tubo di scappamento** (*Aut*) exhaust pipe
tuffarsi *vpr* to plunge, dive
'**tuffo** *sm* dive; (*breve bagno*) dip
tuli'pano *sm* tulip
tu'more *sm* (*Med*) tumour
Tuni'sia *sf* **la ~** Tunisia
'**tuo** (*f* '**tua**, *pl* **tu'oi, 'tue**) *det* **il ~, la tua** *ecc* your ▷ *pron* **il ~, la tua** *ecc* yours
tuo'nare *vi* to thunder; **tuona** it is thundering, there's some thunder
tu'ono *sm* thunder
tu'orlo *sm* yolk
tur'bante *sm* turban
tur'bare *vt* to disturb, trouble
tur'bato, -a *ag* upset; (*preoccupato, ansioso*) anxious
turbo'lenza [turbo'lɛntsa] *sf* turbulence
tur'chese [tur'kese] *sf* turquoise
Tur'chia [tur'kia] *sf* **la ~** Turkey
'**turco, -a, -chi, -che** *ag* Turkish ▷ *sm/f* Turk/Turkish woman ▷ *sm* (*Ling*) Turkish; **parlare ~** (*fig*) to talk double-dutch
tu'rismo *sm* tourism; tourist industry; **tu'rista, -i, -e** *sm/f* tourist; **turismo sessuale** sex tourism; **tu'ristico, -a, -ci, -che** *ag* tourist *cpd*
'**turno** *sm* turn; (*di lavoro*) shift; **di ~** (*soldato, medico, custode*) on duty; **a ~** (*rispondere*) in turn; (*lavorare*) in shifts; **fare a ~ a fare qc** to take turns to do sth; **è il suo ~** it's your (*o* his *ecc*) turn
'**turpe** *ag* filthy, vile
'**tuta** *sf* overalls *pl*; (*Sport*) tracksuit
tu'tela *sf* (*Dir: di minore*) guardianship; (: *protezione*) protection; (*difesa*) defence

tutta'via *cong* nevertheless, yet

 PAROLA CHIAVE

'tutto, -a *det* 1 (*intero*) all; **tutto il latte** all the milk; **tutta la notte** all night, the whole night; **tutto il libro** the whole book; **tutta una bottiglia** a whole bottle
2 (*pl, collettivo*) all; every; **tutti i libri** all the books; **tutte le notti** every night; **tutti i venerdì** every Friday; **tutti gli uomini** all the men; (*collettivo*) all men; **tutto l'anno** all year long; **tutti e due** both *o* each of us (*o* them *o* you); **tutti e cinque** all five of us (*o* them *o* you)
3 (*completamente*): **era tutta sporca** she was all dirty; **tremava tutto** he was trembling all over; **è tutta sua madre** she's just *o* exactly like her mother
4: **a tutt'oggi** so far, up till now; **a tutta velocità** at full *o* top speed
▷ *pron* 1 (*ogni cosa*) everything, all; (*qualsiasi cosa*) anything; **ha mangiato tutto** he's eaten everything; **tutto considerato** all things considered; **in tutto: 5 euro in tutto** 5 euros in all; **in tutto eravamo 50** there were 50 of us in all
2: **tutti, e** (*ognuno*) all, everybody; **vengono tutti** they are all coming, everybody's coming; **tutti quanti** all and sundry
▷ *av* (*completamente*) entirely, quite; **è tutto il contrario** it's quite *o* exactly the opposite; **tutt'al più: saranno stati tutt'al più una cinquantina** there were about fifty of them at (the very) most; **tutt'al più possiamo prendere un treno** if the worst comes to the worst we can take a train; **tutt'altro** on the contrary; **è tutt'altro che felice** he's anything but happy; **tutt'a un tratto** suddenly ▷ *sm* **il tutto** the whole lot, all of it

tut'tora *av* still
TV [ti'vu] *sf inv* (= televisione) TV ▷ *sigla* = Treviso

ubbidi'ente *ag* obedient
ubbi'dire *vi* to obey; **~ a** to obey; (*veicolo, macchina*) to respond to
ubria'care *vt* **~ qn** to get sb drunk; (*alcool*) to make sb drunk; (*fig*) to make sb's head spin *o* reel; **ubriacarsi** *vpr* to get drunk; **ubriacarsi di** (*fig*) to become intoxicated with
ubri'aco, -a, -chi, -che *ag, sm/f* drunk
uc'cello [ut'tʃɛllo] *sm* bird
uc'cidere [ut'tʃidere] *vt* to kill; **uccidersi** *vpr* (*suicidarsi*) to kill o s.; (*perdere la vita*) to be killed
u'dito *sm* (sense of) hearing
UE *sigla f* (= Unione Europea) EU
UEM *sigla f* (= Unione economica e monetaria) EMU
'uffa *escl* tut!
uffici'ale [uffi'tʃale] *ag* official ▷ *sm* (*Amm*) official, officer; (*Mil*) officer; **~ di stato civile** registrar
uf'ficio [uf'fitʃo] *sm* (*gen*) office; (*dovere*) duty; (*mansione*) task, function, job; (*agenzia*) agency, bureau; (*Rel*) service; **d'~** *ag* office *cpd*; official ▷ *av* officially; **ufficio di collocamento** employment office; **ufficio informazioni** information bureau; **ufficio oggetti smarriti** lost property office (BRIT), lost and found (US); **ufficio (del) personale** personnel department;

ufficio postale post office
uffici'oso, -a [uffi'tʃoso] *ag* unofficial
uguagli'anza [ugwaʎ'ʎantsa] *sf* equality
uguagli'are [ugwaʎ'ʎare] *vt* to make
equal; (*essere uguale*) to equal, be equal to;
(*livellare*) to level; **uguagliarsi a o con qn**
(*paragonarsi*) to compare o s. to sb
ugu'ale *ag* equal; (*identico*) identical, the
same; (*uniforme*) level, even ▷ *av* **costano
~** they cost the same; **sono bravi ~** they're
equally good
UIL *sigla f* (= Unione Italiana del Lavoro) *trade
union federation*
'ulcera ['ultʃera] *sf* ulcer
U'livo *sm* **l'~** centre-left Italian political
grouping
u'livo = **olivo**
ulteri'ore *ag* further
ultima'mente *av* lately, of late
ulti'mare *vt* to finish, complete
'ultimo, -a *ag* (*finale*) last; (*estremo*)
farthest, utmost; (*recente: notizia, moda*)
latest; (*fig: sommo, fondamentale*) ultimate
▷ *sm/f* last (one); **fino all'~** to the last,
until the end; **da ~, in ~** in the end; **abitare
all'~ piano** to live on the top floor; **per ~**
(*entrare, arrivare*) last
ulu'lare *vi* to howl
umanità *sf* humanity
u'mano, -a *ag* human; (*comprensivo*)
humane
umidità *sf* dampness; humidity
'umido, -a *ag* damp; (*mano, occhi*) moist;
(*clima*) humid ▷ *sm* dampness, damp;
carne in ~ stew
'umile *ag* humble
umili'are *vt* to humiliate; **umiliarsi** *vpr* to
humble o.s.
u'more *sm* (*disposizione d'animo*) mood;
(*carattere*) temper; **di buon/cattivo ~** in a
good/bad mood
umo'rismo *sm* humour; **avere il senso
dell'~** to have a sense of humour;
umo'ristico, -a, -ci, -che *ag* humorous,
funny
u'nanime *ag* unanimous
unci'netto [untʃi'netto] *sm* crochet hook
un'cino [un'tʃino] *sm* hook
undi'cenne [undi'tʃɛnne] *ag, sm/f* eleven-
year-old
undi'cesimo, -a [undi'tʃɛzimo] *num*
eleventh
'undici ['unditʃi] *num* eleven
'ungere ['undʒere] *vt* to grease, oil; (*Rel*) to
anoint; (*fig*) to flatter, butter up
unghe'rese [unge'rese] *ag, sm/f, sm*
Hungarian
Unghe'ria [unge'ria] *sf* **l'~** Hungary
'unghia ['ungja] *sf* (*Anat*) nail; (*di animale*)

claw; (*di rapace*) talon; (*di cavallo*) hoof
ungu'ento *sm* ointment
'unico, -a, -ci, -che *ag* (*solo*) only;
(*ineguagliabile*) unique; (*singolo: binario*)
single; **figlio(a) ~(a)** only son/daughter,
only child
unifi'care *vt* to unite, unify; (*sistemi*) to
standardize; **unificazi'one** *sf* uniting;
unification; standardization
uni'forme *ag* uniform; (*superficie*) even ▷ *sf*
(*divisa*) uniform
uni'one *sf* union; (*fig: concordia*) unity,
harmony; **Unione europea** European
Union; **ex Unione Sovietica** former
Soviet Union
u'nire *vt* to unite; (*congiungere*) to join,
connect; (: *ingredienti, colori*) to combine;
(*in matrimonio*) to unite, join together;
unirsi *vpr* to unite; (*in matrimonio*) to be
joined together; **~ qc a** to unite sth with;
to join o connect sth with; to combine sth
with; **unirsi a** (*gruppo, società*) to join
unità *sf inv* (*unione, concordia*) unity; (*Mat,
Mil, Comm, di misura*) unit; **unità di misura**
unit of measurement
u'nito, -a *ag* (*paese*) united; (*amici, famiglia*)
close; **in tinta unita** plain, self-coloured
univer'sale *ag* universal; general
università *sf inv* university
uni'verso *sm* universe

PAROLA CHIAVE

'uno, -a (*dav sm* **un** + C, V, **uno** + *s impura, gn,
pn, ps, x, z; dav sf* **un'** + V, **una** + C) *art indef* **1**
a; (*dav vocale*) an; **un bambino** a child; **una
strada** a street; **uno zingaro** a gypsy
2 (*intensivo*): **ho avuto una paura!** I got
such a fright!
▷ *pron* **1** one; **prendine uno** take one (of
them); **l'uno o l'altro** either (of them);
l'uno e l'altro both (of them); **aiutarsi
l'un l'altro** to help one another o each
other; **sono entrati l'uno dopo l'altro**
they came in one after the other
2 (*un tale*) someone, somebody
3 (*con valore impersonale*) one, you; **se uno
vuole** if one wants, if you want
▷ *num* one; **una mela e due pere** one
apple and two pears; **uno più uno fa due**
one plus one equals two, one and one are
two ▷ *sf* **è l'una** it's one (o'clock)

'unsi *ecc vb vedi* **ungere**
'unto, -a *pp di* **ungere** ▷ *ag* greasy, oily
▷ *sm* grease
u'omo (*pl* **u'omini**) *sm* man; **da ~** (*abito,
scarpe*) men's, for men; **uomo d'affari**
businessman; **uomo di paglia** stooge;

uomo politico politician; **uomo rana** frogman

u'ovo (pl(f) **u'ova**) sm egg; **uovo affogato/alla coque** poached/boiled egg; **uovo bazzotto/sodo** soft-/hard-boiled egg; **uovo di Pasqua** Easter egg; **uovo in camicia** poached egg; **uova strapazzate/al tegame** scrambled/fried eggs

ura'gano sm hurricane

urba'nistica sf town planning

ur'bano, -a ag urban, city cpd, town cpd; (Tel: chiamata) local; (fig) urbane

ur'gente [ur'dʒɛnte] ag urgent; **ur'genza** sf urgency; **in caso d'urgenza** in (case of) an emergency; **d'urgenza** ag emergency ▷ av urgently, as a matter of urgency

ur'lare vi (persona) to scream, yell; (animale, vento) to howl ▷ vt to scream, yell

'urlo (pl(m) **'urli**, pl(f) **'urla**) sm scream, yell; howl

urrà escl hurrah!

U.R.S.S. abbr f **l'U.R.S.S.** the USSR

ur'tare vt to bump into, knock against; (fig: irritare) to annoy ▷ vi **~ contro** o **in** to bump into, knock against, crash into; (fig: imbattersi) to come up against; **urtarsi** vpr (reciproco: scontrarsi) to collide; (: fig) to clash; (irritarsi) to get annoyed

'U.S.A. ['uza] smpl **gli U.S.A.** the USA

u'sanza [u'zantsa] sf custom; (moda) fashion

u'sare vt to use, employ ▷ vi (servirsi): **~ di** to use; (: diritto) to exercise; (essere di moda) to be fashionable; (essere solito): **~ fare** to be in the habit of doing, be accustomed to doing ▷ vb impers **qui usa così** it's the custom round here; **u'sato, -a** ag used; (consumato) worn; (di seconda mano) used, second-hand ▷ sm second-hand goods pl

u'scire [uʃʃire] vi (gen) to come out; (partire, andare a passeggio, a uno spettacolo ecc) to go out; (essere sorteggiato: numero) to come up; **~ da** (gen) to leave; (posto) to go (o come) out of, leave; (solco, vasca ecc) to come out of; (muro) to stick out of; (competenza ecc) to be outside; (infanzia, adolescenza) to leave behind; (famiglia nobile ecc) to come from; **~ da** o **di casa** to go out; (fig) to leave home; **~ in automobile** to go out in the car, go for a drive; **~ di strada** (Aut) to go off o leave the road

u'scita [uʃʃita] sf (passaggio, varco) exit, way out; (per divertimento) outing; (Econ: somma) expenditure; (Teatro) entrance; (fig: battuta) witty remark; **dov'è l'~?** where's the exit?; **uscita di sicurezza** emergency exit

usi'gnolo [uziɲ'nɔlo] sm nightingale

'uso sm (utilizzazione) use; (esercizio) practice; (abitudine) custom; **a ~ di** for (the use of); **d'~** (corrente) in use; **fuori ~** out of use; **uso esterno**; **per ~ esterno** for external use only

usti'one sf burn

usu'ale ag common, everyday

u'sura sf usury; (logoramento) wear (and tear)

uten'sile sm tool, implement; **utensili da cucina** kitchen utensils

u'tente sm/f user

'utero sm uterus

'utile ag useful ▷ sm (vantaggio) advantage, benefit; (Econ: profitto) profit

utiliz'zare [utilid'dzare] vt to use, make use of, utilize

'uva sf grapes pl; **uva passa** raisins pl; **uva spina** gooseberry

UVA abbr (= ultravioletto prossimo) UVA

UVB abbr (= ultravioletto remoto) UVB

V

v. *abbr* (= *vedi*) v

va, va' *vb vedi* **andare**

va'cante *ag* vacant

va'canza [va'kantsa] *sf* (*riposo, ferie*) holiday(s) *pl* (BRIT), vacation (US); (*giorno di permesso*) day off, holiday; **vacanze** *sfpl* (*periodo di ferie*) holidays (BRIT), vacation *sg* (US); **essere/andare in ~** to be/go on holiday *o* vacation; **sono qui in ~** I'm on holiday here; **vacanze estive** summer holiday(s) *o* vacation; **vacanze natalizie** Christmas holidays *o* vacation

Attenzione! In inglese esiste la parola *vacancy* che però indica un posto vacante o una camera disponibile.

'vacca, -che *sf* cow

vacci'nare [vattʃi'nare] *vt* to vaccinate

vac'cino [vat'tʃino] *sm* (*Med*) vaccine

vacil'lare [vatʃil'lare] *vi* to sway, wobble; (*luce*) to flicker; (*fig: memoria, coraggio*) to be failing, falter

'vacuo, -a *ag* (*fig*) empty, vacuous

'vado *ecc vb vedi* **andare**

vaga'bondo, -a *sm/f* tramp, vagrant

va'gare *vi* to wander

vagherò *ecc* [vage'rɔ] *vb vedi* **vagare**

va'gina [va'dʒina] *sf* vagina

'vaglia ['vaʎʎa] *sm inv* money order; **vaglia postale** postal order

vagli'are [vaʎ'ʎare] *vt* to sift; (*fig*) to weigh up

'vago, -a, -ghi, -ghe *ag* vague

va'gone *sm* (*Ferr: per passeggeri*) coach; (: *per merci*) truck, wagon; **vagone letto** sleeper, sleeping car; **vagone ristorante** dining *o* restaurant car

'vai *vb vedi* **andare**

vai'olo *sm* smallpox

va'langa, -ghe *sf* avalanche

va'lere *vi* (*avere forza, potenza*) to have influence; (*essere valido*) to be valid; (*avere vigore, autorità*) to hold, apply; (*essere capace: poeta, studente*) to be good, be able ▷ *vt* (*prezzo, sforzo*) to be worth; (*corrispondere*) to correspond to; (*procurare*): **~ qc a qn** to earn sb sth; **valersi di** to make use of, take advantage of; **far ~** (*autorità ecc*) to assert; **vale a dire** that is to say; **~ la pena** to be worth the effort *o* worth it

'valgo *ecc vb vedi* **valere**

vali'care *vt* to cross

'valico, -chi *sm* (*passo*) pass

'valido, -a *ag* valid; (*rimedio*) effective; (*aiuto*) real; (*persona*) worthwhile

vali'getta [vali'dʒetta] *sf* briefcase; **valigetta ventiquattrore** overnight bag *o* case

va'ligia, -gie *o* **ge** [va'lidʒa] *sf* (suit)case; **fare le valigie** to pack (up)

'valle *sf* valley; **a ~** (*di fiume*) downstream; **scendere a ~** to go downhill

va'lore *sm* (*gen*) value; (*merito*) merit, worth; (*coraggio*) valour, courage; (*Comm: titolo*) security; **valori** *smpl* (*oggetti preziosi*) valuables

valoriz'zare [valorid'dzare] *vt* (*terreno*) to develop; (*fig*) to make the most of

va'luta *sf* currency, money; (*Banca*): **~ 15 gennaio** interest to run from January 15th

valu'tare *vt* (*casa, gioiello, fig*) to value; (*stabilire: peso, entrate, fig*) to estimate

'valvola *sf* (*Tecn, Anat*) valve; (*Elettr*) fuse

valzer ['valtser] *sm inv* waltz

vam'pata *sf* (*di fiamma*) blaze; (*di calore*) blast; (: *al viso*) flush

vam'piro *sm* vampire

vanda'lismo *sm* vandalism

'vandalo *sm* vandal

vaneggi'are [vaned'dʒare] *vi* to rave

'vanga, -ghe *sf* spade

van'gelo [van'dʒɛlo] *sm* gospel

va'niglia [va'niʎʎa] *sf* vanilla

vanità *sf* vanity; (*di promessa*) emptiness; (*di sforzo*) futility; **vani'toso, -a** *ag* vain, conceited

'vanno *vb vedi* **andare**

'vano, -a *ag* vain ▷ *sm* (*spazio*) space; (*apertura*) opening; (*stanza*) room

van'taggio [van'taddʒo] *sm* advantage; **essere/portarsi in ~** (*Sport*) to be in/take the lead; **vantaggi'oso, -a** *ag* advantageous; favourable

vantarsi *vpr* **~ (di/di aver fatto)** to boast *o* brag (about/about having done)

'vanvera *sf* **a ~** haphazardly; **parlare a ~** to talk nonsense

va'pore *sm* vapour; (*anche*: **~ acqueo**) steam; (*nave*) steamer; **a ~** (*turbina ecc*) steam *cpd*; **al ~** (*Cuc*) steamed

va'rare *vt* (*Naut, fig*) to launch; (*Dir*) to pass

var'care *vt* to cross

'varco, -chi *sm* passage; **aprirsi un ~ tra la folla** to push one's way through the crowd

vare'china [vare'kina] *sf* bleach

vari'abile *ag* variable; (*tempo, umore*) changeable, variable ▷ *sf* (*Mat*) variable

vari'cella [vari'tʃella] *sf* chickenpox

vari'coso, -a *ag* varicose

varietà *sf inv* variety ▷ *sm inv* variety show

'vario, -a *ag* varied; (*parecchi: col sostantivo al pl*) various; (*mutevole: umore*) changeable

'varo *sm* (*Naut: fig*) launch; (*di leggi*) passing

varrò *ecc vb vedi* **valere**

Var'savia *sf* Warsaw

va'saio *sm* potter

'vasca, -sche *sf* basin; **vasca da bagno** bathtub, bath

vas'chetta [vas'ketta] *sf* (*per gelato*) tub; (*per sviluppare fotografie*) dish

vase'lina *sf* Vaseline®

'vaso *sm* (*recipiente*) pot; (: *barattolo*) jar; (: *decorativo*) vase; (*Anat*) vessel; **vaso da fiori** vase; (*per piante*) flowerpot

vas'soio *sm* tray

'vasto, -a *ag* vast, immense

Vati'cano *sm* **il ~** the Vatican

ve *pron, av vedi* **vi**

vecchi'aia [vek'kjaja] *sf* old age

'vecchio, -a ['vɛkkjo] *ag* old ▷ *sm/f* old man/woman; **i vecchii** the old

ve'dere *vt, vi* to see; **vedersi** *vpr* to meet, see one another; **avere a che ~ con** to have something to do with; **far ~ qc a qn** to show sb sth; **farsi ~** to show *o* s.; (*farsi vivo*) to show one's face; **vedi di non farlo** make sure *o* see you don't do it; **non (ci) si vede** (*è buio ecc*) you can't see a thing; **non lo posso ~** (*fig*) I can't stand him

ve'detta *sf* (*sentinella, posto*) look-out; (*Naut*) patrol boat

'vedovo, -a *sm/f* widower/widow

vedrò *ecc vb vedi* **vedere**

ve'duta *sf* view; **vedute** *sfpl* (*fig: opinioni*) views; **di larghe** *o* **ampie vedute** broad-minded; **di vedute limitate** narrow-minded

vege'tale [vedʒe'tale] *ag, sm* vegetable

vegetari'ano, -a [vedʒeta'rjano] *ag, sm/f* vegetarian; **avete piatti vegetariani?** do you have any vegetarian dishes?

vegetazi'one [vedʒetat'tsjone] *sf* vegetation

'vegeto, -a ['vɛdʒeto] *ag* (*pianta*) thriving; (*persona*) strong, vigorous

'veglia ['veʎʎa] *sf* wakefulness; (*sorveglianza*) watch; (*trattenimento*) evening gathering; **fare la ~ a un malato** to watch over a sick person

vegli'one [veʎ'ʎone] *sm* ball, dance; **veglione di Capodanno** New Year's Eve party

ve'icolo *sm* vehicle

'vela *sf* (*Naut: tela*) sail; (*Sport*) sailing

ve'leno *sm* poison; **vele'noso, -a** *ag* poisonous

veli'ero *sm* sailing ship

vel'luto *sm* velvet; **velluto a coste** cord

'velo *sm* veil; (*tessuto*) voile

ve'loce [ve'lotʃe] *ag* fast, quick ▷ *av* fast, quickly; **velocità** *sf* speed; **a forte velocità** at high speed; **velocità di crociera** cruising speed

'vena *sf* (*gen*) vein; (*filone*) vein, seam; (*fig: ispirazione*) inspiration; (: *umore*) mood; **essere in ~ di qc** to be in the mood for sth

ve'nale *ag* (*prezzo, valore*) market *cpd*; (*fig*) venal; mercenary

ven'demmia *sf* (*raccolta*) grape harvest; (*quantità d'uva*) grape crop, grapes *pl*; (*vino ottenuto*) vintage

'vendere *vt* to sell; **"vendesi"** "for sale"

ven'detta *sf* revenge

vendicarsi *vpr* **~ (di)** to avenge o.s. (for); (*per rancore*) to take one's revenge (for); **~ su qn** to revenge o.s. on sb

'vendita *sf* sale; **la ~** (*attività*) selling; (*smercio*) sales *pl*; **in ~** on sale; **vendita all'asta** sale by auction; **vendita per telefono** telesales *sg*

vene'rare *vt* to venerate

venerdì *sm inv* Friday; **di** *o* **il ~** on Fridays; **V~ Santo** Good Friday

ve'nereo, -a *ag* venereal

Ve'nezia [ve'nɛttsja] *sf* Venice

'vengo *ecc vb vedi* **venire**

veni'ale *ag* venial

ve'nire *vi* to come; (*riuscire: dolce, fotografia*) to turn out; (*come ausiliare: essere*): **viene ammirato da tutti** he is admired by everyone; **~ da** to come from; **quanto viene?** how much does it cost?; **far ~** (*mandare a chiamare*) to send for; **~ giù** to come down; **~ meno** (*svenire*) to faint; **~ meno a qc** not to fulfil sth; **~ su** to come up; **~ a trovare qn** to come and see sb; **~**

via to come away

'venni ecc vb vedi **venire**

ven'taglio [ven'taλλo] sm fan

ven'tata sf gust (of wind)

ven'tenne ag **una ragazza ~** a twenty-year-old girl, a girl of twenty

ven'tesimo, -a num twentieth

'venti num twenty

venti'lare vt (stanza) to air, ventilate; (fig: idea, proposta) to air; **ventila'tore** sm ventilator, fan

ven'tina sf **una ~ (di)** around twenty, twenty or so

'vento sm wind

'ventola sf (Aut, Tecn) fan

ven'tosa sf (Zool) sucker; (di gomma) suction pad

ven'toso, -a ag windy

'ventre sm stomach

'vera sf wedding ring

vera'mente av really

ve'randa sf veranda(h)

ver'bale ag verbal ▷ sm (di riunione) minutes pl

'verbo sm (Ling) verb; (parola) word; (Rel): **il V~** the Word

'verde ag, sm green; **essere al ~** to be broke; **verde bottiglia/oliva** bottle/olive green

ver'detto sm verdict

ver'dura sf vegetables pl

'vergine ['verdʒine] sf virgin; (dello zodiaco): **V~** Virgo ▷ ag virgin; (ragazza): **essere ~** to be a virgin

ver'gogna [ver'goɲɲa] sf shame; (timidezza) shyness, embarrassment; **vergo'gnarsi** vpr **vergognarsi (di)** to be ofeel ashamed (of); to be shy (about), be embarrassed (about); **vergo'gnoso, -a** ag ashamed; (timido) shy, embarrassed; (causa di vergogna: azione) shameful

ve'rifica, -che sf checking no pl, check

verifi'care vt (controllare) to check; (confermare) to confirm, bear out

verità sf inv truth

'verme sm worm

ver'miglio [ver'miλλo] sm vermilion, scarlet

ver'nice [ver'nitʃe] sf (colorazione) paint; (trasparente) varnish; (pelle) patent leather; **"~ fresca"** "wet paint"; **vernici'are** vt to paint; to varnish

'vero, -a ag (veridico: fatti, testimonianza) true; (autentico) real ▷ sm (verità) truth; (realtà) (real) life; **un ~ e proprio delinquente** a real criminal, an out-and-out criminal

vero'simile ag likely, probable

verrò ecc vb vedi **venire**

ver'ruca, -che sf wart

versa'mento sm (pagamento) payment; (deposito di denaro) deposit

ver'sante sm slopes pl, side

ver'sare vt (fare uscire: vino, farina) to pour (out); (spargere: lacrime, sangue) to shed; (rovesciare) to spill; (Econ) to pay; (: depositare) to deposit, pay in

versa'tile ag versatile

versi'one sf version; (traduzione) translation

'verso sm (di poesia) verse, line; (di animale, uccello) cry; (direzione) direction; (modo) way; (di foglio di carta) verso; (di moneta) reverse; **versi** smpl (poesia) verse sg; **non c'è ~ di persuaderlo** there's no way of persuading him, he can't be persuaded prep (in direzione di) toward(s); (nei pressi di) near, around (about); (in senso temporale) about, around; (nei confronti di) for; **~ di me** towards me; **~ sera** towards evening

'vertebra sf vertebra

verte'brale ag vertebral; **colonna ~** spinal column, spine

verti'cale ag, sf vertical

'vertice ['vertitʃe] sm summit, top; (Mat) vertex; **conferenza al ~** (Pol) summit conference

ver'tigine [ver'tidʒine] sf dizziness no pl; dizzy spell; (Med) vertigo; **avere le vertigini** to feel dizzy

ve'scica, -che [veʃʃika] sf (Anat) bladder; (Med) blister

'vescovo sm bishop

'vespa sf wasp

ves'taglia [ves'taλλa] sf dressing gown

ves'tire vt (bambino, malato) to dress; (avere indosso) to have on, wear; **vestirsi** vpr to dress, get dressed; **ves'tito, -a** ag dressed ▷ sm garment; (da donna) dress; (da uomo) suit; **vestiti** smpl (indumenti) clothes; **vestito di bianco** dressed in white

veteri'nario, -a ag veterinary ▷ sm veterinary surgeon (BRIT), veterinarian (US), vet

'veto sm inv veto

ve'traio sm glassmaker; glazier

ve'trata sf glass door (o window); (di chiesa) stained glass window

ve'trato, -a ag (porta, finestra) glazed; (che contiene vetro) glass cpd ▷ sf glass door (o window); (di chiesa) stained glass window; **carta vetrata** sandpaper

ve'trina sf (di negozio) (shop) window; (armadio) display cabinet; **vetri'nista, -i, -e** sm/f window dresser

'vetro sm glass; (per finestra, porta) pane (of glass)

'vetta sf peak, summit, top

vet'tura sf (carrozza) carriage; (Ferr) carriage (BRIT), car (US); (auto) car (BRIT), automobile (US)

vezzeggia'tivo [vettseddʒa'tivo] sm (Ling) term of endearment

vi (dav lo, la, li, le, ne diventa **ve**) pron (oggetto) you; (complemento di termine) (to) you; (riflessivo) yourselves; (reciproco) each other ▷ av (lì) here; (qui) here; (per questo/quel luogo) through here/there; **vi è/sono** there is/are

'via sf (gen) way; (strada) street; (sentiero, pista) path, track; (Amm: procedimento) channels pl ▷ prep (passando per) via, by way of ▷ av away ▷ escl go away!; (suvvia) come on!; (Sport) go! ▷ sm (Sport) starting signal; **in ~ di guarigione** on the road to recovery; **per ~ di** (a causa di) because of, on account of; **in o per ~** on the way; **per ~ aerea** by air; (lettere) by airmail; **andare/essere ~** to go/be away; **~ ~ che** (a mano a mano) as; **dare il ~** (Sport) to give the starting signal; **dare il ~ a** (fig) to start; **in ~ provvisoria** provisionally; **Via lattea** (Astr) Milky Way; **via di mezzo** middle course; **via d'uscita** (fig) way out

via'dotto sm viaduct

viaggi'are [viad'dʒare] vi to travel; **viaggia'tore, -'trice** ag travelling ▷ sm traveller; (passeggero) passenger

vi'aggio ['viaddʒo] sm travel(ling); (tragitto) journey, trip; **buon ~!** have a good trip!; **com'è andato il ~?** how was your journey?; **il ~ dura due ore** the journey takes two hours; **viaggio di nozze** honeymoon; **siamo in ~ di nozze** we're on honeymoon

vi'ale sm avenue

via'vai sm coming and going, bustle

vi'brare vi to vibrate

'vice ['vitʃe] sm/f deputy

vi'cenda [vi'tʃɛnda] sf event; **a ~** in turn

vice'versa [vitʃe'vɛrsa] av vice versa; **da Roma a Pisa e ~** from Rome to Pisa and back

vici'nanza [vitʃi'nantsa] sf nearness, closeness

vi'cino, -a [vi'tʃino] ag (gen) near; (nello spazio) near, nearby; (accanto) next; (nel tempo) near, close at hand ▷ av near, close; **da ~** (guardare) close up; (esaminare, seguire) closely; (conoscere) well, intimately; **~ a** near (to), close to; (accanto a) beside; **c'è una banca qui ~?** is there a bank nearby?; **~ di casa** neighbour

'vicolo sm alley; **vicolo cieco** blind alley

'video sm inv (TV: schermo) screen; **video'camera** sf camcorder;

videocas'setta sf videocassette;

videoclip [video'klip] sm inv videoclip;

videogi'oco, -chi [video'dʒɔko] sm video game; **videoregistra'tore** sm video (recorder); **videote'lefono** sm videophone

'vidi ecc vb vedi **vedere**

vie'tare vt to forbid; (Amm) to prohibit; **~ a qn di fare** to forbid sb to do; to prohibit sb from doing; **"vietato fumare/l'ingresso"** "no smoking/admittance"

vie'tato, -a ag (vedi vb) forbidden; prohibited; banned; **"~ fumare/l'ingresso"** "no smoking/admittance"; **~ ai minori di 14/18 anni** prohibited to children under 14/18; **"senso ~"** (Aut) "no entry"; **"sosta vietata"** (Aut) "no parking"

Viet'nam sm il ~ Vietnam; **vietna'mita, -i, -e** ag, sm/f, sm Vietnamese inv

vi'gente [vi'dʒɛnte] ag in force

'vigile ['vidʒile] ag watchful ▷ sm (anche: ~ urbano) policeman (in towns); **vigile del fuoco** fireman

vi'gilia [vi'dʒilja] sf (giorno antecedente) eve; **la ~ di Natale** Christmas Eve

vigli'acco, -a, -chi, -che [viʎ'ʎakko] ag cowardly ▷ sm/f coward

vi'gneto [viɲ'ɲeto] sm vineyard

vi'gnetta [viɲ'ɲetta] sf cartoon

vi'gore sm vigour; (Dir): **essere/entrare in ~** to be in/come into force

'vile ag (spregevole) low, mean, base; (codardo) cowardly

'villa sf villa

vil'laggio [vil'laddʒo] sm village; **villaggio turistico** holiday village

vil'lano, -a ag rude, ill-mannered

villeggia'tura [villeddʒa'tura] sf holiday(s) pl (BRIT), vacation (US)

vil'letta sf, **vil'lino** ▷ sm small house (with a garden), cottage

'vimini smpl di **~** wicker

'vincere ['vintʃere] vt (in guerra, al gioco, a una gara) to defeat, beat; (premio, guerra, partita) to win; (fig) to overcome, conquer ▷ vi to win; **~ qn in bellezza** to be better-looking than sb; **vinci'tore** sm winner; (Mil) victor

vi'nicolo, -a ag wine cpd

'vino sm wine; **vino bianco/rosato/rosso** white/rosé/red wine; **vino da pasto** table wine

'vinsi ecc vb vedi **vincere**

vi'ola sf (Bot) violet; (Mus) viola ▷ ag, sm inv (colore) purple

vio'lare vt (chiesa) to desecrate, violate; (giuramento, legge) to violate

violen'tare vt to use violence on; (donna) to rape

vio'lento, -a ag violent; **vio'lenza** sf violence; **violenza carnale** rape

vio'letta sf (Bot) violet

vio'letto, -a ag, sm (colore) violet

violi'nista, -i, -e sm/f violinist

vio'lino sm violin

violon'cello [violon't∫ɛllo] sm cello

vi'ottolo sm path, track

vip [vip] sigla m (= very important person) VIP

'vipera sf viper, adder

vi'rare vi (Naut, Aer) to turn; (Fot) to tone; **~ di bordo** (Naut) to tack

'virgola sf (Ling) comma; (Mat) point; **virgo'lette** sfpl inverted commas, quotation marks

vi'rile ag (proprio dell'uomo) masculine; (non puerile, da uomo) manly, virile

virtù sf inv virtue; **in o per ~ di** by virtue of, by

virtu'ale ag virtual

'virus sm inv (anche Inform) virus

'viscere [vi∫∫ere] sfpl (di animale) entrails pl; (fig) bowels pl

'vischio ['viskjo] sm (Bot) mistletoe; (pania) birdlime

'viscido, -a [vi∫∫ido] ag slimy

vi'sibile ag visible

visibilità sf visibility

visi'era sf (di elmo) visor; (di berretto) peak

visi'one sf vision; **prendere ~ di qc** to examine sth, look sth over; **prima/seconda ~** (Cinema) first/second showing

'visita sf visit; (Med) visit, call; (: esame) examination; **visita guidata** guided tour; **a che ora comincia la ~ guidata?** what time does the guided tour start?; **visita medica** medical examination; **visi'tare** vt to visit; (Med) to visit, call on; (: esaminare) to examine; **visita'tore, -'trice** sm/f visitor

vi'sivo, -a ag visual

'viso sm face

vi'sone sm mink

'vispo, -a ag quick, lively

'vissi ecc vb vedi **vivere**

'vista sf (facoltà) (eye)sight; (fatto di vedere): **la ~ di** the sight of; (veduta) view; **sparare a ~** to shoot on sight; **in ~** in sight; **perdere qn di ~** to lose sight of sb; (fig) to lose touch with sb; **a ~ d'occhio** as far as the eye can see; (fig) before one's very eyes; **far ~ di fare** to pretend to do

'visto, -a pp di **vedere** ▷ sm visa; **~ che** seeing (that)

vis'toso, -a ag gaudy, garish; (ingente) considerable

visu'ale ag visual

'vita sf life; (Anat) waist; **a ~** for life

vi'tale ag vital

vita'mina sf vitamin

'vite sf (Bot) vine; (Tecn) screw

vi'tello sm (Zool) calf; (carne) veal; (pelle) calfskin

'vittima sf victim

'vitto sm food; (in un albergo ecc) board; **vitto e alloggio** board and lodging

vit'toria sf victory

'viva escl **~ il re!** long live the king!

vi'vace [vi'vat∫e] ag (vivo, animato) lively; (: mente) lively, sharp; (colore) bright

vi'vaio sm (di pesci) hatchery; (Agr) nursery

vivavoce [viva'vot∫e] sm inv (dispositivo) loudspeaker; **mettere il ~** to switch on the loudspeaker

vi'vente ag living, alive; **i viventi** the living

'vivere vi to live ▷ vt to live; (passare: brutto momento) to live through, go through; (sentire: gioie, pene di qn) to share ▷ sm life; (anche: **modo di ~**) way of life; **viveri** smpl (cibo) food sg, provisions; **~ di** to live on

'vivido, -a ag (colore) vivid, bright

vivisezi'one [viviset'tsjone] sf vivisection

'vivo, -a ag (vivente) alive, living; (: animale) live; (fig) lively; (: colore) bright, brilliant; **i vivi** the living; **~ e vegeto** hale and hearty; **farsi ~** to show one's face; to be heard from; **ritrarre dal ~** to paint from life; **pungere qn nel ~** (fig) to cut sb to the quick

vivrò ecc vb vedi **vivere**

vizi'are [vit'tsjare] vt (bambino) to spoil; (corrompere moralmente) to corrupt; **vizi'ato, -a** ag spoilt; (aria, acqua) polluted

'vizio ['vittsjo] sm (morale) vice; (cattiva abitudine) bad habit; (imperfezione) flaw, defect; (errore) fault, mistake

V.le abbr = **viale**

vocabo'lario sm (dizionario) dictionary; (lessico) vocabulary

vo'cabolo sm word

vo'cale ag vocal ▷ sf vowel

vocazi'one [vokat'tsjone] sf vocation; (fig) natural bent

'voce ['vot∫e] sf voice; (diceria) rumour; (di un elenco, in bilancio) item; **aver ~ in capitolo** (fig) to have a say in the matter

'voga sf (Naut) rowing; (usanza): **essere in ~** to be in fashion o in vogue

vo'gare vi to row

vogherò ecc [voge'rɔ] vb vedi **vogare**

'voglia ['vɔʎʎa] sf desire, wish; (macchia) birthmark; **aver ~ di qc/di fare** to feel like sth/like doing; (più forte) to want sth/to do

'voglio ecc ['vɔʎʎo] vb vedi **volere**

'voi pron you; **voi'altri** pron you

vo'lante ag flying ▷ sm (steering) wheel

volan'tino sm leaflet

vo'lare vi (uccello, aereo, fig) to fly; (cappello)

to blow away o off, fly away o off; **~ via** to fly away o off
vo'latile ag (Chim) volatile ▷ sm (Zool) bird
volente'roso, -a ag willing
volenti'eri av willingly; **"~"** "with pleasure", "I'd be glad to"

 PAROLA CHIAVE

vo'lere sm will, wish(es); **contro il volere di** against the wishes of; **per volere di qn** in obedience to sb's will o wishes
▷ vt **1** (esigere, desiderare) to want; **voler fare/che qn faccia** to want to do/sb to do; **volete del caffè?** would you like o do you want some coffee?; **vorrei questo/fare** I would o I'd like this/to do; **come vuoi** as you like; **senza volere** (inavvertitamente) without meaning to, unintentionally
2 (consentire): **vogliate attendere, per piacere** please wait; **vogliamo andare?** shall we go?; **vuole essere così gentile da …?** would you be so kind as to …?; **non ha voluto ricevermi** he wouldn't see me
3: **volerci** (essere necessario: materiale, attenzione) to need; (: tempo) to take; **quanta farina ci vuole per questa torta?** how much flour do you need for this cake?; **ci vuole un'ora per arrivare a Venezia** it takes an hour to get to Venice
4: **voler bene a qn** (amore) to love sb; (affetto) to be fond of sb, like sb very much; **voler male a qn** to dislike sb; **volerne a qn** to bear sb a grudge; **voler dire** to mean

vol'gare ag vulgar
voli'era sf aviary
voli'tivo, -a ag strong-willed
'volli ecc vb vedi **volere**
'volo sm flight; **al ~: colpire qc al ~** to hit sth as it flies past; **capire al ~** to understand straight away; **volo charter** charter flight; **volo di linea** scheduled flight
volontà sf will; **a ~** (mangiare, bere) as much as one likes; **buona/cattiva ~** goodwill/lack of goodwill
volon'tario, -a ag voluntary ▷ sm (Mil) volunteer
'volpe sf fox
'volta sf (momento, circostanza) time; (turno, giro) turn; (curva) turn, bend; (Archit) vault; (direzione): **partire alla ~ di** to set off for; **a mia (o tua ecc) ~** in turn; **una ~** once; **una ~ sola** only once; **due volte** twice; **una cosa per ~** one thing at a time; **una ~ per tutte** once and for all; **a volte** at times, sometimes; **una ~ che** (temporale) once;

(causale) since; **3 volte 4** 3 times 4
volta'faccia [volta'fattʃa] sm inv (fig) volte-face
vol'taggio [vol'taddʒo] sm (Elettr) voltage
vol'tare vt to turn; (girare: moneta) to turn over; (rigirare) to turn round ▷ vi to turn; **voltarsi** vpr to turn; to turn over; to turn round
voltas'tomaco sm nausea; (fig) disgust
'volto, -a pp di **volgere** ▷ sm face
vo'lubile ag changeable, fickle
vo'lume sm volume
vomi'tare vt, vi to vomit; **'vomito** sm vomiting no pl; vomit
'vongola sf clam
vo'race [vo'ratʃe] ag voracious, greedy
vo'ragine [vo'radʒine] sf abyss, chasm
vorrò ecc vb vedi **volere**
'vortice ['vɔrtitʃe] sm whirlwind; whirlpool; (fig) whirl
'vostro, -a det il(la) ~(a) ecc your ▷ pron il(la) ~(a) ecc yours
vo'tante sm/f voter
vo'tare vi to vote ▷ vt (sottoporre a votazione) to take a vote on; (approvare) to vote for; (Rel): **~ qc a** to dedicate sth to
'voto sm (Pol) vote; (Ins) mark; (Rel) vow; (: offerta) votive offering; **aver voti belli/brutti** (Ins) to get good/bad marks
vs. abbr (Comm) = **vostro**
vul'cano sm volcano
vulne'rabile ag vulnerable
vu'oi, vu'ole vb vedi **volere**
vuo'tare vt to empty; **vuotarsi** vpr to empty
vu'oto, -a ag empty; (fig: privo): **~ di** (senso ecc) devoid of ▷ sm empty space, gap; (spazio in bianco) blank; (Fisica) vacuum; (fig: mancanza) gap, void; **a mani vuote** empty-handed; **vuoto d'aria** air pocket; **vuoto a rendere** returnable bottle

W   X

'wafer ['vafer] *sm inv (Cuc, Elettr)* wafer
'water ['wɔːtər] *sm inv* toilet
watt [vat] *sm inv* watt
W.C. *sm inv* WC
web [ueb] *sm* **il ~** the Web; **cercare nel ~**
   to search the Web ▷ *ag inv* **pagina ~** web
   page
'weekend ['wiːkend] *sm inv* weekend
'western ['western] *ag (Cinema)* cowboy
   cpd ▷ *sm inv* western, cowboy film;
   western all'italiana spaghetti western
'whisky ['wiski] *sm inv* whisky
'windsurf ['windsəːf] *sm inv (tavola)*
   windsurfer; *(sport)* windsurfing
'würstel ['vyrstəl] *sm inv* frankfurter

xe'nofobo, -a [kse'nɔfobo] *ag* xenophobic
   ▷ *sm/f* xenophobe
xi'lofono [ksi'lɔfono] *sm* xylophone

y z

yacht [jɔt] sm inv yacht
'yoga ['jɔga] ag inv, sm yoga (cpd)
yogurt ['jɔgurt] sm inv yog(h)urt

zabai'one [dzaba'jone] sm dessert made of egg yolks, sugar and marsala
zaf'fata [tsaf'fata] sf (tanfo) stench
zaffe'rano [dzaffe'rano] sm saffron
zaf'firo [dzaf'firo] sm sapphire
'zaino ['dzaino] sm rucksack
'zampa ['tsampa] sf (di animale: gamba) leg; (: piede) paw; **a quattro zampe** on all fours
zampil'lare [tsampil'lare] vi to gush, spurt
zan'zara [dzan'dzara] sf mosquito; **zanzari'era** sf mosquito net
'zappa ['tsappa] sf hoe
'zapping ['tsapiŋ] sm (TV) channel-hopping
zar, za'rina [tsar, tsa'rina] sm/f tsar/tsarina
'zattera ['dzattera] sf raft
'zebra ['dzɛbra] sf zebra; **zebre** sfpl (Aut) zebra crossing sg (BRIT), crosswalk sg (US)
'zecca, -che ['tsekka] sf (Zool) tick; (officina di monete) mint
'zelo ['dzɛlo] sm zeal
'zenzero ['dzendzero] sm ginger
'zeppa ['tseppa] sf wedge
'zeppo, -a ['tseppo] ag ~ **di** crammed o packed with
zer'bino [dzer'bino] sm doormat
'zero ['dzɛro] sm zero, nought; **vincere per**

tre a ~ (*Sport*) to win three-nil

'zia ['tsia] *sf* aunt

zibel'lino [dzibel'lino] *sm* sable

'zigomo ['dzigomo] *sm* cheekbone

zig'zag [dzig'dzag] *sm inv* zigzag; **andare a ~** to zigzag

Zimbabwe [tsim'babwe] *sm* **lo ~** Zimbabwe

'zinco ['dzinko] *sm* zinc

'zingaro, -a ['dzingaro] *sm/f* gipsy

'zio ['tsio] (*pl* **'zii**) *sm* uncle

zip'pare *vt* (*Inform: file*) to zip

zi'tella [dzi'tella] *sf* spinster; (*peg*) old maid

'zitto, -a ['tsitto] *ag* quiet, silent; **sta' ~!** be quiet!

'zoccolo ['tsɔkkolo] *sm* (*calzatura*) clog; (*di cavallo ecc*) hoof; (*basamento*) base; plinth

zodia'cale [dzodia'kale] *ag* zodiac *cpd*; **segno ~** sign of the zodiac

zo'diaco [dzo'diako] *sm* zodiac

'zolfo ['tsolfo] *sm* sulphur

'zolla ['dzɔlla] *sf* clod (of earth)

zol'letta [dzol'letta] *sf* sugar lump

'zona ['dzɔna] *sf* zone, area; **zona di depressione** (*Meteor*) trough of low pressure; **zona disco** (*Aut*) ≈ meter zone; **zona industriale** industrial estate; **zona pedonale** pedestrian precinct; **zona verde** (*di abitato*) green area

'zonzo ['dzondzo]: **a ~** *av*, **andare a ~** to wander about, stroll about

zoo ['dzɔo] *sm inv* zoo

zoolo'gia [dzoolo'dʒia] *sf* zoology

zoppi'care [tsoppi'kare] *vi* to limp; to be shaky, rickety

'zoppo, -a ['tsɔppo] *ag* lame; (*fig: mobile*) shaky, rickety

Z.T.L. *sigla f* (= *Zona a Traffico Limitato*) *controlled traffic zone*

'zucca, -che ['tsukka] *sf* (*Bot*) marrow; pumpkin

zucche'rare [tsukke'rare] *vt* to put sugar in; **zucche'rato, -a** *ag* sweet, sweetened

zuccheri'era [tsukke'rjɛra] *sf* sugar bowl

'zucchero ['tsukkero] *sm* sugar; **zucchero di canna** cane sugar; **zucchero filato** candy floss, cotton candy (*us*)

zuc'china [tsuk'kina] *sf* courgette (*BRIT*), zucchini (*us*)

'zuffa ['tsuffa] *sf* brawl

'zuppa ['tsuppa] *sf* soup; (*fig*) mixture, muddle; **zuppa inglese** (*Cuc*) *dessert made with sponge cake, custard and chocolate,* ≈ trifle (*BRIT*)

'zuppo, -a ['tsuppo] *ag* **~ (di)** drenched (with), soaked (with)

A [eɪ] n (Mus) la m

 KEYWORD

a [ə] (before vowel or silent h **an**) indef art **1** un (uno + s impure, gn, pn, ps, x, z), una f (un' + vowel); **a book** un libro; **a mirror** uno specchio; **an apple** una mela; **she's a doctor** è medico
2 (instead of the number "one") un(o), f una; **a year ago** un anno fa; **a hundred/ thousand** etc **pounds** cento/mille etc sterline
3 (in expressing ratios, prices etc) a, per; **3 a day/week** 3 al giorno/alla settimana; **10 km an hour** 10 km all'ora; **£5 a person** 5 sterline a persona or per persona

A.A. n abbr (= Alcoholics Anonymous) AA; (BRIT = Automobile Association) ≈ A.C.I. m
A.A.A. (US) n abbr (= American Automobile Association) ≈ A.C.I. m
aback [ə'bæk] adv **to be taken ~** essere sbalordito(-a)
abandon [ə'bændən] vt abbandonare ▷ n **with ~** sfrenatamente, spensieratamente
abattoir ['æbətwɑː'] (BRIT) n mattatoio
abbey ['æbɪ] n abbazia, badia
abbreviation [əbriːvɪ'eɪʃən] n abbreviazione f

abdomen ['æbdəmən] n addome m
abduct [æb'dʌkt] vt rapire
abide [ə'baɪd] vt **I can't ~ it/him** non lo posso soffrire or sopportare; **abide by** vt fus conformarsi a
ability [ə'bɪlɪtɪ] n abilità f inv
able ['eɪbl] adj capace; **to be ~ to do sth** essere capace di fare qc, poter fare qc
abnormal [æb'nɔːməl] adj anormale
aboard [ə'bɔːd] adv a bordo ▷ prep a bordo di
abolish [ə'bɒlɪʃ] vt abolire
abolition [æbəʊ'lɪʃən] n abolizione f
abort [ə'bɔːt] vt abortire; **abortion** [ə'bɔː ʃən] n aborto; **to have an abortion** abortire

 KEYWORD

about [ə'baʊt] adv **1** (approximately) circa, quasi; **about a hundred/thousand** etc un centinaio/migliaio etc, circa cento/mille etc; **it takes about 10 hours** ci vogliono circa 10 ore; **at about 2 o'clock** verso le 2; **I've just about finished** ho quasi finito
2 (referring to place) qua e là, in giro; **to leave things lying about** lasciare delle cose in giro; **to run about** correre qua e là; **to walk about** camminare
3: **to be about to do sth** stare per fare qc ▷ prep **1** (relating to) su, di; **a book about London** un libro su Londra; **what is it about?** di che si tratta?; (book, film etc) di cosa tratta?; **we talked about it** ne abbiamo parlato; **what or how about doing this?** che ne dici di fare questo?
2 (referring to place): **to walk about the town** camminare per la città; **her clothes were scattered about the room** i suoi vestiti erano sparsi or in giro per tutta la stanza

above [ə'bʌv] adv, prep sopra; **mentioned ~** suddetto; **~ all** soprattutto
abroad [ə'brɔːd] adv all'estero
abrupt [ə'brʌpt] adj (sudden) improvviso(-a); (gruff, blunt) brusco(-a)
abscess ['æbsɪs] n ascesso
absence ['æbsəns] n assenza
absent ['æbsənt] adj assente; **absent-minded** adj distratto(-a)
absolute ['æbsəluːt] adj assoluto(-a); **absolutely** [-'luːtlɪ] adv assolutamente
absorb [əb'zɔːb] vt assorbire; **to be ~ed in a book** essere immerso in un libro; **absorbent cotton** [əb'zɔːbənt-] (US) n cotone m idrofilo; **absorbing** adj avvincente, molto interessante
abstain [əb'steɪn] vi **to ~ (from)**

astenersi (da)

abstract ['æbstrækt] *adj* astratto(-a)

absurd [əb'sə:d] *adj* assurdo(-a)

abundance [ə'bʌndəns] *n* abbondanza

abundant [ə'bʌndənt] *adj* abbondante

abuse [*n* ə'bju:s, *vb* ə'bju:z] *n* abuso; (*insults*) ingiurie *fpl* ▷ *vt* abusare di; **abusive** *adj* ingiurioso(-a)

abysmal [ə'bɪzməl] *adj* spaventoso(-a)

academic [ækə'dɛmɪk] *adj* accademico(-a); (*pej: issue*) puramente formale ▷ *n* universitario(-a); **academic year** *n* anno accademico

academy [ə'kædəmɪ] *n* (*learned body*) accademia; (*school*) scuola privata; **academy of music** *n* conservatorio

accelerate [æk'sɛləreɪt] *vt, vi* accelerare; **acceleration** *n* accelerazione *f*; **accelerator** *n* acceleratore *m*

accent ['æksɛnt] *n* accento

accept [ək'sɛpt] *vt* accettare; **acceptable** *adj* accettabile; **acceptance** *n* accettazione *f*

access ['æksɛs] *n* accesso; **accessible** [æk'sɛsəbl] *adj* accessibile

accessory [æk'sɛsərɪ] *n* accessorio; (*Law*): **~ to** complice *m/f* di

accident ['æksɪdənt] *n* incidente *m*; (*chance*) caso; **I've had an ~** ho avuto un incidente; **by ~** per caso; **accidental** [-'dɛntl] *adj* accidentale; **accidentally** [-'dɛntəlɪ] *adv* per caso; **Accident and Emergency Department** *n* (BRIT) pronto soccorso; **accident insurance** *n* assicurazione *f* contro gli infortuni

acclaim [ə'kleɪm] *n* acclamazione *f*

accommodate [ə'kɔmədeɪt] *vt* alloggiare; (*oblige, help*) favorire

accommodation [əkɔmə'deɪʃən] (US **accommodations**) *n* alloggio

accompaniment [ə'kʌmpənɪmənt] *n* accompagnamento

accompany [ə'kʌmpənɪ] *vt* accompagnare

accomplice [ə'kʌmplɪs] *n* complice *m/f*

accomplish [ə'kʌmplɪʃ] *vt* compiere; (*goal*) raggiungere; **accomplishment** *n* compimento; realizzazione *f*

accord [ə'kɔ:d] *n* accordo ▷ *vt* accordare; **of his own ~** di propria iniziativa; **accordance**: **in accordance with** in conformità con; **according**: **according to** *prep* secondo; **accordingly** *adv* in conformità

account [ə'kaunt] *n* (Comm) conto; (*report*) descrizione *f*; **~s** *npl* (Comm) conti *mpl*; **of no ~** di nessuna importanza; **on ~** in acconto; **on no ~** per nessun motivo; **on ~ of** a causa di; **to take into ~, take**

~ of tener conto di; **account for** *vt fus* spiegare; giustificare; **accountable** *adj* **accountable (to)** responsabile (verso); **accountant** [ə'kauntənt] *n* ragioniere(-a); **account number** *n* numero di conto

accumulate [ə'kju:mjuleɪt] *vt* accumulare ▷ *vi* accumularsi

accuracy ['ækjurəsɪ] *n* precisione *f*

accurate ['ækjurɪt] *adj* preciso(-a); **accurately** *adv* precisamente

accusation [ækju'zeɪʃən] *n* accusa

accuse [ə'kju:z] *vt* accusare; **accused** *n* accusato(-a)

accustomed [ə'kʌstəmd] *adj* **~ to** abituato(-a) a

ace [eɪs] *n* asso

ache [eɪk] *n* male *m*, dolore *m* ▷ *vi* (*be sore*) far male, dolere; **my head ~s** mi fa male la testa

achieve [ə'tʃi:v] *vt* (*aim*) raggiungere; (*victory, success*) ottenere; **achievement** *n* compimento; successo

acid ['æsɪd] *adj* acido(-a) ▷ *n* acido

acknowledge [ək'nɔlɪdʒ] *vt* (*letter: also:* **~ receipt of**) confermare la ricevuta di; (*fact*) riconoscere; **acknowledgement** *n* conferma; riconoscimento

acne ['æknɪ] *n* acne *f*

acorn ['eɪkɔ:n] *n* ghianda

acoustic [ə'ku:stɪk] *adj* acustico(-a)

acquaintance [ə'kweɪntəns] *n* conoscenza; (*person*) conoscente *m/f*

acquire [ə'kwaɪər] *vt* acquistare; **acquisition** [ækwɪ'zɪʃən] *n* acquisto

acquit [ə'kwɪt] *vt* assolvere; **to ~ o.s. well** comportarsi bene

acre ['eɪkər] *n* acro, ≈ 4047 m²

acronym ['ækrənɪm] *n* acronimo

across [ə'krɔs] *prep* (*on the other side*) dall'altra parte di; (*crosswise*) attraverso ▷ *adv* dall'altra parte; in larghezza; **to run/swim ~** attraversare di corsa/a nuoto; **~ from** di fronte a

acrylic [ə'krɪlɪk] *adj* acrilico(-a)

act [ækt] *n* atto; (*in music-hall etc*) numero; (*Law*) decreto ▷ *vi* agire; (*Theatre*) recitare; (*pretend*) fingere ▷ *vt* (*part*) recitare; **to ~ as** agire da; **act up** (*inf*) *vi* (*person*) comportarsi male; (*knee, back, injury*) fare male; (*machine*) non funzionare; **acting** *adj* che fa le funzioni di ▷ *n* (*of actor*) recitazione *f*; (*activity*): **to do some acting** fare del teatro (or del cinema)

action ['ækʃən] *n* azione *f*; (Mil) combattimento; (Law) processo; **out of ~** fuori combattimento; fuori servizio; **to take ~** agire; **action replay** *n* (TV) replay *m inv*

activate ['æktɪveɪt] vt (mechanism) attivare

active ['æktɪv] adj attivo(-a); **actively** adv (participate) attivamente; (discourage, dislike) vivamente

activist ['æktɪvɪst] n attivista m/f

activity [æk'tɪvɪtɪ] n attività f inv; **activity holiday** n vacanza organizzata con attività ricreative per ragazzi

actor ['æktə'] n attore m

actress ['æktrɪs] n attrice f

actual ['æktjuəl] adj reale, effettivo(-a)
▨ Be careful not to translate **actual** by the Italian word **attuale**.

actually ['æktjuəlɪ] adv veramente; (even) addirittura
▨ Be careful not to translate **actually** by the Italian word **attualmente**.

acupuncture ['ækjupʌŋktfə'] n agopuntura

acute [ə'kju:t] adj acuto(-a); (mind, person) perspicace

ad [æd] n abbr = **advertisement**

A.D. adv abbr (= Anno Domini) d.C.

adamant ['ædəmənt] adj irremovibile

adapt [ə'dæpt] vt adattare ▷ vi **to ~ (to)** adattarsi (a); **adapter, adaptor** n (Elec) adattatore m

add [æd] vt aggiungere ▷ vi **to ~ to** (increase) aumentare; **add up** vt (figures) addizionare ▷ vi (fig): **it doesn't ~ up** non ha senso; **add up to** vt fus (Math) ammontare a; (fig: mean) significare; **it doesn't ~ up to much** non è un granché

addict ['ædɪkt] n tossicomane m/f; (fig) fanatico(-a); **addicted** [ə'dɪktɪd] adj **to be addicted to** (drink etc) essere dedito(-a) a; (fig: football etc) essere tifoso(-a) di; **addiction** [ə'dɪkfən] n (Med) tossicodipendenza; **addictive** [ə'dɪktɪv] adj che dà assuefazione

addition [ə'dɪfən] n addizione f; (thing added) aggiunta; **in ~** inoltre; **in ~ to** oltre; **additional** adj supplementare

additive ['ædɪtɪv] n additivo

address [ə'drɛs] n indirizzo; (talk) discorso ▷ vt indirizzare; (speak to) fare un discorso a; (issue) affrontare; **my ~ is ...** il mio indirizzo è...; **address book** n rubrica

adequate ['ædɪkwɪt] adj adeguato(-a), sufficiente

adhere [əd'hɪə'] vi **to ~ to** aderire a; (fig: rule, decision) seguire

adhesive [əd'hi:zɪv] n adesivo; **adhesive tape** n (BRIT: for parcels etc) nastro adesivo; (US Med) cerotto adesivo

adjacent [ə'dʒeɪsənt] adj adiacente; **~ to** accanto a

adjective ['ædʒɛktɪv] n aggettivo

adjoining [ə'dʒɔɪnɪŋ] adj accanto inv, adiacente

adjourn [ə'dʒə:n] vt rimandare ▷ vi essere aggiornato(-a)

adjust [ə'dʒʌst] vt aggiustare; (change) rettificare ▷ vi **to ~ (to)** adattarsi (a); **adjustable** adj regolabile; **adjustment** n (Psych) adattamento; (of machine) regolazione f; (of prices, wages) modifica

administer [əd'mɪnɪstə'] vt amministrare; (justice, drug) somministrare; **administration** [ədmɪnɪs'treɪfən] n amministrazione f; **administrative** [əd'mɪnɪstrətɪv] adj amministrativo(-a)

administrator [əd'mɪnɪstreɪtə'] n amministratore(-trice)

admiral ['ædmərəl] n ammiraglio

admiration [ædmə'reɪfən] n ammirazione f

admire [əd'maɪə'] vt ammirare; **admirer** n ammiratore(-trice)

admission [əd'mɪfən] n ammissione f; (to exhibition, nightclub etc) ingresso; (confession) confessione f

admit [əd'mɪt] vt ammettere; far entrare; (agree) riconoscere; **admit to** vt fus riconoscere; **admittance** n ingresso; **admittedly** adv bisogna pur riconoscere (che)

adolescent [ædəu'lɛsnt] adj, n adolescente m/f

adopt [ə'dɔpt] vt adottare; **adopted** adj adottivo(-a); **adoption** [ə'dɔpfən] n adozione f

adore [ə'dɔ:'] vt adorare

adorn [ə'dɔ:n] vt ornare

Adriatic [eɪdrɪ'ætɪk] n **the ~ (Sea)** il mare Adriatico, l'Adriatico

adrift [ə'drɪft] adv alla deriva

adult ['ædʌlt] adj adulto(-a); (work, education) per adulti ▷ n adulto(-a); **adult education** n scuola per adulti

adultery [ə'dʌltərɪ] n adulterio

advance [əd'vɑ:ns] n avanzamento; (money) anticipo ▷ adj (booking etc) in anticipo ▷ vt (money) anticipare ▷ vi avanzare; **in ~** in anticipo; **do I need to book in ~?** occorre che prenoti in anticipo?; **advanced** adj avanzato(-a); (Scol: studies) superiore

advantage [əd'vɑ:ntɪdʒ] n (also Tennis) vantaggio; **to take ~ of** approfittarsi di

advent ['ædvənt] n avvento; (Rel): **A~** Avvento

adventure [əd'vɛntfə'] n avventura; **adventurous** [əd'vɛntfərəs] adj avventuroso(-a)

adverb ['ædvə:b] n avverbio

adversary ['ædvəsərɪ] n avversario(-a)
adverse ['ædvəːs] adj avverso(-a)
advert ['ædvəːt] (BRIT) n abbr
= **advertisement**
advertise ['ædvətaɪz] vi, vt fare pubblicità
or réclame (a); fare un'inserzione (per
vendere); **to ~ for** (staff) mettere un
annuncio sul giornale per trovare;
advertisement [əd'vəːtɪsmənt] n
(Comm) réclame f inv, pubblicità f inv; (in
classified ads) inserzione f; **advertiser** n
azienda che reclamizza un prodotto; (in
newspaper) inserzionista m/f; **advertising**
['ædvətaɪzɪŋ] n pubblicità
advice [əd'vaɪs] n consigli mpl; **piece of ~**
consiglio; **to take legal ~** consultare un
avvocato
advisable [əd'vaɪzəbl] adj consigliabile
advise [əd'vaɪz] vt consigliare; **to ~ sb of**
sth informare qn di qc; **to ~ sb against**
sth/doing sth sconsigliare qc a qn/a qn
di fare qc; **adviser** n consigliere(-a); (in
business) consulente m/f, consigliere(-a);
advisory [-ərɪ] adj consultivo(-a)
advocate [n 'ædvəkɪt, vb 'ædvəkeɪt]
n (upholder) sostenitore(-trice); (Law)
avvocato (difensore) ▷ vt propugnare
Aegean [ɪ'dʒɪːən] n **the ~ (Sea)** il mar
Egeo, l'Egeo
aerial ['ɛərɪəl] n antenna ▷ adj aereo(-a)
aerobics [ɛə'rəubɪks] n aerobica
aeroplane ['ɛərəpleɪn] (BRIT) n aeroplano
aerosol ['ɛərəsɔl] (BRIT) n aerosol m inv
affair [ə'fɛəˈ] n affare m; (also: **love ~**)
relazione f amorosa; **~s** (business) affari
affect [ə'fɛkt] vt toccare; (influence)
influire su, incidere su; (feign) fingere;
affected [ə'fɛktɪd] adj affettato(-a),
affection [ə'fɛkʃən] n affezione f; **affectionate** adj
affettuoso(-a)
afflict [ə'flɪkt] vt affliggere
affluent ['æfluənt] adj ricco(-a); **the ~**
society la società del benessere
afford [ə'fɔːd] vt permettersi; (provide)
fornire; **affordable** adj (che ha un prezzo)
abbordabile
Afghanistan [æf'gænɪstɑːn] n Afganistan
m
afraid [ə'freɪd] adj impaurito(-a); **to be ~**
of or **to/that** aver paura di/che; **I am ~**
so/not ho paura di sì/no
Africa ['æfrɪkə] n Africa; **African** adj, n
africano(-a); **African-American** adj, n
afroamericano(-a)
after ['ɑːftəˈ] prep, adv dopo ▷ conj dopo
che; **what/who are you ~?** che/chi
cerca?; **~ he left/having done** dopo
che se ne fu andato/dopo aver fatto; **to**
name sb ~ sb dare a qn il nome di qn; **it's**

twenty ~ eight (US) sono le otto e venti;
to ask ~ sb chiedere di qn; **~ all** dopo
tutto; **~ you!** dopo di lei!; **after-effects**
npl consequenze fpl; (of illness) postumi
mpl; **aftermath** n consequenze fpl; **in**
the aftermath of nel periodo dopo;
afternoon n pomeriggio; **after-shave**
(lotion) ['ɑːftəʃeɪv-] n dopobarba m inv;
aftersun (lotion/cream) n doposole m
inv; **afterwards** (US **afterward**) adv dopo
again [ə'gɛn] adv di nuovo; **to begin/see ~**
ricominciare/rivedere; **not ... ~** non ... più;
~ and ~ ripetutamente
against [ə'gɛnst] prep contro
age [eɪdʒ] n età f inv ▷ vt, vi invecchiare;
it's been ~s since sono secoli che; **he is**
20 years of ~ ha 20 anni; **to come of ~**
diventare maggiorenne; **~d 10** di 10 anni;
the ~d ['eɪdʒɪd] gli anziani; **age group** n
generazione f; **age limit** n limite m d'età
agency ['eɪdʒənsɪ] n agenzia
agenda [ə'dʒɛndə] n ordine m del giorno
agent ['eɪdʒənt] n agente m
aggravate ['ægrəveɪt] vt aggravare;
(person) irritare
aggression [ə'grɛʃən] n aggressione f
aggressive [ə'grɛsɪv] adj aggressivo(-a)
agile ['ædʒaɪl] adj agile
agitated ['ædʒɪteɪtɪd] adj agitato(-a),
turbato(-a)
AGM n abbr = **annual general meeting**
ago [ə'gəu] adv **2 days ~** 2 giorni fa; **not**
long ~ poco tempo fa; **how long ~?**
quanto tempo fa?
agony ['ægənɪ] n dolore m atroce; **to be in**
~ avere dolori atroci
agree [ə'griː] vt (price) pattuire ▷ vi **to**
~ (with) essere d'accordo (con); (Ling)
concordare (con); **to ~ to sth/to do sth**
accettare qc/di fare qc; **to ~ that** (admit)
ammettere che; **to ~ on sth** accordarsi su
qc; **garlic doesn't ~ with me** l'aglio non
mi va; **agreeable** adj gradevole; (willing)
disposto(-a); **agreed** adj (time, place)
stabilito(-a); **agreement** n accordo; **in**
agreement d'accordo
agricultural [ægrɪ'kʌltʃərəl] adj
agricolo(-a)
agriculture ['ægrɪkʌltʃəˈ] n agricoltura
ahead [ə'hɛd] adv avanti; davanti; **~ of**
davanti a; (fig: schedule etc) in anticipo su;
~ of time in anticipo; **go right** or **straight**
~ tiri diritto
aid [eɪd] n aiuto ▷ vt aiutare; **in ~ of** a
favore di
aide [eɪd] n (person) aiutante m/f
AIDS [eɪdz] n abbr (= acquired immune
deficiency syndrome) AIDS f
ailing ['eɪlɪŋ] adj sofferente; (fig: economy,

industry etc) in difficoltà

ailment ['eɪlmənt] *n* indisposizione *f*

aim [eɪm] *vt* **to ~ sth at** (*such as gun*) mirare qc a, puntare qc a; (*camera*) rivolgere qc a; (*missile*) lanciare qc contro ▷ *vi* (*also:* **to take ~**) prendere la mira ▷ *n* mira; **to ~ at** mirare; **to ~ to do** aver l'intenzione di fare

ain't [eɪnt] (*inf*) = **am not; aren't; isn't**

air [ɛə'] *n* aria ▷ *vt* (*room*) arieggiare; (*clothes*) far prendere aria a; (*grievances, ideas*) esprimere pubblicamente ▷ *cpd* (*currents*) d'aria; (*attack*) aereo(-a); **to throw sth into the ~** lanciare qc in aria; **by ~** (*travel*) in aereo; **on the ~** (*Radio, TV*) in onda; **airbag** *n* airbag *m inv*; **airbed** (*BRIT*) *n* materassino; **airborne** ['ɛəbɔ:n] *adj* (*plane*) in volo; (*troops*) aerotrasportato(-a); **as soon as the plane was airborne** appena l'aereo ebbe decollato; **air-conditioned** *adj* con *or* ad aria condizionata; **air conditioning** *n* condizionamento d'aria; **aircraft** *n inv* apparecchio; **airfield** *n* campo d'aviazione; **Air Force** *n* aviazione *f* militare; **air hostess** (*BRIT*) *n* hostess *f inv*; **airing cupboard** ['ɛərɪŋ-] *n* armadio riscaldato per asciugare panni.; **airlift** *n* ponte *m* aereo; **airline** *n* linea aerea; **airliner** *n* aereo di linea; **airmail** *n* **by airmail** per via aerea; **airplane** (*US*) *n* aeroplano; **airport** *n* aeroporto; **air raid** *n* incursione *f* aerea; **airsick** *adj* **to be airsick** soffrire di mal d'aria; **airspace** *n* spazio aereo; **airstrip** *n* pista d'atterraggio; **air terminal** *n* air-terminal *m inv*; **airtight** *adj* ermetico(-a); **air-traffic controller** *n* controllore *m* del traffico aereo; **airy** *adj* arioso(-a); (*manners*) noncurante

aisle [aɪl] *n* (*of church*) navata laterale; navata centrale; (*of plane*) corridoio; **aisle seat** *n* (*on plane*) posto sul corridoio

ajar [ə'dʒɑ:'] *adj* socchiuso(-a)

à la carte [ɑ:lɑ:'kɑ:t] *adv* alla carta

alarm [ə'lɑ:m] *n* allarme *m* ▷ *vt* allarmare; **alarm call** *n* (*in hotel etc*) sveglia; **could I have an alarm call at 7 am, please?** vorrei essere svegliato alle 7, per favore; **alarm clock** *n* sveglia; **alarmed** *adj* (*person*) allarmato(-a); (*house, car etc*) dotato(-a) di allarme; **alarming** *adj* allarmante, preoccupante

Albania [æl'beɪnɪə] *n* Albania

albeit [ɔ:l'bi:ɪt] *conj* sebbene + *sub*, benché + *sub*

album ['ælbəm] *n* album *m inv*

alcohol ['ælkəhɔl] *n* alcool *m*; **alcohol-free** *adj* analcolico(-a); **alcoholic** [-'hɔlɪk] *adj* alcolico(-a) ▷ *n* alcolizzato(-a)

alcove ['ælkəʊv] *n* alcova

ale [eɪl] *n* birra

alert [ə'lə:t] *adj* vigile ▷ *n* allarme *m* ▷ *vt* avvertire; mettere in guardia; **on the ~** all'erta

algebra ['ældʒɪbrə] *n* algebra

Algeria [æl'dʒɪərɪə] *n* Algeria

alias ['eɪlɪəs] *adv* alias ▷ *n* pseudonimo, falso nome *m*

alibi ['ælɪbaɪ] *n* alibi *m inv*

alien ['eɪlɪən] *n* straniero(-a); (*extraterrestrial*) alieno(-a) ▷ *adj* **~ (to)** estraneo(-a) (a); **alienate** *vt* alienare

alight [ə'laɪt] *adj* acceso(-a) ▷ *vi* scendere; (*bird*) posarsi

align [ə'laɪn] *vt* allineare

alike [ə'laɪk] *adj* simile ▷ *adv* sia … sia; **to look ~** assomigliarsi

alive [ə'laɪv] *adj* vivo(-a); (*lively*) vivace

🔵 **KEYWORD**

all [ɔ:l] *adj* tutto(-a); **all day** tutto il giorno; **all night** tutta la notte; **all men** tutti gli uomini; **all five came** sono venuti tutti e cinque; **all the books** tutti i libri; **all the food** tutto il cibo; **all the time** sempre; tutto il tempo; **all his life** tutta la vita ▷ *pron* **1** tutto(-a); **I ate it all, I ate all of it** l'ho mangiato tutto; **all of us went** tutti noi siamo andati; **all of the boys went** tutti i ragazzi sono andati

2 (*in phrases*): **above all** soprattutto; **after all** dopotutto; **at all: not at all** (*in answer to question*) niente affatto; (*in answer to thanks*) prego!, di niente!, s'immagini!; **I'm not at all tired** non sono affatto stanco(-a); **anything at all will do** andrà bene qualsiasi cosa; **all in all** tutto sommato

▷ *adv* **all alone** tutto(-a) solo(-a); **it's not as hard as all that** non è poi così difficile; **all the more/the better** tanto più/meglio; **all but** quasi; **the score is two all** il punteggio è di due a due

Allah ['ælə] *n* Allah *m*

allegation [ælɪ'geɪʃən] *n* asserzione *f*

alleged [ə'lɛdʒd] *adj* presunto(-a); **allegedly** [ə'lɛdʒɪdlɪ] *adv* secondo quanto si asserisce

allegiance [ə'li:dʒəns] *n* fedeltà

allergic [ə'lə:dʒɪk] *adj* **~ to** allergico(-a) a; **I'm ~ to penicillin** sono allergico alla penicillina

allergy ['ælədʒɪ] *n* allergia

alleviate [ə'li:vɪeɪt] *vt* sollevare

alley ['ælɪ] *n* vicolo

alliance [ə'laɪəns] *n* alleanza

allied [ˈælaɪd] adj alleato(-a)

alligator [ˈælɪɡeɪtə^r] n alligatore m

all-in [ˈɔːlɪn] adj (BRIT: also adv: charge) tutto compreso

allocate [ˈæləkeɪt] vt assegnare

allot [əˈlɔt] vt assegnare

all-out [ˈɔːlaut] adj (effort etc) totale ▷ adv **to go all out for** mettercela tutta per

allow [əˈlau] vt (practice, behaviour) permettere; (sum to spend etc) accordare; (sum, time estimated) dare; (concede): **to ~ that** ammettere che; **to ~ sb to do** permettere a qn di fare; **he is ~ed to do** lo può fare; **allow for** vt fus tener conto di; **allowance** n (money received) assegno; indennità f inv; (Tax) detrazione f di imposta; **to make allowances for** tener conto di

all right adv (feel, work) bene; (as answer) va bene

ally [ˈælaɪ] n alleato

almighty [ɔːlˈmaɪtɪ] adj onnipotente; (row etc) colossale

almond [ˈɑːmənd] n mandorla

almost [ˈɔːlməust] adv quasi

alone [əˈləun] adj, adv solo(-a); **to leave sb ~** lasciare qn in pace; **to leave sth ~** lasciare qc; **let ~ ...** figuriamoci poi ..., tanto meno ...

along [əˈlɔŋ] prep lungo ▷ adv **is he coming ~?** viene con noi?; **he was limping ~** veniva zoppicando; **~ with** insieme con; **all ~** (all the time) sempre, fin dall'inizio; **alongside** prep accanto a; lungo ▷ adv accanto

aloof [əˈluːf] adj distaccato(-a) ▷ adv **to stand ~** tenersi a distanza or in disparte

aloud [əˈlaud] adv ad alta voce

alphabet [ˈælfəbɛt] n alfabeto

Alps [ælps] npl **the ~** le Alpi

already [ɔːlˈrɛdɪ] adv già

alright [ɔːlˈraɪt] (BRIT) adv = **all right**

also [ˈɔːlsəu] adv anche

altar [ˈɔltə^r] n altare m

alter [ˈɔltə^r] vt, vi alterare; **alteration** [ɔltəˈreɪʃən] n modificazione f, alterazione f; **alterations** (Sewing, Archit) modifiche fpl; **timetable subject to alteration** orario soggetto a variazioni

alternate [adj ɔlˈtəːnɪt, vb ˈɔltəːneɪt] adj alterno(-a); (US: plan etc) alternativo(-a) ▷ vi **to ~ (with)** alternarsi (a); **on ~ days** ogni due giorni

alternative [ɔlˈtəːnətɪv] adj alternativo(-a) ▷ n (choice) alternativa f; **alternatively** adv **alternatively one could ...** come alternativa si potrebbe ...

although [ɔːlˈðəu] conj benché + sub, sebbene + sub

altitude [ˈæltɪtjuːd] n altitudine f

altogether [ɔːltəˈɡɛðə^r] adv del tutto, completamente; (on the whole) tutto considerato; (in all) in tutto

aluminium [æljuˈmɪnɪəm] (BRIT), **aluminum** [əˈluːmɪnəm] (US) n alluminio

always [ˈɔːlweɪz] adv sempre

Alzheimer's (disease) [ˈæltshaɪməz-] n (malattia di) Alzheimer

am [æm] vb see **be**

amalgamate [əˈmælɡəmeɪt] vt amalgamare ▷ vi amalgamarsi

amass [əˈmæs] vt ammassare

amateur [ˈæmətə^r] n dilettante m/f ▷ adj (Sport) dilettante

amaze [əˈmeɪz] vt stupire; **amazed** adj sbalordito(-a); **to be amazed (at)** essere sbalordito (da); **amazement** n stupore m; **amazing** adj sorprendente, sbalorditivo(-a)

Amazon [ˈæməzən] n (Mythology) Amazzone f; (river): **the ~** il Rio delle Amazzoni ▷ cpd (basin, jungle) amazzonico(-a)

ambassador [æmˈbæsədə^r] n ambasciatore(-trice)

amber [ˈæmbə^r] n ambra; **at ~** (BRIT Aut) giallo

ambiguous [æmˈbɪɡjuəs] adj ambiguo(-a)

ambition [æmˈbɪʃən] n ambizione f; **ambitious** [æmˈbɪʃəs] adj ambizioso(-a)

ambulance [ˈæmbjuləns] n ambulanza; **call an ~!** chiamate un'ambulanza!

ambush [ˈæmbuʃ] n imboscata

amen [ˈɑːˈmɛn] excl così sia, amen

amend [əˈmɛnd] vt (law) emendare; (text) correggere; **to make ~s** fare ammenda; **amendment** n emendamento, correzione f

amenities [əˈmiːnɪtɪz] npl attrezzature fpl ricreative e culturali

America [əˈmɛrɪkə] n America; **American** adj, n americano(-a); **American football** n (BRIT) football m americano

amicable [ˈæmɪkəbl] adj amichevole

amid(st) [əˈmɪd(st)] prep in mezzo a

ammunition [æmjuˈnɪʃən] n munizioni fpl

amnesty [ˈæmnɪstɪ] n amnistia; **to grant an ~ to** concedere l'amnistia a, amnistiare

among(st) [əˈmʌŋ(st)] prep fra, tra, in mezzo a

amount [əˈmaunt] n somma; ammontare m; quantità f inv ▷ vi **to ~ to** (total) ammontare a; (be same as) essere come

amp(ère) [ˈæmp(ɛə^r)] n ampère m inv

ample [ˈæmpl] adj ampio(-a); spazioso(-a); (enough): **this is ~** questo è più che sufficiente

amplifier ['æmplɪfaɪəʳ] n amplificatore m

amputate ['æmpjuteɪt] vt amputare

Amtrak ['æmtræk] (US) n società ferroviaria americana

amuse [ə'mjuːz] vt divertire; **amusement** n divertimento; **amusement arcade** n sala giochi; **amusement park** n luna park m inv

amusing [ə'mjuːzɪŋ] adj divertente

an [æn] indef art see **a**

anaemia [ə'niːmɪə] (US **anemia**) n anemia

anaemic [ə'niːmɪk] (US **anemic**) adj anemico(-a)

anaesthetic [ænɪs'θetɪk] (US **anesthetic**) adj anestetico(-a) ▷ n anestetico

analog(ue) ['ænəlɔg] adj (watch, computer) analogico(-a)

analogy [ə'nælədʒɪ] n analogia; **to draw an ~ between** fare un'analogia tra

analyse ['ænəlaɪz] (US **analyze**) vt analizzare; **analysis** [ə'næləsɪs] (pl **analyses**) n analisi f inv; **analyst** ['ænəlɪst] n (Pol etc) analista m/f; (US) (psic)analista m/f

analyze ['ænəlaɪz] (US) vt = **analyse**

anarchy ['ænəkɪ] n anarchia

anatomy [ə'nætəmɪ] n anatomia

ancestor ['ænsɪstəʳ] n antenato(-a)

anchor ['æŋkəʳ] n ancora ▷ vi (also: **to drop ~**) gettare l'ancora ▷ vt ancorare; **to weigh ~** salpare or levare l'ancora

anchovy ['æntʃəvɪ] n acciuga

ancient ['eɪnʃənt] adj antico(-a); (person, car) vecchissimo(-a)

and [ænd] conj e; (often ed before vowel): **~ so on** e così via; **try ~ come** cerca di venire; **he talked ~ talked** non la finiva di parlare; **better ~ better** meglio e meglio

Andes ['ændiːz] npl **the ~** le Ande

anemia etc [ə'niːmɪə] (US) = **anaemia** etc

anesthetic [ænɪs'θetɪk] (US) adj, n = **anaesthetic**

angel ['eɪndʒəl] n angelo

anger ['æŋgəʳ] n rabbia

angina [æn'dʒaɪnə] n angina pectoris

angle ['æŋgl] n angolo; **from their ~** dal loro punto di vista

angler ['æŋgləʳ] n pescatore m con la lenza

Anglican ['æŋglɪkən] adj, n anglicano(-a)

angling ['æŋglɪŋ] n pesca con la lenza

angrily ['æŋgrɪlɪ] adv con rabbia

angry ['æŋgrɪ] adj arrabbiato(-a), furioso(-a); (wound) infiammato(-a); **to be ~ with sb/at sth** essere in collera con qn/per qc; **to get ~** arrabbiarsi; **to make sb ~** fare arrabbiare qn

anguish ['æŋgwɪʃ] n angoscia

animal ['ænɪməl] adj animale ▷ n animale m

animated ['ænɪmeɪtɪd] adj animato(-a)

animation [ænɪ'meɪʃən] n animazione f

aniseed ['ænɪsiːd] n semi mpl di anice

ankle ['æŋkl] n caviglia

annex [n 'æneks, vb ə'neks] n (BRIT: also: **~e**) (edificio) annesso ▷ vt annettere

anniversary [ænɪ'vəːsərɪ] n anniversario

announce [ə'nauns] vt annunciare; **announcement** n annuncio; (letter, card) partecipazione f; **announcer** n (Radio, TV: between programmes) annunciatore(-trice); (: in a programme) presentatore(-trice)

annoy [ə'nɔɪ] vt dare fastidio a; **don't get ~ed!** non irritarti!; **annoying** adj noioso(-a)

annual ['ænjuəl] adj annuale ▷ n (Bot) pianta annua; (book) annuario; **annually** adv annualmente

annum ['ænəm] n see **per**

anonymous [ə'nɔnɪməs] adj anonimo(-a)

anorak ['ænəræk] n giacca a vento

anorexia [ænə'reksɪə] n (Med: also: **~ nervosa**) anoressia

anorexic [ænə'reksɪk] adj, n anoressico(-a)

another [ə'nʌðəʳ] adj **~ book** (one more) un altro libro, ancora un libro; (a different one) un altro libro ▷ pron un altro(un'altra), ancora uno(-a); see also **one**

answer ['ɑːnsəʳ] n risposta; soluzione f ▷ vi rispondere ▷ vt (reply to) rispondere a; (problem) risolvere; (prayer) esaudire; **in ~ to your letter** in risposta alla sua lettera; **to ~ the phone** rispondere (al telefono); **to ~ the bell** rispondere al campanello; **to ~ the door** aprire la porta; **answer back** vi ribattere; **answerphone** n (esp BRIT) segreteria telefonica

ant [ænt] n formica

Antarctic [ænt'ɑːktɪk] n **the ~** l'Antartide f

antelope ['æntɪləup] n antilope f

antenatal ['æntɪ'neɪtl] adj prenatale

antenna [æn'tenə, -niː] (pl **antennae**) n antenna

anthem ['ænθəm] n **national ~** inno nazionale

anthology [æn'θɔlədʒɪ] n antologia

anthrax ['ænθræks] n antrace m

anthropology [ænθrə'pɔlədʒɪ] n antropologia

anti [ænt] prefix anti; **antibiotic** ['æntɪbaɪ'ɔtɪk] n antibiotico; **antibody** ['æntɪbɔdɪ] n anticorpo

anticipate [æn'tɪsɪpeɪt] vt prevedere; pregustare; (wishes, request) prevenire; **anticipation** [æntɪsɪ'peɪʃən] n anticipazione f; (expectation) aspettative fpl

anticlimax ['æntɪ'klaɪmæks] n **it was an ~** fu una completa delusione

anticlockwise ['æntɪ'klɔkwaɪz] *adj, adv* in senso antiorario

antics ['æntɪks] *npl* buffonerie *fpl*

anti: **antidote** ['æntɪdəut] *n* antidoto; **antifreeze** ['æntɪ'fri:z] *n* anticongelante *m*; **anti-globalization** [æntɪgləubəlaɪ'zeɪʃən] *n* antiglobalizzazione *f*; **antihistamine** [æntɪ'hɪstəmɪn] *n* antistaminico; **antiperspirant** ['æntɪ'pə:spərənt] *adj* antitraspirante

antique [æn'ti:k] *n* antichità *f inv* ▷ *adj* antico(-a); **antique shop** *n* negozio d'antichità

antiseptic [æntɪ'sɛptɪk] *n* antisettico

antisocial ['æntɪ'səuʃəl] *adj* asociale

antlers ['æntləz] *npl* palchi *mpl*

anxiety [æŋ'zaɪətɪ] *n* ansia; (*keenness*): ~ **to do** smania di fare

anxious ['æŋkʃəs] *adj* ansioso(-a), inquieto(-a); (*worrying*) angosciante; (*keen*): ~ **to do/that** impaziente di fare/che + *sub*

 KEYWORD

any ['ɛnɪ] *adj* **1** (*in questions etc*): **have you any butter?** hai del burro?, hai un po' di burro?; **have you any children?** hai bambini?; **if there are any tickets left** se ci sono ancora (dei) biglietti, se c'è ancora qualche biglietto
2 (*with negative*): **I haven't any money/ books** non ho soldi/libri
3 (*no matter which*) qualsiasi, qualunque; **choose any book you like** scegli un libro qualsiasi
4 (*in phrases*): **in any case** in ogni caso; **any day now** da un giorno all'altro; **at any moment** in qualsiasi momento, da un momento all'altro; **at any rate** ad ogni modo
▷ *pron* **1** (*in questions, with negative*): **have you got any?** ne hai?; **can any of you sing?** qualcuno di voi sa cantare?; **I haven't any (of them)** non ne ho
2 (*no matter which one(s)*): **take any of those books (you like)** prendi uno qualsiasi di quei libri
▷ *adv* **1** (*in questions etc*): **do you want any more soup/sandwiches?** vuoi ancora un po' di minestra/degli altri panini?; **are you feeling any better?** ti senti meglio?
2 (*with negative*): **I can't hear him any more** non lo sento più; **don't wait any longer** non aspettare più

any: **anybody** ['ɛnɪbɔdɪ] *pron* (*in questions etc*) qualcuno, nessuno; (*with negative*)

nessuno; (*no matter who*) chiunque; **can you see anybody?** vedi qualcuno or nessuno?; **if anybody should phone ...** se telefona qualcuno ...; **I can't see anybody** non vedo nessuno; **anybody could do it** chiunque potrebbe farlo; **anyhow** ['ɛnɪhau] *adv* (*at any rate*) ad ogni modo, comunque; (*haphazard*): **do it anyhow you like** fallo come ti pare; **I shall go anyhow** ci andrò lo stesso or comunque; **she leaves things just anyhow** lascia tutto come capita; **anyone** ['ɛnɪwan] *pron* = **anybody**; **anything** ['ɛnɪθɪŋ] *pron* (*in question etc*) qualcosa, niente; (*with negative*) niente; (*no matter what*): **you can say anything you like** puoi dire quello che ti pare; **can you see anything?** vedi niente or qualcosa?; **if anything happens to me ...** se mi dovesse succedere qualcosa ...; **I can't see anything** non vedo niente; **anything will do** va bene qualsiasi cosa or tutto; **anytime** *adv* in qualunque momento; quando vuole; **anyway** ['ɛnɪweɪ] *adv* (*at any rate*) ad ogni modo, comunque; (*besides*) ad ogni modo; **anywhere** ['ɛnɪwɛəʳ] *adv* (*in questions etc*) da qualche parte; (*with negative*) da nessuna parte; (*no matter where*) da qualsiasi or qualunque parte, dovunque; **can you see him anywhere?** lo vedi da qualche parte?; **I can't see him anywhere** non lo vedo da nessuna parte; **anywhere in the world** dovunque nel mondo

apart [ə'pɑ:t] *adv* (*to one side*) a parte; (*separately*) separatamente; **with one's legs ~** con le gambe divaricate; **10 miles ~** a 10 miglia di distanza (l'uno dall'altro); **to take ~** smontare; **~ from** a parte, eccetto

apartment [ə'pɑ:tmənt] (*us*) *n* appartamento; (*room*) locale *m*; **apartment building** (*us*) *n* stabile *m*, caseggiato

apathy ['æpəθɪ] *n* apatia

ape [eɪp] *n* scimmia ▷ *vt* scimmiottare

aperitif [ə'pɛrɪti:f] *n* aperitivo

aperture ['æpətʃjuəʳ] *n* apertura

APEX *n abbr* (= *advance purchase excursion*) APEX *m inv*

apologize [ə'pɔlədʒaɪz] *vi* **to ~ (for sth to sb)** scusarsi (di qc a qn), chiedere scusa (a qn per qc)

apology [ə'pɔlədʒɪ] *n* scuse *fpl*

apostrophe [ə'pɔstrəfɪ] *n* (*sign*) apostrofo

appal [ə'pɔ:l] (*us* **appall**) *vt* scioccare; **appalling** *adj* spaventoso(-a)

apparatus [æpə'reɪtəs] *n* apparato; (*in gymnasium*) attrezzatura

apparent [ə'pærənt] *adj* evidente; **apparently** *adv* evidentemente

appeal [ə'pi:l] vi (Law) appellarsi alla legge ▷ n (Law) appello; (request) richiesta; (charm) attrattiva; **to ~ for** chiedere (con insistenza); **to ~ to** (person) appellarsi a; (thing) piacere a; **it doesn't ~ to me** mi dice poco; **appealing** adj (nice) attraente

appear [ə'pɪə¹] vi apparire; (Law) comparire; (publication) essere pubblicato(-a); (seem) sembrare; **it would ~ that** sembra che; **appearance** n apparizione f; apparenza; (look, aspect) aspetto

appendicitis [əpɛndɪ'saɪtɪs] n appendicite f

appendix [ə'pɛndɪks] (pl **appendices**) n appendice f

appetite ['æpɪtaɪt] n appetito

appetizer ['æpɪtaɪzə¹] n stuzzichino

applaud [ə'plɔːd] vt, vi applaudire

applause [ə'plɔːz] n applauso

apple ['æpl] n mela; **apple pie** n torta di mele

appliance [ə'plaɪəns] n apparecchio

applicable [ə'plɪkəbl] adj applicabile; **to be ~ to** essere valido per; **the law is ~ from January** la legge entrerà in vigore in gennaio

applicant ['æplɪkənt] n candidato(-a)

application [æplɪ'keɪʃən] n applicazione f; (for a job, a grant etc) domanda; **application form** n modulo per la domanda

apply [ə'plaɪ] vt **to ~ (to)** (paint, ointment) dare (a); (theory, technique) applicare (a) ▷ vi **to ~ to** (ask) rivolgersi a; (be suitable for, relevant to) riguardare, riferirsi a; **to ~ (for)** (permit, grant, job) fare domanda (per); **to ~ o.s. to** dedicarsi a

appoint [ə'pɔɪnt] vt nominare; **appointment** n nomina; (arrangement to meet) appuntamento; **I have an appointment (with)** ... ho un appuntamento (con) ...; **I'd like to make an appointment (with)** vorrei prendere un appuntamento (con)

appraisal [ə'preɪzl] n valutazione f

appreciate [ə'priːʃɪeɪt] vt (like) apprezzare; (be grateful for) essere riconoscente di; (be aware of) rendersi conto di ▷ vi (Finance) aumentare; **I'd ~ your help** ti sono grato per l'aiuto; **appreciation** [əpriːʃɪ'eɪʃən] n apprezzamento; (Finance) aumento del valore

apprehension [æprɪ'hɛnʃən] n (fear) inquietudine f

apprehensive [æprɪ'hɛnsɪv] adj apprensivo(-a)

apprentice [ə'prɛntɪs] n apprendista m/f

approach [ə'prəʊtʃ] vi avvicinarsi ▷ vt

(come near) avvicinarsi a; (ask, apply to) rivolgersi a; (subject, passer-by) avvicinare ▷ n approccio; accesso; (to problem) modo di affrontare

appropriate [adj ə'prəʊprɪɪt, vb ə'prəʊprɪeɪt] adj appropriato(-a), adatto(-a) ▷ vt (take) appropriarsi

approval [ə'pruːvəl] n approvazione f; **on ~** (Comm) in prova, in esame

approve [ə'pruːv] vt, vi approvare; **approve of** vt fus approvare

approximate [ə'prɒksɪmɪt] adj approssimativo(-a); **approximately** adv circa

Apr. abbr (= April) apr.

apricot ['eɪprɪkɔt] n albicocca

April ['eɪprəl] n aprile m; **~ fool!** pesce d'aprile!; **April Fools' Day** n vedi nota nel riquadro

⬥ **APRIL FOOLS' DAY**
⬥
⬥ **April Fool's Day** è il primo aprile, il
⬥ giorno degli scherzi e delle burle. Il nome
⬥ deriva dal fatto che, se una persona
⬥ cade nella trappola che gli è stata tesa,
⬥ fa la figura del "fool", cioè dello sciocco.
⬥ Tradizionalmente, gli scherzi vengono
⬥ fatti entro mezzogiorno.

apron ['eɪprən] n grembiule m

apt [æpt] adj (suitable) adatto(-a); (able) capace; (likely): **to be ~ to do** avere tendenza a fare

aquarium [ə'kwɛərɪəm] n acquario

Aquarius [ə'kwɛərɪəs] n Acquario

Arab ['ærəb] adj, n arabo(-a)

Arabia [ə'reɪbɪə] n Arabia; **Arabian** [ə'reɪbɪən] adj arabo(-a); **Arabic** ['ærəbɪk] adj arabico(-a), arabo(-a) ▷ n arabo; **Arabic numerals** n numeri mpl arabi, numerazione f araba

arbitrary ['ɑːbɪtrərɪ] adj arbitrario(-a)

arbitration [ɑːbɪ'treɪʃən] n (Law) arbitrato; (Industry) arbitraggio

arc [ɑːk] n arco

arcade [ɑː'keɪd] n portico; (passage with shops) galleria

arch [ɑːtʃ] n arco; (of foot) arco plantare ▷ vt inarcare

archaeology [ɑːkɪ'ɒlədʒɪ] (us **archeology**) n archeologia

archbishop [ɑːtʃ'bɪʃəp] n arcivescovo

archeology etc [ɑːkɪ'ɒlədʒɪ] (us) = **archaeology** etc

architect ['ɑːkɪtɛkt] n architetto; **architectural** [ɑːkɪ'tɛktʃərəl] adj architettonico(-a); **architecture** ['ɑːkɪtɛktʃə¹] n architettura

archive ['ɑːkaɪv] n (often pl: also Comput)
archivio
Arctic ['ɑːktɪk] adj artico(-a) ▷ n **the ~**
l'Artico
are [ɑːʳ] vb see **be**
area ['ɛərɪə] n (Geom) area; (zone) zona;
(: smaller) settore m; **area code** (US) n (Tel)
prefisso
arena [əˈriːnə] n arena
aren't [ɑːnt] = **are not**
Argentina [ɑːdʒənˈtiːnə] n Argentina;
Argentinian [-ˈtɪnɪən] adj, n
argentino(-a)
arguably ['ɑːgjuəblɪ] adv **it is ~ ...** si può
sostenere che sia ...
argue ['ɑːgjuː] vi (quarrel) litigare; (reason)
ragionare; **to ~ that** sostenere che
argument ['ɑːgjumənt] n (reasons)
argomento; (quarrel) lite f
Aries ['ɛərɪz] n Ariete m
arise [əˈraɪz] (pt **arose**, pp **arisen**) vi
(opportunity, problem) presentarsi
arithmetic [əˈrɪθmətɪk] n aritmetica
arm [ɑːm] n braccio ▷ vt armare; **~s** npl
(weapons) armi fpl; **~ in ~** a braccetto;
armchair n poltrona
armed [ɑːmd] adj armato(-a); **armed
robbery** n rapina a mano armata
armour ['ɑːməʳ] (US **armor**) n armatura;
(Mil: tanks) mezzi mpl blindati
armpit ['ɑːmpɪt] n ascella
armrest ['ɑːmrɛst] n bracciolo
army ['ɑːmɪ] n esercito
A road n strada statale
aroma [əˈrəumə] n aroma; **aromatherapy**
n aromaterapia
arose [əˈrəuz] pt of **arise**
around [əˈraund] adv attorno, intorno
▷ prep intorno a; (fig: about): **~ £5/3
o'clock** circa 5 sterline/le 3; **is he ~?** è in
giro?
arouse [əˈrauz] vt (sleeper) svegliare;
(curiosity, passions) suscitare
arrange [əˈreɪndʒ] vt sistemare;
(programme) preparare; **to ~ to do
sth** mettersi d'accordo per fare qc;
arrangement n sistemazione f;
(agreement) accordo; **arrangements** npl
(plans) progetti mpl, piani mpl
array [əˈreɪ] n **~ of** fila di
arrears [əˈrɪəz] npl arretrati mpl; **to be in
~ with one's rent** essere in arretrato con
l'affitto
arrest [əˈrɛst] vt arrestare; (sb's attention)
attirare ▷ n arresto; **under ~** in arresto
arrival [əˈraɪvəl] n arrivo; (person)
arrivato(-a); **a new ~** un nuovo venuto;
(baby) un neonato
arrive [əˈraɪv] vi arrivare; **what time does**

the train from Rome ~? a che ora arriva il
treno da Roma?; **arrive at** vt fus arrivare a
arrogance ['ærəgəns] n arroganza
arrogant ['ærəgənt] adj arrogante
arrow ['ærəu] n freccia
arson ['ɑːsn] n incendio doloso
art [ɑːt] n arte f; (craft) mestiere m; **art
college** n scuola di belle arti
artery ['ɑːtərɪ] n arteria
art gallery n galleria d'arte
arthritis [ɑːˈθraɪtɪs] n artrite f
artichoke ['ɑːtɪtʃəuk] n carciofo;
Jerusalem ~ topinambur m inv
article ['ɑːtɪkl] n articolo
articulate [adj ɑːˈtɪkjulɪt, vb ɑːˈtɪkjuleɪt]
adj (person) che si esprime forbitamente;
(speech) articolato(-a) ▷ vi articolare
artificial [ɑːtɪˈfɪʃəl] adj artificiale
artist ['ɑːtɪst] n artista m/f; **artistic**
[ɑːˈtɪstɪk] adj artistico(-a)
art school n scuola d'arte

 KEYWORD

as [æz] conj **1** (referring to time) mentre;
as the years went by col passare degli
anni; **he came in as I was leaving**
arrivò mentre stavo uscendo; **as from
tomorrow** da domani
2 (in comparisons): **as big as** grande come;
twice as big as due volte più grande di;
as much/many as tanto quanto/tanti
quanti; **as soon as possible** prima
possibile
3 (since, because) dal momento che,
siccome
4 (referring to manner, way) come; **do as
you wish** fa' come vuoi; **as she said** come
ha detto lei
5 (concerning): **as for** or **to that** per quanto
riguarda or quanto a quello
6: **as if** or **as though** come se; **he looked
as if he was ill** sembrava stare male; see
also **long; such; well**
▷ prep **he works as a driver** fa l'autista; **as
chairman of the company he ...** come
presidente della compagnia lui ...; **he gave
me it as a present** me lo ha regalato

a.s.a.p. abbr = **as soon as possible**
asbestos [æzˈbɛstəs] n asbesto, amianto
ascent [əˈsɛnt] n salita
ash [æʃ] n (dust) cenere f; (wood, tree)
frassino
ashamed [əˈʃeɪmd] adj vergognoso(-a); **to
be ~ of** vergognarsi di
ashore [əˈʃɔːʳ] adv a terra
ashtray ['æʃtreɪ] n portacenere m
Ash Wednesday n mercoledì m inv delle

Ceneri

Asia ['eɪʃə] n Asia; **Asian** adj, n asiatico(-a)
aside [ə'saɪd] adv da parte ▷ n a parte m
ask [ɑ:sk] vt (question) domandare; (invite) invitare; **to ~ sb sth/sb to do sth** chiedere qc a qn/a qn di fare qc; **to ~ sb about sth** chiedere a qn di qc; **to ~ (sb) a question** fare una domanda (a qn); **to ~ sb out to dinner** invitare qn a mangiare fuori; **ask for** vt fus chiedere; (trouble etc) cercare
asleep [ə'sli:p] adj addormentato(-a); **to be ~** dormire; **to fall ~** addormentarsi
asparagus [əs'pærəgəs] n asparagi mpl
aspect ['æspekt] n aspetto
aspirations [æspə'reɪʃənz] npl aspirazioni fpl
aspire [əs'paɪər] vi **to ~ to** aspirare a
aspirin ['æsprɪn] n aspirina
ass [æs] n asino; (inf) scemo(-a); (US: inf!) culo (!)
assassin [ə'sæsɪn] n assassino; **assassinate** [ə'sæsɪneɪt] vt assassinare
assault [ə'sɔ:lt] n (Mil) assalto; (gen: attack) aggressione f ▷ vt assaltare; aggredire; (sexually) violentare
assemble [ə'sɛmbl] vt riunire; (Tech) montare ▷ vi riunirsi
assembly [ə'sɛmblɪ] n (meeting) assemblea; (construction) montaggio
assert [ə'sə:t] vt asserire; (insist on) far valere; **assertion** [ə'sə:ʃən] n asserzione f
assess [ə'sɛs] vt valutare; **assessment** n valutazione f
asset ['æsɛt] n vantaggio; **~s** npl (Finance: of individual) beni mpl; (: of company) attivo
assign [ə'saɪn] vt **to ~ (to)** (task) assegnare (a); (resources) riservare (a); (cause, meaning) attribuire (a); **to ~ a date to sth** fissare la data di qc; **assignment** n compito
assist [ə'sɪst] vt assistere, aiutare; **assistance** n assistenza, aiuto; **assistant** n assistente m/f; (BRIT: also: **shop assistant**) commesso(-a)
associate [adj, n ə'səʊʃɪɪt, vb ə'səʊʃɪeɪt] adj associato(-a); (member) aggiunto(-a) ▷ n collega m/f ▷ vt associare ▷ vi **to ~ with sb** frequentare qn
association [əsəʊsɪ'eɪʃən] n associazione f
assorted [ə'sɔ:tɪd] adj assortito(-a)
assortment [ə'sɔ:tmənt] n assortimento
assume [ə'sju:m] vt supporre; (responsibilities etc) assumere; (attitude, name) prendere
assumption [ə'sʌmpʃən] n supposizione f, ipotesi f inv; (of power) assunzione f
assurance [ə'ʃuərəns] n assicurazione f; (self-confidence) fiducia in se stesso
assure [ə'ʃuər] vt assicurare

---

219 | **atlas**

asterisk ['æstərɪsk] n asterisco
asthma ['æsmə] n asma
astonish [ə'stɔnɪʃ] vt stupire; **astonished** adj stupito(-a), sorpreso(-a); **to be astonished (at)** essere stupito(-a) (da); **astonishing** adj sorprendente, stupefacente; **I find it astonishing that ...** mi stupisce che ...; **astonishment** n stupore m
astound [ə'staund] vt sbalordire
astray [ə'streɪ] adv **to go ~** smarrirsi; **to lead ~** portare sulla cattiva strada
astrology [əs'trɔlədʒɪ] n astrologia
astronaut ['æstrənɔ:t] n astronauta m/f
astronomer [əs'trɔnəmər] n astronomo(-a)
astronomical [æstrə'nɔmɪkl] adj astronomico(-a)
astronomy [əs'trɔnəmɪ] n astronomia
astute [əs'tju:t] adj astuto(-a)
asylum [ə'saɪləm] n (politico) asilo; (per malati) manicomio

 KEYWORD

at [æt] prep **1** (referring to position, direction) a; **at the top** in cima; **at the desk** al banco, alla scrivania; **at home/school** a casa/scuola; **at the baker's** dal panettiere; **to look at sth** guardare qc; **to throw sth at sb** lanciare qc a qn
2 (referring to time) a; **at 4 o'clock** alle 4; **at night** di notte; **at Christmas** a Natale; **at times** a volte
3 (referring to rates, speed etc) a; **at £1 a kilo** a 1 sterlina al chilo; **two at a time** due alla volta, due per volta; **at 50 km/h** a 50 km/h
4 (referring to manner): **at a stroke** d'un solo colpo; **at peace** in pace
5 (referring to activity): **to be at work** essere al lavoro; **to play at cowboys** giocare ai cowboy; **to be good at sth/doing sth** essere bravo in qc/fare qc
6 (referring to cause): **shocked/surprised/ annoyed at sth** colpito da/sorpreso da/arrabbiato per qc; **I went at his suggestion** ci sono andato dietro suo consiglio

ate [eɪt] pt of **eat**
atheist ['eɪθɪɪst] n ateo(-a)
Athens ['æθɪnz] n Atene f
athlete ['æθli:t] n atleta m/f
athletic [æθ'lɛtɪk] adj atletico(-a); **athletics** n atletica
Atlantic [ət'læntɪk] adj atlantico(-a) ▷ n **the ~ (Ocean)** l'Atlantico, l'Oceano Atlantico
atlas ['ætləs] n atlante m

A.T.M. n abbr (= automated telling machine) cassa automatica prelievi, sportello automatico

atmosphere ['ætməsfɪə'] n atmosfera

atom ['ætəm] n atomo; **atomic** [ə'tɔmɪk] adj atomico(-a); **atom(ic) bomb** n bomba atomica

A to Z® n (map) stradario

atrocity [ə'trɔsɪtɪ] n atrocità f inv

attach [ə'tætʃ] vt attaccare; (document, letter) allegare; (importance etc) attribuire; **to be ~ed to sb/sth** (to like) essere affezionato(-a) a qn/qc; **attachment** [ə'tætʃmənt] n (tool) accessorio; (love): **attachment (to)** affetto (per)

attack [ə'tæk] vt attaccare; (person) aggredire; (task etc) iniziare; (problem) affrontare ▷ n attacco; **heart ~** infarto; **attacker** n aggressore m

attain [ə'teɪn] vt (also: **to ~ to**) arrivare a, raggiungere

attempt [ə'tempt] n tentativo ▷ vt tentare; **to make an ~ on sb's life** attentare alla vita di qn

attend [ə'tend] vt frequentare; (meeting, talk) andare a; (patient) assistere; **attend to** vt fus (needs, affairs etc) prendersi cura di; (customer) occuparsi di; **attendance** n (being present) presenza; (people present) gente f presente; **attendant** n custode m/f, persona di servizio ▷ adj concomitante

▮ Be careful not to translate attend by the Italian word attendere.

attention [ə'tenʃən] n attenzione f ▷ excl (Mil) attenti!; **for the ~ of** (Admin) per l'attenzione di

attic ['ætɪk] n soffitta

attitude ['ætɪtjuːd] n atteggiamento; posa

attorney [ə'təːnɪ] n (lawyer) avvocato; (having proxy) mandatario; **Attorney General** n (BRIT) Procuratore m Generale; (US) Ministro della Giustizia

attract [ə'trækt] vt attirare; **attraction** [ə'trækʃən] n (gen pl: pleasant things) attrattiva; (Physics, fig: towards sth) attrazione f; **attractive** adj attraente

attribute [n 'ætrɪbjuːt, vb ə'trɪbjuːt] n attributo ▷ vt **to ~ sth to** attribuire qc a

aubergine ['əubəʒiːn] n melanzana

auburn ['ɔːbən] adj tizianesco(-a)

auction ['ɔːkʃən] n (also: **sale by ~**) asta ▷ vt (also: **to sell by ~**) vendere all'asta; (also: **to put up for ~**) mettere all'asta

audible ['ɔːdɪbl] adj udibile

audience ['ɔːdɪəns] n (people) pubblico; spettatori mpl; ascoltatori mpl; (interview) udienza

audit ['ɔːdɪt] vt rivedere, verificare

audition [ɔː'dɪʃən] n audizione f

auditor ['ɔːdɪtə'] n revisore m

auditorium [ɔːdɪ'tɔːrɪəm] n sala, auditorio

Aug. abbr (= August) ago., ag.

August ['ɔːgəst] n agosto

aunt [ɑːnt] n zia; **auntie** n zietta; **aunty** n zietta

au pair ['əu'pɛə'] n (also: **~ girl**) (ragazza f) alla pari inv

aura ['ɔːrə] n aura

austerity [ɔs'terɪtɪ] n austerità f inv

Australia [ɔs'treɪlɪə] n Australia; **Australian** adj, n australiano(-a)

Austria ['ɔstrɪə] n Austria; **Austrian** adj, n austriaco(-a)

authentic [ɔː'θentɪk] adj autentico(-a)

author ['ɔːθə'] n autore(-trice)

authority [ɔː'θɔrɪtɪ] n autorità f inv; (permission) autorizzazione f; **the authorities** npl (government etc) le autorità

authorize ['ɔːθəraɪz] vt autorizzare

auto ['ɔːtəu] (US) n auto f inv; **autobiography** [ɔːtəbaɪ'ɔgrəfɪ] n autobiografia; **autograph** ['ɔːtəgrɑːf] n autografo ▷ vt firmare; **automatic** [ɔːtə'mætɪk] adj automatico(-a) ▷ n (gun) arma automatica; (washing machine) lavatrice f automatica; (car) automobile f con cambio automatico; **automatically** adv automaticamente; **automobile** ['ɔːtəməbiːl] (US) n automobile f; **autonomous** [ɔː'tɔnəməs] adj autonomo(-a); **autonomy** [ɔː'tɔnəmɪ] n autonomia

autumn ['ɔːtəm] n autunno

auxiliary [ɔːg'zɪlɪərɪ] adj ausiliario(-a) ▷ n ausiliare m/f

avail [ə'veɪl] vt **to ~ o.s. of** servirsi di; approfittarsi di ▷ n **to no ~** inutilmente

availability [əveɪlə'bɪlɪtɪ] n disponibilità

available [ə'veɪləbl] adj disponibile

avalanche ['ævəlɑːnʃ] n valanga

Ave. abbr = **avenue**

avenue ['ævənjuː] n viale m; (fig) strada, via

average ['ævərɪdʒ] n media ▷ adj medio(-a) ▷ vt (a certain figure) fare di or in media; **on ~** in media

avert [ə'vəːt] vt evitare, prevenire; (one's eyes) distogliere

avid ['ævɪd] adj (supporter etc) accanito(-a)

avocado [ævə'kɑːdəu] n (BRIT: also: **~ pear**) avocado m inv

avoid [ə'vɔɪd] vt evitare

await [ə'weɪt] vt aspettare

awake [ə'weɪk] (pt **awoke**, pp **awoken**, **awaked**) adj sveglio(-a) ▷ vt svegliare ▷ vi

svegliarsi

award [əˈwɔːd] *n* premio; (*Law*)
risarcimento ▷ *vt* assegnare; (*Law:*
damages) accordare

aware [əˈwɛəʳ] *adj* **~ of** (*conscious*)
conscio(-a) di; (*informed*) informato(-a) di;
to become ~ of accorgersi di; **awareness**
n consapevolezza

away [əˈweɪ] *adj, adv* via; lontano(-a); **two
kilometres ~** a due chilometri di distanza;
two hours ~ by car a due ore di distanza
in macchina; **the holiday was two weeks
~** mancavano due settimane alle vacanze;
he's ~ for a week è andato via per una
settimana; **to take ~** togliere; **he was
working/pedalling** *etc* **~** (*la particella
indica la continuità e l'energia dell'azione*)
lavorava/pedalava *etc* più che poteva; **to
fade/wither** *etc* **~** (*la particella rinforza
l'idea della diminuzione*)

awe [ɔː] *n* timore *m*; **awesome** *adj*
imponente

awful [ˈɔːfəl] *adj* terribile; **an ~ lot of**
un mucchio di; **awfully** *adv* (*very*)
terribilmente

awkward [ˈɔːkwəd] *adj* (*clumsy*) goffo(-a);
(*inconvenient*) scomodo(-a); (*embarrassing*)
imbarazzante

awoke [əˈwəuk] *pt of* **awake**

awoken [əˈwəukn] *pp of* **awake**

axe [æks] (*us* **ax**) *n* scure *f* ▷ *vt* (*project etc*)
abolire; (*jobs*) sopprimere

axle [ˈæksl] *n* (*also:* **~-tree**) asse *m*

ay(e) [aɪ] *excl* (*yes*) sì

azalea [əˈzeɪlɪə] *n* azalea

B [biː] *n* (*Mus*) si *m*

B.A. *n abbr* = **Bachelor of Arts**

baby [ˈbeɪbɪ] *n* bambino(-a); **baby
carriage** (*us*) *n* carrozzina; **baby-sit** *vi*
fare il (*or* la) baby-sitter; **baby-sitter** *n*
baby-sitter *m/f inv*; **baby wipe** *n* salvietta
umidificata

bachelor [ˈbætʃələʳ] *n* scapolo; **B~ of Arts/
Science** = laureato(-a) in lettere/scienze

back [bæk] *n* (*of person, horse*) dorso,
schiena; (*as opposed to front*) dietro; (*of
hand*) dorso; (*of train*) coda; (*of chair*)
schienale *m*; (*of page*) rovescio; (*of book*)
retro; (*Football*) difensore *m* ▷ *vt* (*candidate*)
appoggiare; (*horse: at races*) puntare
su; (*car*) guidare a marcia indietro ▷ *vi*
indietreggiare; (*car etc*) fare marcia
indietro ▷ *cpd* posteriore, di dietro; (*Aut:
seat, wheels*) posteriore ▷ *adv* (*not forward*)
indietro; (*returned*): **he's ~** è tornato; **he
ran ~** tornò indietro di corsa; (*restitution*):
throw the ball ~ ritira la palla; **can I have
it ~?** posso riaverlo?; (*again*): **he called
~** ha richiamato; **back down** *vi* fare
marcia indietro; **back out** *vi* (*of promise*)
tirarsi indietro; **back up** *vt* (*support*)
appoggiare, sostenere; (*Comput*) fare una
copia di riserva di; **backache** *n* mal *m* di
schiena; **backbencher** (*BRIT*) *n* membro
del Parlamento senza potere amministrativo;

backbone n spina dorsale; **back door** n porta sul retro; **backfire** vi (Aut) dar ritorni di fiamma; (plans) fallire; **backgammon** n tavola reale; **background** n sfondo; (of events) background m inv; (basic knowledge) base f; (experience) esperienza; **family background** ambiente m familiare; **backing** n (fig) appoggio; **backlog** n **backlog of work** lavoro arretrato; **backpack** n zaino; **backpacker** n chi viaggia con zaino e sacco a pelo; **backslash** n backslash m inv, barra obliqua inversa; **backstage** adv nel retroscena; **backstroke** n nuoto sul dorso; **backup** adj (train, plane) supplementare; (Comput) di riserva ▷ n (support) appoggio, sostegno; (also: **backup file**) file m inv di riserva; **backward** adj (movement) indietro inv; (person) tardivo(-a); (country) arretrato(-a); **backwards** adv indietro; (fall, walk) all'indietro; **backyard** n cortile m dietro la casa

bacon ['beɪkən] n pancetta

bacteria [bæk'tɪərɪə] npl batteri mpl

bad [bæd] adj cattivo(-a); (accident, injury) brutto(-a); (meat, food) andato(-a) a male; **his ~ leg** la sua gamba malata; **to go ~** andare a male

badge [bædʒ] n insegna; (of policeman) stemma m

badger ['bædʒəʳ] n tasso

badly ['bædlɪ] adv (work, dress etc) male; **~ wounded** gravemente ferito; **he needs it ~** ne ha un gran bisogno

badminton ['bædmɪntən] n badminton m

bad-tempered ['bæd'tɛmpəd] adj irritabile; di malumore

bag [bæg] n sacco; (handbag etc) borsa; **~s of** (inf: lots of) un sacco di; **baggage** n bagagli mpl; **baggage allowance** n franchigia f bagaglio inv; **baggage reclaim** n ritiro m bagaglio inv; **baggy** adj largo(-a), sformato(-a); **bagpipes** npl cornamusa

bail [beɪl] n cauzione f ▷ vt (prisoner: also: **grant ~ to**) concedere la libertà provvisoria su cauzione a; (boat: also: **~ out**) aggottare; **on ~** in libertà provvisoria su cauzione

bait [beɪt] n esca ▷ vt (hook) innescare; (trap) munire di esca; (fig) tormentare

bake [beɪk] vt cuocere al forno ▷ vi cuocersi al forno; **baked beans** [-bi:nz] npl fagioli mpl in salsa di pomodoro; **baked potato** n patata cotta al forno con la buccia; **baker** n fornaio(-a), panettiere(-a); **bakery** n panetteria;

baking n cottura (al forno); **baking powder** n lievito in polvere

balance ['bæləns] n equilibrio; (Comm: sum) bilancio; (remainder) resto; (scales) bilancia ▷ vt tenere in equilibrio; (budget) far quadrare; (account) pareggiare; (compensate) contrappesare; **~ of trade/payments** bilancia commerciale/dei pagamenti; **balanced** adj (personality, diet) equilibrato(-a); **balance sheet** n bilancio

balcony ['bælkənɪ] n balcone m; (in theatre) balconata; **do you have a room with a ~?** avete una camera con balcone?

bald [bɔːld] adj calvo(-a); (tyre) liscio(-a)

Balearics [bælɪ'ærɪks] npl **the ~** le Baleari fpl

ball [bɔːl] n palla; (football) pallone m; (for golf) pallina; (of wool, string) gomitolo; (dance) ballo; **to play ~** (fig) stare al gioco

ballerina [bælə'riːnə] n ballerina

ballet ['bæleɪ] n balletto; **ballet dancer** n ballerino(-a) classico(-a)

balloon [bə'luːn] n pallone m

ballot ['bælət] n scrutinio

ballpoint (pen) ['bɔːlpɔɪnt(-)] n penna a sfera

ballroom ['bɔːlrum] n sala da ballo

Baltic ['bɔːltɪk] adj, n **the ~ Sea** il (mar) Baltico

bamboo [bæm'buː] n bambù m

ban [bæn] n interdizione f ▷ vt interdire

banana [bə'nɑːnə] n banana

band [bænd] n banda; (at a dance) orchestra; (Mil) fanfara

bandage ['bændɪdʒ] n benda, fascia

Band-Aid® ['bændeɪd] (US) n cerotto

B. & B. n abbr = **bed and breakfast**

bandit ['bændɪt] n bandito

bang [bæŋ] n (of door) lo sbattere; (of gun, blow) colpo ▷ vt battere (violentemente); (door) sbattere ▷ vi scoppiare; sbattere

Bangladesh [bɑːŋglə'dɛʃ] n Bangladesh m

bangle ['bæŋgl] n braccialetto

bangs [bæŋz] (US) npl (fringe) frangia, frangetta

banish ['bænɪʃ] vt bandire

banister(s) ['bænɪstə(z)] n(pl) ringhiera

banjo ['bændʒəu] (pl **banjoes** or **banjos**) n banjo m inv

bank [bæŋk] n banca, banco; (of river, lake) riva, sponda; (of earth) banco ▷ vi (Aviat) inclinarsi in virata; **bank on** vt fus contare su; **bank account** n conto in banca; **bank balance** n saldo; **a healthy bank balance** un solido conto in banca; **bank card** n carta f assegni inv; **bank charges** npl (BRIT) spese fpl bancarie; **banker** n banchiere m; **bank holiday** (BRIT) n giorno di festa; vedi nota nel riquadro; **banking**

n attività bancaria; professione *f* di banchiere; **bank manager** *n* direttore *m* di banca; **banknote** *n* banconota

⬦ **BANK HOLIDAY**
⬦
⬦ Una **bank holiday**, in Gran Bretagna,
⬦ è una giornata in cui banche e molti
⬦ negozi sono chiusi. Generalmente le
⬦ **bank holidays** cadono di lunedì e molti
⬦ ne approfittano per fare una breve
⬦ vacanza fuori città.

bankrupt ['bæŋkrʌpt] *adj* fallito(-a); **to go ~** fallire; **bankruptcy** *n* fallimento
bank statement *n* estratto conto
banner ['bænə^r] *n* striscione *m*
bannister(s) ['bænɪstə(z)] *n(pl)* see **banister(s)**
banquet ['bæŋkwɪt] *n* banchetto
baptism ['bæptɪzəm] *n* battesimo
baptize [bæp'taɪz] *vt* battezzare
bar [bɑ:^r] *n (place)* bar *m inv; (counter)* banco; *(rod)* barra; *(of window etc)* sbarra; *(of chocolate)* tavoletta; *(fig)* ostacolo; restrizione *f; (Mus)* battuta ▷ *vt (road, window)* sbarrare; *(person)* escludere; *(activity)* interdire; **~ of soap** saponetta; **the B~** *(Law)* l'Ordine *m* degli avvocati; **behind ~s** *(prisoner)* dietro le sbarre; **~ none** senza eccezione
barbaric [bɑ:'bærɪk] *adj* barbarico(-a)
barbecue ['bɑ:bɪkju:] *n* barbecue *m inv*
barbed wire ['bɑ:bd-] *n* filo spinato
barber ['bɑ:bə^r] *n* barbiere *m*; **barber's (shop)** *(US* **barber (shop))** *n* barbiere *m*
bar code *n (on goods)* codice *m* a barre
bare [bɛə^r] *adj* nudo(-a) ▷ *vt* scoprire, denudare; *(teeth)* mostrare; **the ~ necessities** lo stretto necessario; **barefoot** *adj, adv* scalzo(-a); **barely** *adv* appena
bargain ['bɑ:gɪn] *n (transaction)* contratto; *(good buy)* affare *m* ▷ *vi* trattare; **into the ~** per giunta; **bargain for** *vt fus* **he got more than he ~ed for** gli è andata peggio di quel che si aspettasse
barge [bɑ:dʒ] *n* chiatta; **barge in** *vi (walk in)* piombare dentro; *(interrupt talk)* intromettersi a sproposito
bark [bɑ:k] *n (of tree)* corteccia; *(of dog)* abbaio ▷ *vi* abbaiare
barley ['bɑ:lɪ] *n* orzo
barmaid ['bɑ:meɪd] *n* cameriera al banco
barman ['bɑ:mən] *(irreg) n* barista *m*
barn [bɑ:n] *n* granaio
barometer [bə'rɔmɪtə^r] *n* barometro
baron ['bærən] *n* barone *m*; **baroness** *n* baronessa

barracks ['bærəks] *npl* caserma
barrage ['bærɑ:ʒ] *n (Mil, dam)* sbarramento; *(fig)* fiume *m*
barrel ['bærəl] *n* barile *m*; *(of gun)* canna
barren ['bærən] *adj* sterile; *(soil)* arido(-a)
barrette [bə'rɛt] *(US)* *n* fermaglio per capelli
barricade [bærɪ'keɪd] *n* barricata
barrier ['bærɪə^r] *n* barriera
barring ['bɑ:rɪŋ] *prep* salvo
barrister ['bærɪstə^r] *(BRIT) n* avvocato(-essa) *(con diritto di parlare davanti a tutte le corti)*
barrow ['bærəu] *n (cart)* carriola
bartender ['bɑ:tɛndə^r] *(US)* *n* barista *m*
base [beɪs] *n* base *f* ▷ *vt* **to ~ sth on** basare qc su ▷ *adj* vile
baseball ['beɪsbɔ:l] *n* baseball *m*; **baseball cap** *n* berretto da baseball
basement ['beɪsmənt] *n* seminterrato; *(of shop)* interrato
bases¹ ['beɪsi:z] *npl of* **basis**
bases² ['beɪsɪz] *npl of* **base**
bash [bæʃ] *(inf) vt* picchiare
basic ['beɪsɪk] *adj* rudimentale; essenziale; **basically** [-lɪ] *adv* fondamentalmente; sostanzialmente; **basics** *npl* **the basics** l'essenziale *m*
basil ['bæzl] *n* basilico
basin ['beɪsn] *n (vessel: also Geo)* bacino; *(also:* **wash~)** lavabo
basis ['beɪsɪs] *(pl* **bases**) *n* base *f*; **on a part-time ~** part-time; **on a trial ~** in prova
basket ['bɑ:skɪt] *n* cesta; *(smaller)* cestino; *(with handle)* paniere *m*; **basketball** *n* pallacanestro *f*
bass [beɪs] *n (Mus)* basso
bastard ['bɑ:stəd] *n* bastardo(-a); *(inf!)* stronzo *(!)*
bat [bæt] *n* pipistrello; *(for baseball etc)* mazza; *(BRIT: for table tennis)* racchetta ▷ *vt* **he didn't ~ an eyelid** non battè ciglio
batch [bætʃ] *n (of bread)* infornata; *(of papers)* cumulo
bath [bɑ:θ] *n* bagno; *(bathtub)* vasca da bagno ▷ *vt* far fare il bagno a; **to have a ~** fare un bagno; *see also* **baths**
bathe [beɪð] *vi* fare il bagno ▷ *vt (wound)* lavare
bathing ['beɪðɪŋ] *n* bagni *mpl*; **bathing costume** *(US* **bathing suit)** *n* costume *m* da bagno
bath: **bathrobe** ['bɑ:θrəub] *n* accappatoio; **bathroom** ['bɑ:θrum] *n* stanza da bagno; **baths** [bɑ:ðz] *npl* bagni *mpl* pubblici; **bath towel** *n* asciugamano da bagno; **bathtub** *n (vasca da)* bagno
baton ['bætən] *n (Mus)* bacchetta;

(*Athletics*) testimone *m*; (*club*) manganello

batter ['bætə^r] *vt* battere ▷ *n* pastetta;
battered *adj* (*hat*) sformato(-a); (*pan*)
ammaccato(-a)

battery ['bætərɪ] *n* batteria; (*of torch*) pila;
battery farming *n* allevamento in batteria

battle ['bætl] *n* battaglia ▷ *vi* battagliare,
lottare; **battlefield** *n* campo di battaglia

bay [beɪ] *n* (*of sea*) baia; **to hold sb at ~**
tenere qn a bada

bazaar [bə'zɑ:^r] *n* bazar *m inv*; vendita di
beneficenza

BBC *n abbr* (= *British Broadcasting
Corporation*) rete nazionale di radiotelevisione
in Gran Bretagna

- **BBC**
- La **BBC** è l'azienda statale che fornisce
- il servizio radiofonico e televisivo in
- Gran Bretagna. Ha due reti televisive
- terrestri (BBC1 e BBC2), e cinque
- stazioni radiofoniche nazionali. Oggi
- la BBC ha anche diverse stazioni
- digitali radiofoniche e televisive. Da
- molti anni fornisce inoltre un servizio
- di intrattenimento e informazione
- internazionale, il "BBC World Service",
- trasmesso in tutto il mondo.

B.C. *adv abbr* (= *before Christ*) a.C.

 KEYWORD

be [bi:] (*pt* **was, were**, *pp* **been**) *aux vb* **1**
(*with present participle: forming continuous
tenses*): **what are you doing?** che fa?, che
sta facendo?; **they're coming tomorrow**
vengono domani; **I've been waiting for
her for hours** sono ore che l'aspetto
2 (*with pp: forming passives*) essere; **to be
killed** essere *or* venire ucciso(-a); **the box
had been opened** la scatola era stata
aperta; **the thief was nowhere to be
seen** il ladro non si trovava da nessuna
parte
3 (*in tag questions*): **it was fun, wasn't it?** è
stato divertente, no?; **he's good-looking,
isn't he?** è un bell'uomo, vero?; **she's
back, is she?** così è tornata, eh?
4 (+ *to + infinitive*): **the house is
to be sold** abbiamo *or* hanno *etc*
intenzione di vendere casa; **you're to
be congratulated for all your work**
dovremo farvi i complimenti per tutto il
vostro lavoro; **he's not to open it** non
deve aprirlo
▷ *vb + complement* **1** (*gen*) essere; **I'm
English** sono inglese; **I'm tired** sono

stanco(-a); **I'm hot/cold** ho caldo/freddo;
he's a doctor è medico; **2 and 2 are 4** 2
più 2 fa 4; **be careful!** sta attento(-a)!; **be
good** sii buono(-a)
2 (*of health*) stare; **how are you?** come
sta?; **he's very ill** sta molto male
3 (*of age*): **how old are you?** quanti anni
hai?; **I'm sixteen (years old)** ho sedici
anni
4 (*cost*) costare; **how much was the
meal?** quant'era *or* quanto costava il
pranzo?; **that'll be £5, please** (fa) 5
sterline, per favore
▷ *vi* **1** (*exist, occur etc*) essere, esistere; **the
best singer that ever was** il migliore
cantante mai esistito *or* di tutti i tempi; **be
that as it may** comunque sia, sia come
sia; **so be it** sia pure, e sia
2 (*referring to place*) essere, trovarsi; **I won't
be here tomorrow** non ci sarò domani;
Edinburgh is in Scotland Edimburgo si
trova in Scozia
3 (*referring to movement*): **where have you
been?** dov'è stato?; **I've been to China**
sono stato in Cina
▷ *impers vb* **1** (*referring to time, distance*)
essere; **it's 5 o'clock** sono le 5; **it's the
28th of April** è il 28 aprile; **it's 10 km to
the village** di qui al paese sono 10 km
2 (*referring to the weather*) fare; **it's too
hot/cold** fa troppo caldo/freddo; **it's
windy** c'è vento
3 (*emphatic*): **it's me** sono io; **it was Maria
who paid the bill** è stata Maria che ha
pagato il conto

beach [bi:tʃ] *n* spiaggia ▷ *vt* tirare in secco

beacon ['bi:kən] *n* (*lighthouse*) faro;
(*marker*) segnale *m*

bead [bi:d] *n* perlina; **~s** *npl* (*necklace*)
collana

beak [bi:k] *n* becco

beam [bi:m] *n* trave *f*; (*of light*) raggio ▷ *vi*
brillare

bean [bi:n] *n* fagiolo; (*of coffee*) chicco;
runner ~ fagiolino; **beansprouts** *npl*
germogli *mpl* di soia

bear [bɛə^r] (*pt* **bore**, *pp* **borne**) *n* orso ▷ *vt*
portare; (*endure*) sopportare; (*produce*)
generare ▷ *vi* **to ~ right/left** piegare a
destra/sinistra

beard [bɪəd] *n* barba

bearer ['bɛərə^r] *n* portatore *m*

bearing ['bɛərɪŋ] *n* portamento;
(*connection*) rapporto

beast [bi:st] *n* bestia

beat [bi:t] (*pt* **beat**, *pp* **beaten**) *n* colpo;
(*of heart*) battito; (*Mus*) tempo; battuta;
(*of policeman*) giro ▷ *vt* battere; (*eggs,*

cream) sbattere ▷ *vi* battere; **off the ~en track** fuori mano; **~ it!** (*inf*) fila!, fuori dai piedi!; **beat up** *vt* (*person*) picchiare; (*eggs*) sbattere; **beating** *n* bastonata

beautiful ['bju:tɪful] *adj* bello(-a); **beautifully** *adv* splendidamente

beauty ['bju:tɪ] *n* bellezza; **beauty parlour** [-'pɑːlə^r] (*us* **beauty parlor**) *n* salone *m* di bellezza; **beauty salon** *n* istituto di bellezza; **beauty spot** (*BRIT*) *n* (*Tourism*) luogo pittoresco

beaver ['biːvə^r] *n* castoro

became [bɪ'keɪm] *pt of* **become**

because [bɪ'kɔz] *conj* perché; **~ of** a causa di

beckon ['bɛkən] *vt* (*also:* **~ to**) chiamare con un cenno

become [bɪ'kʌm] (*irreg: like* **come**) *vt* diventare; **to ~ fat/thin** ingrassarsi/ dimagrire

bed [bɛd] *n* letto; (*of flowers*) aiuola; (*of coal, clay*) strato; **single/double ~** letto a una piazza/a due piazze *or* matrimoniale; **bed and breakfast** *n* (*place*) ≈ pensione *f* familiare; (*terms*) camera con colazione; *vedi nota nel riquadro;* **bedclothes** ['bɛdkləʊðz] *npl* biancheria e coperte *fpl* da letto; **bedding** *n* coperte e lenzuola *fpl*; **bed linen** *n* biancheria da letto; **bedroom** *n* camera da letto; **bedside** *n* **at sb's bedside** al capezzale di qn; **bedside lamp** *n* lampada da comodino; **bedside table** *n* comodino; **bedsit(ter)** (*BRIT*) *n* monolocale *m*; **bedspread** *n* copriletto; **bedtime** *n* **it's bedtime** è ora di andare a letto

BED AND BREAKFAST

I **bed and breakfasts**, anche **B & Bs**, sono piccole pensioni a conduzione familiare, più economiche rispetto agli alberghi, dove al mattino viene servita la tradizionale colazione all'inglese.

bee [biː] *n* ape *f*

beech [biːtʃ] *n* faggio

beef [biːf] *n* manzo; **roast ~** arrosto di manzo; **beefburger** *n* hamburger *m inv*; **Beefeater** *n* guardia della Torre di Londra

been [biːn] *pp of* **be**

beer [bɪə^r] *n* birra; **beer garden** *n* (*BRIT*) giardino (*di pub*)

beet [biːt] (*us*) *n* (*also:* **red ~**) barbabietola rossa

beetle ['biːtl] *n* scarafaggio; coleottero

beetroot ['biːtruːt] (*BRIT*) *n* barbabietola

before [bɪ'fɔː^r] *prep* (*in time*) prima di; (*in space*) davanti a ▷ *conj* prima che + *sub*;

prima di ▷ *adv* prima; **~ going** prima di andare; **~ she goes** prima che vada; **the week ~** la settimana prima; **I've seen it ~** l'ho già visto; **I've never seen it ~** è la prima volta che lo vedo; **beforehand** *adv* in anticipo

beg [bɛg] *vi* chiedere l'elemosina ▷ *vt* (*also:* **~ for**) chiedere in elemosina; (*favour*) chiedere; **to ~ sb to do sth** pregare qn di fare

began [bɪ'gæn] *pt of* **begin**

beggar ['bɛgə^r] *n* mendicante *m/f*

begin [bɪ'gɪn] (*pt* **began**, *pp* **begun**) *vt*, *vi* cominciare; **to ~ doing** *or* **to do sth** incominciare *or* iniziare a fare qc; **beginner** *n* principiante *m/f*; **beginning** *n* inizio, principio

begun [bɪ'gʌn] *pp of* **begin**

behalf [bɪ'hɑːf] *n* **on ~ of** per conto di; a nome di

behave [bɪ'heɪv] *vi* comportarsi; (*well: also:* **~ o.s.**) comportarsi bene; **behaviour** [bɪ'heɪvjə^r] (*us* **behavior**) *n* comportamento, condotta

behind [bɪ'haɪnd] *prep* dietro; (*followed by pronoun*) dietro di; (*time*) in ritardo con ▷ *adv* dietro; (*leave, stay*) indietro ▷ *n* didietro; **to be ~ (schedule)** essere in ritardo rispetto al programma; **~ the scenes** (*fig*) dietro le quinte

beige [beɪʒ] *adj* beige *inv*

Beijing ['beɪ'dʒɪŋ] *n* Pechino *f*

being ['biːɪŋ] *n* essere *m*

belated [bɪ'leɪtɪd] *adj* tardo(-a)

belch [bɛltʃ] *vi* ruttare ▷ *vt* (*gen: belch out: smoke/etc*) eruttare

Belgian ['bɛldʒən] *adj*, *n* belga *m/f*

Belgium ['bɛldʒəm] *n* Belgio

belief [bɪ'liːf] *n* (*opinion*) opinione *f*, convinzione *f*; (*trust, faith*) fede *f*

believe [bɪ'liːv] *vt*, *vi* credere; **to ~ in** (*God*) credere in; (*ghosts*) credere a; (*method*) avere fiducia in; **believer** *n* (*Rel*) credente *m/f*; (*in idea, activity*): **to be a believer in** credere in

bell [bɛl] *n* campana; (*small, on door, electric*) campanello

bellboy ['bɛlbɔɪ, (*us* **bellhop**) 'bɛlhɔp] *n* ragazzo d'albergo, fattorino d'albergo

bellow ['bɛləʊ] *vi* muggire

bell pepper (*esp us*) *n* peperone *m*

belly ['bɛlɪ] *n* pancia; **belly button** *n* ombelico

belong [bɪ'lɔŋ] *vi* **to ~ to** appartenere a; (*club etc*) essere socio di; **this book ~s here** questo libro va qui; **belongings** *npl* cose *fpl*, roba

beloved [bɪ'lʌvɪd] *adj* adorato(-a)

below [bɪ'ləʊ] *prep* sotto, al di sotto di ▷ *adv* sotto, di sotto; giù; **see ~** vedi sotto *or* oltre

belt [bɛlt] *n* cintura; (*Tech*) cinghia ▷ *vt* (*thrash*) picchiare ▷ *vi* (*inf*) filarsela; **beltway** (*US*) *n* (*Aut: ring road*) circonvallazione *f*; (: *motorway*) autostrada

bemused [bɪˈmjuːzd] *adj* perplesso(-a), stupito(-a)

bench [bɛntʃ] *n* panca; (*in workshop, Pol*) banco; **the B~** (*Law*) la Corte

bend [bɛnd] (*pt, pp* **bent**) *vt* curvare; (*leg, arm*) piegare ▷ *vi* curvarsi; piegarsi ▷ *n* (*BRIT: in road*) curva; (*in pipe, river*) gomito; **bend down** *vi* chinarsi; **bend over** *vi* piegarsi

beneath [bɪˈniːθ] *prep* sotto, al di sotto di; (*unworthy of*) indegno(-a) di ▷ *adv* sotto, di sotto

beneficial [bɛnɪˈfɪʃəl] *adj* che fa bene; vantaggioso(-a)

benefit [ˈbɛnɪfɪt] *n* beneficio, vantaggio; (*allowance of money*) indennità *f inv* ▷ *vt* far bene a ▷ *vi* **he'll ~ from it** ne trarrà beneficio *or* profitto

benign [bɪˈnaɪn] *adj* (*person, smile*) benevolo(-a); (*Med*) benigno(-a)

bent [bɛnt] *pt, pp of* **bend** ▷ *n* inclinazione *f* ▷ *adj* (*inf: dishonest*) losco(-a); **to be ~ on** essere deciso(-a) a

bereaved [bɪˈriːvd] *n* **the ~** i familiari in lutto

beret [ˈbɛreɪ] *n* berretto

Berlin [bəːˈlɪn] *n* Berlino *f*

Bermuda [bəːˈmjuːdə] *n* le Bermude

berry [ˈbɛrɪ] *n* bacca

berth [bəːθ] *n* (*bed*) cuccetta; (*for ship*) ormeggio ▷ *vi* (*in harbour*) entrare in porto; (*at anchor*) gettare l'ancora

beside [bɪˈsaɪd] *prep* accanto a; **to be ~ o.s. (with anger)** essere fuori di sé (dalla rabbia); **that's ~ the point** non c'entra; **besides** [bɪˈsaɪdz] *adv* inoltre, per di più ▷ *prep* oltre a; a parte

best [bɛst] *adj* migliore ▷ *adv* meglio; **the ~ part of** (*quantity*) la maggior parte di; **at ~** tutt'al più; **to make the ~ of sth** cavare il meglio possibile da qc; **to do one's ~** fare del proprio meglio; **to the ~ of my knowledge** per quel che ne so; **to the ~ of my ability** al massimo delle mie capacità; **best-before date** *n* scadenza; **best man** (*irreg*) *n* testimone *m* dello sposo; **bestseller** *n* bestseller *m inv*

bet [bɛt] (*pt, pp* **bet** *or* **betted**) *n* scommessa ▷ *vt, vi* scommettere; **to ~ sb sth** scommettere qc con qn

betray [bɪˈtreɪ] *vt* tradire

better [ˈbɛtəʳ] *adj* migliore ▷ *adv* meglio ▷ *vt* migliorare ▷ *n* **to get the ~ of** avere la meglio su; **you had ~ do it** è meglio che lo meglio su; **you had ~ do it** è meglio che lo

faccia; **he thought ~ of it** cambiò idea; **to get ~** migliorare

betting [ˈbɛtɪŋ] *n* scommesse *fpl*; **betting shop** (*BRIT*) *n* ufficio dell'allibratore

between [bɪˈtwiːn] *prep* tra ▷ *adv* in mezzo, nel mezzo

beverage [ˈbɛvərɪdʒ] *n* bevanda

beware [bɪˈwɛəʳ] *vt, vi* **to ~ (of)** stare attento(-a) (a); **"~ of the dog"** "attenti al cane"

bewildered [bɪˈwɪldəd] *adj* sconcertato(-a), confuso(-a)

beyond [bɪˈjɔnd] *prep* (*in space*) oltre; (*exceeding*) al di sopra di ▷ *adv* di là; **~ doubt** senza dubbio; **~ repair** irreparabile

bias [ˈbaɪəs] *n* (*prejudice*) pregiudizio; (*preference*) preferenza; **bias(s)ed** *adj* parziale

bib [bɪb] *n* bavaglino

Bible [ˈbaɪbl] *n* Bibbia

bicarbonate of soda [baɪˈkɑːbənɪt-] *n* bicarbonato (di sodio)

biceps [ˈbaɪsɛps] *n* bicipite *m*

bicycle [ˈbaɪsɪkl] *n* bicicletta; **bicycle pump** *n* pompa della bicicletta

bid [bɪd] (*pt* **bade** *or* **bid**, *pp* **bidden** *or* **bid**) *n* offerta; (*attempt*) tentativo ▷ *vi* fare un'offerta ▷ *vt* fare un'offerta di; **to ~ sb good day** dire buon giorno a qn; **bidder** *n* **the highest bidder** il maggior offerente

bidet [ˈbiːdeɪ] *n* bidè *m inv*

big [bɪg] *adj* grande; grosso(-a); **Big Apple** *n vedi nota nel riquadro*; **bigheaded** [ˈbɪgˈhɛdɪd] *adj* presuntuoso(-a); **big toe** *n* alluce *m*

⬥ **BIG APPLE**
⬥
⬥ Tutti sanno che **The Big Apple**, la
⬥ Grande Mela, è New York ("apple"
⬥ in gergo significa grande città), ma
⬥ sicuramente i soprannomi di altre città
⬥ americane non sono così conosciuti.
⬥ Chicago è soprannominata "the Windy
⬥ City" perché è ventosa, New Orleans
⬥ si chiama "the Big Easy" per il modo di
⬥ vivere tranquillo e rilassato dei suoi
⬥ abitanti, e l'industria automobilistica
⬥ ha fatto sì che Detroit fosse
⬥ soprannominata "Motown".

bike [baɪk] *n* bici *f inv*; **bike lane** *n* pista ciclabile

bikini [bɪˈkiːnɪ] *n* bikini *m inv*

bilateral [baɪˈlætərl] *adj* bilaterale

bilingual [baɪˈlɪŋgwəl] *adj* bilingue

bill [bɪl] *n* conto; (*Pol*) atto; (*US: banknote*) banconota; (*of bird*) becco; (*of show*) locandina; **can I have the ~, please** il

conto, per favore; **put it on my ~** lo metta
sul mio conto; **"post no ~s"** "divieto di
affissione"; **to fit** or **fill the ~** (fig) fare al
caso; **billboard** n tabellone m; **billfold**
['bɪlfəʊld] (us) n portafoglio
billiards ['bɪljədz] n biliardo
billion ['bɪljən] num (BRIT) bilione m; (US)
miliardo
bin [bɪn] n (for coal, rubbish) bidone m; (for
bread) cassetta; (dustbin) pattumiera; (litter
bin) cestino
bind [baɪnd] (pt, pp bound) vt legare;
(oblige) obbligare ▷ n (inf) scocciatura
binge [bɪndʒ] (inf) n **to go on a ~** fare
baldoria
bingo ['bɪŋgəʊ] n gioco simile alla tombola
binoculars [bɪ'nɔkjʊləz] npl binocolo
bio... [baɪə'...] prefix; **biochemistry**
n biochimica; **biodegradable** adj
biodegradabile; **biography** [baɪ'ɔgrəfɪ]
n biografia; **biological** adj biologico(-a);
biology [baɪ'ɔlədʒɪ] n biologia
birch [bəːtʃ] n betulla
bird [bəːd] n uccello; (BRIT: inf: girl)
bambola; **bird of prey** n (uccello) rapace
m; **birdwatching** n birdwatching m
Biro® ['baɪrəʊ] n biro® f inv
birth [bəːθ] n nascita; **to give ~ to**
partorire; **birth certificate** n certificato
di nascita; **birth control** n controllo
delle nascite; contraccezione f; **birthday**
n compleanno ▷ cpd di compleanno;
birthmark n voglia; **birthplace** n luogo
di nascita
biscuit ['bɪskɪt] (BRIT) n biscotto
bishop ['bɪʃəp] n vescovo
bistro ['biːstrəʊ] n bistrò m inv
bit [bɪt] n of bite ▷ n pezzo; (Comput) bit
m inv; (of horse) morso; **a ~ of** un po' di; **a ~
mad** un po' matto; **~ by ~** a poco a poco
bitch [bɪtʃ] n (dog) cagna; (inf!) vacca
bite [baɪt] (pt, pp bit, bitten) vt, vi mordere;
(insect) pungere ▷ n morso; (insect bite)
puntura; (mouthful) boccone m; **let's have
a ~ to eat** mangiamo un boccone; **to ~
one's nails** mangiarsi le unghie
bitten ['bɪtn] pp of bite
bitter ['bɪtər] adj amaro(-a); (wind, criticism)
pungente ▷ n (BRIT: beer) birra amara
bizarre [bɪ'zaː] adj bizzarro(-a)
black [blæk] adj nero(-a) ▷ n nero;
(person): **B~** negro(-a) ▷ vt (BRIT Industry)
boicottare; **to give sb a ~ eye** fare un
occhio nero a qn; **in the ~** (bank account)
in attivo; **black out** vi (faint) svenire;
blackberry n mora; **blackbird** n merlo;
blackboard n lavagna; **black coffee** n
caffè m inv nero; **blackcurrant** n ribes
m inv; **black ice** n strato trasparente

di ghiaccio; **blackmail** n ricatto ▷ vt
ricattare; **black market** n mercato nero;
blackout n oscuramento; (TV, Radio)
interruzione f delle trasmissioni; (fainting)
svenimento; **black pepper** n pepe m nero;
black pudding n sanguinaccio; **Black
Sea** n **the Black Sea** il Mar Nero
bladder ['blædər] n vescica
blade [bleɪd] n lama; (of oar) pala; **~ of
grass** filo d'erba
blame [bleɪm] n colpa ▷ vt **to ~ sb/sth for
sth** dare la colpa di qc a qn/qc; **who's to ~?**
chi è colpevole?
bland [blænd] adj mite; (taste) blando(-a)
blank [blæŋk] adj bianco(-a); (look)
distratto(-a) ▷ n spazio vuoto; (cartridge)
cartuccia a salve
blanket ['blæŋkɪt] n coperta
blast [blɑːst] n (of wind) raffica; (of bomb
etc) esplosione f ▷ vt far saltare
blatant ['bleɪtənt] adj flagrante
blaze [bleɪz] n (fire) incendio; (fig)
vampata; splendore m ▷ vi (fire) ardere,
fiammeggiare; (guns) sparare senza sosta;
(fig: eyes) ardere ▷ vt **to ~ a trail** (fig)
tracciare una via nuova; **in a ~ of publicity**
circondato da grande pubblicità
blazer ['bleɪzər] n blazer m inv
bleach [bliːtʃ] n (also: **household ~**)
varechina ▷ vt (material) candeggiare;
bleachers (US) npl (Sport) posti mpl di
gradinata
bleak [bliːk] adj tetro(-a)
bled [blɛd] pt, pp of bleed
bleed [bliːd] (pt, pp bled) vi sanguinare;
my nose is ~ing mi viene fuori sangue
dal naso
blemish ['blɛmɪʃ] n macchia
blend [blɛnd] n miscela ▷ vt mescolare
▷ vi (colours etc: also: **~ in**) armonizzare;
blender n (Culin) frullatore m
bless [blɛs] (pt, pp blessed or blest) vt
benedire; **~ you!** (after sneeze) salute!;
blessing n benedizione f; fortuna
blew [bluː] pt of blow
blight [blaɪt] vt (hopes etc) deludere; (life)
rovinare
blind [blaɪnd] adj cieco(-a) ▷ n (for window)
avvolgibile m; (Venetian blind) veneziana
▷ vt accecare; **the ~** npl i ciechi; **blind
alley** n vicolo cieco; **blindfold** n benda
▷ adj, adv bendato(-a) ▷ vt bendare gli
occhi a
blink [blɪŋk] vi battere gli occhi; (light)
lampeggiare
bliss [blɪs] n estasi f
blister ['blɪstər] n (on skin) vescica; (on
paintwork) bolla ▷ vi (paint) coprirsi di bolle
blizzard ['blɪzəd] n bufera di neve

bloated ['bləutɪd] adj gonfio(-a)
blob [blɔb] n (drop) goccia; (stain, spot) macchia
block [blɔk] n blocco; (in pipes) ingombro; (toy) cubo; (of buildings) isolato ▷ vt bloccare; **the sink is ~ed** il lavandino è otturato; **block up** vt bloccare; (pipe) ingorgare, intasare; **blockade** [-'keɪd] n blocco; **blockage** n ostacolo; **blockbuster** n (film, book) grande successo; **block capitals** npl stampatello; **block letters** npl stampatello
bloke [bləuk] (BRIT: inf) n tizio
blond(e) [blɔnd] adj, n biondo(-a)
blood [blʌd] n sangue m; **blood donor** n donatore(-trice) di sangue; **blood group** n gruppo sanguigno; **blood poisoning** n setticemia; **blood pressure** n pressione f sanguigna; **bloodshed** n spargimento di sangue; **bloodshot** adj **bloodshot eyes** occhi iniettati di sangue; **bloodstream** n flusso del sangue; **blood test** n analisi f inv del sangue; **blood transfusion** n trasfusione f di sangue; **blood type** n gruppo sanguigno; **blood vessel** n vaso sanguigno; **bloody** adj (fight) sanguinoso(-a); (nose) sanguinante; (BRIT: inf!) **this bloody ...** questo maledetto ...; **bloody awful/good** (inf!) veramente terribile/forte
bloom [bluːm] n fiore m ▷ vi (tree) essere in fiore; (flower) aprirsi
blossom ['blɔsəm] n fiore m; (with pl sense) fiori mpl ▷ vi essere in fiore
blot [blɔt] n macchia ▷ vt macchiare
blouse [blauz] n (feminine garment) camicetta
blow [bləu] (pt blew, pp blown) n colpo ▷ vi soffiare ▷ vt (fuse) far saltare; (wind) spingere; (instrument) suonare; **to ~ one's nose** soffiarsi il naso; **to ~ a whistle** fischiare; **blow away** vt portare via; **blow out** vi scoppiare; **blow up** vi saltare in aria ▷ vt far saltare in aria; (tyre) gonfiare; (Phot) ingrandire; **blow-dry** n messa in piega a föhn
blown [bləun] pp of **blow**
blue [bluː] adj azzurro(-a); (depressed) giù inv; **~ film/joke** film/barzelletta pornografico(-a); **out of the ~** (fig) all'improvviso; **bluebell** n giacinto dei boschi; **blueberry** n mirtillo; **blue cheese** n formaggio tipo gorgonzola; **blues** npl **the blues** (Mus) il blues; **to have the blues** (inf: feeling) essere a terra; **bluetit** n cinciarella
bluff [blʌf] vi bluffare ▷ n bluff m inv ▷ adj (person) brusco(-a); **to call sb's ~** mettere alla prova il bluff di qn

blunder ['blʌndər] n abbaglio ▷ vi prendere un abbaglio
blunt [blʌnt] adj smussato(-a); spuntato(-a); (person) brusco(-a)
blur [bləːr] n forma indistinta ▷ vt offuscare; **blurred** adj (photo) mosso(-a); (TV) sfuocato(-a)
blush [blʌʃ] vi arrossire ▷ n rossore m; **blusher** n fard m inv
board [bɔːd] n tavola; (on wall) tabellone m; (committee) consiglio, comitato; (in firm) consiglio d'amministrazione; (Naut, Aviat): **on ~** a bordo ▷ vt (ship) salire a bordo di; (train) salire su; **full ~** (BRIT) pensione completa; **half ~** (BRIT) mezza pensione; **~ and lodging** vitto e alloggio; **which goes by the ~** (fig) che viene abbandonato; **board game** n gioco da tavolo; **boarding card** n = **boarding pass**; **boarding pass** n (Aviat, Naut) carta d'imbarco; **boarding school** n collegio; **board room** n sala del consiglio
boast [bəust] vi **to ~ (about or of)** vantarsi (di)
boat [bəut] n nave f; (small) barca
bob [bɔb] vi (boat, cork on water: also: **~ up and down**) andare su e giù
bobby pin ['bɔbɪ-] (US) n fermaglio per capelli
body ['bɔdɪ] n corpo; (of car) carrozzeria; (of plane) fusoliera; (fig: group) gruppo; (: organization) organizzazione f; (: quantity) quantità f inv; **body-building** n culturismo; **bodyguard** n guardia del corpo; **bodywork** n carrozzeria
bog [bɔg] n palude f ▷ vt **to get ~ged down** (fig) impantanarsi
bogus ['bəugəs] adj falso(-a); finto(-a)
boil [bɔɪl] vt, vi bollire ▷ n (Med) foruncolo; **to come to the** (BRIT) or **a** (US) **~** raggiungere l'ebollizione; **boil over** vi traboccare (bollendo); **boiled egg** n uovo alla coque; **boiled potatoes** npl patate fpl bollite or lesse; **boiler** n caldaia; **boiling** adj bollente; **I'm boiling (hot)** (inf) sto morendo di caldo; **boiling point** n punto di ebollizione
bold [bəuld] adj audace; (child) impudente; (colour) deciso(-a)
Bolivia [bə'lɪvɪə] n Bolivia
Bolivian [bə'lɪvɪən] adj, n boliviano(-a)
bollard ['bɔləd] (BRIT) n (Aut) colonnina luminosa
bolt [bəult] n chiavistello; (with nut) bullone m ▷ adv **~ upright** diritto(-a) come un fuso ▷ vt serrare; (also: **~ together**) imbullonare; (food) mangiare in fretta ▷ vi scappare via
bomb [bɔm] n bomba ▷ vt bombardare;

bombard [bɔm'bɑːd] vt bombardare;
bomber n (Aviat) bombardiere m; **bomb
scare** n stato di allarme (per sospetta
presenza di una bomba)

bond [bɔnd] n legame m; (binding promise,
Finance) obbligazione f; (Comm): **in ~** in
attesa di sdoganamento

bone [bəun] n osso; (of fish) spina, lisca ▷ vt
disossare; togliere le spine a

bonfire ['bɔnfaɪə'] n falò m inv

bonnet ['bɔnɪt] n cuffia; (BRIT: of car)
cofano

bonus ['bəunəs] n premio; (fig) sovrappiù
m inv

boo [buː] excl ba! ▷ vt fischiare

book [buk] n libro; (of stamps etc)
blocchetto ▷ vt (ticket, seat, room)
prenotare; (driver) multare; (football
player) ammonire; **~s** npl (Comm) conti
mpl; **I'd like to ~ a double room** vorrei
prenotare una camera doppia; **I ~ed a
table in the name of ...** ho prenotato un
tavolo al nome di...; **book in** vi (BRIT: at
hotel) prendere una camera; **book up** vt
riservare, prenotare; **the hotel is ~ed up**
l'albergo è al completo; **all seats are ~ed
up** è tutto esaurito; **bookcase** n scaffale
m; **booking** n (BRIT) prenotazione f; **I
confirmed my booking by fax/e-mail**
ho confermato la mia prenotazione
tramite fax/e-mail; **booking office** (BRIT)
n (Rail) biglietteria; (Theatre) botteghino;
book-keeping n contabilità; **booklet**
n libricino; **bookmaker** n allibratore m;
bookmark (also Comput) n segnalibro
▷ vt (Comput) mettere un segnalibro a;
(Internet Explorer) aggiungere a "Preferiti";
bookseller n libraio; **bookshelf** n
mensola (per libri); **bookshop, bookstore**
n libreria

boom [buːm] n (noise) rimbombo; (in prices
etc) boom m inv ▷ vi rimbombare; andare
a gonfie vele

boost [buːst] n spinta ▷ vt spingere

boot [buːt] n stivale m; (for hiking) scarpone
m da montagna; (for football etc) scarpa;
(BRIT: of car) portabagagli m inv ▷ vt
(Comput) inizializzare; **to ~** (in addition) per
giunta, in più

booth [buːð] n cabina; (at fair) baraccone m

booze [buːz] (inf) n alcool m

border ['bɔːdə'] n orlo; margine m; (of
a country) frontiera; (for flowers) aiuola
(laterale) ▷ vt (road) costeggiare; (another
country: also: **~ on**) confinare con; **the B~s**
la zona di confine tra l'Inghilterra e la Scozia;
borderline n (fig): **on the borderline**
incerto(-a)

bore [bɔːʳ] pt of **bear** ▷ vt (hole etc)

scavare; (person) annoiare ▷ n (person)
seccatore(-trice); (of gun) calibro; **bored**
adj annoiato(-a); **to be bored** annoiarsi;
he's bored to tears or **to death** or **stiff** è
annoiato a morte; **boredom** n noia

boring ['bɔːrɪŋ] adj noioso(-a)

born [bɔːn] adj: **to be ~** nascere; **I was ~ in
1960** sono nato nel 1960

borne [bɔːn] pp of **bear**

borough ['bʌrə] n comune m

borrow ['bɔrəu] vt **to ~ sth (from sb)**
prendere in prestito qc (da qn)

Bosnia(-Herzegovina)
['bɔznɪə(hɜːtsə'gəuviːnə)] n Bosnia-
Erzegovina; **Bosnian** ['bɔznɪən] n, adj
bosniaco(-a) m/f

bosom ['buzəm] n petto; (fig) seno

boss [bɔs] n capo ▷ vt comandare; **bossy**
adj prepotente

both [bəuθ] adj entrambi(-e), tutt'e due
▷ pron **~ of them** entrambi(-e); **~ of us
went, we ~ went** ci siamo andati tutt'e
due ▷ adv **they sell ~ meat and poultry**
vendono insieme la carne ed il pollame

bother ['bɔðə'] vt (worry) preoccupare;
(annoy) infastidire ▷ vi (also: **~ o.s.**)
preoccuparsi ▷ n **it is a ~ to have to do** è
una seccatura dover fare; **it was no ~** non
c'era problema; **to ~ doing sth** darsi la
pena di fare qc

bottle ['bɔtl] n bottiglia; (baby's) biberon
m inv ▷ vt imbottigliare; **bottle bank** n
contenitore m per la raccolta del vetro;
bottle-opener n apribottiglie m inv

bottom ['bɔtəm] n fondo; (buttocks) sedere
m ▷ adj più basso(-a); ultimo(-a); **at the ~
of** in fondo a

bought [bɔːt] pt, pp of **buy**

boulder ['bəuldə'] n masso (tondeggiante)

bounce [bauns] vi (ball) rimbalzare;
(cheque) essere restituito(-a) ▷ vt far
rimbalzare ▷ n (rebound) rimbalzo;
bouncer (inf) n buttafuori m inv

bound [baund] pt, pp of **bind** ▷ n (gen pl)
limite m; (leap) salto ▷ vi saltare ▷ vt (limit)
delimitare ▷ adj: **~ by law** obbligato(-a) per
legge; **to be ~ to do sth** (obliged) essere
costretto(-a) a fare qc; **he's ~ to fail** (likely)
fallirà di certo; **~ for** diretto(-a) a; **out of ~s**
il cui accesso è vietato

boundary ['baundrɪ] n confine m

bouquet ['bukeɪ] n bouquet m inv

bourbon ['buəbən] (us) n (also: **~ whiskey**)
bourbon m inv

bout [baut] n periodo; (of malaria etc)
attacco; (Boxing etc) incontro

boutique [buː'tiːk] n boutique f inv

bow¹ [bəu] n nodo; (weapon) arco; (Mus)
archetto

bow² [bau] n (with body) inchino; (Naut: also: ~s) prua ▷ vi inchinarsi; (yield): **to ~ to** or **before** sottomettersi a

bowels ['bauəlz] npl intestini mpl; (fig) viscere fpl

bowl [bəul] n (for eating) scodella; (for washing) bacino; (ball) boccia ▷ vi (Cricket) servire (la palla); **bowler** ['bəulər] n (Cricket, Baseball) lanciatore m; (BRIT: also: **bowler hat**) bombetta; **bowling** ['bəulɪŋ] n (game) gioco delle bocce; **bowling alley** n pista da bowling; **bowling green** n campo di bocce; **bowls** [bəulz] n gioco delle bocce

bow tie n cravatta a farfalla

box [bɔks] n ~scatola; (also: **cardboard ~**) cartone m; (Theatre) palco ▷ vt inscatolare ▷ vi fare del pugilato; **boxer** n (person) pugile m; **boxer shorts** ['bɔksəfɔːts] pl n boxer; **a pair of boxer shorts** un paio di boxer; **boxing** n (Sport) pugilato; **Boxing Day** (BRIT) n ≈ Santo Stefano; vedi nota nel riquadro; **boxing gloves** npl guantoni mpl da pugile; **boxing ring** n ring m inv; **box office** n biglietteria

❖ **BOXING DAY**
❖
❖ Il **Boxing Day** è un giorno di festa e
❖ cade in genere il 26 dicembre. Prende
❖ il nome dalla tradizionale usanza di
❖ donare pacchi regalo natalizi, chiamati
❖ "Christmas boxes", a fornitori e
❖ dipendenti.

boy [bɔɪ] n ragazzo

boycott ['bɔɪkɔt] n boicottaggio ▷ vt boicottare

boyfriend ['bɔɪfrɛnd] n ragazzo

bra [brɑː] n reggipetto, reggiseno

brace [breɪs] n (on teeth) apparecchio correttore; (tool) trapano ▷ vt rinforzare, sostenere; **~s** (BRIT) npl (Dress) bretelle fpl; **to ~ o.s.** (also fig) tenersi forte

bracelet ['breɪslɪt] n braccialetto

bracket ['brækɪt] n (Tech) mensola; (group) gruppo; (Typ) parentesi f inv ▷ vt mettere fra parentesi

brag [bræg] vi vantarsi

braid [breɪd] n (trimming) passamano; (of hair) treccia

brain [breɪn] n cervello; **~s** npl (intelligence) cervella fpl; **he's got ~s** è intelligente

braise [breɪz] vt brasare

brake [breɪk] n (on vehicle) freno ▷ vi frenare; **brake light** n (fanalino dello) stop m inv

bran [bræn] n crusca

branch [brɑːntʃ] n ramo; (Comm)

succursale f; **branch off** vi diramarsi; **branch out** vi (fig) intraprendere una nuova attività

brand [brænd] n marca; (fig) tipo ▷ vt (cattle) marcare (a ferro rovente); **brand name** n marca; **brand-new** adj nuovo(-a) di zecca

brandy ['brændɪ] n brandy m inv

brash [bræʃ] adj sfacciato(-a)

brass [brɑːs] n ottone m; **the ~** (Mus) gli ottoni; **brass band** n fanfara

brat [bræt] (pej) n marmocchio, monello(-a)

brave [breɪv] adj coraggioso(-a) ▷ vt affrontare; **bravery** n coraggio

brawl [brɔːl] n rissa

Brazil [brə'zɪl] n Brasile m; **Brazilian** adj, n brasiliano(-a)

breach [briːtʃ] vt aprire una breccia in ▷ n (gap) breccia, varco; (breaking): **~ of contract** rottura di contratto; **~ of the peace** violazione f dell'ordine pubblico

bread [brɛd] n pane m; **breadbin** n cassetta f portapane inv; **breadbox** (US) n cassetta f portapane inv; **breadcrumbs** npl briciole fpl; (Culin) pangrattato

breadth [brɛtθ] n larghezza; (fig: of knowledge etc) ampiezza

break [breɪk] (pt broke, pp broken) vt rompere; (law) violare; (record) battere ▷ vi rompersi; (storm) scoppiare; (weather) cambiare; (dawn) spuntare; (news) saltare fuori ▷ n (gap) breccia; (fracture) rottura; (rest, also Scol) intervallo; (: short) pausa; (chance) possibilità f inv; **to ~ one's leg** rompersi la gamba ecc; **to ~ the news to sb** comunicare per primo la notizia a qn; **to ~ even** coprire le spese; **to ~ free** or **loose** spezzare i legami; **to ~ open** (door etc) sfondare; **break down** vt (figures, data) analizzare ▷ vi (person) avere un esaurimento (nervoso); (Aut) guastarsi; **my car has broken down** mi si è rotta la macchina; **break in** vt (horse etc) domare ▷ vi (burglar) fare irruzione; (interrupt) interrompere; **break into** vt fus (house) fare irruzione in; **break off** vi (speaker) interrompersi; (branch) troncarsi; **break out** vi evadere; (war, fight) scoppiare; **to ~ out in spots** coprirsi di macchie; **break up** vi (ship) sfondarsi; (meeting) sciogliersi; (crowd) disperdersi; (marriage) andare a pezzi; (Scol) chiudere ▷ vt fare a pezzi, spaccare; (fight etc) interrompere, far cessare; **breakdown** n (Aut) guasto; (in communications) interruzione f; (of marriage) rottura; (Med: also: **nervous breakdown**) esaurimento nervoso; (of statistics) resoconto; **breakdown truck,**

breakdown van n carro m attrezzi inv
breakfast ['brɛkfəst] n colazione f; **what time is ~?** a che ora è servita la colazione?
break: **break-in** n irruzione f; **breakthrough** n (fig) passo avanti
breast [brɛst] n (of woman) seno; (chest, Culin) petto; **breast-feed** (irreg: like feed) vt, vi allattare (al seno); **breast-stroke** n nuoto a rana
breath [brɛθ] n respiro; **out of ~** senza fiato
Breathalyser® ['brɛθəlaɪzəʳ] (BRIT) n alcoltest m inv
breathe [bri:ð] vt, vi respirare; **breathe in** vt respirare ▷ vi inspirare; **breathe out** vt, vi espirare; **breathing** n respiro, respirazione f
breath: **breathless** ['brɛθlɪs] adj senza fiato; **breathtaking** ['brɛθteɪkɪŋ] adj mozzafiato inv; **breath test** n ≈ prova del palloncino
bred [brɛd] pt, pp of **breed**
breed [bri:d] (pt, pp bred) vt allevare ▷ vi riprodursi ▷ n razza; (type, class) varietà f inv
breeze [bri:z] n brezza
breezy ['bri:zɪ] adj allegro(-a), ventilato(-a)
brew [bru:] vt (tea) fare un infuso di; (beer) fare ▷ vi (storm, fig: trouble etc) prepararsi; **brewery** n fabbrica di birra
bribe [braɪb] n bustarella ▷ vt comprare; **bribery** n corruzione f
bric-a-brac ['brɪkəbræk] n bric-a-brac m
brick [brɪk] n mattone m; **bricklayer** n muratore m
bride [braɪd] n sposa; **bridegroom** n sposo; **bridesmaid** n damigella d'onore
bridge [brɪdʒ] n ponte m; (Naut) ponte di comando; (of nose) dorso; (Cards) bridge m inv ▷ vt (fig: gap) colmare
bridle ['braɪdl] n briglia
brief [bri:f] adj breve ▷ n (Law) comparsa; (gen) istruzioni fpl ▷ vt mettere al corrente; **~s** npl (underwear) mutande fpl; **briefcase** n cartella; **briefing** n briefing m inv; **briefly** adv (glance) di sfuggita; (explain, say) brevemente
brigadier [brɪgə'dɪəʳ] n generale m di brigata
bright [braɪt] adj luminoso(-a); (clever) sveglio(-a); (lively) vivace
brilliant ['brɪljənt] adj brillante; (light, smile) radioso(-a); (inf) splendido(-a)
brim [brɪm] n orlo
brine [braɪn] n (Culin) salamoia
bring [brɪŋ] (pt, pp brought) vt portare; **bring about** vt causare; **bring back** vt riportare; **bring down** vt portare giù; abbattere; **bring in** vt (person)

fare entrare; (object) portare; (Pol: bill) presentare; (: legislation) introdurre; (Law: verdict) emettere; (produce: income) rendere; **bring on** vt (illness, attack) causare, provocare; (player, substitute) far scendere in campo; **bring out** vt tirar fuori; (meaning) mettere in evidenza; (book, album) far uscire; **bring up** vt (carry up) portare su; (child) allevare; (question) introdurre; (food: vomit) rimettere, rigurgitare
brink [brɪŋk] n orlo
brisk [brɪsk] adj (manner) spiccio(-a); (trade) vivace; (pace) svelto(-a)
bristle ['brɪsl] n setola ▷ vi rizzarsi; **bristling with** irto(-a) di
Brit [brɪt] n abbr (inf: = British person) britannico(-a)
Britain ['brɪtən] n (also: **Great ~**) Gran Bretagna
British ['brɪtɪʃ] adj britannico(-a); **British Isles** npl Isole Britanniche
Briton ['brɪtən] n britannico(-a)
brittle ['brɪtl] adj fragile
broad [brɔ:d] adj largo(-a); (distinction) generale; (accent) spiccato(-a); **in ~ daylight** in pieno giorno; **broadband** adj (Comput) a banda larga ▷ n banda larga; **broad bean** n fava; **broadcast** (pt, pp broadcast) n trasmissione f ▷ vt trasmettere per radio (or per televisione) ▷ vi fare una trasmissione; **broaden** vt allargare ▷ vi allargarsi; **broadly** adv (fig) in generale; **broad-minded** adj di mente aperta
broccoli ['brɔkəlɪ] n broccoli mpl
brochure ['brəuʃjuəʳ] n dépliant m inv
broil [brɔɪl] vt cuocere a fuoco vivo
broiler ['brɔɪləʳ] (US) n (grill) griglia
broke [brəuk] pt of **break** ▷ adj (inf) squattrinato(-a)
broken ['brəukn] pp of **break** ▷ adj rotto(-a); **a ~ leg** una gamba rotta; **in ~ English** in un inglese stentato
broker ['brəukəʳ] n agente m
bronchitis [brɔŋ'kaɪtɪs] n bronchite f
bronze [brɔnz] n bronzo
brooch [brəutʃ] n spilla
brood [bru:d] n covata ▷ vi (person) rimuginare
broom [brum] n scopa; (Bot) ginestra
Bros. abbr (= Brothers) F.lli
broth [brɔθ] n brodo
brothel ['brɔθl] n bordello
brother ['brʌðəʳ] n fratello; **brother-in-law** n cognato
brought [brɔ:t] pt, pp of **bring**
brow [brau] n fronte f; (rare, gen: eyebrow) sopracciglio; (of hill) cima

brown [braun] adj bruno(-a), marrone; (tanned) abbronzato(-a) ▷ n (colour) color m bruno or marrone ▷ vt (Culin) rosolare; **brown bread** n pane m integrale, pane nero

Brownie ['braunı] n giovane esploratrice f

brown rice n riso greggio

brown sugar n zucchero greggio

browse [brauz] vi (among books) curiosare fra i libri; **to ~ through a book** sfogliare un libro; **browser** n (Comput) browser m inv

bruise [bru:z] n (on person) livido ▷ vt farsi un livido a

brunette [bru:'nɛt] n bruna

brush [brʌʃ] n (for painting, shaving) pennello; (quarrel) schermaglia ▷ vt spazzolare; (also: ~ against) sfiorare

Brussels ['brʌslz] n Bruxelles f

Brussels sprout [spraut] n cavolo di Bruxelles

brutal ['bru:tl] adj brutale

B.Sc. n abbr (Univ) = **Bachelor of Science**

BSE n abbr (= bovine spongiform encephalopathy) encefalite f bovina spongiforme

bubble ['bʌbl] n bolla ▷ vi ribollire; (sparkle: fig) essere effervescente; **bubble bath** n bagnoschiuma m inv; **bubble gum** n gomma americana

buck [bʌk] n maschio (di camoscio, caprone, coniglio ecc); (Us: inf) dollaro ▷ vi sgroppare; **to pass the ~ to sb** scaricare (su di qn) la propria responsabilità

bucket ['bʌkɪt] n secchio

buckle ['bʌkl] n fibbia ▷ vt allacciare ▷ vi (wheel etc) piegarsi

bud [bʌd] n gemma; (of flower) bocciolo ▷ vi germogliare; (flower) sbocciare

Buddhism ['budɪzəm] n buddismo

Buddhist ['budɪst] adj, n buddista (m/f)

buddy ['bʌdɪ] (Us) n compagno

budge [bʌdʒ] vt scostare; (fig) smuovere ▷ vi spostarsi; smuoversi

budgerigar ['bʌdʒərɪgɑ:ʳ] n pappagallino

budget ['bʌdʒɪt] n bilancio preventivo ▷ vi **to ~ for sth** fare il bilancio per qc

budgie ['bʌdʒɪ] n = **budgerigar**

buff [bʌf] adj color camoscio ▷ n (inf: enthusiast) appassionato(-a)

buffalo ['bʌfələu] (pl **buffalo** or **buffaloes**) n bufalo; (Us) bisonte m

buffer ['bʌfəʳ] n respingente m; (Comput) memoria tampone, buffer m inv

buffet[1] ['bʌfɪt] vt sferzare

buffet[2] ['bufeɪ] n (food, BRIT: bar) buffet m inv; **buffet car** (BRIT) n (Rail) ≈ servizio ristoro

bug [bʌg] n (esp Us: insect) insetto; (Comput fig: germ) virus m inv; (spy device) microfono spia ▷ vt mettere sotto controllo; (inf: annoy) scocciare

buggy ['bʌgɪ] n (baby buggy) passeggino

build [bɪld] (pt, pp **built**) n (of person) corporatura ▷ vt costruire; **build up** vt accumulare; aumentare; **builder** n costruttore m; **building** n costruzione f; edificio; (industry) edilizia; **building site** n cantiere m di costruzione; **building society** (BRIT) n società f inv immobiliare

built [bɪlt] pt, pp of **build**; **built-in** adj (cupboard) a muro; (device) incorporato(-a) **built-up** adj **built-up area** abitato

bulb [bʌlb] n (Bot) bulbo; (Elec) lampadina

Bulgaria [bʌl'gɛərɪə] n Bulgaria; **Bulgarian** adj bulgaro(-a) ▷ n bulgaro(-a); (Ling) bulgaro

bulge [bʌldʒ] n rigonfiamento ▷ vi essere protuberante or rigonfio(-a); **to be bulging with** essere pieno(-a) or zeppo(-a) di

bulimia [bə'lɪmɪə] n bulimia

bulimic [bju:'lɪmɪk] adj, n bulimico(-a)

bulk [bʌlk] n massa, volume m; **in ~** a pacchi or cassette etc; (Comm) all'ingrosso; **the ~ of** il grosso di; **bulky** adj grosso(-a), voluminoso(-a)

bull [bul] n toro; (male elephant, whale) maschio

bulldozer ['buldəuzəʳ] n bulldozer m inv

bullet ['bulɪt] n pallottola

bulletin ['bulɪtɪn] n bollettino; **bulletin board** n (Comput) bulletin board m inv

bullfight ['bulfaɪt] n corrida; **bullfighter** n torero; **bullfighting** n tauromachia

bully ['bulɪ] n prepotente m ▷ vt angariare; (frighten) intimidire

bum [bʌm] (inf) n (backside) culo; (tramp) vagabondo(-a)

bumblebee ['bʌmblbi:] n bombo

bump [bʌmp] n (in car) piccolo tamponamento; (jolt) scossa; (on road etc) protuberanza; (on head) bernoccolo ▷ vt battere; **bump into** vt fus scontrarsi con; (person) imbattersi in; **bumper** n paraurti m inv ▷ adj **bumper harvest** raccolto eccezionale; **bumpy** ['bʌmpɪ] adj (road) dissestato(-a)

bun [bʌn] n focaccia; (of hair) crocchia

bunch [bʌntʃ] n (of flowers, keys) mazzo; (of bananas) casco; (of people) gruppo; **~ of grapes** grappolo d'uva; **~es** npl (in hair) codine fpl

bundle ['bʌndl] n fascio ▷ vt (also: ~ up) legare in un fascio; (put): **to ~ sth/sb into** spingere qc/qn in

bungalow ['bʌŋgələu] n bungalow m inv

bungee jumping [ˈbʌndʒiːˈdʒʌmpɪŋ] *n* salto nel vuoto da ponti, grattacieli etc con un cavo fissato alla caviglia

bunion [ˈbʌnjən] *n* callo (al piede)

bunk [bʌŋk] *n* cuccetta; **bunk beds** *npl* letti *mpl* a castello

bunker [ˈbʌŋkəʳ] *n* (coal store) ripostiglio per il carbone; (Mil, Golf) bunker *m inv*

bunny [ˈbʌnɪ] *n* (also: ~ **rabbit**) coniglietto

buoy [bɔɪ] *n* boa; **buoyant** *adj* galleggiante; (fig) vivace

burden [ˈbəːdn] *n* carico, fardello ▷ *vt* **to ~ sb with** caricare qn di

bureau [bjuəˈrəu] (*pl* **bureaux**) *n* (BRIT: writing desk) scrivania; (US: chest of drawers) cassettone *m*; (office) ufficio, agenzia

bureaucracy [bjuəˈrɔkrəsɪ] *n* burocrazia

bureaucrat [ˈbjuərəkræt] *n* burocrate *m/f*

bureau de change [-dəˈʃɑːʒ] (*pl* **bureaux de change**) *n* cambiavalute *m inv*

bureaux [bjuəˈrəuz] *npl of* **bureau**

burger [ˈbəːgəʳ] *n* hamburger *m inv*

burglar [ˈbəːgləʳ] *n* scassinatore *m*; **burglar alarm** *n* campanello antifurto; **burglary** *n* furto con scasso

burial [ˈbɛrɪəl] *n* sepoltura

burn [bəːn] (*pt, pp* **burned** *or* **burnt**) *vt, vi* bruciare ▷ *n* bruciatura, scottatura; **burn down** *vt* distruggere col fuoco; **burn out** *vt* (writer etc): **to ~ o.s. out** esaurirsi; **burning** *adj* in fiamme; (sand) che scotta; (ambition) bruciante

Burns Night *n* vedi nota nel riquadro

burnt [bəːnt] *pt, pp of* **burn**

burp [bəːp] (inf) *n* rutto ▷ *vi* ruttare

burrow [ˈbʌrəu] *n* tana ▷ *vt* scavare

burst [bəːst] (*pt, pp* **burst**) *vt* far scoppiare ▷ *vi* esplodere; (tyre) scoppiare ▷ *n* scoppio; (also: ~ **pipe**) rottura nel tubo, perdita; **a ~ of speed** uno scatto di velocità; **to ~ into flames/tears** scoppiare in fiamme/lacrime; **to ~ out laughing** scoppiare a ridere; **to be ~ing with** scoppiare di; **burst into** *vt fus* (room etc) irrompere in

bury [ˈbɛrɪ] *vt* seppellire

bus [bʌs] (*pl* **buses**) *n* autobus *m inv*; **bus**

conductor *n* autista *m/f* (dell'autobus)

bush [buʃ] *n* cespuglio; (scrub land) macchia; **to beat about the ~** menare il cane per l'aia

business [ˈbɪznɪs] *n* (matter) affare *m*; (trading) affari *mpl*; (firm) azienda; (job, duty) lavoro; **to be away on ~** essere andato via per affari; **it's none of my ~** questo non mi riguarda; **he means ~** non scherza; **business class** *n* (Aer) business class *f*; **businesslike** *adj* serio(-a), efficiente; **businessman** (irreg) *n* uomo d'affari; **business trip** *n* viaggio d'affari; **businesswoman** (irreg) *n* donna d'affari

busker [ˈbʌskəʳ] (BRIT) *n* suonatore(-trice) ambulante

bus: **bus pass** *n* tessera dell'autobus; **bus shelter** *n* pensilina (alla fermata dell'autobus); **bus station** *n* stazione *f* delle corriere, autostazione *f*; **bus-stop** *n* fermata d'autobus

bust [bʌst] *n* busto; (Anat) seno ▷ *adj* (inf: broken) rotto(-a); **to go ~** fallire

bustling [ˈbʌslɪŋ] *adj* movimentato(-a)

busy [ˈbɪzɪ] *adj* occupato(-a); (shop, street) molto frequentato(-a) ▷ *vt* **to ~ o.s.** darsi da fare; **busy signal** (US) *n* (Tel) segnale *m* di occupato

 KEYWORD

but [bʌt] *conj* ma; **I'd love to come, but I'm busy** vorrei tanto venire, ma ho da fare ▷ *prep* (apart from, except) eccetto, tranne, meno; **he was nothing but trouble** non dava altro che guai; **no-one but him can do it** nessuno può farlo tranne lui; **but for you/your help** se non fosse per te/per il tuo aiuto; **anything but that** tutto ma non questo
▷ *adv* (just, only) solo, soltanto; **she's but a child** è solo una bambina; **had I but known** se solo avessi saputo; **I can but try** tentar non nuoce; **all but finished** quasi finito

butcher [ˈbutʃəʳ] *n* macellaio ▷ *vt* macellare; **butcher's (shop)** *n* macelleria

butler [ˈbʌtləʳ] *n* maggiordomo

butt [bʌt] *n* (cask) grossa botte *f*; (of gun) calcio; (of cigarette) mozzicone *m*; (BRIT: fig: target) oggetto ▷ *vt* cozzare

butter [ˈbʌtəʳ] *n* burro ▷ *vt* imburrare; **buttercup** *n* ranuncolo

butterfly [ˈbʌtəflaɪ] *n* farfalla; (Swimming: also: ~ **stroke**) (nuoto a) farfalla

buttocks [ˈbʌtəks] *npl* natiche *fpl*

button [ˈbʌtn] *n* bottone *m*; (US: badge)

distintivo ▷ *vt* (*also*: ~ **up**) abbottonare ▷ *vi* abbottonarsi

buy [baɪ] (*pt, pp* **bought**) *vt* comprare ▷ *n* acquisto; **where can I ~ some postcards?** dove posso comprare delle cartoline?; **to ~ sb sth/sth from sb** comprare qc per qn/qc da qn; **to ~ sb a drink** offrire da bere a qn; **buy out** *vt* (*business*) rilevare; **buy up** *vt* accaparrare; **buyer** *n* compratore(-trice)

buzz [bʌz] *n* ronzio; (*inf*: *phone call*) colpo di telefono ▷ *vi* ronzare; **buzzer** [ˈbʌzəʳ] *n* cicalino

 KEYWORD

by [baɪ] *prep* **1** (*referring to cause, agent*) da; **killed by lightning** ucciso da un fulmine; **surrounded by a fence** circondato da uno steccato; **a painting by Picasso** un quadro di Picasso

2 (*referring to method, manner, means*): **by bus/car/train** in autobus/macchina/treno, con l'autobus/la macchina/il treno; **to pay by cheque** pagare con (un) assegno; **by moonlight** al chiaro di luna; **by saving hard, he ...** risparmiando molto, lui ...

3 (*via, through*) per; **we came by Dover** siamo venuti via Dover

4 (*close to, past*) accanto a; **the house by the river** la casa sul fiume; **a holiday by the sea** una vacanza al mare; **she sat by his bed** si sedette accanto al suo letto; **she rushed by me** mi è passata accanto correndo; **I go by the post office every day** passo davanti all'ufficio postale ogni giorno

5 (*not later than*) per, entro; **by 4 o'clock** per *or* entro le 4; **by this time tomorrow** domani a quest'ora; **by the time I got here it was too late** quando sono arrivato era ormai troppo tardi

6 (*during*): **by day/night** di giorno/notte

7 (*amount*) a; **by the kilo/metre** a chili/metri; **paid by the hour** pagato all'ora; **one by one** uno per uno; **little by little** a poco a poco

8 (*Math, measure*): **to divide/multiply by 3** dividere/moltiplicare per 3; **it's broader by a metre** è un metro più largo, è più largo di un metro

9 (*according to*) per; **to play by the rules** attenersi alle regole; **it's all right by me** per me va bene

10: **(all) by oneself** *etc* (tutto(-a)) solo(-a); **he did it (all) by himself** lo ha fatto (tutto) da solo

11: **by the way** a proposito; **this wasn't**

my idea by the way tra l'altro l'idea non è stata mia

▷ *adv* **1** *see* **go**; **pass** *etc*

2: **by and by** (*in past*) poco dopo; (*in future*) fra breve; **by and large** nel complesso

bye(-bye) [ˈbaɪ(ˈbaɪ)] *excl* ciao!, arrivederci!

by-election [ˈbaɪɪlɛkʃən] (*BRIT*) *n* elezione *f* straordinaria

bypass [ˈbaɪpɑːs] *n* circonvallazione *f*; (*Med*) by-pass *m inv* ▷ *vt* fare una deviazione intorno a

byte [baɪt] *n* (*Comput*) byte *m inv*, bicarattere *m*

C

C [siː] n (Mus) do

cab [kæb] n taxi m inv; (of train, truck) cabina

cabaret ['kæbəreɪ] n cabaret m inv

cabbage ['kæbɪdʒ] n cavolo

cabin ['kæbɪn] n capanna; (on ship) cabina; **cabin crew** n equipaggio

cabinet ['kæbɪnɪt] n (Pol) consiglio dei ministri; (furniture) armadietto; (also: **display ~**) vetrinetta; **cabinet minister** n ministro (membro del Consiglio)

cable ['keɪbl] n cavo; fune f; (Tel) cablogramma m ▷ vt telegrafare; **cable car** n funivia; **cable television** n televisione f via cavo

cactus ['kæktəs] (pl **cacti**) n cactus m inv

café ['kæfeɪ] n caffè m inv

cafeteria [kæfɪ'tɪərɪə] n self-service m inv

caffein(e) ['kæfiːn] n caffeina

cage [keɪdʒ] n gabbia

cagoule [kə'guːl] n K-way® m inv

cake [keɪk] n (large) torta; (small) pasticcino; **cake of soap** n saponetta

calcium ['kælsɪəm] n calcio

calculate ['kælkjuleɪt] vt calcolare; **calculation** [-'leɪʃən] n calcolo; **calculator** n calcolatrice f

calendar ['kæləndəʳ] n calendario

calf [kɑːf] (pl **calves**) n (of cow) vitello; (of other animals) piccolo; (also: **~skin**) (pelle f di) vitello; (Anat) polpaccio

calibre ['kælɪbəʳ] (US **caliber**) n calibro

call [kɔːl] vt (gen: also Tel) chiamare; (meeting) indire ▷ vi chiamare; (visit: also: **~ in, ~ round**) passare ▷ n (shout) grido, urlo; (Tel) telefonata; **to be ~ed** (person, object) chiamarsi; **can you ~ back later?** può richiamare più tardi?; **can I make a ~ from here?** posso telefonare da qui?; **to be on ~** essere a disposizione; **call back** vi (return) ritornare; (Tel) ritelefonare, richiamare; **call for** vt fus richiedere; (fetch) passare a prendere; **call in** vt (doctor, expert, police) chiamare, far venire; **call off** vt disdire; **call on** vt fus (visit) passare da; (appeal to) chiedere a; **call out** vi (in pain) urlare; (to person) chiamare; **call up** vt (Mil) richiamare; (Tel) telefonare a; **callbox** (BRIT) n cabina telefonica; **call centre** (US **call center**) n centro informazioni telefoniche; **caller** n persona che chiama, visitatore(-trice)

callous ['kæləs] adj indurito(-a), insensibile

calm [kɑːm] adj calmo(-a) ▷ n calma ▷ vt calmare; **calm down** vi calmarsi ▷ vt calmare; **calmly** adv con calma

Calor gas® ['kæləʳ-] n butano

calorie ['kælərɪ] n caloria

calves [kɑːvz] npl of **calf**

camcorder ['kæmkɔːdəʳ] n camcorder f inv

came [keɪm] pt of **come**

camel ['kæməl] n cammello

camera ['kæmərə] n macchina fotografica; (Cinema, TV) cinepresa; **in ~** a porte chiuse; **cameraman** (irreg) n cameraman m inv

camouflage ['kæməflɑːʒ] n (Mil, Zool) mimetizzazione f ▷ vt mimetizzare

camp [kæmp] n campeggio; (Mil) campo ▷ vi accamparsi ▷ adj effeminato(-a)

campaign [kæm'peɪn] n (Mil, Pol etc) campagna ▷ vi (also fig) fare una campagna; **campaigner** n **campaigner for** fautore(-trice) di; **campaigner against** oppositore(-trice) di

camp: **campbed** n (BRIT) brandina; **camper** ['kæmpəʳ] n campeggiatore(-trice); (vehicle) camper m inv; **campground** (US) n campeggio; **camping** ['kæmpɪŋ] n campeggio; **to go camping** andare in campeggio; **campsite** ['kæmpsaɪt] n campeggio

campus ['kæmpəs] n campus m inv

can¹ [kæn] n (of milk) scatola; (of oil) bidone m; (of water) tanica; (tin) scatola ▷ vt

mettere in scatola

 KEYWORD

can² [kæn] (*negative* **cannot, can't**, *conditional and pt* **could**) *aux vb* **1** (*be able to*) potere; **I can't go any further** non posso andare oltre; **you can do it if you try** sei in grado di farlo — basta provarci; **I'll help you all I can** ti aiuterò come potrò; **I can't see you** non ti vedo **2** (*know how to*) sapere, essere capace di; **I can swim** so nuotare; **can you speak French?** parla francese? **3** (*may*) potere; **could I have a word with you?** posso parlarle un momento? **4** (*expressing disbelief, puzzlement etc*): **it can't be true!** non può essere vero!; **what can he want?** cosa può mai volere? **5** (*expressing possibility, suggestion etc*): **he could be in the library** può darsi che sia in biblioteca; **she could have been delayed** può aver avuto un contrattempo

Canada ['kænədə] *n* Canada *m*; **Canadian** [kə'neɪdɪən] *adj, n* canadese *m/f*
canal [kə'næl] *n* canale *m*
canary [kə'nɛərɪ] *n* canarino *m*
Canary Islands, Canaries [kə'nɛərɪz] *npl* **the ~** le (isole) Canarie
cancel ['kænsəl] *vt* annullare; (*train*) sopprimere; (*cross out*) cancellare; **I want to ~ my booking** vorrei disdire la mia prenotazione; **cancellation** [-'leɪʃən] *n* annullamento; soppressione *f*; cancellazione *f*; (*Tourism*) prenotazione *f* annullata
cancer ['kænsər] *n* cancro *m*
Cancer ['kænsər] *n* (*sign*) Cancro
candidate ['kændɪdeɪt] *n* candidato(-a)
candle ['kændl] *n* candela; (*in church*) cero; **candlestick** *n* bugia; (*bigger, ornate*) candeliere *m*
candy ['kændɪ] *n* zucchero candito; (*us*) caramella; caramelle *fpl*; **candy bar** (*us*) *n* lungo biscotto, in genere ricoperto di cioccolata; **candyfloss** ['kændɪflɔs] *n* (*brit*) zucchero filato
cane [keɪn] *n* canna; (*for furniture*) bambù *m*; (*stick*) verga ▷ *vt* (*brit Scol*) punire a colpi di verga
canister ['kænɪstər] *n* scatola metallica
cannabis ['kænəbɪs] *n* canapa indiana
canned ['kænd] *adj* (*food*) in scatola
cannon ['kænən] (*pl* **cannon** *or* **cannons**) *n* (*gun*) cannone *m*
cannot ['kænɔt] = **can not**

canoe [kə'nuː] *n* canoa; **canoeing** *n* canottaggio
canon ['kænən] *n* (*clergyman*) canonico; (*standard*) canone *m*
can-opener ['kænəupnər] *n* apriscatole *m inv*
can't [kænt] = **can not**
canteen [kæn'tiːn] *n* mensa; (*brit: of cutlery*) portaposate *m inv*

> Be careful not to translate *canteen* by the Italian word *cantina*.

canter ['kæntər] *vi* andare al piccolo galoppo
canvas ['kænvəs] *n* tela
canvass ['kænvəs] *vi* (*Pol*): **to ~ for** raccogliere voti per ▷ *vt* fare un sondaggio di
canyon ['kænjən] *n* canyon *m inv*
cap [kæp] *n* (*hat*) berretto; (*of pen*) coperchio; (*of bottle, toy gun*) tappo; (*contraceptive*) diaframma *m* ▷ *vt* (*outdo*) superare; (*limit*) fissare un tetto (a)
capability [keɪpə'bɪlɪtɪ] *n* capacità *f inv*, abilità *f inv*
capable ['keɪpəbl] *adj* capace
capacity [kə'pæsɪtɪ] *n* capacità *f inv*; (*of lift etc*) capienza
cape [keɪp] *n* (*garment*) cappa; (*Geo*) capo
caper ['keɪpər] *n* (*Culin*) cappero; (*prank*) scherzetto
capital ['kæpɪtl] *n* (*also:* **~ city**) capitale *f*; (*money*) capitale *m*; (*also:* **~ letter**) (*lettera*) maiuscola; **capitalism** *n* capitalismo; **capitalist** *adj, n* capitalista *m/f*; **capital punishment** *n* pena capitale
Capitol ['kæpɪtl] *n* **the ~** il Campidoglio
Capricorn ['kæprɪkɔːn] *n* Capricorno
capsize [kæp'saɪz] *vt* capovolgere ▷ *vi* capovolgersi
capsule ['kæpsjuːl] *n* capsula
captain ['kæptɪn] *n* capitano
caption ['kæpʃən] *n* leggenda
captivity [kæp'tɪvɪtɪ] *n* cattività
capture ['kæptʃər] *vt* catturare; (*Comput*) registrare ▷ *n* cattura; (*data*) registrazione *f* or rilevazione *f* di dati
car [kɑːr] *n* (*Aut*) macchina, automobile *f*; (*Rail*) vagone *m*
carafe [kə'ræf] *n* caraffa
caramel ['kærəməl] *n* caramello
carat ['kærət] *n* carato; **18 ~ gold** oro a 18 carati
caravan ['kærəvæn] *n* (*brit*) roulotte *f inv*; (*of camels*) carovana; **caravan site** (*brit*) *n* campeggio per roulotte
carbohydrate [kɑːbəu'haɪdreɪt] *n* carboidrato
carbon ['kɑːbən] *n* carbonio; **carbon dioxide** [-daɪ'ɔksaɪd] *n* diossido di

carbonio; **carbon monoxide** [-mɔ'nɔksaɪd] *n* monossido di carbonio

car boot sale *n vedi nota nel riquadro*

◈ **CAR BOOT SALE**
◈
◈ Il **car boot sale** è un mercatino
◈ dell'usato molto popolare in Gran
◈ Bretagna. Normalmente ha luogo in
◈ un parcheggio o in un grande spiazzo,
◈ e la merce viene in genere esposta nei
◈ bagagliai, in inglese appunto "boots",
◈ aperti delle macchine.

carburettor [kɑː'bjuˈrɛtəʳ] (*US* **carburetor**) *n* carburatore *m*

card [kɑːd] *n* carta; (*visiting card etc*) biglietto; (*Christmas card etc*) cartolina; **cardboard** *n* cartone *m*; **card game** *n* gioco di carte

cardigan ['kɑːdɪɡən] *n* cardigan *m inv*

cardinal ['kɑːdɪnl] *adj* cardinale ▷ *n* cardinale *m*

cardphone ['kɑːdfəun] *n* telefono a scheda

care [kɛəʳ] *n* cura, attenzione *f*; (*worry*) preoccupazione *f* ▷ *vi* **to ~ about** curarsi di; (*thing, idea*) interessarsi di; **~ of** presso; **in sb's ~** alle cure di qn; **to take ~ (to do)** fare attenzione (a fare); **to take ~ of** curarsi di; (*bill, problem*) occuparsi di; **I don't ~** non me ne importa; **I couldn't ~ less** non m'interessa affatto; **care for** *vt fus* aver cura di; (*like*) volere bene a

career [kə'rɪəʳ] *n* carriera ▷ *vi* (*also:* **~ along**) andare di (gran) carriera

care: **carefree** ['kɛəfriː] *adj* sgombro(-a) di preoccupazioni; **careful** ['kɛəful] *adj* attento(-a); (*cautious*) cauto(-a); **(be) careful!** attenzione!; **carefully** *adv* con cura; cautamente; **caregiver** (*US*) *n* (*professional*) badante *m/f*; (*unpaid*) persona che si prende cura di un parente malato o anziano; **careless** ['kɛəlɪs] *adj* negligente; (*heedless*) spensierato(-a); **carelessness** *n* negligenza; mancanza di tatto; **carer** ['kɛərəʳ] *n* assistente *m/f* (*di persone malata o handicappata*); **caretaker** ['kɛəteɪkəʳ] *n* custode *m*

car-ferry ['kɑːfɛrɪ] *n* traghetto

cargo ['kɑːɡəu] (*pl* **cargoes**) *n* carico

car hire *n* autonoleggio

Caribbean [kærɪ'biːən] *adj* **the ~ Sea** il Mar dei Caraibi

caring ['kɛərɪŋ] *adj* (*person*) premuroso(-a); (*society, organization*) umanitario(-a)

carnation [kɑː'neɪʃən] *n* garofano

carnival ['kɑːnɪvəl] *n* (*public celebration*) carnevale *m*; (*US: funfair*) luna park *m inv*

carol ['kærəl] *n* **Christmas ~** canto di Natale

carousel [kærə'sɛl] (*US*) *n* giostra

car park (*BRIT*) *n* parcheggio

carpenter ['kɑːpɪntəʳ] *n* carpentiere *m*

carpet ['kɑːpɪt] *n* tappeto ▷ *vt* coprire con tappeto

car rental (*US*) *n* autonoleggio

carriage ['kærɪdʒ] *n* vettura; (*of goods*) trasporto; **carriageway** (*BRIT*) *n* (*part of road*) carreggiata

carrier ['kærɪəʳ] *n* (*of disease*) portatore(-trice); (*Comm*) impresa di trasporti; **carrier bag** (*BRIT*) *n* sacchetto

carrot ['kærət] *n* carota

carry ['kærɪ] *vt* (*person*) portare; (: *vehicle*) trasportare; (*involve: responsibilities etc*) comportare; (*Med*) essere portatore(-trice) di ▷ *vi* (*sound*) farsi sentire; **to be** *or* **get carried away** (*fig*) entusiasmarsi; **carry on** *vi* **to ~ on with sth/doing** continuare qc/a fare ▷ *vt* mandare avanti; **carry out** *vt* (*orders*) eseguire; (*investigation*) svolgere

cart [kɑːt] *n* carro ▷ *vt* (*inf*) trascinare

carton ['kɑːtən] *n* (*box*) scatola di cartone; (*of yogurt*) cartone *m*; (*of cigarettes*) stecca

cartoon [kɑː'tuːn] *n* (*Press*) disegno umoristico; (*comic strip*) fumetto; (*Cinema*) disegno animato

cartridge ['kɑːtrɪdʒ] *n* (*for gun, pen*) cartuccia; (*music tape*) cassetta

carve [kɑːv] *vt* (*meat*) trinciare; (*wood, stone*) intagliare; **carving** *n* (*in wood etc*) scultura

car wash *n* lavaggio auto

case [keɪs] *n* caso; (*Law*) causa, processo; (*box*) scatola; (*BRIT: also:* **suit~**) valigia; **in ~ of** in caso di; **in ~ he** caso mai lui; **in any ~** in ogni caso; **just in ~** in caso di bisogno

cash [kæʃ] *n* denaro; (*coins, notes*) denaro liquido ▷ *vt* incassare; **I haven't got any ~** non ho contanti; **to pay (in) ~** pagare in contanti; **~ on delivery** pagamento alla consegna; **cashback** *n* (*discount*) sconto; (*at supermarket etc*) anticipo di contanti ottenuto presso la cassa di un negozio tramite una carta di debito; **cash card** (*BRIT*) *n* tesserino di prelievo; **cash desk** (*BRIT*) *n* cassa; **cash dispenser** (*BRIT*) *n* sportello automatico

cashew [kæ'ʃuː] *n* (*also:* **~ nut**) anacardio

cashier [kæ'ʃɪəʳ] *n* cassiere(-a)

cashmere ['kæʃmɪəʳ] *n* cachemire *m*

cash point *n* sportello bancario automatico, Bancomat® *m inv*

cash register *n* registratore *m* di cassa

casino [kə'siːnəu] *n* casinò *m inv*

casket ['kɑːskɪt] *n* cofanetto; (*US: coffin*) bara

casserole ['kæsərəʊl] *n* casseruola; (*food*): **chicken ~** pollo in casseruola

cassette [kæ'sɛt] *n* cassetta; **cassette player** *n* riproduttore *m* a cassette

cast [kɑːst] (*pt, pp* **cast**) *vt* (*throw*) gettare; (*metal*) gettare, fondere; (*Theatre*): **to ~ sb as Hamlet** scegliere qn per la parte di Amleto ▷ *n* (*Theatre*) cast *m inv*; (*also: plaster ~*) ingessatura; **to ~ one's vote** votare, dare il voto; **cast off** *vi* (*Naut*) salpare; (*Knitting*) calare

castanets [kæstə'nɛts] *npl* castagnette *fpl*

caster sugar ['kɑːstə^r-] (*BRIT*) *n* zucchero semolato

cast-iron ['kɑːstaɪən] *adj* (*lit*) di ghisa; (*fig: case*) di ferro

castle ['kɑːsl] *n* castello

casual ['kæʒjul] *adj* (*chance*) casuale, fortuito(-a); (*: work etc*) avventizio(-a); (*unconcerned*) noncurante, indifferente; **~ wear** casual *m*

casualty ['kæʒjultɪ] *n* ferito(-a); (*dead*) morto(-a), vittima; (*Med: department*) pronto soccorso

cat [kæt] *n* gatto

catalogue ['kætəlɔg] (*US* **catalog**) *n* catalogo ▷ *vt* catalogare

catalytic converter [kætəlɪtɪk-] *n* marmitta catalitica, catalizzatore *m*

cataract ['kætərækt] *n* (*also Med*) cateratta

catarrh [kə'tɑː^r] *n* catarro

catastrophe [kə'tæstrəfɪ] *n* catastrofe *f*

catch [kætʃ] (*pt, pp* **caught**) *vt* prendere; (*ball*) afferrare; (*surprise: person*) sorprendere; (*attention*) attirare; (*comment, whisper*) cogliere; (*person*) raggiungere ▷ *vi* (*fire*) prendere ▷ *n* (*fish etc caught*) retata; (*of ball*) presa; (*trick*) inganno; (*Tech*) gancio; (*game*) catch *m inv*; **to ~ fire** prendere fuoco; **to ~ sight of** scorgere; **catch up** *vi* mettersi in pari ▷ *vt* (*also: ~ up with*) raggiungere; **catching** ['kætʃɪŋ] *adj* (*Med*) contagioso(-a)

category ['kætɪgərɪ] *n* categoria

cater ['keɪtə^r] *vi* **~ for** (*BRIT: needs*) provvedere a; (*: readers, consumers*) incontrare i gusti di; (*Comm: provide food*) provvedere alla ristorazione di

caterpillar ['kætəpɪlə^r] *n* bruco

cathedral [kə'θiːdrəl] *n* cattedrale *f*, duomo

Catholic ['kæθəlɪk] *adj, n* (*Rel*) cattolico(-a)

Catseye® [kæts'aɪ] (*BRIT*) *n* (*Aut*) catarifrangente *m*

cattle ['kætl] *npl* bestiame *m*, bestie *fpl*

catwalk ['kætwɔːk] *n* passerella

caught [kɔːt] *pt, pp of* **catch**

cauliflower ['kɔlɪflauə^r] *n* cavolfiore *m*

cause [kɔːz] *n* causa ▷ *vt* causare

caution ['kɔːʃən] *n* prudenza; (*warning*) avvertimento ▷ *vt* avvertire; ammonire; **cautious** ['kɔːʃəs] *adj* cauto(-a), prudente

cave [keɪv] *n* caverna, grotta; **cave in** *vi* (*roof etc*) crollare

caviar(e) ['kævɪɑː^r] *n* caviale *m*

cavity ['kævɪtɪ] *n* cavità *f inv*

cc *abbr* = **cubic centimetres**; **carbon copy**

CCTV *n abbr* (= *closed-circuit television*) televisione *f* a circuito chiuso

CD *n abbr* (*disc*) CD *m inv*; (*player*) lettore *m* CD *inv*; **CD player** *n* lettore *m* CD; **CD-ROM** [-rɔm] *n abbr* CD-ROM *m inv*

cease [siːs] *vt, vi* cessare; **ceasefire** *n* cessate il fuoco *m inv*

cedar ['siːdə^r] *n* cedro

ceilidh ['keɪlɪ] *n* festa con musiche e danze popolari scozzesi o irlandesi

ceiling ['siːlɪŋ] *n* soffitto; (*on wages etc*) tetto

celebrate ['sɛlɪbreɪt] *vt, vi* celebrare; **celebration** [-'breɪʃən] *n* celebrazione *f*

celebrity [sɪ'lɛbrɪtɪ] *n* celebrità *f inv*

celery ['sɛlərɪ] *n* sedano

cell [sɛl] *n* cella; (*of revolutionaries, Biol*) cellula; (*Elec*) elemento (di batteria)

cellar ['sɛlə^r] *n* sottosuolo; cantina

cello ['tʃɛləʊ] *n* violoncello

Cellophane® ['sɛləfeɪn] *n* cellophane® *m inv*

cellphone ['sɛləfeɪn] *n* cellulare *m*

Celsius ['sɛlsɪəs] *adj* Celsius *inv*

Celtic ['kɛltɪk, 'sɛltɪk] *adj* celtico(-a)

cement [sə'mɛnt] *n* cemento

cemetery ['sɛmɪtrɪ] *n* cimitero

censor ['sɛnsə^r] *n* censore *m* ▷ *vt* censurare; **censorship** *n* censura

census ['sɛnsəs] *n* censimento

cent [sɛnt] *n* (*US: coin*) centesimo (= 1:100 di un dollaro); (*unit of euro*) centesimo; *see also* **per**

centenary [sɛn'tiːnərɪ] *n* centenario

centennial [sɛn'tɛnɪəl] (*US*) *n* centenario

center ['sɛntə^r] (*US*) *n, vt* = **centre**

centi... ['sɛntɪ] *prefix*: **centigrade** ['sɛntɪgreɪd] *adj* centigrado(-a); **centimetre** ['sɛntɪmiːtə^r] (*US* **centimeter**) *n* centimetro; **centipede** ['sɛntɪpiːd] *n* centopiedi *m inv*

central ['sɛntrəl] *adj* centrale; **Central America** *n* America centrale; **central heating** *n* riscaldamento centrale; **central reservation** *n* (*BRIT Aut*) banchina *f* spartitraffico *inv*

centre ['sɛntə^r] (*US* **center**) *n* centro ▷ *vt* centrare; **centre-forward** *n* (*Sport*) centroavanti *m inv*; **centre-half** *n* (*Sport*) centromediano

century ['sɛntjurɪ] *n* secolo; **twentieth ~**

ventesimo secolo

CEO *n abbr* = **chief executive officer**
ceramic [sɪˈræmɪk] *adj* ceramico(-a)
cereal [ˈsiːrɪəl] *n* cereale *m*
ceremony [ˈsɛrɪmənɪ] *n* cerimonia; **to stand on ~** fare complimenti
certain [ˈsəːtən] *adj* certo(-a); **to make ~ of** assicurarsi di; **for ~** per certo, di sicuro; **certainly** *adv* certamente, certo; **certainty** *n* certezza
certificate [səˈtɪfɪkɪt] *n* certificato; diploma *m*
certify [ˈsəːtɪfaɪ] *vt* certificare; (*award diploma to*) conferire un diploma a; (*declare insane*) dichiarare pazzo(-a)
cf. *abbr* (= *compare*) cfr.
CFC *n* (= *chlorofluorocarbon*) CFC *m inv*
chain [tʃeɪn] *n* catena ▷ *vt* (*also*: **~ up**) incatenare; **chain-smoke** *vi* fumare una sigaretta dopo l'altra
chair [tʃɛəʳ] *n* sedia; (*armchair*) poltrona; (*of university*) cattedra; (*of meeting*) presidenza ▷ *vt* (*meeting*) presiedere; **chairlift** *n* seggiovia; **chairman** (*irreg*) *n* presidente *m*; **chairperson** *n* presidente(-essa); **chairwoman** (*irreg*) *n* presidentessa
chalet [ˈʃæleɪ] *n* chalet *m inv*
chalk [tʃɔːk] *n* gesso; **chalkboard** (*US*) *n* lavagna
challenge [ˈtʃælɪndʒ] *n* sfida ▷ *vt* sfidare; (*statement, right*) mettere in dubbio; **to ~ sb to do** sfidare qn a fare; **challenging** *adj* (*task*) impegnativo(-a); (*look*) di sfida
chamber [ˈtʃeɪmbəʳ] *n* camera; **chambermaid** *n* cameriera
champagne [ʃæmˈpeɪn] *n* champagne *m inv*
champion [ˈtʃæmpɪən] *n* campione(-essa); **championship** *n* campionato
chance [tʃɑːns] *n* caso; (*opportunity*) occasione *f*; (*likelihood*) possibilità *f inv* ▷ *vt* **to ~ it** rischiare, provarci ▷ *adj* fortuito(-a); **to take a ~** rischiare; **by ~** per caso
chancellor [ˈtʃɑːnsələʳ] *n* cancelliere *m*; **Chancellor of the Exchequer** [-ɪksˈtʃɛkəʳ] (*BRIT*) *n* Cancelliere dello Scacchiere
chandelier [ʃændəˈlɪəʳ] *n* lampadario
change [tʃeɪndʒ] *vt* cambiare; (*transform*): **to ~ sb into** trasformare qn in ▷ *vi* cambiare; (*change one's clothes*) cambiarsi; (*be transformed*): **to ~ into** trasformarsi in ▷ *n* cambiamento; (*of clothes*) cambio; (*money returned*) resto; (*coins*) spiccioli; **where can I ~ some money?** dove posso cambiare dei soldi?; **to ~ one's mind** cambiare idea; **keep the ~!** tenga pure il resto!; **sorry, I don't have any ~** mi dispiace, non ho spiccioli; **for a ~** tanto per

cambiare; **change over** *vi* (*from sth to sth*) passare; (*players etc*) scambiarsi (*di posto o di campo*) ▷ *vt* cambiare; **changeable** *adj* (*weather*) variabile; **change machine** *n* distributore automatico di monete; **changing room** *n* (*BRIT: in shop*) camerino; (: *Sport*) spogliatoio
channel [ˈtʃænl] *n* canale *m*; (*of river, sea*) alveo ▷ *vt* canalizzare; **Channel Tunnel** *n* **the Channel Tunnel** il tunnel sotto la Manica
chant [tʃɑːnt] *n* canto; salmodia ▷ *vt* cantare; salmodiare
chaos [ˈkeɪɔs] *n* caos *m*
chaotic [keɪˈɔtɪk] *adj* caotico(-a)
chap [tʃæp] (*BRIT: inf*) *n* (*man*) tipo
chapel [ˈtʃæpəl] *n* cappella
chapped [tʃæpt] *adj* (*skin, lips*) screpolato(-a)
chapter [ˈtʃæptəʳ] *n* capitolo
character [ˈkærɪktəʳ] *n* carattere *m*; (*in novel, film*) personaggio; **characteristic** [-ˈrɪstɪk] *adj* caratteristico(-a) ▷ *n* caratteristica; **characterize** [ˈkærɪktəraɪz] *vt* caratterizzare; (*describe*): **to characterize (as)** descrivere (come)
charcoal [ˈtʃɑːkəul] *n* carbone *m* di legna
charge [tʃɑːdʒ] *n* accusa; (*cost*) prezzo; (*responsibility*) responsabilità ▷ *vt* (*gun, battery, Mil: enemy*) caricare; (*customer*) fare pagare a; (*sum*) fare pagare; (*Law*): **to ~ sb (with)** accusare qn (di) ▷ *vi* (*gen with: up, along etc*) lanciarsi; **charge card** *n* carta *f* clienti *inv*; **charger** *n* (*also*: **battery charger**) caricabatterie *m inv*; (*old: warhorse*) destriero
charismatic [kærɪzˈmætɪk] *adj* carismatico(-a)
charity [ˈtʃærɪtɪ] *n* carità; (*organization*) opera pia; **charity shop** *n* (*BRIT*) negozi che vendono articoli di seconda mano e devolvono il ricavato in beneficenza
charm [tʃɑːm] *n* fascino; (*on bracelet*) ciondolo ▷ *vt* affascinare, incantare; **charming** *adj* affascinante
chart [tʃɑːt] *n* tabella; grafico; (*map*) carta nautica ▷ *vt* fare una carta nautica di; **~s** *npl* (*Mus*) hit parade *f*
charter [ˈtʃɑːtəʳ] *vt* (*plane*) noleggiare ▷ *n* (*document*) carta; **chartered accountant** [ˈtʃɑːtəd-] (*BRIT*) *n* ragioniere(-a) professionista; **charter flight** *n* volo *m* charter *inv*
chase [tʃeɪs] *vt* inseguire; (*also*: **~ away**) cacciare ▷ *n* caccia
chat [tʃæt] *vi* (*also*: **have a ~**) chiacchierare ▷ *n* chiacchierata; **chat up** *vt* (*BRIT inf: girl*) abbordare; **chat room** *n* (*Internet*) chat room *f inv*; **chat show** (*BRIT*) *n* talk

show *m inv*

chatter ['tʃætəʳ] *vi* (*person*) ciarlare; (*bird*) cinguettare; (*teeth*) battere ▷ *n* ciarle *fpl*; cinguettio

chauffeur ['ʃəufəʳ] *n* autista *m*

chauvinist ['ʃəuvɪnɪst] *n* (*male chauvinist*) maschilista *m*; (*nationalist*) sciovinista *m/f*

cheap [tʃi:p] *adj* economico(-a); (*joke*) grossolano(-a); (*poor quality*) di cattiva qualità ▷ *adv* a buon mercato; **can you recommend a ~ hotel/restaurant, please?** potrebbe indicarmi un albergo/ ristorante non troppo caro?; **cheap day return** *n* biglietto ridotto di andata e ritorno valido in giornata; **cheaply** *adv* a buon prezzo, a buon mercato

cheat [tʃi:t] *vi* imbrogliare; (*at school*) copiare ▷ *vt* ingannare ▷ *n* imbroglione *m*; **to ~ sb out of sth** defraudare qn di qc; **cheat on** *vt fus* (*husband, wife*) tradire

Chechnya [tʃɪtʃ'njɑ:] *n* Cecenia

check [tʃɛk] *vt* verificare; (*passport, ticket*) controllare; (*halt*) fermare; (*restrain*) contenere ▷ *n* verifica; (*control*) controllo; (*curb*) freno; (*us*: *bill*) conto; (*pattern: gen pl*) quadretti *mpl*; (*us*) = **cheque** ▷ *adj* (*pattern, cloth*) a quadretti; **check in** *vi* (*in hotel*) registrare; (*at airport*) presentarsi all'accettazione ▷ *vt* (*luggage*) depositare; **check off** *vt* segnare; **check out** *vi* (*in hotel*) saldare il conto; **check up** *vi* **to ~ up (on sth)** investigare (qc); **to ~ up on sb** informarsi sul conto di qn; **checkbook** (*us*) *n* = **chequebook**; **checked** *adj* a quadretti; **checkers** (*us*) *n* dama; **check-in** *n* (*also:* **check-in desk**: *at airport*) check-in *m inv*, accettazione *f* (*bagagli inv*); **checking account** (*us*) *n* conto corrente; **checklist** *n* lista di controllo; **checkmate** *n* scaccomatto; **checkout** *n* (*in supermarket*) cassa; **checkpoint** *n* posto di blocco; **checkroom** (*us*) *n* deposito *m* bagagli *inv*; **checkup** *n* (*Med*) controllo medico

cheddar ['tʃɛdəʳ] *n* formaggio duro di latte di mucca di colore bianco o arancione

cheek [tʃi:k] *n* guancia; (*impudence*) faccia tosta; **cheekbone** *n* zigomo; **cheeky** *adj* sfacciato(-a)

cheer [tʃɪəʳ] *vt* applaudire; (*gladden*) rallegrare ▷ *vi* applaudire ▷ *n* grido (di incoraggiamento); **cheer up** *vi* rallegrarsi, farsi animo ▷ *vt* rallegrare; **cheerful** *adj* allegro(-a)

cheerio ['tʃɪərɪ'əu] (*BRIT*) *excl* ciao!

cheerleader ['tʃɪəliːdəʳ] *n* cheerleader *f inv*

cheese [tʃi:z] *n* formaggio; **cheeseburger**

n cheeseburger *m inv*; **cheesecake** *n* specie di torta di ricotta, a volte con frutta

chef [ʃɛf] *n* capocuoco

chemical ['kɛmɪkəl] *adj* chimico(-a) ▷ *n* prodotto chimico

chemist ['kɛmɪst] *n* (*BRIT*: *pharmacist*) farmacista *m/f*; (*scientist*) chimico(-a); **chemistry** *n* chimica; **chemist's (shop)** (*BRIT*) *n* farmacia

cheque [tʃɛk] (*us* **check**) *n* assegno; **chequebook** *n* libretto degli assegni; **cheque card** *n* carta *f* assegni *inv*

cherry ['tʃɛrɪ] *n* ciliegia; (*also:* **~ tree**) ciliegio

chess [tʃɛs] *n* scacchi *mpl*

chest [tʃɛst] *n* petto; (*box*) cassa

chestnut ['tʃɛsnʌt] *n* castagna; (*also:* **~ tree**) castagno

chest of drawers *n* cassettone *m*

chew [tʃu:] *vt* masticare; **chewing gum** *n* chewing gum *m*

chic [ʃi:k] *adj* elegante

chick [tʃɪk] *n* pulcino; (*inf*) pollastrella

chicken ['tʃɪkɪn] *n* pollo; (*inf*: *coward*) coniglio; **chicken out** (*inf*) *vi* avere fifa; **chickenpox** *n* varicella

chickpea ['tʃɪkpi:] *n* cece *m*

chief [tʃi:f] *n* capo ▷ *adj* principale; **chief executive (officer)** *n* direttore *m* generale; **chiefly** *adv* per lo più, soprattutto

child [tʃaɪld] (*pl* **children**) *n* bambino(-a); **child abuse** *n* molestie *fpl* a minori; **child benefit** *n* (*BRIT*) ≈ assegni *mpl* familiari; **childbirth** *n* parto; **child-care** *n* il badare ai bambini; **childhood** *n* infanzia; **childish** *adj* puerile; **child minder** [-'maɪndəʳ] (*BRIT*) *n* bambinaia; **children** ['tʃɪldrən] *npl of* **child**

Chile ['tʃɪlɪ] *n* Cile *m*

Chilean ['tʃɪlɪən] *adj*, *n* cileno(-a)

chill [tʃɪl] *n* freddo; (*Med*) infreddatura ▷ *vt* raffreddare; **chill out** (*esp us*) *vi* (*inf*) darsi una calmata

chil(l)i ['tʃɪlɪ] *n* peperoncino

chilly ['tʃɪlɪ] *adj* freddo(-a), fresco(-a); **to feel ~** sentirsi infreddolito(-a)

chimney ['tʃɪmnɪ] *n* camino

chimpanzee [tʃɪmpæn'zi:] *n* scimpanzé *m inv*

chin [tʃɪn] *n* mento

China ['tʃaɪnə] *n* Cina

china ['tʃaɪnə] *n* porcellana

Chinese [tʃaɪ'ni:z] *adj* cinese ▷ *n inv* cinese *m/f*; (*Ling*) cinese *m*

chip [tʃɪp] *n* (*gen pl: Culin*) patatina fritta; (: *us*: *also:* **potato ~**) patatina; (*of wood, glass, stone*) scheggia; (*also:* **micro~**) chip *m inv* ▷ *vt* (*cup, plate*) scheggiare; **chip**

shop n (BRIT) vedi nota nel riquadro

● CHIP SHOP
●
● I **chip shops**, anche chiamati "fish
● and chip shops", sono friggitorie che
● vendono principalmente filetti di pesce
● impanati e patatine fritte.

chiropodist [kɪ'rɔpədɪst] (BRIT) n pedicure
m/f inv

chisel ['tʃɪzl] n cesello

chives [tʃaɪvz] npl erba cipollina

chlorine ['klɔ:ri:n] n cloro

choc-ice ['tʃɔkaɪs] n (BRIT) gelato ricoperto
al cioccolato

chocolate ['tʃɔklɪt] ▷ n (substance)
cioccolato, cioccolata; (drink) cioccolata;
(a sweet) cioccolatino

choice [tʃɔɪs] n scelta ▷ adj scelto(-a)

choir ['kwaɪə'] n coro

choke [tʃəʊk] vi soffocare ▷ vt soffocare;
(block): **to be ~d with** essere intasato(-a) di
▷ n (Aut) valvola dell'aria

cholesterol [kə'lestərɔl] n colesterolo

choose [tʃu:z] (pt **chose,**, pp **chosen**)
vt scegliere; **to ~ to do** decidere di fare;
preferire fare

chop [tʃɔp] vt (wood) spaccare; (Culin:
also: ~ **up**) tritare ▷ n (Culin) costoletta;
chop down vt (tree) abbattere; **chop off**
vt tagliare; **chopsticks** ['tʃɔpstɪks] npl
bastoncini mpl cinesi

chord [kɔ:d] n (Mus) accordo

chore [tʃɔ:'] n faccenda; **household ~s**
faccende fpl domestiche

chorus ['kɔ:rəs] n coro; (repeated part of
song: also fig) ritornello

chose [tʃəʊz] pt of **choose**

chosen ['tʃəʊzn] pp of **choose**

Christ [kraɪst] n Cristo

christen ['krɪsn] vt battezzare;
christening n battesimo

Christian ['krɪstɪən] adj, n cristiano(-a);
Christianity [-'ænɪtɪ] n cristianesimo;
Christian name n nome m (di battesimo)

Christmas ['krɪsməs] n Natale m; **Merry
~!** Buon Natale!; **Christmas card** n
cartolina di Natale; **Christmas carol**
n canto natalizio; **Christmas Day** n il
giorno di Natale; **Christmas Eve** n la
vigilia di Natale; **Christmas pudding** n
(esp BRIT) specie di budino con frutta secca,
spezie e brandy; **Christmas tree** n albero
di Natale

chrome [krəʊm] n cromo

chronic ['krɔnɪk] adj cronico(-a)

chrysanthemum [krɪ'sænθəməm] n
crisantemo

chubby ['tʃʌbɪ] adj paffuto(-a)

chuck [tʃʌk] (inf) vt buttare, gettare; (BRIT:
also: ~ **up**) piantare; **chuck out** vt buttar
fuori

chuckle ['tʃʌkl] vi ridere sommessamente

chum [tʃʌm] n compagno(-a)

chunk [tʃʌŋk] n pezzo

church [tʃə:tʃ] n chiesa; **churchyard** n
sagrato

churn [tʃə:n] n (for butter) zangola; (for milk)
bidone m

chute [ʃu:t] n (also: **rubbish** ~) canale m di
scarico; (BRIT: children's slide) scivolo

chutney ['tʃʌtnɪ] n salsa piccante (di frutta,
zucchero e spezie)

CIA (US) n abbr (= Central Intelligence Agency)
CIA f

CID (BRIT) n abbr (= Criminal Investigation
Department) ≈ polizia giudiziaria

cider ['saɪdə'] n sidro

cigar [sɪ'gɑ:'] n sigaro

cigarette [sɪgə'rɛt] n sigaretta; **cigarette
lighter** n accendino

cinema ['sɪnəmə] n cinema m inv

cinnamon ['sɪnəmən] n cannella

circle ['sə:kl] n cerchio; (of friends etc)
circolo; (in cinema) galleria ▷ vi girare in
circolo ▷ vt (surround) circondare; (move
round) girare intorno a

circuit ['sə:kɪt] n circuito

circular ['sə:kjulə'] adj circolare ▷ n
circolare f

circulate ['sə:kjuleɪt] vi circolare ▷ vt
far circolare; **circulation** [-'leɪʃən] n
circolazione f; (of newspaper) tiratura

circumstances ['sə:kəmstənsɪz] npl
circostanze fpl; (financial condition)
condizioni fpl finanziarie

circus ['sə:kəs] n circo

cite [saɪt] vt citare

citizen ['sɪtɪzn] n (of country) cittadino(-a);
(of town) abitante m/f; **citizenship** n
cittadinanza

citrus fruits ['sɪtrəs-] npl agrumi mpl

city ['sɪtɪ] n città f inv; **the C~** la Città di
Londra (centro commerciale); **city centre**
n centro della città; **city technology
college** n (BRIT) istituto tecnico superiore
(finanziato dall'industria)

civic ['sɪvɪk] adj civico(-a)

civil ['sɪvɪl] adj civile; **civilian** [sɪ'vɪlɪən]
adj, n borghese m/f

civilization [sɪvɪlaɪ'zeɪʃən] n civiltà f inv

civilized ['sɪvɪlaɪzd] adj civilizzato(-a); (fig)
cortese

civil: civil law n codice m, civile; (study)
diritto civile; **civil rights** npl diritti mpl
civili; **civil servant** n impiegato(-a)
statale; **Civil Service** n amministrazione f

statale; **civil war** n guerra civile

CJD abbr (= Creutzfeld Jacob disease) malattia di Creutzfeldt-Jacob

claim [kleɪm] vt (assert): **to ~ (that)/to be** sostenere (che)/di essere; (credit, rights etc) rivendicare; (damages) richiedere ▷ vi (for insurance) fare una domanda d'indennizzo ▷ n pretesa; rivendicazione f; richiesta; **claim form** n (gen) modulo di richiesta; (for expenses) modulo di rimborso spese

clam [klæm] n vongola

clamp [klæmp] n pinza; morsa ▷ vt stringere con una morsa; (Aut: wheel) applicare i ceppi bloccaruote a

clan [klæn] n clan m inv

clap [klæp] vi applaudire

claret ['klærət] n vino di Bordeaux

clarify ['klærɪfaɪ] vt chiarificare, chiarire

clarinet [klærɪ'nɛt] n clarinetto

clarity ['klærɪtɪ] n clarità

clash [klæʃ] n frastuono; (fig) scontro ▷ vi scontrarsi; cozzare

clasp [klɑːsp] n (hold) stretta; (of necklace, bag) fermaglio, fibbia ▷ vt stringere

class [klɑːs] n classe f ▷ vt classificare

classic ['klæsɪk] adj classico(-a) ▷ n classico; **classical** adj classico(-a)

classification [klæsɪfɪ'keɪʃən] n classificazione f

classify ['klæsɪfaɪ] vt classificare

classmate ['klɑːsmeɪt] n compagno(-a) di classe

classroom ['klɑːsrum] n aula

classy ['klɑːsɪ] adj (inf) chic inv, elegante

clatter ['klætəʳ] n tintinnio; scalpitio ▷ vi tintinnare; scalpitare

clause [klɔːz] n clausola; (Ling) proposizione f

claustrophobic [klɔːstrə'fəubɪk] adj claustrofobico(-a)

claw [klɔː] n (of bird of prey) artiglio; (of lobster) pinza

clay [kleɪ] n argilla

clean [kliːn] adj pulito(-a); (clear, smooth) liscio(-a) ▷ vt pulire; **clean up** vt (also fig) ripulire; **cleaner** n (person) donna delle pulizie; **cleaner's** n (also: **dry cleaner's**) tintoria; **cleaning** n pulizia

cleanser ['klɛnzəʳ] n detergente m

clear [klɪəʳ] adj chiaro(-a); (glass etc) trasparente; (road, way) libero(-a); (conscience) pulito(-a) ▷ vt sgombrare; liberare; (table) sparecchiare; (cheque) fare la compensazione di; (Law: suspect) discolpare; (obstacle) superare ▷ vi (weather) rasserenarsi; (fog) andarsene ▷ adv **~ of** distante da; **clear away** vt (things, clothes etc) mettere a posto; **to ~ away the dishes** sparecchiare la tavola;

clear up vt mettere in ordine; (mystery) risolvere; **clearance** n (removal) sgombro; (permission) autorizzazione f, permesso; **clear-cut** adj ben delineato(-a), distinto(-a); **clearing** n radura; **clearly** adv chiaramente; **clearway** (BRIT) n strada con divieto di sosta

clench [klɛntʃ] vt stringere

clergy ['klɜːdʒɪ] n clero

clerk [klɑːk, (US) klɜːrk] n (BRIT) impiegato(-a); (US) commesso(-a)

clever ['klɛvəʳ] adj (mentally) intelligente; (deft, skilful) abile; (device, arrangement) ingegnoso(-a)

cliché ['kliːʃeɪ] n cliché m inv

click [klɪk] vi scattare ▷ vt (heels etc) battere; (tongue) far schioccare

client ['klaɪənt] n cliente m/f

cliff [klɪf] n scogliera scoscesa, rupe f

climate ['klaɪmɪt] n clima m

climax ['klaɪmæks] n culmine m; (sexual) orgasmo

climb [klaɪm] vi salire; (clamber) arrampicarsi ▷ vt salire; (Climbing) scalare ▷ n salita; arrampicata; scalata; **climb down** vi scendere; (BRIT fig) far marcia indietro; **climber** n rocciatore(-trice); alpinista m/f; **climbing** n alpinismo

clinch [klɪntʃ] vt (deal) concludere

cling [klɪŋ] (pt, pp clung) vi **to ~ (to)** aggrapparsi (a); (of clothes) aderire strettamente (a)

Clingfilm® ['klɪŋfɪlm] n pellicola trasparente (per alimenti)

clinic ['klɪnɪk] n clinica

clip [klɪp] n (for hair) forcina; (also: **paper ~**) graffetta; (TV, Cinema) sequenza ▷ vt attaccare insieme; (hair, nails) tagliare; (hedge) tosare; **clipping** n (from newspaper) ritaglio

cloak [kləuk] n mantello ▷ vt avvolgere; **cloakroom** n (for coats etc) guardaroba m inv; (BRIT: W.C.) gabinetti mpl

clock [klɔk] n orologio; **clock in or on** vi timbrare il cartellino (all'entrata); **clock off or out** vi timbrare il cartellino (all'uscita); **clockwise** adv in senso orario; **clockwork** n movimento or meccanismo a orologeria ▷ adj a molla

clog [klɔg] n zoccolo ▷ vt intasare ▷ vi (also: **~ up**) intasarsi, bloccarsi

clone [kləun] n clone m

close¹ [kləus] adj **~ (to)** vicino(-a) (a); (watch, link, relative) stretto(-a); (examination) attento(-a); (contest) combattuto(-a); (weather) afoso(-a) ▷ adv vicino, dappresso; **~ to** vicino a; **~ by, ~ at hand** a portata di mano; **a ~ friend** un amico intimo; **to have a ~ shave** (fig) scamparla bella

close² [kləuz] vt chiudere ▷ vi (shop etc) chiudere; (lid, door etc) chiudersi; (end) finire ▷ n (end) fine f; **what time do you ~?** a che ora chiudete?; **close down** vi cessare (definitivamente); **closed** adj chiuso(-a)

closely ['kləuslı] adv (examine, watch) da vicino; (related) strettamente

closet ['klɔzɪt] n (cupboard) armadio

close-up ['kləusʌp] n primo piano

closing time n orario di chiusura

closure ['kləuʒəʳ] n chiusura

clot [klɔt] n (also: **blood ~**) coagulo; (inf: idiot) scemo(-a) ▷ vi coagularsi

cloth [klɔθ] n (material) tessuto, stoffa; (rag) strofinaccio

clothes [kləuðz] npl abiti mpl, vestiti mpl; **clothes line** n corda (per stendere il bucato); **clothes peg** (US **clothes pin**) n molletta

clothing ['kləuðɪŋ] n = **clothes**

cloud [klaud] n nuvola; **cloud over** vi rannuvolarsi; (fig) offuscarsi; **cloudy** adj nuvoloso(-a); (liquid) torbido(-a)

clove [kləuv] n chiodo di garofano; **clove of garlic** n spicchio d'aglio

clown [klaun] n pagliaccio ▷ vi (also: **~ about, ~ around**) fare il pagliaccio

club [klʌb] n (society) club m inv, circolo; (weapon, Golf) mazza ▷ vt bastonare ▷ vi **to ~ together** associarsi; **~s** npl (Cards) fiori mpl; **club class** n (Aviat) classe f club inv

clue [kluː] n indizio; (in crosswords) definizione f; **I haven't a ~** non ho la minima idea

clump [klʌmp] n (of flowers, trees) gruppo; (of grass) ciuffo

clumsy ['klʌmzɪ] adj goffo(-a)

clung [klʌŋ] pt, pp of **cling**

cluster ['klʌstəʳ] n gruppo ▷ vi raggrupparsi

clutch [klʌtʃ] n (grip, grasp) presa, stretta; (Aut) frizione f ▷ vt afferrare, stringere forte

cm abbr (= centimetre) cm

Co. abbr = **county**; **company**

c/o abbr (= care of) presso

coach [kəutʃ] n (bus) pullman m inv; (horse-drawn, of train) carrozza; (Sport) allenatore(-trice); (tutor) chi dà ripetizioni ▷ vt allenare; dare ripetizioni a; **coach station** (BRIT) n stazione f delle corriere; **coach trip** n viaggio in pullman

coal [kəul] n carbone m

coalition [kəuə'lɪʃən] n coalizione f

coarse [kɔːs] adj (salt, sand etc) grosso(-a); (cloth, person) rozzo(-a)

coast [kəust] n costa ▷ vi (with cycle etc) scendere a ruota libera; **coastal** adj costiero(-a); **coastguard** n guardia costiera; **coastline** n linea costiera

coat [kəut] n cappotto; (of animal) pelo; (of paint) mano f ▷ vt coprire; **coat hanger** n attaccapanni m inv; **coating** n rivestimento

coax [kəuks] vt indurre (con moine)

cob [kɔb] n see **corn**

cobbled ['kɔbld] adj **~ street** strada pavimentata a ciottoli

cobweb ['kɔbwɛb] n ragnatela

cocaine [kə'keɪn] n cocaina

cock [kɔk] n (rooster) gallo; (male bird) maschio ▷ vt (gun) armare; **cockerel** n galletto

cockney ['kɔknı] n cockney m/f inv (abitante dei quartieri popolari dell'East End di Londra)

cockpit ['kɔkpɪt] n abitacolo

cockroach ['kɔkrəutʃ] n blatta

cocktail ['kɔkteɪl] n cocktail m inv

cocoa ['kəukəu] n cacao

coconut ['kəukənʌt] n noce f di cocco

cod [kɔd] n merluzzo

C.O.D. abbr = **cash on delivery**

code [kəud] n codice m

coeducational ['kəuɛdju'keɪʃənl] adj misto(-a)

coffee ['kɔfɪ] n caffè m inv; **coffee bar** (BRIT) n caffè m inv; **coffee bean** n grano or chicco di caffè; **coffee break** n pausa per il caffè; **coffee maker** n bollitore m per il caffè; **coffeepot** n caffettiera; **coffee shop** n ≈ caffè m inv; **coffee table** n tavolino

coffin ['kɔfɪn] n bara

cog [kɔg] n dente m

cognac ['kɔnjæk] n cognac m inv

coherent [kəu'hɪərənt] adj coerente

coil [kɔɪl] n rotolo; (Elec) bobina; (contraceptive) spirale f ▷ vt avvolgere

coin [kɔɪn] n moneta ▷ vt (word) coniare

coincide [kəuɪn'saɪd] vi coincidere; **coincidence** [kəu'ɪnsɪdəns] n combinazione f

Coke® [kəuk] n coca

coke [kəuk] n coke m

colander ['kɔləndəʳ] n colino

cold [kəuld] adj freddo(-a) ▷ n freddo; (Med) raffreddore m; **it's ~** fa freddo; **to be ~** (person) aver freddo; (object) essere freddo(-a); **to catch ~** prendere freddo; **to catch a ~** prendere un raffreddore; **in ~ blood** a sangue freddo; **cold sore** n erpete m

coleslaw ['kəulslɔː] n insalata di cavolo bianco

colic ['kɔlɪk] n colica

collaborate [kəˈlæbəreɪt] vi collaborare
collapse [kəˈlæps] vi crollare ▷ n crollo; (Med) collasso
collar [ˈkɒləʳ] n (of coat, shirt) colletto; (of dog, cat) collare m; **collarbone** n clavicola
colleague [ˈkɒliːg] n collega m/f
collect [kəˈlɛkt] vt (gen) raccogliere; (as a hobby) fare collezione di; (BRIT: call and pick up) prendere; (money owed, pension) riscuotere; (donations, subscriptions) fare una colletta di ▷ vi adunarsi, riunirsi; ammucchiarsi; **to call ~** (US Tel) fare una chiamata a carico del destinatario; **collection** [kəˈlɛkʃən] n raccolta; collezione f; (for money) colletta; **collective** adj collettivo(-a) ▷ n collettivo; **collector** [kəˈlɛktəʳ] n collezionista m/f
college [ˈkɒlɪdʒ] n college m inv; (of technology etc) istituto superiore
collide [kəˈlaɪd] vi **to ~ with** scontrarsi (con)
collision [kəˈlɪʒən] n collisione f, scontro
cologne [kəˈləʊn] n (also: **eau de ~**) acqua di colonia
Colombia [kəˈlɒmbɪə] n Colombia; **Colombian** adj, n colombiano(-a)
colon [ˈkəʊlən] n (sign) due punti mpl; (Med) colon m inv
colonel [ˈkɜːnl] n colonnello
colonial [kəˈləʊnɪəl] adj coloniale
colony [ˈkɒlənɪ] n colonia
colour etc [ˈkʌləʳ] (US color) n colore m ▷ vt colorare; (tint, dye) tingere; (fig: affect) influenzare ▷ vi (blush) arrossire; **colour in** vt colorare; **colour-blind** adj daltonico(-a); **coloured** adj (photo) a colori; (person) di colore; **colour film** n (for camera) pellicola a colori; **colourful** adj pieno(-a) di colore, a vivaci colori; (personality) colorato(-a); **colouring** n (substance) colorante m; (complexion) colorito; **colour television** n televisione f a colori
column [ˈkɒləm] n colonna
coma [ˈkəʊmə] n coma m inv
comb [kəʊm] n pettine m ▷ vt (hair) pettinare; (area) battere a tappeto
combat [ˈkɒmbæt] n combattimento ▷ vt combattere, lottare contro
combination [kɒmbɪˈneɪʃən] n combinazione f
combine [vb kəmˈbaɪn, n ˈkɒmbaɪn] vt **to ~ (with)** combinare (con); (one quality with another) unire (a) ▷ vi unirsi; (Chem) combinarsi ▷ n (Econ) associazione f
come [kʌm] (pt came, pp come) vi venire; arrivare; **to ~ to** (decision etc) raggiungere; **I've ~ to like him** ha cominciato a piacermi; **to ~ undone** slacciarsi; **to ~**
loose allentarsi; **come across** vt fus trovare per caso; **come along** vi (pupil, work) fare progressi; **~ along!** andiamo!, forza!; **come back** vi ritornare; **come down** vi scendere; (prices) calare; (buildings) essere demolito(-a); **come from** vt fus venire da; provenire da; **come in** vi entrare; **come off** vi (button) staccarsi; (stain) andar via; (attempt) riuscire; **come on** vi (pupil, work, project) fare progressi; (lights) accendersi; (electricity) entrare in funzione; **~ on!** avanti!, andiamo!, forza!; **come out** vi uscire; (stain) andare via; **come round** vi (after faint, operation) riprendere conoscenza, rinvenire; **come to** vi rinvenire; **come up** vi (sun) salire; (problem) sorgere; (event) essere in arrivo; (in conversation) saltar fuori; **come up with** vt fus **he came up with an idea** venne fuori con un'idea
comeback [ˈkʌmbæk] n (Theatre etc) ritorno
comedian [kəˈmiːdɪən] n comico
comedy [ˈkɒmɪdɪ] n commedia
comet [ˈkɒmɪt] n cometa
comfort [ˈkʌmfət] n comodità f inv, benessere m; (relief) consolazione f, conforto ▷ vt consolare, confortare; **comfortable** adj comodo(-a); (financially) agiato(-a); **comfort station** (US) n gabinetti mpl
comic [ˈkɒmɪk] adj (also: **~al**) comico(-a) ▷ n comico; (BRIT: magazine) giornaletto; **comic book** (US) n giornalino (a fumetti); **comic strip** n fumetto
comma [ˈkɒmə] n virgola
command [kəˈmɑːnd] n ordine m, comando; (Mil: authority) comando; (mastery) padronanza ▷ vt comandare; **to ~ sb to do** ordinare a qn di fare; **commander** n capo; (Mil) comandante m
commemorate [kəˈmɛməreɪt] vt commemorare
commence [kəˈmɛns] vt, vi cominciare; **commencement** (US) n (Univ) cerimonia di consegna dei diplomi
commend [kəˈmɛnd] vt lodare; raccomandare
comment [ˈkɒmɛnt] n commento ▷ vi **to ~ (on)** fare commenti (su); **commentary** [ˈkɒməntərɪ] n commentario; (Sport) radiocronaca; telecronaca; **commentator** [ˈkɒmənteɪtəʳ] n commentatore(-trice); radiocronista m/f; telecronista m/f
commerce [ˈkɒmɜːs] n commercio
commercial [kəˈmɜːʃəl] adj commerciale ▷ n (TV, Radio: advertisement) pubblicità f inv; **commercial break** n intervallo pubblicitario

commission [kə'mɪʃən] n commissione
f ▷ vt (work of art) commissionare; **out
of ~** (Naut) in disarmo; **commissioner** n
(Police) questore m

commit [kə'mɪt] vt (act) commettere;
(to sb's care) affidare; **to ~ o.s. to do**
impegnarsi (a fare); **to ~ suicide** suicidarsi;
commitment n impegno; promessa

committee [kə'mɪtɪ] n comitato

commodity [kə'mɔdɪtɪ] n prodotto,
articolo

common ['kɔmən] adj comune; (pej)
volgare; (usual) normale ▷ n terreno
comune; **the C~s** (BRIT) ▷ npl la Camera
dei Comuni; **in ~** in comune; **commonly**
adv comunemente, usualmente;
commonplace adj banale, ordinario(-a);
Commons npl (BRIT Pol): **the (House
of) Commons** la Camera dei Comuni;
common sense n buon senso;
Commonwealth n the **Commonwealth**
il Commonwealth

🔹 **COMMONWEALTH**
🔹
🔹 Il **Commonwealth** è un'associazione
🔹 di stati sovrani indipendenti e di
🔹 alcuni territori annessi che facevano
🔹 parte dell'antico Impero Britannico.
🔹 Nel 1931 questi assunsero il nome
🔹 di "Commonwealth of Nations",
🔹 denominazione successivamente
🔹 semplificata in "Commonwealth".
🔹 Attualmente gli stati del
🔹 "Commonwealth" riconoscono ancora il
🔹 proprio capo di stato.

communal ['kɔmjuːnl] adj (for common
use) pubblico(-a)

commune [n 'kɔmjuːn, vb kə'mjuːn] n
(group) comune f ▷ vi **to ~ with** mettersi in
comunione con

communicate [kə'mjuːnɪkeɪt] vt
comunicare, trasmettere ▷ vi **to ~ with**
comunicare (con)

communication [kəmjuːnɪ'keɪʃən] n
comunicazione f

communion [kə'mjuːnɪən] n (also: **Holy
C~**) comunione f

communism ['kɔmjunɪzəm] n
comunismo; **communist** adj, n
comunista m/f

community [kə'mjuːnɪtɪ] n comunità f
inv; **community centre** (US **community
center**) n circolo ricreativo; **community
service** n (BRIT) ≈ lavoro sostitutivo

commute [kə'mjuːt] vi fare il pendolare
▷ vt (Law) commutare; **commuter** n
pendolare m/f

compact [adj kəm'pækt, n 'kɔmpækt]
adj compatto(-a) ▷ n (also: **powder
~**) portacipria m inv; **compact disc** n
compact disc m inv; **compact disc player**
n lettore m CD inv

companion [kəm'pænɪən] n
compagno(-a)

company ['kʌmpənɪ] n (also Comm,
Mil, Theatre) compagnia; **to keep sb ~**
tenere compagnia a qn; **company car**
n macchina (di proprietà) della ditta;
company director n amministratore m,
consigliere m di amministrazione

comparable ['kɔmpərəbl] adj simile

comparative [kəm'pærətɪv] adj
relativo(-a); (adjective etc) comparativo(-a);
comparatively adv relativamente

compare [kəm'pɛə^r] vt **to ~ sth/sb
with/to** confrontare qc/qn con/a ▷ vi
to ~ (with) reggere il confronto (con);
comparison [-'pærɪsn] n confronto; **in
comparison (with)** in confronto (a)

compartment [kəm'pɑːtmənt] n
compartimento; (Rail) scompartimento; **a
non-smoking ~** uno scompartimento per
non-fumatori

compass ['kʌmpəs] n bussola; **~es** npl
(Math) compasso

compassion [kəm'pæʃən] n compassione
f

compatible [kəm'pætɪbl] adj compatibile

compel [kəm'pɛl] vt costringere,
obbligare; **compelling** adj (fig: argument)
irresistibile

compensate ['kɔmpənseɪt] vt risarcire
▷ vi **to ~ for** compensare; **compensation**
[-'seɪʃən] n compensazione f; (money)
risarcimento

compete [kəm'piːt] vi (take part)
concorrere; (vie): **to ~ with** fare
concorrenza (a)

competent ['kɔmpɪtənt] adj competente

competition [kɔmpɪ'tɪʃən] n gara;
concorso; (Econ) concorrenza

competitive [kəm'pɛtɪtɪv] adj (Econ)
concorrenziale; (sport) agonistico(-a);
(person) che ha spirito di competizione; che
ha spirito agonistico

competitor [kəm'pɛtɪtə^r] n concorrente
m/f

complacent [kəm'pleɪsnt] adj
compiaciuto(-a) di sé

complain [kəm'pleɪn] vi lagnarsi,
lamentarsi; **complaint** n lamento; (in
shop etc) reclamo; (Med) malattia

complement [n 'kɔmplɪmənt, vb
'kɔmplɪmənt] n complemento; (especially
of ship's crew etc) effettivo ▷ vt (enhance)
accompagnarsi bene a; **complementary**

[kɔmplɪˈmɛntərɪ] adj complementare
complete [kəmˈpliːt] adj completo(-a)
▷ vt completare; (a form) riempire;
completely adv completamente;
completion n completamento
complex [ˈkɔmplɛks] adj complesso(-a)
▷ n (Psych, of buildings etc) complesso
complexion [kəmˈplɛkʃən] n (of face)
carnagione f
compliance [kəmˈplaɪəns] n
acquiescenza; **in ~ with** (orders, wishes etc)
in conformità con
complicate [ˈkɔmplɪkeɪt] vt complicare;
complicated adj complicato(-a);
complication [-ˈkeɪʃən] n complicazione f
compliment [n ˈkɔmplɪmənt, vb
ˈkɔmplɪmɛnt] n complimento ▷ vt fare
un complimento a; **complimentary**
[-ˈmɛntərɪ] adj complimentoso(-a),
elogiativo(-a); (free) in omaggio
comply [kəmˈplaɪ] vi **to ~ with** assentire
a; conformarsi a
component [kəmˈpəunənt] adj
componente ▷ n componente m
compose [kəmˈpəuz] vt (form): **to be ~d
of** essere composto di; (music, poem etc)
comporre; **to ~ o.s.** ricomporsi; **composer**
n (Mus) compositore(-trice); **composition**
[kɔmpəˈzɪʃən] n composizione f
composure [kəmˈpəuʒəʳ] n calma
compound [ˈkɔmpaund] n (Chem, Ling)
composto; (enclosure) recinto ▷ adj
composto(-a)
comprehension [kɔmprɪˈhɛnʃən] n
comprensione f
comprehensive [kɔmprɪˈhɛnsɪv] adj
completo(-a); **comprehensive (school)**
(BRIT) n scuola secondaria aperta a tutti

> Be careful not to translate
> *comprehensive* by the Italian word
> *comprensivo*.

compress [vb kəmˈprɛs, n ˈkɔmprɛs] vt
comprimere ▷ n (Med) compressa
comprise [kəmˈpraɪz] vt (also: **be ~d**)
comprendere
compromise [ˈkɔmprəmaɪz] n
compromesso ▷ vt compromettere ▷ vi
venire a un compromesso
compulsive [kəmˈpʌlsɪv] adj (liar, gambler)
che non riesce a controllarsi; (viewing,
reading) cui non si può fare a meno
compulsory [kəmˈpʌlsərɪ] adj
obbligatorio(-a)
computer [kəmˈpjuːtəʳ] n computer
m inv, elaboratore m elettronico;
computer game n gioco per computer;
computer-generated adj realizzato(-a)
al computer; **computerize** vt
computerizzare; **computer programmer**

n programmatore(-trice); **computer
programming** n programmazione
f di computer; **computer science** n
informatica; **computer studies** npl
informatica; **computing** n informatica
con [kɔn] (inf) vt truffare ▷ n truffa
conceal [kənˈsiːl] vt nascondere
concede [kənˈsiːd] vt ammettere
conceited [kənˈsiːtɪd] adj
presuntuoso(-a), vanitoso(-a)
conceive [kənˈsiːv] vt concepire ▷ vi
concepire un bambino
concentrate [ˈkɔnsəntreɪt] vi
concentrarsi ▷ vt concentrare
concentration [kɔnsənˈtreɪʃən] n
concentrazione f
concept [ˈkɔnsɛpt] n concetto
concern [kənˈsəːn] n affare m; (Comm)
azienda, ditta; (anxiety) preoccupazione
f ▷ vt riguardare; **to be ~ed (about)**
preoccuparsi (di); **concerning** prep
riguardo a, circa
concert [ˈkɔnsət] n concerto; **concert
hall** n sala da concerti
concerto [kənˈtʃəːtəu] n concerto
concession [kənˈsɛʃən] n concessione f
concise [kənˈsaɪs] adj conciso(-a)
conclude [kənˈkluːd] vt concludere;
conclusion [-ˈkluːʒən] n conclusione f
concrete [ˈkɔŋkriːt] n calcestruzzo ▷ adj
concreto(-a), di calcestruzzo
concussion [kənˈkʌʃən] n commozione
f cerebrale
condemn [kənˈdɛm] vt condannare;
(building) dichiarare pericoloso(-a)
condensation [kɔndɛnˈseɪʃən] n
condensazione f
condense [kənˈdɛns] vi condensarsi ▷ vt
condensare
condition [kənˈdɪʃən] n condizione f;
(Med) malattia ▷ vt condizionare; **on ~
that** a condizione che + sub, a condizione
di; **conditional** adj condizionale; **to
be conditional upon** dipendere da;
conditioner n (for hair) balsamo; (for
fabrics) ammorbidente m
condo [ˈkɔndəu] (US) n abbr (inf)
= **condominium**
condom [ˈkɔndəm] n preservativo
condominium [kɔndəˈmɪnɪəm] (US) n
condominio
condone [kənˈdəun] vt condonare
conduct [n ˈkɔndʌkt, vb kənˈdʌkt]
n condotta ▷ vt condurre; (manage)
dirigere; amministrare; (Mus) dirigere;
to ~ o.s. comportarsi; **conducted tour**
[kənˈdʌktɪd-] n gita accompagnata;
conductor n (of orchestra) direttore m
d'orchestra; (on bus) bigliettaio; (us: on

train) controllore *m*; (*Elec*) conduttore *m*

cone [kəʊn] *n* cono; (*Bot*) pigna; (*traffic cone*) birillo

confectionery [kənˈfɛkʃənrɪ] *n* dolciumi *mpl*

confer [kənˈfəːʳ] *vt* **to ~ sth on** conferire qc a ▷ *vi* conferire

conference [ˈkɒnfərns] *n* congresso

confess [kənˈfɛs] *vt* confessare, ammettere ▷ *vi* confessare; **confession** [kənˈfɛʃən] *n* confessione *f*

confide [kənˈfaɪd] *vi* **to ~ in** confidarsi con

confidence [ˈkɒnfɪdns] *n* confidenza; (*trust*) fiducia; (*self-assurance*) sicurezza di sé; **in ~** (*speak, write*) in confidenza, confidenzialmente; **confident** *adj* sicuro(-a), sicuro(-a) di sé; **confidential** [kɒnfɪˈdɛnʃəl] *adj* riservato(-a), confidenziale

confine [kənˈfaɪn] *vt* limitare; (*shut up*) rinchiudere; **confined** *adj* (*space*) ristretto(-a)

confirm [kənˈfəːm] *vt* confermare; **confirmation** [kɒnfəˈmeɪʃən] *n* conferma; (*Rel*) cresima

confiscate [ˈkɒnfɪskeɪt] *vt* confiscare

conflict [*n* ˈkɒnflɪkt, *vb* kənˈflɪkt] *n* conflitto ▷ *vi* essere in conflitto

conform [kənˈfɔːm] *vi* **to ~ to** conformarsi (a)

confront [kənˈfrʌnt] *vt* (*enemy, danger*) affrontare; **confrontation** [kɒnfrənˈteɪʃən] *n* scontro

confuse [kənˈfjuːz] *vt* (*one thing with another*) confondere; **confused** *adj* confuso(-a); **confusing** *adj* che fa confondere; **confusion** [-ˈfjuːʒən] *n* confusione *f*

congestion [kənˈdʒɛstʃən] *n* congestione *f*

congratulate [kənˈɡrætjuleɪt] *vt* **to ~ sb (on)** congratularsi con qn (per *or* di); **congratulations** [-ˈleɪʃənz] *npl* auguri *mpl*; (*on success*) complimenti *mpl*, congratulazioni *fpl*

congregation [kɒŋɡrɪˈɡeɪʃən] *n* congregazione *f*

congress [ˈkɒŋɡrɛs] *n* congresso; **congressman** (*irreg*: *US*) *n* membro del Congresso; **congresswoman** (*irreg*: *US*) *n* (donna) membro del Congresso

conifer [ˈkɒnɪfəʳ] *n* conifero

conjugate [ˈkɒndʒugeɪt] *vt* coniugare

conjugation [kɒndʒəˈɡeɪʃən] *n* coniugazione *f*

conjunction [kənˈdʒʌŋkʃən] *n* congiunzione *f*

conjure [ˈkʌndʒəʳ] *vi* fare giochi di prestigio

connect [kəˈnɛkt] *vt* connettere, collegare; (*Elec, Tel*) collegare; (*fig*) associare ▷ *vi* (*train*): **to ~ with** essere in coincidenza con; **to be ~ed with** (*associated*) aver rapporti con; **connecting flight** *n* volo in coincidenza; **connection** [-ʃən] ▷ *n* relazione *f*, rapporto; (*Elec*) connessione *f*; (*train, plane*) coincidenza; (*Tel*) collegamento

conquer [ˈkɒŋkəʳ] *vt* conquistare; (*feelings*) vincere

conquest [ˈkɒŋkwɛst] *n* conquista

cons [kɒnz] *npl see* **convenience**; **pro**

conscience [ˈkɒnʃəns] *n* coscienza

conscientious [kɒnʃɪˈɛnʃəs] *adj* coscienzioso(-a)

conscious [ˈkɒnʃəs] *adj* consapevole; (*Med*) cosciente; **consciousness** *n* consapevolezza; coscienza

consecutive [kənˈsɛkjutɪv] *adj* consecutivo(-a); **on 3 ~ occasions** 3 volte di fila

consensus [kənˈsɛnsəs] *n* consenso; **the ~ of opinion** l'opinione *f* unanime *or* comune

consent [kənˈsɛnt] *n* consenso ▷ *vi* **to ~ (to)** acconsentire (a)

consequence [ˈkɒnsɪkwəns] *n* conseguenza, risultato; importanza

consequently [ˈkɒnsɪkwəntlɪ] *adv* di conseguenza, dunque

conservation [kɒnsəˈveɪʃən] *n* conservazione *f*

conservative [kənˈsəːvətɪv] *adj* conservatore(-trice); (*cautious*) cauto(-a); **Conservative** (*BRIT*) *adj*, *n* (*Pol*) conservatore(-trice)

conservatory [kənˈsəːvətrɪ] *n* (*greenhouse*) serra; (*Mus*) conservatorio

consider [kənˈsɪdəʳ] *vt* considerare; (*take into account*) tener conto di; **to ~ doing sth** considerare la possibilità di fare qc; **considerable** [kənˈsɪdərəbl] *adj* considerevole, notevole; **considerably** *adv* notevolmente, decisamente; **considerate** [kənˈsɪdərɪt] *adj* premuroso(-a); **consideration** [kənsɪdəˈreɪʃən] *n* considerazione *f*; **considering** [kənˈsɪdərɪŋ] *prep* in considerazione di

consignment [kənˈsaɪnmənt] *n* (*of goods*) consegna; spedizione *f*

consist [kənˈsɪst] *vi* **to ~ of** constare di, essere composto(-a) di

consistency [kənˈsɪstənsɪ] *n* consistenza; (*fig*) coerenza

consistent [kənˈsɪstənt] *adj* coerente

consolation [kɒnsəˈleɪʃən] *n* consolazione *f*

console¹ [kənˈsəʊl] *vt* consolare

console² [ˈkɔnsəul] n quadro di comando
consonant [ˈkɔnsənənt] n consonante f
conspicuous [kənˈspɪkjuəs] adj
cospicuo(-a)
conspiracy [kənˈspɪrəsɪ] n congiura,
cospirazione f
constable [ˈkʌnstəbl] (BRIT) n ≈ poliziotto,
agente m di polizia; **chief ~ =** questore m
constant [ˈkɔnstənt] adj costante,
continuo(-a); **constantly** adv
costantemente; continuamente
constipated [ˈkɔnstɪpeɪtɪd] adj
stitico(-a); **constipation** [kɔnstɪˈpeɪʃən]
n stitichezza
constituency [kənˈstɪtjuənsɪ] n collegio
elettorale
constitute [ˈkɔnstɪtjuːt] vt costituire
constitution [kɔnstɪˈtjuːʃən] n
costituzione f
constraint [kənˈstreɪnt] n costrizione f
construct [kənˈstrʌkt] vt costruire;
construction [-ʃən] n costruzione f;
constructive adj costruttivo(-a)
consul [ˈkɔnsl] n console m; **consulate**
[ˈkɔnsjulɪt] n consolato
consult [kənˈsʌlt] vt consultare;
consultant n (Med) consulente m medico;
(other specialist) consulente; **consultation**
[-ˈteɪʃən] n (Med) consulto; (discussion)
consultazione f; **consulting room**
[kənˈsʌltɪŋ-] (BRIT) n ambulatorio
consume [kənˈsjuːm] vt consumare;
consumer n consumatore(-trice)
consumption [kənˈsʌmpʃən] n consumo
cont. abbr **= continued**
contact [ˈkɔntækt] n contatto; (person)
conoscenza ▷ vt mettersi in contatto con;
contact lenses npl lenti fpl a contatto
contagious [kənˈteɪdʒəs] adj (also fig)
contagioso(-a)
contain [kənˈteɪn] vt contenere; **to ~ o.s.**
contenersi; **container** n recipiente m; (for
shipping etc) container m inv
contaminate [kənˈtæmɪneɪt] vt
contaminare
cont'd abbr **= continued**
contemplate [ˈkɔntəmpleɪt] vt
contemplare; (consider) pensare a (or di)
contemporary [kənˈtɛmpərərɪ] adj, n
contemporaneo(-a)
contempt [kənˈtɛmpt] n disprezzo; **~ of**
court (Law) oltraggio alla Corte
contend [kənˈtɛnd] vt **to ~ that** sostenere
che ▷ vi **to ~ with** lottare contro
content¹ [ˈkɔntɛnt] n contenuto; **~s** npl
(of box, case etc) contenuto; **(table of) ~s**
indice m
content² [kənˈtɛnt] adj contento(-a),
soddisfatto(-a) ▷ vt contentare,

soddisfare; **contented** adj contento(-a),
soddisfatto(-a)
contest [n ˈkɔntɛst, vb kənˈtɛst] n
lotta; (competition) gara, concorso
▷ vt contestare; impugnare; (compete
for) essere in lizza per; **contestant**
[kənˈtɛstənt] n concorrente m/f; (in fight)
avversario(-a)
context [ˈkɔntɛkst] n contesto
continent [ˈkɔntɪnənt] n continente
m; **the C~** (BRIT) l'Europa continentale;
continental [-ˈnɛntl] adj continentale;
continental breakfast n colazione f
all'europea (senza piatti caldi); **continental
quilt** (BRIT) n piumino
continual [kənˈtɪnjuəl] adj continuo(-a);
continually adv di continuo
continue [kənˈtɪnjuː] vi continuare ▷ vt
continuare; (start again) riprendere
continuity [kɔntɪˈnjuːɪtɪ] n continuità;
(TV, Cinema) (ordine m della) sceneggiatura
continuous [kənˈtɪnjuəs] adj
continuo(-a), ininterrotto(-a); **continuous
assessment** n (BRIT) valutazione f
continua; **continuously** adv (repeatedly)
continuamente; (uninterruptedly)
ininterrottamente
contour [ˈkɔntuəʳ] n contorno, profilo;
(also: ~ **line**) curva di livello
contraception [kɔntrəˈsɛpʃən] n
contraccezione f
contraceptive [kɔntrəˈsɛptɪv] adj
contraccettivo(-a) ▷ n contraccettivo
contract [n ˈkɔntrækt, vb kənˈtrækt] n
contratto ▷ vi (become smaller) contrarsi;
(Comm): **to ~ to do sth** fare un contratto
per fare qc ▷ vt (illness) contrarre;
contractor n imprenditore m
contradict [kɔntrəˈdɪkt] vt contraddire;
contradiction [kɔntrəˈdɪkʃən] n
contraddizione f; **to be in contradiction
with** discordare con
contrary¹ [ˈkɔntrərɪ] adj contrario(-a);
(unfavourable) avverso(-a), contrario(-a)
▷ n contrario; **on the ~** al contrario;
unless you hear to the ~ salvo
contrordine
contrary² [kənˈtrɛərɪ] adj (perverse)
bisbetico(-a)
contrast [n ˈkɔntrɑːst, vb kənˈtrɑːst] n
contrasto ▷ vt mettere in contrasto; **in ~
to** contrariamente a
contribute [kənˈtrɪbjuːt] vi contribuire
▷ vt **to ~ £10/an article to** dare
10 sterline/un articolo a; **to ~ to**
contribuire a; (newspaper) scrivere
per; **contribution** [kɔntrɪˈbjuːʃən] n
contributo; **contributor** n (to newspaper)
collaboratore(-trice)

control [kən'trəul] vt controllare; (firm, operation etc) dirigere ▷ n controllo; **~s** npl (of vehicle etc) comandi mpl; (governmental) controlli mpl; **under ~** sotto controllo; **to be in ~ of** avere il controllo di; **to go out of ~** (car) non rispondere ai comandi; (situation) sfuggire di mano; **control tower** n (Aviat) torre f di controllo

controversial [kɔntrə'vəːʃl] adj controverso(-a), polemico(-a)

controversy ['kɔntrəvəːsɪ] n controversia, polemica

convenience [kən'viːnɪəns] n comodità f inv; **at your ~** a suo comodo; **all modern ~s** (BRIT), **all mod cons** tutte le comodità moderne

convenient [kən'viːnɪənt] adj comodo(-a)

Be careful not to translate *convenient* by the Italian word *conveniente*.

convent ['kɔnvənt] n convento

convention [kən'venʃən] n convenzione f; (meeting) convegno; **conventional** adj convenzionale

conversation [kɔnvə'seɪʃən] n conversazione f

conversely [kɔn'vəːslɪ] adv al contrario, per contro

conversion [kən'vəːʃən] n conversione f; (BRIT: of house) trasformazione f, rimodernamento

convert [vb kən'vəːt, n 'kɔnvəːt] vt (Comm, Rel) convertire; (alter) trasformare ▷ n convertito(-a); **convertible** n macchina decappottabile

convey [kən'veɪ] vt trasportare; (thanks) comunicare; (idea) dare; **conveyor belt** [kən'veɪəʳ-] n nastro trasportatore

convict [vb kən'vɪkt, n 'kɔnvɪkt] vt dichiarare colpevole ▷ n carcerato(-a); **conviction** [-ʃən] n condanna; (belief) convinzione f

convince [kən'vɪns] vt convincere, persuadere; **convinced** adj **convinced of/that** convinto(-a) di/che; **convincing** adj convincente

convoy ['kɔnvɔɪ] n convoglio

cook [kuk] vt cucinare, cuocere ▷ vi cuocere; (person) cucinare ▷ n cuoco(-a); **cook book** n libro di cucina; **cooker** n fornello, cucina; **cookery** n cucina; **cookery book** (BRIT) n = **cook book**; **cookie** (US) n biscotto; **cooking** n cucina

cool [kuːl] adj fresco(-a); (not afraid, calm) calmo(-a); (unfriendly) freddo(-a) ▷ vt raffreddare; (room) rinfrescare ▷ vi (water) raffreddarsi; (air) rinfrescarsi; **cool down** vi raffreddarsi; (fig: person, situation) calmarsi; **cool off** vi (become

calmer) calmarsi; (lose enthusiasm) perdere interesse

cop [kɔp] (inf) n sbirro

cope [kəup] vi **to ~ with** (problems) far fronte a

copper ['kɔpəʳ] n rame m; (inf: policeman) sbirro

copy ['kɔpɪ] n copia ▷ vt copiare; **copyright** n diritto d'autore

coral ['kɔrəl] n corallo

cord [kɔːd] n corda; (Elec) filo; **~s** npl (trousers) calzoni mpl (di velluto) a coste; **cordless** adj senza cavo

corduroy ['kɔːdərɔɪ] n fustagno

core [kɔːʳ] n (of fruit) torsolo; (of organization etc) cuore m ▷ vt estrarre il torsolo da

coriander [kɔrɪ'ændəʳ] n coriandolo

cork [kɔːk] n sughero; (of bottle) tappo; **corkscrew** n cavatappi m inv

corn [kɔːn] n (BRIT: wheat) grano; (US: maize) granturco; (on foot) callo; **~ on the cob** (Culin) pannocchia cotta

corned beef ['kɔːnd-] n carne f di manzo in scatola

corner ['kɔːnəʳ] n angolo; (Aut) curva ▷ vt intrappolare; mettere con le spalle al muro; (Comm: market) accaparrare ▷ vi prendere una curva

corner shop (BRIT) n piccolo negozio di generi alimentari

cornflakes ['kɔːnfleɪks] npl fiocchi mpl di granturco

cornflour ['kɔːnflauəʳ] (BRIT) n farina finissima di granturco

cornstarch ['kɔːnstɑːtʃ] (US) n = **cornflour**

Cornwall ['kɔːnwəl] n Cornovaglia

coronary ['kɔrənərɪ] n **~ (thrombosis)** trombosi f coronaria

coronation [kɔrə'neɪʃən] n incoronazione f

coroner ['kɔrənəʳ] n magistrato incaricato di indagare la causa di morte in circostanze sospette

corporal ['kɔːpərl] n caporalmaggiore m ▷ adj **~ punishment** pena corporale

corporate ['kɔːpərɪt] adj costituito(-a) (in corporazione), comune

corporation [kɔːpə'reɪʃən] n (of town) consiglio comunale; (Comm) ente m

corps [kɔː, pl kɔːz] n inv corpo

corpse [kɔːps] n cadavere m

correct [kə'rɛkt] adj (accurate) corretto(-a), esatto(-a); (proper) corretto(-a) ▷ vt correggere; **correction** [-ʃən] n correzione f

correspond [kɔrɪs'pɔnd] vi corrispondere; **correspondence** n corrispondenza; **correspondent** n corrispondente m/f; **corresponding** adj corrispondente

corridor ['kɔrɪdɔːʳ] n corridoio

corrode [kə'rəud] vt corrodere ▷ vi corrodersi

corrupt [kə'rʌpt] adj corrotto(-a); (Comput) alterato(-a) ▷ vt corrompere; **corruption** n corruzione f

Corsica ['kɔ:sɪkə] n Corsica

cosmetic [kɔz'mɛtɪk] n cosmetico ▷ adj (fig: measure etc) superficiale; **cosmetic surgery** n chirurgia plastica

cosmopolitan [kɔzmə'pɔlɪtn] adj cosmopolita

cost [kɔst] (pt, pp **cost**) n costo ▷ vt costare; (find out the cost of) stabilire il prezzo di; **~s** npl (Comm, Law) spese fpl; **how much does it ~?** quanto costa?; **at all ~s** a ogni costo

co-star ['kəusta:ʳ] n attore/trice della stessa importanza del protagonista

Costa Rica ['kɔstə'ri:kə] n Costa Rica

costly ['kɔstlɪ] adj costoso(-a), caro(-a)

cost of living adj **~ allowance** indennità f inv di contingenza

costume ['kɔstju:m] n costume m; (lady's suit) tailleur m inv; (BRIT: also: **swimming ~**) costume m da bagno

cosy ['kəuzɪ] (US **cozy**) adj intimo(-a); **I'm very ~ here** sto proprio bene qui

cot [kɔt] n (BRIT: child's) lettino; (US: campbed) brandina

cottage ['kɔtɪdʒ] n cottage m inv; **cottage cheese** n fiocchi mpl di latte magro

cotton ['kɔtn] n cotone m; **cotton on** vi (inf): **to ~ on (to sth)** afferrare (qc); **cotton bud** n (BRIT) cotton fioc® m inv; **cotton candy** (US) n zucchero filato; **cotton wool** (BRIT) n cotone idrofilo

couch [kautʃ] n sofà m inv

cough [kɔf] vi tossire ▷ n tosse f; **I've got a ~** ho la tosse; **cough mixture, cough syrup** n sciroppo per la tosse

could [kud] pt of **can²**

couldn't = **could not**

council ['kaunsl] n consiglio; **city or town ~** consiglio comunale; **council estate** (BRIT) n quartiere m di case popolari; **council house** (BRIT) n casa popolare; **councillor** (US **councilor**) n consigliere(-a); **council tax** n (BRIT) tassa comunale sulla proprietà

counsel ['kaunsl] n avvocato; consultazione f ▷ vt consigliare; **counselling** (US **counseling**) n (Psych) assistenza psicologica; **counsellor** (US **counselor**) n consigliere(-a); (US) avvocato

count [kaunt] vt, vi contare ▷ n (of votes etc) conteggio; (of pollen etc) livello; (nobleman) conte m; **count in** (inf) vt includere; **~ me**

in ci sto anch'io; **count on** vt fus contare su; **countdown** n conto alla rovescia

counter ['kauntəʳ] n banco ▷ vt opporsi a ▷ adv **~ to** contro; in opposizione a; **counter clockwise** [-'klɔkwaɪz] (US) adv in senso antiorario

counterfeit ['kauntəfɪt] n contraffazione f, falso ▷ vt contraffare, falsificare ▷ adj falso(-a)

counterpart ['kauntəpa:t] n (of document etc) copia; (of person) corrispondente m/f

countess ['kauntɪs] n contessa

countless ['kauntlɪs] adj innumerevole

country ['kʌntrɪ] n paese m; (native land) patria; (as opposed to town) campagna; (region) regione f; **country and western (music)** n musica country e western, country m; **country house** n villa in campagna; **countryside** n campagna

county ['kauntɪ] n contea

coup [ku:] (pl **coups**) n colpo; (also: **~ d'état**) colpo di Stato

couple ['kʌpl] n coppia; **a ~ of** un paio di

coupon ['ku:pɔn] n buono; (detachable form) coupon m inv

courage ['kʌrɪdʒ] n coraggio; **courageous** adj coraggioso(-a)

courgette [kuə'ʒɛt] (BRIT) n zucchina

courier ['kurɪəʳ] n corriere m; (for tourists) guida

course [kɔ:s] n corso; (of ship) rotta; (for golf) campo; (part of meal) piatto; **of ~** senz'altro, naturalmente; **~ of action** modo d'agire; **a ~ of treatment** (Med) una cura

court [kɔ:t] n corte f; (Tennis) campo ▷ vt (woman) fare la corte a; **to take to ~** citare in tribunale

courtesy ['kɔ:təsɪ] n cortesia; **(by) ~ of** per gentile concessione di; **courtesy bus, courtesy coach** n autobus m inv gratuito (di hotel, aeroporto)

court: **court-house** (US) n palazzo di giustizia; **courtroom** n tribunale m; **courtyard** n cortile m

cousin ['kʌzn] n cugino(-a); **first ~** cugino di primo grado

cover ['kʌvəʳ] vt coprire; (book, table) rivestire; (include) comprendere; (Press) fare un servizio su ▷ n (of pan) coperchio; (over furniture) fodera; (of bed) copriletto; (of book) copertina; (shelter) riparo; (Comm, Insurance, of spy) copertura; **~s** npl (on bed) lenzuola fpl e coperte fpl; **to take ~** (shelter) ripararsi; **under ~** al riparo; **under ~ of darkness** protetto dall'oscurità; **under separate ~** (Comm) a parte, in plico separato; **cover up** vi **to ~ up for sb** coprire qn; **coverage** n (Press, Radio,

TV): **to give full coverage to sth** fare un ampio servizio su qc; **cover charge** *n* coperto; **cover-up** *n* occultamento (di informazioni)

cow [kau] *n* vacca ▷ *vt* (*person*) intimidire

coward ['kauəd] *n* vigliacco(-a); **cowardly** *adj* vigliacco(-a)

cowboy ['kaubɔɪ] *n* cow-boy *m inv*

cozy ['kəuzɪ] (*US*) *adj* = **cosy**

crab [kræb] *n* granchio

crack [kræk] *n* fessura, crepa; incrinatura; (*noise*) schiocco; (: *of gun*) scoppio; (*drug*) crack *m inv* ▷ *vt* spaccare; incrinare; (*whip*) schioccare; (*nut*) schiacciare; (*problem*) risolvere; (*code*) decifrare ▷ *adj* (*troops*) fuori classe; **to ~ a joke** fare una battuta; **crack down on** *vt fus* porre freno a; **cracked** *adj* (*inf*) matto(-a); **cracker** *n* cracker *m inv*; petardo

crackle ['krækl] *vi* crepitare

cradle ['kreɪdl] *n* culla

craft [krɑːft] *n* mestiere *m*; (*cunning*) astuzia; (*boat*) naviglio; **craftsman** (*irreg*) *n* artigiano; **craftsmanship** *n* abilità

cram [kræm] *vt* (*fill*): **to ~ sth with** riempire qc di; (*put*): **to ~ sth into** stipare qc in ▷ *vi* (*for exams*) prepararsi (in gran fretta)

cramp [kræmp] *n* crampo; **I've got ~ in my leg** ho un crampo alla gamba; **cramped** *adj* ristretto(-a)

cranberry ['krænbərɪ] *n* mirtillo

crane [kreɪn] *n* gru *f inv*

crash [kræʃ] *n* fragore *m*; (*of car*) incidente *m*; (*of plane*) caduta; (*of business etc*) crollo ▷ *vt* fracassare ▷ *vi* (*plane*) fracassarsi; (*car*) avere un incidente; (*two cars*) scontrarsi; (*business etc*) fallire, andare in rovina; **crash course** *n* corso intensivo; **crash helmet** *n* casco

crate [kreɪt] *n* cassa

crave [kreɪv] *vt*, *vi* **to ~ (for)** desiderare ardentemente

crawl [krɔːl] *vi* strisciare carponi; (*vehicle*) avanzare lentamente ▷ *n* (*Swimming*) crawl *m*

crayfish ['kreɪfɪʃ] *n inv* (*freshwater*) gambero (d'acqua dolce); (*saltwater*) gambero

crayon ['kreɪən] *n* matita colorata

craze [kreɪz] *n* mania

crazy ['kreɪzɪ] *adj* matto(-a); (*inf*: *keen*): **~ about sb** pazzo(-a) di qn; **~ about sth** matto(-a) per qc

creak [kriːk] *vi* cigolare, scricchiolare

cream [kriːm] *n* crema; (*fresh*) panna ▷ *adj* (*colour*) color crema *inv*; **cream cheese** *n* formaggio fresco; **creamy** *adj* cremoso(-a)

crease [kriːs] *n* grinza; (*deliberate*) piega ▷ *vt* sgualcire ▷ *vi* sgualcirsi

create [kriːˈeɪt] *vt* creare; **creation** [-ʃən] *n* creazione *f*; **creative** *adj* creativo(-a); **creator** *n* creatore(-trice)

creature ['kriːtʃə*] *n* creatura

crèche [krɛʃ] *n* asilo infantile

credentials [krɪˈdɛnʃlz] *npl* credenziali *fpl*

credibility [krɛdɪˈbɪlɪtɪ] *n* credibilità

credible ['krɛdɪbl] *adj* credibile; (*witness*, *source*) attendibile

credit ['krɛdɪt] *n* credito; onore *m* ▷ *vt* (*Comm*) accreditare; (*believe*: *also*: **give ~ to**) credere, prestar fede a; **~s** *npl* (*Cinema*) titoli *mpl*; **to ~ sb with** (*fig*) attribuire a qn; **to be in ~** (*person*) essere creditore(-trice); (*bank account*) essere coperto(-a); **credit card** *n* carta di credito; **do you take credit cards?** accettate carte di credito?

creek [kriːk] *n* insenatura; (*us*) piccolo fiume *m*

creep [kriːp] (*pt, pp* **crept**) *vi* avanzare furtivamente (*or* pian piano)

cremate [krɪˈmeɪt] *vt* cremare

crematorium [krɛməˈtɔːrɪəm] (*pl* **crematoria**) *n* forno crematorio

crept [krɛpt] *pt, pp of* **creep**

crescent ['krɛsnt] *n* (*shape*) mezzaluna; (*street*) strada semicircolare

cress [krɛs] *n* crescione *m*

crest [krɛst] *n* cresta; (*of coat of arms*) cimiero

crew [kruː] *n* equipaggio; **crew-neck** *n* girocollo

crib [krɪb] *n* culla ▷ *vt* (*inf*) copiare

cricket ['krɪkɪt] *n* (*insect*) grillo; (*game*) cricket *m*; **cricketer** *n* giocatore *m* di cricket

crime [kraɪm] *n* crimine *m*; **criminal** ['krɪmɪnl] *adj*, *n* criminale *m/f*

crimson ['krɪmzn] *adj* color cremisi *inv*

cringe [krɪndʒ] *vi* acquattarsi; (*in embarrassment*) sentirsi sprofondare

cripple ['krɪpl] *n* zoppo(-a) ▷ *vt* azzoppare

crisis ['kraɪsɪs] (*pl* **crises**) *n* crisi *f inv*

crisp [krɪsp] *adj* croccante; (*fig*) frizzante; vivace; deciso(-a); **crispy** *adj* croccante

criterion [kraɪˈtɪərɪən] (*pl* **criteria**) *n* criterio

critic ['krɪtɪk] *n* critico; **critical** *adj* critico(-a); **criticism** ['krɪtɪsɪzm] *n* critica; **criticize** ['krɪtɪsaɪz] *vt* criticare

Croat ['krəuæt] *adj*, *n* = **Croatian**

Croatia [krəuˈeɪʃə] *n* Croazia; **Croatian** *adj* croato(-a) ▷ *n* croato(-a); (*Ling*) croato

crockery ['krɔkərɪ] *n* vasellame *m*

crocodile ['krɔkədaɪl] *n* coccodrillo

crocus ['krəukəs] n croco

croissant ['krwas] n brioche f inv, croissant m inv

crook [kruk] n truffatore m; (of shepherd) bastone m; **crooked** ['krukɪd] adj curvo(-a), storto(-a); (action) disonesto(-a)

crop [krɒp] n (produce) coltivazione f; (amount produced) raccolto; (riding crop) frustino ▷ vt (hair) rapare; **crop up** vi presentarsi

cross [krɒs] n croce f; (Biol) incrocio ▷ vt (street etc) attraversare; (arms, legs, Biol) incrociare; (cheque) sbarrare ▷ adj di cattivo umore; **cross off** vt cancellare (tirando una riga con la penna); **cross out** vt cancellare; **cross over** vi attraversare; **cross-Channel ferry** ['krɒs'tʃænl-] n traghetto che attraversa la Manica; **crosscountry (race)** n cross-country m inv; **crossing** n incrocio; (sea passage) traversata; (also: **pedestrian crossing**) passaggio pedonale; **how long does the crossing take?** quanto dura la traversata?; **crossing guard** (us) n dipendente comunale che aiuta i bambini ad attraversare la strada; **crossroads** n incrocio; **crosswalk** (us) n strisce fpl pedonali, passaggio pedonale; **crossword** n cruciverba m inv

crotch [krɒtʃ] n (Anat) inforcatura; (of garment) pattina

crouch [krautʃ] vi acquattarsi, rannicchiarsi

crouton ['kru:tɒn] n crostino

crow [krəu] n (bird) cornacchia; (of cock) canto del gallo ▷ vi (cock) cantare

crowd [kraud] n folla ▷ vt affollare, stipare ▷ vi **to ~ round/in** affollarsi intorno a/in; **crowded** adj affollato(-a); **crowded with** stipato(-a) di

crown [kraun] n corona; (of head) calotta cranica; (of hat) cocuzzolo; (of hill) cima ▷ vt incoronare; (fig: career) coronare; **crown jewels** npl gioielli mpl della Corona

crucial ['kru:ʃl] adj cruciale, decisivo(-a)

crucifix ['kru:sɪfɪks] n crocifisso

crude [kru:d] adj (materials) greggio(-a), non raffinato(-a); (fig: basic) primitivo(-a); (: vulgar) rozzo(-a), grossolano(-a); **crude (oil)** n (petrolio) greggio

cruel ['kruəl] adj crudele; **cruelty** n crudeltà f inv

cruise [kru:z] n crociera ▷ vi andare a velocità di crociera; (taxi) circolare

crumb [krʌm] n briciola

crumble ['krʌmbl] vt sbriciolare ▷ vi sbriciolarsi; (plaster etc) sgrettolarsi; (land, earth) franare; (building, fig) crollare

crumpet ['krʌmpɪt] n specie di frittella

crumple ['krʌmpl] vt raggrinzare, spiegazzare

crunch [krʌntʃ] vt sgranocchiare; (underfoot) scricchiolare ▷ n (fig) punto or momento cruciale; **crunchy** adj croccante

crush [krʌʃ] n folla; (love): **to have a ~ on sb** avere una cotta per qn; (drink): **lemon ~** spremuta di limone ▷ vt schiacciare; (crumple) sgualcire

crust [krʌst] n crosta; **crusty** adj (bread) croccante; (person) brontolone(-a); (remark) brusco(-a)

crutch [krʌtʃ] n gruccia

cry [kraɪ] vi piangere; (shout) urlare ▷ n urlo, grido; **cry out** vi, vt gridare

crystal ['krɪstl] n cristallo

cub [kʌb] n cucciolo; (also: **~ scout**) lupetto

Cuba ['kju:bə] n Cuba

Cuban ['kju:bən] adj, n cubano(-a)

cube [kju:b] n cubo ▷ vt (Math) elevare al cubo; **cubic** adj cubico(-a); (metre, foot) cubo(-a)

cubicle ['kju:bɪkl] n scompartimento separato; cabina

cuckoo ['kuku:] n cucù m inv

cucumber ['kju:kʌmbə'] n cetriolo

cuddle ['kʌdl] vt abbracciare, coccolare ▷ vi abbracciarsi

cue [kju:] n (snooker cue) stecca; (Theatre etc) segnale m

cuff [kʌf] n (BRIT: of shirt, coat etc) polsino; (us: of trousers) risvolto; **off the ~** improvvisando; **cufflinks** npl gemelli mpl

cuisine [kwɪ'zi:n] n cucina

cul-de-sac ['kʌldəsæk] n vicolo cieco

cull [kʌl] vt (ideas etc) scegliere ▷ n (of animals) abbattimento selettivo

culminate ['kʌlmɪneɪt] vi **to ~ in** culminare con

culprit ['kʌlprɪt] n colpevole m/f

cult [kʌlt] n culto

cultivate ['kʌltɪveɪt] vt (also fig) coltivare

cultural ['kʌltʃərəl] adj culturale

culture ['kʌltʃə'] n (also fig) cultura

cumin ['kʌmɪn] n (spice) cumino

cunning ['kʌnɪŋ] n astuzia, furberia ▷ adj astuto(-a), furbo(-a)

cup [kʌp] n tazza; (prize, of bra) coppa

cupboard ['kʌbəd] n armadio

cup final n (BRIT Football) finale f di coppa

curator [kjuə'reɪtə'] n direttore m (di museo ecc)

curb [kə:b] vt tenere a freno ▷ n freno; (us) bordo del marciapiede

curdle ['kə:dl] vi cagliare

cure [kjuə'] vt guarire; (Culin) trattare; affumicare; essiccare ▷ n rimedio

curfew ['kə:fju:] n coprifuoco

curiosity [kjuərɪ'ɒsɪtɪ] n curiosità

curious ['kjuərɪəs] *adj* curioso(-a)

curl [kəːl] *n* riccio ▷ *vt* ondulare; (*tightly*) arricciare ▷ *vi* arricciarsi; **curl up** *vi* rannicchiarsi; **curler** *n* bigodino; **curly** ['kəːlɪ] *adj* ricciuto(-a)

currant ['kʌrnt] *n* (*dried*) sultanina; (*bush, fruit*) ribes *m inv*

currency ['kʌrnsɪ] *n* moneta; **to gain ~** (*fig*) acquistare larga diffusione

current ['kʌrnt] *adj* corrente ▷ *n* corrente *f*; **current account** (*BRIT*) *n* conto corrente; **current affairs** *npl* attualità *fpl*; **currently** *adv* attualmente

curriculum [kə'rɪkjuləm] (*pl* **curriculums** *or* **curricula**) *n* curriculum *m inv*; **curriculum vitae** [-'viːtaɪ] *n* curriculum vitae *m inv*

curry ['kʌrɪ] *n* curry *m inv* ▷ *vt* **to ~ favour with** cercare di attirarsi i favori di; **curry powder** *n* curry *m*

curse [kəːs] *vt* maledire ▷ *vi* bestemmiare ▷ *n* maledizione *f*; bestemmia

cursor ['kəːsəʳ] *n* (*Comput*) cursore *m*

curt [kəːt] *adj* secco(-a)

curtain ['kəːtn] *n* tenda; (*Theatre*) sipario

curve [kəːv] *n* curva ▷ *vi* curvarsi; **curved** *adj* curvo(-a)

cushion ['kuʃən] *n* cuscino ▷ *vt* (*shock*) fare da cuscinetto a

custard ['kʌstəd] *n* (*for pouring*) crema

custody ['kʌstədɪ] *n* (*of child*) tutela; **to take into ~** (*suspect*) mettere in detenzione preventiva

custom ['kʌstəm] *n* costume *m*, consuetudine *f*; (*Comm*) clientela

customer ['kʌstəməʳ] *n* cliente *m/f*

customized ['kʌstəmaɪzd] *adj* (*car etc*) fuoriserie *inv*

customs ['kʌstəmz] *npl* dogana; **customs officer** *n* doganiere *m*

cut [kʌt] (*pt, pp* **cut**) *vt* tagliare; (*shape, make*) intagliare; (*reduce*) ridurre ▷ *vi* tagliare ▷ *n* taglio; (*in salary etc*) riduzione *f*; **I've ~ myself** mi sono tagliato; **to ~ a tooth** mettere un dente; **cut back** *vt* (*plants*) tagliare; (*production, expenditure*) ridurre; **cut down** *vt* (*tree etc*) abbattere ▷ *vt fus* (*also*: **~ down on**) ridurre; **cut off** *vt* tagliare; (*fig*) isolare; **cut out** *vt* tagliare fuori; eliminare; ritagliare; **cut up** *vt* tagliare a pezzi; **cutback** *n* riduzione *f*

cute [kjuːt] *adj* (*sweet*) carino(-a)

cutlery ['kʌtlərɪ] *n* posate *fpl*

cutlet ['kʌtlɪt] *n* costoletta; (*nut etc cutlet*) cotoletta vegetariana

cut: **cut-price** (*BRIT*) *adj* a prezzo ridotto; **cut-rate** (*US*) *adj* = **cut-price**; **cutting** ['kʌtɪŋ] *adj* tagliente ▷ *n* (*from newspaper*) ritaglio (di giornale); (*from plant*) talea

CV *n abbr* = **curriculum vitae**

cwt *abbr* = **hundredweight(s)**

cybercafé ['saɪbəkaefeɪ] *n* cybercaffè *m inv*

cyberspace ['saɪbəspeɪs] *n* ciberspazio

cycle ['saɪkl] *n* ciclo; (*bicycle*) bicicletta ▷ *vi* andare in bicicletta; **cycle hire** *n* noleggio *m* biciclette *inv*; **cycle lane** *n* pista ciclabile; **cycle path** *n* pista ciclabile; **cycling** ['saɪklɪŋ] *n* ciclismo; **cyclist** ['saɪklɪst] *n* ciclista *m/f*

cyclone ['saɪkləun] *n* ciclone *m*

cylinder ['sɪlɪndəʳ] *n* cilindro

cymbal ['sɪmbl] *n* piatto

cynical ['sɪnɪkl] *adj* cinico(-a)

Cypriot ['sɪprɪət] *adj, n* cipriota (*m/f*)

Cyprus ['saɪprəs] *n* Cipro

cyst [sɪst] *n* cisti *f inv*; **cystitis** [sɪs'taɪtɪs] *n* cistite *f*

czar [zɑːʳ] *n* zar *m inv*

Czech [tʃɛk] *adj* ceco(-a) ▷ *n* ceco(-a); (*Ling*) ceco; **Czech Republic** *n* **the Czech Republic** la Repubblica Ceca

D [diː] n (Mus) re m

dab [dæb] vt (eyes, wound) tamponare; (paint, cream) applicare (con leggeri colpetti)

dad, daddy [dæd, 'dædɪ] n babbo, papà m inv

daffodil ['dæfədɪl] n trombone m, giunchiglia

daft [dɑːft] adj sciocco(-a)

dagger ['dægəʳ] n pugnale m

daily ['deɪlɪ] adj quotidiano(-a), giornaliero(-a) ▷ n quotidiano ▷ adv tutti i giorni

dairy ['dɛərɪ] n (BRIT: shop) latteria; (on farm) caseificio ▷ adj caseario(-a); **dairy produce** npl latticini mpl

daisy ['deɪzɪ] n margherita

dam [dæm] n diga ▷ vt sbarrare; costruire dighe su

damage ['dæmɪdʒ] n danno, danni mpl; (fig) danno ▷ vt danneggiare; **~s** npl (Law) danni

damn [dæm] vt condannare; (curse) maledire ▷ n (inf): **I don't give a ~** non me ne frega niente ▷ adj (inf: also: **~ed**): **this ~ ...** questo maledetto ...; **~ it!** accidenti!

damp [dæmp] adj umido(-a) ▷ n umidità, umido ▷ vt (also: **~en**: cloth, rag) inumidire, bagnare; (: enthusiasm etc) spegnere

dance [dɑːns] n danza, ballo; (ball) ballo ▷ vi ballare; **dance floor** n pista da ballo; **dancer** n danzatore(-trice); (professional) ballerino(-a); **dancing** ['dɑːnsɪŋ] n danza, ballo

dandelion ['dændɪlaɪən] n dente m di leone

dandruff ['dændrəf] n forfora

Dane [deɪn] n danese m/f

danger ['deɪndʒəʳ] n pericolo; **there is a ~ of fire** c'è pericolo di incendio; **in ~** in pericolo; **he was in ~ of falling** rischiava di cadere; **dangerous** adj pericoloso(-a)

dangle ['dæŋgl] vt dondolare; (fig) far balenare ▷ vi pendolare

Danish ['deɪnɪʃ] adj danese ▷ n (Ling) danese m

dare [dɛəʳ] vt **to ~ sb to do** sfidare qn a fare ▷ vi **to ~ do sth** osare fare qc; **I ~ say** (I suppose) immagino (che); **daring** adj audace, ardito(-a) ▷ n audacia

dark [dɑːk] adj (night, room) buio(-a), scuro(-a); (colour, complexion) scuro(-a); (fig) cupo(-a), tetro(-a), nero(-a) ▷ n **in the ~** al buio; **in the ~ about** (fig) all'oscuro di; **after ~** a notte fatta; **darken** vt (colour) scurire ▷ vi (sky, room) oscurarsi; **darkness** n oscurità, buio; **darkroom** n camera oscura

darling ['dɑːlɪŋ] adj caro(-a) ▷ n tesoro

dart [dɑːt] n freccetta; (Sewing) pince f inv ▷ vi **to ~ towards** precipitarsi verso; **to ~ away/along** sfrecciare via/lungo; **dartboard** n bersaglio (per freccette); **darts** n tiro al bersaglio (con freccette)

dash [dæʃ] n (sign) lineetta; (small quantity) punta ▷ vt (missile) gettare; (hopes) infrangere ▷ vi **to ~ towards** precipitarsi verso

dashboard ['dæʃbɔːd] n (Aut) cruscotto

data ['deɪtə] npl dati mpl; **database** n base f di dati, data base m inv; **data processing** n elaborazione f (elettronica) dei dati

date [deɪt] n data; appuntamento; (fruit) dattero ▷ vt datare; (person) uscire con; **what's the ~ today?** quanti ne abbiamo oggi?; **~ of birth** data di nascita; **to ~** (until now) fino a oggi; **dated** adj passato(-a) di moda

daughter ['dɔːtəʳ] n figlia; **daughter-in-law** n nuora

daunting ['dɔːntɪŋ] adj non invidiabile

dawn [dɔːn] n alba ▷ vi (day) spuntare; (fig): **it ~ed on him that ...** gli è venuto in mente che ...

day [deɪ] n giorno; (as duration) giornata; (period of time, age) tempo, epoca; **the ~ before** il giorno avanti or prima; **the ~ after, the following ~** il giorno dopo *or* seguente; **the ~ after tomorrow** dopodomani; **the ~ before yester~** l'altroieri; **by ~** di giorno; **day-care centre** n scuola materna; **daydream** vi sognare a occhi aperti; **daylight** n luce f del giorno; **day return** (BRIT) n biglietto giornaliero di andata e ritorno; **daytime** n giorno; **day-to-day** adj (life, organization) quotidiano(-a); **day trip** n gita (di un giorno)

dazed [deɪzd] adj stordito(-a)

dazzle ['dæzl] vt abbagliare; **dazzling** adj (light) abbagliante; (colour) violento(-a); (smile) smagliante

DC abbr (= direct current) c.c.

dead [dɛd] adj morto(-a); (numb) intirizzito(-a); (telephone) muto(-a); (battery) scarico(-a) ▷ adv assolutamente, perfettamente ▷ npl **the ~** i morti; **he was shot ~** fu colpito a morte; **~ tired** stanco(-a) morto(-a); **to stop ~** fermarsi di colpo; **dead end** n vicolo cieco; **deadline** n scadenza; **deadly** adj mortale; (weapon, poison) micidiale; **Dead Sea** n the Dead Sea il mar Morto

deaf [dɛf] adj sordo(-a); **deafen** vt assordare; **deafening** adj fragoroso(-a), assordante

deal [diːl] (pt, pp **dealt**) n accordo; (business deal) affare m ▷ vt (blow, cards) dare; **a great ~ (of)** molto(-a); **deal with** vt fus (Comm) fare affari con, trattare con; (handle) occuparsi di; (be about: book etc) trattare di; **dealer** n commerciante m/f; **dealings** npl (Comm) relazioni fpl; (relations) rapporti mpl

dealt [dɛlt] pt, pp of **deal**

dean [diːn] n (Rel) decano; (Scol) preside m di facoltà (or di collegio)

dear [dɪəʳ] adj caro(-a) ▷ n **my ~** caro mio/ cara mia ▷ excl **~ me!** Dio mio!; **D~ Sir/ Madam** (in letter) Egregio Signore/Egregia Signora; **D~ Mr/Mrs X** Gentile Signor/ Signora X; **dearly** adv (love) moltissimo; (pay) a caro prezzo

death [dɛθ] n morte f; (Admin) decesso; **death penalty** n pena di morte; **death sentence** n condanna a morte

debate [dɪ'beɪt] n dibattito ▷ vt dibattere; discutere

debit ['dɛbɪt] n debito ▷ vt **to ~ a sum to sb** or **to sb's account** addebitare una somma a qn; **debit card** n carta di debito

debris ['dɛbriː] n detriti mpl

debt [dɛt] n debito; **to be in ~** essere indebitato(-a)

debut ['deɪbjuː] n debutto

Dec. abbr (= December) dic.

decade ['dɛkeɪd] n decennio

decaffeinated [dɪ'kæfɪneɪtɪd] adj decaffeinato(-a)

decay [dɪ'keɪ] n decadimento; (also: **tooth ~**) carie f ▷ vi (rot) imputridire

deceased [dɪ'siːst] n defunto(-a)

deceit [dɪ'siːt] n inganno; **deceive** [dɪ'siːv] vt ingannare

December [dɪ'sɛmbəʳ] n dicembre m

decency ['diːsənsɪ] n decenza

decent ['diːsənt] adj decente; (respectable) per bene; (kind) gentile

deception [dɪ'sɛpʃən] n inganno

deceptive [dɪ'sɛptɪv] adj ingannevole

decide [dɪ'saɪd] vt (person) far prendere una decisione a; (question, argument) risolvere, decidere ▷ vi decidere, decidersi; **to ~ to do/that** decidere di fare/che; **to ~ on** decidere per

decimal ['dɛsɪməl] adj decimale ▷ n decimale m

decision [dɪ'sɪʒən] n decisione f

decisive [dɪ'saɪsɪv] adj decisivo(-a); (person) deciso(-a)

deck [dɛk] n (Naut) ponte m; (of bus): **top ~** imperiale m; (record deck) piatto; (of cards) mazzo; **deckchair** n sedia a sdraio

declaration [dɛklə'reɪʃən] n dichiarazione f

declare [dɪ'klɛəʳ] vt dichiarare

decline [dɪ'klaɪn] n (decay) declino; (lessening) ribasso ▷ vt declinare; rifiutare ▷ vi declinare; diminuire

decorate ['dɛkəreɪt] vt (adorn, give a medal to) decorare; (paint and paper) tinteggiare e tappezzare; **decoration** [-'reɪʃən] n (medal etc, adornment) decorazione f; **decorator** n decoratore m

decrease [n 'diːkriːs, vb diː'kriːs] n diminuzione f ▷ vt, vi diminuire

decree [dɪ'kriː] n decreto

dedicate ['dɛdɪkeɪt] vt consacrare; (book etc) dedicare; **dedicated** adj coscienzioso(-a); (Comput) specializzato(-a), dedicato(-a); **dedication** [dɛdɪ'keɪʃən] n (devotion) dedizione f; (in book etc) dedica

deduce [dɪ'djuːs] vt dedurre

deduct [dɪ'dʌkt] vt **to ~ sth from** dedurre qc (da); **deduction** [dɪ'dʌkʃən] n deduzione f

deed [diːd] n azione f, atto; (Law) atto

deem [diːm] vt (formal) giudicare, ritenere; **to ~ it wise to do** ritenere prudente fare

deep [diːp] adj profondo(-a); **4 metres ~** profondo(-a) 4 metri ▷ adv **spectators stood 20 ~** c'erano 20 file di spettatori; **how ~ is the water?** quanto è profonda l'acqua?; **deep-fry** vt friggere in olio abbondante; **deeply** adv profondamente

deer [dɪəʳ] n inv cervo; **(fallow) ~** daino; **roe ~** capriolo

default [dɪˈfɔːlt] n (Comput: also: **~ value**) default m inv; **by ~** (Sport) per abbandono

defeat [dɪˈfiːt] n sconfitta ▷ vt (team, opponents) sconfiggere

defect [n ˈdiːfɛkt, vb dɪˈfɛkt] n difetto ▷ vi **to ~ to the enemy** passare al nemico; **defective** [dɪˈfɛktɪv] adj difettoso(-a)

defence [dɪˈfɛns] (US **defense**) n difesa

defend [dɪˈfɛnd] vt difendere; **defendant** n imputato(-a); **defender** n difensore(-a)

defense [dɪˈfɛns] (US) n = **defence**

defensive [dɪˈfɛnsɪv] adj difensivo(-a) ▷ n **on the ~** sulla difensiva

defer [dɪˈfəːʳ] vt (postpone) differire, rinviare

defiance [dɪˈfaɪəns] n sfida; **in ~ of** a dispetto di; **defiant** [dɪˈfaɪənt] adj (attitude) di sfida; (person) ribelle

deficiency [dɪˈfɪʃənsɪ] n deficienza, carenza; **deficient** adj deficiente; insufficiente; **to be deficient in** mancare di

deficit [ˈdɛfɪsɪt] n deficit m inv

define [dɪˈfaɪn] vt definire

definite [ˈdɛfɪnɪt] adj (fixed) definito(-a), preciso(-a); (clear, obvious) ben definito(-a), esatto(-a); (Ling) determinativo(-a); **he was ~ about it** ne era sicuro; **definitely** adv indubbiamente

definition [dɛfɪˈnɪʃən] n definizione f

deflate [diːˈfleɪt] vt sgonfiare

deflect [dɪˈflɛkt] vt deflettere, deviare

defraud [dɪˈfrɔːd] vt defraudare

defrost [diːˈfrɔst] vt (fridge) disgelare

defuse [diːˈfjuːz] vt disinnescare; (fig) distendere

defy [dɪˈfaɪ] vt sfidare; (efforts etc) resistere a; **it defies description** supera ogni descrizione

degree [dɪˈgriː] n grado; (Scol) laurea (universitaria); **a first ~ in maths** una laurea in matematica; **by ~s** (gradually) gradualmente, a poco a poco; **to some ~** fino a un certo punto, in certa misura

dehydrated [diːhaɪˈdreɪtɪd] adj disidratato(-a); (milk, eggs) in polvere

de-icer [diːˈaɪsəʳ] n sbrinatore m

delay [dɪˈleɪ] vt ritardare ▷ vi **to ~ (in doing sth)** ritardare (a fare qc) ▷ n ritardo; **to be ~ed** subire un ritardo; (person) essere trattenuto(-a)

delegate [n ˈdɛlɪgɪt, vb ˈdɛlɪgeɪt] n delegato(-a) ▷ vt delegare

delete [dɪˈliːt] vt cancellare

deli [ˈdɛlɪ] n = **delicatessen**

deliberate [adj dɪˈlɪbərɪt, vb dɪˈlɪbəreɪt]

adj (intentional) intenzionale; (slow) misurato(-a) ▷ vi deliberare, riflettere; **deliberately** adv (on purpose) deliberatamente

delicacy [ˈdɛlɪkəsɪ] n delicatezza

delicate [ˈdɛlɪkɪt] adj delicato(-a)

delicatessen [dɛlɪkəˈtɛsn] n ≈ salumeria

delicious [dɪˈlɪʃəs] adj delizioso(-a), squisito(-a)

delight [dɪˈlaɪt] n delizia, gran piacere m ▷ vt dilettare; **to take (a) ~ in** dilettarsi in; **delighted** adj **delighted (at or with)** contentissimo(-a) (di), felice (di); **delighted to do** felice di fare; **delightful** adj delizioso(-a), incantevole

delinquent [dɪˈlɪŋkwənt] adj, n delinquente m/f

deliver [dɪˈlɪvəʳ] vt (mail) distribuire; (goods) consegnare; (speech) pronunciare; (Med) far partorire; **delivery** n distribuzione f; consegna; (of speaker) dizione f; (Med) parto

delusion [dɪˈluːʒən] n illusione f

de luxe [dəˈlʌks] adj di lusso

delve [dɛlv] vi **to ~ into** frugare in; (subject) far ricerche in

demand [dɪˈmɑːnd] vt richiedere; (rights) rivendicare ▷ n domanda; (claim) rivendicazione f; **in ~** ricercato(-a), richiesto(-a); **on ~** a richiesta; **demanding** adj (boss) esigente; (work) impegnativo(-a)

demise [dɪˈmaɪz] n decesso

demo [ˈdɛməu] (inf) n abbr (= demonstration) manifestazione f

democracy [dɪˈmɔkrəsɪ] n democrazia; **democrat** [ˈdɛməkræt] n democratico(-a); **democratic** [dɛməˈkrætɪk] adj democratico(-a)

demolish [dɪˈmɔlɪʃ] vt demolire

demolition [dɛməˈlɪʃən] n demolizione f

demon [ˈdiːmən] n (also fig) demonio ▷ cpd **a ~ squash player** un mago dello squash; **a ~ driver** un guidatore folle

demonstrate [ˈdɛmənstreɪt] vt dimostrare, provare ▷ vi dimostrare, manifestare; **demonstration** [-ˈstreɪʃən] n dimostrazione f; (Pol) dimostrazione, manifestazione f; **demonstrator** n (Pol) dimostrante m/f; (Comm) dimostratore(-trice)

demote [dɪˈməut] vt far retrocedere

den [dɛn] n tana, covo; (room) buco

denial [dɪˈnaɪəl] n diniego; rifiuto

denim [ˈdɛnɪm] n tessuto di cotone ritorto; **~s** npl (jeans) blue jeans mpl

Denmark [ˈdɛnmɑːk] n Danimarca

denomination [dɪnɔmɪˈneɪʃən] n (money) valore m; (Rel) confessione f

denounce [dɪ'nauns] vt denunciare

dense [dɛns] adj fitto(-a); (smoke) denso(-a); (inf: person) ottuso(-a), duro(-a)

density ['dɛnsɪtɪ] n densità f inv

dent [dɛnt] n ammaccatura ▷ vt (also: **make a ~ in**) ammaccare

dental ['dɛntl] adj dentale; **dental floss** [-flɔs] n filo interdentale; **dental surgery** n ambulatorio del dentista

dentist ['dɛntɪst] n dentista m/f

dentures ['dɛntʃəz] npl dentiera

deny [dɪ'naɪ] vt negare; (refuse) rifiutare

deodorant [di:'əudərənt] n deodorante m

depart [dɪ'pɑ:t] vi partire; **to ~ from** (fig) deviare da

department [dɪ'pɑ:tmənt] n (Comm) reparto; (Scol) sezione f, dipartimento; (Pol) ministero; **department store** n grande magazzino

departure [dɪ'pɑ:tʃə'] n partenza; (fig): **~ from** deviazione f da; **a new ~** una svolta (decisiva); **departure lounge** n (at airport) sala d'attesa

depend [dɪ'pɛnd] vi **to ~ on** dipendere da; (rely on) contare su; **it ~s** dipende; **~ing on the result ...** a seconda del risultato ...; **dependant** n persona a carico; **dependent** adj **to be dependent on** dipendere da; (child, relative) essere a carico di ▷ n = **dependant**

depict [dɪ'pɪkt] vt (in picture) dipingere; (in words) descrivere

deport [dɪ'pɔ:t] vt deportare; espellere

deposit [dɪ'pɔzɪt] n (Comm, Geo) deposito; (of ore, oil) giacimento; (Chem) sedimento; (part payment) acconto; (for hired goods etc) cauzione f ▷ vt depositare; dare in acconto; mettere or lasciare in deposito; **deposit account** n conto vincolato

depot ['dɛpəu] n deposito; (US) stazione f ferroviaria

depreciate [dɪ'pri:ʃɪeɪt] vi svalutarsi

depress [dɪ'prɛs] vt deprimere; (price, wages) abbassare; (press down) premere; **depressed** adj (person) depresso(-a), abbattuto(-a); (price) in ribasso; (industry) in crisi; **depressing** adj deprimente; **depression** [dɪ'prɛʃən] n depressione f

deprive [dɪ'praɪv] vt **to ~ sb of** privare qn di; **deprived** adj disgraziato(-a)

dept. abbr = **department**

depth [dɛpθ] n profondità f inv; **in the ~s of** nel profondo di; nel cuore di; **out of one's ~** (in water) dove non si tocca; (fig) a disagio

deputy ['dɛpjutɪ] adj **~ head** (BRIT Scol) vicepreside m/f ▷ n (assistant) vice m/f inv; (US: also: **~ sheriff**) vice-sceriffo

derail [dɪ'reɪl] vt **to be ~ed** deragliare

derelict ['dɛrɪlɪkt] adj abbandonato(-a)

derive [dɪ'raɪv] vt **to ~ sth from** derivare qc da; trarre qc da ▷ vi **to ~ from** derivare da

descend [dɪ'sɛnd] vt, vi discendere, scendere; **to ~ from** discendere da; **to ~ to** (lying, begging) abbassarsi a; **descendant** n discendente m/f; **descent** [dɪ'sɛnt] n discesa; (origin) discendenza, famiglia

describe [dɪs'kraɪb] vt descrivere; **description** [-'krɪpʃən] n descrizione f; (sort) genere m, specie f

desert [n 'dɛzət, vb dɪ'zə:t] n deserto ▷ vt lasciare, abbandonare ▷ vi (Mil) disertare; **deserted** [dɪ'zə:tɪd] adj deserto(-a)

deserve [dɪ'zə:v] vt meritare

design [dɪ'zaɪn] n (art, sketch) disegno; (layout, shape) linea; (pattern) fantasia; (intention) intenzione f ▷ vt disegnare; progettare

designate [vb 'dɛzɪgneɪt, adj 'dɛzɪgnɪt] designare ▷ adj designato(-a)

designer [dɪ'zaɪnə'] n (Art, Tech) disegnatore(-trice); (of fashion) modellista m/f

desirable [dɪ'zaɪərəbl] adj desiderabile; **it is ~ that** è opportuno che + sub

desire [dɪ'zaɪə'] n desiderio, voglia ▷ vt desiderare, volere

desk [dɛsk] n (in office) scrivania; (for pupil) banco; (BRIT: in shop, restaurant) cassa; (in hotel) ricevimento; (at airport) accettazione f; **desk-top publishing** n desktop publishing m

despair [dɪs'pɛə'] n disperazione f ▷ vi **to ~ of** disperare di

despatch [dɪs'pætʃ] n, vt = **dispatch**

desperate ['dɛspərɪt] adj disperato(-a); (fugitive) capace di tutto; **to be ~ for sth/to do** volere disperatamente qc/fare; **desperately** adv disperatamente; (very) terribilmente, estremamente; **desperation** [dɛspə'reɪʃən] n disperazione f

despise [dɪs'paɪz] vt disprezzare, sdegnare

despite [dɪs'paɪt] prep malgrado, a dispetto di, nonostante

dessert [dɪ'zə:t] n dolce m; frutta; **dessertspoon** n cucchiaio da dolci

destination [dɛstɪ'neɪʃən] n destinazione f

destined ['dɛstɪnd] adj **to be ~ to do/for** essere destinato(-a) a fare/per

destiny ['dɛstɪnɪ] n destino

destroy [dɪs'trɔɪ] vt distruggere

destruction [dɪs'trʌkʃən] n distruzione f

destructive [dɪs'trʌktɪv] adj distruttivo(-a)

detach [dɪ'tætʃ] vt staccare, distaccare; **detached** adj (attitude) distante;

detached house *n* villa

detail ['di:teɪl] *n* particolare *m*, dettaglio
▷ *vt* dettagliare, particolareggiare;
in ~ nei particolari; **detailed** *adj*
particolareggiato(-a)

detain [dɪ'teɪn] *vt* trattenere; (*in captivity*)
detenere

detect [dɪ'tɛkt] *vt* scoprire, scorgere; (*Med,
Police, Radar etc*) individuare; **detection**
[dɪ'tɛkʃən] *n* scoperta; individuazione
f; **detective** *n* investigatore(-trice);
detective story *n* giallo

detention [dɪ'tɛnʃən] *n* detenzione *f*; (*Scol*)
permanenza forzata per punizione

deter [dɪ'tə:ʳ] *vt* dissuadere

detergent [dɪ'tə:dʒənt] *n* detersivo

deteriorate [dɪ'tɪərɪəreɪt] *vi* deteriorarsi

determination [dɪtə:mɪ'neɪʃən] *n*
determinazione *f*

determine [dɪ'tə:mɪn] *vt* determinare;
determined *adj* (*person*) risoluto(-a),
deciso(-a); **determined to do** deciso(-a)
a fare

deterrent [dɪ'tɛrənt] *n* deterrente *m*; **to
act as a ~** fungere da deterrente

detest [dɪ'tɛst] *vt* detestare

detour ['di:tuəʳ] *n* deviazione *f*

detract [dɪ'trækt] *vi* **to ~ from** detrarre da

detrimental [dɛtrɪ'mɛntl] *adj* **~ to**
dannoso(-a) a, nocivo(-a) a

devastating ['dɛvəsteɪtɪŋ] *adj*
devastatore(-trice), sconvolgente

develop [dɪ'vɛləp] *vt* sviluppare; (*habit*)
prendere (gradualmente) ▷ *vi* svilupparsi;
(*facts, symptoms: appear*) manifestarsi,
rivelarsi; **can you ~ this film?** può
sviluppare questo rullino?; **developing
country** *n* paese *m* in via di sviluppo;
development *n* sviluppo

device [dɪ'vaɪs] *n* (*apparatus*) congegno

devil ['dɛvl] *n* diavolo; demonio

devious [dɪ'vi:əs] *adj* (*person*) subdolo(-a)

devise [dɪ'vaɪz] *vt* escogitare, concepire

devote [dɪ'vəut] *vt* **to ~ sth to** dedicare qc
a; **devoted** *adj* devoto(-a); **to be devoted
to sb** essere molto affezionato(-a) a qn;
devotion [dɪ'vəuʃən] *n* devozione *f*,
attaccamento; (*Rel*) atto di devozione,
preghiera

devour [dɪ'vauəʳ] *vt* divorare

devout [dɪ'vaut] *adj* pio(-a), devoto(-a)

dew [dju:] *n* rugiada

diabetes [daɪə'bi:ti:z] *n* diabete *m*

diabetic [daɪə'bɛtɪk] *adj, n* diabetico(-a)

diagnose [daɪəg'nəuz] *vt* diagnosticare

diagnosis [daɪəg'nəusɪs] (*pl* **diagnoses**) *n*
diagnosi *f inv*

diagonal [daɪ'ægənl] *adj* diagonale ▷ *n*
diagonale *f*

diagram ['daɪəgræm] *n* diagramma *m*

dial ['daɪəl] *n* quadrante *m*; (*on radio*)
lancetta; (*on telephone*) disco combinatore
▷ *vt* (*number*) fare

dialect ['daɪəlɛkt] *n* dialetto

dialling code, (*us* **area code**) *n* prefisso;
what's the ~ for Paris? qual è il prefisso
telefonico di Parigi?

dialling tone ['daɪəlɪŋ-] (*us* **dial tone**) *n*
segnale *m* di linea libera

dialogue ['daɪəlɔg] (*us* **dialog**) *n* dialogo

diameter [daɪ'æmɪtəʳ] *n* diametro

diamond ['daɪəmənd] *n* diamante *m*;
(*shape*) rombo; **~s** *npl* (*Cards*) quadri *mpl*

diaper ['daɪəpəʳ] (*us*) *n* pannolino

diarrhoea [daɪə'ri:ə] (*us* **diarrhea**) *n*
diarrea

diary ['daɪərɪ] *n* (*daily account*) diario; (*book*)
agenda

dice [daɪs] *n inv* dado ▷ *vt* (*Culin*) tagliare
a dadini

dictate [dɪk'teɪt] *vt* dettare; **dictation**
[dɪk'teɪʃən] *n* dettatura; (*Scol*) dettato

dictator [dɪk'teɪtəʳ] *n* dittatore *m*

dictionary ['dɪkʃənrɪ] *n* dizionario

did [dɪd] *pt of* **do**

didn't [dɪdnt] = **did not**

die [daɪ] *vi* morire; **to be dying for sth/to
do sth** morire dalla voglia di qc/di fare
qc; **die down** *vi* abbassarsi; **die out** *vi*
estinguersi

diesel ['di:zəl] *n* (*vehicle*) diesel *m inv*

diet ['daɪət] *n* alimentazione *f*; (*restricted
food*) dieta ▷ *vi* (*also:* **be on a ~**) stare a
dieta

differ ['dɪfəʳ] *vi* **to ~ from sth** differire
da qc, essere diverso(-a) da qc; **to ~
from sb over sth** essere in disaccordo
con qn su qc; **difference** *n* differenza;
(*disagreement*) screzio; **different** *adj*
diverso(-a); **differentiate** [-'rɛnʃɪeɪt] *vi*
to differentiate between discriminare
or fare differenza fra; **differently** *adv*
diversamente

difficult ['dɪfɪkəlt] *adj* difficile; **difficulty** *n*
difficoltà *f inv*

dig [dɪg] (*pt, pp* **dug**) *vt* (*hole*) scavare;
(*garden*) vangare ▷ *n* (*prod*) gomitata;
(*archaeological*) scavo; (*fig*) frecciata; **dig
up** *vt* (*tree etc*) sradicare; (*information*)
scavare fuori

digest [*vb* daɪ'dʒɛst, *n* 'daɪdʒɛst] *vt* digerire
▷ *n* compendio; **digestion** [dɪ'dʒɛstʃən] *n*
digestione *f*

digit ['dɪdʒɪt] *n* cifra; (*finger*) dito; **digital**
adj digitale; **digital camera** *n* macchina
fotografica digitale; **digital TV** *n*
televisione *f* digitale

dignified ['dɪgnɪfaɪd] *adj* dignitoso(-a)

dignity ['dɪgnɪtɪ] n dignità
digs [dɪgz] (BRIT: inf) npl camera
ammobiliata
dilemma [daɪ'lɛmə] n dilemma m
dill [dɪl] n aneto
dilute [daɪ'luːt] vt diluire; (with water)
annacquare
dim [dɪm] adj (light) debole; (shape etc)
vago(-a); (room) in penombra; (inf: person)
tonto(-a) ▷ vt (light) abbassare
dime [daɪm] (US) n = 10 cents
dimension [daɪ'mɛnʃən] n dimensione f
diminish [dɪ'mɪnɪʃ] vt, vi diminuire
din [dɪn] n chiasso, fracasso
dine [daɪn] vi pranzare; **diner** n (person)
cliente m/f; (US: place) tavola calda
dinghy ['dɪŋgɪ] n battello pneumatico;
(also: **rubber ~**) gommone m
dingy ['dɪndʒɪ] adj grigio(-a)
dining car ['daɪnɪŋ-] (BRIT) n vagone m
ristorante
dining room n sala da pranzo
dining table n tavolo da pranzo
dinner ['dɪnər] n (lunch) pranzo; (evening
meal) cena; (public) banchetto; **dinner
jacket** n smoking m inv; **dinner party**
n cena; **dinner time** n ora di pranzo (or
cena)
dinosaur ['daɪnəsɔːr] n dinosauro
dip [dɪp] n discesa; (in sea) bagno; (Culin)
salsetta ▷ vt immergere; bagnare; (BRIT
Aut: lights) abbassare ▷ vi abbassarsi
diploma [dɪ'pləumə] n diploma m
diplomacy [dɪ'pləuməsɪ] n diplomazia
diplomat ['dɪpləmæt] n diplomatico;
diplomatic [dɪplə'mætɪk] adj
diplomatico(-a)
dipstick ['dɪpstɪk] n (Aut) indicatore m di
livello dell'olio
dire [daɪər] adj terribile; estremo(-a)
direct [daɪ'rɛkt] adj diretto(-a) ▷ vt
dirigere; (order): **to ~ sb to do sth**
dare direttive a qn di fare qc ▷ adv
direttamente; **can you ~ me to ...?** mi può
indicare la strada per ...?; **direct debit** n
(Banking) addebito effettuato per ordine di
un cliente di banca
direction [dɪ'rɛkʃən] n direzione f; **~s** npl
(advice) chiarimenti mpl; **sense of ~** senso
dell'orientamento; **~s for use** istruzioni fpl
directly [dɪ'rɛktlɪ] adv (in straight line)
direttamente; (at once) subito
director [dɪ'rɛktər] n direttore(-trice),
amministratore(-trice); (Theatre, Cinema)
regista m/f
directory [dɪ'rɛktərɪ] n elenco; **directory
enquiries** (us **directory assistance**) n
informazioni fpl elenco abbonati inv
dirt [dəːt] n sporcizia; immondizia; (earth)

terra; **dirty** adj sporco(-a) ▷ vt sporcare
disability [dɪsə'bɪlɪtɪ] n invalidità f inv;
(Law) incapacità f inv
disabled [dɪs'eɪbld] adj invalido(-a);
(mentally) ritardato(-a) ▷ npl **the ~** gli
invalidi
disadvantage [dɪsəd'vɑːntɪdʒ] n
svantaggio
disagree [dɪsə'griː] vi (differ) discordare;
(be against, think otherwise): **to ~ (with)**
essere in disaccordo (con), dissentire
(da); **disagreeable** adj sgradevole;
(person) antipatico(-a); **disagreement** n
disaccordo; (argument) dissapore m
disappear [dɪsə'pɪər] vi scomparire;
disappearance n scomparsa
disappoint [dɪsə'pɔɪnt] vt deludere;
disappointed adj deluso(-a);
disappointing adj deludente;
disappointment n delusione f
disapproval [dɪsə'pruːvəl] n
disapprovazione f
disapprove [dɪsə'pruːv] vi **to ~ of**
disapprovare
disarm [dɪs'ɑːm] vt disarmare;
disarmament n disarmo
disaster [dɪ'zɑːstər] n disastro; **disastrous**
[dɪ'zɑːstrəs] adj disastroso(-a)
disbelief ['dɪsbə'liːf] n incredulità
disc [dɪsk] n disco; (Comput) = **disk**
discard [dɪs'kɑːd] vt (old things) scartare;
(fig) abbandonare
discharge [vb dɪs'tʃɑːdʒ, n 'dɪstʃɑːdʒ]
vt (duties) compiere; (Elec, waste etc)
scaricare; (Med) emettere; (patient)
dimettere; (employee) licenziare; (soldier)
congedare; (defendant) liberare ▷ n (Elec)
scarica; (Med) emissione f; (dismissal)
licenziamento; congedo;
liberazione f
discipline ['dɪsɪplɪn] n disciplina ▷ vt
disciplinare; (punish) punire
disc jockey n disc jockey m inv
disclose [dɪs'kləuz] vt rivelare, svelare
disco ['dɪskəu] n abbr discoteca
discoloured [dɪs'kʌləd] (US **discolored**)
adj scolorito(-a), ingiallito(-a)
discomfort [dɪs'kʌmfət] n disagio; (lack of
comfort) scomodità f inv
disconnect [dɪskə'nɛkt] vt sconnettere,
staccare; (Elec, Radio) staccare; (gas, water)
chiudere
discontent [dɪskən'tɛnt] n
scontentezza
discontinue [dɪskən'tɪnjuː] vt smettere,
cessare; **"~d"** (Comm) "fuori produzione"
discount [n 'dɪskaunt, vb dɪs'kaunt] n
sconto ▷ vt scontare; (idea) non badare a;
are there ~s for students? ci sono sconti

per studenti?

discourage [dɪsˈkʌrɪdʒ] vt scoraggiare

discover [dɪsˈkʌvəʳ] vt scoprire; **discovery** n scoperta

discredit [dɪsˈkrɛdɪt] vt screditare; mettere in dubbio

discreet [dɪˈskriːt] adj discreto(-a)

discrepancy [dɪˈskrɛpənsɪ] n discrepanza

discretion [dɪˈskrɛʃən] n discrezione f; **use your own ~** giudichi lei

discriminate [dɪˈskrɪmɪneɪt] vi **to ~ between** distinguere tra; **to ~ against** discriminare contro; **discrimination** [-ˈneɪʃən] n discriminazione f; (judgment) discernimento

discuss [dɪˈskʌs] vt discutere; (debate) dibattere; **discussion** [dɪˈskʌʃən] n discussione f

disease [dɪˈziːz] n malattia

disembark [dɪsɪmˈbɑːk] vt, vi sbarcare

disgrace [dɪsˈɡreɪs] n vergogna; (disfavour) disgrazia ▷ vt disonorare, far cadere in disgrazia; **disgraceful** adj scandaloso(-a), vergognoso(-a)

disgruntled [dɪsˈɡrʌntld] adj scontento(-a), di cattivo umore

disguise [dɪsˈɡaɪz] n travestimento ▷ vt **to ~ (as)** travestire (da); **in ~** travestito(-a)

disgust [dɪsˈɡʌst] n disgusto, nausea ▷ vt disgustare, far schifo a; **disgusted** [dɪsˈɡʌstɪd] adj indignato(-a); **disgusting** [dɪsˈɡʌstɪŋ] adj disgustoso(-a), ripugnante

dish [dɪʃ] n piatto; **to do** or **wash the ~es** fare i piatti; **dishcloth** n strofinaccio

dishonest [dɪsˈɔnɪst] adj disonesto(-a)

dishtowel [ˈdɪʃtauəl] (us) n strofinaccio dei piatti

dishwasher [ˈdɪʃwɔʃəʳ] n lavastoviglie f inv

disillusion [dɪsɪˈluːʒən] vt disilludere, disingannare

disinfectant [dɪsɪnˈfɛktənt] n disinfettante m

disintegrate [dɪsˈɪntɪɡreɪt] vi disintegrarsi

disk [dɪsk] n (Comput) disco; **single-/ double-sided ~** disco a facciata singola/ doppia; **disk drive** n lettore m; **diskette** (us) n = disk

dislike [dɪsˈlaɪk] n antipatia, avversione f; (gen pl) cosa che non piace ▷ vt **he ~s it** non gli piace

dislocate [ˈdɪsləkeɪt] vt slogare

disloyal [dɪsˈlɔɪəl] adj sleale

dismal [ˈdɪzml] adj triste, cupo(-a)

dismantle [dɪsˈmæntl] vt (machine) smontare

dismay [dɪsˈmeɪ] n costernazione f ▷ vt sgomentare

dismiss [dɪsˈmɪs] vt congedare; (employee) licenziare; (idea) scacciare; (Law) respingere; **dismissal** n congedo; licenziamento

disobedient [dɪsəˈbiːdɪənt] adj disubbidiente

disobey [dɪsəˈbeɪ] vt disubbidire a

disorder [dɪsˈɔːdəʳ] n disordine m; (rioting) tumulto; (Med) disturbo

disorganized [dɪsˈɔːɡənaɪzd] adj (person, life) disorganizzato(-a); (system, meeting) male organizzato(-a)

disown [dɪsˈəun] vt rinnegare

dispatch [dɪsˈpætʃ] vt spedire, inviare ▷ n spedizione f, invio; (Mil, Press) dispaccio

dispel [dɪsˈpɛl] vt dissipare, scacciare

dispense [dɪsˈpɛns] vt distribuire, amministrare; **dispense with** vt fus fare a meno di; **dispenser** n (container) distributore m

disperse [dɪsˈpəːs] vt disperdere; (knowledge) disseminare ▷ vi disperdersi

display [dɪsˈpleɪ] n esposizione f; (of feeling etc) manifestazione f; (screen) schermo ▷ vt mostrare; (goods) esporre; (pej) ostentare

displease [dɪsˈpliːz] vt dispiacere a, scontentare; **~d with** scontento di

disposable [dɪsˈpəuzəbl] adj (pack etc) a perdere; (income) disponibile

disposal [dɪsˈpəuzl] n eliminazione f; (of property) cessione f; **at one's ~** alla sua disposizione

dispose [dɪsˈpəuz] vi **~ of** sbarazzarsi di; **disposition** [-ˈzɪʃən] n disposizione f; (temperament) carattere m

disproportionate [dɪsprəˈpɔːʃənət] adj sproporzionato(-a)

dispute [dɪsˈpjuːt] n disputa; (also: **industrial ~**) controversia (sindacale) ▷ vt contestare; (matter) discutere; (victory) disputare

disqualify [dɪsˈkwɔlɪfaɪ] vt (Sport) squalificare; **to ~ sb from sth/from doing** rendere qn incapace a qc/a fare; squalificare qn da qc/da fare; **to ~ sb from driving** ritirare la patente a qn

disregard [dɪsrɪˈɡɑːd] vt non far caso a, non badare a

disrupt [dɪsˈrʌpt] vt disturbare; creare scompiglio in; **disruption** [dɪsˈrʌpʃən] n disordine m; interruzione f

dissatisfaction [dɪssætɪsˈfækʃən] n scontentezza, insoddisfazione f

dissatisfied [dɪsˈsætɪsfaɪd] adj **~ (with)** scontento(a) or insoddisfatto(a) (di)

dissect [dɪˈsɛkt] vt sezionare

dissent [dɪ'sɛnt] *n* dissenso
dissertation [dɪsə'teɪʃən] *n* tesi *f inv*, dissertazione *f*
dissolve [dɪ'zɔlv] *vt* dissolvere, sciogliere; (*Pol, marriage etc*) sciogliere ▷ *vi* dissolversi, sciogliersi
distance ['dɪstns] *n* distanza; **in the ~** in lontananza
distant ['dɪstnt] *adj* lontano(-a), distante; (*manner*) riservato(-a), freddo(-a)
distil [dɪs'tɪl] (*us* **distill**) *vt* distillare; **distillery** *n* distilleria
distinct [dɪs'tɪŋkt] *adj* distinto(-a); **as ~ from** a differenza di; **distinction** [dɪs'tɪŋkʃən] *n* distinzione *f*; (*in exam*) lode *f*; **distinctive** *adj* distintivo(-a)
distinguish [dɪs'tɪŋgwɪʃ] *vt* distinguere; discernere; **distinguished** *adj* (*eminent*) eminente
distort [dɪs'tɔːt] *vt* distorcere; (*Tech*) deformare
distract [dɪs'trækt] *vt* distrarre; **distracted** *adj* distratto(-a); **distraction** [dɪs'trækʃən] *n* distrazione *f*
distraught [dɪs'trɔːt] *adj* stravolto(-a)
distress [dɪs'trɛs] *n* angoscia ▷ *vt* affliggere; **distressing** *adj* doloroso(-a)
distribute [dɪs'trɪbjuːt] *vt* distribuire; **distribution** [-'bjuːʃən] *n* distribuzione *f*; **distributor** *n* distributore *m*
district ['dɪstrɪkt] *n* (*of country*) regione *f*; (*of town*) quartiere *m*; (*Admin*) distretto; **district attorney** (*us*) *n* ≈ sostituto procuratore *m* della Repubblica
distrust [dɪs'trʌst] *n* diffidenza, sfiducia ▷ *vt* non aver fiducia in
disturb [dɪs'təːb] *vt* disturbare; **disturbance** *n* disturbo; (*political etc*) disordini *mpl*; **disturbed** *adj* (*worried, upset*) turbato(-a); **emotionally disturbed** con turbe emotive; **disturbing** *adj* sconvolgente
ditch [dɪtʃ] *n* fossa ▷ *vt* (*inf*) piantare in asso
ditto ['dɪtəu] *adv* idem
dive [daɪv] *n* tuffo; (*of submarine*) immersione *f* ▷ *vi* tuffarsi; immergersi; **diver** *n* tuffatore(-trice), palombaro
diverse [daɪ'vəːs] *adj* vario(-a)
diversion [daɪ'vəːʃən] *n* (*brit Aut*) deviazione *f*; (*distraction*) divertimento
diversity [daɪ'vəːsɪtɪ] *n* diversità *f inv*, varietà *f inv*
divert [daɪ'vəːt] *vt* deviare
divide [dɪ'vaɪd] *vt* dividere; (*separate*) separare ▷ *vi* dividersi; **divided highway** (*us*) *n* strada a doppia carreggiata
divine [dɪ'vaɪn] *adj* divino(-a)
diving ['daɪvɪŋ] *n* tuffo; **diving board** *n*

trampolino
division [dɪ'vɪʒən] *n* divisione *f*; separazione *f*; (*esp Football*) serie *f*
divorce [dɪ'vɔːs] *n* divorzio ▷ *vt* divorziare da; (*dissociate*) separare; **divorced** *adj* divorziato(-a); **divorcee** [-'siː] *n* divorziato(-a)
D.I.Y. (*brit*) *n abbr* = **do-it-yourself**
dizzy ['dɪzɪ] *adj* **to feel ~** avere il capogiro
DJ *n abbr* = **disc jockey**
DNA *n abbr* (= *deoxyribonucleic acid*) DNA *m*; **DNA test** *n* test *m inv* del DNA

 KEYWORD

do [duː] (*pt* **did**, *pp* **done**) *n* (*inf: party etc*) festa; **it was rather a grand do** è stato un ricevimento piuttosto importante ▷ *vb* **1** (*in negative constructions: non tradotto*): **I don't understand** non capisco
2 (*to form questions: non tradotto*): **didn't you know?** non lo sapevi?; **why didn't you come?** perché non sei venuto?
3 (*for emphasis, in polite expressions*): **she does seem rather late** sembra essere piuttosto in ritardo; **do sit down** si accomodi la prego, prego si sieda; **do take care!** mi raccomando, sta attento!
4 (*used to avoid repeating vb*): **she swims better than I do** lei nuota meglio di me; **do you agree?** — **yes, I do/no, I don't** sei d'accordo? — sì/no; **she lives in Glasgow** — **so do I** lei vive a Glasgow — anch'io; **he asked me to help him and I did** mi ha chiesto di aiutarlo ed io l'ho fatto
5 (*in question tags*): **you like him, don't you?** ti piace, vero?; **I don't know him, do I?** non lo conosco, vero?
▷ *vt* (*gen, carry out, perform etc*) fare; **what are you doing tonight?** che fa stasera?; **to do the cooking** cucinare; **to do the washing-up** fare i piatti; **to do one's teeth** lavarsi i denti; **to do one's hair/ nails** farsi i capelli/le unghie; **the car was doing 100** la macchina faceva i 100 all'ora
▷ *vi* **1** (*act, behave*) fare; **do as I do** faccia come me, faccia come faccio io
2 (*get on, fare*) andare; **he's doing well/ badly at school** va bene/male a scuola; **how do you do?** piacere!
3 (*suit*) andare bene; **this room will do** questa stanza va bene
4 (*be sufficient*) bastare; **will £10 do?** basteranno 10 sterline?; **that'll do** basta così; **that'll do!** (*in annoyance*) ora basta!; **to make do (with)** arrangiarsi (con)
do away with *vt fus* (*kill*) far fuori; (*abolish*) abolire

dock | 262

do up vt (laces) allacciare; (dress, buttons) abbottonare; (renovate: room, house) rimettere a nuovo, rifare
do with vt fus (need) aver bisogno di; (be connected): **what has it got to do with you?** e tu che c'entri?; **I won't have anything to do with it** non voglio avere niente a che farci; **it has to do with money** si tratta di soldi
do without vi fare senza ▷ vt fus fare a meno di

dock [dɔk] n (Naut) bacino; (Law) banco degli imputati ▷ vi entrare in bacino; (Space) agganciarsi; **~s** npl (Naut) dock m inv
doctor ['dɔktə'] n medico(-a); (Ph.D. etc) dottore(-essa) ▷ vt (drink etc) adulterare; **call a ~!** chiamate un dottore!; **Doctor of Philosophy** n dottorato di ricerca; (person) titolare m/f di un dottorato di ricerca
document ['dɔkjumənt] n documento; **documentary** [-'mɛntərɪ] adj (evidence) documentato(-a) ▷ n documentario; **documentation** [dɔkjumən'teɪʃən] n documentazione f
dodge [dɔdʒ] n trucco; schivata ▷ vt schivare, eludere
dodgy ['dɔdʒɪ] adj (inf: uncertain) rischioso(-a); (untrustworthy) sospetto(-a)
does [dʌz] vb see do
doesn't ['dʌznt] = does not
dog [dɔg] n cane m ▷ vt (follow closely) pedinare; (fig: memory etc) perseguitare; **doggy bag** n sacchetto per gli avanzi (da portare a casa)
do-it-yourself ['duːɪtjɔː'sɛlf] n il far da sé
dole [dəul] (BRIT) n sussidio di disoccupazione; **to be on the ~** vivere del sussidio
doll [dɔl] n bambola
dollar ['dɔlə'] n dollaro
dolphin ['dɔlfɪn] n delfino
dome [dəum] n cupola
domestic [də'mɛstɪk] adj (duty, happiness, animal) domestico(-a); (policy, affairs, flights) nazionale; **domestic appliance** n elettrodomestico
dominant ['dɔmɪnənt] adj dominante
dominate ['dɔmɪneɪt] vt dominare
domino ['dɔmɪnəu] (pl **dominoes**) n domino; **dominoes** n (game) gioco del domino
donate [də'neɪt] vt donare; **donation** [də'neɪʃən] n donazione f
done [dʌn] pp of **do**
donkey ['dɔŋkɪ] n asino

donor ['dəunə'] n donatore(-trice); **donor card** n tessera di donatore di organi
don't [dəunt] = do not
donut ['dəunʌt] (US) n = **doughnut**
doodle ['duːdl] vi scarabocchiare
doom [duːm] n destino; rovina ▷ vt **to be ~ed (to failure)** essere predestinato(-a) (a fallire)
door [dɔː'] n porta; **doorbell** n campanello; **door handle** n maniglia; **doorknob** ['dɔːnɔb] n pomello, maniglia; **doorstep** n gradino della porta; **doorway** n porta
dope [dəup] n (inf: drugs) roba ▷ vt (horse etc) drogare
dormitory ['dɔːmɪtrɪ] n dormitorio; (US) casa dello studente
DOS [dɔs] n abbr (= disk operating system) DOS m
dosage ['dəusɪdʒ] n posologia
dose [dəus] n dose f; (bout) attacco
dot [dɔt] n punto; macchiolina ▷ vt **~ted with** punteggiato(-a) di; **on the ~** in punto; **dotted line** ['dɔtɪd-] n linea punteggiata
double ['dʌbl] adj doppio(-a) ▷ adv (twice): **to cost ~ sth** costare il doppio (di qc) ▷ n sosia m inv ▷ vt raddoppiare; (fold) piegare doppio or in due ▷ vi raddoppiarsi; **at the ~** (BRIT), **on the ~** a passo di corsa; **double back** vi (person) tornare sui propri passi; **double bass** n contrabbasso; **double bed** n letto matrimoniale; **double-check** vt, vi ricontrollare; **double-click** vi (Comput) fare doppio click; **double-cross** vt fare il doppio gioco con; **doubledecker** n autobus m inv a due piani; **double glazing** (BRIT) n doppi vetri mpl; **double room** n camera matrimoniale; **doubles** n (Tennis) doppio; **double yellow lines** npl (BRIT: Aut) linea gialla doppia continua che segnala il divieto di sosta
doubt [daut] n dubbio ▷ vt dubitare di; **to ~ that** dubitare che + sub; **doubtful** adj dubbioso(-a), incerto(-a); (person) equivoco(-a); **doubtless** adv indubbiamente
dough [dəu] n pasta, impasto; **doughnut** (US **donut**) n bombolone m
dove [dʌv] n colombo(-a)
down [daun] n piume fpl ▷ adv giù, di sotto ▷ prep giù per ▷ vt (inf: drink) scolarsi; **~ with X!** abbasso X!; **down-and-out** n barbone m; **downfall** n caduta; rovina; **downhill** adv **to go downhill** andare in discesa; (fig) lasciarsi andare; andare a rotoli

Downing Street ['dauniŋ-] n **lo ~**
residenza del primo ministro inglese

⬡ **DOWNING STREET**
⬡
⬡ Al numero 10 di **Downing Street**, nel
⬡ quartiere di Westminster a Londra, si
⬡ trova la residenza del primo ministro
⬡ inglese, al numero 11 quella del
⬡ **Chancellor of the Exchequer**.

down: **download** vt (Comput) scaricare;
   downright adj franco(-a); (refusal)
   assoluto(-a)
Down's syndrome n sindrome f di Down
down: **downstairs** adv di sotto; al
   piano inferiore; **down-to-earth** adj
   pratico(-a); **downtown** adv in città; **down
   under** adv (Australia etc) agli antipodi;
   downward ['daunwəd] adj, adv in giù, in
   discesa; **downwards** ['daunwədz] adv
   =**downward**
doz. abbr =**dozen**
doze [dəuz] vi sonnecchiare
dozen ['dʌzn] n dozzina; **a ~ books** una
   dozzina di libri; **~s of** decine fpl di
Dr. abbr (= doctor) dott.; (in street names)
   =**drive**
drab [dræb] adj tetro(-a), grigio(-a)
draft [drɑːft] n abbozzo; (Pol) bozza;
   (Comm) tratta; (us: call-up) leva ▷ vt
   abbozzare; see also **draught**
drag [dræg] vt trascinare; (river) dragare
   ▷ vi trascinarsi ▷ n (inf) noioso(-a); noia,
   fatica; (women's clothing): **in ~** travestito
   (da donna)
dragon ['drægən] n drago
dragonfly ['drægənflaɪ] n libellula
drain [dreɪn] n (for sewage) fogna; (on
   resources) salasso ▷ vt (land, marshes)
   prosciugare; (vegetables) scolare ▷ vi
   (water) defluire (via); **drainage** n
   prosciugamento; fognatura; **drainpipe** n
   tubo di scarico
drama ['drɑːmə] n (art) dramma
   m, teatro; (play) commedia; (event)
   dramma; **dramatic** [drə'mætɪk] adj
   drammatico(-a)
drank [dræŋk] pt of **drink**
drape [dreɪp] vt drappeggiare; **~s** (us) npl
   (curtains) tende fpl
drastic ['dræstɪk] adj drastico(-a)
draught [drɑːft] (us **draft**) n corrente f
   d'aria; (Naut) pescaggio; **on ~** (beer) alla
   spina; **draught beer** n birra alla spina;
   draughts (BRIT) n (gioco della) dama
draw [drɔː] (pt **drew**, pp **drawn**) vt tirare;
   (take out) estrarre; (attract) attirare;
   (picture) disegnare; (line, circle) tracciare;

(money) ritirare ▷ vi (Sport) pareggiare
   ▷ n pareggio; (in lottery) estrazione f; **to ~
   near** avvicinarsi; **draw out** vi (lengthen)
   allungarsi ▷ vt (money) ritirare; **draw
   up** vi (stop) arrestarsi, fermarsi ▷ vt
   (chair) avvicinare; (document) compilare;
   drawback n svantaggio, inconveniente m
drawer [drɔːʳ] n cassetto
drawing ['drɔːɪŋ] n disegno; **drawing pin**
   (BRIT) n puntina da disegno; **drawing
   room** n salotto
drawn [drɔːn] pp of **draw**
dread [drɛd] n terrore m ▷ vt tremare
   all'idea di; **dreadful** adj terribile
dream [driːm] (pt, pp **dreamed** or **dreamt**)
   n sogno ▷ vt, vi sognare; **dreamer** n
   sognatore(-trice)
dreamt [drɛmt] pt, pp of **dream**
dreary ['drɪərɪ] adj tetro(-a);
   monotono(-a)
drench [drɛntʃ] vt inzuppare
dress [drɛs] n vestito; (no pl: clothing)
   abbigliamento ▷ vt vestire; (wound)
   fasciare ▷ vi vestirsi; **to get ~ed** vestirsi;
   dress up vi vestirsi a festa; (in fancy dress)
   vestirsi in costume; **dress circle** (BRIT) n
   prima galleria; **dresser** n (BRIT: cupboard)
   credenza; (us) cassettone m; **dressing** n
   (Med) benda; (Culin) condimento; **dressing
   gown** (BRIT) n vestaglia; **dressing
   room** n (Theatre) camerino; (Sport)
   spogliatoio; **dressing table** n toilette f
   inv; **dressmaker** n sarta
drew [druː] pt of **draw**
dribble ['drɪbl] vi (baby) sbavare ▷ vt (ball)
   dribblare
dried [draɪd] adj (fruit, beans) secco(-a);
   (eggs, milk) in polvere
drier ['draɪəʳ] n =**dryer**
drift [drɪft] n (of current etc) direzione
   f; forza; (of snow) cumulo; turbine m;
   (general meaning) senso ▷ vi (boat) essere
   trasportato(-a) dalla corrente; (sand, snow)
   ammucchiarsi
drill [drɪl] n trapano; (Mil) esercitazione f
   ▷ vt trapanare; (troops) addestrare ▷ vi (for
   oil) fare trivellazioni
drink [drɪŋk] (pt **drank**, pp **drunk**)
   n bevanda, bibita; (alcoholic drink)
   bicchierino; (sip) sorso ▷ vt, vi bere; **to
   have a ~** bere qualcosa; **would you
   like a ~?** vuoi qualcosa da bere?; **a ~ of
   water** un po' d'acqua; **drink-driving** n
   guida in stato di ebbrezza; **drinker** n
   bevitore(-trice); **drinking water** n acqua
   potabile
drip [drɪp] n goccia; gocciolamento;
   (Med) fleboclisi f inv ▷ vi gocciolare; (tap)
   sgocciolare

drive [draɪv] (pt **drove**, pp **driven**) n
passeggiata or giro in macchina; (also:
~way) viale m d'accesso; (energy) energia;
(campaign) campagna; (also: **disk ~**) lettore
m ▷ vt guidare; (nail) piantare; (push)
cacciare, spingere; (Tech: motor) azionare;
far funzionare ▷ vi (Aut: at controls)
guidare; (: travel) andare in macchina; **left-
/right-hand ~** guida a sinistra/destra; **to
~ sb mad** far impazzire qn; **drive out** vt
(force out) cacciare, mandare via; **drive-in**
(esp US) adj, n drive-in (m inv)

driven ['drɪvn] pp of **drive**

driver ['draɪvəʳ] n conducente m/f; (of taxi)
tassista m; (chauffeur: of bus) autista m/f;
driver's license (US) n patente f di guida

driveway ['draɪvweɪ] n viale m d'accesso

driving ['draɪvɪŋ] n guida; **driving
instructor** n istruttore(-trice) di scuola
guida; **driving lesson** n lezione f di guida;
driving licence (BRIT) n patente f di guida;
driving test n esame m di guida

drizzle ['drɪzl] n pioggerella

droop [dru:p] vi (flower) appassire; (head,
shoulders) chinarsi

drop [drɔp] n (of water) goccia; (lessening)
diminuzione f; (fall) caduta ▷ vt lasciare
cadere; (voice, eyes, price) abbassare; (set
down from car) far scendere; (name from
list) lasciare fuori ▷ vi cascare; (wind)
abbassarsi; **drop in** vi (inf: visit): **to ~
in (on)** fare un salto (da), passare (da);
drop off vi (sleep) addormentarsi ▷ vt
(passenger) far scendere; **drop out** vi
(withdraw) ritirarsi; (student etc) smettere
di studiare

drought [draut] n siccità f inv

drove [drəuv] pt of **drive**

drown [draun] vt affogare; (fig: noise)
soffocare ▷ vi affogare

drowsy ['drauzɪ] adj sonnolento(-a),
assonnato(-a)

drug [drʌg] n farmaco; (narcotic) droga
▷ vt drogare; **to be on ~s** drogarsi; (Med)
prendere medicinali; **hard/soft ~s**
droghe pesanti/leggere; **drug addict**
n tossicomane m/f; **drug dealer** n
trafficante m/f di droga; **druggist** (US) n
persona che gestisce un drugstore; **drugstore**
(US) n drugstore m inv

drum [drʌm] n tamburo; (for oil, petrol)
fusto ▷ vi tamburellare; **~s** npl (set of
drums) batteria; **drummer** n batterista
m/f

drunk [drʌŋk] pp of **drink** ▷ adj
ubriaco(-a); ebbro(-a) ▷ n (also: **~ard**)
ubriacone(-a); **drunken** adj ubriaco(-a);
da ubriaco

dry [draɪ] adj secco(-a); (day, clothes)

asciutto(-a) ▷ vt seccare; (clothes, hair,
hands) asciugare ▷ vi asciugarsi; **dry off**
vi asciugarsi ▷ vt asciugare; **dry up** vi
seccarsi; **dry-cleaner's** n lavasecco m inv;
dry-cleaning n pulitura a secco; **dryer** n
(for hair) föhn m inv, asciugacapelli m inv;
(for clothes) asciugabiancheria; (US: spin-
dryer) centrifuga

DSS n abbr (= Department of Social Security)
ministero della Previdenza sociale

DTP n abbr (= desk-top publishing) desktop
publishing m inv

dual ['djuəl] adj doppio(-a); **dual
carriageway** (BRIT) n strada a doppia
carreggiata

dubious ['dju:bɪəs] adj dubbio(-a)

Dublin ['dʌblɪn] n Dublino f

duck [dʌk] n anatra ▷ vi abbassare la testa

due [dju:] adj dovuto(-a); (expected)
atteso(-a); (fitting) giusto(-a) ▷ n dovuto
▷ adv **~ north** diritto verso nord

duel ['djuəl] n duello

duet [dju:'ɛt] n duetto

dug [dʌg] pt, pp of **dig**

duke [dju:k] n duca m

dull [dʌl] adj (light) debole; (boring)
noioso(-a); (slow-witted) ottuso(-a); (sound,
pain) sordo(-a); (weather, day) fosco(-a),
scuro(-a) ▷ vt (pain, grief) attutire; (mind,
senses) intorpidire

dumb [dʌm] adj muto(-a); (pej) stupido(-a)

dummy ['dʌmɪ] n (tailor's model)
manichino; (Tech, Comm) riproduzione f;
(BRIT: for baby) tettarella ▷ adj falso(-a),
finto(-a)

dump [dʌmp] n (also: **rubbish ~**) discarica
di rifiuti; (inf: place) buco ▷ vt (put down)
scaricare; mettere giù; (get rid of) buttar via

dumpling ['dʌmplɪŋ] n specie di gnocco

dune [dju:n] n duna

dungarees [dʌŋgə'ri:z] npl tuta

dungeon ['dʌndʒən] n prigione f
sotterranea

duplex ['dju:plɛks] (US) n (house) casa
con muro divisorio in comune con un'altra;
(apartment) appartamento su due piani

duplicate [n 'dju:plɪkət, vb 'dju:plɪkeɪt] n
doppio ▷ vt duplicare; **in ~** in doppia copia

durable ['djuərəbl] adj durevole; (clothes,
metal) resistente

duration [djuə'reɪʃən] n durata

during ['djuərɪŋ] prep durante, nel corso di

dusk [dʌsk] n crepuscolo

dust [dʌst] n polvere f ▷ vt (furniture)
spolverare; (cake etc): **to ~ with** cospargere
con; **dustbin** (BRIT) n pattumiera; **duster**
n straccio per la polvere; **dustman**
(irreg: BRIT) n netturbino; **dustpan** n
pattumiera; **dusty** adj polveroso(-a)

Dutch [dʌtʃ] *adj* olandese ▷ *n* (*Ling*) olandese *m*; **the ~** *npl* gli Olandesi; **to go ~** (*inf*) fare alla romana; **Dutchman, Dutchwoman** (*irreg*) *n* olandese *m/f*

duty ['dju:tɪ] *n* dovere *m*; (*tax*) dazio, tassa; **on ~** di servizio; **off ~** libero(-a), fuori servizio; **duty-free** *adj* esente da dazio

duvet ['du:veɪ] (*BRIT*) *n* piumino, piumone *m*

DVD *n abbr* (= digital versatile *or* video disk) DVD *m inv*; **DVD player** *n* lettore *m* DVD

dwarf [dwɔ:f] *n* nano(-a) ▷ *vt* far apparire piccolo

dwell [dwɛl] (*pt, pp* **dwelt**) *vi* dimorare; **dwell on** *vt fus* indugiare su

dwelt [dwɛlt] *pt, pp of* **dwell**

dwindle ['dwɪndl] *vi* diminuire

dye [daɪ] *n* tinta ▷ *vt* tingere

dying ['daɪɪŋ] *adj* morente, moribondo(-a)

dynamic [daɪ'næmɪk] *adj* dinamico(-a)

dynamite ['daɪnəmaɪt] *n* dinamite *f*

dyslexia [dɪs'lɛksɪə] *n* dislessia

dyslexic [dɪs'lɛksɪk] *adj, n* dislessico(-a)

E [i:] *n* (*Mus*) mi *m*

E111 *n abbr* (*also:* **form ~**) E111 (*modulo CEE per rimborso spese mediche*)

each [i:tʃ] *adj* ogni, ciascuno(-a) ▷ *pron* ciascuno(-a), ognuno(-a); **~ one** ognuno(-a); **~ other** si *or* ci *etc*; **they hate ~ other** si odiano (l'un l'altro); **you are jealous of ~ other** siete gelosi l'uno dell'altro; **they have 2 books ~** hanno 2 libri ciascuno

eager ['i:gəʳ] *adj* impaziente, desideroso(-a); ardente; **to be ~ for** essere desideroso di, aver gran voglia di

eagle ['i:gl] *n* aquila

ear [ɪəʳ] *n* orecchio; (*of corn*) pannocchia; **earache** *n* mal *m* d'orecchi; **eardrum** *n* timpano

earl [ə:l] (*BRIT*) *n* conte *m*

earlier ['ə:lɪəʳ] *adj* precedente ▷ *adv* prima

early ['ə:lɪ] *adv* presto, di buon'ora; (*ahead of time*) in anticipo ▷ *adj* (*near the beginning*) primo(-a); (*sooner than expected*) prematuro(-a); (*quick: reply*) veloce; **at an ~ hour** di buon'ora; **to have an ~ night** andare a letto presto; **in the ~** *or* **~ in the spring/19th century** all'inizio della primavera/dell'Ottocento; **early retirement** *n* ritiro anticipato

earmark ['ɪəmɑ:k] *vt* **to ~ sth for** destinare qc a

earn [əːn] vt guadagnare; (rest, reward) meritare

earnest ['əːnɪst] adj serio(-a); **in ~** sul serio

earnings ['əːnɪŋz] npl guadagni mpl; (salary) stipendio

ear: **earphones** ['ɪəfəʊnz] npl cuffia; **earplugs** npl tappi mpl per le orecchie; **earring** ['ɪərɪŋ] n orecchino

earth [əːθ] n terra ▷ vt (BRIT Elec) mettere a terra; **earthquake** n terremoto

ease [iːz] n agio, comodo ▷ vt (soothe) calmare; (loosen) allentare; **to ~ sth out/in** tirare fuori/infilare qc con delicatezza; facilitare l'uscita/l'entrata di qc; **at ~** a proprio agio; (Mil) a riposo

easily ['iːzɪlɪ] adv facilmente

east [iːst] n est m ▷ adj dell'est ▷ adv a oriente; **the E~** l'Oriente m; (Pol) l'Est; **eastbound** ['iːstbaʊnd] adj (traffic) diretto(-a) a est; (carriageway) che porta a est

Easter ['iːstər] n Pasqua; **Easter egg** n uovo di Pasqua

eastern ['iːstən] adj orientale, d'oriente; dell'est

Easter Sunday n domenica di Pasqua

easy ['iːzɪ] adj facile; (manner) disinvolto(-a) ▷ adv **to take it** or **things ~** prendersela con calma; **easy-going** adj accomodante

eat [iːt] (pt ate, pp eaten) vt, vi mangiare; **can we have something to ~?** possiamo mangiare qualcosa?; **eat out** vi mangiare fuori

eavesdrop ['iːvzdrɒp] vi **to ~ (on a conversation)** origliare (una conversazione)

e-book ['iːbuk] n libro elettronico

e-business ['iːbɪznɪs] n (company) azienda che opera in Internet; (commerce) commercio elettronico

EC n abbr (= European Community) CE f

eccentric [ɪk'sɛntrɪk] adj, n eccentrico(-a)

echo ['ɛkəʊ] (pl **echoes**) n eco m or f ▷ vt ripetere; fare eco a ▷ vi echeggiare; dare un eco

eclipse [ɪ'klɪps] n eclissi f inv

eco-friendly [iːkəʊ'frɛndlɪ] adj ecologico(-a)

ecological [iːkə'lɒdʒɪkəl] adj ecologico(-a)

ecology [ɪ'kɒlədʒɪ] n ecologia

e-commerce [iːkɒməːs] n commercio elettronico

economic [iːkə'nɒmɪk] adj economico(-a); **economical** adj economico(-a); (person) economo(-a); **economics** n economia ▷ npl lato finanziario

economist [ɪ'kɒnəmɪst] n economista m/f

economize [ɪ'kɒnəmaɪz] vi risparmiare, fare economia

economy [ɪ'kɒnəmɪ] n economia; **economy class** n (Aviat) classe f turistica; **economy class syndrome** n sindrome f della classe economica

ecstasy ['ɛkstəsɪ] n estasi f inv; **ecstatic** [ɛks'tætɪk] adj estatico(-a), in estasi

eczema ['ɛksɪmə] n eczema m

edge [ɛdʒ] n margine m; (of table, plate, cup) orlo; (of knife etc) taglio ▷ vt bordare; **on ~** (fig) = **edgy**; **to edge away from** sgattaiolare da

edgy ['ɛdʒɪ] adj nervoso(-a)

edible ['ɛdɪbl] adj commestibile; (meal) mangiabile

Edinburgh ['ɛdɪnbərə] n Edimburgo f

edit ['ɛdɪt] vt curare; **edition** [ɪ'dɪʃən] n edizione f; **editor** n (in newspaper) redattore(-trice), redattore(-trice) capo; (of sb's work) curatore(-trice); **editorial** [-'tɔːrɪəl] adj redazionale, editoriale ▷ n editoriale m

> Be careful not to translate *editor* by the Italian word *editore*.

educate ['ɛdjukeɪt] vt istruire; educare; **educated** adj istruito(-a)

education [ɛdju'keɪʃən] n educazione f; (schooling) istruzione f; **educational** adj pedagogico(-a); scolastico(-a); istruttivo(-a)

eel [iːl] n anguilla

eerie ['ɪərɪ] adj che fa accapponare la pelle

effect [ɪ'fɛkt] n effetto ▷ vt effettuare; **to take ~** (law) entrare in vigore; (drug) fare effetto; **in ~** effettivamente; **~s** npl (Theat) effetti mpl scenici; (property) effetti mpl; **effective** adj efficace; (actual) effettivo(-a); **effectively** adv efficacemente; effettivamente

efficiency [ɪ'fɪʃənsɪ] n efficienza; rendimento effettivo

efficient [ɪ'fɪʃənt] adj efficiente; **efficiently** adv efficientemente; efficacemente

effort ['ɛfət] n sforzo; **effortless** adj senza sforzo, facile

e.g. adv abbr (= exempli gratia) per esempio, p.es.

egg [ɛg] n uovo; **hard-boiled/soft-boiled ~** uovo sodo/alla coque; **eggcup** n portauovo m inv; **eggplant** (esp us) n melanzana; **eggshell** n guscio d'uovo; **egg white** n albume m, bianco d'uovo; **egg yolk** n tuorlo, rosso (d'uovo)

ego ['iːgəu] n ego m inv

Egypt ['iːdʒɪpt] n Egitto; **Egyptian** [ɪ'dʒɪpʃən] adj, n egiziano(-a)

eight [eɪt] num otto; **eighteen** num diciotto; **eighteenth** num diciottesimo(-a); **eighth** [eɪtθ] num

ottavo(-a); **eightieth** ['eɪtɪɪθ] *num*
ottantesimo(-a); **eighty** *num* ottanta
Eire ['eərə] *n* Repubblica d'Irlanda
either ['aɪðə'] *adj* l'uno(-a) o l'altro(-a);
(*both, each*) ciascuno(-a) ▷ *pron* **~ (of
them)** (o) l'uno(-a) o l'altro(-a) ▷ *adv*
neanche ▷ *conj* **~ good or bad** o buono o
cattivo; **on ~ side** su ciascun lato; **I don't
like ~** non mi piace né l'uno né l'altro; **no, I
don't ~** no, neanch'io
eject [ɪ'dʒɛkt] *vt* espellere; lanciare
elaborate [*adj* ɪ'læbərɪt, *vb* ɪ'læbəreɪt]
adj elaborato(-a), minuzioso(-a) ▷ *vt*
elaborare ▷ *vi* fornire i particolari
elastic [ɪ'læstɪk] *adj* elastico(-a) ▷ *n*
elastico; **elastic band** (BRIT) *n* elastico
elbow ['ɛlbəʊ] *n* gomito
elder ['ɛldə'] *adj* maggiore, più vecchio(-a)
▷ *n* (*tree*) sambuco; **one's ~s** i più anziani;
elderly *adj* anziano(-a) ▷ *npl* **the elderly**
gli anziani
eldest ['ɛldɪst] *adj, n* **the ~ (child)** il(la)
maggiore (dei bambini)
elect [ɪ'lɛkt] *vt* eleggere ▷ *adj* **the ~
president** ~ il presidente designato; **to ~
to do** decidere di fare; **election** [ɪ'lɛkʃən]
n elezione *f*; **electoral** [ɪ'lɛktərəl] *adj*
elettorale; **electorate** *n* elettorato
electric [ɪ'lɛktrɪk] *adj* elettrico(-a);
electrical *adj* elettrico(-a); **electric
blanket** *n* coperta elettrica; **electric fire**
n stufa elettrica; **electrician** [ɪlɛk'trɪʃən]
n elettricista *m*; **electricity** [ɪlɛk'trɪsɪtɪ]
n elettricità; **electric shock** *n* scossa
(elettrica); **electrify** [ɪ'lɛktrɪfaɪ] *vt* (*Rail*)
elettrificare; (*audience*) elettrizzare
electronic [ɪlɛk'trɒnɪk] *adj* elettronico(-a);
electronic mail *n* posta elettronica;
electronics *n* elettronica
elegance ['ɛlɪɡəns] *n* eleganza
elegant ['ɛlɪɡənt] *adj* elegante
element ['ɛlɪmənt] *n* elemento; (*of heater,
kettle etc*) resistenza
elementary [ɛlɪ'mɛntərɪ] *adj* elementare;
elementary school (US) *n* scuola
elementare
elephant ['ɛlɪfənt] *n* elefante(-essa)
elevate ['ɛlɪveɪt] *vt* elevare
elevator ['ɛlɪveɪtə'] *n* elevatore *m*; (US: *lift*)
ascensore *m*
eleven [ɪ'lɛvn] *num* undici; **eleventh** *adj*
undicesimo(-a)
eligible ['ɛlɪdʒəbl] *adj* eleggibile; (*for
membership*) che ha i requisiti
eliminate [ɪ'lɪmɪneɪt] *vt* eliminare
elm [ɛlm] *n* olmo
eloquent ['ɛləkwənt] *adj* eloquente
else [ɛls] *adv* altro; **something ~**
qualcos'altro; **somewhere ~** altrove;

everywhere ~ in qualsiasi altro luogo;
nobody ~ nessun altro; **where ~?** in quale
altro luogo?; **little ~** poco altro; **elsewhere**
adv altrove
elusive [ɪ'lu:sɪv] *adj* elusivo(-a)
e-mail *n abbr* (= *electronic mail*) posta
elettronica ▷ *vt* mandare un messaggio
di posta elettronica a; **e-mail address** *n*
indirizzo di posta elettronica
embankment [ɪm'bæŋkmənt] *n* (*of road,
railway*) terrapieno
embargo [ɪm'bɑ:ɡəʊ] *n* (*pl* **embargoes**)
(*Comm, Naut*) embargo ▷ *vt* mettere
l'embargo su; **to put an ~ on sth** mettere
l'embargo su qc
embark [ɪm'bɑ:k] *vi* **to ~ (on)** imbarcarsi
(su) ▷ *vt* imbarcare; **to ~ on** (*fig*)
imbarcarsi in
embarrass [ɪm'bærəs] *vt* imbarazzare;
embarrassed *adj* imbarazzato(-a);
embarrassing *adj* imbarazzante;
embarrassment *n* imbarazzo
embassy ['ɛmbəsɪ] *n* ambasciata
embrace [ɪm'breɪs] *vt* abbracciare ▷ *vi*
abbracciarsi ▷ *n* abbraccio
embroider [ɪm'brɔɪdə'] *vt* ricamare;
embroidery *n* ricamo
embryo ['ɛmbrɪəʊ] *n* embrione *m*
emerald ['ɛmərəld] *n* smeraldo
emerge [ɪ'mə:dʒ] *vi* emergere
emergency [ɪ'mə:dʒənsɪ] *n* emergenza;
in an ~ in caso di emergenza; **emergency
brake** (US) *n* freno a mano; **emergency
exit** *n* uscita di sicurezza; **emergency
landing** *n* atterraggio forzato;
emergency room (US: *Med*) *n* pronto
soccorso; **emergency services** *npl* (*fire,
police, ambulance*) servizi *mpl* di pronto
intervento
emigrate ['ɛmɪɡreɪt] *vi* emigrare;
emigration [ɛmɪ'ɡreɪʃən] *n* emigrazione *f*
eminent ['ɛmɪnənt] *adj* eminente
emissions [ɪ'mɪʃənz] *npl* emissioni *fpl*
emit [ɪ'mɪt] *vt* emettere
emotion [ɪ'məʊʃən] *n* emozione *f*;
emotional *adj* (*person*) emotivo(-a);
(*scene*) commovente; (*tone, speech*)
carico(-a) d'emozione
emperor ['ɛmpərə'] *n* imperatore *m*
emphasis ['ɛmfəsɪs] *n* (*pl* -**ases**) enfasi *f*
inv; importanza
emphasize ['ɛmfəsaɪz] *vt* (*word, point*)
sottolineare; (*feature*) mettere in evidenza
empire ['ɛmpaɪə'] *n* impero
employ [ɪm'plɔɪ] *vt* impiegare; **employee**
[-'i:] *n* impiegato(-a); **employer** *n*
principale *m/f*, datore *m* di lavoro;
employment *n* impiego; **employment
agency** *n* agenzia di collocamento

empower [ɪm'pauəʳ] vt **to ~ sb to do** concedere autorità a qn di fare

empress ['ɛmprɪs] n imperatrice f

emptiness ['ɛmptɪnɪs] n vuoto

empty ['ɛmptɪ] adj vuoto(-a); (threat, promise) vano(-a) ▷ vt vuotare ▷ vi vuotarsi; (liquid) scaricarsi; **empty-handed** adj a mani vuote

EMU n abbr (= economic and monetary union) unione f economica e monetaria

emulsion [ɪ'mʌlʃən] n emulsione f

enable [ɪ'neɪbl] vt **to ~ sb to do** permettere a qn di fare

enamel [ɪ'næməl] n smalto; (also: ~ **paint**) vernice f a smalto

enchanting [ɪn'tʃɑːntɪŋ] adj incantevole, affascinante

encl. abbr (= enclosed) all.

enclose [ɪn'kləuz] vt (land) circondare, recingere; (letter etc): **to ~ (with)** allegare (con); **please find ~d** trovi qui accluso

enclosure [ɪn'kləuʒəʳ] n recinto

encore [ɔŋ'kɔːʳ] excl bis ▷ n bis m inv

encounter [ɪn'kauntəʳ] n incontro ▷ vt incontrare

encourage [ɪn'kʌrɪdʒ] vt incoraggiare; **encouragement** n incoraggiamento

encouraging [ɪn'kʌrɪdʒɪŋ] adj incoraggiante

encyclop(a)edia [ɛnsaɪkləu'piːdɪə] n enciclopedia

end [ɛnd] n fine f; (aim) fine m; (of table) bordo estremo; (of pointed object) punta ▷ vt finire; (also: **bring to an ~, put an ~ to**) mettere fine a ▷ vi finire; **in the ~** alla fine; **on ~** (object) ritto(-a); **to stand on ~** (hair) rizzarsi; **for hours on ~** per ore ed ore; **end up** vi **to ~ up in** finire in

endanger [ɪn'deɪndʒəʳ] vt mettere in pericolo

endearing [ɪn'dɪərɪŋ] adj accattivante

endeavour [ɪn'dɛvəʳ] (us **endeavor**) n sforzo, tentativo ▷ vi **to ~ to do** cercare or sforzarsi di fare

ending ['ɛndɪŋ] n fine f, conclusione f; (Ling) desinenza

endless ['ɛndlɪs] adj senza fine

endorse [ɪn'dɔːs] vt (cheque) girare; (approve) approvare, appoggiare; **endorsement** n approvazione f; (on driving licence) contravvenzione registrata sulla patente

endurance [ɪn'djuərəns] n resistenza; pazienza

endure [ɪn'djuəʳ] vt sopportare, resistere a ▷ vi durare

enemy ['ɛnəmɪ] adj, n nemico(-a)

energetic [ɛnə'dʒɛtɪk] adj energico(-a), attivo(-a)

energy ['ɛnədʒɪ] n energia

enforce [ɪn'fɔːs] vt (Law) applicare, far osservare

engaged [ɪn'geɪdʒd] adj (BRIT: busy, in use) occupato(-a); (betrothed) fidanzato(-a); **the line's ~** la linea è occupata; **to get ~** fidanzarsi; **engaged tone** (BRIT) n (Tel) segnale m di occupato

engagement [ɪn'geɪdʒmənt] n impegno, obbligo; appuntamento; (to marry) fidanzamento; **engagement ring** n anello di fidanzamento

engaging [ɪn'geɪdʒɪŋ] adj attraente

engine ['ɛndʒɪn] n (Aut) motore m; (Rail) locomotiva

engineer [ɛndʒɪ'nɪəʳ] n ingegnere m; (BRIT: for repairs) tecnico; (on ship: us: Rail) macchinista m; **engineering** n ingegneria

England ['ɪŋglənd] n Inghilterra

English ['ɪŋglɪʃ] adj inglese ▷ n (Ling) inglese m; **the ~** npl gli Inglesi; **English Channel** n **the English Channel** la Manica; **Englishman** (irreg) n inglese m; **Englishwoman** (irreg) n inglese f

engrave [ɪn'greɪv] vt incidere

engraving [ɪn'greɪvɪŋ] n incisione f

enhance [ɪn'hɑːns] vt accrescere

enjoy [ɪn'dʒɔɪ] vt godere; (have: success, fortune) avere; **to ~ o.s.** godersela, divertirsi; **enjoyable** adj piacevole; **enjoyment** n piacere m, godimento

enlarge [ɪn'lɑːdʒ] vt ingrandire ▷ vi **to ~ on** (subject) dilungarsi su; **enlargement** n (Phot) ingrandimento

enlist [ɪn'lɪst] vt arruolare; (support) procurare ▷ vi arruolarsi

enormous [ɪ'nɔːməs] adj enorme

enough [ɪ'nʌf] adj, n **~ time/books** assai tempo/libri; **have you got ~?** ne ha abbastanza or a sufficienza? ▷ adv **big ~** abbastanza grande; **he has not worked ~** non ha lavorato abbastanza; **~!** basta!; **that's ~, thanks** basta così, grazie; **I've had ~ of him** ne ho abbastanza di lui; ... **which, funnily** or **oddly ~** ... che, strano a dirsi

enquire [ɪn'kwaɪəʳ] vt, vi (esp BRIT) = **inquire**

enquiry [ɪn'kwaɪərɪ] n (esp BRIT) = **inquiry**

enrage [ɪn'reɪdʒ] vt fare arrabbiare

enrich [ɪn'rɪtʃ] vt arricchire

enrol [ɪn'rəul] (us **enroll**) vt iscrivere ▷ vi iscriversi; **enrolment** (us **enrollment**) n iscrizione f

en route [ɔn'ruːt] adv **~ for/from/to** in viaggio per/da/a

en suite [ɔn'swiːt] adj **room with ~**

bathroom camera con bagno

ensure [ɪn'ʃʊəʳ] vt assicurare; garantire

entail [ɪn'teɪl] vt comportare

enter ['ɛntəʳ] vt entrare in; (army) arruolarsi in; (competition) partecipare a; (sb for a competition) iscrivere; (write down) registrare; (Comput) inserire ▷ vi entrare

enterprise ['ɛntəpraɪz] n (undertaking, company) impresa; (spirit) iniziativa; **free ~** liberalismo economico; **private ~** iniziativa privata; **enterprising** ['ɛntəpraɪzɪŋ] adj intraprendente

entertain [ɛntə'teɪn] vt divertire; (invite) ricevere; (idea, plan) nutrire; **entertainer** n comico(-a); **entertaining** adj divertente; **entertainment** n (amusement) divertimento; (show) spettacolo

enthusiasm [ɪn'θu:zɪæzəm] n entusiasmo

enthusiast [ɪn'θu:zɪæst] n entusiasta m/f; **enthusiastic** [-'æstɪk] adj entusiasta, entusiastico(-a); **to be enthusiastic about sth/sb** essere appassionato(-a) di qc/entusiasta di qn

entire [ɪn'taɪəʳ] adj intero(-a); **entirely** adv completamente, interamente

entitle [ɪn'taɪtl] vt (give right) **to ~ sb to sth/to do** dare diritto a qn a qc/a fare; **entitled** adj (book) che si intitola; **to be entitled to do** avere il diritto di fare

entrance [n 'ɛntrns, vb ɪn'trɑ:ns] n entrata, ingresso; (of person) entrata ▷ vt incantare, rapire; **where's the ~?** dov'è l'entrata?; **to gain ~ to** (university etc) essere ammesso a; **entrance examination** n esame m di ammissione; **entrance fee** n tassa d'iscrizione; (to museum etc) prezzo d'ingresso; **entrance ramp** (us) n (Aut) rampa di accesso; **entrant** ['ɛntrnt] n partecipante m/f; concorrente m/f

entrepreneur [ɔntrəprə'nə:ʳ] n imprenditore m

entrust [ɪn'trʌst] vt **to ~ sth to** affidare qc a

entry ['ɛntrɪ] n entrata; (way in) entrata, ingresso; (item: on list) iscrizione f; (in dictionary) voce f; **no ~** vietato l'ingresso; (Aut) divieto di accesso; **entry phone** n citofono

envelope ['ɛnvələup] n busta

envious ['ɛnvɪəs] adj invidioso(-a)

environment [ɪn'vaɪrnmənt] n ambiente m; **environmental** [-'mɛntl] adj ecologico(-a); ambientale; **environmentally** [ɪnvaɪərən'mɛntəlɪ] adv **environmentally sound/friendly** che rispetta l'ambiente

envisage [ɪn'vɪzɪdʒ] vt immaginare; prevedere

envoy ['ɛnvɔɪ] n inviato(-a)

envy ['ɛnvɪ] n invidia ▷ vt invidiare; **to ~ sb sth** invidiare qn per qc

epic ['ɛpɪk] n poema m epico ▷ adj epico(-a)

epidemic [ɛpɪ'dɛmɪk] n epidemia

epilepsy ['ɛpɪlɛpsɪ] n epilessia

epileptic [ɛpɪ'lɛptɪk] adj, n epilettico(-a); **epileptic fit** n attacco epilettico

episode ['ɛpɪsəud] n episodio

equal ['i:kwl] adj uguale ▷ n pari m/f inv ▷ vt uguagliare; **~ to** (task) all'altezza di; **equality** [i:'kwɔlɪtɪ] n uguaglianza; **equalize** vi pareggiare; **equally** adv ugualmente

equation [ɪ'kweɪʃən] n (Math) equazione f

equator [ɪ'kweɪtəʳ] n equatore m

equip [ɪ'kwɪp] vt equipaggiare, attrezzare; **to ~ sb/sth with** fornire qn/qc di; **to be well ~ped** (office etc) essere ben attrezzato(-a); **he is well ~ped for the job** ha i requisiti necessari per quel lavoro; **equipment** n attrezzatura; (electrical etc) apparecchiatura

equivalent [ɪ'kwɪvələnt] adj equivalente ▷ n equivalente m; **to be ~ to** equivalere a

ER abbr (BRIT) = Elizabeth Regina (US: Med) = **emergency room**

era ['ɪərə] n era, età f inv

erase [ɪ'reɪz] vt cancellare; **eraser** n gomma

erect [ɪ'rɛkt] adj eretto(-a) ▷ vt costruire; (assemble) montare; **erection** [ɪ'rɛkʃən] n costruzione f; montaggio; (Physiol) erezione f

ERM n (= Exchange Rate Mechanism) ERM m

erode [ɪ'rəud] vt erodere; (metal) corrodere

erosion [ɪ'rəuʒən] n erosione f

erotic [ɪ'rɔtɪk] adj erotico(-a)

errand ['ɛrnd] n commissione f

erratic [ɪ'rætɪk] adj imprevedibile; (person, mood) incostante

error ['ɛrəʳ] n errore m

erupt [ɪ'rʌpt] vi (volcano) mettersi (or essere) in eruzione; (war, crisis) scoppiare; **eruption** [ɪ'rʌpʃən] n eruzione f; scoppio

escalate ['ɛskəleɪt] vi intensificarsi

escalator ['ɛskəleɪtəʳ] n scala mobile

escape [ɪ'skeɪp] n evasione f; fuga; (of gas etc) fuga, fuoriuscita ▷ vi fuggire; (from jail) evadere, scappare; (leak) uscire ▷ vt sfuggire a; **to ~ from** (place) fuggire da; (person) sfuggire a

escort [n 'ɛskɔ:t, vb ɪ'skɔ:t] n scorta; (male companion) cavaliere m ▷ vt scortare; accompagnare

especially [ɪ'spɛʃlɪ] adv specialmente;

soprattutto; espressamente

espionage ['ɛspɪənɑːʒ] *n* spionaggio

essay ['eseɪ] *n* (*Scol*) composizione *f*; (*Literature*) saggio

essence ['ɛsns] *n* essenza

essential [ɪ'sɛnʃl] *adj* essenziale ▷ *n* elemento essenziale; **essentially** *adv* essenzialmente; **essentials** *npl* **the essentials** l'essenziale *msg*

establish [ɪ'stæblɪʃ] *vt* stabilire; (*business*) mettere su; (*one's power etc*) affermare; **establishment** *n* stabilimento; **the Establishment** la classe dirigente, l'establishment *m*

estate [ɪ'steɪt] *n* proprietà *f inv*; beni *mpl*, patrimonio; (*BRIT: also:* **housing ~**) complesso edilizio; **estate agent** (*BRIT*) *n* agente *m* immobiliare; **estate car** (*BRIT*) *n* giardiniera

estimate [*n* 'ɛstɪmət, *vb* 'ɛstɪmeɪt] *n* stima; (*Comm*) preventivo ▷ *vt* stimare, valutare

etc *abbr* (= *et cetera*) etc., ecc.

eternal [ɪ'təːnl] *adj* eterno(-a)

eternity [ɪ'təːnɪtɪ] *n* eternità

ethical ['ɛθɪkl] *adj* etico(-a), morale; **ethics** ['ɛθɪks] *n* etica ▷ *npl* morale *f*

Ethiopia [iːθɪ'əupɪə] *n* Etiopia

ethnic ['ɛθnɪk] *adj* etnico(-a); **ethnic minority** *n* minoranza etnica

etiquette ['ɛtɪkɛt] *n* etichetta

EU *n abbr* (= *European Union*) UE *f*

euro ['juərəu] *n* (*currency*) euro *m inv*

Europe ['juərəp] *n* Europa; **European** [-'piːən] *adj*, *n* europeo(-a); **European Community** *n* Comunità Europea; **European Union** *n* Unione *f* europea

Eurostar® ['juərəustɑːʳ] *n* Eurostar® *m inv*

evacuate [ɪ'vækjueɪt] *vt* evacuare

evade [ɪ'veɪd] *vt* (*tax*) evadere; (*duties etc*) sottrarsi a; (*person*) schivare

evaluate [ɪ'væljueɪt] *vt* valutare

evaporate [ɪ'væpəreɪt] *vi* evaporare

eve [iːv] *n* **on the ~ of** alla vigilia di

even ['iːvn] *adj* regolare; (*number*) pari *inv* ▷ *adv* anche, perfino; **~ if, ~ though** anche se; **~ more** ancora di più; **~ so** ciò nonostante; **not ~** nemmeno; **to get ~ with sb** dare la pari a qn

evening ['iːvnɪŋ] *n* sera; (*as duration, event*) serata; **in the ~** la sera; **evening class** *n* corso serale; **evening dress** *n* (*woman's*) abito da sera; **in evening dress** (*man*) in abito scuro; (*woman*) in abito lungo

event [ɪ'vɛnt] *n* avvenimento; (*Sport*) gara; **in the ~ of** in caso di; **eventful** *adj* denso(-a) di eventi

eventual [ɪ'vɛntʃuəl] *adj* finale

▨ Be careful not to translate *eventual* by the Italian word *eventuale*.

eventually [ɪ'vɛntʃuəlɪ] *adv* alla fine

▨ Be careful not to translate *eventually* by the Italian word *eventualmente*.

ever ['ɛvəʳ] *adv* mai; (*at all times*) sempre; **the best ~** il migliore che ci sia mai stato; **have you ~ seen it?** l'ha mai visto?; **~ since** *adv* da allora ▷ *conj* sin da quando; **~ so pretty** così bello(-a); **evergreen** *n* sempreverde *m*

every ['ɛvrɪ] *adj* ogni; **~ day** tutti i giorni, ogni giorno; **~ other/third day** ogni due/tre giorni; **~ other car** una macchina su due; **~ now and then** ogni tanto, di quando in quando; **everybody** *pron* = **everyone**; **everyday** *adj* quotidiano(-a); di ogni giorno; **everyone** *pron* ognuno, tutti *pl*; **everything** *pron* tutto, ogni cosa; **everywhere** *adv* (*gen*) dappertutto; (*wherever*) ovunque

evict [ɪ'vɪkt] *vt* sfrattare

evidence ['ɛvɪdns] *n* (*proof*) prova; (*of witness*) testimonianza; (*sign*): **to show ~ of** dare segni di; **to give ~** deporre

evident ['ɛvɪdnt] *adj* evidente; **evidently** *adv* evidentemente

evil ['iːvl] *adj* cattivo(-a), maligno(-a) ▷ *n* male *m*

evoke [ɪ'vəuk] *vt* evocare

evolution [iːvə'luːʃən] *n* evoluzione *f*

evolve [ɪ'vɔlv] *vt* elaborare ▷ *vi* svilupparsi, evolversi

ewe [juː] *n* pecora

ex (*inf*) [ɛks] *n* **my ex** il (la) mio(-a) ex

ex- [ɛks] *prefix* ex

exact [ɪg'zækt] *adj* esatto(-a) ▷ *vt* **to ~ sth (from)** estorcere qc (da); esigere qc (da); **exactly** *adv* esattamente

exaggerate [ɪg'zædʒəreɪt] *vt, vi* esagerare; **exaggeration** [-'reɪʃən] *n* esagerazione *f*

exam [ɪg'zæm] *n abbr* (*Scol*) = **examination**

examination [ɪgzæmɪ'neɪʃən] *n* (*Scol*) esame *m*; (*Med*) controllo

examine [ɪg'zæmɪn] *vt* esaminare; **examiner** *n* esaminatore(-trice)

example [ɪg'zɑːmpl] *n* esempio; **for ~** ad or per esempio

exasperated [ɪg'zɑːspəreɪtɪd] *adj* esasperato(-a)

excavate ['ɛkskəveɪt] *vt* scavare

exceed [ɪk'siːd] *vt* superare; (*one's powers, time limit*) oltrepassare; **exceedingly** *adv* eccessivamente

excel [ɪk'sɛl] *vi* eccellere ▷ *vt* sorpassare; **to ~ o.s** (*BRIT*) superare se stesso

excellence ['ɛksələns] *n* eccellenza

excellent ['ɛksələnt] *adj* eccellente

except [ɪk'sɛpt] *prep (also:* ~ **for, ~ing)** salvo, all'infuori di, eccetto ▷ *vt* escludere; ~ **if/when** salvo se/quando; ~ **that** salvo che; **exception** [ɪk'sɛpʃən] *n* eccezione *f*; **to take exception to** trovare a ridire su; **exceptional** [ɪk'sɛpʃənl] *adj* eccezionale; **exceptionally** [ɪk'sɛpʃənəlɪ] *adv* eccezionalmente

excerpt ['ɛksəːpt] *n* estratto

excess [ɪk'sɛs] *n* eccesso; **excess baggage** *n* bagaglio in eccedenza; **excessive** *adj* eccessivo(-a)

exchange [ɪks'tʃeɪndʒ] *n* scambio; *(also:* **telephone ~)** centralino ▷ *vt* **to ~ (for)** scambiare (con); **could I ~ this, please?** posso cambiarlo, per favore?; **exchange rate** *n* tasso di cambio

excite [ɪk'saɪt] *vt* eccitare; **to get ~d** eccitarsi; **excited** *adj* **to get excited** essere elettrizzato(-a); **excitement** *n* eccitazione *f*; agitazione *f*; **exciting** *adj* avventuroso(-a); *(film, book)* appassionante

exclaim [ɪk'skleɪm] *vi* esclamare; **exclamation** [ɛkskləˈmeɪʃən] *n* esclamazione *f*; **exclamation mark** *(us* **exclamation point)** *n* punto esclamativo

exclude [ɪk'skluːd] *vt* escludere

excluding [ɪk'skluːdɪŋ] *prep* ~ **VAT** IVA esclusa

exclusion [ɪk'skluːʒən] *n* esclusione *f*; **to the ~ of** escludendo

exclusive [ɪk'skluːsɪv] *adj* esclusivo(-a); ~ **of VAT** I.V.A. esclusa; **exclusively** *adv* esclusivamente

excruciating [ɪk'skruːʃɪeɪtɪŋ] *adj* straziante, atroce

excursion [ɪk'skəːʃən] *n* escursione *f*, gita

excuse [*n* ɪk'skjuːs, *vb* ɪk'skjuːz] *n* scusa ▷ *vt* scusare; **to ~ sb from** *(activity)* dispensare qn da; ~ **me!** mi scusi!; **now, if you will ~ me ...** ora, mi scusi ma ...

ex-directory ['ɛksdɪ'rɛktərɪ] *(BRIT) adj (Tel)* **to be ~** non essere sull'elenco

execute ['ɛksɪkjuːt] *vt (prisoner)* giustiziare; *(plan etc)* eseguire; **execution** [ɛksɪ'kjuːʃən] *n* esecuzione *f*

executive [ɪg'zɛkjutɪv] *n (Comm)* dirigente *m*; *(Pol)* esecutivo *n* ▷ *adj* esecutivo(-a)

exempt [ɪg'zɛmpt] *adj* esentato(-a) ▷ *vt* **to ~ sb from** esentare qn da

exercise ['ɛksəsaɪz] *n (keep fit)* moto; *(Scol, Mil etc)* esercizio ▷ *vt* esercitare; *(patience)* usare; *(dog)* portar fuori ▷ *vi (also:* **take ~)** fare del moto; **exercise book** *n* quaderno

exert [ɪg'zəːt] *vt* esercitare; **to ~ o.s.** sforzarsi; **exertion** [-ʃən] *n* sforzo

exhale [ɛks'heɪl] *vt, vi* espirare

exhaust [ɪg'zɔːst] *n (also:* ~ **fumes)** scappamento; *(also:* ~ **pipe)** tubo di scappamento ▷ *vt* esaurire; **exhausted** *adj* esaurito(-a); **exhaustion** [ɪg'zɔːstʃən] *n* esaurimento; **nervous exhaustion** sovraffaticamento mentale

exhibit [ɪg'zɪbɪt] *n (Art)* oggetto esposto; *(Law)* documento *or* oggetto esibito ▷ *vt* esporre; *(courage, skill)* dimostrare; **exhibition** [ɛksɪ'bɪʃən] *n* mostra, esposizione *f*

exhilarating [ɪg'zɪləreɪtɪŋ] *adj* esilarante; stimolante

exile ['ɛksaɪl] *n* esilio; *(person)* esiliato(-a) ▷ *vt* esiliare

exist [ɪg'zɪst] *vi* esistere; **existence** *n* esistenza; **existing** *adj* esistente

exit ['ɛksɪt] *n* uscita ▷ *vi (Theatre, Comput)* uscire; **where's the ~?** dov'è l'uscita?; **exit ramp** *(us) n (Aut)* rampa di uscita

exotic [ɪg'zɔtɪk] *adj* esotico(-a)

expand [ɪk'spænd] *vt* espandere; estendere; allargare ▷ *vi (business, gas)* espandersi; *(metal)* dilatarsi

expansion [ɪk'spænʃən] *n (gen)* espansione *f*; *(of town, economy)* sviluppo; *(of metal)* dilatazione *f*

expect [ɪk'spɛkt] *vt (anticipate)* prevedere, aspettarsi, prevedere *or* aspettarsi che + *sub*; *(require)* richiedere, esigere; *(suppose)* supporre; *(await, also baby)* aspettare ▷ *vi* **to be ~ing** essere in stato interessante; **to ~ sb to do** aspettarsi che qn faccia; **expectation** [ɛkspɛk'teɪʃən] *n* aspettativa; speranza

expedition [ɛkspə'dɪʃən] *n* spedizione *f*

expel [ɪk'spɛl] *vt* espellere

expenditure [ɪk'spɛndɪtʃəʳ] *n* spesa

expense [ɪk'spɛns] *n* spesa; *(high cost)* costo; ~**s** *npl (Comm)* spese *fpl*, indennità *fpl*; **at the ~ of** a spese di; **expense account** *n* conto *m* spese *inv*

expensive [ɪk'spɛnsɪv] *adj* caro(-a), costoso(-a); **it's too ~** è troppo caro

experience [ɪk'spɪərɪəns] *n* esperienza ▷ *vt (pleasure)* provare; *(hardship)* soffrire; **experienced** *adj* esperto(-a)

experiment [*n* ɪk'spɛrɪmənt, *vb* ɪk'spɛrɪment] *n* esperimento, esperienza ▷ *vi* **to ~ (with/on)** fare esperimenti (con/su); **experimental** [ɪkspɛrɪ'mɛntl] *adj* sperimentale; **at the experimental stage** in via di sperimentazione

expert ['ɛkspəːt] *adj, n* esperto(-a); **expertise** [-'tiːz] *n* competenza

expire [ɪk'spaɪəʳ] *vi (period of time, licence)* scadere; **expiry** *n* scadenza; **expiry date** *n (of medicine, food item)* data di scadenza

explain [ɪk'spleɪn] *vt* spiegare;

explanation [ɛksplə'neɪʃən] n spiegazione f

explicit [ɪk'splɪsɪt] adj esplicito(-a)

explode [ɪk'spləud] vi esplodere

exploit [n 'ɛksplɔɪt, vb ɪk'splɔɪt] n impresa ▷ vt sfruttare; **exploitation** [-'teɪʃən] n sfruttamento

explore [ɪk'splɔːʳ] vt esplorare; (possibilities) esaminare; **explorer** n esploratore(-trice)

explosion [ɪk'spləuʒən] n esplosione f; **explosive** [ɪk'spləusɪv] adj esplosivo(-a) ▷ n esplosivo

export [vb ɛk'spɔːt, n 'ɛkspɔːt] vt esportare ▷ n esportazione f; articolo di esportazione ▷ cpd d'esportazione; **exporter** n esportatore m

expose [ɪk'spəuz] vt esporre; (unmask) smascherare; **exposed** adj (position) esposto(-a); **exposure** [ɪk'spəuʒəʳ] n esposizione f; (Phot) posa; (Med) assideramento

express [ɪk'sprɛs] adj (definite) chiaro(-a), espresso(-a); (BRIT: letter etc) espresso inv ▷ n (train) espresso ▷ vt esprimere; **expression** [ɪk'sprɛʃən] n espressione f; **expressway** (US) n (urban motorway) autostrada che attraversa la città

exquisite [ɛk'skwɪzɪt] adj squisito(-a)

extend [ɪk'stɛnd] vt (visit) protrarre; (road, deadline) prolungare; (building) ampliare; (offer) offrire, porgere ▷ vi (land, period) estendersi; **extension** [ɪk'stɛnʃən] n (of road, term) prolungamento; (of contract, deadline) proroga; (building) annesso; (to wire, table) prolunga; (telephone) interno; (: in private house) apparecchio supplementare; **extension lead** n prolunga

extensive [ɪk'stɛnsɪv] adj esteso(-a), ampio(-a); (damage) su larga scala; (coverage, discussion) esauriente; (use) grande

extent [ɪk'stɛnt] n estensione f; **to some ~** fino a un certo punto; **to such an ~ that ...** a un tal punto che ...; **to what ~?** fino a che punto?; **to the ~ of ...** fino al punto di ...

exterior [ɛk'stɪərɪəʳ] adj esteriore, esterno(-a) ▷ n esteriore m, esterno; aspetto (esteriore)

external [ɛk'stəːnl] adj esterno(-a), esteriore

extinct [ɪk'stɪŋkt] adj estinto(-a); **extinction** [ɪk'stɪŋkʃən] n estinzione f

extinguish [ɪk'stɪŋgwɪʃ] vt estinguere

extra ['ɛkstrə] adj extra inv, supplementare ▷ adv (in addition) di più ▷ n extra m inv; (surcharge) supplemento; (Cinema, Theatre) comparsa

extract [vb ɪk'strækt, n 'ɛkstrækt] vt estrarre; (money, promise) strappare ▷ n estratto; (passage) brano

extradite ['ɛkstrədaɪt] vt estradare

extraordinary [ɪk'strɔːdnrɪ] adj straordinario(-a)

extravagance [ɪk'strævəgəns] n sperpero; stravaganza

extravagant [ɪk'strævəgənt] adj (lavish) prodigo(-a); (wasteful) dispendioso(-a)

⬛ Be careful not to translate *extravagant* by the Italian word *stravagante*.

extreme [ɪk'striːm] adj estremo(-a) ▷ n estremo; **extremely** adv estremamente

extremist [ɪk'striːmɪst] adj, n estremista (m/f)

extrovert ['ɛkstrəvəːt] n estroverso(-a)

eye [aɪ] n occhio; (of needle) cruna ▷ vt osservare; **to keep an ~ on** tenere d'occhio; **eyeball** n globo dell'occhio; **eyebrow** n sopracciglio; **eyedrops** npl gocce fpl oculari, collirio; **eyelash** n ciglio; **eyelid** n palpebra; **eyeliner** n eye-liner m inv; **eyeshadow** n ombretto; **eyesight** n vista; **eye witness** n testimone m/f oculare

f

F [ɛf] *n* (*Mus*) fa *m*

fabric ['fæbrɪk] *n* stoffa, tessuto

fabulous ['fæbjuləs] *adj* favoloso(-a); (*super*) favoloso(-a), fantastico(-a)

face [feɪs] *n* faccia, viso, volto; (*expression*) faccia; (*of clock*) quadrante *m*; (*of building*) facciata ▷ *vt* essere di fronte a; (*facts, situation*) affrontare; **~ down** a faccia in giù; **to make** *or* **pull a ~** fare una smorfia; **in the ~ of** (*difficulties etc*) di fronte a; **on the ~ of it** a prima vista; **~ to ~** faccia a faccia; **face up to** *vt fus* affrontare, far fronte a; **face cloth** (*BRIT*) *n* guanto di spugna; **face pack** *n* (*BRIT*) maschera di bellezza

facial ['feɪʃəl] *adj* del viso

facilitate [fə'sɪlɪteɪt] *vt* facilitare

facilities [fə'sɪlɪtɪz] *npl* attrezzature *fpl*; **credit ~** facilitazioni *fpl* di credito

fact [fækt] *n* fatto; **in ~** in effetti

faction ['fækʃən] *n* fazione *f*

factor ['fæktə'] *n* fattore *m*; **I'd like a ~ 15 suntan lotion** vorrei una crema solare con fattore di protezione 15

factory ['fæktərɪ] *n* fabbrica, stabilimento
 Be careful not to translate *factory* by the Italian word *fattoria*.

factual ['fæktjuəl] *adj* che si attiene ai fatti

faculty ['fækəltɪ] *n* facoltà *f inv*; (*US*) corpo insegnante

fad [fæd] *n* mania; capriccio

fade [feɪd] *vi* sbiadire, sbiadirsi; (*light, sound, hope*) attenuarsi, affievolirsi; (*flower*) appassire; **fade away** *vi* (*sound*) affievolirsi

fag [fæg] (*BRIT: inf*) *n* (*cigarette*) cicca

Fahrenheit ['fɑːrənhaɪt] *n* Fahrenheit *m inv*

fail [feɪl] *vt* (*exam*) non superare; (*candidate*) bocciare; (*courage, memory*) mancare a ▷ *vi* fallire; (*student*) essere respinto(-a); (*eyesight, health, light*) venire a mancare; **to ~ to do sth** (*neglect*) mancare di fare qc; (*be unable*) non riuscire a fare qc; **without ~** senza fallo; certamente; **failing** *n* difetto ▷ *prep* in mancanza di; **failure** ['feɪljə'] *n* fallimento; (*person*) fallito(-a); (*mechanical etc*) guasto

faint [feɪnt] *adj* debole; (*recollection*) vago(-a); (*mark*) indistinto(-a) ▷ *n* (*Med*) svenimento ▷ *vi* svenire; **to feel ~** sentirsi svenire; **faintest** *adj* **I haven't the faintest idea** non ho la più pallida idea; **faintly** *adv* debolmente; vagamente

fair [fɛə'] *adj* (*person, decision*) giusto(-a), equo(-a); (*quite large, quite good*) discreto(-a); (*hair etc*) biondo(-a); (*skin, complexion*) chiaro(-a); (*weather*) bello(-a), clemente ▷ *adv* (*play*) lealmente ▷ *n* fiera; (*BRIT: funfair*) luna park *m inv*; **fairground** *n* luna park *m inv*; **fair-haired** [fɛə'hɛəd] *adj* (*person*) biondo(-a); **fairly** *adv* equamente; (*quite*) abbastanza; **fairway** *n* (*Golf*) fairway *m inv*

fairy ['fɛərɪ] *n* fata; **fairy tale** *n* fiaba

faith [feɪθ] *n* fede *f*; (*trust*) fiducia; (*sect*) religione *f*, fede *f*; **faithful** *adj* fedele; **faithfully** *adv* fedelmente; **yours faithfully** (*BRIT: in letters*) distinti saluti

fake [feɪk] *n* imitazione *f*; (*picture*) falso; (*person*) impostore(-a) ▷ *adj* falso(-a) ▷ *vt* (*accounts*) falsificare; (*illness*) fingere; (*painting*) contraffare

falcon ['fɔːlkən] *n* falco, falcone *m*

fall [fɔːl] (*pt* **fell**, *pp* **fallen**) *n* caduta; (*in temperature*) abbassamento; (*in price*) ribasso; (*US: autumn*) autunno ▷ *vi* cadere; (*temperature, price, night*) scendere; **~s** *npl* (*waterfall*) cascate *fpl*; **to ~ flat** (*on one's face*) cadere bocconi; (*joke*) fare cilecca; (*plan*) fallire; **fall apart** *vi* cadere a pezzi; **fall down** *vi* (*person*) cadere; (*building*) crollare; **fall for** *vt fus* (*person*) prendere una cotta per; **to ~ for a trick** (*or a story etc*) cascarci; **fall off** *vi* cadere; (*diminish*) diminuire, abbassarsi; **fall out** *vi* (*hair, teeth*) cadere; (*friends etc*) litigare; **fall over** *vi* cadere; **fall through** *vi* (*plan, project*) fallire

fallen ['fɔːlən] pp of **fall**

fallout ['fɔːlaut] n fall-out m

false [fɔːls] adj falso(-a); **under ~ pretences** con l'inganno; **false alarm** n falso allarme m; **false teeth** (BRIT) npl denti mpl finti

fame [feɪm] n fama, celebrità

familiar [fə'mɪlɪəʳ] adj familiare; (close) intimo(-a); **to be ~ with** (subject) conoscere; **familiarize** [fə'mɪlɪəraɪz] vt **to familiarize o.s. with** familiarizzare con

family ['fæmɪlɪ] n famiglia; **family doctor** n medico di famiglia; **family planning** n pianificazione f familiare

famine ['fæmɪn] n carestia

famous ['feɪməs] adj famoso(-a)

fan [fæn] n (folding) ventaglio; (Elec) ventilatore m; (person) ammiratore(-trice), tifoso(-a) ▷ vt far vento a; (fire, quarrel) alimentare

fanatic [fə'nætɪk] n fanatico(-a)

fan belt n cinghia del ventilatore

fan club n fan club m inv

fancy ['fænsɪ] n immaginazione f, fantasia; (whim) capriccio ▷ adj (hat) stravagante; (hotel, food) speciale ▷ vt (feel like, want) aver voglia di; (imagine, think) immaginare; **to take a ~ to** incapricciarsi di; **he fancies her** (inf) gli piace; **fancy dress** n costume m (per maschera)

fan heater n (BRIT) stufa ad aria calda

fantasize ['fæntəsaɪz] vi fantasticare, sognare

fantastic [fæn'tæstɪk] adj fantastico(-a)

fantasy ['fæntəsɪ] n fantasia, immaginazione f; fantasticheria; chimera

fanzine ['fænziːn] n rivista specialistica (per appassionati)

FAQs abbr (= frequently asked questions) FAQ fpl

far [fɑːʳ] adj lontano(-a) ▷ adv lontano; (much, greatly) molto; **is it ~ from here?** è molto lontano da qui?; **how ~?** quanto lontano?; (referring to activity etc) fino a dove?; **how ~ is the town centre?** quanto dista il centro da qui?; **~ away, ~ off** lontano, distante; **~ better** assai migliore; **~ from** lontano da; **by ~** di gran lunga; **go as ~ as the farm** vada fino alla fattoria; **as ~ as I know** per quel che so

farce [fɑːs] n farsa

fare [fɛəʳ] n (on trains, buses) tariffa; (in taxi) prezzo della corsa; (food) vitto, cibo; **half ~** metà tariffa; **full ~** tariffa intera

Far East n the **~** l'Estremo Oriente m

farewell [fɛə'wɛl] excl, n addio

farm [fɑːm] n fattoria, podere m ▷ vt coltivare; **farmer** n coltivatore(-trice), agricoltore(-trice); **farmhouse** n fattoria;

farming n (gen) agricoltura; (of crops) coltivazione f; (of animals) allevamento; **farmyard** n aia

far-reaching [fɑː'riːtʃɪŋ] adj di vasta portata

farther ['fɑːðəʳ] adv più lontano ▷ adj più lontano(-a)

farthest ['fɑːðɪst] superl of **far**

fascinate ['fæsɪneɪt] vt affascinare; **fascinated** adj affascinato(-a); **fascinating** adj affascinante; **fascination** [-'neɪʃən] n fascino

fascist ['fæʃɪst] adj, n fascista (m/f)

fashion ['fæʃən] n moda; (manner) maniera, modo ▷ vt foggiare, formare; **in ~** alla moda; **out of ~** passato(-a) di moda; **fashionable** adj alla moda, di moda; **fashion show** n sfilata di moda

fast [fɑːst] adj rapido(-a), svelto(-a), veloce; (clock): **to be ~** andare avanti; (dye, colour) solido(-a) ▷ adv rapidamente; (stuck, held) saldamente ▷ n digiuno ▷ vi digiunare; **~ asleep** profondamente addormentato

fasten ['fɑːsn] vt chiudere, fissare; (coat) abbottonare, allacciare ▷ vi chiudersi, fissarsi; abbottonarsi, allacciarsi

fast food n fast food m

fat [fæt] adj grasso(-a); (book, profit etc) grosso(-a) ▷ n grasso

fatal ['feɪtl] adj fatale, mortale; disastroso(-a); **fatality** [fə'tælɪtɪ] n (road death etc) morto(-a), vittima; **fatally** adv a morte

fate [feɪt] n destino; (of person) sorte f

father ['fɑːðəʳ] n padre m; **Father Christmas** n Babbo Natale; **father-in-law** n suocero

fatigue [fə'tiːg] n stanchezza

fattening ['fætnɪŋ] adj (food) che fa ingrassare

fatty ['fætɪ] adj (food) grasso(-a) ▷ n (inf) ciccione(-a)

faucet ['fɔːsɪt] (US) n rubinetto

fault [fɔːlt] n colpa; (Tennis) fallo; (defect) difetto; (Geo) faglia ▷ vt criticare; **it's my ~** è colpa mia; **to find ~ with** trovare da ridire su; **at ~** in fallo; **faulty** adj difettoso(-a)

fauna ['fɔːnə] n fauna

favour etc ['feɪvəʳ] (US **favor**) n favore m ▷ vt (proposition) favorire, essere favorevole a; (pupil etc) favorire; (team, horse) dare per vincente; **to do sb a ~** fare un favore or una cortesia a qn; **to find ~ with** (person) entrare nelle buone grazie di; (: suggestion) avere l'approvazione di; **in ~ of** in favore di; **favourable** adj favorevole; **favourite** [-rɪt] adj, n favorito(-a)

fawn [fɔ:n] n daino ▷ adj (also: **~-coloured**) marrone chiaro inv ▷ vi **to ~ (up)on** adulare servilmente

fax [fæks] n (document) facsimile m inv, telecopia; (machine) telecopiatrice f ▷ vt telecopiare, trasmettere in facsimile

FBI (US) n abbr (= Federal Bureau of Investigation) F.B.I. f

fear [fɪəʳ] n paura, timore m ▷ vt aver paura di, temere; **for ~ of** per paura di; **fearful** adj pauroso(-a); (sight, noise) terribile, spaventoso(-a); **fearless** adj intrepido(-a), senza paura

feasible ['fi:zəbl] adj possibile, realizzabile

feast [fi:st] n festa, banchetto; (Rel: also: **~day**) festa ▷ vi banchettare

feat [fi:t] n impresa, fatto insigne

feather ['fɛðəʳ] n penna

feature ['fi:tʃəʳ] n caratteristica; (Press, TV) articolo ▷ vt (film) avere come protagonista ▷ vi figurare; **~s** npl (of face) fisionomia; **feature film** n film m inv principale

Feb. [fɛb] abbr (= February) feb

February ['fɛbruərɪ] n febbraio

fed [fɛd] pt, pp of **feed**

federal ['fɛdərəl] adj federale

federation [fɛdə'reɪʃən] n federazione f

fed up adj **to be ~** essere stufo(-a)

fee [fi:] n pagamento; (of doctor, lawyer) onorario; (for examination) tassa d'esame; **school ~s** tasse fpl scolastiche

feeble ['fi:bl] adj debole

feed [fi:d] (pt, pp **fed**) n (of baby) pappa; (of animal) mangime m; (on printer) meccanismo di alimentazione ▷ vt nutrire; (baby) allattare; (horse etc) dare da mangiare a; (fire, machine) alimentare; (data, information): **to ~ into** inserire in; **feedback** n feed-back m

feel [fi:l] (pt, pp **felt**) n consistenza; (sense of touch) tatto ▷ vt toccare; palpare; tastare; (cold, pain, anger) sentire; (think, believe): **to ~ (that)** pensare che; **to ~ hungry/cold** aver fame/freddo; **to ~ lonely/better** sentirsi solo/meglio; **I don't ~ well** non mi sento bene; **it ~s soft** è morbido al tatto; **to ~ like** (want) aver voglia di; **to ~ about** or **around for** cercare a tastoni; **feeling** n sensazione f; (emotion) sentimento

feet [fi:t] npl of **foot**

fell [fɛl] pt of **fall** ▷ vt (tree) abbattere

fellow ['fɛləu] n individuo, tipo; compagno; (of learned society) membro cpd; **fellow citizen** n concittadino(-a); **fellow countryman** (irreg) n compatriota m; **fellow men** npl simili mpl; **fellowship** n associazione f; compagnia; specie di borsa di studio universitaria

felony ['fɛlənɪ] n reato, crimine m

felt [fɛlt] pt, pp of **feel** ▷ n feltro

female ['fi:meɪl] n (Zool) femmina; (pej: woman) donna, femmina ▷ adj (Biol, Elec) femmina inv; (sex, character) femminile; (vote etc) di donne

feminine ['fɛmɪnɪn] adj femminile

feminist ['fɛmɪnɪst] n femminista m/f

fence [fɛns] n recinto ▷ vt (also: **~ in**) recingere ▷ vi (Sport) tirare di scherma; **fencing** n (Sport) scherma

fend [fɛnd] vi **to ~ for o.s.** arrangiarsi; **fend off** vt (attack, questions) respingere, difendersi da

fender ['fɛndəʳ] n parafuoco; (on boat) parabordo; (US) parafango; paraurti m inv

fennel ['fɛnl] n finocchio

ferment [vb fə'mɛnt, n 'fə:mɛnt] vi fermentare ▷ n (fig) agitazione f, eccitazione f

fern [fə:n] n felce f

ferocious [fə'rəuʃəs] adj feroce

ferret ['fɛrɪt] n furetto

ferry ['fɛrɪ] n (small) traghetto; (large: also: **~boat**) nave f traghetto inv ▷ vt traghettare

fertile ['fə:taɪl] adj fertile; (Biol) fecondo(-a); **fertilize** ['fə:tɪlaɪz] vt fertilizzare; fecondare; **fertilizer** ['fə:tɪlaɪzə] n fertilizzante m

festival ['fɛstɪvəl] n (Rel) festa; (Art, Mus) festival m inv

festive ['fɛstɪv] adj di festa; **the ~ season** (BRIT: Christmas) il periodo delle feste

fetch [fɛtʃ] vt andare a prendere; (sell for) essere venduto(-a) per

fête [feɪt] n festa

fetus ['fi:təs] (US) n = **foetus**

feud [fju:d] n contesa, lotta

fever ['fi:vəʳ] n febbre f; **feverish** adj febbrile

few [fju:] adj pochi(-e); **a ~** adj qualche inv ▷ pron alcuni(-e); **fewer** adj meno inv, meno numerosi(-e); **fewest** adj il minor numero di

fiancé [fɪ'ã:ŋseɪ] n fidanzato; **fiancée** n fidanzata

fiasco [fɪ'æskəu] n fiasco

fib [fɪb] n piccola bugia

fibre ['faɪbəʳ] (us **fiber**) n fibra; **Fibreglass®** ['faɪbəglɑ:s] (us **fiberglass**) n fibra di vetro

fickle ['fɪkl] adj incostante, capriccioso(-a)

fiction ['fɪkʃən] n narrativa, romanzi mpl; (sth made up) finzione f; **fictional** adj immaginario(-a)

fiddle ['fɪdl] n (Mus) violino; (cheating) imbroglio; truffa ▷ vt (BRIT: accounts) falsificare, falsare; **fiddle with** vt fus gingillarsi con

fidelity [fɪ'dɛlɪtɪ] n fedeltà; (accuracy) esattezza

field [fiːld] n campo; **field marshal** n feldmaresciallo

fierce [fɪəs] adj (animal, person, fighting) feroce; (loyalty) assoluto(-a); (wind) furioso(-a); (heat) intenso(-a)

fifteen [fɪf'tiːn] num quindici; **fifteenth** num quindicesimo(-a)

fifth [fɪfθ] num quinto(-a)

fiftieth ['fɪftɪɪθ] num cinquantesimo(-a)

fifty ['fɪftɪ] num cinquanta; **fifty-fifty** adj **a fifty-fifty chance** una possibilità su due ▷ adv fifty-fifty, metà per ciascuno

fig [fɪg] n fico

fight [faɪt] (pt, pp **fought**) n zuffa, rissa; (Mil) battaglia, combattimento; (against cancer etc) lotta ▷ vt (person) azzuffarsi con; (enemy: also Mil) combattere; (cancer, alcoholism, emotion) lottare contro, combattere; (election) partecipare a ▷ vi combattere; **fight back** vi difendersi; (Sport, after illness) riprendersi ▷ vt (tears) ricacciare; **fight off** vt (attack, attacker) respingere; (disease, sleep, urge) lottare contro; **fighting** n combattimento

figure ['fɪgə'] n figura; (number, cipher) cifra ▷ vt (think: esp us) pensare ▷ vi (appear) figurare; **figure out** vt riuscire a capire; calcolare

file [faɪl] n (tool) lima; (dossier) incartamento; (folder) cartellina; (Comput) archivio; (row) fila ▷ vt (nails, wood) limare; (papers) archiviare; (Law: claim) presentare; passare agli atti; **filing cabinet** ['faɪlɪŋ-] n casellario

Filipino [fɪlɪ'piːnəu] n filippino(-a); (Ling) tagal m

fill [fɪl] vt riempire; (job) coprire ▷ n **to eat one's ~** mangiare a sazietà; **fill in** vt (hole) riempire; (form) compilare; **fill out** vt (form, receipt) riempire; **fill up** vt riempire; **~ it up, please** (Aut) il pieno, per favore

fillet ['fɪlɪt] n filetto; **fillet steak** n bistecca di filetto

filling ['fɪlɪŋ] n (Culin) impasto, ripieno; (for tooth) otturazione f; **filling station** n stazione f di rifornimento

film [fɪlm] n (Cinema) film m inv; (Phot) pellicola, rullino; (of powder, liquid) sottile strato ▷ vt, vi girare; **I'd like a 36-exposure ~** vorrei un rullino da 36 pose; **film star** n divo(-a) dello schermo

filter ['fɪltə'] n filtro ▷ vt filtrare; **filter lane** (BRIT) n (Aut) corsia di svincolo

filth [fɪlθ] n sporcizia; **filthy** adj lordo(-a), sozzo(-a); (language) osceno(-a)

fin [fɪn] n (of fish) pinna

final ['faɪnl] adj finale, ultimo(-a); definitivo(-a) ▷ n (Sport) finale f; **~s** npl (Scol) esami mpl finali; **finale** [fɪ'nɑːlɪ] n finale m; **finalist** ['faɪnəlɪst] n (Sport) finalista m/f; **finalize** ['faɪnəlaɪz] vt mettere a punto; **finally** ['faɪnəlɪ] adv (lastly) alla fine; (eventually) finalmente

finance [faɪ'næns] n finanza; (capital) capitale m ▷ vt finanziare; **~s** npl (funds) finanze fpl; **financial** [faɪ'nænʃəl] adj finanziario(-a); **financial year** n anno finanziario, esercizio finanziario

find [faɪnd] (pt, pp **found**) vt trovare; (lost object) ritrovare ▷ n trovata, scoperta; **to ~ sb guilty** (Law) giudicare qn colpevole; **find out** vt (truth, secret) scoprire; (person) cogliere in fallo; **to ~ out about** informarsi su; (by chance) scoprire; **findings** npl (Law) sentenza, conclusioni fpl; (of report) conclusioni

fine [faɪn] adj bello(-a); ottimo(-a); (thin, subtle) fine ▷ adv (well) molto bene ▷ n (Law) multa ▷ vt (Law) multare; **to be ~** (person) stare bene; (weather) far bello; **fine arts** npl belle arti fpl

finger ['fɪŋgə'] n dito ▷ vt toccare, tastare; **little/index ~** mignolo/(dito) indice m; **fingernail** n unghia; **fingerprint** n impronta digitale; **fingertip** n punta del dito

finish ['fɪnɪʃ] n fine f; (polish etc) finitura ▷ vt, vi finire; **when does the show ~?** quando finisce lo spettacolo?; **to ~ doing sth** finire di fare qc; **to ~ third** arrivare terzo(-a); **finish off** vt compiere; (kill) uccidere; **finish up** vi, vt finire

Finland ['fɪnlənd] n Finlandia; **Finn** [fɪn] n finlandese m/f; **Finnish** adj finlandese ▷ n (Ling) finlandese m

fir [fəː'] n abete m

fire [faɪə'] n fuoco; (destructive) incendio; (gas fire, electric fire) stufa ▷ vt (gun) far fuoco con; (arrow) sparare; (fig) infiammare; (inf: dismiss) licenziare ▷ vi sparare, far fuoco; **~!** al fuoco!; **on ~** in fiamme; **fire alarm** n allarme m d'incendio; **firearm** n arma da fuoco; **fire brigade** [-brɪ'geɪd] (us **fire department**) n (corpo dei) pompieri mpl; **fire engine** n autopompa; **fire escape** n scala di sicurezza; **fire exit** n uscita di sicurezza; **fire extinguisher** [-ɪk'stɪŋgwɪʃə'] n estintore m; **fireman** (irreg) n pompiere m; **fireplace** n focolare m; **fire station** n caserma dei pompieri; **firetruck** (us) n = **fire engine**; **firewall** n (Internet) firewall m inv; **firewood** n legna; **fireworks** npl fuochi mpl d'artificio

firm [fəːm] adj fermo(-a) ▷ n ditta,

azienda; **firmly** adv fermamente
first [fəːst] adj primo(-a) ▷ adv (before others) il primo, la prima; (before other things) per primo; (when listing reasons etc) per prima cosa ▷ n (person: in race) primo(-a); (BRIT Scol) laurea con lode; (Aut) prima; **at ~** dapprima, all'inizio; **~ of all** prima di tutto; **first aid** n pronto soccorso; **first-aid kit** n cassetta pronto soccorso; **first-class** adj di prima classe; **first-hand** adj di prima mano; **first lady** (US) n moglie f del presidente; **firstly** adv in primo luogo; **first name** n prenome m; **first-rate** adj di prima qualità, ottimo(-a)
fiscal ['fɪskəl] adj fiscale; **fiscal year** n anno fiscale
fish [fɪʃ] n inv pesce m ▷ vt (river, area) pescare in ▷ vi pescare; **to go ~ing** andare a pesca; **fish and chip shop** n see **chip shop**; **fisherman** (irreg) n pescatore m; **fish fingers** (BRIT) npl bastoncini mpl di pesce (surgelati); **fishing** n pesca; **fishing boat** n barca da pesca; **fishing line** n lenza; **fishmonger** n pescivendolo; **fishmonger's (shop)** n pescheria; **fish sticks** (US) npl = **fish fingers**; **fishy** (inf) adj (tale, story) sospetto(-a)
fist [fɪst] n pugno
fit [fɪt] adj (Med, Sport) in forma; (proper) adatto(-a), appropriato(-a); conveniente ▷ vt (clothes) stare bene a; (put in, attach) mettere; installare; (equip) fornire, equipaggiare ▷ vi (clothes) stare bene; (parts) andare bene, adattarsi; (in space, gap) entrare ▷ n (Med) accesso, attacco; **~ to** in grado di; **~ for** adatto(-a) a, degno(-a) di; **a ~ of anger** un accesso d'ira; **this dress is a good ~** questo vestito sta bene; **by ~s and starts** a sbalzi; **fit in** vi accordarsi; adattarsi; **fitness** n (Med) forma fisica; **fitted** adj **fitted cupboards** armadi mpl a muro; **fitted carpet** moquette f inv; **fitted kitchen** (BRIT) cucina componibile; **fitting** adj appropriato(-a) ▷ n (of dress) prova; (of piece of equipment) montaggio, aggiustaggio; **fitting room** n camerino; **fittings** npl (in building) impianti mpl
five [faɪv] num cinque; **fiver** (inf) n (BRIT) biglietto da cinque sterline; (US) biglietto da cinque dollari
fix [fɪks] vt fissare; (mend) riparare; (meal, drink) preparare ▷ n **to be in a ~** essere nei guai; **fix up** vt (meeting) fissare; **to ~ sb up with sth** procurare qc a qn; **fixed** [fɪkst] adj (prices etc) fisso(-a); **fixture** ['fɪkstʃər] n impianto (fisso); (Sport) incontro (del calendario sportivo)
fizzy ['fɪzɪ] adj frizzante; gassato(-a)
flag [flæg] vt fissare; (also: **~stone**) pietra

da lastricare ▷ vi stancarsi; affievolirsi; **flagpole** ['flægpəʊl] n albero
flair [flɛər] n (for business etc) fiuto; (for languages etc) facilità; (style) stile m
flak [flæk] n (Mil) fuoco d'artiglieria; (inf: criticism) critiche fpl
flake [fleɪk] n (of rust, paint) scaglia; (of snow, soap powder) fiocco ▷ vi (also: **~ off**) sfaldarsi
flamboyant [flæm'bɔɪənt] adj sgargiante
flame [fleɪm] n fiamma
flamingo [flə'mɪŋɡəʊ] n fenicottero, fiammingo
flammable ['flæməbl] adj infiammabile
flan [flæn] (BRIT) n flan m inv
flank [flæŋk] n fianco ▷ vt fiancheggiare
flannel ['flænl] n (BRIT: also: **face ~**) guanto di spugna; (fabric) flanella
flap [flæp] n (of pocket) patta; (of envelope) lembo ▷ vt (wings) battere ▷ vi (sail, flag) sbattere; (inf: also: **be in a ~**) essere in agitazione
flare [flɛər] n razzo; (in skirt etc) svasatura; **~s** (trousers) pantaloni mpl a zampa d'elefante; **flare up** vi andare in fiamme; (fig: person) infiammarsi di rabbia; (: revolt) scoppiare
flash [flæʃ] n vampata; (also: **news ~**) notizia flampo inv; (Phot) flash m inv ▷ vt accendere e spegnere; (send: message) trasmettere; (: look, smile) lanciare ▷ vi brillare; (light on ambulance, eyes etc) lampeggiare; **in a ~** in un lampo; **to ~ one's headlights** lampeggiare; **he ~ed by** or **past** ci passò davanti come un lampo; **flashback** n flashback m inv; **flashbulb** n cubo m flash inv; **flashlight** n lampadina tascabile
flask [flɑːsk] n fiasco; (also: **vacuum ~**) Thermos® m inv
flat [flæt] adj piatto(-a); (tyre) sgonfio(-a), a terra; (battery) scarico(-a); (beer) svampito(-a); (denial) netto(-a); (Mus) bemolle inv; (: voice) stonato(-a); (rate, fee) unico(-a) ▷ n (BRIT: rooms) appartamento; (Aut) pneumatico sgonfio; (Mus) bemolle m; **to work ~ out** lavorare a più non posso; **flatten** vt (also: **flatten out**) appiattire; (building, city) spianare
flatter ['flætər] vt lusingare; **flattering** adj lusinghiero(-a); (dress) che dona
flaunt [flɔːnt] vt fare mostra di
flavour etc ['fleɪvər] (US **flavor**) n gusto ▷ vt insaporire, aggiungere sapore a; **what ~s do you have?** che gusti avete?; **strawberry-~ed** al gusto di fragola; **flavouring** n essenza (artificiale)
flaw [flɔː] n difetto; **flawless** adj senza difetti

flea [fliː] *n* pulce *f*; **flea market** *n* mercato delle pulci

flee [fliː] (*pt, pp* **fled**) *vt* fuggire da ▷ *vi* fuggire, scappare

fleece [fliːs] *n* vello ▷ *vt* (*inf*) pelare

fleet [fliːt] *n* flotta; (*of lorries etc*) convoglio; parco

fleeting ['fliːtɪŋ] *adj* fugace, fuggitivo(-a); (*visit*) volante

Flemish ['flɛmɪʃ] *adj* fiammingo(-a)

flesh [flɛʃ] *n* carne *f*; (*of fruit*) polpa

flew [fluː] *pt of* **fly**

flex [flɛks] *n* filo (flessibile) ▷ *vt* flettere; (*muscles*) contrarre; **flexibility** *n* flessibilità; **flexible** *adj* flessibile; **flexitime** ['flɛksɪtaɪm] *n* orario flessibile

flick [flɪk] *n* colpetto; scarto ▷ *vt* dare un colpetto a; **flick through** *vt fus* sfogliare

flicker ['flɪkər] *vi* tremolare

flies [flaɪz] *npl of* **fly**

flight [flaɪt] *n* volo; (*escape*) fuga; (*also*: **~ of steps**) scalinata; **flight attendant** (*us*) *n* steward *m inv*, hostess *f inv*

flimsy ['flɪmzɪ] *adj* (*shoes, clothes*) leggero(-a); (*building*) poco solido(-a); (*excuse*) che non regge

flinch [flɪntʃ] *vi* ritirarsi; **to ~ from** tirarsi indietro di fronte a

fling [flɪŋ] (*pt, pp* **flung**) *vt* lanciare, gettare

flint [flɪnt] *n* selce *f*; (*in lighter*) pietrina

flip [flɪp] *vt* (*switch*) far scattare; (*coin*) lanciare in aria

flip-flops ['flɪpflɔps] *npl* (*esp BRIT: sandals*) infradito *mpl*

flipper ['flɪpər] *n* pinna

flirt [fləːt] *vi* flirtare ▷ *n* civetta

float [fləut] *n* galleggiante *m*; (*in procession*) carro; (*money*) somma ▷ *vi* galleggiare

flock [flɔk] *n* (*of sheep, Rel*) gregge *m*; (*of birds*) stormo ▷ *vi* **to ~ to** accorrere in massa a

flood [flʌd] *n* alluvione *m*; (*of letters etc*) marea ▷ *vt* allagare; (*people*) invadere ▷ *vi* (*place*) allagarsi; (*people*): **to ~ into** riversarsi in; **flooding** *n* inondazione *f*; **floodlight** *n* riflettore *m* ▷ *vt* illuminare a giorno

floor [flɔːr] *n* pavimento; (*storey*) piano; (*of sea, valley*) fondo ▷ *vt* (*blow*) atterrare; (: *question*) ridurre al silenzio; **which ~ is it on?** a che piano si trova?; **ground ~** (*BRIT*), **first ~** (*us*) pianterreno; **first ~** (*BRIT*), **second ~** (*us*) primo piano; **floorboard** *n* tavellone *m* di legno; **flooring** *n* (*floor*) pavimento; (*material*) materiale *m* per pavimentazioni; **floor show** *n* spettacolo di varietà

flop [flɔp] *n* fiasco ▷ *vi* far fiasco; (*fall*)

lasciarsi cadere; **floppy** ['flɔpɪ] *adj* floscio(-a), molle

floral ['flɔːrl] *adj* floreale

Florence ['flɔrəns] *n* Firenze *f*

Florentine ['flɔrəntaɪn] *adj* fiorentino(-a)

florist ['flɔrɪst] *n* fioraio(-a); **florist's (shop)** *n* fioraio(-a)

flotation [fləu'teɪʃən] *n* (*Comm*) lancio

flour ['flauər] *n* farina

flourish ['flʌrɪʃ] *vi* fiorire ▷ *n* (*bold gesture*): **with a ~** con ostentazione

flow [fləu] *n* flusso; circolazione *f* ▷ *vi* fluire; (*traffic, blood in veins*) circolare; (*hair*) scendere

flower ['flauər] *n* fiore *m* ▷ *vi* fiorire; **flower bed** *n* aiuola; **flowerpot** *n* vaso da fiori

flown [fləun] *pp of* **fly**

fl. oz. *abbr* = **fluid ounce**

flu [fluː] *n* influenza

fluctuate ['flʌktjueɪt] *vi* fluttuare, oscillare

fluent ['fluːənt] *adj* (*speech*) facile, sciolto(-a); corrente; **he speaks ~ Italian, he's ~ in Italian** parla l'italiano correntemente

fluff [flʌf] *n* lanugine *f*; **fluffy** *adj* lanuginoso(-a); (*toy*) di peluche

fluid ['fluːɪd] *adj* fluido(-a) ▷ *n* fluido; **fluid ounce** *n* = 0.028 l; 0.05 pints

fluke [fluːk] (*inf*) *n* colpo di fortuna

flung [flʌŋ] *pt, pp of* **fling**

fluorescent [fluə'rɛsnt] *adj* fluorescente

fluoride ['fluəraɪd] *n* fluoruro

flurry ['flʌrɪ] *n* (*of snow*) tempesta; **a ~ of activity** uno scoppio di attività

flush [flʌʃ] *n* rossore *m*; (*fig: of youth, beauty etc*) rigoglio, pieno vigore ▷ *vt* ripulire con un getto d'acqua ▷ *vi* arrossire ▷ *adj* **~ with** a livello di, pari a; **to ~ the toilet** tirare l'acqua

flute [fluːt] *n* flauto

flutter ['flʌtər] *n* agitazione *f*; (*of wings*) battito ▷ *vi* (*bird*) battere le ali

fly [flaɪ] (*pt* **flew**, *pp* **flown**) *n* (*insect*) mosca; (*on trousers: also*: **flies**) chiusura ▷ *vt* pilotare; (*passengers, cargo*) trasportare (in aereo); (*distances*) percorrere ▷ *vi* volare; (*passengers*) andare in aereo; (*escape*) fuggire; (*flag*) sventolare; **fly away** *vi* volar via; **fly-drive** *n* fly-drive holiday *fly and drive m inv*; **flying** *n* (*activity*) aviazione *f*; (*action*) volo ▷ *adj* **flying visit** visita volante; **with flying colours** con risultati brillanti; **flying saucer** *n* disco volante; **flyover** (*BRIT*) *n* (*bridge*) cavalcavia *m inv*

FM *abbr* (= *frequency modulation*) FM

foal [fəul] *n* puledro

foam [fəum] *n* schiuma; (*also*: **~ rubber**)

gommapiuma® ⊳ vi schiumare; (*soapy water*) fare la schiuma

focus ['fəukəs] (*pl* **focuses**) *n* fuoco; (*of interest*) centro ⊳ *vt* (*field glasses etc*) mettere a fuoco ⊳ *vi* to ~ **on** (*with camera*) mettere a fuoco; (*person*) fissare lo sguardo su; **in ~ a** fuoco; **out of ~** sfocato(-a)

foetus ['fiːtəs] (*us* **fetus**) *n* feto

fog [fɔg] *n* nebbia; **foggy** *adj* **it's foggy** c'è nebbia; **fog lamp** (*us* **fog light**) *n* (*Aut*) faro *m* antinebbia *inv*

foil [fɔil] *vt* confondere, frustrare ⊳ *n* lamina di metallo; (*kitchen foil*) foglio di alluminio; (*Fencing*) fioretto; **to act as a ~ to** (*fig*) far risaltare

fold [fəuld] *n* (*bend, crease*) piega; (*Agr*) ovile *m*; (*fig*) gregge *m* ⊳ *vt* piegare; (*arms*) incrociare; **fold up** *vi* (*map, bed, table*) piegarsi; (*business*) crollare ⊳ *vt* (*map etc*) piegare, ripiegare; **folder** *n* (*for papers*) cartella; cartellina; **folding** *adj* (*chair, bed*) pieghevole

foliage ['fəuliːidʒ] *n* fogliame *m*

folk [fəuk] *npl* gente *f* ⊳ *adj* popolare; ~**s** *npl* (*family*) famiglia; **folklore** ['fəuklɔːʳ] *n* folclore *m*; **folk music** *n* musica folk *inv*; **folk song** *n* canto popolare

follow ['fɔləu] *vt* seguire ⊳ *vi* seguire; (*result*) conseguire, risultare; **to ~ suit** fare lo stesso; **follow up** *vt* (*letter, offer*) fare seguito a; (*case*) seguire; **follower** *n* seguace *m/f*, discepolo(-a); **following** *adj* seguente ⊳ *n* seguito, discepoli *mpl*; **follow-up** *n* seguito

fond [fɔnd] *adj* (*memory, look*) tenero(-a), affettuoso(-a); **to be ~ of sb** volere bene a qn; **he's ~ of walking** gli piace fare camminate

food [fuːd] *n* cibo; **food mixer** *n* frullatore *m*; **food poisoning** *n* intossicazione *f*; **food processor** [-'prəusesə] *n* tritatutto *m* inv elettrico; **food stamp** (*us*) *n* buono alimentare dato agli indigenti

fool [fuːl] *n* sciocco(-a); (*Culin*) frullato ⊳ *vt* ingannare ⊳ *vi* (*gen: fool around*) fare lo sciocco; **fool about, fool around** *vi* (*waste time*) perdere tempo; **foolish** *adj* scemo(-a), stupido(-a); imprudente; **foolproof** *adj* (*plan etc*) sicurissimo(-a)

foot [fut] (*pl* **feet**) *n* piede *m*; (*measure*) piede (= 304 mm; 12 inches); (*of animal*) zampa ⊳ *vt* (*bill*) pagare; **on ~ a** piedi; **footage** *n* (*Cinema: length*) ≈ metraggio; (*: material*) sequenza; **foot-and-mouth (disease)** [futənd'mauθ-] *n* afta epizootica; **football** *n* pallone *m*; (*sport: BRIT*) calcio; (*: us*) football *m* americano; **footballer** *n* (*BRIT*) = **football player**; **football match** *n* (*BRIT*) partita di calcio;

football player *n* (*BRIT: also:* **footballer**) calciatore *m*; (*us*) giocatore *m* di football americano; **footbridge** *n* passerella; **foothills** *npl* contrafforti *fpl*; **foothold** *n* punto d'appoggio; **footing** *n* (*fig*) posizione *f*; **to lose one's footing** mettere un piede in fallo; **footnote** *n* nota (a piè di pagina); **footpath** *n* sentiero; (*in street*) marciapiede *m*; **footprint** *n* orma, impronta; **footstep** *n* passo; (*footprint*) orma, impronta; **footwear** *n* calzatura

KEYWORD

for [fɔːʳ] *prep* **1** (*indicating destination, intention, purpose*) per; **the train for London** il treno per Londra; **he went for the paper** è andato a prendere il giornale; **it's time for lunch** è ora di pranzo; **what's it for?** a che serve?; **what for?** (*why*) perché?

2 (*on behalf of, representing*) per; **to work for sb/sth** lavorare per qn/qc; **I'll ask him for you** glielo chiederò a nome tuo; **G for George** G come George

3 (*because of*) a causa di; **for this reason** per questo motivo

4 (*with regard to*) per; **it's cold for July** è freddo per luglio; **for everyone who voted yes, 50 voted no** per ogni voto a favore ce n'erano 50 contro

5 (*in exchange for*) per; **I sold it for £5** l'ho venduto per 5 sterline

6 (*in favour of*) per, a favore di; **are you for or against us?** è con noi o contro di noi?; **I'm all for it** sono completamente a favore

7 (*referring to distance, time*) per; **there are roadworks for 5 km** ci sono lavori in corso per 5 km; **he was away for 2 years** è stato via per 2 anni; **she will be away for a month** starà via un mese; **it hasn't rained for 3 weeks** non piove da 3 settimane; **can you do it for tomorrow?** può farlo per domani?

8 (*with infinitive clauses*): **it is not for me to decide** non sta a me decidere; **it would be best for you to leave** sarebbe meglio che lei se ne andasse; **there is still time for you to do it** ha ancora tempo per farlo; **for this to be possible ...** perché ciò sia possibile ...

9 (*in spite of*) nonostante; **for all his complaints, he's very fond of her** nonostante tutte le sue lamentele, le vuole molto bene

⊳ *conj* (*since, as: rather formal*) dal momento che, poiché

forbid [fə'bɪd] (*pt* **forbad(e)**, *pp* **forbidden**) *vt* vietare, interdire; **to ~ sb to do sth** proibire a qn di fare qc; **forbidden** *pt of* **forbid** ▷ *adj* (*food*) proibito(-a); (*area, territory*) vietato(-a); (*word, subject*) tabù *inv*

force [fɔːs] *n* forza ▷ *vt* forzare; **forced** *adj* forzato(-a); **forceful** *adj* forte, vigoroso(-a)

ford [fɔːd] *n* guado

fore [fɔːˈ] *n* **to come to the ~** mettersi in evidenza; **forearm** [ˈfɔːrɑːm] *n* avambraccio; **forecast** [ˈfɔːkɑːst] (*irreg: like* **cast**) *n* previsione *f* ▷ *vt* prevedere; **forecourt** [ˈfɔːkɔːt] *n* (*of garage*) corte *f* esterna; **forefinger** [ˈfɔːfɪŋgəˈ] *n* (*dito*) indice *m*; **forefront** [ˈfɔːfrʌnt] *n* **in the forefront of** all'avanguardia in; **foreground** [ˈfɔːɡraʊnd] *n* primo piano; **forehead** [ˈfɔrɪd] *n* fronte *f*

foreign [ˈfɒrɪn] *adj* straniero(-a); (*trade*) estero(-a); (*object, matter*) estraneo(-a); **foreign currency** *n* valuta estera; **foreigner** *n* straniero(-a); **foreign exchange** *n* cambio con l'estero; (*currency*) valuta estera; **Foreign Office** (BRIT) *n* Ministero degli Esteri; **Foreign Secretary** (BRIT) *n* ministro degli Affari esteri

fore: **foreman** [ˈfɔːmən] (*irreg*) *n* caposquadra *m*; **foremost** [ˈfɔːməʊst] *adj* principale; più in vista ▷ *adv* **first and foremost** innanzitutto; **forename** *n* nome *m* di battesimo

forensic [fəˈrɛnsɪk] *adj* **~ medicine** medicina legale

foresee [fɔːˈsiː] (*irreg: like* **see**) *vt* prevedere; **foreseeable** *adj* prevedibile

forest [ˈfɒrɪst] *n* foresta; **forestry** [ˈfɒrɪstrɪ] *n* silvicoltura

forever [fəˈrɛvəˈ] *adv* per sempre; (*endlessly*) sempre, di continuo

foreword [ˈfɔːwəːd] *n* prefazione *f*

forfeit [ˈfɔːfɪt] *vt* perdere; (*one's happiness, health*) giocarsi

forgave [fəˈɡeɪv] *pt of* **forgive**

forge [fɔːdʒ] *n* fucina ▷ *vt* (*signature, money*) contraffare, falsificare; (*wrought iron*) fucinare, foggiare; **forger** *n* contraffattore *m*; **forgery** *n* falso; (*activity*) contraffazione *f*

forget [fəˈɡɛt] (*pt* **forgot**, *pp* **forgotten**) *vt, vi* dimenticare; **I've forgotten my key/passport** ho dimenticato la chiave/il passaporto; **forgetful** *adj* di corta memoria; **forgetful of** dimentico(-a) di

forgive [fəˈɡɪv] (*pt* **forgave**, *pp* **forgiven**) *vt* perdonare; **to ~ sb for sth** perdonare qc a qn

forgot [fəˈɡɒt] *pt of* **forget**

forgotten [fəˈɡɒtn] *pp of* **forget**

fork [fɔːk] *n* (*for eating*) forchetta; (*for gardening*) forca; (*of roads, rivers, railways*) biforcazione *f* ▷ *vi* (*road etc*) biforcarsi

forlorn [fəˈlɔːn] *adj* (*person*) sconsolato(-a); (*place*) abbandonato(-a); (*attempt*) disperato(-a); (*hope*) vano(-a)

form [fɔːm] *n* forma; (*Scol*) classe *f*; (*questionnaire*) scheda ▷ *vt* formare; **in top ~** in gran forma

formal [ˈfɔːməl] *adj* formale; (*gardens*) simmetrico(-a), regolare; **formality** [fɔːˈmælɪtɪ] *n* formalità *f inv*

format [ˈfɔːmæt] *n* formato ▷ *vt* (*Comput*) formattare

formation [fɔːˈmeɪʃən] *n* formazione *f*

former [ˈfɔːməˈ] *adj* vecchio(-a); (*before ~*) ex *inv* (*before n*); **the ~ ... the latter** quello ... questo; **formerly** *adv* in passato

formidable [ˈfɔːmɪdəbl] *adj* formidabile

formula [ˈfɔːmjʊlə] *n* formula

fort [fɔːt] *n* forte *m*

forthcoming [fɔːθˈkʌmɪŋ] *adj* (*event*) prossimo(-a); (*help*) disponibile; (*character*) aperto(-a), comunicativo(-a)

fortieth [ˈfɔːtɪɪθ] *num* quarantesimo(-a)

fortify [ˈfɔːtɪfaɪ] *vt* (*city*) fortificare; (*person*) armare

fortnight [ˈfɔːtnaɪt] (BRIT) *n* quindici giorni *mpl*, due settimane *fpl*; **fortnightly** *adj* bimensile ▷ *adv* ogni quindici giorni

fortress [ˈfɔːtrɪs] *n* fortezza, rocca

fortunate [ˈfɔːtʃənɪt] *adj* fortunato(-a); **it is ~ that** è una fortuna che; **fortunately** *adv* fortunatamente

fortune [ˈfɔːtʃən] *n* fortuna; **fortune-teller** *n* indovino(-a)

forty [ˈfɔːtɪ] *num* quaranta

forum [ˈfɔːrəm] *n* foro

forward [ˈfɔːwəd] *adj* (*ahead of schedule*) in anticipo; (*movement, position*) in avanti; (*not shy*) aperto(-a), diretto(-a) ▷ *n* (*Sport*) avanti *m inv* ▷ *vt* (*letter*) inoltrare; (*parcel, goods*) spedire; (*career, plans*) promuovere, appoggiare; **to move ~** avanzare; **forwarding address** *n* nuovo recapito cui spedire la posta; **forward(s)** *adv* avanti; **forward slash** *n* barra obliqua

fossil [ˈfɒsl] *adj* fossile ▷ *n* fossile *m*

foster [ˈfɒstəˈ] *vt* incoraggiare, nutrire; (*child*) avere in affidamento; **foster child** *n* bambino(-a) preso(-a) in affidamento; **foster mother** *n* madre f'affidataria

fought [fɔːt] *pt, pp of* **fight**

foul [faʊl] *adj* (*smell, food, temper etc*) cattivo(-a); (*weather*) brutto(-a); (*language*) osceno(-a) ▷ *n* (*Sport*) fallo ▷ *vt* sporcare; **foul play** *n* (*Law*): **the police suspect foul play** la polizia sospetta un atto criminale

found [faund] *pt, pp of* **find** ▷ *vt* (*establish*)
fondare; **foundation** [-'deɪʃən] *n*
(*act*) fondazione *f*; (*base*) base *f*; (*also*:
foundation cream) fondo tinta;
foundations *npl* (*of building*) fondamenta
fpl

founder ['faundəʳ] *n* fondatore(-trice) ▷ *vi*
affondare

fountain ['fauntɪn] *n* fontana; **fountain
pen** *n* penna stilografica

four [fɔːʳ] *num* quattro; **on all ~s** a
carponi; **four-letter word** ['fɔːlɛtə-] *n*
parolaccia; **four-poster** *n* (*also*: **four-
poster bed**) letto a quattro colonne;
fourteen *num* quattordici; **fourteenth**
num quattordicesimo(-a); **fourth** *num*
quarto(-a); **four-wheel drive** ['fɔːwiːl-] *n*
(*Aut*): **with four-wheel drive** con quattro
ruote motrici

fowl [faul] *n* pollame *m*; volatile *m*

fox [fɔks] *n* volpe *f* ▷ *vt* confondere

foyer ['fɔɪeɪ] *n* atrio; (*Theatre*) ridotto

fraction ['frækʃən] *n* frazione *f*

fracture ['fræktʃəʳ] *n* frattura

fragile ['frædʒaɪl] *adj* fragile

fragment ['frægmənt] *n* frammento

fragrance ['freɪgrəns] *n* fragranza,
profumo

frail [freɪl] *adj* debole, delicato(-a)

frame [freɪm] *n* (*of building*) armatura;
(*of human, animal*) ossatura, corpo; (*of
picture*) cornice *f*; (*of door, window*) telaio;
(*of spectacles*: *also*: **~s**) montatura ▷ *vt*
(*picture*) incorniciare; **framework** *n*
struttura

France [frɑːns] *n* Francia

franchise ['fræntʃaɪz] *n* (*Pol*) diritto di
voto; (*Comm*) concessione *f*

frank [fræŋk] *adj* franco(-a), aperto(-a)
▷ *vt* (*letter*) affrancare; **frankly** *adv*
francamente, sinceramente

frantic ['fræntɪk] *adj* frenetico(-a)

fraud [frɔːd] *n* truffa; (*Law*) frode *f*; (*person*)
impostore(-a)

fraught [frɔːt] *adj* **~ with** pieno(-a) di,
intriso(-a) da

fray [freɪ] *vt* logorare ▷ *vi* logorarsi

freak [friːk] *n* fenomeno, mostro

freckle ['frɛkl] *n* lentiggine *f*

free [friː] *adj* libero(-a); (*gratis*) gratuito(-a)
▷ *vt* (*prisoner, jammed person*) liberare;
(*jammed object*) districare; **is this seat ~?**
è libero questo posto?; **~ of charge, for
~** gratuitamente; **freedom** ['friːdəm]
n libertà; **Freefone®** *n* numero verde;
free gift *n* regalo, omaggio; **free kick** *n*
calcio libero; **freelance** *adj* indipendente;
freely *adv* liberamente; (*liberally*)

liberalmente; **Freepost®** *n* affrancatura
a carico del destinatario; **free-range** *adj*
(*hen*) ruspante; (*eggs*) di gallina ruspante;
freeway (*us*) *n* superstrada; **free will** *n*
libero arbitrio; **of one's own free will** di
spontanea volontà

freeze [friːz] (*pt* **froze**, *pp* **frozen**) *vi* gelare
▷ *vt* gelare; (*food*) congelare; (*prices,
salaries*) bloccare ▷ *n* gelo; blocco; **freezer**
n congelatore *m*; **freezing** ['friːzɪŋ] *adj*
(*wind, weather*) gelido(-a); **freezing point**
n punto di congelamento; **3 degrees
below freezing point** 3 gradi sotto zero

freight [freɪt] *n* (*goods*) merce *f*, merci
fpl; (*money charged*) spese *fpl* di trasporto;
freight train (*us*) *n* treno *m* merci *inv*

French [frɛntʃ] *adj* francese ▷ *n* (*Ling*)
francese *m*; **the ~** *npl* i Francesi; **French
bean** *n* fagiolino; **French bread** *n*
baguette *f inv*; **French dressing** *n* (*Culin*)
condimento per insalata; **French fried
potatoes** (*us* **French fries**) *npl* patate
fpl fritte; **Frenchman** (*irreg*) *n* francese
m; **French stick** *n* baguette *f inv*; **French
window** *n* portafinestra; **Frenchwoman**
(*irreg*) *n* francese *f*

frenzy ['frɛnzɪ] *n* frenesia

frequency ['friːkwənsɪ] *n* frequenza

frequent [*adj* 'friːkwənt, *vb* frɪ'kwɛnt] *adj*
frequente ▷ *vt* frequentare; **frequently**
adv frequentemente, spesso

fresh [frɛʃ] *adj* fresco(-a); (*new*) nuovo(-a);
(*cheeky*) sfacciato(-a); **freshen** *vi*
(*wind, air*) rinfrescare; **freshen up** *vi*
rinfrescarsi; **fresher** (*BRIT: inf*) *n* (*Scol*)
matricola; **freshly** *adv* di recente, di
fresco; **freshman** (*irreg*: *us*) *n* = **fresher**;
freshwater *adj* (*fish*) d'acqua dolce

fret [frɛt] *vi* agitarsi, affliggersi

Fri. *abbr* (= *Friday*) ven.

friction ['frɪkʃən] *n* frizione *f*, attrito

Friday ['fraɪdɪ] *n* venerdì *m inv*

fridge [frɪdʒ] (*BRIT*) *n* frigo, frigorifero

fried [fraɪd] *pt, pp of* **fry** ▷ *adj* fritto(-a)

friend [frɛnd] *n* amico(-a); **friendly** *adj*
amichevole; **friendship** *n* amicizia

fries [fraɪz] (*esp us*) *npl* patate *fpl* fritte

frigate ['frɪgɪt] *n* (*Naut: modern*) fregata

fright [fraɪt] *n* paura, spavento; **to take ~**
spaventarsi; **frighten** *vt* spaventare, far
paura a; **frightened** *adj* spaventato(-a);
frightening *adj* spaventoso(-a),
pauroso(-a); **frightful** *adj* orribile

frill [frɪl] *n* balza

fringe [frɪndʒ] *n* (*decoration*: BRIT: *of hair*)
frangia; (*edge: of forest etc*) margine *m*

Frisbee® ['frɪzbɪ] *n* frisbee® *m inv*

fritter ['frɪtəʳ] *n* frittella

frivolous ['frɪvələs] *adj* frivolo(-a)

fro [frəu] *see* **to**

frock [frɔk] *n* vestito

frog [frɔg] *n* rana; **frogman** (*irreg*) *n* uomo *m* rana *inv*

KEYWORD

from [frɔm] *prep* **1** (*indicating starting place, origin etc*) da; **where do you come from?, where are you from?** da dove viene?, di dov'è?; **from London to Glasgow** da Londra a Glasgow; **a letter from my sister** una lettera a mia sorella; **tell him from me that …** gli dica da parte mia che …

2 (*indicating time*) da; **from one o'clock to** *or* **until** *or* **till two** dall'una alle due; **from January (on)** da gennaio, a partire da gennaio

3 (*indicating distance*) da; **the hotel is 1 km from the beach** l'albergo è a 1 km dalla spiaggia

4 (*indicating price, number etc*) da; **prices range from £10 to £50** i prezzi vanno dalle 10 alle 50 sterline

5 (*indicating difference*) da; **he can't tell red from green** non sa distinguere il rosso dal verde

6 (*because of, on the basis of*): **from what he says** da quanto dice lui; **weak from hunger** debole per la fame

front [frʌnt] *n* (*of house, dress*) davanti *m inv*; (*of train*) testa; (*of book*) copertina; (*promenade: also:* **sea ~**) lungomare *m*; (*Mil, Pol, Meteor*) fronte *m*; (*fig: appearances*) fronte *f* ▷ *adj* primo(-a); anteriore, davanti *inv*; **in ~ of** davanti a; **front door** *n* porta d'entrata; (*of car*) sportello anteriore; **frontier** [ˈfrʌntɪəʳ] *n* frontiera; **front page** *n* prima pagina; **front-wheel drive** [ˈfrʌntwiːl-] *n* trasmissione *f* anteriore

frost [frɔst] *n* gelo; (*also:* **hoar~**) brina; **frostbite** *n* congelamento; **frosting** (*us*) *n* (*on cake*) glassa; **frosty** *adj* (*weather, look*) gelido(-a)

froth [frɔθ] *n* spuma; schiuma

frown [fraun] *vi* acciglliarsi

froze [frəuz] *pt of* **freeze**

frozen [ˈfrəuzn] *pp of* **freeze**

fruit [fruːt] *n inv* (*also fig*) frutto; (*collectively*) frutta; **fruit juice** *n* succo di frutta; **fruit machine** (*BRIT*) *n* macchina *f* mangiasoldi *inv*; **fruit salad** *n* macedonia

frustrate [frʌsˈtreɪt] *vt* frustrare; **frustrated** *adj* frustrato(-a)

fry [fraɪ] (*pt, pp* **fried**) *vt* friggere; *see also* **small**; **frying pan** *n* padella

ft. *abbr* = **foot; feet**

fudge [fʌdʒ] *n* (*Culin*) specie di caramella a base di latte, burro e zucchero

fuel [fjuəl] *n* (*for heating*) combustibile *m*; (*for propelling*) carburante *m*; **fuel tank** *n* deposito *m* nafta *inv*; (*on vehicle*) serbatoio (della benzina)

fulfil [fulˈfɪl] *vt* (*function*) compiere; (*order*) eseguire; (*wish, desire*) soddisfare, appagare

full [ful] *adj* pieno(-a); (*details, skirt*) ampio(-a) ▷ *adv* **to know ~ well that** sapere benissimo che; **I'm ~ (up)** sono sazio; **a ~ two hours** due ore intere; **at ~ speed** a tutta velocità; **in ~** per intero; **full-length** *adj* (*film*) a lungometraggio; (*coat, novel*) lungo(-a); (*portrait*) in piedi; **full moon** *n* luna piena; **full-scale** *adj* (*attack, war*) su larga scala; (*model*) in grandezza naturale; **full stop** *n* punto; **full-time** *adj, adv* (*work*) a tempo pieno; **fully** *adv* interamente, pienamente, completamente; (*at least*) almeno

fumble [ˈfʌmbl] *vi* **to ~ with sth** armeggiare con qc

fume [fjuːm] *vi* essere furioso(-a); **fumes** *npl* esalazioni *fpl*, vapori *mpl*

fun [fʌn] *n* divertimento, spasso; **to have ~** divertirsi; **for ~** per scherzo; **to make ~ of** prendersi gioco di

function [ˈfʌŋkʃən] *n* funzione *f*; cerimonia, ricevimento ▷ *vi* funzionare

fund [fʌnd] *n* fondo, cassa; (*source*) fondo; (*store*) riserva; **~s** *npl* (*money*) fondi *mpl*

fundamental [fʌndəˈmɛntl] *adj* fondamentale

funeral [ˈfjuːnərəl] *n* funerale *m*; **funeral director** *n* impresario di pompe funebri; **funeral parlour** [-ˈpɑːləʳ] *n* impresa di pompe funebri

funfair [ˈfʌnfɛəʳ] *n* luna park *m inv*

fungus [ˈfʌŋgəs] (*pl* **fungi**) *n* fungo; (*mould*) muffa

funnel [ˈfʌnl] *n* imbuto; (*of ship*) ciminiera

funny [ˈfʌnɪ] *adj* divertente, buffo(-a); (*strange*) strano(-a), bizzarro(-a)

fur [fəːʳ] *n* pelo; pelliccia; (*BRIT: in kettle etc*) deposito calcareo; **fur coat** *n* pelliccia

furious [ˈfjuərɪəs] *adj* furioso(-a); (*effort*) accanito(-a)

furnish [ˈfəːnɪʃ] *vt* ammobiliare; (*supply*) fornire; **furnishings** *npl* mobili *mpl*, mobilia

furniture [ˈfəːnɪtʃəʳ] *n* mobili *mpl*; **piece of ~** mobile *m*

furry [ˈfəːrɪ] *adj* (*animal*) peloso(-a)

further [ˈfəːðəʳ] *adj* supplementare, altro(-a); nuovo(-a); più lontano(-a) ▷ *adv* più lontano; (*more*) di più; (*moreover*) inoltre ▷ *vt* favorire, promuovere; **further**

education *n* ≈ corsi *mpl* di formazione;
college of further education istituto
statale con corsi specializzati (di formazione
professionale, aggiornamento professionale
ecc); **furthermore** [fəˈðəˈmɔːʳ] adv inoltre,
per di più
furthest [ˈfəːðɪst] superl of **far**
fury [ˈfjuərɪ] n furore m
fuse [fjuːz] (US **fuze**) n fusibile m; (for bomb
etc) miccia, spoletta ▷ vt fondere ▷ vi
fondersi; **to ~ the lights** (BRIT Elec) far
saltare i fusibili; **fuse box** n cassetta dei
fusibili
fusion [ˈfjuːʒən] n fusione f
fuss [fʌs] n agitazione f; (complaining) storie
fpl; **to make a ~** fare delle storie; **fussy** adj
(person) puntiglioso(-a), esigente; che fa le
storie; (dress) carico(-a) di fronzoli; (style)
elaborato(-a)
future [ˈfjuːtʃəʳ] adj futuro(-a) ▷ n futuro,
avvenire m; (Ling) futuro; **in ~** in futuro; **-s**
npl (Comm) operazioni fpl a termine
fuze [fjuːz] (US) = **fuse**
fuzzy [ˈfʌzɪ] adj (Phot) indistinto(-a),
sfocato(-a); (hair) crespo(-a)

G [dʒiː] n (Mus) sol m
g. abbr (= gram, gravity) g.
gadget [ˈgædʒɪt] n aggeggio
Gaelic [ˈgeɪlɪk] adj gaelico(-a) ▷ n (Ling)
gaelico
gag [gæg] n bavaglio; (joke) facezia,
scherzo ▷ vt imbavagliare
gain [geɪn] n guadagno, profitto ▷ vt
guadagnare ▷ vi (clock, watch) andare
avanti; (benefit): **to ~ (from)** trarre
beneficio (da); **to ~ 3lbs (in weight)**
aumentare di 3 libbre; **to ~ on sb** (in race
etc) guadagnare su qn
gal. abbr = **gallon**
gala [ˈgɑːlə] n gala; **swimming ~**
manifestazione f di nuoto
galaxy [ˈgæləksɪ] n galassia
gale [geɪl] n vento forte; burrasca
gall bladder [ˈgɔːl-] n cistifellea
gallery [ˈgælərɪ] n galleria
gallon [ˈgælən] n gallone m (= 8 pints; BRIT
= 4.543l; US = 3.785l)
gallop [ˈgæləp] n galoppo ▷ vi galoppare
gallstone [ˈgɔːlstəun] n calcolo biliare
gamble [ˈgæmbl] n azzardo, rischio
calcolato ▷ vt, vi giocare; **to ~ on** (fig)
giocare su; **gambler** n giocatore(-trice)
d'azzardo; **gambling** n gioco d'azzardo
game [geɪm] n gioco; (event) partita;
(Tennis) game m inv; (Culin, Hunting)

selvaggina ▷ *adj* (*ready*): **to be ~ (for sth/ to do)** essere pronto(-a) (a qc/a fare); **big ~** selvaggina grossa; **~s** *npl* (*Scol*) attività *fpl* sportive; **big ~** selvaggina grossa; **games console** [geɪmz-] *n* console *f inv* dei videogame; **game show** ['geɪmʃəʊ] *n* gioco a premi

gammon ['gæmən] *n* (*bacon*) quarto di maiale; (*ham*) prosciutto affumicato

gang [gæŋ] *n* banda, squadra ▷ *vi* **to ~ up on sb** far combutta contro qn

gangster ['gæŋstər] *n* gangster *m inv*

gap [gæp] *n* (*space*) buco; (*in time*) intervallo; (*difference*): **~ (between)** divario (tra)

gape [geɪp] *vi* (*person*) restare a bocca aperta; (*shirt, hole*) essere spalancato(-a)

gap year *n* (*Scol*) anno di pausa durante il quale gli studenti viaggiano o lavorano

garage ['gæraːʒ] *n* garage *m inv*; **garage sale** *n* vendita di oggetti usati nel garage di un privato

garbage ['gaːbɪdʒ] (*US*) *n* immondizie *fpl*, rifiuti *mpl*; (*inf*) sciocchezze *fpl*; **garbage can** (*US*) *n* bidone *m* della spazzatura; **garbage collector** (*US*) *n* spazzino(-a)

garden ['gaːdn] *n* giardino; **~s** *npl* (*public park*) giardini pubblici; **garden centre** *n* vivaio; **gardener** *n* giardiniere(-a); **gardening** *n* giardinaggio

garlic ['gaːlɪk] *n* aglio

garment ['gaːmənt] *n* indumento

garnish ['gaːnɪʃ] *vt* (*food*) guarnire

garrison ['gærɪsn] *n* guarnigione *f*

gas [gæs] *n* gas *m inv*; (*US*: *gasoline*) benzina ▷ *vt* asfissiare con il gas; **I can smell ~** sento odore di gas; **gas cooker** (*BRIT*) *n* cucina a gas; **gas cylinder** *n* bombola del gas; **gas fire** (*BRIT*) *n* radiatore *m* a gas

gasket ['gæskɪt] *n* (*Aut*) guarnizione *f*

gasoline ['gæsəliːn] (*US*) *n* benzina

gasp [gaːsp] *n* respiro affannoso, ansito ▷ *vi* ansare, ansimare; (*in surprise*) restare senza fiato

gas: **gas pedal** (*esp US*) *n* pedale *m* dell'acceleratore; **gas station** (*US*) *n* distributore *m* di benzina; **gas tank** (*US*) *n* (*Aut*) serbatoio (di benzina)

gate [geɪt] *n* cancello; (*at airport*) uscita

gateau ['gætəʊ, -z] (*pl* **gateaux**) *n* torta

gatecrash ['geɪtkræʃ] (*BRIT*) *vt* partecipare senza invito a

gateway ['geɪtweɪ] *n* porta

gather ['gæðər] *vt* (*flowers, fruit*) cogliere; (*pick up*) raccogliere; (*assemble*) radunare; raccogliere; (*understand*) capire; (*Sewing*) increspare ▷ *vi* (*assemble*) radunarsi; **to ~ speed** acquistare velocità; **gathering** *n* adunanza

gauge [geɪdʒ] *n* (*instrument*) indicatore *m* ▷ *vt* misurare; (*fig*) valutare

gave [geɪv] *pt of* **give**

gay [geɪ] *adj* (*homosexual*) omosessuale; (*cheerful*) gaio(-a), allegro(-a); (*colour*) vivace, vivo(-a)

gaze [geɪz] *n* sguardo fisso ▷ *vi* **to ~ at** guardare fisso

GB *abbr* = **Great Britain**

GCSE (*BRIT*) *n abbr* General Certificate of Secondary Education

gear [gɪər] *n* attrezzi *mpl*, equipaggiamento *m*; (*Tech*) ingranaggio; (*Aut*) marcia ▷ *vt* (*fig*: *adapt*): **to ~ sth to** adattare qc a; **in top** *or* (*US*) **high/low ~** in quarta (*or* quinta)/seconda; **in ~** in marcia; **gear up** *vi* **to ~ up (to do)** prepararsi (a fare); **gear box** *n* scatola del cambio; **gear lever** *n* leva del cambio; **gear shift** (*US*), **gear stick** (*BRIT*) *n* = **gear lever**

geese [giːs] *npl of* **goose**

gel [dʒɛl] *n* gel *m inv*

gem [dʒɛm] *n* gemma

Gemini ['dʒɛmɪnaɪ] *n* Gemelli *mpl*

gender ['dʒɛndər] *n* genere *m*

gene [dʒiːn] *n* (*Biol*) gene *m*

general ['dʒɛnərl] *n* generale *m* ▷ *adj* generale; **in ~** in genere; **general anaesthetic** (*US* **general anesthetic**) *n* anestesia totale; **general election** *n* elezioni *fpl* generali; **generalize** *vi* generalizzare; **generally** *adv* generalmente; **general practitioner** *n* medico generico; **general store** *n* emporio

generate ['dʒɛnəreɪt] *vt* generare

generation [dʒɛnə'reɪʃən] *n* generazione *f*

generator ['dʒɛnəreɪtər] *n* generatore *m*

generosity [dʒɛnə'rɔsɪtɪ] *n* generosità

generous ['dʒɛnərəs] *adj* generoso(-a); (*copious*) abbondante

genetic [dʒɪ'nɛtɪk] *adj* genetico(-a); **~ engineering** ingegneria genetica; **genetically modified** *adj* geneticamente modificato(-a), transgenico(-a); **genetics** *n* genetica

Geneva [dʒɪ'niːvə] *n* Ginevra

genitals ['dʒɛnɪtlz] *npl* genitali *mpl*

genius ['dʒiːnɪəs] *n* genio

Genoa ['dʒɛnəʊə] *n* Genova

gent [dʒɛnt] *n abbr* = **gentleman**

gentle ['dʒɛntl] *adj* delicato(-a); (*person*) dolce

▮▮ Be careful not to translate *gentle* by the Italian word *gentile*.

gentleman ['dʒɛntlmən] (*irreg*) *n* signore *m*; (*well-bred man*) gentiluomo

gently ['dʒɛntlɪ] *adv* delicatamente

gents [dʒɛnts] n W.C. m (per signori)
genuine ['dʒɛnjuɪn] adj autentico(-a); sincero(-a); **genuinely** adv genuinamente
geographic(al) [dʒɪə'græfɪk(l)] adj geografico(-a)
geography [dʒɪ'ɔgrəfɪ] n geografia
geology [dʒɪ'ɔlədʒɪ] n geologia
geometry [dʒɪ'ɔmətrɪ] n geometria
geranium [dʒɪ'reɪnjəm] n geranio
geriatric [dʒɛrɪ'ætrɪk] adj geriatrico(-a)
germ [dʒə:m] n (Med) microbo; (Biol, fig) germe m
German ['dʒə:mən] adj tedesco(-a) ▷ n tedesco(-a); (Ling) tedesco; **German measles** (BRIT) n rosolia
Germany ['dʒə:mənɪ] n Germania
gesture ['dʒɛstjə*] n gesto

 KEYWORD

get [gɛt] (pt, pp **got**, (US) pp **gotten**) vi **1** (become, be) diventare, farsi; **to get old** invecchiare; **to get tired** stancarsi; **to get drunk** ubriacarsi; **to get killed** venire or rimanere ucciso(-a); **when do I get paid?** quando mi pagate?; **it's getting late** si sta facendo tardi
2 (go): **to get to/from** andare a/da; **to get home** arrivare or tornare a casa; **how did you get here?** come sei venuto?
3 (begin) mettersi a, cominciare a; **to get to know sb** incominciare a conoscere qn; **let's get going** or **started** muoviamoci
4 (modal aux vb): **you've got to do it** devi farlo
▷ vt **1**: **to get sth done** (do) fare qc; (have done) far fare qc; **to get one's hair cut** farsi tagliare i capelli; **to get sb to do sth** far fare qc a qn
2 (obtain: money, permission, results) ottenere; (find: job, flat) trovare; (fetch: person, doctor) chiamare; (: object) prendere; **to get sth for sb** prendere or procurare qc a qn; **get me Mr Jones, please** (Tel) mi passi il signor Jones, per favore; **can I get you a drink?** le posso offrire da bere?
3 (receive: present, letter, prize) ricevere; (acquire: reputation) farsi; **how much did you get for the painting?** quanto le hanno dato per il quadro?
4 (catch) prendere; (hit: target etc) colpire; **to get sb by the arm/throat** afferrare qn per un braccio/alla gola; **get him!** prendetelo!
5 (take, move) portare; **to get sth to sb** far avere qc a qn; **do you think we'll get it through the door?** pensi che riusciremo a farlo passare per la porta?

6 (catch, take: plane, bus etc) prendere; **where do we get the ferry to ...?** dove si prende il traghetto per ...?
7 (understand) afferrare; (hear) sentire; **I've got it!** ci sono arrivato!, ci sono!; **I'm sorry, I didn't get your name** scusi, non ho capito (or sentito) il suo nome
8 (have, possess): **to have got** avere; **how many have you got?** quanti ne ha?
get along vi (agree) andare d'accordo; (depart) andarsene; (manage) = **get by**
get at vt fus (attack) prendersela con; (reach) raggiungere, arrivare a
get away vi partire, andarsene; (escape) scappare
get away with vt fus cavarsela; farla franca
get back vi (return) ritornare, tornare ▷ vt riottenere, riavere; **when do we get back?** quando ritorniamo?
get by vi (pass) passare; (manage) farcela
get down vi, vt fus scendere ▷ vt far scendere; (depress) buttare giù
get down to vt fus (work) mettersi a (fare)
get in vi (enter) entrare; (train) arrivare; (arrive home) ritornare, tornare
get into vt fus entrare in; **to get into a rage** incavolarsi
get off vi (from train etc) scendere; (depart: person, car) andare via; (escape) cavarsela ▷ vt (remove: clothes, stain) levare ▷ vt fus (train, bus) scendere da; **where do I get off?** dove devo scendere?
get on vi (at exam etc) andare; (agree): **to get on (with)** andare d'accordo (con) ▷ vt fus montare in; (horse) montare su
get out vi uscire; (of vehicle) scendere ▷ vt tirar fuori, far uscire
get out of vt fus uscire da; (duty etc) evitare
get over vt fus (illness) riaversi da
get round vt fus aggirare; (fig: person) rigirare
get through vi (Tel) avere la linea
get through to vt fus (Tel) parlare a
get together vi riunirsi ▷ vt raccogliere; (people) adunare
get up vi (rise) alzarsi ▷ vt fus salire su per
get up to vt fus (reach) raggiungere; (prank etc) fare

getaway ['gɛtəweɪ] n fuga
Ghana ['gɑ:nə] n Ghana m
ghastly ['gɑ:stlɪ] adj orribile, orrendo(-a); (pale) spettrale
ghetto ['gɛtəu] n ghetto
ghost [gəust] n fantasma m, spettro
giant ['dʒaɪənt] n gigante m ▷ adj gigantesco(-a), enorme

gift [gɪft] n regalo; (donation, ability) dono; **gifted** adj dotato(-a); **gift shop** (us **gift store**) n negozio di souvenir

gift token, gift voucher n buono m omaggio inv

gig [gɪg] n (inf: of musician) serata

gigabyte [giːgəbaɪt] n gigabyte m inv

gigantic [dʒaɪˈgæntɪk] adj gigantesco(-a)

giggle [ˈgɪgl] vi ridere scioccamente

gills [gɪlz] npl (of fish) branchie fpl

gilt [gɪlt] n doratura ▷ adj dorato(-a)

gimmick [ˈgɪmɪk] n trucco

gin [dʒɪn] n (liquor) gin m inv

ginger [ˈdʒɪndʒəʳ] n zenzero

gipsy [ˈdʒɪpsɪ] n zingaro(-a)

giraffe [dʒɪˈrɑːf] n giraffa

girl [gəːl] n ragazza; (young unmarried woman) signorina; (daughter) figlia, figliola; **girlfriend** n (of girl) amica; (of boy) ragazza; **Girl Scout** (us) n Giovane Esploratrice f

gist [dʒɪst] n succo

give [gɪv] (pt **gave**, pp **given**) vt dare ▷ vi cedere; **to ~ sb sth, ~ sth to sb** dare qc a qn; **I'll ~ you £5 for it** te lo pago 5 sterline; **to ~ a cry/sigh** emettere un grido/sospiro; **to ~ a speech** fare un discorso; **give away** vt dare via; (disclose) rivelare; (bride) condurre all'altare; **give back** vt rendere; **give in** vi cedere ▷ vt consegnare; **give out** vt distribuire; annunciare; **give up** vi rinunciare ▷ vt rinunciare a; **to ~ up smoking** smettere di fumare; **to ~ o.s. up** arrendersi

given [ˈgɪvn] pp of **give** ▷ adj (fixed: time, amount) dato(-a), determinato(-a) ▷ conj **~ (that) ...** dato che ...; **~ the circumstances ...** date le circostanze ...

glacier [ˈglæsɪəʳ] n ghiacciaio

glad [glæd] adj lieto(-a), contento(-a); **gladly** [ˈglædlɪ] adv volentieri

glamorous [ˈglæmərəs] adj affascinante, seducente

glamour [ˈglæməʳ] (us **glamor**) n fascino

glance [glɑːns] n occhiata, sguardo ▷ vi **to ~ at** dare un'occhiata a; **to ~ off** (bullet) rimbalzare su

gland [glænd] n ghiandola

glare [glɛəʳ] n (of anger) sguardo furioso; (of light) riverbero, luce f abbagliante; (of publicity) chiasso ▷ vi abbagliare; **to ~ at** guardare male; **glaring** adj (mistake) madornale

glass [glɑːs] n (substance) vetro; (tumbler) bicchiere m; **~es** npl (spectacles) occhiali mpl

glaze [gleɪz] vt (door) fornire di vetri; (pottery) smaltare ▷ n smalto

gleam [gliːm] vi luccicare

glen [glɛn] n valletta

glide [glaɪd] vi scivolare; (Aviat, birds) planare; **glider** n (Aviat) aliante m

glimmer [ˈglɪməʳ] n barlume m

glimpse [glɪmps] n impressione f fugace ▷ vt vedere al volo

glint [glɪnt] vi luccicare

glisten [ˈglɪsn] vi luccicare

glitter [ˈglɪtəʳ] vi scintillare

global [ˈgləʊbl] adj globale; **global warming** n effetto m serra inv

globe [gləʊb] n globo, sfera

gloom [gluːm] n oscurità, buio; (sadness) tristezza, malinconia; **gloomy** adj scuro(-a), fosco(-a), triste

glorious [ˈglɔːrɪəs] adj glorioso(-a), magnifico(-a)

glory [ˈglɔːrɪ] n gloria; splendore m

gloss [glɔs] n (shine) lucentezza; (also: ~ paint) vernice f a olio

glossary [ˈglɔsərɪ] n glossario

glossy [ˈglɔsɪ] adj lucente

glove [glʌv] n guanto; **glove compartment** n (Aut) vano portaoggetti

glow [gləʊ] vi ardere; (face) essere luminoso(-a)

glucose [ˈgluːkəʊs] n glucosio

glue [gluː] n colla ▷ vt incollare

GM adj abbr (= genetically modified) geneticamente modificato(-a)

gm abbr = **gram**

GMO n abbr (= genetically modified organism) OGM m inv

GMT abbr (= Greenwich Mean Time) T.M.G.

gnaw [nɔː] vt rodere

go [gəʊ] (pt **went**, pp **gone**) (pl **goes**) vi andare; (depart) partire, andarsene; (work) funzionare; (time) passare; (break etc) rompersi; (be sold): **to go for £10** essere venduto per 10 sterline; (fit, suit): **to go with** andare bene con; (become): **to go pale** diventare pallido(-a); **to go mouldy** ammuffire ▷ n **to have a go (at)** provare; **to be on the go** essere in moto; **whose go is it?** a chi tocca?; **he's going to do it** sta per fare; **to go for a walk** andare a fare una passeggiata; **to go dancing/ shopping** andare a ballare/fare la spesa; **just then the bell went** proprio allora suonò il campanello; **how did it go?** com'è andato?; **to go round the back/by the shop** passare da dietro/davanti al negozio; **go ahead** vi andare avanti; **go away** vi partire, andarsene; **go back** vi tornare, ritornare; **go by** vi (years, time) scorrere ▷ vt fus attenersi a, seguire (alla lettera); prestar fede a; **go down** vi scendere; (ship) affondare; (sun) tramontare ▷ vt fus scendere; **go for** vt fus (fetch) andare a prendere; (*like*) andar matto(-a) per; (*attack*) attaccare; saltare addosso a; **go in** *vi* entrare; **go into** *vt fus* entrare in; (*investigate*) indagare, esaminare; (*embark on*) lanciarsi in; **go off** *vi* partire, andar via; (*food*) guastarsi; (*explode*) esplodere, scoppiare; (*event*) passare ▷ *vt fus* **I've ~ne off chocolate** la cioccolata non mi piace più; **the gun went off** il fucile si scaricò; **go on** *vi* continuare; (*happen*) succedere; **to ~ on doing** continuare a fare; **go out** *vi* uscire; (*couple*): **they went out for 3 years** sono stati insieme per 3 anni; (*fire, light*) spegnersi; **go over** *vi* (*ship*) ribaltarsi ▷ *vt fus* (*check*) esaminare; **go past** *vi* passare ▷ *vt fus* passare davanti a; **go round** *vi* (*circulate: news, rumour*) circolare; (*revolve*) girare; (*visit*): **to ~ round (to sb's)** passare (da qn); (*make a detour*): **to ~ round (by)** passare (per); (*suffice*) bastare (per tutti); **go through** *vt fus* (*town etc*) attraversare; (*files, papers*) passare in rassegna; (*examine: list etc*) leggere da cima a fondo; **go up** *vi* salire; **go with** *vt fus* (*accompany*) accompagnare; **go without** *vt fus* fare a meno di

go-ahead ['gəuəhɛd] *adj* intraprendente ▷ *n* via *m*

goal [gəul] *n* (*Sport*) gol *m*, rete *f*; (: *place*) porta; (*fig: aim*) fine *m*, scopo; **goalkeeper** *n* portiere *m*; **goal-post** *n* palo (della porta)

goat [gəut] *n* capra

gobble ['gɔbl] *vt* (*also: ~ down, ~ up*) ingoiare

god [gɔd] *n* dio; **G~** Dio; **godchild** *n* figlioccio(-a); **goddaughter** *n* figlioccia; **goddess** *n* dea; **godfather** *n* padrino; **godmother** *n* madrina; **godson** *n* figlioccio

goggles ['gɔglz] *npl* occhiali *mpl* (di protezione)

going ['gəuɪŋ] *n* (*conditions*) andare *m*, stato del terreno ▷ *adj* **the ~ rate** la tariffa in vigore

gold [gəuld] *n* oro ▷ *adj* d'oro; **golden** *adj* (*made of gold*) d'oro; (*gold in colour*) dorato(-a); **goldfish** *n* pesce *m* dorato *or* rosso; **goldmine** *n* (*also fig*) miniera d'oro; **gold-plated** *adj* placcato(-a) oro *inv*

golf [gɔlf] *n* golf *m*; **golf ball** *n* (*for game*) pallina da golf; (*on typewriter*) pallina; **golf club** *n* circolo di golf; (*stick*) bastone *m or* mazza da golf; **golf course** *n* campo di golf; **golfer** *n* giocatore(-trice) di golf

gone [gɔn] *pp of* **go** ▷ *adj* partito(-a)

gong [gɔŋ] *n* gong *m*

good [gud] *adj* buono(-a); (*kind*) buono(-a), gentile; (*child*) bravo(-a) ▷ *n* bene *m*; **~s** *npl* (*Comm etc*) beni *mpl*; merci *fpl*; **~!** bene!, ottimo!; **to be ~ at** essere bravo(-a) in; **to be ~ for** andare bene per; **it's ~ for you** fa bene; **would you be ~ enough to ...?** avrebbe la gentilezza di ...?; **a ~ deal (of)** molto(-a), una buona quantità (di); **a ~ many** molti(-e); **to make ~** (*loss, damage*) compensare; **it's no ~ complaining** brontolare non serve a niente; **for ~** per sempre, definitivamente; **~ morning!** buon giorno!; **~ afternoon/evening!** buona sera!; **~ night!** buona notte!; **goodbye** *excl* arrivederci!; **Good Friday** *n* Venerdì Santo; **good-looking** *adj* bello(-a); **good-natured** *adj* affabile; **goodness** *n* (*of person*) bontà; **for goodness sake!** per amor di Dio!; **goodness gracious!** santo cielo!, mamma mia!; **goods train** (*BRIT*) *n* treno *m* merci *inv*; **goodwill** *n* amicizia, benevolenza

goose [gu:s] (*pl* **geese**) *n* oca

gooseberry ['guzbəri] *n* uva spina; **to play ~** (*BRIT*) tenere la candela

goose bumps, goose pimples *npl* pelle *f* d'oca

gorge [gɔ:dʒ] *n* gola ▷ *vt* **to ~ o.s. (on)** ingozzarsi (di)

gorgeous ['gɔ:dʒəs] *adj* magnifico(-a)

gorilla [gə'rɪlə] *n* gorilla *m inv*

gosh (*inf*) [gɔʃ] *excl* perdinci!

gospel ['gɔspl] *n* vangelo

gossip ['gɔsɪp] *n* chiacchiere *fpl*; pettegolezzi *mpl*; (*person*) pettegolo(-a) ▷ *vi* chiacchierare; **gossip column** *n* cronaca mondana

got [gɔt] *pt, pp of* **get**

gotten ['gɔtn] (*US*) *pp of* **get**

gourmet ['guəmeɪ] *n* buongustaio(-a)

govern ['gʌvən] *vt* governare; **government** ['gʌvnmənt] *n* governo; **governor** ['gʌvənəʳ] *n* (*of state, bank*) governatore *m*; (*of school, hospital*) amministratore *m*; (*BRIT: of prison*) direttore(-trice)

gown [gaun] *n* vestito lungo; (*of teacher, BRIT: of judge*) toga

G.P. *n abbr* = **general practitioner**

grab [græb] *vt* afferrare, arraffare; (*property, power*) impadronirsi di ▷ *vi* **to ~ at** cercare di afferrare

grace [greɪs] *n* grazia ▷ *vt* onorare; **5 days' ~** dilazione *f* di 5 giorni; **graceful** *adj* elegante, aggraziato(-a); **gracious** ['greɪʃəs] *adj* grazioso(-a), misericordioso(-a)

grade [greɪd] *n* (*Comm*) qualità *f inv*; classe *f*; categoria; (*in hierarchy*) grado; (*Scol: mark*) voto; (*US: school class*) classe ▷ *vt* classificare; ordinare; graduare; **grade**

crossing (US) n passaggio a livello; **grade school** (US) n scuola elementare
gradient ['greɪdɪənt] n pendenza, inclinazione f
gradual ['grædjʊəl] adj graduale; **gradually** adv man mano, a poco a poco
graduate [n 'grædjʊɪt, vb 'grædjʊeɪt] n (of university) laureato(-a); (US: of high school) diplomato(-a) ▷ vi laurearsi; diplomarsi; **graduation** [-'eɪʃən] n (ceremony) consegna delle lauree (or dei diplomi)
graffiti [grə'fiːti] npl graffiti mpl
graft [grɑːft] n (Agr, Med) innesto; (bribery) corruzione f; (BRIT: hard work): **it's hard ~** è un lavoraccio ▷ vt innestare
grain [greɪn] n grano; (of sand) granello; (of wood) venatura
gram [græm] n grammo
grammar ['græmə'] n grammatica; **grammar school** (BRIT) n ≈ liceo
gramme [græm] n = **gram**
gran [ɡræn] (inf) (BRIT) nonna
grand [grænd] adj grande, magnifico(-a); grandioso(-a); **grandad** (inf) n = **granddad**; **grandchild** (pl -children) n nipote m; **granddad** (inf) n nonno; **granddaughter** n nipote f; **grandfather** n nonno; **grandma** (inf) n nonna; **grandmother** n nonna; **grandpa** (inf) n = **granddad**; **grandparents** npl nonni mpl; **grand piano** n pianoforte m a coda; **Grand Prix** ['grɑ̃'priː] n (Aut) Gran Premio, Grand Prix m inv; **grandson** n nipote m
granite ['grænɪt] n granito
granny ['grænɪ] (inf) n nonna
grant [grɑːnt] vt accordare; (a request) accogliere; (admit) ammettere, concedere ▷ n (Scol) borsa; (Admin) sussidio, sovvenzione f; **to take sth for ~ed** dare qc per scontato; **to take sb for ~ed** dare per scontata la presenza di qn
grape [greɪp] n chicco d'uva, acino
grapefruit ['greɪpfruːt] n pompelmo
graph [grɑːf] n grafico; **graphic** adj grafico(-a); (vivid) vivido(-a); **graphics** n grafica ▷ npl illustrazioni fpl
grasp [grɑːsp] vt afferrare ▷ n (grip) presa; (fig) potere m; comprensione f
grass [grɑːs] n erba; **grasshopper** n cavalletta
grate [greɪt] n graticola (del focolare) ▷ vi cigolare, stridere ▷ vt (Culin) grattugiare
grateful ['greɪtful] adj grato(-a), riconoscente
grater ['greɪtə'] n grattugia
gratitude ['grætɪtjuːd] n gratitudine f
grave [greɪv] n tomba ▷ adj grave, serio(-a)

gravel ['grævl] n ghiaia
gravestone ['greɪvstəun] n pietra tombale
graveyard ['greɪvjɑːd] n cimitero
gravity ['grævɪtɪ] n (Physics) gravità; pesantezza; (seriousness) gravità, serietà
gravy ['greɪvɪ] n intingolo della carne; salsa
gray [greɪ] adj = **grey**
graze [greɪz] vi pascolare, pascere ▷ vt (touch lightly) sfiorare; (scrape) escoriare ▷ n (Med) escoriazione f
grease [griːs] n (fat) grasso; (lubricant) lubrificante m ▷ vt ingrassare; lubrificare; **greasy** adj grasso(-a), untuoso(-a)
great [greɪt] adj grande, (inf) magnifico(-a), meraviglioso(-a); **Great Britain** n Gran Bretagna; **great-grandfather** n bisnonno; **great-grandmother** n bisnonna; **greatly** adv molto
Greece [griːs] n Grecia
greed [griːd] n (also: ~iness) avarizia; (for food) golosità, ghiottoneria; **greedy** adj avido(-a); goloso(-a), ghiotto(-a)
Greek [griːk] adj greco(-a) ▷ n greco(-a); (Ling) greco
green [griːn] adj verde; (inexperienced) inesperto(-a), ingenuo(-a) ▷ n verde m; (stretch of grass) prato; (on golf course) green m inv; **~s** npl (vegetables) verdura; **green card** n (BRIT Aut) carta verde; (US Admin) permesso di soggiorno e di lavoro; **greengage** ['griːngeɪdʒ] n susina Regina Claudia; **greengrocer** (BRIT) n fruttivendolo(-a), erbivendolo(-a); **greenhouse** n serra; **greenhouse effect** n effetto serra
Greenland ['griːnlənd] n Groenlandia
green salad n insalata verde
greet [griːt] vt salutare; **greeting** n saluto; **greeting(s) card** n cartolina d'auguri
grew [gruː] pt of **grow**
grey [greɪ] (US gray) adj grigio(-a); **grey-haired** adj dai capelli grigi; **greyhound** n levriere m
grid [grɪd] n grata; (Elec) rete f; **gridlock** ['grɪdlʊk] n (traffic jam) paralisi f inv del traffico; **gridlocked** adj paralizzato(-a) dal traffico; (talks etc) in fase di stallo
grief [griːf] n dolore m
grievance ['griːvəns] n lagnanza
grieve [griːv] vi addolorarsi; rattristarsi ▷ vt addolorare; **to ~ for sb** (dead person) piangere qn
grill [grɪl] n (on cooker) griglia; (also: **mixed ~**) grigliata mista ▷ vt (BRIT) cuocere ai ferri; (inf: question) interrogare senza sosta
grille [grɪl] n grata; (Aut) griglia

grim [grɪm] *adj* sinistro(-a), brutto(-a)

grime [graɪm] *n* sudiciume *m*

grin [grɪn] *n* sorriso smagliante ▷ *vi* fare un gran sorriso

grind [graɪnd] (*pt, pp* **ground**) *vt* macinare; (*make sharp*) arrotare ▷ *n* (*work*) sgobbata

grip [grɪp] *n* impugnatura; presa; (*holdall*) borsa da viaggio ▷ *vt* (*object*) afferrare; (*attention*) catturare; **to come to ~s with** affrontare; cercare di risolvere; **gripping** ['grɪpɪŋ] *adj* avvincente

grit [grɪt] *n* ghiaia; (*courage*) fegato ▷ *vt* (*road*) coprire di sabbia; **to ~ one's teeth** stringere i denti

grits [grɪts] (*us*) *npl* macinato grosso (di avena *etc*)

groan [grəʊn] *n* gemito ▷ *vi* gemere

grocer ['grəʊsəʳ] *n* negoziante *m* di generi alimentari; **groceries** *npl* provviste *fpl*; **grocer's (shop)** *n* negozio di (generi) alimentari

grocery ['grəʊsərɪ] *n* (*shop*) (negozio di) alimentari

groin [grɔɪn] *n* inguine *m*

groom [gru:m] *n* palafreniere *m*; (*also*: **bride~**) sposo ▷ *vt* (*horse*) strigliare; (*fig*): **to ~ sb for** avviare qn a; **well-~ed** (*person*) curato(-a)

groove [gru:v] *n* scanalatura, solco

grope [grəʊp] *vi* **to ~ for** cercare a tastoni

gross [grəʊs] *adj* grossolano(-a); (*Comm*) lordo(-a); **grossly** *adv* (*greatly*) molto

grotesque [grəʊˈtɛsk] *adj* grottesco(-a)

ground [graʊnd] *pt, pp of* **grind** ▷ *n* suolo, terra; (*land*) terreno; (*Sport*) campo; (*reason: gen pl*) ragione *f*; (*us: also*: **~ wire**) terra ▷ *vt* (*plane*) tenere a terra; (*us Elec*) mettere la presa a terra a; **~s** *npl* (*of coffee etc*) fondi *mpl*; (*gardens etc*) terreno, giardini *mpl*; **on/to the ~** per/a terra; **to gain/lose ~** guadagnare/perdere terreno; **ground floor** *n* pianterreno; **groundsheet** (*BRIT*) *n* telone *m* impermeabile; **groundwork** *n* preparazione *f*

group [gru:p] *n* gruppo ▷ *vt* (*also*: **~ together**) raggruppare ▷ *vi* (*also*: **~ together**) raggrupparsi

grouse [graʊs] *n inv* (*bird*) tetraone *m* ▷ *vi* (*complain*) brontolare

grovel ['grɔvl] *vi* (*fig*): **to ~ (before)** strisciare (di fronte a)

grow [grəʊ] (*pt* **grew,**, *pp* **grown**) *vi* crescere; (*increase*) aumentare; (*develop*) svilupparsi; (*become*): **to ~ rich/weak** arricchirsi/indebolirsi ▷ *vt* coltivare, far crescere; **grow on** *vt fus* **that painting is ~ing on me** quel quadro più lo guardo più mi piace; **grow up** *vi* farsi grande, crescere

growl [graʊl] *vi* ringhiare

grown [grəʊn] *pp of* **grow**; **grown-up** *n* adulto(-a), grande *m/f*

growth [grəʊθ] *n* crescita, sviluppo; (*what has grown*) crescita; (*Med*) escrescenza, tumore *m*

grub [grʌb] *n* larva; (*inf: food*) roba (da mangiare)

grubby ['grʌbɪ] *adj* sporco(-a)

grudge [grʌdʒ] *n* rancore *m* ▷ *vt* **to ~ sb sth** dare qc a qn di malavoglia; invidiare qc a qn; **to bear sb a ~ (for)** serbar rancore a qn (per)

gruelling ['gruəlɪŋ] (*us* **grueling**) *adj* estenuante

gruesome ['gru:səm] *adj* orribile

grumble ['grʌmbl] *vi* brontolare, lagnarsi

grumpy ['grʌmpɪ] *adj* scorbutico(-a)

grunt [grʌnt] *vi* grugnire

guarantee [gærən'ti:] *n* garanzia ▷ *vt* garantire

guard [gɑ:d] *n* guardia; (*one man*) guardia, sentinella; (*BRIT Rail*) capotreno; (*on machine*) schermo protettivo; (*also*: **fire~**) parafuoco ▷ *vt* fare la guardia a; (*protect*): **to ~ (against)** proteggere (da); **to be on one's ~** stare in guardia; **guardian** *n* custode *m*; (*of minor*) tutore(-trice)

guerrilla [gə'rɪlə] *n* guerrigliero

guess [gɛs] *vi* indovinare ▷ *vt* indovinare; (*us*) credere, pensare ▷ *n* **to take** *or* **have a ~** provare a indovinare

guest [gɛst] *n* ospite *m/f*; (*in hotel*) cliente *m/f*; **guest house** *n* pensione *f*; **guest room** *n* camera degli ospiti

guidance ['gaɪdəns] *n* guida, direzione *f*

guide [gaɪd] *n* (*person, book etc*) guida; (*BRIT: also*: **girl ~**) giovane esploratrice *f* ▷ *vt* guidare; **is there an English-speaking ~?** c'è una guida che parla inglese?; **guidebook** *n* guida; **do you have a guidebook in English?** avete una guida in inglese?; **guide dog** *n* cane *m* guida *inv*; **guided tour** *n* visita guidata; **what time does the guided tour start?** a che ora comincia la visita guidata?; **guidelines** *npl* (*fig*) indicazioni *fpl*, linee *fpl* direttive

guild [gɪld] *n* arte *f*, corporazione *f*, associazione *f*

guilt [gɪlt] *n* colpevolezza; **guilty** *adj* colpevole

guinea pig ['gɪnɪ-] *n* cavia

guitar [gɪˈtɑːʳ] *n* chitarra; **guitarist** *n* chitarrista *m/f*

gulf [gʌlf] *n* golfo; (*abyss*) abisso

gull [gʌl] *n* gabbiano

gulp [gʌlp] *vi* deglutire; (*from emotion*) avere il nodo in gola ▷ *vt* (*also*: **~ down**) tracannare, inghiottire

gum [gʌm] n (Anat) gengiva; (glue) colla; (also: **~drop**) caramella gommosa; (also: **chewing ~**) chewing-gum m inv ▷ vt **to ~ (together)** incollare

gun [gʌn] n fucile m; (small) pistola, rivoltella; (rifle) carabina; (shotgun) fucile da caccia; (cannon) cannone m; **gunfire** n spari mpl; **gunman** (irreg) n bandito armato; **gunpoint** n **at gunpoint** sotto minaccia di fucile; **gunpowder** n polvere f da sparo; **gunshot** n sparo

gush [gʌʃ] vi sgorgare; (fig) abbandonarsi ad effusioni

gust [gʌst] n (of wind) raffica; (of smoke) buffata

gut [gʌt] n intestino, budello; **~s** npl (Anat) interiora fpl; (courage) fegato

gutter ['gʌtə'] n (of roof) grondaia; (in street) cunetta

guy [gaɪ] n (inf: man) tipo, elemento; (also: **~rope**) cavo or corda di fissaggio; (figure) effigie di Guy Fawkes

Guy Fawkes Night [-'fɔːks-] n (BRIT) vedi nota nel riquadro

> ▓ **Guy Fawkes Night**
> ▓
> ▓ La sera del 5 novembre, in occasione
> ▓ della **Guy Fawkes Night**, altrimenti
> ▓ chiamata **Bonfire Night**, viene
> ▓ commemorato con falò e fuochi
> ▓ d'artificio il fallimento della Congiura
> ▓ delle Polveri contro Giacomo I nel 1605.
> ▓ La festa prende il nome dal principale
> ▓ congiurato della cospirazione, Guy
> ▓ Fawkes, la cui effigie viene bruciata
> ▓ durante i festeggiamenti.

gym [dʒɪm] n (also: **~nasium**) palestra; (also: **~nastics**) ginnastica; **gymnasium** [dʒɪm'neɪzɪəm] n palestra; **gymnast** ['dʒɪmnæst] n ginnasta m/f; **gymnastics** [-'næstɪks] n, npl ginnastica; **gym shoes** npl scarpe fpl da ginnastica

gynaecologist [gaɪnɪ'kɔlədʒɪst] (US **gynecologist**) n ginecologo(-a)

gypsy ['dʒɪpsɪ] n = **gipsy**

haberdashery ['hæbə'dæʃərɪ] (BRIT) n merceria

habit ['hæbɪt] n abitudine f; (costume) abito; (Rel) tonaca

habitat ['hæbɪtæt] n habitat m inv

hack [hæk] vt tagliare, fare a pezzi ▷ n (pej: writer) scribacchino(-a); **hacker** ['hækə'] n (Comput) pirata m informatico

had [hæd] pt, pp of **have**

haddock ['hædək] (pl **haddock** or **haddocks**) n eglefino

hadn't ['hædnt] = **had not**

haemorrhage ['hɛmərɪdʒ] (US **hemorrhage**) n emorragia

haemorrhoids ['hɛmərɔɪdz] (US **hemorrhoids**) npl emorroidi fpl

haggle ['hægl] vi mercanteggiare

Hague [heɪg] n **The ~** L'Aia

hail [heɪl] n grandine f; (of criticism etc) pioggia ▷ vt (call) chiamare; (flag down: taxi) fermare; (greet) salutare ▷ vi grandinare; **hailstone** n chicco di grandine

hair [hɛə'] n capelli mpl; (single hair: on head) capello; (: on body) pelo; **to do one's ~** pettinarsi; **hairband** ['hɛəbænd] n (elastic) fascia per i capelli; (rigid) cerchietto; **hairbrush** n spazzola per capelli; **haircut** n taglio di capelli; **hairdo** ['hɛəduː] n acconciatura, pettinatura;

hairdresser *n* parrucchiere(-a);
hairdresser's *n* parrucchiere(-a); **hair
dryer** *n* asciugacapelli *m inv*; **hair gel** *n*
gel *m inv* per capelli; **hair spray** *n* lacca
per capelli; **hairstyle** *n* pettinatura,
acconciatura; **hairy** *adj* irsuto(-a),
peloso(-a); (*inf: frightening*) spaventoso(-a)
hake [heɪk] (*pl* **hake** *or* **hakes**) *n* nasello
half [hɑːf] (*pl* **halves**) *n* mezzo, metà
f inv ▷ *adj* mezzo(-a) ▷ *adv* a mezzo, a
metà; **~ an hour** mezz'ora; **~ a dozen**
mezza dozzina; **~ a pound** mezza libbra;
two and a ~ due e mezzo; **a week and
a ~** una settimana e mezza; **~ (of it)** la
metà; **~ (of)** la metà di; **to cut sth in ~**
tagliare qc in due; **~ asleep** mezzo(-a)
addormentato(-a); **half board** (BRIT)
n mezza pensione; **half-brother** *n*
fratellastro; **half day** *n* mezza giornata;
half fare *n* tariffa a metà prezzo; **half-
hearted** *adj* tiepido(-a); **half-hour** *n*
mezz'ora; **half-price** *adj, adv* a metà
prezzo; **half term** (BRIT) *n* (Scol) vacanza
a *or* di metà trimestre; **half-time** *n* (Sport)
intervallo; **halfway** *adv* a metà strada
hall [hɔːl] *n* sala, salone *m*; (*entrance way*)
entrata
hallmark ['hɔːlmɑːk] *n* marchio di
garanzia; (*fig*) caratteristica
hallo [hə'ləu] *excl* = **hello**
hall of residence (BRIT) *n* casa dello
studente
Halloween [hæləu'iːn] *n* vigilia
d'Ognissanti

> ⬧ **HALLOWEEN**
> ⬧
> ⬧ Negli Stati Uniti e in Gran Bretagna il
> ⬧ 31 ottobre si festeggia **Halloween**, la
> ⬧ notte delle streghe e dei fantasmi. I
> ⬧ bambini, travestiti da fantasmi, streghe
> ⬧ o mostri, bussano alle porte e ricevono
> ⬧ dolci e piccoli doni.

hallucination [həluːsɪ'neɪʃən] *n*
allucinazione *f*
hallway ['hɔːlweɪ] *n* corridoio; (*entrance*)
ingresso
halo ['heɪləu] *n* (*of saint etc*) aureola
halt [hɔːlt] *n* fermata ▷ *vt* fermare ▷ *vi*
fermarsi
halve [hɑːv] *vt* (*apple etc*) dividere a metà;
(*expense*) ridurre di metà
halves [hɑːvz] *npl of* **half**
ham [hæm] *n* prosciutto
hamburger ['hæmbəːgəʳ] *n* hamburger
m inv
hamlet ['hæmlɪt] *n* paesetto
hammer ['hæməʳ] *n* martello ▷ *vt*

martellare ▷ *vi* **to ~ on** *or* **at the door**
picchiare alla porta
hammock ['hæmək] *n* amaca
hamper ['hæmpəʳ] *vt* impedire ▷ *n* cesta
hamster ['hæmstəʳ] *n* criceto
hamstring ['hæmstrɪŋ] *n* (Anat) tendine
m del ginocchio
hand [hænd] *n* mano *f*; (*of clock*) lancetta;
(*handwriting*) scrittura; (*at cards*) mano;
(: *game*) partita; (*worker*) operaio(-a) ▷ *vt*
dare, passare; **to give sb a ~** dare una
mano a qn; **at ~** a portata di mano; **in
~** a disposizione; (*work*) in corso; **on ~**
(*person*) disponibile; (*services*) pronto(-a)
a intervenire; **to ~** (*information etc*) a
portata di mano; **on the one ~ ...**, **on
the other ~** da un lato ..., dall'altro;
hand down *vt* passare giù; (*tradition,
heirloom*) tramandare; (*us: sentence, verdict*)
emettere; **hand in** *vt* consegnare; **hand
out** *vt* distribuire; **hand over** *vt* passare;
cedere; **handbag** *n* borsetta; **hand
baggage** *n* bagaglio a mano; **handbook**
n manuale *m*; **handbrake** *n* freno a mano;
handcuffs *npl* manette *fpl*; **handful** *n*
manciata, pugno
handicap ['hændɪkæp] *n* handicap *m inv*
▷ *vt* handicappare; **to be physically ~ped**
essere handicappato(-a); **to be mentally
~ped** essere un(a) handicappato(-a)
mentale
handkerchief ['hæŋkətʃɪf] *n* fazzoletto
handle ['hændl] *n* (*of door etc*) maniglia; (*of
cup etc*) ansa; (*of knife etc*) impugnatura; (*of
saucepan*) manico; (*for winding*) manovella
▷ *vt* toccare, maneggiare; (*deal with*)
occuparsi di; (*treat: people*) trattare; "**~
with care**" "fragile"; **to fly off the ~** (*fig*)
perdere le staffe, uscire dai gangheri;
handlebar(s) *n(pl)* manubrio
hand: **hand luggage** *n* bagagli *mpl* a
mano; **handmade** *adj* fatto(-a) a mano;
handout *n* (*money, food*) elemosina;
(*leaflet*) volantino; (*at lecture*) prospetto
handsome ['hænsəm] *adj* bello(-a); (*profit,
fortune*) considerevole
handwriting ['hændraɪtɪŋ] *n* scrittura
handy ['hændɪ] *adj* (*person*) bravo(-a);
(*close at hand*) a portata di mano;
(*convenient*) comodo(-a)
hang [hæŋ] (*pt, pp* **hung**) *vt* appendere;
(*criminal: pt, pp* **hanged**) impiccare ▷ *vi*
(*painting*) essere appeso(-a); (*hair*)
scendere; (*drapery*) cadere; **to get the
~ of sth** (*inf*) capire come qc funziona;
hang about *or* **around** *vi* bighellonare,
ciondolare; **hang down** *vi* ricadere;
hang on *vi* (*wait*) aspettare; **hang out**
vt (*washing*) stendere (fuori); (*inf: live*)

stare ▷ vi penzolare, pendere; **hang round** vi = **hang around**; **hang up** vi (Tel) riattaccare ▷ vt appendere

hanger ['hæŋər] n gruccia

hang-gliding ['-glaɪdɪŋ] n volo col deltaplano

hangover ['hæŋəuvər] n (after drinking) postumi mpl di sbornia

hankie ['hæŋkɪ] n abbr = **handkerchief**

happen ['hæpən] vi accadere, succedere; (chance): **to ~ to do sth** fare qc per caso; **what ~ed?** cos'è successo?; **as it ~s** guarda caso

happily ['hæpɪlɪ] adv felicemente; fortunatamente

happiness ['hæpɪnɪs] n felicità, contentezza

happy ['hæpɪ] adj felice, contento(-a); **~ with** (arrangements etc) soddisfatto(-a) di; **to be ~ to do** (willing) fare volentieri; **~ birthday!** buon compleanno!

harass ['hærəs] vt molestare; **harassment** n molestia

harbour ['hɑ:bər] (us **harbor**) n porto ▷ vt (hope, fear) nutrire; (criminal) dare rifugio a

hard [hɑ:d] adj duro(-a) ▷ adv (work) sodo; (think, try) bene; **to look ~ at** guardare fissamente; esaminare attentamente; **no ~ feelings!** senza rancore!; **to be ~ of hearing** essere duro(-a) d'orecchio; **to be ~ done by** essere trattato(-a) ingiustamente; **hardback** n libro rilegato; **hardboard** n legno precompresso; **hard disk** n (Comput) disco rigido; **harden** vt, vi indurire

hardly ['hɑ:dlɪ] adv (scarcely) appena; **it's ~ the case** non è proprio il caso; **~ anyone/ anywhere** quasi nessuno/da nessuna parte; **~ ever** quasi mai

hard: **hardship** ['hɑ:dʃɪp] n avversità f inv; privazioni fpl; **hard shoulder** (BRIT) n (Aut) corsia d'emergenza; **hard-up** (inf) adj al verde; **hardware** ['hɑ:dwɛər] n ferramenta fpl; (Comput) hardware m; (Mil) armamenti mpl; **hardware shop** (us **hardware store**) n (negozio di) ferramenta fpl; **hard-working** [-'wə:kɪŋ] adj lavoratore(-trice)

hardy ['hɑ:dɪ] adj robusto(-a); (plant) resistente al gelo

hare [hɛər] n lepre f

harm [hɑ:m] n male m; (wrong) danno ▷ vt (person) fare male a; (thing) danneggiare; **out of ~'s way** al sicuro; **harmful** adj dannoso(-a); **harmless** adj innocuo(-a), inoffensivo(-a)

harmony ['hɑ:mənɪ] n armonia

harness ['hɑ:nɪs] n (for horse) bardatura, finimenti mpl; (for child) briglie fpl; (safety harness) imbracatura ▷ vt (horse) bardare; (resources) sfruttare

harp [hɑ:p] n arpa ▷ vi **to ~ on about** insistere tediosamente su

harsh [hɑ:ʃ] adj (life, winter) duro(-a); (judge, criticism) severo(-a); (sound) rauco(-a); (light) violento(-a)

harvest ['hɑ:vɪst] n raccolto; (of grapes) vendemmia ▷ vt fare il raccolto di, raccogliere; vendemmiare

has [hæz] vb see **have**

hasn't ['hæznt] = **has not**

hassle ['hæsl] (inf) n sacco di problemi

haste [heɪst] n fretta; precipitazione f; **hasten** ['heɪsn] vt affrettare ▷ vi **to hasten (to)** affrettarsi (a); **hastily** adv in fretta; precipitosamente; **hasty** adj affrettato(-a), precipitoso(-a)

hat [hæt] n cappello

hatch [hætʃ] n (Naut: also: **~way**) boccaporto; (also: **service ~**) portello di servizio ▷ vi (bird) uscire dal guscio; (egg) schiudersi

hatchback ['hætʃbæk] n (Aut) tre (or cinque) porte f inv

hate [heɪt] vt odiare, detestare ▷ n odio; **hatred** ['heɪtrɪd] n odio

haul [hɔ:l] vt trascinare, tirare ▷ n (of fish) pescata; (of stolen goods etc) bottino

haunt [hɔ:nt] vt (fear) pervadere; (person) frequentare ▷ n rifugio; **this house is ~ed** questa casa è abitata da un fantasma; **haunted** adj (castle etc) abitato(-a) dai fantasmi or dagli spiriti; (look) ossessionato(-a), tormentato(-a)

 KEYWORD

have [hæv] (pt, pp **had**) aux vb **1** (gen) avere; essere; **to have arrived/gone** essere arrivato(-a)/andato(-a); **to have eaten/slept** avere mangiato/dormito; **he has been kind/promoted** è stato gentile/promosso; **having finished** or **when he had finished, he left** dopo aver finito, se n'è andato

2 (in tag questions): **you've done it, haven't you?** l'ha fatto, (non è) vero?; **he hasn't done it, has he?** non l'ha fatto, vero?

3 (in short answers and questions): **you've made a mistake — no I haven't/so I have** ha fatto un errore — ma no, niente affatto/sì, è vero; **we haven't paid — yes we have!** non abbiamo pagato — ma sì che abbiamo pagato!; **I've been there before, have you?** ci sono già stato, e lei? ▷ modal aux vb (be obliged): **to have (got) to do sth** dover fare qc; **I haven't got**

or **I don't have to wear glasses** non ho bisogno di portare gli occhiali ▷ *vt* **1** (*possess, obtain*) avere; **he has (got) blue eyes/dark hair** ha gli occhi azzurri/i capelli scuri; **do you have** *or* **have you got a car/phone?** ha la macchina/il telefono?; **may I have your address?** potrebbe darmi il suo indirizzo?; **you can have it for £5** te lo lascio per 5 sterline **2** (+ *noun: take, hold etc*): **to have breakfast/a swim/a bath** fare colazione/una nuotata/un bagno; **to have lunch** pranzare; **to have dinner** cenare; **to have a drink** bere qualcosa; **to have a cigarette** fumare una sigaretta **3**: **to have sth done** far fare qc; **to have one's hair cut** farsi tagliare i capelli; **to have sb do sth** far fare qc a qn **4** (*experience, suffer*) avere; **to have a cold/flu** avere il raffreddore/l'influenza; **she had her bag stolen** le hanno rubato la borsa **5** (*inf: dupe*): **you've been had!** ci sei cascato!

have out *vt* **to have it out with sb** (*settle a problem etc*) mettere le cose in chiaro con qn

haven ['heɪvn] *n* porto; (*fig*) rifugio
haven't ['hævnt] = **have not**
havoc ['hævək] *n* caos *m*
Hawaii [həˈwaɪ:] *n* le Hawaii
hawk [hɔːk] *n* falco
hawthorn ['hɔːθɔːn] *n* biancospino
hay [heɪ] *n* fieno; **hay fever** *n* febbre *f* da fieno; **haystack** *n* pagliaio
hazard ['hæzəd] *n* azzardo, ventura; pericolo, rischio ▷ *vt* (*guess etc*) azzardare; **hazardous** *adj* pericoloso(-a); **hazard warning lights** *npl* (*Aut*) luci *fpl* di emergenza
haze [heɪz] *n* foschia
hazel ['heɪzl] *n* (*tree*) nocciolo ▷ *adj* (*eyes*) (*color*) nocciola *inv*; **hazelnut** ['heɪzlnʌt] *n* nocciola
hazy ['heɪzɪ] *adj* fosco(-a); (*idea*) vago(-a)
he [hiː] *pron* lui, egli; **it is he who ...** è lui che ...

head [hɛd] *n* testa; (*leader*) capo; (*of school*) preside *m/f* ▷ *vt* (*list*) essere in testa a; (*group*) essere a capo di; **~s or tails** testa (o croce), pari (o dispari); **~ first** a capofitto, di testa; **~ over heels in love** pazzamente innamorato(-a); **to ~ the ball** colpire una palla di testa; **head for** *vt fus* dirigersi verso; **head off** *vt* (*threat, danger*) sventare; **headache** *n* mal *m* di testa; **heading** *n* titolo; intestazione *f*; **headlamp** (BRIT) *n*

= **headlight**; **headlight** *n* fanale *m*; **headline** *n* titolo; **head office** *n* sede *f* (centrale); **headphones** *npl* cuffia; **headquarters** *npl* ufficio centrale; (*Mil*) quartiere *m* generale; **headroom** *n* (*in car*) altezza dell'abitacolo; (*under bridge*) altezza limite; **headscarf** *n* foulard *m inv*; **headset** *n* = **headphones**; **headteacher** *n* (*of primary school*) direttore(-trice); (*of secondary school*) preside; **head waiter** *n* capocameriere *m*
heal [hiːl] *vt, vi* guarire
health [hɛlθ] *n* salute *f*; **health care** *n* assistenza sanitaria; **health centre** (BRIT) *n* poliambulatorio; **health food** *n* cibo macrobiotico; **Health Service** (BRIT) *n* **the Health Service** ≈ il Servizio Sanitario Statale; **healthy** *adj* (*person*) sano(-a), in buona salute; (*climate*) salubre; (*appetite, economy etc*) sano(-a)
heap [hiːp] *n* mucchio ▷ *vt* (*stones, sand*): **to ~ (up)** ammucchiare; (*plate, sink*): **to ~ sth with** riempire qc di; **~s of** (*inf*) un mucchio di
hear [hɪəʳ] (*pt, pp* **heard**) *vt* sentire; (*news*) ascoltare ▷ *vi* sentire; **to ~ about** avere notizie di; sentire parlare di; **to ~ from sb** ricevere notizie da qn
hearing ['hɪərɪŋ] *n* (*sense*) udito; (*of witnesses*) audizione *f*; (*of a case*) udienza; **hearing aid** *n* apparecchio acustico
hearse [hɜːs] *n* carro funebre
heart [hɑːt] *n* cuore *m*; **~s** *npl* (*Cards*) cuori *mpl*; **to lose ~** scoraggiarsi; **to take ~** farsi coraggio; **at ~** in fondo; **by ~** (*learn, know*) a memoria; **heart attack** *n* attacco di cuore; **heartbeat** *n* battito del cuore; **heartbroken** *adj* **to be heartbroken** avere il cuore spezzato; **heartburn** *n* bruciore *m* di stomaco; **heart disease** *n* malattia di cuore
hearth [hɑːθ] *n* focolare *m*
heartless ['hɑːtlɪs] *adj* senza cuore
hearty ['hɑːtɪ] *adj* caloroso(-a); robusto(-a), sano(-a); vigoroso(-a)
heat [hiːt] *n* calore *m*; (*fig*) ardore *m*; fuoco; (*Sport: also:* **qualifying ~**) prova eliminatoria ▷ *vt* scaldare; **heat up** *vi* (*liquids*) scaldarsi; (*room*) riscaldarsi ▷ *vt* riscaldare; **heated** *adj* riscaldato(-a); (*argument*) acceso(-a); **heater** *n* radiatore *m*; (*stove*) stufa
heather ['hɛðəʳ] *n* erica
heating ['hiːtɪŋ] *n* riscaldamento
heatwave ['hiːtweɪv] *n* ondata di caldo
heaven ['hɛvn] *n* paradiso, cielo; **heavenly** *adj* divino(-a), celeste
heavily ['hɛvɪlɪ] *adv* pesantemente; (*drink, smoke*) molto

heavy ['hɛvɪ] *adj* pesante; (*sea*) grosso(-a); (*rain, blow*) forte; (*weather*) afoso(-a); (*drinker, smoker*) gran (*before noun*); **it's too ~** è troppo pesante

Hebrew ['hi:bru:] *adj* ebreo(-a) ▷ *n* (*Ling*) ebraico

hectare ['hɛktɑ:ʳ] *n* (BRIT) ettaro

hectic ['hɛktɪk] *adj* movimentato(-a)

he'd [hi:d] = **he would**; **he had**

hedge [hɛdʒ] *n* siepe *f* ▷ *vi* essere elusivo(-a); **to ~ one's bets** (*fig*) coprirsi dai rischi

hedgehog ['hɛdʒhɔg] *n* riccio

heed [hi:d] *vt* (*also*: **take ~ of**) badare a, far conto di

heel [hi:l] *n* (*Anat*) calcagno; (*of shoe*) tacco ▷ *vt* (*shoe*) rifare i tacchi a

hefty ['hɛftɪ] *adj* (*person*) robusto(-a); (*parcel*) pesante; (*profit*) grosso(-a)

height [haɪt] *n* altezza, (*high ground*) altura; (*fig: of glory*) apice *m*; (: *of stupidity*) colmo; **heighten** *vt* (*fig*) accrescere

heir [ɛəʳ] *n* erede *m*; **heiress** *n* erede *f*

held [hɛld] *pt, pp of* **hold**

helicopter ['hɛlɪkɔptəʳ] *n* elicottero

hell [hɛl] *n* inferno; **~!** (*inf*) porca miseria!, accidenti!

he'll [hi:l] = **he will**; **he shall**

hello [hə'ləu] *excl* buon giorno!; ciao! (*to sb one addresses as "tu"*); (*surprise*) ma guarda!

helmet ['hɛlmɪt] *n* casco

help [hɛlp] *n* aiuto; (*charwoman*) donna di servizio ▷ *vt* aiutare; **~!** aiuto!; **can you ~ me?** può aiutarmi?; **~ yourself (to bread)** si serva (del pane); **he can't ~ it** non ci può far niente; **help out** *vi* aiutare ▷ *vt* **to ~ sb out** aiutare qn; **helper** *n* aiutante *m/f*, assistente *m/f*; **helpful** *adj* di grande aiuto; (*useful*) utile; **helping** *n* porzione *f*; **helpless** *adj* impotente; debole; **helpline** *n* ≈ telefono amico; (*Comm*) servizio *m* informazioni *inv* (*a pagamento*)

hem [hɛm] *n* orlo ▷ *vt* fare l'orlo a

hemisphere ['hɛmɪsfɪəʳ] *n* emisfero

hemorrhage ['hɛmərɪdʒ] (US) *n* = **haemorrhage**

hemorrhoids ['hɛmərɔɪdz] (US) *npl* = **haemorrhoids**

hen [hɛn] *n* gallina; (*female bird*) femmina

hence [hɛns] *adv* (*therefore*) dunque; **2 years ~** di qui a 2 anni

hen night *n* (*inf*) addio al nubilato

hepatitis [hɛpə'taɪtɪs] *n* epatite *f*

her [hə:ʳ] *pron* (*direct*) la, l' + *vowel*; (*indirect*) le; (*stressed, after prep*) lei ▷ *adj* il (la) suo(-a), i (le) suoi (sue); *see also* **me**; **my**

herb [hə:b] *n* erba; **herbal** *adj* di erbe; **herbal tea** *n* tisana

herd [hə:d] *n* mandria

here [hɪəʳ] *adv* qui, qua ▷ *excl* ehi!; **~!** (*at roll-call*) presente!; **~ is/are** ecco; **~ he/she is** eccolo/eccola

hereditary [hɪ'rɛdɪtrɪ] *adj* ereditario(-a)

heritage ['hɛrɪtɪdʒ] *n* eredità; (*fig*) retaggio

hernia ['hə:nɪə] *n* ernia

hero ['hɪərəu] (*pl* **heroes**) *n* eroe *m*; **heroic** [hɪ'rəuɪk] *adj* eroico(-a)

heroin ['hɛrəuɪn] *n* eroina

heroine ['hɛrəuɪn] *n* eroina

heron ['hɛrən] *n* airone *m*

herring ['hɛrɪŋ] *n* aringa

hers [hə:z] *pron* il (la) suo(-a), i (le) suoi (sue); *see also* **mine¹**

herself [hə:'sɛlf] *pron* (*reflexive*) si; (*emphatic*) lei stessa; (*after prep*) sé stessa, sé; *see also* **oneself**

he's [hi:z] = **he is**; **he has**

hesitant ['hɛzɪtənt] *adj* esitante, indeciso(-a)

hesitate ['hɛzɪteɪt] *vi* **to ~ (about/to do)** esitare (su/a fare); **hesitation** [-'teɪʃən] *n* esitazione *f*

heterosexual ['hɛtərəu'sɛksjuəl] *adj, n* eterosessuale *m/f*

hexagon ['hɛksəgən] *n* esagono

hey [heɪ] *excl* ehi!

heyday ['heɪdeɪ] *n* **the ~ of** i bei giorni di, l'età d'oro di

HGV *n abbr* = **heavy goods vehicle**

hi [haɪ] *excl* ciao!

hibernate ['haɪbəneɪt] *vi* ibernare

hiccough ['hɪkʌp] *vi* singhiozzare

hiccup ['hɪkʌp] *n* = **hiccough**

hid [hɪd] *pt of* **hide**

hidden ['hɪdn] *pp of* **hide**

hide [haɪd] (*pt* **hid**, *pp* **hidden**) *n* (*skin*) pelle *f* ▷ *vt* **to ~ sth (from sb)** nascondere qc (a qn) ▷ *vi* **to ~ (from sb)** nascondersi (da qn)

hideous ['hɪdɪəs] *adj* laido(-a); orribile

hiding ['haɪdɪŋ] *n* (*beating*) bastonata; **to be in ~** (*concealed*) tenersi nascosto(-a)

hi-fi ['haɪfaɪ] *n* stereo ▷ *adj* ad alta fedeltà, hi-fi *inv*

high [haɪ] *adj* alto(-a); (*speed, respect, number*) grande; (*wind*) forte; (*voice*) acuto(-a) ▷ *adv* alto, in alto; **20m ~** alto(-a) 20m; **highchair** *n* seggiolone *m*; **high-class** *adj* (*neighbourhood*) elegante; (*hotel*) di prim'ordine; (*person*) di gran classe; (*food*) raffinato(-a); **higher education** *n* studi *mpl* superiori; **high heels** *npl* (*heels*) tacchi *mpl* alti; (*shoes*) scarpe *fpl* con i tacchi alti; **high jump** *n* (*Sport*) salto in alto; **highlands** *npl* zona montuosa; **the Highlands** le Highlands scozzesi; **highlight** *n* (*fig: of event*) momento culminante; (*in hair*) colpo di sole ▷ *vt* mettere in evidenza; **highlights** npl (in hair) colpi mpl di sole; **highlighter** n (pen) evidenziatore m; **highly** adv molto; **to speak highly of** parlare molto bene di; **highness** n **Her Highness** Sua Altezza; **high-rise** n (also: **high-rise block, high-rise building**) palazzone m; **high school** n scuola secondaria; (US) istituto superiore d'istruzione; **high season** (BRIT) n alta stagione; **high street** (BRIT) n strada principale; **high-tech** (inf) adj high-tech inv; **highway** ['haɪweɪ] n strada maestra; **Highway Code** (BRIT) n codice m della strada

hijack ['haɪdʒæk] vt dirottare; **hijacker** n dirottatore(-trice)

hike [haɪk] vi fare un'escursione a piedi ▷ n escursione f a piedi; **hiker** n escursionista m/f; **hiking** n escursioni fpl a piedi

hilarious [hɪ'lɛərɪəs] adj (behaviour, event) spassosissimo(-a)

hill [hɪl] n collina, colle m; (fairly high) montagna; (on road) salita; **hillside** n fianco della collina; **hill walking** n escursioni fpl in collina; **hilly** adj collinoso(-a); montagnoso(-a)

him [hɪm] pron (direct) lo, l' + vowel; (indirect) gli; (stressed, after prep) lui; see also **me**; **himself** pron (reflexive) si; (emphatic) lui stesso; (after prep) se stesso, sé; see also **oneself**

hind [haɪnd] adj posteriore ▷ n cerva

hinder ['hɪndər] vt ostacolare

hindsight ['haɪndsaɪt] n **with ~** con il senno di poi

Hindu ['hɪnduː] n indù m/f inv; **Hinduism** n (Rel) induismo

hinge [hɪndʒ] n cardine m ▷ vi (fig): **to ~ on** dipendere da

hint [hɪnt] n (suggestion) allusione f; (advice) consiglio; (sign) accenno ▷ vt **to ~ that** lasciar capire che ▷ vi **to ~ at** alludere a

hip [hɪp] n anca, fianco

hippie ['hɪpɪ] n hippy m/f inv

hippo ['hɪpəu] (pl **hippos**) n ippopotamo

hippopotamus [hɪpə'pɔtəməs] (pl **hippopotamuses** or **hippopotami**) n ippopotamo

hippy ['hɪpɪ] n = **hippie**

hire ['haɪər] vt (BRIT: car, equipment) noleggiare; (worker) assumere, dare lavoro a ▷ n nolo, noleggio; **for ~** da nolo; (taxi) libero(-a); **I'd like to ~ a car** vorrei noleggiare una macchina; **hire(d) car** (BRIT) n macchina a nolo; **hire purchase** (BRIT) n acquisto (or vendita) rateale

his [hɪz] adj, pron il (la) suo (sua), i (le) suoi (sue); see also **my**; **mine¹**

Hispanic [hɪs'pænɪk] adj ispanico(-a)

hiss [hɪs] vi fischiare; (cat, snake) sibilare

historian [hɪ'stɔːrɪən] n storico(-a)

historic(al) [hɪ'stɔrɪk(l)] adj storico(-a)

history ['hɪstərɪ] n storia

hit [hɪt] (pt, pp **hit**) vt colpire, picchiare; (knock against) battere; (reach: target) raggiungere; (collide with: car) urtare contro; (fig: affect) colpire; (find: problem etc) incontrare ▷ n colpo; (success, song) successo; **to ~ it off with sb** andare molto d'accordo con qn; **hit back** vi **to ~ back at sb** restituire il colpo a qn

hitch [hɪtʃ] vt (fasten) attaccare; (also: **~ up**) tirare su ▷ n (difficulty) intoppo, difficoltà f inv; **to ~ a lift** fare l'autostop; **hitch-hike** vi fare l'autostop; **hitch-hiker** n autostoppista m/f; **hitch-hiking** n autostop m

hi-tech ['haɪ'tɛk] adj high-tech inv

hitman ['hɪtmæn] (irreg) n (inf) sicario

HIV abbr **~-negative/-positive** adj sieronegativo(-a)/sieropositivo(-a)

hive [haɪv] n alveare m

hoard [hɔːd] n (of food) provviste fpl; (of money) gruzzolo ▷ vt ammassare

hoarse [hɔːs] adj rauco(-a)

hoax [həuks] n scherzo; falso allarme

hob [hɔb] n piastra (con fornelli)

hobble ['hɔbl] vi zoppicare

hobby ['hɔbɪ] n hobby m inv, passatempo

hobo ['həubəu] (US) n vagabondo

hockey ['hɔkɪ] n hockey m; **hockey stick** n bastone m da hockey

hog [hɔg] n maiale m ▷ vt (fig) arraffare; **to go the whole ~** farlo fino in fondo

Hogmanay [hɔgmə'neɪ] n (Scottish) ≈ San Silvestro

hoist [hɔɪst] n paranco ▷ vt issare

hold [həuld] (pt, pp **held**) vt tenere; (contain) contenere; (keep back) trattenere; (believe) mantenere; considerare; (possess) avere, possedere; detenere ▷ vi (withstand pressure) tenere; (be valid) essere valido(-a) ▷ n presa; (control): **to have a ~ over** avere controllo su; (Naut) stiva; **~ the line!** (Tel) resti in linea!; **to ~ one's own** (fig) difendersi bene; **to catch** or **get (a) ~ of** afferrare; **hold back** vt trattenere; (secret) tenere celato(-a); **hold on** vi tener fermo; (wait) aspettare; **~ on!** (Tel) resti in linea!; **hold out** vt offrire ▷ vi (resist) resistere; **hold up** vt (raise) alzare; (support) sostenere; (delay) ritardare; (rob) assaltare; **holdall** (BRIT) n borsone m; **holder** n (container) contenitore m; (of ticket, title) possessore/posseditrice; (of office etc) incaricato(-a); (of record) detentore(-trice)

hole [həul] n buco, buca

holiday ['hɒlədɪ] n vacanza; (day off)
giorno di vacanza; (public) giorno festivo;
on ~ in vacanza; **I'm on ~ here** sono qui
in vacanza; **holiday camp** (BRIT) n (also:
holiday centre) ≈ villaggio (di vacanze);
holiday job n (BRIT) ≈ lavoro estivo;
holiday-maker (BRIT) n villeggiante m/f;
holiday resort n luogo di villeggiatura
Holland ['hɒlənd] n Olanda
hollow ['hɒləu] adj cavo(-a); (country,
claim) vuoto(-a); (laugh, sound) cupo(-a) ▷ n
cavità f inv; (in land) valletta, depressione f
▷ vt **to ~ out** scavare
holly ['hɒlɪ] n agrifoglio
Hollywood ['hɒlɪwud] n Hollywood f
holocaust ['hɒləkɔːst] n olocausto
holy ['həulɪ] adj santo(-a); (bread, ground)
benedetto(-a), consacrato(-a)
home [həum] n casa; (country) patria·
(institution) casa, ricovero ▷ cpd familiare;
(cooking etc) casalingo(-a); (Econ, Pol)
nazionale, interno(-a); (Sport) di casa ▷ adv
a casa, in patria; (right in: nail etc) fino in
fondo; **at ~** a casa; (in situation) a proprio
agio; **to go** or **come ~** tornare a casa (or
in patria); **make yourself at ~** si metta
a suo agio; **home address** n indirizzo
di casa; **homeland** n patria; **homeless**
adj senza tetto; spatriato(-a); **homely**
adj semplice, alla buona; accogliente;
home-made adj casalingo(-a); **home
match** n partita in casa; **Home Office**
(BRIT) n ministero degli Interni; **home
owner** n proprietario(-a) di casa; **home
page** n (Comput) home page f inv; **Home
Secretary** (BRIT) n ministro degli Interni;
homesick adj **to be homesick** avere la
nostalgia; **home town** n città f inv natale;
homework n compiti mpl (per casa)
homicide ['hɒmɪsaɪd] (US) n omicidio
homoeopathic [həumɪə'pæθɪk] (US
homeopathic) adj omeopatico(-a)
homoeopathy [həumɪ'ɔpəθɪ] (US
homeopathy) n omeopatia
homosexual [hɒmə'sɛksjuəl] adj, n
omosessuale m/f
honest ['ɒnɪst] adj onesto(-a);
sincero(-a); **honestly** adv onestamente;
sinceramente; **honesty** n onestà
honey ['hʌnɪ] n miele m; **honeymoon**
n luna di miele, viaggio di nozze; **we're
on honeymoon** siamo in luna di miele;
honeysuckle n (Bot) caprifoglio
Hong Kong ['hɒŋ'kɒŋ] n Hong Kong f
honorary ['ɒnərərɪ] adj onorario(-a); (duty,
title) onorifico(-a)
honour ['ɒnəʳ] (US **honor**) vt onorare ▷ n
onore m; **honourable** (US **honorable**) adj
onorevole; **honours degree** n (Scol) laurea

specializzata
hood [hud] n cappuccio; (on cooker) cappa
(BRIT Aut) capote f; (US Aut) cofano
hoof [huːf] (pl **hooves**) n zoccolo
hook [huk] n gancio; (for fishing) amo ▷ vt
uncinare; (dress) agganciare
hooligan ['huːlɪgən] n giovinastro,
teppista m
hoop [huːp] n cerchio
hooray [huː'reɪ] excl = **hurray**
hoot [huːt] vi (Aut) suonare il clacson;
(siren) ululare; (owl) gufare
Hoover® ['huːvəʳ] (BRIT) n aspirapolvere
inv ▷ vt **hoover** pulire con l'aspirapolvere
hooves [huːvz] npl of **hoof**
hop [hɒp] vi saltellare, saltare; (on one foot)
saltare su una gamba
hope [həup] vt **to ~ that/to do** sperare
che/di fare ▷ vi sperare ▷ n speranza;
I ~ so/not spero di sì/no; **hopeful** adj
(person) pieno(-a) di speranza; (situation)
promettente; **hopefully** adv con
speranza; **hopefully he will recover**
speriamo che si riprenda; **hopeless** adj
senza speranza, disperato(-a); (useless)
inutile
hops [hɒps] npl luppoli mpl
horizon [hə'raɪzn] n orizzonte m;
horizontal [hɒrɪ'zɒntl] adj orizzontale
hormone ['hɔːməun] n ormone m
horn [hɔːn] n (Zool, Mus) corno; (Aut)
clacson m inv
horoscope ['hɒrəskəup] n oroscopo
horrendous [hə'rɛndəs] adj orrendo(-a)
horrible ['hɒrɪbl] adj orribile, tremendo(-
horrid ['hɒrɪd] adj orrido(-a); (person)
odioso(-a)
horrific [hɒ'rɪfɪk] adj (accident)
spaventoso(-a); (film) orripilante
horrifying ['hɒrɪfaɪɪŋ] adj terrificante
horror ['hɒrəʳ] n orrore m; **horror film** n
film m inv dell'orrore
hors d'œuvre [ɔː'dəːvrə] n antipasto
horse [hɔːs] n cavallo; **horseback: on
horseback** adj, adv a cavallo; **horse
chestnut** n ippocastano; **horsepower**
cavallo (vapore); **horse-racing** n ippica;
horseradish n rafano; **horse riding** n
(BRIT) equitazione f
hose [həuz] n (also: **~pipe**) tubo; (also:
garden ~) tubo per annaffiare
hospital ['hɒspɪtl] n ospedale m; **where
the nearest ~?** dov'è l'ospedale più vicin
hospitality [hɒspɪ'tælɪtɪ] n ospitalità
host [həust] n ospite m; (Rel) ostia; (large
number): **a ~ of** una schiera di
hostage ['hɒstɪdʒ] n ostaggio(-a)
hostel ['hɒstl] n ostello; (also: **youth ~**)
ostello della gioventù

hostess ['həustɪs] n ospite f; (BRIT: air hostess) hostess f inv

hostile ['hɔstaɪl] adj ostile

hostility [hɔ'stɪlɪtɪ] n ostilità f inv

hot [hɔt] adj caldo(-a); (as opposed to only warm) molto caldo(-a); (spicy) piccante; (fig) accanito(-a); ardente; violento(-a), focoso(-a); **to be ~** (person) aver caldo; (object) essere caldo(-a); (weather) far caldo; **hot dog** n hot dog m inv

hotel [həu'tɛl] n albergo

hot-water bottle [hɔt'wɔːtə-] n borsa dell'acqua calda

hound [haund] vt perseguitare ▷ n segugio

hour ['auə'] n ora; **hourly** adj all'ora

house [n haus, pl 'hauzɪz] [vb hauz] n (also: firm) casa; (Pol) camera; (Theatre) sala; pubblico; spettacolo; (dynasty) casata ▷ vt (person) ospitare, alloggiare; **on the ~** (fig) offerto(-a) dalla casa; **household** n famiglia; casa; **householder** n padrone(-a) di casa; (head of house) capofamiglia m/f; **housekeeper** n governante f; **housekeeping** n (work) governo della casa; (money) soldi mpl per le spese di casa; **housewife** (irreg) n massaia, casalinga; **house wine** n vino della casa; **housework** n faccende fpl domestiche

housing ['hauzɪŋ] n alloggio; **housing development** (BRIT), **housing estate** n zona residenziale con case popolari e/o private

hover ['hɔvə'] vi (bird) librarsi; **hovercraft** n hovercraft m inv

how [hau] adv come; **~ are you?** come sta?; **~ do you do?** piacere!; **~ far is it to the river?** quanto è lontano il fiume?; **~ long have you been here?** da quando è qui?; **~ lovely!/awful!** che bello!/orrore!; **~ many?** quanti(-e)?; **~ much?** quanto(-a)?; **~ much milk?** quanto latte?; **~ many people?** quante persone?; **~ old are you?** quanti anni ha?

however [hau'ɛvə'] adv in qualsiasi modo o maniera che; (+ adjective) per quanto + sub; (in questions) come ▷ conj comunque, però

howl [haul] vi ululare; (baby, person) urlare

H.P. abbr = **hire purchase**; **horsepower**

h.p. n abbr = **H.P**

HQ n, abbr = **headquarters**

hr(s) abbr (= hour(s)) h

HTML abbr (= hypertext markup language) HTML m inv

hubcap ['hʌbkæp] n coprimozzo

huddle ['hʌdl] vi: **to ~ together** rannicchiarsi l'uno contro l'altro

huff [hʌf] n: **in a ~** stizzito(-a)

hug [hʌg] vt abbracciare; (shore, kerb) stringere

huge [hjuːdʒ] adj enorme, immenso(-a)

hull [hʌl] n (of ship) scafo

hum [hʌm] vt (tune) canticchiare ▷ vi canticchiare; (insect, plane, tool) ronzare

human ['hjuːmən] (irreg) adj umano(-a) ▷ n essere m umano

humane [hjuː'meɪn] adj umanitario(-a)

humanitarian [hjuːmænɪ'tɛərɪən] adj umanitario(-a)

humanity [hjuː'mænɪtɪ] n umanità

human rights npl diritti mpl dell'uomo

humble ['hʌmbl] adj umile, modesto(-a) ▷ vt umiliare

humid ['hjuːmɪd] adj umido(-a); **humidity** [hjuː'mɪdɪtɪ] n umidità

humiliate [hjuː'mɪlɪeɪt] vt umiliare; **humiliating** adj umiliante; **humiliation** [-'eɪʃən] n umiliazione f

hummus ['huməs] n purè di ceci

humorous ['hjuːmərəs] adj umoristico(-a); (person) buffo(-a)

humour ['hjuːmə'] (US **humor**) n umore m ▷ vt accontentare

hump [hʌmp] n gobba

hunch [hʌntʃ] n (premonition) intuizione f

hundred ['hʌndrəd] num cento; **~s of** centinaia fpl di; **hundredth** [-ɪdθ] num centesimo(-a)

hung [hʌŋ] pt, pp of **hang**

Hungarian [hʌŋ'gɛərɪən] adj ungherese ▷ n ungherese m/f; (Ling) ungherese m

Hungary ['hʌŋgərɪ] n Ungheria

hunger ['hʌŋgə'] n fame f ▷ vi: **to ~ for** desiderare ardentemente

hungry ['hʌŋgrɪ] adj affamato(-a); **to be ~** aver fame

hunt [hʌnt] vt (seek) cercare; (Sport) cacciare ▷ vi: **to ~ (for)** andare a caccia (di); ▷ n caccia; **hunter** n cacciatore m; **hunting** n caccia

hurdle ['həːdl] n (Sport, fig) ostacolo

hurl [həːl] vt lanciare con violenza

hurrah [hu'rɑː] excl = **hurray**

hurray [hu'reɪ] excl urra!, evviva!

hurricane ['hʌrɪkən] n uragano

hurry ['hʌrɪ] n fretta ▷ vi (also: ~ up) affrettarsi ▷ vt (also: ~ up: person) affrettare; (work) far in fretta; **to be in a ~** aver fretta; **hurry up** vi sbrigarsi

hurt [həːt] (pt, pp **hurt**) vt (cause pain to) far male a; (injure, fig) ferire ▷ vi far male

husband ['hʌzbənd] n marito

hush [hʌʃ] n silenzio, calma ▷ vt zittire

husky ['hʌskɪ] adj roco(-a) ▷ n cane m eschimese

hut [hʌt] n rifugio; (shed) ripostiglio

hyacinth ['haɪəsɪnθ] n giacinto

hydrangea [haɪ'dreɪnʒə] *n* ortensia
hydrofoil ['haɪdrəʊfɔɪl] *n* aliscafo
hydrogen ['haɪdrədʒən] *n* idrogeno
hygiene ['haɪdʒiːn] *n* igiene *f*; **hygienic**
[haɪ'dʒiːnɪk] *adj* igienico(-a)
hymn [hɪm] *n* inno; cantica
hype [haɪp] (*inf*) *n* campagna pubblicitaria
hyphen ['haɪfn] *n* trattino
hypnotize ['hɪpnətaɪz] *vt* ipnotizzare
hypocrite ['hɪpəkrɪt] *n* ipocrita *m/f*
hypocritical [hɪpə'krɪtɪkl] *adj* ipocrita
hypothesis [haɪ'pɔθɪsɪs] (*pl* **hypotheses**)
n ipotesi *f inv*
hysterical [hɪ'stɛrɪkl] *adj* isterico(-a)
hysterics [hɪ'stɛrɪks] *npl* accesso di
isteria; (*laughter*) attacco di riso

I [aɪ] *pron* io
ice [aɪs] *n* ghiaccio; (*on road*) gelo; (*ice
cream*) gelato ▷ *vt* (*cake*) glassare ▷ *vi*
(*also*: **~ over**) ghiacciare; (*also*: **~ up**)
gelare; **iceberg** *n* iceberg *m inv*; **ice
cream** *n* gelato; **ice cube** *n* cubetto
di ghiaccio; **ice hockey** *n* hockey *m* su
ghiaccio
Iceland ['aɪslənd] *n* Islanda; **Icelander** *n*
islandese *m/f*; **Icelandic** [aɪs'lændɪk] *adj*
islandese ▷ *n* (*Ling*) islandese *m*
ice: ice lolly (BRIT) *n* ghiacciolo; **ice rink**
n pista di pattinaggio; **ice skating** *n*
pattinaggio sul ghiaccio
icing ['aɪsɪŋ] *n* (*Culin*) glassa; **icing sugar**
(BRIT) *n* zucchero a velo
icon ['aɪkɔn] *n* icona
icy ['aɪsɪ] *adj* ghiacciato(-a); (*weather,
temperature*) gelido(-a)
I'd [aɪd] = **I would**; **I had**
ID card *n* = **identity card**
idea [aɪ'dɪə] *n* idea
ideal [aɪ'dɪəl] *adj* ideale ▷ *n* ideale *m*;
ideally [aɪ'dɪəlɪ] *adv* perfettamente,
assolutamente; **ideally the book
should have …** l'ideale sarebbe che il
libro avesse …
identical [aɪ'dɛntɪkl] *adj* identico(-a)
identification [aɪdɛntɪfɪ'keɪʃən] *n*
identificazione *f*; **(means of) ~** carta

d'identità
identify [aɪ'dɛntɪfaɪ] vt identificare
identity [aɪ'dɛntɪtɪ] n identità f inv;
 identity card n carta d'identità
ideology [aɪdɪ'ɔlədʒɪ] n ideologia
idiom ['ɪdɪəm] n idioma m; (phrase)
 espressione f idiomatica
idiot ['ɪdɪət] n idiota m/f
idle ['aɪdl] adj inattivo(-a); (lazy) pigro(-a),
 ozioso(-a); (unemployed) disoccupato(-a);
 (question, pleasures) ozioso(-a) ▷ vi (engine)
 girare al minimo
idol ['aɪdl] n idolo
idyllic [ɪ'dɪlɪk] adj idillico(-a)
i.e. adv abbr (= that is) cioè
if [ɪf] conj se; **if I were you** ... se fossi in te
 ..., io al tuo posto ...; **if so** se è così; **if not** se
 no; **if only** se solo or soltanto
ignite [ɪg'naɪt] vt accendere ▷ vi
 accendersi
ignition [ɪg'nɪʃən] n (Aut) accensione f; **to
 switch on/off the ~** accendere/spegnere
 il motore
ignorance ['ɪgnərəns] n ignoranza; **to
 keep sb in ~ of sth** tenere qn all'oscuro
 di qc
ignorant ['ɪgnərənt] adj ignorante; **to be
 ~ of** (subject) essere ignorante in; (events)
 essere ignaro(-a) di
ignore [ɪg'nɔː] vt non tener conto di;
 (person, fact) ignorare
I'll [aɪl] = **I will; I shall**
ill [ɪl] adj (sick) malato(-a); (bad) cattivo(-a)
 ▷ n male m ▷ adv **to speak** etc **~ of sb**
 parlare etc male di qn; **to take** or **be taken
 ~** ammalarsi
illegal [ɪ'liːgl] adj illegale
illegible [ɪ'lɛdʒɪbl] adj illeggibile
illegitimate [ɪlɪ'dʒɪtɪmət] adj
 illegittimo(-a)
ill health n problemi mpl di salute
illiterate [ɪ'lɪtərət] adj analfabeta,
 illetterato(-a); (letter) scorretto(-a)
illness ['ɪlnɪs] n malattia
illuminate [ɪ'luːmɪneɪt] vt illuminare
illusion [ɪ'luːʒən] n illusione f
illustrate ['ɪləstreɪt] vt illustrare
illustration [ɪlə'streɪʃən] n illustrazione f
I'm [aɪm] = **I am**
image ['ɪmɪdʒ] n immagine f; (public face)
 immagine (pubblica)
imaginary [ɪ'mædʒɪnərɪ] adj
 immaginario(-a)
imagination [ɪmædʒɪ'neɪʃən] n
 immaginazione f, fantasia
imaginative [ɪ'mædʒɪnətɪv] adj
 immaginoso(-a)
imagine [ɪ'mædʒɪn] vt immaginare
imbalance [ɪm'bæləns] n squilibrio

imitate ['ɪmɪteɪt] vt imitare; **imitation**
 [-'teɪʃən] n imitazione f
immaculate [ɪ'mækjulət] adj
 immacolato(-a); (dress, appearance)
 impeccabile
immature [ɪmə'tjuəʳ] adj immaturo(-a)
immediate [ɪ'miːdɪət] adj immediato(-a);
 immediately adv (at once) subito,
 immediatamente; **immediately next to**
 proprio accanto a
immense [ɪ'mɛns] adj immenso(-a);
 enorme; **immensely** adv
 immensamente
immerse [ɪ'məːs] vt immergere
immigrant ['ɪmɪgrənt] n immigrante
 m/f; immigrato(-a); **immigration**
 [ɪmɪ'greɪʃən] n immigrazione f
imminent ['ɪmɪnənt] adj imminente
immoral [ɪ'mɔrl] adj immorale
immortal [ɪ'mɔːtl] adj, n immortale m/f
immune [ɪ'mjuːn] adj **~ (to)** immune
 (da); **immune system** n sistema m
 immunitario
immunize ['ɪmjunaɪz] vt immunizzare
impact ['ɪmpækt] n impatto
impair [ɪm'pɛəʳ] vt danneggiare
impartial [ɪm'pɑːʃl] adj imparziale
impatience [ɪm'peɪʃəns] n impazienza
impatient [ɪm'peɪʃənt] adj impaziente; **to
 get** or **grow ~** perdere la pazienza
impeccable [ɪm'pɛkəbl] adj impeccabile
impending [ɪm'pɛndɪŋ] adj imminente
imperative [ɪm'pɛrətɪv] adj
 imperativo(-a); necessario(-a), urgente;
 (voice) imperioso(-a)
imperfect [ɪm'pəːfɪkt] adj imperfetto(-a);
 (goods etc) difettoso(-a) ▷ n (Ling: also: **~
 tense**) imperfetto
imperial [ɪm'pɪərɪəl] adj imperiale;
 (measure) legale
impersonal [ɪm'pəːsənl] adj
 impersonale
impersonate [ɪm'pəːsəneɪt] vt
 impersonare; (Theatre) fare la mimica di
impetus ['ɪmpətəs] n impeto
implant [ɪm'plɑːnt] vt (Med) innestare;
 (fig: idea, principle) inculcare
implement [n 'ɪmplɪmənt, vb 'ɪmplɪment]
 n attrezzo; (for cooking) utensile m ▷ vt
 effettuare
implicate ['ɪmplɪkeɪt] vt implicare
implication [ɪmplɪ'keɪʃən] n implicazione
 f; **by ~** implicitamente
implicit [ɪm'plɪsɪt] adj implicito(-a);
 (complete) completo(-a)
imply [ɪm'plaɪ] vt insinuare; suggerire
impolite [ɪmpə'laɪt] adj scortese
import [vb ɪm'pɔːt, n 'ɪmpɔːt] vt importare
 ▷ n (Comm) importazione f

importance [ɪmˈpɔːtns] n importanza
important [ɪmˈpɔːtnt] adj importante;
it's not ~ non ha importanza
importer [ɪmˈpɔːtəʳ] n
importatore(-trice)
impose [ɪmˈpəʊz] vt imporre ▷ vi **to ~
on sb** sfruttare la bontà di qn; **imposing**
[ɪmˈpəʊzɪŋ] adj imponente
impossible [ɪmˈpɔsɪbl] adj impossibile
impotent [ˈɪmpətnt] adj impotente
impoverished [ɪmˈpɔvərɪʃt] adj
impoverito(-a)
impractical [ɪmˈpræktɪkl] adj non
pratico(-a)
impress [ɪmˈprɛs] vt impressionare; (mark)
imprimere, stampare; **to ~ sth on sb** far
capire qc a qn
impression [ɪmˈprɛʃən] n impressione
f; **to be under the ~ that** avere
l'impressione che
impressive [ɪmˈprɛsɪv] adj notevole
imprison [ɪmˈprɪzn] vt imprigionare;
imprisonment n imprigionamento
improbable [ɪmˈprɔbəbl] adj improbabile;
(excuse) inverosimile
improper [ɪmˈprɔpəʳ] adj scorretto(-a);
(unsuitable) inadatto(-a), improprio(-a),
sconveniente, indecente
improve [ɪmˈpruːv] vt migliorare ▷ vi
migliorare; (pupil etc) fare progressi;
improvement n miglioramento;
progresso
improvise [ˈɪmprəvaɪz] vt, vi improvvisare
impulse [ˈɪmpʌls] n impulso; **on ~**
d'impulso, impulsivamente; **impulsive**
[ɪmˈpʌlsɪv] adj impulsivo(-a)

KEYWORD

in [ɪn] prep **1** (indicating place, position) in;
in the house/garden in casa/giardino;
in the box nella scatola; **in the fridge**
nel frigorifero; **I have it in my hand** ce
l'ho in mano; **in town/the country** in
città/campagna; **in school** a scuola; **in
here/there** qui/lì dentro
2 (with place names: of town, region,
country): **in London** a Londra; **in England**
in Inghilterra; **in the United States** negli
Stati Uniti; **in Yorkshire** nello Yorkshire
3 (indicating time: during, in the space of) in;
in spring/summer in primavera/estate;
in 1988 nel 1988; **in May** in o a maggio; **I'll
see you in July** ci vediamo a luglio; **in the
afternoon** nel pomeriggio; **at 4 o'clock
in the afternoon** alle 4 del pomeriggio;
I did it in 3 hours/days l'ho fatto in 3
ore/giorni; **I'll see you in 2 weeks** or **in 2
weeks' time** ci vediamo tra 2 settimane

4 (indicating manner etc) a; **in a loud/soft
voice** a voce alta/bassa; **in pencil** a
matita; **in English/French** in inglese/
francese; **the boy in the blue shirt** il
ragazzo con la camicia blu
5 (indicating circumstances): **in the sun**
al sole; **in the shade** all'ombra; **in the
rain** sotto la pioggia; **a rise in prices** un
aumento dei prezzi
6 (indicating mood, state): **in tears** in
lacrime; **in anger** per la rabbia; **in
despair** disperato(-a); **in good condition**
in buono stato, in buone condizioni; **to
live in luxury** vivere nel lusso
7 (with ratios, numbers): **1 in 10** 1 su 10;
20 pence in the pound 20 pence per
sterlina; **they lined up in twos** si misero
in fila a due a due
8 (referring to people, works) in; **the
disease is common in children** la
malattia è comune nei bambini; **in (the
works of) Dickens** in Dickens
9 (indicating profession etc) in; **to be in
teaching** fare l'insegnante, insegnare; **to
be in publishing** essere nell'editoria
10 (after superlative) di; **the best in the
class** il migliore della classe
11 (with present participle): **in saying this**
dicendo questo, nel dire questo
▷ adv **to be in** (person: at home, work)
esserci; (train, ship, plane) essere
arrivato(-a); (in fashion) essere di moda; **to
ask sb in** invitare qn ad entrare; **to run/
limp etc in** entrare di corsa/zoppicando
etc
▷ n **the ins and outs of the problem**
tutti i particolari del problema

inability [ɪnəˈbɪlɪtɪ] n **~ (to do)** incapacità
(di fare)
inaccurate [ɪnˈækjʊrət] adj inesatto(-a),
impreciso(-a)
inadequate [ɪnˈædɪkwət] adj
insufficiente
inadvertently [ɪnədˈvəːtntlɪ] adv senza
volerlo
inappropriate [ɪnəˈprəʊprɪət] adj
non adatto(-a); (word, expression)
improprio(-a)
inaugurate [ɪˈnɔːgjʊreɪt] vt inaugurare;
(president, official) insediare
Inc. (us) abbr (= incorporated) S.A.
incapable [ɪnˈkeɪpəbl] adj incapace
incense [n ɪnˈsɛns, vb ɪnˈsɛns] n incenso
▷ vt (anger) infuriare
incentive [ɪnˈsɛntɪv] n incentivo
inch [ɪntʃ] n pollice m (25 mm, 12 in a foot);
within an ~ of a un pelo da; **he didn't give
an ~** non ha ceduto di un millimetro

incidence ['ɪnsɪdns] n (of crime, disease) incidenza

incident ['ɪnsɪdnt] n incidente m; (in book) episodio

incidentally [ɪnsɪ'dɛntəlɪ] adv (by the way) a proposito

inclination [ɪnklɪ'neɪʃən] n inclinazione f

incline [n 'ɪnklaɪn, vb ɪn'klaɪn] n pendenza, pendio ▷ vt inclinare ▷ vi (surface) essere inclinato(-a); **to be ~d to do** tendere a fare; essere propenso(-a) a fare

include [ɪn'kluːd] vt includere, comprendere; **is service ~d?** il servizio è compreso?; **including** prep compreso(-a), incluso(-a); **inclusion** [ɪn'kluːʒən] n inclusione f; **inclusive** [ɪn'kluːsɪv] adj incluso(-a), compreso(-a); **inclusive of tax** etc tasse etc comprese

income ['ɪnkʌm] n reddito; **income support** n (BRIT) sussidio di indigenza or povertà; **income tax** n imposta sul reddito

incoming ['ɪnkʌmɪŋ] adj (flight, mail) in arrivo; (government) subentrante; (tide) montante

incompatible [ɪnkəm'pætɪbl] adj incompatibile

incompetence [ɪn'kɔmpɪtns] n incompetenza, incapacità

incompetent [ɪn'kɔmpɪtnt] adj incompetente, incapace

incomplete [ɪnkəm'pliːt] adj incompleto(-a)

inconsistent [ɪnkən'sɪstənt] adj incoerente; **~ with** non coerente con

inconvenience [ɪnkən'viːnjəns] n inconveniente m; (trouble) disturbo ▷ vt disturbare

inconvenient [ɪnkən'viːnjənt] adj scomodo(-a)

incorporate [ɪn'kɔːpəreɪt] vt incorporare; (contain) contenere

incorrect [ɪnkə'rɛkt] adj scorretto(-a); (statement) inesatto(-a)

increase [n 'ɪnkriːs, vb ɪn'kriːs] n aumento ▷ vi, vt aumentare; **increasingly** adv sempre più

incredible [ɪn'krɛdɪbl] adj incredibile; **incredibly** adv incredibilmente

incur [ɪn'kəː] vt (expenses) incorrere; (anger, risk) esporsi a; (debt) contrarre; (loss) subire

indecent [ɪn'diːsnt] adj indecente

indeed [ɪn'diːd] adv infatti; veramente; **yes ~!** certamente!

indefinitely [ɪn'dɛfɪnɪtlɪ] adv (wait) indefinitamente

independence [ɪndɪ'pɛndns] n

indipendenza; **Independence Day** (US) n vedi nota nel riquadro

independent [ɪndɪ'pɛndnt] adj indipendente; **independent school** n (BRIT) istituto scolastico indipendente che si autofinanzia

index ['ɪndɛks] (pl **indexes**) n (in book) indice m; (: in library etc) catalogo; (pl **indices**: ratio, sign) indice m

India ['ɪndɪə] n India; **Indian** adj, n indiano(-a)

indicate ['ɪndɪkeɪt] vt indicare; **indication** [-'keɪʃən] n indicazione f, segno; **indicative** [ɪn'dɪkətɪv] adj **indicative of** indicativo(-a) di; **indicator** ['ɪndɪkeɪtə'] n indicatore m; (Aut) freccia

indices ['ɪndɪsiːz] npl of **index**

indict [ɪn'daɪt] vt accusare; **indictment** [ɪn'daɪtmənt] n accusa

indifference [ɪn'dɪfrəns] n indifferenza

indifferent [ɪn'dɪfrənt] adj indifferente; (poor) mediocre

indigenous [ɪn'dɪdʒɪnəs] adj indigeno(-a)

indigestion [ɪndɪ'dʒɛstʃən] n indigestione f

indignant [ɪn'dɪgnənt] adj **~ (at sth/with sb)** indignato(-a) (per qc/contro qn)

indirect [ɪndɪ'rɛkt] adj indiretto(-a)

indispensable [ɪndɪ'spɛnsəbl] adj indispensabile

individual [ɪndɪ'vɪdjuəl] n individuo ▷ adj individuale; (characteristic) particolare, originale; **individually** adv singolarmente, uno(-a) per uno(-a)

Indonesia [ɪndə'niːzɪə] n Indonesia

indoor ['ɪndɔː'] adj da interno; (plant) d'appartamento; (swimming pool) coperto(-a); (sport, games) fatto(-a) al coperto; **indoors** [ɪn'dɔːz] adv all'interno

induce [ɪn'djuːs] vt persuadere; (bring about, Med) provocare

indulge [ɪn'dʌldʒ] vt (whim) compiacere, soddisfare; (child) viziare ▷ vi **to ~ in sth** concedersi qc; abbandonarsi a qc; **indulgent** adj indulgente

industrial [ɪn'dʌstrɪəl] adj industriale; (injury) sul lavoro; **industrial estate** (BRIT) n zona industriale; **industrialist**

[ɪn'dʌstrɪəlɪst] n industriale m; **industrial park** (US) n = **industrial estate**
industry ['ɪndəstrɪ] n industria; (diligence) operosità
inefficient [ɪnɪ'fɪʃənt] adj inefficiente
inequality [ɪnɪ'kwɒlɪtɪ] n ineguaglianza
inevitable [ɪn'evɪtəbl] adj inevitabile; **inevitably** adv inevitabilmente
inexpensive [ɪnɪk'spensɪv] adj poco costoso(-a)
inexperienced [ɪnɪks'pɪərɪənst] adj inesperto(-a), senza esperienza
inexplicable [ɪnɪk'splɪkəbl] adj inesplicabile
infamous ['ɪnfəməs] adj infame
infant ['ɪnfənt] n bambino(-a)
infantry ['ɪnfəntrɪ] n fanteria
infant school n (BRIT) scuola elementare (per bambini dall'età di 5 a 7 anni)
infect [ɪn'fekt] vt infettare; **infection** [ɪn'fekʃən] n infezione f; **infectious** [ɪn'fekʃəs] adj (disease) infettivo(-a), contagioso(-a); (person: fig: enthusiasm) contagioso(-a)
infer [ɪn'fəːʳ] vt inferire, dedurre
inferior [ɪn'fɪərɪəʳ] adj inferiore; (goods) di qualità scadente ▷ n inferiore m/f; (in rank) subalterno(-a)
infertile [ɪn'fəːtaɪl] adj sterile
infertility [ɪnfəː'tɪlɪtɪ] n sterilità
infested [ɪn'festɪd] adj **~ (with)** infestato(-a) (di)
infinite ['ɪnfɪnɪt] adj infinito(-a); **infinitely** adv infinitamente
infirmary [ɪn'fəːmərɪ] n ospedale m; (in school, factory) infermeria
inflamed [ɪn'fleɪmd] adj infiammato(-a)
inflammation [ɪnflə'meɪʃən] n infiammazione f
inflatable [ɪn'fleɪtəbl] adj gonfiabile
inflate [ɪn'fleɪt] vt (tyre, balloon) gonfiare; (fig) esagerare; gonfiare; **inflation** [ɪn'fleɪʃən] n (Econ) inflazione f
inflexible [ɪn'fleksɪbl] adj inflessibile, rigido(-a)
inflict [ɪn'flɪkt] vt **to ~ on** infliggere a
influence ['ɪnfluəns] n influenza ▷ vt influenzare; **under the ~ of alcohol** sotto l'effetto dell'alcool; **influential** [ɪnflu'enʃl] adj influente
influx ['ɪnflʌks] n afflusso
info (inf) ['ɪnfəu] n = **information**
inform [ɪn'fɔːm] vt **to ~ sb (of)** informare qn (di) ▷ vi **to ~ on sb** denunciare qn
informal [ɪn'fɔːml] adj informale; (announcement, invitation) non ufficiale
information [ɪnfə'meɪʃən] n informazioni fpl; particolari mpl; **a piece of ~** un'informazione; **information office** n

ufficio m informazioni inv; **information technology** n informatica
informative [ɪn'fɔːmətɪv] adj istruttivo(-a)
infra-red [ɪnfrə'red] adj infrarosso(-a)
infrastructure ['ɪnfrəstrʌktʃəʳ] n infrastruttura
infrequent [ɪn'friːkwənt] adj infrequente, raro(-a)
infuriate [ɪn'fjuərɪeɪt] vt rendere furioso(-a)
infuriating [ɪn'fjuərɪeɪtɪŋ] adj molto irritante
ingenious [ɪn'dʒiːnjəs] adj ingegnoso(-a)
ingredient [ɪn'griːdɪənt] n ingrediente m; elemento
inhabit [ɪn'hæbɪt] vt abitare; **inhabitant** [ɪn'hæbɪtnt] n abitante m/f
inhale [ɪn'heɪl] vt inalare ▷ vi (in smoking) aspirare; **inhaler** n inalatore m
inherent [ɪn'hɪərənt] adj **~ (in or to)** inerente (a)
inherit [ɪn'herɪt] vt ereditare; **inheritance** n eredità
inhibit [ɪn'hɪbɪt] vt (Psych) inibire; **inhibition** [-'bɪʃən] n inibizione f
initial [ɪ'nɪʃl] adj iniziale ▷ n iniziale f ▷ vt siglare; **~s** npl (of name) iniziali fpl; (as signature) sigla; **initially** adv inizialmente, all'inizio
initiate [ɪ'nɪʃɪeɪt] vt (start) avviare; intraprendere; iniziare; (person) iniziare; **to ~ sb into a secret** mettere qn a parte di un segreto; **to ~ proceedings against sb** (Law) intentare causa contro qn
initiative [ɪ'nɪʃətɪv] n iniziativa
inject [ɪn'dʒekt] vt (liquid) iniettare; (patient): **to ~ sb with sth** fare a qn un'iniezione di qc; (funds) immettere; **injection** [ɪn'dʒekʃən] n iniezione f, puntura
injure ['ɪndʒəʳ] vt ferire; (damage: reputation etc) nuocere a; **injured** adj ferito(-a); **injury** ['ɪndʒərɪ] n ferita
injustice [ɪn'dʒʌstɪs] n ingiustizia
ink [ɪŋk] n inchiostro; **ink-jet printer** ['ɪŋkdʒet-] n stampante f a getto d'inchiostro
inland [adj 'ɪnlənd, adv ɪn'lænd] adj interno(-a) ▷ adv all'interno; **Inland Revenue** (BRIT) n Fisco
in-laws ['ɪnlɔːz] npl suoceri mpl; famiglia del marito (or della moglie)
inmate ['ɪnmeɪt] n (in prison) carcerato(-a); (in asylum) ricoverato(-a)
inn [ɪn] n locanda
inner ['ɪnəʳ] adj interno(-a), interiore; **inner-city** n centro di una zona urbana
inning ['ɪnɪŋ] n (US: Baseball) ripresa; **~s**

(*Cricket*) turno di battuta

innocence ['ɪnəsns] *n* innocenza

innocent ['ɪnəsnt] *adj* innocente

innovation [ɪnəʊ'veɪʃən] *n* innovazione *f*

innovative ['ɪnəʊveɪtɪv] *adj* innovativo(-a)

in-patient ['ɪnpeɪʃənt] *n* ricoverato(-a)

input ['ɪnput] *n* input *m*

inquest ['ɪnkwɛst] *n* inchiesta

inquire [ɪn'kwaɪə'] *vi* informarsi ▷ *vt* domandare, informarsi su; **inquiry** *n* domanda; (*Law*) indagine *f*, investigazione *f*, **"inquiries"** "informazioni"

ins. *abbr* = **inches**

insane [ɪn'seɪn] *adj* matto(-a), pazzo(-a); (*Med*) alienato(-a)

insanity [ɪn'sænɪtɪ] *n* follia; (*Med*) alienazione *f* mentale

insect ['ɪnsɛkt] *n* insetto; **insect repellent** *n* insettifugo

insecure [ɪnsɪ'kjuə'] *adj* malsicuro(-a); (*person*) insicuro(-a)

insecurity [ɪnsɪ'kjuərɪtɪ] *n* mancanza di sicurezza

insensitive [ɪn'sɛnsɪtɪv] *adj* insensibile

insert [ɪn'sə:t] *vt* inserire, introdurre

inside ['ɪn'saɪd] *n* interno, parte *f* interiore ▷ *adj* interno(-a), interiore ▷ *adv* dentro, all'interno ▷ *prep* dentro, all'interno di; (*of time*): **~ 10 minutes** entro 10 minuti; **inside lane** *n* (*Aut*) corsia di marcia; **inside out** *adv* (*turn*) a rovescio; (*know*) in fondo

insight ['ɪnsaɪt] *n* acume *m*, perspicacia; (*glimpse, idea*) percezione *f*

insignificant [ɪnsɪg'nɪfɪknt] *adj* insignificante

insincere [ɪnsɪn'sɪə'] *adj* insincero(-a)

insist [ɪn'sɪst] *vi* insistere; **to ~ on doing** insistere per fare; **to ~ that** insistere perché + *sub*; (*claim*) sostenere che; **insistent** *adj* insistente

insomnia [ɪn'sɔmnɪə] *n* insonnia

inspect [ɪn'spɛkt] *vt* ispezionare; (*BRIT: ticket*) controllare; **inspection** [ɪn'spɛkʃən] *n* ispezione *f*, controllo; **inspector** *n* ispettore(-trice); (*BRIT: on buses, trains*) controllore *m*

inspiration [ɪnspə'reɪʃən] *n* ispirazione *f*; **inspire** [ɪn'spaɪə'] *vt* ispirare; **inspiring** *adj* stimolante

instability [ɪnstə'bɪlɪtɪ] *n* instabilità

install [ɪn'stɔ:l] (*us* **instal**) *vt* installare; **installation** [ɪnstə'leɪʃən] *n* installazione *f*

instalment [ɪn'stɔ:lmənt] (*us* **installment**) *n* rata; (*of TV serial etc*) puntata; **in ~s** (*pay*) a rate; (*receive*) una parte per volta; (*: publication*) a fascicoli

instance ['ɪnstəns] *n* esempio, caso; **for ~**

per *or* ad esempio; **in the first ~** in primo luogo

instant ['ɪnstənt] *n* istante *m*, attimo ▷ *adj* immediato(-a); urgente; (*coffee, food*) in polvere; **instantly** *adv* immediatamente, subito

instead [ɪn'stɛd] *adv* invece; **~ of** invece di

instinct ['ɪnstɪŋkt] *n* istinto; **instinctive** *adj* istintivo(-a)

institute ['ɪnstɪtju:t] *n* istituto ▷ *vt* istituire, stabilire; (*inquiry*) avviare; (*proceedings*) iniziare

institution [ɪnstɪ'tju:ʃən] *n* istituzione *f*; (*educational institution, mental institution*) istituto

instruct [ɪn'strʌkt] *vt* **to ~ sb in sth** insegnare qc a qn; **to ~ sb to do** dare ordini a qn di fare; **instruction** [ɪn'strʌkʃən] *n* istruzione *f*; **instructions (for use)** istruzioni per l'uso; **instructor** *n* istruttore(-trice); (*for skiing*) maestro(-a)

instrument ['ɪnstrəmənt] *n* strumento; **instrumental** [-'mɛntl] *adj* (*Mus*) strumentale; **to be instrumental in** essere d'aiuto in

insufficient [ɪnsə'fɪʃənt] *adj* insufficiente

insulate ['ɪnsjuleɪt] *vt* isolare; **insulation** [-'leɪʃən] *n* isolamento

insulin ['ɪnsjulɪn] *n* insulina

insult [*n* 'ɪnsʌlt, *vb* ɪn'sʌlt] *n* insulto, affronto ▷ *vt* insultare; **insulting** *adj* offensivo(-a), ingiurioso(-a)

insurance [ɪn'ʃuərəns] *n* assicurazione *f*; **fire/life ~** assicurazione contro gli incendi/sulla vita; **insurance company** *n* società di assicurazioni; **insurance policy** *n* polizza d'assicurazione

insure [ɪn'ʃuə'] *vt* assicurare

intact [ɪn'tækt] *adj* intatto(-a)

intake ['ɪnteɪk] *n* (*Tech*) immissione *f*; (*of food*) consumo; (*BRIT: of pupils etc*) afflusso

integral ['ɪntɪgrəl] *adj* integrale; (*part*) integrante

integrate ['ɪntɪgreɪt] *vt* integrare ▷ *vi* integrarsi

integrity [ɪn'tɛgrɪtɪ] *n* integrità

intellect ['ɪntəlɛkt] *n* intelletto; **intellectual** [-'lɛktjuəl] *adj, n* intellettuale *m/f*

intelligence [ɪn'tɛlɪdʒəns] *n* intelligenza; (*Mil etc*) informazioni *fpl*

intelligent [ɪn'tɛlɪdʒənt] *adj* intelligente

intend [ɪn'tɛnd] *vt* (*gift etc*): **to ~ sth for** destinare qc a; **to ~ to do** aver l'intenzione di fare

intense [ɪn'tɛns] *adj* intenso(-a); (*person*) di forti sentimenti

intensify [ɪn'tɛnsɪfaɪ] *vt* intensificare

intensity [ɪn'tɛnsɪtɪ] *n* intensità

intensive [ɪn'tɛnsɪv] *adj* intensivo(-a);
intensive care *n* terapia intensiva;
intensive care unit (ICU) *n* reparto
terapia intensiva

intent [ɪn'tɛnt] *n* intenzione *f* ▷ *adj* ~ **(on)**
intento(-a) (a), immerso(-a) (in); **to all ~s
and purposes** a tutti gli effetti; **to be ~ on
doing sth** essere deciso a fare qc

intention [ɪn'tɛnʃən] *n* intenzione
f; **intentional** *adj* intenzionale,
deliberato(-a)

interact [ɪntər'ækt] *vi* interagire;
interaction [ɪntər'ækʃən] *n* azione *f*
reciproca, interazione *f*; **interactive** *adj*
(*Comput*) interattivo(-a)

intercept [ɪntə'sɛpt] *vt* intercettare;
(*person*) fermare

interchange ['ɪntətʃeɪndʒ] *n* (*exchange*)
scambio; (*on motorway*) incrocio
pluridirezionale

intercourse ['ɪntəkɔːs] *n* rapporti *mpl*

interest ['ɪntrɪst] *n* interesse *m*; (*Comm:
stake, share*) interessi *mpl* ▷ *vt* interessare;
interested *adj* interessato(-a); **to be
interested in** interessarsi di; **interesting**
adj interessante; **interest rate** *n* tasso di
interesse

interface ['ɪntəfeɪs] *n* (*Comput*) interfaccia

interfere [ɪntə'fɪəʳ] *vi* **to ~ in** (*quarrel, other
people's business*) immischiarsi in; **to ~ with**
(*object*) toccare; (*plans, duty*) interferire
con; **interference** [ɪntə'fɪərəns] *n*
interferenza

interim ['ɪntərɪm] *adj* provvisorio(-a) ▷ *n*
in the ~ nel frattempo

interior [ɪn'tɪərɪəʳ] *n* interno; (*of
country*) entroterra ▷ *adj* interno(-a);
(*minister*) degli Interni; **interior design** *n*
architettura d'interni

intermediate [ɪntə'miːdɪət] *adj*
intermedio(-a)

intermission [ɪntə'mɪʃən] *n* pausa;
(*Theatre, Cinema*) intermissione *f*, intervallo

intern [*vb* ɪn'təːn, *n* 'ɪntəːn] *vt* internare
▷ *n* (*US*) medico interno

internal [ɪn'təːnl] *adj* interno(-a); **Internal
Revenue Service** (*US*) *n* Fisco

international [ɪntə'næʃənl] *adj*
internazionale ▷ *n* (*BRIT Sport*) incontro
internazionale

Internet ['ɪntənɛt] *n* **the ~** Internet *f*;
Internet café *n* cybercaffè *m inv*; **Internet
Service Provider** *n* Provider *m inv*;
Internet user *n* utente *m/f* di Internet

interpret [ɪn'təːprɪt] *vt* interpretare
▷ *vi* fare da interprete; **interpretation**
[ɪntəːprɪ'teɪʃən] *n* interpretazione *f*;
interpreter *n* interprete *m/f*; **could you
act as an interpreter for us?** ci potrebbe

fare da interprete?

interrogate [ɪn'tɛrəugeɪt] *vt* interrogare;
interrogation [-'geɪʃən] *n* interrogazione
f; (*of suspect etc*) interrogatorio

interrogative [ɪntə'rɔgətɪv] *adj*
interrogativo(-a) ▷ *n* (*Ling*) interrogativo

interrupt [ɪntə'rʌpt] *vt, vi* interrompere;
interruption [-'rʌpʃən] *n* interruzione *f*

intersection [ɪntə'sɛkʃən] *n* intersezione
f; (*of roads*) incrocio

interstate ['ɪntəsteɪt] (*US*) *n* fra stati

interval ['ɪntəvl] *n* intervallo; **at ~s** a
intervalli

intervene [ɪntə'viːn] *vi* (*time*) intercorrere;
(*event, person*) intervenire

interview ['ɪntəvjuː] *n* (*Radio, TV
etc*) intervista; (*for job*) colloquio ▷ *vt*
intervistare; avere un colloquio con;
interviewer *n* intervistatore(-trice)

intimate [*adj* 'ɪntɪmət, *vb* 'ɪntɪmeɪt] *adj*
intimo(-a); (*knowledge*) profondo(-a) ▷ *vt*
lasciar capire

intimidate [ɪn'tɪmɪdeɪt] *vt* intimidire,
intimorire

intimidating [ɪn'tɪmɪdeɪtɪŋ] *adj* (*sight*)
spaventoso(-a); (*appearance, figure*)
minaccioso(-a)

into ['ɪntuː] *prep* dentro, in; **come ~ the
house** entra in casa; **he worked late ~ the
night** lavorò fino a tarda notte; **~ Italian**
in italiano

intolerant [ɪn'tɔlərnt] *adj* **~ of**
intollerante di

intranet ['ɪntrənɛt] *n* intranet *f*

intransitive [ɪn'trænsɪtɪv] *adj*
intransitivo(-a)

intricate ['ɪntrɪkət] *adj* intricato(-a),
complicato(-a)

intrigue [ɪn'triːg] *n* intrigo ▷ *vt*
affascinare; **intriguing** *adj* affascinante

introduce [ɪntrə'djuːs] *vt* introdurre;
to ~ sb (to sb) presentare qn (a qn); **to
~ sb to** (*pastime, technique*) iniziare qn a;
introduction [-'dʌkʃən] *n* introduzione
f; (*of person*) presentazione *f*; (*to new
experience*) iniziazione *f*; **introductory** *adj*
introduttivo(-a)

intrude [ɪn'truːd] *vi* (*person*) **to ~ (on)**
intromettersi (in); **intruder** *n* intruso(-a)

intuition [ɪntjuː'ɪʃən] *n* intuizione *f*

inundate ['ɪnʌndeɪt] *vt* **to ~ with**
inondare di

invade [ɪn'veɪd] *vt* invadere

invalid [*n* 'ɪnvəlɪd, *adj* ɪn'vælɪd] *n*
malato(-a); (*with disability*) invalido(-a)
▷ *adj* (*not valid*) invalido(-a), non valido(-a)

invaluable [ɪn'væljuəbl] *adj* prezioso(-a);
inestimabile

invariably [ɪn'vɛərɪəblɪ] *adv*

invariabilmente; sempre
invasion [ɪnˈveɪʒən] n invasione f
invent [ɪnˈvɛnt] vt inventare; **invention** [ɪnˈvɛnʃən] n invenzione f; **inventor** n inventore m
inventory [ˈɪnvəntrɪ] n inventario
inverted commas [ɪnˈvəːtɪd-] (BRIT) npl virgolette fpl
invest [ɪnˈvɛst] vt investire ▷ vi **to ~ (in)** investire (in)
investigate [ɪnˈvɛstɪgeɪt] vt investigare, indagare; (crime) fare indagini su; **investigation** [-ˈgeɪʃən] n investigazione f; (of crime) indagine f
investigator [ɪnˈvɛstɪgeɪtəʳ] n investigatore(-trice); **a private ~** un investigatore privato, un detective
investment [ɪnˈvɛstmənt] n investimento
investor [ɪnˈvɛstəʳ] n investitore(-trice); azionista m/f
invisible [ɪnˈvɪzɪbl] adj invisibile
invitation [ɪnvɪˈteɪʃən] n invito
invite [ɪnˈvaɪt] vt invitare; (opinions etc) sollecitare; **inviting** adj invitante, attraente
invoice [ˈɪnvɔɪs] n fattura ▷ vt fatturare
involve [ɪnˈvɔlv] vt (entail) richiedere, comportare; (associate): **to ~ sb (in)** implicare qn (in); coinvolgere qn (in); **involved** adj involuto(-a), complesso(-a); **to be involved in** essere coinvolto(-a) in; **involvement** n implicazione f; coinvolgimento
inward [ˈɪnwəd] adj (movement) verso l'interno; (thought, feeling) interiore, intimo(-a); **inward(s)** adv verso l'interno
IQ n abbr (= intelligence quotient) quoziente m d'intelligenza
IRA n abbr (= Irish Republican Army) IRA f
Iran [ɪˈrɑːn] n Iran m; **Iranian** adj, n iraniano(-a)
Iraq [ɪˈrɑːk] n Iraq m; **Iraqi** adj, n iracheno(-a)
Ireland [ˈaɪələnd] n Irlanda
iris [ˈaɪrɪs] n (pl irises) n iride f; (Bot) giaggiolo, iride
Irish [ˈaɪrɪʃ] adj irlandese ▷ npl **the ~** gli Irlandesi; **Irishman** (irreg) n irlandese m; **Irish Sea** n Mar m d'Irlanda; **Irishwoman** (irreg) n irlandese f
iron [ˈaɪən] n ferro; (for clothes) ferro da stiro ▷ adj di or in ferro ▷ vt (clothes) stirare
ironic(al) [aɪˈrɔnɪk(l)] adj ironico(-a); **ironically** adv ironicamente
ironing [ˈaɪənɪŋ] n (act) stirare m; (clothes) roba da stirare; **ironing board** n asse f da stiro
irony [ˈaɪrənɪ] n ironia

irrational [ɪˈræʃənl] adj irrazionale
irregular [ɪˈrɛgjuləʳ] adj irregolare
irrelevant [ɪˈrɛləvənt] adj non pertinente
irresistible [ɪrɪˈzɪstɪbl] adj irresistibile
irresponsible [ɪrɪˈspɔnsɪbl] adj irresponsabile
irrigation [ɪrɪˈgeɪʃən] n irrigazione f
irritable [ˈɪrɪtəbl] adj irritabile
irritate [ˈɪrɪteɪt] vt irritare; **irritating** adj (person, sound etc) irritante; **irritation** [-ˈteɪʃən] n irritazione f
IRS (US) n abbr = **Internal Revenue Service**
is [ɪz] vb see **be**
ISDN n abbr (= Integrated Services Digital Network) I.S.D.N. f
Islam [ˈɪzlɑːm] n Islam m; **Islamic** [ɪzˈlæmɪk] adj islamico(-a)
island [ˈaɪlənd] n isola; **islander** n isolano(-a)
isle [aɪl] n isola
isn't [ˈɪznt] = **is not**
isolated [ˈaɪsəleɪtɪd] adj isolato(-a)
isolation [aɪsəˈleɪʃən] n isolamento
ISP n abbr (= Internet Service Provider) provider m inv
Israel [ˈɪzreɪl] n Israele m; **Israeli** [ɪzˈreɪlɪ] adj, n israeliano(-a)
issue [ˈɪʃjuː] n questione f, problema m; (of banknotes etc) emissione f; (of newspaper etc) numero ▷ vt (statement) rilasciare; (rations, equipment) distribuire; (book) pubblicare; (banknotes, cheques, stamps) emettere; **at ~** in gioco, in discussione; **to take ~ with sb (over sth)** prendere posizione contro qn (riguardo a qc); **to make an ~ of sth** fare un problema di qc

 KEYWORD

it [ɪt] pron **1** (specific: subject) esso(-a); (: direct object) lo (la), l'; (: indirect object) gli (le); **where's my book? — it's on the table** dov'è il mio libro? — è sulla tavola; **I can't find it** non lo (or la) trovo; **give it to me** dammelo (or dammela); **about/from/of it** ne; **I spoke to him about it** gliene ho parlato; **what did you learn from it?** quale insegnamento ne hai tratto?; **I'm proud of it** ne sono fiero; **did you go to it?** ci sei andato?; **put the book in it** mettici il libro

2 (impers): **it's raining** piove; **it's Friday tomorrow** domani è venerdì; **it's 6 o'clock** sono le 6; **who is it? — it's me** chi è? — sono io

IT n abbr see **information technology**
Italian [ɪˈtæljən] adj italiano(-a) ▷ n

italiano(-a); (*Ling*) italiano; **the ~s** gli
Italiani; **what's the ~ (word) for ...?** come
si dice in italiano ...?
italics [ɪˈtælɪks] *npl* corsivo
Italy [ˈɪtəlɪ] *n* Italia
itch [ɪtʃ] *n* prurito ▷ *vi* (*person*) avere il
prurito; (*part of body*) prudere; **to ~ to do
sth** aver una gran voglia di fare qc; **itchy**
adj che prude; **to be itchy = to itch**
it'd [ɪtd] = **it would**; **it had**
item [ˈaɪtəm] *n* articolo; (*on agenda*) punto;
(*also*: **news ~**) notizia
itinerary [aɪˈtɪnərərɪ] *n* itinerario
it'll [ˈɪtl] = **it will**; **it shall**
its [ɪts] *adj* il (la) suo(-a), i (le) suoi (sue)
it's [ɪts] = **it is**; **it has**
itself [ɪtˈsɛlf] *pron* (*emphatic*) esso(-a)
stesso(-a); (*reflexive*) si
ITV (BRIT) *n abbr* (= *Independent Television*)
rete televisiva in concorrenza con la BBC
I've [aɪv] = **I have**
ivory [ˈaɪvərɪ] *n* avorio
ivy [ˈaɪvɪ] *n* edera

J

jab [dʒæb] *vt* dare colpetti a ▷ *n* (*Med*:
inf) puntura; **to ~ sth into** affondare *or*
piantare qc dentro
jack [dʒæk] *n* (*Aut*) cricco; (*Cards*) fante *m*
jacket [ˈdʒækɪt] *n* giacca; (*of book*)
copertura; **jacket potato** *n* patata cotta al
forno con la buccia
jackpot [ˈdʒækpɒt] *n* primo premio (in
denaro)
Jacuzzi® [dʒəˈkuːzɪ] *n* vasca per
idromassaggio Jacuzzi®
jagged [ˈdʒægɪd] *adj* seghettato(-a); (*cliffs
etc*) frastagliato(-a)
jail [dʒeɪl] *n* prigione *f* ▷ *vt* mandare in
prigione; **jail sentence** *n* condanna al
carcere
jam [dʒæm] *n* marmellata; (*also*: **traffic
~**) ingorgo; (*inf*) pasticcio ▷ *vt* (*passage
etc*) ingombrare, ostacolare; (*mechanism,
drawer etc*) bloccare; (*Radio*) disturbare con
interferenze ▷ *vi* incepparsi; **to ~ sth into**
forzare qc dentro; infilare qc a forza dentro
Jamaica [dʒəˈmeɪkə] *n* Giamaica
jammed [dʒæmd] *adj* (*door*) bloccato(-a);
(*rifle, printer*) inceppato(-a)
Jan. *abbr* (= *January*) gen., genn.
janitor [ˈdʒænɪtəʳ] *n* (*caretaker*) portiere *m*;
(: *Scol*) bidello
January [ˈdʒænjuərɪ] *n* gennaio
Japan [dʒəˈpæn] *n* Giappone *m*; **Japanese**

[dʒæpə'niːz] adj giapponese ▷ n inv
giapponese m/f; (Ling) giapponese m

jar [dʒɑːʳ] n (glass) barattolo, vasetto ▷ vi
(sound) stridere; (colours etc) stonare

jargon ['dʒɑːgən] n gergo

javelin ['dʒævlɪn] n giavellotto

jaw [dʒɔː] n mascella

jazz [dʒæz] n jazz m

jealous ['dʒɛləs] adj geloso(-a); **jealousy**
n gelosia

jeans [dʒiːnz] npl (blue-)jeans mpl

Jello® ['dʒɛləu] (us) n gelatina di frutta

jelly ['dʒɛlɪ] n gelatina; **jellyfish** n medusa

jeopardize ['dʒɛpədaɪz] vt mettere in
pericolo

jerk [dʒəːk] n (of gas, liquid) getto; (Aviat)
sobbalzo, scossa; sussulto;
(inf: idiot) tonto(-a) ▷ vt dare una scossa a
▷ vi (vehicles) sobbalzare

Jersey ['dʒəːzɪ] n Jersey m

jersey ['dʒəːzɪ] n maglia; (fabric) jersey m

Jesus ['dʒiːzəs] n Gesù m

jet [dʒɛt] n (of gas, liquid) getto; (Aviat)
aviogetto; **jet lag** n (problemi mpl
dovuti allo) sbalzo dei fusi orari; **jet-ski** vi
acquascooter m inv

jetty ['dʒɛtɪ] n molo

Jew [dʒuː] n ebreo

jewel ['dʒuːəl] n gioiello; **jeweller** (us
jeweler) n orefice m, gioielliere(-a);
jeweller's (shop) (us **jewelry store**)
n oreficeria, gioielleria; **jewellery** (us
jewelry) n gioielli mpl

Jewish ['dʒuːɪʃ] adj ebreo(-a), ebraico(-a)

jigsaw ['dʒɪgsɔː] n (also: ~ puzzle) puzzle
m inv

job [dʒɔb] n lavoro; (employment) impiego,
posto; **it's not my ~** (duty) non è compito
mio; **it's a good ~ that ...** meno male
che ...; **just the ~!** proprio quello che
ci vuole; **job centre** (BRIT) n ufficio di
collocamento; **jobless** adj senza lavoro,
disoccupato(-a)

jockey ['dʒɔkɪ] n fantino, jockey m inv
▷ vi **to ~ for position** manovrare per una
posizione di vantaggio

jog [dʒɔg] vt urtare ▷ vi (Sport) fare footing,
fare jogging; **to ~ sb's memory** rinfrescare
la memoria a qn; **to ~ along** trottare; (fig)
andare avanti piano piano; **jogging** n
footing m, jogging m

join [dʒɔɪn] vt unire, congiungere; (become
member of) iscriversi a; (meet) raggiungere;
riunirsi a ▷ vi (roads, rivers) confluire ▷ n
giuntura; **join in** vi partecipare ▷ vt
fus unirsi a; **join up** vi incontrarsi; (Mil)
arruolarsi

joiner ['dʒɔɪnəʳ] (BRIT) n falegname m

joint [dʒɔɪnt] n (Tech) giuntura; giunto;
(Anat) articolazione f, giuntura; (BRIT Culin)

arrosto; (inf: place) locale m; (: of cannabis)
spinello ▷ adj comune; **joint account** n
(at bank etc) conto in partecipazione, conto
comune; **jointly** adv in comune, insieme

joke [dʒəuk] n scherzo; (funny story)
barzelletta; (also: **practical ~**) beffa ▷ vi
scherzare; **to play a ~ on sb** fare uno
scherzo a qn; **joker** n (Cards) matta, jolly
m inv

jolly ['dʒɔlɪ] adj allegro(-a), gioioso(-a)
▷ adv (BRIT: inf) veramente, proprio

jolt [dʒəult] n scossa, sobbalzo ▷ vt urtare

Jordan ['dʒɔːdən] n (country) Giordania;
(river) Giordano

journal ['dʒəːnl] n giornale m; rivista;
diario; **journalism** n giornalismo;
journalist n giornalista m/f

journey ['dʒəːnɪ] n viaggio; (distance
covered) tragitto; **how was your ~?** com'è
andato il viaggio?; **the ~ takes two hours**
il viaggio dura due ore

joy [dʒɔɪ] n gioia; **joyrider** n chi ruba
un'auto per farvi un giro; **joy stick** n (Aviat)
barra di comando; (Comput) joystick m inv

Jr abbr = **junior**

judge [dʒʌdʒ] n giudice m/f ▷ vt giudicare

judo ['dʒuːdəu] n judo

jug [dʒʌg] n brocca, bricco

juggle ['dʒʌgl] vi fare giochi di destrezza;
juggler n giocoliere(-a)

juice [dʒuːs] n succo; **juicy** ['dʒuːsɪ] adj
succoso(-a)

Jul. abbr (= July) lug., lu.

July [dʒuː'laɪ] n luglio

jumble ['dʒʌmbl] n miscuglio ▷ vt (also:
~ **up**) mischiare; **jumble sale** (BRIT) n
vendita di beneficenza

⬤ **JUMBLE SALE**
⬤
⬤ Una **jumble sale** è un mercatino di
⬤ oggetti di seconda mano organizzato
⬤ in chiese, scuole o in circoli ricreativi,
⬤ i cui proventi vengono devoluti in
⬤ beneficenza.

jumbo ['dʒʌmbəu] adj ~ **jet** jumbo-jet m
inv; ~ **size** formato gigante

jump [dʒʌmp] vi saltare, balzare; (start)
sobbalzare; (increase) rincarare ▷ vt saltare
▷ n salto, balzo; sobbalzo

jumper ['dʒʌmpəʳ] n (BRIT: pullover)
maglione m, pullover m inv; (us: dress)
scamiciato

jumper cables (us) npl = **jump leads**

jump leads (BRIT) npl cavi mpl per batteria

Jun. abbr = **junior**

junction ['dʒʌŋkʃən] n (BRIT: of roads)
incrocio; (of rails) nodo ferroviario

June [dʒuːn] n giugno
jungle ['dʒʌŋgl] n giungla
junior ['dʒuːnɪəʳ] adj, n **he's ~ to me by 2 years, he's my ~ by 2 years** è più giovane di me (di 2 anni); **he's ~ to me** (seniority) è al di sotto di me, ho più anzianità di lui; **junior high school** (us) n scuola media (da 12 a 15 anni); **junior school** (BRIT) n scuola elementare (da 8 a 11 anni)
junk [dʒʌŋk] n cianfrusaglie fpl; (cheap goods) robaccia; **junk food** n porcherie fpl
junkie ['dʒʌŋkɪ] (inf) n drogato(-a)
junk mail n stampe fpl pubblicitarie
Jupiter ['dʒuːpɪtəʳ] n (planet) Giove m
jurisdiction [dʒuərɪs'dɪkʃən] n giurisdizione f; **it falls** or **comes within/outside our ~** è/non è di nostra competenza
jury ['dʒuərɪ] n giuria
just [dʒʌst] adj giusto(-a) ▷ adv **he's ~ done it/left** lo ha appena fatto/è appena partito; **~ right** proprio giusto; **~ 2 o'clock** le 2 precise; **she's ~ as clever as you** è in gamba proprio quanto te; **it's ~ as well that ...** meno male che ...; **~ as I arrived** proprio mentre arrivavo; **it was ~ before/enough/here** era poco prima/appena assai/proprio qui; **it's ~ me** sono solo io; **~ missed/caught** appena perso/preso; **~ listen to this!** senta un po' questo!
justice ['dʒʌstɪs] n giustizia
justification [dʒʌstɪfɪ'keɪʃən] n giustificazione f; (Typ) giustezza
justify ['dʒʌstɪfaɪ] vt giustificare
jut [dʒʌt] vi (also: **~ out**) sporgersi
juvenile ['dʒuːvənaɪl] adj giovane, giovanile; (court) dei minorenni; (books) per ragazzi ▷ n giovane m/f, minorenne m/f

K abbr (= one thousand) mille; (= kilobyte) K
kangaroo [kæŋgə'ruː] n canguro
karaoke [kɑːrə'əʊkɪ] n karaoke m inv
karate [kə'rɑːtɪ] n karatè m
kebab [kə'bæb] n spiedino
keel [kiːl] n chiglia; **on an even ~** (fig) in uno stato normale
keen [kiːn] adj (interest, desire) vivo(-a); (eye, intelligence) acuto(-a); (competition) serrato(-a); (edge) affilato(-a); (eager) entusiasta; **to be ~ to do** or **on doing sth** avere una gran voglia di fare qc; **to be ~ on sth** essere appassionato(-a) di qc; **to be ~ on sb** avere un debole per qn
keep [kiːp] (pt, pp **kept**) vt tenere; (hold back) trattenere; (feed: one's family etc) mantenere, sostentare; (a promise) mantenere; (chickens, bees, pigs etc) allevare ▷ vi (food) mantenersi; (remain: in a certain state or place) restare ▷ n (of castle) maschio; (food etc): **enough for his ~** abbastanza per vitto e alloggio; (inf): **for ~s** per sempre; **to ~ doing sth** continuare a fare qc; fare qc di continuo; **to ~ sb from doing** impedire a qn di fare; **to ~ sb busy/a place tidy** tenere qn occupato(-a)/un luogo in ordine; **to ~ sth to o.s.** tenere qc per sé; **to ~ sth (back) from sb** celare qc a qn; **to ~ time** (clock) andar bene; **keep away** vt **to ~ sth/sb away from sb**

tenere qc/qn lontano da qn ▷ vi **to ~ away (from)** stare lontano (da); **keep back** vt (crowds, tears, money) trattenere ▷ vi tenersi indietro; **keep off** vt (dog, person) tenere lontano da ▷ vi stare alla larga; **~ your hands off!** non toccare!, giù le mani!; **"~ off the grass"** "non calpestare l'erba"; **keep on** vi **to ~ on doing** continuare a fare; **to ~ on (about sth)** continuare a insistere (su qc); **keep out** vt tener fuori; **"~ out"** "vietato l'accesso"; **keep up** vt continuare, mantenere ▷ vi **to ~ up with** tener dietro a, andare di pari passo con; (work etc) farcela a seguire; **keeper** n custode m/f, guardiano(-a); **keeping** n (care) custodia; **in keeping with** in armonia con; in accordo con

kennel ['kɛnl] n canile m; **~s** npl canile m; **to put a dog in ~s** mettere un cane al canile

Kenya ['kɛnjə] n Kenia m

kept [kɛpt] pt, pp of **keep**

kerb [kə:b] (BRIT) n orlo del marciapiede

kerosene ['kɛrəsi:n] n cherosene m

ketchup ['kɛtʃəp] n ketchup m inv

kettle ['kɛtl] n bollitore m

key [ki:] n (gen, Mus) chiave f; (of piano, typewriter) tasto ▷ adj chiave inv ▷ vt (also: **~ in**) digitare; **can I have my ~?** posso avere la mia chiave?; **keyboard** n tastiera; **keyhole** n buco della serratura; **keyring** n portachiavi m inv

kg abbr (= kilogram) Kg

khaki ['kɑːkɪ] adj cachi ▷ n cachi m

kick [kɪk] vt calciare, dare calci a; (inf: habit etc) liberarsi di ▷ vi (horse) tirar calci ▷ n calcio; (thrill): **he does it for ~s** lo fa giusto per il piacere di farlo; **kick off** vi (Sport) dare il primo calcio; **kick-off** n (Sport) calcio d'inizio

kid [kɪd] n (inf: child) ragazzino(-a); (animal, leather) capretto ▷ vi (inf) scherzare

kidnap ['kɪdnæp] vt rapire, sequestrare; **kidnapping** n sequestro (di persona)

kidney ['kɪdnɪ] n (Anat) rene m; (Culin) rognone m; **kidney bean** n fagiolo borlotto

kill [kɪl] vt uccidere, ammazzare ▷ n uccisione f; **killer** n uccisore m, killer m inv; assassino(-a); **killing** n assassinio; **to make a killing** (inf) fare un bel colpo

kiln [kɪln] n forno

kilo ['kiːləu] n chilo; **kilobyte** n (Comput) kilobyte m inv; **kilogram(me)** ['kɪləugræm] n chilogrammo; **kilometre** ['kɪləmiːtəʳ] (us **kilometer**) n chilometro; **kilowatt** ['kɪləuwɔt] n chilowatt m inv

kilt [kɪlt] n gonnellino scozzese

kin [kɪn] n see **next**; **kith**

kind [kaɪnd] adj gentile, buono(-a) ▷ n sorta, specie f; (species) genere m; **what ~ of ...?** che tipo di ...?; **to be two of a ~** essere molto simili; **in ~** (Comm) in natura

kindergarten ['kɪndəgɑːtn] n giardino d'infanzia

kindly ['kaɪndlɪ] adj pieno(-a) di bontà, benevolo(-a) ▷ adv con bontà, gentilmente; **will you ~ ...** vuole ... per favore

kindness ['kaɪndnɪs] n bontà, gentilezza

king [kɪŋ] n re m inv; **kingdom** n regno, reame m; **kingfisher** n martin m inv pescatore; **king-size(d) bed** n letto king-size

kiosk ['kiːɔsk] n edicola, chiosco; (BRIT Tel) cabina (telefonica)

kipper ['kɪpəʳ] n aringa affumicata

kiss [kɪs] n bacio ▷ vt baciare; **to ~ (each other)** baciarsi; **kiss of life** n respirazione f bocca a bocca

kit [kɪt] n equipaggiamento, corredo; (set of tools etc) attrezzi mpl; (for assembly) scatola di montaggio

kitchen ['kɪtʃɪn] n cucina

kite [kaɪt] n (toy) aquilone m

kitten ['kɪtn] n gattino(-a), micino(-a)

kiwi ['kiːwiː] n (also: **~ fruit**) kiwi m inv

km abbr (= kilometre) km

km/h abbr (= kilometres per hour) km/h

knack [næk] n **to have the ~ of** avere l'abilità di

knee [niː] n ginocchio; **kneecap** n rotula

kneel [niːl] (pt, pp **knelt**) vi (also: **~ down**) inginocchiarsi

knelt [nɛlt] pt, pp of **kneel**

knew [njuː] pt of **know**

knickers ['nɪkəz] (BRIT) npl mutandine fpl

knife [naɪf] (pl **knives**) n coltello ▷ vt accoltellare, dare una coltellata a

knight [naɪt] n cavaliere m; (Chess) cavallo

knit [nɪt] vt fare a maglia ▷ vi lavorare a maglia; (broken bones) saldarsi; **to ~ one's brows** aggrottare le sopracciglia; **knitting** n lavoro a maglia; **knitting needle** n ferro (da calza); **knitwear** n maglieria

knives [naɪvz] npl of **knife**

knob [nɔb] n bottone m; manopola

knock [nɔk] vt colpire; urtare; (fig: inf) criticare ▷ vi (at door etc): **to ~ at/on** bussare a ▷ n bussata; colpo, botta; **knock down** vt abbattere; **knock off** vi (inf: finish) smettere (di lavorare) ▷ vt (from price) far abbassare; (inf: steal) sgraffignare; **knock out** vt stendere; (Boxing) mettere K.O.; (defeat) battere; **knock over** vt (person) investire; (object) far cadere; **knockout** n (Boxing) knock out m inv ▷ cpd a eliminazione

knot [nɔt] *n* nodo ▷ *vt* annodare
know [nəu] (*pt* **knew**, *pp* **known**) *vt*
sapere; (*person, author, place*) conoscere;
I don't ~ non lo so; **do you ~ where
I can ...?** sa dove posso ...?; **to ~ how
to do** sapere fare; **to ~ about** *or* **of
sth/sb** conoscere qc/qn; **know-
all** *n* sapientone(-a); **know-how** *n*
tecnica; pratica; **knowing** *adj* (*look etc*)
d'intesa; **knowingly** *adv* (*purposely*)
consapevolmente; (*smile, look*) con aria
d'intesa; **know-it-all** (*us*) *n* = **know-all**
knowledge ['nɔlɪdʒ] *n* consapevolezza;
(*learning*) conoscenza, sapere *m*;
knowledgeable *adj* ben informato(-a)
known [nəun] *pp of* **know**
knuckle ['nʌkl] *n* nocca
koala [kəu'ɑːlə] *n* (*also: ~ bear*) koala *m inv*
Koran [kɔ'rɑːn] *n* Corano
Korea [kə'rɪə] *n* Corea; **Korean** *adj, n*
coreano(-a)
kosher ['kəuʃəʳ] *adj* kasher *inv*
Kosovar, Kosovan ['kɔsəvaʳ, 'kɔsəvən]
adj kosovaro(-a)
Kosovo ['kusəvəu] *n* Kosovo
Kremlin ['krɛmlɪn] *n* **the ~** il Cremlino
Kuwait [ku'weɪt] *n* Kuwait *m*

L (*BRIT*) *abbr* = **learner driver**
l. *abbr* (= *litre*) l
lab [læb] *n abbr* (= *laboratory*) laboratorio
label ['leɪbl] *n* etichetta, cartellino; (*brand:
of record*) casa ▷ *vt* etichettare
labor *etc* ['leɪbəʳ] (*us*) = **labour** *etc*
laboratory [lə'bɔrətərɪ] *n* laboratorio
Labor Day (*us*) *n* festa del lavoro

❦ **LABOR DAY**
❦
❦ Negli Stati Uniti e nel Canada il **Labor
❦ Day**, la festa del lavoro, cade il primo
❦ lunedì di settembre, contrariamente a
❦ quanto accade nella maggior parte dei
❦ paesi europei dove tale celebrazione ha
❦ luogo il primo maggio.

labor union (*us*) *n* sindacato
labour ['leɪbəʳ] (*us* **labor**) *n* (*task*) lavoro;
(*workmen*) manodopera; (*Med*): **to be in
~** avere le doglie ▷ *vi* **to ~ (at)** lavorare
duro (a); **L~, the L~ party** (*BRIT*) il partito
laburista, i laburisti; **hard ~** lavori *mpl*
forzati; **labourer** *n* manovale *m*; **farm
labourer** lavoratore *m* agricolo
lace [leɪs] *n* merletto, pizzo; (*of shoe etc*)
laccio ▷ *vt* (*shoe: also: ~ up*) allacciare
lack [læk] *n* mancanza ▷ *vt* mancare di;
through *or* **for ~ of** per mancanza di; **to be**

~ing mancare; **to be ~ing in** mancare di
lacquer ['lækə'] n lacca
lacy ['leɪsɪ] adj (like lace) che sembra un
pizzo
lad [læd] n ragazzo, giovanotto
ladder ['lædə'] n scala; (BRIT: in tights)
smagliatura
ladle ['leɪdl] n mestolo
lady ['leɪdɪ] n signora; dama; **L~ Smith**
lady Smith; **the ladies' (room)** i gabinetti
per signore; **ladybird** (US **ladybug**) n
coccinella
lag [læg] n (of time) lasso, intervallo ▷ vi
(also: **~ behind**) trascinarsi ▷ vt (pipes)
rivestire di materiale isolante
lager ['lɑːgə'] n lager m inv
lagoon [lə'guːn] n laguna
laid [leɪd] pt, pp of **lay; laid back** (inf) adj
rilassato(-a), tranquillo(-a)
lain [leɪn] pp of **lie**
lake [leɪk] n lago
lamb [læm] n agnello
lame [leɪm] adj zoppo(-a); (excuse etc)
zoppicante
lament [lə'mɛnt] n lamento ▷ vt
lamentare, piangere
lamp [læmp] n lampada; **lamppost**
['læmppəʊst] (BRIT) n lampione m;
lampshade ['læmpʃeɪd] n paralume m
land [lænd] n (as opposed to sea) terra
(ferma); (country) paese m; (soil) terreno;
suolo; (estate) terreni mpl, terre fpl ▷ vi
(from ship) sbarcare; (Aviat) atterrare; (fig:
fall) cadere ▷ vt (passengers) sbarcare;
(goods) scaricare; **to ~ sb with sth**
affibbiare qc a qn; **landing** n atterraggio;
(of staircase) pianerottolo; **landing card**
n carta di sbarco; **landlady** n padrona or
proprietaria di casa; **landlord** n padrone m
or proprietario di casa; (of pub etc) padrone
m; **landmark** n punto di riferimento;
(fig) pietra miliare; **landowner** n
proprietario(-a) terriero(-a); **landscape** n
paesaggio; **landslide** n (Geo) frana; (fig:
Pol) valanga
lane [leɪn] n stradina; (Aut, in race) corsia;
"get in ~" "immettersi in corsia"
language ['læŋgwɪdʒ] n lingua; (way
one speaks) linguaggio; **what ~s do you
speak?** che lingue parla?; **bad ~** linguaggio
volgare; **language laboratory** n
laboratorio linguistico
lantern ['læntn] n lanterna
lap [læp] n (of track) giro; (of body): **in** or
on one's ~ in grembo ▷ vt (also: **~ up**)
papparsi, leccare ▷ vi (waves) sciabordare
lapel [lə'pɛl] n risvolto
lapse [læps] n lapsus m inv; (longer) caduta
▷ vi (law) cadere; (membership, contract)

scadere; **to ~ into bad habits** pigliare
cattive abitudini; **~ of time** spazio di
tempo
laptop (computer) ['læptɔp-] n laptop
m inv
lard [lɑːd] n lardo
larder ['lɑːdə'] n dispensa
large [lɑːdʒ] adj grande; (person, animal)
grosso(-a); **at ~** (free) in libertà; (generally)
in generale; nell'insieme; **largely** adv in
gran parte; **large-scale** adj (map, drawing
etc) in grande scala; (reforms, business
activities) su vasta scala
lark [lɑːk] n (bird) allodola; (joke) scherzo,
gioco
laryngitis [lærɪn'dʒaɪtɪs] n laringite f
lasagne [lə'zænjə] n lasagne fpl
laser ['leɪzə'] n laser m; **laser printer** n
stampante f laser inv
lash [læʃ] n frustata; (also: **eye~**) ciglio ▷ vt
frustare; (tie): **to ~ to/together** legare
a insieme; **lash out** vi **to ~ out (at** or
against sb) attaccare violentemente (qn)
lass [læs] n ragazza
last [lɑːst] adj ultimo(-a); (week, month,
year) scorso(-a), passato(-a) ▷ adv per
ultimo ▷ vi durare; **~ week** la settimana
scorsa; **~ night** ieri sera, la notte scorsa;
at ~ finalmente, alla fine; **~ but one**
penultimo(-a); **lastly** adv infine, per finire;
last-minute adj fatto(-a) (or preso(-a) etc)
all'ultimo momento
latch [lætʃ] n chiavistello; **latch onto** vt fus
(cling to: person) attaccarsi a, appiccicarsi a;
(: idea) afferrare, capire
late [leɪt] adj (not on time) in ritardo; (far
on in day etc) tardi inv; tardo(-a); (former)
ex; (dead) defunto(-a) ▷ adv tardi; (behind
time, schedule) in ritardo; **sorry I'm ~** scusi il
ritardo; **the flight is two hours ~** il volo ha
due ore di ritardo; **it's too ~** è troppo tardi;
of ~ di recente; **in the ~ afternoon** nel
tardo pomeriggio; **in ~ May** verso la fine
di maggio; **latecomer** n ritardatario(-a);
lately adv recentemente; **later** ['leɪtə']
adj (date etc) posteriore; (version etc)
successivo(-a) ▷ adv più tardi; **later on** più
avanti; **latest** ['leɪtɪst] adj ultimo(-a), più
recente; **at the latest** al più tardi
lather ['lɑːðə'] n schiuma di sapone ▷ vt
insaponare
Latin ['lætɪn] n latino ▷ adj latino(-a);
Latin America n America Latina; **Latin
American** adj sudamericano(-a)
latitude ['lætɪtjuːd] n latitudine f; (fig)
libertà d'azione
latter ['lætə'] adj secondo(-a), più recente
▷ n **the ~** quest'ultimo, il secondo
laugh [lɑːf] n risata ▷ vi ridere; **laugh at**

vt fus (misfortune etc) ridere di; **laughter** *n* riso; risate *fpl*

launch [lɔːntʃ] *n (of rocket, Comm)* lancio; *(of new ship)* varo; *(also:* **motor ~**) lancia ▷ *vt (rocket, Comm)* lanciare; *(ship, plan)* varare; **launch into** *vt fus* lanciarsi in

launder ['lɔːndə'] *vt* lavare e stirare

Launderette® [lɔːn'drɛt] (BRIT) *n* lavanderia (automatica)

Laundromat® ['lɔːndrəmæt] (US) *n* lavanderia automatica

laundry ['lɔːndrɪ] *n* lavanderia; *(clothes)* biancheria; (: *dirty)* panni *mpl* da lavare

lava ['lɑːvə] *n* lava

lavatory ['lævətərɪ] *n* gabinetto

lavender ['lævəndə'] *n* lavanda

lavish ['lævɪʃ] *adj* copioso(-a), abbondante; *(giving freely):* **~ with** prodigo(-a) di, largo(-a) in ▷ *vt* **to ~ sth on sb** colmare qn di qc

law [lɔː] *n* legge *f;* **civil/criminal ~** diritto civile/penale; **lawful** *adj* legale, lecito(-a); **lawless** *adj* che non conosce nessuna legge

lawn [lɔːn] *n* tappeto erboso; **lawnmower** *n* tosaerba *m or f inv*

lawsuit ['lɔːsuːt] *n* processo, causa

lawyer ['lɔːjə'] *n (for sales, wills etc)* ≈ notaio; *(partner, in court)* ≈ avvocato(-essa)

lax [læks] *adj* rilassato(-a), negligente

laxative ['læksətɪv] *n* lassativo

lay [leɪ] *(pt, pp laid) pt of lie* ▷ *adj* laico(-a); *(not expert)* profano(-a) ▷ *vt* posare, mettere; *(eggs)* fare; *(trap)* tendere; *(plans)* fare, elaborare; **to ~ the table** apparecchiare la tavola; **lay down** *vt* mettere giù; *(rules etc)* formulare, fissare; **to ~ down the law** dettar legge; **to ~ down one's life** dare la propria vita; **lay off** *vt (workers)* licenziare; **lay on** *vt (provide)* fornire; **lay out** *vt (display)* presentare, disporre; **lay-by** (BRIT) *n* piazzola (di sosta)

layer ['leɪə'] *n* strato

layman ['leɪmən] *(irreg) n* laico; profano

layout ['leɪaut] *n* lay-out *m inv,* disposizione *f; (Press)* impaginazione *f*

lazy ['leɪzɪ] *adj* pigro(-a)

lb. *abbr* = **pound** *(weight)*

lead¹ [liːd] *(pt, pp led) n (front position)* posizione *f* di testa; *(distance, time ahead)* vantaggio; *(clue)* indizio; *(Elec)* filo (elettrico); *(for dog)* guinzaglio; *(Theatre)* parte *f* principale ▷ *vt* guidare, condurre; *(induce)* indurre; *(be leader of)* essere a capo di ▷ *vi* condurre; *(Sport)* essere in testa; **in the ~** in testa; **to ~ the way** fare strada; **lead up to** *vt fus* portare a

lead² [lɛd] *n (metal)* piombo; *(in pencil)* mina

leader ['liːdə'] *n* capo; leader *m inv; (in newspaper)* articolo di fondo; *(Sport)* chi è in testa; **leadership** *n* direzione *f;* capacità di comando

lead-free ['lɛdfriː] *adj* senza piombo

leading ['liːdɪŋ] *adj* primo(-a), principale

lead singer *n* cantante alla testa di un gruppo

leaf [liːf] *(pl leaves) n* foglia ▷ *vi* **to ~ through sth** sfogliare qc; **to turn over a new ~** cambiar vita

leaflet ['liːflɪt] *n* dépliant *m inv; (Pol, Rel)* volantino

league [liːg] *n* lega; *(Football)* campionato; **to be in ~ with** essere in lega con

leak [liːk] *n (out)* fuga; *(in)* infiltrazione *f, (security leak)* fuga d'informazioni ▷ *vi (roof, bucket)* perdere; *(liquid)* uscire; *(shoes)* lasciar passare l'acqua ▷ *vt (information)* divulgare

lean [liːn] *(pt, pp leaned or leant) adj* magro(-a) ▷ *vt* **to ~ sth on sth** appoggiare qc su qc ▷ *vi (slope)* pendere; *(rest):* **to ~ against** appoggiarsi contro; essere appoggiato(-a) a; **to ~ on** appoggiarsi a; **lean forward** *vi* sporgersi in avanti; **lean over** *vi* inclinarsi; **leaning** *n* **leaning (towards)** propensione *f* (per)

leant [lɛnt] *pt, pp of* **lean**

leap [liːp] *(pt, pp leaped or leapt) n* salto, balzo ▷ *vi* saltare, balzare

leapt [lɛpt] *pt, pp of* **leap**

leap year *n* anno bisestile

learn [ləːn] *(pt, pp learned or learnt) vt, vi* imparare; **to ~ about sth** *(hear, read)* apprendere qc; **to ~ to do sth** imparare a fare qc; **learner** *n* principiante *m/f;* apprendista *m/f; (BRIT: also:* **learner driver**) guidatore(-a) principiante; **learning** *n* erudizione *f,* sapienza

learnt [ləːnt] *pt, pp of* **learn**

lease [liːs] *n* contratto d'affitto ▷ *vt* affittare

leash [liːʃ] *n* guinzaglio

least [liːst] *adj* **the ~** *(+ noun)* il (la) più piccolo(-a), il (la) minimo(-a); *(smallest amount of)* il (la) meno ▷ *adv (+ verb)* meno; **the ~** *(+ adjective):* **the ~ beautiful girl** la ragazza meno bella; **the ~ possible effort** il minimo sforzo possibile; **I have the ~ money** ho meno denaro di tutti; **at ~** almeno; **not in the ~** affatto, per nulla

leather ['lɛðə'] *n* cuoio

leave [liːv] *(pt, pp left) vt* lasciare; *(go away from)* partire da ▷ *vi* partire, andarsene; *(bus, train)* partire ▷ *n (time off)* congedo; *(Mil, consent)* licenza; **what time does the train/bus ~?** a che ora parte il treno/

l'autobus?; **to be left** rimanere; **there's some milk left over** c'è rimasto del latte; **on ~** in congedo; **leave behind** vt (person, object) lasciare; (: forget) dimenticare; **leave out** vt omettere, tralasciare

leaves [liːvz] npl of **leaf**

Lebanon ['lebənən] n Libano

lecture ['lektʃə^r] n conferenza; (Scol) lezione f ▷ vi fare conferenze; fare lezioni ▷ vt (scold): **to ~ sb on** or **about sth** rimproverare qn or fare una ramanzina a qn per qc; **to give a ~ on** tenere una conferenza su; **lecture hall** n aula magna; **lecturer** ['lektʃərə^r] (BRIT) n (at university) professore(-essa), docente m/f; **lecture theatre** = **lecture hall**

led [led] pt, pp of **lead**

ledge [ledʒ] n (of window) davanzale m; (on wall etc) sporgenza; (of mountain) cornice f, cengia

leek [liːk] n porro

left [left] pt, pp of **leave** ▷ adj sinistro(-a) ▷ adv a sinistra ▷ n sinistra; **on the ~, to the ~** a sinistra; **the L~** (Pol) la sinistra; **left-hand** adj **the left-hand side** il lato sinistro; **left-hand drive** adj guida a sinistra; **left-handed** adj mancino(-a); **left-luggage locker** n armadietto per deposito bagagli; **left-luggage (office)** (BRIT) n deposito m bagagli inv; **left-overs** npl avanzi mpl, resti mpl; **left-wing** adj (Pol) di sinistra

leg [leg] n gamba; (of animal) zampa; (of furniture) piede m; (Culin: of chicken) coscia; (of journey) tappa; **1st/2nd ~** (Sport) partita di andata/ritorno

legacy ['legəsɪ] n eredità f inv

legal ['liːgl] adj legale; **legal holiday** (US) n giorno festivo, festa nazionale; **legalize** vt legalizzare; **legally** adv legalmente; **legally binding** legalmente vincolante

legend ['ledʒənd] n leggenda; **legendary** ['ledʒəndərɪ] adj leggendario(-a)

leggings ['legɪŋz] npl ghette fpl

legible ['ledʒəbl] adj leggibile

legislation [ledʒɪs'leɪʃən] n legislazione f

legislative ['ledʒɪslətɪv] adj legislativo(-a)

legitimate [lɪ'dʒɪtɪmət] adj legittimo(-a)

leisure ['leʒə^r] n agio, tempo libero; ricreazioni fpl; **at ~** con comodo; **leisure centre** n centro di ricreazione; **leisurely** adj tranquillo(-a), fatto(-a) con comodo or senza fretta

lemon ['lemən] n limone m; **lemonade** [-'neɪd] n limonata; **lemon tea** n tè m inv al limone

lend [lend] (pt, pp lent) vt **to ~ sth (to sb)** prestare qc (a qn); **could you ~ me some**

money? mi può prestare dei soldi?

length [leŋθ] n lunghezza; (distance) distanza; (section: of road, pipe etc) pezzo, tratto; (of time) periodo; **at ~** (at last) finalmente, alla fine; (lengthily) a lungo; **lengthen** vt allungare, prolungare ▷ vi allungarsi; **lengthways** adv per il lungo; **lengthy** adj molto lungo(-a)

lens [lenz] n lente f; (of camera) obiettivo

Lent [lent] n Quaresima

lent [lent] pt, pp of **lend**

lentil ['lentl] n lenticchia

Leo ['liːəu] n Leone m

leopard ['lepəd] n leopardo

leotard ['liːətɑːd] n calzamaglia

leprosy ['leprəsɪ] n lebbra

lesbian ['lezbɪən] n lesbica

less [les] adj, pron, adv meno ▷ prep ~ **tax/10% discount** meno tasse/il 10% di sconto; ~ **than ever** meno che mai; ~ **than half** meno della metà; ~ **and** ~ sempre meno; **the ~ he works ...** meno lavora ...; **lessen** ['lesn] vi diminuire, attenuarsi ▷ vt diminuire, ridurre; **lesser** ['lesə^r] adj minore, più piccolo(-a); **to a lesser extent** in grado or misura minore

lesson ['lesn] n lezione f; **to teach sb a ~** dare una lezione a qn

let [let] (pt, pp let) vt lasciare; (BRIT: lease) dare in affitto; **to ~ sb do sth** lasciar fare qc a qn, lasciare che qn faccia qc; **to ~ sb know sth** far sapere qc a qn; ~**'s go** andiamo; ~ **him come** lo lasci venire; **"to ~"** "affittasi"; **let down** vt (lower) abbassare; (dress) allungare; (hair) sciogliere; (tyre) sgonfiare; (disappoint) deludere; **let in** vt lasciare entrare; (visitor etc) far entrare; **let off** vt (allow to go) lasciare andare; (firework etc) far partire; **let out** vt lasciare uscire; (scream) emettere

lethal ['liːθl] adj letale, mortale

letter ['letə^r] n lettera; **letterbox** (BRIT) n buca delle lettere

lettuce ['letɪs] n lattuga, insalata

leukaemia [luː'kiːmɪə] (US leukemia) n leucemia

level ['levl] adj piatto(-a), piano(-a); orizzontale ▷ adv **to draw ~ with** mettersi alla pari di ▷ n livello ▷ vt livellare, spianare; **to be ~ with** essere alla pari di; **level crossing** (BRIT) n passaggio a livello

lever ['liːvə^r] n leva; **leverage** n leverage **(on** or **with)** forza (su); (fig) ascendente m (su)

levy ['levɪ] n tassa, imposta ▷ vt imporre

liability [laɪə'bɪlətɪ] n responsabilità f inv; (handicap) peso

liable ['laɪəbl] adj (subject): ~ **to**

soggetto(-a) a; passibile di; (*responsible*):
~ for responsabile (di); (*likely*): **~ to do**
propenso(-a) a fare
liaise [lɪ'eɪz] *vi* **to ~ (with)** mantenere i
contatti (con)
liar ['laɪə'] *n* bugiardo(-a)
liberal ['lɪbərl] *adj* liberale;
(*generous*): **to be ~ with** distribuire
liberalmente; **Liberal Democrat** *n*
liberaldemocratico(-a)
liberate ['lɪbəreɪt] *vt* liberare
liberation [lɪbə'reɪʃən] *n* liberazione *f*
liberty ['lɪbətɪ] *n* libertà *f inv*; **at ~** (*criminal*)
in libertà; **at ~ to do** libero(-a) di fare
Libra ['li:brə] *n* Bilancia
librarian [laɪ'brɛərɪən] *n* bibliotecario(-a)
library ['laɪbrərɪ] *n* biblioteca
Libya ['lɪbɪə] *n* Libia
lice [laɪs] *npl of* **louse**
licence ['laɪsns] (*US* **license**) *n*
autorizzazione *f*, permesso; (*Comm*)
licenza; (*Radio, TV*) canone *m*,
abbonamento; (*also*: **driving ~**: *US*: *also*:
driver's license) patente *f* di guida;
(*excessive freedom*) licenza
license ['laɪsns] *n* (*US*) = **licence** ▷ *vt* dare
una licenza a; **licensed** *adj* (*for alcohol*) che
ha la licenza di vendere bibite alcoliche;
license plate (*esp US*) *n* (*Aut*) targa
(automobilistica); **licensing hours** (*BRIT*)
npl orario d'apertura (*di un pub*)
lick [lɪk] *vt* leccare; (*inf: defeat*) stracciare;
to ~ one's lips (*fig*) leccarsi i baffi
lid [lɪd] *n* coperchio; (*eyelid*) palpebra
lie [laɪ] (*pt* **lay**, *pp* **lain**) *vi* (*rest*) giacere, star
disteso(-a); (*of object: be situated*) trovarsi,
essere; (*tell lies*: *pt*, *pp* **lied**) mentire, dire
bugie ▷ *n* bugia, menzogna; **to ~ low** (*fig*)
latitare; **lie about** *or* **around** *vi* (*things*)
essere in giro; (*person*) bighellonare; **lie
down** *vi* stendersi, sdraiarsi
Liechtenstein ['lɪktənstaɪn] *n*
Liechtenstein *m*
lie-in ['laɪɪn] (*BRIT*) *n* **to have a ~** rimanere
a letto
lieutenant [lɛf'tɛnənt, (*US*) lu:'tɛnənt] *n*
tenente *m*
life [laɪf] (*pl* **lives**) *n* vita ▷ *cpd* di vita; della
vita; a vita; **to come to ~** rianimarsi; **life
assurance** (*BRIT*) *n* = **life insurance**;
lifeboat *n* scialuppa di salvataggio;
lifeguard *n* bagnino; **life insurance**
n assicurazione *f* sulla vita; **life jacket**
n giubbotto di salvataggio; **lifelike**
adj verosimile; rassomigliante; **life
preserver** [-prɪ'zɜ:və'] (*US*) *n* salvagente
m; giubbotto di salvataggio; **life
sentence** *n* ergastolo; **lifestyle** *n* stile *m*
di vita; **lifetime** *n* **in his lifetime** durante

la sua vita; **once in a lifetime** una volta
nella vita

lift [lɪft] *vt* sollevare; (*ban, rule*) levare ▷ *vi*
(*fog*) alzarsi ▷ *n* (*BRIT: elevator*) ascensore
m; **to give sb a ~** (*BRIT*) dare un passaggio
a qn; **can you give me a ~ to the station?**
può darmi un passaggio fino alla stazione?;
lift up *vt* sollevare, alzare; **lift-off** *n*
decollo
light [laɪt] (*pt*, *pp* **lighted** *or* **lit**) *n* luce *f*,
lume *m*; (*daylight*) luce *f*, giorno; (*lamp*)
lampada; (*Aut: rear light*) luce *f* di posizione;
(: *headlamp*) fanale *m*; (*for cigarette etc*):
have you got a ~? ha da accendere?;
~s *npl* (*Aut: traffic lights*) semaforo *sg*
(*candle, cigarette, fire*) accendere; (*room*):
to be lit by essere illuminato(-a) da *adj*
(*room, colour*) chiaro(-a); (*not heavy, also*
fig) leggero(-a); **to come to ~** venire alla
luce, emergere; **light up** *vi* illuminarsi
▷ *vt* illuminare; **light bulb** *n* lampadina;
lighten *vt* (*make less heavy*) alleggerire;
lighter *n* (*also: cigarette lighter*)
accendino; **light-hearted** *adj* gioioso(-a),
gaio(-a); **lighthouse** *n* faro; **lighting** *n*
illuminazione *f*; **lightly** *adv* leggermente;
to get off lightly cavarsela a buon
mercato
lightning ['laɪtnɪŋ] *n* lampo, fulmine *m*
lightweight ['laɪtweɪt] *adj* (*suit*)
leggero(-a) ▷ *n* (*Boxing*) peso leggero
like [laɪk] *vt* (*person*) volere bene a;
(*activity, object, food*): **I ~ swimming/
that book/chocolate** mi piace
nuotare/quel libro/il cioccolato ▷ *prep*
come ▷ *adj* simile, uguale ▷ *n* **the ~**
uno(-a) uguale; **his ~s and dis~s** i suoi
gusti; **I would ~, I'd ~** mi piacerebbe,
vorrei; **would you ~ a coffee?**
gradirebbe un caffè?; **to be/look ~**
sb/sth somigliare a qn/qc; **what does**
it look/taste ~? che aspetto/gusto ha?;
what does it sound ~? come fa?; **that's**
just ~ him è proprio da lui; **do it ~ this**
fallo così; **it is nothing ~ ...** non è affatto
come ...; **likeable** *adj* simpatico(-a)
likelihood ['laɪklɪhud] *n* probabilità
likely ['laɪklɪ] *adj* probabile; plausibile;
he's ~ to leave probabilmente partirà, è
probabile che parta; **not ~!** neanche per
sogno!
likewise ['laɪkwaɪz] *adv* similmente, nello
stesso modo
liking ['laɪkɪŋ] *n* **~ (for)** debole *m* (per); **to**
be to sb's ~ piacere a qn
lilac ['laɪlək] *n* lilla *m inv*
Lilo® ['laɪləu] *n* materassino gonfiabile
lily ['lɪlɪ] *n* giglio
limb [lɪm] *n* arto

limbo ['lɪmbəʊ] *n* **to be in ~** (*fig*) essere lasciato(-a) nel dimenticatoio

lime [laɪm] *n* (*tree*) tiglio; (*fruit*) limetta; (*Geo*) calce *f*

limelight ['laɪmlaɪt] *n* **in the ~** (*fig*) alla ribalta, in vista

limestone ['laɪmstəʊn] *n* pietra calcarea; (*Geo*) calcare *m*

limit ['lɪmɪt] *n* limite *m* ▷ *vt* limitare; **limited** *adj* limitato(-a), ristretto(-a); **to be limited to** limitarsi a

limousine ['lɪməziːn] *n* limousine *f inv*

limp [lɪmp] *n* **to have a ~** zoppicare ▷ *vi* zoppicare ▷ *adj* floscio(-a), flaccido(-a)

line [laɪn] *n* linea; (*rope*) corda; (*for fishing*) lenza; (*wire*) filo; (*of poem*) verso; (*row, series*) fila, riga; coda; (*on face*) ruga ▷ *vt* (*clothes*): **to ~ (with)** foderare (di); (*box*): **to ~ (with)** rivestire *or* foderare (di); (*trees, crowd*) fiancheggiare; **~ of business** settore *m or* ramo d'attività; **in ~ with** in linea con; **line up** *vi* allinearsi, mettersi in fila ▷ *vt* mettere in fila; (*event, celebration*) preparare

linear ['lɪnɪəʳ] *adj* lineare

linen ['lɪnɪn] *n* biancheria, panni *mpl*; (*cloth*) tela di lino

liner ['laɪnəʳ] *n* nave *f* di linea; (*for bin*) sacchetto

line-up ['laɪnʌp] *n* allineamento, fila; (*Sport*) formazione *f* di gioco

linger ['lɪŋgəʳ] *vi* attardarsi; indugiare; (*smell, tradition*) persistere

lingerie ['lænʒəriː] *n* biancheria intima femminile

linguist ['lɪŋgwɪst] *n* linguista *m/f*; poliglotta *m/f*; **linguistic** *adj* linguistico(-a)

lining ['laɪnɪŋ] *n* fodera

link [lɪŋk] *n* (*of a chain*) anello; (*relationship*) legame *m*; (*connection*) collegamento ▷ *vt* collegare, unire, congiungere; (*associate*): **to ~ with** *or* **to** collegare a; **~s** *npl* (*Golf*) pista *or* terreno da golf; **link up** *vt* collegare, unire ▷ *vi* riunirsi; associarsi

lion ['laɪən] *n* leone *m*; **lioness** *n* leonessa

lip [lɪp] *n* labbro; (*of cup etc*) orlo; **lip-read** *vi* leggere sulle labbra; **lip salve** [-sælv] *n* burro di cacao; **lipstick** *n* rossetto

liqueur [lɪˈkjuəʳ] *n* liquore *m*

liquid ['lɪkwɪd] *n* liquido ▷ *adj* liquido(-a); **liquidizer** *n* frullatore *m* (a brocca)

liquor ['lɪkəʳ] *n* alcool *m*; **liquor store** (*us*) *n* negozio di liquori

Lisbon ['lɪzbən] *n* Lisbona

lisp [lɪsp] *n* pronuncia blesa della "s"

list [lɪst] *n* lista, elenco ▷ *vt* (*write down*) mettere in lista; fare una lista di; (*enumerate*) elencare

listen ['lɪsn] *vi* ascoltare; **to ~ to** ascoltare; **listener** *n* ascoltatore(-trice)

lit [lɪt] *pt, pp of* **light**

liter ['liːtəʳ] (*us*) *n* = **litre**

literacy ['lɪtərəsɪ] *n* il sapere leggere e scrivere

literal ['lɪtərl] *adj* letterale; **literally** *adv* alla lettera, letteralmente

literary ['lɪtərərɪ] *adj* letterario(-a)

literate ['lɪtərət] *adj* che sa leggere e scrivere

literature ['lɪtərɪtʃəʳ] *n* letteratura; (*brochures etc*) materiale *m*

litre ['liːtəʳ] (*us* **liter**) *n* litro

litter ['lɪtəʳ] *n* (*rubbish*) rifiuti *mpl*; (*young animals*) figliata; **litter bin** (*brit*) *n* cestino per rifiuti; **littered** *adj* **littered with** coperto(-a) di

little ['lɪtl] *adj* (*small*) piccolo(-a); (*not much*) poco(-a) ▷ *adv* poco; **a ~** un po' (di); **a ~ bit** un pochino; **~ by ~** a poco a poco; **little finger** *n* mignolo

live¹ [lɪv] *vi* vivere; (*reside*) vivere, abitare; **where do you ~?** dove abita?; **live together** *vi* vivere insieme, convivere; **live up to** *vt fus* tener fede a, non venir meno a

live² [laɪv] *adj* (*animal*) vivo(-a); (*wire*) sotto tensione; (*bullet, missile*) inesploso(-a); (*broadcast*) diretto(-a); (*performance*) dal vivo

livelihood ['laɪvlɪhʊd] *n* mezzi *mpl* di sostentamento

lively ['laɪvlɪ] *adj* vivace, vivo(-a)

liven up ['laɪvnʌp] *vt* (*discussion, evening*) animare ▷ *vi* ravvivarsi

liver ['lɪvəʳ] *n* fegato

lives [laɪvz] *npl of* **life**

livestock ['laɪvstɔk] *n* bestiame *m*

living ['lɪvɪŋ] *adj* vivo(-a), vivente ▷ *n* **to earn** *or* **make a ~** guadagnarsi la vita; **living room** *n* soggiorno

lizard ['lɪzəd] *n* lucertola

load [ləʊd] *n* (*weight*) peso; (*thing carried*) carico ▷ *vt* (*also:* **~ up**): **to ~ (with)** (*lorry, ship*) caricare (di); (*gun, camera, Comput*) caricare (con); **a ~ of**, **~s of** (*fig*) un sacco di; **loaded** *adj* (*vehicle*): **loaded (with)** carico(-a) (di); (*question*) capzioso(-a); (*inf: rich*) carico(-a) di soldi

loaf [ləʊf] (*pl* **loaves**) *n* pane *m*, pagnotta

loan [ləʊn] *n* prestito ▷ *vt* dare in prestito; **on ~** in prestito

loathe [ləʊð] *vt* detestare, aborrire

loaves [ləʊvz] *npl of* **loaf**

lobby ['lɔbɪ] *n* atrio, vestibolo; (*Pol: pressure group*) gruppo di pressione ▷ *vt* fare pressione su

lobster ['lɔbstəʳ] n aragosta
local ['ləukl] adj locale ▷ n (BRIT: pub)
≈ bar m inv all'angolo; **the ~s** npl (local
inhabitants) la gente della zona; **local
anaesthetic** n anestesia locale; **local
authority** n ente m locale; **local
government** n amministrazione f locale;
locally ['ləukəlı] adv da queste parti; nel
vicinato
locate [ləu'keɪt] vt (find) trovare; (situate)
collocare; situare
location [ləu'keɪʃən] n posizione f; **on ~**
(Cinema) all'esterno
loch [lɔx] n lago
lock [lɔk] n (of door, box) serratura; (of
canal) chiusa; (of hair) ciocca, riccio ▷ vt
(with key) chiudere a chiave ▷ vi (door etc)
chiudersi; (wheels) bloccarsi, incepparsi;
lock in vt chiudere dentro (a chiave);
lock out vt chiudere fuori; **lock up** vt
(criminal, mental patient) rinchiudere;
(house) chiudere (a chiave) ▷ vi chiudere
tutto (a chiave)
locker ['lɔkəʳ] n armadietto; **locker-room**
(us) n (Sport) spogliatoio
locksmith ['lɔksmɪθ] n magnano
locomotive [ləukə'məutɪv] n
locomotiva
lodge [lɔdʒ] n casetta, portineria; (hunting
lodge) casino di caccia ▷ vi (person): **to
~ (with)** essere a pensione (presso or
da); (bullet etc) conficcarsi ▷ vt (appeal
etc) presentare, fare; **to ~ a complaint**
presentare un reclamo; **lodger** n
affittuario(-a); (with room and meals)
pensionante m/f
lodging ['lɔdʒɪŋ] n alloggio; see also
board
loft [lɔft] n solaio, soffitta
log [lɔg] n (of wood) ceppo; (also: ~book:
Naut, Aviat) diario di bordo; (Aut) libretto
di circolazione ▷ vt registrare; **log in** vi
(Comput) aprire una sessione (con codice
di riconoscimento); **log off** vi (Comput)
terminare una sessione
logic ['lɔdʒɪk] n logica; **logical** adj
logico(-a)
logo ['ləugəu] n logo m inv
lollipop ['lɔlɪpɔp] n lecca lecca m inv
lolly ['lɔlɪ] (inf) n lecca lecca m inv; (also: **ice
~**) ghiacciolo; (money) grana
London ['lʌndən] n Londra; **Londoner** n
londinese m/f
lone [ləun] adj solitario(-a)
loneliness ['ləunlınıs] n solitudine f,
isolamento
lonely ['ləunlı] adj solo(-a); solitario(-a),
isolato(-a)
long [lɔŋ] adj lungo(-a) ▷ adv a lungo,

per molto tempo ▷ vi **to ~ for sth/to do**
desiderare qc/di fare, non veder l'ora di
aver qc/di fare; **so** or **as ~ as** (while) finché;
(provided that) sempre che + sub; **don't be
~!** fai presto!; **how ~ is this river/course?**
quanto è lungo questo fiume/corso?;
6 metres ~ lungo 6 metri; **6 months ~**
che dura 6 mesi, di 6 mesi; **all night ~**
tutta la notte; **he no ~er comes** non
viene più; **~ before** molto tempo prima;
before ~ (+ future) presto, fra poco; (+ past)
poco tempo dopo; **at ~ last** finalmente;
long-distance adj (race) di fondo; (call)
interurbano(-a); **long-haul** ['lɔŋ hɔːl] adj
(flight) a lunga percorrenza inv; **longing** n
desiderio, voglia, brama
longitude ['lɔŋgɪtjuːd] n longitudine f
long: **long jump** n salto in lungo; **long-
life** adj (milk) a lunga conservazione;
(batteries) di lunga durata; **long-sighted**
adj presbite; **long-standing** adj di
vecchia data; **long-term** adj a lungo
termine
loo [luː] (BRIT: inf) n W.C. m inv, cesso
look [luk] vi guardare; (seem) sembrare,
parere; (building etc): **to ~ south/on
to the sea** dare a sud/sul mare ▷ n
sguardo; (appearance) aspetto, aria;
~s npl (good looks) bellezza; **look after**
vt fus occuparsi di, prendere cura di;
(keep an eye on) guardare, badare a; **look
around** vi guardarsi intorno; **look at** vt
fus guardare; **look back** vi **to ~ back on**
(event etc) ripensare a; **look down on** vt
fus (fig) guardare dall'alto, disprezzare;
look for vt fus cercare; **we're ~ing for a
hotel/restaurant** stiamo cercando un
albergo/ristorante; **look forward to** vt fus
non veder l'ora di; (in letters): **we ~ forward
to hearing from you** in attesa di una
vostra gentile risposta; **look into** vt fus
esaminare; **look out** vi (beware): **to ~ out
(for)** stare in guardia (per); **look out for** vt
fus cercare; **look round** vi (turn) girarsi,
voltarsi; (in shop) dare un'occhiata; **look
through** vt fus (papers, book) scorrere;
(telescope) guardare attraverso; **look up**
vi alzare gli occhi; (improve) migliorare
▷ vt (word) cercare; (friend) andare a
trovare; **look up to** vt fus avere rispetto
per; **lookout** n posto d'osservazione;
guardia; **to be on the lookout (for)** stare
in guardia (per)
loom [luːm] n telaio ▷ vi (also: **~ up**)
apparire minaccioso(-a); (event) essere
imminente
loony ['luːnɪ] (inf) n pazzo(-a)
loop [luːp] n cappio ▷ vt **to ~ sth round
sth** passare qc intorno a qc; **loophole** n

via d'uscita; scappatoia

loose [lu:s] *adj* (*knot*) sciolto(-a); (*screw*) allentato(-a); (*stone*) cadente; (*clothes*) ampio(-a), largo(-a); (*animal*) in libertà, scappato(-a); (*life, morals*) dissoluto(-a) ▷ *n* **to be on the ~** essere in libertà; **loosely** *adv* senza stringere; approssimativamente; **loosen** *vt* sciogliere; (*belt etc*) allentare

loot [lu:t] *n* bottino ▷ *vt* saccheggiare

lop-sided ['lɔp'saɪdɪd] *adj* non equilibrato(-a), asimmetrico(-a)

lord [lɔ:d] *n* signore *m*; **L~ Smith** lord Smith; **the L~** il Signore; **good L~!** buon Dio!; **the (House of) L~s** (BRIT) la Camera dei Lord

lorry ['lɔrɪ] (BRIT) *n* camion *m inv*; **lorry driver** (BRIT) *n* camionista *m*

lose [lu:z] (*pt, pp* **lost**) *vt* perdere ▷ *vi* perdere; **I've lost my wallet/passport** ho perso il portafoglio/passaporto; **to ~ (time)** (*clock*) ritardare; **lose out** *vi* rimetterci; **loser** *n* perdente *m/f*

loss [lɔs] *n* perdita; **to be at a ~** essere perplesso(-a)

lost [lɔst] *pt, pp* of **lose** ▷ *adj* perduto(-a); **I'm ~** mi sono perso; **lost property** (US **lost and found**) *n* oggetti *mpl* smarriti

lot [lɔt] *n* (*at auctions*) lotto; (*destiny*) destino, sorte *f*; **the ~** tutto(-a) quanto(-a); tutti(-e) quanti(-e); **a ~** molto; **a ~ of** una gran quantità di, un sacco di; **~s of** molto(-i); **to draw ~s (for sth)** tirare a sorte (per qc)

lotion ['ləuʃən] *n* lozione *f*

lottery ['lɔtərɪ] *n* lotteria

loud [laud] *adj* forte, alto(-a); (*gaudy*) vistoso(-a), sgargiante ▷ *adv* (*speak etc*) forte; **out ~** (*read etc*) ad alta voce; **loudly** *adv* fortemente, ad alta voce; **loudspeaker** *n* altoparlante *m*

lounge [laundʒ] *n* salotto, soggiorno; (*at airport, station*) sala d'attesa; (BRIT: *also:* **~ bar**) bar *m inv* con servizio a tavolino ▷ *vi* oziare

louse [laus] (*pl* **lice**) *n* pidocchio

lousy ['lauzɪ] (*inf*) *adj* orrendo(-a), schifoso(-a); **to feel ~** stare da cani

love [lʌv] *n* amore *m* ▷ *vt* amare; voler bene a; **to ~ to do: I ~ to do** mi piace fare; **to be/fall in ~ with** essere innamorato(-a)/innamorarsi di; **to make ~** fare l'amore; **"15 ~"** (*Tennis*) "15 a zero"; **love affair** *n* relazione *f*; **love life** *n* vita sentimentale

lovely ['lʌvlɪ] *adj* bello(-a); (*delicious: smell, meal*) buono(-a)

lover ['lʌvəʳ] *n* amante *m/f*; (*person in love*) innamorato(-a); (*amateur*): **a ~ of** un(-un')

amante di; un(-un') appassionato(-a) di

loving ['lʌvɪŋ] *adj* affettuoso(-a)

low [ləu] *adj* basso(-a) ▷ *adv* in basso ▷ *n* (*Meteor*) depressione *f*; **to be ~ on** (*supplies etc*) avere scarsità di; **to feel ~** sentirsi giù; **low-alcohol** *adj* a basso contenuto alcolico; **low-calorie** *adj* a basso contenuto calorico

lower ['ləuəʳ] *adj* (*bottom: of 2 things*) più basso; (*less important*) meno importante ▷ *vt* calare; (*prices, eyes, voice*) abbassare

low-fat ['ləu'fæt] *adj* magro(-a)

loyal ['lɔɪəl] *adj* fedele, leale; **loyalty** *n* fedeltà, lealtà; **loyalty card** *n* carta che offre sconti a clienti abituali

L.P. *n abbr* = **long-playing record**

L-plates ['ɛlpleɪts] (BRIT) *npl* contrassegno P principiante

Lt *abbr* (= *lieutenant*) Ten.

Ltd *abbr* (= *limited*) ≈ S.r.l.

luck [lʌk] *n* fortuna, sorte *f*; **bad ~** sfortuna, mala sorte; **good ~!** buona fortuna!; **luckily** *adv* fortunatamente, per fortuna; **lucky** *adj* fortunato(-a); (*number etc*) che porta fortuna

lucrative ['lu:krətɪv] *adj* lucrativo(-a), lucroso(-a), profittevole

ludicrous ['lu:dɪkrəs] *adj* ridicolo(-a)

luggage ['lʌgɪdʒ] *n* bagagli *mpl*; **our ~ hasn't arrived** i nostri bagagli non sono arrivati; **luggage rack** *n* portabagagli *m inv*

lukewarm ['lu:kwɔ:m] *adj* tiepido(-a)

lull [lʌl] *n* intervallo di calma ▷ *vt* **to ~ sb to sleep** cullare qn finché si addormenta

lullaby ['lʌləbaɪ] *n* ninnananna

lumber ['lʌmbəʳ] *n* (*wood*) legname *m*; (*junk*) roba vecchia

luminous ['lu:mɪnəs] *adj* luminoso(-a)

lump [lʌmp] *n* pezzo; (*in sauce*) grumo; (*swelling*) gonfiore *m*; (*also:* **sugar ~**) zolletta ▷ *vt* (*also:* **~ together**) riunire, mettere insieme; **lump sum** *n* somma globale; **lumpy** *adj* (*sauce*) pieno(-a) di grumi; (*bed*) bitorzoluto(-a)

lunatic ['lu:nətɪk] *adj* pazzo(-a), matto(-a)

lunch [lʌntʃ] *n* pranzo, colazione *f*; **lunch break** *n* intervallo del pranzo; **lunch time** *n* ora di pranzo

lung [lʌŋ] *n* polmone *m*

lure [luəʳ] *n* richiamo; lusinga ▷ *vt* attirare (con l'inganno)

lurk [lə:k] *vi* stare in agguato

lush [lʌʃ] *adj* lussureggiante

lust [lʌst] *n* lussuria; cupidigia; desiderio; (*fig*): **~ for** sete *f* di

Luxembourg ['lʌksəmbə:g] *n* (*state*) Lussemburgo *m*; (*city*) Lussemburgo *f*

luxurious [lʌɡˈzjuərɪəs] *adj* sontuoso(-a), di lusso
luxury [ˈlʌkʃərɪ] *n* lusso ▷ *cpd* di lusso
▌ Be careful not to translate *luxury* by the Italian word *lussuria*.
Lycra® [ˈlaɪkrə] *n* lycra® *f inv*
lying [ˈlaɪɪŋ] *n* bugie *fpl*, menzogne *fpl* ▷ *adj* bugiardo(-a)
lyrics [ˈlɪrɪks] *npl* (*of song*) parole *fpl*

m. *abbr* = **metre**; **mile**; **million**
M.A. *abbr* = **Master of Arts**
ma (*inf*) [mɑː] *n* mamma
mac [mæk] (*BRIT*) *n* impermeabile *m*
macaroni [mækəˈrəʊnɪ] *n* maccheroni *mpl*
Macedonia [mæsɪˈdəʊnɪə] *n* Macedonia;
Macedone [mæsɪˈdəʊnɪən] *adj* macedone ▷ *n* macedone *m/f*; (*Ling*) macedone *m*
machine [məˈʃiːn] *n* macchina ▷ *vt* (*Tech*) lavorare a macchina; (*dress etc*) cucire a macchina; **machine gun** *n* mitragliatrice *f*; **machinery** *n* macchinario, macchine *fpl*; (*fig*) macchina; **machine washable** *adj* lavabile in lavatrice
macho [ˈmætʃəʊ] *adj* macho *inv*
mackerel [ˈmækrl] *n inv* sgombro
mackintosh [ˈmækɪntɔʃ] (*BRIT*) *n* impermeabile *m*
mad [mæd] *adj* matto(-a), pazzo(-a); (*foolish*) sciocco(-a); (*angry*) furioso(-a); **to be ~ about** (*keen*) andare pazzo(-a) per
Madagascar [mædəˈɡæskəʳ] *n* Madagascar *m*
madam [ˈmædəm] *n* signora
mad cow disease *n* encefalite *f* bovina spongiforme
made [meɪd] *pt, pp of* **make**; **made-to-measure** (*BRIT*) *adj* fatto(-a) su

misura; **made-up** ['meɪdʌp] adj (story) inventato(-a)

madly ['mædlɪ] adv follemente

madman ['mædmən] (irreg) n pazzo, alienato

madness ['mædnɪs] n pazzia

Madrid [mə'drɪd] n Madrid f

Mafia ['mæfɪə] n mafia f

mag [mæg] n abbr (BRIT inf) = **magazine** (Press)

magazine [mægə'ziːn] n (Press) rivista; (Radio, TV) rubrica

Be careful not to translate *magazine* by the Italian word *magazzino*.

maggot ['mægət] n baco, verme m

magic ['mædʒɪk] n magia ▷ adj magico(-a); **magical** adj magico(-a); **magician** [mə'dʒɪʃən] n mago(-a)

magistrate ['mædʒɪstreɪt] n magistrato; giudice m/f

magnet ['mægnɪt] n magnete m, calamita; **magnetic** [-'nɛtɪk] adj magnetico(-a)

magnificent [mæg'nɪfɪsnt] adj magnifico(-a)

magnify ['mægnɪfaɪ] vt ingrandire; **magnifying glass** n lente f d'ingrandimento

magpie ['mægpaɪ] n gazza

mahogany [mə'hɔgənɪ] n mogano

maid [meɪd] n domestica; (in hotel) cameriera

maiden name ['meɪdn-] n nome m da nubile or da ragazza

mail [meɪl] n posta ▷ vt spedire (per posta); **mailbox** (US) n cassetta delle lettere; **mailing list** n elenco d'indirizzi; **mailman** (irreg: US) n portalettere m inv, postino; **mail-order** n vendita (or acquisto) per corrispondenza

main [meɪn] adj principale ▷ n (pipe) conduttura principale; **main course** n (Culin) piatto principale, piatto forte; **mainland** n continente m; **mainly** adv principalmente, soprattutto; **main road** n strada principale; **mainstream** n (fig) corrente f principale; **main street** n strada principale

maintain [meɪn'teɪn] vt mantenere; (affirm) sostenere; **maintenance** ['meɪntənəns] n manutenzione f; (alimony) alimenti mpl

maisonette [meɪzə'nɛt] n (BRIT) appartamento a due piani

maize [meɪz] n granturco, mais m

majesty ['mædʒɪstɪ] n maestà f inv

major ['meɪdʒəʳ] n (Mil) maggiore m ▷ adj (greater, Mus) maggiore; (in importance) principale, importante

Majorca [mə'jɔːkə] n Maiorca

majority [mə'dʒɔrɪtɪ] n maggioranza

make [meɪk] (pt, pp **made**) vt fare; (manufacture) fare, fabbricare; (cause to be): **to ~ sb sad** etc rendere qn triste etc; (force): **to ~ sb do sth** costringere qn a fare qc, far fare qc a qn; (equal): **2 and 2 ~ 4** 2 più 2 fa 4 ▷ n fabbricazione f; (brand) marca; **to ~ a fool of sb** far fare a qn la figura dello scemo; **to ~ a profit** realizzare un profitto; **to ~ a loss** subire una perdita; **to ~ it** (arrive) arrivare; (achieve sth) farcela; **what time do you ~ it?** che ora fai?; **to ~ do with** arrangiarsi con; **make off** vi svignarsela; **make out** vt (write out) scrivere; (: cheque) emettere; (understand) capire; (see) distinguere; (: numbers) decifrare; **make up** vt (constitute) formare; (invent) inventare; (parcel) fare ▷ vi conciliarsi; (with cosmetics) truccarsi; **make up for** vt fus compensare; ricuperare; **makeover** ['meɪkəuvəʳ] n (change of image) cambiamento di immagine; (of room, house) trasformazione f; **maker** n (of programme etc) creatore(-trice); (manufacturer) fabbricante m; **makeshift** adj improvvisato(-a); **make-up** n trucco

making ['meɪkɪŋ] n (fig): **in the ~** in formazione; **to have the ~s of** (actor, athlete etc) avere la stoffa di

malaria [mə'lɛərɪə] n malaria

Malaysia [mə'leɪzɪə] n Malaysia

male [meɪl] n (Biol) maschio ▷ adj maschile; maschio(-a)

malicious [mə'lɪʃəs] adj malevolo(-a); (Law) doloso(-a)

malignant [mə'lɪgnənt] adj (Med) maligno(-a)

mall [mɔːl] n (also: **shopping ~**) centro commerciale

mallet ['mælɪt] n maglio

malnutrition [mælnjuː'trɪʃən] n denutrizione f

malpractice [mæl'præktɪs] n prevaricazione f; negligenza

malt [mɔːlt] n malto

Malta ['mɔːltə] n Malta; **Maltese** [mɔːl'tiːz] adj, n (pl inv) maltese (m/f); (Ling) maltese m

mammal ['mæml] n mammifero

mammoth ['mæməθ] adj enorme, gigantesco(-a)

man [mæn] (pl **men**) n uomo ▷ vt fornire d'uomini; stare a; **an old ~** un vecchio; **~ and wife** marito e moglie

manage ['mænɪdʒ] vi farcela ▷ vt (be in charge of) occuparsi di; gestire; **to ~ to do sth** riuscire a far qc; **manageable** adj maneggevole; fattibile; **management** n

amministrazione f, direzione f; **manager**
n direttore m; (of shop, restaurant)
gerente m; (of artist, Sport) manager m
inv; **manageress** [-ə'rɛs] n direttrice
f; gerente f; **managerial** [-ə'dʒɪərɪəl]
adj dirigenziale; **managing director** n
amministratore m delegato
mandarin ['mændərɪn] n (person, fruit)
mandarino
mandate ['mændeɪt] n mandato
mandatory ['mændətərɪ] adj
obbligatorio(-a), ingiuntivo(-a)
mane [meɪn] n criniera
mangetout ['mɔnʒ'tu:] n pisello dolce,
taccola
mango ['mæŋgəu] (pl **mangoes**) n mango
man: **manhole** ['mænhəul] n botola
stradale; **manhood** ['mænhud] n età
virile; virilità
mania ['meɪnɪə] n mania; **maniac**
['meɪnɪæk] n maniaco(-a)
manic ['mænɪk] adj (behaviour, activity)
maniacale
manicure ['mænɪkjuəʳ] n manicure f inv
manifest ['mænɪfɛst] vt manifestare ▷ adj
manifesto(-a), palese
manifesto [mænɪ'fɛstəu] n manifesto
manipulate [mə'nɪpjuleɪt] vt manipolare
man: **mankind** [mæn'kaɪnd] n umanità,
genere m umano; **manly** ['mænlɪ] adj
virile; coraggioso(-a); **man-made** adj
sintetico(-a); artificiale
manner ['mænəʳ] n maniera, modo;
(behaviour) modo di fare; (type, sort):
all ~ of things ogni genere di cosa;
~s npl (conduct) maniere fpl; **bad ~s**
maleducazione f
manoeuvre ['mænpauəʳ] (us **maneuver**)
vt manovrare ▷ vi far manovre ▷ n
manovra
manpower ['mænpauəʳ] n manodopera
mansion ['mænʃən] n casa signorile
manslaughter ['mænslɔ:təʳ] n omicidio
preterintenzionale
mantelpiece ['mæntlpi:s] n mensola del
caminetto
manual ['mænjuəl] adj manuale ▷ n
manuale m
manufacture [mænju'fæktʃəʳ]
vt fabbricare ▷ n fabbricazione
f, manifattura; **manufacturer** n
fabbricante m
manure [mə'njuəʳ] n concime m
manuscript ['mænjuskrɪpt] n
manoscritto
many ['mɛnɪ] adj molti(-e) ▷ pron
molti(-e); **a great ~** moltissimi(-e), un gran
numero (di); **~ a time** molte volte
map [mæp] n carta (geografica); (of city)

cartina; **can you show it to me on the ~?**
può indicarmelo sulla cartina?
maple ['meɪpl] n acero
mar [mɑːʳ] vt sciupare
Mar. abbr (= March) mar.
marathon ['mærəθən] n maratona
marble ['mɑːbl] n marmo; (toy) pallina,
bilia
March [mɑːtʃ] n marzo
march [mɑːtʃ] vi marciare; sfilare ▷ n
marcia
mare [mɛəʳ] n giumenta
margarine [mɑːdʒə'riːn] n margarina
margin ['mɑːdʒɪn] n margine m; **marginal**
adj marginale; **marginal seat** (Pol)
seggio elettorale ottenuto con una stretta
maggioranza; **marginally** adv (bigger,
better) lievemente, di poco; (different) un po'
marigold ['mærɪgəuld] n calendola
marijuana [mærɪ'wɑːnə] n marijuana
marina [mə'riːnə] n marina
marinade n [mærɪ'neɪd] marinata ▷ vt
['mærɪneɪd] = **marinate**
marinate ['mærɪneɪt] vt marinare
marine [mə'riːn] adj (animal, plant)
marino(-a); (forces, engineering)
marittimo(-a) ▷ n (brit) fante m di marina;
(us) marine m inv
marital ['mærɪtl] adj maritale, coniugale;
marital status n stato civile
maritime ['mærɪtaɪm] adj marittimo(-a)
marjoram ['mɑːdʒərəm] n maggiorana
mark [mɑːk] n segno; (stain) macchia; (of
skid etc) traccia; (brit Scol) voto; (Sport)
bersaglio; (currency) marco ▷ vt segnare;
(stain) macchiare; (indicate) indicare; (brit
Scol) dare un voto a; correggere; **to ~ time**
segnare il passo; **marked** adj spiccato(-a),
chiaro(-a); **marker** n (sign) segno;
(bookmark) segnalibro
market ['mɑːkɪt] n mercato ▷ vt (Comm)
mettere in vendita; **marketing** n
marketing m; **marketplace** n (piazza del)
mercato; (world of trade) piazza, mercato;
market research n indagine f or ricerca
di mercato
marmalade ['mɑːməleɪd] n marmellata
d'arance
maroon [mə'ruːn] vt (also fig): **to be ~ed**
(in or **at)** essere abbandonato(-a) (in) ▷ adj
bordeaux inv
marquee [mɑː'kiː] n padiglione m
marriage ['mærɪdʒ] n matrimonio;
marriage certificate n certificato di
matrimonio
married ['mærɪd] adj sposato(-a); (life,
love) coniugale, matrimoniale
marrow ['mærəu] n midollo; (vegetable)
zucca

marry ['mærɪ] vt sposare, sposarsi con; (vicar, priest etc) dare in matrimonio ▷ vi (also: **get married**) sposarsi

Mars [mɑːz] n (planet) Marte m

marsh [mɑːʃ] n palude f

marshal ['mɑːʃl] n maresciallo; (us: fire) capo; (: police) capitano ▷ vt (thoughts, support) ordinare; (soldiers) adunare

martyr ['mɑːtəˈ] n martire m/f

marvel ['mɑːvl] n meraviglia ▷ vi to ~ **(at)** meravigliarsi (di); **marvellous** (us **marvelous**) adj meraviglioso(-a)

Marxism ['mɑːksɪzəm] n marxismo

Marxist ['mɑːksɪst] adj, n marxista m/f

marzipan ['mɑːzɪpæn] n marzapane m

mascara [mæs'kɑːrə] n mascara m

mascot ['mæskət] n mascotte f inv

masculine ['mæskjulɪn] adj maschile; (woman) mascolino(-a)

mash [mæʃ] vt passare, schiacciare; **mashed potatoes** npl purè m di patate

mask [mɑːsk] n maschera ▷ vt mascherare

mason ['meɪsn] n (also: **stone~**) scalpellino; (also: **free~**) massone m; **masonry** n muratura

mass [mæs] n moltitudine f, massa; (Physics) massa; (Rel) messa ▷ cpd di massa ▷ vi ammassarsi; **the ~es** npl (ordinary people) le masse; **~es of** (inf) una montagna di

massacre ['mæsəkəˈ] n massacro

massage ['mæsɑːʒ] n massaggio

massive ['mæsɪv] adj enorme, massiccio(-a)

mass media npl mass media mpl

mass-produce ['mæsprə'djuːs] vt produrre in serie

mast [mɑːst] n albero

master ['mɑːstəˈ] n padrone m; (Art etc, teacher: in primary school) maestro; (: in secondary school) professore m; (title for boys): **M~ X** Signorino X ▷ vt domare; (learn) imparare a fondo; (understand) conoscere a fondo; **mastermind** n mente f superiore ▷ vt essere il cervello di; **Master of Arts/Science** n Master m in/v in lettere/scienze; **masterpiece** n capolavoro

masturbate ['mæstəbeɪt] vi masturbare

mat [mæt] n stuoia; (also: **door~**) stoino, zerbino; (also: **table ~**) sottopiatto ▷ adj = **matt**

match [mætʃ] n fiammifero; (game) partita, incontro; (fig) uguale m/f; matrimonio; partito ▷ vt intonare; (go well with) andare benissimo con; (equal) uguagliare; (correspond to) corrispondere a; (pair: also: **~ up**) accoppiare ▷ vi combaciare; **to be a good ~** andare bene; **matchbox** n scatola per fiammiferi; **matching** adj ben assortito(-a)

mate [meɪt] n compagno(-a) di lavoro; (inf: friend) amico(-a); (animal) compagno(-a); (in merchant navy) secondo ▷ vi accoppiarsi

material [mə'tɪərɪəl] n (substance) materiale m, materia; (cloth) stoffa ▷ adj materiale; **~s** npl (equipment) materiali mpl

materialize [mə'tɪərɪəlaɪz] vi materializzarsi, realizzarsi

maternal [mə'tə:nl] adj materno(-a)

maternity [mə'tə:nɪtɪ] n maternità; **maternity hospital** n ≈ clinica ostetrica; **maternity leave** n congedo di maternità

math [mæθ] (us) n = **maths**

mathematical [mæθə'mætɪkl] adj matematico(-a)

mathematician [mæθəmə'tɪʃən] n matematico(-a)

mathematics [mæθə'mætɪks] n matematica

maths [mæθs] (us **math**) n matematica

matinée ['mætɪneɪ] n matinée f inv

matron ['meɪtrən] n (in hospital) capoinfermiera; (in school) infermiera

matt [mæt] adj opaco(-a)

matter ['mætəˈ] n questione f; (Physics) materia, sostanza; (content) contenuto; (Med: pus) pus m ▷ vi importare; **it doesn't ~** non importa; (I don't mind) non fa niente; **what's the ~?** che cosa c'è?; **no ~ what** qualsiasi cosa accada; **as a ~ of course** come cosa naturale; **as a ~ of fact** in verità; **~s** npl (affairs) questioni

mattress ['mætrɪs] n materasso

mature [mə'tjuəˈ] adj maturo(-a); (cheese) stagionato(-a) ▷ vi maturare; stagionare; **mature student** n studente universitario che ha più di 25 anni; **maturity** n maturità

maul [mɔːl] vt lacerare

mauve [məuv] adj malva inv

max. abbr = **maximum**

maximize ['mæksɪmaɪz] vt (profits etc) massimizzare; (chances) aumentare al massimo

maximum ['mæksɪməm] (pl **maxima**) adj massimo(-a) ▷ n massimo

May [meɪ] n maggio

may [meɪ] (conditional **might**) vi (indicating possibility): **he ~ come** può darsi che venga; (be allowed to): **~ I smoke?** posso fumare?; (wishes): **~ God bless you!** Dio la benedica!; **you ~ as well go** tanto vale che tu te ne vada

maybe ['meɪbiː] adv forse, può darsi; **~ he'll ...** può darsi che lui ... + sub, forse lui ...

May Day n il primo maggio

mayhem ['meɪhɛm] n cagnara

mayonnaise [meɪəˈneɪz] n maionese f

mayor [mɛəʳ] n sindaco; **mayoress** n sindaco (donna); moglie f del sindaco

maze [meɪz] n labirinto, dedalo

MD n abbr (= Doctor of Medicine) titolo di studio; (Comm) see **managing director**

me [miː] pron mi, m' + vowel or silent "h"; (stressed, after prep) me; **he heard me** mi ha or m'ha sentito; **give me a book** dammi (or mi dia) un libro; **it's me** sono io; **with me** con me; **without me** senza di me

meadow [ˈmɛdəu] n prato

meagre [ˈmiːgəʳ] (US **meager**) adj magro(-a)

meal [miːl] n pasto; (flour) farina; **mealtime** n l'ora di mangiare

mean [miːn] (pt, pp **meant**) adj (with money) avaro(-a), gretto(-a); (unkind) meschino(-a), maligno(-a); (shabby) misero(-a); (average) medio(-a) ▷ vt (signify) significare, voler dire; (intend): **to ~ to do** aver l'intenzione di fare ▷ n mezzo; (Math) media; **~s** npl (way, money) mezzi mpl; **by ~s of** per mezzo di; **by all ~s** ma certo, prego; **to be ~t for** essere destinato(-a) a; **do you ~ it?** dice sul serio?; **what do you ~?** che cosa vuol dire?

meaning [ˈmiːnɪŋ] n significato, senso; **meaningful** adj significativo(-a); **meaningless** adj senza senso

meant [mɛnt] pt, pp of **mean**

meantime [ˈmiːntaɪm] adv (also: **in the ~**) nel frattempo

meanwhile [ˈmiːnwaɪl] adv nel frattempo

measles [ˈmiːzlz] n morbillo

measure [ˈmɛʒəʳ] vt, vi misurare ▷ n misura; (also: **tape ~**) metro

measurement [ˈmɛʒəmənt] n (act) misurazione f; (measure) misura; **chest/hip ~** giro petto/fianchi; **to take sb's ~s** prendere le misure di qn

meat [miːt] n carne f; **I don't eat ~** non mangio carne; **cold ~** affettato; **meatball** n polpetta di carne

Mecca [ˈmɛkə] n (also fig) la Mecca

mechanic [mɪˈkænɪk] n meccanico; **can you send a ~?** può mandare un meccanico?; **mechanical** adj meccanico(-a)

mechanism [ˈmɛkənɪzəm] n meccanismo

medal [ˈmɛdl] n medaglia; **medallist** (US **medalist**) n (Sport): **to be a gold medallist** essere medaglia d'oro

meddle [ˈmɛdl] vi **to ~ in** immischiarsi in, mettere le mani in; **to ~ with** toccare

media [ˈmiːdɪə] npl media mpl

mediaeval [mɛdɪˈiːvl] adj = **medieval**

mediate [ˈmiːdɪeɪt] vi fare da mediatore(-trice)

medical [ˈmɛdɪkl] adj medico(-a) ▷ n visita medica; **medical certificate** n certificato medico

medicated [ˈmɛdɪkeɪtɪd] adj medicato(-a)

medication [mɛdɪˈkeɪʃən] n medicinali mpl, farmaci mpl

medicine [ˈmɛdsɪn] n medicina

medieval [mɛdɪˈiːvl] adj medievale

mediocre [miːdɪˈəukəʳ] adj mediocre

meditate [ˈmɛdɪteɪt] vi **to ~ (on)** meditare (su)

meditation [mɛdɪˈteɪʃən] n meditazione f

Mediterranean [mɛdɪtəˈreɪnɪən] adj mediterraneo(-a); **the ~ (Sea)** il (mare) Mediterraneo

medium [ˈmiːdɪəm] (pl media) adj medio(-a) ▷ n (means) mezzo; (pl mediums: person) medium m inv; **medium-sized** adj (tin etc) di grandezza media; (clothes) di taglia media; **medium wave** n onde fpl medie

meek [miːk] adj dolce, umile

meet [miːt] (pt, pp **met**) vt incontrare; (for the first time) fare la conoscenza di; (go and fetch) andare a prendere; (fig) affrontare; soddisfare; raggiungere ▷ vi incontrarsi; (in session) riunirsi; (join: objects) unirsi; **nice to ~ you** piacere (di conoscerla); **meet up** vi **to ~ up with sb** incontrare qn; **meet with** vt fus incontrare; **meeting** n incontro; (session: of club etc) riunione f; (interview) intervista; **she's at a meeting** (Comm) è in riunione; **meeting place** n luogo d'incontro

megabyte [ˈmɛgəbaɪt] n (Comput) megabyte m inv

megaphone [ˈmɛgəfəun] n megafono

melancholy [ˈmɛlənkəlɪ] n malinconia ▷ adj malinconico(-a)

melody [ˈmɛlədɪ] n melodia

melon [ˈmɛlən] n melone m

melt [mɛlt] vi (gen) sciogliersi, struggersi; (metals) fondersi ▷ vt sciogliere, struggere; fondere

member [ˈmɛmbəʳ] n membro; **Member of Congress** (US) n membro del Congresso; **Member of Parliament** (BRIT) n deputato(-a); **Member of the European Parliament** (BRIT) n eurodeputato(-a); **Member of the Scottish Parliament** (BRIT) n deputato(-a) del Parlamento scozzese; **membership** n iscrizione f, (numero d')iscritti mpl, membri mpl; **membership card** n tessera (di iscrizione)

memento [məˈmɛntəu] n ricordo, souvenir m inv

memo [ˈmɛməu] n appunto; (Comm etc) comunicazione f di servizio

memorable [ˈmɛmərəbl] adj memorabile

memorandum [mɛməˈrændəm] (*pl*
memoranda) *n* appunto; (*Comm etc*)
comunicazione *f* di servizio
memorial [mɪˈmɔːrɪəl] *n*
monumento commemorativo ▷ *adj*
commemorativo(-a)
memorize [ˈmɛməraɪz] *vt* memorizzare
memory [ˈmɛmərɪ] *n* (*also Comput*)
memoria; (*recollection*) ricordo
men [mɛn] *npl of* **man**
menace [ˈmɛnəs] *n* minaccia ▷ *vt*
minacciare
mend [mɛnd] *vt* aggiustare, riparare;
(*darn*) rammendare ▷ *n* **on the ~** in via di
guarigione
meningitis [mɛnɪnˈdʒaɪtɪs] *n* meningite *f*
menopause [ˈmɛnəupɔːz] *n* menopausa
men's room *n* **the men's room** (*esp US*) la
toilette degli uomini
menstruation [mɛnstruˈeɪʃən] *n*
mestruazione *f*
menswear [ˈmɛnzwɛər] *n* abbigliamento
maschile
mental [ˈmɛntl] *adj* mentale; **mental
hospital** *n* ospedale *m* psichiatrico;
mentality [mɛnˈtælɪtɪ] *n* mentalità
f inv; **mentally** *adv* **to be mentally
handicapped** essere minorato psichico
menthol [ˈmɛnθɔl] *n* mentolo
mention [ˈmɛnʃən] *n* menzione *f* ▷ *vt*
menzionare, far menzione di; **don't ~ it!**
non c'è di che!, prego!
menu [ˈmɛnjuː] *n* (*set menu, Comput*) menù
m inv; (*printed*) carta; **could we see the ~?**
ci può portare il menù?
MEP *n abbr* = **Member of the European
Parliament**
mercenary [ˈmɜːsɪnərɪ] *adj* venale ▷ *n*
mercenario
merchandise [ˈmɜːtʃəndaɪz] *n* merci *fpl*
merchant [ˈmɜːtʃənt] *n* mercante *m*,
commerciante *m*; **merchant navy** (*US*
merchant marine) *n* marina mercantile
merciless [ˈmɜːsɪlɪs] *adj* spietato(-a)
mercury [ˈmɜːkjurɪ] *n* mercurio
mercy [ˈmɜːsɪ] *n* pietà; (*Rel*) misericordia;
at the ~ of alla mercé di
mere [mɪər] *adj* semplice; **by a ~
chance** per mero caso; **merely** *adv*
semplicemente, non ... che
merge [mɜːdʒ] *vt* unire ▷ *vi* fondersi,
unirsi; (*Comm*) fondersi; **merger** *n* (*Comm*)
fusione *f*
meringue [məˈræŋ] *n* meringa
merit [ˈmɛrɪt] *n* merito, valore *m* ▷ *vt*
meritare
mermaid [ˈmɜːmeɪd] *n* sirena
merry [ˈmɛrɪ] *adj* gaio(-a), allegro(-a); **M~
Christmas!** Buon Natale!; **merry-go-**

round *n* carosello
mesh [mɛʃ] *n* maglia; rete *f*
mess [mɛs] *n* confusione *f*, disordine *m*;
(*fig*) pasticcio; (*dirt*) sporcizia; (*Mil*) mensa;
mess about *or* **around** (*inf*) *vi* trastullarsi;
mess with (*inf*) *vt fus* (*challenge, confront*)
litigare con; (*drugs, drinks*) abusare di;
mess up *vt* sporcare; fare un pasticcio di;
rovinare
message [ˈmɛsɪdʒ] *n* messaggio; **can I
leave a ~?** posso lasciare un messaggio?;
are there any ~s for me? ci sono
messaggi per me?
messenger [ˈmɛsɪndʒər] *n*
messaggero(-a)
Messrs [ˈmɛsəz] *abbr* (*on letters*) Spett.
messy [ˈmɛsɪ] *adj* sporco(-a),
disordinato(-a)
met [mɛt] *pt, pp of* **meet**
metabolism [mɛˈtæbəlɪzəm] *n*
metabolismo
metal [ˈmɛtl] *n* metallo; **metallic** [-ˈtælɪk]
adj metallico(-a)
metaphor [ˈmɛtəfər] *n* metafora
meteor [ˈmiːtɪər] *n* meteora; **meteorite**
[ˈmiːtɪəraɪt] *n* meteorite *m*
meteorology [miːtɪəˈrɔlədʒɪ] *n*
meteorologia
meter [ˈmiːtər] *n* (*instrument*) contatore
m; (*parking meter*) parchimetro; (*US: unit*)
= **metre**
method [ˈmɛθəd] *n* metodo; **methodical**
[mɪˈθɔdɪkl] *adj* metodico(-a)
meths [mɛθs] (*BRIT*) *n* alcool *m* denaturato
meticulous [mɛˈtɪkjuləs] *adj*
meticoloso(-a)
metre [ˈmiːtər] (*US* **meter**) *n* metro
metric [ˈmɛtrɪk] *adj* metrico(-a)
metro [ˈmɛtrəu] *n* metro *m inv*
metropolitan [mɛtrəˈpɔlɪtən] *adj*
metropolitano(-a)
Mexican [ˈmɛksɪkən] *adj, n* messicano(-a)
Mexico [ˈmɛksɪkəu] *n* Messico
mg *abbr* (= *milligram*) mg
mice [maɪs] *npl of* **mouse**
micro... [ˈmaɪkrəu] *prefix* micro...;
microchip *n* microcircuito integrato;
microphone *n* microfono; **microscope**
n microscopio; **microwave** *n* (*also:*
microwave oven) forno a microonde
mid [mɪd] *adj* **~ May** metà maggio; **~
afternoon** metà pomeriggio; **in ~ air** a
mezz'aria; **midday** *n* mezzogiorno
middle [ˈmɪdl] *n* mezzo; centro; (*waist*)
vita ▷ *adj* di mezzo; **in the ~ of the night**
nel bel mezzo della notte; **middle-aged**
adj di mezza età; **Middle Ages** *npl* **the
Middle Ages** il Medioevo; **middle-class**
adj ≈ borghese; **Middle East** *n* Medio

Oriente *m*; **middle name** *n* secondo nome *m*; **middle school** *n* (US) scuola media per ragazzi dagli 11 ai 14 anni; (BRIT) scuola media per ragazzi dagli 8 o 9 ai 12 o 13 anni

midge [mɪdʒ] *n* moscerino

midget ['mɪdʒɪt] *n* nano(-a)

midnight ['mɪdnaɪt] *n* mezzanotte *f*

midst [mɪdst] *n* **in the - of** in mezzo a

midsummer [mɪd'sʌmə^r] *n* mezza or piena estate *f*

midway [mɪd'weɪ] *adj, adv* **- (between)** a mezza strada (fra); **- (through)** a metà (di)

midweek [mɪd'wi:k] *adv* metà settimana

midwife ['mɪdwaɪf] (*pl* **midwives**) *n* levatrice *f*

midwinter [mɪd'wɪntə^r] *n* pieno inverno

might [maɪt] *vb see* **may** ▷ *n* potere *m*, forza; **mighty** *adj* forte, potente

migraine ['mi:greɪn] *n* emicrania

migrant ['maɪgrənt] *adj* (*bird*) migratore(-trice); (*worker*) emigrato(-a)

migrate [maɪ'greɪt] *vi* (*bird*) migrare; (*person*) emigrare

migration [maɪ'greɪʃən] *n* migrazione *f*

mike [maɪk] *n abbr* (= *microphone*) microfono

Milan [mɪ'læn] *n* Milano *f*

mild [maɪld] *adj* mite; (*person, voice*) dolce; (*flavour*) delicato(-a); (*illness*) leggero(-a); (*interest*) blando(-a) ▷ *n* (*beer*) birra leggera; **mildly** ['maɪldlɪ] *adv* mitemente; dolcemente; delicatamente; leggermente; blandamente; **to put it mildly** a dire poco

mile [maɪl] *n* miglio; **mileage** *n* distanza in miglia, ≈ chilometraggio; **mileometer** [maɪ'lɔmɪtə^r] *n* ≈ contachilometri *m inv*; **milestone** ['maɪlstəun] *n* pietra miliare

military ['mɪlɪtərɪ] *adj* militare

militia [mɪ'lɪʃə] *n* milizia

milk [mɪlk] *n* latte *m* ▷ *vt* (*cow*) mungere; (*fig*) sfruttare; **milk chocolate** *n* cioccolato al latte; **milkman** (*irreg*) *n* lattaio; **milky** *adj* lattiginoso(-a); (*colour*) latteo(-a)

mill [mɪl] *n* mulino; (*small: for coffee, pepper etc*) macinino; (*factory*) fabbrica; (*spinning mill*) filatura ▷ *vt* macinare ▷ *vi* (*also:* **- about**) brulicare

millennium [mɪ'lenɪəm] (*pl* **millenniums** *or* **millennia**) *n* millennio

milli... ['mɪlɪ] *prefix*: **milligram(me)** *n* milligrammo; **millilitre** ['mɪlɪli:tə^r] (US **milliliter**) *n* millilitro; **millimetre** (US **millimeter**) *n* millimetro

million ['mɪljən] *num* milione *m*; **millionaire** *n* milionario, ≈ miliardario; **millionth** *num* milionesimo(-a)

milometer [maɪ'lɔmɪtə^r] *n* = **mileometer**

mime [maɪm] *n* mimo ▷ *vt, vi* mimare

mimic ['mɪmɪk] *n* imitatore(-trice) ▷ *vt* fare la mimica di

min. *abbr* = **minute(s)**; **minimum**

mince [mɪns] *vt* tritare, macinare ▷ *n* (BRIT Culin) carne *f* tritata or macinata; **mincemeat** *n* frutta secca tritata per uso in pasticceria; (US) carne *f* tritata or macinata; **mince pie** *n* specie di torta con frutta secca

mind [maɪnd] *n* mente *f* ▷ *vt* (*attend to, look after*) badare a, occuparsi di; (*be careful*) fare attenzione a, stare attento(-a) a; (*object to*): **I don't - the noise** il rumore non mi dà alcun fastidio; **I don't -** non m'importa; **do you - if ...?** le dispiace se...?; **it is on my -** mi preoccupa; **to my -** secondo me, a mio parere; **to be out of one's -** essere uscito(-a) di mente; **to keep** or **bear sth in -** non dimenticare qc; **to make up one's -** decidersi; **- you, ...** sì, però va detto che ...; **never -** non importa, non fa niente; (*don't worry*) non preoccuparti; **"- the step"** "attenzione allo scalino"; **mindless** *adj* idiota

mine¹ [maɪn] *pron* il (la) mio(-a); (*pl*) i (le) miei (mei); **that book is -** quel libro è mio; **yours is red, - is green** il tuo è rosso, il mio è verde; **a friend of -** un mio amico

mine² [maɪn] *n* miniera; (*explosive*) mina ▷ *vt* (*coal*) estrarre; (*ship, beach*) minare; **minefield** *n* (*also fig*) campo minato; **miner** ['maɪnə^r] *n* minatore *m*

mineral ['mɪnərəl] *adj* minerale ▷ *n* minerale *m*; **mineral water** *n* acqua minerale

mingle ['mɪŋgl] *vi* **to - with** mescolarsi a, mischiarsi con

miniature ['mɪnətʃə^r] *adj* in miniatura ▷ *n* miniatura

minibar ['mɪnɪbɑ:^r] *n* minibar *m inv*

minibus ['mɪnɪbʌs] *n* minibus *m inv*

minicab ['mɪnɪkæb] *n* (BRIT) ≈ taxi *m inv*

minimal ['mɪnɪml] *adj* minimo(-a)

minimize ['mɪnɪmaɪz] *vt* minimizzare

minimum ['mɪnɪməm] (*pl* **minima**) *n* minimo ▷ *adj* minimo(-a)

mining ['maɪnɪŋ] *n* industria mineraria

miniskirt ['mɪnɪskə:t] *n* minigonna

minister ['mɪnɪstə^r] *n* (BRIT Pol) ministro; (Rel) pastore *m*

ministry ['mɪnɪstrɪ] *n* ministero

minor ['maɪnə^r] *adj* minore, di poca importanza; (*Mus*) minore ▷ *n* (Law) minorenne *m/f*

Minorca [mɪ'nɔ:kə] *n* Minorca

minority [maɪ'nɔrɪtɪ] *n* minoranza

mint [mɪnt] *n* (*plant*) menta; (*sweet*) pasticca di menta ▷ *vt* (*coins*) battere; **the (Royal) M-** (BRIT), **the (US) M-** (US) la Zecca; **in ~ condition** come nuovo(-a) di zecca

minus ['maɪnəs] n (also: **~ sign**) segno meno ▷ prep meno

minute [adj maɪ'njuːt, n 'mɪnɪt] adj minuscolo(-a); (detail) minuzioso(-a) ▷ n minuto; **~s** npl (of meeting) verbale m

miracle ['mɪrəkl] n miracolo

miraculous [mɪ'rækjuləs] adj miracoloso(-a)

mirage ['mɪrɑːʒ] n miraggio

mirror ['mɪrəʳ] n specchio; (in car) specchietto

misbehave [mɪsbɪ'heɪv] vi comportarsi male

misc. abbr = **miscellaneous**; **miscarriage** ['mɪskærɪdʒ] n (Med) aborto spontaneo; **miscarriage of justice** errore m giudiziario

miscellaneous [mɪsɪ'leɪnɪəs] adj (items) vario(-a); (selection) misto(-a)

mischief ['mɪstʃɪf] n (naughtiness) birichineria; (maliciousness) malizia; **mischievous** adj birichino(-a)

misconception ['mɪskən'sɛpʃən] n idea sbagliata

misconduct [mɪs'kɒndʌkt] n cattiva condotta; **professional ~** reato professionale

miser ['maɪzəʳ] n avaro

miserable ['mɪzərəbl] adj infelice; (wretched) miserabile; (weather) deprimente; (offer, failure) misero(-a)

misery ['mɪzərɪ] n (unhappiness) tristezza; (wretchedness) miseria

misfortune [mɪs'fɔːtʃən] n sfortuna

misgiving [mɪs'gɪvɪŋ] n apprensione f; **to have ~s about** avere dei dubbi per quanto riguarda

misguided [mɪs'gaɪdɪd] adj sbagliato(-a), poco giudizioso(-a)

mishap ['mɪshæp] n disgrazia

misinterpret [mɪsɪn'təːprɪt] vt interpretare male

misjudge [mɪs'dʒʌdʒ] vt giudicare male

mislay [mɪs'leɪ] (irreg) vt smarrire

mislead [mɪs'liːd] (irreg) vt sviare; **misleading** adj ingannevole

misplace [mɪs'pleɪs] vt smarrire

misprint ['mɪsprɪnt] n errore m di stampa

misrepresent [mɪsrɛprɪ'zɛnt] vt travisare

Miss [mɪs] n Signorina

miss [mɪs] vt (fail to get) perdere; (fail to hit) mancare; (fail to see): **you can't ~ it** non puoi non vederlo; (regret the absence of): **I ~ him** sento la sua mancanza ▷ vi mancare ▷ n (shot) colpo mancato; **we ~ed our train** abbiamo perso il treno; **miss out** (BRIT) vt omettere; **miss out on**

vt fus (fun, party) perdersi; (chance, bargain) lasciarsi sfuggire

missile ['mɪsaɪl] n (Mil) missile m; (object thrown) proiettile m

missing ['mɪsɪŋ] adj perso(-a), smarrito(-a); (person) scomparso(-a); (: after disaster, Mil) disperso(-a); (removed) mancante; **to be ~** mancare

mission ['mɪʃən] n missione f; **missionary** n missionario(-a)

misspell [mɪs'spɛl] vt (irreg: like **spell**) sbagliare l'ortografia di

mist [mɪst] n nebbia, foschia ▷ vi (also: **~ over, ~ up**) annebbiarsi; (: BRIT: windows) appannarsi

mistake [mɪs'teɪk] (irreg: like **take**) n sbaglio, errore m ▷ vt sbagliarsi di; fraintendere; **to make a ~** fare uno sbaglio, sbagliare; **there must be some ~** ci dev'essere un errore; **by ~** per sbaglio; **to ~ for** prendere per; **mistaken** pp of **mistake** ▷ adj (idea etc) sbagliato(-a); **to be mistaken** sbagliarsi

mister ['mɪstəʳ] (inf) n signore m; see **Mr**

mistletoe ['mɪsltəu] n vischio

mistook [mɪs'tuk] pt of **mistake**

mistress ['mɪstrɪs] n padrona; (lover) amante f; (BRIT Scol) insegnante f

mistrust [mɪs'trʌst] vt diffidare di

misty ['mɪstɪ] adj nebbioso(-a), brumoso(-a)

misunderstand [mɪsʌndə'stænd] (irreg) vt, vi capire male, fraintendere; **misunderstanding** n malinteso, equivoco; **there's been a misunderstanding** c'è stato un malinteso

misunderstood [mɪsʌndə'stud] pt, pp of **misunderstand**

misuse [n mɪs'juːs, vb mɪs'juːz] n cattivo uso; (of power) abuso ▷ vt far cattivo uso di; abusare di

mitt(en) ['mɪt(n)] n mezzo guanto; manopola

mix [mɪks] vt mescolare ▷ vi (people): **to ~ with** avere a che fare con ▷ n mescolanza, preparato; **mix up** vt mescolare; (confuse) confondere; **mixed** adj misto(-a); **mixed grill** n (BRIT) misto alla griglia; **mixed salad** n insalata mista; **mixed-up** adj (confused) confuso(-a); **mixer** n (for food: electric) frullatore m; (: hand) frullino; (person): **he is a good mixer** è molto socievole; **mixture** n mescolanza; (blend: of tobacco etc) miscela; (Med) sciroppo; **mix-up** n confusione f

ml abbr (= millilitre(s)) ml

mm abbr (= millimetre) mm

moan [məun] n gemito ▷ vi (inf: complain): **to ~ (about)** lamentarsi (di)

moat [məut] *n* fossato

mob [mɔb] *n* calca ▷ *vt* accalcarsi intorno a

mobile ['məubaɪl] *adj* mobile ▷ *n* (*decoration*) mobile *m*; **mobile home** *n* grande roulotte *f inv* (utilizzata come domicilio); **mobile phone** *n* telefono portatile, telefonino

mobility [məu'bɪlɪtɪ] *n* mobilità; (*of applicant*) disponibilità a viaggiare

mobilize ['məubɪlaɪz] *vt* mobilitare ▷ *vi* mobilitarsi

mock [mɔk] *vt* deridere, burlarsi di ▷ *adj* falso(-a); **~s** *npl* (BRIT: *Scol: inf*) simulazione *f* degli esami; **mockery** *n* derisione *f*; **to make a mockery of** burlarsi di; (*exam*) rendere una farsa

mod cons ['mɔd'kɔnz] *npl abbr* (BRIT) = **modern conveniences**; *see* **convenience**

mode [məud] *n* modo

model ['mɔdl] *n* modello; (*person: for fashion*) indossatore(-trice); (: *for artist*) modello(-a) ▷ *adj* (*small-scale: railway etc*) in miniatura; (*child, factory*) modello *inv* ▷ *vt* modellare ▷ *vi* fare l'indossatore (*or* l'indossatrice); **to ~ clothes** presentare degli abiti

modem ['məudɛm] *n* modem *m inv*

moderate [*adj* 'mɔdərət, *vb* 'mɔdəreɪt] *adj* moderato(-a) ▷ *vi* moderarsi, placarsi ▷ *vt* moderare

moderation [mɔdə'reɪʃən] *n* moderazione *f*, misura; **in ~** in quantità moderata, con moderazione

modern ['mɔdən] *adj* moderno(-a); **mod cons** comodità *fpl* moderne; **modernize** *vt* modernizzare; **modern languages** *npl* lingue *fpl* moderne

modest ['mɔdɪst] *adj* modesto(-a); **modesty** *n* modestia

modification [mɔdɪfɪ'keɪʃən] *n* modificazione *f*; **to make ~s** fare *or* apportare delle modifiche

modify ['mɔdɪfaɪ] *vt* modificare

module ['mɔdjuːl] *n* modulo

mohair ['məuhɛəʳ] *n* mohair *m*

Mohammed [məu'hæmɪd] *n* Maometto

moist [mɔɪst] *adj* umido(-a); **moisture** ['mɔɪstʃəʳ] *n* umidità; (*on glass*) goccioline *fpl* di vapore; **moisturizer** ['mɔɪstʃəraɪzəʳ] *n* idratante *f*

mold *etc* [məuld] (US) *n*, *vt* = **mould**

mole [məul] *n* (*animal, fig*) talpa; (*spot*) neo

molecule ['mɔlɪkjuːl] *n* molecola

molest [məu'lɛst] *vt* molestare

molten ['məultən] *adj* fuso(-a)

mom [mɔm] (US) *n* = **mum**

moment ['məumənt] *n* momento, istante *m*; **at that ~** in quel momento; **at the ~** al momento, in questo momento; **momentarily** ['məuməntərɪlɪ] *adv* per un momento; (US: *very soon*) da un momento all'altro; **momentary** *adj* momentaneo(-a), passeggero(-a); **momentous** [-'mɛntəs] *adj* di grande importanza

momentum [məu'mɛntəm] *n* (*Physics*) momento; (*fig*) impeto; **to gather ~** aumentare di velocità

mommy ['mɔmɪ] (US) *n* = **mummy**

Mon. *abbr* (= *Monday*) lun.

Monaco ['mɔnəkəu] *n* Principato di Monaco

monarch ['mɔnək] *n* monarca *m*; **monarchy** *n* monarchia

monastery ['mɔnəstərɪ] *n* monastero

Monday ['mʌndɪ] *n* lunedì *m inv*

monetary ['mʌnɪtərɪ] *adj* monetario(-a)

money ['mʌnɪ] *n* denaro, soldi *mpl*; **I haven't got any ~** non ho soldi; **money belt** *n* marsupio (*per soldi*); **money order** *n* vaglia *m inv*

mongrel ['mʌŋgrəl] *n* (*dog*) cane *m* bastardo

monitor ['mɔnɪtəʳ] *n* (TV, *Comput*) monitor *m inv* ▷ *vt* controllare

monk [mʌŋk] *n* monaco

monkey ['mʌŋkɪ] *n* scimmia

monologue ['mɔnələg] *n* monologo

monopoly [mə'nɔpəlɪ] *n* monopolio

monosodium glutamate [mɔnə'səudɪəm'gluːtəmeɪt] *n* glutammato di sodio

monotonous [mə'nɔtənəs] *adj* monotono(-a)

monsoon [mɔn'suːn] *n* monsone *m*

monster ['mɔnstəʳ] *n* mostro

month [mʌnθ] *n* mese *m*; **monthly** *adj* mensile ▷ *adv* al mese; ogni mese

monument ['mɔnjumənt] *n* monumento

mood [muːd] *n* umore *m*; **to be in a good/ bad ~** essere di buon/cattivo umore; **moody** *adj* (*variable*) capriccioso(-a), lunatico(-a); (*sullen*) imbronciato(-a)

moon [muːn] *n* luna; **moonlight** *n* chiaro di luna

moor [muəʳ] *n* brughiera ▷ *vt* (*ship*) ormeggiare ▷ *vi* ormeggiarsi

moose [muːs] *n inv* alce *m*

mop [mɔp] *n* lavapavimento *m inv*; (*also: ~ of hair*) zazzera ▷ *vt* lavare con lo straccio; (*face*) asciugare; **mop up** *vt* asciugare con uno straccio

mope [məup] *vi* fare il broncio

moped ['məupɛd] *n* (BRIT) ciclomotore *m*

moral ['mɔrl] *adj* morale ▷ *n* morale *f*; **~s** *npl* (*principles*) moralità

morale [mɔ'rɑːl] *n* morale *m*

morality [mə'ræliti] n moralità
morbid ['mɔːbid] adj morboso(-a)

 KEYWORD

more [mɔːʳ] adj **1** (greater in number etc)
più; **more people/letters than we
expected** più persone/lettere di quante
ne aspettavamo; **I have more wine/
money than you** ho più vino/soldi di te;
I have more wine than beer ho più vino
che birra
2 (additional) altro(-a), ancora; **do you
want (some) more tea?** vuole dell'altro
tè?, vuole ancora del tè?; **I have no** or **I
don't have any more money** non ho
più soldi
▷ pron **1** (greater amount) più; **more than 10**
più di 10; **it cost more than we expected**
ha costato più di quanto ci aspettavamo
2 (further or additional amount) ancora;
is there any more? ce n'è ancora?;
there's no more non ce n'è più; **a little
more** ancora un po'; **many/much more**
molti(-e)/molto(-a) di più
▷ adv **more dangerous/easily (than)**
più pericoloso/facilmente (di); **more and
more** sempre di più; **more and more
difficult** sempre più difficile; **more or less**
più o meno; **more than ever** più che mai

moreover [mɔː'rəuvəʳ] adv inoltre, di più
morgue [mɔːg] n obitorio
morning ['mɔːnɪŋ] n mattina, mattino;
(duration) mattinata ▷ cpd del mattino;
in the ~ la mattina; **7 o'clock in the ~** le 7
di or della mattina; **morning sickness** n
nausee fpl mattutine
Moroccan [mə'rɔkən] adj, n
marocchino(-a)
Morocco [mə'rɔkəu] n Marocco
moron ['mɔːrɔn] (inf) n deficiente m/f
morphine ['mɔːfiːn] n morfina
morris dancing n vedi nota nel riquadro

⁂ **MORRIS DANCING**
⁂
⁂ Il **morris dancing** è una danza
⁂ folcloristica inglese tradizionalmente
⁂ riservata agli uomini. Vestiti di bianco
⁂ e con dei campanelli attaccati alle
⁂ caviglie, i ballerini eseguono una danza
⁂ tenendo in mano dei fazzoletti bianchi
⁂ e lunghi bastoni. Questa danza è molto
⁂ popolare nelle feste paesane.

Morse [mɔːs] n (also: **~ code**) alfabeto
Morse
mortal ['mɔːtl] adj mortale ▷ n mortale m

mortar ['mɔːtəʳ] n (Constr) malta; (dish)
mortaio
mortgage ['mɔːgidʒ] n ipoteca; (loan)
prestito ipotecario ▷ vt ipotecare
mortician [mɔː'tɪʃən] (us) n impresario di
pompe funebri
mortified ['mɔːtɪfaɪd] adj umiliato(-a)
mortuary ['mɔːtjuəri] n camera
mortuaria; obitorio
mosaic [məu'zeiik] n mosaico
Moscow ['mɔskəu] n Mosca
Moslem ['mɔzləm] adj, n = **Muslim**
mosque [mɔsk] n moschea
mosquito [mɔs'kiːtəu] (pl **mosquitoes**)
n zanzara
moss [mɔs] n muschio
most [məust] adj (almost all) la maggior
parte di; (largest, greatest): **who has (the)
~ money?** chi ha più soldi di tutti? ▷ pron
la maggior parte ▷ adv più; (work, sleep
etc) di più; (very) molto, estremamente;
the ~ (also: **+ adjective**) il(-la) più; **~ of** la
maggior parte di; **~ of them** quasi tutti; **I
saw (the) ~** ho visto più io; **at the (very)
~** al massimo; **to make the ~ of** trarre il
massimo vantaggio da; **a ~ interesting
book** un libro estremamente interessante;
mostly adv per lo più
MOT (BRIT) n abbr = **Ministry of
Transport; the ~ (test)** revisione annuale
obbligatoria degli autoveicoli
motel [məu'tɛl] n motel m inv
moth [mɔθ] n farfalla notturna; tarma
mother ['mʌðəʳ] n madre f ▷ vt (care
for) fare da madre a; **motherhood** n
maternità; **mother-in-law** n suocera;
mother-of-pearl [mʌðərəv'pəːl] n
madreperla; **Mother's Day** n la festa della
mamma; **mother-to-be** [mʌðətə'biː]
n futura mamma; **mother tongue** n
madrelingua
motif [məu'tiːf] n motivo
motion ['məuʃən] n movimento, moto;
(gesture) gesto; (at meeting) mozione f ▷ vt,
vi **to ~ (to) sb to do** fare cenno a qn di
fare; **motionless** adj immobile; **motion
picture** n film m inv
motivate ['məutɪveɪt] vt (act, decision)
dare origine a, motivare; (person) spingere
motivation [məutɪ'veɪʃən] n motivazione
f
motive ['məutɪv] n motivo
motor ['məutəʳ] n motore m;
(BRIT: inf: vehicle) macchina ▷ cpd
automobilistico(-a); **motorbike** n moto f
inv; **motorboat** n motoscafo; **motorcar**
(BRIT) n automobile f; **motorcycle**
n motocicletta; **motorcyclist** n
motociclista m/f; **motoring** (BRIT) n

turismo automobilistico; **motorist** n
automobilista m/f; **motor racing** (BRIT)
n corse fpl automobilistiche; **motorway**
(BRIT) n autostrada
motto ['mɔtəu] (pl **mottoes**) n motto
mould [məuld] (US **mold**) n forma,
stampo; (mildew) muffa ▷ vt formare;
(fig) foggiare; **mouldy** adj ammuffito(-a);
(smell) di muffa
mound [maund] n rialzo, collinetta; (heap)
mucchio
mount [maunt] n (Geo) monte m ▷ vt
montare; (horse) montare a ▷ vi (increase)
aumentare; **mount up** vi (build up)
accumularsi
mountain ['mauntɪn] n montagna
▷ cpd di montagna; **mountain bike**
n mountain bike f inv; **mountaineer**
[-'nɪəʳ] n alpinista m/f; **mountaineering**
[-'nɪətɪŋ] n alpinismo; **mountainous**
adj montagnoso(-a); **mountain range** n
catena montuosa
mourn [mɔ:n] vt piangere, lamentare ▷ vi
to ~ (for sb) piangere (la morte di qn);
mourner n parente m/f or amico(-a) del
defunto; **mourning** n lutto; **in mourning**
in lutto
mouse [maus] (pl **mice**) n topo; (Comput)
mouse m inv; **mouse mat, mouse pad** n
(Comput) tappetino del mouse
moussaka [mu'sɑ:kə] n moussaka
mousse [mu:s] n mousse f inv
moustache [məs'tɑ:ʃ] (US **mustache**) n
baffi mpl
mouth [mauθ, pl mauðz] n bocca; (of river)
bocca, foce f; (opening) orifizio; **mouthful**
n boccata; **mouth organ** n armonica;
mouthpiece n (Mus) imboccatura,
bocchino; (spokesman) portavoce m/f inv;
mouthwash n collutorio
move [mu:v] n (movement) movimento; (in
game) mossa; (: turn to play) turno; (change:
of house) trasloco; (: of job) cambiamento
▷ vt muovere; (change position of) spostare;
(emotionally) commuovere; (Pol: resolution
etc) proporre ▷ vi (gen) muoversi,
spostarsi; (also: ~ house) cambiar casa,
traslocare; **to get a ~ on** affrettarsi,
sbrigarsi; **can you ~ your car, please?**
può spostare la macchina, per favore?;
to ~ sb to do sth indurre or spingere qn
a fare qc; **to ~ towards** andare verso;
move back vi (return) ritornare; **move
in** vi (to a house) entrare (in una nuova
casa); (police etc) intervenire; **move off** vi
partire; **move on** vi riprendere la strada;
move out vi (of house) sgombrare; **move
over** vi spostarsi; **move up** vi avanzare;
movement ['mu:vmənt] n (gen)

movimento; (gesture) gesto; (of stars, water,
physical) moto
movie ['mu:vɪ] n film m inv; **the ~s** il
cinema; **movie theater** (US) n cinema
m inv
moving ['mu:vɪŋ] adj mobile; (causing
emotion) commovente
mow [məu] (pt mowed, pp mowed or
mown) vt (grass) tagliare; (corn) mietere;
mower n (also: **lawnmower**) tagliaerba
m inv
Mozambique [məuzəm'bi:k] n
Mozambico
MP n abbr = **Member of Parliament**
MP3 n abbr M3; **MP3 player** n lettore m
MP3
mpg n abbr = **miles per gallon** (30 mpg
= 9.4 l. per 100 km)
m.p.h. n abbr = **miles per hour** (60 m.p.h
= 96 km/h)
Mr ['mɪstəʳ] (US **Mr.**) n **Mr X** Signor X, Sig. X
Mrs ['mɪsɪz] (US **Mrs.**) n **Mrs X** Signora X,
Sig.ra X
Ms [mɪz] (US **Ms.**) n = **Miss or Mrs**; **Ms X**
≈ Signora X, ≈ Sig.ra X

> 🔹 **Ms**
> 🔹
> 🔹 In inglese si usa **Ms** al posto di "Mrs"
> 🔹 (Signora) o "Miss" (Signorina) per evitare
> 🔹 la distinzione tradizionale tra le donne
> 🔹 sposate e quelle nubili.

MSP n abbr = **Member of the Scottish
Parliament**
Mt abbr (Geo: = mount) M.

KEYWORD

much [mʌtʃ] adj, pron molto(-a); **he's done
so much work** ha lavorato così tanto; **I
have as much money as you** ho tanti
soldi quanti ne hai tu; **how much is it?**
quant'è?; **it costs too much** costa troppo;
as much as you want quanto vuoi
▷ adv 1 (greatly) molto, tanto; **thank you
very much** molte grazie; **he's very much
the gentleman** è il vero gentiluomo;
I read as much as I can leggo quanto
posso; **as much as you** tanto quanto te
2 (by far) molto; **it's much the biggest
company in Europe** è di gran lunga la più
grossa società in Europa
3 (almost) grossomodo, praticamente;
they're much the same sono
praticamente uguali

muck [mʌk] n (dirt) sporcizia; **muck up**
(inf) vt (ruin) rovinare; **mucky** adj (dirty)

sporco(-a), lordo(-a)

mucus ['mju:kəs] n muco

mud [mʌd] n fango

muddle ['mʌdl] n confusione f, disordine m; pasticcio ▷ vt (also: **~ up**) confondere

muddy ['mʌdɪ] adj fangoso(-a)

mudguard ['mʌdgɑ:d] n parafango

muesli ['mju:zlɪ] n muesli m

muffin ['mʌfɪn] n specie di pasticcino soffice da tè

muffled ['mʌfld] adj smorzato(-a), attutito(-a)

muffler ['mʌflə'] (us) n (Aut) marmitta; (: on motorbike) silenziatore m

mug [mʌg] n (cup) tazzone m; (for beer) boccale m; (inf: face) muso; (: fool) scemo(-a) ▷ vt (assault) assalire; **mugger** ['mʌgə'] n aggressore m; **mugging** n assalto

muggy ['mʌgɪ] adj afoso(-a)

mule [mju:l] n mulo

multicoloured ['mʌltɪkʌləd] (us **multicolored**) adj multicolore, variopinto(-a)

multimedia ['mʌltɪ'mi:dɪə] adj multimedia inv

multinational [mʌltɪ'næʃənl] adj, n multinazionale (f)

multiple ['mʌltɪpl] adj multiplo(-a), molteplice ▷ n multiplo; **multiple choice (test)** n esercizi mpl a scelta multipla; **multiple sclerosis** [-sklɪ'rəusɪs] n sclerosi f a placche

multiplex cinema ['mʌltɪplɛks-] n cinema m inv multisala inv

multiplication [mʌltɪplɪ'keɪʃən] n moltiplicazione f

multiply ['mʌltɪplaɪ] vt moltiplicare ▷ vi moltiplicarsi

multistorey ['mʌltɪ'stɔ:rɪ] (BRIT) adj (building, car park) a più piani

mum [mʌm] (BRIT: inf) n mamma ▷ adj **to keep ~** non aprire bocca

mumble ['mʌmbl] vt, vi borbottare

mummy ['mʌmɪ] n (BRIT: mother) mamma; (embalmed) mummia

mumps [mʌmps] n orecchioni mpl

munch [mʌntʃ] vt, vi sgranocchiare

municipal [mju:'nɪsɪpl] adj municipale

mural ['mjuərl] n dipinto murale

murder ['mə:də'] n assassinio, omicidio ▷ vt assassinare; **murderer** n omicida m, assassino

murky ['mə:kɪ] adj tenebroso(-a)

murmur ['mə:mə'] n mormorio ▷ vt, vi mormorare

muscle ['mʌsl] n muscolo; (fig) forza; **muscular** ['mʌskjulə'] adj muscolare; (person, arm) muscoloso(-a)

museum [mju:'zɪəm] n museo

mushroom ['mʌʃrum] n fungo ▷ vi crescere in fretta

music ['mju:zɪk] n musica; **musical** adj musicale; (person) portato(-a) per la musica ▷ n (show) commedia musicale; **musical instrument** n strumento musicale; **musician** [-'zɪʃən] n musicista m/f

Muslim ['mʌzlɪm] adj, n musulmano(-a)

muslin ['mʌzlɪn] n mussola

mussel ['mʌsl] n cozza

must [mʌst] aux vb (obligation): **I ~ do it** devo farlo; (probability): **he ~ be there by now** dovrebbe essere arrivato ormai; **I ~ have made a mistake** devo essermi sbagliato ▷ n **it's a ~** è d'obbligo

mustache ['mʌstæʃ] (us) n = **moustache**

mustard ['mʌstəd] n senape f, mostarda

mustn't ['mʌsnt] = **must not**

mute [mju:t] adj, n muto(-a)

mutilate ['mju:tɪleɪt] vt mutilare

mutiny ['mju:tɪnɪ] n ammutinamento

mutter ['mʌtə'] vt, vi borbottare, brontolare

mutton ['mʌtn] n carne f di montone

mutual ['mju:tʃuəl] adj mutuo(-a), reciproco(-a)

muzzle ['mʌzl] n muso; (protective device) museruola; (of gun) bocca ▷ vt mettere la museruola a

my [maɪ] adj il (la) mio(-a); (pl) i (le) miei (mie); **my house** la mia casa; **my books** i miei libri; **my brother** mio fratello; **I've washed my hair/cut my finger** mi sono lavato i capelli/tagliato il dito

myself [maɪ'sɛlf] pron (reflexive) mi; (emphatic) io stesso(-a); (after prep) me; see also **oneself**

mysterious [mɪs'tɪərɪəs] adj misterioso(-a)

mystery ['mɪstərɪ] n mistero

mystical ['mɪstɪkəl] adj mistico(-a)

mystify ['mɪstɪfaɪ] vt mistificare; (puzzle) confondere

myth [mɪθ] n mito; **mythology** [mɪ'θɔlədʒɪ] n mitologia

n

narrative ['nærətiv] *n* narrativa
narrator [nə'reitə'] *n* narratore(-trice)
narrow ['nærəʊ] *adj* stretto(-a); (*fig*)
limitato(-a), ristretto(-a) ▷ *vi* restringersi;
to have a ~ escape farcela per un pelo;
narrow down *vt* (*search, investigation,
possibilities*) restringere; (*list*) ridurre;
narrowly *adv* per un pelo; (*time*) per poco;
narrow-minded *adj* meschino(-a)
nasal ['neizl] *adj* nasale
nasty ['nɑːsti] *adj* (*person, remark:
unpleasant*) cattivo(-a); (: *rude*) villano(-a);
(*smell, wound, situation*) brutto(-a)
nation ['neiʃən] *n* nazione *f*
national ['næʃənl] *adj* nazionale ▷ *n*
cittadino(-a); **national anthem** *n* inno
nazionale; **national dress** *n* costume
m nazionale; **National Health Service**
(*BRIT*) *n* servizio nazionale di assistenza
sanitaria, ≈ S.S.N. *m*; **National Insurance**
(*BRIT*) *n* ≈ Previdenza Sociale; **nationalist**
adj, *n* nazionalista (*m/f*); **nationality**
[-'næliti] *n* nazionalità *f* inv; **nationalize**
vt nazionalizzare; **national park** *n*
parco nazionale; **National Trust** *n*
sovrintendenza ai beni culturali e ambientali

⬚ **NATIONAL TRUST**

⬚ Fondato nel 1895, il **National Trust** è
⬚ un'organizzazione che si occupa della
⬚ tutela e della salvaguardia di luoghi
⬚ di interesse storico o ambientale nel
⬚ Regno Unito.

nationwide ['neiʃənwaid] *adj* diffuso(-a)
in tutto il paese ▷ *adv* in tutto il paese
native ['neitiv] *n* abitante *m/f* del paese
▷ *adj* indigeno(-a); (*country*) natio(-a);
(*ability*) innato(-a); **a ~ of Russia** un nativo
della Russia; **a ~ speaker of French** una
persona di madrelingua francese; **Native
American** *n* discendente di tribù dell'America
settentrionale
NATO ['neitəʊ] *n abbr* (= *North Atlantic
Treaty Organization*) N.A.T.O. *f*
natural ['nætʃrəl] *adj* naturale; (*ability*)
innato(-a); (*manner*) semplice; **natural gas**
n gas *m* metano; **natural history** *n* storia
naturale; **naturally** *adv* naturalmente;
(*by nature: gifted*) di natura; **natural
resources** *npl* risorse *fpl* naturali
nature ['neitʃə'] *n* natura; (*character*)
natura, indole *f*; **by ~** di natura; **nature
reserve** (*BRIT*) parco naturale
naughty ['nɔːti] *adj* (*child*) birichino(-a),
cattivello(-a); (*story, film*) spinto(-a)
nausea ['nɔːsiə] *n* (*Med*) nausea; (*fig:
disgust*) schifo

n/a *abbr* = **not applicable**
nag [næg] *vt* tormentare ▷ *vi* brontolare in
continuazione
nail [neil] *n* (*human*) unghia; (*metal*) chiodo
▷ *vt* inchiodare; **to ~ sb down to (doing)
sth** costringere qn a (fare) qc; **nailbrush**
n spazzolino da or per unghie; **nailfile** *n*
lima da or per unghie; **nail polish** *n* smalto
da or per unghie; **nail polish remover** *n*
acetone *m*, solvente *m*; **nail scissors** *npl*
forbici *fpl* da or per unghie; **nail varnish**
(*BRIT*) *n* = **nail polish**
naïve [nai'iːv] *adj* ingenuo(-a)
naked ['neikid] *adj* nudo(-a)
name [neim] *n* nome *m*; (*reputation*) nome,
reputazione *f* ▷ *vt* (*baby etc*) chiamare;
(*plant, illness*) nominare; (*person, object*)
identificare; (*price, date*) fissare; **what's
your ~?** come si chiama?; **by ~** di nome;
she knows them all by ~ li conosce tutti
per nome; **namely** *adv* cioè
nanny ['næni] *n* bambinaia
nap [næp] *n* (*sleep*) pisolino; (*of cloth*)
peluria; **to be caught ~ping** essere preso
alla sprovvista
napkin ['næpkin] *n* (*also: table ~*)
tovagliolo
nappy ['næpi] (*BRIT*) *n* pannolino
narcotics [nɑː'kɔtikz] *npl* (*drugs*)
narcotici, stupefacenti *mpl*

naval ['neɪvl] adj navale
navel ['neɪvl] n ombelico
navigate ['nævɪgeɪt] vt percorrere navigando ▷ vi navigare; (Aut) fare da navigatore; **navigation** [-'geɪʃən] n navigazione f
navy ['neɪvɪ] n marina
Nazi ['nɑːtsɪ] n nazista m/f
NB abbr (= nota bene) N.B.
near [nɪəʳ] adj vicino(-a); (relation) prossimo(-a) ▷ adv vicino ▷ prep (also: ~ to) vicino a, presso; (: time) verso ▷ vt avvicinarsi a; **nearby** [nɪə'baɪ] adj vicino(-a) ▷ adv vicino; **is there a bank nearby?** c'è una banca qui vicino?; **nearly** adv quasi; **I nearly fell** per poco non sono caduto; **near-sighted** [nɪə'saɪtɪd] adj miope
neat [niːt] adj (person, room) ordinato(-a); (work) pulito(-a); (solution, plan) ben indovinato(-a), azzeccato(-a); (spirits) liscio(-a); **neatly** adv con ordine; (skilfully) abilmente
necessarily ['nɛsɪsrɪlɪ] adv necessariamente
necessary ['nɛsɪsrɪ] adj necessario(-a)
necessity [nɪ'sɛsɪtɪ] n necessità f inv
neck [nɛk] n collo; (of garment) colletto ▷ vi (inf) pomiciare, sbaciucchiarsi; **~ and ~** testa a testa; **necklace** ['nɛklɪs] n collana; **necktie** ['nɛktaɪ] n cravatta
nectarine ['nɛktərɪn] n nocepesca
need [niːd] n bisogno ▷ vt aver bisogno di; **do you ~ anything?** ha bisogno di qualcosa?; **to ~ to do** dover fare; aver bisogno di fare; **you don't ~ to go** non devi andare, non c'è bisogno che tu vada
needle ['niːdl] n ago; (on record player) puntina ▷ vt punzecchiare
needless ['niːdlɪs] adj inutile
needlework ['niːdlwəːk] n cucito
needn't ['niːdnt] = need not
needy ['niːdɪ] adj bisognoso(-a)
negative ['nɛgətɪv] n (Ling) negazione f; (Phot) negativo ▷ adj negativo(-a)
neglect [nɪ'glɛkt] vt trascurare ▷ n (of person, duty) negligenza; (of child, house etc) scarsa cura; **state of ~** stato di abbandono
negotiate [nɪ'gəʊʃɪeɪt] vi **to ~ (with)** negoziare (con) ▷ vt (Comm) negoziare; (obstacle) superare; **negotiations** [nɪgəʊʃɪ'eɪʃənz] pl n trattative fpl, negoziati mpl
negotiator [nɪ'gəʊʃɪeɪtəʳ] n negoziatore(-trice)
neighbour ['neɪbəʳ] (US **neighbor**) n vicino(-a); **neighbourhood** n vicinato; **neighbouring** adj vicino(-a)

neither ['naɪðəʳ] adj, pron né l'uno(-a) né l'altro(-a), nessuno(-a) dei (delle) due ▷ conj neanche, nemmeno, neppure ▷ adv **~ good nor bad** né buono né cattivo; **I didn't move and ~ did Claude** io non mi mossi e nemmeno Claude; **..., ~ did I refuse ...**, ma non ho nemmeno rifiutato
neon ['niːɔn] n neon m
Nepal [nɪ'pɔːl] n Nepal m
nephew ['nɛvjuː] n nipote m
nerve [nəːv] n nervo; (fig) coraggio; (impudence) faccia tosta; **~s** (nervousness) nervoso; **a fit of ~s** una crisi di nervi
nervous ['nəːvəs] adj nervoso(-a); (anxious) agitato(-a), in apprensione; **nervous breakdown** n esaurimento nervoso
nest [nɛst] n nido ▷ vi fare il nido, nidificare
net [nɛt] n rete f ▷ adj netto(-a) ▷ vt (fish etc) prendere con la rete; (profit) ricavare un utile netto di; **the N~** (Internet) Internet f; **netball** n specie di pallacanestro
Netherlands ['nɛðələndz] npl **the ~** i Paesi Bassi
nett [nɛt] adj = net
nettle ['nɛtl] n ortica
network ['nɛtwəːk] n rete f
neurotic [njuə'rɔtɪk] adj, n nevrotico(-a)
neuter ['njuːtəʳ] adj neutro(-a) ▷ vt (cat etc) castrare
neutral ['njuːtrəl] adj neutro(-a); (person, nation) neutrale ▷ n (Aut): **in ~** in folle
never ['nɛvəʳ] adv (non...) mai; **I've ~ been to Spain** non sono mai stato in Spagna; **~ again** mai più; **I'll ~ go there again** non ci vado più; **~ in my life** mai in vita mia; see also **mind**; **never-ending** adj interminabile; **nevertheless** [nɛvəðə'lɛs] adv tuttavia, ciò nonostante, ciò nondimeno
new [njuː] adj nuovo(-a); (brand new) nuovo(-a) di zecca; **New Age** n New Age f inv; **newborn** adj neonato(-a); **newcomer** ['njuːkʌməʳ] n nuovo(-a) venuto(-a); **newly** adv di recente
news [njuːz] n notizie fpl; (Radio) giornale m radio; (TV) telegiornale m; **a piece of ~** una notizia; **news agency** n agenzia di stampa; **newsagent** (BRIT) n giornalaio; **newscaster** n (Radio, TV) annunciatore(-trice); **news dealer** (US) = **newsagent**; **newsletter** n bollettino; **newspaper** n giornale m; **newsreader** n = **newscaster**
newt [njuːt] n tritone m
New Year n Anno Nuovo; **New Year's Day** n il Capodanno; **New Year's Eve** n la vigilia di Capodanno

New York [-'jɔːk] n New York f

New Zealand [-'ziːlənd] n Nuova Zelanda; **New Zealander** n neozelandese m/f

next [nɛkst] adj prossimo(-a) ▷ adv accanto; (in time) dopo; **the ~ day** il giorno dopo, l'indomani; **~ time** la prossima volta; **~ year** l'anno prossimo; **when do we meet ~?** quando ci rincontriamo?; **~ to** accanto a; **~ to nothing** quasi niente; **~ please!** (avanti) il prossimo!; **next door** adv, adj accanto inv; **next-of-kin** n parente m/f prossimo(-a)

NHS n abbr = **National Health Service**

nibble ['nɪbl] vt mordicchiare

nice [naɪs] adj (holiday, trip) piacevole; (flat, picture) bello(-a); (person) simpatico(-a), gentile; **nicely** adv bene

niche [niːʃ] n (Archit) nicchia

nick [nɪk] n taglietto; tacca ▷ vt (inf) rubare; **in the ~ of time** appena in tempo

nickel ['nɪkl] n nichel m; (US) moneta da cinque centesimi di dollaro

nickname ['nɪkneɪm] n soprannome m

nicotine ['nɪkətiːn] n nicotina

niece [niːs] n nipote f

Nigeria [naɪ'dʒɪərɪə] n Nigeria

night [naɪt] n notte f; (evening) sera; **at ~** la sera; **by ~** di notte; **the ~ before last** l'altro ieri notte (or sera); **night club** n locale m notturno; **nightdress** n camicia da notte; **nightie** ['naɪtɪ] n = **nightdress**; **nightlife** ['naɪtlaɪf] n vita notturna; **nightly** ['naɪtlɪ] adj di ogni notte or sera; (by night) notturno(-a) ▷ adv ogni notte or sera; **nightmare** ['naɪtmɛəʳ] n incubo

night: **night school** n scuola serale; **night shift** n turno di notte; **night-time** n notte f

nil [nɪl] n nulla m; (BRIT Sport) zero

nine [naɪn] num nove; **nineteen** num diciannove; **nineteenth** [naɪn'tiːnθ] num diciannovesimo(-a); **ninetieth** ['naɪntɪɪθ] num novantesimo(-a); **ninety** num novanta; **ninth** [naɪnθ] num nono(-a)

nip [nɪp] vt pizzicare; (bite) mordere

nipple ['nɪpl] n (Anat) capezzolo

nitrogen ['naɪtrədʒən] n azoto

 KEYWORD

no [nəu] (pl **noes**) adv (opposite of "yes") no; **are you coming? — no (I'm not)** viene? — no (non vengo); **would you like some more? — no thank you** ne vuole ancora un po'? — no, grazie

▷ adj (not any) nessuno(-a); **I have no money/time/books** non ho soldi/

tempo/libri; **no student would have done it** nessuno studente lo avrebbe fatto; **"no parking"** "divieto di sosta"; **"no smoking"** "vietato fumare"

▷ n no m inv

nobility [nəu'bɪlɪtɪ] n nobiltà

noble ['nəubl] adj nobile

nobody ['nəubədɪ] pron nessuno

nod [nɔd] vi accennare col capo, fare un cenno; (in agreement) annuire con un cenno del capo; (sleep) sonnecchiare ▷ vt **to ~ one's head** fare di sì col capo ▷ n cenno; **nod off** vi assopirsi

noise [nɔɪz] n rumore m; (din, racket) chiasso; **I can't sleep for the ~** non riesco a dormire a causa del rumore; **noisy** adj (street, car) rumoroso(-a); (person) chiassoso(-a)

nominal ['nɔmɪnl] adj nominale; (rent) simbolico(-a)

nominate ['nɔmɪneɪt] vt (propose) proporre come candidato; (elect) nominare; **nomination** [nɔmɪ'neɪʃən] n nomina; candidatura; **nominee** [nɔmɪ'niː] n persona nominata, candidato(-a)

none [nʌn] pron (not one thing) niente; (not one person) nessuno(-a); **~ of you** nessuno(-a) di voi; **I've ~ left** non ne ho più; **he's ~ the worse for it** non ne ha risentito

nonetheless [nʌnðə'lɛs] adv nondimeno

non-fiction [nɔn'fɪkʃən] n saggistica

nonsense ['nɔnsəns] n sciocchezze fpl

non: **non-smoker** n non fumatore(-trice); **non-smoking** adj (person) che non fuma; (area, section) per non fumatori; **non-stick** adj antiaderente, antiadesivo(-a)

noodles ['nuːdlz] npl taglierini mpl

noon [nuːn] n mezzogiorno

no-one ['nəuwʌn] pron = **nobody**

nor [nɔːʳ] conj = **neither** ▷ adv see **neither**

norm [nɔːm] n norma

normal ['nɔːml] adj normale; **normally** adv normalmente

north [nɔːθ] n nord m, settentrione m ▷ adj nord inv, del nord, settentrionale ▷ adv verso nord; **North America** n America del Nord; **North American** adj, n nordamericano(-a); **northbound** ['nɔːθbaund] adj (traffic) diretto(-a) a nord; (carriageway) che va verso nord; **north-east** n nord-est m; **northeastern** adj nordorientale; **northern** ['nɔːðən] adj del nord, settentrionale; **Northern Ireland** n Irlanda del Nord; **North Korea** n Corea del Nord; **North Pole** n Polo Nord; **North**

Sea n Mare m del Nord; **north-west** n nord-ovest m; **northwestern** adj nordoccidentale

Norway ['nɔːweɪ] n Norvegia; **Norwegian** [nɔː'wiːdʒən] adj norvegese ▷ n norvegese m/f; (Ling) norvegese m

nose [nəuz] n naso; (of animal) muso ▷ vi **to ~ about** aggirarsi; **nosebleed** n emorragia nasale; **nosey** (inf) adj = **nosy**

nostalgia [nɔs'tældʒɪə] n nostalgia

nostalgic [nɔs'tældʒɪk] adj nostalgico(-a)

nostril ['nɔstrɪl] n narice f; (of horse) frogia

nosy ['nəuzɪ] (inf) adj curioso(-a)

not [nɔt] adv non; **he is ~ or isn't here** non è qui, non c'è; **you must ~ or you mustn't do that** non devi fare quello; **it's too late, isn't it** or **is it ~?** è troppo tardi, vero?; **~ that I don't like him** non che (lui) non mi piaccia; **~ yet/now** non ancora/ora; see also **all**; **only**

notable ['nəutəbl] adj notevole; **notably** ['nəutəblɪ] adv (markedly) notevolmente; (particularly) in particolare

notch [nɔtʃ] n tacca; (in saw) dente m

note [nəut] n nota; (letter, banknote) biglietto ▷ vt (also: **~ down**) prendere nota di; **to take ~s** prendere appunti; **notebook** n taccuino; **noted** ['nəutɪd] adj celebre; **notepad** n bloc-notes m inv; **notepaper** n carta da lettere

nothing ['nʌθɪŋ] n nulla m, niente m; (zero) zero; **he does ~** non fa niente; **~ new/much** etc niente di nuovo/speciale etc; **for ~** per niente

notice ['nəutɪs] n avviso; (of leaving) preavviso ▷ vt notare, accorgersi di; **to take ~ of** fare attenzione a; **to bring sth to sb's ~** far notare qc a qn; **at short ~** con un breve preavviso; **until further ~** fino a nuovo avviso; **to hand in one's ~** licenziarsi; **noticeable** adj evidente

notify ['nəutɪfaɪ] vt **to ~ sth to sb** far sapere qc a qn; **to ~ sb of sth** avvisare qn di qc

notion ['nəuʃən] n idea; (concept) nozione f; **~s** npl (US: haberdashery) merceria

notorious [nəu'tɔːrɪəs] adj famigerato(-a)

notwithstanding [nɔtwɪθ'stændɪŋ] adv nondimeno ▷ prep nonostante, malgrado

nought [nɔːt] n zero

noun [naun] n nome m, sostantivo

nourish ['nʌrɪʃ] vt nutrire; **nourishment** n nutrimento

Nov. abbr (= November) nov.

novel ['nɔvl] n romanzo ▷ adj nuovo(-a); **novelist** n romanziere(-a); **novelty** n

novità f inv

November [nəu'vɛmbər] n novembre m

novice ['nɔvɪs] n principiante m/f; (Rel) novizio(-a)

now [nau] adv ora, adesso ▷ conj **~ (that)** adesso che, ora che; **by ~** ormai; **just ~** proprio ora; **right ~** subito, immediatamente; **~ and then, ~ and again** ogni tanto; **from ~ on** da ora in poi; **nowadays** ['nauədeɪz] adv oggidì

nowhere ['nəuwɛər] adv in nessun luogo, da nessuna parte

nozzle ['nɔzl] n (of hose etc) boccaglio; (of fire extinguisher) lancia

nr abbr (BRIT) = **near**

nuclear ['njuːklɪər] adj nucleare

nucleus ['njuːklɪəs] (pl nuclei) n nucleo

nude [njuːd] adj nudo(-a) ▷ n (Art) nudo; **in the ~** tutto(-a) nudo(-a)

nudge [nʌdʒ] vt dare una gomitata a

nudist ['njuːdɪst] n nudista m/f

nudity ['njuːdɪtɪ] n nudità

nuisance ['njuːsns] n **it's a ~** è una seccatura; **he's a ~** è uno scocciatore

numb [nʌm] adj **~ (with)** intorpidito(-a) (da); (with fear) impietrito(-a) (da); **~ with cold** intirizzito(-a) (dal freddo)

number ['nʌmbər] n numero ▷ vt numerare; (include) contare; **a ~ of** un certo numero di; **to be ~ed among** venire annoverato(-a) tra; **they were 10 in ~** erano in tutto 10; **number plate** (BRIT) n (Aut) targa; **Number Ten** n (BRIT: = 10 Downing Street) residenza del Primo Ministro del Regno Unito

numerical [njuː'mɛrɪkl] adj numerico(-a)

numerous ['njuːmərəs] adj numeroso(-a)

nun [nʌn] n suora, monaca

nurse [nəːs] n infermiere(-a); (also: **~maid**) bambinaia ▷ vt (patient, cold) curare; (baby: BRIT) cullare; (: US) allattare, dare il latte a

nursery ['nəːsərɪ] n (room) camera dei bambini; (institution) asilo; (for plants) vivaio; **nursery rhyme** n filastrocca; **nursery school** n scuola materna; **nursery slope** (BRIT) n (Ski) pista per principianti

nursing ['nəːsɪŋ] n (profession) professione f di infermiere (or di infermiera); (care) cura; **nursing home** n casa di cura

nurture ['nəːtʃər] vt allevare; nutrire

nut [nʌt] n (of metal) dado; (fruit) noce f

nutmeg ['nʌtmɛg] n noce f moscata

nutrient ['njuːtrɪənt] adj nutriente ▷ n sostanza nutritiva

nutrition [nju:'trɪʃən] *n* nutrizione *f*
nutritious [nju:'trɪʃəs] *adj* nutriente
nuts [nʌts] (*inf*) *adj* matto(-a)
NVQ *n abbr* (BRIT) = **National Vocational
Qualification**
nylon ['naɪlɔn] *n* nailon *m* ▷ *adj* di nailon

oak [əuk] *n* quercia ▷ *adj* di quercia
O.A.P. (BRIT) *n, abbr* = **old age pensioner**
oar [ɔ:ʳ] *n* remo
oasis [əu'eɪsɪs] (*pl* **oases**) *n* oasi *f inv*
oath [əuθ] *n* giuramento; (*swear word*)
  bestemmia
oatmeal ['əutmi:l] *n* farina d'avena
oats [əuts] *npl* avena
obedience [ə'bi:dɪəns] *n* ubbidienza
obedient [ə'bi:dɪənt] *adj* ubbidiente
obese [əu'bi:s] *adj* obeso(-a)
obesity [əu'bi:sɪtɪ] *n* obesità
obey [ə'beɪ] *vt* ubbidire a; (*instructions,
  regulations*) osservare
obituary [ə'bɪtjuərɪ] *n* necrologia
object [*n* 'ɔbdʒɪkt, *vb* əb'dʒɛkt] *n*
  oggetto; (*purpose*) scopo, intento;
  (*Ling*) complemento oggetto ▷ *vi* **to
  ~ to** (*attitude*) disapprovare; (*proposal*)
  protestare contro, sollevare delle obiezioni
  contro; **expense is no ~** non si bada a
  spese; **to ~ that** obiettare che; **objection**
  [əb'dʒɛkʃən] *n* obiezione *f*; **objective** *n*
  obiettivo
obligation [ɔblɪ'geɪʃən] *n* obbligo, dovere
  m; **without ~** senza impegno
obligatory [ə'blɪgətərɪ] *adj*
  obbligatorio(-a)
oblige [ə'blaɪdʒ] *vt* (*force*): **to ~ sb to do**
  costringere qn a fare; (*do a favour*) fare una

cortesia a; **to be ~d to sb for sth** essere
grato a qn per qc
oblique [ə'bli:k] *adj* obliquo(-a); *(allusion)*
indiretto(-a)
obliterate [ə'blɪtəreɪt] *vt* cancellare
oblivious [ə'blɪvɪəs] *adj* ~ **of** incurante di;
inconscio(-a) di
oblong ['ɔblɔŋ] *adj* oblungo(-a) ▷ *n*
rettangolo
obnoxious [əb'nɔkʃəs] *adj* odioso(-a);
(smell) disgustoso(-a), ripugnante
oboe ['əubəu] *n* oboe *m*
obscene [əb'si:n] *adj* osceno(-a)
obscure [əb'skjuə'] *adj* oscuro(-a) ▷ *vt*
oscurare; *(hide: sun)* nascondere
observant [əb'zə:vnt] *adj* attento(-a)

> ▪ Be careful not to translate *observant*
> by the Italian word *osservante*.

observation [ɔbzə'veɪʃən] *n* osservazione
f; *(by police etc)* sorveglianza
observatory [əb'zə:vətrɪ] *n*
osservatorio
observe [əb'zə:v] *vt* osservare;
(remark) fare osservare; **observer** *n*
osservatore(-trice)
obsess [əb'sɛs] *vt* ossessionare; **obsession**
[əb'sɛʃən] *n* ossessione *f*; **obsessive** *adj*
ossessivo(-a)
obsolete ['ɔbsəli:t] *adj* obsoleto(-a)
obstacle ['ɔbstəkl] *n* ostacolo
obstinate ['ɔbstɪnɪt] *adj* ostinato(-a)
obstruct [əb'strʌkt] *vt* *(block)* ostruire,
ostacolare; *(halt)* fermare; *(hinder)*
impedire; **obstruction** [əb'strʌkʃən] *n*
ostruzione *f*; ostacolo
obtain [əb'teɪn] *vt* ottenere
obvious ['ɔbvɪəs] *adj* ovvio(-a), evidente;
obviously *adv* ovviamente; certo
occasion [ə'keɪʒən] *n* occasione *f*;
(event) avvenimento; **occasional** *adj*
occasionale; **occasionally** *adv* ogni
tanto
occult [ɔ'kʌlt] *adj* occulto(-a) ▷ *n* **the ~**
l'occulto
occupant ['ɔkjupənt] *n* occupante *m/f*; *(of
boat, car etc)* persona a bordo
occupation [ɔkju'peɪʃən] *n* occupazione *f*;
(job) mestiere *m*, professione *f*
occupy ['ɔkjupaɪ] *vt* occupare; **to ~ o.s. in
doing** occuparsi a fare
occur [ə'kə:'] *vi* succedere, capitare; **to ~
to sb** venire in mente a qn; **occurrence** *n*
caso, fatto; presenza

> ▪ Be careful not to translate *occur* by
> the Italian word *occorrere*.

ocean ['əuʃən] *n* oceano
o'clock [ə'klɔk] *adv* **it is 5 o'clock** sono le 5
Oct. *abbr* (= *October*) ott.
October [ɔk'təubə'] *n* ottobre *m*

octopus ['ɔktəpəs] *n* polpo, piovra
odd [ɔd] *adj* *(strange)* strano(-a),
bizzarro(-a); *(number)* dispari *inv*; *(not of a
set)* spaiato(-a); **60-~** 60 e oltre; **at ~ times**
di tanto in tanto; **the ~ one out** l'eccezione
f; **oddly** *adv* stranamente; **odds** *npl* *(in
betting)* quota
odometer [ɔ'dɔmɪtə'] *n* odometro
odour ['əudə'] *(us* **odor***) n* odore *m*;
(unpleasant) cattivo odore

KEYWORD

of [ɔv, əv] *prep* **1** *(gen)* di; **a boy of 10** un
ragazzo di 10 anni; **a friend of ours** un
nostro amico; **that was kind of you** è
stato molto gentile da parte sua
2 *(expressing quantity, amount, dates etc)*
di; **a kilo of flour** un chilo di farina; **how
much of this do you need?** quanto gliene
serve?; **there were 3 of them** *(people)*
erano in 3; *(objects)* ce n'erano 3; **3 of us
went** 3 di noi sono andati; **the 5th of July**
il 5 luglio
3 *(from, out of)* di, in; **of made of wood**
(fatto) di or in legno

KEYWORD

off [ɔf] *adv* **1** *(distance, time)*: **it's a long way
off** è lontano; **the game is 3 days off** la
partita è tra 3 giorni
2 *(departure, removal)* via; **to go off to
Paris** andarsene a Parigi; **I must be off**
devo andare via; **to take off one's coat**
togliersi il cappotto; **the button came off**
il bottone è venuto via *or* si è staccato; **10%
off** con lo sconto del 10%
3 *(not at work)*: **to have a day off** avere un
giorno libero; **to be off sick** essere assente
per malattia
▷ *adj* *(engine)* spento(-a); *(tap)* chiuso(-a);
(cancelled) sospeso(-a); (BRIT: *food*)
andato(-a) a male; **on the off chance**
nel caso; **to have an off day** non essere
in forma
▷ *prep* **1** *(motion, removal etc)* da; *(distant
from)* a poca distanza da; **a street off the
square** una strada che parte dalla piazza
2: **to be off meat** non mangiare più la
carne

offence [ə'fɛns] *(us* **offense***) n* (LAW)
contravvenzione *f*; (: *more serious*) reato; **to
take ~ at** offendersi per
offend [ə'fɛnd] *vt* *(person)* offendere;
offender *n* delinquente *m/f*; *(against
regulations)* contravventore(-trice)
offense [ə'fɛns] *(us) n* = **offence**

offensive [ə'fɛnsɪv] *adj* offensivo(-a);
(*smell etc*) sgradevole, ripugnante ▷ *n* (*Mil*)
offensiva

offer ['ɔfə^r] *n* offerta, proposta ▷ *vt*
offrire; **"on ~"** (*Comm*) "in offerta
speciale"

offhand [ɔf'hænd] *adj* disinvolto(-a),
noncurante ▷ *adv* su due piedi

office ['ɔfɪs] *n* (*place*) ufficio; (*position*)
carica; **doctor's ~** (*us*) studio; **to take ~**
entrare in carica; **office block** (*us* **office
building**) *n* complesso di uffici; **office
hours** *npl* orario d'ufficio; (*us Med*) orario
di visite

officer ['ɔfɪsə^r] *n* (*Mil etc*) ufficiale *m*;
(*also*: **police ~**) agente *m* di polizia; (*of
organization*) funzionario

office worker *n* impiegato(-a) d'ufficio

official [ə'fɪʃl] *adj* (*authorized*) ufficiale ▷ *n*
ufficiale *m*; (*civil servant*) impiegato(-a)
statale; funzionario

off: **off-licence** (*BRIT*) *n* (*shop*) spaccio
di bevande alcoliche; **off-line** *adj, adv*
(*Comput*) off-line *inv*, fuori linea;
(: *switched off*) spento(-a); **off-peak** *adj*
(*ticket, heating etc*) a tariffa ridotta; (*time*)
non di punta; **off-putting** (*BRIT*) *adj*
sgradevole, antipatico(-a); **off-season**
adj, adv fuori stagione; **offset** ['ɔfsɛt]
(*irreg*) *vt* (*counteract*) controbilanciare,
compensare; **offshore** [ɔf'ɔ:^r] *adj* (*breeze*)
di terra; (*island*) vicino alla costa; (*fishing*)
costiero(-a); **offside** ['ɔf'saɪd] *adj* (*Sport*)
fuori gioco; (*Aut: in Britain*) destro(-a); (: *in
Italy etc*) sinistro(-a); **offspring** ['ɔfsprɪŋ] *n
inv* prole *f*, discendenza

often ['ɔfn] *adv* spesso; **how ~ do you go?**
quanto spesso ci vai?

oh [əu] *excl* oh!

oil [ɔɪl] *n* olio; (*petroleum*) petrolio; (*for
central heating*) nafta ▷ *vt* (*machine*)
lubrificare; **oil filter** *n* (*Aut*) filtro dell'olio;
oil painting *n* quadro a olio; **oil refinery**
n raffineria di petrolio; **oil rig** *n* derrick *m*
inv; (*at sea*) piattaforma per trivellazioni
subacquee; **oil slick** *n* chiazza d'olio;
oil tanker *n* (*ship*) petroliera; (*truck*)
autocisterna per petrolio; **oil well** *n* pozzo
petrolifero; **oily** *adj* unto(-a), oleoso(-a);
(*food*) grasso(-a)

ointment ['ɔɪntmənt] *n* unguento

O.K. ['əu'keɪ] *excl* d'accordo! ▷ *adj* non
male *inv* ▷ *vt* approvare; **is it O.K.?**, **are
you O.K.?** tutto bene?

old [əuld] *adj* vecchio(-a); (*ancient*)
antico(-a), vecchio(-a); (*person*)
vecchio(-a), anziano(-a); **how ~ are you?**
quanti anni ha?; **he's 10 years ~** ha 10 anni;
~er brother fratello maggiore; **old age** *n*

vecchiaia; **old-age pension** ['əuldeɪdʒ-]
n (*BRIT*) pensione *f* di vecchiaia; **old-age
pensioner** (*BRIT*) *n* pensionato(-a); **old-
fashioned** *adj* antiquato(-a), fuori moda;
(*person*) all'antica; **old people's home** *n*
ricovero per anziani

olive ['ɔlɪv] *n* (*fruit*) oliva; (*tree*) olivo ▷ *adj*
(*also*: **~-green**) verde oliva *inv*; **olive oil** *n*
olio d'oliva

Olympic [əu'lɪmpɪk] *adj* olimpico(-a);
the ~ Games, the ~s i giochi olimpici, le
Olimpiadi

omelet(te) ['ɔmlɪt] *n* omelette *f inv*

omen ['əumən] *n* presagio, augurio

ominous ['ɔmɪnəs] *adj* minaccioso(-a);
(*event*) di malaugurio

omit [əu'mɪt] *vt* omettere

 KEYWORD

on [ɔn] *prep* **1** (*indicating position*) su; **on
the wall** sulla parete; **on the left** a *or*
sulla sinistra

2 (*indicating means, method, condition
etc*): **on foot** a piedi; **on the train/plane**
in treno/aereo; **on the telephone** al
telefono; **on the radio/television**
alla radio/televisione; **to be on drugs**
drogarsi; **on holiday** in vacanza

3 (*of time*): **on Friday** venerdì; **on Fridays**
il *or* di venerdì; **on June 20th** il 20 giugno;
on Friday, June 20th venerdì, 20 giugno;
a week on Friday venerdì a otto; **on
his arrival** al suo arrivo; **on seeing this**
vedendo ciò

4 (*about, concerning*) su, di; **information
on train services** informazioni sui
collegamenti ferroviari; **a book on
Goldoni/physics** un libro su Goldoni/di
or sulla fisica

▷ *adv* **1** (*referring to dress, covering*): **to
have one's coat on** avere indosso il
cappotto; **to put one's coat on** mettersi
il cappotto; **what's she got on?** cosa
indossa?; **she put her boots/gloves/
hat on** si mise gli stivali/i guanti/il
cappello; **screw the lid on tightly** avvita
bene il coperchio

2 (*further, continuously*): **to walk on, go
on** *etc* continuare, proseguire *etc*; **to read
on** continuare a leggere; **on and off** ogni
tanto

▷ *adj* **1** (*in operation: machine, TV, light*)
acceso(-a); (: *tap*) aperto(-a); (: *brake*)
inserito(-a); **is the meeting still on?** (*in
progress*) la riunione è ancora in corso?;
(*not cancelled*) è confermato l'incontro?;
there's a good film on at the cinema
danno un buon film al cinema

2 (*inf*): **that's not on!** (*not acceptable*) non si fa così!; (*not possible*) non se ne parla neanche!

once [wʌns] *adv* una volta ▷ *conj* non appena, quando; **~ he had left/it was done** dopo che se n'era andato/fu fatto; **at ~** subito; (*simultaneously*) a un tempo; **~ a week** una volta per settimana; **~ more** ancora una volta; **~ and for all** una volta per sempre; **~ upon a time** c'era una volta

oncoming [ˈɔnkʌmɪŋ] *adj* (*traffic*) che viene in senso opposto

 KEYWORD

one [wʌn] *num* uno(-a); **one hundred and fifty** centocinquanta; **one day** un giorno ▷ *adj* **1** (*sole*) unico(-a); **the one book which** l'unico libro che; **the one man who** l'unico che

2 (*same*) stesso(-a); **they came in the one car** sono venuti nella stessa macchina ▷ *pron* **1**: **this one** questo(-a); **that one** quello(-a); **I've already got one/a red one** ne ho già uno/uno rosso; **one by one** uno per uno

2: **one another** l'un l'altro; **to look at one another** guardarsi; **to help one another** auitarsi l'un l'altro or a vicenda

3 (*impersonal*) si; **one never knows** non si sa mai; **to cut one's finger** tagliarsi un dito; **one needs to eat** bisogna mangiare

one: **one-off** (*BRIT*: *inf*) *n* fatto eccezionale
oneself [wʌnˈsɛlf] *pron* (*reflexive*) si; (*after prep*) se stesso(-a), sé; **to do sth (by) ~** fare qc da sé; **to hurt ~** farsi male; **to keep sth for ~** tenere qc per sé; **to talk to ~** parlare da solo

one: **one-shot** [wʌnˈʃɔt] (*US*) *n* = **one-off**; **one-sided** *adj* (*argument*) unilaterale; **one-to-one** *adj* (*relationship*) univoco(-a); **one-way** *adj* (*street*, *traffic*) a senso unico
ongoing [ˈɔngəuɪŋ] *adj* in corso; in attuazione
onion [ˈʌnjən] *n* cipolla
on-line [ˈɔnlaɪn] *adj*, *adv* (*Comput*) on-line *inv*
onlooker [ˈɔnlukəʳ] *n* spettatore(-trice)
only [ˈəunlɪ] *adv* solo, soltanto ▷ *adj* solo(-a), unico(-a) ▷ *conj* solo che, ma; **an ~ child** un figlio unico; **not ~ ... but also** non solo ... ma anche
on-screen [ɔnˈskriːn] *adj* sullo schermo *inv*
onset [ˈɔnsɛt] *n* inizio
onto [ˈɔntu] *prep* = **on to**
onward(s) [ˈɔnwəd(z)] *adv* (*move*) in avanti; **from that time onward(s)** da

quella volta in poi

oops [ups] *excl* ops! (*esprimere rincrescimento per un piccolo contrattempo*); **~-a-daisy!** oplà!
ooze [uːz] *vi* stillare
opaque [əuˈpeɪk] *adj* opaco(-a)
open [ˈəupn] *adj* aperto(-a); (*road*) libero(-a); (*meeting*) pubblico(-a) ▷ *vt* aprire ▷ *vi* (*eyes*, *door*, *debate*) aprirsi; (*flower*) sbocciare; (*shop*, *bank*, *museum*) aprire; (*book etc*: *commence*) cominciare; **is it ~ to the public?** è aperto al pubblico?; **in the ~ (air)** all'aperto; **what time do you ~?** a che ora aprite?; **open up** *vt* aprire; (*blocked road*) sgombrare ▷ *vi* (*shop*, *business*) aprire; **open-air** *adj* all'aperto; **opening** *adj* (*speech*) di apertura ▷ *n* apertura; (*opportunity*) occasione *f*, opportunità *f inv*; sbocco; **opening hours** *npl* orario d'apertura; **open learning** *n* sistema educativo secondo il quale lo studente ha maggior controllo e gestione delle modalità di apprendimento; **openly** *adv* apertamente; **open-minded** *adj* che ha la mente aperta; **open-necked** *adj* col collo slacciato; **open-plan** *adj* senza pareti divisorie; **Open University** *n* (*BRIT*) vedi nota nel riquadro

◈ OPEN UNIVERSITY
◈
◈ La **Open University**, fondata in Gran
◈ Bretagna nel 1969, organizza corsi
◈ di laurea per corrispondenza o via
◈ Internet. Alcune lezioni possono venir
◈ seguite per radio o alla televisione e
◈ vengono organizzati regolari corsi
◈ estivi.

opera [ˈɔpərə] *n* opera; **opera house** *n* opera; **opera singer** *n* cantante *m/f* d'opera or lirico(-a)
operate [ˈɔpəreɪt] *vt* (*machine*) azionare, far funzionare; (*system*) usare ▷ *vi* funzionare; (*drug*) essere efficace; **to ~ on sb (for)** (*Med*) operare qn (di)
operating room (*US*) *n* = **operating theatre**
operating theatre *n* (*Med*) sala operatoria
operation [ɔpəˈreɪʃən] *n* operazione *f*; **to be in ~** (*machine*) essere in azione or funzionamento; (*system*) essere in vigore; **to have an ~** (*Med*) subire un'operazione; **operational** *adj* in funzione; d'esercizio
operative [ˈɔpərətɪv] *adj* (*measure*) operativo(-a)
operator [ˈɔpəreɪtəʳ] *n* (*of machine*) operatore(-trice); (*Tel*) centralinista *m/f*

opinion [ə'pɪnɪən] *n* opinione *f*, parere *m*;
in my ~ secondo me, a mio avviso; **opinion
poll** *n* sondaggio di opinioni

opponent [ə'pəunənt] *n* avversario(-a)

opportunity [ɔpə'tjuːnɪtɪ] *n* opportunità
f inv, occasione *f*; **to take the ~ of doing**
cogliere l'occasione per fare

oppose [ə'pəuz] *vt* opporsi a; **~d to**
contrario(-a) a; **as ~d to** in contrasto con

opposite ['ɔpəzɪt] *adj* opposto(-a); *(house
etc)* di fronte ▷ *adv* di fronte, dirimpetto
▷ *prep* di fronte a ▷ *n* **the ~** il contrario,
l'opposto; **the ~ sex** l'altro sesso

opposition [ɔpə'zɪʃən] *n* opposizione *f*

oppress [ə'prɛs] *vt* opprimere

opt [ɔpt] *vi* **to ~ for** optare per; **to ~ to do**
scegliere di fare; **opt out** *vi* **to ~ out of**
ritirarsi da

optician [ɔp'tɪʃən] *n* ottico

optimism ['ɔptɪmɪzəm] *n* ottimismo

optimist ['ɔptɪmɪst] *n* ottimista *m/f*;
optimistic [-'mɪstɪk] *adj* ottimistico(-a)

optimum ['ɔptɪməm] *adj* ottimale

option ['ɔpʃən] *n* scelta; *(Scol)* materia
facoltativa; *(Comm)* opzione *f*; **optional**
adj facoltativo(-a); *(Comm)* a scelta

or [ɔːʳ] *conj* o, oppure; *(with negative)*: **he
hasn't seen or heard anything** non
ha visto né sentito niente; **or else** se no,
altrimenti; oppure

oral ['ɔːrəl] *adj* orale ▷ *n* esame *m* orale

orange ['ɔrɪndʒ] *n (fruit)* arancia ▷ *adj*
arancione; **orange juice** *n* succo
d'arancia; **orange squash** *n* succo
d'arancia *(da diluire con l'acqua)*

orbit ['ɔːbɪt] *n* orbita ▷ *vt* orbitare intorno
a

orchard ['ɔːtʃəd] *n* frutteto

orchestra ['ɔːkɪstrə] *n* orchestra; *(us:
seating)* platea

orchid ['ɔːkɪd] *n* orchidea

ordeal [ɔː'diːl] *n* prova, travaglio

order ['ɔːdəʳ] *n* ordine *m*; *(Comm)*
ordinazione *f* ▷ *vt* ordinare; **can I ~ now,
please?** posso ordinare, per favore?; **in
~** in ordine, *(of document)* in regola; **in
(working) ~** funzionante; **in ~ to do** per
fare; **in ~ that** affinché + *sub*; **on ~** *(Comm)*
in ordinazione; **out of ~** non in ordine, *(not
working)* guasto; **to ~ sb to do** ordinare
a qn di fare; **order form** *n* modulo
d'ordinazione; **orderly** *n (Mil)* attendente
m; *(Med)* inserviente *m* ▷ *adj (room)* in
ordine; *(mind)* metodico(-a); *(person)*
ordinato(-a), metodico(-a)

ordinary ['ɔːdnrɪ] *adj* normale, comune;
(pej) mediocre; **out of the ~** diverso dal
solito, fuori dell'ordinario

ore [ɔːʳ] *n* minerale *m* grezzo

oregano [ɔrɪ'gɑːnəu] *n* origano

organ ['ɔːgən] *n* organo; **organic**
[ɔː'gænɪk] *adj* organico(-a); *(of food)*
biologico(-a); **organism** *n* organismo

organization [ɔːgənaɪ'zeɪʃən] *n*
organizzazione *f*

organize ['ɔːgənaɪz] *vt* organizzare;
to get ~d organizzarsi; **organized** ['ɔː
gənaɪzd] *adj* organizzato(-a); **organizer**
n organizzatore(-trice)

orgasm ['ɔːgæzəm] *n* orgasmo

orgy ['ɔːdʒɪ] *n* orgia

oriental [ɔːrɪ'ɛntl] *adj, n* orientale *m/f*

orientation [ɔːrɪen'teɪʃən] *n*
orientamento

origin ['ɔrɪdʒɪn] *n* origine *f*

original [ə'rɪdʒɪnl] *adj* originale; *(earliest)*
originario(-a) ▷ *n* originale *m*; **originally**
adv (at first) all'inizio

originate [ə'rɪdʒɪneɪt] *vi* **to ~ from** essere
originario(-a) di; *(suggestion)* provenire da;
to ~ in avere origine in

Orkneys ['ɔːknɪz] *npl* **the ~** *(also:* **the
Orkney Islands)** le Orcadi

ornament ['ɔːnəmənt] *n* ornamento;
(trinket) ninnolo; **ornamental** [-'mɛntl]
adj ornamentale

ornate [ɔː'neɪt] *adj* molto ornato(-a)

orphan ['ɔːfn] *n* orfano(-a)

orthodox ['ɔːθədɔks] *adj* ortodosso(-a)

orthopaedic [ɔːθə'piːdɪk] *(us* **orthopedic)**
adj ortopedico(-a)

osteopath ['ɔstɪəpæθ] *n* specialista *m/f* di
osteopatia

ostrich ['ɔstrɪtʃ] *n* struzzo

other ['ʌðəʳ] *adj* altro(-a) ▷ *pron* **the ~
(one)** l'altro(-a); **~s** *(other people)* altri *mpl*;
~ than altro che; a parte; **otherwise** *adv*,
conj altrimenti

otter ['ɔtəʳ] *n* lontra

ouch [autʃ] *excl* ohi!, ahi!

ought [ɔːt] *(pt* ought) *aux vb* **I ~ to do
it** dovrei farlo; **this ~ to have been
corrected** questo avrebbe dovuto essere
corretto; **he ~ to win** dovrebbe vincere

ounce [auns] *n* oncia *(= 28.35 g, 16 in a
pound)*

our ['auəʳ] *adj* il (la) nostro(-e); *(pl)* i (le)
nostri(-e); *see also* **my**; **ours** *pron* il (la)
nostro(-a); *(pl)* i (le) nostri(-e); *see also*
mine; **ourselves** *pron pl (reflexive)* ci; *(after
preposition)* noi; *(emphatic)* noi stessi(-e);
see also **oneself**

oust [aust] *vt* cacciare, espellere

out [aut] *adv (gen)* fuori; **~ here/there**
qui/là fuori; **to speak ~ loud** parlare
forte; **to have a night ~** uscire una sera;
the boat was 10 km ~ la barca era a 10
km dalla costa; **3 days ~ from Plym~h** a 3

giorni da Plymouth; **~ of** (*outside*) fuori di; (*because of*) per; **~ of 10** su 10; **~ of petrol** senza benzina; **outback** ['autbæk] *n* (*in Australia*) interno, entroterra; **outbound** *adj* **outbound (for** *or* **from)** in partenza (per *or* da); **outbreak** ['autbreɪk] *n* scoppio; epidemia; **outburst** ['autbə:st] *n* scoppio; **outcast** ['autka:st] *n* esule *m/f*; (*socially*) paria *m inv*; **outcome** ['autkʌm] *n* esito, risultato; **outcry** ['autkraɪ] *n* protesta, clamore *m*; **outdated** [aut'deɪtd] *adj* (*custom, clothes*) fuori moda; (*idea*) sorpassato(-a); **outdoor** [aut'dɔ:ʳ] *adj* all'aperto; **outdoors** *adv* fuori; all'aria aperta

outer ['autəʳ] *adj* esteriore; **outer space** *n* spazio cosmico

outfit ['autfɪt] *n* (*clothes*) completo; (: *for sport*) tenuta

out: **outgoing** ['autgəuɪŋ] *adj* (*character*) socievole; **outgoings** (BRIT) *npl* (*expenses*) spese *fpl*, uscite *fpl*; **outhouse** ['authaus] *n* costruzione *f* annessa

outing ['autɪŋ] *n* gita; escursione *f*

out: **outlaw** ['autlɔ:] *n* fuorilegge *m/f* ▷ *vt* bandire; **outlay** ['autleɪ] *n* spese *fpl*; (*investment*) sborsa, spesa; **outlet** ['autlet] *n* (*for liquid etc*) sbocco, scarico; (us Elec) presa di corrente; (*also*: **retail outlet**) punto di vendita; **outline** ['autlaɪn] *n* contorno, profilo; (*summary*) abbozzo, grandi linee *fpl* ▷ *vt* (*fig*) descrivere a grandi linee; **outlook** ['autluk] *n* prospettiva, vista; **outnumber** [aut'nʌmbəʳ] *vt* superare in numero; **out-of-date** *adj* (*passport*) scaduto(-a); (*clothes*) fuori moda *inv*; **out-of-doors** [autəv'dɔ: z] *adv* all'aperto; **out-of-the-way** *adj* (*place*) fuori mano *inv*; **out-of-town** [autəv'taun] *adj* (*shopping centre etc*) fuori città; **outpatient** ['autpeɪʃənt] *n* paziente *m/f* esterno(-a); **outpost** ['autpəust] *n* avamposto; **output** ['autput] *n* produzione *f*, (*Comput*) output *m inv*

outrage ['autreɪdʒ] *n* oltraggio; scandalo ▷ *vt* oltraggiare; **outrageous** [-'reɪdʒəs] *adj* oltraggioso(-a), scandaloso(-a)

outright [*adv* aut'raɪt, *adj* 'autraɪt] *adv* completamente; schiettamente, apertamente; sul colpo ▷ *adj* completo(-a), schietto(-a) e netto(-a)

outset ['autset] *n* inizio

outside [aut'saɪd] *n* esterno, esteriore *m* ▷ *adj* esterno(-a), esteriore ▷ *adv* fuori, all'esterno ▷ *prep* fuori di, all'esterno di; **at the ~** (*fig*) al massimo; **outside lane** *n* (Aut) corsia di sorpasso; **outside line** *n* (Tel) linea esterna; **outsider** *n* (*in race etc*) outsider *m inv*; (*stranger*) estraneo(-a)

out: **outsize** ['autsaɪz] *adj* (*clothes*) per taglie forti; **outskirts** ['autskə:ts] *npl* sobborghi *mpl*; **outspoken** [aut'spəukən] *adj* molto franco(-a); **outstanding** [aut'stændɪŋ] *adj* eccezionale, di rilievo; (*unfinished*) non completo(-a); non evaso(-a); non regolato(-a)

outward ['autwəd] *adj* (*sign, appearances*) esteriore; (*journey*) d'andata; **outwards** ['autwədz] *adv* (*esp* BRIT) = **outward**

outweigh [aut'weɪ] *vt* avere maggior peso di

oval ['əuvl] *adj* ovale ▷ *n* ovale *m*

ovary ['əuvərɪ] *n* ovaia

oven ['ʌvn] *n* forno; **oven glove** *n* guanto da forno; **ovenproof** *adj* da forno; **oven-ready** *adj* pronto(-a) da infornare

over ['əuvəʳ] *adv* al di sopra ▷ *adj* (*or adv*) (*finished*) finito(-a), terminato(-a); (*too*) troppo; (*remaining*) che avanza ▷ *prep* su; sopra; (*above*) al di sopra di; (*on the other side of*) di là di; (*more than*) più di; (*during*) durante; **~ here** qui; **~ there** là; **all ~** (*everywhere*) dappertutto; (*finished*) tutto(-a) finito(-a); **~ and ~ (again)** più e più volte; **~ and above** oltre (a); **to ask sb ~** invitare qn (a passare)

overall [*adj, n* 'əuvərɔ:l, *adv* əuvər'ɔ:l] *adj* totale ▷ *n* (BRIT) grembiule *m* ▷ *adv* nell'insieme, complessivamente; **~s** *npl* (*worker's overalls*) tuta (da lavoro)

overboard ['əuvəbɔ:d] *adv* (Naut) fuori bordo, in mare

overcame [əuvə'keɪm] *pt of* **overcome**

overcast ['əuvəka:st] *adj* (*sky*) coperto(-a)

overcharge [əuvə'tʃa:dʒ] *vt* **to ~ sb for sth** far pagare troppo caro a qn per qc

overcoat ['əuvəkəut] *n* soprabito, cappotto

overcome [əuvə'kʌm] (*irreg*) *vt* superare; sopraffare

over: **overcrowded** [əuvə'kraudɪd] *adj* sovraffollato(-a); **overdo** [əuvə'du:] (*irreg*) *vt* esagerare; (*overcook*) cuocere troppo; **overdone** [əuvə'dʌn] *adj* troppo cotto(-a); **overdose** ['əuvədəus] *n* dose *f* eccessiva; **overdraft** ['əuvədra:ft] *n* scoperto (di conto); **overdrawn** [əuvə'drɔ: n] *adj* (*account*) scoperto(-a); **overdue** [əuvə'dju:] *adj* in ritardo; **overestimate** [əuvər'estɪmeɪt] *vt* sopravvalutare

overflow [*vb* əuvə'fləu, *n* 'əuvəfləu] *vi* traboccare ▷ *n* (*also*: **~ pipe**) troppopieno

overgrown [əuvə'grəun] *adj* (*garden*) ricoperto(-a) di vegetazione

overhaul [*vb* əuvə'hɔ:l, *n* 'əuvəhɔ:l] *vt* revisionare ▷ *n* revisione *f*

overhead [*adv* əuvə'hed, *adj, n* 'əuvəhed] *adv* di sopra ▷ *adj* aereo(-a); (*lighting*)

verticale ▷ *n* (*us*) = **overheads**;
overhead projector *n* lavagna luminosa;
overheads *npl* spese *fpl* generali

over: **overhear** [əuvə'hɪəʳ] (*irreg*) *vt* sentire
(per caso); **overheat** [əuvə'hi:t] *vi* (*engine*)
surriscaldare; **overland** *adj, adv* per via di
terra; **overlap** [əuvə'læp] *vi* sovrapporsi;
overleaf [əuvə'li:f] *adv* a tergo; **overload**
[əuvə'ləud] *vt* sovraccaricare; **overlook**
[əuvə'luk] *vt* (*have view of*) dare su; (*miss*)
trascurare; (*forgive*) passare sopra a

overnight [əuvə'naɪt] *adv* (*happen*)
durante la notte; (*fig*) tutto ad un tratto
▷ *adj* di notte; **he stayed there ~** ci ha
passato la notte; **overnight bag** *n* borsa
da viaggio

overpass ['əuvəpɑ:s] *n* cavalcavia *m inv*

overpower [əuvə'pauəʳ] *vt* sopraffare;
overpowering *adj* irresistibile; (*heat,
stench*) soffocante

over: **overreact** [əuvəri:'ækt] *vi* reagire
in modo esagerato; **overrule** [əuvə'ru:l]
vt (*decision*) annullare; (*claim*) respingere;
overrun [əuvə'rʌn] (*irreg: like* run) *vt*
(*country*) invadere; (*time limit*) superare

overseas [əuvə'si:z] *adv* oltremare;
(*abroad*) all'estero ▷ *adj* (*trade*) estero(-a);
(*visitor*) straniero(-a)

oversee [əuvə'si:] *vt irreg* sorvegliare

overshadow [əuvə'ʃædəu] *vt* far ombra
su; (*fig*) eclissare

oversight ['əuvəsaɪt] *n* omissione *f*, svista

oversleep [əuvə'sli:p] (*irreg*) *vi* dormire
troppo a lungo

overspend [əuvə'spɛnd] *vi irreg* spendere
troppo; **we have overspent by 5000
dollars** abbiamo speso 5000 dollari di
troppo

overt [əu'və:t] *adj* palese

overtake [əuvə'teɪk] (*irreg*) *vt* sorpassare

over: **overthrow** [əuvə'θrəu] (*irreg*)
vt (*government*) rovesciare; **overtime**
['əuvətaɪm] *n* (*lavoro*) straordinario

overtook [əuvə'tuk] *pt of* **overtake**

over: **overturn** [əuvə'tə:n] *vt* rovesciare
▷ *vi* rovesciarsi; **overweight** [əuvə'weɪt]
adj (*person*) troppo grasso(-a); **overwhelm**
[əuvə'wɛlm] *vt* sopraffare; sommergere;
schiacciare; **overwhelming** *adj* (*victory,
defeat*) schiacciante; (*heat, desire*)
intenso(-a)

ow [au] *excl* ahi!

owe [əu] *vt* **to ~ sb sth, to ~ sth to sb**
dovere qc a qn; **how much do I ~ you?**
quanto le devo?; **owing to** *prep* a causa di

owl [aul] *n* gufo

own [əun] *vt* possedere ▷ *adj* proprio(-a);
a room of my ~ la mia propria camera; **to
get one's ~ back** vendicarsi; **on one's ~**

tutto(-a) solo(-a); **own up** *vi* confessare;
owner *n* proprietario(-a); **ownership** *n*
possesso

ox [ɔks] (*pl* **oxen**) *n* bue *m*

Oxbridge ['ɔksbrɪdʒ] *n* le università di
Oxford e/o Cambridge

oxen ['ɔksn] *npl of* **ox**

oxygen ['ɔksɪdʒən] *n* ossigeno

oyster ['ɔɪstəʳ] *n* ostrica

oz. *abbr* = **ounce(s)**

ozone ['əuzəun] *n* ozono; **ozone friendly**
adj che non danneggia l'ozono; **ozone
layer** *n* fascia d'ozono

P

p [piː] abbr = **penny; pence**

P.A. n abbr = **personal assistant; public address system**

p.a. abbr = **per annum**

pace [peɪs] n passo; (speed) passo; velocità ▷ vi **to ~ up and down** camminare su e giù; **to keep ~ with** camminare di pari passo a; (events) tenersi al corrente di; **pacemaker** n (Med) segnapasso; (Sport: also: **pace setter**) battistrada m inv

Pacific [pəˈsɪfɪk] n **the ~ (Ocean)** il Pacifico, l'Oceano Pacifico

pacifier [ˈpæsɪfaɪər] (US) n (dummy) succhiotto, ciuccio (col)

pack [pæk] n pacco; (US: of cigarettes) pacchetto; (backpack) zaino; (of hounds) muta; (of thieves etc) banda; (of cards) mazzo ▷ vt (in suitcase etc) mettere; (box) riempire; (cram) stipare, pigiare; **to ~ (one's bags)** fare la valigia; **to ~ sb off** spedire via qn; **~ it in!** (inf) dacci un taglio!; **pack in** (BRIT inf) vi (watch, car) guastarsi ▷ vt mollare, piantare; **~ it in!** piantala!; **pack up** vi (BRIT inf: machine) guastarsi; (: person) far fagotto ▷ vt (belongings, clothes) mettere in una valigia; (goods, presents) imballare

package [ˈpækɪdʒ] n pacco; balla; (also: **~ deal**) pacchetto; forfait m inv; **package holiday** n vacanza organizzata; **package tour** n viaggio organizzato

packaging [ˈpækɪdʒɪŋ] n confezione f, imballo

packed [pækt] adj (crowded) affollato(-a); **packed lunch** n pranzo al sacco

packet [ˈpækɪt] n pacchetto

packing [ˈpækɪŋ] n imballaggio

pact [pækt] n patto, accordo; trattato

pad [pæd] n blocco; (to prevent friction) cuscinetto; (inf: flat) appartamentino ▷ vt imbottire; **padded** adj imbottito(-a)

paddle [ˈpædl] n (oar) pagaia; (US: for table tennis) racchetta da ping-pong ▷ vi sguazzare ▷ vt **to ~ a canoe** etc vogare con la pagaia; **paddling pool** (BRIT) n piscina per bambini

paddock [ˈpædək] n prato recintato; (at racecourse) paddock m inv

padlock [ˈpædlɔk] n lucchetto

paedophile [ˈpiːdəufaɪl] (US **pedophile**) adj, n pedofilo(-a)

page [peɪdʒ] n pagina; (also: **~ boy**) paggio ▷ vt (in hotel etc) (far) chiamare

pager [ˈpeɪdʒər] n (Tel) cercapersone m inv

paid [peɪd] pt, pp of **pay** ▷ adj (work, official) rimunerato(-a); **to put ~ to** (BRIT) mettere fine a

pain [peɪn] n dolore m; **to be in ~** soffrire, aver male; **to take ~s to do** mettercela tutta per fare; **painful** adj doloroso(-a), che fa male; difficile, penoso(-a); **painkiller** n antalgico, antidolorifico; **painstaking** [ˈpeɪnzteɪkɪŋ] adj (person) sollecito(-a); (work) accurato(-a)

paint [peɪnt] n vernice f, colore m ▷ vt dipingere; (walls, door etc) verniciare; **to ~ the door blue** verniciare la porta di azzurro; **paintbrush** n pennello; **painter** n (artist) pittore m; (decorator) imbianchino; **painting** n pittura; verniciatura; (picture) dipinto, quadro

pair [pɛər] n (of shoes, gloves etc) paio; (of people) coppia; duo m inv; **a ~ of scissors/ trousers** un paio di forbici/pantaloni

pajamas [pɪˈdʒɑːməz] (US) npl pigiama m

Pakistan [pɑːkɪˈstɑːn] n Pakistan m; **Pakistani** adj, n pakistano(-a)

pal [pæl] (inf) n amico(-a), compagno(-a)

palace [ˈpæləs] n palazzo

pale [peɪl] adj pallido(-a) ▷ n **to be beyond the ~** aver oltrepassato ogni limite

Palestine [ˈpælɪstaɪn] n Palestina; **Palestinian** [-ˈtɪnɪən] adj, n palestinese m/f

palm [pɑːm] n (Anat) palma, palmo; (also: **~ tree**) palma ▷ vt **to ~ sth off on sb** (inf) rifilare qc a qn

pamper [ˈpæmpər] vt viziare, coccolare

pamphlet [ˈpæmflət] n dépliant m inv

pan [pæn] n (also: **sauce~**) casseruola; (also: **frying ~**) padella

pancake ['pænkeɪk] n frittella

panda ['pændə] n panda m inv

pane [peɪn] n vetro

panel ['pænl] n (of wood, cloth etc) pannello; (Radio, TV) giuria

panhandler ['pænhændlə^r] (US) n (inf) accattone(-a)

panic ['pænɪk] n panico ▷ vi perdere il sangue freddo

panorama [pænə'rɑːmə] n panorama m

pansy ['pænzɪ] n (Bot) viola del pensiero, pensée f inv; (inf: pej) femminuccia

pant [pænt] vi ansare

panther ['pænθə^r] n pantera

panties ['pæntɪz] npl slip m, mutandine fpl

pantomime ['pæntəmaɪm] (BRIT) n pantomima

⬥ **PANTOMIME**
⬥
⬥ In Gran Bretagna la **pantomime** è una
⬥ sorta di libera interpretazione delle
⬥ favole più conosciute, che vengono
⬥ messe in scena a teatro durante il
⬥ periodo natalizio. È uno spettacolo
⬥ per tutta la famiglia che prevede la
⬥ partecipazione del pubblico.

pants [pænts] npl mutande fpl, slip m; (US: trousers) pantaloni mpl

paper ['peɪpə^r] n carta; (also: **wall~**) carta da parati, tappezzeria; (also: **news~**) giornale m; (study, article) saggio; (exam) prova scritta ▷ adj di carta ▷ vt tappezzare; **~s** npl (also: **identity ~s**) carte fpl, documenti mpl; **paperback** n tascabile m; edizione f economica; **paper bag** n sacchetto di carta; **paper clip** n graffetta, clip f inv; **paper shop** n (BRIT) giornalaio (negozio); **paperwork** n lavoro amministrativo

paprika ['pæprɪkə] n paprica

par [pɑː^r] n parità, pari f; (Golf) norma; **on a ~ with** alla pari con

paracetamol [pærə'siːtəmɔl] (BRIT) n paracetamolo

parachute ['pærəʃuːt] n paracadute m inv

parade [pə'reɪd] n parata ▷ vt (fig) fare sfoggio di ▷ vi sfilare in parata

paradise ['pærədaɪs] n paradiso

paradox ['pærədɔks] n paradosso

paraffin ['pærəfɪn] (BRIT) n **~ (oil)** paraffina

paragraph ['pærəɡrɑːf] n paragrafo

parallel ['pærəlɛl] adj parallelo(-a); (fig) analogo(-a) ▷ n (line) parallela; (fig, Geo) parallelo

paralysed ['pærəlaɪzd] adj paralizzato(-a)

paralysis [pə'rælɪsɪs] n paralisi f inv

paramedic [pærə'mɛdɪk] n paramedico

paranoid ['pærənɔɪd] adj paranoico(-a)

parasite ['pærəsaɪt] n parassita m

parcel ['pɑːsl] n pacco, pacchetto ▷ vt (also: **~ up**) impaccare

pardon ['pɑːdn] n perdono; grazia ▷ vt perdonare; (Law) graziare; **~ me!** mi scusi!; **I beg your ~!** scusi!; **I beg your ~?** (BRIT), **~ me?** (US) prego?

parent ['pɛərənt] n genitore m; **~s** npl (mother and father) genitori mpl; **parental** [pə'rɛntl] adj dei genitori

▨ Be careful not to translate **parent** by the Italian word **parente**.

Paris ['pærɪs] n Parigi f

parish ['pærɪʃ] n parrocchia; (BRIT: civil) ≈ municipio

Parisian [pə'rɪzɪən] adj, n parigino(-a)

park [pɑːk] n parco ▷ vt, vi parcheggiare; **can I ~ here?** posso parcheggiare qui?

parking ['pɑːkɪŋ] n parcheggio; **"no ~"** "sosta vietata"; **parking lot** (US) n posteggio, parcheggio; **parking meter** n parchimetro; **parking ticket** n multa per sosta vietata

parkway ['pɑːkweɪ] (US) n viale m

parliament ['pɑːləmənt] n parlamento; **parliamentary** [pɑːlə'mɛntərɪ] adj parlamentare

Parmesan [pɑːmɪ'zæn] n (also: **~ cheese**) parmigiano

parole [pə'rəul] n **on ~** in libertà per buona condotta

parrot ['pærət] n pappagallo

parsley ['pɑːslɪ] n prezzemolo

parsnip ['pɑːsnɪp] n pastinaca

parson ['pɑːsn] n prete m; (Church of England) parroco

part [pɑːt] n parte f; (of machine) pezzo; (US: in hair) scriminatura ▷ adj in parte ▷ adv = **partly** ▷ vt separare ▷ vi (people) separarsi; **to take ~ in** prendere parte a; **for my ~** per parte mia; **to take sth in good ~** prendere bene qc; **to take sb's ~** parteggiare per or prendere le parti di qn; **for the most ~** in generale; nella maggior parte dei casi; **part with** vt fus separarsi da; rinunciare a

partial ['pɑːʃl] adj parziale; **to be ~ to** avere un debole per

participant [pɑː'tɪsɪpənt] n **~ (in)** partecipante m/f (a)

participate [pɑː'tɪsɪpeɪt] vi **to ~ (in)** prendere parte (a), partecipare (a)

particle ['pɑːtɪkl] n particella

particular [pə'tɪkjulə^r] adj particolare;

speciale; (*fussy*) difficile; meticoloso(-a);
in ~ in particolare, particolarmente;
particularly *adv* particolarmente; in
particolare; **particulars** *npl* particolari
mpl, dettagli *mpl*; (*information*)
informazioni *fpl*

parting ['pɑːtɪŋ] *n* separazione *f*; (BRIT: *in
hair*) scriminatura ▷ *adj* d'addio

partition [pɑː'tɪʃən] *n* (*Pol*) partizione *f*;
(*wall*) tramezzo

partly ['pɑːtlɪ] *adv* parzialmente; in parte

partner ['pɑːtnəʳ] *n* (*Comm*) socio(-a);
(*wife, husband etc, Sport*) compagno(-a);
(*at dance*) cavaliere/dama; **partnership** *n*
associazione *f*; (*Comm*) società *f inv*

part of speech *n* parte *f* del discorso

partridge ['pɑːtrɪdʒ] *n* pernice *f*

part-time ['pɑːt'taɪm] *adj, adv* a orario
ridotto

party ['pɑːtɪ] *n* (*Pol*) partito; (*group*)
gruppo; (*Law*) parte *f*; (*celebration*)
ricevimento; serata; festa ▷ *cpd* (*Pol*) del
partito, di partito

pass [pɑːs] *vt* (*gen*) passare; (*place*) passare
davanti a; (*exam*) passare, superare;
(*candidate*) promuovere; (*overtake, surpass*)
sorpassare, superare; (*approve*) approvare
▷ *vi* passare ▷ *n* (*permit*) lasciapassare
m inv; permesso; (*in mountains*) passo,
gola; (*Sport*) passaggio; (*Scol*): **to get a ~**
prendere la sufficienza; **could you ~ the
salt/oil, please?** mi passa il sale/l'olio,
per favore?; **to ~ sth through a hole** *etc*
far passare qc attraverso un buco *etc*; **to
make a ~ at sb** (*inf*) fare delle proposte *or*
delle avances a qn; **pass away** *vi* morire;
pass by *vi* passare ▷ *vt* trascurare; **pass
on** *vt* passare; **pass out** *vi* svenire; **pass
over** *vi* (*die*) spirare ▷ *vt* lasciare da parte;
pass up *vt* (*opportunity*) lasciarsi sfuggire,
perdere; **passable** *adj* (*road*) praticabile;
(*work*) accettabile

passage ['pæsɪdʒ] *n* (*gen*) passaggio; (*also:
~way*) corridoio; (*in book*) brano, passo; (*by
boat*) traversata

passenger ['pæsɪndʒəʳ] *n* passeggero(-a)

passer-by [pɑːsə'baɪ] *n* passante *m/f*

passing place *n* (*Aut*) piazzola di sosta

passion ['pæʃən] *n* passione *f*, amore
m; **passionate** *adj* appassionato(-a);
passion fruit *n* frutto della passione

passive ['pæsɪv] *adj* (*also Ling*) passivo(-a)

passport ['pɑːspɔːt] *n* passaporto;
passport control *n* controllo *m*
passaporti *inv*; **passport office** *n* ufficio
m, passaporti *inv*

password ['pɑːswəːd] *n* parola d'ordine

past [pɑːst] *prep* (*further than*) oltre, di là di;
dopo; (*later than*) dopo ▷ *adj* passato(-a);

(*president etc*) ex *inv* ▷ *n* passato; **he's ~
forty** ha più di quarant'anni; **ten ~ eight** le
otto e dieci; **for the ~ few days** da qualche
giorno; in questi ultimi giorni; **to run ~**
passare di corsa

pasta ['pæstə] *n* pasta

paste [peɪst] *n* (*glue*) colla; (*Culin*) pâté *m
inv*; pasta ▷ *vt* collare

pastel ['pæstl] *adj* pastello *inv*

pasteurized ['pæstəraɪzd] *adj*
pastorizzato(-a)

pastime ['pɑːstaɪm] *n* passatempo

pastor ['pɑːstəʳ] *n* pastore *m*

past participle [-'pɑːtɪsɪpl] *n* (*Ling*)
participio passato

pastry ['peɪstrɪ] *n* pasta

pasture ['pɑːstʃəʳ] *n* pascolo

pasty[1] ['pæstɪ] *n* pasticcio di carne

pasty[2] ['peɪstɪ] *adj* (*face etc*) smorto(-a)

pat [pæt] *vt* accarezzare, dare un colpetto
(affettuoso) a

patch [pætʃ] *n* (*of material, on tyre*) toppa;
(*eye patch*) benda; (*spot*) macchia ▷ *vt*
(*clothes*) rattoppare; **(to go through) a
bad ~** (attraversare) un brutto periodo;
patchy *adj* irregolare

pâté ['pæteɪ] *n* pâté *m inv*

patent ['peɪtnt] *n* brevetto ▷ *vt* brevettare
▷ *adj* patente, manifesto(-a)

paternal [pə'təːnl] *adj* paterno(-a)

paternity leave [pə'təːnɪtɪ-] *n* congedo
di paternità

path [pɑːθ] *n* sentiero, viottolo; viale
m; (*fig*) via, strada; (*of planet, missile*)
traiettoria

pathetic [pə'θetɪk] *adj* (*pitiful*)
patetico(-a); (*very bad*) penoso(-a)

pathway ['pɑːθweɪ] *n* sentiero

patience ['peɪʃns] *n* pazienza; (BRIT *Cards*)
solitario

patient ['peɪʃnt] *n* paziente *m/f*,
malato(-a) ▷ *adj* paziente

patio ['pætɪəu] *n* terrazza

patriotic [pætrɪ'ɔtɪk] *adj* patriottico(-a)

patrol [pə'trəul] *n* pattuglia ▷ *vt*
pattugliare; **patrol car** *n* autoradio *f inv*
(della polizia)

patron ['peɪtrən] *n* (*in shop*) cliente *m/f*; (*of
charity*) benefattore(-trice); **~ of the arts**
mecenate *m/f*

patronizing ['pætrənaɪzɪŋ] *adj*
condiscendente

pattern ['pætən] *n* modello; (*design*)
disegno, motivo; **patterned** *adj* a disegni,
a motivi; (*material*) fantasia *inv*

pause [pɔːz] *n* pausa ▷ *vi* fare una pausa,
arrestarsi

pave [peɪv] *vt* pavimentare; **to ~ the way
for** aprire la via a

pavement ['peɪvmənt] (BRIT) n
marciapiede m

Be careful not to translate *pavement*
by the Italian word *pavimento*.

pavilion [pə'vɪlɪən] n (Sport) edificio
annesso a campo sportivo

paving ['peɪvɪŋ] n pavimentazione f

paw [pɔː] n zampa

pawn [pɔːn] n (Chess) pedone m; (fig)
pedina ▷ vt dare in pegno; **pawn broker** n
prestatore m su pegno

pay [peɪ] (pt, pp paid) n stipendio; paga
▷ vt pagare ▷ vi (be profitable) rendere;
can I ~ by credit card? posso pagare
con la carta di credito?; **to ~ attention
(to)** fare attenzione (a); **to ~ sb a visit**
far visita a qn; **to ~ one's respects to sb**
porgere i propri rispetti a qn; **pay back** vt
rimborsare; **pay for** vt fus pagare; **pay
in** vt versare; **pay off** vt (debt) saldare;
(person) pagare; (employee) pagare e
licenziare ▷ vi (scheme, decision) dare
dei frutti; **pay out** vt (money) sborsare,
tirar fuori; (rope) far allentare; **pay up** vt
saldare; **payable** adj pagabile; **pay day**
n giorno di paga; **pay envelope** (US) n
= **pay packet**; **payment** n pagamento;
versamento; saldo; **payout** n pagamento;
(in competition) premio; **pay packet** (BRIT)
n busta f paga inv; **pay phone** n cabina
telefonica; **payroll** n ruolo (organico); **pay
slip** n foglio m paga inv; **pay television** n
televisione f a pagamento, pay-tv f inv

PC n abbr = **personal computer** ▷ adv abbr
= **politically correct**

p.c. abbr = **per cent**

PDA n abbr (= personal digital assistant) PDA
m inv

PE n abbr (= physical education) ed. fisica

pea [piː] n pisello

peace [piːs] n pace f; **peaceful** adj
pacifico(-a), calmo(-a)

peach [piːtʃ] n pesca

peacock ['piːkɔk] n pavone m

peak [piːk] n (of mountain) cima, vetta;
(mountain itself) picco; (of cap) visiera; (fig)
apice m, culmine m; **peak hours** npl ore
fpl di punta

peanut ['piːnʌt] n arachide f, nocciolina
americana; **peanut butter** n burro di
arachidi

pear [pɛəʳ] n pera

pearl [pɜːl] n perla

peasant ['pɛznt] n contadino(-a)

peat [piːt] n torba

pebble ['pɛbl] n ciottolo

peck [pɛk] vt (also: ~ at) beccare ▷ n colpo
di becco; (kiss) bacetto; **peckish** (BRIT: inf)
adj **I feel peckish** ho un languorino

peculiar [pɪ'kjuːlɪəʳ] adj strano(-a),
bizzarro(-a); peculiare; **~ to** peculiare di

pedal ['pɛdl] n pedale m ▷ vi pedalare

pedalo ['pɛdələu] n pedalò m inv

pedestal ['pɛdəstl] n piedestallo

pedestrian [pɪ'dɛstrɪən] n pedone(-a)
▷ adj pedonale; (fig) prosaico(-a),
pedestre; **pedestrian crossing** (BRIT) n
passaggio pedonale; **pedestrianized**
adj **a pedestrianized street** una zona
pedonalizzata; **pedestrian precinct**
(BRIT), **pedestrian zone** (US) n zona
pedonale

pedigree ['pɛdɪgriː] n (of animal) pedigree
m inv; (fig) background m inv ▷ cpd (animal)
di razza

pedophile ['piːdəufaɪl] (US) n
= **paedophile**

pee [piː] (inf) vi pisciare

peek [piːk] vi guardare furtivamente

peel [piːl] n buccia; (of orange, lemon) scorza
▷ vt sbucciare ▷ vi (paint etc) staccarsi

peep [piːp] n (BRIT: look) sguardo furtivo,
sbirciata; (sound) pigolìo ▷ vi (BRIT)
guardare furtivamente

peer [pɪəʳ] vi **to ~ at** scrutare ▷ n (noble)
pari m inv; (equal) pari m/f inv, uguale m/f;
(contemporary) contemporaneo(-a)

peg [pɛg] n caviglia; (for coat etc)
attaccapanni m inv; (BRIT: also: **clothes ~**)
molletta

pelican ['pɛlɪkən] n pellicano; **pelican
crossing** (BRIT) n (Aut) attraversamento
pedonale con semaforo a controllo manuale

pelt [pɛlt] vt **to ~ sb (with)** bombardare qn
(con) ▷ vi (rain) piovere a dirotto; (inf: run)
filare ▷ n pelle f

pelvis ['pɛlvɪs] n pelvi f inv, bacino

pen [pɛn] n penna; (for sheep) recinto

penalty ['pɛnltɪ] n penalità f inv;
sanzione f penale; (fine) ammenda; (Sport)
penalizzazione f

pence [pɛns] (BRIT) npl of **penny**

pencil ['pɛnsl] n matita; **pencil in**
vt scrivere a matita; **pencil case** n
astuccio per matite; **pencil sharpener** n
temperamatite m inv

pendant ['pɛndnt] n pendaglio

pending ['pɛndɪŋ] prep in attesa di ▷ adj
in sospeso

penetrate ['pɛnɪtreɪt] vt penetrare

penfriend ['pɛnfrɛnd] (BRIT) n
corrispondente m/f

penguin ['pɛŋgwɪn] n pinguino

penicillin [pɛnɪ'sɪlɪn] n penicillina

peninsula [pə'nɪnsjulə] n penisola

penis ['piːnɪs] n pene m

penitentiary [pɛnɪ'tɛnʃərɪ] (US) n carcere
m

penknife ['pɛnnaɪf] n temperino
penniless ['pɛnɪlɪs] adj senza un soldo
penny ['pɛnɪ] (pl **pennies** or **pence**) (BRIT) n penny m; (US) centesimo
penpal ['pɛnpæl] n corrispondente m/f
pension ['pɛnʃən] n pensione f; **pensioner** (BRIT) n pensionato(-a)
pentagon ['pɛntəgən] n pentagono; **the P~** (US Pol) il Pentagono
penthouse ['pɛnthaʊs] n appartamento (di lusso) nell'attico
penultimate [pɪ'nʌltɪmət] adj penultimo(-a)
people ['piːpl] npl gente f; persone fpl; (citizens) popolo ▷ n (nation, race) popolo; **4/several ~ came** 4/parecchie persone sono venute; **~ say that ...** si dice che ...
pepper ['pɛpəʳ] n pepe m; (vegetable) peperone m ▷ vt (fig): **to ~ with** spruzzare di; **peppermint** n (sweet) pasticca di menta
per [pəːʳ] prep per; a; **~ hour** all'ora; **~ kilo etc** il chilo etc; **~ day** al giorno
perceive [pə'siːv] vt percepire; (notice) accorgersi di
per cent adv per cento
percentage [pə'sɛntɪdʒ] n percentuale f
perception [pə'sɛpʃən] n percezione f; sensibilità; perspicacia
perch [pəːtʃ] n (fish) pesce m persico; (for bird) sostegno, ramo ▷ vi appollaiarsi
percussion [pə'kʌʃən] n percussione f; (Mus) strumenti mpl a percussione
perfect [adj, n 'pəːfɪkt, vb pə'fɛkt] adj perfetto(-a) ▷ n (also: **~ tense**) perfetto, passato prossimo ▷ vt perfezionare; mettere a punto; **perfection** [pə'fɛkʃən] n perfezione f; **perfectly** adv perfettamente, alla perfezione
perform [pə'fɔːm] vt (carry out) eseguire, fare; (symphony etc) suonare; (play, ballet) dare; (opera) fare ▷ vi suonare; recitare; **performance** n esecuzione f; (at theatre etc) rappresentazione f, spettacolo; (of an artist) interpretazione f; (of player etc) performance f; (of car, engine) prestazione f; **performer** n artista m/f
perfume ['pəːfjuːm] n profumo
perhaps [pə'hæps] adv forse
perimeter [pə'rɪmɪtəʳ] n perimetro
period ['pɪərɪəd] n periodo; (History) epoca; (Scol) lezione f; (full stop) punto; (Med) mestruazioni fpl ▷ adj (costume, furniture) d'epoca; **periodical** [-'ɔdɪkl] n periodico; **periodically** adv periodicamente
perish ['pɛrɪʃ] vi perire, morire; (decay) deteriorarsi
perjury ['pəːdʒərɪ] n spergiuro
perk [pəːk] (inf) n vantaggio

perm [pəːm] n (for hair) permanente f
permanent ['pəːmənənt] adj permanente; **permanently** adv definitivamente
permission [pə'mɪʃən] n permesso
permit [n 'pəːmɪt, vb pə'mɪt] n permesso ▷ vt permettere; **to ~ sb to do** permettere a qn di fare
perplex [pə'plɛks] vt lasciare perplesso(-a)
persecute ['pəːsɪkjuːt] vt perseguitare
persecution [pəːsɪ'kjuːʃən] n persecuzione f
persevere [pəːsɪ'vɪəʳ] vi perseverare
Persian ['pəːʃən] adj persiano(-a) ▷ n (Ling) persiano; **the (~) Gulf** n il Golfo Persico
persist [pə'sɪst] vi **to ~ (in doing)** persistere (nel fare); ostinarsi (a fare); **persistent** adj persistente; ostinato(-a)
person ['pəːsn] n persona; **in ~** di or in persona, personalmente; **personal** adj personale; individuale; **personal assistant** n segretaria personale; **personal computer** n personal computer m inv; **personality** [-'nælɪtɪ] n personalità f inv; **personally** adv personalmente; **to take sth personally** prendere qc come una critica personale; **personal organizer** n (Filofax®) Fulltime®; (electronic) agenda elettronica; **personal stereo** n Walkman® m inv
personnel [pəːsə'nɛl] n personale m
perspective [pə'spɛktɪv] n prospettiva
perspiration [pəːspɪ'reɪʃən] n traspirazione f, sudore m
persuade [pə'sweɪd] vt **to ~ sb to do sth** persuadere qn a fare qc
persuasion [pə'sweɪʒən] n persuasione f; (creed) convinzione f, credo
persuasive [pə'sweɪsɪv] adj persuasivo(-a)
perverse [pə'vəːs] adj perverso(-a)
pervert [n 'pəːvəːt, vb pə'vəːt] n pervertito(-a) ▷ vt pervertire
pessimism ['pɛsɪmɪzəm] n pessimismo
pessimist ['pɛsɪmɪst] n pessimista m/f; **pessimistic** [-'mɪstɪk] adj pessimistico(-a)
pest [pɛst] n animale m (or insetto) pestifero; (fig) peste f
pester ['pɛstəʳ] vt tormentare, molestare
pesticide ['pɛstɪsaɪd] n pesticida m
pet [pɛt] n animale m domestico ▷ cpd favorito(-a) ▷ vt accarezzare; **teacher's ~** favorito(-a) del maestro
petal ['pɛtl] n petalo
petite [pə'tiːt] adj piccolo(-a) e aggraziato(-a)
petition [pə'tɪʃən] n petizione f
petrified ['pɛtrɪfaɪd] adj (fig) morto(-a) di paura

petrol ['pɛtrəl] (BRIT) n benzina; **two/four-star ~** = benzina normale/super; **I've run out of ~** sono rimasto senza benzina

⬛ Be careful not to translate *petrol* by the Italian word *petrolio*.

petroleum [pə'trəulɪəm] n petrolio
petrol: **petrol pump** (BRIT) n (in car, at garage) pompa di benzina; **petrol station** (BRIT) n stazione f di rifornimento; **petrol tank** (BRIT) n serbatoio della benzina
petticoat ['pɛtɪkəut] n sottana
petty ['pɛtɪ] adj (mean) meschino(-a); (unimportant) insignificante
pew [pjuː] n panca (di chiesa)
pewter ['pjuːtə^r] n peltro
phantom ['fæntəm] n fantasma m
pharmacist ['fɑːməsɪst] n farmacista m/f
pharmacy ['fɑːməsɪ] n farmacia
phase [feɪz] n fase f, periodo; **phase in** vt introdurre gradualmente; **phase out** vt (machinery) eliminare gradualmente; (product) ritirare gradualmente; (job, subsidy) abolire gradualmente
Ph.D. n abbr = **Doctor of Philosophy**
pheasant ['fɛznt] n fagiano
phenomena [fə'nɔmɪnə] npl of **phenomenon**
phenomenal [fɪ'nɔmɪnl] adj fenomenale
phenomenon [fə'nɔmɪnən] (pl **phenomena**) n fenomeno
Philippines ['fɪlɪpiːnz] npl **the ~** le Filippine
philosopher [fɪ'lɔsəfə^r] n filosofo(-a)
philosophical [fɪlə'sɔfɪkl] adj filosofico(-a)
philosophy [fɪ'lɔsəfɪ] n filosofia
phlegm [flɛm] n flemma
phobia ['fəubjə] n fobia
phone [fəun] n telefono ▷ vt telefonare; **to be on the ~** avere il telefono; (be calling) essere al telefono; **phone back** vt, vi richiamare; **phone up** vt telefonare a ▷ vi telefonare; **phone book** n guida del telefono, elenco telefonico; **phone booth** n = **phone box**; **phone box** n cabina telefonica; **phone call** n telefonata; **phonecard** n scheda telefonica; **phone number** n numero di telefono
phonetics [fə'nɛtɪks] n fonetica
phoney ['fəunɪ] adj falso(-a), fasullo(-a)
photo ['fəutəu] n foto f inv
photo... ['fəutəu] prefix: **photo album** n (new) album m inv per fotografie; (containing photos) album m inv delle fotografie; **photocopier** n fotocopiatrice f; **photocopy** n fotocopia ▷ vt fotocopiare
photograph ['fəutəgræf] n fotografia ▷ vt fotografare; **photographer** [fə'tɔgrəfə^r]

n fotografo; **photography** [fə'tɔgrəfɪ] n fotografia
phrase [freɪz] n espressione f; (Ling) locuzione f; (Mus) frase f ▷ vt esprimere; **phrase book** n vocabolarietto
physical ['fɪzɪkl] adj fisico(-a); **physical education** n educazione f fisica; **physically** adv fisicamente
physician [fɪ'zɪʃən] n medico
physicist ['fɪzɪsɪst] n fisico
physics ['fɪzɪks] n fisica
physiotherapist [fɪzɪəu'θɛrəpɪst] n fisioterapista m/f
physiotherapy [fɪzɪəu'θɛrəpɪ] n fisioterapia
physique [fɪ'ziːk] n fisico; costituzione f
pianist ['piːənɪst] n pianista m/f
piano [pɪ'ænəu] n pianoforte m
pick [pɪk] n (tool: also: **~-axe**) piccone m ▷ vt scegliere; (gather) cogliere; (remove) togliere; (lock) far scattare; **take your ~** scelga; **the ~ of** il fior fiore di; **to ~ one's nose** mettersi le dita nel naso; **to ~ one's teeth** pulirsi i denti con lo stuzzicadenti; **to ~ a quarrel** attaccar briga; **pick on** vt fus (person) avercela con; **pick out** vt scegliere; (distinguish) distinguere; **pick up** vi (improve) migliorarsi ▷ vt raccogliere; (Police, Radio) prendere; (collect) passare a prendere; (Aut: give lift to) far salire; (person: for sexual encounter) rimorchiare; (learn) imparare; **to ~ up speed** acquistare velocità; **to ~ o.s. up** rialzarsi
pickle ['pɪkl] n (also: **~s**: as condiment) sottaceti mpl; (fig: mess) pasticcio ▷ vt mettere sottaceto; mettere in salamoia
pickpocket ['pɪkpɔkɪt] n borsaiolo
pick-up ['pɪkʌp] n (BRIT: on record player) pick-up m inv; (small truck: also: **~ truck, ~ van**) camioncino
picnic ['pɪknɪk] n picnic m inv; **picnic area** n area per il picnic
picture ['pɪktʃə^r] n quadro; (painting) pittura; (photograph) foto(grafia); (drawing) disegno; (film) film m inv ▷ vt raffigurarsi; **~s** (BRIT) npl (cinema): **the ~s** il cinema; **would you take a ~ of us, please?** può farci una foto, per favore?; **picture frame** n cornice m inv; **picture messaging** n picture messaging m, invio di messaggini con disegni
picturesque [pɪktʃə'rɛsk] adj pittoresco(-a)
pie [paɪ] n torta; (of meat) pasticcio
piece [piːs] n pezzo; (of land) appezzamento; (item): **a ~ of furniture/advice** un mobile/consiglio ▷ vt **to ~ together** mettere insieme; **to take to ~s** smontare

pie chart n grafico a torta
pier [pɪəʳ] n molo; (of bridge etc) pila
pierce [pɪəs] vt forare; (with arrow etc) trafiggere; **pierced** adj **I've got pierced ears** ho i buchi per gli orecchini
pig [pɪg] n maiale m, porco
pigeon ['pɪdʒən] n piccione m
piggy bank ['pɪgɪ-] n salvadanaro
pigsty ['pɪgstaɪ] n porcile m
pigtail ['pɪgteɪl] n treccina
pike [paɪk] n (fish) luccio
pilchard ['pɪltʃəd] n specie di sardina
pile [paɪl] n (pillar, of books) pila; (heap) mucchio; (of carpet) pelo; **to ~ into** (car) stiparsi or ammucchiarsi in; **pile up** vt ammucchiare ▷ vi ammucchiarsi; **piles** [paɪlz] npl emorroidi fpl; **pile-up** ['paɪlʌp] n (Aut) tamponamento a catena
pilgrimage ['pɪlgrɪmɪdʒ] n pellegrinaggio
pill [pɪl] n pillola; **the ~** la pillola
pillar ['pɪləʳ] n colonna
pillow ['pɪləu] n guanciale m; **pillowcase** n federa
pilot ['paɪlət] n pilota m/f ▷ cpd (scheme etc) pilota inv ▷ vt pilotare; **pilot light** n fiamma pilota
pimple ['pɪmpl] n foruncolo
pin [pɪn] n spillo; (Tech) perno ▷ vt attaccare con uno spillo; **~s and needles** formicolio; **to ~ sb down** (fig) obbligare qn a pronunziarsi; **to ~ sth on sb** (fig) addossare la colpa di qc a qn
PIN n abbr (= personal identification number) codice m segreto
pinafore ['pɪnəfɔːʳ] n (also: **~ dress**) grembiule m (senza maniche)
pinch [pɪntʃ] n pizzicotto, pizzico ▷ vt pizzicare; (inf: steal) grattare; **at a ~** in caso di bisogno
pine [paɪn] n (also: **~ tree**) pino ▷ vi **to ~ for** struggersi dal desiderio di
pineapple ['paɪnæpl] n ananas m inv
ping [pɪŋ] n (noise) tintinnio; **ping-pong®** n ping-pong® m
pink [pɪŋk] adj rosa inv ▷ n (colour) rosa m inv; (Bot) garofano
pinpoint ['pɪnpɔɪnt] vt indicare con precisione
pint [paɪnt] n pinta (BRIT = 0.57l; US = 0.47l); (BRIT: inf) ≈ birra da mezzo
pioneer [paɪə'nɪəʳ] n pioniere(-a)
pious ['paɪəs] adj pio(-a)
pip [pɪp] n (seed) seme m; (BRIT: time signal on radio) segnale m orario
pipe [paɪp] n tubo; (for smoking) pipa ▷ vt portare per mezzo di tubazione; **pipeline** n conduttura; (for oil) oleodotto; **piper** n piffero; suonatore(-trice) di cornamusa

pirate ['paɪərət] n pirata m ▷ vt riprodurre abusivamente
Pisces ['paɪsiːz] n Pesci mpl
pistol ['pɪstl] n pistola
piston ['pɪstən] n pistone m
pit [pɪt] n buca, fossa; (also: **coal ~**) miniera; (quarry) cava ▷ vt **to ~ sb against sb** opporre qn a qn
pitch [pɪtʃ] n (BRIT Sport) campo; (Mus) tono; (tar) pece f; (fig) grado, punto ▷ vt (throw) lanciare ▷ vi (fall) cascare; **to ~ a tent** piantare una tenda; **pitch-black** adj nero(-a) come la pece
pitfall ['pɪtfɔːl] n trappola
pith [pɪθ] n (of plant) midollo; (of orange) parte f interna della scorza; (fig) essenza, succo; vigore m
pitiful ['pɪtɪful] adj (touching) pietoso(-a)
pity ['pɪtɪ] n pietà ▷ vt aver pietà di; **what a ~!** che peccato!
pizza ['piːtsə] n pizza
placard ['plækɑːd] n affisso
place [pleɪs] n posto, luogo; (proper position, rank, seat) posto; (house) casa, alloggio; (home) **at/to his ~** a casa sua ▷ vt (object) posare, mettere; (identify) riconoscere; individuare; **to take ~** aver luogo; succedere; **to change ~s with sb** scambiare il posto con qn; **out of ~** (not suitable) inopportuno(-a); **in the first ~** in primo luogo; **to ~ an order** dare un'ordinazione; **to be ~d** (in race, exam) classificarsi; **place mat** n sottopiatto; (in linen etc) tovaglietta; **placement** n collocamento; (job) lavoro
placid ['plæsɪd] adj placido(-a), calmo(-a)
plague [pleɪg] n peste f ▷ vt tormentare
plaice [pleɪs] n inv pianuzza
plain [pleɪn] adj (clear) chiaro(-a), palese; (simple) semplice; (frank) franco(-a), aperto(-a); (not handsome) bruttino(-a); (without seasoning etc) scondito(-a); naturale; (in one colour) tinta unita inv ▷ adv francamente, chiaramente ▷ n pianura; **plain chocolate** n cioccolato fondente; **plainly** adv chiaramente; (frankly) francamente
plaintiff ['pleɪntɪf] n attore(-trice)
plait [plæt] n treccia
plan [plæn] n pianta; (scheme) progetto, piano ▷ vt (think in advance) progettare; (prepare) organizzare ▷ vi far piani or progetti; **to ~ to do** progettare di fare
plane [pleɪn] n (Aviat) aereo; (tree) platano; (tool) pialla; (Art, Math etc) piano ▷ adj piano(-a), piatto(-a) ▷ vt (with tool) piallare
planet ['plænɪt] n pianeta m
plank [plæŋk] n tavola, asse f

planning ['plænɪŋ] n progettazione f; **family ~** pianificazione f delle nascite

plant [plɑːnt] n pianta; (machinery) impianto; (factory) fabbrica ▷ vt piantare; (bomb) mettere

plantation [plæn'teɪʃən] n piantagione f

plaque [plæk] n placca

plaster ['plɑːstə'] n intonaco; (also: ~ **of Paris**) gesso; (BRIT: also: **sticking ~**) cerotto ▷ vt intonacare; ingessare; (cover): **to ~ with** coprire di; **plaster cast** n (Med) ingessatura, gesso; (model, statue) modello in gesso

plastic ['plæstɪk] n plastica ▷ adj (made of plastic) di or in plastica; **plastic bag** n sacchetto di plastica; **plastic surgery** n chirurgia plastica

plate [pleɪt] n (dish) piatto; (in book) tavola; (dental plate) dentiera; **gold/silver ~** vasellame m d'oro/d'argento

plateau ['plætəʊ] n (pl **plateaus** or **plateaux**) n altipiano

platform ['plætfɔːm] n (stage, at meeting) palco; (Rail) marciapiede m; (BRIT: of bus) piattaforma; **which ~ does the train for Rome go from?** da che binario parte il treno per Roma?

platinum ['plætɪnəm] n platino

platoon [plə'tuːn] n plotone m

platter ['plætə'] n piatto

plausible ['plɔːzɪbl] adj plausibile, credibile; (person) convincente

play [pleɪ] n gioco; (Theatre) commedia ▷ vt (game) giocare a; (team, opponent) giocare contro; (instrument, piece of music) suonare; (record, tape) ascoltare; (role, part) interpretare ▷ vi giocare; suonare; recitare; **to ~ safe** giocare sul sicuro; **play back** vt riascoltare, risentire; **play up** vi (cause trouble) fare i capricci; **player** n giocatore(-trice); (Theatre) attore(-trice); (Mus) musicista m/f; **playful** adj giocoso(-a); **playground** n (in school) cortile m per la ricreazione; (in park) parco m giochi inv; **playgroup** n giardino d'infanzia; **playing card** n carta da gioco; **playing field** n campo sportivo; **playschool** n = **playgroup**; **playtime** n (Scol) ricreazione f; **playwright** n drammaturgo(-a)

plc abbr (= public limited company) società per azioni a responsabilità limitata quotata in borsa

plea [pliː] n (request) preghiera, domanda; (Law) (argomento di) difesa

plead [pliːd] vt patrocinare; (give as excuse) addurre a pretesto ▷ vi (Law) perorare la causa; (beg): **to ~ with sb** implorare qn

pleasant ['plɛznt] adj piacevole, gradevole

please [pliːz] excl per piacere!, per favore!; (acceptance): **yes, ~** sì, grazie ▷ vt piacere a ▷ vi piacere; (think fit): **do as you ~** faccia come le pare; **~ yourself!** come ti (or le) pare!; **pleased** adj **pleased (with)** contento(-a) (di); **pleased to meet you!** piacere!

pleasure ['plɛʒə'] n piacere m; **"it's a ~"** "prego"

pleat [pliːt] n piega

pledge [plɛdʒ] n pegno; (promise) promessa ▷ vt impegnare; promettere

plentiful ['plɛntɪful] adj abbondante, copioso(-a)

plenty ['plɛntɪ] n **~ of** tanto(-a), molto(-a); un'abbondanza di

pliers ['plaɪəz] npl pinza

plight [plaɪt] n situazione f critica

plod [plɔd] vi camminare a stento; (fig) sgobbare

plonk [plɔŋk] (inf) n (BRIT: wine) vino da poco ▷ vt **to ~ sth down** buttare giù qc bruscamente

plot [plɔt] n congiura, cospirazione f; (of story, play) trama; (of land) lotto ▷ vt (mark out) fare la pianta di; rilevare; (: diagram etc) tracciare; (conspire) congiurare, cospirare ▷ vi congiurare

plough [plaʊ] (US **plow**) n aratro ▷ vt (earth) arare; **to ~ money into** (company etc) investire danaro in; **ploughman's lunch** ['plaʊmənz-] (BRIT) n pasto a base di pane, formaggio e birra

plow [plaʊ] (US) = **plough**

ploy [plɔɪ] n stratagemma m

pluck [plʌk] vt (fruit) cogliere; (musical instrument) pizzicare; (bird) spennare; (hairs) togliere ▷ n coraggio, fegato; **to ~ up courage** farsi coraggio

plug [plʌg] n tappo; (Elec) spina; (Aut: also: **spark(ing) ~**) candela ▷ vt (hole) tappare; (inf: advertise) spingere; **plug in** vt (Elec) attaccare a una presa; **plughole** n (BRIT) scarico

plum [plʌm] n (fruit) susina

plumber ['plʌmə'] n idraulico

plumbing ['plʌmɪŋ] n (trade) lavoro di idraulico; (piping) tubature fpl

plummet ['plʌmɪt] vi **to ~ (down)** cadere a piombo

plump [plʌmp] adj grassoccio(-a) ▷ vi **to ~ for** (inf: choose) decidersi per

plunge [plʌndʒ] n tuffo; (fig) caduta ▷ vt immergere ▷ vi (fall) cadere, precipitare; (dive) tuffarsi; **to take the ~** saltare il fosso

plural ['plʊərl] adj plurale ▷ n plurale m

plus [plʌs] n (also: **~ sign**) segno più ▷ prep più; **ten/twenty ~** più di dieci/venti

ply [plaɪ] vt (a trade) esercitare ▷ vi (ship)

fare il servizio ▷ n (of wool, rope) capo; **to ~ sb with drink** dare di bere continuamente a qn; **plywood** n legno compensato

P.M. n abbr = **prime minister**

p.m. adv abbr (= post meridiem) del pomeriggio

PMS n abbr (= premenstrual syndrome) sindrome f premestruale

PMT n abbr (= premenstrual tension) sindrome f premestruale

pneumatic drill [nju:'mætɪk-] n martello pneumatico

pneumonia [nju:'məʊnɪə] n polmonite f

poach [pəʊtʃ] vt (cook: egg) affogare; (: fish) cuocere in bianco; (steal) cacciare (or pescare) di frodo ▷ vi fare il bracconiere; **poached** adj (egg) affogato(-a)

P.O. Box n abbr = **Post Office Box**

pocket ['pɔkɪt] n tasca ▷ vt intascare; **to be out of ~** (BRIT) rimetterci; **pocketbook** (US) n (wallet) portafoglio; **pocket money** n paghetta, settimana

pod [pɔd] n guscio

podiatrist [pɔ'di:ətrɪst] (US) n callista m/f, pedicure m/f

podium ['pəʊdɪəm] n podio

poem ['pəʊɪm] n poesia

poet ['pəʊɪt] n poeta/essa; **poetic** [-'ɛtɪk] adj poetico(-a); **poetry** n poesia

poignant ['pɔɪnjənt] adj struggente

point [pɔɪnt] n (gen) punto; (tip: of needle etc) punta; (in time) punto, momento; (Scol) voto; (main idea, important part) nocciolo; (Elec) presa (di corrente); (also: **decimal ~**): **2 ~ 3 (2.3)** 2 virgola 3 (2 3) ▷ vt (show) indicare; (gun etc) **to ~ sth at** puntare qc contro ▷ vi **to ~ at** mostrare a dito; **~s** npl (Aut) puntine fpl; (Rail) scambio; **to be on the ~ of doing sth** essere sul punto di or stare per fare qc; **to make a ~** fare un'osservazione; **to get/miss the ~** capire/non capire; **to come to the ~** venire al fatto; **there's no ~ in doing** è inutile (fare); **point out** vt far notare; **point-blank** adv (also: **at point-blank range**) a bruciapelo; (fig) categoricamente; **pointed** adj (shape) aguzzo(-a), appuntito(-a); (remark) specifico(-a); **pointer** n (needle) lancetta; (fig) indicazione f, consiglio; **pointless** adj inutile, vano(-a); **point of view** n punto di vista

poison ['pɔɪzn] n veleno ▷ vt avvelenare; **poisonous** adj velenoso(-a)

poke [pəʊk] vt (fire) attizzare; (jab with finger, stick etc) punzecchiare; (put): **to ~ sth in(to)** spingere qc dentro; **poke about** or **around** vi frugare; **poke out** vi (stick out) sporger fuori

poker ['pəʊkəʳ] n attizzatoio; (Cards) poker m

Poland ['pəʊlənd] n Polonia

polar ['pəʊlə'] adj polare; **polar bear** n orso bianco

Pole [pəʊl] n polacco(-a)

pole [pəʊl] n (of wood) palo; (Elec, Geo) polo; **pole bean** (US) n (runner bean) fagiolino; **pole vault** n salto con l'asta

police [pə'li:s] n polizia ▷ vt mantenere l'ordine in; **police car** n macchina della polizia; **police constable** (BRIT) n agente m di polizia; **police force** n corpo di polizia, polizia; **policeman** (irreg) n poliziotto, agente m di polizia; **police officer** n = **police constable**; **police station** n posto di polizia; **policewoman** (irreg) n donna f poliziotto inv

policy ['pɔlɪsɪ] n politica; (also: **insurance ~**) polizza (d'assicurazione)

polio ['pəʊlɪəʊ] n polio f

Polish ['pəʊlɪʃ] adj polacco(-a) ▷ n (Ling) polacco

polish ['pɔlɪʃ] n (for shoes) lucido; (for floor) cera; (for nails) smalto; (shine) lucentezza, lustro; (fig: refinement) raffinatezza ▷ vt lucidare; (fig: improve) raffinare; **polish off** vt (food) mangiarsi; **polished** adj (fig) raffinato(-a)

polite [pə'laɪt] adj cortese; **politeness** n cortesia

political [pə'lɪtɪkl] adj politico(-a); **politically** adv politicamente; **politically correct** politicamente corretto(-a)

politician [pɔlɪ'tɪʃən] n politico

politics ['pɔlɪtɪks] n politica ▷ npl (views, policies) idee fpl politiche

poll [pəʊl] n scrutinio; (votes cast) voti mpl; (also: **opinion ~**) sondaggio (d'opinioni) ▷ vt ottenere

pollen ['pɔlən] n polline m

polling station ['pəʊlɪŋ-] (BRIT) n sezione f elettorale

pollute [pə'lu:t] vt inquinare

pollution [pə'lu:ʃən] n inquinamento

polo ['pəʊləʊ] n polo; **polo-neck** n collo alto; (also: **polo-neck sweater**) dolcevita ▷ adj a collo alto; **polo shirt** n polo f inv

polyester [pɔlɪ'estə'] n poliestere m

polystyrene [pɔlɪ'staɪri:n] n polistirolo

polythene ['pɔlɪθi:n] n politene m; **polythene bag** n sacco di plastica

pomegranate ['pɔmɪgrænɪt] n melagrana

pompous ['pɔmpəs] adj pomposo(-a)

pond [pɔnd] n pozza; stagno

ponder ['pɔndə'] vt ponderare, riflettere su

pony ['pəʊnɪ] n pony m inv; **ponytail** n coda di cavallo; **pony trekking**

[-trɛkɪŋ] (BRIT) n escursione f a cavallo
poodle ['puːdl] n barboncino, barbone m
pool [puːl] n (puddle) pozza; (pond) stagno;
(also: **swimming ~**) piscina; (fig: of light)
cerchio; (billiards) specie di biliardo a buca
▷ vt mettere in comune; **~s** npl (football
pools) ≈ totocalcio; **typing ~** servizio
comune di dattilografia
poor [puə⁴] adj povero(-a); (mediocre)
mediocre, cattivo(-a) ▷ npl **the ~** i poveri; **~
in** povero(-a) di; **poorly** adv poveramente;
male ▷ adj indisposto(-a), malato(-a)
pop [pɔp] n (noise) schiocco; (Mus) musica
pop; (drink) bibita gasata; (us: inf: father)
babbo ▷ vt (put) mettere (in fretta) ▷ vi
scoppiare; (cork) schioccare; **pop in** vi
passare; **pop out** vi fare un salto fuori;
popcorn n pop-corn m
poplar ['pɔplə⁴] n pioppo
popper ['pɔpə⁴] n bottone m a pressione
poppy ['pɔpɪ] n papavero
Popsicle® ['pɔpsɪkl] (us) n (ice lolly)
ghiacciolo
pop star n pop star f inv
popular ['pɔpjulə⁴] adj popolare;
(fashionable) in voga; **popularity** [-'lærɪtɪ]
n popolarità
population [pɔpju'leɪʃən] n popolazione f
porcelain ['pɔːslɪn] n porcellana
porch [pɔːtʃ] n veranda
pore [pɔː⁴] n poro ▷ vi **to ~ over** essere
immerso(-a) in
pork [pɔːk] n carne f di maiale; **pork chop**
n braciola or costoletta di maiale; **pork pie**
n (BRIT: Culin) pasticcio di maiale in crosta
porn [pɔːn] (inf) n pornografia ▷ adj
porno inv; **pornographic** [pɔːnə'græfɪk]
adj pornografico(-a); **pornography**
[pɔː'nɔgrəfɪ] n pornografia
porridge ['pɔrɪdʒ] n porridge m
port [pɔːt] n (gen, wine) porto; (Naut: left
side) babordo
portable ['pɔːtəbl] adj portatile
porter ['pɔːtə⁴] n (for luggage) facchino,
portabagagli m inv; (doorkeeper) portiere
m, portinaio
portfolio [pɔːt'fəuliəu] n (case) cartella;
(Pol, Finance) portafoglio; (of artist) raccolta
dei propri lavori
portion ['pɔːʃən] n porzione f
port of call n (porto di) scalo
portrait ['pɔːtreɪt] n ritratto
portray [pɔː'treɪ] vt fare il ritratto di;
(character on stage) rappresentare; (in
writing) ritrarre
Portugal ['pɔːtjugl] n Portogallo
Portuguese [pɔːtju'giːz] adj portoghese
▷ n inv portoghese m/f; (Ling) portoghese
m

pose [pəuz] n posa ▷ vi posare; (pretend):
to ~ as atteggiarsi a, posare a ▷ vt porre
posh [pɔʃ] (inf) adj elegante; (family) per
bene
position [pə'zɪʃən] n posizione f; (job)
posto ▷ vt sistemare
positive ['pɔzɪtɪv] adj positivo(-a); (certain)
sicuro(-a), certo(-a); (definite) preciso(-a),
definitivo(-a); **positively** adv (affirmatively,
enthusiastically) positivamente; (decisively)
decisamente; (really) assolutamente
possess [pə'zɛs] vt possedere; **possession**
[pə'zɛʃən] n possesso; **possessions** npl
(belongings) beni mpl; **possessive** adj
possessivo(-a)
possibility [pɔsɪ'bɪlɪtɪ] n possibilità f inv
possible ['pɔsɪbl] adj possibile; **as big as ~**
il più grande possibile; **possibly** ['pɔsɪblɪ]
adv (perhaps) forse; **if you possibly can**
se le è possibile, **I cannot possibly come**
proprio non posso venire
post [pəust] n (BRIT) posta; (: collection)
levata; (job, situation) posto; (Mil)
postazione f; (pole) palo ▷ vt (BRIT:
send by post) imbucare; (: appoint): **to ~
to** assegnare a; **where can I ~ these
cards?** dove posso imbucare queste
cartoline?; **postage** n affrancatura;
postal adj postale; **postal order** n vaglia
m inv postale; **postbox** (BRIT) n cassetta
postale; **postcard** n cartolina; **postcode**
n (BRIT) codice m (di avviamento) postale
poster ['pəustə⁴] n manifesto, affisso
postgraduate ['pəust'grædjuət] n
laureato/a che continua gli studi
postman ['pəustmən] (irreg) n postino
postmark ['pəustmɑːk] n bollo or timbro
postale
post-mortem [-'mɔːtəm] n autopsia
post office n (building) ufficio postale;
(organization): **the Post Office** ≈ le Poste e
Telecomunicazioni
postpone [pəs'pəun] vt rinviare
posture ['pɔstʃə⁴] n portamento; (pose)
posa, atteggiamento
postwoman ['pəustwumən] (BRIT: irreg)
n postina
pot [pɔt] n (for cooking) pentola; casseruola;
(teapot) teiera; (coffeepot) caffettiera; (for
plants, jam) vaso; (inf: marijuana) erba
▷ vt (plant) piantare in vaso; **a ~ of tea
for two** tè per due; **to go to ~** (inf: work,
performance) andare in malora
potato [pə'teɪtəu] (pl potatoes) n patata;
potato peeler n sbucciapatate m inv
potent ['pəutnt] adj potente, forte
potential [pə'tɛnʃl] adj potenziale ▷ n
possibilità fpl
pothole ['pɔthəul] n (in road) buca; (BRIT:

underground) caverna
pot plant *n* pianta in vaso
potter ['pɔtəʳ] *n* vasaio ▷ *vi* **to ~ around,
~ about** (BRIT) lavoracchiare; **pottery**
n ceramiche *fpl*; (*factory*) fabbrica di
ceramiche
potty ['pɔtɪ] *adj* (*inf: mad*) tocco(-a) ▷ *n*
(*child's*) vasino
pouch [pautʃ] *n* borsa; (*Zool*) marsupio
poultry ['pəultrɪ] *n* pollame *m*
pounce [pauns] *vi* **to ~ (on)** piombare (su)
pound [paund] *n* (*weight*) libbra; (*money*)
(*lira*) sterlina ▷ *vt* (*beat*) battere; (*crush*)
pestare, polverizzare ▷ *vi* (*beat*) battere,
martellare; **pound sterling** *n* sterlina
(inglese)
pour [pɔːʳ] *vt* versare ▷ *vi* riversarsi; (*rain*)
piovere a dirotto; **pour in** *vi* affluire in
gran quantità; **pour out** *vi* (*people*) uscire
a fiumi ▷ *vt* vuotare; versare; (*fig*) sfogare;
pouring *adj* **pouring rain** pioggia
torrenziale
pout [paut] *vi* sporgere le labbra; fare il
broncio
poverty ['pɔvətɪ] *n* povertà, miseria
powder ['paudəʳ] *n* polvere *f* ▷ *vt* **to ~
one's face** incipriarsi il viso; **powdered
milk** *n* latte *m* in polvere
power ['pauəʳ] *n* (*strength*) potenza, forza;
(*ability, Pol: of party, leader*) potere *m*; (*Elec*)
corrente *f*; **to be in ~** (*Pol etc*) essere al
potere; **power cut** (BRIT) *n* interruzione
f or mancanza di corrente; **power
failure** *n* interruzione *f* della corrente
elettrica; **powerful** *adj* potente, forte;
powerless *adj* impotente; **powerless to
do** impossibilitato(-a) a fare; **power point**
(BRIT) *n* presa di corrente; **power station**
n centrale *f* elettrica
p.p. *abbr* = **per procurationem; p.p. J.
Smith** per J. Smith; = (*pages*) p.p.
PR *abbr* = **public relations**
practical ['præktɪkl] *adj* pratico(-a);
practical joke *n* beffa; **practically** *adv*
praticamente
practice ['præktɪs] *n* pratica; (*of profession*)
esercizio; (*at football etc*) allenamento;
(*business*) gabinetto; clientela ▷ *vt, vi* (*US*)
= **practise; in ~** (*in reality*) in pratica; **out of
~** fuori esercizio
practise ['præktɪs] (*US* **practice**) *vt* (*work
at: piano, one's backhand etc*) esercitarsi a;
(*train for: skiing, running etc*) allenarsi a; (*a
sport, religion*) praticare; (*method*) usare;
(*profession*) esercitare ▷ *vi* esercitarsi;
(*train*) allenarsi; (*lawyer, doctor*) esercitare;
practising *adj* (*Christian etc*) praticante;
(*lawyer*) che esercita la professione
practitioner [præk'tɪʃənəʳ] *n*

professionista *m/f*
pragmatic [præg'mætɪk] *adj*
pragmatico(-a)
prairie ['prɛərɪ] *n* prateria
praise [preɪz] *n* elogio, lode *f* ▷ *vt* elogiare,
lodare
pram [præm] (BRIT) *n* carrozzina
prank [præŋk] *n* burla
prawn [prɔːn] *n* gamberetto; **prawn
cocktail** *n* cocktail *m inv* di gamberetti
pray [preɪ] *vi* pregare; **prayer** [prɛəʳ] *n*
preghiera
preach [priːtʃ] *vt, vi* predicare; **preacher** *n*
predicatore(-trice); (*US: minister*) pastore *m*
precarious [prɪ'kɛərɪəs] *adj* precario(-a)
precaution [prɪ'kɔːʃən] *n* precauzione *f*
precede [prɪ'siːd] *vt* precedere; **precedent**
['prɛsɪdənt] *n* precedente *m*; **preceding**
[prɪ'siːdɪŋ] *adj* precedente
precinct ['priːsɪŋkt] (*US*) *n* circoscrizione *f*
precious ['prɛʃəs] *adj* prezioso(-a)
precise [prɪ'saɪs] *adj* preciso(-a); **precisely**
adv precisamente
precision [prɪ'sɪʒən] *n* precisione *f*
predator ['prɛdətəʳ] *n* predatore *m*
predecessor ['priːdɪsɛsəʳ] *n*
predecessore(-a)
predicament [prɪ'dɪkəmənt] *n* situazione
f difficile
predict [prɪ'dɪkt] *vt* predire; **predictable**
adj prevedibile; **prediction** [prɪ'dɪkʃən] *n*
predizione *f*
predominantly [prɪ'dɔmɪnəntlɪ] *adv* in
maggior parte; soprattutto
preface ['prɛfəs] *n* prefazione *f*
prefect ['priːfɛkt] *n* (BRIT: *in school*)
studente(-essa) con funzioni disciplinari;
(*French etc, Admin*) prefetto
prefer [prɪ'fɜːʳ] *vt* preferire; **to ~ doing** or
to do preferire fare; **preferable** ['prɛfrəbl]
adj preferibile; **preferably** ['prɛfrəblɪ] *adv*
preferibilmente; **preference** ['prɛfrəns] *n*
preferenza
prefix ['priːfɪks] *n* prefisso
pregnancy ['prɛgnənsɪ] *n* gravidanza
pregnant ['prɛgnənt] *adj* incinta *ag*
prehistoric ['priːhɪs'tɔrɪk] *adj*
preistorico(-a)
prejudice ['prɛdʒudɪs] *n* pregiudizio;
(*harm*) torto, danno; **prejudiced** *adj*
prejudiced (against) prevenuto(-a)
(contro); **prejudiced (in favour of)** ben
disposto(-a) (verso)
preliminary [prɪ'lɪmɪnərɪ] *adj* preliminare
prelude ['prɛljuːd] *n* preludio
premature ['prɛmətʃuəʳ] *adj*
prematuro(-a)
premier ['prɛmɪəʳ] *adj* primo(-a) ▷ *n* (*Pol*)
primo ministro

première [ˈprɛmɪɛəʳ] n prima
Premier League n ≈ serie A
premises [ˈprɛmɪsɪz] npl locale m; **on the ~** sul posto; **business ~** locali commerciali
premium [ˈpriːmɪəm] n premio; **to be at a ~** essere ricercatissimo
premonition [prɛməˈnɪʃən] n premonizione f
preoccupied [priːˈɔkjupaɪd] adj preoccupato(-a)
prepaid [priːˈpeɪd] adj pagato(-a) in anticipo
preparation [prɛpəˈreɪʃən] n preparazione f; **~s** npl (for trip, war) preparativi mpl
preparatory school [prɪˈpærətərɪ-] n scuola elementare privata
prepare [prɪˈpɛəʳ] vt preparare ▷ vi **to ~ for** prepararsi a; **~d to** pronto(-a) a
preposition [prɛpəˈzɪʃən] n preposizione f
prep school n = **preparatory school**
prerequisite [priːˈrɛkwɪzɪt] n requisito indispensabile
preschool [ˈpriːˈskuːl] adj (age) prescolastico(-a); (child) in età prescolastica
prescribe [prɪˈskraɪb] vt (Med) prescrivere
prescription [prɪˈskrɪpʃən] n prescrizione f; (Med) ricetta; **could you write me a ~?** mi può fare una ricetta medica?
presence [ˈprɛzns] n presenza; **~ of mind** presenza di spirito
present [adj, n ˈprɛznt, vb prɪˈzɛnt] adj presente; (wife, residence, job) attuale ▷ n (actuality): **the ~** il presente; (gift) regalo ▷ vt presentare; (give): **to ~ sb with sth** offrire qc a qn; **to give sb a ~** fare un regalo a qn; **at ~** al momento; **presentable** [prɪˈzɛntəbl] adj presentabile; **presentation** [-ˈteɪʃən] n presentazione f; (ceremony) consegna ufficiale; **present-day** adj attuale, d'oggigiorno; **presenter** n (Radio, TV) presentatore(-trice); **presently** adv (soon) fra poco, presto; (at present) al momento; **present participle** n participio presente
preservation [prɛzəˈveɪʃən] n preservazione f, conservazione f
preservative [prɪˈzəːvətɪv] n conservante m
preserve [prɪˈzəːv] vt (keep safe) preservare, proteggere; (maintain) conservare; (food) mettere in conserva ▷ n (often pl: jam) marmellata; (: fruit) frutta sciroppata
preside [prɪˈzaɪd] vi **to ~ (over)** presiedere (a)
president [ˈprɛzɪdənt] n presidente m; **presidential** [-ˈdɛnʃl] adj presidenziale

press [prɛs] n (newspapers etc): **the P~** la stampa; (tool, machine) pressa; (for wine) torchio ▷ vt (push) premere, pigiare; (squeeze) spremere; (: hand) stringere; (clothes: iron) stirare; (pursue) incalzare; (insist): **to ~ sth on sb** far accettare qc da qn ▷ vi premere; accalcare; **we are ~ed for time** ci manca il tempo; **to ~ for sth** insistere per avere qc; **press conference** n conferenza f stampa inv; **pressing** adj urgente; **press stud** (BRIT) n bottone m a pressione; **press-up** (BRIT) n flessione f sulle braccia
pressure [ˈprɛʃəʳ] n pressione f; **to put ~ on sb (to do)** mettere qn sotto pressione (affinché faccia); **pressure cooker** n pentola a pressione; **pressure group** n gruppo di pressione
prestige [prɛsˈtiːʒ] n prestigio
prestigious [prɛsˈtɪdʒəs] adj prestigioso(-a)
presumably [prɪˈzjuːməblɪ] adv presumibilmente
presume [prɪˈzjuːm] vt supporre
pretence [prɪˈtɛns] (us **pretense**) n (claim) pretesa; **to make a ~ of doing** far finta di fare; **under false ~s** con l'inganno
pretend [prɪˈtɛnd] vt (feign) fingere ▷ vi far finta; **to ~ to do** far finta di fare
pretense [prɪˈtɛns] (us) n = **pretence**
pretentious [prɪˈtɛnʃəs] adj pretenzioso(-a)
pretext [ˈpriːtɛkst] n pretesto
pretty [ˈprɪtɪ] adj grazioso(-a), carino(-a) ▷ adv abbastanza, assai
prevail [prɪˈveɪl] vi (win, be usual) prevalere; (persuade): **to ~ (up)on sb to do** persuadere qn a fare; **prevailing** adj dominante
prevalent [ˈprɛvələnt] adj (belief) predominante; (customs) diffuso(-a); (fashion) corrente; (disease) comune
prevent [prɪˈvɛnt] vt **to ~ sb from doing** impedire a qn di fare; **to ~ sth from happening** impedire che qc succeda; **prevention** [-ˈvɛnʃən] n prevenzione f; **preventive** adj preventivo(-a)
preview [ˈpriːvjuː] n (of film) anteprima
previous [ˈpriːvɪəs] adj precedente; anteriore; **previously** adv prima
prey [preɪ] n preda ▷ vi **to ~ on** far preda di; **it was ~ing on his mind** lo stava ossessionando
price [praɪs] n prezzo ▷ vt (goods) fissare il prezzo di; valutare; **priceless** adj inapprezzabile; **price list** n listino (dei) prezzi
prick [prɪk] n puntura ▷ vt pungere; **to ~ up one's ears** drizzare gli orecchi

prickly ['prɪklɪ] *adj* spinoso(-a)
pride [praɪd] *n* orgoglio; superbia ▷ *vt* **to ~ o.s. on** essere orgoglioso(-a) di, vantarsi di
priest [priːst] *n* prete *m*, sacerdote *m*
primarily ['praɪmərɪlɪ] *adv* principalmente, essenzialmente
primary ['praɪmərɪ] *adj* primario(-a); (*first in importance*) primo(-a) ▷ *n* (*us: election*) primarie *fpl*; **primary school** (BRIT) *n* scuola elementare
prime [praɪm] *adj* primario(-a), fondamentale; (*excellent*) di prima qualità ▷ *vt* (*wood*) preparare; (*fig*) mettere al corrente ▷ *n* **in the ~ of life** nel fiore della vita; **Prime Minister** *n* primo ministro
primitive ['prɪmɪtɪv] *adj* primitivo(-a)
primrose ['prɪmrəuz] *n* primavera
prince [prɪns] *n* principe *m*
princess [prɪn'sɛs] *n* principessa
principal ['prɪnsɪpl] *adj* principale ▷ *n* (*headmaster*) preside *m*; **principally** *adv* principalmente
principle ['prɪnsɪpl] *n* principio; **in ~** in linea di principio; **on ~** per principio
print [prɪnt] *n* (*mark*) impronta; (*letters*) caratteri *mpl*; (*fabric*) tessuto stampato; (*Art, Phot*) stampa ▷ *vt* imprimere; (*publish*) stampare, pubblicare; (*write in capitals*) scrivere in stampatello; **out of ~** esaurito(-a); **print out** *vt* (*Comput*) stampare; **printer** *n* tipografo; (*machine*) stampante *f*; **printout** *n* tabulato
prior ['praɪər] *adj* precedente; (*claim etc*) più importante; **~ to doing** prima di fare
priority [praɪ'ɔrɪtɪ] *n* priorità *f inv*; precedenza
prison ['prɪzn] *n* prigione *f* ▷ *cpd* (*system*) carcerario(-a); (*conditions, food*) nelle or delle prigioni; **prisoner** *n* prigioniero(-a); **prisoner-of-war** *n* prigioniero(-a) di guerra
pristine ['prɪstiːn] *adj* immacolato(-a)
privacy ['prɪvəsɪ] *n* solitudine *f*, intimità
private ['praɪvɪt] *adj* privato(-a); personale ▷ *n* soldato semplice; **"~"** (*on envelope*) "riservata"; (*on door*) "privato"; **in ~** in privato; **privately** *adv* in privato; (*within oneself*) dentro di sé; **private property** *n* proprietà privata; **private school** *n* scuola privata
privatize ['praɪvɪtaɪz] *vt* privatizzare
privilege ['prɪvɪlɪdʒ] *n* privilegio
prize [praɪz] *n* premio ▷ *adj* (*example, idiot*) perfetto(-a); (*bull, novel*) premiato(-a) ▷ *vt* apprezzare, pregiare; **prize-giving** *n* premiazione *f*; **prizewinner** *n* premiato(-a)
pro [prəu] *n* (*Sport*) professionista *m/f* ▷ *prep* pro; **the ~s and cons** il pro e il contro

probability [prɔbə'bɪlɪtɪ] *n* probabilità *f inv*; **in all ~** con tutta probabilità
probable ['prɔbəbl] *adj* probabile
probably ['prɔbəblɪ] *adv* probabilmente
probation [prə'beɪʃən] *n* **on ~** (*employee*) in prova; (*Law*) in libertà vigilata
probe [prəub] *n* (*Med, Space*) sonda; (*enquiry*) indagine *f*, investigazione *f* ▷ *vt* sondare, esplorare; indagare
problem ['prɔbləm] *n* problema *m*
procedure [prə'siːdʒər] *n* (*Admin, Law*) procedura; (*method*) metodo, procedimento
proceed [prə'siːd] *vi* (*go forward*) avanzare, andare avanti; (*go about it*) procedere; (*continue*): **to ~ (with)** continuare; **to ~ to** andare a; passare a; **to ~ to do** mettersi a fare; **proceedings** *npl* misure *fpl*; (*Law*) procedimento; (*meeting*) riunione *f*; (*records*) rendiconti *mpl*; atti *mpl*; **proceeds** ['prəusiːdz] *npl* profitto, incasso
process ['prəusɛs] *n* processo; (*method*) metodo, sistema *m* ▷ *vt* trattare; (*information*) elaborare
procession [prə'sɛʃən] *n* processione *f*, corteo; **funeral ~** corteo funebre
proclaim [prə'kleɪm] *vt* proclamare, dichiarare
prod [prɔd] *vt* dare un colpetto a; pungolare ▷ *n* colpetto
produce [*n* 'prɔdjuːs, *vb* prə'djuːs] *n* (*Agr*) prodotto, prodotti *mpl* ▷ *vt* produrre; (*show*) esibire, mostrare; (*cause*) cagionare, causare; **producer** *n* (*Theatre*) regista *m/f*; (*Agr, Cinema*) produttore *m*
product ['prɔdʌkt] *n* prodotto; **production** [prə'dʌkʃən] *n* produzione *f*; **productive** [prə'dʌktɪv] *adj* produttivo(-a); **productivity** [prɔdʌk'tɪvɪtɪ] *n* produttività
Prof. *abbr* (= *professor*) Prof.
profession [prə'fɛʃən] *n* professione *f*; **professional** *n* professionista *m/f* ▷ *adj* professionale; (*work*) da professionista
professor [prə'fɛsər] *n* professore *m* (*titolare di una cattedra*); (*us*) professore(-essa)
profile ['prəufaɪl] *n* profilo
profit ['prɔfɪt] *n* profitto; beneficio ▷ *vi* **to ~ (by** *or* **from)** approfittare (di); **profitable** *adj* redditizio(-a)
profound [prə'faund] *adj* profondo(-a)
programme ['prəugræm] (*us* **program**) *n* programma *m* ▷ *vt* programmare; **programmer** (*us* **programer**) *n* programmatore(-trice); **programming** (*us* **programing**) *n* programmazione *f*
progress [*n* 'prəugrɛs, *vb* prə'grɛs] *n*

progresso ▷ vi avanzare, procedere;
in ~ in corso; **to make ~** far progressi;
progressive [-'grɛsɪv] adj progressivo(-a);
(person) progressista
prohibit [prə'hɪbɪt] vt proibire, vietare
project [n 'prɔdʒɛkt, vb prə'dʒɛkt] n (plan)
piano; (venture) progetto; (Scol) studio
▷ vt proiettare ▷ vi (stick out) sporgere;
projection [prə'dʒɛkʃən] n proiezione
f; sporgenza; **projector** [prə'dʒɛktəʳ] n
proiettore m
prolific [prə'lɪfɪk] adj (artist etc)
fecondo(-a)
prolong [prə'lɔŋ] vt prolungare
prom [prɔm] n abbr = **promenade**; (US:
ball) ballo studentesco

promenade [prɔmə'nɑːd] n (by sea)
lungomare m
prominent ['prɔmɪnənt] adj
(standing out) prominente; (important)
importante
promiscuous [prə'mɪskjuəs] adj (sexually)
di facili costumi
promise ['prɔmɪs] n promessa ▷ vt,
vi promettere; **to ~ sb sth, ~ sth to sb**
promettere qc a qn; **to ~ (sb) that/to**
do sth promettere (a qn) che/di fare qc;
promising adj promettente
promote [prə'məut] vt promuovere;
(venture, event) organizzare; **promotion**
[-'məuʃən] n promozione f
prompt [prɔmpt] adj rapido(-a),
svelto(-a); puntuale; (reply) sollecito(-a)
▷ adv (punctually) in punto ▷ n (Comput)
prompt m ▷ vt incitare; provocare;
(Theatre) suggerire a; **to ~ sb to do** incitare
qn a fare; **promptly** adv prontamente;
puntualmente
prone [prəun] adj (lying) prono(-a); **~ to**
propenso(-a) a, incline a
prong [prɔŋ] n rebbio, punta
pronoun ['prəunaun] n pronome m
pronounce [prə'nauns] vt pronunciare;

how do you ~ it? come si pronuncia?
pronunciation [prənʌnsɪ'eɪʃən] n
pronuncia
proof [pruːf] n prova; (of book) bozza; (Phot)
provino ▷ adj **~ against** a prova di
prop [prɔp] n sostegno, appoggio ▷ vt
(also: **~ up**) sostenere, appoggiare; (lean):
to ~ sth against appoggiare qc contro
or a; **~s** oggetti m inv di scena; **prop up** vt
sostenere, appoggiare
propaganda [prɔpə'gændə] n
propaganda
propeller [prə'pɛləʳ] n elica
proper ['prɔpəʳ] adj (suited, right)
adatto(-a), appropriato(-a); (seemly)
decente; (authentic) vero(-a); (inf: real:
noun) + vero(-a) e proprio(-a); **properly**
['prɔpəlɪ] adv (eat, study) bene; (behave)
come si deve; **proper noun** n nome m
proprio
property ['prɔpətɪ] n (things owned) beni
mpl; (land, building) proprietà f inv; (Chem
etc: quality) proprietà
prophecy ['prɔfɪsɪ] n profezia
prophet ['prɔfɪt] n profeta m
proportion [prə'pɔːʃən] n proporzione f;
(share) parte f; **~s** npl (size) proporzioni fpl;
proportional adj proporzionale
proposal [prə'pəuzl] n proposta; (plan)
progetto; (of marriage) proposta di
matrimonio
propose [prə'pəuz] vt proporre, suggerire
▷ vi fare una proposta di matrimonio; **to**
~ to do proporsi di fare, aver l'intenzione
di fare
proposition [prɔpə'zɪʃən] n proposizione
f; (offer) proposta
proprietor [prə'praɪətəʳ] n
proprietario(-a)
prose [prəuz] n prosa
prosecute ['prɔsɪkjuːt] vt processare;
prosecution [-'kjuːʃən] n processo;
(accusing side) accusa; **prosecutor** n (also:
public prosecutor) ≈ procuratore m della
Repubblica
prospect [n 'prɔspɛkt, vb prə'spɛkt] n
prospettiva; (hope) speranza ▷ vi **to ~ for**
cercare; **~s** npl (for work etc) prospettive
fpl; **prospective** [-'spɛktɪv] adj possibile;
futuro(-a)
prospectus [prə'spɛktəs] n prospetto,
programma m
prosper ['prɔspəʳ] vi prosperare;
prosperity [prɔ'spɛrɪtɪ] n prosperità;
prosperous adj prospero(-a)
prostitute ['prɔstɪtjuːt] n prostituta;
male ~ uomo che si prostituisce
protect [prə'tɛkt] vt proteggere,
salvaguardare; **protection** n protezione f;

protective *adj* protettivo(-a)

protein ['prəʊtiːn] *n* proteina

protest [*n* 'prəʊtɛst, *vb* prə'tɛst] *n* protesta ▷ *vt, vi* protestare

Protestant ['prɒtɪstənt] *adj, n* protestante *m/f*

protester [prə'tɛstə^r] *n* dimostrante *m/f*

protractor [prə'træktə^r] *n* (*Geom*) goniometro

proud [praʊd] *adj* fiero(-a), orgoglioso(-a); (*pej*) superbo(-a)

prove [pruːv] *vt* provare, dimostrare ▷ *vi* **to ~ (to be) correct** *etc* risultare vero(-a) *etc*; **to ~ o.s.** mostrare le proprie capacità

proverb ['prɒvəːb] *n* proverbio

provide [prə'vaɪd] *vt* fornire, provvedere; **to ~ sb with sth** fornire *or* provvedere qn di qc; **provide for** *vt fus* provvedere a; (*future event*) prevedere; **provided** *conj* **provided (that)** purché + *sub*, a condizione che + *sub*; **providing** [prə'vaɪdɪŋ] *conj* purché +*sub*, a condizione che +*sub*

province ['prɒvɪns] *n* provincia; **provincial** [prə'vɪnʃəl] *adj* provinciale

provision [prə'vɪʒən] *n* (*supply*) riserva; (*supplying*) provvista; rifornimento; (*stipulation*) condizione *f*; **~s** *npl* (*food*) provviste *fpl*; **provisional** *adj* provvisorio(-a)

provocative [prə'vɒkətɪv] *adj* (*aggressive*) provocatorio(-a); (*thought-provoking*) stimolante; (*seductive*) provocante

provoke [prə'vəʊk] *vt* provocare; incitare

prowl [praʊl] *vi* (*also*: **~ about, ~ around**) aggirarsi ▷ *n* **to be on the ~** aggirarsi

proximity [prɒk'sɪmɪtɪ] *n* prossimità

proxy ['prɒksɪ] *n* **by ~** per procura

prudent ['pruːdnt] *adj* prudente

prune [pruːn] *n* prugna secca ▷ *vt* potare

pry [praɪ] *vi* **to ~ into** ficcare il naso in

PS *abbr* (= *postscript*) P.S.

pseudonym ['sjuːdənɪm] *n* pseudonimo

psychiatric [saɪkɪ'ætrɪk] *adj* psichiatrico(-a)

psychiatrist [saɪ'kaɪətrɪst] *n* psichiatra *m/f*

psychic ['saɪkɪk] *adj* (*also*: **~al**) psichico(-a); (*person*) dotato(-a) di qualità telepatiche

psychoanalysis [saɪkəʊə'nælɪsɪs, -siːz] (*pl* **-ses**) *n* psicanalisi *f inv*

psychological [saɪkə'lɔdʒɪkl] *adj* psicologico(-a)

psychologist [saɪ'kɔlədʒɪst] *n* psicologo(-a)

psychology [saɪ'kɔlədʒɪ] *n* psicologia

psychotherapy [saɪkəʊ'θɛrəpɪ] *n* psicoterapia

pt *abbr* (= *pint*; *point*) pt.

PTO *abbr* (= *please turn over*) v.r.

pub [pʌb] *n abbr* (= *public house*) pub *m inv*

puberty ['pjuːbətɪ] *n* pubertà

public ['pʌblɪk] *adj* pubblico(-a) ▷ *n* pubblico; **in ~** in pubblico

publication [pʌblɪ'keɪʃən] *n* pubblicazione *f*

public: public company *n* società *f inv* per azioni (*costituita tramite pubblica sottoscrizione*); **public convenience** (BRIT) *n* gabinetti *mpl*; **public holiday** *n* giorno festivo, festa nazionale; **public house** (BRIT) *n* pub *m inv*

publicity [pʌb'lɪsɪtɪ] *n* pubblicità

publicize ['pʌblɪsaɪz] *vt* rendere pubblico(-a)

public: public limited company *n* = società per azioni a responsabilità limitata (*quotata in Borsa*); **publicly** ['pʌblɪklɪ] *adv* pubblicamente; **public opinion** *n* opinione *f* pubblica; **public relations** *n* pubbliche relazioni *fpl*; **public school** *n* (BRIT) scuola privata; (US) scuola statale; **public transport** *n* mezzi *mpl* pubblici

publish ['pʌblɪʃ] *vt* pubblicare; **publisher** *n* editore *m*; **publishing** *n* (*industry*) editoria; (*of a book*) pubblicazione *f*

pub lunch *n* pranzo semplice ed economico servito nei pub

pudding ['pudɪŋ] *n* budino; (BRIT: *dessert*) dolce *m*; **black ~**, (US) **blood ~** sanguinaccio

puddle ['pʌdl] *n* pozza, pozzanghera

Puerto Rico ['pwəːtəʊ'riːkəʊ] *n* Portorico

puff [pʌf] *n* sbuffo ▷ *vt* **to ~ one's pipe** tirare sboccate di fumo ▷ *vi* (*pant*) ansare; **puff pastry** *n* pasta sfoglia

pull [pul] *n* (*tug*) **to give sth a ~** tirare su qc ▷ *vt* tirare; (*muscle*) strappare; (*trigger*) premere ▷ *vi* tirare; **to ~ to pieces** fare a pezzi; **to ~ one's punches** (*Boxing*) risparmiare l'avversario; **to ~ one's weight** dare il proprio contributo; **to ~ o.s. together** ricomporsi, riprendersi; **to ~ sb's leg** prendere in giro qn; **pull apart** *vt* (*break*) fare a pezzi; **pull away** *vi* (*move off: vehicle*) muoversi, partire; (*boat*) staccarsi dal molo, salpare; (*draw back: person*) indietreggiare; **pull back** *vt* (*lever etc*) tirare indietro; (*curtains*) aprire ▷ *vi* (*from confrontation etc*) tirarsi indietro; (*Mil: withdraw*) ritirarsi; **pull down** *vt* (*house*) demolire; (*tree*) abbattere; **pull in** *vi* (*Aut: at the kerb*) accostarsi; (*Rail*) entrare in stazione; **pull off** *vt* (*clothes*) togliere; (*deal etc*) portare a compimento; **pull out** *vi* partire; (*Aut: come out of line*) spostarsi sulla mezzeria ▷ *vt* staccare; far uscire; (*withdraw*) ritirare; **pull over** *vi* (*Aut*) accostare; **pull up** vi (stop) fermarsi ▷ vt (raise) sollevare; (uproot) sradicare

pulley ['pulɪ] n puleggia, carrucola

pullover ['puləuvəʳ] n pullover m inv

pulp [pʌlp] n (of fruit) polpa

pulpit ['pulpɪt] n pulpito

pulse [pʌls] n polso; (Bot) legume m; **~s** npl (Culin) legumi mpl

puma ['pjuːmə] n puma m inv

pump [pʌmp] n pompa; (shoe) scarpetta ▷ vt pompare; **pump up** vt gonfiare

pumpkin ['pʌmpkɪn] n zucca

pun [pʌn] n gioco di parole

punch [pʌntʃ] n (blow) pugno; (tool) punzone m; (drink) ponce m ▷ vt (hit): **to ~ sb/sth** dare un pugno a qn/qc; **punch-up** (BRIT: inf) n rissa

punctual ['pʌŋktjuəl] adj puntuale

punctuation [pʌŋktju'eɪʃən] n interpunzione f, punteggiatura

puncture ['pʌŋktʃəʳ] n foratura ▷ vt forare

Be careful not to translate *puncture* by the Italian word *puntura*.

punish ['pʌnɪʃ] vt punire; **punishment** n punizione f

punk [pʌŋk] n (also: **~ rocker**) punk m/f inv; (also: **~ rock**) musica punk, punk rock m; (US: inf: hoodlum) teppista m

pup [pʌp] n cucciolo(-a)

pupil ['pjuːpl] n allievo(-a); (Anat) pupilla

puppet ['pʌpɪt] n burattino

puppy ['pʌpɪ] n cucciolo(-a), cagnolino(-a)

purchase ['pəːtʃɪs] n acquisto, compera ▷ vt comprare

pure [pjuəʳ] adj puro(-a); **purely** ['pjuəlɪ] adv puramente

purify ['pjuərɪfaɪ] vt purificare

purity ['pjuərɪtɪ] n purezza

purple ['pəːpl] adj di porpora; viola inv

purpose ['pəːpəs] n intenzione f, scopo; **on ~** apposta

purr [pəːʳ] vi fare le fusa

purse [pəːs] n (BRIT) borsellino; (US) borsetta ▷ vt contrarre

pursue [pə'sjuː] vt inseguire; (fig: activity etc) continuare con; (: aim etc) perseguire

pursuit [pə'sjuːt] n inseguimento; (fig) ricerca; (pastime) passatempo

pus [pʌs] n pus m

push [puʃ] n spinta; (effort) grande sforzo; (drive) energia ▷ vt spingere; (button) premere; (thrust): **to ~ sth (into)** ficcare qc (in); (fig) fare pubblicità a ▷ vi spingere; premere; **to ~ for** (fig) insistere per; **push in** vi introdursi a forza; **push off** (inf) vi filare; **push on** vi (continue) continuare; **push over** vt far cadere; **push through** vi farsi largo spingendo ▷ vt (measure) far approvare; **pushchair** (BRIT)

n passeggino; **pusher** n (drug pusher) spacciatore(-trice); **push-up** (US) n (press-up) flessione f sulle braccia

pussy(-cat) ['pusɪ(-)] (inf) n micio

put [put] (pt, pp put) vt mettere, porre; (say) dire, esprimere; (a question) fare; (estimate) stimare; **put away** vt (return) mettere a posto; **put back** vt (replace) rimettere (a posto); (postpone) rinviare; (delay) ritardare; **put by** vt (money) mettere da parte; **put down** vt (parcel etc) posare, mettere giù; (pay) versare; (in writing) mettere per iscritto; (revolt, animal) sopprimere; (attribute) attribuire; **put forward** vt (ideas) avanzare, proporre; **put in** vt (application, complaint) presentare; (time, effort) mettere; **put off** vt (postpone) rimandare, rinviare; (discourage) dissuadere; **put on** vt (clothes, lipstick etc) mettere; (light etc) accendere; (play etc) mettere in scena; (food, meal) mettere su; (brake) mettere; **to ~ on weight** ingrassare; **to ~ on airs** darsi delle arie; **put out** vt mettere fuori; (one's hand) porgere; (light etc) spegnere; (person: inconvenience) scomodare; **put through** vt (Tel: call) passare; (: person) mettere in comunicazione; (plan) far approvare; **put up** vt (raise) sollevare, alzare; (: umbrella) aprire; (: tent) montare; (pin up) affiggere; (hang) appendere; (build) costruire, erigere; (increase) aumentare; (accommodate) alloggiare; **put aside** vt (lay down: book etc) mettere da una parte, posare; (save) mettere da parte; (in shop) tenere da parte; **put together** vt mettere insieme, riunire; (assemble: furniture) montare; (: meal) improvvisare; **put up with** vt fus sopportare

putt [pʌt] n colpo leggero; **putting green** n green m inv; campo da putting

puzzle ['pʌzl] n enigma m, mistero; (jigsaw) puzzle m; (also: **crossword ~**) parole fpl incrociate, cruciverba m inv ▷ vt confondere, rendere perplesso(-a) ▷ vi scervellarsi; **puzzled** adj perplesso(-a); **puzzling** adj (question) poco chiaro(-a); (attitude, set of instructions) incomprensibile

pyjamas [pɪ'dʒɑːməz] (BRIT) npl pigiama m

pylon ['paɪlən] n pilone m

pyramid ['pɪrəmɪd] n piramide f

Pyrenees [pɪrɪ'niːz] npl **the ~** i Pirenei

quack [kwæk] n (of duck) qua qua m inv; (pej: doctor) dottoruccio(-a)

quadruple [kwɔ'druːpl] vt quadruplicare ▷ vi quadruplicarsi

quail [kweɪl] n (Zool) quaglia ▷ vi (person): **to ~ at** or **before** perdersi d'animo davanti a

quaint [kweɪnt] adj bizzarro(-a); (old-fashioned) antiquato(-a); grazioso(-a), pittoresco(-a)

quake [kweɪk] vi tremare ▷ n abbr = **earthquake**

qualification [kwɔlɪfɪ'keɪʃən] n (degree etc) qualifica, titolo; (ability) competenza, qualificazione f; (limitation) riserva, restrizione f

qualified ['kwɔlɪfaɪd] adj qualificato(-a); (able): **~ to** competente in, qualificato(-a) a; (limited) condizionato(-a)

qualify ['kwɔlɪfaɪ] vt abilitare; (limit: statement) modificare, precisare ▷ vi **to ~ (as)** qualificarsi (come); **to ~ (for)** acquistare i requisiti necessari (per); (Sport) qualificarsi (per or a)

quality ['kwɔlɪtɪ] n qualità f inv

qualm [kwɑːm] n dubbio; scrupolo

quantify ['kwɔntɪfaɪ] vt quantificare

quantity ['kwɔntɪtɪ] n quantità f inv

quarantine ['kwɔrəntiːn] n quarantena

quarrel ['kwɔrl] n lite f, disputa ▷ vi litigare

quarry ['kwɔrɪ] n (for stone) cava; (animal) preda

quart [kwɔːt] n ≈ litro

quarter ['kwɔːtəʳ] n quarto; (us: coin) quarto di dollaro; (of year) trimestre m; (district) quartiere m ▷ vt dividere in quattro; (Mil) alloggiare; **~s** npl (living quarters) alloggio; (Mil) alloggi mpl, quadrato; **a ~ of an hour** un quarto d'ora; **quarter final** n quarto di finale; **quarterly** adj trimestrale ▷ adv trimestralmente

quartet(te) [kwɔː'tɛt] n quartetto

quartz [kwɔːts] n quarzo

quay [kiː] n (also: **~side**) banchina

queasy ['kwiːzɪ] adj (stomach) delicato(-a); **to feel ~** aver la nausea

queen [kwiːn] n (gen) regina; (Cards etc) regina, donna

queer [kwɪəʳ] adj strano(-a), curioso(-a) ▷ n (inf) finocchio

quench [kwɛntʃ] vt **to ~ one's thirst** dissetarsi

query ['kwɪərɪ] n domanda, questione f ▷ vt mettere in questione

quest [kwɛst] n cerca, ricerca

question ['kwɛstʃən] n domanda, questione f ▷ vt (person) interrogare; (plan, idea) mettere in questione or in dubbio; **it's a ~ of doing** si tratta di fare; **beyond ~** fuori di dubbio; **out of the ~** fuori discussione, impossibile; **questionable** adj discutibile; **question mark** n punto interrogativo; **questionnaire** [kwɛstʃə'nɛəʳ] n questionario

queue [kjuː] (BRIT) n coda, fila ▷ vi fare la coda

quiche [kiːʃ] n torta salata a base di uova, formaggio, prosciutto o altro

quick [kwɪk] adj rapido(-a), veloce; (reply) pronto(-a); (mind) pronto(-a), acuto(-a) ▷ n **cut to the ~** (fig) toccato(-a) sul vivo; **be ~!** fa presto!; **quickly** adv rapidamente, velocemente

quid [kwɪd] (BRIT: inf) n inv sterlina

quiet ['kwaɪət] adj tranquillo(-a), quieto(-a); (ceremony) semplice ▷ n tranquillità, calma ▷ vt, vi (us) = **quieten**; **keep ~!** sta zitto!; **quieten** (also: **quieten down**) vi calmarsi, chetarsi ▷ vt calmare, chetare; **quietly** adv tranquillamente, calmamente, sommessamente

quilt [kwɪlt] n trapunta; (continental quilt) piumino

quirky ['kwəːkɪ] adj stravagante

quit [kwɪt] (pt, pp **quit** or **quitted**) vt mollare; (premises) lasciare, partire da ▷ vi (give up) mollare; (resign) dimettersi

quite [kwaɪt] *adv* (*rather*) assai; (*entirely*)
completamente, del tutto; **I ~ understand**
capisco perfettamente; **that's not ~ big
enough** non è proprio sufficiente; **~ a few
of them** non pochi di loro; **~ (so)!** esatto!

quits [kwɪts] *adj* **~ (with)** pari (con); **let's
call it ~** adesso siamo pari

quiver ['kwɪvəʳ] *vi* tremare, fremere

quiz [kwɪz] *n* (*game*) quiz *m inv*; indovinello
▷ *vt* interrogare

quota ['kwəutə] *n* quota

quotation [kwəu'teɪʃən] *n* citazione
f; (*of shares etc*) quotazione *f*; (*estimate*)
preventivo; **quotation marks** *npl*
virgolette *fpl*

quote [kwəut] *n* citazione *f* ▷ *vt* (*sentence*)
citare; (*price*) dare, fissare; (*shares*) quotare
▷ *vi* **to ~ from** citare; **~s** *npl* = **quotation
marks**

r

rabbi ['ræbaɪ] *n* rabbino

rabbit ['ræbɪt] *n* coniglio

rabies ['reɪbiːz] *n* rabbia

RAC (*BRIT*) *n abbr* = **Royal Automobile
Club**

rac(c)oon [rə'kuːn] *n* procione *m*

race [reɪs] *n* razza; (*competition, rush*) corsa
▷ *vt* (*horse*) far correre ▷ *vi* correre; (*engine*)
imballarsi; **race car** (*US*) *n* = **racing car**;
racecourse *n* campo di corse, ippodromo;
racehorse *n* cavallo da corsa; **racetrack**
n pista

racial ['reɪʃl] *adj* razziale

racing ['reɪsɪŋ] *n* corsa; **racing car** (*BRIT*) *n*
macchina da corsa; **racing driver** (*BRIT*) *n*
corridore *m* automobilista

racism ['reɪsɪzəm] *n* razzismo; **racist** *adj*,
n razzista *m/f*

rack [ræk] *n* rastrelliera; (*also:* **luggage
~**) rete *f*, portabagagli *m inv*; (*also:* **roof ~**)
portabagagli; (*dish rack*) scolapiatti *m inv*
▷ *vt* **~ed by** torturato(-a) da; **to ~ one's
brains** scervellarsi

racket ['rækɪt] *n* (*for tennis*) racchetta;
(*noise*) fracasso; baccano; (*swindle*)
imbroglio, truffa; (*organized crime*) racket
m inv

racquet ['rækɪt] *n* racchetta

radar ['reɪdɑːʳ] *n* radar *m*

radiation [reɪdɪ'eɪʃən] *n* irradiamento;

(*radioactive*) radiazione *f*
radiator ['reɪdɪeɪtə'] *n* radiatore *m*
radical ['rædɪkl] *adj* radicale
radio ['reɪdɪəʊ] *n* radio *f inv*; **on the ~** alla radio; **radioactive** [reɪdɪəʊ'æktɪv] *adj* radioattivo(-a); **radio station** *n* stazione *f* radio *inv*
radish ['rædɪʃ] *n* ravanello
RAF *n abbr* = **Royal Air Force**
raffle ['ræfl] *n* lotteria
raft [rɑːft] *n* zattera; (*also:* **life ~**) zattera di salvataggio
rag [ræg] *n* straccio, cencio; (*pej: newspaper*) giornalaccio, bandiera; (*for charity*) iniziativa studentesca a scopo benefico; **~s** *npl* (*torn clothes*) stracci *mpl*, brandelli *mpl*
rage [reɪdʒ] *n* (*fury*) collera, furia ▷ *vi* (*person*) andare su tutte le furie; (*storm*) infuriare; **it's all the ~** fa furore
ragged ['rægɪd] *adj* (*edge*) irregolare; (*clothes*) logoro(-a); (*appearance*) pezzente
raid [reɪd] *n* (*Mil*) incursione *f*; (*criminal*) rapina; (*by police*) irruzione *f* ▷ *vt* fare un'incursione in; rapinare; fare irruzione in
rail [reɪl] *n* (*on stair*) ringhiera; (*on bridge, balcony*) parapetto; (*of ship*) battagliola; **railcard** (*BRIT*) tessera di riduzione ferroviaria; **railing(s)** *n(pl)* ringhiere *fpl*; **railroad** (*US*) *n* = **railway**; **railway** (*BRIT: irreg*) *n* ferrovia; **railway line** (*BRIT*) *n* linea ferroviaria; **railway station** (*BRIT*) *n* stazione *f* ferroviaria
rain [reɪn] *n* pioggia ▷ *vi* piovere; **in the ~** sotto la pioggia; **it's ~ing** piove; **rainbow** *n* arcobaleno; **raincoat** *n* impermeabile *m*; **raindrop** *n* goccia di pioggia; **rainfall** *n* pioggia; (*measurement*) piovosità; **rainforest** *n* foresta pluviale; **rainy** *adj* piovoso(-a)
raise [reɪz] *n* aumento ▷ *vt* (*lift*) alzare; sollevare; (*increase*) aumentare; (*a protest, doubt, question*) sollevare; (*cattle, family*) allevare; (*crop*) coltivare; (*army, funds*) raccogliere; (*loan*) ottenere; **to ~ one's voice** alzare la voce
raisin ['reɪzn] *n* uva secca
rake [reɪk] *n* (*tool*) rastrello ▷ *vt* (*garden*) rastrellare
rally ['rælɪ] *n* (*Pol etc*) riunione *f*; (*Aut*) rally *m inv*; (*Tennis*) scambio ▷ *vt* riunire, radunare ▷ *vi* (*sick person, Stock Exchange*) riprendersi
RAM [ræm] *n abbr* (= *random access memory*) memoria ad accesso casuale
ram [ræm] *n* montone *m*, ariete *m* ▷ *vt* conficcare; (*crash into*) cozzare, sbattere contro; percuotere; speronare
Ramadan [ræmə'dæn] *n* Ramadan *m inv*

ramble ['ræmbl] *n* escursione *f* ▷ *vi* (*pej: also:* **~ on**) divagare; **rambler** *n* escursionista *m/f*; (*Bot*) rosa rampicante; **rambling** *adj* (*speech*) sconnesso(-a); (*house*) tutto(-a) a nicchie e corridoi; (*Bot*) rampicante
ramp [ræmp] *n* rampa; **on/off ~** (*US Aut*) raccordo di entrata/uscita
rampage [ræm'peɪdʒ] *n* **to go on the ~** scatenarsi in modo violento
ran [ræn] *pt of* **run**
ranch [rɑːntʃ] *n* ranch *m inv*
random ['rændəm] *adj* fatto(-a) *or* detto(-a) per caso; (*Comput, Math*) casuale ▷ *n* **at ~** a casaccio
rang [ræŋ] *pt of* **ring**
range [reɪndʒ] *n* (*of mountains*) catena; (*of missile, voice*) portata; (*of proposals, products*) gamma; (*Mil: also:* **shooting ~**) campo di tiro; (*also:* **kitchen ~**) fornello, cucina economica ▷ *vt* disporre ▷ *vi* **to ~ over** coprire; **to ~ from ... to** andare da ... a
ranger ['reɪndʒə'] *n* guardia forestale
rank [ræŋk] *n* fila; (*status, Mil*) grado; (*BRIT: also:* **taxi ~**) posteggio di taxi ▷ *vi* **to ~ among** essere tra ▷ *adj* puzzolente; vero(-a) e proprio(-a); **the ~ and file** (*fig*) la gran massa
ransom ['rænsəm] *n* riscatto; **to hold sb to ~** (*fig*) esercitare pressione su qn
rant [rænt] *vi* vociare
rap [ræp] *vt* bussare a; picchiare su ▷ *n* (*music*) rap *m inv*
rape [reɪp] *n* violenza carnale, stupro; (*Bot*) ravizzone *m* ▷ *vt* violentare
rapid ['ræpɪd] *adj* rapido(-a); **rapidly** *adv* rapidamente; **rapids** *npl* (*Geo*) rapida
rapist ['reɪpɪst] *n* violentatore *m*
rapport [ræ'pɔː'] *n* rapporto
rare [rɛə'] *adj* raro(-a); (*Culin: steak*) al sangue; **rarely** *adv* raramente
rash [ræʃ] *adj* imprudente, sconsiderato(-a) ▷ *n* (*Med*) eruzione *f*; (*of events etc*) scoppio
rasher ['ræʃə'] *n* fetta sottile (di lardo *or* prosciutto)
raspberry ['rɑːzbərɪ] *n* lampone *m*
rat [ræt] *n* ratto
rate [reɪt] *n* (*proportion*) tasso, percentuale *f*; (*speed*) velocità *f inv*; (*price*) tariffa ▷ *vt* giudicare; stimare; **~s** *npl* (*BRIT: property tax*) imposte *fpl* comunali; (*fees*) tariffe *fpl*; **to ~ sb/sth as** valutare qn/qc come
rather ['rɑːðə'] *adv* piuttosto; **it's ~ expensive** è piuttosto caro; (*too*) è un po' caro; **there's ~ a lot** ce n'è parecchio; **I would** *or* **I'd ~ go** preferirei andare
rating ['reɪtɪŋ] *n* (*assessment*) valutazione *f*; (*score*) punteggio di merito; **~s** *npl* (*Radio,*

TV) indice *m* di ascolto

ratio ['reɪʃɪəu] *n* proporzione *f*, rapporto

ration ['ræʃən] *n (gen pl)* razioni *fpl* ▷ *vt* razionare; **~s** *npl* razioni *fpl*

rational ['ræʃənl] *adj* razionale, ragionevole; *(solution, reasoning)* logico(-a)

rattle ['rætl] *n* tintinnio; *(louder)* strepito; *(for baby)* sonaglino ▷ *vi* risuonare, tintinnare; fare un rumore di ferraglia ▷ *vt* scuotere (con strepito)

rave [reɪv] *vi (in anger)* infuriarsi; *(with enthusiasm)* andare in estasi; *(Med)* delirare ▷ *n (BRIT: inf: party)* rave *m inv*

raven ['reɪvən] *n* corvo

ravine [rə'viːn] *n* burrone *m*

raw [rɔː] *adj (uncooked)* crudo(-a); *(not processed)* greggio(-a); *(sore)* vivo(-a); *(inexperienced)* inesperto(-a); *(weather, day)* gelido(-a)

ray [reɪ] *n* raggio; **a ~ of hope** un barlume di speranza

razor ['reɪzər] *n* rasoio; **razor blade** *n* lama di rasoio

Rd *abbr* = **road**

re [riː] *prep* con riferimento a

RE *n abbr (BRIT Mil: = Royal Engineers)* ≈ G. M. *(Genio Militare)*; *(BRIT)* = **religious education**

reach [riːtʃ] *n* portata; *(of river etc)* tratto ▷ *vt* raggiungere; arrivare a ▷ *vi* stendersi; **out of/within ~** fuori/a portata di mano; **within ~ of the shops/station** vicino ai negozi/alla stazione; **reach out** *vt (hand)* allungare ▷ *vi* **to ~ out for** stendere la mano per prendere

react [riː'ækt] *vi* reagire; **reaction** [-'ækʃən] *n* reazione *f*; **reactor** [riː'æktər] *n* reattore *m*

read [riːd, *pt, pp* red] *(pt, pp* **read**) *vi* leggere ▷ *vt* leggere; *(understand)* intendere, interpretare; *(study)* studiare; **read out** *vt* leggere ad alta voce; **reader** *n* lettore(-trice); *(BRIT: at university)* professore con funzioni preminenti di ricerca

readily ['redɪlɪ] *adv* volentieri; *(easily)* facilmente; *(quickly)* prontamente

reading ['riːdɪŋ] *n* lettura; *(understanding)* interpretazione *f*; *(on instrument)* indicazione *f*

ready ['redɪ] *adj* pronto(-a); *(willing)* pronto(-a), disposto(-a); *(available)* disponibile ▷ *n* **at the ~** *(Mil)* pronto a sparare; **when will my photos be ~?** quando saranno pronte le mie foto?; **to get ~** *vi* prepararsi ▷ *vt* preparare; **ready-made** *adj* prefabbricato(-a); *(clothes)* confezionato(-a)

real [rɪəl] *adj* reale; vero(-a); **in ~ terms** in realtà; **real ale** *n* birra ad effervescenza

naturale; **real estate** *n* beni *mpl* immobili; **realistic** [-'lɪstɪk] *adj* realistico(-a); **reality** [riː'ælɪtɪ] *n* realtà *f inv*

realization [rɪəlaɪ'zeɪʃən] *n* presa di coscienza; realizzazione *f*

realize ['rɪəlaɪz] *vt (understand)* rendersi conto di

really ['rɪəlɪ] *adv* veramente, davvero; **~!** *(indicating annoyance)* oh, insomma!

realm [rɛlm] *n* reame *m*, regno

Realtor® ['rɪəltɔːr] *(US)* *n* agente *m* immobiliare

reappear [riːə'pɪər] *vi* ricomparire, riapparire

rear [rɪər] *adj* di dietro; *(Aut: wheel etc)* posteriore ▷ *n* didietro, parte *f* posteriore ▷ *vt (cattle, family)* allevare ▷ *vi (also: ~ up: animal)* impennarsi

rearrange [riːə'reɪndʒ] *vt* riordinare

rear: rear-view mirror ['rɪəvjuː-] *n (Aut)* specchio retrovisore; **rear-wheel drive** *n* trazione *fpl* posteriore

reason ['riːzn] *n* ragione *f*; *(cause, motive)* ragione, motivo ▷ *vi* **to ~ with sb** far ragionare qn; **it stands to ~ that** è ovvio che; **reasonable** *adj* ragionevole; *(not bad)* accettabile; **reasonably** *adv* ragionevolmente; **reasoning** *n* ragionamento

reassurance [riːə'ʃuərəns] *n* rassicurazione *f*

reassure [riːə'ʃuər] *vt* rassicurare; **to ~ sb of** rassicurare qn di or su

rebate ['riːbeɪt] *n (on tax etc)* sgravio

rebel [*n* 'rɛbl, *vb* rɪ'bɛl] *n* ribelle *m/f* ▷ *vi* ribellarsi; **rebellion** *n* ribellione *f*; **rebellious** *adj* ribelle

rebuild [riː'bɪld] *vt irreg* ricostruire

recall [rɪ'kɔːl] *vt* richiamare; *(remember)* ricordare, richiamare alla mente ▷ *n* richiamo

rec'd *abbr* = **received**

receipt [rɪ'siːt] *n (document)* ricevuta; *(act of receiving)* ricevimento; **~s** *npl (Comm)* introiti *mpl*; **can I have a ~, please?** posso avere una ricevuta, per favore?

receive [rɪ'siːv] *vt* ricevere; *(guest)* ricevere, accogliere; **receiver** [rɪ'siː-vər] *n (Tel)* ricevitore *m*; *(Radio, TV)* apparecchio ricevente; *(of stolen goods)* ricettatore(-trice); *(Comm)* curatore *m* fallimentare

recent ['riːsnt] *adj* recente; **recently** *adv* recentemente

reception [rɪ'sɛpʃən] *n* ricevimento; *(welcome)* accoglienza; *(TV etc)* ricezione *f*; **reception desk** *n (in hotel)* reception *f inv*; *(in hospital, at doctor's)* accettazione *f*; *(in offices etc)* portineria; **receptionist** *n* receptionist *m/f* inv

recession [rɪ'sɛʃən] *n* recessione *f*

recharge [riː'tʃɑːdʒ] *vt* (*battery*) ricaricare

recipe ['rɛsɪpɪ] *n* ricetta

recipient [rɪ'sɪpɪənt] *n* beneficiario(-a); (*of letter*) destinatario(-a)

recital [rɪ'saɪtl] *n* recital *m* inv

recite [rɪ'saɪt] *vt* (*poem*) recitare

reckless ['rɛkləs] *adj* (*driver etc*) spericolato(-a); (*spending*) folle

reckon ['rɛkən] *vt* (*count*) calcolare; (*think*): **I ~ that ...** penso che ...

reclaim [rɪ'kleɪm] *vt* (*demand back*) richiedere, reclamare; (*land*) bonificare; (*materials*) recuperare

recline [rɪ'klaɪn] *vi* stare sdraiato(-a)

recognition [rɛkəg'nɪʃən] *n* riconoscimento; **transformed beyond ~** irriconoscibile

recognize ['rɛkəgnaɪz] *vt* **to ~ (by/as)** riconoscere (a or da/come)

recollection [rɛkə'lɛkʃən] *n* ricordo

recommend [rɛkə'mɛnd] *vt* raccomandare; (*advise*) consigliare; **can you ~ a good restaurant?** mi può consigliare un buon ristorante?; **recommendation** [rɛkəmɛn'deɪʃən] *n* raccomandazione *f*; consiglio

reconcile ['rɛkənsaɪl] *vt* (*two people*) riconciliare; (*two facts*) conciliare, quadrare; **to ~ o.s. to** rassegnarsi a

reconsider [riːkən'sɪdəʳ] *vt* riconsiderare

reconstruct [riːkən'strʌkt] *vt* ricostruire

record [*n* 'rɛkɔːd, *vb* rɪ'kɔːd] *n* ricordo, documento; (*of meeting etc*) nota, verbale *m*; (*register*) registro; (*file*) pratica, dossier *m* inv; (*Comput*) record *m* inv; (*also*: **criminal ~**) fedina penale sporca; (*Mus*: *disc*) disco; (*Sport*) record *m* inv, primato ▷ *vt* (*set down*) prendere nota di, registrare; (*Mus*: *song etc*) registrare; **in ~ time** a tempo di record; **off the ~** *adj* ufficioso(-a) ▷ *adv* ufficiosamente; **recorded delivery** (BRIT) *n* (*Post*) **recorded delivery letter** *etc* lettera *etc* raccomandata; **recorder** *n* (*Mus*) flauto diritto; **recording** *n* (*Mus*) registrazione *f*; **record player** *n* giradischi *m* inv

recount [rɪ'kaʊnt] *vt* raccontare, narrare

recover [rɪ'kʌvəʳ] *vt* ricuperare ▷ *vi* **to ~ (from)** riprendersi (da); **recovery** [rɪ'kʌvərɪ] *n* ricupero; ristabilimento; ripresa

> Be careful not to translate *recover* by the Italian word *ricoverare*.

recreate [riːkrɪ'eɪt] *vt* ricreare

recreation [rɛkrɪ'eɪʃən] *n* ricreazione *f*; svago; **recreational drug** [rɛkrɪ'eɪʃənl-] *n* sostanza stupefacente usata a scopo ricreativo;

recreational vehicle (US) *n* camper *m* inv

recruit [rɪ'kruːt] *n* recluta; (*in company*) nuovo(-a) assunto(-a) ▷ *vt* reclutare; **recruitment** *n* reclutamento

rectangle ['rɛktæŋgl] *n* rettangolo; **rectangular** [-'tæŋgjuləʳ] *adj* rettangolare

rectify ['rɛktɪfaɪ] *vt* (*error*) rettificare; (*omission*) riparare

rector ['rɛktəʳ] *n* (Rel) parroco (*anglicano*)

recur [rɪ'kəːʳ] *vi* riaccadere; (*symptoms*) ripresentarsi; **recurring** *adj* (Math) periodico(-a)

recyclable [riː'saɪkləbl] *adj* riciclabile

recycle [riː'saɪkl] *vt* riciclare

recycling [riː'saɪklɪŋ] *n* riciclaggio

red [rɛd] *n* rosso; (Pol: *pej*) rosso(-a) ▷ *adj* rosso(-a); **in the ~** (*account*) scoperto; (*business*) in deficit; **Red Cross** *n* Croce *f* Rossa; **redcurrant** *n* ribes *m* inv

redeem [rɪ'diːm] *vt* (*debt*) riscattare; (*sth in pawn*) ritirare; (*fig*, *also* Rel) redimere

red: red-haired [-'hɛəd] *adj* dai capelli rossi; **redhead** ['rɛdhɛd] *n* rosso(-a); **red-hot** *adj* arroventato(-a); **red light** *n* **to go through a red light** (Aut) passare col rosso; **red-light district** ['rɛdlaɪt-] *n* quartiere *m* a luci rosse; **red meat** *n* carne *f* rossa

reduce [rɪ'djuːs] *vt* ridurre; (*lower*) ridurre, abbassare; **"~ speed now"** (Aut) "rallentare"; **at a ~d price** scontato(-a); **reduced** *adj* (*decreased*) ridotto(-a); **at a reduced price** a prezzo ribassato or ridotto; **"greatly reduced prices"** "grandi ribassi"; **reduction** [rɪ'dʌkʃən] *n* riduzione *f*; (*of price*) ribasso; (*discount*) sconto; **is there a reduction for children/ students?** ci sono riduzioni per i bambini/ gli studenti?

redundancy [rɪ'dʌndənsɪ] *n* licenziamento

redundant [rɪ'dʌndnt] *adj* (*worker*) licenziato(-a); (*detail*, *object*) superfluo(-a); **to be made ~** essere licenziato (per eccesso di personale)

reed [riːd] *n* (Bot) canna; (Mus: *of clarinet etc*) ancia

reef [riːf] *n* (*at sea*) scogliera

reel [riːl] *n* bobina, rocchetto; (Fishing) mulinello; (Cinema) rotolo; (*dance*) danza veloce scozzese ▷ *vi* (*sway*) barcollare

ref [rɛf] (*inf*) *n* abbr (= *referee*) arbitro

refectory [rɪ'fɛktərɪ] *n* refettorio

refer [rɪ'fəːʳ] *vt* **to ~ sth to** (*dispute*, *decision*) deferire qc a; **to ~ sb to** (*inquirer*, Med: *patient*) indirizzare qn a; (*reader: to text*) rimandare qn a ▷ *vi* **to ~ to** (*allude to*) accennare a; (*consult*) rivolgersi a

referee [rɛfə'riː] n arbitro; (BRIT: for job application) referenza ▷ vt arbitrare

reference ['rɛfrəns] n riferimento; (mention) menzione f, allusione f; (for job application) referenza; **with ~ to** (Comm: in letter) in or con riferimento a; **reference number** n numero di riferimento

refill [vb riː'fɪl, n'riː'fɪl] vt riempire di nuovo; (pen, lighter etc) ricaricare ▷ n (for pen etc) ricambio

refine [rɪ'faɪn] vt raffinare; **refined** adj (person, taste) raffinato(-a); **refinery** n raffineria

reflect [rɪ'flɛkt] vt (light, image) riflettere; (fig) rispecchiare ▷ vi (think) riflettere, considerare; **it ~s badly/well on him** si ripercuote su di lui in senso negativo/positivo; **reflection** [-'flɛkʃən] n riflessione f, (image) riflesso; (criticism): **reflection on** giudizio su; attacco a; **on reflection** pensandoci sopra

reflex ['riːflɛks] adj riflesso(-a) ▷ n riflesso

reform [rɪ'fɔːm] n (of sinner etc) correzione f; (of law etc) riforma ▷ vt correggere; riformare

refrain [rɪ'freɪn] vi **to ~ from doing** trattenersi dal fare ▷ n ritornello

refresh [rɪ'frɛʃ] vt rinfrescare; (food, sleep) ristorare; **refreshing** adj (drink) rinfrescante; (sleep) riposante, ristoratore(-trice); **refreshments** npl rinfreschi mpl

refrigerator [rɪ'frɪdʒəreɪtəʳ] n frigorifero

refuel [riː'fjuəl] vi far rifornimento (di carburante)

refuge ['rɛfjuːdʒ] n rifugio; **to take ~ in** rifugiarsi in; **refugee** [rɛfju'dʒiː] n rifugiato(-a), profugo(-a)

refund [n'riːfʌnd, vb rɪ'fʌnd] n rimborso ▷ vt rimborsare

refurbish [riː'fəːbɪʃ] vt rimettere a nuovo

refusal [rɪ'fjuːzəl] n rifiuto; **to have first ~ on** avere il diritto d'opzione su

refuse [n'rɛfjuːs, vb rɪ'fjuːz] n rifiuti mpl ▷ vt, vi rifiutare; **to ~ to do** rifiutare di fare

regain [rɪ'geɪn] vt riguadagnare; riacquistare, recuperare

regard [rɪ'gɑːd] n riguardo, stima ▷ vt considerare, stimare; **to give one's ~s to** porgere i suoi saluti a; **"with kindest ~s"** "cordiali saluti"; **regarding** prep riguardo a, per quanto riguarda; **regardless** adv lo stesso; **regardless of** a dispetto di, nonostante

regenerate [rɪ'dʒɛnəreɪt] vt rigenerare

reggae ['rɛgeɪ] n reggae m

regiment ['rɛdʒɪmənt] n reggimento

region ['riːdʒən] n regione f; **in the ~ of** (fig) all'incirca di; **regional** adj regionale

register ['rɛdʒɪstəʳ] n registro; (also: **electoral ~**) lista elettorale ▷ vt registrare (vehicle) immatricolare; (letter) assicurare; (instrument) segnare ▷ vi iscriversi; (at hotel) firmare il registro; (make impression) entrare in testa; **registered** (BRIT) adj (letter) assicurato(-a)

registrar ['rɛdʒɪstrɑːʳ] n ufficiale m di stato civile; segretario

registration [rɛdʒɪs'treɪʃən] n (act) registrazione f; iscrizione f; (Aut: also: **~ number**) numero di targa

registry office (BRIT) n anagrafe f; **to get married in a ~** ≈ sposarsi in municipio

regret [rɪ'grɛt] n rimpianto, rincrescimento ▷ vt rimpiangere; **regrettable** adj deplorevole

regular ['rɛgjuləʳ] adj regolare; (usual) abituale, normale; (soldier) dell'esercito regolare ▷ n (client etc) cliente m/f abituale; **regularly** adv regolarmente

regulate ['rɛgjuleɪt] vt regolare; **regulation** [-'leɪʃən] n regolazione f; (rule) regola, regolamento

rehabilitation ['riːhəbɪlɪ'teɪʃən] n (of offender) riabilitazione f; (of disabled) riadattamento

rehearsal [rɪ'həːsəl] n prova

rehearse [rɪ'həːs] vt provare

reign [reɪn] n regno ▷ vi regnare

reimburse [riːɪm'bəːs] vt rimborsare

rein [reɪn] n (for horse) briglia

reincarnation [riːɪnkɑː'neɪʃən] n reincarnazione f

reindeer ['reɪndɪəʳ] n inv renna

reinforce [riːɪn'fɔːs] vt rinforzare; **reinforcements** npl (Mil) rinforzi mpl

reinstate [riːɪn'steɪt] vt reintegrare

reject [n'riːdʒɛkt, vb rɪ'dʒɛkt] n (Comm) scarto ▷ vt rifiutare, respingere; (Comm: goods) scartare; **rejection** [rɪ'dʒɛkʃən] n rifiuto

rejoice [rɪ'dʒɔɪs] vi **to ~ (at or over)** provare diletto in

relate [rɪ'leɪt] vt (tell) raccontare; (connect) collegare ▷ vi **to ~ to** (connect) riferirsi a; (get on with) stabilire un rapporto con; **relating to** che riguarda, rispetto a; **related** adj **related (to)** imparentato(-a) (con); collegato(-a) or connesso(-a) (a)

relation [rɪ'leɪʃən] n (person) parente m/f; (link) rapporto, relazione f; **~s** npl (relatives) parenti mpl; **relationship** n rapporto; (personal ties) rapporti mpl, relazioni fpl; (also: **family relationship**) legami mpl di parentela

relative ['rɛlətɪv] n parente m/f ▷ adj relativo(-a); (respective) rispettivo(-a); **relatively** adv relativamente; (fairly, *rather*) abbastanza

relax [rɪ'læks] vi rilasciarsi; (*person: unwind*) rilassarsi ▷ vt rilasciare; (*mind, person*) rilassare; **relaxation** [ri:læk'seɪʃən] n rilasciamento; rilassamento; (*entertainment*) ricreazione f, svago; **relaxed** *adj* rilassato(-a); **relaxing** *adj* rilassante

relay ['ri:leɪ] n (*Sport*) corsa a staffetta ▷ vt (*message*) trasmettere

release [rɪ'li:s] n (*from prison*) rilascio; (*from obligation*) liberazione f; (*of gas etc*) emissione f; (*of film etc*) distribuzione f; (*record*) disco; (*device*) disinnesto ▷ vt (*prisoner*) rilasciare; (*from obligation, wreckage etc*) liberare; (*book, film*) fare uscire; (*news*) rendere pubblico(-a); (*gas etc*) emettere; (*Tech: catch, spring etc*) disinnestare

relegate ['rɛləgeɪt] vt relegare; (*BRIT Sport*): **to be ~d** essere retrocesso(-a)

relent [rɪ'lɛnt] vi cedere; **relentless** *adj* implacabile

relevant ['rɛləvənt] *adj* pertinente; (*chapter*) in questione; **~ to** pertinente a

▌ Be careful not to translate *relevant* by the Italian word *rilevante*.

reliable [rɪ'laɪəbl] *adj* (*person, firm*) fidato(-a), che dà affidamento; (*method*) sicuro(-a); (*machine*) affidabile

relic ['rɛlɪk] n (*Rel*) reliquia; (*of the past*) resto

relief [rɪ'li:f] n (*from pain, anxiety*) sollievo; (*help, supplies*) soccorsi mpl; (*Art, Geo*) rilievo

relieve [rɪ'li:v] vt (*pain, patient*) sollevare; (*bring help*) soccorrere; (*take over from: gen*) sostituire; (: *guard*) rilevare; **to ~ sb of sth** (*load*) alleggerire qn di qc; **to ~ o.s.** fare i propri bisogni; **relieved** *adj* sollevato(-a); **to be relieved that ...** essere sollevato(-a) (dal fatto) che ...; **I'm relieved to hear it** mi hai tolto un peso con questa notizia

religion [rɪ'lɪdʒən] n religione f

religious [rɪ'lɪdʒəs] *adj* religioso(-a); **religious education** n religione f

relish ['rɛlɪʃ] n (*Culin*) condimento; (*enjoyment*) gran piacere m ▷ vt (*food etc*) godere; **to ~ doing** adorare fare

relocate ['ri:ləu'keɪt] vt trasferire ▷ vi trasferirsi

reluctance [rɪ'lʌktəns] n riluttanza

reluctant [rɪ'lʌktənt] *adj* riluttante, mal disposto(-a); **reluctantly** *adv* di mala voglia, a malincuore

rely [rɪ'laɪ]: **to ~ on** vt fus contare su; (*be dependent*) dipendere da

remain [rɪ'meɪn] vi restare, rimanere; **remainder** n resto; (*Comm*) rimanenza; **remaining** *adj* che rimane; **remains** npl resti mpl

remand [rɪ'mɑ:nd] n **on ~** in detenzione preventiva ▷ vt **to ~ in custody** rinviare in carcere; trattenere a disposizione della legge

remark [rɪ'mɑ:k] n osservazione f ▷ vt osservare, dire; **remarkable** *adj* notevole; eccezionale

remarry [ri:'mærɪ] vi risposarsi

remedy ['rɛmədɪ] n **~ (for)** rimedio (per) ▷ vt rimediare a

remember [rɪ'mɛmbə'] vt ricordare, ricordarsi di; **~ me to him** salutalo da parte mia; **Remembrance Day** [rɪ'mɛmbrəns-] n 11 novembre, giorno della commemorazione dei caduti in guerra

⬧ **REMEMBRANCE DAY**

⬧
⬧ In Gran Bretagna, il **Remembrance**
⬧ **Day** è un giorno di commemorazione
⬧ dei caduti in guerra. Si celebra ogni anno
⬧ la domenica più vicina all'11 novembre,
⬧ anniversario della firma dell'armistizio
⬧ con la Germania nel 1918.

remind [rɪ'maɪnd] vt **to ~ sb of sth** ricordare qc a qn; **to ~ sb to do** ricordare a qn di fare; **reminder** n richiamo; (*note etc*) promemoria m inv

reminiscent [rɛmɪ'nɪsnt] *adj* **~ of** che fa pensare a, che richiama

remnant ['rɛmnənt] n resto, avanzo

remorse [rɪ'mɔ:s] n rimorso

remote [rɪ'məut] *adj* remoto(-a), lontano(-a); (*person*) distaccato(-a); **remote control** n telecomando; **remotely** *adv* remotamente; (*slightly*) vagamente

removal [rɪ'mu:vəl] n (*taking away*) rimozione f; soppressione f; (*BRIT: from house*) trasloco; (*from office: dismissal*) destituzione f; (*Med*) ablazione f; **removal man** (*irreg*) n (*BRIT*) addetto ai traslochi; **removal van** (*BRIT*) n furgone m per traslochi

remove [rɪ'mu:v] vt togliere, rimuovere; (*employee*) destituire; (*stain*) far sparire; (*doubt, abuse*) sopprimere, eliminare

Renaissance [rɪ'neɪsɑ̃:ns] n **the ~** il Rinascimento

rename [ri:'neɪm] vt ribattezzare

render ['rɛndə'] vt rendere

rendezvous ['rɔndɪvu:] n appuntamento; (*place*) luogo d'incontro; (*meeting*) incontro

renew [rɪ'nju:] vt rinnovare; (*negotiations*) riprendere

renovate ['rɛnəveɪt] vt rinnovare; (*art work*) restaurare

renowned [rɪ'naund] *adj* rinomato(-a)
rent [rɛnt] *n* affitto ▷ *vt* (*take for rent*) prendere in affitto; (*also*: ~ **out**) dare in affitto; **rental** *n* (*for television, car*) fitto
reorganize [riː'ɔːɡənaɪz] *vt* riorganizzare
rep [rɛp] *n abbr* (*Comm*: = *representative*) rappresentante *m/f*; (*Theatre*: = *repertory*) teatro di repertorio
repair [rɪ'pɛəʳ] *n* riparazione *f* ▷ *vt* riparare; **in good/bad ~** in buone/cattive condizioni; **where can I get this ~ed?** dove lo posso far riparare?; **repair kit** *n* corredo per riparazioni
repay [riː'peɪ] (*irreg*) *vt* (*money, creditor*) rimborsare, ripagare; (*sb's efforts*) ricompensare; (*favour*) ricambiare; **repayment** *n* pagamento; rimborso
repeat [rɪ'piːt] *n* (*Radio, TV*) replica ▷ *vt* ripetere; (*pattern*) riprodurre; (*promise, attack, also Comm: order*) rinnovare ▷ *vi* ripetere; **can you ~ that, please?** può ripetere, per favore?; **repeatedly** *adv* ripetutamente, spesso; **repeat prescription** *n* (BRIT) ricetta ripetibile
repellent [rɪ'pɛlənt] *adj* repellente ▷ *n* **insect ~** prodotto *m* anti-insetti *inv*
repercussions [riːpə'kʌʃənz] *npl* ripercussioni *fpl*
repetition [rɛpɪ'tɪʃən] *n* ripetizione *f*
repetitive [rɪ'pɛtɪtɪv] *adj* (*movement*) che si ripete; (*work*) monotono(-a); (*speech*) pieno(-a) di ripetizioni
replace [rɪ'pleɪs] *vt* (*put back*) rimettere a posto; (*take the place of*) sostituire; **replacement** *n* rimessa; sostituzione *f*; (*person*) sostituto(-a)
replay ['riːpleɪ] *n* (*of match*) partita ripetuta; (*of tape, film*) replay *m inv*
replica ['rɛplɪkə] *n* replica, copia
reply [rɪ'plaɪ] *n* risposta ▷ *vi* rispondere
report [rɪ'pɔːt] *n* rapporto; (*Press etc*) cronaca; (BRIT: *also*: **school ~**) pagella; (*of gun*) sparo ▷ *vt* riportare; (*Press etc*) fare una cronaca su; (*bring to notice: occurrence*) segnalare; (: *person*) denunciare ▷ *vi* (*make a report*) fare un rapporto (o una cronaca); (*present o.s.*): **to ~ (to sb)** presentarsi (a qn); **I'd like to ~ a theft** vorrei denunciare un furto; **report card** (US, Scottish) *n* pagella; **reportedly** *adv* stando a quanto si dice; **he reportedly told them to ...** avrebbe detto loro di ...; **reporter** *n* reporter *m inv*
represent [rɛprɪ'zɛnt] *vt* rappresentare; **representation** [-'teɪʃən] *n* rappresentazione *f*; (*petition*) rappresentanza; **representative** *n* rappresentante *m/f*; (US Pol) deputato(-a) ▷ *adj* rappresentativo(-a)

repress [rɪ'prɛs] *vt* reprimere; **repression** [-'prɛʃən] *n* repressione *f*
reprimand ['rɛprɪmɑːnd] *n* rimprovero ▷ *vt* rimproverare
reproduce [riːprə'djuːs] *vt* riprodurre ▷ *vi* riprodursi; **reproduction** [-'dʌkʃən] *n* riproduzione *f*
reptile ['rɛptaɪl] *n* rettile *m*
republic [rɪ'pʌblɪk] *n* repubblica; **republican** *adj*, *n* repubblicano(-a)
reputable ['rɛpjutəbl] *adj* di buona reputazione; (*occupation*) rispettabile
reputation [rɛpju'teɪʃən] *n* reputazione *f*
request [rɪ'kwɛst] *n* domanda; (*formal*) richiesta ▷ *vt* **to ~ (of or from sb)** chiedere (a qn); **request stop** (BRIT) *n* (*for bus*) fermata facoltativa or a richiesta
require [rɪ'kwaɪəʳ] *vt* (*need: person*) aver bisogno di; (: *thing, situation*) richiedere; (*want*) volere, esigere; (*order*): **to ~ sb to do sth** ordinare a qn di fare qc; **requirement** *n* esigenza; bisogno; requisito
resat [riː'sæt] *pt, pp of* **resit**
rescue ['rɛskjuː] *n* salvataggio; (*help*) soccorso ▷ *vt* salvare
research [rɪ'səːtʃ] *n* ricerca, ricerche *fpl* ▷ *vt* fare ricerche su
resemblance [rɪ'zɛmbləns] *n* somiglianza
resemble [rɪ'zɛmbl] *vt* assomigliare a
resent [rɪ'zɛnt] *vt* risentirsi di; **resentful** *adj* pieno(-a) di risentimento; **resentment** *n* risentimento
reservation [rɛzə'veɪʃən] *n* (*booking*) prenotazione *f*; (*doubt*) dubbio; (*protected area*) riserva; (BRIT: *on road: also*: **central ~**) spartitraffico *m inv*; **reservation desk** (US) *n* (*in hotel*) reception *f inv*
reserve [rɪ'zəːv] *n* riserva ▷ *vt* (*seats etc*) prenotare; **reserved** *adj* (*shy*) riservato(-a)
reservoir ['rɛzəvwɑːʳ] *n* serbatoio
residence ['rɛzɪdəns] *n* residenza; **residence permit** (BRIT) *n* permesso di soggiorno
resident ['rɛzɪdənt] *n* residente *m/f*; (*in hotel*) cliente *m/f* fisso(-a) ▷ *adj* residente; (*doctor*) fisso(-a); (*course, college*) a tempo pieno con pernottamento; **residential** [-'dɛnʃəl] *adj* di residenza; (*area*) residenziale
residue ['rɛzɪdjuː] *n* resto; (Chem, Physics) residuo
resign [rɪ'zaɪn] *vt* (*one's post*) dimettersi da ▷ *vi* dimettersi; **to ~ o.s. to** rassegnarsi a; **resignation** [rɛzɪɡ'neɪʃən] *n* dimissioni *fpl*; rassegnazione *f*
resin ['rɛzɪn] *n* resina
resist [rɪ'zɪst] *vt* resistere a; **resistance** *n* resistenza
resit ['riːsɪt] (BRIT) (*pt, pp* **resat**) *vt* (*exam*) ripresentarsi a; (*subject*) ridare l'esame di

▷ *n* **he's got his French ~ on Friday** deve ridare l'esame di francese venerdì

resolution [rezə'luːʃən] *n* risoluzione *f*

resolve [rɪ'zɔlv] *n* risoluzione *f* ▷ *vi* (*decide*): **to ~ to do** decidere di fare ▷ *vt* (*problem*) risolvere

resort [rɪ'zɔːt] *n* (*town*) stazione *f*; (*recourse*) ricorso ▷ *vi* **to ~ to** aver ricorso a; **in the last ~** come ultima risorsa

resource [rɪ'sɔːs] *n* risorsa; **resourceful** *adj* pieno(-a) di risorse, intraprendente

respect [rɪs'pɛkt] *n* rispetto ▷ *vt* rispettare; **respectable** *adj* rispettabile; **respectful** *adj* rispettoso(-a); **respective** [rɪs'pɛktɪv] *adj* rispettivo(-a); **respectively** *adv* rispettivamente

respite ['rɛspaɪt] *n* respiro, tregua

respond [rɪs'pɔnd] *vi* rispondere; **response** [rɪs'pɔns] *n* risposta

responsibility [rɪspɔnsɪ'bɪlɪtɪ] *n* responsabilità *f inv*

responsible [rɪs'pɔnsɪbl] *adj* (*trustworthy*) fidato(-a); (*job*) di (grande) responsabilità; **~ (for)** responsabile (di); **responsibly** *adv* responsabilmente

responsive [rɪs'pɔnsɪv] *adj* che reagisce

rest [rɛst] *n* riposo; (*stop*) sosta, pausa; (*Mus*) pausa; (*object: to support sth*) appoggio, sostegno; (*remainder*) resto, avanzi *mpl* ▷ *vi* riposarsi; (*remain*) rimanere, restare; (*be supported*) **to ~ on** appoggiarsi su ▷ *vt* (*far*) riposare; (*lean*): **to ~ sth on/against** appoggiare qc su/contro; **the ~ of them** gli altri; **it ~s with him to decide** sta a lui decidere

restaurant ['rɛstərɔŋ] *n* ristorante *m*; **restaurant car** (*BRIT*) *n* vagone *m* ristorante

restless ['rɛstlɪs] *adj* agitato(-a), irrequieto(-a)

restoration [rɛstə'reɪʃən] *n* restauro; restituzione *f*

restore [rɪ'stɔːʳ] *vt* (*building, to power*) restaurare; (*sth stolen*) restituire; (*peace, health*) ristorare

restrain [rɪs'treɪn] *vt* (*feeling, growth*) contenere, frenare; (*person*): **to ~ (from doing)** trattenere (dal fare); **restraint** *n* (*restriction*) limitazione *f*; (*moderation*) ritegno; (*of style*) contenutezza

restrict [rɪs'trɪkt] *vt* restringere, limitare; **restriction** [-kʃən] *n* **restriction (on)** restrizione *f* (di), limitazione *f*

rest room (*US*) *n* toletta

restructure [riː'strʌktʃəʳ] *vt* ristrutturare

result [rɪ'zʌlt] *n* risultato ▷ *vi* **to ~ in** avere per risultato; **as a ~ of** in or di conseguenza a, in seguito a

resume [rɪ'zjuːm] *vt, vi* (*work, journey*) riprendere

résumé ['reɪzjumeɪ] *n* riassunto; (*US*) curriculum *m inv* vitae

resuscitate [rɪ'sʌsɪteɪt] *vt* (*Med*) risuscitare

retail ['riːteɪl] *adj, adv* al minuto ▷ *vt* vendere al minuto; **retailer** *n* commerciante *m/f* al minuto, dettagliante *m/f*

retain [rɪ'teɪn] *vt* (*keep*) tenere, serbare

retaliation [rɪtælɪ'eɪʃən] *n* rappresaglie *fpl*

retarded [rɪ'tɑːdɪd] *adj* ritardato(-a)

retire [rɪ'taɪəʳ] *vi* (*give up work*) andare in pensione; (*withdraw*) ritirarsi, andarsene; (*go to bed*) andare a letto, ritirarsi; **retired** *adj* (*person*) pensionato(-a); **retirement** *n* pensione *f*; (*act*) pensionamento

retort [rɪ'tɔːt] *vi* rimbeccare

retreat [rɪ'triːt] *n* ritirata; (*place*) rifugio ▷ *vi* battere in ritirata

retrieve [rɪ'triːv] *vt* (*sth lost*) ricuperare, ritrovare; (*situation, honour*) salvare; (*error, loss*) rimediare a

retrospect ['rɛtrəspɛkt] *n* **in ~** guardando indietro; **retrospective** [-'spɛktɪv] *adj* retrospettivo(-a); (*law*) retroattivo(-a)

return [rɪ'təːn] *n* (*going or coming back*) ritorno; (*of sth stolen*) restituzione *f*; (*Finance: from land, shares*) profitto, reddito ▷ *cpd* (*journey, match*) di ritorno; (*BRIT: ticket*) di andata e ritorno ▷ *vi* tornare, ritornare ▷ *vt* rendere, restituire; (*bring back*) riportare; (*send back*) mandare indietro; (*put back*) rimettere; (*Pol: candidate*) eleggere; **~s** *npl* (*Comm*) incassi *mpl*; profitti *mpl*; **in ~ (for)** in cambio (di); **by ~ of post** a stretto giro di posta; **many happy ~s (of the day)!** cento di questi giorni!; **return ticket** *n* (*esp BRIT*) biglietto di andata e ritorno

reunion [riː'juːnɪən] *n* riunione *f*

reunite [riːjuː'naɪt] *vt* riunire

revamp ['riː'væmp] *vt* (*firm*) riorganizzare

reveal [rɪ'viːl] *vt* (*make known*) rivelare, svelare; (*display*) rivelare, mostrare; **revealing** *adj* rivelatore(-trice); (*dress*) scollato(-a)

revel ['rɛvl] *vi* **to ~ in sth/in doing** dilettarsi di qc/a fare

revelation [rɛvə'leɪʃən] *n* rivelazione *f*

revenge [rɪ'vɛndʒ] *n* vendetta ▷ *vt* vendicare; **to take ~ on** vendicarsi di

revenue ['rɛvənjuː] *n* reddito

Reverend ['rɛvərənd] *adj* (*in titles*) reverendo(-a)

reversal [rɪ'vəːsl] *n* capovolgimento

reverse [rɪ'vəːs] *n* il contrario, opposto; (*back, defeat*) rovescio; (*Aut: also: ~ gear*) marcia indietro ▷ *adj* (*order, direction*)

contrario(-a), opposto(-a) ▷ *vt* (*turn*)
invertire, rivoltare; (*change*) capovolgere,
rovesciare; (*Law: judgment*) cassare; (*car*)
fare marcia indietro con ▷ *vi* (BRIT *Aut*,
person etc) fare marcia indietro; **reverse-
charge call** [rɪ'vəːstʃɑːdʒ-] (BRIT) *n* (*Tel*)
telefonata con addebito al ricevente;
reversing lights (BRIT) *npl* (*Aut*) luci *fpl* per
la retromarcia

revert [rɪ'vəːt] *vi* **to ~ to** tornare a

review [rɪ'vjuː] *n* rivista; (*of book, film*)
recensione *f*; (*of situation*) esame *m* ▷ *vt*
passare in rivista; fare la recensione di; fare
il punto di

revise [rɪ'vaɪz] *vt* (*manuscript*) rivedere,
correggere; (*opinion*) emendare,
modificare; (*study: subject, notes*) ripassare;
revision [rɪ'vɪʒən] *n* revisione *f*; ripasso

revival [rɪ'vaɪvəl] *n* ripresa; ristabilimento;
(*of faith*) risveglio

revive [rɪ'vaɪv] *vt* (*person*) rianimare;
(*custom*) far rivivere; (*hope, courage,
economy*) ravvivare; (*play, fashion*)
riesumare ▷ *vi* (*person*) rianimarsi; (*hope*)
ravvivarsi; (*activity*) riprendersi

revolt [rɪ'vəult] *n* rivolta, ribellione *f* ▷ *vi*
rivoltarsi, ribellarsi ▷ *vt* (far) rivoltare;
revolting *adj* ripugnante

revolution [rɛvə'luːʃən] *n* rivoluzione *f*; (*of
wheel etc*) rivoluzione, giro; **revolutionary**
adj, n rivoluzionario(-a)

revolve [rɪ'vɔlv] *vi* girare

revolver [rɪ'vɔlvə*] *n* rivoltella

reward [rɪ'wɔːd] *n* ricompensa, premio
▷ *vt* **to ~ (for)** ricompensare (per);
rewarding *adj* (*fig*) gratificante

rewind [riː'waɪnd] (*irreg*) *vt* (*watch*)
ricaricare; (*ribbon etc*) riavvolgere

rewrite [riː'raɪt] *vt irreg* riscrivere

rheumatism ['ruːmətɪzəm] *n*
reumatismo

rhinoceros [raɪ'nɔsərəs] *n* rinoceronte *m*

rhubarb ['ruːbɑːb] *n* rabarbaro

rhyme [raɪm] *n* rima; (*verse*) poesia

rhythm ['rɪðm] *n* ritmo

rib [rɪb] *n* (*Anat*) costola ▷ *vt* (*tease*)
punzecchiare

ribbon ['rɪbən] *n* nastro; **in ~s** (*torn*) a
brandelli

rice [raɪs] *n* riso; **rice pudding** *n* budino
di riso

rich [rɪtʃ] *adj* ricco(-a); (*clothes*)
sontuoso(-a); (*abundant*): **~ in** ricco(-a) di

rid [rɪd] (*pt, pp* **rid**) *vt* **to ~ sb of** sbarazzare
or liberare qn di; **to get ~ of** sbarazzarsi di

riddle ['rɪdl] *n* (*puzzle*) indovinello ▷ *vt* **to
be ~d with** (*holes*) essere crivellato(-a) di;
(*doubts*) essere pieno(-a) di

ride [raɪd] (*pt* **rode**, *pp* **ridden**) *n* (*on horse*)

cavalcata; (*outing*) passeggiata; (*distance
covered*) cavalcata; corsa ▷ *vi* (*as sport*)
cavalcare; (*go somewhere: on horse, bicycle*)
andare (a cavallo or in bicicletta *etc*);
(*journey: on bicycle, motorcycle, bus*) andare,
viaggiare ▷ *vt* (*a horse*) montare, cavalcare;
to take sb for a ~ (*fig*) prendere in giro qn;
fregare qn; **to ~ a horse/bicycle/camel**
montare a cavallo/in bicicletta/in groppa a
un cammello; **rider** *n* cavalcatore(-trice);
(*in race*) fantino; (*on bicycle*) ciclista *m/f*; (*on
motorcycle*) motociclista *m/f*

ridge [rɪdʒ] *n* (*of hill*) cresta; (*of roof*) colmo;
(*on object*) riga (in rilievo)

ridicule ['rɪdɪkjuːl] *n* ridicolo; scherno
▷ *vt* mettere in ridicolo; **ridiculous**
[rɪ'dɪkjuləs] *adj* ridicolo(-a)

riding ['raɪdɪŋ] *n* equitazione *f*; **riding
school** *n* scuola d'equitazione

rife [raɪf] *adj* diffuso(-a); **to be ~ with**
abbondare di

rifle ['raɪfl] *n* carabina ▷ *vt* vuotare

rift [rɪft] *n* fessura, crepatura; (*fig:
disagreement*) incrinatura, disaccordo

rig [rɪg] *n* (*also:* **oil ~**: *on land*) derrick *m inv*;
(*: at sea*) piattaforma di trivellazione ▷ *vt*
(*election etc*) truccare

right [raɪt] *adj* giusto(-a); (*suitable*)
appropriato(-a); (*not left*) destro(-a)
▷ *n* giusto; (*title, claim*) diritto; (*not left*)
destra ▷ *adv* (*answer*) correttamente;
(*not on the left*) a destra ▷ *vt* raddrizzare;
(*fig*) riparare ▷ *excl* bene!; **to be ~** (*person*)
aver ragione; (*answer*) essere giusto(-a) or
corretto(-a); **by ~s** di diritto; **on the ~** a
destra; **to be in the ~** aver ragione, essere
nel giusto; **~ now** proprio adesso; subito;
~ away subito; **right angle** *n* angolo
retto; **rightful** *adj* (*heir*) legittimo(-a);
right-hand *adj* **right-hand drive** guida
a destra; **the right-hand side** il lato
destro; **right-handed** *adj* (*person*) che
adopera la mano destra; **rightly** *adv* bene,
correttamente; (*with reason*) a ragione;
right of way *n* diritto di passaggio; (*Aut*)
precedenza; **right-wing** *adj* (*Pol*) di destra

rigid ['rɪdʒɪd] *adj* rigido(-a); (*principle*)
rigoroso(-a)

rigorous ['rɪgərəs] *adj* rigoroso(-a)

rim [rɪm] *n* orlo; (*of spectacles*) montatura;
(*of wheel*) cerchione *m*

rind [raɪnd] *n* (*of bacon*) cotenna; (*of lemon
etc*) scorza

ring [rɪŋ] (*pt* **rang**, *pp* **rung**) *n* anello; (*of
people, objects*) cerchio; (*of spies*) giro;
(*of smoke etc*) spirale *m*; (*arena*) pista,
arena; (*for boxing*) ring *m inv*; (*sound of bell*)
scampanio ▷ *vi* (*person, bell, telephone*)
suonare; (*also:* **~ out**: *voice, words*)

risuonare; (*Tel*) telefonare; (*ears*) fischiare ▷ *vt* (BRIT *Tel*) telefonare a; (: *bell, doorbell*) suonare; **to give sb a ~** (BRIT *Tel*) dare un colpo di telefono a qn; **ring back** *vt, vi* (*Tel*) richiamare; **ring off** (BRIT) *vi* (*Tel*) mettere giù, riattaccare; **ring up** (BRIT) *vt* (*Tel*) telefonare a; **ringing tone** (BRIT) *n* (*Tel*) segnale *m* di libero; **ringleader** *n* (*of gang*) capobanda *m*; **ring road** (BRIT) *n* raccordo anulare

ring tone *n* suoneria

rink [rɪŋk] *n* (*also:* **ice ~**) pista di pattinaggio

rinse [rɪns] *n* risciacquatura; (*hair tint*) cachet *m* *inv* ▷ *vt* sciacquare

riot ['raɪət] *n* sommossa, tumulto; (*of colours*) orgia ▷ *vi* tumultuare; **to run ~** creare disordine

rip [rɪp] *n* strappo ▷ *vt* strappare ▷ *vi* strapparsi; **rip off** *vt* (*inf: cheat*) fregare; **rip up** *vt* stracciare

ripe [raɪp] *adj* (*fruit, grain*) maturo(-a); (*cheese*) stagionato(-a)

rip-off ['rɪpɔf] *n* (*inf*): **it's a ~!** è un furto!

ripple ['rɪpl] *n* increspamento, ondulazione *f*; mormorio ▷ *vi* incresparsi

rise [raɪz] (*pt* **rose**, *pp* **risen**) *n* (*slope*) salita, pendio; (*hill*) altura; (*increase: in wages: BRIT*) aumento; (: *in prices, temperature*) rialzo, aumento; (*fig: to power etc*) ascesa ▷ *vi* alzarsi, levarsi; (*prices*) aumentare; (*waters, river*) crescere (*sun, wind, person: from chair, bed*) levarsi; (*also:* **~ up**: *building*) ergersi; (: *rebel*) insorgere; ribellarsi; (*in rank*) salire; **to ~ to the occasion** essere all'altezza; **risen** ['rɪzn] *pp of* **rise**; **rising** *adj* (*increasing: number*) sempre crescente; (: *prices*) in aumento; (*tide*) montante; (*sun, moon*) nascente, che sorge

risk [rɪsk] *n* rischio; pericolo ▷ *vt* rischiare; **to take** *or* **run the ~ of doing** correre il rischio di fare; **at ~** in pericolo; **at one's own ~** a proprio rischio e pericolo; **risky** *adj* rischioso(-a)

rite [raɪt] *n* rito; **last ~s** l'estrema unzione

ritual ['rɪtjuəl] *adj* rituale ▷ *n* rituale *m*

rival ['raɪvl] *n* rivale *m/f*; (*in business*) concorrente *m/f* ▷ *adj* rivale; che fa concorrenza ▷ *vt* essere in concorrenza con; **to ~ sb/sth in** competere con qn/qc in; **rivalry** *n* rivalità; concorrenza

river ['rɪvər] *n* fiume *m* ▷ *cpd* (*port, traffic*) fluviale; **up/down ~** a monte/valle; **riverbank** *n* argine *m*

rivet ['rɪvɪt] *n* ribattino, rivetto ▷ *vt* (*fig*) concentrare, fissare

Riviera [rɪvɪ'eərə] *n* **the (French) ~** la Costa Azzurra; **the Italian ~** la Riviera

road [rəʊd] *n* strada; (*small*) cammino; (*in town*) via ▷ *cpd* stradale; **major/minor ~** strada con/senza diritto di precedenza; **which ~ do I take for ...?** che strada devo prendere per andare a...?; **roadblock** *n* blocco stradale; **road map** *n* carta stradale; **road rage** *n* comportamento aggressivo al volante; **road safety** *n* sicurezza sulle strade; **roadside** *n* margine *m* della strada; **roadsign** *n* cartello stradale; **road tax** *n* (BRIT) tassa di circolazione; **roadworks** *npl* lavori *mpl* stradali

roam [rəʊm] *vi* errare, vagabondare

roar [rɔːr] *n* ruggito; (*of crowd*) tumulto; (*of thunder, storm*) muggito; (*of laughter*) scoppio ▷ *vi* ruggire; tumultuare; muggire; **to ~ with laughter** scoppiare dalle risa; **to do a ~ing trade** fare affari d'oro

roast [rəʊst] *n* arrosto ▷ *vt* arrostire; (*coffee*) tostare, torrefare; **roast beef** *n* arrosto di manzo

rob [rɔb] *vt* (*person*) rubare; (*bank*) svaligiare; **to ~ sb of sth** derubare qn di qc; (*fig: deprive*) privare qn di qc; **robber** *n* ladro; (*armed*) rapinatore *m*; **robbery** *n* furto; rapina

robe [rəʊb] *n* (*for ceremony etc*) abito; (*also:* **bath ~**) accappatoio; (*US: also:* **lap ~**) coperta

robin ['rɔbɪn] *n* pettirosso

robot ['rəʊbɔt] *n* robot *m* *inv*

robust [rəʊ'bʌst] *adj* robusto(-a); (*economy*) solido(-a)

rock [rɔk] *n* (*substance*) roccia; (*boulder*) masso; roccia; (*in sea*) scoglio; (*US: pebble*) ciottolo; (BRIT: *sweet*) zucchero candito ▷ *vt* (*swing gently: cradle*) dondolare; (: *child*) cullare; (*shake*) scrollare, far tremare ▷ *vi* dondolarsi; scrollarsi, tremare; **on the ~s** (*drink*) col ghiaccio; (*marriage etc*) in crisi; **rock and roll** *n* rock and roll *m*; **rock climbing** *n* roccia

rocket ['rɔkɪt] *n* razzo

rocking chair *n* sedia a dondolo

rocky ['rɔkɪ] *adj* (*hill*) roccioso(-a); (*path*) sassoso(-a); (*marriage etc*) instabile

rod [rɔd] *n* (*metallic, Tech*) asta; (*wooden*) bacchetta; (*also:* **fishing ~**) canna da pesca

rode [rəʊd] *pt of* **ride**

rodent ['rəʊdnt] *n* roditore *m*

rogue [rəʊg] *n* mascalzone *m*

role [rəʊl] *n* ruolo; **role-model** *n* modello (di comportamento)

roll [rəʊl] *n* rotolo; (*of banknotes*) mazzo; (*also:* **bread ~**) panino; (*register*) lista; (*sound: of drums etc*) rullo ▷ *vt* rotolare; (*also:* **~ up**: *string*) aggomitolare; (: *sleeves*) rimboccare; (*cigarettes*) arrotolare; (*eyes*) roteare; (*also:* **~ out:** *pastry*) stendere; (*lawn, road etc*) spianare ▷ *vi* rotolare; (*wheel*) girare; (*drum*) rullare; (*vehicle: also:* **~ along**) avanzare; (*ship*) rollare; **roll over** *vi* rivoltarsi; **roll up** (*inf*) *vi* (*arrive*) arrivare ▷ *vt* (*carpet*) arrotolare; **roller** *n* rullo; (*wheel*) rotella; (*for hair*) bigodino; **Rollerblades®** *npl* pattini *mpl* in linea; **roller coaster** [-ˈkəustə*] *n* montagne *fpl* russe; **roller skates** *npl* pattini *mpl* a rotelle; **roller-skating** *n* pattinaggio a rotelle; **to go roller-skating** andare a pattinare (*con i pattini a rotelle*); **rolling pin** *n* matterello

ROM [rɔm] *n abbr* (= *read only memory*) memoria di sola lettura

Roman [ˈrəumən] *adj, n* romano(-a); **Roman Catholic** *adj, n* cattolico(-a)

romance [rəˈmæns] *n* storia (*or avventura or film m inv*) romantico(-a); (*charm*) poesia; (*love affair*) idillio

Romania [rəuˈmeɪnɪə] *n* Romania

Romanian [rəuˈmeɪnɪən] *adj* romeno(-a) ▷ *n* romeno; (*Ling*) romeno

Roman numeral *n* numero romano

romantic [rəˈmæntɪk] *adj* romantico(-a); sentimentale

Rome [rəum] *n* Roma

roof [ruːf] *n* tetto; (*of tunnel, cave*) volta ▷ *vt* coprire (con un tetto); **~ of the mouth** palato; **roof rack** *n* (*Aut*) portabagagli *m inv*

rook [ruk] *n* (*bird*) corvo nero; (*Chess*) torre *f*

room [ruːm] *n* (*in house*) stanza; (*bedroom, in hotel*) camera; (*in school etc*) sala; (*space*) posto, spazio; **roommate** *n* compagno(-a) di stanza; **room service** *n* servizio da camera; **roomy** *adj* spazioso(-a); (*garment*) ampio(-a)

rooster [ˈruːstə*] *n* gallo

root [ruːt] *n* radice *f* ▷ *vi* (*plant, belief*) attecchire

rope [rəup] *n* corda, fune *f*; (*Naut*) cavo ▷ *vt* (*box*) legare; (*climbers*) legare in cordata; (*area: also:* **~ off**) isolare cingendo con cordoni; **to know the ~s** (*fig*) conoscere i trucchi del mestiere

rose [rəuz] *pt of* **rise** ▷ *n* rosa; (*also:* **~ bush**) rosaio; (*on watering can*) rosetta

rosé [ˈrəuzeɪ] *n* vino rosato

rosemary [ˈrəuzmərɪ] *n* rosmarino

rosy [ˈrəuzɪ] *adj* roseo(-a)

rot [rɔt] *n* (*decay*) putrefazione *f*; (*inf: nonsense*) stupidaggini *fpl* ▷ *vt, vi* imputridire, marcire

rota [ˈrəutə] *n* tabella dei turni

rotate [rəuˈteɪt] *vt* (*revolve*) far girare; (*change round: jobs*) fare a turno ▷ *vi* (*revolve*) girare

rotten [ˈrɔtn] *adj* (*decayed*) putrido(-a), marcio(-a); (*dishonest*) corrotto(-a); (*inf: bad*) brutto(-a); (: *action*) vigliacco(-a); **to feel ~** (*ill*) sentirsi da cani

rough [rʌf] *adj* (*skin, surface*) ruvido(-a); (*terrain, road*) accidentato(-a); (*voice*) rauco(-a); (*person, manner: coarse*) rozzo(-a), aspro(-a); (: *violent*) brutale; (*district*) malfamato(-a); (*weather*) cattivo(-a); (*sea*) mosso(-a); (*plan*) abbozzato(-a); (*guess*) approssimativo(-a) ▷ *n* (*Golf*) macchia; **to ~ it** far vita dura; **to sleep ~** (BRIT) dormire all'addiaccio; **roughly** *adv* (*handle*) rudemente, brutalmente; (*make*) grossolanamente; (*speak*) bruscamente; (*approximately*) approssimativamente

roulette [ruːˈlet] *n* roulette *f*

round [raund] *adj* rotondo(-a); (*figures*) tondo(-a) ▷ *n* (BRIT: *of toast*) fetta; (*duty: of policeman, milkman etc*) giro; (: *of doctor*) visite *fpl*; (*game: of cards, golf, in competition*) partita; (*of ammunition*) cartuccia; (*Boxing*) round *m inv*; (*of talks*) serie *f inv* ▷ *vt* (*corner*) girare; (*bend*) prendere ▷ *prep* intorno a ▷ *adv* **all** ~ tutt'attorno; **to go the long way** ~ fare il giro più lungo; **all the year** ~ tutto l'anno; **it's just** ~ **the corner** (*also fig*) è dietro l'angolo; **~ the clock** ininterrottamente; **to go ~ to sb's house** andare da qn; **go ~ the back** passi dietro; **enough to go** ~ abbastanza per tutti; **~ of applause** applausi *mpl*; **~ of drinks** giro di bibite; **~ of sandwiches** sandwich *m inv*; **round off** *vt* (*speech etc*) finire; **round up** *vt* radunare; (*criminals*) fare una retata di; (*prices*) arrotondare; **roundabout** *n* (BRIT Aut) rotatoria; (: *at fair*) giostra ▷ *adj* (*route, means*) indiretto(-a); **round trip** *n* (*viaggio di*) andata e ritorno; **roundup** *n* raduno; (*of criminals*) retata

rouse [rauz] *vt* (*wake up*) svegliare; (*stir up*) destare; provocare; risvegliare

route [ruːt] *n* itinerario; (*of bus*) percorso

routine [ruːˈtiːn] *adj* (*work*) corrente, abituale; (*procedure*) solito(-a) ▷ *n* (*pej*) routine *f*, tran tran *m*; (*Theatre*) numero

row¹ [rəu] *n* (*line*) riga, fila; (*Knitting*) ferro; (*behind one another: of cars, people*) fila; (*in boat*) remata ▷ *vi* (*in boat*) remare; (*as sport*) vogare ▷ *vt* (*boat*) manovrare a remi; **in a ~** (*fig*) di fila

row² [rau] *n* (*racket*) baccano, chiasso; (*dispute*) lite *f*; (*scolding*) sgridata ▷ *vi* (*argue*) litigare

rowboat [ˈrəubəut] (US) *n* barca a remi

rowing [ˈrəuɪŋ] *n* canottaggio; **rowing boat** (BRIT) *n* barca a remi

royal [ˈrɔɪəl] *adj* reale; **royalty** [ˈrɔɪəltɪ] *n* (*royal persons*) (membri *mpl* della) famiglia reale; (*payment: to author*) diritti *mpl* d'autore

rpm *abbr* (= *revolutions per minute*) giri/min.

R.S.V.P. *abbr* (= *répondez s'il vous plaît*) R.S.V.P.

Rt. Hon. (BRIT) *abbr* (= *Right Honourable*) ≈ Onorevole

rub [rʌb] *n* **to give sth a ~** strofinare qc; (*sore place*) massaggiare qc ▷ *vt* strofinare; massaggiare; (*hands: also:* **~ together**) sfregarsi; **to ~ sb up** (BRIT) *or* **~ sb the wrong way** (US) lisciare qn contro pelo; **rub in** *vt* (*ointment*) far penetrare (massaggiando *or* frizionando); **rub off** *vi* andare via; **rub out** *vt* cancellare

rubber [ˈrʌbəʳ] *n* gomma; **rubber band** *n* elastico; **rubber gloves** *npl* guanti *mpl* di gomma

rubbish [ˈrʌbɪʃ] *n* (*from household*) immondizie *fpl*, rifiuti *mpl*; (*fig, pej*) cose *fpl* senza valore; robaccia; sciocchezze *fpl*; **rubbish bin** (BRIT) *n* pattumiera; **rubbish dump** *n* (*in town*) immondezzaio

rubble [ˈrʌbl] *n* macerie *fpl*; (*smaller*) pietrisco

ruby [ˈruːbɪ] *n* rubino

rucksack [ˈrʌksæk] *n* zaino

rudder [ˈrʌdəʳ] *n* timone *m*

rude [ruːd] *adj* (*impolite: person*) scortese, rozzo(-a); (: *word, manners*) grossolano(-a), rozzo(-a); (*shocking*) indecente

ruffle [ˈrʌfl] *vt* (*hair*) scompigliare; (*clothes, water*) increspare; (*fig: person*) turbare

rug [rʌg] *n* tappeto; (BRIT: *for knees*) coperta

rugby [ˈrʌgbɪ] *n* (*also:* **~ football**) rugby *m*

rugged [ˈrʌgɪd] *adj* (*landscape*) aspro(-a); (*features, determination*) duro(-a); (*character*) brusco(-a)

ruin [ˈruːɪn] *n* rovina ▷ *vt* rovinare; **~s** *npl* (*of building, castle etc*) rovine *fpl*, ruderi *mpl*

rule [ruːl] *n* regola; (*regulation*) regolamento, regola; (*government*) governo; (*ruler*) riga ▷ *vt* (*country*) governare; (*person*) dominare ▷ *vi* regnare; decidere; (*Law*) dichiarare; **as a ~** normalmente; **rule out** *vt* escludere; **ruler** *n* (*sovereign*) sovrano(-a); (*for measuring*) regolo, riga; **ruling** *adj* (*party*) al potere; (*class*) dirigente ▷ *n* (*Law*) decisione *f*

rum [rʌm] *n* rum *m*

Rumania *etc* [ruːˈmeɪnɪə] *n* = **Romania** *etc*

rumble [ˈrʌmbl] *n* rimbombo; brontolio ▷ *vi* rimbombare; (*stomach, pipe*) brontolare

rumour [ˈruːməʳ] (US **rumor**) *n* voce *f* ▷ *vt*

it is **~ed that** corre voce che

▐ Be careful not to translate **rumour** by the Italian word **rumore**.

rump steak [rʌmp-] *n* bistecca di girello

run [rʌn] (*pt* **ran**, *pp* **run**) *n* corsa; (*outing*) gita (in macchina); (*distance travelled*) percorso, tragitto; (*Ski*) pista; (*Cricket, Baseball*) meta; (*series*) serie *f*; (*Theatre*) periodo di rappresentazione; (*in tights, stockings*) smagliatura ▷ *vt* (*distance*) correre; (*operate: business*) gestire, dirigere; (: *competition, course*) organizzare; (: *hotel*) gestire; (: *house*) governare; (*Comput*) eseguire; (*water, bath*) far scorrere; (*force through: rope, pipe*) **to ~ sth through** far passare qc attraverso; (*pass: hand, finger*) **to ~ sth over** passare qc su; (*Press: feature*) presentare ▷ *vi* correre; (*flee*) scappare; (*pass: road etc*) passare; (*work: machine, factory*) funzionare, andare; (*bus, train: operate*) far servizio; (: *travel*) circolare; (*continue: play, contract*) durare; (*slide: drawer; flow: river, bath*) scorrere; (*colours, washing*) stemperarsi; (*in election*) presentarsi candidato; (*nose*) colare; **there was a ~ on ...** c'era una corsa a ...; **in the long ~** a lungo andare; **on the ~** in fuga; **to ~ a race** partecipare ad una gara; **I'll ~ you to the station** la porto alla stazione; **to ~ a risk** correre un rischio; **run after** *vt fus* (*to catch up*) rincorrere; (*chase*) correre dietro a; **run away** *vi* fuggire; **run down** *vt* (*production*) ridurre gradualmente; (*factory*) rallentare l'attività di; (*Aut*) investire; (*criticize*) criticare; **to be ~ down** (*person: tired*) essere esausto(-a); **run into** *vt fus* (*meet: person*) incontrare per caso; (: *trouble*) incontrare, trovare; (*collide with*) andare a sbattere contro; **run off** *vi* fuggire ▷ *vt* (*water*) far scolare; (*copies*) fare; **run out** *vi* (*person*) uscire di corsa; (*liquid*) colare; (*lease*) scadere; (*money*) esaurirsi; **run out of** *vt fus* rimanere a corto di; **run over** *vt* (*Aut*) investire, mettere sotto ▷ *vt fus* (*revise*) rivedere; **run through** *vt fus* (*instructions*) dare una scorsa a; (*rehearse: play*) riprovare, ripetere; **run up** *vt* (*debt*) lasciar accumulare; **to ~ up against** (*difficulties*) incontrare; **runaway** *adj* (*person*) fuggiasco(-a); (*horse*) partente *m/f*; (*truck*) fuori controllo

rung [rʌŋ] *pp of* **ring** ▷ *n* (*of ladder*) piolo

runner [ˈrʌnəʳ] *n* (*in race*) corridore *m*; (: *horse*) partente *m/f*; (*on sledge*) pattino; (*for drawer etc*) guida; **runner bean** (BRIT) *n* fagiolo rampicante; **runner-up** *n* secondo(-a) arrivato(-a)

running [ˈrʌnɪŋ] *n* corsa; direzione *f*; organizzazione *f*; funzionamento

▷ *adj* (*water*) corrente; (*commentary*) simultaneo(-a); **to be in/out of the ~ for sth** essere/non essere più in lizza per qc; **6 days ~** 6 giorni di seguito

runny ['rʌnɪ] *adj* che cola

run-up ['rʌnʌp] *n* **~ to** (*election etc*) periodo che precede

runway ['rʌnweɪ] *n* (*Aviat*) pista (di decollo)

rupture ['rʌptʃər] *n* (*Med*) ernia

rural ['rʊrəl] *adj* rurale

rush [rʌʃ] *n* corsa precipitosa; (*hurry*) furia, fretta; (*sudden demand*): **~ for** corsa a; (*current*) flusso; (*of emotion*) impeto; (*Bot*) giunco ▷ *vt* mandare *or* spedire velocemente; (*attack: town etc*) prendere d'assalto ▷ *vi* precipitarsi; **rush hour** *n* ora di punta

Russia ['rʌʃə] *n* Russia; **Russian** *adj* russo(-a) ▷ *n* russo(-a); (*Ling*) russo

rust [rʌst] *n* ruggine *f* ▷ *vi* arrugginirsi

rusty ['rʌstɪ] *adj* arrugginito(-a)

ruthless ['ruːθlɪs] *adj* spietato(-a)

RV *abbr* (= revised version) versione riveduta della Bibbia ▷ *n abbr* (US) see **recreational vehicle**

rye [raɪ] *n* segale *f*

S

Sabbath ['sæbəθ] *n* (*Jewish*) sabato; (*Christian*) domenica

sabotage ['sæbətɑːʒ] *n* sabotaggio ▷ *vt* sabotare

saccharin(e) ['sækərɪn] *n* saccarina

sachet ['sæʃeɪ] *n* bustina

sack [sæk] *n* (*bag*) sacco ▷ *vt* (*dismiss*) licenziare, mandare a spasso; (*plunder*) saccheggiare; **to get the ~** essere mandato a spasso

sacred ['seɪkrɪd] *adj* sacro(-a)

sacrifice ['sækrɪfaɪs] *n* sacrificio ▷ *vt* sacrificare

sad [sæd] *adj* triste

saddle ['sædl] *n* sella ▷ *vt* (*horse*) sellare; **to be ~d with sth** (*inf*) avere qc sulle spalle

sadistic [sə'dɪstɪk] *adj* sadico(-a)

sadly ['sædlɪ] *adv* tristemente; (*regrettably*) sfortunatamente; **~ lacking in** penosamente privo di

sadness ['sædnɪs] *n* tristezza

s.a.e. *n abbr* (= stamped addressed envelope) busta affrancata e con indirizzo

safari [sə'fɑːrɪ] *n* safari *m inv*

safe [seɪf] *adj* sicuro(-a); (*out of danger*) salvo(-a), al sicuro; (*cautious*) prudente ▷ *n* cassaforte *f*; **~ from** al sicuro da; **~ and sound** sano(-a) e salvo(-a); **(just) to be on the ~ side** per non correre rischi; **could you put this in the ~, please?** lo potrebbe mettere nella cassaforte, per favore?; **safely** *adv* sicuramente; sano(-a) e salvo(-a); prudentemente; **safe sex** *n* sesso sicuro

safety ['seɪftɪ] *n* sicurezza; **safety belt** *n* cintura di sicurezza; **safety pin** *n* spilla di sicurezza

saffron ['sæfrən] *n* zafferano

sag [sæg] *vi* incurvarsi; afflosciarsi

sage [seɪdʒ] *n* (*herb*) salvia; (*man*) saggio

Sagittarius [sædʒɪˈtɛərɪəs] *n* Sagittario

Sahara [səˈhɑːrə] *n* **the ~ (Desert)** il (deserto del) Sahara

said [sɛd] *pt, pp of* **say**

sail [seɪl] *n* (*on boat*) vela; (*trip*): **to go for a ~** fare un giro in barca a vela ▷ *vt* (*boat*) condurre, governare ▷ *vi* (*travel: ship*) navigare; (: *passenger*) viaggiare per mare; (*set off*) salpare; (*sport*) fare della vela; **they ~ed into Genoa** entrarono nel porto di Genova; **sailboat** (*us*) *n* barca a vela; **sailing** *n* (*sport*) vela; **to go sailing** fare della vela; **sailing boat** *n* barca a vela; **sailor** *n* marinaio

saint [seɪnt] *n* santo(-a)

sake [seɪk] *n* **for the ~ of** per, per amore di

salad ['sæləd] *n* insalata; **salad cream** (*BRIT*) *n* (tipo di) maionese *f*; **salad dressing** *n* condimento per insalata

salami [səˈlɑːmɪ] *n* salame *m*

salary ['sælərɪ] *n* stipendio

sale [seɪl] *n* vendita; (*at reduced prices*) svendita, liquidazione *f*; (*auction*) vendita all'asta; **"for ~"** "in vendita"; **on ~** in vendita; **on ~ or return** da vendere o rimandare; **~s** *npl* (*total amount sold*) vendite *fpl*; **sales assistant** (*us* **sales clerk**) *n* commesso(-a); **salesman/woman** (*irreg*) *n* commesso(-a); (*representative*) rappresentante *m/f*; **salesperson** (*irreg*) *n* (*in shop*) commesso; (*representative*) rappresentante *m/f* di commercio; **sales rep** *n* rappresentante *m/f* di commercio

saline ['seɪlaɪn] *adj* salino(-a)

saliva [səˈlaɪvə] *n* saliva

salmon ['sæmən] *n inv* salmone *m*

salon ['sælɒn] *n* (*hairdressing salon*) parrucchiere(-a); (*beauty salon*) salone *m* di bellezza

saloon [səˈluːn] *n* (*us*) saloon *m inv*, bar *m inv*; (*BRIT: Aut*) berlina; (*ship's lounge*) salone *m*

salt [sɔːlt] *n* sale *m* ▷ *vt* salare; **saltwater** *adj* di mare; **salty** *adj* salato(-a)

salute [səˈluːt] *n* saluto ▷ *vt* salutare

salvage ['sælvɪdʒ] *n* (*saving*) salvataggio; (*things saved*) beni *mpl* salvati *or* recuperati ▷ *vt* salvare, mettere in salvo

Salvation Army [sælˈveɪʃən-] *n* Esercito della Salvezza

same [seɪm] *adj* stesso(-a), medesimo(-a) ▷ *pron* **the ~** lo (la) stesso(-a), gli (le) stessi(-e); **the ~ book as** lo stesso libro di (o che); **at the ~ time** allo stesso tempo; **all** *or* **just the ~** tuttavia; **to do the ~ as sb** fare come qn; **the ~ to you!** altrettanto a te!

sample ['sɑːmpl] *n* campione *m* ▷ *vt* (*food*) assaggiare; (*wine*) degustare

sanction ['sæŋkʃən] *n* sanzione *f* ▷ *vt* sancire, sanzionare; **~s** *npl* (*Pol*) sanzioni *fpl*

sanctuary ['sæŋktjuərɪ] *n* (*holy place*) santuario; (*refuge*) rifugio; (*for wildlife*) riserva

sand [sænd] *n* sabbia ▷ *vt* (*also*: **~ down**) cartavetrare

sandal ['sændl] *n* sandalo

sand: **sandbox** ['sændbɒks] (*us*) *n* = **sandpit**; **sandcastle** ['sændkɑːsl] *n* castello di sabbia; **sand dune** *n* duna di sabbia; **sandpaper** ['sændpeɪpəʳ] *n* carta vetrata; **sandpit** ['sændpɪt] *n* (*for children*) buca di sabbia; **sands** *npl* spiaggia; **sandstone** ['sændstəun] *n* arenaria

sandwich ['sændwɪtʃ] *n* tramezzino, panino, sandwich *m inv* ▷ *vt*: **~ed between** incastrato(-a) fra; **cheese/ham ~** sandwich al formaggio/prosciutto

sandy ['sændɪ] *adj* sabbioso(-a); (*colour*) color sabbia *inv*, biondo(-a) rossiccio(-a)

sane [seɪn] *adj* (*person*) sano(-a) di mente; (*outlook*) sensato(-a)

sang [sæŋ] *pt of* **sing**

sanitary towel ['sænɪtərɪ-] (*us* **sanitary napkin**) *n* assorbente *m* (igienico)

sanity ['sænɪtɪ] *n* sanità mentale; (*common sense*) buon senso

sank [sæŋk] *pt of* **sink**

Santa Claus [sæntəˈklɔːz] *n* Babbo Natale

sap [sæp] *n* (*of plants*) linfa ▷ *vt* (*strength*) fiaccare

sapphire ['sæfaɪəʳ] *n* zaffiro

sarcasm ['sɑːkæzm] *n* sarcasmo

sarcastic [sɑːˈkæstɪk] *adj* sarcastico(-a); **to be ~** fare del sarcasmo

sardine [sɑːˈdiːn] *n* sardina

Sardinia [sɑːˈdɪnɪə] *n* Sardegna

SASE (*us*) *n abbr* (= *self-addressed stamped envelope*) busta affrancata e con indirizzo

sat [sæt] *pt, pp of* **sit**

Sat. *abbr* (= *Saturday*) sab.

satchel ['sætʃl] *n* cartella

satellite ['sætəlaɪt] *adj* satellite ▷ *n* satellite *m*; **satellite dish** *n* antenna parabolica; **satellite television** *n* televisione *f* via satellite

satin ['sætɪn] n raso ▷ adj di raso
satire ['sætaɪəʳ] n satira
satisfaction [sætɪs'fækʃən] n soddisfazione f
satisfactory [sætɪs'fæktərɪ] adj soddisfacente
satisfied ['sætɪsfaɪd] adj (customer) soddisfatto(-a); **to be ~ (with sth)** essere soddisfatto(-a) (di qc)
satisfy ['sætɪsfaɪ] vt soddisfare; (convince) convincere
Saturday ['sætədɪ] n sabato
sauce [sɔːs] n salsa; (containing meat, fish) sugo; **saucepan** n casseruola
saucer ['sɔːsəʳ] n sottocoppa m, piattino
Saudi Arabia ['saʊdɪ-] n Arabia Saudita
sauna ['sɔːnə] n sauna
sausage ['sɔsɪdʒ] n salsiccia; **sausage roll** n rotolo di pasta sfoglia ripieno di salsiccia
sautéed ['səʊteɪd] adj saltato(-a)
savage ['sævɪdʒ] adj (cruel, fierce) selvaggio(-a), feroce; (primitive) primitivo(-a) ▷ n selvaggio(-a) ▷ vt attaccare selvaggiamente
save [seɪv] vt (person, belongings, Comput) salvare; (money) risparmiare, mettere da parte; (time) risparmiare; (food) conservare; (avoid: trouble) evitare; (Sport) parare ▷ vi (also: ~ up) economizzare ▷ n (Sport) parata ▷ prep salvo, a eccezione di
savings ['seɪvɪŋz] npl (money) risparmi mpl; **savings account** n libretto di risparmio; **savings and loan association** (us) n ≈ società di credito immobiliare
savoury ['seɪvərɪ] (us **savory**) adj (dish: not sweet) salato(-a)
saw [sɔː] (pt sawed, pp sawed or sawn) pt of **see** ▷ n (tool) sega ▷ vt segare; **sawdust** n segatura
sawn [sɔːn] pp of **saw**
saxophone ['sæksəfəun] n sassofono
say [seɪ] (pt, pp **said**) n **to have one's ~** fare sentire il proprio parere; **to have a** or **some ~** avere voce in capitolo ▷ vt dire; **could you ~ that again?** potrebbe ripeterlo?; **that goes without ~ing** va da sé; **saying** n proverbio, detto
scab [skæb] n crosta; (pej) crumiro(-a)
scaffolding ['skæfəldɪŋ] n impalcatura
scald [skɔːld] n scottatura ▷ vt scottare
scale [skeɪl] n scala; (of fish) squama ▷ vt (mountain) scalare; **~s** npl (for weighing) bilancia; **on a large ~** su vasta scala; **~ of charges** tariffa
scallion ['skæljən] n cipolla; (us: shallot) scalogna; (: leek) porro
scallop ['skɔləp] n (Zool) pettine m; (Sewing) smerlo
scalp [skælp] n cuoio capelluto ▷ vt

scotennare
scalpel ['skælpl] n bisturi m inv
scam [skæm] n (inf) truffa
scampi ['skæmpɪ] npl scampi mpl
scan [skæn] vt scrutare; (glance at quickly) scorrere, dare un'occhiata a; (TV) analizzare; (Radar) esplorare ▷ n (Med) ecografia
scandal ['skændl] n scandalo; (gossip) pettegolezzi mpl
Scandinavia [skændɪ'neɪvɪə] n Scandinavia; **Scandinavian** adj, n scandinavo(-a)
scanner ['skænəʳ] n (Radar, Med) scanner m inv
scapegoat ['skeɪpgəut] n capro espiatorio
scar [skɑː] n cicatrice f ▷ vt sfregiare
scarce [skɛəs] adj scarso(-a); (copy, edition) raro(-a); **to make o.s. ~** (inf) squagliarsela; **scarcely** adv appena
scare [skɛəʳ] n spavento; panico ▷ vt spaventare, atterrire; **there was a bomb ~ at the bank** hanno evacuato la banca per paura di un attentato dinamitardo; **to ~ sb stiff** spaventare a morte qn; **scarecrow** n spaventapasseri m inv; **scared** adj **to be ~ scared** aver paura
scarf [skɑːf] (pl scarves or scarfs) n (long) sciarpa; (square) fazzoletto da testa, foulard m inv
scarlet ['skɑːlɪt] adj scarlatto(-a)
scarves [skɑːvz] npl of **scarf**
scary ['skɛərɪ] adj che spaventa
scatter ['skætəʳ] vt spargere; (crowd) disperdere ▷ vi disperdersi
scenario [sɪ'nɑːrɪəu] n (Theatre, Cinema) copione m; (fig) situazione f
scene [siːn] n (Theatre, fig etc) scena; (of crime, accident) scena, luogo; (sight, view) vista, veduta; **scenery** n (Theatre) scenario; (landscape) panorama m; **scenic** adj scenico(-a); panoramico(-a)
scent [sɛnt] n profumo; (sense of smell) olfatto, odorato; (fig: track) pista
sceptical ['skɛptɪkəl] (us **skeptical**) adj scettico(-a)
schedule ['ʃɛdjuːl, (us) 'skɛdjuːl] n programma m, piano; (of trains) orario; (of prices etc) lista, tabella ▷ vt fissare; **on ~** in orario; **to be ahead of/behind ~** essere in anticipo/ritardo sul previsto; **scheduled flight** n volo di linea
scheme [skiːm] n piano, progetto; (method) sistema m; (dishonest plan, plot) intrigo, trama; (arrangement) disposizione f, sistemazione f; (pension scheme etc) programma m ▷ vi fare progetti; (intrigue) complottare
schizophrenic [skɪtsə'frɛnɪk] adj, n

schizofrenico(-a)

scholar ['skɒləʳ] n (expert) studioso(-a); **scholarship** n erudizione f; (grant) borsa di studio

school [sku:l] n (primary, secondary) scuola; (university: US) università f inv ▷ cpd scolare, scolastico(-a) ▷ vt (animal) addestrare; **schoolbook** n libro scolastico; **schoolboy** n scolaro; **school children** npl scolari mpl; **schoolgirl** n scolara; **schooling** n istruzione f; **schoolteacher** n insegnante m/f, docente m/f; (primary) maestro(-a)

science ['saɪəns] n scienza; **science fiction** n fantascienza; **scientific** [-'tɪfɪk] adj scientifico(-a); **scientist** n scienziato(-a)

sci-fi ['saɪfaɪ] n abbr (inf) = **science fiction**

scissors ['sɪzəz] npl forbici fpl

scold [skəuld] vt rimproverare

scone [skɒn] n focaccina da tè

scoop [sku:p] n mestolo; (for ice cream) cucchiaio dosatore; (Press) colpo giornalistico, notizia (in) esclusiva

scooter ['sku:təʳ] n (motor cycle) motoretta, scooter m inv; (toy) monopattino

scope [skəup] n (capacity: of plan, undertaking) portata; (: of person) capacità fpl; (opportunity) possibilità fpl

scorching ['skɔ:tʃɪŋ] adj cocente, scottante

score [skɔ:ʳ] n i punti mpl, punteggio; (Mus) partitura, spartito; (twenty) venti ▷ vt (goal, point) segnare, fare; (success) ottenere ▷ vi segnare; (Football) fare un goal; (keep score) segnare i punti; **~s of** (very many) un sacco di; **on that ~** a questo riguardo; **to ~ 6 out of 10** prendere 6 su 10; **score out** vt cancellare con un segno; **scoreboard** n tabellone m segnapunti; **scorer** n marcatore(-trice); (keeping score) segnapunti m inv

scorn [skɔ:n] n disprezzo ▷ vt disprezzare

Scorpio ['skɔ:pɪəu] n Scorpione m

scorpion ['skɔ:pɪən] n scorpione m

Scot [skɒt] n scozzese m/f

Scotch tape® n scotch® m

Scotland ['skɒtlənd] n Scozia

Scots [skɒts] adj scozzese; **Scotsman** (irreg) n scozzese m; **Scotswoman** (irreg) n scozzese f; **Scottish** ['skɒtɪʃ] adj scozzese; **Scottish Parliament** n Parlamento scozzese

scout [skaut] n (Mil) esploratore m; (also: **boy ~**) giovane esploratore, scout m inv

scowl [skaul] vi accigliarsi, aggrottare le sopracciglia; **to ~ at** guardare torvo

scramble ['skræmbl] n arrampicata ▷ vi inerpicarsi; **to ~ out** etc uscire etc in fretta; **to ~ for** azzuffarsi per; **scrambled eggs** npl uova fpl strapazzate

scrap [skræp] n pezzo, pezzetto; (fight) zuffa; (also: **~ iron**) rottami mpl di ferro, ferraglia ▷ vt demolire; (fig) scartare ▷ vi **to ~ (with sb)** fare a botte (con qn); **~s** npl (waste) scarti mpl; **scrapbook** n album m inv di ritagli

scrape [skreɪp] vt, vi raschiare, grattare ▷ n **to get into a ~** cacciarsi in un guaio

scrap paper n cartaccia

scratch [skrætʃ] n graffio ▷ cpd **~ team** squadra raccogliticcia ▷ vt graffiare, rigare ▷ vi grattare; (paint, car) graffiare; **to start from ~** cominciare or partire da zero; **to be up to ~** essere all'altezza; **scratch card** n (BRIT) cartolina f gratta e vinci

scream [skri:m] n grido, urlo ▷ vi urlare, gridare

screen [skri:n] n schermo; (fig) muro, cortina, velo ▷ vt schermare, fare schermo a; (from the wind etc) riparare; (film) proiettare; (book) adattare per lo schermo; (candidates etc) selezionare; **screening** n (Med) dépistage m inv; **screenplay** n sceneggiatura; **screen saver** n (Comput) screen saver m inv

screw [skru:] n vite f ▷ vt avvitare; **screw up** vt (paper etc) spiegazzare; (inf: ruin) rovinare; **to ~ up one's eyes** strizzare gli occhi; **screwdriver** n cacciavite m

scribble ['skrɪbl] n scarabocchio ▷ vt scribacchiare in fretta ▷ vi scarabocchiare

script [skrɪpt] n (Cinema etc) copione m; (in exam) elaborato or compito d'esame

scroll [skrəul] n rotolo di carta

scrub [skrʌb] n (land) boscaglia ▷ vt pulire strofinando; (reject) annullare

scruffy ['skrʌfɪ] adj sciatto(-a)

scrum(mage) ['skrʌm(ɪdʒ)] n mischia

scrutiny ['skru:tɪnɪ] n esame m accurato

scuba diving ['sku:bə-] n immersioni fpl subacquee

sculptor ['skʌlptəʳ] n scultore m

sculpture ['skʌlptʃəʳ] n scultura

scum [skʌm] n schiuma; (pej: people) feccia

scurry ['skʌrɪ] vi sgambare, affrettarsi

sea [si:] n mare m ▷ cpd marino(-a), del mare; (bird, fish) di mare; (route, transport) marittimo(-a); **by ~** (travel) per mare; **on the ~** (boat) in mare; (town) di mare; **to be all at ~** (fig) non sapere che pesci pigliare; **out to ~** al largo; (out) at **~** in mare; **seafood** n frutti mpl di mare; **sea front** n lungomare m; **seagull** n gabbiano

seal [si:l] n (animal) foca; (stamp) sigillo;

(*impression*) impronta del sigillo ▷ *vt*
sigillare; **seal off** *vt* (*close*) sigillare; (*forbid entry to*) bloccare l'accesso a
sea level *n* livello del mare
seam [si:m] *n* cucitura; (*of coal*) filone *m*
search [sə:tʃ] *n* ricerca; (*Law: at sb's home*)
perquisizione *f* ▷ *vt* frugare ▷ *vi* **to ~ for**
ricercare; **in ~ of** alla ricerca di; **search
engine** *n* (*Comput*) motore *m* di ricerca;
search party *n* squadra di soccorso
sea: **seashore** ['si:ʃɔ:ʳ] *n* spiaggia; **seasick**
['si:sɪk] *adj* che soffre il mal di mare;
seaside ['si:saɪd] *n* spiaggia; **seaside
resort** *n* stazione *f* balneare
season ['si:zn] *n* stagione *f* ▷ *vt* condire,
insaporire; **seasonal** *adj* stagionale;
seasoning *n* condimento; **season ticket**
n abbonamento
seat [si:t] *n* sedile *m*; (*in bus, train: place*)
posto; (*Parliament*) seggio; (*buttocks*)
didietro; (*of trousers*) fondo ▷ *vt* far
sedere; (*have room for*) avere *or* essere
fornito(-a) di posti a sedere per; **I'd like to
book two ~s** vorrei prenotare due posti;
to be ~ed essere seduto(-a); **seat belt** *n*
cintura di sicurezza; **seating** *n* posti *mpl*
a sedere
sea: **sea water** *n* acqua di mare; **seaweed**
['si:wi:d] *n* alghe *fpl*
sec. *abbr* = **second(s)**
secluded [sɪ'klu:dɪd] *adj* isolato(-a),
appartato(-a)
second ['sɛkənd] *num* secondo(-a) ▷ *adv*
(*in race etc*) al secondo posto ▷ *n* (*unit of
time*) secondo; (*Aut: also: ~ gear*) seconda;
(*Comm: imperfect*) scarto; (*BRIT: Scol:
degree*) laurea con punteggio discreto ▷ *vt*
(*motion*) appoggiare; **secondary** *adj*
secondario(-a); **secondary school** *n*
scuola secondaria; **second-class** *adj* di
seconda classe ▷ *adv* in seconda classe;
secondhand *adj* di seconda mano,
usato(-a); **secondly** *adv* in secondo
luogo; **second-rate** *adj* scadente; **second
thoughts** *npl* ripensamenti *mpl*; **on
second thoughts** (*BRIT*) *or* **thought** (*US*)
ripensandoci bene
secrecy ['si:krəsɪ] *n* segretezza
secret ['si:krɪt] *adj* segreto(-a) ▷ *n* segreto;
in ~ in segreto
secretary ['sɛkrətrɪ] *n* segretario(-a); **S~
of State (for)** (*BRIT: Pol*) ministro (di)
secretive ['si:krətɪv] *adj* riservato(-a)
secret service *n* servizi *mpl* segreti
sect [sɛkt] *n* setta
section ['sɛkʃən] *n* sezione *f*
sector ['sɛktəʳ] *n* settore *m*
secular ['sɛkjuləʳ] *adj* secolare
secure [sɪ'kjuəʳ] *adj* sicuro(-a); (*firmly fixed*)

assicurato(-a), ben fermato(-a); (*in safe
place*) al sicuro ▷ *vt* (*fix*) fissare, assicurare;
(*get*) ottenere, assicurarsi; **securities** *npl*
(*Stock Exchange*) titoli *mpl*
security [sɪ'kjuərɪtɪ] *n* sicurezza; (*for
loan*) garanzia; **security guard** *n* guardia
giurata
sedan [sə'dæn] (*US*) *n* (*Aut*) berlina
sedate [sɪ'deɪt] *adj* posato(-a), calmo(-a)
▷ *vt* calmare
sedative ['sɛdɪtɪv] *n* sedativo, calmante *m*
seduce [sɪ'dju:s] *vt* sedurre; **seductive**
[-'dʌktɪv] *adj* seducente
see [si:] (*pt* **saw**, *pp* **seen**) *vt* vedere;
(*accompany*): **to ~ sb to the door**
accompagnare qn alla porta ▷ *vi* vedere;
(*understand*) capire ▷ *n* sede *f* vescovile;
to ~ that (*ensure*) badare che + *sub*, fare in
modo che + *sub*; **~ you soon!** a presto!; **see
off** *vt* salutare alla partenza; **see out** *vt*
(*take to the door*) accompagnare alla porta;
see through *vt* portare a termine ▷ *vt fus*
non lasciarsi ingannare da; **see to** *vt fus*
occuparsi di
seed [si:d] *n* seme *m*; (*fig*) germe *m*; (*Tennis
etc*) testa di serie; **to go to ~** fare seme;
(*fig*) scadere
seeing ['si:ɪŋ] *conj*: **~ (that)** visto che
seek [si:k] (*pt, pp* **sought**) *vt* cercare
seem [si:m] *vi* sembrare, parere; **there ~s
to be ...** sembra che ci sia ...; **seemingly**
adv apparentemente
seen [si:n] *pp* of **see**
seesaw ['si:sɔ:] *n* altalena a bilico
segment ['sɛgmənt] *n* segmento
segregate ['sɛgrɪgeɪt] *vt* segregare,
isolare
seize [si:z] *vt* (*grasp*) afferrare; (*take
possession of*) impadronirsi di; (*Law*)
sequestrare
seizure ['si:ʒəʳ] *n* (*Med*) attacco; (*Law*)
confisca, sequestro
seldom ['sɛldəm] *adv* raramente
select [sɪ'lɛkt] *adj* scelto(-a) ▷ *vt* scegliere,
selezionare; **selection** [-'lɛkʃən]
n selezione *f*, scelta; **selective** *adj*
selettivo(-a)
self [sɛlf] *n* **the ~** l'io *m* ▷ *prefix* auto-...;
self-assured *adj* sicuro(-a) di sé; **self-
catering** (*BRIT*) *adj* in cui ci si cucina
da sé; **self-centred** (*US* **self-centered**)
adj egocentrico(-a); **self-confidence**
n sicurezza di sé; **self-confident** *adj*
sicuro(-a) di sé; **self-conscious** *adj*
timido(-a); **self-contained** (*BRIT*) *adj*
(*flat*) indipendente; **self-control** *n*
autocontrollo; **self-defence** (*US* **self-
defense**) *n* autodifesa; (*Law*) legittima
difesa; **self-drive** *adj* (*BRIT*: *rented car*)

senza autista; **self-employed** adj che lavora in proprio; **self-esteem** n amor proprio m; **self-indulgent** adj indulgente verso se stesso(-a); **self-interest** n interesse m personale; **selfish** adj egoista; **self-pity** n autocommiserazione f; **self-raising** (US **self-rising**) adj **self-raising flour** miscela di farina e lievito; **self-respect** n rispetto di sé, amor proprio; **self-service** n autoservizio, self-service m

sell [sɛl] (pt, pp **sold**) vt vendere ▷ vi vendersi; **to ~ at** or **for 1000 euros** essere in vendita a 1000 euro; **sell off** vt svendere, liquidare; **sell out** vi **to ~ out (of sth)** esaurire (qc); **the tickets are all sold out** i biglietti sono esauriti; **sell-by date** ['sɛlbaɪ-] n data di scadenza; **seller** n venditore(-trice)

Sellotape® ['sɛləuteɪp] (BRIT) n nastro adesivo, scotch® m

selves [sɛlvz] npl of **self**

semester [sɪ'mɛstəʳ] (US) n semestre m

semi... ['sɛmɪ] prefix semi...; **semicircle** n semicerchio; **semidetached (house)** [sɛmɪdɪ'tætʃt-] (BRIT) n casa gemella; **semi-final** n semifinale f

seminar ['sɛmɪnɑːʳ] n seminario

semi-skimmed ['sɛmɪ'skɪmd] adj (milk) parzialmente scremato(-a)

senate ['sɛnɪt] n senato; **senator** n senatore(-trice)

send [sɛnd] (pt, pp **sent**) vt mandare; **send back** vt rimandare; **send for** vt fus mandare a chiamare, far venire; **send in** vt (report, application, resignation) presentare; **send off** vt (goods) spedire; (BRIT: Sport: player) espellere; **send on** vt (BRIT: letter) inoltrare; (luggage etc: in advance) spedire in anticipo; **send out** vt (invitation) diramare; **send up** vt (person, price) far salire; (BRIT: parody) mettere in ridicolo; **sender** n mittente m/f; **send-off** n **to give sb a good send-off** festeggiare la partenza di qn

senile ['siːnaɪl] adj senile

senior ['siːnɪəʳ] adj (older) più vecchio(-a); (of higher rank) di grado più elevato; **senior citizen** n persona anziana; **senior high school** (US) n = liceo

sensation [sɛn'seɪʃən] n sensazione f; **sensational** adj sensazionale; (marvellous) eccezionale

sense [sɛns] n senso; (feeling) sensazione f, senso; (meaning) senso, significato; (wisdom) buonsenso ▷ vt sentire, percepire; **it makes ~** ha senso; **senseless** adj sciocco(-a); (unconscious) privo(-a) di sensi; **sense of humour** (BRIT) n senso dell'umorismo

sensible ['sɛnsɪbl] adj sensato(-a), ragionevole

Be careful not to translate **sensible** by the Italian word **sensibile**.

sensitive ['sɛnsɪtɪv] adj sensibile; (skin, question) delicato(-a)

sensual ['sɛnsjuəl] adj sensuale

sensuous ['sɛnsjuəs] adj sensuale

sent [sɛnt] pt, pp of **send**

sentence ['sɛntns] n (Ling) frase f; (Law: judgment) sentenza; (: punishment) condanna ▷ vt **to ~ sb to death/to 5 years** condannare qn a morte/a 5 anni

sentiment ['sɛntɪmənt] n sentimento; (opinion) opinione f; **sentimental** [-'mɛntl] adj sentimentale

Sep. abbr (= September) Sett.

separate [adj 'sɛprɪt, vb 'sɛpəreɪt] adj separato(-a) ▷ vt separare ▷ vi separarsi; **separately** adv separatamente; **separates** npl (clothes) coordinati mpl; **separation** [-'reɪʃən] n separazione f

September [sɛp'tɛmbəʳ] n settembre m

septic ['sɛptɪk] adj settico(-a); (wound) infettato(-a); **septic tank** n fossa settica

sequel ['siːkwl] n conseguenza; (of story) seguito; (of film) sequenza

sequence ['siːkwəns] n (series) serie f; (order) ordine m

sequin ['siːkwɪn] n lustrino, paillette f inv

Serb [səːb] adj, n = **Serbian**

Serbia ['səːbɪə] n Serbia

Serbian ['səːbɪən] adj serbo(-a) ▷ n serbo(-a); (Ling) serbo

sergeant ['sɑːdʒənt] n sergente m; (Police) brigadiere m

serial ['sɪərɪəl] n (Press) romanzo a puntate; (Radio, TV) trasmissione f a puntate, serial m inv; **serial killer** n serial-killer m/f inv; **serial number** n numero di serie

series ['sɪəriːz] n inv serie f inv; (Publishing) collana

serious ['sɪərɪəs] adj serio(-a), grave; **seriously** adv seriamente

sermon ['səːmən] n sermone m

servant ['səːvənt] n domestico(-a)

serve [səːv] vt (employer etc) servire, essere a servizio di; (purpose) servire a; (customer, food, meal) servire; (apprenticeship) fare; (prison term) scontare ▷ vi (also Tennis) servire; (be useful): **to ~ as/for/to do** servire da/per/per fare ▷ n (Tennis) servizio; **it ~s him right** ben gli sta, se l'è meritata; **server** n (Comput) server m inv

service ['səːvɪs] n servizio; (Aut: maintenance) assistenza, revisione f ▷ vt (car, washing machine) revisionare; **to be of ~ to sb** essere d'aiuto a qn; **~ included/**

not included servizio compreso/escluso; **~s** (BRIT: on motorway) stazione f di servizio; (Mil): **the S~s** le Forze Armate; **service area** n (on motorway) area di servizio; **service charge** (BRIT) n servizio; **serviceman** (irreg) n militare m; **service station** n stazione f di servizio

serviette [səːviˈɛt] (BRIT) n tovagliolo

session [ˈsɛʃən] n (sitting) seduta, sessione f; (Scol) anno scolastico (or accademico)

set [sɛt] (pt, pp **set**) n serie f inv; (of cutlery etc) servizio; (Radio, TV) apparecchio; (Tennis) set m inv; (group of people) mondo, ambiente m; (Cinema) scenario; (Theatre: stage) scene fpl; (: scenery) scenario; (Math) insieme m; (Hairdressing) messa in piega ▷ adj (fixed) stabilito(-a), determinato(-a); (ready) pronto(-a) ▷ vt (place) posare, mettere; (arrange) sistemare; (fix) fissare; (adjust) regolare; (decide: rules etc) stabilire, fissare ▷ vi (sun) tramontare; (jam, jelly) rapprendersi; (concrete) fare presa; **to be ~ on doing** essere deciso a fare; **to ~ to music** mettere in musica; **to ~ on fire** dare fuoco a; **to ~ free** liberare; **to ~ sth going** mettere in moto qc; **to ~ sail** prendere il mare; **set aside** vt mettere da parte; **set down** vt (bus, train) lasciare; **set in** vi (infection) svilupparsi; (complications) intervenire; **the rain has ~ in for the day** ormai pioverà tutto il giorno; **set off** vi partire ▷ vt (bomb) far scoppiare; (cause to start) mettere in moto; (show up well) dare risalto a; **set out** vi partire ▷ vt (arrange) disporre; (state) esporre, presentare; **to ~ out to do** proporsi di fare; **set up** vt (organization) fondare, costituire; **setback** n (hitch) contrattempo, inconveniente m; **set menu** n menù m inv fisso

settee [sɛˈtiː] n divano, sofà m inv

setting [ˈsɛtɪŋ] n (background) ambiente m; (of controls) posizione f; (of sun) tramonto; (of jewel) montatura

settle [ˈsɛtl] vt (argument, matter) appianare; (accounts) regolare; (Med: calm) calmare ▷ vi (bird, dust etc) posarsi; (sediment) depositarsi; **to ~ for sth** accontentarsi di qc; **to ~ on sth** decidersi per qc; **settle down** vi (get comfortable) sistemarsi; (calm down) calmarsi; (get back to normal: situation) tornare alla normalità; **settle in** vi sistemarsi; **settle up** vi **to ~ up with sb** regolare i conti con qn; **settlement** n (payment) pagamento, saldo; (agreement) accordo; (colony) colonia; (village etc) villaggio, comunità f inv

setup [ˈsɛtʌp] n (arrangement) sistemazione f; (situation) situazione f

seven [ˈsɛvn] num sette; **seventeen** num diciassette; **seventeenth** [sɛvnˈtiːθ] num diciassettesimo(-a); **seventh** num settimo(-a); **seventieth** [ˈsɛvntɪɪθ] num settantesimo(-a); **seventy** num settanta

sever [ˈsɛvəʳ] vt recidere, tagliare; (relations) troncare

several [ˈsɛvərl] adj, pron alcuni(-e), diversi(-e); **~ of us** alcuni di noi

severe [sɪˈvɪəʳ] adj severo(-a); (serious) serio(-a), grave; (hard) duro(-a); (plain) semplice, sobrio(-a)

sew [səu] (pt **sewed**, pp **sewn**) vt, vi cucire

sewage [ˈsuːɪdʒ] n acque fpl di scolo

sewer [ˈsuːəʳ] n fogna

sewing [ˈsəuɪŋ] n cucitura; cucito; **sewing machine** n macchina da cucire

sewn [səun] pp of **sew**

sex [sɛks] n sesso; **to have ~ with** avere rapporti sessuali con; **sexism** [ˈsɛksɪzəm] n sessismo; **sexist** adj, n sessista m/f; **sexual** [ˈsɛksjuəl] adj sessuale; **sexual intercourse** n rapporti mpl sessuali; **sexuality** [sɛksjuˈælɪtɪ] n sessualità f; **sexy** [ˈsɛksɪ] adj provocante, sexy inv

shabby [ˈʃæbɪ] adj malandato(-a); (behaviour) vergognoso(-a)

shack [ʃæk] n baracca, capanna

shade [ʃeɪd] n ombra; (for lamp) paralume m; (of colour) tonalità f inv; (small quantity): **a ~ (more/too large)** un po' (di più/ troppo grande) ▷ vt ombreggiare, fare ombra; **in the ~** all'ombra; **~s** (US) npl (sunglasses) occhiali mpl da sole

shadow [ˈʃædəu] n ombra ▷ vt (follow) pedinare; **shadow cabinet** (BRIT) n (Pol) governo m ombra inv

shady [ˈʃeɪdɪ] adj ombroso(-a); (fig: dishonest) losco(-a), equivoco(-a)

shaft [ʃɑːft] n (of arrow, spear) asta; (Aut, Tech) albero; (of mine) pozzo; (of lift) tromba; (of light) raggio

shake [ʃeɪk] (pt **shook**, pp **shaken**) vt scuotere; (bottle, cocktail) agitare ▷ vi tremare; **to ~ one's head** (in refusal, dismay) scuotere la testa; **to ~ hands with sb** stringere or dare la mano a qn; **shake off** vt scrollare (via); (fig) sbarazzarsi di; **shake up** vt scuotere; **shaky** adj (hand, voice) tremante; (building) traballante

shall [ʃæl] aux vb **I ~ go** andrò; **~ I open the door?** apro io la porta?; **I'll get some, ~ I?** ne prendo un po', va bene?

shallow [ˈʃæləu] adj poco profondo(-a); (fig) superficiale

sham [ʃæm] n finzione f, messinscena; (jewellery, furniture) imitazione f

shambles [ˈʃæmblz] n confusione f,

baraonda, scompiglio

shame [ʃeɪm] n vergogna ▷ vt far vergognare; **it is a ~ (that/to do)** è un peccato (che + sub/fare); **what a ~!** che peccato!; **shameful** adj vergognoso(-a); **shameless** adj sfrontato(-a); (immodest) spudorato(-a)

shampoo [ʃæm'puː] n shampoo m inv ▷ vt fare lo shampoo a

shandy ['ʃændɪ] n birra con gassosa

shan't [ʃɑːnt] = **shall not**

shape [ʃeɪp] n forma ▷ vt formare; (statement) formulare; (sb's ideas) condizionare; **to take ~** prendere forma

share [ʃɛəʳ] n (thing received, contribution) parte f; (Comm) azione f ▷ vt dividere; (have in common) condividere, avere in comune; **shareholder** n azionista m/f

shark [ʃɑːk] n squalo, pescecane m

sharp [ʃɑːp] adj (razor, knife) affilato(-a); (point) acuto(-a), acuminato(-a); (nose, chin) aguzzo(-a); (outline, contrast) netto(-a); (cold, pain) pungente; (voice) stridulo(-a); (person: quick-witted) sveglio(-a); (: unscrupulous) disonesto(-a); (Mus): **C ~** do chiesis ▷ n (Mus) diesis m inv ▷ adv **at 2 o'clock ~** alle due in punto; **sharpen** vt affilare; (pencil) fare la punta a; (fig) acuire; **sharpener** n (also: **pencil sharpener**) temperamatite m inv; **sharply** adv (turn, stop) bruscamente; (stand out, contrast) nettamente; (criticize, retort) duramente, aspramente

shatter ['ʃætəʳ] vt mandare in frantumi, frantumare; (fig: upset) distruggere; (: ruin) rovinare ▷ vi frantumarsi, andare in pezzi; **shattered** adj (grief-stricken) sconvolto(-a); (exhausted) a pezzi, distrutto(-a)

shave [ʃeɪv] vt radere, rasare ▷ vi radersi, farsi la barba ▷ n **to have a ~** farsi la barba; **shaver** n (also: **electric shaver**) rasoio elettrico

shaving cream n crema da barba

shaving foam n = **shaving cream**

shavings ['ʃeɪvɪŋz] npl (of wood etc) trucioli mpl

shawl [ʃɔːl] n scialle m

she [ʃiː] pron ella, lei; **~-cat** gatta; **~-elephant** elefantessa

sheath [ʃiːθ] n fodero, guaina; (contraceptive) preservativo

shed [ʃɛd] (pt, pp **shed**) n capannone m ▷ vt (leaves, fur etc) perdere; (tears, blood) versare; (workers) liberarsi di

she'd [ʃiːd] = **she had**; **she would**

sheep [ʃiːp] n inv pecora; **sheepdog** n cane m da pastore; **sheepskin** n pelle f di pecora

sheer [ʃɪəʳ] adj (utter) vero(-a) (e proprio(-a)); (steep) a picco, perpendicolare; (almost transparent) sottile ▷ adv a picco

sheet [ʃiːt] n (on bed) lenzuolo; (of paper) foglio; (of glass, ice) lastra; (of metal) foglio, lamina

sheik(h) [ʃeɪk] n sceicco

shelf [ʃɛlf] (pl **shelves**) n scaffale m, mensola

shell [ʃɛl] n (on beach) conchiglia; (of egg, nut etc) guscio; (explosive) granata; (of building) scheletro ▷ vt (peas) sgranare; (Mil) bombardare

she'll [ʃiːl] = **she will**; **she shall**

shellfish ['ʃɛlfɪʃ] n inv (crab etc) crostaceo; (scallop etc) mollusco; (as food) crostacei; molluschi

shelter ['ʃɛltəʳ] n riparo, rifugio ▷ vt riparare, proteggere; (give lodging to) dare rifugio or asilo a ▷ vi ripararsi, mettersi al riparo; **sheltered** adj riparato(-a)

shelves ['ʃɛlvz] npl of **shelf**

shelving ['ʃɛlvɪŋ] n scaffalature fpl

shepherd ['ʃɛpəd] n pastore m ▷ vt (guide) guidare; **shepherd's pie** (BRIT) n timballo di carne macinata e purè di patate

sheriff ['ʃɛrɪf] (US) n sceriffo

sherry ['ʃɛrɪ] n sherry m inv

she's [ʃiːz] = **she is**; **she has**

Shetland ['ʃɛtlənd] n (also: **the ~s, the ~ Isles**) le isole Shetland, le Shetland

shield [ʃiːld] n scudo; (trophy) scudetto; (protection) schermo ▷ vt **to ~ (from)** riparare (da), proteggere (da or contro)

shift [ʃɪft] n (change) cambiamento; (of workers) turno ▷ vt spostare, muovere; (remove) rimuovere ▷ vi spostarsi, muoversi

shin [ʃɪn] n tibia

shine [ʃaɪn] (pt, pp **shone**) n splendore m, lucentezza ▷ vi (ri)splendere, brillare ▷ vt far brillare, far risplendere; (torch): **to ~ sth on** puntare qc verso

shingles ['ʃɪŋglz] n (Med) herpes zoster m

shiny ['ʃaɪnɪ] adj lucente, lucido(-a)

ship [ʃɪp] n nave f ▷ vt trasportare (via mare); (send) spedire (via mare); **shipment** n carico; **shipping** n (ships) naviglio; (traffic) navigazione f; **shipwreck** n relitto; (event) naufragio ▷ vt **to be shipwrecked** naufragare, fare naufragio; **shipyard** n cantiere m navale

shirt [ʃəːt] n camicia; **in ~ sleeves** in maniche di camicia

shiver ['ʃɪvəʳ] n brivido ▷ vi rabbrividire, tremare

shock [ʃɔk] n (impact) urto, colpo; (Elec) scossa; (emotional) colpo, shock m inv;

(*Med*) shock ▷ *vt* colpire, scioccare; scandalizzare; **shocking** *adj* scioccante, traumatizzante; scandaloso(-a)

shoe [ʃuː] (*pt, pp* **shod**) *n* scarpa; (*also:* **horse~**) ferro di cavallo ▷ *vt* (*horse*) ferrare; **shoelace** *n* stringa; **shoe polish** *n* lucido per scarpe; **shoeshop** *n* calzoleria

shone [ʃɔn] *pt, pp of* **shine**

shook [ʃuk] *pt of* **shake**

shoot [ʃuːt] (*pt, pp* **shot**) *n* (*on branch, seedling*) germoglio ▷ *vt* (*game*) cacciare, andare a caccia di; (*person*) sparare a; (*execute*) fucilare; (*film*) girare ▷ *vi* (*with gun*): **to ~ (at)** sparare (a), fare fuoco (su); (*with bow*): **to ~ (at)** tirare (su); (*Football*) sparare, tirare (forte); **shoot down** *vt* (*plane*) abbattere; **shoot up** *vi* (*fig*) salire alle stelle; **shooting** *n* (*shots*) sparatoria; (*Hunting*) caccia

shop [ʃɔp] *n* negozio; (*workshop*) officina ▷ *vi* (*also:* **go ~ping**) fare spese; **shop assistant** (*BRIT*) *n* commesso(-a); **shopkeeper** *n* negoziante *m/f*, bottegaio(-a); **shoplifting** *n* taccheggio; **shopping** *n* (*goods*) spesa, acquisti *mpl*; **shopping bag** *n* borsa per la spesa; **shopping centre** (*US* **shopping center**) *n* centro commerciale; **shopping mall** *n* centro commerciale; **shopping trolley** *n* (*BRIT*) carrello del supermercato; **shop window** *n* vetrina

shore [ʃɔː] *n* (*of sea*) riva, spiaggia; (*of lake*) riva ▷ *vt* **to ~ (up)** puntellare; **on ~** a riva

short [ʃɔːt] *adj* (*not long*) corto(-a); (*soon finished*) breve; (*person*) basso(-a); (*curt*) brusco(-a), secco(-a); (*insufficient*) insufficiente ▷ *n* (*also:* **~ film**) cortometraggio; **to be ~ of sth** essere a corto di *or* mancare di qc; **in ~** in breve; **~ of doing** a meno che non si faccia; **everything ~ of** tutto fuorché; **it is ~ for** è l'abbreviazione *or* il diminutivo di; **to cut ~** (*speech, visit*) accorciare, abbreviare; **to fall ~ of** venir meno a; non soddisfare; **to run ~ of** rimanere senza; **to stop ~** fermarsi di colpo; **to stop ~ of** non arrivare fino a; **shortage** *n* scarsezza, carenza; **shortbread** *n* biscotto di pasta frolla; **shortcoming** *n* difetto; **short(crust) pastry** (*BRIT*) *n* pasta frolla; **shortcut** *n* scorciatoia; **shorten** *vt* accorciare, ridurre; **shortfall** *n* deficit *m*; **shorthand** (*BRIT*) *n* stenografia; **short-lived** *adj* di breve durata; **shortly** *adv* fra poco; **shorts** *npl* (*also:* **a pair of shorts**) i calzoncini; **short-sighted** (*BRIT*) *adj* miope; **short-sleeved** [ˈʃɔːtsliːvd] *adj* a maniche corte; **short story** *n* racconto, novella; **short-tempered** *adj* irascibile;

short-term *adj* (*effect*) di *or* a breve durata; (*borrowing*) a breve scadenza

shot [ʃɔt] *pt, pp of* **shoot** ▷ *n* sparo, colpo; (*try*) prova; (*Football*) tiro; (*injection*) iniezione *f*; (*Phot*) foto *f inv*; **like a ~** come un razzo; (*very readily*) immediatamente; **shotgun** *n* fucile *m* da caccia

should [ʃud] *aux vb* **I ~ go now** dovrei andare ora; **he ~ be there now** dovrebbe essere arrivato ora; **I ~ go if I were you** se fossi in te andrei; **I ~ like to** mi piacerebbe

shoulder [ˈʃəʊldə^r] *n* spalla; (*BRIT: of road*): **hard ~** banchina ▷ *vt* (*fig*) addossarsi, prendere sulle proprie spalle; **shoulder blade** *n* scapola

shouldn't [ˈʃudnt] = **should not**

shout [ʃaut] *n* urlo, grido ▷ *vt* gridare ▷ *vi* (*also:* **~ out**) urlare, gridare

shove [ʃʌv] *vt* spingere; (*inf: put*): **to ~ sth in** ficcare qc in

shovel [ˈʃʌvl] *n* pala ▷ *vt* spalare

show [ʃəʊ] (*pt* **showed**, *pp* **shown**) *n* (*of emotion*) dimostrazione *f*, manifestazione *f*; (*semblance*) apparenza; (*exhibition*) mostra, esposizione *f*; (*Theatre, Cinema*) spettacolo ▷ *vt* far vedere, mostrare; (*courage etc*) dimostrare, dar prova di; (*exhibit*) esporre ▷ *vi* vedersi, essere visibile; **for ~** per fare scena; **on ~** (*exhibits etc*) esposto(-a); **can you ~ me where it is, please?** può mostrarmi dov'è, per favore?; **show in** *vt* (*person*) far entrare; **show off** *vi* (*pej*) esibirsi, mettersi in mostra ▷ *vt* (*display*) mettere in risalto; (*pej*) mettere in mostra; **show out** *vt* (*person*) accompagnare alla porta; **show up** *vi* (*stand out*) essere ben visibile; (*inf: turn up*) farsi vedere ▷ *vt* mettere in risalto; **show business** *n* industria dello spettacolo

shower [ˈʃauə^r] *n* (*rain*) acquazzone *m*; (*of stones etc*) pioggia; (*also:* **~-bath**) doccia ▷ *vi* fare la doccia ▷ *vt* **to ~ sb with** (*gifts, abuse etc*) coprire qn di; (*missiles*) lanciare contro qn una pioggia di; **to have a ~** fare la doccia; **shower cap** *n* cuffia da doccia; **shower gel** *n* gel *m* doccia *inv*

showing [ˈʃəʊɪŋ] *n* (*of film*) proiezione *f*

show jumping *n* concorso ippico (di salto ad ostacoli)

shown [ʃəʊn] *pp of* **show**

show: **show-off** (*inf*) *n* (*person*) esibizionista *m/f*; **showroom** *n* sala d'esposizione

shrank [ʃræŋk] *pt of* **shrink**

shred [ʃred] *n* (*gen pl*) brandello ▷ *vt* fare a brandelli; (*Culin*) sminuzzare, tagliuzzare

shrewd [ʃruːd] *adj* astuto(-a), scaltro(-a)

shriek [ʃriːk] *n* strillo ▷ *vi* strillare

shrimp [ʃrimp] *n* gamberetto

shrine [ʃraɪn] n reliquario; (place) santuario

shrink [ʃrɪŋk] (pt **shrank**, pp **shrunk**) vi restringersi; (fig) ridursi; (also: **~ away**) ritrarsi ▷ vt (wool) far restringere ▷ n (inf: pej) psicanalista m/f; **to ~ from doing sth** rifuggire dal fare qc

shrivel ['ʃrɪvl] (also: **~ up**) vt raggrinzare, avvizzire ▷ vi raggrinzirsi, avvizzire

shroud [ʃraud] n lenzuolo funebre ▷ vt **~ed in mystery** avvolto(-a) nel mistero

Shrove Tuesday ['ʃrəuv-] n martedì m grasso

shrub [ʃrʌb] n arbusto

shrug [ʃrʌg] n scrollata di spalle ▷ vt, vi to **~ (one's shoulders)** alzare le spalle, fare spallucce; **shrug off** vt passare sopra a

shrunk [ʃrʌŋk] pp of **shrink**

shudder ['ʃʌdə'] n brivido ▷ vi rabbrividire

shuffle ['ʃʌfl] vt (cards) mescolare; **to ~ (one's feet)** strascicare i piedi

shun [ʃʌn] vt sfuggire, evitare

shut [ʃʌt] (pt, pp **shut**) vt chiudere ▷ vi chiudersi, chiudere; **shut down** vt, vi chiudere definitivamente; **shut up** vi (inf: keep quiet) stare zitto(-a), fare silenzio ▷ vt (close) chiudere; (silence) far tacere; **shutter** n imposta; (Phot) otturatore m

shuttle ['ʃʌtl] n spola, navetta; (space shuttle) navetta (spaziale); (also: **~ service**) servizio m navetta inv; **shuttlecock** ['ʃʌtlkɔk] n volano

shy [ʃaɪ] adj timido(-a)

sibling ['sɪblɪŋ] n (formal) fratello/sorella

Sicily ['sɪsɪlɪ] n Sicilia

sick [sɪk] adj (ill) malato(-a); (vomiting): **to be ~** vomitare; (humour) macabro(-a); **to feel ~** avere la nausea; **to be ~ of** (fig) averne abbastanza di; **sickening** adj (fig) disgustoso(-a), rivoltante; **sick leave** n congedo per malattia; **sickly** adj malaticcio(-a); (causing nausea) nauseante; **sickness** n malattia; (vomiting) vomito

side [saɪd] n lato; (of lake) riva; (team) squadra ▷ cpd (door, entrance) laterale ▷ vi **to ~ with sb** parteggiare per qn, prendere le parti di qn; **by the ~ of** a fianco di; (road) sul ciglio di; **by ~** fianco a fianco; **from ~ to ~** da una parte all'altra; **to take ~s (with)** schierarsi (con); **sideboard** n credenza; **sideboards** (BRIT), **sideburns** ['saɪdbə:nz] npl (whiskers) basette fpl; **sidelight** n (Aut) luce f di posizione; **sideline** n (Sport) linea laterale; (fig) attività secondaria; **side order** n contorno (pietanza); **side road** n strada secondaria; **side street** n traversa; **sidetrack** vt (fig) distrarre; **sidewalk** (US) n marciapiede m; **sideways** adv (move) di lato, di fianco

siege [si:dʒ] n assedio

sieve [sɪv] n setaccio ▷ vt setacciare

sift [sɪft] vt passare al crivello; (fig) vagliare

sigh [saɪ] n sospiro ▷ vi sospirare

sight [saɪt] n (faculty) vista; (spectacle) spettacolo; (on gun) mira ▷ vt avvistare; **in ~** in vista; **on ~** a vista; **out of ~** non visibile; **sightseeing** n giro turistico; **to go sightseeing** visitare una località

sign [saɪn] n segno; (with hand etc) segno, gesto; (notice) insegna, cartello ▷ vt firmare; (player) ingaggiare; **where do I ~?** dove devo firmare?; **sign for** vt fus (item) firmare per l'accettazione di; **sign in** vi firmare il registro (all'arrivo); **sign on** vi (Mil) arruolarsi; (as unemployed) iscriversi sulla lista (dell'ufficio di collocamento) ▷ vt (Mil) arruolare; (employee) assumere; **sign up** vi (Mil) arruolarsi; (for course) iscriversi ▷ vt (player) ingaggiare; (recruits) reclutare

signal ['sɪgnl] n segnale m ▷ vi (Aut) segnalare, mettere la freccia ▷ vt (person) fare segno a; (message) comunicare per mezzo di segnali

signature ['sɪgnətʃə'] n firma

significance [sɪg'nɪfɪkəns] n significato; importanza

significant [sɪg'nɪfɪkənt] adj significativo(-a)

signify ['sɪgnɪfaɪ] vt significare

sign language n linguaggio dei muti

signpost ['saɪnpəust] n cartello indicatore

Sikh [si:k] adj, n sikh (m/f) inv

silence ['saɪlns] n silenzio ▷ vt far tacere, ridurre al silenzio

silent ['saɪlnt] adj silenzioso(-a); (film) muto(-a); **to remain ~** tacere, stare zitto

silhouette [sɪlu:'ɛt] n silhouette f inv

silicon chip ['sɪlɪkən-] n piastrina di silicio

silk [sɪlk] n seta ▷ adj di seta

silly ['sɪlɪ] adj stupido(-a), sciocco(-a)

silver ['sɪlvə'] n argento; (money) monete da 5, 10, 20 or 50 pence; (also: **~ware**) argenteria ▷ adj d'argento; **silver-plated** adj argentato(-a)

similar ['sɪmɪlə'] adj **~ (to)** simile (a); **similarity** [sɪmɪ'lærɪtɪ] n somiglianza, rassomiglianza; **similarly** adv allo stesso modo; così pure

simmer ['sɪmə'] vi cuocere a fuoco lento

simple ['sɪmpl] adj semplice; **simplicity** [-'plɪsɪtɪ] n semplicità; **simplify** vt semplificare; **simply** adv semplicemente

simulate ['sɪmjuleɪt] vt fingere, simulare

simultaneous [sɪməl'teɪnɪəs] adj simultaneo(-a); **simultaneously** adv simultaneamente, contemporaneamente

sin [sɪn] n peccato ▷ vi peccare

since [sɪns] adv da allora ▷ prep da ▷ conj

(time) da quando; (because) poiché, dato che; **~ then, ever ~ da** allora

sincere [sɪn'sɪə'] adj sincero(-a); **sincerely** adv **yours sincerely** (in letters) distinti saluti

sing [sɪŋ] (pt **sang**, pp **sung**) vt, vi cantare

Singapore [sɪŋgə'pɔː'] n Singapore f

singer ['sɪŋə'] n cantante m/f

singing ['sɪŋɪŋ] n canto

single ['sɪŋgl] adj solo(-a), unico(-a); (unmarried: man) celibe; (: woman) nubile; (not double) semplice ▷ n (BRIT: also: **~ ticket**) biglietto m di (sola) andata; (record) 45 giri m; **~s** n (Tennis) singolo; **single out** vt scegliere; (distinguish) distinguere; **single bed** n letto singolo; **single file** n **in single file** in fila indiana; **single-handed** adv senza aiuto, da solo(-a); **single-minded** adj tenace, risoluto(-a); **single parent** n (mother) ragazza f madre inv; (father) ragazzo m padre inv; **single-parent family** famiglia monoparentale; **single room** n camera singola

singular ['sɪŋgjulə'] adj (exceptional, Ling) singolare ▷ n (Ling) singolare m

sinister ['sɪnɪstə'] adj sinistro(-a)

sink [sɪŋk] (pt **sank**, pp **sunk**) n lavandino, acquaio ▷ vt (ship) (fare) affondare, colare a picco; (foundations) scavare; (piles etc): **to ~ sth into** conficcare qc in ▷ vi affondare, andare a fondo; (ground etc) cedere, avvallarsi; **my heart sank** mi sentii venir meno; **sink in** vi penetrare

sinus ['saɪnəs] n (Anat) seno

sip [sɪp] n sorso ▷ vt sorseggiare

sir [sə'] n signore m; **S~ John Smith** Sir John Smith; **yes ~** sì, signore

siren ['saɪərn] n sirena

sirloin ['sə:lɔɪn] n controfiletto

sister ['sɪstə'] n sorella; (nun) suora; (BRIT: nurse) infermiera f caposala inv; **sister-in-law** n cognata

sit [sɪt] (pt, pp **sat**) vi sedere, sedersi; (assembly) essere in seduta; (for painter) posare ▷ vt (exam) sostenere, dare; **sit back** vi (in seat) appoggiarsi allo schienale; **sit down** vi sedersi; **sit on** vt fus (jury, committee) far parte di; **sit up** vi tirarsi su a sedere; (not go to bed) stare alzato(-a) fino a tardi

sitcom ['sɪtkɔm] n abbr (= situation comedy) commedia di situazione; (TV) telefilm m inv comico d'interni

site [saɪt] n posto; (also: **building ~**) cantiere m ▷ vt situare

sitting ['sɪtɪŋ] n (of assembly etc) seduta; (in canteen) turno; **sitting room** n soggiorno

situated ['sɪtjueɪtɪd] adj situato(-a)

situation [sɪtju'eɪʃən] n situazione f; (job)

lavoro; (location) posizione f; **"~s vacant"** (BRIT) "offerte fpl di impiego"

six [sɪks] num sei; **sixteen** num sedici; **sixteenth** [sɪks'ti:nθ] num sedicesimo(-a); **sixth** num sesto(-a); **sixth form** n (BRIT) ultimo biennio delle scuole superiori; **sixth-form college** n istituto che offre corsi di preparazione all'esame di maturità per ragazzi dai 16 ai 18 anni; **sixtieth** ['sɪkstɪɪθ] num sessantesimo(-a) ▷ pron (in series) sessantesimo(-a); (fraction) sessantesimo; **sixty** num sessanta

size [saɪz] n dimensioni fpl; (of clothing) taglia, misura; (of shoes) numero; (glue) colla; **sizeable** adj considerevole

sizzle ['sɪzl] vi sfrigolare

skate [skeɪt] n pattino; (fish: pl inv) razza ▷ vi pattinare; **skateboard** n skateboard m inv; **skateboarding** n skateboard m inv; **skater** n pattinatore(-trice); **skating** n pattinaggio; **skating rink** n pista di pattinaggio

skeleton ['skɛlɪtn] n scheletro

skeptical ['skɛptɪkl] (US) adj = **sceptical**

sketch [skɛtʃ] n (drawing) schizzo, abbozzo; (Theatre) scenetta comica, sketch m inv ▷ vt abbozzare, schizzare

skewer ['skjuːə'] n spiedo

ski [skiː] n sci m inv ▷ vi sciare; **ski boot** n scarpone m da sci

skid [skɪd] n slittamento ▷ vi slittare

ski: skier ['skiːə'] n sciatore(-trice); **skiing** ['skiːɪŋ] n sci m

skilful ['skɪlful] (US **skillful**) adj abile

ski lift n sciovia

skill [skɪl] n abilità f inv, capacità f inv; **skilled** adj esperto(-a); (worker) qualificato(-a), specializzato(-a)

skim [skɪm] vt (milk) scremare; (glide over) sfiorare ▷ vi **to ~ through** (fig) scorrere, dare una scorsa a; **skimmed milk** (US **skim milk**) n latte m scremato

skin [skɪn] n pelle f ▷ vt (fruit etc) sbucciare; (animal) scuoiare, spellare; **skinhead** n skinhead m/f inv; **skinny** adj molto magro(-a), pelle e ossa inv

skip [skɪp] n saltello, balzo; (BRIT: container) benna ▷ vi saltare; (with rope) saltare la corda ▷ vt saltare

ski: ski pass n ski pass m; **ski pole** n racchetta (da sci)

skipper ['skɪpə'] n (Naut, Sport) capitano

skipping rope ['skɪpɪŋ-] (US **skip rope**) n corda per saltare

skirt [skə:t] n gonna, sottana ▷ vt fiancheggiare, costeggiare

skirting board (BRIT) n zoccolo

ski slope n pista da sci

ski suit n tuta da sci

skull [skʌl] *n* cranio, teschio

skunk [skʌŋk] *n* moffetta

sky [skaɪ] *n* cielo; **skyscraper** *n* grattacielo

slab [slæb] *n* lastra; (*of cake, cheese*) fetta

slack [slæk] *adj* (*loose*) allentato(-a); (*slow*) lento(-a); (*careless*) negligente; **slacks** *npl* (*trousers*) pantaloni *mpl*

slain [sleɪn] *pp of* **slay**

slam [slæm] *vt* (*door*) sbattere; (*throw*) scaraventare; (*criticize*) stroncare ▷ *vi* sbattere

slander ['slɑːndər] *n* calunnia; diffamazione *f*

slang [slæŋ] *n* gergo, slang *m*

slant [slɑːnt] *n* pendenza, inclinazione *f*; (*fig*) angolazione *f*, punto di vista

slap [slæp] *n* manata, pacca; (*on face*) schiaffo ▷ *vt* dare una manata a; (*on face*) schiaffeggiare ▷ *adv* (*directly*) in pieno; **~ a coat of paint on it** dagli una mano di vernice

slash [slæʃ] *vt* tagliare; (*face*) sfregiare; (*fig: prices*) ridurre drasticamente, tagliare

slate [sleɪt] *n* ardesia; (*piece*) lastra di ardesia ▷ *vt* (*fig: criticize*) stroncare, distruggere

slaughter ['slɔːtər] *n* strage *f*, massacro ▷ *vt* (*animal*) macellare; (*people*) trucidare, massacrare; **slaughterhouse** *n* macello, mattatoio

Slav [slɑːv] *adj, n* slavo(-a)

slave [sleɪv] *n* schiavo(-a) ▷ *vi* (*also: ~ away*) lavorare come uno schiavo; **slavery** *n* schiavitù *f*

slay [sleɪ] (*pt* **slew**, *pp* **slain**) *vt* (*formal*) uccidere

sleazy ['sliːzɪ] *adj* trasandato(-a)

sled [slɛd] (*US*) = **sledge**

sledge [slɛdʒ] *n* slitta

sleek [sliːk] *adj* (*hair, fur*) lucido(-a), lucente; (*car, boat*) slanciato(-a), affusolato(-a)

sleep [sliːp] (*pt, pp* **slept**) *n* sonno ▷ *vi* dormire; **to go to ~** addormentarsi; **sleep in** *vi* (*oversleep*) dormire fino a tardi; **sleep together** *vi* (*have sex*) andare a letto insieme; **sleeper** (*BRIT*) *n* (*Rail: on track*) traversina; (*: train*) treno di vagoni letto; **sleeping bag** *n* sacco a pelo; **sleeping car** *n* vagone *m* letto *inv*, carrozza *f* letto *inv*; **sleeping pill** *n* sonnifero; **sleepover** *n* notte *f* che un ragazzino passa da amici; **sleepwalk** *vi* camminare nel sonno; (*as a habit*) essere sonnambulo(-a); **sleepy** *adj* assonnato(-a), sonnolento(-a); (*fig*) addormentato(-a)

sleet [sliːt] *n* nevischio

sleeve [sliːv] *n* manica; (*of record*)

copertina; **sleeveless** *adj* (*garment*) senza maniche

sleigh [sleɪ] *n* slitta

slender ['slɛndər] *adj* snello(-a), sottile; (*not enough*) scarso(-a), esiguo(-a)

slept [slɛpt] *pt, pp of* **sleep**

slew [sluː] *pt of* **slay** ▷ *vi* (*BRIT*) girare

slice [slaɪs] *n* fetta ▷ *vt* affettare, tagliare a fette

slick [slɪk] *adj* (*skilful*) brillante; (*clever*) furbo(-a) ▷ *n* (*also:* **oil ~**) chiazza di petrolio

slide [slaɪd] (*pt, pp* **slid**) *n* scivolone *m*; (*in playground*) scivolo; (*Phot*) diapositiva; (*BRIT: also:* **hair ~**) fermaglio (per capelli) ▷ *vt* far scivolare ▷ *vi* scivolare; **sliding** *adj* (*door*) scorrevole

slight [slaɪt] *adj* (*slim*) snello(-a), sottile; (*frail*) delicato(-a), fragile; (*trivial*) insignificante; (*small*) piccolo(-a) ▷ *n* offesa, affronto; **not in the ~est** affatto, neppure per sogno; **slightly** *adv* lievemente, un po'

slim [slɪm] *adj* magro(-a), snello(-a) ▷ *vi* dimagrire; fare (*or* seguire) una dieta dimagrante; **slimming** ['slɪmɪŋ] *adj* (*diet*) dimagrante; (*food*) ipocalorico(-a)

slimy ['slaɪmɪ] *adj* (*also fig: person*) viscido(-a); (*covered with mud*) melmoso(-a)

sling [slɪŋ] (*pt, pp* **slung**) *n* (*Med*) fascia al collo; (*for baby*) marsupio ▷ *vt* lanciare, tirare

slip [slɪp] *n* scivolata, scivolone *m*; (*mistake*) errore *m*, sbaglio; (*underskirt*) sottoveste *f*; (*of paper*) striscia di carta; tagliando, scontrino ▷ *vt* (*slide*) far scivolare ▷ *vi* (*slide*) scivolare; (*move smoothly*): **to ~ into/out of** scivolare in/fuori da; (*decline*) declinare; **to ~ sth on/off** infilarsi/ togliersi qc; **to give sb the ~** sfuggire qn; **a ~ of the tongue** un lapsus linguae; **slip up** *vi* sbagliarsi

slipper ['slɪpər] *n* pantofola

slippery ['slɪpərɪ] *adj* scivoloso(-a)

slip road (*BRIT*) *n* (*to motorway*) rampa di accesso

slit [slɪt] (*pt, pp* **slit**) *n* fessura, fenditura; (*cut*) taglio ▷ *vt* fendere; tagliare

slog [slɔg] (*BRIT*) *n* faticata ▷ *vi* lavorare con accanimento, sgobbare

slogan ['sləʊgən] *n* motto, slogan *m inv*

slope [sləʊp] *n* pendio; (*side of mountain*) versante *m*; (*ski slope*) pista; (*of roof*) pendenza; (*of floor*) inclinazione *f* ▷ *vi* **to ~ down** declinare; **to ~ up** essere in salita; **sloping** *adj* inclinato(-a)

sloppy ['slɔpɪ] *adj* (*work*) tirato(-a) via; (*appearance*) sciatto(-a)

slot [slɔt] *n* fessura ▷ *vt* **to ~ sth into** infilare qc in; **slot machine** *n*

(BRIT: *vending machine*) distributore *m* automatico; (*for gambling*) slot-machine *f inv*

Slovakia [sləʊˈvækɪə] *n* Slovacchia

Slovene [ˈsləʊviːn] *adj* sloveno(-a) ▷ *n* sloveno(-a); (*Ling*) sloveno

Slovenia [sləʊˈviːnɪə] *n* Slovenia; **Slovenian** *adj, n* = **Slovene**

slow [sləʊ] *adj* (*watch*): **to be ~** essere indietro ▷ *adv* lentamente ▷ *vt, vi* (*also*: **~ down, ~ up**) rallentare; **"~"** (*road sign*) "rallentare"; **slow down** *vi* rallentare; **slowly** *adv* lentamente; **slow motion** *n* **in slow motion** al rallentatore

slug [slʌg] *n* lumaca; (*bullet*) pallottola; **sluggish** *adj* lento(-a); (*trading*) stagnante

slum [slʌm] *n* catapecchia

slump [slʌmp] *n* crollo, caduta; (*economic*) depressione *f*, crisi *f inv* ▷ *vi* crollare

slung [slʌn] *pt, pp of* **sling**

slur [sləːʳ] *n* (*fig*): **~ (on)** calunnia (su) ▷ *vt* pronunciare in modo indistinto

sly [slaɪ] *adj* (*smile, remark*) sornione(-a); (*person*) furbo(-a)

smack [smæk] *n* (*slap*) pacca; (*on face*) schiaffo ▷ *vt* schiaffeggiare; (*child*) picchiare ▷ *vi* **to ~ of** puzzare di

small [smɔːl] *adj* piccolo(-a); **small ads** (BRIT) *npl* piccola pubblicità; **small change** *n* moneta, spiccioli *mpl*

smart [smɑːt] *adj* elegante; (*fashionable*) alla moda; (*clever*) intelligente; (*quick*) sveglio(-a) ▷ *vi* bruciare; **smartcard** [ˈsmɑːtkɑːd] *n* smartcard *f inv*, carta intelligente

smash [smæʃ] *n* (*also*: **~-up**) scontro, collisione *f*; (*smash hit*) successone *m* ▷ *vt* frantumare, fracassare; (*Sport: record*) battere ▷ *vi* frantumarsi, andare in pezzi; **smashing** (*inf*) *adj* favoloso(-a), formidabile

smear [smɪəʳ] *n* macchia; (*Med*) striscio ▷ *vt* spalmare; (*make dirty*) sporcare; **smear test** *n* (BRIT *Med*) Pap-test *m inv*

smell [smɛl] (*pt* **smelt** *or* **smelled**) *n* odore *m*; (*sense*) olfatto, odorato ▷ *vt* sentire (l')odore di ▷ *vi* (*food etc*) avere odore (di); (*pej*) puzzare, avere un cattivo odore di); **smelly** *adj* puzzolente

smelt [smɛlt] *pt, pp of* **smell** ▷ *vt* (*ore*) fondere

smile [smaɪl] *n* sorriso ▷ *vi* sorridere

smirk [sməːk] *n* sorriso furbo; sorriso compiaciuto

smog [smɔg] *n* smog *m*

smoke [sməʊk] *n* fumo ▷ *vt, vi* fumare; **do you mind if I ~?** le dà fastidio se fumo?; **smoke alarm** *n* rivelatore *f* di fumo; **smoked** *adj* (*bacon, glass*) affumicato(-a);

smoker *n* (*person*) fumatore(-trice); (*Rail*) carrozza per fumatori; **smoking** *n* fumo; **"no smoking"** (*sign*) "vietato fumare"; **smoky** *adj* fumoso(-a); (*taste*) affumicato(-a)

smooth [smuːð] *adj* liscio(-a); (*sauce*) omogeneo(-a); (*flavour, whisky*) amabile; (*movement*) regolare; (*person*) mellifluo(-a) ▷ *vt* (*also*: **~ out**) lisciare, spianare; (: *difficulties*) appianare

smother [ˈsmʌðəʳ] *vt* soffocare

SMS *abbr* (= *short message service*) SMS; **SMS message** *n* SMS *m inv*, messaggino

smudge [smʌdʒ] *n* macchia; sbavatura ▷ *vt* imbrattare, sporcare

smug [smʌg] *adj* soddisfatto(-a), compiaciuto(-a)

smuggle [ˈsmʌgl] *vt* contrabbandare; **smuggling** *n* contrabbando

snack [snæk] *n* spuntino; **snack bar** *n* tavola calda, snack bar *m inv*

snag [snæg] *n* intoppo, ostacolo imprevisto

snail [sneɪl] *n* chiocciola

snake [sneɪk] *n* serpente *m*

snap [snæp] *n* (*sound*) schianto, colpo secco; (*photograph*) istantanea ▷ *adj* improvviso(-a) ▷ *vt* (*far*) schioccare; (*break*) spezzare di netto ▷ *vi* spezzarsi con un rumore secco; (*fig: person*) parlare con tono secco; **to ~ shut** chiudersi di scatto; **snap at** *vt fus* (*dog*) cercare di mordere; **snap up** *vt* afferrare; **snapshot** *n* istantanea

snarl [snɑːl] *vi* ringhiare

snatch [snætʃ] *n* (*small amount*) frammento ▷ *vt* strappare (con violenza); (*fig*) rubare

sneak [sniːk] (*pt* (US) **snuck**) *vi* **to ~ in/out** entrare/uscire di nascosto ▷ *n* spione(-a); **to ~ up on sb** avvicinarsi quatto quatto a qn; **sneakers** *npl* scarpe *fpl* da ginnastica

sneer [snɪəʳ] *vi* sogghignare; **to ~ at** farsi beffe di

sneeze [sniːz] *n* starnuto ▷ *vi* starnutire

sniff [snɪf] *n* fiutata, annusata ▷ *vi* tirare su col naso ▷ *vt* fiutare, annusare

snigger [ˈsnɪgəʳ] *vi* ridacchiare, ridere sotto i baffi

snip [snɪp] *n* pezzetto; (*bargain*) (buon) affare *m*, occasione *f* ▷ *vt* tagliare

sniper [ˈsnaɪpəʳ] *n* (*marksman*) franco tiratore *m*, cecchino

snob [snɔb] *n* snob *m/f inv*

snooker [ˈsnuːkəʳ] *n* tipo di gioco del biliardo

snoop [ˈsnuːp] *vi* **to ~ about** curiosare

snooze [snuːz] *n* sonnellino, pisolino ▷ *vi* fare un sonnellino

snore [snɔːʳ] *vi* russare

snorkel [ˈsnɔːkl] *n* (*of swimmer*) respiratore

m a tubo

snort [snɔːt] *n* sbuffo ▷ *vi* sbuffare

snow [snəu] *n* neve *f* ▷ *vi* nevicare;
snowball *n* palla di neve ▷ *vi* (*fig*) crescere
a vista d'occhio; **snowstorm** *n* tormenta

snub [snʌb] *vt* snobbare ▷ *n* offesa,
affronto

snug [snʌg] *adj* comodo(-a); (*room, house*)
accogliente, comodo(-a)

 KEYWORD

so [səu] *adv* **1** (*thus, likewise*) così; **if so** se è
così, quand'è così; **I didn't do it — you did
so!** non l'ho fatto io — sì che l'hai fatto!;
so do I, so am I *etc* anch'io; **it's 5 o'clock
— so it is!** sono le 5 — davvero!; **I hope
so** lo spero; **I think so** penso di sì; **so far**
finora, fin qui; (*in past*) fino ad allora
2 (*in comparisons etc: to such a degree*) così;
so big (that) così grande (che); **she's not
so clever as her brother** lei non è (così)
intelligente come suo fratello
3: **so much** *adj* tanto(-a)
▷ *adv* tanto; **I've got so much work/
money** ho tanto lavoro/tanti soldi; **I love
you so much** ti amo tanto; **so many**
tanti(-e)
4 (*phrases*): **10 or so** circa 10; **so long!** (*inf:
goodbye*) ciao!, ci vediamo!
▷ *conj* **1** (*expressing purpose*): **so as to do**
in modo or così da fare; **we hurried so as
not to be late** ci affrettammo per non fare
tardi; **so (that)** affinché + *sub*, perché + *sub*
2 (*expressing result*): **he didn't arrive so I
left** non è venuto così me ne sono andata;
so you see, I could have gone vedi, sarei
potuto andare

soak [səuk] *vt* inzuppare; (*clothes*) mettere
a mollo ▷ *vi* (*clothes etc*) essere a mollo;
soak up *vt* assorbire; **soaking** *adj* (*also:*
soaking wet) fradicio(-a)

so-and-so ['səuənsəu] *n* (*somebody*) un
tale; **Mr/Mrs ~** signor/signora tal dei tali

soap [səup] *n* sapone *m*; **soap opera** *n*
soap opera *f inv*; **soap powder** *n* detersivo

soar [sɔːʳ] *vi* volare in alto; (*price etc*) salire
alle stelle; (*building*) ergersi

sob [sɔb] *n* singhiozzo ▷ *vi* singhiozzare

sober ['səubəʳ] *adj* sobrio(-a); (*not drunk*)
non ubriaco(-a); (*moderate*) moderato(-a);
sober up *vt* far passare la sbornia a ▷ *vi*
farsi passare la sbornia

so-called ['səu'kɔːld] *adj* cosiddetto(-a)

soccer ['sɔkəʳ] *n* calcio

sociable ['səuʃəbl] *adj* socievole

social ['səuʃl] *adj* sociale ▷ *n* festa, serata;
socialism *n* socialismo; **socialist** *adj, n*

socialista *m/f*; **socialize** *vi* **to socialize
(with)** socializzare (con); **social life** *n*
vita sociale; **socially** *adv* socialmente,
in società; **social security** (BRIT) *n*
previdenza sociale; **social services** *npl*
servizi *mpl* sociali; **social work** *n* servizio
sociale; **social worker** *n* assistente *m/f*
sociale

society [sə'saɪətɪ] *n* società *f inv*; (*club*)
società, associazione *f*; (*also:* **high ~**) alta
società

sociology [səusɪ'ɔlədʒɪ] *n* sociologia

sock [sɔk] *n* calzino

socket ['sɔkɪt] *n* cavità *f inv*; (*of eye*) orbita;
(BRIT: *Elec: also:* **wall ~**) presa di corrente

soda ['səudə] *n* (*Chem*) soda; (*also:* **~
water**) acqua di seltz; (US: *also:* **~ pop**)
gassosa

sodium ['səudɪəm] *n* sodio

sofa ['səufə] *n* sofà *m inv*; **sofa bed** *n*
divano *m* letto *inv*

soft [sɔft] *adj* (*not rough*) morbido(-a); (*not
hard*) soffice; (*not loud*) sommesso(-a); (*not
bright*) tenue; (*kind*) gentile; **soft drink**
n analcolico; **soft drugs** *npl* droghe *fpl*
leggere; **soften** ['sɔfn] *vt* ammorbidire;
addolcire; attenuare ▷ *vi* ammorbidirsi;
addolcirsi; attenuarsi; **softly** *adv*
dolcemente; morbidamente; **software**
['sɔftwɛəʳ] *n* (*Comput*) software *m*

soggy ['sɔgɪ] *adj* inzuppato(-a)

soil [sɔɪl] *n* terreno ▷ *vt* sporcare

solar ['səuləʳ] *adj* solare; **solar power** *n*
energie solari; **solar system** *n* sistema
m solare

sold [səuld] *pt, pp of* **sell**

soldier ['səuldʒəʳ] *n* soldato, militare *m*

sold out *adj* (*Comm*) esaurito(-a)

sole [səul] *n* (*of foot*) pianta (del piede);
(*of shoe*) suola; (*fish: pl inv*) sogliola
▷ *adj* solo(-a), unico(-a); **solely** *adv*
solamente, unicamente; **I will hold you
solely responsible** la considererò il solo
responsabile

solemn ['sɔləm] *adj* solenne

solicitor [sə'lɪsɪtəʳ] (BRIT) *n* (*for wills etc*)
≈ notaio; (*in court*) ≈ avvocato

solid ['sɔlɪd] *adj* solido(-a); (*not hollow*)
pieno(-a); (*meal*) sostanzioso(-a) ▷ *n*
solido

solitary ['sɔlɪtərɪ] *adj* solitario(-a)

solitude ['sɔlɪtjuːd] *n* solitudine *f*

solo ['səuləu] *n* assolo; **soloist** *n* solista
m/f

soluble ['sɔljubl] *adj* solubile

solution [sə'luːʃən] *n* soluzione *f*

solve [sɔlv] *vt* risolvere

solvent ['sɔlvənt] *adj* (*Comm*) solvibile ▷ *n*
(*Chem*) solvente *m*

sombre ['sɒmbə'] (US **somber**) adj
scuro(-a); (mood, person) triste

 KEYWORD

some [sʌm] adj **1** (a certain amount or number
of): **some tea/water/cream** del tè/
dell'acqua/della panna; **some children/
apples** dei bambini/delle mele
2 (certain: in contrasts) certo(-a); **some
people say that …** alcuni dicono che …,
certa gente dice che …
3 (unspecified) un(a) certo(-a), qualche;
some woman was asking for you una
tale chiedeva di lei; **some day** un giorno;
some day next week un giorno della
prossima settimana
▷ pron **1** (a certain number) alcuni(-e),
certi(-e); **I've got some** (books etc) ne ho
alcuni; **some (of them) have been sold**
alcuni sono stati venduti
2 (a certain amount) un po'; **I've got some**
(money, milk) ne ho un po'; **I've read some
of the book** ho letto parte del libro
▷ adv **some 10 people** circa 10 persone

some: somebody ['sʌmbədɪ] pron
= **someone; somehow** ['sʌmhau] adv
in un modo o nell'altro, in qualche modo;
(for some reason) per qualche ragione;
someone ['sʌmwʌn] pron qualcuno;
someplace ['sʌmpleɪs] (US) adv
= **somewhere; something** ['sʌmθɪŋ]
pron qualcosa, qualche cosa; **something
nice** qualcosa di bello; **something to do**
qualcosa da fare; **sometime** ['sʌmtaɪm]
adv (in future) una volta o l'altra; (in past):
sometime last month durante il mese
scorso; **sometimes** ['sʌmtaɪmz] adv
qualche volta; **somewhat** ['sʌmwɔt] adv
piuttosto; **somewhere** ['sʌmwɛə'] adv in
or da qualche parte
son [sʌn] n figlio
song [sɒŋ] n canzone f
son-in-law ['sʌnɪnlɔ:] n genero
soon [su:n] adv presto, fra poco; (early, a
short time after) presto; **~ afterwards** poco
dopo; see also **as; sooner** adv (time) prima;
(preference): **I would sooner do** preferirei
fare; **sooner or later** prima o poi
soothe [su:ð] vt calmare
sophisticated [sə'fɪstɪkeɪtɪd]
adj sofisticato(-a); raffinato(-a);
complesso(-a)
sophomore ['sɒfəmɔ:'] (US) n
studente(-essa) del secondo anno
soprano [sə'prɑ:nəu] n (voice) soprano m;
(singer) soprano m/f
sorbet ['sɔ:beɪ] n sorbetto

sordid ['sɔ:dɪd] adj sordido(-a)
sore [sɔ:'] adj (painful) dolorante ▷ n piaga
sorrow ['sɒrəu] n dolore m
sorry ['sɒrɪ] adj spiacente; (condition,
excuse) misero(-a); **~!** scusa! (or scusi! or
scusate!); **to feel ~ for sb** rincrescersi
per qn
sort [sɔ:t] n specie f, genere m; **sort out** vt
(papers) classificare; ordinare; (: letters etc)
smistare; (: problems) risolvere; (Comput)
ordinare
SOS n abbr (= save our souls) S.O.S. m inv
so-so ['səusəu] adv così così
sought [sɔ:t] pt, pp of **seek**
soul [səul] n anima
sound [saund] adj (healthy) sano(-a); (safe,
not damaged) solido(-a), in buono stato;
(reliable, not superficial) solido(-a); (sensible)
giudizioso(-a), di buon senso ▷ adv **~
asleep** profondamente addormentato
▷ n suono; (noise) rumore m; (Geo) stretto
▷ vt (alarm) suonare ▷ vi suonare; (fig:
seem) sembrare; **to ~ like** rassomigliare a;
soundtrack n (of film) colonna sonora
soup [su:p] n minestra; brodo; zuppa
sour ['sauə'] adj aspro(-a); (fruit)
acerbo(-a); (milk) acido(-a); (fig)
arcigno(-a); acido(-a); **it's ~ grapes** è
soltanto invidia
source [sɔ:s] n fonte f, sorgente f; (fig)
fonte
south [sauθ] n sud m, meridione m,
mezzogiorno ▷ adj del sud, sud inv,
meridionale ▷ adv verso sud; **South
Africa** n Sudafrica m; **South African**
adj, n sudafricano(-a); **South America** n
Sudamerica m, America del sud; **South
American** adj, n sudamericano(-a);
southbound ['sauθbaund] adj (gen)
diretto(-a) a sud; (carriageway) sud
inv; **southeastern** [sauθ'i:stən] adj
sudorientale; **southern** ['sʌðən] adj
del sud, meridionale; esposto(-a) a sud;
South Korea n Corea f del Sud; **South
Pole** n Polo Sud; **southward(s)** adv
verso sud; **south-west** n sud-ovest
m; **southwestern** [sauθ'westən] adj
sudoccidentale
souvenir [su:və'nɪə'] n ricordo, souvenir
m inv
sovereign ['sɒvrɪn] adj, n sovrano(-a)
sow¹ [səu] (pt **sowed**, pp **sown**) vt
seminare
sow² [sau] n scrofa
soya [sɔɪə] (US **soy**) n **~ bean** n seme m di
soia; **soya sauce** n salsa di soia
spa [spɑ:] n (resort) stazione f termale; (US:
also: **health ~**) centro di cure estetiche
space [speɪs] n spazio; (room) posto;

spazio; (*length of time*) intervallo ▷ *cpd*
spaziale ▷ *vt* (*also:* ~ **out**) distanziare;
spacecraft *n inv* veicolo spaziale;
spaceship = **spacecraft**
spacious ['speɪʃəs] *adj* spazioso(-a),
ampio(-a)
spade [speɪd] *n* (*tool*) vanga; pala; (*child's*)
paletta; ~**s** *npl* (*Cards*) picche *fpl*
spaghetti [spə'gɛtɪ] *n* spaghetti *mpl*
Spain [speɪn] *n* Spagna
spam [spæm] (*Comput*) *n* spamming ▷ *vt*
to ~ **sb** inviare a qn messaggi pubblicitari
non richiesti via email
span [spæn] *n* (*of bird, plane*) apertura
alare; (*of arch*) campata; (*in time*) periodo;
durata ▷ *vt* attraversare; (*fig*) abbracciare
Spaniard ['spænjəd] *n* spagnolo(-a)
Spanish ['spænɪʃ] *adj* spagnolo(-a) ▷ *n*
(*Ling*) spagnolo; **the** ~ *npl* gli Spagnoli
spank [spæŋk] *vt* sculacciare
spanner ['spænər] (*BRIT*) *n* chiave *f* inglese
spare [speər] *adj* di riserva, di scorta;
(*surplus*) in più, d'avanzo ▷ *n* (*part*) pezzo
di ricambio ▷ *vt* (*do without*) fare a meno
di; (*afford to give*) concedere; (*refrain from
hurting, using*) risparmiare; **to** ~ (*surplus*)
d'avanzo; **spare part** *n* pezzo di ricambio;
spare room *n* stanza degli ospiti; **spare
time** *n* tempo libero; **spare tyre** (*US* **spare
tire**) *n* (*Aut*) gomma di scorta; **spare
wheel** *n* (*Aut*) ruota di scorta
spark [spɑːk] *n* scintilla; **spark(ing) plug**
n candela
sparkle ['spɑːkl] *n* scintillio, sfavillio ▷ *vi*
scintillare, sfavillare
sparrow ['spærəu] *n* passero
sparse [spɑːs] *adj* sparso(-a), rado(-a)
spasm ['spæzəm] *n* (*Med*) spasmo; (*fig*)
accesso, attacco
spat [spæt] *pt, pp of* **spit**
spate [speɪt] *n* (*fig*): ~ **of** diluvio *or* fiume
m di
spatula ['spætjulə] *n* spatola
speak [spiːk] (*pt* **spoke**, *pp* **spoken**) *vt*
(*language*) parlare; (*truth*) dire ▷ *vi* parlare;
I don't ~ **Italian** non parlo italiano; **do you**
~ **English?** parla inglese?; **to** ~ **to sb/of** *or*
about sth parlare a qn/di qc; **can I** ~ **to ...?**
posso parlare con ...?; ~ **up!** parla più forte!;
speaker *n* (*in public*) oratore(-trice);
(*also:* **loudspeaker**) altoparlante *m*; (*Pol*):
the Speaker il presidente della Camera dei
Comuni (*BRIT*) *or* dei Rappresentanti (*US*)
spear [spɪər] *n* lancia ▷ *vt* infilzare
special ['spɛʃl] *adj* speciale; **special
delivery** *n* (*Post*): **by special delivery**
per espresso; **special effects** *npl*
(*Cine*) effetti *mpl* speciali; **specialist** *n*
specialista *m/f*; **speciality** [spɛʃɪ'ælɪtɪ]

n specialità *f inv*; **I'd like to try a local
speciality** vorrei assaggiare una specialità
del posto; **specialize** *vi* **to specialize
(in)** specializzarsi (in); **specially** *adv*
specialmente, particolarmente;
special needs *adj* **special needs
children** bambini *mpl* con difficoltà di
apprendimento; **special offer** *n* (*Comm*)
offerta speciale; **special school** *n* (*BRIT*)
scuola speciale (*per portatori di handicap*);
specialty (*US*) *n* = **speciality**
species ['spiːʃiːz] *n inv* specie *f inv*
specific [spə'sɪfɪk] *adj* specifico(-a);
preciso(-a); **specifically** *adv*
esplicitamente; (*especially*) appositamente
specify ['spɛsɪfaɪ] *vt* specificare, precisare;
unless otherwise specified salvo
indicazioni contrarie
specimen ['spɛsɪmən] *n* esemplare *m*,
modello; (*Med*) campione *m*
speck [spɛk] *n* puntino, macchiolina;
(*particle*) granello
spectacle ['spɛktəkl] *n* spettacolo; ~**s**
npl (*glasses*) occhiali *mpl*; **spectacular**
[-'tækjulər] *adj* spettacolare
spectator [spɛk'teɪtər] *n* spettatore *m*
spectrum ['spɛktrəm] (*pl* **spectra**) *n*
spettro
speculate ['spɛkjuleɪt] *vi* speculare; (*try to
guess*): **to** ~ **about** fare ipotesi su
sped [spɛd] *pt, pp of* **speed**
speech [spiːtʃ] *n* (*faculty*) parola; (*talk,
Theatre*) discorso; (*manner of speaking*)
parlata; **speechless** *adj* ammutolito(-a),
muto(-a)
speed [spiːd] *n* velocità *f inv*; (*promptness*)
prontezza; **at full** *or* **top** ~ a tutta velocità;
speed up *vi, vt* accelerare; **speedboat** *n*
motoscafo; **speeding** *n* (*Aut*) eccesso
di velocità; **speed limit** *n* limite *m* di
velocità; **speedometer** [spɪ'dɔmɪtər] *n*
tachimetro; **speedy** *adj* veloce, rapido(-a);
pronto(-a)
spell [spɛl] (*pt, pp* **spelt** (*BRIT*) *or* **spelled**) *n*
(*also:* **magic** ~) incantesimo; (*period of time*)
(*breve*) periodo ▷ *vt* (*in writing*) scrivere
(*lettera per lettera*); (*aloud*) dire lettera per
lettera; (*fig*) significare; **to cast a** ~ **on sb**
fare un incantesimo a qn; **he can't** ~ fa
errori di ortografia; **spell out** *vt* (*letter by
letter*) dettare lettera per lettera; (*explain*):
to ~ **sth out for sb** spiegare qc a qn per
filo e per segno; **spellchecker** ['spɛltʃɛkər]
n correttore *m* ortografico; **spelling** *n*
ortografia
spelt [spɛlt] (*BRIT*) *pt, pp of* **spell**
spend [spɛnd] (*pt, pp* **spent**) *vt* (*money*)
spendere; (*time, life*) passare; **spending** *n*
government spending spesa pubblica

spent [spɛnt] *pt, pp of* **spend**

sperm [spəːm] *n* sperma *m*

sphere [sfɪəʳ] *n* sfera

spice [spaɪs] *n* spezia ▷ *vt* aromatizzare

spicy ['spaɪsɪ] *adj* piccante

spider ['spaɪdəʳ] *n* ragno

spike [spaɪk] *n* punta

spill [spɪl] (*pt, pp* **spilt** *or* **spilled**) *vt* versare, rovesciare ▷ *vi* versarsi, rovesciarsi

spin [spɪn] (*pt, pp* **spun**) *n* (*revolution of wheel*) rotazione *f*; (*Aviat*) avvitamento; (*trip in car*) giretto ▷ *vt* (*wool etc*) filare; (*wheel*) far girare ▷ *vi* girare

spinach ['spɪnɪtʃ] *n* spinacio; (*as food*) spinaci *mpl*

spinal ['spaɪnl] *adj* spinale

spin doctor (*inf*) *n* esperto di comunicazioni responsabile dell'immagine di un partito politico

spin-dryer [spɪn'draɪəʳ] (BRIT) *n* centrifuga

spine [spaɪn] *n* spina dorsale; (*thorn*) spina

spiral ['spaɪərl] *n* spirale *f* ▷ *vi* (*fig*) salire a spirale

spire ['spaɪəʳ] *n* guglia

spirit ['spɪrɪt] *n* spirito; (*ghost*) spirito, fantasma *m*; (*mood*) stato d'animo, umore *m*; (*courage*) coraggio; **~s** *npl* (*drink*) alcolici *mpl*; **in good ~s** di buon umore

spiritual ['spɪrɪtjuəl] *adj* spirituale

spit [spɪt] (*pt, pp* **spat**) *n* (*for roasting*) spiedo; (*saliva*) sputo; saliva ▷ *vi* sputare; (*fire, fat*) scoppiettare

spite [spaɪt] *n* dispetto ▷ *vt* contrariare, far dispetto a; **in ~ of** nonostante, malgrado; **spiteful** *adj* dispettoso(-a)

splash [splæʃ] *n* spruzzo; (*sound*) splash *m inv*; (*of colour*) schizzo ▷ *vt* spruzzare ▷ *vi* (*also*: **~ about**) sguazzare; **splash out** (*inf*) *vi* (BRIT) fare spese folli

splendid ['splɛndɪd] *adj* splendido(-a), magnifico(-a)

splinter ['splɪntəʳ] *n* scheggia ▷ *vi* scheggiarsi

split [splɪt] (*pt, pp* **split**) *n* spaccatura; (*fig: division, quarrel*) scissione *f* ▷ *vt* spaccare; (*party*) dividere; (*work, profits*) spartire, ripartire ▷ *vi* (*divide*) dividersi; **split up** *vi* (*couple*) separarsi, rompere; (*meeting*) sciogliersi

spoil [spɔɪl] (*pt, pp* **spoilt** *or* **spoiled**) *vt* (*damage*) rovinare, guastare; (*mar*) sciupare; (*child*) viziare

spoilt [spɔɪlt] *pt, pp of* **spoil**

spoke [spəʊk] *pt of* **speak** ▷ *n* raggio

spoken ['spəʊkn] *pp of* **speak**

spokesman ['spəʊksmən] (*irreg*) *n* portavoce *m inv*

spokesperson ['spəʊkspəːsn] *n* portavoce *m/f*

spokeswoman ['spəʊkswumən] (*irreg*) *n* portavoce *f inv*

sponge [spʌndʒ] *n* spugna; (*also*: **~ cake**) pan *m* di spagna ▷ *vt* spugnare, pulire con una spugna ▷ *vi* **to ~ off** *or* **on** scroccare a; **sponge bag** (BRIT) *n* nécessaire *m inv*

sponsor ['spɒnsəʳ] *n* (*Radio, TV, Sport etc*) sponsor *m inv*; (*Pol: of bill*) promotore(-trice) ▷ *vt* sponsorizzare; (*bill*) presentare; **sponsorship** *n* sponsorizzazione *f*

spontaneous [spɒn'teɪnɪəs] *adj* spontaneo(-a)

spooky ['spuːkɪ] (*inf*) *adj* che fa accapponare la pelle

spoon [spuːn] *n* cucchiaio; **spoonful** *n* cucchiaiata

sport [spɔːt] *n* sport *m inv*; (*person*) persona di spirito *m* ▷ *vt* sfoggiare; **sport jacket** (US) *n* = **sports jacket**; **sports car** *n* automobile *f* sportiva; **sports centre** (BRIT) *n* centro sportivo; **sports jacket** (BRIT) *n* giacca sportiva; **sportsman** (*irreg*) *n* sportivo; **sportswear** *n* abiti *mpl* sportivi; **sportswoman** (*irreg*) *n* sportiva; **sporty** *adj* sportivo(-a)

spot [spɒt] *n* punto; (*mark*) macchia; (*dot: on pattern*) pallino; (*pimple*) foruncolo; (*place*) posto; (*Radio, TV*) spot *m inv*; (*small amount*): **a ~ of** un po' di ▷ *vt* (*notice*) individuare, distinguere; **on the ~** sul posto; (*immediately*) su due piedi; (*in difficulty*) nei guai; **spotless** *adj* immacolato(-a); **spotlight** *n* proiettore *m*; (*Aut*) faro ausiliario

spouse [spauz] *n* sposo(-a)

sprain [spreɪn] *n* storta, distorsione *f* ▷ *vt* **to ~ one's ankle** storcersi una caviglia

sprang [spræŋ] *pt of* **spring**

sprawl [sprɔːl] *vi* sdraiarsi (in modo scomposto); (*place*) estendersi (disordinatamente)

spray [spreɪ] *n* spruzzo; (*container*) nebulizzatore *m*, spray *m inv*; (*of flowers*) mazzetto ▷ *vt* spruzzare; (*crops*) irrorare

spread [sprɛd] (*pt, pp* **spread**) *n* diffusione *f*; (*distribution*) distribuzione *f*; (*Culin*) pasta (da spalmare); (*inf: food*) banchetto ▷ *vt* (*cloth*) stendere, distendere; (*butter etc*) spalmare; (*disease, knowledge*) propagare, diffondere ▷ *vi* stendersi, distendersi; spalmarsi; propagarsi, diffondersi; **spread out** *vi* (*move apart*) separarsi; **spreadsheet** *n* foglio elettronico ad espansione

spree [spriː] *n* **to go on a ~** fare baldoria

spring [sprɪŋ] (*pt* **sprang**, *pp* **sprung**) *n* (*leap*) salto, balzo; (*coiled metal*) molla;

(*season*) primavera; (*of water*) sorgente
f ▷ vi saltare, balzare; **spring up** vi
(*problem*) presentarsi; **spring onion** n
(BRIT) cipollina

sprinkle ['sprɪŋkl] vt spruzzare; spargere;
to ~ water etc **on, ~ with water** etc
spruzzare dell'acqua etc su

sprint [sprɪnt] n scatto ▷ vi scattare

sprung [sprʌŋ] pp of **spring**

spun [spʌn] pt, pp of **spin**

spur [spəː] n sperone m; (*fig*) sprone m,
incentivo ▷ vt (*also: ~ on*) spronare; **on the
~ of the moment** lì per lì

spurt [spəːt] n (*of water*) getto; (*of energy*)
scatto ▷ vi sgorgare

spy [spaɪ] n spia ▷ vi **to ~ on** spiare ▷ vt
(*see*) scorgere

sq. abbr = **square**

squabble ['skwɔbl] vi bisticciarsi

squad [skwɔd] n (*Mil*) plotone m; (*Police*)
squadra

squadron ['skwɔdrn] n (*Mil*) squadrone m;
(*Aviat, Naut*) squadriglia

squander ['skwɔndəˀ] vt dissipare

square [skwɛəˀ] n quadrato; (*in town*)
piazza ▷ adj quadrato(-a); (*inf: ideas,
person*) di vecchio stampo ▷ vt (*arrange*)
regolare; (*Math*) elevare al quadrato;
(*reconcile*) conciliare; **all ~** pari; **a ~ meal** un
pasto abbondante; **2 metres ~** di 2 metri
per 2; **1 ~ metre** 1 metro quadrato; **square
root** n radice f quadrata

squash [skwɔʃ] n (*Sport*) squash m; (BRIT:
drink): **lemon/orange ~** sciroppo di
limone/arancia; (*us*) zucca; (*Sport*) squash
m ▷ vt schiacciare

squat [skwɔt] adj tarchiato(-a), tozzo(-a)
▷ vi (*also: ~ down*) accovacciarsi; **squatter**
n occupante m/f abusivo(-a)

squeak [skwiːk] vi squittire

squeal [skwiːl] vi strillare

squeeze [skwiːz] n pressione f; (*also Econ*)
stretta ▷ vt premere; (*hand, arm*) stringere

squid [skwɪd] n calamaro

squint [skwɪnt] vi essere strabico(-a) ▷ n
he has a ~ è strabico

squirm [skwəːm] vi contorcersi

squirrel ['skwɪrəl] n scoiattolo

squirt [skwəːt] vi schizzare; zampillare
▷ vt spruzzare

Sr abbr = **senior**

Sri Lanka [srɪ'læŋkə] n Sri Lanka m

St abbr = **saint**; **street**

stab [stæb] n (*with knife etc*) pugnalata; (*of
pain*) fitta; (*inf: try*): **to have a ~ at (doing)
sth** provare (a fare) qc ▷ vt pugnalare

stability [stə'bɪlɪtɪ] n stabilità

stable ['steɪbl] n (*for horses*) scuderia; (*for
cattle*) stalla ▷ adj stabile

stack [stæk] n catasta, pila ▷ vt
accatastare, ammucchiare

stadium ['steɪdɪəm] n stadio

staff [stɑːf] n (*work force: gen*) personale
m; (: BRIT: Scol) personale insegnante ▷ vt
fornire di personale

stag [stæg] n cervo

stage [steɪdʒ] n palcoscenico; (*profession*):
the ~ il teatro, la scena; (*point*) punto;
(*platform*) palco ▷ vt (*play*) allestire,
mettere in scena; (*demonstration*)
organizzare; **in ~s** per gradi; a tappe

stagger ['stægəˀ] vi barcollare ▷ vt (*person*)
sbalordire; (*hours, holidays*) scaglionare;
staggering adj (*amazing*) sbalorditivo(-a)

stagnant ['stægnənt] adj stagnante

stag night, stag party n festa di addio
al celibato

stain [steɪn] n macchia; (*colouring*)
colorante m ▷ vt macchiare; (*wood*)
tingere; **stained glass** [steɪnd'glɑːs] n
vetro colorato; **stainless steel** n acciaio
inossidabile

staircase ['stɛəkeɪs] n scale fpl, scala

stairs [stɛəz] npl (*flight of stairs*) scale fpl,
scala

stairway ['stɛəweɪ] n = **staircase**

stake [steɪk] n palo, piolo; (*Comm*)
interesse m; (*Betting*) puntata, scommessa
▷ vt (*bet*) scommettere; (*risk*) rischiare; **to
be at ~** essere in gioco

stale [steɪl] adj (*bread*) raffermo(-a);
(*food*) stantio(-a); (*air*) viziato(-a); (*beer*)
svaporato(-a); (*smell*) di chiuso

stalk [stɔːk] n gambo, stelo ▷ vt inseguire

stall [stɔːl] n bancarella; (*in stable*) box m
inv di stalla ▷ vt (*Aut*) far spegnere; (*fig*)
bloccare ▷ vi (*Aut*) spegnersi, fermarsi; (*fig*)
temporeggiare

stamina ['stæmɪnə] n vigore m, resistenza

stammer ['stæməˀ] n balbuzie f ▷ vi
balbettare

stamp [stæmp] n (*postage stamp*)
francobollo; (*implement*) timbro; (*mark,
also fig*) marchio, impronta; (*on document*)
bollo; timbro ▷ vi (*also: ~ one's foot*)
battere il piede ▷ vt battere; (*letter*)
affrancare; (*mark with a stamp*) timbrare;
stamp out vt (*fire*) estinguere; (*crime*)
eliminare; (*opposition*) soffocare; **stamped
addressed envelope** n (BRIT) busta
affrancata e indirizzata

▌ Be careful not to translate *stamp* the
Italian word by *stampa*.

stampede [stæm'piːd] n fuggi fuggi m inv

stance [stæns] n posizione f

stand [stænd] n (*pt, pp* **stood**) n (*position*)
posizione f; (*for taxis*) posteggio; (*structure*)
supporto, sostegno; (*at exhibition*)

stand *m inv*; (*in shop*) banco; (*at market*) bancarella; (*booth*) chiosco; (*Sport*) tribuna ▷ *vi* stare in piedi; (*rise*) alzarsi in piedi; (*be placed*) trovarsi ▷ *vt* (*place*) mettere, porre; (*tolerate, withstand*) resistere, sopportare; (*treat*) offrire; **to make a ~** prendere posizione; **to ~ for parliament** (BRIT) presentarsi come candidato (per il parlamento); **stand back** *vi* prendere le distanze; **stand by** *vi* (*be ready*) tenersi pronto(-a) ▷ *vt fus* (*opinion*) sostenere; **stand down** *vi* (*withdraw*) ritirarsi; **stand for** *vt fus* (*signify*) rappresentare, significare; (*tolerate*) sopportare, tollerare; **stand in for** *vt fus* sostituire; **stand out** *vi* (*be prominent*) spiccare; **stand up** *vi* (*rise*) alzarsi in piedi; **stand up for** *vt fus* difendere; **stand up to** *vt fus* tener testa a, resistere a

standard ['stændəd] *n* modello, standard *m inv*; (*level*) livello; (*flag*) stendardo ▷ *adj* (*size etc*) normale, standard *inv*; **~s** *npl* (*morals*) principi *mpl*, valori *mpl*; **standard of living** *n* livello di vita

stand-by ['stændbaɪ] *n* riserva, sostituto; **to be on ~** (*gen*) tenersi pronto(-a); (*doctor*) essere di guardia; **stand-by ticket** *n* (*Aviat*) biglietto senza garanzia

standing ['stændɪŋ] *adj* diritto(-a), in piedi; (*permanent*) permanente ▷ *n* rango, condizione *f*, posizione *f*; **of many years' ~** che esiste da molti anni; **standing order** (BRIT) *n* (*at bank*) ordine *m* di pagamento (permanente)

stand: standpoint ['stændpɔɪnt] *n* punto di vista; **standstill** ['stændstɪl] *n* **at a standstill** fermo(-a); (*fig*) a un punto morto; **to come to a standstill** fermarsi; giungere a un punto morto

stank [stæŋk] *pt of* **stink**

staple ['steɪpl] *n* (*for papers*) graffetta ▷ *adj* (*food etc*) di base ▷ *vt* cucire

star [stɑːʳ] *n* stella; (*celebrity*) divo(-a) ▷ *vi* **to ~ (in)** essere il (*or* la) protagonista (di) ▷ *vt* (*Cinema*) essere interpretato(-a) da; **the ~s** *npl* (*Astrology*) le stelle

starboard ['stɑːbəd] *n* dritta

starch [stɑːtʃ] *n* amido

stardom ['stɑːdəm] *n* celebrità

stare [steəʳ] *n* sguardo fisso ▷ *vi* **to ~ at** fissare

stark [stɑːk] *adj* (*bleak*) desolato(-a) ▷ *adv* **~ naked** completamente nudo(-a)

start [stɑːt] *n* inizio; (*of race*) partenza; (*sudden movement*) sobbalzo; (*advantage*) vantaggio ▷ *vt* cominciare, iniziare; (*car*) mettere in moto ▷ *vi* cominciare; (*on journey*) partire, mettersi in viaggio; (*jump*) sobbalzare; **when does the film ~?**

a che ora comincia il film?; **to ~ doing** *or* **to do sth** (in)cominciare a fare qc; **start off** *vi* cominciare; (*leave*) partire; **start out** *vi* (*begin*) cominciare; (*set out*) partire; **start up** *vi* cominciare; (*car*) avviarsi ▷ *vt* iniziare; (*car*) avviare; **starter** *n* (*Aut*) motorino d'avviamento; (*Sport: official*) starter *m inv*; (BRIT: *Culin*) primo piatto; **starting point** *n* punto di partenza

startle ['stɑːtl] *vt* far trasalire; **startling** *adj* sorprendente

starvation [stɑːˈveɪʃən] *n* fame *f*, inedia

starve [stɑːv] *vi* morire di fame; soffrire la fame ▷ *vt* far morire di fame, affamare

state [steɪt] *n* stato ▷ *vt* dichiarare, affermare; annunciare; **the S~s** (USA) gli Stati Uniti; **to be in a ~** essere agitato(-a); **statement** *n* dichiarazione *f*; **state school** *n* scuola statale; **statesman** (*irreg*) *n* statista *m*

static ['stætɪk] *n* (*Radio*) scariche *fpl* ▷ *adj* statico(-a)

station ['steɪʃən] *n* stazione *f* ▷ *vt* collocare, disporre

stationary ['steɪʃənərɪ] *adj* fermo(-a), immobile

stationer's (shop) *n* cartoleria

stationery ['steɪʃnərɪ] *n* articoli *mpl* di cancelleria

station wagon (US) *n* giardinetta

statistic [stəˈtɪstɪk] *n* statistica; **statistics** *n* (*science*) statistica

statue ['stætjuː] *n* statua

stature ['stætʃəʳ] *n* statura

status ['steɪtəs] *n* posizione *f*, condizione *f* sociale; prestigio; stato; **status quo** [-ˈkwəu] *n* **the status quo** lo statu quo

statutory ['stætjutrɪ] *adj* stabilito(-a) dalla legge, statutario(-a)

staunch [stɔːntʃ] *adj* fidato(-a), leale

stay [steɪ] *n* (*period of time*) soggiorno, permanenza ▷ *vi* rimanere; (*reside*) alloggiare, stare; (*spend some time*) trattenersi, soggiornare; **to ~ put** non muoversi; **to ~ the night** fermarsi per la notte; **stay away** *vi* (*from person, building*) stare lontano (*from event*) non andare; **stay behind** *vi* restare indietro; **stay in** *vi* (*at home*) stare in casa; **stay on** *vi* restare, rimanere; **stay out** *vi* (*of house*) rimanere fuori (di casa); **stay up** *vi* (*at night*) rimanere alzato(-a)

steadily ['stɛdɪlɪ] *adv* (*firmly*) saldamente; (*constantly*) continuamente; (*fixedly*) fisso; (*walk*) con passo sicuro

steady ['stɛdɪ] *adj* (*not wobbling*) fermo(-a); (*regular*) costante; (*person, character*) serio(-a); (: *calm*) calmo(-a), tranquillo(-a) ▷ *vt* stabilizzare; calmare

steak [steɪk] *n* (*meat*) bistecca; (*fish*) trancia

steal [stiːl] (*pt* **stole**, *pp* **stolen**) *vt* rubare ▷ *vi* rubare; (*move*) muoversi furtivamente; **my wallet has been stolen** mi hanno rubato il portafoglio

steam [stiːm] *n* vapore *m* ▷ *vt* (*Culin*) cuocere a vapore ▷ *vi* fumare; **steam up** *vi* (*window*) appannarsi; **to get ~ed up about sth** (*fig*) andare in bestia per qc; **steamy** *adj* (*room*) pieno(-a) di vapore; (*window*) appannato(-a)

steel [stiːl] *n* acciaio ▷ *adj* di acciaio

steep [stiːp] *adj* ripido(-a), scosceso(-a); (*price*) eccessivo(-a) ▷ *vt* inzuppare; (*washing*) mettere a mollo

steeple ['stiːpl] *n* campanile *m*

steer [stɪəʳ] *vt* guidare ▷ *vi* (*Naut: person*) governare; (*car*) guidarsi; **steering** *n* (*Aut*) sterzo; **steering wheel** *n* volante *m*

stem [stɛm] *n* (*of flower, plant*) stelo; (*of tree*) fusto; (*of glass*) gambo; (*of fruit, leaf*) picciolo ▷ *vt* contenere, arginare

step [stɛp] *n* passo; (*stair*) gradino, scalino; (*action*) mossa, azione *f* ▷ *vi* **to ~ forward/back** fare un passo avanti/indietro; **~s** *npl* (*BRIT*) = **stepladder**; **to be in/out of ~ (with)** stare/non stare al passo (con); **step down** *vi* (*fig*) ritirarsi; **step in** *vi* fare il proprio ingresso; **step up** *vt* aumentare; intensificare; **stepbrother** *n* fratellastro; **stepchild** *n* figliastro(-a); **stepdaughter** *n* figliastra; **stepfather** *n* patrigno; **stepladder** *n* scala a libretto; **stepmother** *n* matrigna; **stepsister** *n* sorellastra; **stepson** *n* figliastro

stereo ['stɛrɪəʊ] *n* (*system*) sistema *m* stereofonico; (*record player*) stereo *m inv* ▷ *adj* (*also:* **~phonic**) stereofonico(-a)

stereotype ['stɪərɪətaɪp] *n* stereotipo

sterile ['stɛraɪl] *adj* sterile; **sterilize** ['stɛrɪlaɪz] *vt* sterilizzare

sterling ['stəːlɪŋ] *adj* (*gold, silver*) di buona lega ▷ *n* (*Econ*) (*lira*) sterlina; **a pound ~** una lira sterlina

stern [stəːn] *adj* severo(-a) ▷ *n* (*Naut*) poppa

steroid ['stɪərɔɪd] *n* steroide *m*

stew [stjuː] *n* stufato ▷ *vt* cuocere in umido

steward ['stjuːəd] *n* (*Aviat, Naut, Rail*) steward *m inv*; (*in club etc*) dispensiere *m*; **stewardess** *n* assistente *f* di volo, hostess *f inv*

stick [stɪk] (*pt*, *pp* **stuck**) *n* bastone *m*; (*of rhubarb, celery*) gambo; (*of dynamite*) candelotto ▷ *vt* (*glue*) attaccare; (*thrust*): **to ~ sth into** conficcare *or* piantare *or* infiggere qc in; (*inf*: *put*) ficcare; (*inf*:

tolerate) sopportare ▷ *vi* attaccarsi; (*remain*) restare, rimanere; **stick out** *vi* sporgere, spuntare; **stick up** *vi* sporgere, spuntare; **stick up for** *vt fus* difendere; **sticker** *n* cartellino adesivo; **sticking plaster** *n* cerotto adesivo; **stick shift** (*US*) *n* (*Aut*) cambio manuale

sticky ['stɪkɪ] *adj* attaccaticcio(-a), vischioso(-a); (*label*) adesivo(-a); (*fig*: *situation*) difficile

stiff [stɪf] *adj* rigido(-a), duro(-a); (*muscle*) legato(-a), indolenzito(-a); (*difficult*) difficile, arduo(-a); (*cold*) freddo(-a), formale; (*strong*) forte; (*high*: *price*) molto alto(-a) ▷ *adv* **bored ~** annoiato(-a) a morte

stifling ['staɪflɪŋ] *adj* (*heat*) soffocante

stigma ['stɪgmə] *n* (*fig*) stigma *m*

stiletto [stɪ'lɛtəʊ] (*BRIT*) *n* (*also:* **~ heel**) tacco a spillo

still [stɪl] *adj* fermo(-a); silenzioso(-a) ▷ *adv* (*up to this time, even*) ancora; (*nonetheless*) tuttavia, ciò nonostante

stimulate ['stɪmjʊleɪt] *vt* stimolare

stimulus ['stɪmjʊləs] (*pl* **stimuli**) *n* stimolo

sting [stɪŋ] (*pt*, *pp* **stung**) *n* puntura; (*organ*) pungiglione *m* ▷ *vt* pungere

stink [stɪŋk] (*pt* **stank**, *pp* **stunk**) *n* fetore *m*, puzzo ▷ *vi* puzzare

stir [stəːʳ] *n* agitazione *f*, clamore *m* ▷ *vt* mescolare; (*fig*) risvegliare ▷ *vt* muoversi; **stir up** *vt* provocare, suscitare; **stir-fry** *vt* saltare in padella ▷ *n* pietanza al salto

stitch [stɪtʃ] *n* (*Sewing*) punto; (*Knitting*) maglia; (*Med*) punto (di sutura); (*pain*) fitta ▷ *vt* cucire, attaccare; suturare

stock [stɔk] *n* riserva, provvista; (*Comm*) giacenza, stock *m inv*; (*Agr*) bestiame *m*; (*Culin*) brodo; (*descent*) stirpe *f*; (*Finance*) titoli *mpl*; azioni *fpl* ▷ *adj* (*fig*: *reply etc*) consueto(-a); classico(-a) ▷ *vt* (*have in stock*) avere, vendere; **~s and shares** valori *mpl* di borsa; **in ~** in magazzino; **out of ~** esaurito(-a); **stockbroker** ['stɔkbrəʊkəʳ] *n* agente *m* di cambio; **stock cube** (*BRIT*) *n* dado; **stock exchange** *n* Borsa (valori); **stockholder** ['stɔkhəʊldəʳ] *n* (*Finance*) azionista *m/f*

stocking ['stɔkɪŋ] *n* calza

stock market *n* Borsa, mercato finanziario

stole [stəʊl] *pt of* **steal** ▷ *n* stola

stolen ['stəʊln] *pp of* **steal**

stomach ['stʌmək] *n* stomaco; (*belly*) pancia ▷ *vt* sopportare, digerire; **stomachache** *n* mal *m* di stomaco

stone [stəʊn] *n* pietra; (*pebble*) sasso, ciottolo; (*in fruit*) nocciolo; (*Med*) calcolo;

(BRIT: *weight*) = 6.348 kg; 14 *libbre* ▷ *adj*
di pietra ▷ *vt* lapidare; (*fruit*) togliere il
nocciolo a
stood [stud] *pt, pp of* **stand**
stool [stu:l] *n* sgabello
stoop [stu:p] *vi* (*also:* **have a ~**) avere una
curvatura; (*also:* **~ down**) chinarsi, curvarsi
stop [stɔp] *n* arresto; (*stopping place*)
fermata; (*in punctuation*) punto
▷ *vt* arrestare, fermare; (*break off*)
interrompere; (*also:* **put a ~ to**) porre fine
a ▷ *vi* fermarsi; (*rain, noise etc*) cessare,
finire; **to ~ doing sth** cessare *or* finire di
fare qc; **could you ~ here/at the corner?**
può fermarsi qui/all'angolo?; **to ~ dead**
fermarsi di colpo; **stop by** *vi* passare, fare
un salto; **stop off** *vi* sostare brevemente;
stopover *n* breve sosta; (*Aviat*) scalo;
stoppage ['stɔpɪdʒ] *n* arresto, fermata;
(*of pay*) trattenuta; (*strike*) interruzione *f*
del lavoro
storage ['stɔ:rɪdʒ] *n* immagazzinamento
store [stɔ:ʳ] *n* provvista, riserva; (*depot*)
deposito; (BRIT: *department store*) grande
magazzino; (US: *shop*) negozio ▷ *vt*
immagazzinare; **~s** *npl* (*provisions*)
rifornimenti *mpl*, scorte *fpl*; **in ~** di riserva,
in serbo; **storekeeper** (US) *n* negoziante
m/f
storey ['stɔ:rɪ] (US **story**) *n* piano
storm [stɔ:m] *n* tempesta, temporale
m, burrasca; uragano ▷ *vi* (*fig*) infuriarsi
▷ *vt* prendere d'assalto; **stormy** *adj*
tempestoso(-a), burrascoso(-a)
story ['stɔ:rɪ] *n* storia; favola; racconto;
(US) = **storey**
stout [staut] *adj* solido(-a), robusto(-a);
(*friend, supporter*) tenace; (*fat*)
corpulento(-a), grasso(-a) ▷ *n* birra scura
stove [stəuv] *n* (*for cooking*) fornello; (:
small) fornelletto; (*for heating*) stufa
straight [streɪt] *adj* dritto(-a); (*frank*)
onesto(-a), franco(-a); (*simple*) semplice
▷ *adv* diritto; (*drink*) liscio; **to put** *or* **get**
~ mettere in ordine, mettere ordine in; **~**
away, ~ off (*at once*) immediatamente;
straighten *vt* (*also:* **straighten out**)
raddrizzare; **straightforward** *adj*
semplice; onesto(-a), franco(-a)
strain [streɪn] *n* (*Tech*) sollecitazione
f; (*physical*) sforzo; (*mental*) tensione *f*;
(*Med*) strappo; distorsione *f*; (*streak, trace*)
tendenza; elemento ▷ *vt* tendere; (*muscle*)
sforzare; (*ankle*) storcere; (*resources*) pesare
su; (*food*) colare; passare; **strained** *adj*
(*muscle*) stirato(-a); (*laugh etc*) forzato(-a);
(*relations*) teso(-a); **strainer** *n* passino,
colino
strait [streɪt] *n* (*Geo*) stretto; **~s** *npl* **to be**

in dire ~s (*fig*) essere nei guai
strand [strænd] *n* (*of thread*) filo; **stranded**
adj nei guai; senza mezzi di trasporto
strange [streɪndʒ] *adj* (*not known*)
sconosciuto(-a); (*odd*) strano(-a),
bizzarro(-a); **strangely** *adv* stranamente;
stranger *n* sconosciuto(-a); estraneo(-a)
strangle ['stræŋgl] *vt* strangolare
strap [stræp] *n* cinghia; (*of slip, dress*)
spallina, bretella
strategic [strə'ti:dʒɪk] *adj* strategico(-a)
strategy ['strætɪdʒɪ] *n* strategia
straw [strɔ:] *n* paglia; (*drinking straw*)
cannuccia; **that's the last ~!** è la goccia
che fa traboccare il vaso!
strawberry ['strɔ:bərɪ] *n* fragola
stray [streɪ] *adj* (*animal*) randagio(-a);
(*bullet*) vagante; (*scattered*) sparso(-a) ▷ *vi*
perdersi
streak [stri:k] *n* striscia; (*of hair*) mèche
f inv ▷ *vt* striare, screziare ▷ *vi* **to ~ past**
passare come un fulmine
stream [stri:m] *n* ruscello; corrente *f*;
(*of people, smoke etc*) fiume *m* ▷ *vt* (*Scol*)
dividere in livelli di rendimento ▷ *vi*
scorrere; **to ~ in/out** entrare/uscire a fiotti
street [stri:t] *n* strada, via; **streetcar** (US)
n tram *m inv*; **street light** *n* lampione *m*;
street map *n* pianta (di una città)
street plan *n* pianta (di una città)
strength [streŋθ] *n* forza; **strengthen** *vt*
rinforzare; fortificare; consolidare
strenuous ['strenjuəs] *adj* vigoroso(-a),
energico(-a); (*tiring*) duro(-a), pesante
stress [stres] *n* (*force, pressure*) pressione *f*;
(*mental strain*) tensione *f*; (*accent*) accento
▷ *vt* insistere su, sottolineare; accentare;
stressed *adj* (*tense: person*) stressato(-a);
(*Ling, Poetry: syllable*) accentato(-a);
stressful *adj* (*job*) difficile, stressante
stretch [stretʃ] *n* (*of sand etc*) distesa
▷ *vt* stirarsi; (*extend*) **to ~ to** *or* **as far as**
estendersi fino a ▷ *vt* tendere, allungare;
(*spread*) distendere; (*fig*) spingere (al
massimo); **stretch out** *vi* allungarsi,
estendersi ▷ *vt* (*arm etc*) allungare,
tendere; (*to spread*) distendere
stretcher ['stretʃəʳ] *n* barella, lettiga
strict [strɪkt] *adj* (*severe*) rigido(-a),
severo(-a); (*precise*) preciso(-a), stretto(-a);
strictly *adv* severamente; rigorosamente,
strettamente
stride [straɪd] (*pt* **strode**, *pp* **stridden**) *n*
passo lungo ▷ *vi* camminare a grandi passi
strike [straɪk] (*pt, pp* **struck**) *n* sciopero;
(*of oil etc*) scoperta; (*attack*) attacco
▷ *vt* colpire; (*oil etc*) scoprire, trovare;
(*bargain*) fare; (*fig*): **the thought** *or* **it**
~s me that ... mi viene in mente che ...

▷ vi scioperare; (*attack*) attaccare; (*clock*)
suonare; **on ~** (*workers*) in sciopero; **to ~ a
match** accendere un fiammifero; **striker**
n scioperante m/f; (*Sport*) attaccante m;
striking adj che colpisce

string [strɪŋ] (*pt, pp* **strung**) n spago; (*row*)
fila; sequenza; catena; (*Mus*) corda ▷ vt
to ~ out disporre di fianco; **to ~ together**
(*words, ideas*) mettere insieme; **the ~s**
npl (*Mus*) gli archi; **to pull ~s for sb** (*fig*)
raccomandare qn

strip [strɪp] n striscia ▷ vt spogliare; (*paint*)
togliere; (*also:* **~ down**: *machine*) smontare
▷ vi spogliarsi; **strip off** vt (*paint etc*)
staccare ▷ vi (*person*) spogliarsi

stripe [straɪp] n striscia, riga; (*Mil, Police*)
gallone m; **striped** adj a strisce or righe

stripper ['strɪpər] n spogliarellista m/f

strip-search ['strɪpsɑːtʃ] vt **to ~ sb**
perquisire qn facendolo(-a) spogliare ▷ n
perquisizione (*facendo spogliare il perquisito*)

strive [straɪv] (*pt* **strove**, *pp* **striven**) vi **to
~ to do** sforzarsi di fare

strode [strəʊd] pt *of* **stride**

stroke [strəʊk] n colpo; (*Swimming*)
bracciata; (: *style*) stile m; (*Med*) colpo
apoplettico ▷ vt accarezzare; **at a ~** in un
attimo

stroll [strəʊl] n giretto, passeggiatina
▷ vi andare a spasso; **stroller** (*us*) n
passeggino

strong [strɒŋ] adj (*gen*) forte; (*sturdy: table,
fabric etc*) robusto(-a); **they are 50 ~** sono
in 50; **stronghold** n (*also fig*) roccaforte
f; **strongly** adv fortemente, con forza;
energicamente; vivamente

strove [strəʊv] pt *of* **strive**

struck [strʌk] pt, pp *of* **strike**

structure ['strʌktʃər] n struttura; (*building*)
costruzione f, fabbricato

struggle ['strʌgl] n lotta ▷ vi lottare

strung [strʌŋ] pt, pp *of* **string**

stub [stʌb] n mozzicone m; (*of ticket etc*)
matrice f, talloncino ▷ vt **to ~ one's toe**
urtare *or* sbattere il dito del piede; **stub
out** vt schiacciare

stubble ['stʌbl] n stoppia; (*on chin*) barba
ispida

stubborn ['stʌbən] adj testardo(-a),
ostinato(-a)

stuck [stʌk] pt, pp *of* **stick** ▷ adj (*jammed*)
bloccato(-a)

stud [stʌd] n bottoncino; borchia; (*also:*
~ earring) orecchino a pressione; (*also:*
~ farm) scuderia, allevamento di cavalli;
(*also:* **~ horse**) stallone m ▷ vt (*fig*): **~ded
with** tempestato(-a) di

student ['stjuːdənt] n studente(-essa)
▷ cpd studentesco(-a); universitario(-a);

degli studenti; **student driver** (*us*) n
conducente m/f principiante; **students'
union** n (*BRIT: association*) circolo
universitario; (: *building*) sede f del circolo
universitario

studio ['stjuːdɪəʊ] n studio; **studio flat**
(*us* **studio apartment**) n monolocale m

study ['stʌdɪ] n studio ▷ vt studiare;
esaminare ▷ vi studiare

stuff [stʌf] n roba; (*substance*) sostanza,
materiale m ▷ vt imbottire; (*Culin*) farcire;
(*dead animal*) impagliare; (*inf: push*) ficcare;
stuffing n imbottitura; (*Culin*) ripieno;
stuffy adj (*room*) mal ventilato(-a),
senz'aria; (*ideas*) antiquato(-a)

stumble ['stʌmbl] vi inciampare; **to ~
across** (*fig*) imbattersi in

stump [stʌmp] n ceppo; (*of limb*) moncone
m ▷ vt **to be ~ed** essere sconcertato(-a)

stun [stʌn] vt stordire; (*amaze*) sbalordire

stung [stʌŋ] pt, pp *of* **sting**

stunk [stʌŋk] pp *of* **stink**

stunned [stʌnd] adj (*from blow*)
stordito(-a); (*amazed, shocked*)
sbalordito(-a)

stunning ['stʌnɪŋ] adj sbalorditivo(-a);
(*girl etc*) fantastico(-a)

stunt [stʌnt] n bravata; trucco
pubblicitario

stupid ['stjuːpɪd] adj stupido(-a);
stupidity [-'pɪdɪtɪ] n stupidità f inv,
stupidaggine f

sturdy ['stɜːdɪ] adj robusto(-a),
vigoroso(-a); solido(-a)

stutter ['stʌtər] n balbuzie f ▷ vi balbettare

style [staɪl] n stile m; (*distinction*) eleganza,
classe f; **stylish** adj elegante; **stylist** n
hair stylist parrucchiere(-a)

sub... [sʌb] prefix sub..., sotto...;
subconscious adj subcosciente ▷ n
subcosciente m

subdued [səb'djuːd] adj pacato(-a); (*light*)
attenuato(-a)

subject [n 'sʌbdʒɪkt, vb səb'dʒɛkt] n
soggetto; (*citizen etc*) cittadino(-a);
(*Scol*) materia ▷ vt sottomettere
a; esporre a; **to be ~ to** (*law*) essere
sottomesso(-a) a; (*disease*) essere
soggetto(-a) a; **subjective** [-'dʒɛktɪv]
adj soggettivo(-a); **subject matter** n
argomento; contenuto

subjunctive [səb'dʒʌŋktɪv] adj
congiuntivo(-a) ▷ n congiuntivo

submarine [sʌbmə'riːn] n sommergibile
m

submission [səb'mɪʃən] n sottomissione
f; (*claim*) richiesta

submit [səb'mɪt] vt sottomettere ▷ vi
sottomettersi

subordinate [sə'bɔ:dɪnət] *adj, n* subordinato(-a)

subscribe [səb'skraɪb] *vi* contribuire; **to ~ to** (*opinion*) approvare, condividere; (*fund*) sottoscrivere a; (*newspaper*) abbonarsi a; essere abbonato(-a) a

subscription [səb'skrɪpʃən] *n* sottoscrizione *f*; abbonamento

subsequent ['sʌbsɪkwənt] *adj* successivo(-a), seguente; conseguente; **subsequently** *adv* in seguito, successivamente

subside [səb'saɪd] *vi* cedere, abbassarsi; (*flood*) decrescere; (*wind*) calmarsi

subsidiary [səb'sɪdɪərɪ] *adj* sussidiario(-a); accessorio(-a) ▷ *n* filiale *f*

subsidize ['sʌbsɪdaɪz] *vt* sovvenzionare

subsidy ['sʌbsɪdɪ] *n* sovvenzione *f*

substance ['sʌbstəns] *n* sostanza

substantial [səb'stænʃl] *adj* solido(-a); (*amount, progress etc*) notevole; (*meal*) sostanzioso(-a)

substitute ['sʌbstɪtju:t] *n* (*person*) sostituto(-a); (*thing*) succedaneo, surrogato ▷ *vt* **to ~ sth/sb for** sostituire qc/qn a; **substitution** [sʌbstɪ'tju:ʃən] *n* sostituzione *f*

subtle ['sʌtl] *adj* sottile

subtract [səb'trækt] *vt* sottrarre

suburb ['sʌbə:b] *n* sobborgo; **the ~s** la periferia; **suburban** [sə'bə:bən] *adj* suburbano(-a)

subway ['sʌbweɪ] *n* (*US: underground*) metropolitana; (*BRIT: underpass*) sottopassaggio

succeed [sək'si:d] *vi* riuscire; avere successo ▷ *vt* succedere a; **to ~ in doing** riuscire a fare

success [sək'ses] *n* successo; **successful** *adj* (*venture*) coronato(-a) da successo, riuscito(-a); **to be successful (in doing)** riuscire (a fare); **successfully** *adv* con successo

succession [sək'seʃən] *n* successione *f*

successive [sək'sesɪv] *adj* successivo(-a); consecutivo(-a)

successor [sək'sesə'] *n* successore *m*

succumb [sə'kʌm] *vi* soccombere

such [sʌtʃ] *adj* tale; (*of that kind*): **~ a book** un tale libro, un libro di questo genere; **~ books** tali libri, libri di questo genere; (*so much*): **~ courage** tanto coraggio ▷ *adv* talmente, così; **~ a long trip** un viaggio così lungo; **~ a lot of** talmente *or* così tanto(-a); **~ as** (*like*) come; **~ as** come *or* in quanto tale; **such-and-such** *adj* tale (*after noun*)

suck [sʌk] *vt* succhiare; (*breast, bottle*) poppare

Sudan [su:'dɑ:n] *n* Sudan *m*

sudden ['sʌdn] *adj* improvviso(-a); **all of a ~** improvvisamente, all'improvviso; **suddenly** *adv* bruscamente, improvvisamente, di colpo

sue [su:] *vt* citare in giudizio

suede [sweɪd] *n* pelle *f* scamosciata

suffer ['sʌfə'] *vt* soffrire, patire; (*bear*) sopportare, tollerare ▷ *vi* soffrire; **to ~ from** soffrire di; **suffering** *n* sofferenza

suffice [sə'faɪs] *vi* essere sufficiente, bastare

sufficient [sə'fɪʃənt] *adj* sufficiente; **~ money** abbastanza soldi

suffocate ['sʌfəkeɪt] *vi* (*have difficulty breathing*) soffocare; (*die through lack of air*) asfissiare

sugar ['ʃugə'] *n* zucchero ▷ *vt* zuccherare

suggest [sə'dʒest] *vt* proporre, suggerire; indicare; **suggestion** [-'dʒestʃən] *n* suggerimento, proposta; indicazione *f*

suicide ['suɪsaɪd] *n* (*person*) suicida *m/f*; (*act*) suicidio; *see also* **commit**; **suicide bombing** *n* attentato suicida

suit [su:t] *n* (*man's*) vestito; (*woman's*) completo, tailleur *m inv*; (*Law*) causa; (*Cards*) seme *m*, colore *m* ▷ *vt* andar bene a *or* per; essere adatto(-a) a *or* per; (*adapt*): **to ~ sth to** adattare qc a; **well ~ed** ben assortito(-a); **suitable** *adj* adatto(-a); appropriato(-a); **suitcase** ['su:tkeɪs] *n* valigia

suite [swi:t] *n* (*of rooms*) appartamento; (*Mus*) suite *f inv*; (*furniture*): **bedroom/ dining room ~** arredo *or* mobilia per la camera da letto/sala da pranzo

sulfur ['sʌlfə'] (*US*) *n* = **sulphur**

sulk [sʌlk] *vi* fare il broncio

sulphur ['sʌlfə'] (*US* **sulfur**) *n* zolfo

sultana [sʌl'tɑ:nə] *n* (*fruit*) uva (secca) sultanina

sum [sʌm] *n* somma; (*Scol etc*) addizione *f*; **sum up** *vt, vi* riassumere

summarize ['sʌmərɑɪz] *vt* riassumere, riepilogare

summary ['sʌmərɪ] *n* riassunto

summer ['sʌmə'] *n* estate *f* ▷ *cpd* d'estate, estivo(-a); **summer holidays** *npl* vacanze *fpl* estive; **summertime** *n* (*season*) estate *f*

summit ['sʌmɪt] *n* cima, sommità; (*Pol*) vertice *m*

summon ['sʌmən] *vt* chiamare, convocare

Sun. *abbr* (= *Sunday*)

sun [sʌn] *n* sole *m*; **sunbathe** *vi* prendere un bagno di sole; **sunbed** *n* lettino solare; **sunblock** *n* protezione *f* solare totale; **sunburn** *n* (*painful*) scottatura; **sunburned, sunburnt** *adj* abbronzato(-a); (*painfully*) scottato(-a)

Sunday ['sʌndɪ] *n* domenica

Sunday paper n giornale m della domenica

❋ **SUNDAY PAPER**
❋
❋ I **Sunday papers** sono i giornali
❋ che escono di domenica. Sono
❋ generalmente corredati da supplementi
❋ e riviste di argomento culturale,
❋ sportivo e di attualità.

sunflower ['sʌnflauəʳ] n girasole m
sung [sʌŋ] pp of **sing**
sunglasses ['sʌnglɑːsɪz] npl occhiali mpl da sole
sunk [sʌŋk] pp of **sink**
sun: **sunlight** n (luce f del) sole m; **sun lounger** n sedia a sdraio; **sunny** adj assolato(-a), soleggiato(-a); (fig) allegro(-a), felice; **sunrise** n levata del sole, alba; **sun roof** n (Aut) tetto apribile; **sunscreen** n (cream) crema solare protettiva; **sunset** n tramonto; **sunshade** n parasole m; **sunshine** n luce f (del) sole m; **sunstroke** n insolazione f, colpo di sole; **suntan** n abbronzatura; **suntan lotion** n lozione f solare; **suntan oil** n olio solare
super ['suːpəʳ] (inf) adj fantastico(-a)
superb [suːˈpəːb] adj magnifico(-a)
superficial [suːpəˈfɪʃəl] adj superficiale
superintendent [suːpərɪnˈtɛndənt] n direttore(-trice); (Police) ≈ commissario (capo)
superior [suˈpɪərɪəʳ] adj, n superiore m/f
superlative [suˈpəːlətɪv] adj superlativo(-a), supremo(-a) ▷ n (Ling) superlativo
supermarket ['suːpəmɑːkɪt] n supermercato
supernatural [suːpəˈnætʃərəl] adj soprannaturale ▷ n soprannaturale m
superpower ['suːpəpauəʳ] n (Pol) superpotenza
superstition [suːpəˈstɪʃən] n superstizione f
superstitious [suːpəˈstɪʃəs] adj superstizioso(-a)
superstore ['suːpəstɔːʳ] n (Brit) grande supermercato
supervise ['suːpəvaɪz] vt (person etc) sorvegliare; (organization) soprintendere a; **supervision** [-ˈvɪʒən] n sorveglianza; supervisione f; **supervisor** n sorvegliante m/f; soprintendente m/f; (in shop) capocommesso(-a)
supper ['sʌpəʳ] n cena
supple ['sʌpl] adj flessibile; agile
supplement [n 'sʌplɪmənt, vb sʌplɪˈmɛnt]

n supplemento ▷ vt completare, integrare
supplier [səˈplaɪəʳ] n fornitore m
supply [səˈplaɪ] vt (provide) fornire; (equip): **to ~ (with)** approvvigionare (di), attrezzare (con) ▷ n riserva, provvista; (supplying) approvvigionamento; (Tech) alimentazione f; **supplies** npl (food) viveri mpl; (Mil) sussistenza
support [səˈpɔːt] n (moral, financial etc) sostegno, appoggio; (Tech) supporto ▷ vt sostenere; (financially) mantenere; (uphold) sostenere, difendere; **supporter** n (Pol etc) sostenitore(-trice), fautore(-trice); (Sport) tifoso(-a)

▐ Be careful not to translate **support** by the Italian word **sopportare**.

suppose [səˈpəuz] vt supporre; immaginare; **to be ~d to do** essere tenuto(-a) a fare; **supposedly** [səˈpəuzɪdlɪ] adv presumibilmente; **supposing** conj se, ammesso che + sub
suppress [səˈprɛs] vt reprimere; sopprimere; occultare
supreme [suˈpriːm] adj supremo(-a)
surcharge ['səːtʃɑːdʒ] n supplemento
sure [ʃuəʳ] adj sicuro(-a); (definite, convinced) sicuro(-a), certo(-a); **~! (**of course) senz'altro!, certo!; **~ enough** infatti; **to make ~ of sth/that** assicurarsi di qc/che; **surely** adv sicuramente; certamente
surf [səːf] n (waves) cavalloni mpl; (foam) spuma
surface ['səːfɪs] n superficie f ▷ vt (road) asfaltare ▷ vi risalire alla superficie; (fig: news, feeling) venire a galla
surfboard ['səːfbɔːd] n tavola per surfing
surfing ['səːfɪŋ] n surfing m
surge [səːdʒ] n (strong movement) ondata; (of feeling) impeto ▷ vi gonfiarsi; (people) riversarsi
surgeon ['səːdʒən] n chirurgo
surgery ['səːdʒərɪ] n chirurgia; (Brit: room) studio or gabinetto medico, ambulatorio; (: also: **~ hours**) orario delle visite or di consultazione; **to undergo ~** subire un intervento chirurgico
surname ['səːneɪm] n cognome m
surpass [səːˈpɑːs] vt superare
surplus ['səːpləs] n eccedenza; (Econ) surplus m inv ▷ adj eccedente, d'avanzo
surprise [səˈpraɪz] n sorpresa; (astonishment) stupore m ▷ vt sorprendere; stupire; **surprised** [səˈpraɪzd] adj (look, smile) sorpreso(-a); **to be surprised** essere sorpreso, sorprendersi; **surprising** adj sorprendente, stupefacente; **surprisingly** adv (easy, helpful) sorprendentemente
surrender [səˈrɛndəʳ] n resa, capitolazione f ▷ vi arrendersi

surround [sə'raund] vt circondare;
(Mil etc) accerchiare; **surrounding** adj
circostante; **surroundings** npl dintorni
mpl; (fig) ambiente m

surveillance [sə'veɪləns] n sorveglianza,
controllo

survey [n 'sə:veɪ, vb sə:'veɪ] n quadro
generale; (study) esame m; (in housebuying
etc) perizia; (of land) rilevamento, rilievo
topografico ▷ vt osservare; esaminare;
valutare; rilevare; **surveyor** n perito;
geometra m; (of land) agrimensore m

survival [sə'vaɪvl] n sopravvivenza; (relic)
reliquia, vestigio

survive [sə'vaɪv] vi sopravvivere ▷ vt
sopravvivere a; (accident etc) sopravvivere;
survivor n superstite m/f,
sopravvissuto(-a)

suspect [adj, n 'sʌspɛkt, vb səs'pɛkt] adj
sospetto(-a) ▷ n persona sospetta ▷ vt
sospettare; (think likely) supporre; (doubt)
dubitare

suspend [səs'pɛnd] vt sospendere;
suspended sentence n condanna con
la condizionale; **suspenders** npl (BRIT)
giarrettiere fpl; (US) bretelle fpl

suspense [səs'pɛns] n apprensione f; (in
film etc) suspense m; **to keep sb in ~** tenere
qn in sospeso

suspension [səs'pɛnʃən] n (gen Aut)
sospensione f; (of driving licence) ritiro
temporaneo; **suspension bridge** n ponte
m sospeso

suspicion [səs'pɪʃən] n sospetto;
suspicious [səs'pɪʃəs] adj (suspecting)
sospettoso(-a); (causing suspicion)
sospetto(-a)

sustain [səs'teɪn] vt sostenere;
sopportare; (Law: charge) confermare;
(suffer) subire

swallow ['swɔləu] n (bird) rondine f ▷ vt
inghiottire; (fig: story) bere

swam [swæm] pt of **swim**

swamp [swɔmp] n palude f ▷ vt
sommergere

swan [swɔn] n cigno

swap [swɔp] vt **to ~ (for)** scambiare (con)

swarm [swɔ:m] n sciame m ▷ vi (bees)
sciamare; (people) brulicare; (place): **to be
~ing with** brulicare di

sway [sweɪ] vi (tree) ondeggiare; (person)
barcollare ▷ vt (influence) influenzare,
dominare

swear [swɛəʳ] (pt swore, pp sworn) vi
(curse) bestemmiare, imprecare ▷ vt
(promise) giurare; **swear in** vt prestare
giuramento a; **swearword** n parolaccia

sweat [swɛt] n sudore m, traspirazione f
▷ vi sudare

sweater ['swɛtəʳ] n maglione m

sweatshirt ['swɛtʃə:t] n felpa

sweaty ['swɛtɪ] adj sudato(-a),
bagnato(-a) di sudore

Swede [swi:d] n svedese m/f

swede [swi:d] (BRIT) n rapa svedese

Sweden ['swi:dn] n Svezia; **Swedish** ['swi:
dɪʃ] adj svedese ▷ n (Ling) svedese m

sweep [swi:p] (pt, pp swept) n spazzata;
(also: **chimney ~**) spazzacamino ▷ vt
spazzare, scopare; (current) spazzare ▷ vi
(hand) muoversi con gesto ampio; (wind)
infuriare

sweet [swi:t] n (BRIT: pudding) dolce m;
(candy) caramella ▷ adj dolce; (fresh)
fresco(-a); (fig) piacevole; delicato(-a),
grazioso(-a); gentile; **sweetcorn** n
granturco dolce; **sweetener** ['swi:tnəʳ]
n (Culin) dolcificante m; **sweetheart** n
innamorato(-a); **sweetshop** n (BRIT)
= pasticceria

swell [swɛl] (pt swelled, pp swollen,
swelled) n (of sea) mare m lungo ▷ adj (US:
inf: excellent) favoloso(-a) ▷ vt gonfiare,
ingrossare; aumentare ▷ vi gonfiarsi,
ingrossarsi; (sound) crescere; (also: **~ up**)
gonfiarsi; **swelling** n (Med) tumefazione
f, gonfiore m

swept [swɛpt] pt, pp of **sweep**

swerve [swə:v] vi deviare; (driver) sterzare;
(boxer) scartare

swift [swɪft] n (bird) rondone m ▷ adj
rapido(-a), veloce

swim [swɪm] (pt swam, pp swum) n **to
go for a ~** andare a fare una nuotata ▷ vi
nuotare; (Sport) fare del nuoto; (head, room)
girare ▷ vt (river, channel) attraversare
or percorrere a nuoto; (length) nuotare;
swimmer n nuotatore(-trice); **swimming**
n nuoto; **swimming costume** (BRIT) n
costume m da bagno; **swimming pool** n
piscina; **swimming trunks** npl costume
m da bagno (da uomo); **swimsuit** n
costume m da bagno

swing [swɪŋ] (pt, pp swung) n altalena;
(movement) oscillazione f; (Mus) ritmo;
swing m ▷ vt dondolare, far oscillare;
(also: **~ round**) far girare ▷ vi oscillare,
dondolare; (also: **~ round**: object) roteare;
(: person) girarsi, voltarsi; **to be in full ~**
(activity) essere in piena attività; (party etc)
essere nel pieno

swipe card n tessera magnetica

swirl [swə:l] vi turbinare, far mulinello

Swiss [swɪs] adj, n inv svizzero(-a)

switch [swɪtʃ] n (for light, radio etc)
interruttore m; (change) cambiamento
▷ vt (change) cambiare; scambiare; **switch
off** vt spegnere; **could you ~ off the
light?** puoi spegnere la luce?; **switch on**

vt accendere; *(engine, machine)* mettere in moto, avviare; **switchboard** *n* (*Tel*) centralino

Switzerland ['swɪtsələnd] *n* Svizzera

swivel ['swɪvl] *vi (also:* **~ round**) girare

swollen ['swəulən] *pp of* **swell**

swoop [swu:p] *n* incursione *f* ▷ *vi (also:* **~ down**) scendere in picchiata, piombare

swop [swɔp] *n, vt* = **swap**

sword [sɔːd] *n* spada; **swordfish** *n* pesce *m* spada *inv*

swore [swɔːʳ] *pt of* **swear**

sworn [swɔːn] *pp of* **swear** ▷ *adj* giurato(-a)

swum [swʌm] *pp of* **swim**

swung [swʌŋ] *pt, pp of* **swing**

syllable ['sɪləbl] *n* sillaba

syllabus ['sɪləbəs] *n* programma *m*

symbol ['sɪmbl] *n* simbolo; **symbolic(al)** [sɪm'bɔlɪk(l)] *adj* simbolico(-a); **to be symbolic(al) of sth** simboleggiare qc

symmetrical [sɪ'mɛtrɪkl] *adj* simmetrico(-a)

symmetry ['sɪmɪtrɪ] *n* simmetria

sympathetic [sɪmpə'θɛtɪk] *adj (showing pity)* compassionevole; *(kind)* comprensivo(-a); **~ towards** ben disposto(a) verso

> Be careful not to translate *sympathetic* by the Italian word *simpatico*.

sympathize ['sɪmpəθaɪz] *vi* **to ~ with** *(person)* compatire; partecipare al dolore di; *(cause)* simpatizzare per

sympathy ['sɪmpəθɪ] *n* compassione *f*

symphony ['sɪmfənɪ] *n* sinfonia

symptom ['sɪmptəm] *n* sintomo; indizio

synagogue ['sɪnəgɔg] *n* sinagoga

syndicate ['sɪndɪkɪt] *n* sindacato

syndrome ['sɪndrəum] *n* sindrome *f*

synonym ['sɪnənɪm] *n* sinonimo

synthetic [sɪn'θɛtɪk] *adj* sintetico(-a)

Syria ['sɪrɪə] *n* Siria

syringe [sɪ'rɪndʒ] *n* siringa

syrup ['sɪrəp] *n* sciroppo; *(also:* **golden ~**) melassa raffinata

system ['sɪstəm] *n* sistema *m*; *(order)* metodo; *(Anat)* organismo; **systematic** [-'mætɪk] *adj* sistematico(-a); metodico(-a); **systems analyst** *n* analista *m* di sistemi

ta [tɑː] (*BRIT: inf*) *excl* grazie!

tab [tæb] *n (loop on coat etc)* laccetto; *(label)* etichetta; **to keep ~s on** *(fig)* tenere d'occhio

table ['teɪbl] *n* tavolo, tavola; *(Math, Chem etc)* tavola ▷ *vt (BRIT: motion etc)* presentare; **a ~ for 4, please** un tavolo per 4, per favore; **to lay** *or* **set the ~** apparecchiare *or* preparare la tavola; **tablecloth** *n* tovaglia; **table d'hôte** [tɑːbl'dəut] *adj (meal)* a prezzo fisso; **table lamp** *n* lampada da tavolo; **tablemat** *n* sottopiatto; **tablespoon** *n* cucchiaio da tavola; *(also:* **tablespoonful**: *as measurement)* cucchiaiata

tablet ['tæblɪt] *n (Med)* compressa; *(of stone)* targa

table tennis *n* tennis *m* da tavolo, ping-pong® *m*

tabloid ['tæblɔɪd] *n (newspaper)* tabloid *m inv (giornale illustrato di formato ridotto)*; **the ~s, the ~ press** i giornali popolari

taboo [tə'buː] *adj, n* tabù *m inv*

tack [tæk] *n (nail)* bulletta; *(fig)* approccio ▷ *vt* imbullettare; imbastire ▷ *vi* bordeggiare

tackle ['tækl] *n* attrezzatura, equipaggiamento; *(for lifting)* paranco; *(Football)* contrasto; *(Rugby)* placcaggio ▷ *vt (difficulty)* affrontare; *(Football)* contrastare; (*Rugby*) placcare

tacky ['tækɪ] *adj* appiccicaticcio(-a); (*pej*) scadente

tact [tækt] *n* tatto: **tactful** *adj* delicato(-a), discreto(-a)

tactics ['tæktɪks] *n*, *npl* tattica

tactless ['tæktlɪs] *adj* che manca di tatto

tadpole ['tædpəʊl] *n* girino

taffy ['tæfɪ] (*US*) *n* caramella *f* mou *inv*

tag [tæg] *n* etichetta

tail [teɪl] *n* coda; (*of shirt*) falda ▷ *vt* (*follow*) seguire, pedinare; **~s** *npl* (*formal suit*) frac *m inv*

tailor ['teɪlə*] *n* sarto

Taiwan [taɪ'wɑːn] *n* Taiwan *m*; **Taiwanese** [taɪwə'niːz] *adj*, *n* taiwanese

take [teɪk] (*pt* **took**, *pp* **taken**) *vt* prendere; (*gain: prize*) ottenere, vincere; (*require: effort, courage*) occorrere, volerci; (*tolerate*) accettare, sopportare; (*hold: passengers etc*) contenere; (*accompany*) accompagnare; (*bring, carry*) portare; (*exam*) sostenere, presentarsi a; **to ~ a photo/a shower** fare una fotografia/una doccia; **I ~ it that** suppongo che; **take after** *vt fus* assomigliare a; **take apart** *vt* smontare; **take away** *vt* portare via; togliere; **take back** *vt* (*return*) restituire; riportare; (*one's words*) ritirare; **take down** *vt* (*building*) demolire; (*letter etc*) scrivere; **take in** *vt* (*deceive*) imbrogliare, abbindolare; (*understand*) capire; (*include*) comprendere, includere; (*lodger*) prendere, ospitare; **take off** *vi* (*Aviat*) decollare; (*go away*) andarsene ▷ *vt* (*remove*) togliere; **take on** *vt* (*work*) accettare, intraprendere; (*employee*) assumere; (*opponent*) sfidare, affrontare; **take out** *vt* portare fuori; (*remove*) togliere; (*licence*) prendere, ottenere; **to ~ sth out of sth** (*drawer, pocket etc*) tirare qc fuori da qc; estrarre qc da qc; **take over** *vt* (*business*) rilevare ▷ *vi* **to ~ over from sb** prendere le consegne *or* il controllo da qn; **take up** *vt* (*dress*) accorciare; (*occupy: time, space*) occupare; (*engage in: hobby etc*) mettersi a; **to ~ sb up on sth** accettare qc da qn; **takeaway** (*BRIT*) *n* (*shop etc*) ≈ rosticceria; (*food*) pasto per asporto; **taken** *pp* of **take**; **takeoff** *n* (*Aviat*) decollo; **takeout** (*US*) *n* = **takeaway**; **takeover** *n* (*Comm*) assorbimento; **takings** ['teɪkɪŋz] *npl* (*Comm*) incasso

talc [tælk] *n* (*also:* **~um powder**) talco

tale [teɪl] *n* racconto, storia; **to tell ~s** (*fig: to teacher, parent etc*) fare la spia

talent ['tælnt] *n* talento; **talented** *adj* di talento

talk [tɔːk] *n* discorso; (*gossip*) chiacchiere

fpl; (*conversation*) conversazione *f*; (*interview*) discussione *f* ▷ *vi* parlare; **~s** *npl* (*Pol etc*) colloqui *mpl*; **to ~ about** parlare di; **to ~ sb out of/into doing** dissuadere qn da/convincere qn a fare; **to ~ shop** parlare di lavoro *or* di affari; **talk over** *vt* discutere; **talk show** *n* conversazione *f* televisiva, talk show *m inv*

tall [tɔːl] *adj* alto(-a); **to be 6 feet ~** ≈ essere alto 1 metro e 80

tambourine [tæmbə'riːn] *n* tamburello

tame [teɪm] *adj* addomesticato(-a); (*fig: story, style*) insipido(-a), scialbo(-a)

tamper ['tæmpə*] *vi* **to ~ with** manomettere

tampon ['tæmpɔn] *n* tampone *m*

tan [tæn] *n* (*also:* **sun~**) abbronzatura ▷ *vi* abbronzarsi ▷ *adj* (*colour*) marrone rossiccio *inv*

tandem ['tændəm] *n* tandem *m inv*

tangerine [tændʒə'riːn] *n* mandarino

tangle ['tæŋgl] *n* groviglio; **to get into a ~** aggrovigliarsi; (*fig*) combinare un pasticcio

tank [tæŋk] *n* serbatoio; (*for fish*) acquario; (*Mil*) carro armato

tanker ['tæŋkə*] *n* (*ship*) nave *f* cisterna *inv*; (*truck*) autobotte *f*, autocisterna

tanned [tænd] *adj* abbronzato(-a)

tantrum ['tæntrəm] *n* accesso di collera

Tanzania [tænzə'nɪə] *n* Tanzania

tap [tæp] *n* (*on sink etc*) rubinetto; (*gentle blow*) colpetto ▷ *vt* dare un colpetto a; (*resources*) sfruttare, utilizzare; (*telephone*) mettere sotto controllo; **on ~** (*fig: resources*) a disposizione; **tap dancing** *n* tip tap *m*

tape [teɪp] *n* nastro; (*also:* **magnetic ~**) nastro (magnetico); (*sticky tape*) nastro adesivo ▷ *vt* (*record*) registrare (su nastro); (*stick*) attaccare con nastro adesivo; **tape measure** *n* metro a nastro; **tape recorder** *n* registratore *m* (a nastro)

tapestry ['tæpɪstrɪ] *n* arazzo; tappezzeria

tar [tɑː*] *n* catrame *m*

target ['tɑːgɪt] *n* bersaglio; (*fig: objective*) obiettivo

tariff ['tærɪf] *n* tariffa

tarmac ['tɑːmæk] *n* (*BRIT: on road*) macadam *m* al catrame; (*Aviat*) pista di decollo

tarpaulin [tɑː'pɔːlɪn] *n* tela incatramata

tarragon ['tærəgən] *n* dragoncello

tart [tɑːt] *n* (*Culin*) crostata; (*BRIT: inf: pej: woman*) sgualdrina ▷ *adj* (*flavour*) aspro(-a), acido(-a)

tartan ['tɑːtn] *n* tartan *m inv*

tartar(e) sauce *n* salsa tartara

task [tɑːsk] *n* compito; **to take to ~** rimproverare

taste [teɪst] n gusto; (flavour) sapore m, gusto; (sample) assaggio; (fig: glimpse, idea) idea ▷ vt gustare; (sample) assaggiare ▷ vi **to ~ of** or **like** (fish etc) sapere or avere sapore di; **in good/bad ~** di buon/cattivo gusto; **can I have a ~?** posso assaggiarlo?; **you can ~ the garlic (in it)** (ci) si sente il sapore dell'aglio; **tasteful** adj di buon gusto; **tasteless** adj (food) insipido(-a); (remark) di cattivo gusto; **tasty** adj saporito(-a), gustoso(-a)

tatters ['tætəz] npl **in ~ a** brandelli

tattoo [tə'tu:] n tatuaggio; (spectacle) parata militare ▷ vt tatuare

taught [tɔ:t] pt, pp of **teach**

taunt [tɔ:nt] n scherno ▷ vt schernire

Taurus ['tɔ:rəs] n Toro

taut [tɔ:t] adj teso(-a)

tax [tæks] n (on goods) imposta; (on services) tassa; (on income) imposte fpl, tasse fpl ▷ vt tassare; (fig: strain: patience etc) mettere alla prova; **tax-free** adj esente da imposte

taxi ['tæksɪ] n taxi m inv ▷ vi (Aviat) rullare; **can you call me a ~, please?** può chiamarmi un taxi, per favore?; **taxi driver** n tassista m/f; **taxi rank** (BRIT) n = **taxi stand**; **taxi stand** n posteggio dei taxi

tax payer n contribuente m/f

TB n abbr = **tuberculosis**

tea [ti:] n tè m inv; (BRIT: snack: for children) merenda; **high ~** (BRIT) cena leggera (presa nel tardo pomeriggio); **tea bag** n bustina di tè; **tea break** (BRIT) n intervallo per il tè

teach [ti:tʃ] (pt, pp **taught**) vt **to ~ sb sth, ~ sth to sb** insegnare qc a qn ▷ vi insegnare; **teacher** n insegnante m/f; (in secondary school) professore(-essa); (in primary school) maestro(-a); **teaching** n insegnamento

tea: tea cloth n (for dishes) strofinaccio; (BRIT: for trolley) tovaglietta da tè; **teacup** ['ti:kʌp] n tazza da tè

tea leaves npl foglie fpl di tè

team [ti:m] n squadra; (of animals) tiro; **team up** vi **to ~ up (with)** mettersi insieme (a)

teapot ['ti:pɔt] n teiera

tear¹ [tɛə*] (pt **tore**, pp **torn**) n strappo ▷ vt strappare ▷ vi strapparsi; **tear apart** vt (also fig) distruggere; **tear down** vt +adv (building, statue) demolire; (poster, flag) tirare giù; **tear off** vt (sheet of paper etc) strappare; (one's clothes) togliersi di dosso; **tear up** vt (sheet of paper etc) strappare

tear² [tɪə*] n lacrima; **in ~s** in lacrime; **tearful** ['tɪəful] adj piangente, lacrimoso(-a); **tear gas** n gas m lacrimogeno

tearoom ['ti:ru:m] n sala da tè

tease [ti:z] vt canzonare; (unkindly)

tormentare

tea: teaspoon n cucchiaino da tè; (also: **teaspoonful**) as measurement) cucchiaino; **teatime** n ora del tè; **tea towel** (BRIT) n strofinaccio (per i piatti)

technical ['tɛknɪkl] adj tecnico(-a)

technician [tɛk'nɪʃən] n tecnico(-a)

technique [tɛk'ni:k] n tecnica

technology [tɛk'nɔlədʒɪ] n tecnologia

teddy (bear) ['tɛdɪ-] n orsacchiotto

tedious ['ti:dɪəs] adj noioso(-a), tedioso(-a)

tee [ti:] n (Golf) tee m inv

teen [ti:n] adj = **teenage** ▷ n (US) = **teenager**

teenage ['ti:neɪdʒ] adj (fashions etc) per giovani, per adolescenti; **teenager** n adolescente m/f

teens [ti:nz] npl **to be in one's ~** essere adolescente

teeth [ti:θ] npl of **tooth**

teetotal ['ti:'təutl] adj astemio(-a)

telecommunications ['tɛlɪkəmju:nɪ'keɪʃənz] n telecomunicazioni fpl

telegram ['tɛlɪgræm] n telegramma m

telegraph pole n palo del telegrafo

telephone ['tɛlɪfəun] n telefono ▷ vt (person) telefonare a; (message) comunicare per telefono; **telephone book** n elenco telefonico; **telephone booth** (BRIT), **telephone box** n cabina telefonica; **telephone call** n telefonata; **telephone directory** n elenco telefonico; **telephone number** n numero di telefono

telesales ['tɛlɪseɪlz] n vendita per telefono

telescope ['tɛlɪskəup] n telescopio

televise ['tɛlɪvaɪz] vt teletrasmettere

television ['tɛlɪvɪʒən] n televisione f; **on ~** alla televisione; **television programme** n programma m televisivo

tell [tɛl] (pt, pp **told**) vt dire; (relate: story) raccontare; (distinguish): **to ~ sth from** distinguere qc da ▷ vi (talk): **to ~ (of)** parlare (di); (have effect) farsi sentire, avere effetto; **to ~ sb to do** dire a qn di fare; **tell off** vt rimproverare, sgridare; **teller** n (in bank) cassiere(-a)

telly ['tɛlɪ] (BRIT: inf) n abbr (= television) tivù f inv

temp [tɛmp] n abbr (= temporary) segretaria temporanea

temper ['tɛmpə*] n (nature) carattere m; (mood) umore m; (fit of anger) collera ▷ vt (moderate) moderare; **to be in a ~** essere in collera; **to lose one's ~** andare in collera

temperament ['tɛmprəmənt] n (nature) temperamento; **temperamental** [-'mɛntl] adj capriccioso(-a)

temperature ['tɛmprətʃə*] n

temperatura; **to have** or **run a ~** avere la febbre

temple ['tɛmpl] n (building) tempio; (Anat) tempia

temporary ['tɛmpərəri] adj temporaneo(-a); (job, worker) avventizio(-a), temporaneo(-a)

tempt [tɛmpt] vt tentare; **to ~ sb into doing** indurre qn a fare; **temptation** [-'teɪʃən] n tentazione f; **tempting** adj allettante

ten [tɛn] num dieci

tenant ['tɛnənt] n inquilino(-a)

tend [tɛnd] vt badare a, occuparsi di ▷ vi **to ~ to do** tendere a fare; **tendency** ['tɛndənsɪ] n tendenza

tender ['tɛndə^r] adj tenero(-a); (sore) dolorante ▷ n (Comm: offer) offerta; (money): **legal ~** moneta in corso legale ▷ vt offrire

tendon ['tɛndən] n tendine m

tenner ['tɛnə^r] n (BRIT inf) (banconota da) dieci sterline fpl

tennis ['tɛnɪs] n tennis m; **tennis ball** n palla da tennis; **tennis court** n campo da tennis; **tennis match** n partita di tennis; **tennis player** n tennista m/f; **tennis racket** n racchetta da tennis

tenor ['tɛnə^r] n (Mus) tenore m

tenpin bowling ['tɛnpɪn-] n bowling m

tense [tɛns] adj teso(-a) ▷ n (Ling) tempo

tension ['tɛnʃən] n tensione f

tent [tɛnt] n tenda

tentative ['tɛntətɪv] adj esitante, incerto(-a); (conclusion) provvisorio(-a)

tenth [tɛnθ] num decimo(-a)

tent: **tent peg** n picchetto da tenda; **tent pole** n palo da tenda, montante m

tepid ['tɛpɪd] adj tiepido(-a)

term [tə:m] n termine m; (Scol) trimestre m; (Law) sessione f ▷ vt chiamare, definire; **~s** npl (conditions) condizioni fpl; (Comm) prezzi mpl, tariffe fpl; **in the short/long ~** a breve/lunga scadenza; **to be on good ~s with sb** essere in buoni rapporti con qn; **to come to ~s with** (problem) affrontare

terminal ['tə:mɪnl] adj finale, terminale; (disease) terminale ▷ n (Elec) morsetto; (Comput) terminale m; (Aviat, for oil, ore etc) terminal m inv; (BRIT: also: **coach ~**) capolinea m

terminate ['tə:mɪneɪt] vt mettere fine a

termini ['tə:mɪnaɪ] npl of **terminus**

terminology [tə:mɪ'nɔlədʒɪ] n terminologia

terminus ['tə:mɪnəs] (pl **termini**) n (for buses) capolinea m; (for trains) stazione f terminale

terrace ['tɛrəs] n terrazza; (BRIT: row of houses) fila di case a schiera; **terraced** adj (garden) a terrazze

terrain [tɛ'reɪn] n terreno

terrestrial [tɪ'rɛstrɪəl] adj (life) terrestre; (BRIT: channel) terrestre

terrible ['tɛrɪbl] adj terribile; **terribly** adv terribilmente; (very badly) malissimo

terrier ['tɛrɪə^r] n terrier m inv

terrific [tə'rɪfɪk] adj incredibile, fantastico(-a); (wonderful) formidabile, eccezionale

terrified ['tɛrɪfaɪd] adj atterrito(-a)

terrify ['tɛrɪfaɪ] vt terrorizzare; **terrifying** adj terrificante

territorial [tɛrɪ'tɔ:rɪəl] adj territoriale

territory ['tɛrɪtərɪ] n territorio

terror ['tɛrə^r] n terrore m; **terrorism** n terrorismo; **terrorist** n terrorista m/f

test [tɛst] n (trial, check: of courage etc) prova; (Med) esame m; (Chem) analisi f inv; (exam: of intelligence etc) test m inv; (: in school) compito in classe; (also: **driving ~**) esame m di guida ▷ vt provare; esaminare; analizzare; sottoporre ad esame; **to ~ sb in history** esaminare qn in storia

testicle ['tɛstɪkl] n testicolo

testify ['tɛstɪfaɪ] vi (Law) testimoniare, deporre; **to ~ to sth** (Law) testimoniare qc; (gen) comprovare o dimostrare qc

testimony ['tɛstɪmənɪ] n (Law) testimonianza, deposizione f

test: **test match** n (Cricket, Rugby) partita internazionale; **test tube** n provetta

tetanus ['tɛtənəs] n tetano

text [tɛkst] n testo; (on mobile phone) SMS m inv, messaggino ▷ vt **to ~ sb** (inf) mandare un SMS a qn; **textbook** n libro di testo

textile ['tɛkstaɪl] n tessile m

text message n (Tel) SMS m inv, messaggino

text messaging [-'mɛsɪdʒɪŋ] n il mandarsi SMS

texture ['tɛkstʃə^r] n tessitura; (of skin, paper etc) struttura

Thai [taɪ] adj tailandese ▷ n tailandese m/f; (Ling) tailandese m

Thailand ['taɪlænd] n Tailandia

Thames [tɛmz] n **the ~** il Tamigi

than [ðæn, ðən] conj (in comparisons) che; (with numerals, pronouns, proper names) di; **more ~ 10/once** più di 10/una volta; **I have more ~ you** ne ho più/meno di te; **I have more pens ~ pencils** ho più penne che matite; **she is older ~ you think** è più vecchia di quanto tu (non) pensi

thank [θæŋk] vt ringraziare; **~ you (very much)** grazie (tante); **~s** npl ringraziamenti mpl, grazie fpl excl grazie!;

~s to grazie a; **thankfully** adv con riconoscenza; con sollievo; **thankfully there were few victims** grazie al cielo ci sono state poche vittime; **Thanksgiving (Day)** n giorno del ringraziamento

● **THANKSGIVING (DAY)**
●
● Negli Stati Uniti il quarto giovedì di
● novembre ricorre il **Thanksgiving**
● **(Day)**, festa che rievoca la celebrazione
● con cui i Padri Pellegrini, fondatori della
● colonia di Plymouth in Massachusetts,
● ringraziarono Dio del buon raccolto
● del 1621.

 KEYWORD

that [ðæt] (pl **those**) adj (demonstrative) quel (quell', quello) m; quella (quell') f; **that man/woman/book** quell'uomo/quella donna/quel libro; (not "this") quell'uomo/ quella donna/quel libro là; **that one** quello(-a) là
▷ pron **1** (demonstrative) ciò; (not "this one") quello(-a); **who's that?** chi è?; **what's that?** cos'è quello?; **is that you?** sei tu?; **I prefer this to that** preferisco questo a quello; **that's what he said** questo è ciò che ha detto; **what happened after that?** che è successo dopo?; **that is (to say)** cioè **2** (relative: direct) che; (: indirect) cui; **the book (that) I read** il libro che ho letto; **the box (that) I put it in** la scatola in cui l'ho messo; **the people (that) I spoke to** le persone con cui o con le quali ho parlato **3** (relative: of time) in cui; **the day (that) he came** il giorno in cui è venuto
▷ conj che; **he thought that I was ill** pensava che io fossi malato
▷ adv (demonstrative) così; **I can't work that much** non posso lavorare (così) tanto; **that high** così alto; **the wall's about that high and that thick** il muro è alto circa così e spesso circa così

thatched [θætʃt] adj (roof) di paglia
thaw [θɔː] n disgelo ▷ vi (ice) sciogliersi; (food) scongelarsi ▷ vt (food: also: **~ out**) (fare) scongelare

 KEYWORD

the [ðiː, ðə] def art **1** (gen) il (lo, l') m; la (l') f; i (gli) mpl; le fpl; **the boy/girl/ink** il ragazzo/la ragazza/l'inchiostro; **the books/pencils** i libri/le matite; **the history of the world** la storia del mondo; **give it to the postman** dallo al postino;

I haven't the time/money non ho tempo/soldi; **the rich and the poor** i ricchi e i poveri **2** (in titles): **Elizabeth the First** Elisabetta prima; **Peter the Great** Pietro il grande **3** (in comparisons): **the more he works, the more he earns** più lavora più guadagna

theatre ['θɪətə'] (US **theater**) n teatro; (also: **lecture ~**) aula magna; (also: **operating ~**) sala operatoria
theft [θɛft] n furto
their [ðɛə'] adj il (la) loro; (pl) i (le) loro; **theirs** pron il (la) loro; (pl) i (le) loro; see also **my**; **mine**
them [ðɛm, ðəm] pron (direct) li (le); (indirect) gli (loro after vb); (stressed, after prep: people) loro; (: people, things) essi(-e); see also **me**
theme [θiːm] n tema m; **theme park** n parco di divertimenti (intorno a un tema centrale)
themselves [ðəm'sɛlvz] pl pron (reflexive) si; (emphatic) loro stessi(-e); (after prep) se stessi(-e)
then [ðɛn] adv (at that time) allora; (next) poi, dopo; (and also) e poi ▷ conj (therefore) perciò, dunque, quindi ▷ adj **the ~ president** il presidente di allora; **by ~** allora; **from ~ on** da allora in poi
theology [θɪ'ɔlədʒɪ] n teologia
theory ['θɪərɪ] n teoria
therapist ['θɛrəpɪst] n terapista m/f
therapy ['θɛrəpɪ] n terapia

 KEYWORD

there [ðɛə'] adv **1**: **there is, there are** c'è, ci sono; **there are 3 of them** (people) sono in 3; (things) ce ne sono 3; **there's no-one here** non c'è nessuno qui; **there has been an accident** c'è stato un incidente **2** (referring to place) là, lì; **up/in/down there** lassù/là dentro/laggiù; **he went there on Friday** ci è andato venerdì; **I want that book there** voglio quel libro là or lì; **there he is!** eccolo! **3**: **there, there** (esp to child) su, su

there: **thereabouts** [ðɛərə'bauts] adv (place) nei pressi, da quelle parti; (amount) giù di lì, all'incirca; **thereafter** [ðɛər'ɑːftə'] adv da allora in poi; **thereby** [ðɛə'baɪ] adv con ciò; **therefore** ['ðɛəfɔː'] adv perciò, quindi; **there's** [ðɛəz] = **there is**; **there has**
thermal ['θəːml] adj termico(-a)
thermometer [θə'mɔmɪtə'] n

termometro
thermostat ['θəːməstæt] *n* termostato
these [ðiːz] *pl pron, adj* questi(-e)
thesis ['θiːsɪs] (*pl* **theses**) *n* tesi *f inv*
they [ðeɪ] *pl pron* essi (esse); (*people only*)
loro; ~ **say that ...** (*it is said that*) si dice
che ...; **they'd** = **they had**; **they would**;
they'll = **they shall**; **they will**; **they're**
= **they are**; **they've** = **they have**
thick [θɪk] *adj* spesso(-a); (*crowd*)
compatto(-a); (*stupid*) ottuso(-a), lento(-a)
▷ *n* **in the ~ of** nel folto di; **it's 20 cm ~**
ha uno spessore di 20 cm; **thicken** *vi*
ispessire ▷ *vt* (*sauce etc*) ispessire, rendere
più denso(-a); **thickness** *n* spessore *m*
thief [θiːf] (*pl* **thieves**) *n* ladro(-a)
thigh [θaɪ] *n* coscia
thin [θɪn] *adj* sottile; (*person*) magro(-a);
(*soup*) poco denso(-a) ▷ *vt* **to ~ (down)**
(*sauce, paint*) diluire
thing [θɪŋ] *n* cosa; (*object*) oggetto;
(*mania*): **to have a ~ about** essere
fissato(-a) con; **~s** *npl* (*belongings*) cose *fpl*;
poor ~ poverino(-a); **the best ~ would be
to** la cosa migliore sarebbe di; **how are ~s?**
come va?
think [θɪŋk] (*pt, pp* **thought**) *vi* pensare,
riflettere ▷ *vt* pensare, credere; (*imagine*)
immaginare; **to ~ of** pensare a; **what did
you ~ of them?** cosa ne ha pensato?; **to
~ about sth/sb** pensare a qc/qn; **I'll ~
about it** ci penserò; **to ~ of doing** pensare
di fare; **I ~ so/not** penso di sì/no; **to ~ well
of** avere una buona opinione di; **think
over** *vt* riflettere su; **think up** *vt* ideare
third [θəːd] *num* terzo(-a) ▷ *n* terzo(-a);
(*fraction*) terzo, terza parte *f*; (*Aut*) terza;
(BRIT: *Scol: degree*) laurea col minimo dei voti;
thirdly *adv* in terzo luogo; **third party
insurance** (BRIT) *n* assicurazione *f* contro
terzi; **Third World** *n* **the Third World** il
Terzo Mondo
thirst [θəːst] *n* sete *f*; **thirsty** *adj* (*person*)
assetato(-a), che ha sete
thirteen [θəːˈtiːn] *num* tredici; **thirteenth**
[-ˈtiːnθ] *num* tredicesmo(-a)
thirtieth ['θəːtɪɪθ] *num* trentesimo(-a)
thirty ['θəːtɪ] *num* trenta

KEYWORD

this [ðɪs] (*pl* **these**) *adj* (*demonstrative*)
questo(-a); **this man/woman/book**
quest'uomo/questa donna/questo libro;
(*not "that"*) quest'uomo/questa donna/
questo libro qui; **this one** questo(-a) qui
▷ *pron* (*demonstrative*) questo(-a); (*not "that
one"*) questo(-a) qui; **who/what is this?**
chi è/che cos'è questo?; **I prefer this to**

that preferisco questo a quello; **this is
where I live** io abito qui; **this is what he
said** questo è ciò che ha detto; **this is Mr
Brown** (*in introductions, photo*) questo è il
signor Brown; (*on telephone*) sono il signor
Brown
▷ *adv* (*demonstrative*): **this high/long** *etc*
alto/lungo *etc* così; **I didn't know things
were this bad** non sapevo andasse così
male

thistle ['θɪsl] *n* cardo
thorn [θɔːn] *n* spina
thorough ['θʌrə] *adj* (*search*)
minuzioso(-a); (*knowledge, research*)
approfondito(-a), profondo(-a);
(*person*) coscienzioso(-a); (*cleaning*)
a fondo; **thoroughly** *adv* (*search*)
minuziosamente; (*wash, study*) a fondo;
(*very*) assolutamente
those [ðəuz] *pl pron* quelli(-e) ▷ *pl adj* quei
(quegli) *mpl*; quelle *fpl*
though [ðəu] *conj* benché, sebbene ▷ *adv*
comunque
thought [θɔːt] *pt, pp of* **think** ▷ *n* pensiero;
(*opinion*) opinione *f*; **thoughtful** *adj*
pensieroso(-a), pensoso(-a); (*considerate*)
premuroso(-a); **thoughtless** *adj*
sconsiderato(-a); (*behaviour*) scortese
thousand ['θauzənd] *num* mille; **one ~**
mille; **~s of** migliaia di; **thousandth** *num*
millesimo(-a)
thrash [θræʃ] *vt* picchiare; bastonare;
(*defeat*) battere
thread [θrεd] *n* filo; (*of screw*) filetto ▷ *vt*
(*needle*) infilare
threat [θrεt] *n* minaccia; **threaten** *vi*
(*storm*) minacciare ▷ *vt* **to threaten sb
with/to do** minacciare qn con/di fare;
threatening *adj* minaccioso(-a)
three [θriː] *num* tre; **three-
dimensional** *adj* tridimensionale; (*film*)
stereoscopico(-a); **three-piece suite**
['θriːpiːs-] *n* salotto comprendente un
divano e due poltrone; **three-quarters**
npl tre quarti *mpl*; **three-quarters full**
pieno per tre quarti
threshold ['θrεʃhəuld] *n* soglia
threw [θruː] *pt of* **throw**
thrill [θrɪl] *n* brivido ▷ *vt* (*audience*)
elettrizzare; **to be ~ed** (*with gift etc*) essere
elettrizzato(-a); **thrilled** *adj* **I was thrilled
to get your letter** la tua lettera mi ha
fatto veramente piacere; **thriller** *n* thriller
m inv; **thrilling** *adj* (*book*) pieno(-a) di
suspense; (*news, discovery*) elettrizzante
thriving ['θraɪvɪŋ] *adj* fiorente
throat [θrəut] *n* gola; **to have a sore ~**
avere (un or il) mal di gola

throb [θrɔb] vi palpitare; pulsare; vibrare

throne [θrəun] n trono

through [θru:] prep attraverso; (time) per, durante; (by means of) per mezzo di; (owing to) a causa di ▷ adj (ticket, train, passage) diretto(-a) ▷ adv attraverso; **to put sb ~ to sb** (Tel) passare qn a qn; **to be ~** (Tel) ottenere la comunicazione; (have finished) essere finito(-a); **"no ~ road"** (BRIT) "strada senza sbocco"; **throughout** prep (place) dappertutto in; (time) per or durante tutto(-a) ▷ adv dappertutto; sempre

throw [θrəu] (pt **threw**, pp **thrown**) n (Sport) lancio, tiro ▷ vt tirare, gettare; (Sport) lanciare, tirare; (rider) disarcionare; (fig) confondere; **to ~ a party** dare una festa; **throw away** vt gettare or buttare via; **throw in** vt (Sport: ball) rimettere in gioco; (include) aggiungere; **throw off** vt sbarazzarsi di; **throw out** vt buttare fuori; (reject) respingere; **throw up** vi vomitare

thru [θru:] (US) prep, adj, adv = **through**

thrush [θrʌʃ] n tordo

thrust [θrʌst] (pt, pp **thrust**) vt spingere con forza; (push in) conficcare

thud [θʌd] n tonfo

thug [θʌg] n delinquente m

thumb [θʌm] n (Anat) pollice m; **to ~ a lift** fare l'autostop; **thumbtack** (US) n puntina da disegno

thump [θʌmp] n colpo forte; (sound) tonfo ▷ vt (person) picchiare; (object) battere su ▷ vi picchiare; battere

thunder ['θʌndə'] n tuono ▷ vi tuonare; (train etc): **to ~ past** passare con un rombo; **thunderstorm** n temporale m

Thur(s). abbr (= Thursday) gio.

Thursday ['θə:zdɪ] n giovedì m inv

thus [ðʌs] adv così

thwart [θwɔ:t] vt contrastare

thyme [taɪm] n timo

Tiber ['taɪbə'] n **the ~** il Tevere

Tibet [tɪ'bɛt] n Tibet m

tick [tɪk] n (sound: of clock) tic tac m inv; (mark) segno; spunta; (Zool) zecca; (BRIT: inf): **in a ~** in un attimo ▷ vi fare tic tac ▷ vt spuntare; **tick off** vt spuntare; (person) sgridare

ticket ['tɪkɪt] n biglietto; (in shop: on goods) etichetta; (parking ticket) multa; (for library) scheda; **a single/return ~ to ...** un biglietto di sola andata/di andata e ritorno per...; **ticket barrier** n (BRIT: Rail) cancelletto d'ingresso; **ticket collector** n bigliettaio; **ticket inspector** n controllore m; **ticket machine** n distributore m di biglietti; **ticket office** n biglietteria

tickle ['tɪkl] vt fare il solletico a; (fig) solleticare ▷ vi **it ~s** mi (or gli etc) fa il

solletico; **ticklish** [-lɪʃ] adj che soffre il solletico; (problem) delicato(-a)

tide [taɪd] n marea; (fig: of events) corso; **high/low ~** alta/bassa marea

tidy ['taɪdɪ] adj (room) ordinato(-a), lindo(-a); (dress, work) curato(-a), in ordine; (person) ordinato(-a) ▷ vt (also: ~ **up**) riordinare, mettere in ordine

tie [taɪ] n (string etc) legaccio; (BRIT: also: **neck~**) cravatta; (fig: link) legame m; (Sport: draw) pareggio ▷ vt (parcel) legare; (ribbon) annodare ▷ vi (Sport) pareggiare; **to ~ sth in a bow** annodare qc; **to ~ a knot in sth** fare un nodo a qc; **tie down** vt legare; (to price etc) costringere ad accettare; **tie up** vt (parcel, dog) legare; (boat) ormeggiare; (arrangements) concludere; **to be ~d up** (busy) essere occupato(-a) or preso(-a)

tier [tɪə'] n fila; (of cake) piano, strato

tiger ['taɪgə'] n tigre f

tight [taɪt] adj (rope) teso(-a), tirato(-a); (money) poco(-a); (clothes, budget, bend etc) stretto(-a); (control) severo(-a), fermo(-a); (inf: drunk) sbronzo(-a) ▷ adv (squeeze) fortemente; (shut) ermeticamente; **tighten** vt (rope) tendere; (screw) stringere; (control) rinforzare ▷ vi tendersi; stringersi; **tightly** adv (grasp) bene, saldamente; **tights** (BRIT) npl collant m inv

tile [taɪl] n (on roof) tegola; (on wall or floor) piastrella, mattonella

till [tɪl] n registratore m di cassa ▷ vt (land) coltivare ▷ prep, conj = **until**

tilt [tɪlt] vt inclinare, far pendere ▷ vi inclinarsi, pendere

timber ['tɪmbə'] n (material) legname m

time [taɪm] n tempo; (epoch: often pl) epoca, tempo; (by clock) ora; (moment) momento; (occasion) volta; (Mus) tempo ▷ vt (race) cronometrare; (programme) calcolare la durata di; (fix moment for) programmare; (remark etc) dire (or fare) al momento giusto; **a long ~** molto tempo; **what ~ does the museum/shop open?** a che ora apre il museo/negozio?; **for the ~ being** per il momento; **4 at a ~** 4 per or alla volta; **from ~ to ~** ogni tanto; **at ~s** a volte; **in ~** (soon enough) in tempo; (after some time) col tempo; (Mus) a tempo; **in a week's ~** fra una settimana; **in no ~** in un attimo; **any ~** in qualsiasi momento; **on ~** puntualmente; **5 ~s 5** 5 volte 5, 5 per 5; **what ~ is it?** che ora è?, che ore sono?; **to have a good ~** divertirsi; **time limit** n limite m di tempo; **timely** adj opportuno(-a); **timer** n (time switch) temporizzatore m; (in kitchen) contaminuti m inv; **time-share** adj **time-share apartment/villa** appartamento/villa in multiproprietà; **timetable** n orario; **time zone** n fuso orario

timid ['tɪmɪd] adj timido(-a); (easily scared) pauroso(-a)

timing ['taɪmɪŋ] n (Sport) cronometraggio; (fig) scelta del momento opportuno

tin [tɪn] n stagno; (also: ~ **plate**) latta; (container) scatola; (BRIT: can) barattolo (di latta), lattina; **tinfoil** n stagnola

tingle ['tɪŋgl] vi pizzicare

tinker ['tɪŋkəʳ]: ~ **with** vt fus armeggiare intorno a; cercare di riparare

tinned [tɪnd] (BRIT) adj (food) in scatola

tin opener ['-əʊpnəʳ] (BRIT) n apriscatole m inv

tint [tɪnt] n tinta; **tinted** adj (hair) tinto(-a); (spectacles, glass) colorato(-a)

tiny ['taɪnɪ] adj minuscolo(-a)

tip [tɪp] n (end) punta; (gratuity) mancia; (BRIT: for rubbish) immondezzaio; (advice) suggerimento ▷ vt (waiter) dare la mancia a; (tilt) inclinare; (overturn: also: ~ **over**) capovolgere; (empty: also: ~ **out**) scaricare; **how much should I ~?** quanto devo lasciare di mancia?; **tip off** vt fare una soffiata a

tiptoe ['tɪptəʊ] n **on** ~ in punta di piedi

tire ['taɪəʳ] n (US) = tyre ▷ vt stancare ▷ vi stancarsi; **tired** adj stanco(-a); **to be tired of** essere stanco or stufo di; **tire pressure** (US) n = **tyre pressure**; **tiring** adj faticoso(-a)

tissue ['tɪʃuː] n tessuto; (paper handkerchief) fazzoletto di carta; **tissue paper** n carta velina

tit [tɪt] n (bird) cinciallegra; **to give ~ for tat** rendere pan per focaccia

title ['taɪtl] n titolo

T-junction ['tiː'dʒʌŋkʃən] n incrocio a T

TM abbr = trademark

KEYWORD

to [tuː, tə] prep **1** (direction) a; **to go to France/London/school** andare in Francia/a Londra/a scuola; **to go to Paul's/the doctor's** andare da Paul/dal dottore; **the road to Edinburgh** la strada per Edimburgo; **to the left/right** a sinistra/destra

2 (as far as) (fino) a; **from here to London** da qui a Londra; **to count to 10** contare fino a 10; **from 40 to 50 people** da 40 a 50 persone

3 (with expressions of time): **a quarter to 5** le 5 meno un quarto; **it's twenty to 3** sono le 3 meno venti

4 (for, of): **the key to the front door** la chiave della porta d'ingresso; **a letter to**

his wife una lettera per la moglie

5 (expressing indirect object) a; **to give sth to sb** dare qc a qn; **to talk to sb** parlare a qn; **to be a danger to sb/sth** rappresentare un pericolo per qn/qc

6 (in relation to) a; **3 goals to 2** 3 goal a 2; **30 miles to the gallon** ≈ 11 chilometri con un litro

7 (purpose, result): **to come to sb's aid** venire in aiuto a qn; **to sentence sb to death** condannare a morte qn; **to my surprise** con mia sorpresa

▷ with vb **1** (simple infinitive): **to go/eat** etc andare/mangiare etc

2 (following another vb): **to want/try/start to do** volere/cercare di/cominciare a fare

3 (with vb omitted): **I don't want to** non voglio (farlo); **you ought to** devi (farlo)

4 (purpose, result) per; **I did it to help you** l'ho fatto per aiutarti

5 (equivalent to relative clause): **I have things to do** ho da fare; **the main thing is to try** la cosa più importante è provare

6 (after adjective etc): **ready to go** pronto a partire; **too old/young to ...** troppo vecchio/giovane per ...

▷ adv **to push the door to** accostare la porta

---

toad [təʊd] n rospo; **toadstool** n fungo (velenoso)

toast [təʊst] n (Culin) pane m tostato; (drink, speech) brindisi m inv ▷ vt (Culin) tostare; (drink to) brindare a; **a piece** or **slice of ~** una fetta di pane tostato; **toaster** n tostapane m inv

tobacco [tə'bækəʊ] n tabacco

toboggan [tə'bɒgən] n toboga m inv

today [tə'deɪ] adv oggi ▷ n (also fig) oggi m

toddler ['tɒdləʳ] n bambino(-a) che impara a camminare

toe [təʊ] n dito del piede; (of shoe) punta; **to ~ the line** (fig) stare in riga, conformarsi; **toenail** n unghia del piede

toffee ['tɒfɪ] n caramella

together [tə'gɛðəʳ] adv insieme; (at same time) allo stesso tempo; ~ **with** insieme a

toilet ['tɔɪlət] n (BRIT: lavatory) gabinetto ▷ cpd (bag, soap etc) da toletta; **where's the ~?** dov'è il bagno?; **toilet bag** n (BRIT) nécessaire m inv da toilette; **toilet paper** n carta igienica; **toiletries** npl articoli mpl da toletta; **toilet roll** n rotolo di carta igienica

token ['təʊkən] n (sign) segno; (substitute coin) gettone m; **book/record/gift ~** (BRIT) buono-libro/disco/regalo

Tokyo ['təʊkjəʊ] n Tokyo f

told [təʊld] *pt, pp of* **tell**

tolerant ['tɒlərnt] *adj* ~ **(of)** tollerante (nei confronti di)

tolerate ['tɒləreɪt] *vt* sopportare; (*Med, Tech*) tollerare

toll [təʊl] *n* (*tax, charge*) pedaggio ▷ *vi* (*bell*) suonare; **the accident ~ on the roads** il numero delle vittime della strada; **toll call** (*us*) *n* (*Tel*) (telefonata) interurbana; **toll-free** (*us*) *adj* senza addebito, gratuito(-a) ▷ *adv* gratuitamente; **toll-free number** ≈ numero verde

tomato [təˈmɑːtəʊ] (*pl* **tomatoes**) *n* pomodoro; **tomato sauce** *n* salsa di pomodoro

tomb [tuːm] *n* tomba; **tombstone** ['tuːmstəʊn] *n* pietra tombale

tomorrow [təˈmɒrəʊ] *adv* domani ▷ *n* (*also fig*) domani *m inv*; **the day after ~** dopodomani; **~ morning** domani mattina

ton [tʌn] *n* tonnellata; (*BRIT*: 1016 *kg*: *us*: 907 *kg*: *metric* 1000 *kg*); **~s of** (*inf*) un mucchio *or* sacco di

tone [təʊn] *n* tono ▷ *vi* (*also*: ~ **in**) intonarsi; **tone down** *vt* (*colour, criticism, sound*) attenuare

tongs [tɒŋz] *npl* tenaglie *fpl*; (*for coal*) molle *fpl*; (*for hair*) arricciacapelli *m inv*

tongue [tʌŋ] *n* lingua; **~ in cheek** (*say, speak*) ironicamente

tonic ['tɒnɪk] *n* (*Med*) tonico; (*also*: ~ **water**) acqua tonica

tonight [təˈnaɪt] *adv* stanotte; (*this evening*) stasera ▷ *n* questa notte; questa sera

tonne [tʌn] *n* (*BRIT*: *metric ton*) tonnellata

tonsil ['tɒnsl] *n* tonsilla; **tonsillitis** [-'laɪtɪs] *n* tonsillite *f*

too [tuː] *adv* (*excessively*) troppo; (*also*) anche; (*also*: ~ **much**) ▷ *adv* troppo ▷ *adj* troppo(-a); **~ many** troppi(-e)

took [tuk] *pt of* **take**

tool [tuːl] *n* utensile *m*, attrezzo; **tool box** *n* cassetta *f* portautensili; **tool kit** *n* cassetta di attrezzi

tooth [tuːθ] (*pl* **teeth**) *n* (*Anat, Tech*) dente *m*; **toothache** *n* mal *m* di denti; **toothbrush** *n* spazzolino da denti; **toothpaste** *n* dentifricio; **toothpick** *n* stuzzicadenti *m inv*

top [tɒp] *n* (*of mountain, page, ladder*) cima; (*of box, cupboard, table*) sopra *m inv*, parte *f* superiore; (*lid: of box, jar*) coperchio; (: *of bottle*) tappo; (*blouse etc*) sopra *m inv*; (*toy*) trottola ▷ *adj* più alto(-a); (*in rank*) primo(-a); (*best*) migliore ▷ *vt* (*exceed*) superare; (*be first in*) essere in testa a; **on ~ of** sopra, in cima a; (*in addition to*) oltre a; **from ~ to bottom** da cima a fondo;

top up (*us* **top off**) *vt* riempire; (*salary*) integrare; **top floor** *n* ultimo piano; **top hat** *n* cilindro

topic ['tɒpɪk] *n* argomento; **topical** *adj* d'attualità

topless ['tɒplɪs] *adj* (*bather etc*) col seno scoperto

topping ['tɒpɪŋ] *n* (*Culin*) guarnizione *f*

topple ['tɒpl] *vt* rovesciare, far cadere ▷ *vi* cadere; traballare

torch [tɔːtʃ] *n* torcia; (*BRIT*: *electric*) lampadina tascabile

tore [tɔːʳ] *pt of* **tear¹**

torment [*n* 'tɔːmɛnt, *vb* tɔːˈmɛnt] *n* tormento ▷ *vt* tormentare

torn [tɔːn] *pp of* **tear¹**

tornado [tɔːˈneɪdəʊ] (*pl* **tornadoes**) *n* tornado

torpedo [tɔːˈpiːdəʊ] (*pl* **torpedoes**) *n* siluro

torrent ['tɒrnt] *n* torrente *m*; **torrential** [tɔˈrɛnʃl] *adj* torrenziale

tortoise ['tɔːtəs] *n* tartaruga

torture ['tɔːtʃəʳ] *n* tortura ▷ *vt* torturare

Tory ['tɔːrɪ] (*BRIT*: *Pol*) *adj* dei tories, conservatore(-trice) ▷ *n* tory *m/f inv*, conservatore(-trice)

toss [tɒs] *vt* gettare, lanciare; (*one's head*) scuotere; **to ~ a coin** fare a testa o croce; **to ~ up for sth** fare a testa o croce per qc; **to ~ and turn** (*in bed*) girarsi e rigirarsi

total ['təʊtl] *adj* totale ▷ *n* totale *m* ▷ *vt* (*add up*) sommare; (*amount to*) ammontare a

totalitarian [təʊtælɪˈtɛərɪən] *adj* totalitario(-a)

totally ['təʊtəlɪ] *adv* completamente

touch [tʌtʃ] *n* tocco; (*sense*) tatto; (*contact*) contatto ▷ *vt* toccare; **a ~ of** (*fig*) un tocco di; un pizzico di; **to get in ~ with** mettersi in contatto con; **to lose ~** (*friends*) perdersi di vista; **touch down** *vi* (*on land*) atterrare; **touchdown** *n* atterraggio; (*on sea*) ammaraggio; (*us*: Football) meta; **touched** *adj* commosso(-a); **touching** *adj* commovente; **touchline** *n* (*Sport*) linea laterale; **touch-sensitive** *adj* sensibile al tatto

tough [tʌf] *adj* duro(-a); (*resistant*) resistente

tour ['tʊəʳ] *n* viaggio; (*also*: **package ~**) viaggio organizzato *or* tutto compreso; (*of town, museum*) visita; (*by artist*) tournée *f inv* ▷ *vt* visitare; **tour guide** *n* guida turistica

tourism ['tʊərɪzəm] *n* turismo

tourist ['tʊərɪst] *n* turista *m/f* ▷ *adv* (*travel*) in classe turistica ▷ *cpd* turistico(-a); **tourist office** *n* pro loco *f inv*

tournament ['tʊənəmənt] n torneo
tour operator n (BRIT) operatore m
turistico
tow [təʊ] vt rimorchiare; **"on ~"** (BRIT), **"in ~"** (US) "veicolo rimorchiato"; **tow away** vt rimorchiare
toward(s) [tə'wɔːd(z)] prep verso; (of attitude) nei confronti di; (of purpose) per
towel ['taʊəl] n asciugamano; (also: **tea ~**) strofinaccio; **towelling** n (fabric) spugna
tower ['taʊəʳ] n torre f; **tower block** (BRIT) n palazzone m
town [taʊn] n città f inv; **to go to ~** andare in città; (fig) mettercela tutta; **town centre** n centro (città); **town hall** n ≈ municipio
tow truck (US) n carro m, attrezzi inv
toxic ['tɔksɪk] adj tossico(-a)
toy [tɔɪ] n giocattolo; **toy with** vt fus giocare con; (idea) accarezzare, trastullarsi con; **toyshop** n negozio di giocattoli
trace [treɪs] n traccia ▷ vt (draw) tracciare; (follow) seguire; (locate) rintracciare
track [træk] n (of person, animal) traccia; (on tape, Sport, path: gen) pista; (: of bullet etc) traiettoria; (: of suspect, animal) pista, tracce fpl; (Rail) binario, rotaie fpl ▷ vt seguire le tracce di; **to keep ~ of** seguire; **track down** vt (prey) scovare; snidare; (sth lost) rintracciare; **tracksuit** n tuta sportiva
tractor ['træktəʳ] n trattore m
trade [treɪd] n commercio; (skill, job) mestiere m ▷ vi commerciare ▷ vt **to ~ sth (for sth)** barattare qc (con qc); **to ~ with/in** commerciare con/in; **trade in** vt (old car etc) dare come pagamento parziale; **trademark** n marchio di fabbrica; **trader** n commerciante m/f; **tradesman** (irreg) n fornitore m; (shopkeeper) negoziante m; **trade union** n sindacato
trading ['treɪdɪŋ] n commercio
tradition [trə'dɪʃən] n tradizione f; **traditional** adj tradizionale
traffic ['træfɪk] n traffico ▷ vi **to ~ in** (pej: liquor, drugs) trafficare in; **traffic circle** (US) n isola rotatoria; **traffic island** n salvagente m, isola f spartitraffico inv; **traffic jam** n ingorgo (del traffico); **traffic lights** npl semaforo; **traffic warden** n addetto(-a) al controllo del traffico e del parcheggio
tragedy ['trædʒədɪ] n tragedia
tragic ['trædʒɪk] adj tragico(-a)
trail [treɪl] n (tracks) tracce fpl, pista; (path) sentiero; (of smoke etc) scia ▷ vt trascinare,

strascicare; (follow) seguire ▷ vi essere al traino; (dress etc) strusciare; (plant) arrampicarsi; strisciare; (in game) essere in svantaggio; **trailer** n (Aut) rimorchio; (US) roulotte f inv; (Cinema) prossimamente m inv
train [treɪn] n treno; (of dress) coda, strascico ▷ vt (apprentice, doctor etc) formare; (sportsman) allenare; (dog) addestrare; (memory) esercitare; (point: gun etc) **to ~ sth on** puntare qc contro ▷ vi formarsi; allenarsi; **what time does the ~ from Rome get in?** a che ora arriva il treno da Roma?; **is this the ~ for ...?** è questo il treno per...?; **one's ~ of thought** il filo dei propri pensieri; **trainee** [treɪ'niː] n (in trade) apprendista m/f; **trainer** n (Sport) allenatore(-trice), (: shoe) scarpa da ginnastica; (of dogs etc) addestratore(-trice); **trainers** npl (shoes) scarpe fpl da ginnastica; **training** n formazione f; allenamento; addestramento; **in training** (Sport) in allenamento; **training course** n corso di formazione professionale; **training shoes** npl scarpe fpl da ginnastica
trait [treɪt] n tratto
traitor ['treɪtəʳ] n traditore m
tram [træm] (BRIT) n (also: **~car**) tram m inv
tramp [træmp] n (person) vagabondo(-a); (inf: pej: woman) sgualdrina
trample ['træmpl] vt **to ~ (underfoot)** calpestare
trampoline ['træmpəliːn] n trampolino
tranquil ['træŋkwɪl] adj tranquillo(-a); **tranquillizer** (US **tranquilizer**) n (Med) tranquillante m
transaction [træn'zækʃən] n transazione f
transatlantic ['trænzət'læntɪk] adj transatlantico(-a)
transcript ['trænskrɪpt] n trascrizione f
transfer [n 'trænsfəʳ, vb træns'fəʳ] n (gen: also Sport) trasferimento; (Pol: of power) passaggio; (picture, design) decalcomania; (: stick-on) autoadesivo ▷ vt trasferire; passare; **to ~ the charges** (BRIT) fare una chiamata a carico del destinatario
transform [træns'fɔːm] vt trasformare; **transformation** n trasformazione f
transfusion [træns'fjuːʒən] n trasfusione f
transit ['trænzɪt] n **in ~** in transito
transition [træn'zɪʃən] n passaggio, transizione f
transitive ['trænzɪtɪv] adj (Ling) transitivo(-a)
translate [trænz'leɪt] vt tradurre; **can**

you ~ this for me? me lo può tradurre?;
translation [-'leɪʃən] n traduzione f;
translator n traduttore(-trice)
transmission [trænz'mɪʃən] n
trasmissione f
transmit [trænz'mɪt] vt trasmettere;
transmitter n trasmettitore m
transparent [træns'pærnt] adj
trasparente
transplant [vb træns'plɑ:nt, n
'trænsplɑ:nt] vt trapiantare ▷ n (Med)
trapianto
transport [n 'trænspɔ:t, vb træns'pɔ:
t] n trasporto ▷ vt trasportare;
transportation [-'teɪʃən] n (mezzo di)
trasporto
transvestite [trænz'vɛstaɪt] n
travestito(-a)
trap [træp] n (snare, trick) trappola;
(carriage) calesse m ▷ vt prendere in
trappola, intrappolare
trash [træʃ] (pej) n (goods) ciarpame m;
(nonsense) sciocchezze fpl; **trash can** (us) n
secchio della spazzatura
trauma ['trɔ:mə] n trauma m; **traumatic**
[-'mætɪk] adj traumatico(-a)
travel ['trævl] n viaggio; viaggi mpl ▷ vi
viaggiare ▷ vt (distance) percorrere;
travel agency n agenzia (di) viaggi;
travel agent n agente m di viaggio;
travel insurance n assicurazione f
di viaggio; **traveller** (us **traveler**) n
viaggiatore(-trice); **traveller's cheque**
(us **traveler's check**) n assegno turistico;
travelling (us **traveling**) n viaggi mpl;
travel-sick adj **to get travel-sick** (in
vehicle) soffrire di mal d'auto; (in aeroplane)
soffrire di mal d'aria; (in boat) soffrire di mal
di mare; **travel sickness** n mal m d'auto
(or di mare or d'aria)
tray [treɪ] n (for carrying) vassoio; (on desk)
vaschetta
treacherous ['trɛtʃərəs] adj infido(-a)
treacle ['tri:kl] n melassa
tread [trɛd] (pt **trod**, pp **trodden**) n passo;
(sound) rumore m di passi; (of stairs) pedata;
(of tyre) battistrada m inv ▷ vi camminare;
tread on vt fus calpestare
treasure ['trɛʒəʳ] n tesoro ▷ vt (value)
tenere in gran conto, apprezzare molto;
(store) custodire gelosamente; **treasurer**
['trɛʒərəʳ] n tesoriere(-a)
treasury ['trɛʒərɪ] n **the T~** (BRIT), **the T~
Department** (us) il ministero del Tesoro
treat [tri:t] n regalo ▷ vt trattare; (Med)
curare; **to ~ sb to sth** offrire qc a qn;
treatment ['tri:tmənt] n trattamento
treaty ['tri:tɪ] n patto, trattato
treble ['trɛbl] adj triplo(-a), triplice ▷ vt

triplicare ▷ vi triplicarsi
tree [tri:] n albero
trek [trɛk] n escursione f a piedi;
escursione f in macchina; (tiring walk)
camminata sfiancante ▷ vi (as holiday) fare
dell'escursionismo
tremble ['trɛmbl] vi tremare
tremendous [trɪ'mɛndəs] adj (enormous)
enorme; (excellent) fantastico(-a),
strepitoso(-a)

> Be careful not to translate
> *tremendous* by the Italian word
> *tremendo*.

trench [trɛntʃ] n trincea
trend [trɛnd] n (tendency) tendenza; (of
events) corso; (fashion) moda; **trendy** adj
(idea) di moda; (clothes) all'ultima moda
trespass ['trɛspəs] vi **to ~ on** entrare
abusivamente in; **"no ~ing"** "proprietà
privata", "vietato l'accesso"
trial ['traɪəl] n (Law) processo; (test: of
machine etc) collaudo; **on ~** (Law) sotto
processo; **trial period** n periodo di prova
triangle ['traɪæŋgl] n (Math, Mus)
triangolo
triangular [traɪ'æŋgjʊləʳ] adj triangolare
tribe [traɪb] n tribù f inv
tribunal [traɪ'bju:nl] n tribunale m
tribute ['trɪbju:t] n tributo, omaggio; **to
pay ~ to** rendere omaggio a
trick [trɪk] n trucco; (joke) tiro; (Cards) presa
▷ vt imbrogliare, ingannare; **to play a ~
on sb** giocare un tiro a qn; **that should do
the ~** vedrai che funziona
trickle ['trɪkl] n (of water etc) rivolo;
gocciolio ▷ vi gocciolare
tricky ['trɪkɪ] adj difficile, delicato(-a)
tricycle ['traɪsɪkl] n triciclo
trifle ['traɪfl] n sciocchezza; (BRIT: Culin)
≈ zuppa inglese ▷ adv **a ~ long** un po'
lungo
trigger ['trɪgəʳ] n (of gun) grilletto
trim [trɪm] adj (house, garden) ben
tenuto(-a); (figure) snello(-a) ▷ n (haircut
etc) spuntata, regolata; (embellishment)
finiture fpl; (on car) guarnizioni fpl ▷ vt
spuntare; (decorate): **to ~ (with)** decorare
(con); (Naut: a sail) orientare
trio ['tri:əu] n trio
trip [trɪp] n viaggio; (excursion) gita,
escursione f; (stumble) passo falso ▷ vi
inciampare; (go lightly) camminare con
passo leggero; **on ~** in viaggio; **trip up** vi
inciampare ▷ vt fare lo sgambetto a
triple ['trɪpl] adj triplo(-a)
triplets ['trɪplɪts] npl bambini(-e)
trigemini(-e)
tripod ['traɪpɔd] n treppiede m
triumph ['traɪʌmf] n trionfo ▷ vi **to**

~ (over) trionfare (su); **triumphant**
[traɪˈʌmfənt] *adj* trionfante
trivial [ˈtrɪvɪəl] *adj* insignificante;
(*commonplace*) banale

> Be careful not to translate *trivial* by
> the Italian word *triviale*.

trod [trɔd] *pt of* **tread**
trodden [trɔdn] *pp of* **tread**
trolley [ˈtrɔlɪ] *n* carrello
trombone [trɔmˈbəun] *n* trombone *m*
troop [tru:p] *n* gruppo; (*Mil*) squadrone *m*;
~s *npl* (*Mil*) truppe *fpl*
trophy [ˈtrəufɪ] *n* trofeo
tropical [ˈtrɔpɪkl] *adj* tropicale
trot [trɔt] *n* trotto ▷ *vi* trottare; **on the ~**
(*BRIT: fig*) di fila, uno(-a) dopo l'altro(-a)
trouble [ˈtrʌbl] *n* difficoltà *f inv*, problema
m; difficoltà *fpl*, problemi; (*worry*)
preoccupazione *f*; (*bother, effort*) sforzo;
(*Pol*) conflitti *mpl*, disordine *m*; (*Med*):
stomach *etc* **~** disturbi *mpl* gastrici *etc*
▷ *vt* disturbare; (*worry*) preoccupare ▷ *vi*
to ~ to do disturbarsi a fare; **~s** *npl* (*Pol*
etc) disordini *mpl*; **to be in ~** avere dei
problemi; **it's no ~!** di niente!; **what's the
~?** cosa c'è che non va?; **I'm sorry to ~ you**
scusi il disturbo; **troubled** *adj* (*person*)
preoccupato(-a), inquieto(-a); (*epoch, life*)
agitato(-a), difficile; **troublemaker** *n*
elemento disturbatore, agitatore(-trice);
(*child*) disloca(-a); **troublesome** *adj*
fastidioso(-a), seccante
trough [trɔf] *n* (*drinking trough*)
abbeveratoio; (*also*: **feeding ~**) trogolo,
mangiatoia; (*channel*) canale *m*
trousers [ˈtrauzəz] *npl* pantaloni *mpl*,
calzoni *mpl*; **short ~** calzoncini *mpl*
trout [traut] *n inv* trota
trowel [ˈtrauəl] *n* cazzuola
truant [ˈtruənt] (*BRIT*) *n*: **to play ~**
marinare la scuola
truce [tru:s] *n* tregua
truck [trʌk] *n* autocarro, camion *m inv*;
(*Rail*) carro merci aperto; (*for luggage*)
carrello *m* portabagagli *inv*; **truck driver** *n*
camionista *m/f*
true [tru:] *adj* vero(-a); (*accurate*)
accurato(-a), esatto(-a); (*genuine*) reale;
(*faithful*) fedele; **to come ~** avverarsi
truly [ˈtru:lɪ] *adv* veramente; (*truthfully*)
sinceramente; (*faithfully*): **yours ~** (*in letter*)
distinti saluti
trumpet [ˈtrʌmpɪt] *n* tromba
trunk [trʌŋk] *n* (*of tree, person*) tronco; (*of
elephant*) proboscide *f*; (*case*) baule *m*; (*us:
Aut*) bagagliaio; **~s** (*also*: **swimming ~s**)
calzoncini *mpl* da bagno
trust [trʌst] *n* fiducia; (*Law*)
amministrazione *f* fiduciaria; (*Comm*)

trust *m inv* ▷ *vt* (*rely on*) contare su; (*hope*)
sperare; (*entrust*): **to ~ sth to sb** affidare qc
a qn; **trusted** *adj* fidato(-a); **trustworthy**
adj fidato(-a), degno(-a) di fiducia
truth [tru:θ, *pl* tru:ðz] *n* verità *f inv*;
truthful *adj* (*person*) sincero(-a);
(*description*) veritiero(-a), esatto(-a)
try [traɪ] *n* prova, tentativo; (*Rugby*) meta
▷ *vt* (*Law*) giudicare; (*test: also*: **~ out**)
provare; (*strain*) mettere alla prova ▷ *vi*
provare; **to ~ to do** (*seek*) cercare di fare; **try on**
vt (*clothes*) provare; **trying** *adj* (*day,
experience*) logorante, pesante; (*child*)
difficile, insopportabile
T-shirt [ˈti:ʃə:t] *n* maglietta
tub [tʌb] *n* tinozza; mastello; (*bath*)
bagno
tube [tju:b] *n* tubo; (*BRIT: underground*)
metropolitana, metrò *m inv*; (*for tyre*)
camera d'aria
tuberculosis [tjubə:kjuˈləusɪs] *n*
tubercolosi *f inv*
tube station (*BRIT*) *n* stazione *f* della
metropolitana
tuck [tʌk] *vt* (*put*) mettere; **tuck away** *vt*
riporre; (*building*): **to be ~ed away** essere
in un luogo isolato; **tuck in** *vt* mettere
dentro; (*child*) rimboccare ▷ *vi* (*eat*)
mangiare di buon appetito; abbuffarsi;
tuck shop *n* negozio di pasticceria (*in una
scuola*)
Tue(s). *abbr* (= *Tuesday*) mar.
Tuesday [ˈtju:zdɪ] *n* martedì *m inv*
tug [tʌg] *n* (*ship*) rimorchiatore *m* ▷ *vt*
tirare con forza
tuition [tju:ˈɪʃən] *n* (*BRIT*) lezioni *fpl*; (:
private tuition) lezioni *fpl* private; (*us: school
fees*) tasse *fpl* scolastiche
tulip [ˈtju:lɪp] *n* tulipano
tumble [ˈtʌmbl] *n* (*fall*) capitombolo ▷ *vi*
capitombolare, ruzzolare; **to ~ to sth**
(*inf*) realizzare qc; **tumble dryer** (*BRIT*) *n*
asciugatrice *f*
tumbler [ˈtʌmbləʳ] *n* bicchiere *m* (senza
stelo)
tummy [ˈtʌmɪ] (*inf*) *n* pancia
tumour [ˈtju:məʳ] (*us* **tumor**) *n* tumore *m*
tuna [ˈtju:nə] *n inv* (*also*: **~ fish**) tonno
tune [tju:n] *n* (*melody*) melodia, aria
▷ *vt* (*Mus*) accordare; (*Radio, TV, Aut*)
regolare, mettere a punto; **to be in/out
of ~** (*instrument*) essere accordato(-a)/
scordato(-a); (*singer*) essere intonato(-a)/
stonato(-a); **tune in** *vi* (*Radio, TV*): **to ~ in (to)**
(*Radio, TV*) sintonizzarsi (su); **tune up** *vi*
(*musician*) accordare lo strumento
tunic [ˈtju:nɪk] *n* tunica
Tunisia [tju:ˈnɪzɪə] *n* Tunisia

tunnel ['tʌnl] n galleria ▷ vi scavare una galleria

turbulence ['təːbjuləns] n (Aviat) turbolenza

turf [təːf] n terreno erboso; (clod) zolla ▷ vt coprire di zolle erbose

Turin [tjuə'rɪn] n Torino f

Turk [təːk] n turco(-a)

Turkey ['təːkɪ] n Turchia

turkey ['təːkɪ] n tacchino

Turkish ['təːkɪʃ] adj turco(-a) ▷ n (Ling) turco

turmoil ['təːmɔɪl] n confusione f, tumulto

turn [təːn] n giro; (change) cambiamento; (in road) curva; (tendency: of mind, events) tendenza; (performance) numero; (chance) turno; (Med) crisi f inv, attacco ▷ vt girare, voltare; (change): **to ~ sth into** trasformare qc in ▷ vi girare; (person: look back) girarsi, voltarsi; (reverse direction) girare; (change) cambiare; (milk) andare a male; (become) diventare; **a good ~** un buon servizio; **it gave me quite a ~** mi ha fatto prendere un bello spavento; **"no left ~"** (Aut) "divieto di svolta a sinistra"; **it's your ~** tocca a lei; **in ~** a sua volta; a turno; **to take ~s (at sth)** fare (qc) a turno; **~ left/right at the next junction** al prossimo incrocio, giri a sinistra/destra; **turn around** vi (person) girarsi; (rotate) girare ▷ vt (object) girare; **turn away** vi girarsi (dall'altra parte) ▷ vt mandare via; **turn back** vi ritornare, tornare indietro ▷ vt far tornare indietro; (clock) spostare indietro; **turn down** vt (refuse) rifiutare; (reduce) abbassare; (fold) ripiegare; **turn in** vi (inf: go to bed) andare a letto ▷ vt (fold) voltare in dentro; **turn off** vi (from road) girare, voltare ▷ vt (light, radio, engine etc) spegnere; **I can't ~ the heating off** non riesco a spegnere il riscaldamento; **turn on** vt (light, radio etc) accendere; **I can't ~ the heating on** non riesco ad accendere il riscaldamento; **turn out** vt (light, gas) chiudere; spegnere ▷ vi (voters) presentarsi; **to ~ out to be ...** rivelarsi ..., risultare ...; **turn over** vi (person) girarsi ▷ vt girare; **turn round** vi girare; (person) girarsi; **turn to** vt fus **to ~ to sb** girarsi verso qn; **to ~ to sb for help** rivolgersi a qn per aiuto; **turn up** vi (person) arrivare, presentarsi; (lost object) saltar fuori ▷ vt (collar, sound) alzare; **turning** n (in road) curva; **turning point** n (fig) svolta decisiva

turnip ['təːnɪp] n rapa

turn: turnout ['təːnaut] n presenza, affluenza; **turnover** ['təːnəuvəˈ] n (Comm) turnover m inv; (Culin): **apple** etc **turnover**

sfogliatella alle melle ecc; **turnstile** ['təːnstaɪl] n tornella; **turn-up** (BRIT) n (on trousers) risvolto

turquoise ['təːkwɔɪz] n turchese m ▷ adj turchese

turtle ['təːtl] n testuggine f; **turtleneck (sweater)** ['təːtlnɛk-] n maglione m con il collo alto

Tuscany ['tʌskənɪ] n Toscana

tusk [tʌsk] n zanna

tutor ['tjuːtəˈ] n (in college) docente m/f (responsabile di un gruppo di studenti); (private teacher) precettore m; **tutorial** [-'tɔːrɪəl] n (Scol) lezione f con discussione (a un gruppo limitato)

tuxedo [tʌk'siːdəu] (US) n smoking m inv

TV [tiː'viː] n abbr (= television) tivù f inv

tweed [twiːd] n tweed m inv

tweezers ['twiːzəz] npl pinzette fpl

twelfth [twelfθ] num dodicesimo(-a)

twelve [twelv] num dodici; **at ~ o'clock** alle dodici, a mezzogiorno; (midnight) a mezzanotte

twentieth ['twentɪɪθ] num ventesimo(-a)

twenty ['twentɪ] num venti

twice [twaɪs] adv due volte; **~ as much** due volte tanto; **~ a week** due volte alla settimana

twig [twɪg] n ramoscello ▷ vt, vi (inf) capire

twilight ['twaɪlaɪt] n crepuscolo

twin [twɪn] adj, n gemello(-a) ▷ vt **to ~ one town with another** fare il gemellaggio di una città con un'altra; **twin(-bedded) room** n stanza con letti gemelli; **twin beds** npl letti mpl gemelli

twinkle ['twɪŋkl] vi scintillare; (eyes) brillare

twist [twɪst] n torsione f; (in wire, flex) piega; (in road) curva; (in story) colpo di scena ▷ vt attorcigliare; (ankle) slogare; (weave) intrecciare; (roll around) arrotolare; (fig) distorcere ▷ vi (road) serpeggiare

twit [twɪt] (inf) n cretino(-a)

twitch [twɪtʃ] n tiratina; (nervous) tic m inv ▷ vi contrarsi

two [tuː] num due; **to put ~ and ~ together** (fig) fare uno più uno

type [taɪp] n (category) genere m; (model) modello; (example) tipo; (Typ) tipo, carattere m ▷ vt (letter etc) battere (a macchina), dattilografare; **typewriter** n macchina da scrivere

typhoid ['taɪfɔɪd] n tifoidea

typhoon [taɪ'fuːn] n tifone m

typical ['tɪpɪkl] adj tipico(-a); **typically** adv tipicamente; **typically, he arrived**

late come al solito è arrivato tardi
typing ['taɪpɪŋ] *n* dattilografia
typist ['taɪpɪst] *n* dattilografo(-a)
tyre ['taɪər] (*us* **tire**) *n* pneumatico, gomma; **I've got a flat ~** ho una gomma a terra; **tyre pressure** *n* pressione *f* (delle gomme)

UFO ['juːfəu] *n abbr* (= *unidentified flying object*) UFO *m inv*
Uganda [juːˈgændə] *n* Uganda
ugly ['ʌglɪ] *adj* brutto(-a)
UHT *abbr* (= *ultra heat treated*) UHT *inv*, a lunga conservazione
UK *n abbr* = **United Kingdom**
ulcer ['ʌlsər] *n* ulcera; (*also*: **mouth ~**) afta
ultimate ['ʌltɪmət] *adj* ultimo(-a), finale; (*authority*) massimo(-a), supremo(-a); **ultimately** *adv* alla fine; in definitiva, in fin dei conti
ultimatum [ʌltɪˈmeɪtəm, -tə] (*pl* **ultimatums** *or* **ultimata**) *n* ultimatum *m inv*
ultrasound [ʌltrəˈsaund] *n* (*Med*) ultrasuono
ultraviolet ['ʌltrəˈvaɪəlɪt] *adj* ultravioletto(-a)
umbrella [ʌmˈbrɛlə] *n* ombrello
umpire ['ʌmpaɪər] *n* arbitro
UN *n abbr* (= *United Nations*) ONU *f*
unable [ʌnˈeɪbl] *adj* **to be ~ to** non potere, essere nell'impossibilità di; essere incapace di
unacceptable [ʌnəkˈsɛptəbl] *adj* (*proposal, behaviour*) inaccettabile; (*price*) impossibile
unanimous [juːˈnænɪməs] *adj* unanime
unarmed [ʌnˈɑːmd] *adj* (*without a weapon*)

disarmato(-a); (combat) senz'armi
unattended [ʌnəˈtɛndɪd] adj (car, child, luggage) incustodito(-a)
unattractive [ʌnəˈtræktɪv] adj poco attraente
unavailable [ʌnəˈveɪləbl] adj (article, room, book) non disponibile; (person) impegnato(-a)
unavoidable [ʌnəˈvɔɪdəbl] adj inevitabile
unaware [ʌnəˈwɛəᵣ] adj **to be ~ of** non sapere, ignorare; **unawares** adv di sorpresa, alla sprovvista
unbearable [ʌnˈbɛərəbl] adj insopportabile
unbeatable [ʌnˈbiːtəbl] adj imbattibile
unbelievable [ʌnbɪˈliːvəbl] adj incredibile
unborn [ʌnˈbɔːn] adj non ancora nato(-a)
unbutton [ʌnˈbʌtn] vt sbottonare
uncalled-for [ʌnˈkɔːldfɔːᵣ] adj (remark) fuori luogo inv; (action) ingiustificato(-a)
uncanny [ʌnˈkænɪ] adj misterioso(-a), strano(-a)
uncertain [ʌnˈsəːtn] adj incerto(-a); dubbio(-a); **uncertainty** n incertezza
unchanged [ʌnˈtʃeɪndʒd] adj invariato(-a)
uncle [ˈʌŋkl] n zio
unclear [ʌnˈklɪəᵣ] adj non chiaro(-a); **I'm still ~ about what I'm supposed to do** non ho ancora ben capito cosa dovrei fare
uncomfortable [ʌnˈkʌmfətəbl] adj scomodo(-a); (uneasy) a disagio, agitato(-a); (unpleasant) fastidioso(-a)
uncommon [ʌnˈkɔmən] adj raro(-a), insolito(-a), non comune
unconditional [ʌnkənˈdɪʃənl] adj incondizionato(-a), senza condizioni
unconscious [ʌnˈkɔnʃəs] adj privo(-a) di sensi, svenuto(-a); (unaware) inconsapevole, inconscio(-a) ▷ n **the ~** l'inconscio
uncontrollable [ʌnkənˈtrəuləbl] adj incontrollabile; indisciplinato(-a)
unconventional [ʌnkənˈvɛnʃənl] adj poco convenzionale
uncover [ʌnˈkʌvəᵣ] vt scoprire
undecided [ʌndɪˈsaɪdɪd] adj indeciso(-a)
undeniable [ʌndɪˈnaɪəbl] adj innegabile, indiscutibile
under [ˈʌndəᵣ] prep sotto; (less than) meno di; al disotto di; (according to) secondo, in conformità a ▷ adv (al) disotto; **~ there** là sotto; **~ repair** in riparazione; **undercover** adj segreto(-a), clandestino(-a); **underdone** adj (Culin) al sangue; (pej) poco cotto(-a); **underestimate** vt sottovalutare; **undergo** vt (irreg) subire; (treatment) sottoporsi a; **undergraduate** n studente(-essa) universitario(-a); **underground** n (BRIT:

railway) metropolitana; (Pol) movimento clandestino ▷ adj sotterraneo(-a); (fig) clandestino(-a) ▷ adv sottoterra; **to go underground** (fig) darsi alla macchia; **undergrowth** n sottobosco; **underline** vt sottolineare; **undermine** vt minare; **underneath** [ʌndəˈniːθ] adv sotto, disotto ▷ prep sotto, al di sotto di; **underpants** npl mutande fpl, slip m inv; **underpass** (BRIT) n sottopassaggio; **underprivileged** adj non abbiente; meno favorito(-a); **underscore** vt sottolineare; **undershirt** (US) n maglietta; **underskirt** (BRIT) n sottoveste f
understand [ʌndəˈstænd] (irreg: like stand) vt, vi capire, comprendere; **I don't ~** non capisco; **I ~ that ...** sento che ...; credo di capire che ...; **understandable** adj comprensibile; **understanding** adj comprensivo(-a) ▷ n comprensione f; (agreement) accordo
understatement [ʌndəˈsteɪtmənt] n **that's an ~!** a dire poco!
understood [ʌndəˈstud] pt, pp of **understand** ▷ adj inteso(-a); (implied) sottinteso(-a)
undertake [ʌndəˈteɪk] (irreg: like take) vt intraprendere; **to ~ to do sth** impegnarsi a fare qc
undertaker [ˈʌndəteɪkəᵣ] n impresario di pompe funebri
undertaking [ʌndəˈteɪkɪŋ] n impresa; (promise) promessa
under: **underwater** [ʌndəˈwɔːtəᵣ] adv sott'acqua ▷ adj subacqueo(-a); **underway** [ʌndəˈweɪ] adj **to be underway** essere in corso; **underwear** [ˈʌndəwɛəᵣ] n biancheria (intima); **underwent** [ʌndəˈwɛnt] vb see **undergo**; **underworld** [ˈʌndəwəːld] n (of crime) malavita
undesirable [ʌndɪˈzaɪərəbl] adj sgradevole
undisputed [ʌndɪsˈpjuːtɪd] adj indiscusso(-a)
undo [ʌnˈduː] vt (irreg) disfare
undone [ʌnˈdʌn] pp of **undo**; **to come ~** slacciarsi
undoubtedly [ʌnˈdautɪdlɪ] adv senza alcun dubbio
undress [ʌnˈdrɛs] vi spogliarsi
unearth [ʌnˈəːθ] vt dissotterrare; (fig) scoprire
uneasy [ʌnˈiːzɪ] adj a disagio; (worried) preoccupato(-a); (peace) precario(-a)
unemployed [ʌnɪmˈplɔɪd] adj disoccupato(-a) ▷ npl **the ~** i disoccupati
unemployment [ʌnɪmˈplɔɪmənt] n disoccupazione f; **unemployment**

benefit (US **unemployment compensation**) n sussidio di disoccupazione

unequal [ʌnˈiːkwəl] adj (length, objects) disuguale; (amounts) diverso(-a); (division of labour) ineguale

uneven [ʌnˈiːvn] adj ineguale; irregolare

unexpected [ʌnɪkˈspɛktɪd] adj inatteso(-a), imprevisto(-a); **unexpectedly** adv inaspettatamente

unfair [ʌnˈfɛəʳ] adj ~ **(to)** ingiusto(-a) (nei confronti di)

unfaithful [ʌnˈfeɪθful] adj infedele

unfamiliar [ʌnfəˈmɪlɪəʳ] adj sconosciuto(-a), strano(-a); **to be ~ with** non avere familiarità con

unfashionable [ʌnˈfæʃnəbl] adj (clothes) fuori moda; (district) non alla moda

unfasten [ʌnˈfaːsn] vt slacciare; sciogliere

unfavourable [ʌnˈfeɪvərəbl] (US **unfavorable**) adj sfavorevole

unfinished [ʌnˈfɪnɪʃt] adj incompleto(-a)

unfit [ʌnˈfɪt] adj (ill) malato(-a), in cattiva salute; (incompetent): ~ **(for)** incompetente (in); (: work, Mil) inabile (a)

unfold [ʌnˈfəuld] vt spiegare ▷ vi (story, plot) svelarsi

unforgettable [ʌnfəˈgɛtəbl] adj indimenticabile

unfortunate [ʌnˈfɔːtʃnət] adj sfortunato(-a); (event, remark) infelice; **unfortunately** adv sfortunatamente, purtroppo

unfriendly [ʌnˈfrɛndlɪ] adj poco amichevole, freddo(-a)

unfurnished [ʌnˈfəːnɪʃt] adj non ammobiliato(-a)

unhappiness [ʌnˈhæpɪnɪs] n infelicità

unhappy [ʌnˈhæpɪ] adj infelice; ~ **about/with** (arrangements etc) insoddisfatto(-a) di

unhealthy [ʌnˈhɛlθɪ] adj (gen) malsano(-a); (person) malaticcio(-a)

unheard-of [ʌnˈhəːdɔv] adj inaudito(-a), senza precedenti

unhelpful [ʌnˈhɛlpful] adj poco disponibile

unhurt [ʌnˈhəːt] adj illeso(-a)

unidentified [ʌnaɪˈdɛntɪfaɪd] adj non identificato(-a)

uniform [ˈjuːnɪfɔːm] n uniforme f, divisa ▷ adj uniforme

unify [ˈjuːnɪfaɪ] vt unificare

unimportant [ʌnɪmˈpɔːtənt] adj senza importanza, di scarsa importanza

uninhabited [ʌnɪnˈhæbɪtɪd] adj disabitato(-a)

unintentional [ʌnɪnˈtɛnʃənəl] adj involontario(-a)

union [ˈjuːnjən] n unione f; (also: **trade ~**)

sindacato ▷ cpd sindacale, dei sindacati; **Union Jack** n bandiera nazionale britannica

unique [juːˈniːk] adj unico(-a)

unisex [ˈjuːnɪsɛks] adj unisex inv

unit [ˈjuːnɪt] n unità f inv; (section: of furniture etc) elemento; (team, squad) reparto, squadra

unite [juːˈnaɪt] vt unire ▷ vi unirsi; **united** adj unito(-a); unificato(-a); (efforts) congiunto(-a); **United Kingdom** n Regno Unito; **United Nations (Organization)** n (Organizzazione f delle) Nazioni Unite; **United States (of America)** n Stati mpl Uniti (d'America)

unity [ˈjuːnɪtɪ] n unità

universal [juːnɪˈvəːsl] adj universale

universe [ˈjuːnɪvəːs] n universo

university [juːnɪˈvəːsɪtɪ] n università f inv

unjust [ʌnˈdʒʌst] adj ingiusto(-a)

unkind [ʌnˈkaɪnd] adj scortese; crudele

unknown [ʌnˈnəun] adj sconosciuto(-a)

unlawful [ʌnˈlɔːful] adj illecito(-a), illegale

unleaded [ʌnˈlɛdɪd] adj (petrol, fuel) verde, senza piombo

unleash [ʌnˈliːʃ] vt (fig) scatenare

unless [ʌnˈlɛs] conj a meno che (non) + sub

unlike [ʌnˈlaɪk] adj diverso(-a) ▷ prep a differenza di, contrariamente a

unlikely [ʌnˈlaɪklɪ] adj improbabile

unlimited [ʌnˈlɪmɪtɪd] adj illimitato(-a)

unlisted [ʌnˈlɪstɪd] (US) adj (Tel): **to be ~** non essere sull'elenco

unload [ʌnˈləud] vt scaricare

unlock [ʌnˈlɔk] vt aprire

unlucky [ʌnˈlʌkɪ] adj sfortunato(-a); (object, number) che porta sfortuna

unmarried [ʌnˈmærɪd] adj non sposato(-a); (man only) scapolo, celibe; (woman only) nubile

unmistak(e)able [ʌnmɪsˈteɪkəbl] adj inconfondibile

unnatural [ʌnˈnætʃrəl] adj innaturale; contro natura

unnecessary [ʌnˈnɛsəsərɪ] adj inutile, superfluo(-a)

UNO [ˈjuːnəu] n abbr (= United Nations Organization) ONU f

unofficial [ʌnəˈfɪʃl] adj non ufficiale; (strike) non dichiarato(-a) dal sindacato

unpack [ʌnˈpæk] vi disfare la valigia (or le valigie) ▷ vt disfare

unpaid [ʌnˈpeɪd] adj (holiday) non pagato(-a); (work) non retribuito(-a); (bill, debt) da pagare

unpleasant [ʌnˈplɛznt] adj spiacevole

unplug [ʌnˈplʌg] vt staccare

unpopular [ʌnˈpɔpjuləʳ] adj impopolare

unprecedented [ʌnˈprɛsɪdəntɪd] adj senza precedenti

unpredictable [ˌʌnprɪˈdɪktəbl] *adj*
imprevedibile

unprotected [ˈʌnprəˈtɛktɪd] *adj* (*sex*) non
protetto(-a)

unqualified [ʌnˈkwɔlɪfaɪd] *adj* (*teacher*)
non abilitato(-a); (*success*) assoluto(-a),
senza riserve

unravel [ʌnˈrævl] *vt* dipanare, districare

unreal [ʌnˈrɪəl] *adj* irreale

unrealistic [ʌnrɪəˈlɪstɪk] *adj* non
realistico(-a)

unreasonable [ʌnˈriːznəbl] *adj*
irragionevole

unrelated [ʌnrɪˈleɪtɪd] *adj* ~ (**to**) senza
rapporto (con); non imparentato(-a) (con)

unreliable [ʌnrɪˈlaɪəbl] *adj* (*person,
machine*) che non dà affidamento; (*news,
source of information*) inattendibile

unrest [ʌnˈrɛst] *n* agitazione *f*

unroll [ʌnˈrəul] *vt* srotolare

unruly [ʌnˈruːlɪ] *adj* indisciplinato(-a)

unsafe [ʌnˈseɪf] *adj* pericoloso(-a),
rischioso(-a)

unsatisfactory [ˈʌnsætɪsˈfæktərɪ] *adj*
che lascia a desiderare, insufficiente

unscrew [ʌnˈskruː] *vt* svitare

unsettled [ʌnˈsɛtld] *adj* (*person*)
turbato(-a); indeciso(-a); (*weather*)
instabile

unsettling [ʌnˈsɛtlɪŋ] *adj* inquietante

unsightly [ʌnˈsaɪtlɪ] *adj* brutto(-a),
sgradevole a vedersi

unskilled [ʌnˈskɪld] *adj* non
specializzato(-a)

unspoiled [ˈʌnˈspɔɪld], **unspoilt**
[ˈʌnˈspɔɪlt] *adj* (*place*) non deturpato(-a)

unstable [ʌnˈsteɪbl] *adj* (*gen*) instabile;
(*mentally*) squilibrato(-a)

unsteady [ʌnˈstɛdɪ] *adj* instabile,
malsicuro(-a)

unsuccessful [ʌnsəkˈsɛsful] *adj* (*writer,
proposal*) che non ha successo; (*marriage,
attempt*) mal riuscito(-a), fallito(-a); **to be ~**
(*in attempting sth*) non avere successo

unsuitable [ʌnˈsuːtəbl] *adj* inadatto(-a);
inopportuno(-a); sconveniente

unsure [ʌnˈʃuə] *adj* incerto(-a); **to be ~ of
o.s** essere insicuro(-a)

untidy [ʌnˈtaɪdɪ] *adj* (*room*) in disordine;
(*appearance*) trascurato(-a); (*person*)
disordinato(-a)

untie [ʌnˈtaɪ] *vt* (*knot, parcel*) disfare;
(*prisoner, dog*) slegare

until [ʌnˈtɪl] *prep* fino a; (*after negative*)
prima di ▷ *conj* finché, fino a quando; (*in
past, after negative*) prima che + *sub*, prima
di + *infinitive*; **~ he comes** finché *or* fino a
quando non arriva; **~ now** finora; **~ then**
fino ad allora

untrue [ʌnˈtruː] *adj* (*statement*) falso(-a),
non vero(-a)

unused [ʌnˈjuːzd] *adj* nuovo(-a)

unusual [ʌnˈjuːʒuəl] *adj* insolito(-a),
eccezionale, raro(-a); **unusually** *adv*
insolitamente

unveil [ʌnˈveɪl] *vt* scoprire; svelare

unwanted [ʌnˈwɔntɪd] *adj* (*clothing*)
smesso(-a); (*child*) non desiderato(-a)

unwell [ʌnˈwɛl] *adj* indisposto(-a); **to feel
~** non sentirsi bene

unwilling [ʌnˈwɪlɪŋ] *adj* **to be ~ to do** non
voler fare

unwind [ʌnˈwaɪnd] (*irreg: like* **wind¹**) *vt*
svolgere, srotolare ▷ *vi* (*relax*) rilassarsi

unwise [ʌnˈwaɪz] *adj* poco saggio(-a)

unwittingly [ʌnˈwɪtɪŋlɪ] *adv* senza volerlo

unwrap [ʌnˈræp] *vt* disfare; aprire

unzip [ʌnˈzɪp] *vt* aprire (la chiusura lampo
di); (*Comput*) dezippare

KEYWORD

up [ʌp] *prep* **he went up the stairs/the
hill** è salito su per le scale/sulla collina; **the
cat was up a tree** il gatto era su un albero;
they live further up the street vivono un
po' più su nella stessa strada
▷ *adv* **1** (*upwards, higher*) su, in alto; **up in
the sky/the mountains** su nel cielo/in
montagna; **up there** lassù; **up above** su
in alto
2: **to be up** (*out of bed*) essere alzato(-a);
(*prices, level*) essere salito(-a)
3: **up to** (*as far as*) fino a; **up to now** finora
4: **to be up to** (*depending on*): **it's up to
you** sta a lei, dipende da lei; (*equal to*):
he's not up to it (*job, task etc*) non ne è
all'altezza; (*inf: be doing*): **what is he up to?**
cosa sta combinando?
▷ *n* **ups and downs** alti e bassi *mpl*

up-and-coming [ˈʌpəndˈkʌmɪŋ] *adj*
pieno(-a) di promesse, promettente

upbringing [ˈʌpbrɪŋɪŋ] *n* educazione *f*

update [ʌpˈdeɪt] *vt* aggiornare

upfront [ʌpˈfrʌnt] *adj* (*inf*) franco(-a),
aperto(-a) ▷ *adv* (*pay*) subito

upgrade [ʌpˈgreɪd] *vt* (*house, job*)
migliorare; (*employee*) avanzare di grado

upheaval [ʌpˈhiːvl] *n* sconvolgimento;
tumulto

uphill [ʌpˈhɪl] *adj* in salita; (*fig: task*) difficile
▷ *adv* **to go ~** andare in salita, salire

upholstery [ʌpˈhəulstərɪ] *n* tappezzeria

upmarket [ʌpˈmɑːkɪt] *adj* (*product*) che si
rivolge ad una fascia di mercato superiore

upon [əˈpɔn] *prep* su

upper [ˈʌpəʳ] *adj* superiore ▷ *n* (*of shoe*)

tomaia; **upper-class** adj dell'alta borghesia

upright ['ʌpraɪt] adj diritto(-a); verticale; (fig) diritto(-a), onesto(-a)

uprising ['ʌpraɪzɪŋ] n insurrezione f, rivolta

uproar ['ʌprɔːr] n tumulto, clamore m

upset [n 'ʌpsɛt, vb, adj ʌp'sɛt] (irreg: like **set**) n (to plan etc) contrattempo; (stomach upset) disturbo ▷ vt (glass etc) rovesciare; (plan, stomach) scombussolare; (person: offend) contrariare; (: grieve) addolorare; sconvolgere ▷ adj contrariato(-a), addolorato(-a); (stomach) scombussolato(-a)

upside-down [ʌpsaɪd'daun] adv sottosopra

upstairs [ʌp'stɛəz] adv, adj di sopra, al piano superiore ▷ n piano di sopra

up-to-date ['ʌptə'deɪt] adj moderno(-a); aggiornato(-a)

uptown ['ʌptaun] (US) adv verso i quartieri residenziali ▷ adj dei quartieri residenziali

upward ['ʌpwəd] adj ascendente; verso l'alto; **upward(s)** adv in su, verso l'alto

uranium [juə'reɪnɪəm] n uranio

Uranus [juə'reɪnəs] n (planet) Urano

urban ['əːbən] adj urbano(-a)

urge [əːdʒ] n impulso; stimolo; forte desiderio ▷ vt **to ~ sb to do** esortare qn a fare, spingere qn a fare; raccomandare a qn di fare

urgency ['əːdʒənsɪ] n urgenza; (of tone) insistenza

urgent ['əːdʒənt] adj urgente; (voice) insistente

urinal ['juərɪnl] n (BRIT: building) vespasiano; (: vessel) orinale m, pappagallo

urinate ['juərɪneɪt] vi orinare

urine ['juərɪn] n orina

us [ʌs] pron ci; (stressed, after prep) noi; see also **me**

US(A) n abbr (= United States (of America)) USA mpl

use [n juːs, vb juːz] n uso; impiego, utilizzazione f ▷ vt usare, utilizzare, servirsi di; **in ~** in uso; **out of ~** fuori uso; **to be of ~** essere utile, servire; **it's no ~** non serve, è inutile; **she ~d to do it** lo faceva (una volta), era solita farlo; **to be ~d to** avere l'abitudine di; **use up** vt consumare, esaurire; **used** adj (object, car) usato(-a); **useful** adj utile; **useless** adj inutile; (person) inetto(-a); **user** n utente m/f; **user-friendly** adj (computer) di facile uso

usual ['juːʒuəl] adj solito(-a); **as ~** come al solito, come d'abitudine; **usually** adv di solito

utensil [juː'tɛnsl] n utensile m; **kitchen ~s** utensili da cucina

utility [juː'tɪlɪtɪ] n utilità; (also: **public ~**) servizio pubblico

utilize ['juːtɪlaɪz] vt utilizzare; sfruttare

utmost ['ʌtməust] adj estremo(-a) ▷ n **to do one's ~** fare il possibile or di tutto

utter ['ʌtər] adj assoluto(-a), totale ▷ vt pronunciare, proferire; emettere; **utterly** adv completamente, del tutto

U-turn ['juː'təːn] n inversione f a U

V

v. *abbr* = **verse**; **versus**; **volt**; (= *vide*) vedi, vedere

vacancy ['veɪkənsɪ] *n* (BRIT: *job*) posto libero; (*room*) stanza libera; **"no vacancies"** "completo"

> Be careful not to translate *vacancy* by the Italian word *vacanza*.

vacant ['veɪkənt] *adj* (*job, seat etc*) libero(-a); (*expression*) assente

vacate [və'keɪt] *vt* lasciare libero(-a)

vacation [və'keɪʃən] (*esp US*) *n* vacanze *fpl*; **vacationer** (*US* **vacationist**) *n* vacanziere(-a)

vaccination [væksɪ'neɪʃən] *n* vaccinazione *f*

vaccine ['væksiːn] *n* vaccino

vacuum ['vækjum] *n* vuoto; **vacuum cleaner** *n* aspirapolvere *m inv*

vagina [və'dʒaɪnə] *n* vagina

vague [veɪg] *adj* vago(-a); (*blurred: photo, memory*) sfocato(-a)

vain [veɪn] *adj* (*useless*) inutile, vano(-a); (*conceited*) vanitoso(-a); **in ~** inutilmente, invano

Valentine's Day ['væləntaɪnzdeɪ] *n* San Valentino *m*

valid ['vælɪd] *adj* valido(-a), valevole; (*excuse*) valido(-a)

valley ['vælɪ] *n* valle *f*

valuable ['væljuəbl] *adj* (*jewel*) di (grande)

valore; (*time, help*) prezioso(-a); **valuables** *npl* oggetti *mpl* di valore

value ['væljuː] *n* valore *m* ▷ *vt* (*fix price*) valutare, dare un prezzo a; (*cherish*) apprezzare, tenere a; **~s** *npl* (*principles*) valori *mpl*

valve [vælv] *n* valvola

vampire ['væmpaɪə'] *n* vampiro

van [væn] *n* (*Aut*) furgone *m*; (BRIT: *Rail*) vagone *m*

vandal ['vændl] *n* vandalo(-a); **vandalism** *n* vandalismo; **vandalize** *vt* vandalizzare

vanilla [və'nɪlə] *n* vaniglia ▷ *cpd* (*ice cream*) alla vaniglia

vanish ['vænɪʃ] *vi* svanire, scomparire

vanity ['vænɪtɪ] *n* vanità

vapour ['veɪpə'] (*US* **vapor**) *n* vapore *m*

variable ['vɛərɪəbl] *adj* variabile; (*mood*) mutevole

variant ['vɛərɪənt] *n* variante *f*

variation [vɛərɪ'eɪʃən] *n* variazione *f*; (*in opinion*) cambiamento

varied ['vɛərɪd] *adj* vario(-a), diverso(-a)

variety [və'raɪətɪ] *n* varietà *f inv*; (*quantity*) quantità, numero

various ['vɛərɪəs] *adj* vario(-a), diverso(-a); (*several*) parecchi(-e), molti(-e)

varnish ['vɑːnɪʃ] *n* vernice *f*; (*nail varnish*) smalto ▷ *vt* verniciare; mettere lo smalto su

vary ['vɛərɪ] *vt, vi* variare, mutare

vase [vɑːz] *n* vaso

Vaseline® ['væsɪliːn] *n* vaselina

vast [vɑːst] *adj* vasto(-a); (*amount, success*) enorme

VAT [væt] *n abbr* (= *value added tax*) I.V.A. *f*

Vatican ['vætɪkən] *n* **the ~** il Vaticano

vault [vɔːlt] *n* (*of roof*) volta; (*tomb*) tomba; (*in bank*) camera blindata ▷ *vt* (*also: ~ over*) saltare (d'un balzo)

VCR *n abbr* = **video cassette recorder**

VDU *n abbr* = **visual display unit**

veal [viːl] *n* vitello

veer [vɪə'] *vi* girare; virare

vegan ['viːgən] *n* vegetaliano(-a)

vegetable ['vedʒtəbl] *n* verdura, ortaggio ▷ *adj* vegetale

vegetarian [vedʒɪ'tɛərɪən] *adj, n* vegetariano(-a); **do you have any ~ dishes?** avete piatti vegetariani?

vegetation [vedʒɪ'teɪʃən] *n* vegetazione *f*

vehicle ['viːɪkl] *n* veicolo

veil [veɪl] *n* velo

vein [veɪn] *n* vena; (*on leaf*) nervatura

Velcro® ['vɛlkrəu] *n* velcro® *m inv*

velvet ['vɛlvɪt] *n* velluto ▷ *adj* di velluto

vending machine ['vɛndɪŋ-] *n* distributore *m* automatico

vendor ['vɛndə'] *n* venditore(-trice)

vengeance ['vɛndʒəns] n vendetta; **with a ~** (fig) davvero; furiosamente

Venice ['vɛnɪs] n Venezia

venison ['vɛnɪsn] n carne f di cervo

venom ['vɛnəm] n veleno

vent [vɛnt] n foro, apertura; (in dress, jacket) spacco ▷ vt (fig: one's feelings) sfogare, dare sfogo a

ventilation [vɛntɪ'leɪʃən] n ventilazione f

venture ['vɛntʃər] n impresa (rischiosa) ▷ vt rischiare, azzardare ▷ vi avventurarsi; **business ~** iniziativa commerciale

venue ['vɛnju:] n luogo (designato) per l'incontro

Venus ['vi:nəs] n (planet) Venere m

verb [və:b] n verbo; **verbal** adj verbale; (translation) orale

verdict ['və:dɪkt] n verdetto

verge [və:dʒ] (BRIT) n bordo, orlo; **"soft ~s"** (BRIT: Aut) banchine fpl cedevoli; **on the ~ of doing** sul punto di fare

verify ['vɛrɪfaɪ] vt verificare; (prove the truth of) confermare

versatile ['və:sətaɪl] adj (person) versatile; (machine, tool etc) (che si presta) a molti usi

verse [və:s] n versi mpl; (stanza) stanza, strofa; (in bible) versetto

version ['və:ʃən] n versione f

versus ['və:səs] prep contro

vertical ['və:tɪkl] adj verticale ▷ n verticale m

very ['vɛrɪ] adv molto ▷ adj **the ~ book which** proprio il libro che; **the ~ last** proprio l'ultimo; **at the ~ least** almeno; **~ much** moltissimo

vessel ['vɛsl] n (Anat) vaso; (Naut) nave f; (container) recipiente m

vest [vɛst] n (BRIT) maglia; (: sleeveless) canottiera; (US: waistcoat) gilè m inv

vet [vɛt] n abbr (BRIT: = veterinary surgeon) veterinario ▷ vt esaminare minuziosamente

veteran ['vɛtərn] n (also: **war ~**) veterano

veterinary surgeon ['vɛtrɪnərɪ-] (US **veterinarian**) n veterinario

veto ['vi:təu] (pl **vetoes**) n veto ▷ vt opporre il veto a

via ['vaɪə] prep (by way of) via; (by means of) tramite

viable ['vaɪəbl] adj attuabile; vitale

vibrate [vaɪ'breɪt] vi **to ~ (with)** vibrare (di); (resound) risonare (di)

vibration [vaɪ'breɪʃən] n vibrazione f

vicar ['vɪkər] n pastore m

vice [vaɪs] n (evil) vizio; (Tech) morsa; **vice-chairman** (irreg) n vicepresidente m

vice versa ['vaɪsɪ'və:sə] adv viceversa

vicinity [vɪ'sɪnɪtɪ] n vicinanze fpl

vicious ['vɪʃəs] adj (remark, dog) cattivo(-a); (blow) violento(-a)

victim ['vɪktɪm] n vittima

victor ['vɪktər] n vincitore m

Victorian [vɪk'tɔ:rɪən] adj vittoriano(-a)

victorious [vɪk'tɔ:rɪəs] adj vittorioso(-a)

victory ['vɪktərɪ] n vittoria

video ['vɪdɪəu] cpd video... ▷ n (video film) video m inv; (also: **~ cassette**) videocassetta; (also: **~ cassette recorder**) videoregistratore m; **video camera** n videocamera; **video (cassette) recorder** n videoregistratore m; **video game** n videogioco; **video shop** n videonoleggio; **video tape** n videotape m inv; **video wall** n schermo m multivideo inv

vie [vaɪ] vi **to ~ with** competere con, rivaleggiare con

Vienna [vɪ'ɛnə] n Vienna

Vietnam [vjɛt'næm] n Vietnam m; **Vietnamese** adj, n inv vietnamita m/f

view [vju:] n vista, veduta; (opinion) opinione f ▷ vt (look at: also fig) considerare; (house) visitare; **on ~** (in museum etc) esposto(-a); **in full ~ of** sotto gli occhi di; **in ~ of the weather/the fact that** considerato il tempo/che; **in my ~** a mio parere; **viewer** n spettatore(-trice); **viewpoint** n punto di vista; (place) posizione f

vigilant ['vɪdʒɪlənt] adj vigile

vigorous ['vɪgərəs] adj vigoroso(-a)

vile [vaɪl] adj (action) vile; (smell) disgustoso(-a), nauseante; (temper) pessimo(-a)

villa ['vɪlə] n villa

village ['vɪlɪdʒ] n villaggio; **villager** n abitante m/f di villaggio

villain ['vɪlən] n (scoundrel) canaglia; (BRIT: criminal) criminale m; (in novel etc) cattivo

vinaigrette [vɪneɪ'grɛt] n vinaigrette f inv

vine [vaɪn] n vite f; (climbing plant) rampicante m

vinegar ['vɪnɪgər] n aceto

vineyard ['vɪnjɑ:d] n vigna, vigneto

vintage ['vɪntɪdʒ] n (year) annata, produzione f ▷ cpd d'annata

vinyl ['vaɪnl] n vinile m

viola [vɪ'əulə] n viola

violate ['vaɪəleɪt] vt violare

violation [vaɪə'leɪʃən] n violazione f; **in ~ of sth** violando qc

violence ['vaɪələns] n violenza

violent ['vaɪələnt] adj violento(-a)

violet ['vaɪələt] adj (colour) viola inv, violetto(-a) ▷ n (plant) violetta; (colour) violetto

violin [vaɪə'lɪn] n violino

VIP n abbr (= very important person) V.I.P. m/f inv

virgin ['vəːdʒɪn] n vergine f ▷ adj vergine inv

Virgo ['vəːgəu] n (sign) Vergine f

virtual ['vəːtjuəl] adj effettivo(-a), vero(-a); (Comput, Physics) virtuale; (in effect): **it's a ~ impossibility** è praticamente impossibile; **the ~ leader** il capo all'atto pratico; **virtually** ['vəːtjuəlɪ] adv (almost) praticamente; **virtual reality** n (Comput) realtà virtuale

virtue ['vəːtjuː] n virtù f inv; (advantage) pregio, vantaggio; **by ~ of** grazie a

virus ['vaɪərəs] n (also Comput) virus m inv

visa ['viːzə] n visto

vise [vaɪs] (US) n (Tech) = **vice**

visibility [vɪzɪ'bɪlɪtɪ] n visibilità

visible ['vɪzəbl] adj visibile

vision ['vɪʒən] n (sight) vista; (foresight, in dream) visione f

visit ['vɪzɪt] n visita; (stay) soggiorno ▷ vt (person: US: also: ~ **with**) andare a trovare; (place) visitare; **visiting hours** npl (in hospital etc) orario delle visite; **visitor** n visitatore(-trice); (guest) ospite m/f; **visitor centre** (US **visitor center**) n centro informazioni per visitatori di museo, zoo, parco ecc

visual ['vɪzjuəl] adj visivo(-a); visuale; ottico(-a); **visualize** ['vɪzjuəlaɪz] vt immaginare, figurarsi; (foresee) prevedere

vital ['vaɪtl] adj vitale

vitality [vaɪ'tælɪtɪ] n vitalità

vitamin ['vɪtəmɪn] n vitamina

vivid ['vɪvɪd] adj vivido(-a)

V-neck ['viːnɛk] n maglione m con lo scollo a V

vocabulary [vəu'kæbjulərɪ] n vocabolario

vocal ['vəukl] adj (Mus) vocale; (communication) verbale

vocational [vəu'keɪʃənl] adj professionale

vodka ['vɒdkə] n vodka f inv

vogue [vəug] n moda; (popularity) popolarità, voga

voice [vɔɪs] n voce f ▷ vt (opinion) esprimere; **voice mail** n servizio di segreteria telefonica

void [vɔɪd] n vuoto ▷ adj (invalid) nullo(-a); (empty): ~ **of** privo(-a) di

volatile ['vɒlətaɪl] adj volatile; (fig) volubile

volcano [vɒl'keɪnəu] (pl **volcanoes**) n vulcano

volleyball ['vɒlɪbɔːl] n pallavolo f

volt [vəult] n volt m inv; **voltage** n tensione f, voltaggio

volume ['vɒljuːm] n volume m

voluntarily ['vɒləntrɪlɪ] adv volontariamente; gratuitamente

voluntary ['vɒləntərɪ] adj volontario(-a); (unpaid) gratuito(-a), non retribuito(-a)

volunteer [vɒlən'tɪəʳ] n volontario(-a) ▷ vt offrire volontariamente ▷ vi (Mil) arruolarsi volontario; **to ~ to do** offrire (volontariamente) di fare

vomit ['vɒmɪt] n vomito ▷ vt, vi vomitare

vote [vəut] n voto, suffragio; (cast) voto; (franchise) diritto di voto ▷ vt **to be ~d chairman** etc venir eletto presidente etc; (propose): **to ~ that** approvare la proposta che ▷ vi votare; ~ **of thanks** discorso di ringraziamento; **voter** n elettore(-trice); **voting** n scrutinio

voucher ['vautʃəʳ] n (for meal, petrol etc) buono

vow [vau] n voto, promessa solenne ▷ vt **to ~ to do/that** giurare di fare/che

vowel ['vauəl] n vocale f

voyage ['vɔɪɪdʒ] n viaggio per mare, traversata

vulgar ['vʌlgəʳ] adj volgare

vulnerable ['vʌlnərəbl] adj vulnerabile

vulture ['vʌltʃəʳ] n avvoltoio

waddle ['wɒdl] *vi* camminare come una papera

wade [weɪd] *vi* **to ~ through** camminare a stento in; (*fig: book*) leggere con fatica

wafer ['weɪfə'] *n* (*Culin*) cialda

waffle ['wɒfl] *n* (*Culin*) cialda; (*inf*) ciance *fpl* ▷ *vi* cianciare

wag [wæg] *vt* agitare, muovere ▷ *vi* agitarsi

wage [weɪdʒ] *n* (*also: ~s*) salario, paga ▷ *vt* **to ~ war** fare la guerra

wag(g)on ['wægən] *n* (*horse-drawn*) carro; (BRIT: *Rail*) vagone *m* (merci)

wail [weɪl] *n* gemito; (*of siren*) urlo ▷ *vi* gemere; urlare

waist [weɪst] *n* vita, cintola; **waistcoat** (BRIT) *n* panciotto, gilè *m inv*

wait [weɪt] *n* attesa ▷ *vi* aspettare, attendere; **to lie in ~ for** stare in agguato a; **to ~ for** aspettare; **~ for me, please** aspettami, per favore; **I can't ~ to** (*fig*) non vedo l'ora di; **wait on** *vt fus* servire; **waiter** *n* cameriere *m*; **waiting list** *n* lista di attesa; **waiting room** *n* sala d'aspetto *or* d'attesa; **waitress** *n* cameriera

waive [weɪv] *vt* rinunciare a, abbandonare

wake [weɪk] (*pt* **woke**, **waked**, *pp* **woken**, **waked**) *vt* (*also: ~ up*) svegliare ▷ *vi* (*also: ~ up*) svegliarsi ▷ *n* (*for dead person*) veglia funebre; (*Naut*) scia

Wales [weɪlz] *n* Galles *m*

walk [wɔːk] *n* passeggiata; (*short*) giretto; (*gait*) passo, andatura; (*path*) sentiero; (*in park etc*) sentiero, vialetto ▷ *vi* camminare; (*for pleasure, exercise*) passeggiare ▷ *vt* (*distance*) fare *or* percorrere a piedi; (*dog*) accompagnare, portare a passeggiare; **10 minutes' ~ from** 10 minuti di cammino *or* a piedi da; **from all ~s of life** di tutte le condizioni sociali; **walk out** *vi* (*audience*) andarsene; (*workers*) scendere in sciopero; **walker** *n* (*person*) camminatore(-trice); **walkie-talkie** ['wɔːkɪ'tɔːkɪ] *n* walkie-talkie *m inv*; **walking** *n* camminare *m*; **walking shoes** *npl* pedule *fpl*; **walking stick** *n* bastone *m* da passeggio; **Walkman®** ['wɔːkmən] *n* Walkman® *m inv*; **walkway** *n* passaggio pedonale

wall [wɔːl] *n* muro; (*internal, of tunnel, cave*) parete *f*

wallet ['wɒlɪt] *n* portafoglio; **I can't find my ~** non trovo il portafoglio

wallpaper ['wɔːlpeɪpə'] *n* carta da parati ▷ *vt* (*room*) mettere la carta da parati in

walnut ['wɔːlnʌt] *n* noce *f*; (*tree, wood*) noce *m*

walrus ['wɔːlrəs] (*pl* **walrus** *or* **walruses**) *n* tricheco

waltz [wɔːlts] *n* valzer *m inv* ▷ *vi* ballare il valzer

wand [wɒnd] *n* (*also:* **magic ~**) bacchetta (magica)

wander ['wɒndə'] *vi* (*person*) girare senza meta, girovagare; (*thoughts*) vagare ▷ *vt* girovagare per

want [wɒnt] *vt* volere; (*need*) aver bisogno di ▷ *n* **for ~ of** per mancanza di; **wanted** *adj* (*criminal*) ricercato(-a); **"wanted"** (*in adverts*) "cercasi"

war [wɔː'] *n* guerra; **to make ~ (on)** far guerra (a)

ward [wɔːd] *n* (*in hospital: room*) corsia; (: *section*) reparto; (*Pol*) circoscrizione *f*; (*Law: child: also:* **~ of court**) pupillo(-a)

warden ['wɔːdn] *n* (*of park, game reserve, youth hostel*) guardiano(-a); (BRIT: *of institution*) direttore(-trice); (BRIT: *also:* **traffic ~**) addetto(-a) al controllo del traffico e del parcheggio

wardrobe ['wɔːdrəub] *n* (*cupboard*) guardaroba *m inv*, armadio; (*clothes*) guardaroba; (*Cinema, Theatre*) costumi *mpl*

warehouse ['wɛəhaus] *n* magazzino

warfare ['wɔːfɛə'] *n* guerra

warhead ['wɔːhɛd] *n* (*Mil*) testata

warm [wɔːm] *adj* caldo(-a); (*thanks, welcome, applause*) caloroso(-a); (*person*) cordiale; **it's ~** fa caldo; **I'm ~** ho caldo; **warm up** *vi* scaldarsi, riscaldarsi

▷ *vt* scaldare, riscaldare; (*engine*) far scaldare; **warmly** *adv* (*applaud, welcome*) calorosamente; (*dress*) con abiti pesanti; **warmth** *n* calore *m*

warn [wɔːn] *vt* **to ~ sb that/(not) to do/of** avvertire *or* avvisare qn che/di (non) fare/di; **warning** *n* avvertimento; (*notice*) avviso; (*signal*) segnalazione *f*; **warning light** *n* spia luminosa

warrant ['wɔrnt] *n* (*voucher*) buono; (*Law:* *to arrest*) mandato di cattura; (*: to search*) mandato di perquisizione

warranty ['wɔrəntɪ] *n* garanzia

warrior ['wɔrɪər] *n* guerriero(-a)

Warsaw ['wɔːsɔː] *n* Varsavia

warship ['wɔːʃɪp] *n* nave *f* da guerra

wart [wɔːt] *n* verruca

wartime ['wɔːtaɪm] *n* **in ~** in tempo di guerra

wary ['wɛərɪ] *adj* prudente

was [wɔz] *pt of* **be**

wash [wɔʃ] *vt* lavare ▷ *vi* lavarsi; (*sea*) **to ~ over/against sth** infrangersi su/contro qc ▷ *n* lavaggio; (*of ship*) scia; **to give sth a ~** lavare qc, dare una lavata a qc; **to have a ~** lavarsi; **wash up** *vi* (*BRIT*) lavare i piatti; (*US*) darsi una lavata; **washbasin** (*US* **washbowl**) *n* lavabo; **wash cloth** (*US*) *n* pezzuola (per lavarsi); **washer** *n* (*Tech*) rondella; **washing** *n* (*linen etc*) bucato; **washing line** *n* (*BRIT*) corda del bucato; **washing machine** *n* lavatrice *f*; **washing powder** (*BRIT*) *n* detersivo (in polvere)

Washington ['wɔʃɪŋtən] *n* Washington *f*

wash: **washing-up** *n* rigovernatura, lavatura dei piatti; **washing-up liquid** *n* detersivo liquido (per stoviglie); **washroom** *n* gabinetto

wasn't ['wɔznt] = **was not**

wasp [wɔsp] *n* vespa

waste [weɪst] *n* spreco; (*of time*) perdita; (*rubbish*) rifiuti *mpl*; (*also:* **household ~**) immondizie *fpl* ▷ *adj* (*material*) di scarto; (*food*) avanzato(-a); (*land*) incolto(-a) ▷ *vt* sprecare; **waste ground** (*BRIT*) *n* terreno incolto *or* abbandonato; **wastepaper basket** ['weɪstpeɪpə-] *n* cestino per la carta straccia

watch [wɔtʃ] *n* (*also:* **wrist ~**) orologio (da polso); (*act of watching, vigilance*) sorveglianza; (*guard:* Mil, Naut) guardia; (*Naut: spell of duty*) quarto ▷ *vt* (*look at*) osservare; (*: match, programme*) guardare; (*spy on, guard*) sorvegliare, tenere d'occhio; (*be careful of*) fare attenzione a ▷ *vi* osservare, guardare; (*keep guard*) fare *or* montare la guardia; **watch out** *vi* fare attenzione; **watchdog** *n* (*also fig*) cane *m* da guardia; **watch strap** *n* cinturino da

orologio

water ['wɔːtər] *n* acqua ▷ *vt* (*plant*) annaffiare ▷ *vi* (*eyes*) lacrimare; (*mouth*): **to make sb's mouth ~** far venire l'acquolina in bocca a qn; **in British ~s** nelle acque territoriali britanniche; **water down** *vt* (*milk*) diluire; (*fig: story*) edulcorare; **watercolour** (*US* **watercolor**) *n* acquerello; **watercress** *n* crescione *m*; **waterfall** *n* cascata; **watering can** *n* annaffiatoio; **watermelon** *n* anguria, cocomero; **waterproof** *adj* impermeabile; **water-skiing** *n* sci *m* acquatico

watt [wɔt] *n* watt *m inv*

wave [weɪv] *n* onda; (*of hand*) gesto, segno; (*in hair*) ondulazione *f*; (*fig: surge*) ondata ▷ *vi* fare un cenno con la mano; (*branches, grass*) ondeggiare; (*flag*) sventolare ▷ *vt* (*hand*) fare un gesto con; (*handkerchief*) sventolare; (*stick*) brandire; **wavelength** *n* lunghezza d'onda

waver ['weɪvər] *vi* esitare; (*voice*) tremolare

wavy ['weɪvɪ] *adj* ondulato(-a); ondeggiante

wax [wæks] *n* cera ▷ *vt* dare la cera a; (*car*) lucidare ▷ *vi* (*moon*) crescere

way [weɪ] *n* via; (*path, access*) passaggio; (*distance*) distanza; (*direction*) parte *f*, direzione *f*; (*manner*) modo, stile *m*; (*habit*) abitudine *f*; **which ~? — this ~** da che parte *or* in quale direzione? — da questa parte *or* per di qua; **on the ~** (*en route*) per strada; **to be on one's ~** essere in cammino *or* sulla strada; **to be in the ~** bloccare il passaggio; (*fig*) essere tra i piedi *or* d'impiccio; **to go out of one's ~ to do** (*fig*) mettercela tutta *or* fare di tutto per fare; **under ~** (*project*) in corso; **to lose one's ~** perdere la strada; **in a ~** in un certo senso; **in some ~s** sotto certi aspetti; **no ~!** (*inf*) neanche per idea!; **by the ~ ...** a proposito ...; **"~ in"** (*BRIT*) "entrata", "ingresso"; **"~ out"** (*BRIT*) "uscita"; **the ~ back** la strada del ritorno; **"give ~"** (*BRIT: Aut*) "dare la precedenza"

W.C. ['dʌblju:si:] (*BRIT*) *n* W.C. *m inv*, gabinetto

we [wiː] *pl pron* noi

weak [wiːk] *adj* debole; (*health*) precario(-a); (*beam etc*) fragile; (*tea*) leggero(-a); **weaken** *vi* indebolirsi ▷ *vt* indebolire; **weakness** *n* debolezza; (*fault*) punto debole, difetto; **to have a weakness for** avere un debole per

wealth [wɛlθ] *n* (*money, resources*) ricchezza, ricchezze *fpl*; (*of details*) abbondanza, profusione *f*; **wealthy** *adj* ricco(-a)

weapon ['wɛpən] *n* arma; **~s of mass**

destruction armi *mpl* di distruzione di massa

wear [wɛəʳ] (*pt* **wore**, *pp* **worn**) *n* (*use*) uso; (*damage through use*) logorio, usura; (*clothing*): **sports/baby ~** abbigliamento sportivo/per neonati ▷ *vt* (*clothes*) portare; (*put on*) mettersi; (*damage: through use*) consumare ▷ *vi* (*last*) durare; (*rub etc through*) consumarsi; **evening ~** abiti *mpl* or tenuta da sera; **wear off** *vi* sparire lentamente; **wear out** *vt* consumare; (*person, strength*) esaurire

weary ['wɪərɪ] *adj* stanco(-a) ▷ *vi* **to ~ of** stancarsi di

weasel ['wiːzl] *n* (*Zool*) donnola

weather ['wɛðəʳ] *n* tempo ▷ *vt* (*storm, crisis*) superare; **What's the ~ like?** che tempo fa?; **under the ~** (*fig: ill*) poco bene; **weather forecast** *n* previsioni *fpl* del tempo, bollettino meteorologico

weave [wiːv] (*pt* **wove**, *pp* **woven**) *vt* (*cloth*) tessere; (*basket*) intrecciare

web [wɛb] *n* (*of spider*) ragnatela; (*on foot*) palma; (*fabric, also fig*) tessuto; **the (World Wide) W~** la Rete; **web page** *n* (*Comput*) pagina *f* web *inv*; **website** *n* (*Comput*) sito (Internet)

wed [wɛd] (*pt*, *pp* **wedded**) *vt* sposare ▷ *vi* sposarsi

we'd [wiːd] = **we had**; **we would**

Wed. *abbr* (= *Wednesday*) mer.

wedding ['wɛdɪŋ] *n* matrimonio; **wedding anniversary** *n* anniversario di matrimonio; **wedding day** *n* giorno delle nozze or del matrimonio; **wedding dress** *n* abito nuziale; **wedding ring** *n* fede *f*

wedge [wɛdʒ] *n* (*of wood etc*) zeppa; (*of cake*) fetta ▷ *vt* (*fix*) fissare con zeppe; (*pack tightly*) incastrare

Wednesday ['wɛdnzdɪ] *n* mercoledì *m inv*

wee [wiː] (*Scottish*) *adj* piccolo(-a)

weed [wiːd] *n* erbaccia ▷ *vt* diserbare; **weedkiller** *n* diserbante *m*

week [wiːk] *n* settimana; **a ~ today/on Friday** oggi/venerdì a otto; **weekday** *n* giorno feriale; (*Comm*) giornata lavorativa; **weekend** *n* fine settimana *m* or *f inv*, weekend *m inv*; **weekly** *adv* ogni settimana, settimanalmente ▷ *adj* settimanale ▷ *n* settimanale *m*

weep [wiːp] (*pt*, *pp* **wept**) *vi* (*person*) piangere

weigh [weɪ] *vt*, *vi* pesare; **to ~ anchor** salpare l'ancora; **weigh up** *vt* valutare

weight [weɪt] *n* peso; **to lose/put on ~** dimagrire/ingrassare; **weightlifting** *n* sollevamento pesi

weir [wɪəʳ] *n* diga

weird [wɪəd] *adj* strano(-a), bizzarro(-a); (*eerie*) soprannaturale

welcome ['wɛlkəm] *adj* benvenuto(-a) ▷ *n* accoglienza, benvenuto ▷ *vt* dare il benvenuto a; (*be glad of*) rallegrarsi di; **thank you — you're ~!** grazie — prego!

weld [wɛld] *n* saldatura ▷ *vt* saldare

welfare ['wɛlfɛəʳ] *n* benessere *m*; **welfare state** *n* stato assistenziale

well [wɛl] *n* pozzo ▷ *adv* bene ▷ *adj* **to be ~** (*person*) stare bene ▷ *excl* allora!; mal; ebbene!; **as ~** anche; **as ~ as** così come; oltre a; **~ done!** bravo(-a)!; **get ~ soon!** guarisci presto!; **to do ~** andare bene

we'll [wiːl] = **we will**; **we shall**

well: **well-behaved** *adj* ubbidiente; **well-built** *adj* (*person*) ben fatto(-a); **well-dressed** *adj* ben vestito(-a), vestito(-a) bene

wellies (*inf*) ['wɛlɪz] *npl* (*BRIT*) stivali *mpl* di gomma

well: **well-known** *adj* noto(-a), famoso(-a); **well-off** *adj* benestante, danaroso(-a); **well-paid** [wɛl'peɪd] *adj* ben pagato(-a)

Welsh [wɛlʃ] *adj* gallese ▷ *n* (*Ling*) gallese *m*; **Welshman** (*irreg*) *n* gallese *m*; **Welshwoman** (*irreg*) *n* gallese *f*

went [wɛnt] *pt of* **go**

wept [wɛpt] *pt*, *pp of* **weep**

were [wəːʳ] *pt of* **be**

we're [wɪəʳ] = **we are**

weren't [wəːnt] = **were not**

west [wɛst] *n* ovest *m*, occidente *m*, ponente *m* ▷ *adj* (a) ovest *inv*, occidentale ▷ *adv* verso ovest; **the W~** l'Occidente *m*; **westbound** ['wɛstbaund] *adj* (*traffic*) diretto(-a) a ovest; (*carriageway*) ovest *inv*; **western** *adj* occidentale, dell'ovest ▷ *n* (*Cinema*) western *m inv*; **West Indian** *adj* delle Indie Occidentali ▷ *n* abitante *m/f* delle Indie Occidentali; **West Indies** [-'ɪndɪz] *npl* Indie *fpl* Occidentali

wet [wɛt] *adj* umido(-a), bagnato(-a); (*soaked*) fradicio(-a); (*rainy*) piovoso(-a) ▷ *n* (*BRIT: Pol*) politico moderato; **to get ~** bagnarsi; **"~ paint"** "vernice fresca"; **wetsuit** *n* tuta da sub

we've [wiːv] = **we have**

whack [wæk] *vt* picchiare, battere

whale [weɪl] *n* (*Zool*) balena

wharf [wɔːf] (*pl* **wharves**) *n* banchina

 KEYWORD

what [wɔt] *adj* **1** (*in direct/indirect questions*) che; quale; **what size is it?** che taglia è?; **what colour is it?** di che colore è?; **what books do you want?** quali or che libri vuole?

2 (*in exclamations*) che; **what a mess!** che

disordine!

▷ *pron* **1** (*interrogative*) che cosa, cosa, che; **what are you doing?** che or(che) cosa fai?; **what are you talking about?** di che cosa parli?; **what is it called?** come si chiama?; **what about me?** e io?; **what about doing …?** e se facessimo …?
2 (*relative*) ciò che, quello che; **I saw what you did/was on the table** ho visto quello che hai fatto/quello che era sul tavolo
3 (*indirect use*) (che) cosa; **he asked me what she had said** mi ha chiesto che cosa avesse detto; **tell me what you're thinking about** dimmi a cosa stai pensando
▷ *excl* (*disbelieving*) cosa!, come!

whatever [wɔt'ɛvə] *adj* ~ **book** qualunque or qualsiasi libro + *sub* ▷ *pron* **do ~ is necessary/you want** faccia qualunque or qualsiasi cosa sia necessaria/lei voglia; ~ **happens** qualunque cosa accada; **no reason** ~ or **whatsoever** nessuna ragione affatto or al mondo; **nothing** ~ proprio niente
whatsoever [wɔtsəu'ɛvə] *adj* = **whatever**
wheat [wiːt] *n* grano, frumento
wheel [wiːl] *n* ruota; (*Aut: also*: **steering** ~) volante *m*; (*Naut*) (ruota del) timone *m* ▷ *vt* spingere ▷ *vi* (*birds*) roteare; (*also*: ~ **round**) girare; **wheelbarrow** *n* carriola; **wheelchair** *n* sedia a rotelle; **wheel clamp** *n* (*Aut*) morsa che blocca la ruota di una vettura in sosta vietata
wheeze [wiːz] *vi* ansimare

 KEYWORD

when [wɛn] *adv* quando; **when did it happen?** quando è successo?
▷ *conj* **1** (*at, during, after the time that*) quando; **she was reading when I came in** quando sono entrato lei leggeva; **that was when I needed you** era allora che avevo bisogno di te
2 (*on, at which*): **on the day when I met him** il giorno in cui l'ho incontrato; **one day when it was raining** un giorno che pioveva
3 (*whereas*) quando, mentre; **you said I was wrong when in fact I was right** mi hai detto che avevo torto, quando in realtà avevo ragione

whenever [wɛn'ɛvə] *adv* quando mai
▷ *conj* quando; (*every time that*) ogni volta che
where [wɛəʳ] *adv, conj* dove; **this is** ~ è qui che; **whereabouts** *adv* dove ▷ *n* **sb's**

whereabouts luogo dove qn si trova;
whereas *conj* mentre; **whereby** *pron* per cui; **wherever** [-'ɛvəʳ] *conj* dovunque + *sub*; (*interrogative*) dove mai
whether ['wɛðəʳ] *conj* se; **I don't know ~ to accept or not** non so se accettare o no; **it's doubtful ~** è poco probabile che; **~ you go or not** che lei vada o no

 KEYWORD

which [wɪtʃ] *adj* **1** (*interrogative: direct, indirect*) quale; **which picture do you want?** quale quadro vuole?; **which one?** quale?; **which one of you did it?** chi di voi lo ha fatto?
2: **in which case** nel qual caso
▷ *pron* **1** (*interrogative*) quale; **which (of these) are yours?** quali di questi sono suoi?; **which of you are coming?** chi di voi viene?
2 (*relative*) che; (: *indirect*) cui, il (la) quale; **the apple which you ate/which is on the table** la mela che hai mangiato/che è sul tavolo; **the chair on which you are sitting** la sedia sulla quale or su cui sei seduto; **he said he knew, which is true** ha detto che lo sapeva, il che è vero; **after which** dopo di che

whichever [wɪtʃ'ɛvə] *adj* **take ~ book you prefer** prenda qualsiasi libro che preferisce; **~ book you take** qualsiasi libro prenda
while [waɪl] *n* momento ▷ *conj* mentre; (*as long as*) finché; (*although*) sebbene + *sub*; per quanto + *sub*; **for a ~** per un po'
whilst [waɪlst] *conj* = **while**
whim [wɪm] *n* capriccio
whine [waɪn] *n* gemito ▷ *vi* gemere; uggiolare; piagnucolare
whip [wɪp] *n* frusta; (*for riding*) frustino; (*Pol: person*) capogruppo (*che sovrintende alla disciplina dei colleghi di partito*) ▷ *vt* frustare; (*cream, eggs*) sbattere; **whipped cream** *n* panna montata
whirl [wəːl] *vt* (far) girare rapidamente, (far) turbinare ▷ *vi* (*dancers*) volteggiare; (*leaves, water*) sollevarsi in vortice
whisk [wɪsk] *n* (*Culin*) frusta; frullino ▷ *vt* sbattere, frullare; **to ~ sb away** or **off** portar via qn a tutta velocità
whiskers ['wɪskəz] *npl* (*of animal*) baffi *mpl*; (*of man*) favoriti *mpl*
whisky ['wɪskɪ] (*US, Ireland* **whiskey**) *n* whisky *m inv*
whisper ['wɪspəʳ] *n* sussurro ▷ *vt, vi* sussurrare
whistle ['wɪsl] *n* (*sound*) fischio; (*object*)

fischietto ▷ *vi* fischiare

white [waɪt] *adj* bianco(-a); (*with fear*) pallido(-a) ▷ *n* bianco; (*person*) bianco(-a); **White House** *n* Casa Bianca; **whitewash** *n* (*paint*) bianco di calce ▷ *vt* imbiancare; (*fig*) coprire

whiting ['waɪtɪŋ] *n inv* (*fish*) merlango

Whitsun ['wɪtsn] *n* Pentecoste *f*

whittle ['wɪtl] *vt* **to ~ away, ~ down** ridurre, tagliare

whizz [wɪz] *vi* **to ~ past** *or* **by** passare sfrecciando

KEYWORD

who [huː] *pron* **1** (*interrogative*) chi; **who is it?, who's there?** chi è?
2 (*relative*) che; **the man who spoke to me** l'uomo che ha parlato con me; **those who can swim** quelli che sanno nuotare

whoever [huː'ɛvə] *pron* **~ finds it** chiunque lo trovi; **ask ~ you like** lo chieda a chiunque vuole; **~ she marries** chiunque sposerà, non importa chi sposerà; **~ told you that?** chi mai gliel'ha detto?

whole [həʊl] *adj* (*complete*) tutto(-a), completo(-a); (*not broken*) intero(-a), intatto(-a) ▷ *n* (*all*): **the ~ of** tutto(-a) il (la); (*entire unit*) tutto; (*not broken*) tutto; **the ~ of the town** tutta la città, la città intera; **on the ~, as a ~** nel complesso, nell'insieme; **wholefood(s)** *n(pl)* cibo integrale; **wholeheartedly** [həʊl'hɑː tɪdlɪ] *adv* sentitamente, di tutto cuore; **wholemeal** *adj* (*bread, flour*) integrale; **wholesale** *n* commercio *or* vendita all'ingrosso ▷ *adj* all'ingrosso; (*destruction*) totale; **wholewheat** *adj* = **wholemeal**; **wholly** *adv* completamente, del tutto

KEYWORD

whom [huːm] *pron* **1** (*interrogative*) chi; **whom did you see?** chi hai visto?; **to whom did you give it?** a chi lo hai dato?
2 (*relative*) che, *prep* + il (la) quale (*check syntax of Italian verb used*); **the man whom I saw/to whom I spoke** l'uomo che ho visto/al quale ho parlato

whore [hɔː] (*inf: pej*) *n* puttana

KEYWORD

whose [huːz] *adj* **1** (*possessive: interrogative*) di chi; **whose book is this?, whose is this book?** di chi è questo libro?; **whose daughter are you?** di chi sei figlia?

2 (*possessive: relative*): **the man whose son you rescued** l'uomo il cui figlio hai salvato; **the girl whose sister you were speaking to** la ragazza alla cui sorella stavi parlando
▷ *pron* di chi; **whose is this?** di chi è questo?; **I know whose it is** so di chi è

KEYWORD

why [waɪ] *adv* perché; **why not?** perché no?; **why not do it now?** perché non farlo adesso?
▷ *conj* **I wonder why he said that** mi chiedo perché l'abbia detto; **that's not why I'm here** non è questo il motivo per cui sono qui; **the reason why** il motivo per cui
▷ *excl* (*surprise*) ma guarda un po'!; (*remonstrating*) ma (via)!; (*explaining*) ebbene!

wicked ['wɪkɪd] *adj* cattivo(-a), malvagio(-a); maligno(-a); perfido(-a)

wicket ['wɪkɪt] *n* (*Cricket*) porta; area tra le due porte

wide [waɪd] *adj* largo(-a); (*area, knowledge*) vasto(-a); (*choice*) ampio(-a) ▷ *adv* **to open ~** spalancare; **to shoot ~** tirare a vuoto *or* fuori bersaglio; **widely** *adv* (*differing*) molto, completamente; (*travelled, spaced*) molto; (*believed*) generalmente; **widen** *vt* allargare, ampliare; **wide open** *adj* spalancato(-a); **widespread** *adj* (*belief etc*) molto *or* assai diffuso(-a)

widow ['wɪdəʊ] *n* vedova; **widower** *n* vedovo

width [wɪdθ] *n* larghezza

wield [wiːld] *vt* (*sword*) maneggiare; (*power*) esercitare

wife [waɪf] (*pl* **wives**) *n* moglie *f*

wig [wɪg] *n* parrucca

wild [waɪld] *adj* selvatico(-a); selvaggio(-a); (*sea, weather*) tempestoso(-a); (*idea, life*) folle; stravagante; (*applause*) frenetico(-a); **wilderness** ['wɪldənɪs] *n* deserto; **wildlife** *n* natura; **wildly** *adv* selvaggiamente; (*applaud*) freneticamente; (*hit, guess*) a casaccio; (*happy*) follemente

KEYWORD

will [wɪl] (*pt, pp* **willed**) *aux vb* **1** (*forming future tense*): **I will finish it tomorrow** lo finirò domani; **I will have finished it by tomorrow** lo finirò entro domani; **will you do it? — yes I will/no I won't** lo farai? — sì (lo farò)/no (non lo farò)

2 (*in conjectures, predictions*): **he will** or **he'll be there by now** dovrebbe essere arrivato ora; **that will be the postman** sarà il postino

3 (*in commands, requests, offers*): **will you be quiet!** vuoi stare zitto?; **will you come?** vieni anche tu?; **will you help me?** mi aiuti?, mi puoi aiutare?; **will you have a cup of tea?** vorrebbe una tazza di tè?; **I won't put up with it!** non lo accetterò!
▷ vt **to will sb to do** volere che qn faccia; **he willed himself to go on** continuò grazie a un grande sforzo di volontà
▷ n volontà; testamento

willing ['wɪlɪŋ] *adj* volonteroso(-a); **~ to do** disposto(-a) a fare; **willingly** *adv* volentieri

willow ['wɪləʊ] *n* salice *m*

willpower ['wɪlpaʊə*ʳ*] *n* forza di volontà

wilt [wɪlt] *vi* appassire

win [wɪn] (*pt, pp* **won**) *n* (*in sports etc*) vittoria ▷ vt (*battle, prize, money*) vincere; (*popularity*) conquistare ▷ vi vincere; **win over** vt convincere

wince [wɪns] *vi* trasalire

wind¹ [waɪnd] (*pt, pp* **wound**) *vt* attorcigliare; (*wrap*) avvolgere; (*clock, toy*) caricare ▷ vi (*road, river*) serpeggiare; **wind down** vt (*car window*) abbassare; (*fig: production, business*) diminuire; **wind up** vt (*clock*) caricare; (*debate*) concludere

wind² [wɪnd] *n* vento; (*Med*) flatulenza; (*breath*) respiro, fiato ▷ vt (*take breath away*) far restare senza fiato; **~ power** energia eolica

windfall ['wɪndfɔːl] *n* (*money*) guadagno insperato

winding ['waɪndɪŋ] *adj* (*road*) serpeggiante; (*staircase*) a chiocciola

windmill ['wɪndmɪl] *n* mulino a vento

window ['wɪndəʊ] *n* finestra; (*in car, train, plane*) finestrino; (*in shop etc*) vetrina; (*also:* **~ pane**) vetro; **I'd like a ~ seat** vorrei un posto vicino al finestrino; **window box** *n* cassetta da fiori; **window cleaner** *n* (*person*) pulitore *m* di finestre; **window pane** *n* vetro; **window seat** *n* posto finestrino; **windowsill** *n* davanzale *m*

windscreen ['wɪndskriːn] (*us* **windshield**) *n* parabrezza *m inv*; **windscreen wiper** (*us* **windshield wiper**) *n* tergicristallo

windsurfing ['wɪndsəːfɪŋ] *n* windsurf *m inv*

windy ['wɪndɪ] *adj* ventoso(-a); **it's ~** c'è vento

wine [waɪn] *n* vino; **wine bar** *n* enoteca

(*per degustazione*); **wine glass** *n* bicchiere *m* da vino; **wine list** *n* lista dei vini; **wine tasting** *n* degustazione *f* dei vini

wing [wɪŋ] *n* ala; (*Aut*) fiancata; **wing mirror** *n* (*BRIT*) specchietto retrovisore esterno

wink [wɪŋk] *n* ammiccamento ▷ vi ammiccare, fare l'occhiolino; (*light*) baluginare

winner ['wɪnə*ʳ*] *n* vincitore(-trice)

winning ['wɪnɪŋ] *adj* (*team, goal*) vincente; (*smile*) affascinante

winter ['wɪntə*ʳ*] *n* inverno; **winter sports** *npl* sport *mpl* invernali; **wintertime** *n* inverno, stagione *f* invernale

wipe [waɪp] *n* pulita, passata ▷ vt pulire (strofinando); (*erase: tape*) cancellare; **wipe out** vt (*debt*) pagare, liquidare; (*memory*) cancellare; (*destroy*) annientare; **wipe up** vt asciugare

wire ['waɪə*ʳ*] *n* filo; (*Elec*) filo elettrico; (*Tel*) telegramma *m* ▷ vt (*house*) fare l'impianto elettrico di; (*also:* **~ up**) collegare, allacciare; (*person*) telegrafare a

wiring ['waɪərɪŋ] *n* impianto elettrico

wisdom ['wɪzdəm] *n* saggezza; (*of action*) prudenza; **wisdom tooth** *n* dente *m* del giudizio

wise [waɪz] *adj* saggio(-a); prudente; giudizioso(-a)

wish [wɪʃ] *n* (*desire*) desiderio; (*specific desire*) richiesta ▷ vt desiderare, volere; **best ~es** (*on birthday etc*) i migliori auguri; **with best ~es** (*in letter*) cordiali saluti, con i migliori saluti; **to ~ sb goodbye** dire arrivederci a qn; **he ~ed me well** mi augurò di riuscire; **to ~ to do/sb to do** desiderare or volere fare/che qn faccia; **to ~ for** desiderare

wistful ['wɪstful] *adj* malinconico(-a)

wit [wɪt] *n* (*also:* **~s**) intelligenza; presenza di spirito; (*wittiness*) spirito, arguzia; (*person*) bello spirito

witch [wɪtʃ] *n* strega

🔵 **KEYWORD**

with [wɪð, wɪθ] *prep* **1** (*in the company of*) con; **I was with him** ero con lui; **we stayed with friends** siamo stati da amici; **I'll be with you in a minute** vengo subito

2 (*descriptive*) con; **a room with a view** una stanza con vista sul mare (*or* sulle montagne *etc*); **the man with the grey hat/blue eyes** l'uomo con il cappello grigio/gli occhi blu

3 (*indicating manner, means, cause*): **with tears in her eyes** con le lacrime agli occhi; **red with anger** rosso dalla rabbia; **to**

shake with fear tremare di paura
4: **I'm with you** (*I understand*) la seguo;
to be with it (*inf: up-to-date*) essere alla
moda; (: *alert*) essere sveglio(-a)

withdraw [wɪθ'drɔː] (*irreg: like* **draw**) *vt*
ritirare; (*money from bank*) ritirare; prelevare
▷ *vi* ritirarsi; **withdrawal** *n* ritiro; prelievo;
(*of army*) ritirata; **withdrawal symptoms**
n (*Med*) crisi *f* di astinenza; **withdrawn** *adj*
(*person*) distaccato(-a)
withdrew [wɪθ'druː] *pt of* **withdraw**
wither ['wɪðəʳ] *vi* appassire
withhold [wɪθ'həʊld] (*irreg: like* **hold**)
vt (*money*) trattenere; (*permission*): **to ~
(from)** rifiutare (a); (*information*): **to ~
(from)** nascondere (a)
within [wɪð'ɪn] *prep* all'interno, (*in time,
distances*) entro ▷ *adv* all'interno, dentro; **~
reach (of)** alla portata (di); **~ sight (of)** in
vista (di); **~ a mile of** entro un miglio da; **~
the week** prima della fine della settimana
without [wɪð'aʊt] *prep* senza; **to go ~ sth**
fare a meno di qc
withstand [wɪθ'stænd] (*irreg: like* **stand**)
vt resistere a
witness ['wɪtnɪs] *n* (*person, also Law*)
testimone *m/f* ▷ *vt* (*event*) essere
testimone di; (*document*) attestare
l'autenticità di
witty ['wɪtɪ] *adj* spiritoso(-a)
wives [waɪvz] *npl of* **wife**
wizard ['wɪzəd] *n* mago
wk *abbr* = **week**
wobble ['wɒbl] *vi* tremare; (*chair*)
traballare
woe [wəʊ] *n* dolore *m*; disgrazia
woke [wəʊk] *pt of* **wake**
woken ['wəʊkn] *pp of* **wake**
wolf [wʊlf] (*pl* **wolves**) *n* lupo
woman ['wʊmən] (*pl* **women**) *n* donna
womb [wuːm] *n* (*Anat*) utero
women ['wɪmɪn] *npl of* **woman**
won [wʌn] *pt, pp of* **win**
wonder ['wʌndəʳ] *n* meraviglia ▷ *vi* **to ~
whether/why** domandarsi se/perché; **to
~ at** essere sorpreso(-a) di; meravigliarsi
di; **to ~ about** domandarsi di; pensare
a; **it's no ~ that** c'è poco or non c'è da
meravigliarsi che + *sub*; **wonderful** *adj*
meraviglioso(-a)
won't [wəʊnt] = **will not**
wood [wʊd] *n* legno; (*timber*) legname *m*;
(*forest*) bosco; **wooden** *adj* di legno; (*fig*)
rigido(-a); inespressivo(-a); **woodwind** *npl*
(*Mus*): **the woodwind** i legni; **woodwork**
n (*craft, subject*) falegnameria
wool [wʊl] *n* lana; **to pull the ~ over sb's
eyes** (*fig*) imbrogliare qn; **woollen** (*US*

woolen) *adj* di lana; (*industry*) laniero(-a);
woolly (*US* **wooly**) *adj* di lana; (*fig: ideas*)
confuso(-a)
word [wəːd] *n* parola; (*news*) notizie *fpl*
▷ *vt* esprimere, formulare; **in other ~s** in
altre parole; **to break/keep one's ~** non
mantenere/mantenere la propria parola;
to have ~s with sb avere un diverbio con
qn; **wording** *n* formulazione *f*; **word
processing** *n* elaborazione *f* di testi, word
processing *m*; **word processor** *n* word
processor *m inv*
wore [wɔːʳ] *pt of* **wear**
work [wəːk] *n* lavoro; (*Art, Literature*)
opera ▷ *vi* lavorare; (*mechanism, plan etc*)
funzionare; (*medicine*) essere efficace
▷ *vt* (*clay, wood etc*) lavorare; (*mine etc*)
sfruttare; (*machine*) far funzionare;
(*cause: effect, miracle*) fare; **to be out of
~** essere disoccupato(-a); **~s** *n* (*BRIT:
factory*) fabbrica *npl* (*of clock, machine*)
meccanismo; **how does this ~?** come
funziona?; **the TV isn't ~ing** la TV non
funziona; **to ~ loose** allentarsi; **work
out** *vi* (*plans etc*) riuscire, andare bene
▷ *vt* (*problem*) risolvere; (*plan*) elaborare;
it ~s out at £100 fa 100 sterline; **worker**
n lavoratore(-trice), operaio(-a); **work
experience** *n* (*previous jobs*) esperienze
fpl lavorative; (*student training placement*)
tirocinio; **workforce** *n* forza lavoro;
working class *n* classe *f* operaia;
working week *n* settimana lavorativa;
workman (*irreg*) *n* operaio; **work of
art** *n* opera d'arte; **workout** *n* (*Sport*)
allenamento; **work permit** *n* permesso
di lavoro; **workplace** *n* posto di lavoro;
workshop *n* officina; (*practical session*)
gruppo di lavoro; **work station** *n* stazione
f di lavoro; **work surface** *n* piano di
lavoro; **worktop** *n* piano di lavoro
world [wəːld] *n* mondo ▷ *cpd* (*champion*)
del mondo; (*power, war*) mondiale; **to
think the ~ of sb** (*fig*) pensare un gran
bene di qn; **World Cup** *n* (*Football*) Coppa
del Mondo; **world-wide** *adj* universale;
World-Wide Web *n* World Wide Web *m*
worm [wəːm] *n* (*also: earth~*) verme *m*
worn [wɔːn] *pp of* **wear** ▷ *adj* usato(-a);
worn-out *adj* (*object*) consumato(-a),
logoro(-a); (*person*) sfinito(-a)
worried ['wʌrɪd] *adj* preoccupato(-a)
worry ['wʌrɪ] *n* preoccupazione *f* ▷ *vt*
preoccupare ▷ *vi* preoccuparsi; **worrying**
adj preoccupante
worse [wəːs] *adj* peggiore ▷ *adv*, *n* peggio;
a change for the ~ un peggioramento;
worsen *vt*, *vi* peggiorare; **worse off** *adj* in
condizioni (economiche) peggiori

worship ['wəːʃɪp] n culto ▷ vt (God) adorare, venerare; (person) adorare; **Your W~** (BRIT: to mayor) signor sindaco; (: to judge) signor giudice

worst [wəːst] adj il (la) peggiore ▷ adv, n peggio; **at ~** al peggio, per male che vada

worth [wəːθ] n valore m ▷ adj **to be ~** valere; **it's ~ it** ne vale la pena; **it is ~ one's while (to do)** vale la pena (fare); **worthless** adj di nessun valore; **worthwhile** adj (activity) utile; (cause) lodevole

worthy ['wəːðɪ] adj (person) degno(-a); (motive) lodevole; **~ of** degno di

 KEYWORD

would [wud] aux vb **1** (conditional tense): **if you asked him he would do it** se glielo chiedesse lo farebbe; **if you had asked him he would have done it** se glielo avesse chiesto lo avrebbe fatto

2 (in offers, invitations, requests): **would you like a biscuit?** vorrebbe or vuole un biscotto?; **would you ask him to come in?** lo faccia entrare, per cortesia; **would you open the window please?** apra la finestra, per favore

3 (in indirect speech): **I said I would do it** ho detto che l'avrei fatto

4 (emphatic): **it WOULD have to snow today!** doveva proprio nevicare oggi!

5 (insistence): **she wouldn't do it** non ha voluto farlo

6 (conjecture): **it would have been midnight** sarà stato mezzanotte; **it would seem so** sembrerebbe proprio di sì

7 (indicating habit): **he would go there on Mondays** andava lì ogni lunedì

wouldn't ['wudnt] = **would not**

wound¹ [waund] pt, pp of **wind¹**

wound² [wuːnd] n ferita ▷ vt ferire

wove [wəuv] pt of **weave**

woven ['wəuvn] pp of **weave**

wrap [ræp] vt avvolgere; (pack: also: ~ up) incartare; **wrapper** n (on chocolate) carta; (BRIT: of book) copertina; **wrapping** ['ræpɪŋ] n carta; **wrapping paper** n carta da pacchi; (for gift) carta da regali

wreath [riːθ, pl riːðz] n corona

wreck [rɛk] n (sea disaster) naufragio; (ship) relitto; (pej: person) rottame m ▷ vt demolire; (ship) far naufragare; (fig) rovinare; **wreckage** n rottami mpl; (of building) macerie fpl; (of ship) relitti mpl

wren [rɛn] n (Zool) scricciolo

wrench [rɛntʃ] n (Tech) chiave f; (tug) torsione f brusca; (fig) strazio ▷ vt strappare; storcere; **to ~ sth from** strappare qc a or da

wrestle ['rɛsl] vi **to ~ (with sb)** lottare (con qn); **wrestler** n lottatore(-trice); **wrestling** n lotta

wretched ['rɛtʃɪd] adj disgraziato(-a); (inf: weather, holiday) orrendo(-a), orribile; (: child, dog) pestifero(-a)

wriggle ['rɪgl] vi (also: ~ about) dimenarsi; (: snake, worm) serpeggiare, muoversi serpeggiando

wring [rɪŋ] (pt, pp **wrung**) vt torcere; (wet clothes) strizzare; (fig): **to ~ sth out of** strappare qc a

wrinkle ['rɪŋkl] n (on skin) ruga; (on paper etc) grinza ▷ vt (nose) torcere; (forehead) corrugare ▷ vi (skin, paint) raggrinzirsi

wrist [rɪst] n polso

write [raɪt] (pt **wrote**, pp **written**) vt, vi scrivere; **write down** vt annotare; (put in writing) mettere per iscritto; **write off** vt (debt, plan) cancellare; **write out** vt mettere per iscritto; (cheque, receipt) scrivere; **write-off** n perdita completa; **writer** n autore(-trice), scrittore(-trice)

writing ['raɪtɪŋ] n scrittura; (of author) scritto, opera; in ~ per iscritto; **writing paper** n carta da lettere

written ['rɪtn] pp of **write**

wrong [rɒŋ] adj sbagliato(-a); (not suitable) inadatto(-a); (wicked) cattivo(-a); (unfair) ingiusto(-a) ▷ adv in modo sbagliato, erroneamente ▷ n (injustice) torto ▷ vt fare torto a; **I took a ~ turning** ho sbagliato strada; **you are ~ to do it** ha torto a farlo; **you are ~ about that, you've got it ~** si sbaglia; **to be in the ~** avere torto; **what's ~?** cosa c'è che non va?; **to go ~** (person) sbagliarsi; (plan) fallire, non riuscire; (machine) guastarsi; **wrongly** adv (incorrectly, by mistake) in modo sbagliato; **wrong number** n (Tel): **you've got the wrong number** ha sbagliato numero

wrote [rəut] pt of **write**

wrung [rʌŋ] pt, pp of **wring**

WWW n abbr = **World Wide Web**; **the ~** la Rete

X y

XL abbr = **extra large**
Xmas ['ɛksməs] n abbr = **Christmas**
X-ray ['ɛksreɪ] n raggio X; (photograph) radiografia ▷ vt radiografare
xylophone ['zaɪləfəʊn] n xilofono

yacht [jɔt] n panfilo, yacht m inv;
  yachting n yachting m, sport m della vela
yard [jɑːd] n (of house etc) cortile m; (measure) iarda (= 914 mm; 3 feet); **yard sale** (US) n vendita di oggetti usati nel cortile di una casa privata
yarn [jɑːn] n filato; (tale) lunga storia
yawn [jɔːn] n sbadiglio ▷ vi sbadigliare
yd. abbr = **yard(s)**
yeah [jɛə] (inf) adv sì
year [jɪəʳ] n anno; (referring to harvest, wine etc) annata; **he is 8 ~s old** ha 8 anni; **an eight-~-old child** un(a) bambino(-a) di otto anni; **yearly** adj annuale ▷ adv annualmente
yearn [jəːn] vi **to ~ for sth/to do** desiderare ardentemente qc/di fare
yeast [jiːst] n lievito
yell [jɛl] n urlo ▷ vi urlare
yellow ['jɛləʊ] adj giallo(-a); **Yellow Pages®** npl pagine fpl gialle
yes [jɛs] adv sì ▷ n sì m inv; **to say/answer ~** dire/rispondere di sì
yesterday ['jɛstədɪ] adv ieri ▷ n ieri m inv; **~ morning/evening** ieri mattina/sera; **all day ~** ieri per tutta la giornata
yet [jɛt] adv ancora; già ▷ conj ma, tuttavia; **it is not finished ~** non è ancora finito; **the best ~** finora il

migliore; **as ~** finora
yew [ju:] n tasso (albero)
Yiddish ['jɪdɪʃ] n yiddish m
yield [ji:ld] n produzione f, resa; reddito
  ▷ vt produrre, rendere; (surrender)
  cedere ▷ vi cedere; (US: Aut) dare la
  precedenza
yob(bo) ['jɔb(əu)] n (BRIT inf) bullo
yoga ['jəugə] n yoga m
yog(h)urt ['jəugət] n iogurt m inv
yolk [jəuk] n tuorlo, rosso d'uovo

 KEYWORD

you [ju:] pron 1 (subject) tu; (: polite form) lei;
  (: pl) voi; (: very formal) loro; **you Italians
  enjoy your food** a voi Italiani piace
  mangiare bene; **you and I will go** tu ed io
  or lei ed io andiamo
  2 (object: direct) ti; la; vi; loro (after vb); (:
  indirect) ti; le; vi; loro (after vb); **I know you**
  ti or la or vi conosco; **I gave it to you** te
  l'ho dato; gliel'ho dato; ve l'ho dato; l'ho
  dato loro
  3 (stressed, after prep, in comparisons) te; lei;
  voi; loro; **I told you to do it** ho detto a TE
  (or a LEI etc) di farlo; **she's younger than
  you** è più giovane di te (or lei etc)
  4 (impers: one) si; **fresh air does you good**
  l'aria fresca fa bene; **you never know** non
  si sa mai

you'd [ju:d] = **you had**; **you would**
you ll [ju:l] = **you will**; **you shall**
young [jʌŋ] adj giovane ▷ npl (of animal)
  piccoli mpl; (people): **the ~** i giovani, la
  gioventù; **youngster** n giovanotto,
  ragazzo; (child) bambino(-a)
your [jɔːʳ] adj il (la) tuo(-a) pl, i (le) tuoi
  (tue); il (la) suo(-a); (pl) i (le) suoi (sue); il
  (la) vostro(-a); (pl) i (le) vostri(-e); il (la)
  loro; (pl) i (le) loro; see also **my**
you're [juəʳ] = **you are**
yours [jɔːz] pron il (la) tuo(-a); (pl) i (le)
  tuoi (tue); (polite form) il (la) suo(-a); (pl)
  i (le) suoi (sue); (pl) il (la) vostro(-a); (pl)
  i (le) vostri(-e); (: very formal) il (la) loro;
  (pl) i (le) loro; see also **mine**; **faithfully**;
  sincerely
yourself [jɔː'sɛlf] pron (reflexive) ti;
  si; (after prep) te; sé; (emphatic) tu
  stesso(-a); lei stesso(-a); **yourselves** pl
  pron (reflexive) vi; si; (after prep) voi; loro;
  (emphatic) voi stessi(-e); loro stessi(-e); see
  also **oneself**
youth [ju:θ, pl ju:ðz] n gioventù f; (young
  man) giovane m, ragazzo; **youth club** n
  centro giovanile; **youthful** adj giovane;
  da giovane; giovanile; **youth hostel** n

ostello della gioventù
you've [ju:v] = **you have**
Yugoslavia ['ju:gəu'sla:vɪə] n (Hist)
  Jugoslavia

Z

zeal [ziːl] *n* zelo; entusiasmo
zebra ['ziːbrə] *n* zebra; **zebra crossing** (BRIT) *n* (passaggio pedonale a) strisce *fpl*, zebre *fpl*
zero ['zɪərəu] *n* zero
zest [zɛst] *n* gusto; (*Culin*) buccia
zigzag ['zɪgzæg] *n* zigzag *m inv* ▷ *vi* zigzagare
Zimbabwe [zɪm'bɑːbwɪ] *n* Zimbabwe *m*
zinc [zɪŋk] *n* zinco
zip [zɪp] *n* (*also:* ~ **fastener**, (US) **zipper**) chiusura *f* or cerniera *f* lampo *inv* ▷ *vt* (*also:* ~ **up**) chiudere con una cerniera lampo; **zip code** (US) *n* codice *m* di avviamento postale; **zipper** (US) *n* cerniera *f* lampo *inv*
zit [zɪt] *n* brufolo
zodiac ['zəudɪæk] *n* zodiaco
zone [zəun] *n* (*also Mil*) zona
zoo [zuː] *n* zoo *m inv*
zoology [zuːˈɔlədʒɪ] *n* zoologia
zoom [zuːm] *vi* **to ~ past** sfrecciare; **zoom lens** *n* zoom *m inv*, obiettivo a focale variabile
zucchini [zuːˈkiːnɪ] (US) *npl* (*courgettes*) zucchine *fpl*